THE EUROPEAN CONVENTION

JACOBS, WHITE, AND OVEY

THE EUROPEAN CONVENTION ON HUMAN RIGHTS

Sixth Edition

BERNADETTE RAINEY,
ELIZABETH WICKS, AND
CLARE OVEY

OXFORD
UNIVERSITY PRESS

OXFORD
UNIVERSITY PRESS

Great Clarendon Street, Oxford, OX2 6DP,
United Kingdom

Oxford University Press is a department of the University of Oxford. It furthers the University's objective of excellence in research, scholarship, and education by publishing worldwide. Oxford is a registered trade mark of Oxford University Press in the UK and in certain other countries

Impression: 3

Published in the United States of America by Oxford University Press
198 Madison Avenue, New York, NY 10016, United States of America

British Library Cataloguing in Publication Data
Data available

Library of Congress Control Number: 2014930238

ISBN 978–0–19–965508–3

Printed in Great Britain by
Bell and Bain Ltd, Glasgow

To human rights defenders everywhere

CONTENTS

FOREWORD

We are delighted to welcome the sixth edition of this work, which was started by Francis Jacobs in 1975, while Robin White worked on the second to fifth editions. Two new authors, Bernadette Rainey and Elizabeth Wicks, have joined Clare Ovey in preparing this fully revised and updated edition. It is a source of considerable pleasure and pride for both of us that this work has established itself as one of the leading English language texts on the Convention, and that its future is in such safe hands.

The new edition continues to be an accessible yet comprehensive guide to the operation of the European Convention on Human Rights and to the case-law of the Court of Human Rights. The authors have risen to the challenge, in the face of an increasing number of judgments, of avoiding both over-simplification and over-elaboration. They have rightly concentrated on the key principles derived from the case-law, offering the appropriate level of detail for an appreciation not only of the development of the case-law but also its current state. That has always been a key characteristic of this book. The case-law continues to demonstrate the Court's commitment to treating the Convention text as a living instrument, capable of addressing modern concerns within broadly framed rights rather than being locked into the era in which the text was drafted. This has not been entirely uncontroversial in relation to the reception of some judgments in some Contracting Parties.

The challenges presented by new developments, coupled with some examples in the case-law of breaches of the most fundamental of human rights—and not just in the young democracies of central and eastern Europe—show the continuing relevance of a basic regional text protecting human rights. Both the rich history of the Convention system and the evolution of the protected rights are vividly told in this work. There is much in the text both for those coming new to the Convention, whether as students or practitioners of the law, and for those already familiar with its workings and judgments. The case-law of the Court of Human Rights is necessarily casuistic, and there is great value in the skilful synthesis which the authors have provided.

When the fifth edition was published there were real concerns about the ability of the Convention system to cope with its case-load, which threatened to overwhelm the resources available. Although pressures remain, this sixth edition shows that the entry into force of Protocol No. 14 has enabled the Court, through new working methods, to begin to make significant inroads into the backlog of applications. The changes to be found in Protocols 15 and 16, which are fully considered here, will offer some further methods for more effective case management. The focus on subsidiarity in these two new protocols demonstrates the vital contribution national courts can make to the protection of Convention rights. There will, however, no doubt be further developments and future pressures when the accession of the European Union to the Convention system is completed.

This book should be seen as continuing to contribute to the education of human rights defenders everywhere, and as a source of valuable information for those charged with adjudicating on disputes with a human rights element.

Francis Jacobs
Robin White
March 2014

PREFACE TO THE SIXTH EDITION

Much of the work on the preparation of this sixth edition has coincided with a growing debate on the future of the Strasbourg Court. There has been something of an explosion in the case-law over the last few years; the Court gave its 10,000th judgment in 2008. The Court has reached impressive levels of productivity. The number of cases dealt by the Court indicates just how important the European Convention and its Court is for those within the jurisdiction of the Contracting Parties. Even though it still has a backlog of cases, the number of applications waiting to be dealt with by the Court fell in 2013. Protocol 14 came into force in 2010 which has enabled the Court to make the most of its slender resources. There are two strands which can be identified from a global view of the applications made to the Court in recent years. For some States, most notably Russia, Turkey, Serbia, and Ukraine, basic requirements of the Convention are not being met within the national legal orders, and they are producing very large numbers of applications. There is also an alarming number of cases before the Court dealing with ill treatment and discrimination. Elsewhere, the numbers are not so high, and many applications are concerned with novel questions relating to the interpretation and application of Convention rights. Yet overall probably something in the region of 70 per cent of admissible cases are repetitive and can be determined by the application of well-established Convention principles. Such cases could, and should, be resolved within the national legal orders. The development of Protocols 15 and 16 are the products of the reform agenda initiated by the Interlaken process. Both these Protocols and the discussion at the Conferences on further reform of the Court focus on subsidiarity. The role of the Court in relation to the national legal orders is a continuing challenge to both the Court and the Contracting States. Such is the context in which this edition has been prepared.

As with previous editions, this book is explicitly about the European Convention as seen from Strasbourg rather than its implementation in any particular State. It continues to use as its main reference point the public voice of the Court in its judgments on the merits and its decisions on admissibility. Our overall aim has been to provide an accessible and readable account of the current state of Convention case-law, which focuses on the key principles which that case-law establishes. As the case-law grows, such synthesis strikes us as having an increasing role to play in ensuring an accurate overview of the content of Convention rights. We have recast material in the light of case-law developments. Inevitably, the book has increased in length, though we have strived to retain a length of text which does not overwhelm the reader with too much detail. We are supporters of the Strasbourg Court, and have focused on the achievements of this pan-European system of adjudication of human rights questions. We hope our enthusiasm for the Court has not led us to be uncritical where the case-law is not in an entirely satisfactory state. It should be remembered that the role of the Strasbourg Court is casuistic in the sense that it does not control its case-law; it makes determinations on the merits of all those applications, which it finds to be admissible. For big questions, it does have the mechanism of the Grand Chamber to bring the minds of a larger group of judges to such questions. It is perhaps not surprising that judgments of the Grand Chamber are less likely to be unanimous than decisions of Chambers.

The structure of the book is the same as the fifth edition. We have retained a structure which relates our synthesis and analysis to individual articles of the Convention and its Protocols. We continue to believe that this is the most effective way to present Convention rights to those coming to a study of the Convention as a whole for the first time.

The preparation of the first draft of each chapter of this new edition has fallen to either Elizabeth Wicks or Bernadette Rainey. Clare Ovey has read and commented on every draft chapter, and provided significant input into the revision of those early drafts. All three of us take responsibility for the final text you have before you. Robin White, as consultant editor, read all the material in draft and made many helpful comments for our consideration. Francis Jacobs continues to display a paternal pride in a work he started in 1975. His support and encouragement are much appreciated. We are grateful to colleagues who have both consciously and unconsciously contributed to the preparation of this new edition through their responses to ideas we have tried out on them. It is important to stress that we write in our personal capacities. Elizabeth Wicks is Professor of Human Rights Law at the University of Leicester; Bernadette Rainey is a Lecturer at Cardiff Law School; and Clare Ovey is a Head of Division at the Court of Human Rights and the views expressed in this book are her own and not in any sense those of the Court.

The text is intended to be up to date to 1 October 2013.

Bernadette Rainey
Elizabeth Wicks
Clare Ovey
Cardiff, Leicester, and Strasbourg
December 2013

A NOTE ON CITATION CONVENTIONS

COMMISSION DECISIONS AND REPORTS

These are cited by application number in roman, followed by the names of the parties in italics and the date of the decision or report, and, where the decision or report is reported, the relevant report reference.

Example: App. 10581/83, *Norris and National Gay Federation v Ireland*, Decision of 16 May 1984, (1984) 44 DR 132.

COURT JUDGMENTS AND DECISIONS

JUDGMENTS

Older judgments of the Court were give a Series number, but for more modern judgments this practice has been abandoned.

In every case the date of the judgment is given. Where there is a Series number this is used. The application number is also given in parentheses and in roman after the names of the parties to the case. Judgments of the Grand Chamber are indicated by an annotation in square brackets after the date.

Where the case is reported in the *European Human Rights Reports*, a reference to those reports is also given. Where a case is also reported in the Court's official reports, published by Carl Heymanns Verlag KG, this reference is also given in the form recommended by the Strasbourg Court, namely ECHR [Year]-[Part] So a reference reading ECHR 2005-I would indicate that the judgment is reported in Part I of the official reports for the year 2005. A citation ending in 'nyr' means that the judgment will be reported in the official reports but that the case has not yet been allocated to a specific issue of the reports for that year.

Examples:

Cruz Varas v Sweden, (App. 15576/89), 20 March 1991, Series A No 201, (1992) 14 EHRR 1.

Mamatkulov and Askarov v Turkey, (Apps. 46827/99 and 46951/99), 4 February 2005 [GC], (2005) 41 EHRR 494, ECHR 2005-I.

DECISIONS

The Court is now responsible for admissibility decisions as well as judgments. Admissibility decisions are listed separately from judgments, but the structure of the reference follows the same principles: names of the parties followed by the application number and the date of the decision. If there is a report available that is given. The words 'Decision of' appear before the date to indicate that this is an admissibility decision rather than a judgment.

Example: Senator Lines v Austria, Belgium, Denmark, Finland, France, Germany, Greece, Ireland, Italy, Luxembourg, the Netherlands, Portugal, Spain, Sweden and the United Kingdom, (App. 56672/00), Decision of 10 March 2004 [GC] (2004) 39 EHRR SE3, ECHR 2004-IV

Note that nearly all Court decisions and judgments are available on the Court's database HUDOC; see http://echr.coe.int/echr/en/hudoc.

TABLE OF JUDGMENTS AND DECISIONS OF THE COURT OF HUMAN RIGHTS

JUDGMENTS

DECISIONS ON ADMISSIBILITY

TABLE OF DECISIONS AND REPORTS OF THE COMMISSION OF HUMAN RIGHTS

TABLE OF TREATIES AND RELATED DOCUMENTS

References in **bold** indicate that the Article is reproduced in full

MISCELLANEOUS LEGISLATION

Austria

Bosnia and Herzegovina

Europe

Cyprus

France

Germany

Iraq

Latvia

Norway

Russia

Slovakia

Sweden

Switzerland

Turkey

United Kingdom

United States

TABLE OF CASES

ABBREVIATIONS

AC	Appeal Court
AJCL	*American Journal of Comparative Law*
AJIL	*American Journal of International Law*
BYIL	*British Yearbook of International Law*
CD	Collection of Decisions of the Commission of Human Rights
CLP	*Current Legal Problems*
CML Rev	*Common Market Law Review*
Contracting Parties	Parties to the European Convention on Human Rights
Crim LR	*Criminal Law Review*
CSCE	Conference on Security and Co-operation in Europe
CUP	Cambridge University Press
DH	*Droits de l'Homme*
DR	Decisions and Reports of the Commission of Human Rights
ELRev	*European Law Review*
EC	European Community
ECHR	European Convention on Human Rights
ECHR	(in citations to decisions and judgments) Reports of Judgments and Decisions of the European Court of Human Rights, Carl Heymanns Verlag KG.
ECR	European Court Reports
EEC	European Economic Community
EHRLR	*European Human Rights Law Review*
EHRR	European Human Rights Reports
EJIL	*European Journal of International Law*
ELJ	*European Law Journal*
EPL	*European Public Law*
ETS	European Treaty Series
European J of Int'l L	*European Journal of International Law*
EWHC	England and Wales: High Court
GC	Grand Chamber
HRLJ	*Human Rights Law Journal*
HRLRev	*Human Rights Law Review*
HRQ	*Human Rights Quarterly*

HUDOC	HUDOC database: http://echr.coe.int/echr/en/hudoc
ICCPR	International Covenant on Civil and Political Rights
ICLQ	*International and Comparative Law Quarterly*
ILJ	*Industrial Law Journal*
ILO	International Labour Organization
KCLJ	*King's College Law Journal*
LIEI	*Legal Issues of European Integration*
LQR	*Law Quarterly Review*
Luxembourg Court	Court of Justice of the European Communities
Member States	Member States of the European Union
MJ	*Maastricht Journal of European and Comparative Law*
MLR	*Modern Law Review*
MUP	Manchester University Press
NATO	North Atlantic Treaty Organisation
NILR	*Netherlands International Law Review*
NQHR	*Netherlands Quarterly of Human Rights*
OUP	Oxford University Press
PKK	Parti Karkerani Kurdistan (Kurdistan Workers' Party)
PL	*Public Law*
SCR	Supreme Court Reports (Canada)
Strasbourg Court	European Court of Human Rights
Strasbourg organs	Commission, Court, and Committee of Ministers
UNGAOR	*United Nations General Assembly Official Records*
UNESCO	United Nations Educational, Scientific, and Cultural Organisation
WLR	Weekly Law Reports
Yearbook	*Yearbook of the European Convention on Human Rights*
YEL	*Yearbook of European Law*

PART 1

INSTITUTIONS AND PROCEDURES

1

CONTEXT, BACKGROUND, AND INSTITUTIONS

CONTEXT

Although the European Convention was a direct response to a global war which had included the horrors of the holocaust, its origins also belong to a line in the development of human rights which can be traced back much further.[1] It is linked to two centuries of political thought associated with the ideas expressed in the American Declaration of Independence and the French Declaration of the Rights of Man. But it can also be viewed in the context of the much longer struggle to secure respect for personal autonomy, the inherent dignity of persons, and the equality of all men and women.[2] The political philosophy and human rights agenda of the Allied Powers after the Second World War shaped both the selection of rights protected and the machinery for their protection. The United Nations Charter had taken a giant step forward in the protection of human rights in acknowledging in Articles 55 and 56 that the General Assembly should undertake responsibility for ensuring that all members of the United Nations kept the pledge in Article 55 to promote 'universal respect for, and observance of, human rights and fundamental freedoms for all without distinction as to race, sex, language or religion.' The recognition that the way in which a State treats its nationals is a matter for international concern and action was ground-breaking, and paved the way for the introduction of international human rights enforcement mechanisms. There was, however, no catalogue of human rights and fundamental freedoms. Within the United Nations, such a catalogue was established in the Universal Declaration of Human Rights.[3] The rights protected in the European Convention draw their inspiration from the Universal Declaration, but do not simply duplicate the rights referred to there.

There were twin concerns which led the Council of Europe to seize the moment in preparing the European Convention. The first was to provide a means through which it was believed that the most serious human rights violations which had occurred during the Second World War could be avoided in the future. The second was to protect States from Communist subversion. This explains, in part, the constant references to values and principles that are necessary in a democratic society, though the precise nature of those values

[1] See generally P. Lauren, *The Evolution of International Human Rights. Visions Seen* (University of Pennsylvania Press, Philadelphia 2003); M. Ishay, *The History of Human Rights. From Ancient Times to the Globalization Era* (University of California Press, Berkeley 2004); and C. Tomuschat, *Human Rights: Between Idealism and Realism* (OUP, Oxford 2003). See also J. Donnelly, 'Human rights: a new standard of civilization' (1998) 74 *International Affairs* 1.

[2] For a discussion of values and human rights, see D. Feldman, *Civil Liberties and Human Rights in England and Wales* (2nd edn OUP, Oxford 2002), Part I, and H. Fenwick, *Civil Liberties and Human Rights* (4th edn Routledge Cavendish, London 2007), ch.1, and the materials cited there. For a critical account of human rights adjudication under the Convention, see G. Beck, 'Human rights adjudication under the ECHR between value pluralism and essential contestability', [2008] EHRLR 214.

[3] See later in this chapter.

is nowhere described or defined in the Convention text itself. Seizing the moment and securing early agreement among the twelve States[4] which signed the European Convention on 4 November 1950 meant that compromises had to be made in the rights included in the main body of the Convention. Reading the *travaux préparatoires* provides a salutary reminder of the context in which the text of the Convention was prepared.[5] In order to secure speedy acceptance of the text, the rights selected for inclusion were broadly uncontroversial and were related directly to events of the then recent past. In the course of deliberations in the Consultative Assembly, Pierre-Henri Teitgen[6] said:

> Who does not appreciate that these rights are fundamental, essential rights, and that there is no State which can, if it abuses them, claim to respect natural law and the fundamental principle of human dignity? Is there any State which can, by violating these rights and fundamental freedoms, claim that its country enjoys a democratic regime?[7]

The result was the production of a Convention containing civil and political rights considered essential to the provision of a bulwark against the spread of communism, and a guarantee against a repetition of the horrors of the Second World War. Further rights would be added later through a number of protocols, but the organs charged with the interpretation and application of the rights set out in the Convention have never regarded them as static. The Convention is 'a living instrument'.[8] This has resulted in an interpretation which seeks to ensure that the requirements of the Convention are interpreted in a present day context and not locked into a moment in history following the Second World War.

THE STRUCTURE AND AIMS OF THE COUNCIL OF EUROPE

After the Second World War, European movements arose, simultaneously and spontaneously, throughout the European democracies. They arose in response to the threat to fundamental human rights and to political freedom which had all but overwhelmed the European continent in the War, and which reappeared after the War in new forms of totalitarianism. The International Committee of Movements for European Unity, and its Congress at The Hague in May 1948, were the foundation of the Council of Europe established on 5 May 1949 and the drafting by its Contracting Parties of the Convention for the Protection of Human Rights and Fundamental Freedoms of 4 November 1950,[9] generally known as the European Convention on Human Rights. The Convention reflected the concerns and objects of this

[4] Belgium, Denmark, France, Germany, Iceland, Ireland, Italy, Luxembourg, Netherlands, Norway, Turkey, and the United Kingdom.

[5] For a detailed consideration of the background to particular provisions of the Convention, see Council of Europe, *Collected Edition of the Travaux Préparatoires of the European Convention on Human Rights* (Martinus Nijhoff, The Hague 1975 to 1985). See also A. Lester, 'Fundamental Rights: The United Kingdom Isolated?' [1984] PL 46; G. Marston, 'The United Kingdom's Part in the Preparation of the European Convention on Human Rights' (1993) 42 ICLQ 796; E. Wicks, 'The UK Government's Perceptions of the European Convention on Human Rights at the Time of Entry' [2000] PL 438; and A. W. Simpson, *Human Rights and the End of Empire. Britain and the Genesis of the European Convention* (OUP, Oxford 2004).

[6] One of the key figures involved in the drafting of the European Convention.

[7] Council of Europe, *Collected Edition of the Travaux Préparatoires*, Vol. I (Martinus Nijhoff, The Hague 1975), 268–70.

[8] See particularly material on the interpretation of the Convention in ch.4.

[9] ETS 5. The Convention entered into force on 3 September 1953.

novel international organization,[10] as set out in its Constitution, the Statute of the Council of Europe.[11] In the Preamble to the Statute, the Contracting States reaffirmed:

> their devotion to the spiritual and moral values which are the common heritage of their peoples and the true source of individual freedom, political liberty and the rule of law, principles which form the basis of all genuine democracy.

The aim of the Council of Europe was, and remains, 'to achieve a greater unity between its Members for the purpose of safeguarding and realizing the ideals and principles which are their common heritage and facilitating their economic and social progress',[12] and this aim was to be pursued 'through the organs of the Council by discussion of questions of common concern and by agreements and common action in economic, social, cultural, scientific, legal and administrative matters and in the maintenance and further realization of human rights and fundamental freedoms.'[13]

The current political mandate of the Council of Europe was established at a summit which took place in Warsaw in 2005.[14] The agenda is:

- to protect human rights, pluralist democracy, and the rule of law;
- to promote awareness and encourage the development of Europe's cultural identity and diversity;
- to find common solutions to the challenges facing European society: such as discrimination against minorities, xenophobia, intolerance, bioethics and cloning, terrorism, trafficking in human beings, organized crime and corruption, cybercrime, violence against children;
- to consolidate democratic stability in Europe by backing political, legislative and constitutional reform.

The Council operates through three organs. The decision-making body is the Committee of Ministers composed of the foreign ministers of the Contracting Parties. The Parliamentary Assembly,[15] composed of 318 representatives[16] drawn from the national parliaments, is the deliberative body whose debates can lead to recommendations made to the Committee of Ministers. The third organ was added in 1994 and is the Congress of Local and Regional Authorities of Europe, which has consultative functions and is composed of representatives of local and regional authorities. The work of these organs is supported by a Secretariat, headed by a Secretary-General appointed by the Parliamentary Assembly on the recommendation of the Committee of Ministers.[17]

[10] See generally, Council of Europe, *Manual of the Council of Europe. Its Structure, Functions and Achievements* (Stevens, London 1970). See also www.coe.int.

[11] ETS 1.

[12] Art. 1(a) of the Statute.

[13] Art. 1(b). For recent material on the general contribution of the Council of Europe to the development of a common legal system for European States, see Council of Europe, *Towards a pan-European legal area* (Council of Europe Press, Strasbourg 2005); Council of Europe, *European judicial systems—facts and figures* (Strasbourg, 2005); and Council of Europe, *The early settlement of disputes and the role of judges* (Council of Europe Press, Strasbourg 2005).

[14] www.coe.int/t/dcr/summit/20050517_decl_varsovie_en.asp.

[15] Referred to as the Consultative Assembly in the Statute of the Council of Europe, ETS 1: see Arts. 22–35. It styled itself the Parliamentary Assembly in 1974. In February 1994 the Committee of Ministers decided to use the denomination 'Parliamentary Assembly' in all future Council of Europe documents.

[16] With 318 substitutes.

[17] Statute of the Council of Europe, ETS 1, Arts. 36 and 37; and see later in this chapter.

Article 3 of the Statute requires that every Contracting Party 'must accept the principles of the rule of law and of the enjoyment by all persons within its jurisdiction of human rights and fundamental freedoms.' Under Article 8, a Contracting Party which has seriously violated Article 3 of the Statute may be suspended from its rights of representation and requested by the Committee of Ministers to withdraw from the Council of Europe under Article 7 and, if it does not comply, may be expelled.[18] The uniqueness of these provisions lay in the fact that questions of human rights fell traditionally within the domestic jurisdiction of States, and were of concern to international law only if the interests of another State were affected, as, for example, by the treatment of that State's nationals. History had demonstrated the inadequacy of those traditional concepts of international law and State sovereignty which made the protection of individuals the exclusive prerogative of the State of which they were nationals. Their rights may require protection, above all, against their own State. The creation of the Council of Europe and the adoption of the Convention on Human Rights are an acknowledgment that the protection of human rights is viewed as an indispensable element of European democracy.

The principle of respect for human rights had been established in international law by the Charter of the United Nations.[19] The Universal Declaration of Human Rights, adopted by the General Assembly of the United Nations on 10 December 1948, proclaims as a 'common standard of achievement' an extensive list of human rights, which, although the Declaration is not legally binding as such, is an authoritative guide to the interpretation of the Charter.[20] Further work in the United Nations, which led to the adoption in 1966 of two Covenants, the Covenant on Economic, Social and Cultural Rights and the Covenant on Civil and Political Rights, drew a distinction between two different classes of fundamental rights. Social and economic rights, although they appear in the Universal Declaration, are less universal in the sense that they constitute standards to be attained, depending on the level of economic development. They require action by governments, whereas civil and political rights often require protection against executive action. Within the Council of Europe, social and economic rights are mainly the concern of the European Social Charter,[21] which provides for progressive implementation and for supervision by the examination of periodic reports on progress achieved. The European Committee of Social Rights is the body responsible for monitoring compliance in the States party to the Charter under a collective complaints procedure which came into effect in 1998.[22]

The Council of Europe today consists of 47 countries. There are five countries with observer status.[23] The membership of the Council of Europe is broad and now encompasses the new democracies of central and eastern Europe. New members of the Council of

[18] It was in consequence of proceedings started under this provision, following an initiative in the Consultative Assembly, that Greece announced in 1969 its withdrawal from the Council of Europe and denounced the Convention. Greece was readmitted in 1974.

[19] See, in particular, Arts. 55 and 56 of the United Nations Charter.

[20] While the Universal Declaration itself is not a binding instrument of international law, the principles it enshrines may acquire legal force as the 'general principles of law recognized by civilized nations' under Art. 38(1)(c) of the Statute of the International Court of Justice, or as customary law reflecting the general practice of States (see Art. 38(1)(b) of the Statute), or even as 'a peremptory norm of general international law' (*jus cogens*), that is, a norm accepted and recognized by the international community of States as a whole as a norm from which no derogation is permitted (see Art. 53 of the Vienna Convention on the Law of Treaties).

[21] The Charter entered into force on 26 February 1965. See generally D. Harris, *The European Social Charter* (University of Virginia Press, Charlottesville 1984); D. Gomien, D. Harris, and L. Zwaak, *Law and Practice of the European Convention on Human Rights and the European Social Charter* (Council of Europe Press, Strasbourg 1996); and *Fundamental Social Rights: Case Law of the European Social Charter* (Council of Europe Press, Strasbourg 2000).

[22] See www.coe.int/t/dghl/monitoring/socialcharter/default_EN.asp.

[23] Canada, the Holy See, Japan, Mexico, and the United States.

Europe are required to accede to the European Convention, which in its form as amended by Protocol 11 carries with it recognition both of an individual right of application to the Strasbourg Court and of a wholly judicial system for the protection of human rights.

THE CONTENT OF THE EUROPEAN CONVENTION

Human rights can be defined in terms of generations. This taxonomy was introduced by Karel Vasak, when he was Director of the Human Rights and Peace Division of UNESCO. First generation rights are civil and political rights, while second generation rights are social and cultural rights. The third generation of human rights consists of those rights that concern people collectively and include the right to development, to peace, and to a clean environment. Some commentators[24] now refer to a fourth generation of human rights, but there is no consistency over the content of this latest generational identification of human rights, save that they tend to relate to the impact of scientific and technological developments. Examples are communication and information rights, and rights relating to developments in biotechnology. It is sometimes said that it is the inter-generational character of these rights which constitutes the basis for their status as a generation of rights.[25]

The European Convention on Human Rights guarantees, for the most part, civil and political rights. However, Article 1 of the First Protocol, which protects property rights, and Article 2 of the same Protocol, which guarantees the right to education, are limited exceptions to this principle. Section I of the European Convention spells out, generally in more detailed form, most of the basic civil and political rights contained in the Universal Declaration, while the First, Fourth, Sixth, Seventh, Twelfth, and Thirteenth Protocols guarantee certain additional rights and freedoms. The remaining Protocols amended procedural provisions of the Convention. Finally, Protocol 14 (and also Protocols 15 and 16, once they enter into force) introduce a set of changes to improve the efficiency of the measures of implementation under the Convention.[26] The rights set out in the Convention and Protocols are thus derived essentially from the Universal Declaration. The content of these rights, and the circumstances in which limitations might legitimately be imposed on them, are often made more specific.

However, not every Contracting Party has ratified every provision of every protocol to the Convention. As at 1 September 2013, only 14 of the 47 Contracting Parties have ratified all substantive provisions of the Protocols to the Convention. This indicates that, although the provisions of the Convention and its Protocols may seem to be statements of the most basic human rights, they nevertheless present some issues which are controversial within certain Contracting Parties. For example, the UK has not even signed Protocol 7, which contains rights in relation to migration, the criminal law, and equality between spouses, or Protocol 12 on the general prohibition of discrimination. It has signed but not ratified Protocol 4 which is concerned with the prohibition of imprisonment for debt and with provisions related to migration. In both cases, it is concerns about migration rights which explain the absence of ratification of these protocols.

[24] See, for example, D. Otto, 'Rethinking the "universality" of Human Rights Law' (1997) 29 *Columbia Human Rights Law Review* 1.

[25] Though that is true of rights relating to the environment. Such rights transcend the present generation; what is done now may have a significant impact on future generations.

[26] The Protocols are discussed more fully in Chapters 2, 3, and 25.

THE SYSTEM OF PROTECTION

Protocol 11 to the Convention[27] entered into force on 1 November 1998 and restructured the institutional framework of the Convention. However, an understanding of the system of protection prior to 1 November 1998 remains necessary because decisions made by the Strasbourg organs prior to the change continue to have an effect as authorities on the interpretation and application of the Convention.

THE 'OLD' SYSTEM OF PROTECTION

The Convention created two organs 'to ensure the observance of the engagements undertaken by the High Contracting Parties':[28] the European Commission of Human Rights and the European Court of Human Rights. The main function of these two part-time organs, sometimes collectively referred to as the Strasbourg organs,[29] was to deal with applications made by States and by individuals alleging violations of the Convention. Under former Article 24, any Contracting Party could refer to the Commission any alleged breach of the provisions of the Convention by another Contracting Party. Under former Article 25, the Commission could receive applications from any person, non-governmental organization, or group of individuals claiming to be the victim of a violation by one of the Contracting Parties of the rights set forth in the Convention and any relevant Protocols. Initially, acceptance of the jurisdiction of the Commission to receive individual petitions was optional, but in the 1990s came to be an expected requirement of participation in the Convention system. The procedure differs depending on whether the application is made under Article 24 or 25; what follows describes the process in relation to individual applications under former Article 25.

Once an application was registered, the Commission first considered whether the application met the admissibility requirements, and made a *decision* on this question.[30] If the application was declared inadmissible, that was an end of the matter. If the application was declared admissible, the Commission went on to conduct an investigation into the merits of the complaint and to consider whether there had been a violation of the Convention. The result was a *report* from the Commission expressing an opinion[31] as to whether or not there had been a violation. The report was communicated on a confidential basis to the applicant and to the respondent State concerned and was delivered to the Committee of Ministers, the political organ of the Council of Europe. Throughout this time, attempts would have been made to secure a friendly settlement 'on the basis of respect for human rights'.[32]

Final decisions on cases on which the Commission had reported and which had not resulted in a friendly settlement were made by the Committee of Ministers, or the Court

[27] See N. Rowe and V. Schlette, 'The Protection of Human Rights in Europe after the Eleventh Protocol to the ECHR' (1998) 23 ELRev HR/1; A. Drzemczewski, 'The European Human Rights Convention: Protocol No. 11—Entry into force and first year of application' (2000) 21 HRLJ 1; A. Drzemczewski, 'A major overhaul of the European Human Rights Convention control mechanism: Protocol No. 11' in *Collected Courses of the Academy of European Law*, Vol. VI (Martinus Nijhoff, Florence 1997) at 121; H. Schermers, 'The Eleventh Protocol to the European Convention on Human Rights' (1994) 19 ELRev 367; H. Schermers, 'Adaptation of the 11th Protocol to the European Convention on Human Rights' (1995) 20 ELRev 559; and H. Schermers, 'Election of Judges to the European Court of Human Rights' (1998) 23 ELRev 568.

[28] Former Art. 19 ECHR.

[29] Together with the Committee of Ministers: see later in this chapter.

[30] See later in this chapter.

[31] This is not legally binding.

[32] Former Art. 28 ECHR.

of Human Rights. Recognition of the jurisdiction of the Court was technically voluntary under former Article 46 of the Convention, but a clear expectation had arisen that Contracting Parties would recognize the competence of the Court. Within three months of the transmission of the Commission report to the Committee of Ministers, the application could be referred to the Court by the Commission, the respondent State, or the Contracting Party whose national was alleged to be the victim.[33] The applicant had no standing to refer the application to the Court, unless the respondent State was a party to Protocol 9.[34] Where the respondent State had ratified Protocol 9, the applicant could refer the matter to the Court, but (unless it was also referred to the Court by the Commission or a State) it had first to be submitted to a panel of three judges, who could decide unanimously that the application should not be considered by the Court because it did not raise a serious question affecting the interpretation or application of the Convention.

If the case was referred to the Court and heard by it, there was a full judicial procedure, and even where Protocol 9 had not been ratified, some accommodations were made which allowed participation by the applicant, who could submit written pleadings and oral submissions at a hearing. The Court sat in plenary session or in Chambers of nine.[35] Decisions were made by a majority of the judges present and voting, with the President enjoying a casting vote if necessary. This was the judgment of the Court. Separate concurring or dissenting opinions could be attached to the judgment of the Court.

Those cases which were not referred to the Court within three months of transmission of the Commission's report to the Committee of Ministers were automatically decided by the Committee of Ministers. Latterly, the practice of the Committee of Ministers was to endorse the Commission report without any further investigation of the merits of the case. The use of a political organ was a compromise to ensure that all applications resulted in a final determination. In the early years, there were Contracting Parties which had not recognized the competence of the Court; even in respect of Contracting Parties who had accepted the Court's jurisdiction, a sizeable number of applications, particularly those involving repetitive violations (such as Italian length of proceedings cases), were not referred to the Court.

THE 'NEW' SYSTEM OF PROTECTION

Protocol 11 amended the Convention to make provision for a new wholly judicial system of determination of applications. The Commission and the Court were replaced from 1 November 1998 by a new permanent Court, which handles both the admissibility and merits phases of application. The Court is also charged with seeking to secure friendly settlement of matters before it.[36]

Inter-State complaints are made under Article 33. Since it was set up in 1959, the Court has delivered judgment in only three inter-State cases (with two further cases declared admissible).[37] Such cases have invariably been politically motivated, and have

[33] Former Art. 48 ECHR.

[34] 24 Contracting Parties (not including the United Kingdom) ratified Protocol 9.

[35] Former Art. 43 ECHR. [36] Art. 38(1)(b).

[37] *Ireland v United Kingdom*, (App. 5310/71), 18 January 1978, Series A No 25, (1979–80) 2 EHRR 25; ECHR 2001-IV; *Denmark v Turkey*, (App. 34382/97), 5 April 2000, (2000) 29 EHRR CD35; ECHR 2000-IV (struck out of the list); and *Cyprus v Turkey*, (App. 25781/94), 10 May 2001 [GC]; (2001) 35 EHRR 731; ECHR 2001-IV; *Georgia v Russia* (App. 13255/07), 30 June 2009; *Georgia v Russia (II)* (App. 38263/08), 13 December 2011. A further seventeen inter-State applications were dealt with by the former Commission.

had a highly-charged political content. The case brought by Ireland against the United Kingdom concerned the treatment of suspected terrorists in Northern Ireland.[38] The case brought by Cyprus against Turkey[39] raised questions concerning the Turkish intervention in Cyprus in July 1974. Two further inter-State complaints have been declared admissible. In 2009, an application by Georgia against Russia concerning the alleged harassment of the Georgian immigrant population in Russia was declared admissible by the Court.[40] In 2011, a second inter-State application by Georgia against Russia, complaining about the military intervention in South Ossetia, was also declared admissible.[41]

Individual applications are made to the Court under Article 34 and individuals have full standing before the Court. There has continued to be a filtering process by staff in the Registry of the Court before applications are registered. In the calendar year 2012, 65,150 applications were allocated to a judicial formation, and 18,700 disposed of administratively.[42] Applications which are registered are initially considered by a three-judge Committee which will consider whether the complaint meets the Convention's admissibility criteria,[43] but the Committee can only rule an application to be inadmissible if it is unanimous.[44] Those cases which are not ruled inadmissible by the three-judge Committee are put before a seven-judge Chamber of the Court, which will include the judge sitting in respect of the respondent State. The Chamber will consider the written arguments of the parties, investigate the material facts if these are in contention, and may hear oral argument. This stage of the proceedings concludes with a decision whether the complaint is admissible[45] and whether a friendly settlement is possible.[46] There follows a consideration of the merits. In most cases the admissibility and merits phases are joined for reasons of judicial economy. Certain cases of special difficulty can be relinquished or referred by a Chamber to a Grand Chamber of 17 judges.[47]

The limitations of what Protocol 11 could achieve, coupled with the continuing rise in the caseload and the accession of the countries of central and eastern Europe, led to a further round of reform proposals being started in 2000 in order to secure the long-term effectiveness of the machinery of protection offered by the Convention.[48] The result was Protocol 14 of 13 May 2004 which finally entered into force on 1 June 2010.[49] Entry into force was dependent upon ratification of all Contracting Parties and for some time the continuing failure of the Russian Federation to ratify Protocol 14 was a source of frustration for many.[50]

[38] *Ireland v United Kingdom*, (App. 5310/71), 18 January 1978, Series A No 25, (1979–80) 2 EHRR 25; ECHR 2001-IV.

[39] *Cyprus v Turkey*, (App. 25781/94), 10 May 2001 [GC]; (2001) 35 EHRR 731; ECHR 2001-IV.

[40] *Georgia v Russia (I)*, (App. 13255/07), see Decision of 3 July 2009.

[41] *Georgia v Russia (II)*, (App. 38263/08), see Decision of 13 December 2011.

[42] European Court of Human Rights, *Annual Report 2012* (Strasbourg 2013), 149.

[43] Arts. 27–8 ECHR. For a discussion of the conditions of admissibility, see ch.2.

[44] Art. 28 ECHR.

[45] Note that it is open to the Chamber to conclude that the application is inadmissible by majority decision following the deliberations of the three-judge Committee which was not unanimous.

[46] Arts. 29 and 38, ECHR. [47] Arts. 30–1 and 43 ECHR.

[48] Council of Europe, *Reforming the European Convention on Human Rights. A work in progress* (Council of Europe Publishing, Strasbourg 2009).

[49] Protocol 14 to the Convention for the Protection of Human Rights and Fundamental Freedoms, amending the Control System of the Convention, of 13 May 2004, ETS 194. Russia's ratification in 2010 means that the Protocol has now been ratified by all Contracting Parties.

[50] The interim solution adopted in 2009 was Protocol 14bis, which took the provisions on the use of judicial resources from Protocol 14 and enabled them to be applied on a party by party basis. In relation to applications from those Contracting Parties that ratify Protocol 14bis entered into force on 1 October 2009 and enabled the extended jurisdiction of single judges and three-judge Committees to be used for applications from those States that had ratified this Protocol. Upon entry into force of Protocol 14, however, Protocol 14bis ceased to be in force.

Protocol 14 makes important changes to the system for filtering applications. Article 26 of the Convention is amended to add the use of single-judge formations to the existing formations of the Court. The new single-judge formations have competence to declare inadmissible or to strike out applications. In this work they are to be assisted by rapporteurs. Committees of three judges will be able to go on to consider the merits of applications considered admissible where the interpretation of application of the Convention and its Protocols is well established in the case-law of the Court. This provision is designed to enable repetitive cases to be determined rapidly and efficiently.

The admissibility criteria flow from the terms of Articles 34 and 35:[51]

(1) Can the applicant claim to be a victim of a violation of a Convention right?
(2) Is the respondent State a party to the Convention?
(3) Have domestic remedies been exhausted?
(4) Is the application filed within the six-month time limit?
(5) Is the application signed?
(6) Has the application been brought before?
(7) Is the application compatible with the Convention?
(8) Is the application manifestly ill-founded?
(9) Is there an abuse of the right of petition?

The admissibility criteria did not change with Protocol 11, but Protocol 14 introduces a new admissibility criterion. Article 12 of Protocol 14 amends Article 35(3) of the Convention to read as follows:

> The Court shall declare inadmissible any individual application submitted under Article 34 if it considers that:
>
> (a) the application is incompatible with the provisions of the Convention or the Protocols thereto, manifestly ill-founded, or an abuse of the right of individual application; or
> (b) the applicant has not suffered a significant disadvantage, unless respect for human rights as defined in the Convention and the Protocols thereto requires an examination of the application on the merits and provided that no case may be rejected on this ground which has not been duly considered by a domestic tribunal.

The Explanatory Report stresses that the new provision in Article 35(3)(b) does not restrict the right of individuals to apply to the Court, but it is seen as providing the Court with 'an additional tool which would assist in its filtering work'. There are twin safeguards in the application of this ground of inadmissibility; it cannot be used where an examination of the application on the merits is required; and it cannot be used unless the complaint has already been duly considered by a court or tribunal in the national legal order.[52] For a period of two years following the entry into force of the Protocol (until 1 June 2012), Article 20 reserved to the Court's Chambers and the Grand Chamber the application of the new criterion. This meant that single-judge formations and committees of judges were not be able to rule an application inadmissible on this ground during the initial period after the entry into force of the Protocol when it was expected that the Court's Chambers and Grand Chamber would be providing guidance on the circumstances when it is appropriate to use the new inadmissibility criterion. When in force, Protocol 15 will bring

[51] Formerly Arts. 25 and 26.
[52] All of the admissibility criteria will be discussed in more detail in ch.2.

further changes: removing the second safeguard clause from the 'no significant disadvantage' admissibility criterion in Article 35(3)(b) and reducing the time limit for admissibility from six months to four months.

Many of the over 150,000 cases pending before the European Court of Human Rights are so-called repetitive cases, which derive from a common dysfunction at the national level. The impact of these repetitive cases on the Court's workload was widely regarded as intolerable and thus a 'pilot judgment procedure' was developed as a technique of identifying the structural problems underlying repetitive cases and imposing an obligation on States to address those problems. The High Level Conference meeting on the future of the Court held at Interlaken in February 2010 requested the Court to develop clear and predictable standards for its pilot judgment procedure.[53] As a response, in March 2011 the Court added a new rule (Rule 61) to its Rules of Court clarifying how it handles potential systemic or structural violations of human rights. The new rule codifies the Court's existing 'pilot-judgment procedure', applied in cases where there is a systemic or structural dysfunction in the country concerned which has given or could give rise to similar applications before the Court. Where the Court receives several applications that share a root cause, it can select one or more for priority treatment under the pilot procedure. A key feature of the pilot procedure is the possibility of adjourning related cases for a period of time on the condition that the Government act promptly to adopt the national measures required to satisfy the judgment. The Court can, however, resume examining adjourned cases whenever the interests of justice so require.

The Contracting Parties undertake to abide by the final judgment[54] of the Court in any case to which they are parties.[55] The final judgment is transmitted to the Committee of Ministers whose sole role in the process is now to supervise the execution of judgments.[56]

THE ROLE OF THE SECRETARY-GENERAL OF THE COUNCIL OF EUROPE

The Secretary-General is the senior official of the Council of Europe, elected for a period of five years by the Parliamentary Assembly from a list of candidates drawn up by the Committee of Ministers.[57] The Secretary-General is the depository for ratifications of the Convention[58] with all the duties that entails. Denunciations of the Convention and derogations permitted by the Convention, as well as any declarations required under Convention provisions, are filed with the Secretary-General.

[53] High Level Conference on the Future of the European Court of Human Rights (Interlaken Declaration), 19 February 2010 (available at: http://www.eda.admin.ch/etc/medialib/downloads/edazen/topics/europa/euroc.Par.0133.File.tmp/final_en.pdf). For discussion of the Interlaken Declaration, see A. Mowbray, 'The Interlaken Declaration: the beginning of a new era for the European Court of Human Rights?' (2010) 10 HRLRev 519–528.

[54] A judgment by a Chamber becomes final (1) on expiry of the three-month period or (2) earlier if the parties announce that they have no intention of requesting a referral or (3) following a decision of the panel rejecting a request for referral to the Grand Chamber where an application for a referral is made.

[55] Art. 46(1).

[56] Art. 46(2). There has in recent times been concern over the failure of Contracting States to implement final judgments. See T. Barkhuysen, M. van Emmerik, and P. van Kempen, *The Execution of Strasbourg and Geneva Human Rights Decisions in the National Legal Order* (Martinus Nijhoff, The Hague 1999).

[57] Art. 36 of the Statute of the Council of Europe.

[58] Art. 59 ECHR.

The Secretary-General also has an important monitoring function under Article 52,[59] which provides:

> On receipt of a request from the Secretary-General of the Council of Europe any High Contracting Party shall furnish an explanation of the manner in which its internal law ensures the effective implementation of any of the provisions of this Convention.

Reporting systems are, of course, common measures for securing implementation of human rights obligations.[60] Such procedures are proactive, requiring States to examine the state of their own law rather than reactive, requiring responses to alleged violations of international obligations. This kind of self-assessment or compliance audit can be very valuable if undertaken in the spirit required by the Convention.

Article 52 of the Convention is, however, silent on the circumstances in which the Secretary-General will exercise the powers given under the provision. The Secretary-General has stated that it is a matter entirely within 'his own responsibility and at his own discretion'.[61] Contracting Parties have acquiesced in this interpretation.

General practice to date has been to address requests to all Contracting Parties, but in recent years the Secretary-General has put individual questions to Moldova concerning Transdniestria, and to Russia concerning the situation in Chechnya. In October 1964 Contracting Parties were asked to report generally on how their legal systems guaranteed the rights protected in the Convention and First Protocol; in July 1970 on the implementation of the rights protected by Article 5(5); in April 1975 on the application of Articles 8, 9, 10, and 11; in March 1983 on the implementation of the Convention in respect of children and young persons placed in the care of institutions following a decision of the administrative or judicial authorities; and in July 1988 on the rights protected by Article 6(1) and (3).

The Secretary-General has compiled the responses received from the Contracting Parties and brought these to the notice of the Parliamentary Assembly, and more recently also to the Commission (until its abolition) and the Court.[62] The responses are not subject to any critical scrutiny.[63] The responses of the Contracting Parties are published, though each Contracting Party is consulted to seek its views on whether it would wish the information supplied by it not to be published. The Secretary-General has no standing to

[59] Formerly Art. 57. See generally, P. Mahoney, 'Does Article 57 of the European Convention on Human Rights serve any useful purpose?' in F. Matscher and H. Petzold (eds.), *Protecting Human Rights: The European Dimension. Studies in Honour of Gérard J. Wiarda* (Carl Heymanns Verlag, Köln 1988), at 373–93. See also J. Melander, 'Report on "Responses from the Organs of the European Convention including the Committee of Ministers"' and C. Zanghi, 'Written Communication on "Responsibilities Resulting for the Committee of Ministers and the Secretary General of the Council of Europe for the Implementation of the European Convention on Human Rights"' in Council of Europe, *Proceedings of the Sixth Colloquy about the European Convention on Human Rights, 13–16 November 1985* (Martinus Nijhoff, Dordrecht 1988), at 842–904 (esp. 892–904) and 920–64 (esp. 957–64) respectively. For a summary of activities under Article 52 of the Convention, see the annually produced *Yearbook of the European Convention on Human Rights.*

[60] See, for example, Art. 40 of the International Covenant on Civil and Political Rights; Arts. 16–22 of the International Covenant on Economic, Social and Cultural Rights; Arts. 22–3 of the Constitution of the International Labour Organisation; Arts. 42–3 of the American Convention on Human Rights; and Art. 62 of the African Charter on Human and Peoples' Rights.

[61] Statement of Secretary-General to the Legal Committee of the Consultative Assembly in Oslo on 29 August 1964, Council of Europe, *Collected Texts* (Council of Europe Press, Strasbourg 1987), 235–6.

[62] Council of Europe, *Human Rights Information Sheet No. 21* H/INF(87)1, 95 and *Human Rights Information Sheet No. 23* H/INF(88)2, 59.

[63] Compare the procedure under Art. 40 of the International Covenant on Civil and Political Rights where the Human Rights Committee questions States on their responses. See generally, D. McGoldrick, *The Human Rights Committee* (OUP, Oxford 1991), ch.3.

bring violations which might be evidenced in the responses from the Contracting Parties to the attention of the Court, though it would be open to any Contracting Party to the Convention to make a complaint under Article 33[64] provided that the admissibility conditions were met. In cases of the most serious violations, the matter could be referred to the Committee of Ministers with a view to its exercising its powers of suspension and expulsion under Articles 7 and 8 of the Statute of the Council of Europe.

A good example of a more recent initiative has been the inquiry into alleged secret detentions in the Contracting Parties of so-called 'high-value detainees' held by the United States. In November 2005, the Secretary-General, acting under Article 52, sent a questionnaire to all 46 Contracting Parties. The Article 52 inquiry was launched against the background of reports alleging involvement by Contracting Parties in unlawful deprivation of liberty of terrorist suspects and their transport in or through their territory by or at the instigation of foreign agencies; this has come to be known as 'secret detention', and 'extraordinary rendition'. In March 2006, the Secretary-General released his report based on the responses of 36 countries to the questionnaire, which was critical of the incomplete response of some Contracting Parties to the question enquiring whether any public officials had been involved in the unacknowledged deprivation of liberty of any individual, or transport of any individual while so deprived of their liberty. This prompted action within the Committee on Legal Affairs and Human Rights, and a detailed report was prepared for their consideration and presented in turn to the Parliamentary Assembly. The outcome, after further enquiries, was a recommendation of the Parliamentary Assembly declaring that it had established with a high degree of probability that secret detention centres operated by the Central Intelligence Agency of the United States had existed for some years in Poland and Romania. The recommendation also called on Contracting Parties to look into the need for democratic oversight of military intelligence services and foreign intelligence services operating on their territory.[65]

The role of the Secretary-General now overlaps to some extent with that of the Commissioner for Human Rights.

THE COMMISSIONER FOR HUMAN RIGHTS

The Commissioner for Human Rights is an office established by resolution of the Committee of Ministers.[66] The Commissioner[67] is elected by the Parliamentary Assembly and is charged with promoting education in, and awareness of, human rights in the territories of the Contracting Parties. Additionally the Commissioner helps to promote the effective observance and full enjoyment of human rights as embodied in a variety of Council of Europe instruments, as well as identifying possible shortcomings in the law and practice of the Contracting Parties in relation to the protection of human rights. But the Commissioner may not take up any individual complaints. Particular activities to date have included studies of the human rights situation in Georgia, in Chechnya, and in Kosovo. A substantial annual report is submitted to the Committee of Ministers and to

[64] Formerly Art. 24.

[65] Recommendation 1801 (2007); Text adopted by the Assembly on 27 June 2007 (23rd Sitting). For more detail see www.coe.int/T/E/Com/Files/Events/2006-cia/.

[66] Resolution (99) 50 of 7 May 1999, adopted by the Committee of Ministers at its 104th session.

[67] Currently Nils Muižnieks, a Latvian national, elected in 2012.

the Parliamentary Assembly. The Commissioner may also issue recommendations, opinions,[68] and reports on any matters within his competence.[69]

The Commissioner also makes both contact visits and assessment visits to countries who are members of the Council of Europe. Contact visits aim at strengthening the relationships with the authorities and looking into one or several specific issues, while the main goal of assessment visits is to give a comprehensive review of the effectiveness of human rights protection. By 2008, the full cycle of assessment visits was completed with all forty-seven Member States having been visited for the purpose of a comprehensive human rights appraisal. The Commissioner now focuses on more targeted country visits. Each visit is completed by the publication of a report, some of which are made public on the Commissioner's website.

OTHER HUMAN RIGHTS INSTRUMENTS OF THE COUNCIL OF EUROPE

Mention has already been made of the European Social Charter as the Council of Europe instrument which addresses economic, social, and cultural rights. However, there are now over 200 Council of Europe treaties, many of which address human rights issues[70]—the following are of particular significance:

- the European Agreement relating to persons participating in proceedings of the European Commission and Court of Human Rights of 6 May 1969;[71]
- the European Agreement relating to persons participating in proceedings of the European Court of Human Rights of 5 March 1996;[72]
- the European Convention for the Prevention of Torture and Inhuman and Degrading Treatment of 26 November 1987 and its two Protocols;[73]
- the European Charter for Regional or Minority Languages of 5 November 1992;[74]
- the Framework Convention for the Protection of National Minorities of 1 February 1995;[75]
- the Convention on Action against Trafficking in Human Beings;[76] and
- the Convention on the Protection of Children against Sexual Exploitation and Sexual Abuse.[77]

[68] See, for example, Opinion 1/2002 on certain aspects of the United Kingdom 2001 derogation from Article 5 paragraph 1 of the European Convention on Human Rights, 28 August 2002, Comm DH(2002)8 requested by the United Kingdom's Parliamentary Joint Committee on Human Rights.

[69] See generally www.coe.int/t/commissioner/About/welcome_en.asp. The previous Commissioner, Thomas Hammarberg published a series of viewpoints on current issues. Some of these are available in a compilation: T. Hammarberg, *Human Rights in Europe: no ground for complacency* (Council of Europe Press, Strasbourg 2008), and provide an interesting overview of some pressure points in relation to human rights protection in Europe.

[70] For a full list, see www.conventions.coe.int. [71] ETS 67.

[72] ETS 161. [73] ETS 126, ETS 151, and ETS 152. [74] ETS 148.

[75] ETS 157. See also Council of Europe, *Framework Convention for the Protection of National Minorities. Collected Texts* (Council of Europe Press, Strasbourg 2005).

[76] ETS 197. [77] ETS 201.

Though this work is concerned with the European Convention on Human Rights, the contribution of the Council of Europe to the protection of human rights goes far beyond this Convention. Conventions such as the European Convention for the Prevention of Torture are having a significant impact on the work of the Court in dealing with cases involving allegations of violations of Article 3 prohibiting torture, inhuman, and degrading treatment.[78]

RELATIONSHIP WITH OTHER INTERNATIONAL COURTS AND TRIBUNALS

A recent phenomenon has been the referral of the same issue to more than one process of international adjudication. There is a dispersal of responsibility for interpreting international human rights law among different judicial and quasi-judicial bodies. In addition to the International Court of Justice, there are the three major regional systems for the protection of human rights—in Africa, the Americas, and Europe—as well as the bodies responsible for the monitoring and implementation of the provisions of international human right instruments covering both general and particular aspects of human rights. Finally, there are the ad hoc bodies set up to address such matters as mass atrocities in the former Yugoslavia and in Rwanda.

Multiple referrals can happen in relation to the circumstances involved in individual applications, but can be most striking in relation to inter-State cases. The most dramatic contemporary example is the dispute between Georgia and the Russian Federation concerning South Ossetia, which is the subject of two inter-State applications filed with the Strasbourg Court. Contemporaneously Georgia instituted proceedings before the International Court of Justice alleging violations of the Convention on the Elimination of all Forms of Racial Discrimination (CERD). However, in a judgment of 1 April 2011 the International Court of Justice held that it did not have jurisdiction to entertain the application lodged with it by Georgia due to a failure to meet two procedural preconditions provided for in Article 22 of CERD. The Strasbourg Court has declared Georgia's application admissible under the ECHR.[79] In doing so it noted that the admissibility requirement in Article 35(2) that the application has not already been submitted to another procedure of international investigation and settlement applies only to individual applications.[80] The possibility remains, therefore, for a State to lodge multiple applications under different schemes. The risk involved in referral to more than one system of consideration is that of a divergent approach to the same issues.[81] The Strasbourg Court has always stated that interpretation of the Convention must take account of relevant rules of international law.[82] But it has also referred to the special character of the Convention as an instrument of international human rights protection.[83] This can lead to perceived or real divergences of approach to central questions of international law. At a broad level of generality, it can certainly be said that the International Court of Justice and the Strasbourg Court take

[78] See ch.9. [79] *Georgia v Russia (II)* (App. 38263/08), Decision of 13 December 2011.

[80] § 79.

[81] See generally R. Higgins, 'The International Court of Justice and the European Court of Human Rights: Partners for the Protection of Human Rights', Speech at the ceremony marking the fiftieth anniversary of the Strasbourg Court, 30 January 2009, available on the Court's website.

[82] *Loizidou v Turkey*, (App. 15318/89), 18 December 1996, (1996) 23 EHRR 513, ECHR 1996-VI, § 43.

[83] *Cyprus v Turkey*, (App. 25781/94), 10 May 2001, (2001) 35 EHRR 731; ECHR 2001-IV, [GC], § 78.

account of each other's case-law in determining such questions, but nevertheless, the risk of diverging interpretations remains.

A subset of Contracting Parties to the European Convention constitute the European Union (previously known as Community), which is increasingly seeing itself as a human rights organization. This calls for consideration of the relationship between the two organizations and their courts.[84]

The Convention is not formally binding on the Union, but its provisions can and must be given effect as general principles of Union law. The early steps towards the development of the protection of fundamental rights as general principles of Union law can be seen in the case-law of the Luxembourg Court.[85] This approach was endorsed by the political institutions in their Joint Declaration of 5 April 1977 which stressed the importance they attached to the protection of fundamental rights as derived from the constitutions of the Member States and from the European Convention, and confirmed the respect of all the institutions for such rights. This was followed by the inclusion in the Preamble to the Single European Act of 17 February 1986 of a reference to the European Convention. The Treaty on European Union, which entered into force on 1 November 1993, incorporated reference to the European Convention in Article F.2, which reads:

> The Union shall respect fundamental rights, as guaranteed by the European Convention for the Protection of Human Rights and Fundamental Freedoms signed in Rome on 4 November 1950 and as they result from the constitutional traditions common to the Member States, as general principles of Community [now known as Union] law.

It is now the position, therefore, that the Luxembourg Court will review measures of the institutions for their compatibility with fundamental rights protected by the European Convention. It has also not ignored the question of the extent to which the conduct of Member States may be subject to review for compatibility with human rights standards when they are acting within the field of Union law. In such cases, the conduct of Member States can be called to account by the Luxembourg Court where they are directly implementing Union provisions.[86] Where the Member States are implementing Union law, the review may go further. So in the *ERT* case,[87] which concerned a Greek television monopoly, the Court took the view that any derogation by a Member State from the freedom to provide services under the EEC Treaty had to be compatible with the freedom of expression recognized under the European Convention on Human Rights. This formulation suggests that in any regulation by Member States of matters falling within the scope of Union, measures taken by Member States must as a matter of *Union law* comply with the Convention.

The Strasbourg Court has ruled that action by a Member State of the EU in implementation of obligations under Union law is capable of giving rise to a violation by that State of provisions of the Convention.[88] In the *Bosphorus Airways* case,[89] the Grand Chamber

[84] The future of this relationship will be considered further in ch.25.

[85] In such cases as Case 29/69, *Stauder v Ulm*, [1969] ECR 419; Case 11/70, *Internationale Handelsgesell-schaft*, [1970] ECR 1125; Case 4/73, *Nold v Commission*, [1974] ECR 491; Case 36/75, *Rutili*, [1975] ECR 1219; and Case 44/79, *Hauer*, [1979] ECR 3727.

[86] See Case C-5/88, *Wachauf*, [1989] ECR 2609, and cf. Case C-2/92, *Bostock*, [1994] ECR I-955.

[87] Case C-260/89, *ERT*, [1991] ECR I-2925. See also Opinion of Advocate General Jacobs in Case C-168/91, *Konstantinidis v Altensteig-Standesamt*, [1993] ECR I-2755.

[88] *Dangeville SA v France*, (App. 36677/97), 16 April 2002, (2004) 38 EHRR 699.

[89] *'Bosphorus Airways' v Ireland*, (App. 45036/98), 30 June 2005 [GC], (2006) 42 EHRR 1, ECHR 2005-VI; for a penetrating commentary, see C. Costello, 'The *Bosphorus* ruling of the European Court of Human Rights: fundamental rights and blurred boundaries in Europe' (2006) 6 HRLRev 87. See also *Cooperatieve*

was called upon to consider the relationship between the protection of human rights in the EU and such protection under the European Convention. The context was the seizure in Ireland of an aircraft in compliance with the EC Regulation imposing sanctions against Serbia and Montenegro. The Grand Chamber concluded that the Member States of the EU remain individually responsible for compliance with Convention rights where competence has passed to the EU, but the Strasbourg Court would only interfere where the protection afforded by the Union was not equivalent to that provided under the Convention. Equivalence was regarded as comparability rather than congruence. There was a presumption that protection within the Union was equivalent to that under the Convention, and the Strasbourg Court would only interfere if it considered that the protection within the Union was 'manifestly deficient'.[90] The Grand Chamber found that the systems for the protection of human rights under Union law were equivalent to those offered under the European Convention. Hence the presumption of compliance applied, and it had not been rebutted in the case before the Court.

Inevitably the question arose whether the EU should accede to the European Convention. The Council of the European Union asked the Luxembourg Court, in accordance with the procedure in Article 228 of the EC Treaty,[91] for an Opinion on certain questions in connection with the proposed accession.[92] The Luxembourg Court ruled that 'as Community law now stands, the Community has no competence to accede to the European Convention.' The only possible basis for competence was Article 235 (now 308) of the EC Treaty.[93] Accession would, in the Court's view, require the integration of two separate systems for the protection of human rights. Such changes 'would be of constitutional significance and would therefore be such as to go beyond the scope of Article 235' and could only be brought about by way of amendments to the EC Treaty. The Opinion is very clever; it is argued that the response is legally correct in the context of the timing and the question asked. It serves to preserve in full the power of protection of fundamental rights by way of the application of the general principles of law. Few reading the Opinion can be left in any doubt about the complexities of integrating the EU system and the Strasbourg system.[94]

Provision is now made in the Treaty of Lisbon on the EU side, and in Protocol 14 on the Council of Europe side for the Union to accede to the European Convention.[95] Accession is now required under Article 6 of the Lisbon Treaty and foreseen by Article 59 of the ECHR as amended by Protocol 14. Official talks on the European Union's accession to the European Convention of Human Rights (ECHR) started on 7 July 2010. In April 2013, after lengthy negotiations, the draft accession agreement of the EU to

Producentorganisatie van de Nederlandse Kokkelvisserij UA v The Netherlands, (App. 13546/05), Decision of 5 February 2009.

[90] §§ 154–5.

[91] Now Art. 300 of the EC Treaty.

[92] Opinion 2/94 on accession by the Community to the European Convention on Human Rights, [1996] ECR I-1759.

[93] This provides: 'If action by the Community should prove necessary to attain, in the course of the operation of the common market, one of the objectives of the Community and this Treaty has not provided the necessary powers, the Council shall, acting unanimously on a proposal from the Commission and after consulting the European Parliament, take the appropriate measures.'

[94] See also Study of the Technical and Legal Issues of a Possible EC/EU Accession to the European Convention on Human Rights. Report adopted by the Steering Committee for Human Rights (CDDH) at its 53rd meeting 25–28 June 2002, DG-II(2002)006 (CDDH(2002)010 Addendum 2).

[95] Article I-9(2) of the Treaty of Lisbon, and Article 17 of Protocol 14. The Treaty of Lisbon entered into force on 1 December 2009. On whether accession is really necessary, see R. White, 'The Strasbourg Perspective and

the European Convention on Human rights was finalized. The EU Court of Justice in Luxembourg will now be asked to give its opinion on the text.

The Treaty of Lisbon also gives legal status to the European Union's Charter of Fundamental Rights of the European Union. This Charter was adopted by solemn proclamation on 7 December 2000[96] at the Nice Council. There remain intriguing questions about its impact on the protection of fundamental rights within the EU. It is divided into six sections[97] and includes rights for citizens of the EU as well as certain rights which are to be applicable to all within the jurisdiction of the Member States. The rights are said to be based on the rights guaranteed by the European Convention, but in some cases there are significant differences of wording.[98] Its scope is considerably wider than the rights protected in the European Convention. The evolving relationship between the two European systems for human rights protection is a fascinating one that is far from settled.

CONCLUDING REMARKS

The subject of this book brings together a number of threads which, however precariously, have brought developments in the ordering of international society that can only be described as spectacular if compared with the situation in 1945. One of these threads is European integration on a level to serve not only technical needs and economic interests, but also to embody a system of liberal values which crystallize centuries of political development. The second is a continuing concern for the protection of human rights. The international protection of human rights has of course many other dimensions, but it has, arguably, been most fully and systematically developed under the law of the European Convention on Human Rights. European integration, also, has many other facets, but both the construction of the EU, and cooperation in various fields among the States of western Europe, have been progressively based on a set of ideas and values of which the system described here is the most complete expression.[99] The third is the spread of

its Effect on the Court of Justice: Is Mutual Respect Enough?', in A. Arnull and others, *Continuity and Change in EU Law. Essays in Honour of Sir Francis Jacobs* (OUP, Oxford 2008), 130.

[96] Referred to in this chapter as 'the EU Charter'. See, generally, S. Peers and A. Ward, *The EU Charter of Fundamental Rights. Politics, Law and Policy* (Hart, Oxford 2004); N. Isiksel, 'Fundamental Rights in the EU after *Kadi* and *Al Barakaat*' (2010) 16 ELJ 551; R.C.A. White, 'A New Era for Human Rights in the European Union?' (2011) 30 *Yearbook of European Law* 100; K. Lenaerts, 'Exploring the Limits of the EU Charter of Fundamental Rights' (2012) ECL Rev 375; S. Peers et al, *The EU Charter of Fundamental Rights: A Commentary* (Hart, Oxford 2014, forthcoming). On the drafting of the Charter, see G. de Búrca, 'The drafting of the European Union Charter of Fundamental Rights' (2001) 26 ELRev 126. See also speech by P-H. Imbert, Director General of Human Rights of the Council of Europe at the Judge's [sic] Symposium on the relationship between the European Convention on Human Rights and the Charter of Fundamental Rights of the European Union, 16 September 2002: available at www.coe.int.

[97] Dignity, freedoms, equality, solidarity, citizens' rights, and justice.

[98] For example, Art. 9 of the EU Charter provides, 'The right to marry and the right to found a family shall be guaranteed in accordance with the national laws governing the exercise of these rights.' This could be interpreted as decoupling the right to marry and the right to found a family which are coupled in Art. 12 of the Convention. Elsewhere there is a more sweeping approach to limitations which may be applied to certain rights.

[99] See A. Clapham, *Human Rights and the European Community: A Critical Overview* (Nomos, Baden Baden 1991); A. Casese, A. Clapham, and J. Weiler (eds.), *Human Rights and the European Community: Methods of Protection* (Nomos, Baden Baden 1991); and A. Casese, A. Clapham, and J. Weiler (eds.), *Human Rights and the European Community: The Substantive Law* (Nomos, Baden Baden 1991); P. Alston, *The EU and Human Rights* (OUP, Oxford 1999); and A. Williams, *EU Human Rights Policies. A Study in Irony* (OUP, Oxford 2004).

democracy to the countries of central and eastern Europe and their embracing of the system of protection of human rights embodied in the European Convention on Human Rights, which has become a truly pan-European system offering a judicial approach to the protection of the fundamental rights and freedoms listed in the Convention and its Protocols.

2

PROCEEDINGS BEFORE THE COURT

INTRODUCTION

This chapter explains proceedings before the Strasbourg Court, including the application of the admissibility criteria, which results in over nine in every ten applications being rejected as inadmissible.[1]

On 1 November 1998 Protocol 11 to the European Convention came into effect, establishing a new permanent European Court of Human Rights. It has the largest territorial jurisdiction of any permanent court in the world, given that the combined population of the 47 Contracting Parties is over 800 million people; in addition, of course, non-nationals and non-residents can bring cases under the Convention concerning matters within a Contracting State's jurisdiction.[2]

The Strasbourg Court's principal role is to pronounce on applications, brought both by individuals and States, under the European Convention on Human Rights. Its judgments are legally binding on respondent States and are declaratory in nature: that is, the Court can announce that the facts of the application disclose a violation of one or more Articles of the Convention, and, under Article 41 of the Convention, it can award monetary compensation to an individual victim of any such violation.

The Court's caseload is huge. In the calendar year 2012, 65,150 new applications were lodged; there were 1,678 judgments of the Court, including 6 judgments of a Grand Chamber. 87,879 admissibility decisions were made. Yet, as at 1 July 2013, the number of applications awaiting a determination stood at 113,350. The Court is faced with the difficult task of striking a balance between efficiency and speed in dealing with so many applications, while administering justice in each individual case and maintaining the quality of its judgments. Attempts to address some of these problems were made with the entry into force of Protocol 14 in 2010. Further discussions have led to several declarations on the future of the Court system and further reform, which will be discussed at the end of the chapter.

COMPOSITION AND GENERAL PROCEDURE

JUDGES

The Strasbourg Court consists of a number of judges equal to the number of Contracting Parties to the Convention.[3] The judges are elected by the Parliamentary Assembly from a

[1] A flow chart showing how cases are processed in the Strasbourg Court is included as an appendix to this chapter.

[2] See ch.5.

[3] Art. 20 ECHR. For an up-to-date list of judges, see www.echr.coe.int.

list of three candidates nominated by each State.[4] They are required to be of high moral character and must either possess the qualifications required for appointment to high judicial office or be 'jurisconsults' of recognized competence.[5] Before electing a judge, the Parliamentary Assembly appoints delegates to interview the candidates, examine their résumés and report back to the Assembly. The judges are normally, but not necessarily, nationals of the Contracting Party in respect of which they are elected. They are, of course, independent. The judges are currently elected for a non-renewable period of nine years.[6]

Attempts have been made to secure an appropriate gender balance among the judges of the Strasbourg Court. This became contentious in the context of the nominations of persons for consideration as successor to Judge Bonello as judge in respect of Malta, and resulted in an Advisory Opinion of the Court.[7] The Parliamentary Assembly had passed two resolutions seeking to secure better gender balance in the Court by requiring the nomination of at least one candidate of each sex. All the candidates proposed by the Maltese Government were men. Correspondence ensued between the representative of the Parliamentary Assembly and the Maltese Government. The Maltese Government argued that it had done its utmost to find a suitably qualified female candidate, but had failed to do so, and believed that its actions in nominating three men were in compliance with Article 21 of the Convention. The matter could not be resolved. At the request of the Maltese authorities, the Committee of Ministers requested an advisory opinion asking whether 'a list of candidates for the post of judge at the European Court of Human Rights, which satisfies the criteria listed in Article 21 of the Convention' could be refused 'solely on the basis of gender-related issues'. A second question asked whether the two resolutions of the Parliamentary Assembly were compatible with Article 22 of the Convention.[8] While stressing the importance of equality between the sexes in contemporary society, the Court noted that there had been no move to amend the Convention provisions on eligibility to serve as a judge of the Strasbourg Court, and concluded that, where a Contracting Party shows that it has used all due care in seeking to nominate at least one candidate of each sex, it is not open to the Parliamentary Assembly to reject a Contracting Party's lists on the sole ground that no woman candidate is listed.

COMMITTEES, SECTIONS, CHAMBERS, AND GRAND CHAMBERS

Under Article 27, as amended by Protocol 14 of the Convention, the Court may sit in a single judge formation, Committees of three judges, Chambers of seven judges, or in a Grand Chamber of seventeen judges.

The single judge formations are competent only to declare applications inadmissible or strike them off the Court's list of cases,[9] and thus deal only with clearly inadmissible cases

[4] Art. 22 ECHR.

[5] Art. 21(1) ECHR, which is based on Art. 2 of the Statute of the International Court of Justice.

[6] Art. 23 ECHR (as amended by P14, Art 2). Protocol 14 amended the previous term of office, which was a renewable six year period. The retirement age is seventy years old. This will be further amended by Protocol 15, see later in this chapter.

[7] *Advisory Opinion on certain legal questions concerning the lists of candidates submitted with a view to the election of judges to the European Court of Human Rights*, 12 February 2008 [GC], (2009) 49 EHRR 29; see A. Mowbray, 'The Consideration of Gender in the Process of Appointing Judges to the European Court of Human Rights', (2008) 8 HRL Rev 549. For further detail on the Court's jurisdiction to give advisory opinions, see later in this chapter.

[8] In the event, the Court did not find it necessary to provide an answer to this second question.

[9] Art. 28 ECHR.

in the procedure outlined later. The three judge Committees may examine admissibility and the merits of repetitive cases.[10]

The Court is divided into five Sections.[11] The composition of the Sections seeks to achieve geographic and gender balance and to reflect the different legal systems among the Contracting Parties. Within these Sections, the seven-judge Chambers examine the admissibility and merits both of individual applications, which are not prima facie inadmissible, and of inter-State cases.

Under Article 30 of the Convention, where a case pending before a Chamber raises a serious question affecting the interpretation of the Convention or Protocols, or where it appears that the Chamber is likely to reach a decision which would be inconsistent with earlier case-law, the Chamber may relinquish jurisdiction to the Grand Chamber unless one of the parties to the case objects. This proviso, requiring the consent of the parties to relinquishment, places considerable power in the hands of the applicant or respondent State to interfere with the working of the Court. Its force has been slightly mitigated by Rule 72(2), which states that the Registrar shall notify the parties of the Chamber's intention to relinquish jurisdiction, and sets a time limit of one month for objections, which must be 'duly reasoned'. An objection which does not meet these criteria will be considered invalid by the Chamber. The need for consent will be removed by Protocol 15 when it comes into force.[12] This is intended to accelerate the proceedings and enhance consistency in case-law.[13] This modification will reduce applicant and State interference in the referrals. This change should be considered alongside an amendment to the Rules of Court which states the Chamber *shall* refer an application to the Grand Chamber that might have a result inconsistent with the Court's case-law.[14]

The Grand Chamber's other principal role is provided for by Article 43 of the Convention, which allows a party to a case to request that it be referred to the Grand Chamber after the Chamber has given judgment. The request must be submitted within three months of the date of judgment, and a panel of five judges of the Grand Chamber decides whether or not it should be accepted. Article 43(2) states that the panel 'shall accept the request if the case raises a serious question affecting the interpretation or application of the Convention or the protocols thereto, or a serious issue of general importance', but the panel's deliberations are secret and, to date, there has been little guidance as to the type of issues which it considers 'serious'. In 2012, the panel considered requests concerning a total of 185 cases, and accepted referral requests in seven cases.[15]

The judge elected in respect of the respondent State automatically sits as a member of the Chamber or Grand Chamber,[16] and is often referred to as the 'national judge'. It is arguable that greater independence would be achieved by excluding the national judge,[17] but

[10] If admissible, a judgment is given in repetitive cases where the underlying question concerning the interpretation or the application of the Convention or the Protocols, is already the subject of well-established case-law of the Court (Art. 28(1)(b)).

[11] Up-to-date information on the composition of the Court and its Sections can be found at www.echr.coe.int. In 2011, a new filtering section was added. See later in this chapter for more detail.

[12] Protocol 15, Art. 3; see later in this chapter.

[13] Protocol 15 to the Convention for the Protection of Human Rights and Fundamental Freedoms, amending the Control System of the Convention, Explanatory Report §§ 16–20.

[14] Rule 72 (amended 6 February 2013).

[15] European Court of Human Rights, *Annual Report 2012* (Strasbourg 2013), 57.

[16] Art. 27(2).

[17] However, evidence suggests national judges do not tend to dissent. Research has found that a national judge is only rarely the only one to dissent; nor did there appear to be alliances which resulted in the national judge plus one or more others dissenting. See R. White and I. Boussiakou 'Separate opinions in the European Court of Human Rights' (2009) 9 *Human Rights Law Review* 37–60.

the inclusion of the judge in respect of the respondent State has the advantage of ensuring acquaintance with the national legal order of that State.

PRESIDENCY

The Court has a President and two Vice-Presidents, and each Section has a President, elected by the plenary Court for three years. The President of the Strasbourg Court, at present the Luxembourg judge Dean Spielmann, directs the work and administration of the Court and represents it. He sits in the Grand Chamber, but does not take part in the consideration of cases being heard by Chambers except where he is the national judge.[18]

PUBLIC NATURE OF PROCEEDINGS

The judges deliberate in private and details of their deliberations are secret.[19] Apart from that important exception, however, proceedings before the Court are generally public in character, with hearings held in open court.[20] All documents, with the exception of those deposited within the framework of friendly-settlement negotiations, are accessible to the public. In exceptional cases, however, the Rules of Court allow for confidentiality of hearings and documents.[21]

REGISTRY

Article 24 of the Convention states that 'The Court shall have a registry.' It consists of approximately 640 lawyers, translators, and administrative and clerical employees from the Contracting Parties, recruited by the Secretary-General of the Council of Europe.[22] The Registrar and Deputy Registrar are elected by the Court.[23] Because of the Court's heavy caseload, the registry has an important role in case management. Its main functions are to conduct correspondence with applicants and Contracting Parties, to prepare cases for examination, to advise the Court on questions of national law and the law of the Convention, and to assist in the drafting of judgments and decisions. The practice has been for an application to be assigned, as it comes in, to a lawyer in the registry, who will prepare the case for the judge chosen as rapporteur,[24] and attend sessions of the Chamber whenever the case is being examined. With the introduction of single judge formations under Protocol 14, a non-judicial rapporteur is appointed to assist the judge.[25] In a large measure the standard of the Court's work, and its effectiveness, depend on the quality of its registry.

PROCEDURE PRIOR TO THE DECISION ON ADMISSIBILITY

INTRODUCTION OF AN APPLICATION

The Court's procedure is primarily a written one. Most applications originate in a letter to the Registrar setting out the complaint.[26] At this stage the case is given a file number and

[18] Rule 9 of the Rules of Court, which are available on the Court's website: www.echr.coe.int/echr/.
[19] Rule 22. [20] Rules 33 and 63. [21] Rule 63. [22] Rule 18(3).
[23] Rules 15 and 16. [24] Discussed in more detail later in this chapter. [25] Rule 18A.
[26] For an account of taking a case to the Court from an applicant's perspective, see P. Leach, *Taking a Case to the European Court of Human Rights* (OUP, Oxford 2005). See also K. Reid, *A Practitioner's Guide to the*

allocated to a lawyer in the registry from the State against which the complaint is made. Applicants may be represented by lawyers, but they have the option of acting in person until the case is communicated to the respondent State.[27] The Court's procedure in the early stages is designed to facilitate the position of litigants in person as far as possible. Thus, although the Court has only two official languages,[28] applicants may correspond with the Court in the State's official language before notice of the application has been given to the respondent State.[29]

Upon receipt of an introductory letter the registry lawyer will write to the applicant asking for further information and copies of documents and national judgments relevant to the application, and will send him or her an application form.[30] The form must be completed with details such as the applicant's name, age, occupation, and address and that of any representative, the name of the respondent State, the subject matter of the claim, as far as possible the provision of the Convention alleged to have been violated, and a statement of the facts and arguments on which the applicant relies.[31] The Court is now being much more stringent in its application of Rule 47. A failure to comply with Rule 47 will lead to rejection of the application and the applicant will be informed that she must submit a form that is compliant with Rule 47 within eight weeks of the request for a complaint form.[32] From 1 January 2014, the Court will apply Rule 47 so that only an application form properly completed to include all the information required by Rule 47 will interrupt the running of the six months' time limit. The legal role of the 'introductory letter' will no longer exist. Later in 2014 the Court will make available on its website electronic application forms, to assist applicants to comply with the rule.[33]

When the material submitted by the applicant is on its own sufficient to show that the application is inadmissible or should be struck off the Court's list of cases, a single judge formation will examine the file and decide whether or not to declare it inadmissible. Where the application does not appear to be clearly inadmissible, a judge rapporteur will be appointed to conduct an initial examination and to direct the future procedure.[34] In 2009, the Court introduced a priority policy for applications so that very serious allegations of human rights violations would be processed and adjudicated on more quickly.[35] A number of categories were established with priority given to urgent applications (where there is a particularly high risk to the applicant), with the least important being applications that are manifestly inadmissible. A working party has been established to keep the policy under review.

Following the Inter-governmental Conference on Court Reform at Interlaken in 2010,[36] the Court established a Filtering Section. The Section's remit is to examine all applications from the States producing the highest amount of applications.[37] This is to ensure that the

European Convention of Human Rights (3rd edn Sweet & Maxwell, London 2008). A pilot project allowing online applications through the Court's internet site was launched in February 2009 for applicants using the Swedish or Dutch application forms.

[27] Rule 36. [28] English and French: Rule 34(1).

[29] Rule 34. [30] Available online: www.echr.coe.int. [31] Rule 47.

[32] A failure to comply within eight weeks will impact on the six month time limit that an applicant has to apply to the Court, (see admissibility criteria later) see Practice Direction of the Court on the Institution of Proceedings (available at www.echr.coe.int/Documents/PD_institution_proceedings_ENG.pdf).

[33] At present, the Court is providing electronic application forms on a trial basis in Swedish and Dutch.

[34] Rule 49. [35] Rule 41 (as amended).

[36] Council of Europe Conference on the Future of the European Court of Human Rights: Interlaken Declaration, February 2010.

[37] When the filtering section was established the five States with the highest numbers of applications were Russia, Turkey, Romania, Ukraine, and Poland. By the end of 2012, the five States with the highest number of applications were Russia, Turkey, Italy, Ukraine, and Serbia.

proper procedural track is used in accordance with the priority policy. The filtering mechanism seems to have led to the speeding up of the processing of these cases.[38]

LEGAL AID

There are no fees or charges for applications to the Court and its expenses are met, under Article 50 of the Convention, by the Council of Europe. The Court may grant an applicant free legal aid at any stage of the proceedings after the respondent State's observations on admissibility have been received, or the time limit for their submission has expired.[39] Applicants must submit a certified declaration of means, showing that they have insufficient means to meet their costs, and this is sent to the respondent State for comment. Legal aid may be granted to cover lawyers' fees, on a scale fixed by the Registrar, and also other necessary expenses.

INTERIM MEASURES AND THE RIGHT TO COMMUNICATE WITH THE COURT

The Strasbourg Court has no express power under the Convention to order interim or interlocutory measures to safeguard the position of the parties pending a final decision. However, in urgent cases, where there is 'an imminent risk of irreparable damage',[40] the Court may 'at the request of a party or of any other person concerned, or of its own motion, indicate to the parties any interim measure which it considers should be adopted in the interests of the parties or of the proper conduct of the proceedings before it'.[41] This power is most frequently used in deportation cases, where there is a possibility of immediate expulsion to a country where the applicant is likely to be tortured or killed,[42] but it has also been used, for example, to safeguard embryos created by *in vitro* fertilization that would otherwise have to be destroyed in accordance with domestic law.[43] In another case, the Court directed that an applicant detained in hospital as a person with a mental illness be seen by a lawyer.[44]

Initially the Court took the view that, in the absence of any relevant power contained in the Convention, such an indication gave rise to no binding obligation on the part of the State.[45] However, in the *Mamatkulov* case[46] the Grand Chamber overruled the earlier cases and, after making a survey of comparable human rights instruments, concluded that:

> by virtue of Article 34 of the Convention Contracting States undertake to refrain from any act or omission that may hinder the effective exercise of an individual applicant's right of application. A failure by a Contracting State to comply with interim measures is to be regarded as preventing the Court from effectively examining the applicant's complaint

[38] By the end of June 2011, there had been a 42 per cent increase in the number of applications from the five States being dealt with by a single judge compared to 2010.

[39] Rules 91–6.

[40] See *Mamatkulov and Askarov v Turkey*, (Apps. 46827/99 and 46951/99), 4 February 2005 [GC], (2005) 41 EHRR 494, ECHR 2005-I, § 104.

[41] Rule 39(1). In 2012, 1,973 requests were made, of which 103 were allowed: *Analysis of Statistics*, European Court of Human Rights, 2013, 5.

[42] See the examples set out in *Mamatkulov and Askarov v Turkey*, (Apps. 46827/99 and 46951/99), 4 February 2005 [GC], (2005) 41 EHRR 494, ECHR 2005-I, §§ 104–7.

[43] *Evans v United Kingdom*, (App. 6339/05), 10 April 2007 [GC], (2008) 46 EHRR 728, ECHR 2007-IV.

[44] *Shtukaturov v Russia*, (App. 44009/05), 27 March 2008, §§ 31–40.

[45] For example, *Cruz Varas v Sweden*, (App. 15576/89), 20 March 1991, Series A No 201, (1992) 14 EHRR 1; and *Čonka and others v Belgium*, (App. 51564/99), Decision of 13 March 2001.

[46] *Mamatkulov and Askarov v Turkey*, (Apps. 46827/99 and 46951/99), 4 February 2005 [GC], (2005) 41 EHRR 494, ECHR 2005-I.

and as hindering the effective exercise of his or her right and, accordingly, as a violation of Article 34 of the Convention.[47]

This position has been reinforced by the Grand Chamber in the *Paladi* case.[48] The case concerned a Moldovan politician held in pre-trial detention. He had submitted medical reports to the Court which showed that he was seriously ill, and that he would not receive adequate medical treatment in prison. The Court indicated an interim measure to the Moldovan Government, requesting that the applicant should not be transferred from the clinic where he was being treated back to prison. There was a delay of approximately five days during which the interim measure was not complied with and the applicant was removed from the clinic to a prison, before being taken back to the clinic on the fifth day. There was no evidence that the applicant had suffered any irreversible harm to his health as a result of the delay. The Court in its judgment again emphasized the binding nature of interim measures and made it clear that any failure to comply would lead to a violation of Article 34 unless, in an exceptional case, the respondent State could demonstrate that there had been an 'objective impediment which prevented compliance and that the Government took all reasonable steps to remove the impediment and to keep the Court informed about the situation.'[49] The fact that the damage which the interim measure was designed to prevent subsequently turned out not to have occurred, despite the State's failure to act in full compliance with the interim measure, was irrelevant for the assessment of whether the State has fulfilled its obligations under Article 34.

It is not just a failure to comply with an interim measure which will give rise to a breach of Article 34. In the *Assenov* case,[50] for example, the Court found a violation of the right of application based on the fact that the Bulgarian police had visited the applicant's parents, at a time when the applicant was in custody, and put pressure on them to withdraw the application to Strasbourg.

In addition, freedom to correspond with the Court, even in the case of persons in detention whose correspondence is normally subject to control, is protected by the European Agreement relating to persons participating in proceedings of the European Commission and Court of Human Rights.[51] Under this Agreement, parties to the Convention undertake to respect the right of those involved in most capacities before the Court to correspond freely with the Court. Article 3(2) contains special provisions relating to those detained in custody. Article 4 guarantees free movement, subject to certain limitations, in connection with the proceedings. Finally, Article 2 offers immunity from legal process in respect of oral or written statements made before, and documents or other evidence submitted to, the Court.

EXAMINATION OF ADMISSIBILITY: PROCEDURAL ISSUES

SINGLE JUDGE FORMATION AND COMMITTEE PROCEDURE

The admissibility criteria are set out in Article 35 of the Convention.[52] Given the large number of applications which it receives, the Court has had to devise an admissibility

[47] § 128. Article 34 ECHR provides: The Court may receive applications from any person...claiming to be the victim of a violation...of the rights set forth in the Convention.... The High Contracting Parties undertake not to hinder in any way the effective exercise of this right.

[48] *Paladi v Moldova*, (App. 39806/05), 10 March 2009 [GC], ECHR 2009-nyr, §§ 87–92.

[49] § 92.

[50] *Assenov and others v Bulgaria*, (App. 24760/94), 28 October 1998, (1999) 28 EHRR 652, ECHR 1998-VIII, § 169.

[51] ETS 161.

[52] See later in this chapter.

procedure which is economical and efficient, reserving as much time as possible for meritorious cases, but which still ensures that justice is done in each individual case. Thus, all applications which appear to be manifestly inadmissible are referred to a single judge formation. An application may be referred to a Committee of three judges by the judge rapporteur or by the single judge formation.[53] At the end of 2012, 81,700 applications were held inadmissible or struck out by a single judge formation. Of the 128,100 applications pending before a judicial body 43,050 were before the Chamber, 25,200 were before a Committee, and 59,850 applications were before the single judge formation.[54]

The decisions of the single judge formation and the three judge Committees are final with no possibility of appeal. The Committee decisions must be taken unanimously.[55] Until 1 January 2002 applicants were sent a copy of the decision, which included very limited reasoning. From 1 January 2002, those whose applications are found to be inadmissible have received only a letter from the registry stating that the application has been declared inadmissible. The letter states that the registry is not able to give any further information or reasons in connection with the decision. Many applicants no doubt feel aggrieved to have their cases disposed of so summarily by the Court. However, given its vast caseload, it is arguable that the Court is justified in adopting a procedure which is as economic as possible in respect of hopeless applications. Other constitutional courts, such as the German Constitutional Court and the United States Supreme Court, adopt a similar practice.

CHAMBER PROCEDURE

Applications which are not dealt with by a single judge formation or a Committee are considered by a Chamber, on the basis of a report prepared by the judge rapporteur. The Chamber can immediately decide to declare a case inadmissible,[56] but this happens rarely. Once an application has been declared inadmissible, whether by a single judge formation, a Committee or a Chamber, that is the end of the matter. There is no possibility of appeal. However, almost all cases that are referred to a Chamber appear to have some prima facie merit. The Chamber President acting alone will usually decide to communicate the application to the respondent State, and request written observations, unless it is a complex or high profile case which the Section may need to discuss before communicating the application.[57] The Chamber will produce a 'de plano' admissibility decision (i.e. without seeking the observations of the parties) where it considers the case inadmissible but there is value in publishing a reasoned decision.

Again, to save judge time, the Court in most cases considers the admissibility and merits of a case jointly; thus reversing the exceptional rule contained in Article 29(3) of the Convention. Before coming to a conclusion on admissibility or the merits, the Chamber may decide to hold a hearing.[58]

The procedure for inter-State cases is broadly similar to that outlined here. However, any inter-State case is automatically communicated at once to the respondent State for its observations on admissibility.[59]

[53] Rule 49(1) and (2)(b).

[54] European Court of Human Rights, *Annual Report* 2012 (Council of Europe Publishing, Strasbourg 2013), 149.

[55] Art. 28 ECHR, and Rule 52A and 53.

[56] Rule 54(1).

[57] Rule 54(2).

[58] Rule 54(3).

[59] Rule 51.

THIRD-PARTY INTERVENTION

A Contracting Party which is not the respondent State may intervene where an applicant is its national, and must be informed of any such application at the same time as it is communicated to the respondent State.[60] The Council of Europe Commissioner for Human Rights may also intervene in any Chamber or Grand Chamber case.[61]

Once the respondent State has been notified of an application, it is possible, subject to the leave of the President of the Chamber, for a third party to submit written comments or, occasionally, to intervene at the hearing.[62] Third-party comments are usually submitted by non-governmental organizations whose field of expertise touches on the subject matter of the application. However, it is possible for other States and interested individuals to intervene. In the *T and V* cases,[63] for example, which concerned the trial and sentencing of two children who had murdered another child, a non-governmental organization, Justice, was permitted to submit a written brief about the criminal responsibility of children, and the dead child's parents were allowed to submit written and oral comments. In *Saadi v Italy*,[64] which reconsidered and affirmed the rationale in the *Chahal* case[65] that there was an absolute prohibition of treatment contrary to Article 3 which could not involve any weighing of the risk of ill-treatment against reasons of national security of the State in which the person was resident, the United Kingdom intervened to argue for a modification of the principles established in the *Chahal* case.[66]

ESTABLISHMENT OF THE FACTS

Article 38(1)(a) of the Convention provides:

> If the Court declares the application admissible, it shall pursue the examination of the case, together with the representatives of the parties, and if need be, undertake an investigation, for the effective conduct of which the States concerned shall furnish all necessary facilities.

In most cases, the facts will have been established by domestic courts and the task of the Strasbourg Court will be limited to examining these facts to assess compliance with the Convention. The Court also places reliance on the report of the Committee on the Prevention of Torture in cases concerning the conditions of detention.[67] In some cases, however, particularly where the alleged violation arises wholly or in part from a deficiency in the administration of justice in the national legal order, or where, for example, the

[60] Rule 44(1).

[61] Art. 36(3)(as amended by Protocol 14, Art. 13). See Protocol 14 to the Convention for the Protection of Human Rights and Fundamental Freedoms, amending the Control System of the Convention CETS No.194, Explanatory Report § 76. [62] Rule 44.

[63] *T v United Kingdom*, (App. 24724/94); and *V v United Kingdom*, (App. 24888/94), 16 December 1999 [GC], (2000) 30 EHRR 121, ECHR 1999-IX.

[64] *Saadi v Italy*, (App. 37201/06), 28 February 2008 [GC], (2009) 49 EHRR 730, ECHR 2008-nyr.

[65] *Chahal v United Kingdom*, (App. 22414/93), 15 November 1996; (1997) 23 EHRR 413, ECHR 1996-V.

[66] For further examples of third-party submissions, see *Von Hannover v Germany*, (App. 59320/00), 24 June 2004, (2005) 40 EHRR 1, ECHR 2004-VI; *Vo. v France*, (App. 53924/00), 8 July 2004 [GC], (2005) 40 EHRR 259, ECHR 2004-VIII; '*Bosphorus Airways*' *v Ireland*, (App. 45036/98), 30 June 2005 [GC], (2006) 42 EHRR 1, ECHR 2005-VI; and *DH and others v Czech Republic*, (App. 57325/00), 13 November 2007 [GC], (2008) 47 EHRR 59, ECHR 2007-nyr.

[67] See, among the many examples, *Ostrovar v Moldova*, (App. 35207/03), 13 September 2005, (2007) 44 EHRR 378.

applicants are dispensed from exhausting domestic remedies,[68] and the facts are in dispute, the Court will be required to establish them itself.

Under Rule 42 of the Rules of Court, the Chamber may, at the request of a party to the case or a third party, or of its own motion, obtain any evidence which it considers capable of providing clarification of the facts of the case. It may request, but not order, the parties to produce documentary evidence and decide to hear as a witness or expert any person whose evidence or statements seem likely to be of assistance.[69]

Where necessary, the Court may appoint a delegation of judges to conduct an inquiry or carry out an investigation on the spot.[70] Under Article 38 of the Convention, the State concerned must 'furnish all necessary facilities' to enable the Court to conduct any such investigation. In the *Tanrikulu* case,[71] the Commission sent a delegation to south-east Turkey to investigate the alleged killing of the applicant's husband by security forces. The Commission repeatedly requested the Turkish authorities to give it a copy of the full investigation file, but this was not supplied.[72] In addition, the Commission requested the two State prosecutors who had investigated the case on the national level to appear before its delegates to give evidence. Neither of them appeared, and the Turkish authorities provided no satisfactory explanation for their failure to attend.[73] In its judgment, the Court made a separate finding that Turkey had fallen short of its obligations under Article 28 of the Convention (now Article 38).

The Court's approach to such matters is as follows:

> The Court reiterates that it is of the utmost importance for the effective operation of the system of individual petition instituted under Article 34 of the Convention that States should furnish all necessary facilities to make possible a proper and effective examination of applications (see *Tanrıkulu v Turkey* [GC], no. 23763/94, § 70, ECHR 1999-IV). This obligation requires the Contracting States to furnish all necessary facilities to the Court, whether it is conducting a fact-finding investigation or performing its general duties as regards the examination of applications. Failure on a Government's part to submit such information which is in their hands, without a satisfactory explanation, may not only give rise to the drawing of inferences as to the well-foundedness of the applicant's allegations, but may also reflect negatively on the level of compliance by a respondent State with its obligations under Article 38 § 1 (a) of the Convention (see *Timurtaş v Turkey*, no. 23531/94, § 66, ECHR 2000-VI).[74]

An attempt by a delegation from the Strasbourg Court to visit Russia was frustrated in the *Shamayev* case, with the result that the Court abandoned its attempt to visit the applicants in Russia and proceeded on the basis of the evidence before it.[75]

[68] *Akdivar and others v Turkey*, (App. 21893/93), 16 September 1996, (1997) 23 EHRR 143, ECHR 1996-IV, and see also later in this chapter.

[69] For example, in *Khokhlich v Ukraine*, (App. 41707/98), 29 April 2003, the Strasbourg Court decided that it needed a medical opinion to enable it to determine the truth of a complaint that the applicant had been infected with tuberculosis while detained on death row. The costs of the medical examination were borne by the Council of Europe under Rule 42(5).

[70] See the Annex to the Rules of Court. See also P. Leach, C. Paraskeva, and G. Uzelac, *International Human Rights and Fact-Finding. An analysis of the fact-finding missions conducted by the European Commission and Court of Human Rights* (London, 2009) available at www.londonmet.ac.uk/research-units/hrsj/.

[71] *Tanrikulu v Turkey*, (App. 23763/94), 8 July 1999 [GC], (2000) 30 EHRR 950, ECHR 1999-IV.

[72] § 31. [73] § 39.

[74] *Nolan and K v Russia*, (App. 2512/04), 12 February 2009, § 55. See also M. Smith, 'The adjudicatory fact-finding tools of the European Court of Human Rights', [2009] EHRLR 206.

[75] *Shamayev and others v Georgia and Russia*, (App. 36378/02), 12 April 2005, ECHR 2005-III.

CONDITIONS OF ADMISSIBILITY

PRELIMINARY REMARKS

Before the coming into force of Protocol 11, the Commission was primarily responsible for examining the admissibility of applications.[76] On 1 November 1998 the new permanent Court took over this function. The admissibility criteria, governed by Articles 34 and 35 of the Convention, were not altered by the provisions of Protocol 11, and the Court draws on the case-law of the Commission in this respect.[77] However, Protocol 14 has added to the admissibility criteria under Article 35 and these will be further amended by Protocol 15.[78] The principal criteria for admissibility are considered in the following paragraphs.

CAN THE APPLICANT CLAIM TO BE A VICTIM?

The first question to be considered is that of standing: who may bring an application to the Court? Article 33, on inter-State cases, presents no problem in this respect; an application may be brought only by a Contracting Party. Under Article 34, on individual applications, the Strasbourg Court may receive applications:

> from any person, non-governmental organization or group of individuals claiming to be the victim of a violation by one of the High Contracting Parties of the rights set forth in this Convention or the protocols thereto.

This formulation excludes the bringing of individual applications by governmental bodies or public corporations which are under the control of the State.[79]

The term 'person' (*personne physique* in the French text) appears to include only natural persons but an application may be brought also by any corporate or unincorporated body. Thus applications have been brought by companies, trade unions, churches, political parties, and numerous other types of body. A corporate body has some but not all of the rights of individuals; it has the right to a fair trial under Article 6, to protection of its correspondence under Article 8,[80] and is expressly granted property rights under Article 1 of the First Protocol, but it does not have the right to education under Article 2 of Protocol 1.

There are, of course, no restrictions based on residence, nationality, or any other status. Only if the individual applicant does not claim to be a victim, as for example where he or she complains generally of certain legislation,[81] or where he or she simply alleges that a fellow-prisoner has been ill-treated, will the application be outside the Court's competence

[76] See ch.1.

[77] See T. Zwart, *The Admissibility of Human Rights Petitions. The Case Law of the European Commission of Human Rights and the Human Rights Committee* (Martinus Nijhoff, Dordrecht 1994).

[78] See later in this chapter.

[79] See *Islamic Republic of Iran Shipping Lines v Turkey*, (App. 40998/98), 13 December 2007, (2008) 47 EHRR 573, ECHR 2007-nyr, §§ 78–84.

[80] App. 14369/88, *Noviflora Sweden AB v Sweden*; Decision of an unspecified date in 1992, (1993) 15 EHRR CD6.

[81] In *Quardiri v Switzerland*, (App. 65840/09), 28 June 2011 and *Ligue des Musulmans de Suisee and others*, (App. 66272/09), 28 June 2011, the applicants argued that a constitutional amendment banning the building of minarets violated their right to religious belief under Article 9 and was discriminatory under Article 14 with Article 9. The Court rejected the applications, as the applicants could not demonstrate a direct effect on their beliefs. The mere possibility that it might impinge on their beliefs in the future was not enough to make them victims and the current complaint was made in the abstract. However the Court did note that if an applicant's request to build a minaret was refused and domestic remedies were exhausted, then he could be a victim.

ratione personae. The Court has no jurisdiction on an individual application to review national law or practice in the absence of an alleged violation of a Convention provision. Similarly, associations have no capacity to raise general complaints,[82] though they may act in a representative capacity for specific individuals.[83]

Where a violation of the right to life is alleged, the Court must accept an application from close relatives of the dead person. In other cases close relatives have standing to bring an application only in relation to the effect of any alleged violation on themselves. So an application by close relatives of a person accused of crime who dies before final disposition of the case can make a claim based on the loss of reputation of the family.[84] In contrast, a complaint under Article 6 relating to the length and fairness of proceedings is personal to the litigant and an application by relatives will not be admitted.[85] Where the applicant dies in the course of the proceedings under the Convention, the Court will have regard to the wishes of the heirs of the deceased in deciding whether to permit the application to proceed.[86]

Cases concerning children will normally be brought by parents or guardians, but the Court will accept applications from minors if the complaint concerns action by the authorities affecting the relationship of child and parent or guardian.[87] A person who is neither a custodial parent, guardian, nor legal representative of a child will not have standing to make a complaint.[88] There is no bar to applications by persons under a disability.[89]

In certain cases, in order to give effective protection to human rights, the Strasbourg Court has had to give a wide interpretation to the notion of 'victim'. In the *Klass* case,[90] for example, where the applicants complained about legislation in Germany which allowed the State to intercept telephone calls without informing the person concerned, the Court concluded that the applicants could claim to be victims even though they were unable to establish that they had been the subjects of surveillance, since 'in the mere existence of the legislation itself there is involved, for all those to whom the legislation could be applied, a menace of surveillance', which must have placed a restriction on the applicants' confidence freely to use the telephone system. In that case, it would have been virtually impossible for the applicants to adduce evidence of specific measures taken against them—and indeed this very impossibility formed one of the bases of their complaints. However, where the legislation provides for notification of surveillance to a person concerned, a claim that there has been a violation of Article 8 will generally not succeed unless the applicant has received such notification.[91] Moreover, where the applicant complains of a specific

[82] App. 10581/83, *Norris and National Gay Federation v Ireland*, Decision of 16 May 1984, (1984) 44 DR 132.

[83] App. 10983/84, *Confédération des Syndicats médicaux français and Fédération nationale des Infirmiers v France*, Decision of 12 May 1986, (1986) 47 DR 225; see also App. 10733/84, *Associación de Aviadores de la República, Jaime Mata and others v Spain*, Decision of 11 March 1985, (1985) 41 DR 211.

[84] App. 10300/83, *Nölkenbockhoff and Bergemann v Federal Republic of Germany*, Decision of 12 December 1984, (1985) 40 DR 180.

[85] *Nölkenbockhoff and Bergemann*. But note observations of the Chamber in *Micallef v Malta*, (App. 17056/06), 15 January 2008, §§ 23–33 suggesting exceptions to this position: see also the judgment of the Grand Chamber of 15 October 2009, §§ 44–51.

[86] See, for example, *Aksoy v Turkey*, (App. 21987/93), 18 December 1996, (1997) 23 EHRR 553, ECHR 1996-VI, § 2; and *Gładkowski v Poland*, (App. 29697/96), 14 March 2000.

[87] App. 10929/84, *Nielsen v Denmark*, Decision of 10 March 1986, (1986) 46 DR 55; *A. v United Kingdom*,(App. 25599/94), 23 September 1998, (1999) 27 EHRR 611, ECHR 1998-VI.

[88] App. 22920/93, *MB v United Kingdom*, Decision of 6 April 1994, (1994) 77-A DR 42.

[89] App. 527/62, *X v Austria*, Decision of 4 October 1962, (1962) 5 *Yearbook* 238.

[90] *Klass v Germany*, (App. 5029/71), 6 September 1978, Series A No 28, (1979–80) 2 EHRR 214; and see also *Malone v United Kingdom*, (App. 8691/79), 2 August 1984, Series A No 82, (1985) 7 EHRR 14.

[91] Joined Apps. 10439/83, 10440/83, 10441/83, 10452/83, and 10513/83, *Mersch and others v Luxembourg*, Decision of 10 May 1985, (1985) 43 DR 34.

instance of surveillance or telephone-tapping, the Court will require evidence establishing a 'reasonable likelihood' that some such measure was applied to him or her.[92]

In the *Norris* case the Court held that a homosexual man could 'claim to be a victim' of legislation in Ireland which criminalized consensual sex between men, because he either respected the law and suppressed his sexual preferences, or he indulged them and risked prosecution.[93] This was so even though the applicant himself had never been investigated by the police and there was evidence that the Irish authorities had a policy of not bringing prosecutions under the law.[94]

A person will not cease to be a victim by reason of some acknowledgment by the respondent State that there has been a violation of the Convention. The Grand Chamber has ruled:

> The Court also reiterates that a decision or measure favourable to the applicant is not in principle sufficient to deprive him of his status as a 'victim' unless the national authorities have acknowledged, either expressly or in substance, and then afforded redress for, the breach of the Convention.[95]

In order to lose victim status, there must be a remedy which constitutes full redress for the violation which the victim has suffered. This will, obviously, require an exercise of judgment on the part of the Strasbourg Court.

WAS THE ALLEGED VIOLATION COMMITTED BY A CONTRACTING PARTY?

Under Articles 33 and 34 an application may be brought only against a Contracting Party, and only in respect of a breach for which the State is in some way responsible.[96] Otherwise the application will be rejected as being outside the Court's competence *ratione personae*.

The State is directly liable for the acts of the legislature, executive, and judiciary, and also for the acts of other public bodies, for example, public corporations with a certain measure of independence, such as a local health authority or a public corporation under the control of the State.[97] It cannot be held to account for the acts or omissions of private persons, such as private companies, lawyers, or legal professional bodies like the Bar Council. As noted throughout this book, however, many of the substantive Articles of the Convention impose positive obligations on a Contracting Party. Thus the State can, for example, be held responsible under Article 8 for failing to ensure that a privately owned factory does not dangerously pollute the surrounding area[98] or under Article 3 for the lack of adequate protection in its criminal law against violence carried out by a private individual.[99]

[92] *Halford v United Kingdom*, (App. 20605/92), 25 June 1997, (1997) 24 EHRR 523, ECHR 1997-III.

[93] *Norris v Ireland*, (App. 10581/83), 26 October 1988, Series A No 142, (1991) 13 EHRR 186, § 32.

[94] Further examples of where a person is virtually certain to be affected in the future by some national provision can be found in App. 6833/74, *Marckx v Belgium*, Decision of 13 June 1979, Series A No 31, (1979–80) 2 EHRR 330; and App. 13378/05, *Burden v United Kingdom*, Decision of 29 April 2008 [GC], (2007) 47 EHRR 857, ECHR 2008-nyr. Both cases concerned inheritance rights.

[95] *Scordino v Italy (No. 1)*, (App. 36813/97), 29 March 2006 [GC], (2007) 45 EHRR 207, ECHR 2006-V, § 180; see also *Moscow Branch of the Salvation Army v Russia*, (App. 72881/01), 5 October 2006, (2007) 44 EHRR 912, ECHR 2006-XI, §§ 63–70.

[96] See also the discussion on jurisdiction in ch.5.

[97] App. 7601/76, *Young and James v United Kingdom*, Decision of 11 July 1977, (1977) 20 *Yearbook* 520; and App. 7866/76, *Webster v United Kingdom*, Decision of 3 March 1978, (1978) 12 DR 168.

[98] *López Ostra v Spain*, (App. 16798/90), 9 December 1994, Series A No 303-C, (1995) 20 EHRR 277.

[99] *A v United Kingdom*, (App. 25599/94), 23 September 1998, (1999) 27 EHRR 611, ECHR 1998-VI.

An application will be declared inadmissible as incompatible *ratione loci* with the Convention if it relates to an alleged violation of the Convention outside the State's territorial jurisdiction, and incompatible *ratione temporis* if it is based on events which occurred before the respondent State accepted the jurisdiction of the Court, or became a party to the Convention.

DO THE MATTERS COMPLAINED OF FALL WITHIN THE SCOPE OF THE CONVENTION OR PROTOCOLS?

The Court cannot deal with complaints concerning rights not covered by the Convention or Protocols, and a Contracting Party cannot be brought to task in respect of alleged violations of rights included in protocols which it has not ratified. Such complaints are normally rejected under Article 35(3) as incompatible *ratione materiae* with the provisions of the Convention.

It is the duty of the Strasbourg Court to examine an application not only in relation to any rights that may have been invoked by the applicant, but also, of its own motion, in relation to any rights which, on the facts and submissions before it, may appear to have been infringed.

HAVE DOMESTIC REMEDIES BEEN EXHAUSTED?

Contracting Parties quite frequently raise objections that applicants have not exhausted the remedies available to them in the national legal order in order to remedy an alleged violation of Convention rights. According to Article 35(1):

> The Court may only deal with the matter after all domestic remedies have been exhausted, according to the generally recognized rules of international law, and within a period of six months from the date on which the final decision was taken.

In the *Akdivar* case,[100] the Strasbourg Court explained the rationale for this rule:

> [T]he rule of exhaustion of domestic remedies... obliges those seeking to bring their case against the State before an international judicial or arbitral organ to use first the remedies provided by the national legal system. Consequently, States are dispensed from answering before an international body for their acts before they have had an opportunity to put matters right through their own legal system. The rule is based on the assumption, reflected in Article 13 of the Convention—with which it has close affinity—that there is an effective remedy available in respect of the alleged breach in the domestic system whether or not the provisions of the Convention are incorporated in national law. In this way, it is an important aspect of the principle that the machinery of protection established by the Convention is subsidiary to the national systems safeguarding human rights.

But the Court has also said that the application of the requirement must be viewed in context:

> The application of the rule of exhaustion must make due allowance for the fact that it is being applied in the context of machinery for the protection of human rights that the Contracting Parties have agreed to set up. Accordingly, the Court has recognized that Article 35(1) must be applied with some degree of flexibility and without excessive formalism. The rule is neither absolute nor capable of being applied automatically. In reviewing whether it has been

[100] *Akdivar and others v Turkey*, (App. 21893/93), 16 September 1996, (1997) 23 EHRR 143, ECHR 1996-IV.

observed it is essential to have regard to the particular circumstances of each case. This means, amongst other things, that the Court must take realistic account of the general legal and political context in which the remedies operate, as well as the personal circumstances of the applicant.[101]

Under Article 35(1), applicants are under an obligation to use the remedies provided by national law which are sufficient to afford redress in respect of the breaches alleged. The complaint must be made to the appropriate judicial or administrative authorities, and should have been taken to the highest instance available. Applicants will not have complied with the rule if they have been unable to pursue national proceedings because of their own failure to comply with the domestic formal requirements and time limits.[102] In addition, applicants must have raised before the national authorities, if it is possible to do so, the particular complaints which they wish to make before the Court. If they raise only some of their complaints, only those will be admissible.[103]

There is, however, no obligation to attempt to use a remedy which is inadequate or ineffective,[104] but mere doubts will not suffice.[105] In addition, according to the 'generally recognized rules of international law' there may be special circumstances which absolve applicants from the obligation to exhaust the domestic remedies at their disposal. So, for example, in the *Akdivar* case, where the Kurdish applicants complained that their village had been destroyed by Turkish soldiers, and the respondent State was unable to provide evidence of damages having been awarded in a single similar case, the Strasbourg Court held that there was no need for the applicants to bring proceedings in the national courts before complaining in Strasbourg. Again, if the national case-law shows that a remedy, such as an appeal, has no reasonable chance of success, the applicant is not obliged to try it. The Court will accept a lawyer's formal opinion to this effect as a 'final decision' under Article 35. In *LL United Kingdom*,[106] the applicant was convicted of assault and under age consumption of alcohol. She served her sentence in an adult prison despite being under eighteen years old. She appealed her sentence to Jersey's Royal Court which dismissed the appeal. The applicant could then have appealed to the Judicial Committee of the Privy Council (made up of judges of the UK Supreme Court). She did not do so, claiming before the Strasbourg Court that there was no 'reasonable prospect of success,' given it was rare that appeals were allowed to the Privy Council from Jersey. However, the Court noted evidence of previous appeals to the Privy Council and found that the applicant had failed to show that there was 'settled legal opinion at the relevant time' to suggest that there was no prospect of success. Her doubts about the process were not enough to absolve her from attempting to use the remedy.[107]

The domestic remedies rule applies also to inter-State applications under Article 33, unlike the other grounds of inadmissibility specified in Article 35, which are expressly confined to individual applications under Article 34. The rule, however, has only a limited application in inter-State cases: domestic remedies must have been exhausted in respect of

[101] *Foka v Turkey*, (App. 28940/95), Decision of 9 November 2006, 11.

[102] See, for example, *Yahiaoui v France*, (App. 30962/96), 14 January 2000, (2001) 33 EHRR 393.

[103] As in *A and others v United Kingdom*, (App. 3455/05), 19 February 2009 [GC], (2009) 49 EHRR 29, ECHR 2009-nyr, § 122.

[104] Declarations of incompatibility under the Human Rights Act 1998 are not regarded as an effective remedy: *Burden v United Kingdom*, (App. 13378/05), 29 April 2008 [GC], (2007) 47 EHRR 857, ECHR 2008-nyr, §§ 40–4.

[105] *Daddi v Italy*, (App. 15476/09), Decision of 16 June 2009.

[106] App. 39678/09, Decision of 15 January 2013.

[107] §§ 26–8, The Court also found that the applicant could have made a civil claim that may have provided redress for the alleged violation, § 28.

violations of the rights of particular individuals, but not where the scope of the application is to determine the compatibility with the Convention of legislative measures and administrative practices in general.[108]

The applicant must provide, in the application, information enabling it to be shown that the conditions laid down in Article 35 have been satisfied; if this is not done, the Court must examine the question of its own motion. If the respondent State raises the objection of non-exhaustion, it is for that State to prove the existence, in its municipal legal system, of remedies which have not been exercised.[109] If the existence of such a remedy is established, the applicant must show that it has been exhausted, or that it was unlikely to be effective and adequate in regard to the grievance in question, or that in the special circumstances of the case he or she was absolved from compliance with the rule. The rules concerning the burden of proof are based, as is the substantive rule, on the generally recognized rules of international law referred to in Article 35.[110]

A particular issue has arisen in relation to the exhaustion of domestic remedies in cases involving complaints that judgment has not been given in a reasonable time. Several Contracting Parties have put special procedures in place to address the problem. The question arises as to whether such new procedures are effective and whether they must be exhausted before a complaint can be raised that there has been a violation of Article 6. Where Contracting Parties introduce such procedures in response to repeated judgments finding violations of the right to judgment within a reasonable time, the Strasbourg Court will examine such procedures with some care if a complaint is raised that an applicant has not exhausted domestic remedies, since:

> It is also clear that for countries where length-of-proceedings violations already exist, a remedy designed to expedite the proceedings—although desirable for the future—may not be adequate to redress a situation in which the proceedings have clearly already been excessively long.[111]

ESCAPING THE REQUIREMENT TO EXHAUST DOMESTIC REMEDIES: TACKLING ADMINISTRATIVE PRACTICES

The exhaustion rule is inapplicable where an administrative practice is in issue, and this can have implications in both inter-State and individual applications. An administrative practice exists if there is repetition of acts and official tolerance, even if only at a subordinate level, and despite occasional reactions from the authorities.[112] In inter-State cases, there is no requirement in such cases that there should be a victim at all. Thus the rule does not apply if the applicant State can show that the treatment complained of constitutes an administrative practice. It did not apply, for this reason, in the *Irish* case,[113] to the Irish Government's complaints concerning the treatment of persons in custody in Northern Ireland. In applications

[108] App. 788/60, *Pfunders Case, Austria v Italy*, Decision of 11 January 1961, (1961) 4 *Yearbook* 116, at 146–50; and see, more recently, *Cyprus v Turkey*, (App. 25781/94), 10 May 2001 [GC]; (2002) 35 EHRR 30; ECHR 2001-IV. See further later in this chapter.

[109] *Akdivar and others v Turkey*, (App. 21893/93), 16 September 1996, (1997) 23 EHRR 143, ECHR 1996-IV.

[110] *Akdivar and others v Turkey*, (App. 21893/93), 16 September 1996, (1997) 23 EHRR 143, ECHR 1996-IV.

[111] *Scordino v Italy (No. 1)*, (App. 36813/97), 29 March 2006 [GC], (2007) 45 EHRR 207, ECHR 2006-V, § 185; see also *Žunič v Slovenia*, (App. 24342/04), Decision of 18 October 2007.

[112] *Ireland v United Kingdom*, (App. 5310/71), 18 January 1978, Series A No 25, (1979–80) 2 EHRR 25.

[113] App. 5310/71, *Ireland v United Kingdom*, Decision of 1 October 1972, (1972) 15 *Yearbook* 76; see also Joined Apps. 9940–44/82, *France, Norway, Denmark, Sweden, and The Netherlands v Turkey*, Decision of 6 December 1983, (1984) 35 DR 143.

by individuals, there will be a need for the applicant to show that he or she is a victim.[114] But it is not sufficient merely to allege the existence of such legislative measures or administrative practices; their existence must be shown by means of substantial evidence. On this ground, the complaints in the *Irish* case relating to deaths (as distinct from ill-treatment) allegedly caused by the respondent State's security forces were rejected.

The reason for this exception is that, in cases where there is an administrative practice, proceedings to exhaust domestic remedies run the risk of tackling only a single instance of a Convention violation, whereas there is a systemic problem. In the *Caraher* case,[115] the Court summarized the case-law regarding the notion of an administrative practice as follows:

> In the First Greek case (Yearbook 11 p.770), the Commission identified two elements necessary to the existence of an administrative practice: a repetition of acts and official tolerance. Repetition of acts was stated as referring to a substantial number of acts which were linked or connected in some way by the circumstances surrounding them (eg. time and place, or the attitude of persons involved) and which were not simply a number of isolated acts. The Court has stated that a practice incompatible with the Convention consists of an accumulation of identical or analogous breaches which are sufficiently numerous and inter-connected to amount not merely to isolated incidents or exceptions but to a pattern or system (Ireland v. the United Kingdom judgment of 18 January 1978, Series A no. 25, p. 64, § 159). By official tolerance is meant that, though acts are plainly unlawful, they are tolerated in the sense that the superiors of those responsible, though aware of the acts, take no action to punish them or prevent their repetition; or that a higher authority, in the face of numerous allegations, manifests indifference by refusing any inadequate investigation of their truth or falsity; or that in judicial proceedings a fair hearing of such complaints is denied (*mutatis mutandis*, Application Nos. 9940-9944/82, France, Norway, Denmark, Sweden and the Netherlands v. Turkey, dec. 6.12.83, DR 35 p. 143 at p. 163, § 19). However, it may be noted that a practice may be found even where no official tolerance is established at the higher official levels and even where some acts have been prosecuted, since the higher authorities are under a responsibility to take effective steps to bring to an end the repetition of acts (see eg. Ireland v. the United Kingdom judgment, op. cit., § 159).[116]

Most cases involving allegations of an administrative practice have arisen in relation to allegations of violations of the prohibition of torture in Article 3. In certain length of proceedings cases under Article 6, the Strasbourg Court has referred to 'a practice which is incompatible with the Convention'.[117] The Court categorized the situation in the *Kauczor* case[118] in the same way in considering violations of Article 5 involving the length of pre-trial detention. In all three of these cases, this categorization was used more as the basis for ordering general remedial measures under Article 46[119] than as a reason to disapply the rule requiring exhaustion of domestic remedies.

HAS THE APPLICATION BEEN INTRODUCED WITHIN THE SIX-MONTH TIME LIMIT?

Article 35 prescribes a strict period of limitation: an application is inadmissible if it is not brought within six months from the date on which the final decision was taken.[120] Time starts

[114] Apps. 5577–83/72, *Donnelly and others v United Kingdom*, 5 April 1973, (1973) 16 *Yearbook* 212.

[115] *Caraher v United Kingdom*, (App. 24520/94), Decision of 11 January 2000, ECHR 2000-I.

[116] p.18.

[117] *Bottazzi v Italy*, (App. 34884/97), 28 July 1999, ECHR 1999-V, § 22; *Scordino (No. 1) v Italy*, (App. 36813/97), 29 March 2006 [GC], ECHR 2006-V, §§ 229–31.

[118] *Kauczor v Poland*, (App. 45219/06), 3 February 2009, § 60.

[119] See further later in this chapter, and in ch.3.

[120] This period will be reduced to four months when Protocol 15 of the ECHR comes into force. Not yet in force as of October 2013.

running from the day after the applicant became aware of the act or decision of which he or she complains. Where domestic remedies have been completed, this is usually the hearing at which the final domestic judgment is delivered,[121] but where no domestic remedies are available, the six-month period runs from the date of the act alleged to constitute the violation of the Convention. The applicant cannot reopen the period by, for example, subsequently applying for a retrial, as such an application does not constitute an 'effective remedy' for the purposes of Article 35. Where the complaint concerns a continuing situation, time runs from the end of the situation, but as long as the situation continues, the six-months rule cannot bite.[122] The Court has stated:

> that the concept of a 'continuing situation' refers to a state of affairs which operates by continuous activities by or on the part of the State to render the applicants victims.[123]

But the Court went on to state:

> The applicants' complaints have as their source specific events which occurred on identifiable dates... These cannot be construed as a 'continuing situation' for the purposes of the six-month rule. The fact that an event has significant consequences over time... does not mean that the event has produced a 'continuing situation'.[124]

The concept of continuing violations of Convention rights has proved to be problematic.[125] The Court seeks to distinguish instantaneous acts and continuing violations, but this is far from straightforward. Many instantaneous acts have continuing effects. The taking of property provides an excellent example. If property is formally expropriated and so the owner's title to the property has been extinguished, then there is arguably an instantaneous act and time will start running to raise a complaint under the Convention. But if a State acts in a way which adversely affects an owner's enjoyment of their property, perhaps by the exercise of planning controls or threats of compulsory purchase, then there may be a continuing violation of the right to peaceful enjoyment of property. The approach of the Commission was to seek to distinguish between instantaneous acts which might give rise to enduring effects from violations which continue. Only the latter prevent time from running. The Court has not yet elaborated on the distinction. Loucaides is critical of the Court's current approach and proposes a test in which the following factors are relevant considerations:

(a) the nature of the complaint, i.e. the particular act or conduct alleged to be a violation;

(b) the effects of the act or conduct complained of on the rights of the applicant;

(c) the duration of such effects; and

(d) the prolongation of the operation of the relevant act or conduct or the maintenance of the effects in question through the involvement or conduct of the State.

Loucaides then proposes:

> ...there is a 'continuing' violation if the complaint is directed against a constant interference with a right safeguarded by the Convention, which is an extension of an interference caused

[121] *West v United Kingdom*, (App. 34728/97), Decision of 20 October 1997.

[122] *Papamichalopoulos and others v Greece*, (App. 14556/89), 24 June 1993, Series A No 260–B, (1993) 16 EHRR 440; and *Loizidou v Turkey* (App. 15318/89), 18 December 1996, (1996) 23 EHRR 513, ECHR 1996-VI.

[123] *Posti and Rahko v Finland*, (App. 27824/95), 24 September 2002, (2003) 37 EHRR 158, ECHR 2002-VII, § 39.

[124] § 40.

[125] See L. Loucaides, 'The concept of "continuing" violations of human rights' in P. Mahoney and others (eds.), *Protecting Human Rights: The European Perspective. Studies in Memory of Rolv Ryssdal* (Carl Heymanns, Köln 2000), 803.

> by the initial instantaneous act whose effects still subsist as a result of a prolongation of the operation of the act or its effects through an involvement or conduct of the State.[126]

The six-months rule is applied strictly by the Court and cannot be waived by the respondent State.[127] In certain cases it may appear to create injustice—where an application is submitted late through the oversight of the applicant's lawyer, for example—but, like all limitation periods, it is intended to promote legal certainty and finality. Protocol 15 will reduce the six-months rule to a four month period when it comes into force.[128] The change is part of the on-going reform process and is meant to accelerate the process and reflects the greater use of electronic communication.[129] Given that swifter communication is possible, it is arguable that this will not have a significant impact on applicants.

HAS THE APPLICATION BEEN BROUGHT BEFORE?

Article 35(2)(b) provides that an application is inadmissible if it:

> is substantially the same as a matter which has already been examined by the Court or has already been submitted to another procedure of international investigation or settlement and contains no relevant new information.

There is little case-law of the Court or Commission rejecting an application on the ground that it has already been submitted to another procedure of international investigation or settlement. This is principally because the Commission and the Court have viewed the requirement of the alternative procedure as being judicial or quasi-judicial proceedings similar to those set up by the Convention.[130] It follows that the complaints[131] procedure before the United Nations Human Rights Council is not a comparable procedure of international investigation.[132] The same conclusion has been reached in relation to complaints raised before the Human Rights Committee under the International Covenant on Civil and Political Rights.[133] However, the Court has recently rejected an application, finding it had previously been submitted to another international tribunal. In *POA and others United Kingdom*,[134] the POA trade union and several individual applicants alleged a violation of Article 11. However, the POA had already made a complaint about the same issue to the International Labour Organization (ILO) Committee on Freedom of Association. The Court had previously found that the Committee was a comparable procedure of international investigation.[135] It went on to find that the complaint made was sufficiently similar to be the same complaint made to the ILO Committee. This was clear for the POA as

[126] 813–14.

[127] *Walker v United Kingdom*, (App. 34979/97), Decision of 25 January 2000, ECHR 2001-I.

[128] Protocol 15, Article 4.

[129] Protocol 15 to the Convention for the Protection of Human Rights and Fundamental Freedoms, amending the Control System of the Convention, Explanatory Report §§ 21–2.

[130] *Mikolenko v Estonia*, (App. 16944/03), Decision of 5 January 2006.

[131] Formerly known as the Resolution 1053 procedure. The Resolution 1053 procedure was replaced by the complaints procedure in 2007 (Resolution 5/1 of the UN Human Rights Council). This allows for individual complaints known as communications to be made to the Council.

[132] *Mikolenko v Estonia*, (App. 16944/03), Decision of 5 January 2006.

[133] *Folgerø and others v Norway*, (App. 15472/02), Decision of 14 February 2006. See also C. Phuong, 'The relationship between the European Court of Human Rights and the Human Rights Committee: has the "same matter" already been "examined"?' (2007) 7 HRL Rev 385.

[134] App. 59253/11, Decision of 21 May 2013.

[135] *Fédération hellénique des syndicats des employés du secteur bancaire v Greece* (App. 72808/10), 6 December 2011.

it was the complainant to the ILO. However, the individual applicants were not parties to the ILO complaint. Therefore, the Court examined their applications separately. The Court distinguished the case from previous cases held admissible[136] as, in those cases, the applicant's complaints could be separated from the general complaint of a national federation. In the present case, the Court found that their complaints were not distinguishable from the general complaint made by the POA as the individuals were officials of the specific organization before the Court:[137]

> In the present case, it is true the earlier proceedings before the Committee on Freedom of Association did not concern any specific measure taken in respect of the second and third applicants, but focused on the general legislative prohibition of industrial action by prison officers. This is of little consequence, however, since the individual situations of the second and third applicants are not unique in any relevant respect, but simply exemplify the effects of the statutory ban, which is likewise the subject of the present application. Accordingly, to permit them to maintain their action before the Court would be tantamount to circumventing Article 35 § 2(b) of the Convention.[138]

In many cases applicants seek to reopen proceedings after the application has been declared inadmissible, alleging errors in the Court's decision or introducing further details of the same complaints. Since there is no provision for reopening a case, it is necessary to treat the new material as a fresh application. Such an application will be doomed to failure if, for example, the new material does not affect the substance of the previous allegations. In other cases, the new material may remedy the ground on which the previous application was rejected. If, for example, an application is rejected for non-exhaustion of domestic remedies, the applicant may still be able to pursue the domestic remedies and then reintroduce the complaint.

IS THE APPLICATION MANIFESTLY ILL-FOUNDED?

Article 35(3) requires the Strasbourg Court to reject as inadmissible an application which is 'manifestly ill-founded'. This provision requires an initial assessment of the substance of the case and enables the Court to deal effectively with its immense caseload by weeding out at an early stage clearly unmeritorious applications. A complaint will be declared manifestly ill-founded if, for example, the applicant has made wholly unsubstantiated allegations or where the allegations, even if substantiated, would not suffice to establish a violation. For example, complaints by prisoners under Article 3 concerning the conditions of their detention have been rejected as manifestly ill-founded on the ground that, even if the matters complained of were established, they would not constitute 'inhuman or degrading treatment or punishment'. Similarly, complaints about issues which have already been examined by the Court and found not to constitute a violation can be declared inadmissible as manifestly ill-founded.

IS THERE AN ABUSE OF THE RIGHT OF APPLICATION?

Abuse of the right of application, as a ground of rejecting an application, must of course be distinguished from the principle of abuse of rights embodied in Article 17.[139] Article 17 lays down, in effect, that no one may be able to take advantage of the provisions of the

[136] *Council of Civil Service Unions United Kingdom*, (App. 11603/85), Commission Decision of 29 January 1987, Decisions and Reports 50; *Evaldsson and others v Sweden*, (App. 75252/01), 28 March 2006.

[137] The Court followed the Commission decision on admissibility in *Cereceda Martin and others v Spain*, (App. 16358/90), Decision of 12 October 1992, Decisions and Reports 73, at p. 134.

[138] § 32.

[139] See ch.6.

Convention to perform acts aimed at destroying the rights guaranteed. It is thus concerned with preventing abuse of the substantive rights. Abuse of the right of application, on the other hand, may arise where an applicant makes improper use of the procedural rights under Article 34 to bring the complaint before the Court. For example, the Court is the recipient of multiple applications from a number of individuals who would have been (and frequently are), within the English system, subject to vexatious litigant orders. The Commission habitually declared such applications inadmissible for abuse of process, stating:

> It cannot be the task of the Commission, a body which was set up under the Convention 'to ensure the observance of the engagements undertaken by the High Contracting Parties in the present Convention' to deal with a succession of ill-founded and querulous complaints, creating unnecessary work which is incompatible with its real functions, and which hinders it in carrying them out.[140]

The presentation of incomplete and misleading information to the Court will constitute an abuse of the right of application, especially if the information concerns matter highly germane to the application,[141] as will the submission of forged documents.[142]

IS THE APPLICATION ANONYMOUS?

Article 35(2)(a) requires the Strasbourg Court to reject any application which is anonymous. The underlying purpose of this requirement is to preclude applications lodged for improper reasons, but it could be an inhibition to those who do not wish their identity to be revealed to a Contracting Party for fear of repercussions. Indeed the Court does ask applicants whether they are content for their identity to be disclosed to the respondent State, and will not disclose the applicant's identity if so requested.[143] This requirement has not proved to be problematic.

HAS THE APPLICANT SUFFERED A SIGNIFICANT DISADVANTAGE?

Article 35(3)(b) states that an application is inadmissible if the applicant:

> has not suffered a significant disadvantage, unless respect for human rights as defined in the Convention and the Protocols thereto requires an examination of the application on its merits and provided that no case may be rejected on this ground which has not been duly considered by a domestic tribunal.

This criterion was added by Protocol 14, Article 12 in order to allow the Court to further filter out cases where an examination on the merits may not be warranted.[144] Two safeguards were added to ensure that even where the impact of a measure may be viewed as trivial, the measure itself can be examined if it could give rise to a question of interpretation of the

[140] Joined Apps. 5070/71, 5171/71, and 5186/71, *X v Federal Republic of Germany*, Decision of 10 July 1971, (1971) 42 CD 58, 60; cited with approval in Joined Apps. 5145/71, 5246/71, 5333/72, 5586/72, 5587/72, and 5532/72, *Ringeisen v Austria*, Decision of 2 April 1973, (1973) 43 CD 152; and App. 13284/87, *M v United Kingdom*, Decision of 15 October 1987, (1987) 54 DR 214.

[141] *Hadrabovå v Czech Republic*, (App. 42165/02), Decision of 25 September 2007.

[142] *Bagheri and Maliki v The Netherlands*, (App. 30164.06), Decision of 15 May 2007.

[143] Rule 47(3).

[144] Protocol 14 to the Convention for the Protection of Human Rights and Fundamental Freedoms, amending the Control System of the Convention, CETS No.194, Explanatory Report § 39.

Convention or there has been a failure to consider the application properly in national law. As an additional safeguard, the single judge formations and committees were not allowed to use this admissibility criterion for the first two years of its operation (from June 2010 to June 2012).[145] The obvious purpose was to enable Chambers and the Grand Chamber to establish some ground rules on the application of the new criterion before smaller groupings of judges could make use of it.

The case-law that has developed under Article 35(3)(b) has not been extensive[146] but has demonstrated some emerging interpretative principles applied by the Court, albeit on a case by case basis. First, a question arises as to how the three constituents of the criterion interact with each other. Although in some cases the Court did not examine 'significant disadvantage' where it found that the safeguards were not in place,[147] the more common approach has been to deal with each part of the criterion, with 'significant disadvantage' being examined, followed by the safeguards.

What is meant by 'significant disadvantage'?

The interpretation of what is 'significant' is based on the *de minimis* principle, meaning a violation of a right should attain 'a minimum level of severity to warrant consideration by an international court'.[148] In the first case decided under Article 35(3)(c), *Ionescu v Romania*,[149] the Court found that a financial loss of 90 euros did not have a significant impact on the applicant's personal situation. In *Korolev v Russia*,[150] the Court further stated that the interpretation of 'significant disadvantage' depends on both subjective and objective elements:

> The assessment of this minimum level is, in the nature of things, relative and depends on all the circumstances of the case...The severity of a violation should be assessed, taking account of both the applicant's subjective perceptions and what is objectively at stake in a particular case.[151]

The Court has found that the perception of the applicant as to the importance of the right in question is an important factor when deciding the significance of the interference. As well as the context of the financial loss of the applicant. In *Giuran v Romania*,[152] the applicant, a pensioner, had attempted to recover goods stolen from his house worth 350 euros. The applicant's desire to vindicate his right to possessions and home were taken into account as well as the fact that the average pension was worth 50 euros, making the sum significant to him. Conversely, in another case, the Court found that the applicant's feelings of unfair treatment were relevant but not enough on their own to objectively justify a

[145] See note 144, §§ 80–4, Protocol 14, Article 20.

[146] Between June 2010 and June 2012, the new criterion was considered in forty-two applications. Twenty-six of these resulted in the complaint being held inadmissible and, in sixteen cases, the Court rejected the use of the criterion. See the Court's overview of the use of Article 35(3)(b) in European Court of Human Rights Research Report 'The new admissibility criterion under Article 35 S3 (b) of the Convention case –law principles two years on' (Strasbourg 2012).

[147] *Finger v Bulgaria*, (App. 37346/05), 10 May 2011; *Flisar v Slovenia*, (App. 3127/09), Decision of 29 September 2011.

[148] *Korolev v Russia*, (App. 25551/05), 1 July 2010. The Court had not previously made significant use of the *de minimis* principle though the Court had found cases inadmissible under other criteria where there was a relatively minor interference with the right in question, for example see *Bock v Germany*, (App. 22051/07), Decision of 19 January 2010. In this case, the Court used Article 35(3)(a) to find a claim based on the reimbursement of 8 euros for medicines was an abuse of process.

[149] App. 36659/04, Decision of 1 June 2010.

[150] App. 25551/05, 1 July 2010.

[151] App. 25551/05, 1 July 2010.

[152] App. 24360/04, 21 June 2011.

finding of significant disadvantage.[153] In *Giusti v Italy*,[154] the court attempted to clarify the developing interpretation of significant disadvantage by stating that:

> In order to verify whether the violation of a right attained that minimum threshold, it is necessary to take into account *inter alia*: the nature of the right allegedly breached, the seriousness of the impact of the alleged violation on the exercise of the right and/or the potential consequences of the violation on the applicant's personal situation.[155]

Given the focus on the nature of the right, it has been argued that applications based on certain rights such as the non-derogable rights would always raise significant disadvantage.[156] Further, 'significant disadvantage' covers both financial and non-financial disadvantage. As noted, when the issue is based on financial disadvantage the court will consider the context, though in cases where the Court has found that there is no significant disadvantage the amounts at issue have been generally under 500 euros.[157] Non-financial cases have included the communication of information in court proceedings,[158] detention,[159] and expression.[160] In the first case to examine the application of the new criterion to Article 5(3), *Bannikov v Latvia*,[161] the Court found that detention for 1 year, 11 months and 18 days was not insignificant and that, given the length of detention and the importance of personal liberty, the '*de minimis* criterion could hardly be applied'. The concurring opinion went further, stating:

> How the respondent Government could, with a straight face, submit that the applicant was to be considered as having suffered no 'significant disadvantage' according to Article 35 § 3 (b) is beyond my powers of comprehension.[162]

The concurring opinion was also critical of the majority for devoting four paragraphs of the judgment to Article 35(3)(b) and in so doing giving the impression that there may be circumstances were an application under Article 5(1) and (3) may be 'insignificant'. The concurring opinion demonstrates that the meaning of '*de minimis*' is still an area of contention within the Court and as noted, it is arguable that it should not be applied in cases involving non-derogable rights and possibly the non-qualified rights such as Article 5 and Article 6:

> It would be a sad day indeed for fundamental human rights if, in order to reduce its backlog, the Court were to begin applying Article 35 § 3 (b) to Article 5 § 1 situations, instead of confining the said ground of inadmissibility to violations with a financial or patrimonial impact considered to be trivial.[163]

[153] *Ladygin v Russia*, (App. 35365/05), Decision of 30 August 2011. In this case, the applicant had been refused access to a court judge after he had attempted to gain access to the judge ahead of a queue of other people waiting. [154] App. No 13175/03, Decision of 30 August 2011. [155] *Giusti v Italy*, § 34.

[156] See A. Buyse, 'Significantly Insignificant? The Life in the Margins of the Admissibility Criterion in Article 35(3)(b) ECHR' in B. McGonigle Leyh, Y. Haeck, C. Burbano Herrera, and D. Contreras Garduno (eds.) *Liber Amicorum for Leo Zwaak* (Intersentia, Antwerp 2014).

[157] For example *Rinck v France*, (App. 18774/09) Decision of 19 October 2011,which involved a traffic fine of 150 euros. See European Court of Human Rights Research Report 'The new admissibility criterion under Article 35 S3 (b) of the Convention case-law principles two years on' (Strasbourg 2012).

[158] *Holub v Czech Republic*, (App. 24880/05), Decision on 14 December 2010, where it was held that the failure to provide third party information had not impacted a decision of the Constitutional Court. In contrast, the Court found a significant disadvantage in *3A.CZ s.r.o v Czech Republic*, (App. 21835/06), Decision on 10 February 2011, where information not given to the applicants was information of which they were not aware.

[159] In *Van Velden v the Netherlands*, (App. 30666/08), 19 July 2011, the Court held that a period of pre-trial detention amounted to significant disadvantage. [160] *Eon v France*, (App. 26118/10), 14 March 2013.

[161] App. 19279/03, 11 June 2013.

[162] *Bannikov v Latvia*. Concurring judgment of Judge De Gaetano, joined by Judge Ziemele § 1.

[163] *Bannikov v Latvia*, § 3.

In some cases, there may be a combination of a financial penalty and an interference with a non-financial interest. In *Eon v France*,[164]the applicant was convicted of an offence and given a suspended fine of 30 euros for insulting the Head of State. He had waved a placard reading 'Casse toi pov'con' ('Get lost, you sad prick'), a phrase used by the President when a farmer had refused to shake his hand. The phrase was widely disseminated in the media and on the internet, becoming a slogan.The Court, applying *Kolorev*[165] found that although the fine was small, the case was part of a debate of public interest in France and the law in question may have had a chilling effect on freedom of expression.[166]

As noted by the case-law we have examined, 'significant disadvantage' is at the core of the admissibility criterion. However the Court will usually examine whether the safeguards are in place. After finding that there was significant disadvantage in *Eon v France*,[167] the Court went on to note the importance of the matter, both in national debate and in convention terms.[168] The Court in *Bannikov v Latvia*[169] underlined the shortcomings in the domestic examination of the case as well as there being a significant disadvantage.[170]

Where a matter is found to be trivial, the safeguards have been used in a number of cases to allow the application to continue. The first safeguard concerning the importance of the matter for respect of human rights is worded similarly to Article 37 of the Convention which concerns the striking out of applications from the Court's case list and Article 39 concerning friendly settlement. The safeguard has been used to find the application admissible in applications involving a structural deficiency affecting other persons in the same position as the applicant,[171] inconsistent case-law in the State,[172] and the application of new legislation in a State.[173] Conversely, the Court has also held that in some situations respect for human rights does not require an examination of the merits by the Court; where the Court has already dealt with the issue in substantial case-law,[174] where the Court and Committee of Ministers have already addressed the issue as a systematic problem,[175] or where the domestic law has changed and the issue is only of historical interest.[176]

The first safeguard has been used more widely than the second safeguard concerning the examination of the application in national law. This has only been used in a handful of cases.[177] These cases involved procedural failings by the State and the words 'duly examined' in the clause does not require the State to examine the merits of every claim before a national court. This clause reflects the concept of subsidiarity, which requires the states to be primarily responsible for providing an effective remedy for alleged human rights

[164] *Eon v France*, (App. 26118/10), 14 March 2013, §§ 5–7.

[165] App. 25551/05, 1 July 2010. [166] *Eon v France*, (App. 26118/10), 14 March 2013, §§ 35–6.

[167] §§ 35–36. [168] § 35. [169] App. 19279/03, 11 June 2013. [170] § 59.

[171] *Kolorev v Russia*, (App. 25551/05), 1 July 2010.

[172] *Zivic v Serbia*, (App. 37204/08), 13 September 2011.

[173] *Nicoleta Gheeorghe v Romania*, (App. 23470/05), 3 April 2012.

[174] *Rinck v France*, (App. 18774/09) Decision of 19 October 2011.

[175] *Gururyan v Armenia*, (App. 111456/05), Decision of 24 January 2012.

[176] *Ionescu v Romania*, (App. 36659/04), Decision of 1 June 2010, see European Court of Human Rights Research Report 'The new admissibility criterion under Article 35 S3 (b) of the Convention case-law principles two years on' (Strasbourg2012) § 25.

[177] See European Court of Human Rights Research Report 'The new admissibility criterion under Article 35 S3 (b) of the Convention case-law principles two years on' (Strasbourg 2012) § 29. In the first two years of operation, the second safeguard clause had only been used in four cases to prevent the application of the criterion: *Dudek v Germany*, (App. 12977/09), Decision of 23 November 2010; *Finger v Bulgaria*, (App. 37346/05), 10 May 2011; *Flisar v Slovenia*, (App. 3127/09), Decision of 29 September 2011; *Fomin v Moldova*, (App. 36755/06), 11 October 2011.

violations.[178] The relationship between the European Court of Human Rights and national courts encapsulated by the notion of subsidiarity has been the focus of recent discussion on Court reform. The Brighton Declaration on court reform called for the removal of the second safeguard clause to reflect the emphasis on subsidiarity and the need to apply the admissibility criteria strictly.[179] When in force, Protocol 15[180] will remove the second safeguard clause from Article 35(3)(b). How much practical impact this will have is questionable given the low numbers of applicants that have successfully used the second safeguard clause to gain admissibility to the Court.

It is clear that 'insignificant disadvantage' was introduced to increase the efficiency of the Court by reducing the 'less serious' cases that come before the Court. However, it is still unclear how great an impact has been made on applications before the Court. Since the criterion has been fully operational at all levels of the complaints system, it has been used as the primary reason for inadmissibility in only a small number of cases.[181] Indeed, it has been noted that in many cases which could use this criterion, other admissibility criteria have been used more efficiently.[182]

JUDGMENT

Judgments of the Strasbourg Court must contain, *inter alia*, a summary of the facts, the arguments, and the reasons for the Court's decision.[183] Any judge who has taken part in the consideration of the case can annex a separate concurring or dissenting opinion. The names of the judges making up the majority and those annexing separate opinions must be stated. Judgments are structured around a common set of headings, which will typically be as follows:

- Procedure, which provides the details of the application and representation in the case.
- The Facts, which includes the circumstances of the case, and relevant national law and international law.
- The Law, which includes the alleged violation of the relevant Convention provision or provisions together with a summary of the arguments of the parties before concluding with the Court's assessment.
- Application of Article 41 on just satisfaction if that forms part of the Court's Judgment.[184]

[178] This is reflected in Art. 1 of the ECHR and Art. 13, which provides the right to an effective remedy in domestic law.

[179] High Level Conference on the Future of the European Court of Human Rights: Brighton Declaration 2012, § 14 and § 15(c).

[180] Protocol 15, Article 5.

[181] The criterion was used in less than 50 cases during the two years of restricted use (European Court of Human Rights Research Report 'The new admissibility criterion under Article 35 S3 (b) of the Convention case –law principles two years on' (Strasbourg 2012) § 32). From June 2012 until March 2013, the single judge formations have used Article 35(3)(b) in 127 decisions on admissibility, 68 of these were based solely on the criterion. (A. Buyse 'Significantly Insignificant? The Life in the Margins of the Admissibility Criterion in Article 35(3)(b) ECHR' in B. McGonigle Leyh, Y. Haeck, C. Burbano Herrera, and D. Contreras Garduno (eds.) *Liber Amicorum for Leo Zwaak* (Intersentia, Antwerp 2014), fn. 84.

[182] A. Buyse 'Significantly Insignificant? The Life in the Margins of the Admissibility Criterion in Article 35(3)(b) ECHR' in B. McGonigle Leyh, Y. Haeck, C. Burbano Herrera, and D. Contreras Garduno (eds.) *Liber Amicorum for Leo Zwaak* (Intersentia, Antwerp 2014), see Steering Committee for Human Rights (CDDH) 'CDDH report containing elements to contribute to the evaluation of the effects of Protocol No.14 to the Convention and implementation of the Interlaken and Izmir Declaration on the Court's situation' CDDH (2012) R76, Addendum II, November 2012.

[183] Rule 74.

[184] See later in this chapter.

- The *dispositif*, that is, a summary of the Court's rulings on the alleged violations of the Convention.
- Any separate concurring opinions or dissenting opinions.

Chamber judgments are generally delivered in either English or French, although all judgments which are published in the Court's official series of report are translated into the other official language.[185] Grand Chamber judgments are translated into both official languages prior to adoption.

The Court's judgments may be delivered in open court or, more usually, communicated to the parties in writing.[186] Within three months of the date of a Chamber judgment, it is open to the parties to request that the case be referred to the Grand Chamber.[187] A judgment of the Grand Chamber is final. Judgments of the Chambers become final when (1) the parties declare that they will not be seeking a referral; or (2) the three-month period expires without any request having been made; or (3) the panel of the Grand Chamber refuses a request for referral.[188]

A finding by the Court in its judgment of a violation of the Convention or Protocols places an obligation on the respondent State to make the changes required to the domestic legal order to avoid a repetition of the breach. This is inherent in the obligation in Article 46(1) to abide by the decision of the Court in any case to which the State is a party. Where the Strasbourg Court issues pilot judgments,[189] as in the *Kudła*[190] and *Broniowski*[191] cases, this may involve the introduction of new remedies in the national legal order where none exist, or the taking of steps to provide redress to a class of victims in the same position as the applicant in the case before the Court. Under Article 46(2) of the Convention, the Strasbourg Court's judgments are transmitted to the Committee of Ministers of the Council of Europe, which supervises their execution.[192] Protocol 14 has given an additional role to the Grand Chamber in the supervision of judgments. The Committee of Ministers can refer a case back to the Grand Chamber for infringement proceedings under Article 46 of the Convention.[193] A referral has to be agreed by two-thirds of the Committee of Ministers. A case may be referred where a contracting Party has failed to abide by a final judgment of the Court in a case to which it was party.[194] If the Grand Chamber finds that a State has failed to fulfil its obligations under Article 46, it shall refer the case back to the Committee of Ministers to consider further measures. The explanatory report for Protocol 14 noted that this procedure should only be used in exceptional cases but that it is a way of putting political pressure on States to comply with their obligations.[195]

185 Rule 76. In November 2013, the Court launched a Turkish version of the Court's case-law database (HUDOC) and a Russian interface is being completed (as of November 2013). The Court (supported by the Human Rights Trust Fund) has also increased the number of cases translated into the other languages of the Council of Europe. See the European Court of Human Rights Press Release, 335(2013) 14 November 2013. For some reflections on the form of judgments in the Strasbourg Court, see R. White, 'Judgments in the Strasbourg Court: Some Reflections' (July 17, 2009) available at SSRN: http://ssrn.com/abstract=1435197 or http://dx.doi.org/10.2139/ssrn.1435197. See also R. White and I. Boussiakou, 'Separate opinions in the European Court of Human Rights' (2009) 9 *Human Rights Law Review* 37–60.

186 Rule 77. 187 Article 43 ECHR and Rule 73 of the Rules of Court.

188 Article 44 ECHR. 189 See later in this chapter.

190 *Kudła v Poland*, (App. 30210/96), 26 October 2000 [GC], (2002) 35 EHRR 198, ECHR 2000-XI.

191 *Broniowski v Poland*, (App. 31443/96), 22 June 2004 [GC], (2005) 40 EHRR 495, ECHR 2004-V.

192 See ch.3.

193 Article 46 ECHR as amended by Protocol 14, Article 16. The Committee Ministers can also ask the Grand Chamber to clarify any confusion in the interpretation of a judgment. 194 Article 46(4).

195 Protocol 14 to the Convention for the Protection of Human Rights and Fundamental Freedoms, amending the Control System of the Convention, CETS No.194, Explanatory Report, § 100. The proceedings have not been used. However, in 2012 several NGOs submitted a formal request to the Committee of Ministers to initiate

PILOT JUDGMENTS PROCEDURE

Through development of its internal procedures, the Strasbourg Court has introduced pilot judgments as a means of addressing systemic problems in the Contracting Parties which result in multiple applications to the Court.[196] The slender legal base for such judgments is Article 46 under which Contracting Parties agree to 'abide by the final judgment of the Court in any case to which they are parties'. This has been strengthened by introducing a Rule of Court which sets out a regulatory framework for the use of the procedure.[197] The object of the pilot judgment is to set the environment in which the systemic problem can be addressed. Friberg says:

> The specific feature of the PJP [pilot judgments procedure] is that instead of dealing with each individual case, the Court singles out one or a small number of applications for priority treatment and adjourns all the other applications until the pilot case has been decided.[198]

In the judgment in the pilot case, the Strasbourg Court makes clear its expectations about how the respondent State should address the systemic problem and find a remedy not only for the individual applicant in the case, but also for all other applicants in look-alike cases. They would obtain a remedy under the new procedure established in the national legal order when the requirements of the pilot judgment are implemented. Friberg cites three important interests, which are served by the use of pilot judgments: (1) speedier redress for victims; (2) the systemic problem is redressed within the national legal order under guidance from the Strasbourg Court; and (3) the removal from the Strasbourg Court's docket of large numbers of repetitive complaints.

The first pilot judgment was given in the *Broniowski* case,[199] which concerned the operation of a legislative scheme to enable purchases at a discount of land by those who had lost land in the redrawing of the eastern border of Poland after the Second World War.[200]

Variants on the procedure soon grew up to enable Chambers to address some of the issues, as in the *Lukenda* case,[201] though Judge Zagrebelsky, in a partly dissenting opinion, indicated that he believed that the case should have been relinquished in favour of a Grand Chamber.[202]

proceedings against Russia for its failure to comply with the *Isayeva* judgment in 2005. European Human Right Advocacy Centre and Memorial Human Rights Centre *Request for the initiation of Infringement Proceedings by the Committee of Ministers in relation to the judgment of the European Court of Human Rights in Isayeva v Russia (No. 57950/00, 24 February 2005)*, 30 July 2012. At the time of writing this is still pending.

[196] Endorsed by the Committee of Ministers in Resolution DH (2004) 3 of 12 May 2004. See generally E. Friberg, 'Pilot Judgments from the Court's Perspective' in Council of Europe, *Towards Stronger Implementation of the European Convention on Human Rights at National Level* (Council of Europe Publishing, Strasbourg 2008), 86. Friberg is a registar of the Strasbourg Court; V. Colandrea, 'On the Power of the European Court of Human Rights to Order Specific Non-Monetary Measures: Some Remarks in Light of the *Assanidze, Broniowski* and *Sejdovic* Cases' (2007) 7 HRLRev 396; and C. Paraskeva, 'Human Rights Protection Begins and Ends at Home: The "Pilot Judgment Procedure" Developed by the European Court of Human Rights' (2007) 3 *Human Rights Law Commentary*, www.nottingham.ac.uk/law/hrlc/publications/hrlc.php.

[197] Rule 61 introduced in March 2011. This codifies the practice of the Court before 2011. The introduction of the Rule followed a request made in the Interlaken Declaration on the future of the Court, 2010.

[198] E. Friberg, 'Pilot Judgments from the Court's Perspective' in Council of Europe, *Towards Stronger Implementation of the European Convention on Human Rights at National Level* (Council of Europe Publishing, Strasbourg 2008), 87.

[199] *Broniowski v Poland*, (App. 31443/96), 22 June 2004, (2005) 40 EHRR 495; ECHR 2004-X. See also *Hutten-Czapska v Poland*, (App. 35014/97), 19 June 2006 [GC], (2007) 45 EHRR 52, ECHR 2006-VIII.

[200] The so-called Bug River Claims. See ch.20.

[201] *Lukenda v Slovenia*, (App. 23032/02), 6 October 2005, (2008) 47 EHRR 728; ECHR 2005-X; and *Burdov v Russia (No. 2)*, (App. 33509/04), 15 January 2009, (2009) 49 EHRR 22.

[202] For further examples of variants on the pilot judgment procedure, see *Xenides-Arestis v Turkey*, (App. 46347/99), 22 December 2005; *Sejdovic v Italy*, (App. 56581/00), 1 March 2006 [GC], ECHR 2006-II;

The use of pilot judgments continues to be limited despite the codification of the procedure. Between March 2011 and July 2013 there were approximately thirteen pilot judgments delivered by the Court.[203]

The President of the European Court of Human Rights has described the pilot judgment procedure as signifying a 'shift of tone, from the declaratory to the directive.'[204] He believes that the procedure has been successful in dealing with large numbers of cases quickly. However, he notes that the Court has been cautious when using the procedure and has in some cases given the State a wide margin of appreciation when implementing its judgment.[205]

The three judge committee for deciding on the merits of repetitive claims complements the pilot judgment procedure. However, Friberg has suggested that the Court could reduce the burden on itself even more if a more radical solution to repetitive cases was taken:

> What one could envisage is that, instead of delivering judgments in repetitive cases, the Court would simply certify that the case is to be settled in the light of the previous decisive judgment. The follow-up cases would be referred directly to the Committee of Ministers, not as decided cases but certified to be enforced on the basis of that existing judgment.[206]

REMEDIES UNDER ARTICLE 41

Article 41 of the Convention[207] provides that:

> If the Court finds that there has been a violation of the Convention or the protocols thereto, and if the internal law of the High Contracting Party concerned allows only partial reparation to be made, the Court shall, if necessary, afford just satisfaction to the injured party.

Respondent States are in principle free to choose the means whereby they will comply with a judgment in which the Court has found a breach. This discretion as to the manner of execution of a judgment reflects the freedom of choice attaching to the primary obligation of the Contracting States under Article 1 of the Convention to secure the rights and freedoms guaranteed. If the nature of the breach allows for *restitutio in integrum*, it is for

Scordino v Italy (No. 1), (App. 36813/97), 29 March 2006 [GC], (2007) 45 EHRR 207; ECHR 2006-V; *Driza v Albania*, (App. 33771/02), 13 November 2007, (2009) 49 EHRR 779, ECHR 2007-XII; *Urbárska Obec Rенčianske Biskupice v Slovakia*, (App. 74258/01), 27 November 2007, (2009) 48 EHRR 1139, ECHR 2007-nyr; *Gülmez v Turkey*, (App. 16330/02), 20 May 2008; and *Viaşu v Romania*, (App. 79951/01), 9 December 2008.

[203] For example *Ananyev and others v Russia*, (App. 42525/07), 10 January 2012; *Torreggiani and others v Italy*, (App. 43517/09) 8 January 2013 (both dealing with Article 3 and prison conditions); *Rumpf v Germany*, (App. 46344/06), 2 September 2010; *Athanasiou and others v Greece*, (App. 50973/08), 21 December 2010 (both dealing with Articles 6 and 13 and length of proceedings); *Greens and M.T v United Kingdom*, (App. 60041/08), 23 November 2010 (dealing with Protocol 1, Article 3 and prisoners' voting rights).

[204] Judge Dean Spielman, Keynote Speech *Judgments of the European Court of Human Rights Effects and Implementation* Conference at the Paulinerkirche Göttingen Georg-August-University, Göttingen 20 September 2013, 5.

[205] Judge Dean Spielman, Keynote Speech, 5–6, In *Greens and M.T v United Kingdom*, (App. 60041/08), 23 November 2010, the Court requested the UK to initiate legislative proposals on electoral law, but left the detail and scope of the legislation to the State.

[206] E. Friberg, 'Pilot Judgments from the Court's Perspective' in Council of Europe, *Towards Stronger Implementation of the European Convention on Human Rights at National Level* (Strasbourg 2008), 86, 93.

[207] See generally M. Mas, 'Right to Compensation under Article 50' in T. St. J. Macdonald, F. Matscher, and H. Petzold (eds.), *The European System for the Protection of Human Rights*, (Martinus Nijhoff, Dordrecht 1993), 775.

the respondent State to effect it, the Court having neither the power nor the practical possibility of doing so itself.[208]

If, on the other hand, national law does not allow—or allows only partial—reparation to be made for the consequences of the breach, the Strasbourg Court can, under Article 41, afford the injured party such satisfaction as appears to it to be appropriate. The Court's case-law under Article 41 (formerly Article 50) has been criticized for the lack of clear principles as to when damages should be awarded and how they should be measured.[209] Nonetheless, it is possible to identify a few general rules which the Strasbourg Court applies in determining questions of just satisfaction. Awards of financial just satisfaction can be made under three heads: pecuniary loss, non-pecuniary loss, and costs and expenses.

The Court will award damages only in respect of losses which can be shown to have been caused by the violation in question. In the *Kingsley* case,[210] for example, the applicant, who had been stripped of his licence to run a casino by a tribunal which was not independent for the purposes of Article 6(1), claimed compensation for all the losses which he claimed to have resulted from the loss of the licence. The Grand Chamber pointed out that it could not be assumed that a tribunal in compliance with Article 6(1) would have reached a different conclusion and let the applicant keep the licence. It could not, therefore, award financial compensation to the applicant in respect of loss of procedural opportunity or any distress, loss, or damage allegedly flowing from the outcome of the domestic proceedings.[211]

The most frequent award of just satisfaction beyond the declaration of a violation is the award of costs and expenses incurred in the case, either in the domestic proceedings or in Strasbourg. In either event, the costs must have been 'actually and necessarily incurred to prevent or redress the breach of the Convention,... [and] reasonable as to quantum'.[212]

ADVISORY OPINIONS OF THE EUROPEAN COURT OF HUMAN RIGHTS

Under Article 47 of the Convention[213] the Strasbourg Court has jurisdiction to give advisory opinions at the request of the Committee of Ministers[214] on legal questions concerning the interpretation of the Convention and its accompanying Protocols. The Court is required to sit as a Grand Chamber in considering such requests and must deliver a reasoned opinion on the questions referred; separate opinions are permitted.[215] Though a request for an Opinion was made in January 2002, no advisory opinion followed, since the Court decided that the request was outside its competence.[216] The first advisory opinion

208 See generally L. Loucaides, 'Reparation for violations of human rights under the European Convention and restitutio in integrum' [2008] EHRLR 182; and L. Wildhaber, 'Reparations for Internationally Wrongful Acts of States. Article 41 of the European Convention on Human Rights: Just Satisfaction under the European Convention on Human Rights' (2003) 3 *Baltic Yearbook of International Law* 1.

209 See, for example, the report prepared jointly by the English and Scottish Law Commissions, *Damages under the Human Rights Act 1998*, Law Com. No. 266/Scot Law Com. No. 180, §§ 3.4 and following. See also A. Mowbray, 'The European Court of Human Rights' Approach to Just Satisfaction' [1997] PL 647.

210 *Kingsley v United Kingdom*, (App. 35605/97), 28 May 2002 [GC], (2002) 35 EHRR 177, ECHR 2002-IV.

211 § 43. 212 § 49.

213 Formerly the Second Protocol which has been in force since 21 September 1970.

214 Decisions to request an advisory opinion require a majority vote: Art. 47(3) of the Convention.

215 Art. 31b of the Convention. See the Rules of Court for the procedural rules surrounding advisory opinions.

216 *Decision on the competence of the Court to give an advisory opinion*. 2 June 2004 [GC], ECHR 2004-VI.

was delivered in February 2008 on the question of nominations for election as a judge at the Strasbourg Court.[217]

The paucity of advisory opinions is hardly surprising since Article 47(2) provides:

> Such opinions shall not deal with any question relating to the content or scope of the rights or freedoms defined in Section I of the Convention and in the protocols thereto, or with any other questions which the Commission, the Court or the Committee of Ministers might have to consider in consequence of any such proceedings as could be instituted in accordance with the Convention.

On 2 June 2004 the Court decided that the request by the Committee of Ministers for an advisory opinion made in January 2002 concerning the coexistence of the European Convention and the Convention on Human Rights and Fundamental Freedoms of the Commonwealth of Independent States ('the CIS Convention') was outside its competence.[218] The CIS Convention was signed on 26 May 1995 and entered into force on 11 August 1998 on its ratification by Belarus, the Kyrgyz Republic, the Russian Federation, and Tajikistan. Among the Convention's measures of implementation is a CIS Commission with competence to examine individual and collective applications alleging breaches of the Convention provisions. As at the date of the Court's decision, the CIS Commission had not been set up. The existence of the CIS Convention machinery has troubled the Parliamentary Assembly and the Committee of Ministers for some time. Concern was expressed at the potential for conflict between the operation of the CIS Convention and of the European Convention. In January 2002 the Committee of Ministers accepted the recommendation of the Parliamentary Assembly to ask for an advisory opinion.[219]

The Court adopted a narrow view of its jurisdiction to give advisory opinions, noting that the intention was to provide for advisory opinions on questions which could not arise from contentious proceedings. Examples given were such things as the election of judges and the procedure of the Committee of Ministers in exercising its role in the supervision of judgments. In deciding that it lacked competence to provide the requested opinion, the Court said:[220]

> The Court considers that the purpose of the provisions excluding its advisory jurisdiction is to avoid the potential situation in which the Court adopts in an advisory opinion a position which might prejudice its later examination of an application brought under Articles 33 or 34 of the Convention and that it is irrelevant that such an application has not and may never be lodged.

The Court concluded that it might be called upon in contentious proceedings to determine whether the procedures under the CIS Convention constituted 'another procedure of international investigation or settlement' and so it lacked the competence to respond to the request for an advisory opinion.

The restrictive framing of the conditions for advisory opinions of the European Court of Human Rights is in contrast to the much broader advisory opinion procedure under the Inter-American Convention on Human Rights, which is open to Member States of the Organization of American States and has proved to be a particularly fruitful source of

[217] *Advisory Opinion on certain legal questions concerning the lists of candidates submitted with a view to the election of judges to the European Court of Human Rights*, 12 February 2008 [GC], (2009) 49 EHRR 825, ECHR 2008-nyr. See earlier in this chapter.

[218] *Decision on the Competence of the Court to Give an Advisory Opinion*, 2 June 2004; ECHR 2004-VI.

[219] Recommendation 1519 (2001) of 23 May 2001.

[220] § 33 of the Decision of 2 June 2004.

case-law under that Convention.[221] Advisory opinions of the International Court of Justice have also had a significant influence on the development of international law,[222] and the preliminary ruling procedure[223] under Article 267 of the Treaty on the Functioning of the European Union[224] has been an outstanding success in securing both the development of European Community law and its uniform application throughout the Member States.[225]

Given the success of other international courts, a Wise Persons Report from 2006 suggested the extension of the use of advisory opinions as a way of expanding the Strasbourg Court's constitutional role.[226] This discussion was raised again as part of the Izmir Declaration on the future of the Court in 2011.[227] The Brighton Declaration 2012[228] also included a proposal on advisory opinions. A Reflection Paper[229] from the Court followed, which further discussed the objectives and implications of an extended advisory jurisdiction. It highlighted the benefit of creating an institutional dialogue between domestic courts and Strasbourg, furthering subsidiarity.[230] These developments have led to the adoption of Protocol 16,[231] which will come into force after ten States ratify the Protocol.

The new advisory opinion procedure does not replace the Article 47 procedure but complements it. It allows States to refer a case to the Grand Chamber for an advisory opinion on 'questions of principle relating to the interpretation or application of the rights and freedoms defined in the Convention or protocols...' if they wish to do so.[232] The Grand Chamber may refuse a request and must give reasons for doing so.[233] If it accepts a referral then the Grand Chamber's Advisory Opinion is non-binding.[234]

The optional nature of the procedure underlines the principle of subsidiarity; it is the State that is primarily responsible for decisions on human rights violations so advisory opinions should only be of benefit where the State needs clarification or guidance.[235] The non-binding nature of an Advisory Opinion retains the importance of the right to individual petition.

As noted, the development of this new procedure has been influenced by the success of instruments such as the TFEU procedure. However, there are notable differences between the EU and the ECHR procedures. Rulings given by the Court of Justice of the European Union under the Article 267 TFEU procedure are binding on EU national courts, and in

[221] See Art. 64 of the American Convention on Human Rights of 22 November 1969, OAS Treaty Series No 36. As at 31 December 2004, the Inter-American Court had delivered 18 advisory opinions.

[222] See S. Rosenne, *The Law and Practice of the International Court 1920–1996*, Vol. I (3rd edn Martinus Nijhoff, The Hague 1997), ch.5.

[223] The jurisdiction of the Court of Justice is not advisory in the sense used above, though it does operate as an effective partnership between national courts and the Community court by providing national courts with authoritative interpretations of Community law which they must apply to the cases before them.

[224] Formerly Art. 234 of the EC Treaty.

[225] See generally L. Neville Brown and T. Kennedy, *The Court of Justice of the European Communities*, (5th edn Sweet & Maxwell, London 2000), ch.10.

[226] Report of the Group of Wise Persons to the Committee of Ministers, 15 November 2006, CM (2006)203, § 81.

[227] High Level Conference on the Future of the European Court of Human Rights, Izmir Declaration 26-27 April 2011. See ch.25 for a discussion on the Court's role.

[228] High Level Conference on the Future of the European Court of Human Rights, Brighton Declaration 19-20 April 2012, § 12(d).

[229] European Court of Human Rights 'Reflection Paper on the Proposal to extend the Court's jurisdiction' (Strasbourg 2012).

[230] 'Reflection Paper on the Proposal to extend the Court's jurisdiction' § 4–11. There were some dissenting opinions, with concerns raised about the impact on the case load of the Court, § 11. The Paper went on to note the argument that the new mechanisms would reduce workload in the long term, § 16.

[231] Protocol 16 ECHR adopted 6 May 2013, (not yet in force).

[232] Protocol 16, Article 1.

[233] Protocol 16, Article 2.

[234] Protocol 16, Article 3.

[235] European Court of Human Rights 'Reflection Paper on the Proposal to extend the Court's jurisdiction' (Strasbourg 2012) § 32.

certain cases the highest national courts must refer cases to that Court. These differences reflect the different nature of the two systems.[236]

THE REFORM PROCESS: PROTOCOLS 15 AND 16 AND BEYOND

Protocol 14 was designed to enable the Strasbourg Court to streamline some of its procedures in order to make the most effective use possible of the judicial resources available to it. It was opened for signature on 13 May 2004. After a delay caused by Russia's refusal to ratify, the other Forty-six Member States agreed on an interim measure to allow some of the provisions to come into force for those States.[237] Protocol 14 eventually came into force in June 2010, after Russia ratified.[238] As noted, the new admissibility criterion was controversial and was framed against the background of a debate between those who envisaged an increasing constitutional role for the Court and those who perceived the reform as undermining the accessibility of human rights protection to individuals.[239] The reform process has had to tread a narrow path between these two conceptions of the Strasbourg Court's role.

FURTHER REFORM

Despite the changes introduced by Protocol 14, it was recognized that the Protocol would not alone resolve the problems surrounding the volume of applications to the Strasbourg Court.[240] Discussions on further reform have taken place in a series of Inter-governmental Conferences at Interlaken, Izmir, and Brighton. The 'Interlaken Process' of further reform has led to the adoption of Protocol 15 and 16.[241] The practical need to decrease the Court workload in order to maintain the effectiveness of the Court is clearly one reason for ongoing reform. However this practical aim is fuelled by an internal and public debate on the future role of the European Court of Human Rights.[242] During discussion at Brighton in 2012, it was proposed that the margin of appreciation doctrine developed by the Court be included in the ECHR itself.[243] Although it has not been made into a substantive clause, it will be added to the preamble by Protocol 15 to underline the importance of subsidiarity. How this will influence the jurisprudence of the Court is debatable and it may be more symbolic than practical.

[236] For a discussion of the similarities and differences between the European Union preliminary ruling procedure and the European Convention advisory opinion procedure, see P. Gragl, '(Judicial) love is not a one way street: the EU preliminary reference procedure as a model for ECtHR advisory opinions under draft Protocol No. 16' (2013) *European Law Review* 38(2), 229–247.

[237] Protocol 14bis 2009 brought the single judge formation and committees into force for those States who had ratified the protocol.

[238] See L. Caflisch, 'The reform of the European Court of Human Rights: Protocol No. 14 and beyond' (2006) 6 HRLRev 403.

[239] For a general overview of the debates surrounding Protocol 14 see P. Sardaro 'The Right of Individual Petition to the European Court' in P. Lemmens and W. Vanderhole (eds.) *Protocol 14 and the Reform of the European Court of Human Rights* (Intersentia, Antwerp 2005), 44–67.

[240] See ch.25.

[241] Both open for signature as of 2 October 2013.

[242] See ch. 25.

[243] High Level Conference on the Future of the European Court of Human Rights, Brighton Declaration 19–20 April 2012, § 12 (b).

CONCLUDING REMARKS

To a certain extent, the Court had become a victim of its own success. Protocol 11 was adopted to assist the Strasbourg organs to deal effectively with the rapidly increasing caseload, but only a few years after its coming into force, the Court amended its Rules of Procedure to enable Committees to deal with inadmissible cases even more summarily. The changes made by Protocol 14 were designed to reduce the Court's caseload and there is evidence that the changes are beginning to reduce the caseload. In 2012, the Court's backlog has decreased for the first time in several years. At the end of 2012, the backlog of applications was 128,100; a reduction of 23,000 from the previous year and by October 2013, this number has further decreased to 111, 350.[244] Whilst the backlog is still substantial, the evidence suggests it is under control. Despite the continuing reform of the Court, it continues to accept individual applicants who meet the criteria. The right to individual petition is still at the heart of the European Court's complaint system.[245]

However, it is evident from the continuing reform process that the focus is now on the relationship between the International court and domestic jurisdictions. Subsidiarity has been central to the discussion during the High-level conferences at Interlaken, Izmir, and Brighton. This is reflected in Protocols 15 and 16. A constructive dialogue between the Strasbourg Court and domestic courts may help to further decrease the Court's workload. However, in the longer term, further changes may be needed if the Court is to function as effectively in its second fifty years as it has in its first fifty years.

[244] See 2012 Annual Report of the European Court (2013) and Statistics of the European Court, available at http://www.echr.coe.int/Pages/home.aspx?p=reports&c=, see also European Court of Human Rights Press Release 312(2013), 24 October 2013.

[245] See High Level Conference on the Future of the European Court of Human Rights, Brighton Declaration 19-20 April 2012, § 13 "The right of individual application is a cornerstone of the Convention system. The right to present an application to the Court should be practically realisable, and States Parties must ensure that they do not hinder in any way the effective exercise of this right".

APPENDIX

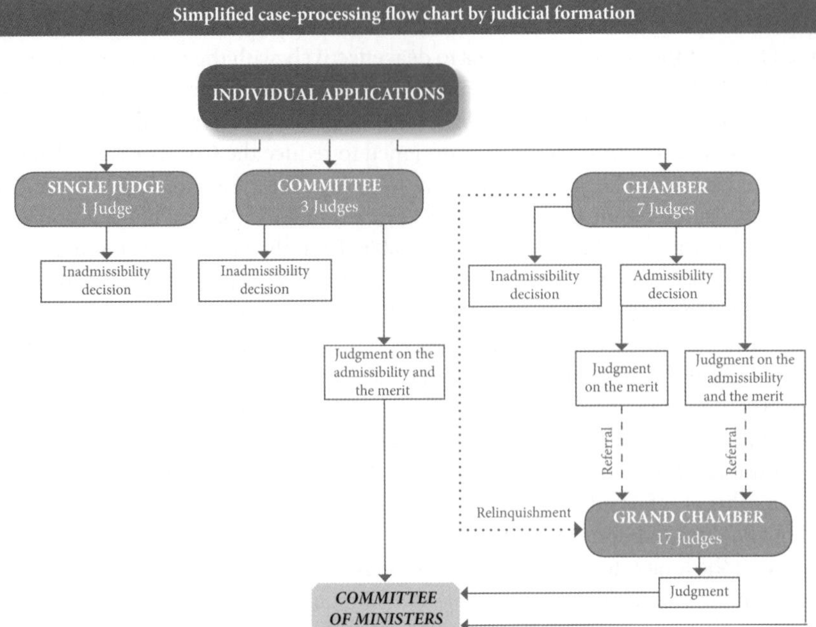

Figure 2.1 Case processing flow chart

Source: Reproduced with the permission of the European Court of Human Rights. This flow chart indicates the progress of a case through the different judicial formations. In the interests of readability, it does not include certain stages in the procedure—such as communication of an application to the respondent State, consideration of a re-hearing request by the Panel of the Grand Chamber and friendly settlement negotiations.

3

SUPERVISING THE ENFORCEMENT OF JUDGMENTS

INTRODUCTION

As mentioned in Chapter 2, the Strasbourg Court's judgments are final[1] and binding on respondent States.[2] It is however evident that, without compliance or enforcement, even the best of judgments is of little value to the victims of human rights violations. As Leni Fischer, the President of the Council of Europe's Parliamentary Assembly, said at the new Court's inauguration ceremony on 3 November 1998:

> What the new European Court of Human Rights needs most is unequivocal respect for and follow-up to its decisions in the Council of Europe member countries. This alone will provide the Court with the authority it needs in order to protect the fundamental rights of our people.[3]

The Committee of Ministers is the organ of the Council of Europe which is alone charged with the task of supervising the execution of these judgments.[4] The Committee of Ministers effectively 'signs off' judgments and friendly settlements;[5] and its manner of exercising this function has increased in rigour over time. Most recently, Protocol 14 introduced some significant changes. The Committee has recently begun producing very informative annual reports on the supervision of the execution of judgments.[6] During the calendar year 2012, 1,438 new judgments finding a violation of a Convention provision were brought before the Committee for supervision of their execution (which represented

[1] Art. 44 ECHR.

[2] Art. 46(1) ECHR provides: 'The High Contracting Parties undertake to abide by the final judgment of the Court in any case to which they are parties'.

[3] Council of Europe Press Release No. 729/98. See also Committee of Ministers Recommendation CM/Rec(2008)2 on efficient domestic capacity for rapid execution of judgments of the European Court of Human Rights, 6 February 2008.

[4] Art. 46(2) of the Convention provides: 'The final judgment of the Court shall be transmitted to the Committee of Ministers, which shall supervise its execution'.

[5] See generally, E. Abdelgawad, *The execution of judgments of the European Court of Human Rights*, 2nd edn Human Rights Files No. 19 (Council of Europe Publishing, Strasbourg 2008); J. Sims, 'Compliance without Remands: The Experience under the European Convention on Human Rights, (2004) 36 *Arizona State Law Journal* 639; M. Marmo, 'The Execution of Judgments of the European Court of Human Rights—A Political Battle' (2008) 15 MJ 235; and L. Miara and V. Prais, 'The Role of Civil Society in the Execution of Judgments of the European Court of Human Rights' [2012] EHRLR 528.

[6] For the latest report, see Committee of Ministers, *Supervision of the Execution of Judgments of the European Court of Human Rights. Sixth Annual Report 2012* (Council of Europe Publishing, Strasbourg 2013) (referred to in this chapter as 'the *Sixth Annual Report*').

a decrease on the previous year's figure of 1,606). As at the end of the calendar year, there were 11,099 judgments still under active consideration by the Committee.[7]

COMPOSITION AND PROCEDURE OF COMMITTEE OF MINISTERS

According to Article 14 of the Statute of the Council of Europe, each of the Contracting Parties is entitled to one representative on the Committee of Ministers, and each representative is entitled to one vote. In principle these representatives are the Ministers of Foreign Affairs of each Contracting Party, but the Ministers themselves usually meet only twice a year. At the bimonthly meetings which the Committee devotes to its tasks under the Convention, the Ministers act through their Deputies, namely their Permanent Representatives[8] in Strasbourg. The Committee is assisted by a Secretariat provided by the Secretary-General of the Council of Europe.

The Committee operates under Rules of Procedure adopted in May 2006 in the exercise of its supervisory function under Article 46(2) of the Convention.[9] Its functions include the supervision of the execution of friendly settlements as well as judgments of the Court. The Committee's deliberations remain confidential, although an increasing amount of information about the execution of judgments is made public, notably on the internet,[10] and through the annual reports.

The first section of the rules covers general provisions. Rules 1 and 2 are concerned with the organization and chairmanship of meetings. The Chair rotates among the Contracting Parties. Rule 3 provides that a judgment of the Court should be included on the Committee's agenda without delay; in practice, this is within six weeks of the Court's judgment. Rule 4 provides that violations which indicate a systemic problem should be given priority in the Committee's work, but not to the detriment of violations which have caused grave consequences for the injured party. Under Rule 5, the Committee adopts an annual report which is sent to the Court, the Secretary-General, the Parliamentary Assembly, and the Commissioner for Human Rights.

The second section of the rules concerns the supervision of the execution of judgments. The Committee invites the respondent State to explain the measures taken as a consequence of the finding of a violation of Convention rights, and this will include the provision of any just satisfaction awarded by the Court. Of particular importance are general measures taken by the Contracting Party to avoid violations in the future in similar situations. Responses are expected promptly. If the respondent State informs the Committee that it is not yet in a position to provide information about measures taken in execution of the judgment, which, because of the shortness of the six-week delay, will frequently occur at the first meeting at which the judgment is placed on the agenda, the case will automatically return to the agenda of the following meeting. The Committee will then re-examine the case at each subsequent meeting until the required individual measures have been

[7] Source: the *Sixth Annual Report*.

[8] Ambassadors.

[9] Rules of the Committee of Ministers for the supervision of the execution of judgments and of the terms of friendly settlements adopted by the Committee of Ministers on 10 May 2006 at the 964th meeting of the Ministers' Deputies, available on the Council of Europe's website dedicated to the supervision of the execution of the Court's judgments: www.coe.int/t/dghl/monitoring/execution/default_en.asp.

[10] www.coe.int/t/dghl/monitoring/execution/default_en.asp.

effected, and every six months until the general measures necessary to ensure compliance with the judgment have been taken.

Since January 2011, the supervision of the adoption and implementation of action plans has followed a new twin-track procedure.[11] Most cases follow the standard procedure. An enhanced procedure is used for cases requiring urgent individual measures or revealing important structural problems (in particular pilot judgments) and for inter-State cases. This enhanced procedure enables priority attention to be given to such cases by the Committee of Ministers. These cases are regularly included on the Committee of Ministers meeting's agenda.

Though the deliberations of the Committee of Ministers on these issues are generally confidential, Rule 8 provides that, unless the Committee decides otherwise in order to protect legitimate public or private interests, the agenda of each meeting and certain information shall be accessible to the public, namely:

- information and documents provided by the respondent State; and
- information supplied by the victim,[12] by a non-governmental organization, or national human rights bodies.

Article 16 of Protocol 14 gives new powers to the Committee of Ministers which are designed to make the execution of judgments of the Court more effective. The Committee of Ministers may apply for an interpretation of a judgment where execution of the judgment is hindered by a problem of interpretation. The Committee of Ministers may also bring infringement proceedings against a Contracting State which it alleges has violated Article 46 of the Convention by failing to implement a judgment of the Court.[13] The Committee must first serve a notice on the recalcitrant State. Such proceedings will be heard by a Grand Chamber. They are also seen as necessary only in 'exceptional circumstances.'[14] Rules 10 and 11 recognize these changes. Rule 10 permits referral back to the Court for interpretation of the judgment. Such decisions require a majority vote of two thirds of the representatives entitled to sit on the Committee. Rule 11 contains the procedure for referring back to the Strasbourg Court a question of refusal to abide by a final judgment of the Court.

The third section of the rules concerns the supervision of the execution of the terms of friendly settlements, and largely parallels the provisions of the second section. Rule 16 allows the Committee to make interim resolutions. An example would be for the respondent State to provide information on the progress of the execution of the judgment, or for the Committee to express concern or to make relevant suggestions with respect to the execution of the judgment. Rule 17 provides that:

> After having established that the High Contracting Party concerned has taken all the necessary measures to abide by the judgment or that the terms of the friendly settlement have

[11] CM/INF/DH(2010)45 final, December 7, 2010, 'Supervision of the execution of the judgments and decision of the European Court of Human Rights: implementation of the Interlaken Action plan—Outstanding issues concerning the practical modalities of implementation of the new twin track supervision system.' Document prepared by the Department for the Execution of Judgments of the European Court of Human Rights (DG-HL) and finalized after the 1,100th meeting (December 2010) (DH) of the Ministers' Deputies.

[12] Whose anonymity will be preserved if anonymity has been granted under Rule 47(3) of the Rules of Court.

[13] But note the ability of an applicant to complain that in a further application that a judgment has not been implemented, as in *Verein Gegen Tierfabriken Schweiz (VgT) v Switzerland (No. 2)*, (App. 32772/02), 30 June 2009 [GC], ECHR 2009, in which the Grand Chamber found a violation of Article 10 arising from the continuing failure of the respondent State to permit the broadcasting of the commercial following an earlier judgment of the Court.

[14] Explanatory Memorandum, § 100.

> been executed, the Committee of Ministers shall adopt a resolution concluding that its functions under Article 46, paragraph 2...of the Convention have been exercised.

The Committee's resolutions are available from the Council of Europe and within HUDOC.

Since 1974, the Rules have permitted a quasi-adversarial process as regards the execution of individual measures, such as the payment of monetary compensation, the grant of a residence permit, or the reopening of court proceedings. The victim of a violation may submit written comments and respond to those of the respondent State in connection with such issues.[15]

However, in a large number of cases brought before the Court, the prime concern of applicants is not just to ameliorate their personal situation, but also to achieve changes to existing domestic law or practice. There is no formal right of access to the Committee's decision-making process as regards the need for general measures, either for the victim or for interested non-governmental organizations or other third parties. It would, however, appear that in practice the Committee's Secretariat will, where necessary, seek and receive information from individual applicants, non-governmental and international organizations[16] to assist in determining the nature and extent of reforms needed to ensure compliance with the Court's judgment and the extent to which measures recommended to the respondent State through interim resolutions have been carried out. Any material received in this way by the Secretariat will not be used directly as a basis for discussion in the Committee, but will instead be forwarded to the respondent State for information.

The Committee's voting procedures are governed by the Statute of the Council of Europe. A quorum consisting of the representatives of two-thirds of the Contracting Parties is necessary before any meeting can proceed. For the adoption of a resolution or interim resolution a simple majority of all the Contracting Parties and a two-thirds majority of all the States present at the meeting is required. For certain matters unanimity is required.[17]

THE EXECUTION OF JUDGMENTS

JUST SATISFACTION

In every case where the Strasbourg Court finds a violation, it has the power under Article 41 of the Convention to award just satisfaction.[18] If the Court decides to make a monetary award, it will require the respondent State to pay the applicant within three months of the delivery of the judgment.[19] After the Committee's first examination at its meeting immediately following the delivery of the judgment, a case involving an award of just satisfaction will usually come up for renewed examination after the expiry of the three-month time limit. If the respondent State is unable to supply proof of payment, the case will return to the agenda at every subsequent meeting until the Committee is satisfied that the money has been paid in full. Since January 1996, to safeguard the value of an award in the case of delayed payment, the Court has included an order to States to pay simple interest,

[15] Rules 9 and 15.

[16] The memorandum prepared by the Committee of Ministers' Secretariat on Cases concerning the action of security forces in Northern Ireland, CM/Inf (2004) 14, 29 October 2004, refers to comments received from, among others, the applicants' lawyers and from the Northern Ireland Human Rights Commission.

[17] Article 20 of the Statute. [18] See ch.2.

[19] In 2012 €176.8 million was awarded to victims by way of compensation, costs, and expenses; source: the *Sixth Annual Report*. This represented a considerable increase on previous years and seems to be largely due to three exceptional cases against Italy in which over €100 million was paid in just satisfaction.

calculated on a daily basis, from the expiry of the three months until payment. To guard against inflation and for ease of comparison, the Court now expresses all monetary awards in euros, to be converted into the national currency at the date of payment.

Until the *Loizidou* case,[20] the most difficult case involving just satisfaction that the Committee of Ministers had had to deal with, and which was, indeed, largely responsible for the introduction of default interest, was the *Stran Greek Refineries* case.[21] The applicant company had entered into a contract with the Greek State (which at the time was governed by the military junta) to build an oil refinery, and had incurred considerable expenditure procuring goods and services for the construction of the refinery. When the democratic Government regained power, they decided that it was not in the national interest for the refinery to be built and they terminated the contract. The company started proceedings against the State for compensation for the expenditure it had incurred under the terms of the contract, and a substantial arbitration award was made against the Government, which appealed to the Court of Cassation. However, the State then asked for the hearing to be postponed on the ground that a draft law concerning the point in issue was just about to go through Parliament. The new legislation in fact made it inevitable that the Court of Cassation would find against the applicant. The Strasbourg Court unanimously found a violation of Article 6(1), and awarded pecuniary damages of almost US$30,000,000, together with simple interest at 6 per cent from 27 February 1984 (the date of the arbitration award) to the date of judgment.

Because of the size of the award, the Greek Government refused to pay within the three-month limit and asked the Committee if it could pay by instalments over a period of five years, without interest. This request was rejected by the Committee; the President at the time[22] wrote to the Greek Minister of Foreign Affairs, stressing that:

> the credibility and effectiveness of the mechanism for the collective enforcement of human rights established under the Convention was based on the respect of the obligations freely entered into by the States and in particular in respect of the supervisory bodies.[23]

In the event, the case was not resolved until 17 January 1997, when, as a result of increasing pressure applied by the Committee, the Greek Government transferred US$30,863,828 to the applicants, corresponding to the just satisfaction awarded by the Court, increased in order to provide compensation for the loss of value caused by the delay in payment.[24]

OTHER INDIVIDUAL MEASURES

In addition to the payment of compensation, individual measures may be required to ensure that the injured party is put, as far as possible, in the same situation as he or she enjoyed prior to the violation of the Convention (*restitutio in integrum*). For example, where the Court has found a violation of Article 8 of the Convention caused by the refusal to allow adequate contact between a parent and a child in public care, the respondent State will be required to facilitate more frequent access visits; in a deportation case under Article 3 or 8, a residence permit should be granted; and so on.

[20] *Loizidou v Turkey*, (App. 15318/89), 23 March 1995 (preliminary objections) Series A No 310, (1995) 20 EHRR 99, 18 December 1996 (merits), (1997) 23 EHRR 513, ECHR 1996-VI; and 28 July 1998 (just satisfaction), ECHR 1998-IV.

[21] *Stran Greek Refineries and Stratis Andreadis v Greece*, (App. 13427/87), 9 December 1994, Series A No 301-B, (1994) 19 EHRR 293.

[22] The Estonian Foreign Minister.

[23] Res. DH (1997) 184, 20 March 1997.

[24] Res. DH (1997) 184, 20 March 1997.

The individual measure most commonly required for *restitutio in integrum* is the reopening of domestic legal proceedings. The need for such a measure arises primarily in respect of criminal proceedings, since problems with civil proceedings can frequently be remedied through financial compensation.[25] But a criminal conviction may need to be quashed, or a retrial ordered, in two types of situation: first, where the Court has found procedural injustice in the original trial giving rise to a violation of Article 6; or, secondly, where it has found that the substantive criminal law of a State is incompatible with one of the provisions of the Convention, for example, where an applicant has been tried and convicted for proselytism, contrary to Article 9,[26] or for exercising his or her right to freedom of expression in some way prohibited by national law.[27]

In its Recommendation No. R (2000) 2, adopted on 19 January 2000, the Committee asked Contracting Parties to provide means of reopening proceedings within their national legal systems following a finding of violation by the Strasbourg Court, particularly where the injured party continues to suffer very serious negative consequences because of the outcome of the domestic decision at issue, which are not adequately remedied by the just satisfaction and cannot be rectified except by re-examination or reopening, or where the judgment of the Court leads to the conclusion that the impugned domestic decision is on the merits contrary to the Convention, or the violation found is based on procedural errors or shortcomings of such gravity that a serious doubt is cast on the outcome of the domestic proceedings complained of. Most Contracting Parties have now incorporated some mechanism into national law to permit criminal proceedings to be reopened in the circumstances outlined above.[28]

GENERAL MEASURES

The aim of general measures is to prevent the recurrence of similar violations of the Convention. There are many examples of States taking action as a result of findings of violations of the Convention, including, in the United Kingdom, changes in military policy to allow homosexuals to serve in the armed forces,[29] amendment of the law so that both men and women become entitled to free bus passes at the age of 60,[30] changes to rules on prisoners' correspondence,[31] the abolition of corporal punishment in schools,[32] and the decriminalization of consensual homosexual acts in Northern Ireland.[33] Sometimes the changes made are less salutary. For example, the Court held in the *Abdulaziz, Cabales and*

[25] As in the *Stran Greek Refineries* case, earlier.

[26] For example, *Kokkinakis v Greece*, (App. 14307/88), 25 May 1993, Series A No 260-A, (1994) 17 EHRR 397: see ch.17.

[27] See ch.18.

[28] In Turkey, the Constitution was amended in 2003 to allow retrials following a finding of violation of Article 6 by the Strasbourg Court, but not for cases pending on that date before the domestic courts; it is thought that the latter exception was adopted to avoid having to give the Kurdish leader Öcalan a retrial: see *Öcalan v Turkey*, (App. 46221/99), 12 May 2005 [GC], (2005) 41 EHRR 985, ECHR 2005-IV.

[29] Following the judgment in *Smith and Grady v United Kingdom*, (Apps. 33985/96 and 33986/96), 27 September 1999, (2000) 29 EHRR 493, ECHR 1999-VI, the 'Armed Forces Code of Social Conduct' was brought into force on 12 January 2000, lifting the ban.

[30] *Matthews v United Kingdom*, (App. 40302/98), 15 July 2002 (friendly settlement).

[31] Following *Silver and others v United Kingdom*, (Apps. 5947/72, 6205/73, 7052/75, 7061/75, 7107/75, 7113/75, and 7136/75), 25 March 1983, Series A No 61, (1983) 5 EHRR 347.

[32] Following *Campbell and Cosans v United Kingdom*, (App. 7511/76 and 7743/76), 25 February 1982, Series A No 48, (1982) 4 EHRR 293.

[33] Following *Dudgeon v United Kingdom*, (App. 7525/76), 22 October 1981, Series A No 45, (1982) 4 EHRR 149.

Balkandali case[34] that immigration rules which permitted men to bring their non-national wives to live with them in the United Kingdom, but did not allow women in the same position to gain entry clearance for their husbands, gave rise to a violation of Articles 8 and 14 taken together. The respondent State's response—accepted, as it had to be, by the Committee of Ministers—was to bring an end to the discrimination by removing the right of entry for husbands and wives alike.

Over half of the general measures taken by respondent States involve changes to legislation. Other general measures include administrative reforms, changes to court practice, or the introduction of human rights training for the police.

As mentioned earlier, the Committee's Rules provide that, until it is satisfied with the general measures taken by a respondent State to comply with a judgment of the Court, the case will return to the Committee's agenda every six months at least. On the whole, States are relatively quick to implement the recommendations of the Committee in respect of general measures, sometimes even adopting the necessary measures before the case in question comes before the Committee or even the Court.[35] When implementation is delayed, this can be for a variety of reasons, including technical problems, economic issues, or political resistance in the respondent State. In the statistics for 2012, Turkey is revealed to be the State with the worst record in terms of the number of cases that took more than five years to execute the judgment (71 such cases, while Russia had 49 cases). Turkey is also the State with the most leading cases still pending for execution under the supervision of the Committee (178 such cases in 2012, with Russia just behind with 157).[36]

Where there might be a delay in setting in place general measures in a national legal order, the Committee is increasingly expecting interim measures to be taken. To give just one example, the Committee approved interim measures taken in Cyprus in response to the Court's judgment in the *Egmez* case pending comprehensive legislative reforms.[37]

Perhaps more serious is the situation where measures are required to remedy a whole series of cases which highlight an ingrained and persistent problem within the respondent State. An example relates to the actions of the Turkish security forces in south-eastern Turkey. In well over 50 judgments, the Court found violations of Articles 2, 3, 5, 6, 8, and 13 of the Convention and Article 1 of Protocol 1, in respect of villages destroyed by security forces,[38] torture or serious ill-treatment of Kurds held in police custody,[39] and breaches of the right to life or disappearances.[40] In almost all of these cases the Court in addition found breaches of the Convention relating to the absence of adequate official investigations into the allegations in question, giving rise to the virtual impunity of agents of the State and a lack of effective domestic remedies for their Kurdish victims.

[34] *Abdulaziz, Cabales and Balkandali v United Kingdom*, (Apps. 9214/80, 9473/81, and 9474/81), 28 May 1985, Series A No 94, (1985) 7 EHRR 471.

[35] For example, the Court 'noted with satisfaction' in *Findlay v United Kingdom*, (App. 22107/93) 25 February 1997; (1997) 24 EHRR 221, that the United Kingdom had implemented changes to its courts martial procedure following the Commission's Report indicating a violation of Article 6.

[36] Committee of Ministers, *Supervision of the Execution of Judgments of the European Court of Human Rights. Sixth Annual Report 2012* (Council of Europe Publishing, Strasbourg 2013).

[37] Res. DH (2006) 13, 12 April 2006.

[38] The first cases of this type were *Akdivar and others v Turkey*, (App. 21893/93), 16 September 1996, (1997) 23 EHRR 143; *Mentes and others v Turkey*, (App. 23186/94), 28 November 1997, (1998) 26 EHRR 595; and *Selçuk and Asker v Turkey*, (Apps. 23184/94 and 23185/94), 24 April 1998, (1998) 26 EHRR 477, ECHR 1998-II.

[39] The first findings of torture against Turkey were in *Aksoy v Turkey*, (App. 21987/93), 18 December 1996, (1997) 23 EHRR 553; *Aydin v Turkey*, (App. 23178/94), 25 September 1997, (1998) 25 EHRR 251, ECHR 1997-VI; and *Tekin v Turkey*, (App. 22496/93), 9 June 1998, (2001) 31 EHRR 95.

[40] The first cases of this type were *Kaya v Turkey*, (App. 22729/93), 19 February 1998; (1999) 28 EHRR 1; and *Kurt v Turkey*, (App. 24276/94), 25 May 1998; (1999) 27 EHRR 373, ECHR 1998-III.

The Committee started its examination of these problems in 1996, and they remain ongoing, although the Committee has decided to close its examination of a number of issues flowing from these cases. But it remains concerned about the procedures which might lead to prosecution of members of the security forces who exceed their official mandate, and has strongly encouraged the authorities to adopt a zero tolerance policy on the use of torture and other forms of ill-treatment.[41]

Another example of persistent and recurring human rights violations is the Italian length of proceedings cases which have persisted for over twenty years. It appears that the problems within the Italian legal system are so deep-rooted and pernicious that there is a limit to what the Italian Government can do to bring about effective reform. But continuing pressure from the Committee does appear to be beginning to bring results, not least in a frank acknowledgment by the highest courts of Italy of the seriousness of the problem for the operation of the rule of law.[42]

Increased use of the now-formalized pilot judgment procedure has given greater emphasis to general measures. For example, the ongoing saga over prisoner voting in the UK has arisen in the context of pilot judgments. In *Greens and M.T. v United Kingdom*,[43] the Court observed that the UK had still not amended its legislation, imposing a blanket ban on voting for convicted prisoners, five years after the *Hirst (No. 2)* judgment found it to be in violation of Article 3 of Protocol 1.[44] Since *Hirst*, the Court had received 2,500 similar applications. The Court found another violation in *Greens and M.T.* and adjourned its examination of all similar applications, while giving the UK Government six months from the date when the judgment became final to introduce legislative proposals for bringing electoral law into line with the *Hirst (No. 2)* judgment. This deadline was then extended until six months after delivery of the Grand Chamber judgment in the similar case of *Scoppola (No. 3) v Italy*[45] in which the UK was an intervening party. The UK Government finally published a draft bill on prisoners' voting eligibility in November 2012 and the Committee has further adjourned the Court's consideration of the pending cases against the UK until the end of September 2013. The issue is being played out against a political, and to some extent popular, backlash against the Convention system. Eight years after the UK was found in violation of Article 3 of Protocol 1, the offending legislation remains in force.

THE ROLE OF THE PARLIAMENTARY ASSEMBLY

The Parliamentary Assembly now includes on the agenda of one its four meetings each year the execution of judgments of the Strasbourg Court.[46] This has evolved from its earlier direction to the Committee on Legal Affairs and Human Rights to report problems which arise in compliance by Contracting Parties with judgments of the Strasbourg Court made against them. It will be recalled that the jurisdiction of the Parliamentary Assembly is purely consultative, but the use of such techniques as written questions to the Committee of Ministers can raise the political temperature in relation to issues flowing from judgments of the Strasbourg Court. Abdelgawad says:

[41] Res. DH (2008) 69, 18 September 2008. [42] Res. DH (2009) 43,19 March 2009.

[43] *Greens and M.T. v United Kingdom*, (App. 60041/08 and 60054/08), 23 November 2010.

[44] *Hirst v The United Kingdom (No. 2)*, (App. 74025/01), 6 October 2005.

[45] *Scoppola v Italy (No. 3)*, (App. 126/05), 22 May 2012.

[46] See E. Abdelgawad, *The execution of judgments of the European Court of Human Rights*, 2nd edn Human Rights Files No. 19 (Council of Europe Publishing, Strasbourg 2008), 59–63.

> The significance of [involvement of the Parliamentary Assembly] lies above all in the ability of members of national parliaments to bring subsequent pressure to bear on the national legislature and executive to adopt the necessary measures, and also in their power to make formal recommendations to the national authorities in charge of policy making.[47]

SANCTIONS

Rolv Ryssdal, former President of the Court, once remarked:

> [the Convention], as an international treaty that encroaches on domestic law, relies for its enforcement on a combination of binding legal obligation and the traditional good faith required of the signatories to an international agreement.[48]

However, in addition to good faith, a number of pressures and interests combine to encourage States to comply with the legal obligation to take measures of restitution created by a finding of a violation by the Court.

The first of these is the common interest in a stable Europe. The Convention was drafted and adopted in the aftermath of the Second World War, when European unity and the promotion and support of strong democracies throughout the continent were seen as essential to the security of all. The Convention system has played some part in the resolution of conflict in Northern Ireland and Cyprus, and in re-establishing democracy in Spain, Portugal, Turkey, and Greece. However, its role in this respect became particularly relevant after the collapse of communism in central and eastern Europe in 1989, when it became apparent that Europe could no longer hope to rely on the Cold War fear of mutual annihilation to maintain order and stability. If the Contracting Parties of the Council of Europe aspire to strengthen democracy and the rule of law in the Balkans or in Turkey, for example, it is essential that every government is seen to comply willingly with the Court's judgments and the Committee's recommendations. This is the very basis of the collective enforcement of human rights.

In addition, in respect of those States which are not yet part of the European Union but that wish to join, a good record in Strasbourg is seen as an important precondition for membership. The Committee of Ministers' powers are thus reinforced by a certain indirect economic incentive.

There are a number of ways in which the Committee can attempt to influence a government. The first of these is confidential peer pressure: the ministers and their representatives are obliged to keep attending the Committee's meetings and will be reluctant to be seen—or rather, to have their governments seen—as unrepentant violators of human rights. The potency of this type of pressure should not be underestimated. In addition, on a more formal and public level, the Chairman of the Committee can make use of bilateral letters to notify the government concerned of the Committee's views on any particular matter.

In recent years the Committee has made increasing use of interim resolutions as a way of directly addressing the State authority competent to resolve the problems it is encountering in the enforcement of judgments. In addition, the Council of Europe's Parliamentary Assembly is taking a greater interest in the Committee's work under the Convention, and, through the use of Parliamentary questions, may elicit information about the progress of a case and highlight a State's failure adequately to cooperate.

[47] *The execution of judgments of the European Court of Human Rights*, 2nd edn Human Rights Files No. 19 (Council of Europe Publishing, Strasbourg 2008), at 61.

[48] Lecture given at Masaryk University, 20 March 1996; and see also R. Ryssdal, 'The Enforcement System set up under the European Convention of Human Rights' in M. Bulterman and K. Kuijer (eds.), *Compliance with Judgments of International Courts: proceedings of the symposium organized in honour of Professor Henry G. Schermers* (Martinus Nijhoff, The Hague 1996).

The ultimate sanction available to the Committee is the threat of expulsion from the Council of Europe under Articles 3 and 8 of the Council's Statute.[49] So far, in the history of the Council, the Committee has never made use of its powers to suspend a Contracting Party, although it came close to doing so in 1970, when the military dictatorship which had seized power in Greece in 1967 declared that it considered the finding by the Commission in an inter-State case of a number of serious human rights violations, including torture, to be 'null and void' and that it '[did] not consider itself legally bound by the conclusions of the said report'.[50] In the event, however, Greece withdrew from the Council of Europe without being expelled, and did not join again until the dictatorship had been overthrown.

The Turkish Government repudiated the Court's judgment in the *Loizidou* case,[51] where the Court found that the denial to a Greek Cypriot of access to her property in northern Cyprus was a breach of Article 1 of the First Protocol to the Convention (right to peaceful enjoyment of property), imputable to Turkey, and ordered the payment of substantial compensation. For many years Turkey refused to pay the just satisfaction awarded by the Court. The Committee of Ministers adopted a number of interim resolutions, the last of which suggested a link between the failure to respect the judgment and Turkey's ambitions for closer relations with the EU.[52] Turkey finally paid the money owing on 2 December 2003.[53]

Protocol 14 to the Convention provides the Committee with an interim sanction to deal with intractable States, short of expulsion. Under Article 16 of the Protocol, Article 46 of the Convention is amended so that, if a State refuses to abide by a final judgment against it, the Committee may, after serving formal notice on the respondent State, refer to the Court the question whether that State has failed to fulfil its obligation.

CONCLUDING REMARKS

In the first few decades of its existence, the organs of the European Convention system, in contrast to those of other regional and international systems for the protection of human rights,[54] were privileged in that their field of application extended, on the whole, to a relatively homogeneous region of Europe where democracy and the rule of law were well established. However, this region has now expanded to the borders of Asia, to incorporate new Contracting Parties which have developed very different cultures and traditions from those prevailing in western Europe. The Committee is increasingly being called upon to deal with grave and endemic breaches of human rights.

Historically, the Committee has largely relied on good faith and diplomatic pressure to ensure compliance with the Strasbourg Court's judgments. Apart from all-out expulsion from the Council of Europe, which risks being counter-productive to the protection of human rights in the offending State, the sanctions available are limited. Recent reforms have sought to streamline the Convention system, at both judgment and execution level, and there is a growing emphasis upon the need for implementation of the rights at national level. Priority is increasingly being given to systematic problems, although with no guarantee that the political will exists to eradicate them. The challenges of properly supervising the enforcement of judgments when there are so many more judgments than in earlier times, and when the range of systemic problems appears to be growing, should not be underestimated.

[49] See ch.1.

[50] Res. DH (1970) 1, 15 April 1970.

[51] *Loizidou v Turkey*, (App. 15318/89), 23 March 1995 (preliminary objections) Series A No 310, (1995) 20 EHRR 99; 18 December 1996 (merits), (1997) 23 EHRR 513, ECHR 1996-VI; and 28 July 1998 (just satisfaction), ECHR 1998-IV.

[52] Res. DH (2001) 80, 26 June 2001.

[53] Res. DH (2003) 190, 2 December 2003.

[54] Such as the Inter-American and African systems.

4

INTERPRETING THE CONVENTION

INTRODUCTORY REMARKS

The Convention, even with its Protocols, is a relatively short document. To be effective, it requires interpretation. The role of the Strasbourg Court is to interpret and apply the Convention.[1] An understanding of the development of the Convention case-law requires an understanding of the Court's approach to its interpretation.[2] The starting point for the Strasbourg Court was the rules of international law on the interpretation of treaties, since the Convention is an international treaty. When the Strasbourg Court first came to consider this question, the Vienna Convention on the Law of Treaties had not entered into force,[3] but the Strasbourg Court decided that its provisions represented customary international law and should be applied to the interpretation of the Convention.[4]

The interpretation of the Convention has been dominated by a purposive approach,[5] drawn from the principles in the Vienna Convention which permit the application of meanings which are consonant with the object and purpose of the treaty. The Strasbourg Court has summarized its approach as follows:

> Under the Vienna Convention on the Law of Treaties, the Court is required to ascertain the ordinary meaning to be given to the words in their context and in the light of the object and purpose of the provision from which they are drawn... The Court must have regard to the fact that the context of the provision is a treaty for the effective protection of individual human rights and that the Convention must be read as a whole, and interpreted in such a way as to promote internal consistency and harmony between its various provisions... The Court must also take into account any relevant rules and principles of international law applicable in relations between the Contracting Parties... Recourse may also

[1] Article 32(1) ECHR.

[2] The material in this chapter draws in particular on material in J. Merrills, *The Development of International Law by the European Court of Human Rights* (MUP, Manchester 1988); M. Delmas-Marty, *The European Convention for the Protection of Human Rights. International Protection versus National Restrictions* (Martinus Nijhoff, Dordrecht 1992), Part III; F. Matscher, 'Methods of Interpretation of the Convention' in R. Macdonald, F. Matscher, and H. Petzold, *The European System for the Protection of Human Rights* (Martinus Nijhoff, Dordrecht 1993), 63; A. Mowbray, 'The Creativity of the European Court of Human Rights' (2005) 5 Human Rights Law Review 57; S. Greer, *The European Convention on Human Rights. Achievements, Problems and Prospects* (CUP, Cambridge 2006); and G. Letsas, *A Theory of Interpretation of the European Convention on Human Rights* (OUP, Oxford 2007).

[3] It entered into force for the States Parties on 27 January 1980. As at 1 September 2013, there were 113 States Parties to the Convention.

[4] *Golder v United Kingdom*, (App. 4451/70), 21 February 1975, Series A No 18, (1979–80) 1 EHRR 524, § 29; and *Al-Adsani v United Kingdom*, (App. 35763/97), 21 November 2001 [GC], (2002) 34 EHRR 273, ECHR 2001-XI, § 55. See also L. Wildhaber, 'The European Convention on Human Rights and International Law' (2007) 56 ICLQ 217. Arts. 31–3 of the Vienna Convention are set out in the appendix to this chapter.

[5] Often referred to as a teleological interpretation.

> be had to supplementary means of interpretation, including the preparatory works to the Convention, either to confirm a meaning determined in accordance with the above steps, or to establish the meaning where it would otherwise be ambiguous, obscure or manifestly absurd or unreasonable ...[6]

The Court has not adopted a hierarchical approach to the application of the principles of interpretation it uses. It has viewed the task of interpretation as a single complex operation, though reference to the object and purpose of the provision in the context of the Convention as a whole has been the most influential of the principles applied by the Court, and has been described as the 'sheet anchor of the Convention's principles of interpretation'.[7] There are, however, a number of supplementary aids to interpretation which have led some to question the coherence of the Strasbourg Court's approach to the interpretation of the Convention. Greer observes:

> It is strange ... that such an unstructured approach should have become so widely and uncritically accepted because some of the interpretive principles (for example, *democracy, effective protection* and *legality*) are obviously more intimately connected with the Convention's core purpose than others (for example, the *margin of appreciation* or *evolutive* and *autonomous* interpretation). This, in itself suggests a more formal and hierarchical structure than has yet been acknowledged.[8]

What no one denies is that the European Convention has a special character. It penetrates the national legal orders by requiring Contracting Parties to behave in a particular way towards their own citizens and those citizens of other countries who are within their jurisdiction. What was previously treated by international law as a matter within the domestic jurisdiction of States is brought within an international system of protection and supervision.

THE INFLUENCE OF THE VIENNA CONVENTION

In the *Golder* case[9] the Strasbourg Court had stated that Articles 31 to 33 of the Vienna Convention on the Law of Treaties of 23 May 1969, notwithstanding that the Vienna Convention was not then yet in force, should guide the Court in its interpretation of the Convention since the principles contained in those Articles were generally regarded as being declaratory of principles of customary international law.[10]

Examination of the principles to be found in Articles 31 to 33 suggests the following propositions.

(1) Terms used in the treaty should be accorded their ordinary meaning.
(2) Regard can be had to the context in which the words appear.
(3) Regard can be had to the object and purpose of the treaty.
(4) The *travaux préparatoires* may be used to help resolve an ambiguity in the text, to confirm a meaning attributed by the use of other rules, or to avoid an absurdity.

[6] *Saadi v United Kingdom*, (App. 13229/03), 29 January 2008 [GC], (2008) 47 EHRR 427, ECHR 2008, § 62.

[7] S. Greer, *The European Convention on Human Rights. Achievements, Problems and Prospects* (CUP, Cambridge 2006), 195.

[8] *The European Convention on Human Rights. Achievements, Problems and Prospects* (CUP, Cambridge 2006), 194.

[9] *Golder v United Kingdom*, (App. 4451/70), 21 February 1975, Series A No 18, (1979–80) 1 EHRR 524, § 29.

[10] Re-affirmed in *Banković and others v Belgium and 16 other Contracting States*, (App. 52207/99), Decision of 12 December 2001 [GC], (2007) 44 EHRR SE5, ECHR 2001-XII, § 35.

(5) The treaty is equally authentic in each official language and any differences of meaning are to be resolved by adopting the meaning which best accords with the object and purpose of the treaty.

How far do these general rules of treaty interpretation apply to the European Convention on Human Rights? While the relevant provisions of the Vienna Convention are sufficiently general to give some guidance, they must be applied with caution in view of the special features of the Convention. Although it is an international treaty, the Convention has a special character which goes beyond merely setting out the rights and obligations of the Contracting Parties. Some specific aspects of the application of principles in the Vienna Convention warrant further comment.

USE OF *TRAVAUX PRÉPARATOIRES*

The special nature of the European Convention means that particular caution is necessary in relying on the preparatory work of the Convention.[11] Preparatory work is notoriously unreliable as a general guide to treaty interpretation, and is hence treated only as a supplementary means of interpretation in Article 32 of the Vienna Convention. But because of the special features of the European Convention, it should be invoked, if at all, as a guide to the general intentions of the Contracting Parties, rather than to delimit strictly the scope of particular Articles. This, too, is in accordance with the real purpose of the Convention. Caution is required in the use of the preparatory work because the Strasbourg Court has repeatedly confirmed that the Convention is a living instrument and has adopted a dynamic interpretation to the substance of its provisions.[12] In the *Sigurjonsson* case[13] the Court noted that the use of the *travaux préparatoires* in the earlier *Young, James and Webster* case[14] was not decisive but merely provided a working hypothesis.[15]

The preparatory work was legitimately invoked by the Commission to show that the provision that 'Everyone shall be free to leave any country, including his own', does not entitle a convicted prisoner to leave the country in which he is lawfully detained. The contrary interpretation would lead, in the words of Article 32 of the Vienna Convention, to a result which is manifestly absurd or unreasonable. On the other hand, in the *Lawless* case, the Court refused to resort to the preparatory work to interpret a provision which was sufficiently clear.[16]

More recently, the Grand Chamber has relied on the *travaux préparatoires* in interpreting Article 3 of Protocol 1[17] on the right to free elections, which at first sight appears to give rise to obligations only between States.[18] In the *Banković* decision,[19] the Grand Chamber found confirmation of its view that the term 'jurisdiction' in Article 1 was an

[11] See the Report of the Commission of 29 August 1973 in the *Golder* case. See also *Banković and others v Belgium and 16 other Contracting States*, (App. 52207/99), Decision of 12 December 2001 [GC], (2007) 44 EHRR SE5, ECHR 2001-XII, especially §§ 17–21 and 58.

[12] See R. Bernhardt, 'Thoughts on the interpretation of human-rights treaties' in F. Matscher and H. Petzold, *Protecting Human Rights: The European Dimension* (Carl Heymanns, Köln 1990), 65, 68–9, and see further later in this chapter.

[13] *Sigurdur A. Sigurjonsson v Iceland*, (App. 16130/90), 30 June 1993, Series A No 264, (1993) 16 EHRR 462.

[14] *Young, James and Webster v United Kingdom*, (Apps. 7601/76 and 7801/77), 13 August 1981, Series A No 44, (1982) 4 EHRR 38.

[15] *Sigurdur A. Sigurjonsson v Iceland*, (App. 16130/90), 30 June 1993, Series A No 264, (1993) 16 EHRR 462, §§ 24–5.

[16] *Lawless v Ireland*, (App. 332/57), 1 July 1961, Series A No 2, (1979–80) 1 EHRR 13, § 14.

[17] See ch.22.

[18] *Yumak and Sadak v Turkey*, (App. 10226/03), 8 July 2008 [GC], (2009) 48 EHRR 61, ECHR 2008-nyr, § 109.

[19] *Banković and others v Belgium and 16 other Contracting States*, (App. 52207/99), Decision of 12 December 2001 [GC], (2007) 44 EHRR SE5, ECHR 2001-XII, § 63.

essentially territorial notion from the *travaux préparatoires*. The Expert Intergovernmental Committee had replaced the words 'all persons within their territories' with a reference to persons 'within their jurisdiction' indicating a wish to include those who were not physically present on the territory of a Contracting Party but had a sufficient legal connection with that Contracting Party. By contrast, in *Hirsi Jamaa v Italy*, the Grand Chamber concluded that the *travaux préparatoires* did not preclude extraterritorial application of the notion of 'expulsion' in Article 4 of Protocol 4.[20] In the *Kudła* case,[21] the Strasbourg Court referred to the *travaux préparatoires* in support of its interpretation of Article 13 as requiring a domestic remedy for complaints about unreasonably long legal proceedings, while in *Bayatyan v Armenia*, the Court used the *travaux préparatoires* to confirm that the sole purpose of sub-paragraph (b) of Article4(3) is to provide a further elucidation of the notion 'forced or compulsory labour' and does not in itself, therefore, either recognize nor exclude a right to conscientious objection.[22]

In recent years, reference to the *travaux préparatoires* has arisen more frequently in dissenting opinions than in the judgments of the Court.[23]

DIFFERENT LANGUAGE VERSIONS

The Convention is equally authentic in the English and in the French texts. Where these texts differ, the meaning which best reconciles the texts, having regard to the object and purpose of the treaty, must be adopted.[24] In the *James* case[25] the applicants sought to challenge provisions of the United Kingdom leasehold enfranchisement legislation as being inconsistent with Article 1 of Protocol 1. The issue raised required the Court to consider whether the deprivation of property suffered by the freeholders who were compelled under the legislation to sell the freehold to their tenants could be said to be 'in the public interest'. It appeared that the French text 'pour cause d'utilité publique' carried a somewhat different connotation from the English text. The Court adopted a definition which 'best reconciles the language of the English and French texts, having regard to the object and purpose of Article 1' and referred explicitly to Article 33 of the Vienna Convention in doing so.[26]

ORDINARY MEANING

The Strasbourg Court has frequently used the ordinary meaning of words in order to interpret provisions of the Convention. This may involve reference to dictionaries to determine the ordinary and natural meaning of the words.[27] In the *Johnston* case[28] the Court ruled

[20] *Hirsi Jamaa v Italy*, (App. 27765/09), 23 February 2012 [GC], ECHR 2012.

[21] *Kudła v Poland*, (App. 30210/96), 26 October 2000 [GC], (2002) 35 EHRR 198, ECHR 2000-XI, § 152.

[22] *Bayatyan v Armenia*, (App. 23459/03), 7 July 2011 [GC], ECHR 2011.

[23] See, for example, *Ždanoka v Latvia*, (App. 58278/00), 16 March 2006 [GC], (2007) 45 EHRR 478, ECHR 2006-IV, dissenting opinion of Judge Rozakis; *Hutten-Czapska v Poland*, (App. 35014/97), 19 June 2006 [GC], ECHR 2006-VIII, partly concurring and partly dissenting opinion of Judge Zupančič; and *Kononov v Latvia*, (App. 36376/04), 24 July 2008 [GC], joint dissenting opinion of Judges Fura-Sandström, Björgvinsson, and Ziemele.

[24] Article 33(4) of the Vienna Convention. See also the *Wemhoff* case, (App. 2122/64), 27 June 1968, Series A No 7, (1979–80) 1 EHRR 55.

[25] *James and others v United Kingdom*, (App. 8793/79), 21 February 1986, Series A No 98, (1986) 8 EHRR 123.

[26] § 42. The Court had earlier taken exactly the same approach to the interpretation of the phrase 'prescribed by law' in Article 10(2) of the Convention in *The Sunday Times v United Kingdom*, (App. 6538/74), 26 April 1979, Series A No 30, (1979–80) 2 EHRR 245, § 48.

[27] *Luedicke, Belkacem and Koç v Germany*, (Apps. 6210/73, 6877/75, and 7132/75), 28 November 1978, Series A No 29, (1981) 2 EHRR 149, § 40.

[28] *Johnston v Ireland*, (App. 9697/82), 18 December 1986, Series A No 112, (1987) 9 EHRR 203.

that the ordinary meaning of the words 'right to marry' did not include a right to divorce; and, in the *Pretty* case,[29] that the right to life in Article 2 could not be read as including a right to die. In the *Lithgow* case[30] the Court ruled that the ordinary meaning of the reference to 'the general principles of international law' in Article 1 of Protocol 1 required that the phrase be given the same meaning as under Article 38(1)(d) of the Statute of the International Court of Justice.

There is one area where the ordinary meaning of words takes on a special significance. Frequently the Convention uses terms which do not have identical scope in the national legal systems. Here a difficulty arises as to the precise scope of the Convention term. If the national definition is determinative of the meaning, there is a risk of variable application of the Convention among the Contracting Parties. Examples of such terms in the Convention are 'civil rights and obligations' and 'criminal charge' in Article 6. The Strasbourg Court has adopted its own rules for determining the meaning of such terms. This has come to be known as the independent classification of terms, or, more usually, as the autonomous meaning of terms. The Court has justified this approach by the need to secure uniformity of treatment among the Contracting Parties. Any other approach would result in the Convention's institutions having to defer to the classification adopted in a particular Contracting Party. The issue of defining 'criminal charge' arose in the *Engel* case[31] which concerned action against persons conscripted into the Netherlands armed forces. The action was classified as disciplinary. If the matter involved consideration of a criminal charge, it was squarely within the scope of Article 6. The Court ruled that a Convention definition must be applied to the proceedings; their classification in the national legal order was only one factor to be taken into account in determining their scope. In the *König* case[32] the applicant claimed a violation arising from proceedings of an administrative nature in which he had sought to challenge the withdrawal of his right to practise medicine. The Court concluded that the proceedings involved the determination of his civil rights and obligations despite the German classification of the proceedings as administrative in nature. The need to secure a uniform interpretation of the Convention in all the Contracting Parties clearly requires that differential application of the Convention protection arising from differences of terminology be avoided. The more controversial issue surrounds the criteria adopted by the Strasbourg Court for the determination of the meaning of the Convention term. Here there can be opportunities for judicial creativity.

The difference between the traditional international treaty and the Convention again becomes apparent. Many of the terms used belong essentially to the domestic legal order and so the Court has used comparative law techniques in assigning the Convention meaning to the terms.[33] Where common approaches or standards emerge from the comparative study, that meaning will be applied. Where common standards do not emerge, then a greater flexibility of standards is accepted which has come to be known as the 'margin of appreciation'.[34]

[29] *Pretty v United Kingdom*, (App. 2346/02), 29 April 2002, (2002) 35 EHRR 1, ECHR 2002-III.

[30] *Lithgow and others v United Kingdom*, (Apps. 9006/80, 9262/81, 9263/81, 9265/81, 9266/81, 9313/81, and 9405/81), 8 July 1986, Series A No 102 (1986) 8 EHRR 329.

[31] *Engel and others v Netherlands*, (Apps. 5100/71, 5101/71, 5102/71, 5354/72, and 5370/72), 8 June 1976, Series A No 22, (1979–80) 1 EHRR 647.

[32] *König v Germany*, (App. 6232/73), 28 June 1978, Series A No 27, (1980) 2 EHRR 170.

[33] See L. Wildhaber, 'Judging in a modern constitutional democracy—Employing the comparative law method in constitutional decision-making', presentation by Judge Wildhaber in Johannesburg on 20 March 2004 to mark the inauguration of the new building for the Constitutional Court of South Africa.

[34] See further later in this chapter.

CONTEXT

In the *Golder* case, the Strasbourg Court said:

> In the way in which it is presented in the 'general rule' in Article 31 of the Vienna Convention, the process of interpretation of a treaty is a unity, a single combined operation; this rule, closely integrated, places on the same footing the various elements enumerated in the four paragraphs of the Article.[35]

Context is defined in Article 31(2) of the Vienna Convention as the whole of the text together with its preamble and annexes, any agreement related to the treaty made by all the parties in connection with the conclusion of the treaty, and any instrument accepted by all the parties as one related to the treaty. In practice, the use of context enables a treaty to be read as a whole and assistance to be derived from the underlying objectives frequently set out in the preamble.

The use of context has most often arisen where applicants are faced with violations which are covered in some detail by provisions in a Protocol which has not been ratified by the respondent State. In such cases the respondent State often seeks to argue that the whole matter is governed by the Protocol, while applicants will argue that aspects of their claim nevertheless fall within Articles of the Convention which are in force as against the respondent State. The Court has concluded in such cases that the presence of detailed rules in a Protocol does not bar the applicability of a more general provision to aspects of the case. So in the *Abdulaziz* case[36] the applicant was able to rely on the right to respect for family life in raising an issue concerning the United Kingdom immigration legislation, even though the UK is not a party to the Fourth Protocol. Similarly, the applicant in the *Rasmussen* case[37] was able to rely on Article 8 of the Convention in a case concerning paternity issues even though Denmark was not a party to the Seventh Protocol which sets out the rights of parents in relation to their children. In the *Guzzardi* case[38] the applicant was able to rely on Article 5 to challenge the requirement that he live on a small island under police supervision even though Italy had not recognized the rights of free movement contained in the Fourth Protocol.

The Court has said that interpretation of Articles of the Convention 'must be in harmony with the logic of the Convention'.[39] So a finding that Article 8 did not require the disclosure of information held in a secret police register which accounted for the applicant's failure to secure employment near a naval base meant that a claim that there had been a failure to provide a remedy under Article 13 could not arise. The reverse situation may also arise; if a right is not part of a more specific provision, it cannot be part of a more general provision. So, since the right to divorce is not part of the right to marry under Article 12, it cannot form part of the rights contained in Article 8, which is of more general purpose and scope.[40]

The *Maaouia* case illustrates how the Court uses context to determine the meaning of terms.[41] The applicant complained at the length of the proceedings for the rescission of the deportation order made against him. The question was whether such proceedings

[35] *Golder v United Kingdom*, (App. 4451/70), 21 February 1975, Series A No 18, (1979–80) 1 EHRR 524, § 30.

[36] *Abdulaziz, Cabales and Balkandali v United Kingdom*, (Apps. 9214/80, 9473/81, and 9474/81), 28 May 1985, Series A No 94, (1985) 7 EHRR 471.

[37] *Rasmussen v Denmark*, (App. 8777/79), 28 November 1984, Series A No 87, (1985) 7 EHRR 372.

[38] *Guzzardi v Italy*, (App. 7367/76), 6 November 1980, Series A No 39, (1981) 3 EHRR 333.

[39] *Leander v Sweden*, (App. 9248/81), 26 March 1987, Series A No 116, (1988) 9 EHRR 433, § 78.

[40] *Johnston v Ireland*, (App. 9697/82), 18 December 1986, Series A No 112, (1987) 9 EHRR 203.

[41] *Maaouia v France*, (App. 39652/98), 5 October 2000 [GC], (2001) 33 EHRR 1037, ECHR 2000-X.

came within the terms 'civil rights and obligation' or constituted a 'criminal charge' against him.[42] The Court stressed that these were autonomous terms and that provisions of the Convention must be construed in the light of the entire Convention system including the Protocols to the Convention. Since Protocol 7 contained certain specific guarantees relating to procedures for the expulsion of aliens, they did not constitute proceedings relating to civil rights and obligations within Article 6(1). Nor did they constitute the determination of a criminal charge against the applicant. Consequently, Article 6(1) did not apply to such proceedings.

A further example can be found in the decision of the Grand Chamber in the *Stec* case.[43] Here the Court considered it to be in the interests of the Convention as a whole that the autonomous concept of possessions in Article 1 of Protocol 1 should be interpreted in a manner which was consistent with the concept of pecuniary rights under Article 6(1). For this reason, it included both contributory and non-contributory social security benefits as within the definition of possessions. In *Hirsi Jamaa v Italy*, the Court again emphasized the principle that the Convention must be interpreted as a whole, and therefore the scope of a particular provision (in this case, Article 4 of Protocol 4), should be the same as the scope of the Convention as a whole. Thus, where the Contracting State has been found to have exercised its jurisdiction outside its national territory, there can be no obstacle to accepting that the exercise of extraterritorial jurisdiction took the form of collective expulsion, even though that concept in Article 4 is principally territorial.[44]

It is easy to make too much of the use of context, whereas examination of the case-law of the Court shows that the context used for reference in interpreting a term can vary considerably. In some cases, the context consists solely of paragraphs of the same Article, while in others the whole Convention, including its Preamble and Protocols, is used. Selection of the context often merges into consideration of the object and purpose of the provision.

OBJECT AND PURPOSE

The Commission's Report on the *Golder* case suggests that particular account should be taken of two features of the European Convention when a question of interpretation arises. First, it provides for a system of international adjudication, while the general rules of treaty interpretation have evolved primarily as guides to interpretation by the parties themselves.[45] Hence, in the *Pfunders* case the Court stated that the Convention should be interpreted objectively:

> ...the obligations undertaken by the High Contracting Parties in the Convention are essentially of an objective character, being designed rather to protect the fundamental rights of individual human beings from infringement by any of the High Contracting Parties than to create subjective and reciprocal rights for the High Contracting Parties themselves.[46]

Secondly, any general presumption that treaty obligations should be interpreted restrictively since they derogate from the sovereignty of States is not applicable to the Convention. This follows indeed from the last words of Article 31(1) of the Vienna

[42] See chs 12 and 13.

[43] *Stec and others v United Kingdom*, (Apps. 65731/01 and 65900/01), Decision of 6 July 2005 [GC], (2005) 41 EHRR SE18, ECHR 2005-X, § 49.

[44] *Hirsi Jamaa v Italy*, (App. 27765/09), 23 February 2012 [GC], ECHR 2012, § 178.

[45] F. Jacobs, 'Varieties of Approach to Treaty Interpretation with Special Reference to the Draft Convention on the Law of Treaties before the Vienna Diplomatic Conference' (1969) 18 ICLQ 318, 341–3.

[46] App. 788/60, *Austria v Italy*, Decision of 11 January 1961, (1962) 4 *Yearbook* 116, 138.

Convention which provides that a treaty is to be interpreted in good faith in accordance with the ordinary meaning to be given to the terms of the treaty in their context and *in the light of its object and purpose*. Thus the Strasbourg Court stated in the *Wemhoff* case that it was necessary:

> to seek the interpretation that is most appropriate in order to realise the aim and achieve the object of the treaty, not that which would restrict to the greatest possible degree the obligations undertaken by the Parties.[47]

These two features of the European Convention suggest that a further conclusion may be drawn as to the appropriate principles of interpretation: that the interpretation of the Convention must be 'dynamic' in the sense that it must be interpreted in the light of developments in social and political attitudes. Its effects cannot be confined to the conceptions of the period when it was drafted or entered into force.[48] Thus the concept of degrading treatment in Article 3 may be interpreted to include racial discrimination, even though this might not have entered the minds of the drafters of the Convention;[49] and the protection of privacy under Article 8 must be developed to meet new technological developments which were not envisaged fifty years ago.[50] But the dynamic or evolutive interpretation of the Convention will not justify reading new rights into the Convention. So the absence of any provision for divorce in the Convention could not be changed by reference to the increased incidence of marriage breakdown since the Convention was drafted. In the *Johnston* case, the Court said:

> It is true that the Convention and its Protocols must be interpreted in the light of present-day conditions. However, the Court cannot, by means of an evolutive interpretation, derive from these instruments a right that was not included therein at the outset.[51]

Perhaps the best example of the dynamic interpretation of the Convention can be found in the line of cases under Article 8 dealing with the rights of transsexuals to recognition of their gender identity.[52] Many other examples of a dynamic interpretation of the Convention will be met in subsequent chapters: changes in the concept of the family, of education, of forced labour, or of trade union freedom. This approach is necessary if effect is to be given to the general intentions of the drafters of the Convention. They did not intend solely to protect the individual against the threats to human rights which were then prevalent, with the result that, as the nature of the threats changed, the protection gradually fell away. Their intention was to protect the individual against the threats of the future, as well as the threats of the past. However, if no consensus emerges from a comparative interpretation[53] and if the issue is a controversial one, the Strasbourg Court will revert to respect for national margins of appreciation in recognizing a diversity of approaches.[54] One writer has described the dynamic or evolutive approach as 'firmly established in

[47] *Wemhoff* case, (App. 2122/64), 27 June 1968, Series A No 7, (1979–80) 1 EHRR 55, § 8.

[48] See S. Prebensen 'Evolutive interpretation of the European Convention on Human Rights' in P. Mahoney and others, *Protecting Human Rights: The European Perspective. Studies in Memory of Rolv Ryssdal*, (Carl Heymanns, Köln 2000), 1123.

[49] See ch.9.

[50] See ch.16; and *The Belgian Linguistic* case, (Apps. 1474/62, 1677/62, 1691/62, 1769/63, 1994/63, and 2126/64), 9 February 1967 and 23 July 1968, Series A Nos 5 and 6, (1979–80) 1 EHRR 241 and 252.

[51] *Johnston v Ireland*, (App. 9697/82), 18 December 1986, Series A No 112, (1987) 9 EHRR 203, § 53.

[52] See especially *Goodwin v United Kingdom*, (App. 28957/95), 11 July 2002 [GC], (2002) 35 EHRR 447, ECHR 2002-VI; and *I v United Kingdom*, (App. 26580/94), 11 July 2002; (2003) 36 EHRR 967. See discussion of these cases in ch.16.

[53] See further later in this chapter.

[54] See, for example, *Vo v France*, (App. 53924/00), 8 July 2004 [GC], (2005) 40 EHRR 259, ECHR 2004-VIII, §§ 81–5, on the question of when the right to life begins.

the Strasbourg jurisprudence as a flexible, albeit a limited, means of adaptation of the Convention law.'[55]

THE PRINCIPLE OF EVOLUTIVE INTERPRETATION

Professor Merrills rightly notes[56] that the case-law of the Strasbourg Court supports the view that, in interpreting the Convention, the Court seeks to give the provisions of the Convention the 'fullest weight and effect consistent with the language used and with the rest of the text and in such a way that every part of it can be given meaning.'[57] It was the use of the object and purpose provisions of the Vienna Convention in the context of the European Convention which opened the door to this approach to interpretation of the Convention.

One of the most dramatic illustrations of the application of the principle of effectiveness arose in the *Airey* case.[58] Johanna Airey wished to seek a decree of judicial separation from her husband on the grounds of his alleged cruelty to her and their children. She is described as coming from a humble background and receiving low wages for her work. Mr Airey had left the matrimonial home, but Mrs Airey feared that he might return and wished to ensure that he had no right to do so. She was unable to find a lawyer to act for her, since no legal aid was available to assist her and she lacked the resources to fund such assistance on a fee-paying basis. She complained to the Commission which unanimously considered that there was a breach of Article 6(1) by reason of the effective denial of access to a court. The respondent State sought to argue, *inter alia*, that there was no bar to Mrs Airey appearing as a litigant in person before the Irish courts to seek a judicial separation. The Strasbourg Court, which by a majority of five to two decided that there was a violation of Article 6(1), considered it important to determine whether any remedy available to Mrs Airey was 'practical and effective' as distinct from being 'theoretical or illusory'.[59] The Court concluded that it was not 'realistic' for Mrs Airey to conduct her own case effectively.

The need for the right to a fair trial to remain effective has also more recently been emphasized in *Salduz v Turkey* where the applicant alleged that Article 6(3)(c) had been violated as he had been denied access to a lawyer during his police custody. While this provision only explicitly requires that everyone charged with a criminal offence has the right 'to defend himself in person or through legal assistance…', the Court held that in order for the right to a fair trial to remain sufficiently 'practical and effective', access to a lawyer should be provided from the first interrogation of a suspect by the police (unless it is demonstrated in the light of the particular circumstances of each case that there are compelling reasons to restrict this right).[60]

[55] S. Prebensen 'Evolutive interpretation of the European Convention on Human Rights' in P. Mahoney and others, *Protecting Human Rights: The European Perspective. Studies in Memory of Rolv Ryssdal* (Carl Heymanns, Köln 2000), 1136.

[56] J. Merrills, *The Development of International Law by the European Court of Human Rights* (MUP, Manchester 1988), ch.5.

[57] 98.

[58] *Airey v Ireland*, (App. 6289/73), 9 October 1979, Series A No 32, (1979–80) 2 EHRR 305, § 24. See also *Artico v Italy*, (App. 6694/74), 13 May 1980, Series A No 37, (1981) 3EHRR 1, § 33.

[59] § 24.

[60] *Salduz v Turkey*, (App. 36391/02), 27 November 2008, [GC], ECHR 2008, § 55.

The Court has contrasted rights which are practical and effective with those that are merely theoretical and illusory in a number of cases.[61] This principle can now be regarded as a general principle applicable whenever Convention rights are in issue.

The phrase 'the Convention is a living instrument' has been used in around 30 cases.[62] It was the *Tyrer* case[63] which first introduced the notion of the Convention as a 'living instrument' to be interpreted in the light of present-day conditions. The context was an application which raised a complaint that judicial corporal punishment in the form of 'birching' in the Isle of Man was degrading treatment prohibited by Article 3 of the Convention. The Court said:

> The Court must also recall that the Convention is a living instrument which... must be interpreted in the light of present-day conditions. In the case now before it the Court cannot but be influenced by the developments and commonly accepted standards in the penal policy of the member States of the Council of Europe in this field.[64]

The requirement that the Convention is interpreted as a living instrument means that it has to be given something of an activist interpretation. The Convention could not be a living instrument if its interpretation remained static; the content of the Convention rights will change over time. Most, but not all, commentators consider that this change must always operate to enhance the content of human rights.[65] Judicial activism is a label used to refer to a judicial approach which seeks to extend or modify existing law especially in cases where policy choices are before a court, while judicial restraint is a label used to refer to a judicial approach which focuses upon the judge applying existing case-law and avoiding developing the law beyond its clearly established parameters. It is sometimes suggested that judicial activism takes the judge into the realm of the policy-maker, while judicial restraint recognizes the separation of law-maker and law-applier. Mahoney comments:

> Judicial activism raises the spectre of judges illegitimately enlarging their role in society to one of legislating on general policy matters and of exceeding their given functions of interpretation, whereas judicial self-restraint carries the risk of judges abdicating their responsibility of independent review of governmental action.[66]

[61] See, for example, *The Belgian Linguistic* case, (Apps. 1474/62, 1677/62, 1691/62, 1769/63, 1994/63, and 2126/64), 23 July 1968, Series A No 6, (1979–80) 1 EHRR 252, §§ 3–4; *Golder v United Kingdom*, (App. 4451/70), 21 February 1975, Series A No 18, (1979–80) 1 EHRR 524, § 35; *Luedicke, Belkacem and Koç v Federal Republic of Germany*, (Apps. 6210/73, 6877/75, and 7132/75), 28 November 1978, Series A No 29, (1980) 2 EHRR 433, § 42; *Marckx v Belgium*, (App. 6833/74), 13 June 1979, Series A No 31, (1979–80) 2 EHRR 330, § 31; *Artico v Italy*, (App. 6694/74), 13 May 1980, Series A No 37, (1981) 3 EHRR 1, § 33; *Kamasinski v Austria*, (App. 9783/82), 19 December 1989, Series A No 168, § 65; *Matthews v United Kingdom*, (App. 24833/94), 18 February 1999 [GC], (1999) 28 EHRR 361, ECHR 1999-I, § 34; *Podkolzina v Latvia*, (App. 46726/99), 9 April 2002, ECHR 2002-II, § 35; *Folgerø v Norway*, (App. 15472/02), 29 June 2007 [GC], (2008) 46 EHRR 1147, ECHR 2007-VIII, § 100; and *Mehmet Eren v Turkey*, (App. 32347/02), 14 October 2008, § 50.

[62] Recently in *EB v France*, (App. 43546/02), 22 January 2008 [GC], § 92; and in *Saadi v United Kingdom*, (App 13229/03), 29 January 2008, ECHR 2008, § 55 where the Court said: '[The Convention]...had to be interpreted in a manner which ensured that rights were given a broad construction and that limitations were narrowly construed, in a manner which gave practical and effective protection to human rights, and as a living instrument, in light of present day conditions and in accordance with developments in international law so as to reflect the increasingly high standard being required in the area of the protection of human rights.' A HUDOC search reveals that the phrase 'a living instrument' has been used in 47 cases.

[63] *Tyrer v United Kingdom*, (App. 5856/72), 25 April 1978, Series A No 26, (1979–80) 12 EHRR 1.

[64] § 31.

[65] See discussion in P. Mahoney, 'Judicial Activism and Judicial Self-Restraint in the European Court of Human Rights: Two Sides of the Same Coin' [1990] HRLJ 57, 66–8.

[66] 'Judicial Activism and Judicial Self-Restraint in the European Court of Human Rights: Two Sides of the Same Coin', 58.

Mahoney argues:

> The conclusion of the present study is that, as far as the European Convention on Human Rights is concerned, the dilemma of activism versus restraint is more apparent than real, in that activism and restraint are complementary components of the methodology of judicial review inherent in the very nature of the Convention as an international treaty intended to secure effective protection of human rights and fundamental freedoms.[67]

Some commentators have observed that a new approach to the interpretation of the Convention can be discerned from some decisions in recent years which extend the evolutive approach.[68] This is an approach which seeks to integrate interpretation of the civil and political rights, which are traditionally considered to be the principal focus of the European Convention, and the interpretation of economic, social, and cultural rights, which are traditionally considered to be the principal focus of the European Social Charter. The integrated approach limits the effect of the division created by two legal instruments. It recognizes that, on the one hand, the enjoyment of civil and political rights requires respect for and promotion of social rights, and, on the other hand, that social rights are not second best to civil and political rights.

Mantouvalou argues convincingly that the *Sidabras and Dziautas* case[69] is an illustration of this method of interpretation. The case concerned limitations on the employment in Lithuania of former KGB employees. Complaints were made of breaches of Articles 8, 10, and 14 of the Convention. In finding by five votes to two, a violation of Article 14 when read in conjunction with Article 8, the Court appears to have been significantly influenced by conclusions of the European Committee on Social Rights in adjudicating on a claim under the European Social Charter, as well as concerns expressed within the International Labour Organization framework concerning restrictions on access to employment in the public sector. According to the Court, it was proper to take a broad view of the scope of the Convention right in order to ensure its consistency with interpretations made in the context of the treaty frameworks concerned primarily with social rights. Mantouvalou concludes:

> The adoption of the integrated approach has not been a matter of conscious choice for the ECtHR. That is why it is still unclear what exactly it entails and what outcomes it may lead to. It has been driven by applicants, who have genuinely believed that they had a claim under the Convention, and has been inspired by declarations that civil and political and economic and social rights are interdependent and indivisible.[70]

It is, however, possible to find authorities which go the other way, such as the Court's decision in the *N* case[71] finding that there would be no violation of Article 3 if the United Kingdom returned an AIDS sufferer to Uganda on the grounds that the circumstances were not wholly exceptional.[72] In coming to this conclusion, the Court had noted the

[67] 'Judicial Activism and Judicial Self-Restraint in the European Court of Human Rights: Two Sides of the Same Coin', 59. For a contrary and critical view, see L. Hoffmann, 'The Universality of Human Rights', Judicial Studies Board Annual lecture, delivered on 19 March 2009. But see also, disagreeing with these views, M. Arden, 'Human Rights and Civil Wrongs: Tort under the Spotlight', Hailsham Lecture 2009, 12 May 2009.

[68] For a useful summary, see V. Mantouvalou, 'Work and Private Life: *Sidabras and Dziautas v Lithuania*', (2005) 30 ELRev 573.

[69] *Sidabras and Dziautas v Lithuania* (Apps. 55480/00 and 593300/00), 27 July 2004, (2004) 42 EHRR 104, ECHR 2004-VIII. See also *Rainys and Gasparavicius v Lithuania* (Apps. 70665/01 and 74345/01), 7 April 2005.

[70] V. Mantouvalou, 'Work and private life: *Sidabras and Dziautas v Lithuania*' (2005) 30 ELRev 573, 583.

[71] *N v United Kingdom*, (App. 26565/05), 27 May 2008 [GC], (2008) 47 EHRR 885, ECHR 2008-nyr.

[72] As they had been in *D v United Kingdom*, (App. 30240/96), 2 May 1997, (1997) 24 EHRR 423, ECHR 1997-III.

advances which had been made in the availability of antiretroviral medication in Uganda, but also noted that the object of Article 3 was not to place an obligation on a Contracting Party to 'alleviate…disparities [in medical treatments] through the provision of free and unlimited health care to all aliens without a right to stay within its jurisdiction.'[73] This was seen to impose too great a burden on the Contracting Parties.

The Grand Chamber considered the practice of interpreting the Convention provisions in the light of other international texts and instruments in some detail in the *Demir and Baykara* case.[74] The context was consideration of the restriction in Turkey on municipal civil servants forming trade unions. The Turkish Government had argued that it was inappropriate for the Strasbourg Court to take account of international agreements to which it was not a party in interpreting Article 11 of the Convention. The Grand Chamber explores its practice in this area,[75] and concludes:

> 85. The Court, in defining the meaning of terms and notions in the text of the Convention, can and must take into account elements of international law other than the Convention, the interpretation of such elements by competent organs, and the practice of European States reflecting their common values. The consensus emerging from specialised international instruments and from the practice of Contracting States may constitute a relevant consideration for the Court when it interprets the provisions of the Convention in specific cases.
>
> 86. In this context, it is not necessary for the respondent State to have ratified the entire collection of instruments that are applicable in respect of the precise subject matter of the case concerned. It will be sufficient for the Court that the relevant international instruments denote a continuous evolution in the norms and principles applied in international law or in the domestic law of the majority of member States of the Council of Europe and show, in a precise area, that there is common ground in modern societies….

The Court used this evidence of common ground between States to reconsider its exclusion of collective bargaining from the ambit of Article 11's right to form and join trade unions, concluding that collective bargaining was now 'one of the essential elements' of the provision.[76]

A similar evolution in the Court's approach to the meaning of a provision was apparent in *Hirsi Jamaa v Italy*, in which the Grand Chamber was called upon to interpret Article 4 of Protocol 4: 'Collective expulsion of aliens is prohibited.'[77] The applicants in this case were Somali and Eritrean nationals, who were part of a group of about 200 migrants who had left Libya aboard three ships with the aim of reaching Italy. The vessels were intercepted by the Italian authorities 35 nautical miles from the Italian coast and the occupants were transferred onto Italian military ships and returned to Libya, where they were handed over to the Libyan authorities. The question for the Court was whether this amounted to an 'expulsion' given that the migrants were outside of Italian territory at the time.

Focusing on the purpose and meaning of the provision, and acknowledging that this must be analysed taking into account the principle that the Convention is a living instrument which must be interpreted in the light of present-day conditions and in such a way that it renders the guarantees practical and effective and not theoretical and illusory, the Court was prepared to permit extraterritorial application for the concept of expulsion. It noted that 'migratory flows in Europe have continued to intensify, with increasing use

[73] § 44.

[74] *Demir and Baykara v Turkey*, (App. 34503/97), 12 November 2008 [GC], (2009) 48 EHRR 1272, ECHR 2008-nyr.

[75] §§ 65–86. [76] § 154.

[77] *Hirsi Jamaa v Italy*, (App. 27765/09), 23 February 2012 [GC], ECHR 2012.

being made of the sea' and that if Article 4 of Protocol 4 were to apply 'only to collective expulsions from the national territory of the States Parties to the Convention, a significant component of contemporary migratory patterns would not fall within the ambit of that provision, notwithstanding the fact that the conduct it is intended to prohibit can occur outside national territory and in particular, as in the instant case, on the high seas. Article 4 would thus be ineffective in practice with regard to such situations, which, however, are on the increase.'[78]

A similar evolutive approach was taken in *Bayatyan v Armenia*.[79] The issue here was whether Article 9 could guarantee a right to refuse military service on conscientious grounds. The applicant was a Jehovah's Witness who refused to perform military service and was arrested, convicted, and imprisoned for doing so. Previous Commission case-law had denied the existence of such a guarantee under Article 9 due to Article 4(3)(b) of the Convention, which provides that forced or compulsory labour should not include 'any service of a military character or, in cases of conscientious objectors, in countries where they are recognized, service exacted instead of compulsory military service.' By including the words 'in countries where they are recognised' the Commission felt that a choice had been left to the Contracting Parties whether or not to recognize conscientious objectors and, therefore, Article 9, as qualified by Article 4(3)(b), did not impose on a State the obligation to recognize conscientious objectors. In *Bayatyan*, however, the Grand Chamber took an evolutive approach to Article 9. The Court recognized a trend among Council of Europe Member States, during the late 1980s and the 1990s, to recognize the right to conscientious objection. By the time the alleged interference with the applicant's rights occurred, namely in 2002–03, only four other Member States, in addition to Armenia, did not provide for the possibility of claiming conscientious objector status. Since that time two other States, and Armenia itself, have recognized a right of conscientious objection, leaving only Azerbaijan and Turkey outside of the consensus.[80] In addition, the Court recognized equally important developments concerning recognition of the right to conscientious objection in various international fora, including in the interpretation by the United Nations Human Rights Council (UNHRC) of the provisions of the International Covenant on Civil and Political Rights (ICCPR) (Articles 8 and 18). The UNHRC had initially taken a similar approach to the Commission but had subsequently modified that approach and recognized a right to conscientious objection could be derived from Article 18 of the ICCPR.[81] Therefore, in accordance with the 'living instrument' approach to interpretation of the Convention, the Court departed from the Commission's case-law and declined to read Article 9 in conjunction with Article 4(3)(b). It proceeded to find a violation of Article 9, holding that the applicant's conviction had constituted an interference which was not necessary in a democratic society within the meaning of Article 9.

Selmouni v France further demonstrates that the 'living instrument' doctrine can be used to update the application of Convention rights to reflect current expectations.[82] In applying Article 3 to forms of ill-treatment of a detainee by police officers, the Court stated that 'certain acts which were classified in the past as "inhuman and degrading treatment" as opposed to "torture" could be classified differently in future.' The Court explained that 'the increasingly high standard being required in the area of the protection of human rights and fundamental liberties correspondingly and inevitably requires greater firmness in assessing breaches of the fundamental values of democratic societies.'[83] It is clear from

[78] § 177. [79] *Bayatyan v Armenia*, (App. 23459/03), 7 July 2011 [GC], ECHR 2011.
[80] § 103–4. [81] § 105.
[82] *Selmouni v France*, (App. 25803/94), 28 July 1999 [GC], ECHR 1999-V.
[83] § 101.

this that the evolutive interpretation of the Convention is not only a response to scientific advances or social changes, but is also a response to the higher standards of compliance with human rights expected of today's State governments. Mowbray makes a sound point about the living instrument doctrine when he argues that a 'greater willingness to elaborate upon the application of the doctrine in specific cases would help to alleviate potential fears that it is simply a cover for subjective ad-hockery.'[84] While the doctrine will be balanced against a reluctance to overrule previous case-law because, as expressed in *Goodwin v United Kingdom*, the Court 'should not depart, without good reason, from precedents laid down in previous cases,'[85] it is clear that the perceived need for an evolutive interpretation will suffice for such a 'good reason' to depart. In *Micallef v Malta*, the Grand Chamber confirmed that:

> While it is in the interests of legal certainty, foreseeability and equality before the law that the Court should not depart, without good reason, from precedents laid down in previous cases, a failure by the Court to maintain a dynamic and evolutive approach would risk rendering it a bar to reform or improvement.[86]

COMPARATIVE INTERPRETATION

One response to suggestions that the Strasbourg judges are too active and make law rather than interpret it has been resort to a search for a common European standard. The standards adopted for interpreting the European Convention may sometimes differ from those applicable to other international instruments. This is because the interpretation of the European Convention may legitimately be based on a common tradition of constitutional laws and a large measure of legal tradition common to the countries of the Council of Europe.[87] Thus the Court and the Commission have relied as a guide to the scope of the rights guaranteed by the Convention, on comparative surveys of the laws of the Contracting Parties: the laws relating to vagrancy,[88] for example, or legislation on the right to respect for family life,[89] or on various aspects of criminal procedure,[90] or on the age of criminal responsibility,[91] or the law relating to recognition of the gender identity of transsexuals.[92]

Reference may be made to the general practice of the Contracting Parties in order to decide what is 'reasonable' or what is 'necessary'—two terms which occur frequently in the Convention—or what constitutes 'normal' civic obligations under Article 4.[93] There may thus be a conflict between two legitimate aims of interpretation: to avoid inconsistencies with other international instruments, and to develop the protection of human rights in Europe on the basis of a common European law.

The yardstick of democratic standards runs through the Convention and has proved to be an important source of inspiration in delimiting the requirements of the Convention.

[84] A. Mowbray, 'The Creativity of the European Court of Human Rights' (2005) 5 HRLR 57, 71.

[85] *Christine Goodwin v United Kingdom*, (App. 28957/95), 11 July 2002 [GC], ECHR 2002-VI, § 74. See also *Mamatkulov & Askarov v Turkey* [GC], (Apps. 46827/99 and 46951/99), § 121, ECHR 2005-I and *Vilho Eskelinen & others v Finland*, (App. 63235/00), 19 April 2007 [GC], ECHR 2007-II. For discussion of this reluctance to overrule previous case-law, see A. Mowbray, 'An Examination of the European Court of Human Rights' Approach to Overruling its Previous Case Law' (2009) 5 HRLR 179.

[86] *Micallef v Malta*, (App. 17056/06), 15 October 2009 [GC], ECHR 2009, § 81.

[87] See generally A. Dremczewski, *European Human Rights Convention in Domestic Law* (OUP, Oxford 1983).

[88] See Appendix IV to the Commission's Report of 19 July 1969 on the *Vagrancy Cases*, entitled 'Outline of Vagrancy legislation in force in European countries'.

[89] See ch.15.

[90] See chs. 12 and 13.

[91] *V v United Kingdom*, (App. 24888/94), 16 December 1999, (2000) 30 EHRR 121, ECHR 1999-IX.

[92] *Goodwin v United Kingdom*, (App. 28957/95), 11 July 2002 [GC], (2002) 35 EHRR 447, ECHR 2002-VI; and *I v United Kingdom*, (App. 26580/94), 11 July 2002, (2003) 36 EHRR 967.

[93] See ch.10.

Certain key features of a democratic society emerge from a significant case-law in which the term has been relevant.[94] Democratic values require respect for the rule of law, which has been reflected in recognition by the Court of a right of access to the courts.[95] In one case, the Grand Chamber of the Court said:

> 89. As has been stated many times in the Court's judgments, not only is political democracy a fundamental feature of the European public order but the Convention was designed to promote and maintain the ideals and values of a democratic society. Democracy, the Court has stressed, is the only political model contemplated in the Convention and the only one compatible with it. By virtue of the wording of the second paragraph of Article 11, and likewise of Articles 8, 9 and 10 of the Convention, the only necessity capable of justifying an interference with any of the rights enshrined in those Articles is one that must claim to spring from 'democratic society'....
>
> 90. Referring to the hallmarks of a 'democratic society', the Court has attached particular importance to pluralism, tolerance and broadmindedness. In that context, it has held that although individual interests must on occasion be subordinated to those of a group, democracy does not simply mean that the views of the majority must always prevail: a balance must be achieved which ensures the fair and proper treatment of minorities and avoids any abuse of a dominant position....[96]

APPROACHES AND IDEOLOGIES, AND THE MARGIN OF APPRECIATION

Fundamental differences of approach to interpretation of the Convention had emerged in the 1975 *Golder* case.[97] The Commission had argued that an important canon of interpretation of international treaties had only very limited application to the European Convention, namely consideration of the intention of the parties at the time of ratification. The Commission argued that the European Convention should not be interpreted in this subjective manner by reference to the intention of the parties, but should be interpreted objectively. The Commission argued:

> The over-riding function of this Convention is to protect the rights of the individual and not to lay down as between States mutual obligations which are to be restrictively interpreted having regard to the sovereignty of these States. On the contrary, the role of the Convention and the function of its interpretation is to make the protection of the individual effective.[98]

This approach to interpretation was adopted by the majority of the Court in its 9–3 decision. The opposing view to interpretation of the Convention was championed by Sir Gerald Fitzmaurice throughout his term as a judge at the Court and an understanding of this approach helps to explain why he was so frequently in the minority in the Court. For Sir Gerald Fitzmaurice, the objective approach to interpretation was fundamentally flawed.

[94] See further discussion in ch.14. See also J. Merrills, *The Development of International Law by the European Court of Human Rights* (MUP, Manchester 1993), ch.6. See also S. Marks, 'The European Convention on Human Rights and its "Democratic Society"' (1995) 66 BYIL 209; and C. Gearty, 'Democracy and Human Rights in the European Court of Human Rights: A Critical Appraisal' (2000) 51 NILQ 381.

[95] *Golder v United Kingdom*, (App. 4451/70), 21 February 1975, Series A No 18, (1979–80) 1 EHRR 524, § 29.

[96] *Gorzelik and others v Poland*, (App. 44158/98), 17 February 2004, (2005) 40 EHRR 76, ECHR 2004-I, §§ 89–90.

[97] *Golder v United Kingdom*, (App. 4451/70), 21 February 1975, Series A No 18, (1979–80) 1 EHRR 524.

[98] *Golder v United Kingdom*, Report of 1 June 1973. Series B, No 16, 40.

Since the Convention made serious inroads into the domestic jurisdiction of States, a restrictive approach to its interpretation was required. He argued in his minority opinion in the *Golder* case that a cautious and conservative approach should be adopted to the interpretation of the Convention, since extensive interpretation could impose on Contracting Parties obligations they had not intended to assume in ratifying the Convention. Therefore doubts should be resolved in favour of the State rather than the individual.

The resolution of doubts in favour of States has found its clearest exposition in the case-law of the Strasbourg Court in the concept of the 'margin of appreciation' which has been used extensively. But the term is used in more than one sense, as Letsas notes;[99] furthermore the Strasbourg Court is criticized for not always distinguishing between different meanings and contexts in which the term is used:

> I propose to analyse the margin of appreciation doctrine, as it figures in the case-law, in a different way by drawing a distinction between two different ways in which it has been used by the Court. The first one, which I shall call the *substantive* concept is to address the relationship between individual freedoms and collective goals. The second one, which I shall call the *structural* concept, is to address the limits or intensity of review of the European Court of Human Rights in view of its status as an international tribunal. It amounts to the claim that the European Court should often *defer* to the judgment of national authorities on the basis that the ECHR is an *international* convention, not a national bill of rights. The ideas of subsidiarity and state consensus are usually invoked to support the structural use of the margin of appreciation.[100]

This is a helpful analysis which enables us to appreciate the different contexts in which the notion operates. In its first sense, it has its greatest application when balancing the rights contained in the first paragraphs of Articles 8 to 11 of the Convention against the permissible interferences which may be justified by resort to the limitations permitted by the second paragraphs of those provisions.[101] In the second sense, the easiest example is the approach of the Strasbourg Court to review of a Contracting Party's claim that there is a public emergency threatening the life of the nation which warrants derogation from one or more provisions of the Convention.[102]

Margins of appreciation are the outer limits of schemes of protection which are acceptable under the Convention.[103] The Court will not interfere with actions which are within the margin of appreciation. So in the *Brannigan* case,[104] the Court affirmed its earlier case-law in considering the validity of the UK's derogation under Article 15 excluding the application of Article 5(3) to the system of detention applicable under the prevention of terrorism legislation. The Court recognized that Contracting Parties are in a better position than the judges to decide both on the presence of an emergency

[99] G. Letsas, *A Theory of Interpretation of the European Convention on Human Rights* (OUP, Oxford 2007), ch.4.

[100] 80–1.

[101] For a further discussion of limitations in this context, see ch.14. The Strasbourg Court has interpreted certain other provisions of the Convention using the same methodology; so, for example, the right to property in Art.1 of Protocol 1 is now applied using this approach.

[102] See ch.6.

[103] See G. van der Meersch, 'Le caractère "autonome" des terms et la "marge d'appreciation" des gouvernements dans l'interprétation de la Convention européenne des Droits de l'Homme' in F. Matscher and H. Petzold, *Protecting Human Rights: The European Dimension. Studies in honour of Gérard J. Wiarda* (Carl Heymanns, Köln 1989), 201; R. Macdonald, 'The margin of appreciation' in R. Macdonald, F. Matscher, and H. Petzold, *The European System for the Protection of Human Rights* (Martinus Nijhoff, Dordrecht 1993), 83; and J.G. Merrills, *The Development of International Law by the European Court of Human Rights* (MUP, Manchester 1993), ch.7.

[104] *Brannigan and McBride v United Kingdom*, (Apps. 14553/89, and 14554/89), 26 May 1993, Series A No 258–B, (1994) 17 EHRR 539.

threatening the life of the nation and on the nature and scope of the derogations necessary to avert it. It was therefore appropriate to leave 'a wide margin of appreciation . . . to the national authorities'.[105] However, even this wide margin of appreciation is subject to the supervision of the Convention organs, since it is for the Court to determine whether the derogation goes beyond the extent strictly required by the exigencies of the situation. It followed that:

> in exercising its supervision the Court must give appropriate weight to such relevant factors as the nature of the rights affected by the derogation, the circumstances leading to, and the duration of, the emergency situation.[106]

The absence of judicial control over the extended period of detention was held not to be beyond the margin of appreciation in this case.

The use of margins of appreciation permits the Court to keep in touch with legal reality where there is scope for differential application of Convention provisions while retaining some control over State conduct.[107] As the concept has evolved in the case-law of the Court, it has become clear that the scope of the margin will vary according to the circumstances, subject matter, and background to the issue before the Court as well as the presence or absence of common ground among the States Parties to the Convention.[108]

Letsas has argued that a proper understanding of the margin of appreciation and of the limits of interpretation will avoid the Convention being extended into areas which are inappropriate for human rights protection; he calls this rights inflation. He uses the example of a right to sleep which he suggests was involved in the litigation concerning airport noise, where the Grand Chamber reversed the Chamber judgment, which had found a violation of Article 8.[109]

CONCLUDING REMARKS

Interpretation of the Convention builds on the rules of public international law on the interpretation of treaties and has remained broadly consistent with those principles. At the same time the approach taken to interpretation has recognized that both the nature of the obligations contained in the Convention and the regional limitation on its application legitimately permit the giving of a particular meaning to words and phrases in the Convention. There would appear to be two core principles of interpretation: that which seeks to effect the object and purpose of the Convention (the teleological approach), and that which seeks to give it a practical and effective application in the light of present-day conditions (the evolutive approach).

The role of the Strasbourg Court is casuistic; deciding individual cases does not lend itself to broad statements of theory, and the Court has never used practice statements

[105] § 43, affirming *Ireland v United Kingdom*, (App. 5310/71), 18 January 1978, Series A No 25, (1979–80) 2 EHRR 25, § 207.

[106] *Brannigan and McBride v United Kingdom*, (Apps. 14553/89, and 14554/89), 26 May 1993, Series A No 258–B, (1994) 17 EHRR 539, § 43.

[107] See generally Y. Arai-Takahashi, *The Margin of Appreciation Doctrine and the Principle of Proportionality in the Jurisprudence of the ECHR* (Intersentia, Antwerp 2002); and H. Yourow, *The Margin of Appreciation Doctrine in the Dynamics of European Human Rights Jurisprudence* (Martinus Nijhoff, Dordrecht 1996).

[108] See *Rasmussen v Denmark*, (App. 8777/79), 28 November 1984, Series A No 87, (1985) 7 EHRR 372.

[109] G. Letsas, *A Theory of Interpretation of the European Convention on Human Rights* (OUP, Oxford 2007), esp. ch.6. See also *Hatton v United Kingdom*, (App. 36022/97), 8 July 2003 [GC], (2003) 37 EHRR 611, ECHR 2003-VIII, discussed in more detail in ch.16.

or practice directions to set out its approach to interpretation. It has, accordingly, been left to commentators to synthesize from the case-law of the Strasbourg Court a set of principles which the Court uses in interpreting the Convention. Its overall approach can perhaps best be summarized as an evolutive approach based upon its understanding of the object and purpose of the Convention, but also reflective of its own role as an international human rights court conscious of its subsidiary role in the protection of human rights.

APPENDIX

EXTRACTS FROM THE VIENNA CONVENTION ON THE LAW OF TREATIES

Article 31
General rule of interpretation

1. A treaty shall be interpreted in good faith in accordance with the ordinary meaning to be given to the terms of the treaty in their context and in the light of its object and purpose.

2. The context for the purpose of the interpretation of a treaty shall comprise, in addition to the text, including its preamble and annexes:

(a) any agreement relating to the treaty which was made between all the parties in connection with the conclusion of the treaty;

(b) any instrument which was made by one or more parties in connection with the conclusion of the treaty and accepted by the other parties as an instrument related to the treaty.

3. There shall be taken into account, together with the context:

(a) any subsequent agreement between the parties regarding the interpretation of the treaty or the application of its provisions;

(b) any subsequent practice in the application of the treaty which establishes the agreement of the parties regarding its interpretation;

(c) any relevant rules of international law applicable in the relations between the parties.

4. A special meaning shall be given to a term if it is established that the parties so intended.

Article 32
Supplementary means of interpretation

Recourse may be had to supplementary means of interpretation, including the preparatory work of the treaty and the circumstances of its conclusion, in order to confirm the meaning resulting from the application of Article 31, or to determine the meaning when the interpretation according to Article 31:

(a) leaves the meaning ambiguous or obscure; or

(b) leads to a result which is manifestly absurd or unreasonable.

Article 33
Interpretation of treaties authenticated in two or more languages

1. When a treaty has been authenticated in two or more languages, the text is equally authoritative in each language, unless the treaty provides or the parties agree that, in case of divergence, a particular text shall prevail.

2. A version of the treaty in a language other than one of those in which the text was authenticated shall be considered an authentic text only if the treaty so provides or the parties so agree.

3. The terms of the treaty are presumed to have the same meaning in each authentic text.

4. Except where a particular text prevails in accordance with paragraph 1, where a comparison of the authentic texts discloses a difference of meaning which the application of Articles 31 and 32 does not remove, the meaning which best reconciles the texts, having regard to the object and purpose of the treaty, shall be adopted.

5

THE SCOPE OF THE CONVENTION

GENERAL SCOPE OF THE CONVENTION

This chapter explores a number of issues arising from the obligation in Article 1 of the Convention, which requires Contracting Parties to secure to everyone within their jurisdiction the Convention rights set out in Section I of the Convention. The whole of Section I, however, does not in terms impose any obligations on States; it takes the form of a declaration of rights. It is Article 1 which transforms this declaration of rights into a set of obligations for the Contracting Parties which ratify the Convention.

The overall approach of the Convention is based on the principles of solidarity and subsidiarity. Solidarity refers to the commitment of the Contracting Parties to secure effective protection of the rights enumerated in the Convention within their national legal orders, while subsidiarity[1] refers to the role of the Strasbourg Court as secondary to the institutions of national legal systems in adjudicating on claims that Convention rights have been violated. It is partly for this reason that a complaint cannot be made to the Strasbourg Court until all efforts to resolve the dispute have been undertaken within the national legal order. This principle also explains why the Strasbourg Court does not regard itself as a court of appeal from decisions of institutions within national legal orders.

Writers have differed on the nature of the guarantee in Article 1. Some have argued that there is an obligation to incorporate the actual text of the Convention, or of Section I at least, into national law.[2] A former President of the Court has spoken of the merits of incorporation in the following terms:

> Incorporation of the Convention into national law, as known in many States, is one of the most effective means of reducing the need for recourse to Strasbourg.[3]

The advantages of incorporation are spelled out in other speeches:

> [Incorporation] has in fact two advantages: it provides the national court with the possibility of taking account of the Convention and the Strasbourg case-law to resolve the dispute before it, and at the same time it gives the European organs an opportunity to discover the

[1] See H. Petzold, 'The Convention and the Principle of Subsidiarity', in R. Macdonald, F. Matscher, and H. Petzold, *The European System for the Protection of Human Rights* (Martinus Nijhoff, Dordrecht 1993), 41.

[2] See T. Buergenthal, 'The effect of the European Convention on Human Rights on the Internal Law of Member States' in *The European Convention on Human Rights*, British Institute of International and Comparative Law, Supplementary Publication No. 11, 1965, 57 *et seq.*, and for the opposite view T. Sørensen, 'Obligations of a State Party to a Treaty as regards its Municipal Law' in A. H. Robertson (ed.), *Human Rights in National and International Law* (MUP, Manchester 1968), 11–31. See also A. Drzemczewski, *European Human Rights Convention in Domestic Law. A Comparative Study* (OUP, Oxford 1983).

[3] R. Ryssdal, Speech to the Informal Ministerial Conference on Human Rights and Celebration of the 40th Anniversary of the European Convention on Human Rights, Rome, 5 November 1990, 2, Council of Europe document Cour (90) 289.

> views of the national courts regarding the interpretation of the Convention and its application to a specific set of circumstances. The dialogue which thus develops between those who are called upon to apply the Convention on the domestic level and those who must do so on the European level is crucial for an effective protection of the rights guaranteed under the Convention.[4]

There is, however, no dispute that national law must give full effect to the rights guaranteed by the Convention. Contracting Parties have in fact chosen to implement its guarantees by different methods, according to their own constitutional practices. Thus the Convention has the status of national law in Germany and of constitutional law in Austria. In France the Convention has an intermediate status, higher than ordinary legislation but lower than the Constitution. Prior to the Human Rights Act 1998, the Convention had not been enacted as part of the law of the United Kingdom and therefore did not have the force of law.[5] It was argued that the general law of the land guaranteed all the rights contained in the Convention. Convention rights[6] were enacted into UK law with the entry into force of the Human Rights Act 1998 on 2 October 2000.[7] The Act is said to give 'further effect' to the Convention in UK law and, in the political rhetoric of the time, to 'bring rights home'.

Incorporation in some form is now the standard means by which effect is given to the Convention in the national legal orders. The protection of the individual is more effective if the substantive rights guaranteed by the Convention can be enforced by the national courts.[8] If the rights are not expressly enacted in national law, or cannot be invoked before the national courts, there is no alternative to the European procedure. The experience of statutory enactment into the law of the UK is that Convention rights gain a much higher profile within the national legal order, as public authorities determine the extent to which any action is compatible with the rights guaranteed in the Convention.

Whether or not Contracting Parties incorporate the actual text of the Convention into national law, they are obliged, by appropriate means, 'to ensure that their domestic legislation is compatible with the Convention and, if need be, to make any necessary adjustments to this end'.[9] Further, the terms of Article 52[10] show that national law must be such as to 'ensure the effective implementation' of all the provisions of the Convention. This does not, however, exhaust the effect of Article 1. Contracting Parties are liable for violations of the Convention which may result not only from legislation incompatible with it, but also from acts of all public authorities, at every level, including the executive and the courts.

Article 1 contains a double obligation. There is, on the one hand, the negative obligation which requires Contracting Parties not to infringe the rights protected in the Convention. There is also, on the other hand, the positive obligation to ensure that the rights protected by the Convention are guaranteed to those within the jurisdiction of Contracting

[4] R. Ryssdal, Speech at the ceremony for the 40th anniversary of the European Convention on Human Rights at Trieste, 18 December 1990, Council of Europe document Cour (90) 318, 2. See also dictum in *Ireland v United Kingdom*, (App. 5310/71), 18 January 1978, Series A No 25; (1979–80) 2 EHRR 25, § 239; and J. Frowein, 'Incorporation of the Convention into Domestic Law' in J. P. Gardner (ed.), *Aspects of Incorporation of the European Convention of Human Rights into Domestic Law* (BIICL, London 1993).

[5] *R v Chief Immigration Officer, Heathrow Airport, ex parte Salamat Bibi*, [1976] 1 WLR 979, [1976] 3 All ER 843, CA; *R v Secretary of State for the Home Department, ex parte Brind*, [1991] 1 AC 696, [1991] 2 WLR 588, HL.

[6] With the exception of Art. 13. [7] See later in this chapter.

[8] It also provides the possibility that national legal orders may more readily develop the protection of human rights beyond the minimum guarantees set out in the Convention.

[9] App. 214/56, *De Becker v Belgium*, Decision of 9 June 1958, (1958–9) 2 *Yearbook* 214, 234.

[10] Formerly Art. 57.

Parties.[11] The extent to which a State may be liable for violations committed outside their territory is considered later in this chapter. But is the liability of a Contracting Party limited to its actions as the State exercising its public authority rather than its actions of a private nature, for example, as an employer?

In both the *Swedish Engine Drivers' Union* case[12] and the *Schmidt and Dahlström* case[13] the applicants' complaints under Articles 11 and 14 were arguably directed partly against the State as employer and partly against the State's exercise of public authority. The Swedish Government contended that the applicants were attacking not the Swedish legislative, executive, and judicial authorities, but rather the National Collective Bargaining Office and thus the 'State as employer'; and that, in the sphere of work and employment conditions, the Convention could not impose upon the State obligations that were not incumbent on private employers. According to the Commission, on the other hand, the disputed decision adopted by the Office could in principle be challenged under Article 11, even if the Office fulfilled typical employer functions. The Court concluded that the Convention was applicable in this situation.

TEMPORAL SCOPE

In the *Nielsen* case, the Commission said:

> Under a generally recognized rule of international law, the Convention only governs for each Contracting Party those facts which are subsequent to the date of its entry into force with regard to the Party in question.[14]

The Convention has no retroactive effect. The Convention entered into force on 3 September 1953.[15] For any State ratifying the Convention and Protocols after these dates, they enter into force on the date of ratification. An application cannot relate back to an event earlier than the entry into force of the instrument in question in respect of a Contracting Party against which the application is brought, unless that event has consequences which may raise the question of a continuing violation.[16]

A different view was taken of the effect of declarations recognizing the competence of the Commission to consider individual applications. The general rule was that, unless the drafting of the recognition of competence precluded it, the Commission was competent to consider matters going back to the date of accession of the Contracting Party.[17]

[11] See, for example, *Z and others v United Kingdom*, (App. 29392/95), 10 May 2001 [GC], (2002) 34 EHRR 97, ECHR 2001-V, § 73.

[12] *Swedish Engine Drivers' Union v Sweden*, (App. 5614/72), 6 February 1976, Series A No. 20, (1979–80) 1 EHRR 617.

[13] *Schmidt and Dahlström v Sweden*, (App. 5589/72), 6 February 1976, Series A No 21, (1979–80) 1 EHRR 637.

[14] App. 343/57, *Nielsen v Denmark*, Decision of 2 September 1959, (1959–60) 2 *Yearbook* 412, 454.

[15] The various Protocols entered into force on the following dates (not necessarily for all Contracting Parties): Protocol 1: 18 May 1954; Protocol 2: 21 September 1970; Protocol 3: 21 September 1970; Protocol 4: 2 May 1968; Protocol 5: 21 December 1971; Protocol 6: 1 March 1985; Protocol 7: 1 November 1988; Protocol 8: 1 January 1990; Protocol 9: 1 October 1994; Protocol 10: not in force (but rendered otiose since the entry into force of Protocol 11); Protocol 11: 1 November 1998; Protocol 12: 1 April 2005; Protocol 13: 1 July 2003; Protocol 14: 1 June 2010.

[16] As in App. 214/56, *De Becker v Belgium*, Decision of 9 June 1958, (1958–9) 2 *Yearbook* 214. See also ch.2 for what constitutes a continuing violation.

[17] App. 6323/73, *X v Italy*, Decision of 4 March 1976, (1976) 3 DR 80 and App. 9587/81, *X v France*, Decision of 13 December 1982, (1983) 29 DR 228.

Similar considerations applied to declarations accepting the compulsory jurisdiction of the Court.[18]

An example of the Court's approach to jurisdiction *ratione temporis* can be found in the *Zana* case.[19] The case concerned a prosecution in relation to remarks made by the former mayor of a Turkish town to journalists expressing support for the PKK in August 1987. In March 1991 he was sentenced to a period of imprisonment. The Turkish Government had accepted the jurisdiction of the Strasbourg Court only in relation to facts and events subsequent to 22 January 1990, and objected to the Court's jurisdiction to decide Zana's application on this basis. But the Court decided that the principal fact which gave rise to the complaint of a violation of Article 10 was the judgment of the Turkish court in March 1991 rather than the applicant's statements to journalists in August 1987. It was this event which interfered with the applicant's freedom of speech. The Turkish objection was rejected.[20]

Similarly in the *Witkowska-Toboła* case[21] the applicant complained about the breach of her property rights in relation to the operation of the compensation scheme for those who had lost land in Poland. Certain events had occurred prior to the entry into force of the Convention for Poland, but the Strasbourg Court ruled that:

> the Court's jurisdiction *ratione temporis* covers the period following the date of ratification, the facts that occurred before that date being considered only inasmuch as they have created a situation extending beyond that date or are relevant for the understanding of the situation obtaining afterwards.[22]

The Grand Chamber reviewed the authorities and confirmed this approach in the *Blečič* case.[23] The key issue is to establish the date of the facts which constitute the interference with a Convention right. The subsequent failure of remedies aimed at addressing the interference cannot alone bring the matter within the temporal jurisdiction of the Strasbourg Court. In order to determine the date of the factual situation which gives rise to the alleged breach of Convention rights, the nature and scope of the Convention right in issue are relevant.

In the *Šilih* case,[24] the Court observed that the procedural obligation to carry out an investigation under Article 2 into a death had evolved into 'a separate and autonomous duty'[25] and, in the particular circumstances of the case, the absence of an investigation into a death which had occurred before the date the Convention became binding for the respondent State did not take the matter outside the jurisdiction of the Court *ratione temporis*. But this was not unqualified. A significant proportion of the procedural steps required to meet the obligation in Article 2 needed to fall within the time frame after the Convention came into force for the Contracting Party. In *Varnava and others v Turkey*,[26]

[18] But it was only necessary for the respondent State to have accepted the Court's competence for this purpose in the context of inter-State applications. A Contracting Party which has not accepted the competence of the Court for this purpose could nevertheless complain about the conduct of a Contracting Party which had: App. 788/60, *Austria v Italy*, Decision of 11 January 1961, (1962) 4 *Yearbook* 116.

[19] *Zana v Turkey*, (App. 18954/91), 25 November 1997, (1999) 27 EHRR 667, ECHR 1997-VII.

[20] Issues of the temporal scope of the Convention were also in issue in *Ilaşcu and others v Moldova and Russia*, (App. 48787/99), 8 July 2004 [GC], (2005) 40 EHRR 1030, ECHR 2004-VII discussed in detail later in this chapter. The Court followed the approach it had adopted in its earlier cases.

[21] *Witkowska-Toboła v Poland*, (App. 11208/02), Decision of 4 December 2007. [22] § 31.

[23] *Blečič v Croatia*, (App. 59532/00), 8 March 2006 [GC], (2006) 43 EHRR 1038, ECHR 2006-III, §§ 63–82, affirmed in *Šilih v Slovenia*, (App. 71463/01), 9 April 2009 [GC], (2009) 49 EHRR 996, ECHR 2009-nyr, §§ 139–47.

[24] *Šilih v Slovenia*, (App. 71463/01), 9 April 2009 [GC], (2009) 49 EHRR 996, ECHR 2009-nyr.

[25] § 159.

[26] *Varnava and others v Turkey*, (App. 16064/90, 16065/90, 16066/90, 16068/90, 16069/90, 16070/90, 16071/90, 16072/90 and 16073/90), 18 September 2009 [GC], ECHR 2009.

however, the Grand Chamber identified an important distinction between investigations into deaths and investigations into disappearances under Article 2. As a disappearance is characterized by an ongoing situation of uncertainty, the procedural obligation continues for as long as the fate of the missing person remains unknown, even if death is presumed after a period of time. Therefore, an ongoing failure to provide the requisite investigation will be regarded as a continuing violation and *ratione temporis* objections will not apply.

This issue of investigations into actions that occurred before the respondent State was committed to the Convention was considered again in *Janowiec and others v Russia*.[27] This case involved a claim by relatives of victims of the Katyń massacre of 1940 in which Polish officers and officials were killed by the Soviet secret police and buried in mass graves in the Katyń forest. The applicants acknowledged that the massacre itself was an act outside the temporal reach of the Convention but argued that the Court could examine the observance by Russia of their right to obtain an effective investigation under the procedural limb of Article 2. The Court followed the approach in *Šilih* and confirmed that the procedural obligation to carry out an effective investigation under Article 2 has evolved into a separate and autonomous duty capable of binding the State even when the death took place before the critical date. However this requires 'a genuine connection between the death and the entry into force of the Convention'.[28] No such connection could be found in this case and so the Court did not have temporal jurisdiction to consider the procedural requirements of Article 2. It did, however, find that it had jurisdiction to consider the Article 3 obligation on the Russian authorities to 'react to the plight of the relatives of the dead or disappeared individual in a humane and compassionate way'.[29] The Court's judgment has been referred to a Grand Chamber. If confirmed it represents a potential relaxation of the approach to temporal scope rules in respect of the treatment of relatives of those who died long before a State's commitment to the Convention.

Denunciation under Article 58[30] does not have immediate effect. When a State ratifies the Convention, there is an initial commitment for five years, and thereafter six months' notice is required to denounce the Convention. The obligations undertaken remain in full effect until the expiry of the period of notice. So the application made by Denmark, Norway, and Sweden against Greece in April 1970, some four months after Greece had denounced the Convention on 12 December 1969, was admissible since the six months' notice period did not expire until 13 June 1970.[31]

THE CONCEPT OF JURISDICTION IN ARTICLE 1 OF THE CONVENTION

The guarantee in Article 1 is to secure Convention rights to those 'within the jurisdiction' of a Contracting Party.[32] Establishing the jurisdiction of a Contracting Party is a threshold which must be reached before the Strasbourg Court can examine a complaint under the

[27] *Janowiec and others v Russia*, (Apps. 55508/07 and 29520/09), 16 April 2012. [28] § 132.

[29] § 152. [30] Formerly Art. 65.

[31] App. 4448/70, *Denmark, Norway and Sweden v Greece*, Decision of 26 May 1970, (1970) 13 *Yearbook* 108. This application was struck out of the Commission's list in 1976 after Greece had again become a party to the Convention: Report of Decision of 4 October 1976 (1976) 6 DR 6.

[32] Compare Art. 2(1) of the International Covenant on Civil and Political Rights, which reads: Each State Party...undertakes to respect and to ensure to all individuals within its territory and subject to its jurisdiction the rights recognized in the present Covenant, without distinction of any kind, such as race, colour, sex, language, religion, political or other opinion, national or social origin, property, birth or other status.

Convention.[33] Two principal questions have arisen in connection with the scope of jurisdiction under Article 1. First, to what extent is a State accountable under the Convention in respect of its acts or omissions which occur, or have effect, outside its territorial boundaries? Secondly, to what extent is a State accountable under the Convention in respect of acts or omissions which occur within its territorial borders but within a region over which the main State organs have no, or only limited, control?

Before considering these issues in detail, it is worth noting that a number of specific provisions of the Convention may have extraterritorial effect. For example, in the *Soering* case,[34] the Court took the view that the extradition of Soering to the United States where he might be exposed to the so-called death row phenomenon would amount to a breach by the UK of its obligations under Article 3. This approach has subsequently been following in many extradition and deportation cases, which are discussed in more detail in Chapter 9. However, this type of case should not be seen as an example of extraterritorial application of the Convention, since the liability under the Convention arises from the decision to remove the person concerned from the territory of the Contracting State and expose him to a risk of ill-treatment in the receiving country. The Contracting State is not liable for what actually befalls the applicant once out of its territory, but instead for making the decision to expel him knowing that there was such a risk.[35]

THE EXTRATERRITORIAL SCOPE OF JURISDICTION

In its admissibility decision in the *Banković* case[36] the Grand Chamber held, unanimously, that 'jurisdiction' was essentially a territorial notion. Much of the reasoning in *Banković* has been superseded by subsequent case law, in particular *Al-Skeini v United Kingdom*.[37] Nonetheless, since the Court has never explicitly overruled *Banković*, and since it forms the starting point of discussion in the later cases, it is important to examine its findings in some depth here. The application was brought against the seventeen NATO States which were also parties to the European Convention by relatives of journalists killed by a NATO air strike on the offices of the Serbian national radio and television network in Belgrade during the Kosovo conflict in 1999. The applicants argued that, as a result of the air strike, the victims had been brought within the 'effective control' of the respondent States and that, in consequence, they were within the 'jurisdiction' of those States. They asked the Strasbourg Court to find that the obligation on those States under Article 1 to secure Convention rights outside their territories was proportionate to the level of control in fact exercised. The fact that the States exercised complete control over their military aircraft

[33] See M. Milanović, 'From Compromise to Principle: Clarifying the Concept of State Jurisdiction in Human Rights Treaties' (2008) 8 HRLRev 411.

[34] *Soering v United Kingdom*, (App. 14038/88), 7 July 1989, Series A No 161, (1989) 11 EHRR 439. See further in ch.9.

[35] *Al-Adsani v United Kingdom*, (App. 35763/97), 21 November 2001, § 39.

[36] *Banković and others v Belgium and 16 other Contracting States*, (App. 52207/99), Decision of 12 December 2001 [GC], (2007) 44 EHRR SE5, ECHR 2001-XII. See R. Lawson, 'Life after *Banković*: On the Extraterritorial Application of the European Convention on Human Rights'; and M. O'Boyle, 'The European Convention on Human Rights and Extraterritorial Jurisdiction: A Comment on Life after *Banković*' both in F. Coomans and M. Kamminga (eds.) *Extraterritorial Application of Human Rights Treaties* (Intersentia, Antwerp 2004), 83 and 125. See also L. Loucaides, 'Determining the extra-territorial effect of the European Convention: facts, jurisprudence and the Banković case' [2006] EHRLR 391; M. Gondek, 'Extraterritorial Application of the European Convention on Human Rights: Territorial Focus in the Age of Globalization?' (2005) 52 *Netherlands International Law Review* 349; J. Altiparmak, '*Banković*: an obstacle to the application of the European Convention on Human Rights', (2004) 9 *Journal of Conflict and Security Law* 213.

[37] *Al-Skeini and others v United Kingdom*, (App. 55721/07), 7 July 2011, ECHR 2011.

and that the bomb dropped from the aircraft caused the deaths meant that the States should be held accountable under the Convention for this act.

The Court, however, rejected this argument and held that 'from the standpoint of public international law, the jurisdictional competence of a State is primarily territorial'[38] and that, since the Convention had to be interpreted in harmony with principles of international law, States could not normally be held to account under the Convention for acts or omissions of their agents outside their territorial borders.

The Court in *Banković* recognized that there were a small number of exceptions to the territorial principle, which included the activities of a State's diplomatic or consular agents abroad;[39] and events on board craft and vessels registered in, or flying the flag of, that State;[40] or situations where agents of the Convention State, with the consent of the Government of the territorial State, exercised public powers normally to be exercised by the territorial Government.[41] In addition, an exception had been established in two cases arising from the invasion of Cyprus by Turkish troops and the subsequent occupation and division of the island. In the *Loizidou (preliminary objections)* judgment,[42] the Strasbourg Court, examining a complaint by a woman living in southern Cyprus who was denied access to her property in northern Cyprus, had found that the responsibility of a Contracting Party was capable of being engaged when, as a consequence of lawful or unlawful military action, it exercised effective control of an area outside its national territory. On the merits,[43] the Court found that it was not necessary to determine whether Turkey actually exercised detailed control over the policies and actions of the authorities of the 'Turkish Republic of Northern Cyprus' ('TRNC'). It was obvious from the large number of troops engaged in active duties in northern Cyprus that Turkey's army exercised 'effective overall control over that part of the island'.[44] Such control, according to the relevant test and in the circumstances of the case, was found to entail the responsibility of Turkey for the policies and actions of the 'TRNC'. The Court concluded that those affected by such policies or actions therefore came within the jurisdiction of Turkey for the purposes of Article 1 of the Convention. Turkey's obligation to secure the rights and freedoms set out in the Convention was found therefore to extend to northern Cyprus. In its subsequent *Cyprus v Turkey* judgment,[45] the Court added that since Turkey had such 'effective control', its responsibility could not be confined to the acts of its own agents but was engaged by the acts of the local administration which survived by virtue of Turkish support.[46] Turkey's jurisdiction under Article 1 was therefore considered to extend to securing the entire range of substantive Convention rights in northern Cyprus.[47]

[38] *Banković*, § 57. [39] See *M v Denmark*, (App. 17392/90), 14 October 1992.

[40] See *Hirsi Jamaa and others v Italy*, (App. 27765/09), 23 February 2012 [GC], ECHR 2012, where the Grand Chamber confirmed that Somalian and Eritrean migrants travelling from Libya who were intercepted at sea by Italian authorities and transferred to vessels flying the Italian flag fell within the jurisdiction of Italy.

[41] This principle was first expressed in *Drozd and Janousek v France and Spain*, (App. 12747/87), 26 June 1992, Series A No 240, (1992) 14 EHRR 745, where the Court examined complaints arising from decisions of French and Spanish judges sitting in Andorran courts. In that case, however, the Court found that, when sitting in the Andorran courts, the French and Spanish judges were acting as Andorran judges and that no responsibility for their actions attached to France or Spain.

[42] *Loizidou v Turkey (Preliminary Objections)*, (App. 15318/89), 23 March 1995, Series A No 310, (1995) 20 EHRR 99.

[43] *Loizidou v Turkey (Merits)*, (App. 15318/89), 18 December 1996, (1996) 23 EHRR 513, ECHR 1996-VI.

[44] § 56.

[45] *Cyprus v Turkey*, (App. 25781/94), 10 May 2001 [GC], (2002) 35 EHRR 731; ECHR 2001-IV.

[46] This point was re-iterated more recently in the admissibility decision in *Andreas Manitaras and others v Turkey* (App. 54591/00), 3 June 2008.

[47] §§ 75–7.

In the *Banković* case, the Strasbourg Court contrasted the situation created by the NATO bombing raids in Belgrade and held that, since the respondent States did not have 'effective' control of the area, it did not fall within their jurisdiction under Article 1 of the Convention. Moreover, the Court introduced a controversial concept known as *espace juridique* which implies that the Convention only applies inside the territorial borders of its Contracting States and not beyond this European 'legal space'. The Court observed that:

> . . . the Convention is a multi-lateral treaty operating, subject to Article 56 of the Convention, in an essentially regional context and notably in the legal space (*espace juridique*) of the Contracting States. The FRY [former Republic of Yugoslavia] clearly does not fall within this legal space. The Convention was not designed to be applied throughout the world, even in respect of the conduct of Contracting States. Accordingly, the desirability of avoiding a gap or vacuum in human rights' protection has so far been relied on by the Court in favour of establishing jurisdiction only when the territory in question was one that, but for the specific circumstances, would normally be covered by the Convention.[48]

In subsequent cases, however, the Court has not applied the rule that Article 1 jurisdiction is limited to the European 'legal space'. The Convention has been considered to apply to the alleged acts of Turkish agents in northern Iraq,[49] Kenya,[50] Iran,[51] and in the UN neutral buffer zone in Cyprus.[52] It has been applied in relation to the acts of the Portuguese authorities having effects on a ship in international waters.[53] It has also applied to the acts of British soldiers during the occupation of Iraq. In *Al-Skeini v United Kingdom*,[54] the Grand Chamber finally clarified that the importance of establishing the occupying State's liability in cases where the territory of one Convention State is occupied by the armed forces of another does not imply, *a contrario*, that jurisdiction under Article 1 can never exist outside the Convention's legal space (*espace juridique*). Thus, this problematic concept seems finally to have been laid to rest.

Other aspects of the approach taken to extraterritorial jurisdiction in *Banković* have also been undermined in subsequent cases. One such example is the Court's retreat from the principle expressed in the *Banković* case that (apart from the limited 'embassies', 'ships', and 'aircraft' exceptions) jurisdiction under the Convention does not apply to acts or omissions of a Contracting State outside its territorial borders unless the State exercises 'effective control' over the region or area in question. The *Issa* judgment,[55] adopted after the Grand Chamber's unanimous decision in *Banković*, concerned claims by the relatives of Iraqi citizens living in Iraq that their husbands and sons had been killed by Turkish troops during an incursion into northern Iraq. While the Turkish Government confirmed that a sizeable military operation had taken place in northern Iraq at the material time aimed at pursuing and eliminating terrorists, it denied any military operations in the area where the applicants claimed their relatives had been killed. Ultimately the decision turned on the inability of the applicants to prove their assertion that the deaths were caused by Turkish military operations and the Court's observations on jurisdiction are, therefore, *obiter*. Nonetheless, it is striking that the Court expressly rejected the

48 § 80.
49 *Issa and others v Turkey*, (App. 31821/96), Decision of 16 November 2004, (2005) 41 EHRR 567.
50 *Öcalan v Turkey*, (App. 46221/99), 12 March 2003, (2005) 41 EHRR 985, ECHR 2005-IV.
51 *Pad and others v Turkey*, (App. 60167/00), Decision of 28 June 2007.
52 *Isaak v Turkey*, (App. 44587/98), 24 June 2008.
53 *Women on Waves and others v Portugal*, (App. 31276/05), 3 February 2009.
54 *Al-Skeini and others v United Kingdom*, (App. 55721/07), 7 July 2011, ECHR 2011.
55 *Issa and others v Turkey*, (App. 31821/96), Decision of 16 November 2004, (2005) 41 EHRR 567.

Turkish Government's submissions based on *Banković* and instead cited decisions of the Inter-American Commission on Human Rights and the United Nations Human Rights Committee[56] in support of the proposition that:

> ...a State may also be held accountable for violation of the Convention rights and freedoms of persons who are in the territory of another State but who are found to be under the former State's authority and control through its agents operating—whether lawfully or unlawfully—in the latter State.... Accountability in such situations stems from the fact that Article 1 of the Convention cannot be interpreted so as to allow a State party to perpetrate violations of the Convention on the territory of another State, which it could not perpetrate on its own territory....[57]

If this approach were to be followed in subsequent cases, it would expand the scope of the Convention dramatically beyond what was decided in the *Banković* case.

The divergence of approach between *Banković* and *Issa* was problematic but the Grand Chamber's judgment in *Al-Skeini v United Kingdom* has now added considerable clarity to the issue of extraterritorial jurisdiction.[58] The case involved six deaths in Al-Basrah, southern Iraq in 2003 while the UK was an occupying power. The relatives of the first four applicants were shot by British soldiers; the son of the fifth applicant was beaten by British soldiers and then forced into a river where he drowned; the son of the sixth applicant died while detained at a British military base. The Grand Chamber confirmed that a state's jurisdictional competence under Article 1 remains primarily territorial, but it proceeded to identify and explain a number of important exceptions to this general principle. These exceptions were classified as falling under two headings: first, there is the concept of effective control over a territory, which had previously been applied in *Lozidou*; second, there is the concept of state agent authority and control. This encompasses the well-established exceptions of acts of diplomatic and consular agents, the exercise of public powers through consent, invitation, or acquiescence of the territorial government, and the use of force by a State's agents operating outside its territory. Such a use of force has previously been recognized as bringing an individual within the jurisdiction of a State, as for example in *Issa* where the applicants' relatives had been taken into custody by Turkish officials, or in *Medvedyev v France*[59] where the French navy seized control of a cargo-vessel. The earlier case of *Al-Saadoon and Mufdhi v United Kingdom*[60] had also established that two Iraqi nationals detained in British-controlled military prisons in Iraq fell within the jurisdiction of the UK. The Grand Chamber in *Al-Skeini* took an important step forward in the development of extraterritorial jurisdiction by emphasizing that it is not the control exercised over the place of detention that establishes jurisdiction in such cases, but rather the control over the individual:

> The Court does not consider that jurisdiction in the above cases arose solely from the control exercised by the Contracting State over the buildings, aircraft or ship in which the

[56] *Coard and others v United States*, Inter-American Commission on Human Rights, Decision of 29 September 1999, Report No 109/99, Case No 10.951, §§ 37, 39, 41, and 43; and the views adopted by the Human Rights Committee on 29 July 1981 in the cases of *Lopez Burgos v Uruguay and Celiberti de Casariego v Uruguay*, Nos 52/1979 and 56/1979, §§ 12.3 and 10.3 respectively.

[57] *Issa*, § 71.

[58] See M. Schaefer, '*Al-Skeini* and the elusive parameters of extraterritorial jurisdiction', (2011) EHRLR. 566; M. Milanovic, '*Al-Skeini* and *Al-Jedda* in Strasbourg', (2012) EJIL 121; C. Mallory, 'Case Comment on *Al-Skeini and others v United Kingdom*', (2012) ICLQ 301.

[59] *Medvedyev and others v France*, (App. 3394/03), 23 March 2010, ECHR 2010.

[60] *Al-Sadoon and Mufdhi v United Kingdom*, (App. 61498/08), 2 March 2010, ECHR 2010 (extracts).

individuals were held. What is decisive in such cases is the exercise of physical power and control over the person in question.[61]

These two main headings for the establishment of extraterritorial jurisdiction, namely effective control over territory, and state agent authority and control, lead to two very different implications for the Contracting State. Where effective control over an area is established, the Controlling State has the responsibility under Article 1 to secure, within the area under its control, the entire range of substantive rights set out in the Convention.[62] (Whether that is a realistic obligation is open to question.) By contrast, and contrary to the Court's previous statements in *Banković*, in situations where the State through its agents exercises control and authority over an individual, the State is only under an obligation under Article 1 to secure to that individual the rights and freedoms under Section 1 that are relevant to the situation of that individual. This is most likely to include the protection offered by Articles 2, 3, and 5 but may also extend beyond those provisions, perhaps to include some elements of Article 8 depending upon the circumstances of the situation in question. Certainly it is now clear that, contrary to *Banković*, Convention rights can be 'divided and tailored in accordance with the particular circumstances of the extra-territorial act in question.'[63]

Returning to the facts of *Al-Skeini*, the Grand Chamber confirmed that the UK's assumption of authority and responsibility for the maintenance of security in south east Iraq meant that it exercised authority and control over individuals killed in the course of security operations in Al-Basrah. All of the applicants' deceased relatives were thus regarded as falling within the jurisdiction of the UK. This case provides some welcome clarity on the interpretation of jurisdiction under Article 1. Nevertheless, as the concurring opinions argue, there remain a series of unnecessarily complex exceptions to the primarily territorial jurisdiction under Article 1. Judge Bonello, in his concurring opinion, proposed a functional test to determine jurisdiction. This would move the focus away from territorial and/or extraterritorial jurisdiction and, instead, focus upon whether the State has the authority and control to perform its functions under the Convention. It would ask whether the alleged violation depended on the agents of the State and whether it was within the power of the State to punish the perpetrators and to compensate the victims? If the answer is yes, then the alleged violation falls within the State's jurisdiction. As a test for jurisdiction, it has some merit, not least for the clarity it would bring to the issue. It is based, as Judge Bonello explains, on a simple proposition: 'The duties assumed through ratifying the Convention go hand in hand with the duty to perform and observe them. Jurisdiction arises from the mere fact of having assumed those obligations and from having the capability to fulfil them (or not to fulfil them).'[64] Whether or not the Court moves in the direction of such a functional test, it is likely that further development of the definition of jurisdiction will be necessary in future cases, particularly given the ever increasing involvement of Contracting States in conflicts beyond their territorial borders.

JURISDICTION OVER BREAK-AWAY OR AUTONOMOUS REGIONS

Since the Contracting States are required under Article 1 to secure the Convention rights and freedoms to everyone 'within their jurisdiction', and since the State's jurisdictional

[61] *Al-Skeini*, § 136. [62] *Al-Skeini*, § 138. [63] *Banković*, § 75.
[64] Concurring opinion of Judge Bonello, § 13.

competence is primarily territorial, it follows that the State is generally under an obligation to apply the Convention in every part of its territory.

The Court has held that 'jurisdiction is presumed to be exercised normally throughout the State's territory.'[65] This presumption may, however, be limited in exceptional circumstances, particularly where a State is prevented from exercising its authority in part of its territory, as a result of military occupation by the armed forces of another State, acts of war or rebellion, or the acts of a foreign State supporting the installation of a separatist State within the territory of the State concerned.[66]

The *Ilaşcu* case[67] concerned the question whether either Moldova and/or Russia could be held accountable under the Convention for the arrest and detention of four Moldovan nationals by the separatist regime which controls the region of Transdniestria, in the eastern part of Moldovan territory. In June 1990, as the Soviet Union began to break up, Moldova proclaimed its sovereignty. Three months later, the Transdniestrian separatist regime declared the existence of the 'Moldavian Republic of Transdniestria' (the 'MRT'). The 'MRT' has not been recognized by the international community. On 27 August 1991 the Moldovan Parliament adopted the Declaration of Independence of the Republic of Moldova, whose territory included Transdniestria. Following this Declaration of Independence, the USSR began withdrawing its army and military equipment from Moldovan territory. Many of the Soviet soldiers who had been stationed in Transdniestria and who came from the region joined the separatist uprising and a large store of armaments fell into 'MRT' hands. During the winter of 1991–1992 there were violent clashes between Transdniestrian separatist forces and the Moldovan security forces. It was alleged that the separatists received military and economic support from Russia, both during the armed conflict, when the separatists were able to retain control over Transdniestria, and subsequently. The applicants were arrested in Transdniestria in June 1992 and subjected to severe ill-treatment. They were convicted by a Transdniestrian court of a number of offences, including offences against the 'national security' of 'the legitimate State of Transdniestria', and sentenced to long periods of imprisonment. The Supreme Court of Moldova quashed the convictions on the basis that they had been rendered by an unconstitutional court and ordered the applicants' release, but the authorities of the 'MRT' did not respond and the applicants remained in detention in appalling conditions.

In order to determine whether the applicants came within the jurisdiction of either Moldova or Russia, the Grand Chamber undertook a remarkable fact-finding mission. A delegation of four judges travelled to Chişinău and Tiraspol and heard evidence from 43 witnesses, including the President of Moldova at the time of the 1991–1992 conflict, a number of former Moldovan ministers, including the former Prime Minister, senior officials and diplomats, the commander of the Moldovan armed forces during the conflict, and a number of senior Russian military personnel.

The Strasbourg Court found, on the basis of all the material in its possession, that the Moldovan Government did not exercise authority over the part of its territory which was under the effective control of the 'MRT'. Nonetheless, the Court held that:

> …even in the absence of effective control over the Transdniestrian region, Moldova still has a positive obligation under Article 1 of the Convention to take the diplomatic, economic, judicial

[65] See *Ilaşcu and others v Moldova and Russia*, (App. 48787/99), 8 July 2004 [GC], (2005) 40 EHRR 1030, ECHR 2004-VII, § 312.

[66] *Ilaşcu*, § 312.

[67] *Ilaşcu and others v Moldova and Russia* (App. 48787/99), 8 July 2004 [GC], (2005) 40 EHRR 1030, ECHR 2004-VII. See also *Von Maltzan and others, von Zitzewitz and others, and Man Ferrostaal and Töpfer Stiftung v Germany*, (Apps. 1916/01, 71916/01 and 10260/02), Decision of 2 March 2005 [GC], (2006) 42 EHRR SE11, ECHR 2005-V.

> or other measures that it is in its power to take and are in accordance with international law to secure to the applicants the rights guaranteed by the Convention.[68]

The Court concluded that Moldova had not complied with this positive obligation because, in its negotiations with Russia and representatives of the 'MRT' for the settlement of the situation in Transdniestria, no specific mention had been made of the applicants' plight with a view to securing their release.

Even more controversially, the Court found that the applicants also fell within the jurisdiction of Russia. On the facts as found by the Court, the USSR, and particularly its 14th Army which had been stationed in Transdniestria, had given substantial support to the separatists during the fighting in 1991–1992. Moreover, following Russia's ratification of the Convention on 5 May 1998, the Russian army remained stationed in Transdniestria, in breach of Russia's undertakings to withdraw, and Russia had also provided considerable economic assistance to the 'MRT'. The Court concluded that 'that there is a continuous and uninterrupted link of responsibility on the part of the Russian Federation for the applicants' fate'.[69]

The Court concluded that there had been violations of Articles 3 and 5 of the Convention against both States and ordered each State to pay substantial awards of damages. The Russian judge was the only dissenter. In his separate opinion he expressed his 'deep disagreement' with the Court's findings and conclusions in respect of Russia.

The applicants in *Ilaşcu* were not released from detention until June 2007, nearly three years after the Court's judgment. The subsequent case of *Ivantoc v Moldova and Russia*[70] dealt with their continued detention. Moldova retained its positive obligation to take diplomatic, judicial, or other measures within its powers to secure the applicants' rights but in *Ivantoc*, unlike in the earlier case, it was held to have met that obligation. The Court recognized that following its previous judgment in 2004, 'the Moldovan authorities constantly raised the issue of the applicants' fate in their bilateral relations with the Russian Federation. Furthermore, they continually sought the assistance of other States and international organisations in obtaining the applicants' release.'[71] Moldova had, therefore, discharged its positive obligation under Article 1 and, due to its lack of effective control in 'MRT', could not be found in breach of any of the Convention rights. The 'MRT' remained under the effective authority, or at least the decisive influence, of the Russian Federation and thus the applicants remained within that State's jurisdiction. In reaching this conclusion, the Court emphasized that in the period 2004–2007, Russia continued to enjoy a close relationship with the 'MRT' amounting to providing political, financial, and economic support to the separatist regime, and the Russian army remained stationed on Moldovan territory. The Court thus found the applicants to be within Russia's jurisdiction and proceeded to find violations of Articles 3, 5, and 8 and, furthermore, regarded these as aggravated violations due to the disregard by the Russian Federation of the Court's injunction in *Ilaşcu* ordering the applicants' release.[72] As in the earlier case, the lone dissenter was the Russian judge.[73]

In the *Assanidze* case,[74] the respondent State was Georgia, and the actions in issue were those of the Ajarian Autonomous Republic, a region of Georgia which enjoyed a high

[68] *Ilaşcu*, § 331. [69] *Ilaşcu*, § 393.

[70] *Ivantoc v Moldova and Russia*, (App. 23687/05), 15 November 2011. [71] *Ivantoc*, § 109.

[72] *Ivantoc*, § 144.

[73] In another case concerning 'MRT', *Catan and others v the Republic of Moldova and Russia*, (Apps. 43370/04, 8252/05 and 18454/06), 19 October 2012 [GC], Russia was found in violation of Article 2 of Protocol 1 while Moldova was again regarded as having discharged its positive obligation as regards Moldovan-language schools threatened with coercive measures by the separatist regime.

[74] *Assanidze v Georgia*, (App. 71503/01), 8 April 2004 [GC], (2004) 39 EHRR 653, ECHR 2004-II.

degree of self-government but which had no separatist ambitions. The applicant had been acquitted in a judgment of the Georgian Supreme Court, but remained in imprisonment in the Ajarian Republic. This was not a case in which a part of the territory of the respondent State was under the effective control of another State, and the Georgian Government accepted that the applicant fell within its jurisdiction. The Court found a violation against Georgia, holding that even where a State encountered real difficulties in securing compliance with the rights guaranteed by the Convention in all parts of its territory, it remained responsible for events occurring anywhere within its borders.

LIABILITY FOR ACTS OF INTERNATIONAL ORGANIZATIONS

Questions have arisen as to whether a Contracting Party can violate the Convention by becoming party to another treaty. In one case, the Commission said:

> If a State contracts treaty obligations and subsequently concludes another international agreement which disables it from performing its obligations under the first treaty, it will be answerable for any resulting breach of its obligations under the treaty.[75]

In another case, the Commission held that the transfer of powers by the Contracting States to an international organization is compatible with the Convention, provided that fundamental rights receive, within that organization, an equivalent protection. In the context of Article 1 of Protocol 1, the European Patents Convention contains detailed safeguards for the protection of intellectual property rights. The transfer of power which it entails is therefore compatible with the Convention. The application was outside the scope of the Convention *ratione personae*.[76]

In the *Matthews* case,[77] the Strasbourg Court was called upon to consider a complaint against the UK about participation in elections to the European Parliament which were set out in an act of the Community's institutions. The Community Act[78] establishing the rules for direct elections provided in Annex II that the United Kingdom would apply the provisions only in respect of the UK. Denise Matthews was a UK national living in Gibraltar, a dependent territory of the UK. She sought to register as a voter in respect of the elections to the European Parliament, but was refused on the grounds that the Community Act did not include Gibraltar within the franchise for these elections. She complained that this refusal violated her rights under Article 3 of Protocol 1 on free elections.[79] The Strasbourg Court decided that the UK remained responsible for securing the rights in Article 3 of Protocol 1 in respect of Community legislation in the same way as if the restriction on the franchise

[75] App. 235/56, X *v Federal Republic of Germany*, Decision of 10 June 1958, (1958–9) 2 *Yearbook* 256, 300.

[76] App. 21090/92, *Heinz v Contracting Parties who are also Parties to the European Patent Convention*, Decision of 10 January 1994, (1994) 76-A DR 125. See also App. 13258/77, *M & Co. v Federal Republic of Germany*, Decision of 9 February 1990, (1990) 64 DR 138, 144, making the same point in connection with the EEC Treaty (as it then was).

[77] *Matthews v United Kingdom*, (App. 24833/94), 18 February 1999 [GC], (1999) 28 EHRR 361, ECHR 1999-I. see also Canor, '*Primus inter pares.* Who is the ultimate guardian of fundamental rights in Europe?' (2000) 25 ELRev 3; T. King, 'Ensuring human rights review of intergovernmental acts in Europe' (2000) 25 ELRev 79; and H. Schermers, 'European Remedies in the Field of Human Rights' in C. Kilpatrick, N. Novitz, and P. Skidmore, *The Future of Remedies in Europe* (Hart, Oxford 2000), 205.

[78] This is a measure adopted by the Community institutions.

[79] See ch.22.

had been included in national law. The Court went on to find that Article 3 applied, since it was possible to interpret the European Parliament as being a legislature within the Article, and concluded that there had been a violation of the Article. The significance of the case is that the Strasbourg Court has stated in the clearest terms that the Contracting Parties remain responsible for guaranteeing the rights contained in the Convention even where they create an international organization and transfer competence to it in particular areas, and that, where no other judicial body is competent to review acts of the international organization, the Strasbourg Court will consider complaints of violations of the Convention's guaranteed rights.[80]

The need for Contracting Parties to take their Convention obligations into account when entering into other international legal commitments was re-iterated in *Al-Saadoon and Mufdhi v United Kingdom*[81] where the UK was found to be in violation of Article 3 for subjecting the applicants to the fear of the death penalty by handing them over to the Iraqi authorities with no guarantee that they would not be executed. The applicants had been arrested by British soldiers during the occupation of Iraq but once that occupation had ended, the Iraqi authorities had requested their transfer to face charges which, under the Iraqi Penal Code, carried a maximum penalty of the death sentence. The UK Government argued that it was not entitled to continue to detain Iraqi nationals on Iraqi territory once Iraq had regained sovereignty and that it had no choice but to transfer the applicants to the custody of the Iraqi courts when requested to do so. The Court was adamant, however, that Contracting Parties should not enter into agreements with other States that violate their own Convention obligations.

The relationship between obligations arising under European Community law and Convention law arose in the *Bosphorus Airways* case.[82] The context was the seizure in Ireland of an aircraft leased by Bosphorus Airways from Yugoslav Airlines[83] under the terms of EC Council Regulation 990/93[84] which was adopted as part of the United Nations sanctions regime against the Federal Republic of Yugoslavia (Serbia and Montenegro). The Strasbourg Court examined the nature of Regulations in European Community law, noting that they were binding in their entirety on the Member States of the European Union, and were directly applicable in the sense that they were immediately binding in the national legal order. The actions taken in pursuance of the Regulation were, however, an interference with property rights covered by Article 1 of Protocol 1. In determining whether such an act violated the Convention, the Grand Chamber took as a starting point that the protection of fundamental rights in European Community law was, at the relevant time, equivalent to that of the Convention system. There was therefore a rebuttable presumption that action taken in compliance with Community law met the requirements of the Convention.[85]

Events in Kosovo have also contributed to the case-law on the liability of international organizations. The decisions in the *Behrami* and *Saramati* cases[86] sit somewhat uneasily

[80] For the 2004 elections to the European Parliament, Gibraltar was added to the constituency which included Cornwall!

[81] *Al-Sadoon and Mufdhi v United Kingdom*, (App. 61498/08), 2 March 2010, ECHR 2010 (extracts).

[82] *'Bosphorus Airways' v Ireland*, (App. 45036/98), 30 June 2005 [GC], (2006) 42 EHRR 1, ECHR 2005-VI.

[83] JAT. [84] [1993] *Official Journal of the European Communities* L102/1.

[85] *'Bosphorus Airways' v Ireland*, (App. 45036/98), 30 June 2005 [GC], (2006) 42 EHRR 1, ECHR 2005-VI, §§ 159–66. See ch.25 for further comment on the relationship between the Convention system and European Community law.

[86] *Behrami v France*, (App. 71412/01), Decision of 2 May 2007 [GC]; and *Saramati v France, Germany and Norway*, (App. 78166/01), Decision of 2 May 2007 [GC], (2007) 45 EHRR SE10; see A. Sari, 'Jurisdiction and International Responsibility in Peace Support Operations: The *Behrami* and *Saramati* Cases' (2008) 8 HRLRev 151, for a description of the Decision and criticism of it.

with the earlier case-law. These cases concerned claims in respect of alleged violations of the Convention by UNMIK[87] and KFOR.[88] UNMIK had been established by the United Nations Security Council acting under Chapter VII of the United Nations Charter. KFOR was part of the United Nations peace plan but was authorized by a Military Technical Agreement signed by the Federal Republic of Yugoslavia and Serbia in which the deployment and operation of KFOR in Kosovo was agreed. Principal contributors to KFOR were NATO members. The facts which gave rise to the cases were as follows. The two Behrami brothers were playing with unexploded cluster bombs; one exploded, killing one brother and seriously injuring the other. The father of the boys complained that the death and injuries had been caused by the failure of French KFOR troops to mark or defuse unexploded cluster bombs when they knew of their existence. Saramati's complaints related to his detention as a threat to the security of KFOR. His claims were made against France, Germany, and Norway as the relevant participating countries in KFOR.

The issue before the Strasbourg Court was whether the actions of which the applicants complained were within the jurisdiction of the Contracting Parties. This involved a consideration of the relationship between the Contracting Parties and the international groupings concerned. But the Strasbourg Court considered that the question concerned less the exercise of extraterritorial jurisdiction by the respondent States and more 'whether this Court is competent to examine under the Convention those States' contribution to the civil and security presences which did exercise the relevant control in Kosovo'.[89] The Strasbourg Court concluded that the acts complained of were attributable to the United Nations, and so were outside the competence of the Strasbourg Court to review *ratione personae*.[90] The Court distinguished the *Bosphorus Airways* case[91] on the grounds that the Irish case had concerned an act of Ireland on its own territory and on the authority of its own Government, albeit in compliance with a Regulation of the European Union which was binding upon it. The Court's approach assumes that responsibility can only be attributed to a single party; in reality it is difficult to see why there cannot be dual attribution of responsibility: that is, both to the international organization and to the individual participating States.

The Court's decision in distinguishing the *Bosphorus Airways* case seemed to close the door to review of any action by a Contracting Party where authority for the action is the United Nations. However, in *Al-Jedda v United Kingdom*,[92] the multinational force in Iraq was not regarded by the Grand Chamber as attributable to the United Nations. The UK and the US had invaded Iraq and assumed governmental responsibilities there in March 2003 independently of any UN Security Council Resolution. While a subsequent Resolution in October 2003 authorized a multinational force to take all measures necessary to contribute to security and stability in Iraq, in the Court's view this did not have the effect of making the acts of soldiers in the multinational force attributable to the UN. The troops remained under the unified command structure of the multinational force and the US and the UK, through the Coalition Provisional Authority, continued to exercise the powers of government in Iraq.

The applicant in *Al-Jedda* had been detained in a British military facility for over three years. His internment was authorized on the basis of 'security reasons' and he was not brought to trial. Far from being attributable to the UN, such security internments had

[87] United Nations Interim Administration Mission in Kosovo.

[88] Kosovo Force.

[89] *Behrami v France*, (App. 71412/01), Decision of 2 May 2007 [GC], and *Saramati v France, Germany and Norway*, (App. 78166/01), Decision of 2 May 2007 [GC], (2007) 45 EHRR SE10, § 71.

[90] §§ 144–52.

[91] See earlier in this chapter.

[92] *Al-Jedda v United Kingdom*, (App. 27021/08), 7 July 2011 [GC], ECHR 2011.

been severely criticized by the UN. The door is certainly left open by this judgment for a Contracting State to avoid jurisdictional liability in the context of a human rights violation attributable to the UN, or required by a UN Resolution. However, in this highly fact-specific judgment, the UK was never likely to be able to avoid liability for this detention given the UN's prior criticisms of it, and the UK's concession before domestic courts that the military prison was within its jurisdiction.

It should also be observed, particularly since the point has been raised regularly by Contracting Parties, that Article 103 of the UN Charter provides:

> In the event of a conflict between the obligations of the Members of the United Nations under the present Charter and their obligations under any other international agreement, their obligations under the present Charter shall prevail.

The Strasbourg Court has alluded to this provision, but has not decided any case solely on its application. In its decision in the *Behrami* and *Saramati* cases, the Court said:

> 147.... More generally, it is further recalled... that the Convention has to be interpreted in the light of any relevant rules and principles of international law applicable in relations between its Contracting Parties. The Court has therefore had regard to two complementary provisions of the Charter, Articles 25 and 103, as interpreted by the International Court of Justice....

The Strasbourg Court recognized the importance of the United Nations system for the protection of international peace and security. Here measures under Chapter VII of the UN Charter had been authorized, and actions in connection with such measures were not susceptible to scrutiny by the Strasbourg Court. This would interfere to an unacceptable extent with the effective conduct of operations by the United Nations.[93] In *Al-Jedda*, the Article 103 point was raised again but was easily dismissed given that there was no UN Resolution requiring the UK's actions in that case. This conclusion was built upon a presumption in favour of the UN seeking to protect, and not violate, human rights, as well as the specific UN objections to security internments without trial relevant to that case.

The same approach was followed in the later case of *Nada v Switzerland*.[94] This case concerned the addition of the applicant's name to the Federal Taliban Ordinance and the resulting ban on international travel. As the applicant resided in the small enclave of Campione d'Italia, his inability to travel to, or through, surrounding Switzerland meant that he was confined to an area of about 1.6 square kilometres. Security Council Resolutions required an entry and transit ban in respect of individuals referred to in a list of individuals and entities associated with Osama bin Laden and al-Qaeda, but the Grand Chamber thought that Switzerland should have made more of an effort to comply with the Resolutions in a way that took into account the applicant's unusual circumstances and avoided infringement of his right to respect for private life. The intervening UK and French governments, as well as some concurring judges (including the President of the Court) disagreed with the majority that the Resolutions left scope for implementation at a national level.

The decision in *Nada* nevertheless shows another means of avoiding the implications of Article 103's priority for UN obligations over those in the Convention. In *Nada*, unlike in *Al-Jedda*, the UN had authorized the human rights infringement, but because it left room for implementation, the Contracting States should have implemented it with their

[93] *Behrami v France*, (App. 71412/01), Decision of 2 May 2007 [GC], and *Saramati v France, Germany and Norway*, (App. 78166/01), Decision of 2 May 2007 [GC], (2007) 45 EHRR SE10, §§ 148–9.

[94] *Nada v Switzerland*, (App. 10593/08), 12 September 2012 [GC], ECHR 2012.

Convention obligations in mind. It appears as if the Court is keen to place the onus of reconciling conflicting international obligations on the States rather than to declare any general rules:

> 197. . . the Court finds that the respondent State could not validly confine itself to relying on the binding nature of Security Council resolutions, but should have persuaded the Court that it had taken – or at least had attempted to take – all possible measures to adapt the sanctions regime to the applicant's individual situation. That finding dispenses the Court from determining the question, raised by the respondent and intervening Governments, of the hierarchy between the obligations of the State Parties to the Convention under that instrument, on the one hand, and those arising from the United Nations Charter, on the other. In the Court's view, the important point is that the respondent Government have failed to show that they attempted, as far as possible, to harmonise the obligations that they regarded as divergent. . .

Such harmonization may prove to be a tough challenge for some Contracting States.

OTHER ISSUES RELATING TO TERRITORIAL SCOPE

Under Article 1, the Contracting Parties guarantee the rights and freedoms defined in Section I to everyone within their jurisdiction. Many aspects of this issue have already been discussed in considering the scope of the concept of the term 'jurisdiction' as used in Article 1. However, there remain one or two issues relating to the territorial scope of the Convention which should be noted.

The guarantee in Article 1 may be subject to certain territorial limits.[95] This follows from the so-called colonial clause in Article 56,[96] which provides that a Contracting Party may, by means of a declaration, extend the Convention to all or any of the territories for whose international relations it is responsible. But for this provision, the Convention would have extended, by the mere act of ratification, to all such territories. It has already been shown that the wording of Article 1 does not introduce any territorial limitation to the Convention. It is introduced, therefore, only by implication in former Article 63, which runs counter to the whole scheme of the Convention, and which can be explained by historical circumstances of little relevance today.[97]

The United Kingdom has extended the Convention to a number of dependent overseas territories, and the Netherlands has extended it to Surinam[98] and the Netherlands Antilles. When such territories become independent, the declaration automatically lapses, and it is unnecessary to denounce the Convention in respect of the territory concerned under Article 58(4).[99] On independence, of course, the State which has made the declaration ceases to be responsible for the international relations of the new State; and there can be no question of the new State remaining a party to the Convention by the law of State succession, since the Convention is confined, by Article 59(1),[100] to Members of the Council of Europe.[101]

[95] App. 1065/61, *X v Belgium*, Decision of 30 May 1961, (1961) 4 *Yearbook* 260, 268.

[96] Formerly Art. 63.

[97] See J. G. Merrills and A. H. Robertson, *Human Rights in Europe* (MUP, Manchester 2001), 26–7.

[98] Until its independence in 1975.

[99] Formerly Art. 65(4).

[100] Formerly Art. 66(1).

[101] See M. Eissen, 'The Independence of Malta and the European Convention on Human Rights' (1965–6) 41 BYIL 401; and 'Malawi and the European Convention on Human Rights' (1968–9) 43 BYIL 190. Malta subsequently became a member of the Council of Europe and a party to the Convention, as did Cyprus.

A declaration under Article 56 may also lapse for a different reason. The Convention was extended by Denmark to Greenland, for whose international relations it was responsible at the time; but subsequently, in 1953, Greenland became part of metropolitan Denmark, so that the Convention automatically applied to Greenland irrespective of the declaration.

Article 56(3) provides that the provisions of the Convention apply to territories to which a declaration under Article 56(1) applies 'with due regard...to local requirements'. The interpretation of this phrase was considered in the *Tyrer* case[102] which concerned corporal punishment in the Isle of Man. The respondent State sought to argue that public opinion on the island which supported the practice of birching was a 'local requirement' which brought the practice within Article 63(3). The Court rejected this, saying that public opinion was insufficient to ground such a claim; positive and conclusive proof would be needed of the requirement.[103]

THE NATURE OF A STATE'S POSITIVE OBLIGATIONS

A difficult question is how far a Contracting Party is responsible for violations of the rights guaranteed by the Convention, committed within its territory by private persons. Where Section I of the Convention is enacted as part of national law, or can be invoked before the national courts, a limited effect on third parties[104] may be allowed, since Section I does not itself confine liability to the State.[105] On the European level, however, the Strasbourg Court can only deal, under Article 34,[106] with an application by an individual claiming to be a victim of a violation by one of the Contracting Parties. If the violation is by a private individual, therefore, a State may have fulfilled its obligations if its law adequately protects the rights guaranteed and provides for an effective remedy in the event of such violation.

Positive obligations is a label used to describe the circumstances in which a Contracting Party is required to take action in order to secure to those within its jurisdiction the rights protected by the Convention.[107] Though positive obligations were once thought to be the exception rather than the rule, there are now hardly any provisions of the Convention under which positive obligations have not been recognized. Clearly one concern is the uncertainty which arises in defining the limits of such obligations, but the Strasbourg Court tends to allow a degree of latitude to Contracting Parties in this area of legal protection afforded by the Convention.

[102] *Tyrer v United Kingdom*, (App. 5856/72), 25 April 1978, Series A No 26, (1980) 2 EHRR 1.

[103] § 38. The Court's comments suggest that corporal punishment as a preventive measure could not be taken out of the application of Article 3 by reason of being a local requirement.

[104] See for this effect on third parties *(Drittwirkung)* in national law, as well as on the European level, M. Eissen, 'The European Convention on Human Rights and the Duties of the Individual' in (1962) 32 *Acta Scandinavica Juris Gentium* 230; A. Drzemczewski, 'The domestic status of the European Convention on Human Rights. New Dimensions' [1977/1] LIEI 1–85; and E. A. Alkema, 'The third party applicability or "Drittwirkung" of the European Convention on Human Rights' in F. Matscher and H. Petzold, *Protecting Human Rights: The European Dimension. Studies in Honour of Gérard J. Wiarda* (Carl Heymanns, Köln 1988), 33–45. See also A. Clapham, *Human Rights in the Private Sphere* (OUP, Oxford 1993).

[105] On the effect of incorporation and the notion of the horizontal effect of the Convention within a national legal order, see M. Hunt, 'The "horizontal effect" of the Human Rights Act' [1998] PL 423.

[106] Formerly Art. 25.

[107] See generally J.-F. Akandji-Kombe, *Positive obligations under the European Convention on Human Rights: a Guide to the implementation of the European Convention on Human Rights*, Human Rights Handbooks, No. 7 (Council of Europe Publishing, Strasbourg 2007); A. Mowbray, *The Development of Positive Obligations under the European Convention on Human Rights by the European Court of Human Rights* (Hart, Oxford 2004).

The requirement to act positively flows from the express terms of some Convention provisions, while in others it is implied and has required careful elaboration by the Strasbourg Court in its case-law. For example, Article 6 on the right to a fair trial expressly requires Contracting Parties to ensure that certain procedural safeguards exist in its national legal order in both civil and criminal procedure. In contrast, it took some time for the Strasbourg Court to read into Article 2 on the right to life an obligation to conduct an investigation into a death which was alleged to have occurred at the hands of the State or through failings of the State.

In the *Ilaşcu* case,[108] the Court summarizes the scope of a State's positive obligations in the following terms:[109]

> In determining the scope of a State's positive obligations, regard must be had to the fair balance that has to be struck between the general interest and the interests of the individual, the diversity of situations obtaining in Contracting States and the choices which must be made in terms of priorities and resources. Nor must these obligations be interpreted in such a way as to impose an impossible or disproportionate burden.

This meant that, in circumstances where a Contracting Party had lost effective control of a part of its territory, that Contracting Party nevertheless had a duty to use all appropriate legal and diplomatic means to continue to guarantee the protection of the rights and freedoms guaranteed by the Convention.[110] The decision of the majority in the *Ilaşcu* case attracted two partly dissenting opinions each joined by four other judges, a partly dissenting opinion, and a dissenting opinion. All these separate or dissenting opinions concerned the extent of positive obligations in situations such as that in this case. This indicates that, at least in the particular circumstances of that case, the conclusions of the majority in relation to Moldova's positive obligations are highly controversial.

However, the particular circumstances and difficulties of the *Ilaşcu* case should not deflect attention away from the pervasive influence of positive obligations under very many provisions the Convention. Indeed, it may be inappropriate to make too sharp a distinction between so-called negative obligations and positive obligations. The terms of many Convention provisions do not easily lend themselves to such analysis. Take Article 2 for example. Its first sentence provides that everyone's right to life shall be protected by law. That clearly requires some action on the part of the State, for example, by setting in place criminal sanctions for the taking of life. The difficulty is in determining the limits of such positive obligations. Does it extend to the provision of health services, and, if so, at what level? The second sentence, which is subject to certain exceptions, provides that no one shall be deprived of life intentionally. That is rather more in the nature of a prohibition than the first sentence of the Article. What is required is a careful analysis of each provision of the Convention. For this reason, the issue of positive obligations is addressed more specifically in the material in Part 2 of this book on Convention rights.

THE STATUS OF THE CONVENTION IN THE UNITED KINGDOM

The enactment of the European Convention on Human Rights into national law in the United Kingdom under the Human Rights Act 1998[111] was an event of major constitutional significance. Statutory enactment means that Convention rights can be argued and considered in national courts and tribunals alongside other issues in cases before them. Incorporation

[108] *Ilaşcu and others v Moldova and Russia*, (App. 48787/99), 8 July 2004 [GC], (2005) 40 EHRR 1030, ECHR 2004-VII.

[109] § 332. [110] § 333.

[111] Which entered into force on 2 October 2000.

has been followed by an energetic focus within the national legal order on compliance with Convention rights of many aspects of UK law. The Act was a clever and elegant piece of legislation which set in place a scheme which preserves the distinct roles of judges and politicians in the constitutional order of the UK.[112]

There is an improved system of pre-legislative scrutiny of legislation. Section 19 of the Act requires the minister introducing a Bill in Parliament to state whether, in his or her view, it is compatible with the European Convention, or to decline to do so but to indicate that the Government nevertheless wishes to proceed with the Bill. Critics have expressed concern that without the support of a national Human Rights Commission,[113] the level of scrutiny may well be inadequate to guarantee compliance with the Convention in every case.

The substantive Articles of the Convention and Protocols to which the UK is party are restated in section 1 and Schedule 1 to the Act as provisions of UK law with the exception of Article 13 of the Convention.[114] The enacted rights are referred to as Convention rights.

Under section 6(1) of the Act, it is unlawful for any public authority to 'act in a way which is incompatible with a Convention right'. Public authorities include a court or tribunal, and 'any person certain of whose functions are of a public nature', but does not include either House of Parliament. There remains considerable uncertainty as to the ambit of the term 'public authority'.[115] Under section 7, any person who claims that a public authority has acted in a manner which is incompatible with a Convention right, may bring proceedings against the authority in a court or tribunal as determined by rules of court made under the Act. If the act complained of is that of a court or tribunal, the matter may only be raised on appeal. Furthermore, any party to proceedings can rely on a Convention right in legal proceedings. Applicants bringing judicial review proceedings will have standing if they are, or would be, considered a victim of a violation under Article 34 of the Convention.[116] Convention case-law has been generous over the matter of standing to raise a complaint of a violation.

Whenever Convention rights are in issue before public authorities, new rules of interpretation come into play. First, in determining whether there has been a violation of a Convention right, a court or tribunal must 'take into account' case-law of the Commission, Court of Human Rights, and the Committee of Ministers. In interpreting any primary or secondary legislation whenever enacted, the court or tribunal must 'so far as it is possible

[112] For a description of preparations for implementation, see generally A. Finlay, 'The Human Rights Act: The Lord Chancellor's Department's Preparations for Implementation' [1999] EHRLR 512. For a judicial comment on the impact of incorporation, see Lord Steyn, 'The New Legal Landscape' [2000] EHRLR 549. For detailed commentaries on the operation of the Human Rights Act 1998, see R. Clayton and H. Tomlinson, *The Law of Human Rights* (2nd edn OUP, Oxford 2009); and I. Leigh and R. Masterman, *Making Rights Real: The Human Rights Act in its First Decade* (Hart, Oxford 2008); and A. Kavanagh, *Constitutional Review under the UK Human Rights Act* (CUP, Cambridge 2009).

[113] The work of the Joint Committee on Human Rights has been invaluable in considering a number of important issues in relation to compliance with the Convention in UK law. On 1 October 2007 a single Equality and Human Rights Commission was established under the Equality Act 2006 and combined the work of the Equal Opportunities Commission, the Commission for Racial Equality, and the Disability Rights Commission which it replaced. See www.equalityhumanrights.com.

[114] Article 13 guarantees an effective remedy before a national authority for a violation of a Convention right. Its omission is seen by some as controversial, see R. White, 'Remedies in a Multi-Level Legal Order: The Strasbourg Court and the UK' in C. Kilpatrick, T. Novitz, and P. Skidmore, *The Future of Remedies in Europe* (Hart, Oxford 2000), 191.

[115] The courts have been called upon to interpret this phrase on numerous occasions. See, for example, *Aston Cantlow and Wilcote with Billesley Parochial Church Council v Wallbank* [2003] UKHL 37, [2004] 1 AC546 and *YL v Birmingham City Council* [2007] UKHL 27, [2008] 1 AC 95.

[116] See ch.2.

to do so, read and give effect to that legislation in a way which is compatible with the Convention rights.'[117]

If a court or tribunal concludes that there has been a violation of a Convention right, 'it may grant such relief or remedy, or make such order, within its jurisdiction as it considers just and appropriate.'[118] This is an enabling provision giving courts and tribunals powers based on, but going beyond, those enjoyed by the Strasbourg Court under Article 41 of the Convention to afford just satisfaction to a victim of a violation.[119] However, damages can only be awarded by those courts or tribunals which have power to award damages, or to order the payment of compensation, in civil proceedings.[120] Significantly, Article 13, which guarantees a right to a remedy in national law, has been omitted from the Convention rights in the Human Rights Act.

Where the new rules of interpretation do not enable a court or tribunal to read and give effect to primary legislation in a way which is compatible with the Convention rights, the declaration of incompatibility comes into play. Section 4(2) of the Act provides that a court which is satisfied that a provision in primary legislation is incompatible with a Convention right 'may make a declaration of incompatibility'.[121] For England and Wales, the following courts have power to make such a declaration: the High Court, Court of Appeal, Supreme Court, Judicial Committee of the Privy Council, and the Courts Martial Appeal Court. Where a lesser court or tribunal[122] is faced with such an issue, it must apply the 'incompatible' legislation and the matter will have to be taken on appeal until a court with the power is reached. All courts and tribunals, however, have the power to rule that subordinate legislation is incompatible with Convention rights unless the primary legislation prevents removal of the incompatibility.[123] The declaration of incompatibility is the solution to the dilemma of having judges declaring primary legislation invalid, which was seen to be an interference by judges in the role of the legislature. The declaration of incompatibility does not affect the validity, continuing operation or enforcement of the provision, and is not binding on the parties to the proceedings in which it is made.[124] Its effect is to prompt the legislature to change the law in response to the political pressure such a declaration creates.[125] To facilitate this, a remedial order may be made under section 10 and Schedule 2 to the Act. This is a fast-track legislative procedure designed to remove the incompatibility at the heart of the court's declaration.

At the time of writing, the future of the Human Rights Act remains uncertain. The Conservative-Liberal Democrat coalition government which took office in 2010 established a Commission on a Bill of Rights to 'to investigate the creation of a UK Bill of Rights

[117] s.3(1) of the Act. There is now a significant case-law on the proper role of the courts in interpreting legislation to secure compatibility: see in particular *Ghaidan v Godin-Mendoza* [2004] UKHL 30, which stresses the primacy of the rule of interpretation in securing the compatibility of UK law with Convention rights.

[118] s.8(1) of the Act. [119] See ch.2. [120] s.8(2) of the Act.

[121] In *Burden v United Kingdom*, (App. 13378/05), 29 April 2008 [GC], (2008) 47 EGRR 857, ECHR 2008, §§ 40–4, the Grand Chamber ruled that a declaration of incompatibility is not currently an effective remedy within the meaning of Article 35 of the Convention for the purpose of the rule requiring an applicant to exhaust domestic remedies.

[122] And there are very many of these. [123] s.4(3) and (4) of the Act.

[124] s.4(6) of the Act.

[125] An example of a declaration of incompatibility which had the desired effect of placing political pressure on government to facilitate a change in the law can be found in *A v Secretary of State* [2005] 3 All ER 169, the so-called 'Belmarsh case'. By contrast, a declaration of incompatibility issued in respect of the blanket ban on prisoner voting in *Smith v Scott* ((2007) SC 345) has not yet heralded a change in the law, as recently discussed by the Supreme Court in *R (on the application of Chester) v Secretary of State for Justice; McGeoch v The Lord President of the Council and another* [2013] UKSC 63.

that incorporates and builds on all our obligations under the European Convention on Human Rights, ensures that these rights continue to be enshrined in UK law, and protects and extend our liberties.'[126] Whether such a Bill of Rights will be enacted and, if so, whether it would supplement or replace the Human Rights Act are questions which remain to be decided.[127] The incorporation of the Convention, whether by means of the Human Rights Act or otherwise, does not in any way deprive those who believe they are victims of violations of the Convention from making applications to the Court in Strasbourg, subject to the Convention's admissibility rules.

CONCLUDING REMARKS

The centrality of Article 1 to the multi-level system of protection set in place by the European Convention has been demonstrated by the material discussed in this chapter. The extension of the Convention to the countries of central and eastern Europe, the ramifications of international action in some parts of Europe and beyond, as well as the continuing failure to find a resolution to the division of Cyprus, have presented the Strasbourg Court with some very difficult factual situations with a heavy political content. It is to the credit of the Court that it has not ducked making decisions in the most difficult cases, though inevitably those judgments have proved to be controversial. While recent cases have sought to provide some much-needed clarity to the issues, questions remain about the precise limits of extraterritorial jurisdiction and responsibility. These questions will only be further complicated by the increased use of drone strikes which present particularly challenging issues for the concept of jurisdiction.

[126] The Commission on a Bill of Rights' report can be found here: www.justice.gov.uk/about/cbr

[127] For discussion of some concerns about a downgrading of rights by means of this process, see H. Fenwick, 'The Human Rights Act or a British Bill of Rights: Creating a Down-grading Recalibration of Rights Against the Counter-terror Backdrop?' [2012] PL 468.

6

RESERVATIONS AND DEROGATIONS

INTRODUCTION

This chapter brings together two principal means by which a Contracting Party can escape the full application of certain provisions of the Convention and two further provisions of the Convention designed to ensure that it is not used for a purpose for which it was not intended.

Article 57 of the Convention permits reservations to certain provisions to the extent that current law in force in the Contracting Party as at the date of ratification of the Convention is not compatible with the Convention. Reservations of a general character are not permitted. Reservations operate, so long as the reservation is in effect, as permanent variations of the obligations arising under the Convention for the Contracting Party making the reservation.

Article 15 of the Convention permits Contracting Parties to exclude on a temporary basis the operation of certain Convention rights in the limited circumstances provided by the Article through the system of derogations.

Articles 17 and 18 seek to ensure that the Convention is not used to undermine the scheme of protection set out in it. Article 17 reflects a concern for the defence of democratic society and its institutions, and precludes actions which might undermine those principles. It is aimed at protection against totalitarian and other deeply offensive activities. The Strasbourg Court has consistently, and rightly, taken a very restrictive view of its application. Finally, Article 18 prohibits the use of the limitations permitted by the Convention provisions for any purpose other than that for which the Convention allows.

RESERVATIONS

International law recognizes that a State, in accepting a treaty, may in certain circumstances attach a reservation, that is, make its acceptance subject to some new term which limits or varies the application of the treaty to that State.[1] The extent to which reservations are appropriate to a human rights instrument has been questioned. Frowein says:[2]

> It is of crucial importance that the member States of the [European] Convention should be willing to exercise their collective responsibility in the matter of reservations and agree that reservations can only be a means whereby a new member can bring its law into line with the

[1] See Art. 19 *et seq*. of the Vienna Convention on the Law of Treaties.

[2] J. Frowein, 'Reservations to the European Convention on Human Rights' in F. Matscher and H. Petzold (eds.), *Protecting Human Rights: The European Dimension. Studies in Honour of Gérard J. Wiarda* (Carl Heymanns, Köln 1990), 193–200, 200.

> Convention. In fact, many of the reservations could easily be made superfluous by sometimes very minor amendments to the legislation in force. The Convention system has in recent years grown more and more into the role of a system of European integration in the sense of its preamble. Unilateral derogations are incompatible with the very idea of such a system.

Article 57[3] of the Convention permits certain reservations and provides:

> 1. Any State may, when signing this Convention or when depositing its instrument of ratification, make a reservation in respect of any particular provision of the Convention to the extent that any law then in force in its territory is not in conformity with the provision. Reservations of a general character shall not be permitted under this Article.
> 2. Any reservation made under this Article shall contain a brief statement of the law concerned.

Reservations must relate to a particular provision of the Convention and to a particular law in force at the time, and they must contain a brief statement of the law concerned. It should be noted that reservations are only permitted in relation to existing laws at the time of ratification; reservations are not permitted where a Contracting Party subsequently wishes to vary its commitments under the Convention.[4] A fair number of reservations have been made to the Convention and Protocols, but these are mainly very limited in scope.[5] Any far-reaching reservation would in any event be illegal as being incompatible with the object and purpose of the Treaty.[6]

Although there is no legal obligation in this respect, and no express provision for withdrawal of a reservation, it would be in accordance with the spirit of the Convention, and with its object and purpose, to envisage that laws which necessitated reservations would progressively be amended or repealed to ensure that the Contracting Parties complied without reservation with all the Convention's provisions. This has certainly happened on some occasions. When ratifying the Convention, Norway found it necessary to make a reservation in respect of Article 9, since the Norwegian Constitution of 1814 provided for a ban on Jesuits. In 1956 this provision was abrogated and the reservation withdrawn. Similarly in Switzerland, a reservation to the same Article was considered necessary pending revision of the denominational Articles of the Federal Constitution. When the revision was made, the reservation was withdrawn.

RESERVATIONS MADE BY CONTRACTING PARTIES

Article 57 of the Convention appears to permit only reservations in respect of those Articles of the Convention which lay down substantive obligations, but Contracting Parties have attempted to qualify declarations relating to the procedural provisions of the Convention, that is, those provisions which dealt with the competence of the Strasbourg organs.

There is no such thing as a 'quasi-reservation'. The Latvian Government argued in the *Slivenko* case[7] that it had ratified the Convention on the assumption that it was entirely

[3] Formerly Art. 64 of the Convention.

[4] Though Article 15 permits derogations from certain Convention provisions in time of war or other public emergency threatening the life of the nation.

[5] See http://conventions.coe.int for a full list of current reservations.

[6] Art. 19 of the Vienna Convention on the Law of Treaties. See also *Reservations to the Convention on Genocide*, [1951] ICJ Rep. 15.

[7] *Slivenko and others v Latvia*, (App. 48321/99), Decision of 23 January 2002 [GC], ECHR 2002-II.

compatible with a treaty it had concluded with Russia of 30 April 1994, and so its ratification of the Convention and its Protocols was subject to a quasi-reservation in respect of that treaty. The Court did not share this view.

At the time of ratifying the Convention in 1990, Finland had lodged a reservation in respect to the right to a public hearing under Article 6(1), since Finnish law at that time did not provide for a public hearing in proceedings before certain courts, including the Supreme Administrative Court. In December 1996, when the law had been amended, Finland withdrew its reservation in respect of the lack of public hearings before the Supreme Administrative Court concerning decisions taken from 1 December 1996. In the *Helle* case,[8] the Court held that, in the light of the reservation, the failure to hold a hearing in relation to decisions reached in 1991 and 1992 did not give rise to a breach of Article 6.

Since recognition of the Court and acceptance of the right of individual petition are now mandatory requirements of the Convention, the matters raised in the following section are of largely historical interest. However, an understanding of the position adopted by some Contracting Parties may be helpful in reading certain significant cases in which the issue arose. There remained some doubt whether reservations could be made in declarations under former Article 25, accepting the competence of the Commission to receive applications from individuals, or under former Article 46, recognizing the compulsory jurisdiction of the Court. However, the Commission did accept that declarations under former Article 25 may be subject to the proviso that they have no retroactive effect. Former Article 46(1), providing for declarations recognizing the Court's jurisdiction 'in all matters', seems to exclude the possibility of a partial recognition, although the second paragraph provides that a declaration may be made on condition of reciprocity or for a limited period. Further, what is now Article 57 seems to envisage only reservations of a substantive character, relating to a specific law in force at the time of signature or ratification; and a reservation is not permissible where a treaty provides for only specified reservations which do not include the reservation in question.[9]

The Turkish Government, however, filed two declarations under former Articles 25(1) and 46 to which conditions are attached that the Commission and Court would almost certainly consider to be attempted reservations. They appear to have been intended to exclude the Commission's competence in complaints concerning its conduct in the northern part of Cyprus, while others seek to exclude the right to complain about the activities of Turkish military personnel. The third, fourth, and fifth qualifications seek to limit the interpretation which may be placed on Articles 8 to 11 of the Convention. The Commission held all these 'qualifications' to be invalid in the *Chrysostomos* case.[10] These declarations were subsequently considered by the Court in the *Loizidou* case.[11] The Court ruled that a territorial limitation is not permissible, but that, notwithstanding the purported territorial restrictions, the declarations contained valid acceptances of the competence of the Commission and the Court.

INTERPRETATION OF RESERVATIONS

Applications which must be excluded because of a reservation made by the respondent State are outside the Strasbourg Court's competence *ratione materiae*. A reservation must be

[8] *Helle v Finland*, (App. 20722/92), 19 December 1997, (1998) 26 EHRR 159. See also *Laukkanen and Manninen v Finland*, (App. 50230/99), 3 February 2004.

[9] Art. 19 of the Vienna Convention on the Law of Treaties.

[10] Apps. 15299–15311/89, *Chrysostomos v Turkey*, Decision of 4 March 1991, (1991) 12 HRLJ 113.

[11] *Loizidou v Turkey*, (App. 15318/89), 23 March 1995, Series A No 310, (1995) 20 EHRR 99, §§ 65–98.

interpreted in the language in which it is made, not in its translation into one of the languages, English or French, of the authentic texts of the Convention.[12] The Commission gave rather extensive interpretations of those reservations which it had to consider, but its approach has now been overtaken by authority from the Court, which is much more robust.

The Commission had held that a reservation may serve to exclude not only measures expressly covered by the reservation, but also other related measures.[13] It may extend to exclude a new law which replaces the law in force at the time of the reservation, provided that the new law does not have the effect of enlarging the scope of the reservation.[14] It may extend to legislative and administrative measures to implement the purpose for which the reservation was made.[15] It may even extend to other provisions of the Convention than those expressly mentioned in the reservation if it is clearly intended to cover the entire operation of national law in the field concerned.[16] Quite apart from this point, it would seem that the Commission has departed from the evident intention of what was then Article 64. That Article refers expressly to laws in force at the time of signature or ratification, and clearly envisages that all subsequent legislation will be in conformity with the Convention. The Commission appears to have gone too far in accepting that a later law in the same field might be brought within the scope of a reservation.

However, both the Commission[17] and the Court have taken the view that it is for them to determine the legal validity of reservations. The Court has been rather more rigorous in its examination of these issues than the Commission. The leading authority is the *Belilos* case.[18] Marlène Belilos had been fined 120 Swiss francs for having taken part in an unauthorized demonstration. She raised a complaint under Article 6 of the Convention. This brought into play a *declaration* made by Switzerland in respect of this Article:

> The Swiss Federal Council considers that the guarantee of fair trial in Article 6, paragraph 1 of the Convention, in the determination of civil rights and obligations or any criminal charge against the person in question is intended solely to ensure ultimate control by the judiciary over the acts or decisions of the public authorities relating to such rights or obligations or the determination of such a charge.

The Strasbourg Court had to consider the effect of this declaration on the claim, which the respondent State argued amounted in substance to a reservation. The Court accepted this argument, noting that the Convention only made provision for reservations. As a reservation its validity fell to be determined against the requirements of former Article 64. The Court asserted jurisdiction relying on what were then Articles 19,[19] 45,[20] and 49.[21] The Court went on to say that reservations of a general character (which are not permitted by the reservations Article of the Convention) were those 'couched in terms that were too vague or broad for it to

[12] App. 1047/61, *X v Austria*, Decision of 15 December 1961, (1961) 4 *Yearbook* 356; App. 1452/62, *X v Austria*, Decision of 18 December 1963, (1963) 6 *Yearbook* 268; App. 2432/65, *X v Austria*, Decision of 7 April 1967, (1967) 22 CD 124.

[13] App. 2432/65, *X v Austria*, Decision of 7 April 1967, (1967) 22 CD 124.

[14] App. 2432/65, *X v Austria*. See also App. 3923/69, *X v Austria*, Decision of 14 December 1970, (1971) 37 CD 10.

[15] App. 2765/66, *X v Austria*, Decision of 15 December 1967, (1967) 10 *Yearbook* 412, 418.

[16] App. 3923/69, *X v Austria*, Decision of 14 December 1970, (1971) 37 CD 10; App. 4002/69, *X v Austria*, Decision of 29 March 1971, (1971) 14 *Yearbook* 178.

[17] Initially in App. 9116/80, *Telemtasch v Switzerland*, Decision of 5 May 1982, (1983) 31 DR 120.

[18] *Belilos v Switzerland*, (App. 10328/83), 29 April 1988, Series A No 132, (1988) 10 EHRR 466.

[19] Which charges the Court with ensuring the observance of the engagements undertaken by the High Contracting Parties.

[20] Giving the Court jurisdiction to consider all cases concerning the interpretation and application of the Convention referred by a State or the Commission under Art. 48.

[21] Providing that in the event of a dispute as to whether the Court has jurisdiction, the matter is to be settled by a decision of the Court.

be possible to determine their exact meaning and scope.'[22] The Court also noted that the validity of a reservation would be dependent upon its being accompanied by a brief statement of the law concerned. Since the Swiss reservation met neither of these conditions it was invalid. In international law, the position under the Vienna Convention in such circumstances would be that the provision in question would not be valid as between the parties.[23] However, the Court rightly, since this was not litigation between two States, decided that the effect of holding the reservation invalid was that the full force of Article 6 applied in the case, and they went on to consider the merits of the case on that basis.

The Strasbourg Court has taken a tough line on the requirement to state the law concerned, and a number of purported reservations have been ruled invalid for a failure to state the law concerned.

A Swiss reservation was in issue in the *Weber* case.[24] Weber had been fined for breaching the confidentiality of a judicial investigation. He complained that his rights under Articles 6 and 10 had been violated. In relation to the complaint under Article 6, the respondent State sought to rely on a reservation in the following terms:

> The rule contained in Article 6(1) of the Convention that hearing shall be in public shall not apply to proceedings relating to the determination…of any criminal charge which, in accordance with cantonal legislation, are heard before an administrative authority. The rule that judgment must be pronounced publicly shall not affect the operation of cantonal legislation on civil or criminal procedure providing that judgment shall not be delivered in public but notified to the parties in writing.

The Court found that this reservation was invalid because it was not accompanied by a brief statement of the law concerned; such an omission was not regarded as a purely formal requirement but a condition of substance. The Court proceeded to test the complaint against Article 6(1).

In a case concerning Austria,[25] a reservation to Article 5 was in issue. The Court noted that the national law in issue was all in force on the date when Austria ratified the Convention, and that its wording was sufficiently specific to meet the requirements of former Article 64(1). The reservation contained a reference to the Bundesgesetzblatt[26] by way of providing a brief statement of the laws affected. The Court amplified its earlier comments on the requirements of former Article 64(2):

> According to the Court's case-law, the 'brief statement' as required by [Article 64(2)] 'both constitutes an evidential factor and contributes to legal certainty'; its purpose 'is to provide a guarantee—in particular for the other Contracting Parties and the Convention institutions—that a reservation does not go beyond the provisions expressly excluded by the State concerned.'…This does not mean that it is necessary under Article 64(2) to provide a description, even a concise one, of the substance of the texts in question.
>
> In this instance, the reference to the Federal Official Gazette—preceded moreover by an indication of the subject-matter of the relevant provisions—makes it possible for everyone to identify the precise laws concerned and to obtain any information regarding them. It

[22] *Belilos v Switzerland*, (App. 10328/83), 29 April 1988, Series A No 132, (1988) 10 EHRR 466, § 55.

[23] Art. 21(3) of the Vienna Convention provides: When a State objecting to a reservation has not opposed the entry into force of the treaty between itself and the reserving State, the provisions to which the reservation relates do not apply as between the two States to the extent of the reservation. See also J. Frowein, 'Reservations to the European Convention on Human Rights' in F. Matscher and H. Petzold (eds.), *Protecting Human Rights: The European Dimension. Studies in Honour of Gérard J. Wiarda* (Carl Heymanns, Köln 1990), 193–200, 197.

[24] *Weber v Switzerland*, (App. 11034/84), 22 May 1990, Series A No 177, (1990) 12 EHRR 508.

[25] *Chorherr v Austria*, (App. 13308/87), 25 August 1993, Series A No 266–B, (1994) 17 EHRR 358.

[26] Federal Official Gazette.

> also provides a safeguard against any interpretation which would unduly extend the field of application of the reservation. Accordingly, that reservation complies with Article 64(2).[27]

A different Austrian reservation was in issue in the *Eisenstecken* case.[28] This reservation was broadly worded and concerned the right to a fair trial in Article 6; it read:

> The provisions of Article 6 of the Convention shall be so applied that there shall be no prejudice to the principles governing public court hearings laid down in Article 90 of the 1929 version of the Federal Constitutional Law.

The applicant complained that there was no public hearing in a dispute concerning real property transactions. The reservation had been considered in a number of earlier cases,[29] and in a remarkably short section of one earlier judgment apparently accepted as valid.[30] The Court in the *Eisenstecken* case observed that the compatibility of the Austrian reservation with the requirements of what is now Article 57 had not previously been tested. The Court goes on to rule the reservation to be invalid for its failure to contain a brief statement of the law which is said not to conform to Article 6 of the Convention, and that it was not necessary to consider its compatibility with other requirements of Article 57.

In two cases against Lithuania,[31] the validity of a reservation in respect of Article 5(3)[32] was in issue. Lithuania had made a reservation for one year after the Convention entered into force in respect of Lithuania. The question was whether on the expiry of the reservation, the obligation to bring a detained person promptly before a judge arose, or whether the opportunity had been missed by reason of the earlier detention. The Court is particularly accommodating (though there is logic in the Court's position) in finding that the obligation arises immediately on entering detention and cannot usefully be resurrected at some time later if the person is still in detention on the expiry of the Lithuanian reservation. There was no renewed obligation after the expiry of the reservation.[33]

Sometimes the reservation is not invalid but does not apply to the circumstances in respect of which it is pleaded. This happened in the *Dacosta Silva* case[34] where the Strasbourg Court determined that Spain's reservation in relation to Articles 5 and 6 in their application to military disciplinary rules did not apply to the disciplinary rules of the Civil Guard, and so could not be relied upon to escape liability under the Convention.

DEROGATIONS IN EMERGENCY SITUATIONS

Article 15 provides:

> 1. In time of war or other public emergency threatening the life of the nation any High Contracting Party may take measures derogating from its obligations under this Convention to the extent strictly required by the exigencies of the situation, provided that such measures are not inconsistent with its other obligations under international law.

[27] § 21.

[28] *Eisenstecken v Austria*, (App. 29477/95), 3 October 2000, (2002) 34 EHRR 860, ECHR 2000-X.

[29] Eisenstecken §§ 24–6.

[30] *Ettl v Austria*, (App. 9273/81), 23 April 1987, Series A No 117, (1988) 10 EHRR 255, § 42.

[31] *Jecius v Lithuania*, (App. 34578/97), 31 July 2000, ECHR 2000-IX; and *Grauslys v Lithuania*, (App. 36743/97), 10 October 2000.

[32] The entitlement of detained persons to be brought promptly before a competent judicial authority.

[33] *Jecius v Lithuania*, (App. 34578/97), 31 July 2000, ECHR 2000-IX, § 86.

[34] *Dacosta Silva v Spain*, (App. 69966/01), 2 February 2007, ECHR 2007-XIII.

2. No derogation from Article 2, except in respect of deaths resulting from lawful acts of war, or from Articles 3, 4 (paragraph 1) and 7 shall be made under this provision.
3. Any High Contracting Party availing itself of this right of derogation shall keep the Secretary-General of the Council of Europe fully informed of the measures which it has taken and the reasons therefor. It shall also inform the Secretary-General of the Council of Europe when such measures have ceased to operate and the provisions of the Convention are again being fully executed.

It is greatly to the credit of the Contracting Parties that, as at 1 September 2013, notwithstanding the problems caused for a number of Contracting Parties by increases in terrorist activity, and the threats of such actions, there are no extant derogations in effect. To date it has been Articles 5 and 6 which have attracted almost all derogations; it is significant that these Articles contain little scope for applying limitations on the sorts of grounds that are specified in, for example, Articles 8 to 11.[35]

Article 15 incorporates, in effect, the principle of necessity common to all legal systems. Most States have provisions for emergency legislation, empowering them to take measures in a state of emergency which would not otherwise be lawful.[36] However, under Article 15, such measures are subject to the control of the organs of the Convention. If a Contracting Party seeks to rely on a derogation in proceedings before the Strasbourg Court, it is for the Court to consider, first, whether a public emergency threatening the life of the nation could be said to exist at the material time; and secondly, whether the measures taken were in fact strictly required by the exigencies of the situation. Thirdly, such measures must be consistent with other obligations under international law. Finally, there must have been timely notification to the Secretary-General of the Council of Europe both of the introduction of derogating measures and of the reasons for them, and, where appropriate, of the lifting of those measures.

Issues relating to Article 15 have normally been examined on the merits and cannot usually be disposed of at the stage of admissibility. In inter-State cases, this is indeed inevitable, since such a case cannot be rejected as being manifestly ill-founded.[37] In the case brought by Ireland against the United Kingdom, the respondent State invoked, at the stage of admissibility, the notification of derogation which it had made in respect of Northern Ireland. The Irish Government accepted that a public emergency within the meaning of Article 15 existed in Northern Ireland, but denied that the measures taken by the respondent State were strictly required by the exigencies of the situation. The Commission held that this question could not be determined at the stage of admissibility.[38] Indeed, even on an individual application, it would be difficult to justify a decision holding that all the conditions of Article 15 were fulfilled at the stage of admissibility; normally such an application should be examined at the merits phase if Article 15 is invoked.[39]

There would seem to be nothing objectionable in a Contracting Party making use of an Article 15 derogation to avoid granting rights under the Convention when it has been held

[35] See, in general, A. Mokhtar, 'Human Rights Obligations *v* Derogations: Article 15 of the European Convention on Human Rights', (2004) 8 *International Journal of Human Rights* 65; and J. Allain, 'Derogations from the European Convention on Human Rights in light of "Other Obligations under International Law"' [2005] EHRLR 480.

[36] See generally Pinheiro Farinha, 'L'article 15 de la Convention' in F. Matscher and H. Petzold (eds.), *Protecting Human Rights: The European Dimension. Essays in honour of Gérard Wiarda* (Carl Heymanns, Köln 1990), 521.

[37] See ch.2.

[38] Apps. 5310/71 and 5151/72, *Ireland v United Kingdom*, Decision of 1 October 1972, (1972) 41 CD 3, 88.

[39] But see App. 493/59, *X v Ireland*, Decision of 27 July 1961, (1961) 4 *Yearbook* 302, 310–16.

to be in violation of the Convention. In the *Brogan* case[40] the United Kingdom was found to be in breach of Article 5(3) of the Convention in the period allowed for questioning before a suspect was brought before a judicial officer under the prevention of terrorism legislation. Prior to the judgment of the Court, it had considered that the legislation met the requirements of Article 5(3). In response to the judgment, instead of amending its legislation to ensure compliance with the period for bringing suspects before a judicial officer, the United Kingdom entered a derogation under Article 15. Obviously, that derogation could not apply retrospectively, and would be subject to assessment in the usual way by the Convention organs for compliance with the requirements of Article 15.[41] Any doubt about the validity of the derogation filed following the judgment in the *Brogan* case was resolved in the *Brannigan and McBride* case.[42] Judge De Meyer's dissent, in which he argued that it was not permissible for the UK Government to try to escape the consequences of the *Brogan* judgment by entering a derogation in response to it, did not gain the support of the majority of the Court which instead simply accepted the validity of the subsequent derogation.

NON-DEROGABLE RIGHTS

Certain rights under the Convention are not susceptible to derogation in any circumstances. Article 2 on the right to life is non-derogable, save to the extent that derogations are permitted 'in respect of deaths resulting from lawful acts of war'.[43] No Contracting State has purported to make such a derogation, however, and so the potentially complex legal issue of distinguishing lawful acts of war from those that are unlawful has not yet arisen. If and when it does so, the resolution will undoubtedly lie in international humanitarian law. Both Protocol 6, which prohibits the death penalty in times of peace,[44] and Protocol 13, which prohibits it in all circumstances,[45] are also non-derogable. Article 3 which prohibits torture and inhuman or degrading punishment or treatment is non-derogable in its entirety. Furthermore, no derogations may be made in respect of the prohibition of slavery and servitude in Article 4(1); nor in respect of the requirement that there be no punishment without law under Article 7; nor in respect of the right not to be tried or punished twice under Article 4 of Protocol 7.[46]

SUBSTANTIVE REQUIREMENTS

Permissible derogations under Article 15 must meet both the substantive requirements of Article 15(1) and the procedural requirements in Article 15(3). The substantive requirements require three conditions to be satisfied:

- there must be a public emergency threatening the life of the nation;
- the measures taken in response to it must be strictly required by the exigencies of the situation; and
- the measures taken must be in compliance with the Contracting Party's other obligations under international law.

[40] *Brogan and others v United Kingdom*, (Apps. 11209/84, 11234/84, 11266/84, and 11386/85), 29 November 1988, Series A No 145–B, (1989) 11 EHRR 117.

[41] This is the view taken in J. Merrills, *Human Rights in Europe* (MUP, Manchester, 2001), 211.

[42] *Brannigan and McBride v United Kingdom*, (Apps. 14533/89, and 14554/89), 26 May 1993, Series A No 253–B, (1994) 17 EHRR 539.

[43] Art. 15(2).

[44] Russia is the only Council of Europe State not to have ratified this additional Protocol.

[45] Neither Russia nor Azerbaijan have signed this Protocol; Poland has signed but not ratified it.

[46] As of September 2013, the UK has not signed this protocol, while Germany, the Netherlands, and Turkey have all signed but not ratified it.

The procedural requirements require that there is some formal or public act of derogation, and that notice of the derogation, measures adopted in consequence of it, and of the ending of the derogation, is communicated to the Secretary-General of the Council of Europe.[47]

The use of derogations under Article 15 arose for the first time in the *Cyprus* cases;[48] two applications were brought by Greece against the UK when Cyprus was still under British rule. The Commission considered that it was 'competent to pronounce on the existence of a public danger which, under Article 15, would grant to the Contracting Party concerned the right to derogate from the obligations laid down in the Convention.' The Commission also considered that it was 'competent to decide whether measures taken by a Party under Article 15 of the Convention had been taken to the extent strictly required by the exigencies of the situation.' It added that 'the Government should be able to exercise a certain measure of discretion in assessing the extent strictly required by the exigencies of the situation.'[49] Subsequently a political solution to the Cyprus problem was reached, and the Committee of Ministers decided that no further action was called for. The notion of a government's 'measure of discretion'[50] was to have an influential career in this context. Its scope in relation to derogations is considered later. The existence of this control was confirmed by the Court in the *Lawless* case.[51] The Strasbourg Court considered, first, whether there could be said to be a public emergency threatening the life of the nation; secondly, whether the measures taken in derogation from obligations under the Convention were 'strictly required by the exigencies of the situation'; and thirdly, whether the measures were consistent with other obligations under international law.

The Commission adopted the position that issues arising under Article 15 will not be examined unless they are raised by the respondent State. The *McVeigh* case[52] concerned the UK anti-terrorist legislation as it had been applied to the three applicants who had arrived in Liverpool on a ferry from Ireland. They were held for 45 hours without charge, questioned, searched, finger-printed, and photographed. They made complaints under Articles 5, 8, and 10. At the material time, various derogations were in effect in respect of the UK, but the UK did not seek to invoke them in respect of the situation in Great Britain, as distinct from Northern Ireland.[53]

THERE MUST BE A PUBLIC EMERGENCY THREATENING THE LIFE OF THE NATION

What constitutes a public emergency? In the *Lawless* case, the Strasbourg Court defined it as:

> an exceptional situation of crisis or emergency which affects the whole population and constitutes a threat to the organized life of the community of which the State is composed.[54]

[47] See Art. 15(3).

[48] App. 176/57, *Greece v United Kingdom*, (1958–9) 2 *Yearbook* 174 and 182; App. 299/57, *Greece v United Kingdom*, (1958–9) 2 *Yearbook* 178 and 186.

[49] App. 176/57, *Greece v United Kingdom*, (1958–9) 2 *Yearbook* 174, 176.

[50] In French *marge d'appreciation*; the term 'margin of appreciation' is now used in preference to 'measures of discretion'.

[51] *Lawless v Ireland*, (App. 332/57), 14 November 1960, 7 April 1961, and 1 July 1961, Series A, Nos 1–3, (1979–80) 1 EHRR 1, 13, and 15, § 22 of the judgment of 1 July 1961.

[52] Apps. 8022/77, 8025/77, and 8027/77, *McVeigh, O'Neil and Evans v United Kingdom*, Report of 18 March 1981, (1982) 25 DR 15.

[53] Derogations made by Turkey have frequently limited their application to parts of the country.

[54] *Lawless v Ireland*, (App. 332/57), 14 November 1960, 7 April 1961, and 1 July 1961, Series A, Nos 1–3, (1979–80) 1 EHRR 1, 13, and 15, § 28 of the judgment of 1 July 1961.

The danger must be exceptional in that the normal measures permitted by the Convention are plainly inadequate to deal with the situation. The Court found that the existence of a public emergency was 'reasonably deduced' by the Irish Government. The Court had regard in particular to three factors: the existence of a secret army (the Irish Republican Army—IRA); the fact that this army was also operating outside the territory of the Contracting Party; and the steady and alarming increase in terrorist activities in the period before the emergency was declared.[55]

In the *Greek* case, the Commission had to consider the validity of a derogation by a revolutionary government. The respondent Government, which had seized power in Greece by a *coup d'état* on 21 April 1967 and had suspended parts of the Constitution, invoked Article 15 of the Convention. The Commission considered that the Convention applied in the same way to a revolutionary as to a constitutional government.[56] As regards the definition of a 'public emergency threatening the life of the nation', the Commission followed the definition given by the Court in the *Lawless* case.[57] Methodologically, too, the Commission followed the Court, but only in part. It sought to answer the question whether there was such a public emergency in Greece by examining the elements indicated by the respondent State as constituting in its view such an emergency.[58] These elements were examined by the Commission under three heads: the danger of a Communist take-over; the crisis of constitutional government; and the breakdown of public order in Greece.[59] The Commission considered that the burden lay upon the respondent State to show that the conditions justifying measures of derogation under Article 15 had been and continued to be met.[60] It concluded that Greece had not satisfied it that there was on 21 April 1967 a public emergency threatening the life of the Greek nation.[61] However, in one respect the Commission did not follow the Court's earlier view of Article 15. The Commission, while referring to the Government's 'margin of appreciation', did not merely consider whether the Greek Government had sufficient reason to believe that a public emergency existed; it considered whether such an emergency existed in fact. This difference of approach is of great importance since it makes more stringent the requirements of Article 15.

In *Ireland v United Kingdom*[62] both the Commission and the Court readily accepted that there was a public emergency threatening the life of the nation because of the terrorist threat from the activities of the IRA. This issue was not contested by Ireland. No argument was made on the basis that—certainly at the time—the major threat related only to a part of the United Kingdom.

A rather different situation was presented in the *Sakik* case.[63] The Turkish Government sought, in responding to the applications alleging violations of Article 5 arising from the length of detention in police custody, to rely on derogations filed in respect of Article 5. But those derogations did not apply to the country as a whole, and did not apply to Ankara, where the facts alleged to have resulted in the violation of Article 5 had occurred. The Court confirmed that derogations would be strictly interpreted and could not extend to part of a territory not mentioned in the notice of derogation.[64]

[55] *Lawless v Ireland*, (App. 332/57), 14 November 1960, 7 April 1961, and 1 July 1961, Series A, Nos 1–3, (1979–80) 1 EHRR 1, 13, and 15, § 28 of the judgment of 1 July 1961.

[56] App. 3321/67, *Denmark v Greece*, App. 3322/67, *Norway v Greece*, App. 3323/67, *Sweden v Greece*, and App. 3344/67, *Netherlands v Greece*, ('the *Greek* case'), Report of 18 November 1969, (1969) 12 Yearbook 1, 32.

[57] The *Greek* case, 71–2.

[58] The *Greek* case, 44.

[59] The *Greek* case, 45.

[60] The *Greek* case, 72.

[61] The *Greek* case, 76.

[62] *Ireland v United Kingdom*, (App. 5310/71), 18 January 1978, Series A No 25, (1979–80) 2 EHRR 25.

[63] *Sakik and others v Turkey*, (Apps. 23878/94–23883/94), 26 November 1997, (1998) 27 EHRR 662, ECHR 1997-VII.

[64] § 39. See also *Abdülsamet Yaman v Turkey*, (App. 32446/96), 2 November 2004, § 69.

The approach of the Court in reviewing whether there is a public emergency threatening the life of the nation is neatly summarized in the *Aksoy* case:

> The Court recalls that it falls to each Contracting State, with its responsibility for 'the life of [its] nation', to determine whether that life is threatened by a 'public emergency' and, if so, how far it is necessary to go in attempting to overcome the emergency. By reason of their direct and continuous contact with the pressing needs of the moment, the national authorities are in principle better placed than the international judge to decide both on the presence of such an emergency and on the nature and scope of the derogations necessary to avert it. Accordingly, in this matter a wide margin of appreciation should be left to the national authorities.[65]

The Court has been called upon to consider whether a UK derogation[66] in respect of Article 5(1) permitting detention without trial of foreign nationals suspected of involvement in terrorist activities was based upon a public emergency threatening the life of the nation in the *A and others* case.[67] The public emergency was said to flow from the terrorist attacks in New York, Washington DC, and Pennsylvania of 11 September 2001. However, no other party to the European Convention had felt it necessary to derogate from Convention rights in relation to those events, and there had, at the time, been no terrorist attacks in the UK attributable to those alleged to be responsible for the attacks of 11 September 2001 in the United States. United Kingdom support for the so-called war on terrorism has, however, had a high visibility, which clearly rendered the UK a *potential* target for such terrorist activity.[68] The House of Lords, by a majority of eight to one, concluded that there was a public emergency threatening the life of the nation, that imprisonment without trial would be a proportionate response to the threat faced, but that its limitation to foreign nationals was discriminatory, and the UK Government had only filed its derogation in respect of Article 5, and not of Article 14.[69] When the Grand Chamber came to consider whether there was a public emergency threatening the life of the nation, it observed that where there has been such a careful consideration of the validity of the derogation in the national courts, it would only interfere if the national court has misinterpreted or misapplied Article 15 as interpreted by the Strasbourg Court or had reached a conclusion which was manifestly unreasonable.[70]

To date, apart from the *Greek* case, which involved a derogation whose underlying purpose was to support a non-democratic government, the Strasbourg Court has accepted the existence of a Contracting Party's assessment of the existence of a public emergency threatening the life of the nation. Some dissenting judgments have suggested that the Strasbourg Court defers too readily to the judgment of Contracting Parties in this context.[71]

[65] *Aksoy v Turkey*, (App. 21987/93), 18 December 1996, (1997) 23 EHRR 553, ECHR 1996-VI, § 68.

[66] See the Human Rights Act 1998 (Designated Derogation) Order 2001, SI 2001, No. 3644. The derogation was withdrawn with effect from 14 March 2005.

[67] *A and others v United Kingdom*, (App. 3455/05), 19 February 2009 [GC], (2009) 49 EHRR 29, ECHR 2009-nyr.

[68] Which, in fact, materialized in July 2005.

[69] *A and others v Secretary of State for the Home Department; X and another v Secretary of State for the Home Department* [2004] UKHL 56.

[70] *A and others v United Kingdom*, (App. 3455/05), 19 February 2009 [GC], (2009) 49 EHRR 29, ECHR 2009-nyr, § 174.

[71] See, for example, the dissenting opinion of Judge Walsh in *Brannigan and McBride v United Kingdom*, (Apps. 14533/89, and 14554/89), 26 May 1993, Series A No 258-B, (1994) 17 EHRR 539.

THE MEASURES TAKEN MUST BE STRICTLY REQUIRED

If it is established that this first condition of Article 15 is satisfied, it must next be asked whether the measures which are the subject of the application were 'strictly required by the exigencies of the situation'. In the *Aksoy* case, the Court said:

> It is for the Court to rule whether, *inter alia*, the States have gone beyond the 'extent strictly required by the exigencies' of the crisis. The domestic margin of appreciation is thus accompanied by a European supervision. In exercising this supervision, the Court must give appropriate weight to such relevant factors as the nature of the rights affected by the derogation and the circumstances leading to, and the duration of, the emergency situation.[72]

In the *Lawless* case, the Strasbourg Court held, following the opinion of the Commission, that detention without trial was justified under Article 15. In considering whether such a measure was strictly required by the exigencies of the situation, the Court had particular regard, not only to the dangers of the situation, but also to the existence of a number of safeguards designed to prevent abuses in the operation of the system of administrative detention.[73] Examination of safeguards where there is a derogation has taken on great significance in cases where the Court is called upon to review the compatibility of derogations with the requirements of Article 15. In *Ireland v United Kingdom*[74] the Court made an independent examination of the circumstances, but in doing so placed considerable emphasis on the margin of appreciation to be accorded to the Contracting Party. The Court found that the system of extrajudicial deprivation of liberty was justified by the circumstances as perceived by the United Kingdom between August 1971 and March 1975.

The determination of whether measures taken are strictly required by the exigencies of the situation requires consideration of three elements. First, are the derogations necessary to cope with the threat to the life of the nation? Secondly, are the measures taken no greater than those required to deal with the emergency? This is a test of proportionality.[75] Finally, how long have the derogating measures been applied? There is no case-law in which duration of the measures has been a crucial issue, but it is certainly arguable that measures, which at their inception were clearly required, could cease to be so if they proved either to be ineffectual or if it could no longer be established that they were strictly required by the situation. The Court said in *Ireland v United Kingdom* that the interpretation of Article 15 must leave a place for progressive adaptation.[76]

It is possible to detect in the *Brannigan and McBride* case[77] a greater willingness by the Court to question the effectiveness of the safeguards which the Contracting Party puts in place to compensate for suspension of the rights required by the Convention provision in respect of which the derogation is filed. This tougher stand on the safeguards required to ensure that the derogations do not go beyond what is strictly required by the exigencies of the situation is supported by the Court's approach in the *Aksoy* case, where the Court declined to accept that the situation required suspects to be held for fourteen days without

[72] *Aksoy v Turkey*, (App. 21987/93), 18 December 1996; (1997) 23 EHRR 553, ECHR 1996-VI, § 68, referring to *Brannigan and McBride v United Kingdom*, (Apps. 14533/89, and 14554/89), 26 May 1993, Series A No 258-B, (1994) 17 EHRR 539, § 43.

[73] *Lawless v Ireland*, (App. 332/57), 14 November 1960, 7 April 1961, and 1 July 1961, Series A Nos 1–3, (1979–80) 1 EHRR 1, 13, and 15, §§ 31–8 of the judgment of 1 July 1961.

[74] *Ireland v United Kingdom*, (App. 5310/71), 18 January 1978, Series A No 25, (1979–80) 2 EHRR 25.

[75] For an example of its application, see *A and others v United Kingdom*, (App. 3455/05), 19 February 2009 [GC], (2009) 49 EHRR 29, ECHR 2009-nyr, §§ 182–90.

[76] § 83. See also *Marshall v United Kingdom*, (App. 41571/98), Decision of 10 July 2001.

[77] *Brannigan and McBride v United Kingdom*, (Apps. 14533/89, and 14554/89), 26 May 1993, Series A No 258-B, (1994) 17 EHRR 539.

judicial intervention, noting that the Turkish Government had not detailed any reasons why judicial intervention was impracticable.[78]

In the *A and others* case,[79] the Strasbourg Court upheld the House of Lords' landmark decision that the extended power of detention was disproportionate and therefore not 'strictly required' since it targeted only foreign nationals while there was evidence that a similar threat came from United Kingdom nationals involved with al-Qaeda and other linked groups. In particular the Court rejected the respondent State's argument that the assessment of what measures were needed to combat the threat was a matter of political rather than judicial judgment. It observed that, particularly where a derogating measure encroached upon a fundamental Convention right, such as the right to liberty, the Court had to be satisfied that it was a genuine response to the emergency situation, that it was fully justified by the special circumstances of the emergency, and that adequate safeguards were provided against abuse.

THE MEASURES MUST COMPLY WITH OTHER OBLIGATIONS UNDER INTERNATIONAL LAW

Measures which may be taken by a Contracting Party under Article 15(1) must not be 'inconsistent with its other obligations under international law'. Thus, they must not conflict with its other treaty obligations, or obligations under customary international law. Any such measures are not permitted under Article 15. Hence, a Contracting Party could not avail itself of Article 15 to release itself from its obligations, for example, under other human rights instruments. This would in any event be precluded by Article 53 of the Convention,[80] which provides:

> Nothing in this Convention shall be construed as limiting or derogating from any of the human rights and fundamental freedoms which may be ensured under the laws of any High Contracting Party or under any other agreement to which it is a Party.

The requirement of consistency with international obligations has played little part in the case-law of the Court on Article 15 so far. In the *Brannigan and McBride* case[81] it was argued that Article 4 of the United Nations International Covenant on Civil and Political Rights required the emergency to be 'officially proclaimed'. Without expressing a view on the precise content of this requirement, the Court observed that the statement of the Home Secretary in Parliament on 22 December 1988 was formal in character and made public the Government's reliance on Article 15, and was 'well in keeping with the notion of an official proclamation'.[82]

PROCEDURAL REQUIREMENTS

Two issues require consideration in addressing the procedural requirements of Article 15. First, is it an inherent requirement that there is some official proclamation of the public emergency threatening the life of the nation? Secondly, what are the notification requirements of Article 15(3), and what is the consequence of any failure to comply with those requirements?

[78] *Aksoy v Turkey*, (App. 21987/93), 18 December 1996; (1997) 23 EHRR 553, ECHR 1996-VI, §§ 78 and 84.

[79] *A and others v United Kingdom*, (App. 3455/05), 19 February 2009 [GC], (2009) 49 EHRR 29, ECHR 2009-nyr.

[80] Formerly Art. 60.

[81] *Brannigan and McBride v United Kingdom*, (Apps. 14533/89, and 14554/89), 26 May 1993, Series A No 253–B, (1994) 17 EHRR 539.

[82] § 72–3.

There is no express requirement in Article 15 that there is an official proclamation of the public emergency in the national legal order. But it seems that some form of public proclamation of the public emergency is an implicit feature of Article 15.[83] Though there is no direct authority on this issue, the implications of the comments of the Court in the *Brannigan and McBride* case noted earlier are to this effect. At the very least, a Contracting Party which had not made any formal announcements within the national legal order might find itself facing greater difficulties in proving the existence of a public emergency before the Court.

Article 15(3) requires notification both of the introduction of derogations and of the lifting of them. The precise nature of the obligation in this paragraph was considered by the Court in the *Lawless* case where it was argued that notification to the Secretary-General in July 1957 did not meet the requirements of the paragraph for three reasons: first, it did not indicate expressly that it was a derogation under Article 15; secondly, it did not refer to the existence of a public emergency threatening the life of the nation; and, thirdly, the matter had not been made public in Ireland until October and so could not be relied upon in respect of acts occurring between July and October. The Court did not consider that any of these factors tainted the notification; it was couched in terms sufficient to enable the Secretary-General to understand the Irish Government's position. Furthermore the paragraph required the matter to be notified to the Secretary-General and did not impose any obligation to publish the derogation within the Contracting Party.[84] Nor did it regard a delay of twelve days between national adoption and notification outside the scope of a requirement of notification as 'without delay'.[85]

In the *Greek* case, there was a four-month delay between the implementation of derogating measures and notification. Even though the derogation was held to be invalid because the Commission was not satisfied that there was a public emergency threatening the life of the nation, the Commission noted that late notification would not justify action taken before the actual notification.[86] In the *Aksoy* case,[87] the Court raised the question that the Turkish derogation notice did not appear to contain sufficient information about the measure in question, but found that it was not necessary to determine whether Turkey had complied with the formal requirements since the power to detain a suspect for fourteen days without charge was disproportionate in any event.

The paragraph contains no sanction, though, in practice, it may well be that a Contracting Party would find great difficulty in proving its case if it failed to notify the Secretary-General of the measures taken. After all, the essence of Article 15 is that the Contracting Party reviews its ability to sustain the protection of the rights guaranteed by the Convention and concludes that certain of them must be limited in order to deal with an extraordinary situation.

PROHIBITION OF ABUSE OF RIGHTS

Article 17 provides:

> Nothing in this Convention may be interpreted as implying for any State, group or person any right to engage in any activity or perform any act aimed at the destruction of any of the

[83] Having regard, in particular, to the requirement under Art. 4 of the International Covenant on Civil and Political Rights.

[84] *Lawless v Ireland*, (App. 332/57), 1 July 1961, Series A No 1, (1979–80) 1 EHRR 15, 62.

[85] *Lawless v Ireland*, (App. 332/57), 1 July 1961, Series A No 1, (1979–80) 1 EHRR 15, 62.

[86] App. 3321/67, *Denmark v Greece*, App. 3322/67, *Norway v Greece*, App. 3323/67, *Sweden v Greece*, and App. 3344/67, *Netherlands v Greece*, ('the *Greek* case'), Report of 18 November 1969, (1969) 12 Yearbook 1, 41–3.

[87] *Aksoy v Turkey*, (App. 21987/93), 18 December 1996, (1997) 23 EHRR 553, ECHR 1996-VI, § 86.

rights and freedoms set forth herein or at their limitation to a greater extent than is provided for in the Convention.

In the *Norwood* case[88] the Court, in ruling the application inadmissible, referred to Article 17 in the following terms:

> The general purpose of Article 17 is to prevent individuals or groups with totalitarian aims from exploiting in their own interests the principles enunciated by the Convention.[89]

THE EARLY COMMISSION DECISIONS

The Commission stated that Article 17 is designed to safeguard the rights listed in the Convention, by protecting the free operation of democratic institutions.[90] In an early case introduced by the German Communist Party, the Commission quoted, from the preparatory work, the statement that the object was to prevent adherents to totalitarian doctrines from exploiting the rights guaranteed by the Convention for the purpose of destroying human rights.[91] The object of Article 17, therefore, is to limit the rights guaranteed only to the extent that such limitation is necessary to prevent their total subversion, and it must be quite narrowly construed in relation to this object.

In the case under discussion, the German Communist Party had, in 1956, been declared 'anti-constitutional' by the Federal Constitutional Court. The Court had consequently dissolved it and ordered the confiscation of its property. The Party challenged this decision as contrary to Articles 9, 10, and 11 of the Convention. The Commission, applying Article 17, rejected the application as incompatible with the provisions of the Convention. The avowed aim of the Communist Party, according to its own declarations, was to establish a communist society by means of a proletarian revolution and the dictatorship of the proletariat. Consequently, even if it sought power by solely constitutional methods, recourse to a dictatorship was incompatible with the Convention because it would involve the suppression of a number of rights and freedoms which the Convention guaranteed.

In a sequel to this case, a company incorporated under Swiss law, Retimag S.A., complained of the confiscation without compensation of two of its properties in Germany.[92] The German court which ordered the confiscation had held that the company was unquestionably a legal front which had the dual purpose of safeguarding real property belonging to the dissolved Communist Party and of continuing communist subversive activities. Article 17 was invoked by the German Government but the application was rejected for non-exhaustion of domestic remedies.

The *Kühnen* case[93] concerned a German journalist, who was accused of trying to reinstitute the National Socialist Party, which was allegedly a neo-Nazi party. He sought to rely on Article 10. The Commission said that Article 17 covers essentially those rights which will facilitate the attempt to derive from them a right to engage personally in activities aimed at the destruction of any of the rights and freedoms set forth in the Convention. In

[88] *Norwood v United Kingdom*, (App. 23131/03), Decision of 16 November 2004, ECHR 2004-XI. See also *Witzsch v Germany*, (App. 7485/03), Decision of 13 December 2005.

[89] *Norwood v United Kingdom*, (App. 23131/03), Decision of 16 November 2004, ECHR 2004-XI, 4.

[90] App. 250/57, *Parti Communiste v Federal Republic of Germany*, 20 July 1957, (1955–7) 1 *Yearbook* 222, 224.

[91] App. 250/57, *Parti Communiste v Federal Republic of Germany*, 20 July 1957, (1955–7) 1 *Yearbook* 222, 224.

[92] App. 712/60, *Retimag S.A. v Federal Republic of Germany*, Decision of 16 December 1961, (1961) 4 *Yearbook* 384.

[93] App. 12194/86, *Kühnen v Federal Republic of Germany*, Decision of 12 May 1988, (1988) 56 DR 205.

particular, the Commission has found that the freedom of expression enshrined in Article 10 of the Convention may not be invoked in a sense contrary to Article 17.[94]

THE STRASBOURG COURT'S CASE-LAW

From the earliest decisions in which Article 17 has been raised, the Court has adopted a much more restrictive view of its application. In the *Lawless* case,[95] the Irish Government maintained that the activities of the IRA, in which Lawless was engaged, fell within the terms of Article 17, and that he was therefore not entitled to rely on Articles 5, 6, 7, or any other Article of the Convention. The Commission expressed the view that Article 17 was not applicable. It stated that the general purpose of Article 17 was to prevent totalitarian groups from exploiting the principles enunciated by the Convention. But to achieve that purpose, it was not necessary to deprive the persons concerned of all the rights and freedoms guaranteed in the Convention. Article 17 covered essentially those rights which, if invoked, would enable them to engage in the activities referred to in Article 17. The Court, in somewhat different language, followed in substance the view of the Commission.[96] Thus Article 17 applies only to rights, such as those in Articles 9, 10, and 11, which entitle a person to engage in activities; it prevents him from relying on those Articles to engage in subversive activities. A person engaging in subversive activities does not, therefore, forfeit the right to a fair trial under Article 6; but he cannot claim the freedom to organize political meetings, for instance, if his or her purpose in using that freedom is to undermine all civil liberties. It is always a question of the purpose for which the rights are used; the principle is that 'no person may be able to take advantage of the provisions of the Convention to perform acts aimed at destroying the aforesaid rights and freedoms.'[97] Hence, Article 17 cannot be used to deprive an individual of his political freedom simply on the ground that he has supported a totalitarian government in the past.[98]

Even persons engaging in terrorist activities for subversive ends cannot be completely deprived of their protection under the Convention. In the result, those who pursue anarchy, for example, by organizing political meetings on a peaceful basis may in a sense be at a disadvantage compared with those who resort to violence. The former may lose, through the application of Article 17, the political freedoms guaranteed by Articles 9, 10, and 11; the latter, since they do not seek to exercise political activities, lose nothing. If, however, the scale of violence is such as to create a national emergency, the rights guaranteed under Articles 5 and 6 may also be suspended in application of Article 15.

The Strasbourg Court gave considerable attention to Article 17 in its judgment in the *Lehideux and Isorni* case.[99] The applicants had been convicted for 'public defence of war crimes or the crimes of collaboration' in relation to the publication of a one-page advertisement in the French newspaper, *Le Monde*, which spoke favourably about Philippe Pétain.[100] A criminal complaint had been filed by the National Association of Former Members of the Resistance, which had initiated the prosecution. The applicants

[94] See also Apps. 8348/78 and 8406/78, *Glimmerveen and Hagenbeek v Netherlands*, Decision of 11 October 1979, (1980) 18 DR 187.

[95] *Lawless v Ireland*, (App. 332/57), 14 November 1960, 7 April 1961, and 1 July 1961, Series A Nos 1–3, (1979–80) 1 EHRR 1, 13, and 15.

[96] *Lawless v Ireland*, (App. 332/57), 14 November 1960, 7 April 1961, and 1 July 1961, Series A Nos 1–3, (1979–80) 1 EHRR 1, 13, and 15.

[97] § 6 of judgment of 1 July 1961.

[98] See *De Becker*, Report of 8 January 1960, Series B No 2, 137–8.

[99] *Lehideux and Isorni v France*, (App. 24662/94), 23 September 1998, (2000) 30 EHRR 665, ECHR 1998-VIII.

[100] A national hero in France for his role in the First World War, who in June 1940 as Vice-Premier surrendered the north and west of France to Germany, but left the rest of France with its capital at Vichy ostensibly

complained of a violation of Article 10 of the Convention on freedom of expression, and the French Government responded by asking the Court to dismiss the application under Article 17. The Commission had concluded that there was nothing in the advertisement in *Le Monde* which constituted racial hatred or other statements calculated to destroy or restrict the rights and freedoms guaranteed by the Convention. Furthermore, it did not consider that the expression of ideas constituted an 'activity' within the meaning of Article 17. The Court first gave consideration to the complaint under Article 10, and ultimately found that there was a breach of Article 10 because the applicants' criminal conviction was disproportionate and, so, unnecessary in a democratic society. Having reached this conclusion, the Court decided that it was not appropriate to apply Article 17.[101]

A number of concurring and dissenting opinions are attached to the judgment. Judge Jambrek in a concurring opinion says:

> In order that Article 17 may be applied, the aim of the offending actions must be to spread violence or hatred, to resort to illegal or undemocratic methods, to encourage the use of violence, to undermine the nation's democratic and pluralist political system, or to pursue objectives that are racist or likely to destroy the rights and freedoms of others... Therefore, the requirements of Article 17 are strictly scrutinized, and rightly so.[102]

This appears to reflect the underlying approach adopted by the Court. The matter could be resolved by applying Article 10 and the repression of this type of publication through the use of criminal sanctions went beyond the requirements of a democratic society. The defenders of Marshall Pétain could not be said to be undermining democracy in the way envisaged by Article 17. It was therefore inappropriate to permit the French Government to plead that provision to excuse their actions.

This approach seems to be confirmed by the way in which the *ÖZDEP* case[103] was argued. The case involved a court order dissolving a political party in Turkey. The Turkish Constitutional Court had concluded that the Freedom and Democracy Party's (ÖZDEP) activities were subject to the restrictions in Articles 11(2) and 17 of the Convention. The application to the Strasbourg organs did not raise issues under Article 17, but considered the matter solely under Article 11.[104] In *Paksas v Lithuania*,[105] the Grand Chamber reiterated that Article 17 is applicable only on an exceptional basis and in extreme cases, and declined to apply it in the context of an impeached President's disqualification from standing for parliamentary election. It was held that the applicant was merely seeking to regain the full enjoyment of a right which the Convention in principle secures to everyone, and that the Lithuanian Government's allegation that his real aim was to be re-elected President of Lithuania was immaterial.

However, some expression is regarded as beyond the pale. An example is denial of the Holocaust; in one case the Strasbourg Court said, 'Its proponents indisputably have designs that fall into the category of aims prohibited by Article 17 of the Convention.'[106] In that case the applicant could not rely on Article 10 on freedom of expression, and his application in this respect was ruled inadmissible.[107] By contrast merely wearing a red

under his own control, whereas in reality he was a close collaborator with Germany. Pétain was subsequently convicted of treason and sentenced to death, but this was commuted to solitary confinement for life. Pétain died in July 1951.

[101] § 58. [102] § 2 of concurring opinion.

[103] *ÖZDEP v Turkey*, (App. 23885/94), 8 December 1999, (2001) 31 EHRR 675, ECHR 1999-VIII.

[104] Thus rendering it, in the view of the Court, unnecessary to consider the applicant's complaints under Articles 9, 10, and 14.

[105] *Paksas v Lithuania*, (App. 34932/04), 6 January 2011 [GC], ECHR 2011 (extracts).

[106] *Garaudy v France*, (App. 65831/01), Decision of 24 June 2003, ECHR 2003-IX.

[107] See also to the same effect *Ivanov v Russia*, (App. 35222/04), Decision of 20 February 2007, ECHR 2007-II.

star as a totalitarian symbol was unrelated to racist propaganda and would not attract the exception in Article 17.[108]

The Court does not always seem to be consistent in its use of Article 17. In recent times, it has been used to dismiss an application without elaboration of possible justifications for a repressive measure taken by a Contracting Party. A good example is the *Norwood* case.[109] This concerned a complaint by a Regional Organizer for the British National Party[110] following his conviction under the public order legislation for the display of a large anti-Islamic poster in the window of his home. He had argued that this was an exercise of his right of freedom of expression. The Court noted that both the Court, and, previously, the Commission, had found that the freedom of expression guaranteed under Article 10 of the Convention may not be invoked in a sense contrary to Article 10. It concluded:

> Such a general, vehement attack against a religious group, linking the group as a whole with a grave act of terrorism, is incompatible with the values proclaimed and guaranteed by the Convention, notably, tolerance, social peace and non-discrimination. The applicant's display of the poster in his window constituted an act within the meaning of Article 17, which did not, therefore, enjoy the protection of Articles 10 or 14.[111]

LIMITATION ON USE OF RESTRICTIONS ON RIGHTS

Article 18 provides:

> The restrictions permitted under this Convention to the said rights and freedoms shall not be applied for any purpose other than those for which they have been prescribed.

This provision shows that there can be no inherent or implied limitations on the rights guaranteed. Each limitation must be express and have an explicit purpose. Article 18 does not have an independent character and will only be relevant in conjunction with an Article which contains limitations, though there does not need to be a violation of that other provision before Article 18 bites. It is not clear why Article 18 was included in the Convention. There is no equivalent provision in the Universal Declaration of Human Rights nor in the United Nations Covenant on Civil and Political Rights, though Article 30 of the American Convention provides:

> The restrictions that, pursuant to this Convention, may be placed on the enjoyment or exercise of the rights or freedoms recognized herein may not be applied except in accordance with the laws enacted for reasons of general interest and in accordance with the purpose for which such restrictions have been established.

There is not much guidance in the preparatory work. Article 18 may seem to add little to the Convention except to make explicit what is either implicit in other provisions or else may be thought to be well established under the general principles recognized by international law. But it is useful as putting beyond doubt the scope of the restrictions permitted, and as making clear the requirement of good faith in the application of these restrictions.

[108] *Vajnai v Hungary*, (App. 33629/06), Decision of 8 July 2008.

[109] *Norwood v United Kingdom*, (App. 23131/03), Decision of 16 November 2004, ECHR 2004-XI.

[110] An extreme right wing political party opposed to immigration into the UK.

[111] *Norwood v United Kingdom*, (App. 23131/03), Decision of 16 November 2004, ECHR 2004-XI, 4.

Article 18 limits the area of discretion of the national authorities. In effect, it excludes *détournement de pouvoir*[112] or abuse of power, notions familiar in many systems of national law. The principle is that where the real purpose of the authorities in imposing a restriction is outside the purposes specified, one of the specified purposes cannot be used as a pretext for imposing that restriction. The restriction may be one which is legitimate in itself, and lawfully imposed in accordance with the proper procedure. But it will still be prohibited if imposed for an improper purpose. For example, where the right of a convicted prisoner to respect for family life is subject to a restriction on the grounds set out in Article 8(2), such a restriction may be imposed only for the purposes there specified, and not, for example, as a punishment.

One difficulty in using Article 18 is its dependence on showing a particular motivation. In the *Handyside* case[113] the applicant sought to argue that the purpose of the seizure of *The Little Red Schoolbook* was not for the protection of morals, but 'to muzzle a small-scale publisher whose political leanings met with the disapproval of a fragment of the public opinion.'[114] The Commission concluded that there was no evidence to sustain this allegation, and the Court considered the matter solely on the limitations in Article 10(2) and did not consider the issue under Article 18. The Court has incorporated its consideration of motivation into its consideration of whether the limitations are necessary in a democratic society.

The provision is cited with some regularity by applicants, but the Court hardly ever finds the need to consider its terms. Other provisions of the Convention are usually sufficient for the application to be determined without recourse to this provision.[115] But the Strasbourg Court did find a violation of Article 18 in the *Gusinskiy* case.[116] The rather complicated saga involved the arrest and detention of the applicant, and an apparent agreement that the charges would be dropped if he sold his shares in a media company to Gazprom, a State-controlled company. The applicant complained that his detention was intended to force him to sell his share-holding on unfavourable terms and conditions and that this violated Article 18. The Strasbourg Court had already found that the applicant's detention had been in breach of Article 5. However, the Court concluded that 'it is not the purpose of such public-law matters as criminal proceedings and detention on remand to be used as part of commercial bargaining strategies'[117] and this further tainted the respondent State's actions; there was a violation of Article 18. It is interesting to note that the Court does not put forward any particular justification for using Article 18 in conjunction with Article 5; almost all the other cases involving Article 18 have been in the context of Articles 8 to 11 which contain specific internal limitations.[118]

In *Khodorkovskiy v Russia*,[119] the applicant maintained that the entire criminal prosecution of himself and other managers of Yukos, a large oil company, had been politically and economically motivated. The Court acknowledged that the evidence raised a suspicion as to the real intent of the authorities, but the burden of proof rests with the applicant and

[112] See App. 753/60, *X v Austria*, Decision of 5 August 1960, (1960) 3 *Yearbook* 310; *Lawless v Ireland*, 14 November 1960, 7 April 1961, and 1 July 1961, Series A Nos 1–3, (1979–80) 1 EHRR 1, 13, and 15.

[113] *Handyside v United Kingdom*, (App. 5493/72), 7 December 1976, Series A No 24, (1979–80) 1 EHRR 737.

[114] *Handyside*, § 52.

[115] See, for example, *Quinn v France*, (App. 18580/91), 22 March 1995, (1996) 21 EHRR 529; *Lukanov v Bulgaria*, (App. 21915/93), 20 March 1997, (1997) 24 EHRR 121, ECHR 1997-II; *Kurt v Turkey* (App. 24276/94), 25 May 1998, (1999) 27 EHRR 373, ECHR 1998-III; and *Beyeler v Italy*, (App. 33202/96), 5 January 2000 [GC], (2001) 33 EHRR 1224, ECHR 2000-I.

[116] *Gusinskiy v Russia*, (App. 70276/01), 19 May 2004, (2005) 41 EHRR 281, ECHR 2004-IV.

[117] § 76. [118] See ch.14. [119] *Khodorkovskiy v Russia*, (App. 5829/04), 31 May 2011.

the evidence was not sufficient for the Court to conclude that the whole legal machinery of the State was misused, that the authorities were acting with bad faith throughout and in blatant disregard of the Convention. The Court emphasized that this was 'a very serious claim which requires an incontrovertible and direct proof.'[120]

The Court was satisfied, however, in the subsequent case of *Lutsenko v Ukraine*.[121] The applicant, who was the leader of an opposition party, complained that his arrest and detention were used by the Ukrainian authorities to exclude him from participation in upcoming parliamentary elections. He did not refer to any specific Convention provision on this point but the Court of its own accord considered this issue under Article 18 and found a violation of that provision. This was based on evidence that the prosecuting authorities had explicitly indicated the applicant's communication with the media as one of the grounds for his arrest which, in the Court's view, suggested that the proceedings against the applicant were an attempt to punish him for publicly disagreeing with accusations against him and asserting his innocence. The Court found, therefore, that the restriction of the applicant's liberty under Article 5(1)(c) was initiated not only for the purpose of bringing him before the competent legal authority on reasonable suspicion of having committed an offence, but also for other reasons which amounted to a violation of Article 18 taken in conjunction with Article 5.

[120] § 260. [121] *Lutsenko v Ukraine*, (App. 6492/11), 3 July 2012.

PART 2

CONVENTION RIGHTS

7

THE RIGHT TO AN EFFECTIVE REMEDY

INTRODUCTION

The essence of Article 13 has been described by the Grand Chamber in the following terms:

> The object of Article 13, as emerges from the *travaux préparatoires*, is to provide a means whereby individuals can obtain relief at national level for violations of their Convention rights before having to set in motion the international machinery of complaint before the Court.[1]

Article 13 provides:

> Everyone whose rights and freedoms as set forth in this Convention are violated shall have an effective remedy before a national authority notwithstanding that the violation has been committed by persons acting in an official capacity.

There are significant differences between Article 13 and the corresponding provisions of other human rights instruments. For example, Article 8 of the Universal Declaration on Human Rights is wider in encompassing rights granted to an individual by the constitution or by law, but potentially narrower in only requiring effective remedies from competent national tribunals.[2]

Until comparatively recently, Article 13 occupied something of a twilight zone in the case-law of the Convention organs.[3] This is somewhat surprising for three reasons: first, the Convention is built upon an obligation that Contracting Parties guarantee to those within their jurisdiction the rights enumerated in the Convention and its Protocols; secondly, the engagement of the Strasbourg organs is subsidiary to the protection of these rights in the national legal orders; and, thirdly, the protection of rights in the national legal order must be dependent upon the remedies available there. These three reasons justify examining Article 13 in advance of other Convention rights, since Article 13 when read with Article 1 imposes an obligation on Contracting Parties to provide remedies in the national legal order. If Contracting Parties accomplished this, then the Strasbourg Court's caseload would be reduced, and its work would become much more focused on big constitutional questions concerning the content of the rights protected by the Convention rather than in consideration of many routine violations of Convention rights which should have been put right within the national legal order. Such an approach is prominent in the Brighton Declaration which emphasizes the need for more effective national implementation which

[1] *Kudła v Poland*, (App. 30210/96), 26 October 2000 [GC], (2002) 35 EHRR 198, ECHR 2002-XI, § 152.

[2] Art. 8 of the Universal Declaration reads: Everyone has the right to an effective remedy by the competent national tribunals for acts violating the fundamental rights granted him by the constitution or by law.

[3] See R. White, 'Remedies in a Multi-Level Legal Order: The Strasbourg Court and the UK' in C. Kilpatrick, T. Novitz, and P. Skidmore, (eds.), *The Future of Remedies in Europe* (Hart, Oxford 2000), 191.

would enable the Court to 'focus its efforts on serious or widespread violations, systemic and structural problems, and important questions of interpretation and application of the Convention, and hence would need to remedy fewer violations itself, and consequently deliver fewer judgments.'[4] The benefits in terms of reduction of workload are obvious, although there is a danger, of course, that such a strategy originating from the Contracting States may seek to exclude the Court from necessary scrutiny of national laws.

One of the reasons for the slow development of Article 13 has been the ambiguities in the drafting of the provision. One ambiguity was whether Article 13 only applied *after* the Convention organs had determined that there had been a breach of the Convention rights.[5] The proper view is, however, that Article 13 is about guaranteeing a process within the national legal order by which a remedy for a violation can be provided at that level. This led to a further difficulty about the use of Article 13 by the Strasbourg organs. Since Article 13 only required a remedy in the national legal order where a person's rights and freedoms as set forth in the Convention are violated, was it necessary to prove a violation of one of the Convention rights before Article 13 could be pleaded? The question was answered in the *Klass* case in 1978, which ruled that Article 13 is an independent provision which can be violated even if there is no violation of another Convention right, although there must be an arguable violation of a Convention right.[6]

In its more recent judgments, the Strasbourg Court is increasingly taking issues of violations of Article 13 in conjunction with specific provisions of the Convention. In this regard, there are some similarities between the Court's approach to alleged violations of Articles 13 and 14, though, under Article 13, the test is whether the applicant has an 'arguable complaint' under one of the substantive Articles.[7]

In the *Čonka* case[8] the Court found a violation of Article 13 when read in conjunction with Article 4 of Protocol 4, but not when taken in conjunction with Article 3 of the Convention; and, in the *Peck* case,[9] the Court found a violation of Article 13 when read in conjunction with Article 8. There are now many judgments reading Article 13 with Article 2 or 3 in finding that the respondent State has failed to conduct an investigation into allegations of a suspicious death or of ill-treatment.[10] The Court has summarized the position as follows:

> The Court reiterates that Article 13 of the Convention guarantees the availability at the national level of a remedy to enforce the substance of the Convention rights and freedoms in whatever form they might happen to be secured in the domestic legal order. Given the fundamental importance of the right to protection of life, Article 13 requires, in addition

[4] High Level Conference on the Future of the European Court of Human Rights: Brighton Declaration (accessible here: www.echr.coe.int/NR/rdonlyres/8AC14EA9-A92B-4875-A76A-4E21A8B3AC5A/0/ENG_20120418_BRIGHTON_DECLARATION_FINALE.pdf), § 33.

[5] See J. Fawcett, *The Application of the European Convention on Human Rights* (OUP, Oxford 1987), 290–1.

[6] *Klass and others v Germany*, (App. 5029/71), 6 September 1978, Series A No 28, (1979–80) 2 EHRR 214, § 63.

[7] Though this is probably not qualitatively that different from the question asked by the Court when dealing with alleged violations of Art. 14, namely, whether the complaint is within the material scope of one of the substantive Articles. See ch.24.

[8] *Čonka v Belgium*, (App. 51564/99), 5 February 2002, (2002) 34 EHRR 1298, ECHR 2002-I.

[9] *Peck v United Kingdom*, (App. 44647/98), 28 January 2003, (2003) 36 EHRR 719, ECHR 2003-I.

[10] As, for example, *Abdurzakova and Abdurzakov v Russia*, (App. 35080/04), 15 January 2009 (Art. 13 in conjunction with Art. 2—disappearances in Chechnya); and *Muminov v Russia*, (App. 42502/06), 11 December 2008 (Art. 13 in conjunction with Art. 3—assessment of risk of ill-treatment of detainees if expelled to Uzbekistan). See further later in this chapter. See also P. van Dijk and others (eds.), *Theory and Practice of the European Convention on Human Rights*, (4th edn Intersentia, Antwerp 2006), 1011–6.

> to the payment of compensation where appropriate, a thorough and effective investigation capable of leading to the identification and punishment of those responsible for the deprivation of life and infliction of treatment contrary to Article 3, including effective access for the complainant to the investigation procedure leading to the identification and punishment of those responsible.... The Court further reiterates that the requirements of Article 13 are broader than a Contracting State's obligation under Article 2 to conduct an effective investigation...[11]

Although the absence of a remedy before the national authorities will normally be a matter subsidiary to the principal complaint, it is appropriate that it should be examined separately where it is alleged that, as a general feature of the national law, there is no effective remedy. For example, it may be suggested that if an applicant complains of an invasion of privacy, and if national law affords no general remedy in such cases, the complaint should be examined under Article 13 as well as under Article 8.[12] On the other hand, where the essence of the principal complaint is the absence of an appropriate remedy required by another provision of the Convention, it is unnecessary to consider Article 13. Thus, in the *Vagrancy* cases,[13] where the Strasbourg Court found that the applicants did not have the necessary judicial guarantees under Article 5(4) to challenge the lawfulness of their detention, the Court did not consider that it had to examine separately the issue under Article 13.[14]

Article 13 does not offer any guarantee of a remedy allowing a State's primary legislation to be challenged before a national authority on the grounds that it is contrary to the Convention.[15] The Grand Chamber has also reiterated that the absence of remedies against decisions of a constitutional court will not normally raise an issue under Article 13, and therefore nor does this Article require the provision of a remedy allowing a constitutional precedent with statutory force to be challenged.[16]

It appeared from the early case-law that the requirements made of the national legal orders were at a relatively low level. It could almost be reduced to the question of whether there was some mechanism, or mechanisms taken together, which might lead to a remedy for the complaint. There are, however, signs in the more recent case-law that new life is being breathed into Article 13.[17]

There are two questions which must always be asked: whether there is an arguable complaint; and whether the remedy in the national legal order is effective.

WHAT IS AN ARGUABLE COMPLAINT?

The Strasbourg Court requires the applicant to show only an arguable case in order to be able to complain of a violation of Article 13. The *Klass* case[18] concerned the availability of

[11] *Lyanova and Aliyeva v Russia*, (Apps. 12713/02 and 28440/03), 2 October 2008, § 134.

[12] As in *Peck v United Kingdom*, (App. 44647/98), 28 January 2003, (2003) 36 EHRR 719, ECHR 2003-I.

[13] *De Wilde, Ooms and Versyp v Belgium*, (Apps. 2832/66, 2835/66, and 2899/66), 18 June 1971, Series A No 12, (1979–80) 1 EHRR 373.

[14] § 95. And see later in this chapter on the relationship between Art. 13 and Art. 6 ECHR.

[15] *James and others v United Kingdom*, (App. 8793/79), 21 February 1986, Series A No 98, (1986) 8 EHRR 123, § 85, confirmed in *Kudła v Poland*, (App. 30210/96), 26 October 2000 [GC], (2002) 35 EHRR 198, ECHR 2002-XI, § 151 and *A and others v. The United Kingdom*, (App. 3455/05), 19 February 2009 [GC].

[16] *Paksas v Lithuania*, (App. 34932/04), 6 January 2011 [GC].

[17] See discussion in ch.12 on the Court's comments on the need for an effective remedy where there are violations of Art. 6 by reason of the excessive length of proceedings.

[18] *Klass v Germany*, (App. 5029/71), 6 September 1978, Series A No 28, (1979–80) 2 EHRR 214.

secret surveillance in Germany. The applicants complained that the legislation authorizing such surveillance violated Articles 6, 8, and 13. The Court differed from the Commission, which had concluded that it must be shown that a substantive provision had been violated before the Article came into play. The test, said the Court, is rather one of whether the applicant has an arguable case.

The precise delimitation of the arguability test remains difficult.[19] The Court itself has indicated that providing an abstract definition would not help and decides the issue on a case-by-case basis.[20] In the *Boyle and Rice* case[21] the Court addressed the tricky question of how a case could be viewed as arguable when the Commission had concluded that it was manifestly ill-founded; all but one of the applicants' complaints under Article 8 had been dismissed as manifestly ill-founded. The answer lies in there being two rather different tests. In deciding that a case is manifestly ill-founded, the Commission is making a judgment on the merits, in that, in effect, the finding means that examination of the merits is not required because the applicant has put forward insufficient evidence to justify doing so. In determining whether a case is arguable, the test is rather one of seeing whether there are the makings of a prima facie case. The Commission suggested before the Court in the *Boyle and Rice* case that to be arguable a case needed only to raise a Convention issue which merits further examination. That is a low threshold.[22] It follows from this that, in all those cases where the Court[23] finds that a complaint is admissible, the arguability threshold is met. The position adopted in the *Boyle and Rice* case was elaborated by the Court in the *Powell and Rayner* case,[24] which concerned complaints under Articles 6, 8, 13, and Article 1 of Protocol 1 in relation to excessive noise from air traffic in the vicinity of Heathrow Airport. The Court suggested that the coherence of the Convention system could be undermined if the test of arguability was set at so low a level that cases where the merits were so weak that the case could be regarded as manifestly ill-founded could nevertheless be considered under Article 13. The threshold should be the same. Now that both admissibility and merits questions are determined by the Strasbourg Court, any risk of inconsistencies of approach would seem to have been removed.

THE NATURE OF THE REMEDIES REQUIRED

BACKGROUND

The current position is neatly recapitulated in the *Iovchev* case:[25]

> The Court reiterates that Article 13 of the Convention guarantees the availability at national level of a remedy to enforce the substance of the Convention rights and freedoms in whatever form they may happen to be secured in the domestic legal order. The effect of

[19] F. Hampson, 'The Concept of an "Arguable Claim" under Article 13 of the European Convention on Human Rights' (1990) 39 ICLQ 891.

[20] *Boyle and Rice v United Kingdom*, (App. 9659/82, and 9658/82), 27 April 1988, Series A No 131, (1988) 10 EHRR 425, § 55.

[21] *Boyle and Rice v United Kingdom*, (App. 9659/82, and 9658/82), 27 April 1988, Series A No 131, (1988) 10 EHRR 425, § 55.

[22] See, for example, *Powell and Rayner v United Kingdom*, (App. 9310/81), 21 February 1990, Series A No 172, (1990) 12 EHRR 355.

[23] Note that, prior to 1 November 1998, admissibility decisions were made by the Commission.

[24] *Powell and Rayner v United Kingdom*, (App. 9310/81), 21 February 1990, Series A No 172, (1990) 12 EHRR 355, § 33.

[25] *Iovchev v Bulgaria*, (App. 41211/98), 2 February 2006, §§ 142–3.

> Article 13 is thus to require the provision of a domestic remedy to deal with the substance of an 'arguable complaint' under the Convention and to grant appropriate relief, although Contracting Parties are afforded some discretion as to the manner in which they conform to their Convention obligations under this provision. The scope of the obligation under Article 13 varies depending on the nature of the applicant's complaint under the Convention. Nevertheless, the remedy required by Article 13 must be 'effective' in practice as well as in law….

Article 13 offers a measure of respect for national procedural autonomy; this refers to the ability of each Contracting Party to determine the form of remedies offered to meet its obligations under the Article. Those remedies need not be judicial, but must be effective. Ombudsman procedures and other non-judicial procedures will be included. Once a remedy is identified, it is not necessary to show the certainty of a favourable outcome.[26] National procedural autonomy does not, however, extend to the very existence of a remedy, since Article 13 requires that there is an effective remedy to enforce the substance of the Convention rights in the national legal order.[27] In the *Silver* case[28] the Court said that the remedy before the national authority should concern both the determination of the claim and any redress. The respondent State will be expected to identify the remedies available to the applicant and to show at least a prima facie case for their effectiveness. So, where respondent States cannot put forward an example of a relevant remedy, they are unlikely to satisfy the Court that there is an effective remedy available.[29]

The process need not be judicial, but, if it is not, consideration should be given to its powers and the guarantees it affords. For example in the *Khan* case,[30] the Strasbourg Court held that the possibility of complaining to the Police Complaints Authority about alleged breaches of the Convention by the police was not an 'effective remedy', because the Authority was not sufficiently independent from either the police or the Home Secretary. Where the process is judicial, there will be a breach of Article 13 if an order of a court is not implemented by the authorities.[31]

ACCESS TO AN EFFECTIVE REMEDY

The tendency of respondent States has been simply to point to some procedure available within the national legal order for raising aspects of the matters covered by the applicant's complaint to the Strasbourg organs. The Court is, however, increasingly considering whether those remedies provide an effective means of raising the substance of the complaints of violations of the particular Convention rights in issue,[32] both as a matter of practice as well as of law.[33] Where irreversible harm might ensue, it will not be sufficient

[26] *Pine Valley Developments v Ireland*, (App. 12742/87), 29 November 1991, Series A No 222, (1992) 14 EHRR 319, § 66; *Costello-Roberts v United Kingdom*, (App. 13134/87), 25 March 1993, Series A No 247-C, (1995) 19 EHRR 112, § 40; and *Lorsé v The Netherlands*, (App. 52750/99), 4 February 2003, (2003) 37 EHRR 105, § 96.

[27] See the discussion of what constitutes a domestic remedy for the purpose of the requirement to exhaust domestic remedies in ch.2.

[28] *Silver v United Kingdom*, (Apps. 5947/72, 6205/73, 7052/75, 7061/75, 7107/75, 7113/75, and 7136/75), 25 March 1983, Series A No 61, (1983) 5 EHRR 347, § 113.

[29] See, for example, *Vereinigung Demokratischer Soldaten Österreichs and Gubi v Austria*, (App. 15153/89), 19 December 1994, Series A No 302, (1995) 20 EHRR 56, § 93.

[30] *Khan v United Kingdom*, (App. 35394/97), 12 May 2000, (2001) 31 EHRR 1016, ECHR 2000-V, §§ 43–7.

[31] *Iatridis v Greece*, (App. 31107/96), 25 March 1999 [GC], (2000) 30 EHRR 97, ECHR 1999-II.

[32] See *Chahal v United Kingdom*, (App. 22414/93), 15 November 1996, (1997) 23 EHRR 413, ECHR 1996-V.

[33] *Metropolitan Church of Bessarabia and others v Moldova*, (App. 45701/99), 14 December 2001, (2002) 35 EHRR 306, ECHR 2002-XII, § 137; see also *Debelić v Croatia*, (App. 2448/03), 26 May 2005.

that the remedies are merely as effective as they can be; they must provide much more certain guarantees of effectiveness.[34] The Court's position was summarized in its judgment in the *Čonka* case:

> The scope of the Contracting Parties' obligations under Article 13 varies depending on the nature of the applicant's complaint; however, the remedy required by Article 13 must be 'effective' in practice as well as in law. The 'effectiveness' of a 'remedy' within the meaning of Article 13 does not depend on the certainty of a favourable outcome for the applicant. Nor does the 'authority' referred to in that provision necessarily have to be a judicial authority; but if it is not, its powers and the guarantees which it affords are relevant in determining whether the remedy before it is effective. Also, even if a single remedy does not by itself entirely satisfy the requirements of Article 13, the aggregate of remedies provided for under domestic law may do so.[35]

This approach is well illustrated in the facts of the *Keenan* case.[36] Keenan had been found hanged in his cell one day after the imposition of punishment of further imprisonment and segregation had been imposed on him. He had a history of mental illness. His mother complained of violations of Articles 2, 3, and 13. No violation of Article 2 was found by the Court, but a violation of Article 3, in the form of inhuman and degrading treatment, was found because of a lack of effective monitoring and supervision of his mental state and the imposition of a punishment which threatened his physical and moral resistance having regard to the state of his mental health. In relation to remedies, the respondent State argued that, during his detention, Mark Keenan had a number of possible remedies open to him: he could have sought judicial review; he could have made a complaint under the prison complaints procedure; he could have begun actions in tort; and he could have brought an action for misfeasance in the exercise of a public office. Furthermore, his mother could, after his death, have brought proceedings in tort in respect of any injury or exacerbation of his mental illness suffered prior to her son's death. The respondent State did, however, concede that an inquest was not an effective remedy since it did not furnish the applicant with the possibility of establishing the responsibility of the prison authorities or of obtaining damages.

The Court held that there was no effective remedy available to Mark Keenan to challenge speedily the imposition of the punishment during which he killed himself. Such remedies as had been identified were not effective: it would not have been possible for Mark Keenan to have obtained legal aid and legal representation, and lodged an application for judicial review in a short period of time; similarly prison complaints typically took six weeks to adjudicate. In relation to the remedies available to the next of kin after the death, the Court concluded that no effective remedy was available to the applicant which would have established where responsibility lay for the death of her son. This was regarded as an essential element of a remedy under Article 13 for a bereaved parent. Furthermore, the Court did not accept that adequate damages would have been recoverable or that legal aid would have been available to pursue the claim. The Court emphasized that in relation to a violation of Article 2 or Article 3, 'compensation for the non-pecuniary damage flowing from the breach should in principle be available as part of the range of possible remedies.'[37]

[34] *Chahal v United Kingdom*, (App. 22414/93), 15 November 1996, (1997) 23 EHRR 413, ECHR 1996-V, §§ 150–2.

[35] *Čonka v Belgium*, (App. 51564/99), 5 February 2002, (2002) 34 EHRR 1298, ECHR 2002-I, § 75.

[36] *Keenan v United Kingdom*, (App. 27229/95), 3 April 2001, (2001) 33 EHRR 913, ECHR 2001-III.

[37] § 129.

This latter point was central in the case of *Stanev v Bulgaria*[38] in which the applicant complained about his placement in a social care home for people with mental disorders, and the living conditions in the home. The Court found a violation of Article 3 and confirmed that, where such a violation is found, compensation for the non-pecuniary damage flowing from the breach should in principle be part of the range of available remedies. As it was not, there had also been a violation of Article 13.

The Strasbourg Court is increasingly indicating what constitutes effectiveness in the remedies available within the national legal order. The remedy must be one which enables the applicants to raise their Convention rights in a timely manner, and to have them considered in the national proceedings.[39] The Court has also indicated that, to be an effective remedy, a process may need to prevent the execution of measures contrary to the Convention. This means that it is not compatible with Article 13 for such measures to be put into effect before the national authorities have examined their compatibility with the Convention.[40]

The *Iovchev* case[41] provides a good example of where the Strasbourg Court will accept that there is a remedy which is effective in law but not in practice. The relevant Bulgarian legislation in principle did not exclude the possibility of compensation being paid where a person had suffered inhuman or degrading treatment while in detention, but the process by which this had to be established was so onerous in the particular circumstances of the case, coupled with the delays which had occurred, that the applicant could not be regarded as having at his disposal an effective remedy for his complaint about the conditions of his detention. There had been a violation of Article 13.[42]

In the *Klass* case[43] the Strasbourg Court indicated that the requirement of effectiveness had to be read in the context of the complaint. An effective remedy in respect of secret surveillance meant a remedy 'that was as effective as could be having regard to the restricted scope for recourse inherent in any system of secret surveillance'. The Court expanded on this in the *Leander* case[44] which concerned secret security checks, making clear that although no single remedy might itself entirely satisfy the requirements of Article 13, the aggregate of remedies under the system might do so.[45]

The *Al-Nashif* case[46] revisited the extent to which considerations of national security imposed limitations on the remedies required by Article 13 in the context of deportation proceedings. While accepting that there will be some limitations, especially where secret surveillance or secret checks are involved, there is nevertheless a minimum standard required by Article 13:

> Even where an allegation of a threat to national security is made, the guarantee of an effective remedy requires as a minimum that the competent independent appeals authority must be informed of the reasons grounding the deportation decision, even if such reasons are not

[38] *Stanev v. Bulgaria*, (App. 36760/06), 17 January 2012 [GC].

[39] *Hatton v United Kingdom*, (App. 36022/97), 8 July 2003 [GC], (2003) 37 EHRR 611, ECHR 2003-VIII, § 140. On the limitations of the remedy of judicial review in England and Wales prior to the entry into force of the Human Rights Act 1998, see *Smith and Grady v United Kingdom*, (Apps. 33985/96 and 33986/96), 27 September 1999, (2000) 29 EHRR 493, ECHR 1999-VI; and *Peck v United Kingdom*, (App. 44647/98), 28 January 2003, (2003) 36 EHRR 719, ECHR 2003-I.

[40] *Čonka v Belgium*, (App. 51564/99), 5 February 2002, (2002) 34 EHRR 1298, ECHR 2002-I, § 79. The case concerned the expulsion of aliens.

[41] *Iovchev v Bulgaria*, (App. 41211/98), 2 February 2006.

[42] §§ 144–8.

[43] *Klass v Germany*, (App. 5029/71), 6 September 1978, Series A No 28, (1979–80) 2 EHRR 214.

[44] *Leander v Sweden*, (Apps. 9248/81), 26 March 1987, Series A No 116, (1987) 9 EHRR 433.

[45] *Chahal v United Kingdom*, (App. 22414/93), 15 November 1996, (1997) 23 EHRR 413, § 145.

[46] *Al-Nashif v Bulgaria*, (App. 50963/99), 20 June 2002, (2003) 36 EHRR 655.

publicly available. The authority must be competent to reject the executive's assertion that there is a threat to national security where it finds it arbitrary or unreasonable. There must be some form of adversarial proceedings, if need be through a special representative after a security clearance. Furthermore, the question whether the impugned measure would interfere with the individual's right to respect for family life and, if so, whether a fair balance is struck between the public interest involved and the individual's rights must be examined.[47]

Deportation cases raise particular issues of concern. In *M. and others v Bulgaria*,[48] the Court reiterated that in the context of deportation the domestic remedy for examination of allegations about serious risks of ill-treatment contrary to Article 3 in the destination country must have automatic suspensive effect.[49] Under Bulgarian law, a deportation order issued on national security grounds could not be stayed nor could an appeal against it have suspensive effect, even if an irreversible risk of death or ill-treatment in the receiving State is claimed. This was contrary to the requirements of Article 13.

In *Hirsi Jamaa and others v Italy*,[50] the Grand Chamber confirmed that where a complaint concerns allegations that the person's expulsion would expose him to a real risk of suffering treatment contrary to Article 3, and also under Article 4 of Protocol 4 (prohibiting the collective expulsion of aliens), effectiveness requires that the person concerned should have access to a remedy with automatic suspensive effect. By contrast, in *De Souza Ribeiro v France*[51] where expulsions were challenged on the basis of alleged interference with private and family life, it was held not to be imperative, in order for a remedy to be effective, that it should have automatic suspensive effect. There were, however, other standard Article 13 requirements:

> ... in immigration matters, where there is an arguable claim that expulsion threatens to interfere with the alien's right to respect for his private and family life, Article 13 in conjunction with Article 8 of the Convention requires that States must make available to the individual concerned the effective possibility of challenging the deportation or refusal-of-residence order and of having the relevant issues examined with sufficient procedural safeguards and thoroughness by an appropriate domestic forum offering adequate guarantees of independence and impartiality.[52]

In the circumstances of *De Souza Ribeiro*, the Court considered that the haste with which the removal order was executed (given that the applicant was removed from French Guiana less than 36 hours after his arrest) had the effect of rendering the available remedies ineffective in practice and therefore inaccessible. While it acknowledged the importance of swift access to a remedy, it insisted that 'speed should not go so far as to constitute an obstacle or unjustified hindrance to making use of it, or take priority over its practical effectiveness.'[53] It therefore concluded that 'the manner in which the applicant's removal was effected was extremely rapid, even perfunctory. In the circumstances, before he was deported, the applicant had no chance of having the lawfulness of the removal order examined sufficiently thoroughly by a national authority offering the requisite procedural guarantees.'[54] While States will be afforded some discretion as to the manner in which they conform to their obligations under Article 13, the Grand Chamber made clear in this case

[47] § 137.

[48] *M. and others v Bulgaria*, (App. 41416/08), 26 July 2011.

[49] See also *Gebremedhin [Gaberamadhien] v France*, (App. 25389/05), 26 April 2007 and *M.S.S. v Belgium and Greece*, (App. 30696/09), ECHR 2011 [GC].

[50] *Hirsi Jamaa and others v Italy*, (App. 27765/09), 23 February 2012, [GC].

[51] *De Souza Ribeiro v France*, (App. 22689/07), 13 December 2012, [GC].

[52] § 83.

[53] § 95.

[54] § 96.

that such discretion must not result in an applicant being denied access in practice to the minimum procedural safeguards needed to protect him against arbitrary expulsion.

In immigration cases, while the Court has emphasized that its sole concern, in keeping with the principle of subsidiarity, is to examine the effectiveness of the domestic procedures and ensure that they respect human rights, this does involve consideration of whether an available remedy is effective in practice. For example, in *M.S.S. v Belgium and Greece*,[55] the Court noted shortcomings in access to the asylum procedure in Greece and in the examination of applications for asylum, including insufficient information for asylum seekers about the procedures to be followed, shortage of interpreters, and lack of training of the staff responsible for conducting the individual interviews, lack of legal aid effectively depriving the asylum seekers of legal counsel, and excessively lengthy delays in receiving a decision.[56] The Court also rejected the Government's argument that an application to the Supreme Administrative Court for judicial review of a possible rejection of the applicant's request for asylum could be considered as a safety net protecting him against arbitrary refoulement. The shortcomings of this procedure led the Court to reiterate that 'the accessibility of a remedy in practice is decisive when assessing its effectiveness.'[57]

In *Nada v Switzerland*,[58] the applicant's name had been added to the Federal Taliban Ordinance and he was therefore banned from international travel, a restriction that infringed his Article 8 rights due to his residence in the small enclave of Campione d'Italia surrounded by Switzerland. Security Council Resolutions required an entry and transit ban in respect of individuals referred to in a list of individuals and entities associated with Osama bin Laden and al-Qaeda. The Swiss Federal Court had taken the view that whilst it could verify whether Switzerland was bound by the Security Council resolutions, it could not lift the sanctions imposed on the applicant on the ground that they did not respect human rights. The Strasbourg Court disagreed, and referred with approval to the finding of the Court of Justice of the European Union (CJEU) that 'it is not a consequence of the principles governing the international legal order under the United Nations that any judicial review of the internal lawfulness of the contested regulation in the light of fundamental freedoms is excluded by virtue of the fact that that measure is intended to give effect to a resolution of the Security Council adopted under Chapter VII of the Charter of the United Nations'.[59] In addition, the Court held that there was nothing in the Security Council resolutions to prevent the Swiss authorities from introducing mechanisms to verify the measures taken at national level pursuant to those resolutions. Its failure to do so amounted to a violation of Article 13, taken together with Article 8.

AN EFFECTIVE REMEDY FOR ALLEGED BREACHES OF ARTICLE 6

For many years, the Strasbourg Court concluded that the provisions of Articles 6 and 13 overlapped, so that if the matter was within Article 6, there was no need to consider any alleged violations of Article 13. In the *Kamasinski* case,[60] the Court said, 'The requirements of Article 13 are less strict than, and are absorbed by, those of Article 6.'[61]

[55] *M.S.S. v Belgium and Greece*, (App. 30696/09), 21 January 2011, ECHR 2011 [GC].

[56] § 301. [57] § 318. [58] *Nada v Switzerland*, (App. 10593/08), 12 September 2012 [GC].

[59] *Yassin Abdullah Kadi and Al Barakaat International Foundation v Council of the European Union and Commission of the European Communities* (joined cases C-402/05 P and C-415/05 P), § 299.

[60] *Kamasinski v Austria*, (App. 9783/82), 19 December 1989, Series A No 168, (1991) 33 EHRR 36.

[61] § 110. See also *Kadubec v Slovakia*, (App. 27061/95), 2 September 1998, § 64; and *Brualla Gomez de la Torre v Spain*, (App. 26737/95), 19 December 1997, (2001) 33 EHRR 1341, § 41.

In the *Kudła* case,[62] the Grand Chamber decided that the case-law in this area should be reviewed in the light of the number of applications the Court received complaining of the failure to ensure a hearing within a reasonable time. The Court reiterated that excessive delays in the administration of justice presented a threat to the rule of law within the national legal order. In a significant development of the case-law on Article 13, the Grand Chamber concluded:

> If Article 13 is, as the respondent State argued, to be interpreted as having no application to the right to a hearing within a reasonable time as safeguarded by Article 6(1), individuals will systematically be forced to refer to the Court in Strasbourg complaints that would otherwise, and in the Court's opinion more appropriately, have to be addressed in the first place within the national legal system. In the long term the effective functioning, on both the national and international level, of the scheme of human rights protection set up by the Convention is liable to be weakened.
>
> In view of the foregoing considerations, the Court considers that the correct interpretation is that that provision guarantees an effective remedy before a national authority for an alleged breach of the requirements under Article 6(1) to hear a case within a reasonable time.[63]

It follows that the national legal orders must ensure that there is a remedy which either ensures that excessive delays are avoided, or provides redress where such delays arise.[64] In the context of the nature of the mischief being remedied, the remedy will almost certainly need to be judicial in nature.[65]

In *McFarlane v Ireland*,[66] the Irish Government argued that the Court's previous judgment in *Barry v Ireland*[67] was incorrect in concluding that an action for damages for a breach of the constitutional right to reasonable expedition did not constitute an effective domestic remedy for delay in criminal proceedings. The Grand Chamber rejected this argument by identifying a number of matters which would cast some doubt on the effectiveness of this proposed remedy. First, there is, in the Court's view, significant uncertainty as to the availability of the proposed constitutional remedy. Secondly, the Court considered that it was not demonstrated that this action could constitute a remedy as regards a judge's delay in delivering a judgment. The Government had accepted that there was likely to be an exception to the right to damages for a breach of a constitutional right when the delay was caused by the failure of an individual judge to deliver judgment within a reasonable time, given the important and established principle of judicial immunity. Since the Court holds a State responsible under the 'reasonable time' aspect of Article 6(1) for delay by judges in delivering their judgments, any remedy which does not apply to this form of delay cannot be considered an effective one within the meaning of Article 13. Thirdly, the proposed constitutional remedy would form part of the High and Supreme Court body of civil litigation for which no specific and streamlined procedures had been developed. One consequence of this was that the speed of the remedial action may be too slow to be effective. A second consequence concerned the legal costs and expenses burden the remedial action could impose. Overall, therefore, the Grand Chamber did not regard

[62] *Kudła v Poland*, (App. 30210/96), 26 October 2000 [GC], (2002) 35 EHRR 198, ECHR 2000-XI.

[63] §§ 155–6.

[64] § 159 refers to the relief being 'either preventive or compensatory'. See also *Krasuski v Poland*, (App. 61444/00), 14 June 2005, § 66.

[65] Examples of violations of Art. 13 in conjunction with Art. 6(1) are: *Čiž v Slovakia*, (App. 66142/01), 14 October 2003; and *Kuzin v Russia*, (App. 22118/02), 9 June 2005.

[66] *McFarlane v Ireland*, (App. 31333/06), 10 September 2010.

[67] *Barry v Ireland*, (App. 18273/04). 15 December 2005.

the possibility of an action for damages for a breach of the constitutional right to reasonable expedition as an effective remedy under Article 13.

In areas other than the excessive length of proceedings, violations of Article 13 will continue to be largely absorbed by Article 6(1).[68]

THE RIGHT TO AN EFFECTIVE INVESTIGATION

In a number of cases,[69] the Court has stated that the exercise of remedies available within the national legal order must not be unjustifiably hindered by the acts or omissions of the authorities of the respondent State. In the *Keenan* case, the Court said:

> Given the fundamental importance of the right to the protection of life, Article 13 requires, in addition to the payment of compensation where appropriate, a thorough and effective investigation capable of leading to the identification and punishment of those responsible for the deprivation of life, including effective access for the complainant to the investigation procedure.[70]

In the *Kaya* case,[71] the applicant's brother had been killed in disputed circumstances by the security forces. A violation of Article 2 was found by reason of the absence of an effective and independent investigation into the death, but the complaint that there was also a violation of Article 13 was then considered. The Court said:

> In particular, where those relatives have an arguable claim that the victim has been unlawfully killed by agents of the State, the notion of an effective remedy for the purposes of Article 13 entails, in addition to the payment of compensation where appropriate, a thorough and effective investigation capable of leading to the identification and punishment of those responsible and including effective access for the relatives to the investigatory procedure. Seen in these terms the requirements of Article 13 are broader than a Contracting State's procedural obligation under Article 2 to conduct an effective investigation.[72]

In *Giuliani and Gaggio v Italy*,[73] however, as the Court had found that an effective domestic investigation satisfying the requirements of promptness and impartiality under Article 2 of the Convention had been conducted into the circumstances surrounding a death, it followed that there had been no violation of Article 13 of the Convention.

What will be crucial is whether the investigation meets the various requirements of effectiveness as a remedy. *El-Masri v The Former Yugoslav Republic of Macedonia*[74] confirms that, where an individual has an arguable claim that he has been ill-treated by agents of the State, the notion of an effective remedy requires a thorough and effective investigation

[68] See, for example, *Mihajlović v Croatia*, (App. 21752/02), 7 July 2005, § 49.

[69] See, for example, *Aksoy v Turkey*, (App. 21987/93), 18 December 1996; (1997) 23 EHRR 553, ECHR 1996-VI, § 95; *Aydin v Turkey*, (App. 23178/94), 25 September 1997; (1998) 25 EHRR 251, ECHR 1997-VI, § 103; and *Kaya v Turkey*, (App. 22729/93), 19 February 1998; (1999) 28 EHRR 1, ECHR 1998-I, § 106.

[70] *Keenan v United Kingdom*, (App. 27229/95), 3 April 2001, (2001) 33 EHRR 913, ECHR 2001-III, § 122.

[71] *Kaya v Turkey*, (App. 22729/93), 19 February 1998; (1999) 28 EHRR 1, ECHR 1998-I. See also *Akdeniz v Turkey*, (App. 25165/94), 31 May 2005; and *Öneryildiz v Turkey*, (App. 48939/99), 30 November 2004 [GC], (2005) 41 EHRR 325, ECHR 2004-XII.

[72] § 107. See also comment in ch.9. A similar approach has been adopted in relation to certain claims falling within Articles 3 (*Assenov and others v Bulgaria*, (App. 24760/94), 28 October 1998, (1999) 28 EHRR 652; ECHR 1998-VIII) and Article 5 (*Kurt v Turkey*, (App. 24276/94), 25 May 1998, (1999) 27 EHRR 373, ECHR 1998-III.) All of these cases have confirmed that the requirements of Article 13 are broader than the procedural obligations under the substantive Articles.

[73] *Giuliani and Gaggio v Italy*, (App. 23458/02), 24 March 2011 [GC].

[74] *El-Masri v The Former Yugoslav Republic Of Macedonia*, (App. 39630/09), 13 December 2012 [GC].

capable of leading to the identification and punishment of those responsible and including effective access for the complainant to the investigatory procedure. In this case, the applicant had been subjected to a secret rendition operation in which the respondent State had arrested him, ill-treated him, and then handed him over to CIA agents who transferred him to a CIA-run secret detention facility in Afghanistan where he was further ill-treated for a number of months. He brought the substance of his grievances to the attention of the public prosecutor but, in the Grand Chamber's view, those complaints were never the subject of any serious investigation and were discounted in favour of a hastily reached explanation that he had never been subjected to the actions of which he complained.[75] It held that the ineffectiveness of the criminal investigation undermined the effectiveness of any other remedy, including a civil action for damages, and found a violation of Article 13, alongside violations of Articles 3, 5, and 8.

These judgments are to be welcomed, since they reflect the realities of the difficulties that are faced by individuals in building a case against powerful State agencies. Those agencies are best placed to collect the information required to determine whether there has been a violation of the rights guaranteed by the Convention. This development in the ambit of Article 13 is a good example of the Court seeking to ensure that Convention rights are practical and effective and not theoretical and illusory. Indeed, in one case,[76] the Court indicated that in some cases only court proceedings might be sufficient to offer sufficiency of redress, noting the strong guarantees of independence offered by such proceedings.

IS COMPENSATION AN INGREDIENT OF AN EFFECTIVE REMEDY?

It is clear that the obligation under Article 13 requires States to provide 'appropriate relief', and that there is some discretion afforded to the Contracting Parties in this regard. The Court has said that the 'nature of the right at stake has implications for the type of remedy' which the State is required to provide.[77] In some cases this must include the possibility of 'compensation for the non-pecuniary damage flowing from the breach' of the Convention. This is particularly so where breaches of Articles 2 and 3 are involved,[78] but would also appear to be a requirement of the remedies available where there has been excessive delay in the administration of justice.[79] The test is whether the remedy is effective in practice, as well as in law. In the *McGlinchey* case,[80] which concerned a death in prison, the respondent State had argued that internal prison remedies met its obligations under Article 13. The Court, however, noted that these would not provide any right to compensation, and that other possible remedies would be ineffective. This was a case in which there had been a breach of Article 3. In such cases compensation for the non-pecuniary damages flowing from the breach should be available as part of the range of possible remedies.[81] A violation of Article 13 in conjunction with Article 3 was found.

[75] § 258.

[76] *Z and others v United Kingdom*, (App. 29392/95), 10 May 2001 [GC], (2002) 34 EHRR 97, ECHR 2001-V, § 110.

[77] *Öneryildiz v Turkey*, (App. 48939/99), 30 November 2004 [GC], (2005) 41 EHRR 325, ECHR 2004-XII, § 147.

[78] *Z and others v United Kingdom*, (App. 29392/95), 10 May 2001, (2002) 34 EHRR 97, ECHR 2001-V, § 109. See also *McGlinchey v United Kingdom*, (App. 50390/99), 29 April 2003, (2003) 37 EHRR 821, ECHR 2003-V, §§ 62–3.

[79] *Kudła v Poland*, (App. 30210/96), 26 October 2000 [GC], (2002) 35 EHRR 198, ECHR 2000-XI; and *Krasuski v Poland*, (App. 61444/00), 14 June 2005.

[80] *McGlinchey v United Kingdom*, (App. 50390/99), 29 April 2003, (2003) 37 EHRR 821, ECHR 2003-V.

[81] § 66.

VIOLATIONS BY PERSONS IN AN OFFICIAL CAPACITY

The last words of Article 13, 'notwithstanding that the violation has been committed by persons acting in an official capacity', show that no defence of State privilege or immunity from suit may be allowed. It has been argued that they also show that the scope of the Convention is not limited to persons exercising public authority.[82]

What is, however, clear is that Article 13 is not concerned with challenges to legislation. Where the source of the grievance is the legislation itself, requiring an effective remedy would be tantamount to allowing judicial review of legislation. The Commission had consistently held that Article 13 has no application in such situations, and the Court has not dissented from that view.[83] To read such a requirement into Article 13 would effectively require the incorporation of the Convention, but where the Convention has been incorporated, there will usually be some process by which the compatibility of legislation can be tested against the requirements of the Convention.[84]

CONCLUDING REMARKS

It has taken longer for real substance to be given to Article 13 through the case-law of the Strasbourg organs than to virtually any other provision of the Convention and its Protocols. In particular, the much more practical approach of the Strasbourg Court in recent years to the determination of whether the remedies allegedly available in the national legal order are, in fact, available as a means of dealing with the alleged violations of Convention rights is to be welcomed.

As Article 13 develops and the Contracting Parties respond, there is scope for its making a contribution to the reduction in the number of cases which result in applications to the Strasbourg Court. Wherever a remedy can be provided for a violation of Convention rights in the national legal order, the matter does not need to be raised at the supranational level. Greater emphasis on remedies in the national legal order will result in the deeper embedding of respect for Convention rights in the national legal orders.[85]

The potential for the development through interpretation of the rights contained in Article 13 remains high. Areas ripe for further interpretation include the determination of compensation where the Court has now said that Article 13 requires compensation to be available within national legal orders; and the extension of the requirement for investigations and remedies that have now been attached to Article 13, particularly in the context

[82] See ch.5.

[83] For example, App. 1080/184, *L v Sweden*, Report of the Commission, 3 October 1988, (1989) 61 DR 62, and see *Leander v Sweden*, (App. 9248/81), 26 March 1987, Series A No 116, (1987) 9 EHRR 433, § 77; *Sigurdur Sigurjonsson v Iceland*, (App. 16130/90), 30 June 1993, Series A No 264, (1993) 16 EHRR 462, § 77 of Commission Opinion, and § 44 of the judgment; and *A v United Kingdom*, (App. 35373/97), 17 December 2002, (2003) 36 EHRR 917, ECHR 2002-X.

[84] See, for example, the possibility of obtaining a declaration of incompatibility in the United Kingdom under s. 4 of the Human Rights Act 1998. The Grand Chamber has confirmed that this does not constitute an effective remedy: *Burden v United Kingdom*, (App. 13378/05), 29 April 2008 [GC], (2008) 47 EHRR 857, ECHR 2008-nyr, §§ 40–4.

[85] L. Helfer, 'Redesigning the European Court of Human Rights: Embeddedness as a Deep Structural Principle of the European Human Rights Regime' (2008) 19 EJIL 125, esp 144–6.

of violations of Articles 2, 3, and 5. This is all about measuring the sufficiency of the guarantees required within the national legal order in order to determine whether what is on offer there constitutes an effective remedy, not only in relation to the substance of the complaints made but also in relation to the relief granted in cases where a violation of a substantive provision is found.

8

THE RIGHT TO LIFE

INTRODUCTION

Article 2 provides:

1. Everyone's right to life shall be protected by law. No-one shall be deprived of his life intentionally save in the execution of a sentence of a court following his conviction of a crime for which this penalty is provided by law.
2. Deprivation of life shall not be regarded as inflicted in contravention of this Article when it results from the use of force which is no more than absolutely necessary:
   (a) in defence of any person from unlawful violence;
   (b) in order to effect a lawful arrest or to prevent the escape of a person lawfully detained;
   (c) in action lawfully taken for the purpose of quelling a riot or insurrection.

The Strasbourg Court observed in the *McCann* case that:

> ... as a provision which not only safeguards the right to life but sets out the circumstances when the deprivation of life may be justified, Article 2 ranks as one of the most fundamental provisions in the Convention.... As such, its provisions must be strictly construed.[1]

It was not until its judgment in the *McCann* case, in September 1994, that the Strasbourg Court had the opportunity to consider the right to life. However, since then an increasingly rich and diverse case-law has developed and the depressingly wide range of circumstances in which the right to life is threatened within modern day Europe has been illustrated.[2] It emerges that a Contracting Party's obligation to safeguard life consists of three main aspects: the duty to refrain from unlawful killing by its agents; the duty to investigate suspicious deaths;[3] and, in certain circumstances, a positive obligation to take steps to prevent the avoidable loss of life.

THE DEATH PENALTY AND THE EXTRATERRITORIAL APPLICATION OF THE RIGHT TO LIFE

In one respect, part of the text of Article 2 has, in practice, been overtaken by provisions in protocols. The second sentence of Article 2(1) reserves the right of Contracting

[1] *McCann and others v United Kingdom*, (App. 18984/91), 27 September 1995, Series A No 324, (1996) 21 EHRR 97, § 97.

[2] On the right to life generally, see D. Korff, *The Right to Life: a Guide to the implementation of Article 2 of the European Convention on Human Rights*, Human Rights Handbooks, No. 8 (Council of Europe Publishing, Strasbourg 2006); B. Mathieu, *The Right to Life* (Council of Europe Publishing, Strasbourg 2006); E. Wicks, *The Right to Life and Conflicting Interests* (OUP, Oxford 2010); and, for some varied legal and ethical perspectives on the right, J. Yorke (ed.), *The Right to Life and the Value of Life: Orientations in Law, Politics and Ethics* (Ashgate, Farnham 2010).

[3] And, if required, to prosecute the perpetrators of an unlawful killing.

Parties to subject convicted criminals to the death penalty.[4] However, Protocol 6 to the Convention abolishes the death penalty in peacetime and Protocol 13 abolishes it in all circumstances. Forty-six Contracting Parties have ratified Protocol 6,[5] and 43 Contracting Parties have ratified Protocol 13.[6] It is the policy of the Council of Europe to require all new Contracting Parties to undertake to abolish capital punishment in peacetime as a condition of their admission into the organization.

In the *Öcalan* case,[7] the Grand Chamber first speculated whether the fact that almost all the Contracting States (at the time) had ratified Protocol 6, and 43 out of 44 of them had abolished capital punishment (with a moratorium on killings in the last remaining Contracting Party, Russia), could be taken as signalling their agreement to modify the second sentence of Article 2(1). In that case it found it unnecessary finally to resolve the point because of its finding that it would be a breach of Article 2 to implement a death sentence after an unfair trial. However, in *Al-Saadoon and Mufdhi v United Kingdom*[8] a Chamber of the Court suggested that the second sentence of Article 2 had now been amended by state practice:

> All but two of the Member States have now signed Protocol No. 13 and all but three of the States which have signed have ratified it. These figures, together with consistent State practice in observing the moratorium on capital punishment, are strongly indicative that Article 2 has been amended so as to prohibit the death penalty in all circumstances. Against this background, the Court does not consider that the wording of the second sentence of Article 2 § 1 continues to act as a bar to its interpreting the words 'inhuman or degrading treatment or punishment' in Article 3 as including the death penalty.[9]

In this case, the Court also declared that, for States bound by the absolute prohibition of the death penalty in all circumstances in Protocol 13, that principle can be regarded as enshrining one of the basic values of the democratic societies making up the Council of Europe (alongside Articles 2 and 3) and therefore its provisions will be strictly construed.

Despite the removal of the death penalty from the European landscape, it remains a potentially live issue before the Court due to the possibility of extradition to States outside Europe where the penalty is retained. If a Contracting Party which has ratified Protocol 6 wishes to extradite an accused to a country where he or she would face judicial execution[10] there will be a risk of a violation of the Protocol,[11] and it may be necessary for the sending State to secure an agreement from the receiving State that the death penalty will not be applied before the extradition can go ahead.

[4] See, on the death penalty generally and human rights, R. Hood and C. Hoyle, *The Death Penalty. A World-Wide Perspective* (4th edn OUP, Oxford 2008); P. Hodgkinson and W.A. Schabas, (eds.), *Capital Punishment: Strategies for Abolition* (CUP, Cambridge 2004); J. Yorke (ed.), *Against the Death Penalty: International Initiatives and Implications* (Ashgate, Farnham 2007); Council of Europe, *Death Penalty. Beyond Abolition* (Council of Europe Publishing, Strasbourg 2004), and J. Yorke, 'The Right to Life and Abolition of the Death Penalty in the Council of Europe' (2009) 34 European Law Review 205.

[5] Protocol 6 had entered into force on receiving five ratifications on 1 March 1985: see http://conventions.coe.int. Russia has signed but not ratified Protocol 6.

[6] Azerbaijan and Russia have not signed the Protocol; Armenia and Poland have signed but not ratified it. Protocol 13 entered into force on 1 July 2003 on receiving ten ratifications.

[7] *Öcalan v Turkey*, (App. 46221/99), 12 May 2005 [GC], (2005) 41 EHRR 985, ECHR 2005-IV, §§ 163–6.

[8] *Al-Saadoon and Mufdhi v United Kingdom*, (App. 61498/08), 2 March 2010 [GC], ECHR 2010 (extracts).

[9] § 120.

[10] As had been the case in *Soering v United Kingdom*, 7 July 1989, Series A No 161, (1989) 11 EHRR 439; see ch.9.

[11] See, for example, *Nivette v France*, (App. 44190/98), Decision of 3 July 2001, ECHR 2001-VII; and *Bader and Kanbor v Sweden*, (App. 13284/04), 8 November 2005, (2008) 46 EHRR 197, ECHR 2005-XI, §§ 41–2.

Furthermore, Article 2 has a general extraterritorial application, to protect those liable to expulsion not just from the death penalty, but from any real risk of deliberate killing.[12]

PROHIBITION OF INTENTIONAL KILLING BY THE STATE

The first and most obvious element of a Contracting Party's obligation under Article 2 is to refrain, through its agents, from deliberate, unjustified killing.

This aspect was considered by the Strasbourg Court in the *McCann* case,[13] which was brought by the relatives of three Irish Republican terrorists who had been killed by members of the British security forces in Gibraltar. It was not disputed that the soldiers had intended to shoot and kill the terrorists; according to the briefing which the soldiers had been given, the terrorists had planted a car bomb in a crowded area and were likely to have been carrying a concealed detonator, which would have allowed them to explode the bomb at the touch of a button. This briefing proved to be based on inaccurate information: they were not carrying a detonator at the time of the shooting. The respondent State claimed that the facts fell within the ambit of paragraph 2(a) of Article 2: killings resulting from the use of force which was no more than absolutely necessary to defend a number of innocent bystanders from unlawful violence. The Court held that the use of the phrase 'absolutely necessary' in paragraph 2 indicated that the force used had to be strictly proportionate to the achievement of one of the aims set out in sub-paragraphs 2(a)–(c). Given this strict test, it was not sufficient for the person administering the force honestly to believe that his or her actions were valid; this belief had also to be based on 'good reasons' in the light of the information available at the relevant time.

The Court accepted that the soldiers were not to blame, in that they honestly and reasonably believed that it was necessary to shoot the suspects to prevent them from detonating a bomb. However, the Court widened the field of scrutiny to look at the security operation in its entirety. The identities of the three members of the terrorist squad were known to the British authorities, and it would have been possible to arrest them as they entered Gibraltar, before there was any risk of their having set a car bomb. Looking at all the facts, therefore, the Court concluded that it had not been necessary to use lethal force and that the killings amounted to a violation of Article 2.

The planning of an operation was also crucial in the interesting case of *Finogenov and others v Russia*[14] concerning events during the hostage crisis in Moscow on 23–26 October 2002 in which a group of terrorists belonging to the Chechen separatist movement, armed with machine-guns and explosives, took hostages in the Dubrovka theatre. For three days more than 900 people were held at gunpoint in the theatre's auditorium. In addition, the theatre building was booby-trapped and eighteen suicide bombers were positioned in the hall among the hostages. In the early morning of 26 October 2002, the Russian security forces pumped an unknown narcotic gas into the main auditorium through the building's ventilation system. A few minutes later, when the terrorists controlling the explosive devices and the suicide bombers in the auditorium lost consciousness under the influence

[12] See also the discussion of the extraterritorial application of Article 3 in ch.9.

[13] *McCann and others v United Kingdom*, (App. 18984/91), (App. 18984/91), 27 September 1995, Series A No 324, (1996) 21 EHRR 97.

[14] *Finogenov and others v Russia*, (App. 18299/03 and 27311/03), 20 December 2011, ECHR 2011 (extracts).

of the gas, the Russian forces stormed the building. Most of the suicide bombers were shot while unconscious; others tried to resist but were killed in the ensuing gunfire. Most of the hostages survived, although exact numbers were unknown. However, a significant number of hostages were affected by the gas, and over 100 died as a result, some because of inadequate medical assistance at the scene.

The applicants alleged that the Russian authorities had applied excessive force, which had resulted in the death of their relatives who were being held hostage by the terrorists in the Dubrovka theatre. The applicants further claimed that the authorities had failed to plan and conduct the rescue operation in such a way as to minimize the risks for the hostages.[15] The Court chose to apply different degrees of scrutiny to different aspects of the situation. As the hostage-taking itself came as a surprise for the authorities, the military preparations for the storming had to be made quickly and in secrecy and the authorities were not in control of the situation inside the building. In such a situation the Court accepted that 'difficult and agonising decisions had to be made by the domestic authorities' and was 'prepared to grant them a margin of appreciation, at least in so far as the military and technical aspects of the situation are concerned, even if now, with hindsight, some of the decisions taken by the authorities may appear open to doubt.'[16] In contrast, the subsequent phases of the operation, especially when no serious time constraints existed and the authorities were in control of the situation, required closer scrutiny by the Court.[17]

The Court concluded that there existed a real, serious, and immediate risk of mass human losses and that therefore the authorities' decision to storm the building could be justified under Article 2(2). Similarly, the use of gas during the storming was not regarded by the Court as a disproportionate measure. The Court took care to distinguish this case from the *Isayeva* one, considered later, in which the indiscriminate use of heavy weapons in anti-terrorist operations was condemned as 'incompatible with the standard of care prerequisite to an operation involving use of lethal force by State agents'.[18]The Court pointed out that the use of airborne bombs to destroy a rebel group which was hiding in a village full of civilians, was very different from the use of gas against a group consisting of hostages and hostage-takers, as even though the gas was potentially lethal, it was not, in the Court's view, used 'indiscriminately' as it left the hostages a high chance of survival, dependent on the efficiency of the authorities' rescue effort.[19] Whether this distinction is merited seems debatable but the implications of it are lessened by the Court's closer scrutiny of the rescue effort.

While acknowledging the need to keep certain aspects of the operation secret, the Court concluded that in the circumstances the rescue operation was not sufficiently prepared, in particular because of the inadequate information exchange between various services, the belated start of the evacuation, limited on-the-field coordination of various services, lack of appropriate medical treatment and equipment on the spot, and inadequate logistics.[20] These failings amounted to a breach of the State's positive obligations under Article 2. Most notably, the mass evacuation of hostages from the theatre started at least one hour and twenty minutes after the gas had been dispersed, which raised unanswered questions about why the evacuation was so delayed and also why additional preparations had not been made during that period, such as informing the medics of the use of gas and preparing appropriate medicines. Thus, while the Court held unanimously that there had been

[15] There was an additional claim relating to the effectiveness of the criminal investigation into the authorities' actions.

[16] § 213. [17] § 214.

[18] *Isayeva v Russia*, (App. 57950/00), 25 February 2005, (2005) 41 EHRR 791, § 191. [19] § 232.

[20] § 266.

no violation of Article 2 in respect of the decision by the Russian authorities to resolve the hostage crisis by force and to use the gas, it did find a violation in respect of the inadequate planning and conduct of the rescue operation.

While the Court is tolerant of honest mistakes, based on good reasons, as to the level of force absolutely necessary in particular circumstances, it is far less likely that an honest mistake as to the very existence of a threat will be regarded as justifying a killing by State agents. This can be demonstrated by *Gül v Turkey*,[21] where police officers opened fire at an unknown target behind a closed door in a residential apartment. While it was possible that the officers had mistaken the sound of the door bolt being drawn back for the sound of the occupant of the flat opening fire at them, their reaction was held to be grossly disproportionate.[22] The Court unanimously found a violation of Article 2 in that case and distinguished it from the earlier case of *Andronicou and Constantinou v Cyprus*[23] where it was held not to be disproportionate for the police to open fire at an identified hostage-taker who was known to be in possession of a gun and had already fired at an officer.[24]

There was also a finding of no violation in the Grand Chamber decision in the controversial case of *Giuliani and Gaggio v Italy*.[25] The applicants were relatives of Carlo Giuliani, who was shot and killed during the demonstrations on the fringes of the G8 summit in Genoa in July 2001. Following numerous clashes between demonstrators and the law-enforcement agencies, a jeep carrying two carabinieri, M.P. and D.R., who were unfit to remain on duty, became isolated amongst the demonstrators, who surrounded and attacked the vehicle. M.P. was injured and panic-stricken in the back of the vehicle and could not see that troops were nearby. He showed his pistol by stretching out his hand in the direction of the jeep's rear window, and shouted at the demonstrators to leave unless they wanted to be killed. As the Grand Chamber explained:

> In this extremely tense situation Carlo Giuliani decided to pick up a fire extinguisher which was lying on the ground, and raised it to chest height with the apparent intention of throwing it at the occupants of the vehicle. His actions could reasonably be interpreted by M.P. as an indication that, despite the latter's shouted warnings and the fact that he had shown his gun, the attack on the jeep was not about to cease or diminish in intensity. Moreover, the vast majority of the demonstrators appeared to be continuing the assault. M.P.'s honest belief that his life was in danger could only have been strengthened as a result. In the Court's view, this served as justification for recourse to a potentially lethal means of defence such as the firing of shots.[26]

M.P fired into the air—the only angle possible from his position in the rear of the vehicle—and apparently a bullet was deflected and hit Carlo Giuliani, killing him. The Court concluded that the use of lethal force had been absolutely necessary in defence of any person from unlawful violence within the meaning of Article 2(2)(a) of the Convention.[27]

Dissenting judges in the case[28] point out that M.P. could not see Carlo Giuliani lifting the fire extinguisher and thus that could not serve as a justification for opening fire. They

[21] *Gül v Turkey*, (App. 22676/93), 14 December 2000. [22] § 82.

[23] *Andronicou and Constantinou v Cyprus*, (App. 25052/94), (1997) 25 EHRR 491; ECHR 1997-VI.

[24] See also *Ramsahai and others v The Netherlands*, (App. 52391/99), 15 May 2007 [GC], (2008) 46 EHRR 983, ECHR 2007; *Huohvainen v Finland*, (App. 57389/00), 13 March 2007, (2008) 47 EHRR 974; *Bubbins v United Kingdom* ECHR 2005–II.

[25] *Giuliani and Gaggio v Italy*, (App. 23458/02), 24 March 2011 [GC], ECHR 2011 (extracts).

[26] § 191.

[27] The Court also found no violation on account of the organization and planning of the policing operations during the G8 summit in Genoa, nor of the procedural aspect of Article 2 in respect of the subsequent investigation. [28] Judges Tulkens, Zupančič, Gyulumyan, and Karakaş.

also note that if the shots were truly fired into the air, they were mere warning shots and justification under Article 2(2) would be unnecessary. On the other hand, if the shots were fired at chest height—and the evidence is unclear—they were not, in the view of the dissenting judges, absolutely necessary under Article 2(2). These judges also, with good reason, criticize the majority for considering only the unlawful violence defence as if this was an individual use of violence. They argue it should instead be set in its proper context of force used to quell a riot or insurrection and its absolute necessity should be assessed in relation to that purpose.

Article 2 can be engaged even where no death actually occurs. In the *Makaratzis* case,[29] the applicant, who drove his car through a red traffic light in the centre of Athens, was chased by several police cars and motorcycles. When he failed to stop, the police shot at his car, hitting him in the right arm, right foot, left buttock, and chest. The Strasbourg Court observed that it was only by sheer good luck that the applicant had not been killed, and that Article 2 therefore applied. It was prepared to accept that the use of lethal force had been reasonable in the circumstances, since the police appeared to believe that the applicant was himself armed and dangerous. However, the Court was 'struck with the chaotic way in which the firearms were actually used', with a large number of officers acting erratically and uncontrollably, without a clear chain of command. The Court also found that the domestic law, as it then stood, contained insufficient guidance as to the use of firearms by the police.

More recently, the Court has again found a violation of Article 2 in circumstances where no death occurred. In *Sašo Gorgiev v The Former Yugoslav Republic of Macedonia*[30] the applicant was shot at close range by a police reservist in a bar where he was working. He was hit in the chest and suffered serious life-threatening injuries but survived. The Court concluded that, in the circumstances of this case, the State was responsible for the unlawful actions of its agents outside their official duties. The incident occurred during the reservist's working hours when he was supposed to be on duty in the police station; he was in uniform, and armed with his service weapon. He had left his place of duty without the authorization of his superiors and, while intoxicated, engaged in dangerous behaviour putting the applicant's life at risk. The State was held responsible under Article 2 for these actions, even though they were not officially sanctioned and did not result in death, arguably a twofold expansion of State liability under the right to life.[31]

Excessive use of force in all the circumstances of the case will result in a finding of a violation of Article 2, as in the *Nikolova and Velichkova* case,[32] in which a 63-year-old man was hit over the head by the police after being spotted by police testing a home-made metal detector; he died from severe cranial and cerebral trauma and internal brain haemorrhaging. It would also seem that suspect restraint techniques used by the police—being handcuffed in front of the body and immobilized by being pinned on the stomach by the use of the combined body weight of a number of officers—coupled with a failure to respond to a medical crisis which led to the death of the victim by slow asphyxia, can give rise to a violation of

[29] *Makaratzis v Greece*, (App. 50385/99), 20 December 2004 [GC], (2005) 41 EHRR 1092, ECHR 2004-XI.

[30] *Sašo Gorgiev v The Former Yugoslav Republic of Macedonia*, (App. 49382/06), 19 April 2012, ECHR 2012 (extracts).

[31] *Gorovenky and Bugara v Ukraine*, (App. 36146/05 and 42418/05), 12 January 2012 is a similar case in which the applicants' relatives were shot by a police officer who was off-duty. The Court again found the State liable on the basis that it had failed to exercise the requisite control over the procedure for equipping police officers with a weapon, in particular by failing to exercise sufficient scrutiny over the selection of agents allowed to carry firearms.

[32] *Nikolova and Velichkova v Bulgaria*, (App. 7888/03), 20 December 2007, (2009) 48 EHRR 915.

Article 2.[33] In relation to Article 2(2)(b), the use of lethal force will not be regarded as absolutely necessary to prevent the escape of a detainee from lawful detention who poses no threat to life or limb and is not suspected of having committed a violent offence.[34]

It appears that the Court will itself examine the circumstances of a killing by State officials only where there is evidence that, for some reason, the domestic judicial system is inadequate or unable to uncover the truth. In the *Hugh Jordan* case,[35] it took into account the fact that civil proceedings brought by the applicant against the police regarding the killing of his son by a police officer in Northern Ireland were still pending, and explained that it would be inappropriate and contrary to its subsidiary role under the Convention to attempt to establish the facts of this case by embarking on a fact-finding exercise of its own by summoning witnesses. Such an exercise would duplicate the proceedings before the civil courts which are better placed and equipped as fact-finding tribunals.[36] The Strasbourg Court distinguished the case from those brought against Turkey where the Commission had embarked on fact-finding missions where there were pending proceedings against the alleged security force perpetrators of unlawful killings. In the *Hugh Jordan* case, there was no evidence to show that the civil courts would be unable to establish the facts and determine whether the killing had been lawful.

DEATH IN CUSTODY AND FORCED DISAPPEARANCE

History has shown that, in the absence of safeguards against abuse of power, it is all too easy for the State to cover up its own unlawful violence, particularly when that violence is carried out behind closed doors. The protection afforded by Article 2 would be of no value if a State could avoid international sanction by concealing the evidence of killings caused by its agents. Where an individual is known to have been taken into custody and subsequently disappears or is found dead, therefore, it is logical that a heavy burden should fall on the State to establish an innocent explanation.[37]

According to Amnesty International, following an analysis of the relevant international instruments, the crime of 'disappearances' has the following elements: (1) a deprivation of liberty, (2) effected by government agents or with their consent or acquiescence, followed by, (3) an absence of information or refusal to acknowledge the deprivation of liberty or refusal to disclose the fate or whereabouts of the person, (4) thereby placing such persons outside the protection of the law.[38] The Inter-American Court of Human Rights has held that 'the phenomenon of disappearances is a complex form of human rights violation', including breaches of the right to life and the right not to be subjected to ill-treatment, 'that must be understood and confronted in an integral fashion'.[39] The gravity of the violations of rights attendant on a disappearance has led the United Nations Human Rights

[33] *Saoud v France*, (App. 9375/02), 9 October 2007, ECHR 2007-XI.

[34] *Nachova and others v Bulgaria*, (App. 43577/98 and 43579/98), ECHR 2005-VII [GC]; *Putintseva v Russia*, (App. 33498/04), 10 May 2012.

[35] *Hugh Jordan v United Kingdom*, (App. 24746/94), 4 May 2001, (2003) 37 EHRR 52, ECHR 2001-III.

[36] § 111.

[37] See the judgment of the Inter-American Court of Human Rights in *Velásquez Rodríguez v Honduras*, 29 July 1988, Inter-Am. Ct. H. R. (Series C) No. 4 (1988).

[38] See Amnesty International's written submissions to the Strasbourg Court in connection with the case of *Kurt v Turkey*, (App. 24276/94), 25 May 1998; (1999) 27 EHRR 373, ECHR 1998-III, §§ 68–71.

[39] *Velásquez Rodríguez v Honduras*, 29 July 1988, Inter-Am. Ct. H. R. (Series C) No. 4 (1988).

Committee to conclude in relation to Article 6 of the International Covenant on Civil and Political Rights that State Parties should take specific and effective measures to prevent them occurring and thoroughly to investigate any case of a missing or disappeared person which may involve a violation of the right to life.[40] Against this background, it is arguable that the Strasbourg organs were disappointingly timid in their treatment of the first case of a disappearance to come before them.[41] The Commission and Court both accepted that it had been proved beyond reasonable doubt that the applicant's son had last been seen some four and a half years earlier surrounded by soldiers during a security operation in his village in south-east Turkey. The Court moreover conceded that in these circumstances the applicant's fears that her son might have died in unacknowledged custody at the hands of his captors could not be said to be without foundation. Nonetheless, it declined to find a breach of Article 2 in the absence of concrete evidence that the young man had been killed by the authorities. Instead, it opted for 'a particularly grave violation of the right to liberty and security of person under Article 5 raising serious concerns about the welfare of [the applicant's son]'.

In more recent cases, however, the Court has been much more robust. In the *Timurtas* case,[42] the applicant alleged that his son had been taken into custody in August 1993 and had subsequently disappeared. He had filed a complaint with the Turkish authorities but the public prosecutor had decided not to investigate, because the applicant was unable to substantiate his allegations and because it was likely that his son was a member of a Kurdish terrorist organization. The respondent State denied that the applicant's son had ever been arrested and produced in support the custody records of the local police station, army headquarters, and interrogation centre—none of which contained any mention of the young man. A delegation from the Commission travelled to south-east Turkey to take evidence. The applicant was unable to find any eyewitness to testify to the arrest and detention of his son. He did, however, produce a photocopy of a document purporting to be an army post-operational report recording his son's arrest. The respondent State disputed the document's authenticity, claiming that the reference number in truth belonged to another, quite different, document, but refusing to produce this second document for security reasons.

The Strasbourg Court acknowledged the risk inherent in relying for proof almost entirely on a photocopy. However, it held that the respondent State's failure, without satisfactory explanation, to disclose evidence which it claimed to hold gave rise to an inference that the photocopied report was genuine, and that the applicant's son had been arrested. The Court next considered whether, in the absence of a body, any issue could arise under Article 2, concluding that this would depend on all the facts of the case, in particular whether there was sufficient circumstantial evidence pointing towards death in custody. In this respect the length of time which had elapsed since the person had been placed in detention, although not decisive, was highly relevant, since the more time which passed without any news, the greater was the likelihood that he had died. Given that more than six and a half years had gone by since the applicant's son had been arrested and that the respondent State was unable to provide any explanation of what had happened to him, the Court found a violation of Article 2.[43]

[40] General Comment 6 (Sixteenth Session 1982), 37 UN GAOR, Supp. No. 40 (A/37/40) Annex V, para. 1.

[41] *Kurt v Turkey*, (App. 24276/94), 25 May 1998, (1999) 27 EHRR 373, ECHR 1998-III.

[42] *Timurtaş v Turkey*, (App. 23531/94), 13 June 2000, (2001) 33 EHRR 121, ECHR 2000-VI.

[43] See also *ER and others v Turkey*, (App. 23016/04), 31 July 2012 in which another disappearance of a person in south-east Turkey in the 1990s after being taken into detention was held to amount to a violation of Article 2 in both substantive and procedural aspects.

The same principle applies *a fortiori* where there is clear evidence of a death in custody. In the *Salman* case,[44] the applicant's husband was arrested at midnight on 28 April 1992 on suspicion of aiding and abetting Kurdish terrorists. Twenty-four hours later he was taken to the State Hospital where he was declared dead on arrival. The hospital autopsy disclosed various marks and bruises, including a broken sternum, but did not determine the cause of death. The case was referred to the Istanbul Forensic Institute which concluded that the applicant's husband had died of a heart attack brought on by the effect of his arrest on a pre-existing heart condition. The applicant claimed that photographs of the corpse taken by the family showed that her husband had been beaten on the soles of his feet. Ten police officers were acquitted of homicide by the Adana Aggravated Felony Court on the basis that there was inadequate evidence of any use of torture. The Strasbourg Court observed that where a person was taken into custody in good health and then died, the obligation on the Contracting Party to provide a satisfactory account was particularly stringent. Since the respondent State was unable to explain how the applicant's husband had come by his injuries and since the evidence did not support the contention that he had died of a heart attack caused by the stress of arrest, the Court found the respondent State to have violated Article 2.

In *Mižigárová v Slovakia*,[45] the applicant's husband died after receiving a fatal gunshot wound while in police custody. The parties disputed whether this was fired by the armed police officer who was interrogating the suspect or was the result of suicide, but the Court took the view that whichever possibility was correct, the State had failed in its Article 2 obligations.

RESPONDING TO INTERNAL ARMED INSURGENCY: THE CASE OF CHECHNYA

In recent years, the Strasbourg Court has delivered many judgments arising from events in what has been labelled the second Chechen War.[46] The first Chechen War began in 1994 when Russian troops acted to restore constitutional order in Chechnya in the face of declared independence by Chechnya following the dissolution of the Soviet Union in 1991. A cease fire agreement in 1996 led to the withdrawal of Russian troops. The constitutional status of Chechnya remained that of part of the Russian Federation but there was no stability following the cease fire and, in 1997, a separatist president was elected in Chechnya. In August and September 1999, Russia conducted a campaign of aerial bombardment over Chechnya, leading to significant civilian loss of life. A land offensive began in October 1999 directed at the main city of Grozny, and at Gudermes, Chechnya's second largest city, as well as other parts of Chechnya. By the spring of 2000, Russian troops were largely in control of Chechnya; and in May 2000 President Putin established direct rule of Chechnya. This did not end the insurgency, which was continued by Chechen separatists.

[44] *Salman v Turkey*, (App. 21986/93), 27 June 2000 [GC], (2002) 34 EHRR 425, ECHR 2000-VII. See also *Abdurrahman Orak v Turkey*, (App. 31889/96), 14 February 2002; and *Anguelova v Bulgaria*, (App. 38361/97), 13 June 2002, (2004) 38 EHRR 659, ECHR 2002-IV. In the latter case, the Court found a separate violation based on the failure of the police to get the applicant speedy medical assistance after he collapsed from a head injury.

[45] *Mižigárová v Slovakia*, (App. 74832/01), 14 December 2010.

[46] For a discussion of the case-law arising from this situation, see P. Leach, 'The Chechen conflict: analysing the oversight of the European Court of Human Rights' [2008] EHRLR 732. An appendix to the article lists the judgments of the Strasbourg Court up to 3 July 2008.

At no time did Russia seek to derogate from any provisions of the Convention. It characterized its actions as 'counter-terrorist operations'.

The human cost of the war was substantial loss of civilian life, displacement of hundreds of thousands of people, allegations of torture and war crimes from both sides in the conflict, and significant violations of international humanitarian law. The character of the Russian action has been described by the Strasbourg Court as a response to an illegal armed insurgency:

> 180. The Court accepts that the situation that existed in Chechnya at the relevant time called for exceptional measures by the State in order to regain control over the Republic and to suppress the illegal armed insurgency. Given the context of the conflict in Chechnya at the relevant time, those measures could presumably include the deployment of army units equipped with combat weapons, including military aviation and artillery. The presence of a very large group of armed fighters in Katyr-Yurt, and their active resistance to the law-enforcement bodies, which are not disputed by the parties, may have justified use of lethal force by the agents of the State, thus bringing the situation within paragraph 2 of Article 2.
>
> 181. Accepting that the use of force may have been justified in the present case, it goes without saying that a balance must be achieved between the aim pursued and the means employed to achieve it. The Court will now consider whether the actions in the present case were no more than absolutely necessary for achieving the declared purpose....[47]

The use of aerial bombardment of an area containing a civilian population requires special justification. The Strasbourg Court said:

> ...According to the servicemen's statements, bombs and other non-guided heavy combat weapons were used against targets both in the centre and on the edges of the village....
>
> 191. The Court considers that using this kind of weapon in a populated area, outside wartime and without prior evacuation of the civilians, is impossible to reconcile with the degree of caution expected from a law-enforcement body in a democratic society. No martial law and no state of emergency has been declared in Chechnya, and no derogation has been made under Article 15 of the Convention...The operation in question therefore has to be judged against a normal legal background. Even when faced with a situation where, as the Government submit, the population of the village had been held hostage by a large group of well-equipped and well-trained fighters, the primary aim of the operation should be to protect lives from unlawful violence. The massive use of indiscriminate weapons stands in flagrant contrast with this aim and cannot be considered compatible with the standard of care prerequisite to an operation of this kind involving the use of lethal force by State agents.[48]

The applications to the Strasbourg Court raising violations of Article 2 have involved complaints of mass killings of civilians, disappearances, extrajudicial executions, and failures to investigate. The response of the Russian authorities has been to deny responsibility and to refuse to cooperate with the Court,[49] although in some cases the respondent State has

[47] *Isayeva v Russia*, (App. 57950/00), 25 February 2005, (2005) 41 EHRR 791, §§ 180–1.

[48] §§ 190–1.

[49] And the respondent State has been found to be in breach of its duties under Article 38 to furnish the Court with all necessary facilities to enable it to pursue the examination of the case in many of the cases coming before the Court. This had led the Court to draw adverse inferences in many of the cases.

suggested that the victims were members of paramilitary groups, but has failed to provide any credible evidence to establish this.[50]

The *Imakayeva* case[51] is a typical disappearance case. The applicant complained of the disappearance of her son and husband. The day after the disappearance, the authorities were asked to assist and to investigate; efforts were made to find the missing men by visiting detention centres and prisons. The applicant was subsequently told that investigations had failed to establish the whereabouts of the missing men, although she was also told that her husband had been detained by military personnel but subsequently released, and her son had been detained on suspicion of being a member of a bandit group. The Strasbourg Court found violations of Article 2 both in respect of the disappearances,[52] and in respect of the failure to conduct an effective investigation into the circumstances in which they had disappeared.[53]

THE POSITIVE OBLIGATION TO PROTECT LIFE

In the *LCB* case,[54] the Strasbourg Court recognized for the first time that the first sentence of Article 2(1) enjoins a Contracting Party not only to refrain from the intentional and unlawful taking of life, but also to take appropriate steps to safeguard the lives of those within their jurisdiction. This was an important statement of principle, despite the fact that the applicant was unable to prove either that her father's service in the Royal Air Force during the United Kingdom's nuclear tests on Christmas Island in 1957–8 had been the cause of her childhood leukaemia or that, had the respondent State provided her family with more information about the tests and the possible health consequences, earlier medical intervention would have mitigated her illness.

More recent cases have demonstrated that the State's duty to safeguard life is extensive.[55] In the *Öneryildiz* case, the Grand Chamber went so far as to hold:

> . . . that this obligation [to take appropriate steps to safeguard the lives of those within the State's jurisdiction] must be construed as applying in the context of any activity, whether public or not, in which the right to life may be at stake, . . .[56]

The obligation entails, at its most basic, a duty to put in place a legislative and administrative framework designed to provide effective deterrence against unlawful killing.[57] Thus, Turkey was at fault in cases involving the murder of a journalist working for a Kurdish separatist newspaper and a doctor known to have treated members of the Kurdish terrorist

[50] In the recent case of *Maskhadova and others v Russia*, (App. 18071/05), 6 June 2013, the applicants alleged that the respondent Government had been directly responsible for the death of Aslan Maskhadov, one of the military and political leaders of the Chechen separatist movement and the elected President of the so-called Chechen Republic of Ichkeriya. However, the Court found no proof to support the applicants' allegations and was satisfied that the official investigation into the death met the procedural requirements of Article 2.

[51] *Imakayeva v Russia*, (App. 7615/02), 9 November 2006, (2008) 47 EHRR 139, ECHR 2006-XIII.

[52] Described as 'life-threatening' in the particular circumstances.

[53] See further later in this chapter on the duty to investigate and the shortcomings of official investigations into disappearances in Chechnya.

[54] *LCB v United Kingdom*, (App. 23413/94), 9 June 1998; (1998) 27 EHRR 212, ECHR 1998-III.

[55] For a parallel obligation under Article 8, see *Guerra v Italy*, (App. 14967/89), 19 February 1998, (1998) 26 EHRR 357, ECHR 1998-I; see ch.16.

[56] *Öneryildiz v Turkey*, (App. 48939/99), 30 November 2004 [GC], (2005) 41 EHRR 325, ECHR 2004-XII, § 72.

[57] § 89.

organization, the PKK.[58] In both cases the applicants alleged that their brothers had been assassinated by members of the State security forces, but this could not be proved. The Strasbourg Court did, however, find that the authorities were aware that journalists, doctors, and others associated with the PKK and Kurdish separatism had been the object of a campaign of serious attacks and threats, possibly emanating from or carried out with the acquiescence of the security forces. Although there was a framework of law in place aimed at the protection of life (criminal law, police, prosecutor, and courts), at the relevant time the implementation of the criminal justice system in south-east Turkey was seriously undermined by various Emergency Rule measures (including the transfer of jurisdiction away from the courts to councils of civil servants and a series of failures to investigate allegations of wrongdoing by the members of the security forces). This situation fostered a dangerous lack of accountability among members of the security forces and removed the protection which the applicants' brothers should have received by law.

In addition, an obligation to take action to avert a specific risk to a particular individual's life may arise in certain, limited circumstances. This can arise in both individual cases, and in more general situations, such as the planning of the policing of a known demonstration at an international event, such as a G8 summit.[59]

The *Osman* case[60] is an example of an individual situation. The applicants' family had become the target of a dangerous stalker, who eventually broke into their home and shot and killed their husband and father. Bearing in mind the difficulties in policing modern society, the unpredictability of human conduct, and the need for the police to act within the confines imposed on them by, *inter alia*, Articles 5 and 8 of the Convention, the Strasbourg Court defined this particular aspect of the duty to protect life rather narrowly. It considered that the authorities could be said to be in breach of Article 2 in this context only if it could be established that they knew or ought to have known at the relevant time of the existence of a real and immediate risk to the life of an identified individual or individuals from the criminal acts of a third party, and that they failed to take measures within the scope of their powers which, judged reasonably, might have been expected to avoid that risk. In the instant case, the applicants were not able to point to any decisive stage in the sequence of events leading to the shooting when it could be said that the police knew or ought to have known that the lives of the Osman family were at real and immediate risk, and the police could not be criticized for attaching weight to the presumption of innocence and the rights of the stalker in the absence of any concrete evidence against him.

By contrast, in *Opuz v Turkey*[61] a violation of Article 2's positive obligation was identified. In this case, the applicant alleged that the Turkish authorities had failed to protect her and her mother from domestic violence which had resulted in the death of her mother. The victims' situations were known to the authorities and the mother had submitted a petition to the Chief Public Prosecutor's Office, stating that her life was in immediate danger and requesting the police to take action. The authorities' only response was to take statements from the perpetuator about the allegations. Two weeks later, he killed the applicant's mother. The Court found that the authorities could have foreseen a lethal attack and thus their responsibility to take reasonable steps to mitigate the harm was engaged.

[58] *Kiliç v Turkey*, (App. 22492/93), 28 March 2000, (2001) 33 EHRR 1357, ECHR 2000-III; and *Mahmut Kaya v Turkey*, (App. 22535/93), 28 March 2000, ECHR 2000-III.

[59] See *Giuliani and Gaggio v Italy*, (App. 23458/02) 24 March 2011 [GC], ECHR 2011 (extracts), discussed earlier, though no violation of the positive obligation to protect life was found in this case, which involved the policing of G8 protests in Genoa in July 2001.

[60] *Osman v United Kingdom*, (App. 23452/94), 28 October 1998, (1998) 29 EHRR 245, ECHR 1998-VIII.

[61] *Opuz v Turkey*, (App. 33401/02), 9 June 2009, ECHR 2009.

The Government claimed that any further interference by the authorities would have amounted to a breach of the victims' Article 8 rights. The Court was very dismissive of this argument, reiterating that sometimes interference with private or family life of individuals might be necessary in order to protect the health and rights of others or to prevent commission of criminal acts. In particular, the Court underlined that 'in domestic violence cases perpetrators' rights cannot supersede victims' human rights to life and to physical and mental integrity'.[62] The Court also reiterated that 'once the situation has been brought to their attention, the national authorities cannot rely on the victim's attitude for their failure to take adequate measures which could prevent the likelihood of an aggressor carrying out his threats against the physical integrity of the victim.'[63] The Turkish authorities were found to have failed in their positive obligation to protect the right to life of the applicant's mother within the meaning of Article 2 (and further violations were found of Article 3 and Article 14).

The Court has also held a State responsible under Article 2 when a death occurs after the premature release of a person from detention without a proper assessment of risk. In *Branko Tomašić and others v Croatia*[64] the applicants were the relatives of M.T. and her infant child, V.T., who were both killed in August 2006 by M. M., the child's father. On 15 March 2006, a court had found M.M. guilty of repeatedly threatening to kill himself, M.T. and their child with a bomb. He was sentenced to five months' imprisonment and ordered to have compulsory psychiatric treatment during his imprisonment and afterwards as necessary (although a second-instance court reduced that treatment to the duration of his prison sentence). M.M. served his sentence, during which no adequate psychiatric treatment was provided to him. He was released on 3 July 2006 but there was no assessment of his condition immediately prior to his release with a view to assessing the risk that he might carry out his previous threats. On 15 August 2006 he fatally shot M.T. and V.T., before committing suicide. The Court considered that no adequate measures were taken to diminish the likelihood of M.M. carrying out his threats upon his release from prison and found that the Croatian authorities had failed in their Article 2 obligations to take all necessary and reasonable steps in the circumstances to protect the lives of M.T. and V.T.

In the *Keenan* case,[65] the risk to life came from the victim himself, a young man with mental health problems who committed suicide in prison. The Strasbourg Court emphasized that prisoners are in a vulnerable position and that the authorities are under a duty to protect them,[66] and noted that this necessity is reflected in English law, where inquests are automatically held following all deaths in custody. In Keenan's case, the prison administration had acted reasonably to protect him from himself. They knew that he was prone to psychotic flare-ups, and during the periods when he appeared to be suicidal, they had placed him on the hospital wing and checked him every fifteen minutes. On the day when he killed himself, he had been returned to an ordinary cell because he did not appear to be in any particular trouble.[67]

In *Reynolds v United Kingdom*[68] the Court accepted there was an 'arguable claim' under Article 2 (and the denial of an effective remedy under Article 13) where the applicant's

[62] § 147. [63] § 153.

[64] *Branko Tomašić and others v Croatia*, (App. 46598/06), 15 January 2009.

[65] *Keenan v United Kingdom*, (App. 27229/95), 3 April 2001, (2001) 33 EHRR 913, ECHR 2001-III.

[66] See also *Paul and Audrey Edwards v United Kingdom*, (App. 46477/99), 14 March 2002, (2002) 35 EHRR 487, ECHR 2002-II, where the Court found a violation of Article 2 based on the prison authorities' negligence in locking the applicants' son in a cell with an extremely violent and mentally ill offender.

[67] See also *Renolde v France*, (App. 5608/05), 16 October 2008, (2009) 48 EHRR 969.

[68] *Reynolds v The United Kingdom*, (App. 2694/08), 13 March 2012.

son, who had a history of schizophrenia, committed suicide after being assessed as a low suicide risk and transferred to a sixth floor psychiatric unit from where he broke a window and fell to his death. The Court accepted that there was an arguable claim that an operational duty had arisen to take reasonable steps to protect the applicant's son from a real and immediate risk of suicide and that that duty was not fulfilled. Domestic case-law at the time in the UK drew a distinction between detained and voluntary mental patients, since removed by a Supreme Court decision.[69] The Court's finding of a violation in this case casts doubts upon the acceptability of such a distinction and yet its removal carries a State duty to prevent suicide beyond the ambit of persons within the control of the State and arguably risks extending a duty to prevent suicide to an arena in which it may conflict with duties under Article 8 to respect autonomous decisions about death.

It may be difficult for an applicant to establish the precise circumstances surrounding a death and thus for the Court to determine whether the State authorities have done all that they reasonably could be expected to do in the circumstances. This was apparent in *Mikayil Mammadov v Azerbaijan*.[70] The applicant's wife committed suicide by pouring a flammable liquid over herself and igniting it. She did this in response to a police operation conducted in an administrative building in which she and her family were, without official authorization, residing. The Court concluded that the aim of this operation had been to evict the applicant's family from the dwelling (although the authorities denied this), but that the authorities could not be considered to have intentionally put the life of the applicant's wife at risk or otherwise caused her to commit suicide. The Court concluded that 'self-immolation as a protest tactic does not constitute predictable or reasonable conduct in the context of eviction from an illegally occupied dwelling, even in a situation involving such a particularly vulnerable sector of the population as refugees and internally displaced persons.'[71] Nevertheless, the Court noted that, once the situation became clear, the authorities would have had an obligation under Article 2 to prevent the threat to life from materializing, by any means which were reasonable and feasible in the circumstances. On the facts of the case, however, the circumstances surrounding the death were disputed and unclear, and thus it was not possible for the Court to determine whether any additional steps should or could have been taken by the authorities. The Court distinguished this situation from a death in custody, where the burden may rest on the State to provide a satisfactory and plausible explanation, in the absence of which inferences unfavourable to the State can be drawn.

The Court has confirmed that a State's obligation to protect life extends to the protection of the lives of persons in custody. This involves providing in a timely manner the medical care necessary to prevent death. In *Jasinskis v Latvia*[72] the applicant's son (who had been deaf and mute since birth) had fallen down some stairs, hit his head, and had been unconscious for some time. The police chose not to wait for the ambulance that had been called and instead took him directly to the police station without any medical attention, believing that he was merely intoxicated. He subsequently died from his head injuries. The Court reiterated that persons in custody are in a vulnerable position and the authorities are under a duty to protect them. Special care should be demonstrated where the authorities decide to place and maintain in detention a person with disabilities to ensure conditions correspond to any special needs resulting from the disability. On the facts of the case, the Court concluded that the authorities had failed in their Article 2 duties which included

[69] *Rabone v Pennine Care NHS Trust* [2012] UKSC 2.

[70] *Mikayil Mammadov v Azerbaijan*, (App. 4762/05), 17 December 2009. [71] § 111.

[72] *Jasinskis v Latvia*, (App. 45744/08), 21 December 2010.

an obligation to protect the life of individuals in custody by providing them with the medical care necessary to safeguard their life. Taking into account the police's knowledge about the applicant's son's fall and his sensory disability, the Court concluded that their failure to seek a medical opinion about his state of health coupled with their failure to react to his knocking on the doors and walls of the sobering-up cell and to call an ambulance for almost seven hours after he could not be woken up in the morning, amounted to a violation of Article 2's duty to safeguard the life of the applicant's son.[73] Due diligence will be expected of the prison authorities to take account of a prisoner's medical condition.[74] The same approach is adopted where medical intervention is undertaken to treat those with alcohol substance abuse.[75]

The Court has been more reluctant to read a more general right to medical treatment into the States' right to life obligations. In *Hristozov and others v Bulgaria*,[76] the applicants argued that the authorities' refusal to give them authorization to use an experimental anti-cancer product (MBVax Coley Fluid) was in breach of their right to life. The product had not been authorized in any country, but had been allowed for so-called 'compassionate use' in a number of countries (including the United Kingdom). The drug company had offered that as part of its pre-clinical development of the product it would be willing to provide the product free of charge for use on cancer patients who could no longer benefit from conventional treatments, in return for data on the treatment's adverse and beneficial effects on each patient. The Bulgarian authorities refused to permit this. The Court found no violation of Article 2, holding that while it may impose a duty on States to put in place an appropriate legal framework, compelling hospitals to adopt appropriate measures for the protection of their patients' lives, Bulgaria did indeed have in place regulations governing access to unauthorized medicinal products. The applicants argued these regulations were too restrictive but in the Court's view Article 2 could not be interpreted as requiring access to unauthorized medicinal products for the terminally ill to be regulated in a particular way.

Where the risk to life arises from an inherently dangerous, but basically lawful, activity, such as, for example, military tests,[77] or the operation of a factory involving toxic emissions,[78] or of a large waste disposal site,[79] there is a duty on the Contracting Party to provide an effective system of regulation, supervision and control, providing for the identification and correction of any dangerous shortcomings.[80] Where appropriate, the Contracting Party must ensure that people whose lives may be put at risk by the process in question are provided with sufficient information to allow them to assess the risk and take preventive measures.[81] These duties arise whether the activity is carried out by the Contracting Party or by private enterprise.

The *Öneryildiz* case[82] concerned a tragic accident at a huge rubbish tip operated by the local authorities on the outskirts of Istanbul. The relevant regulatory law had not been

[73] In *Carabulea v Romania*, (App. 45661/99), 13 July 2010, the Court found that the authorities had not only failed to provide timely medical care to the deceased, but that they had also failed to provide any plausible or satisfactory explanation for the death of a healthy 27-year-old man in police custody. Romania was found to be in violation of Articles 3 and 13, as well as 2.

[74] *Gagiu v Romania*, (App. 63258/00), 24 February 2009.

[75] *Mojsiejew v Poland*, (App. 11818/02), 24 March 2009.

[76] *Hristozov and others v Bulgaria*, (App. 47039/11 and 358/12), 13 November 2012, ECHR 2012.

[77] *LCB v United Kingdom*, (App. 23413/94), 9 June 1998, (1998) 27 EHRR 212, ECHR 1998-III.

[78] *Guerra v Italy*, (App. 14967/89), 19 February 1998, (1998) 26 EHRR 357, ECHR 1998-I.

[79] *Öneryildiz v Turkey*, (App. 48939/99), 30 November 2004 [GC], (2005) 41 EHRR 325, ECHR 2004-XII, § 89.

[80] § 90.

[81] *Öneryildiz v Turkey*, (App. 48939/99), 30 November 2004 [GC], (2005) 41 EHRR 325, ECHR 2004-XII.

[82] *Öneryildiz v Turkey*, (App. 48939/99), 30 November 2004 [GC], (2005) 41 EHRR 325, ECHR 2004-XII

complied with, and no ventilation system was installed. This led to a build-up of methane and other gases, which exploded, causing a landslide which engulfed part of a shanty-town which had sprung up on the slope beneath the tip. The Strasbourg Court held that the Turkish authorities were to blame for the resulting loss of life, because an expert report produced several years before the accident had clearly identified the risk, but no action had been taken. Although the houses which were destroyed had been built illegally, the policy of the authorities was generally tolerant of such breaches of planning controls, and the inhabitants had been provided with an electricity and water supply and required to pay local taxes. Moreover, it would have been relatively simple to make the tip safe by building ventilation ducts.

The positive obligation will extend to natural disasters as well as those resulting from dangerous activities.[83] The *Budayeva* case[84] concerned the response of the authorities to known risks of mudslides, which had occurred in the region every year since 1937. Mudslides in July 2000 caused considerable devastation, and the first applicant's husband had been killed when he had stayed behind in a block of flats to help his parents-in-law, and those flats had collapsed. The Strasbourg Court identified a string of deficiencies in the response of the authorities to the known risk, and found a violation of Article 2 because of the inadequacy of the defence system and the failure to establish any form of warning system. But the Strasbourg Court noted that the burden placed upon a Contracting Party must be reasonable:

> ... an impossible or disproportionate burden must not be imposed on the authorities without consideration being given, in particular, to the operational choices which they must make in terms of priorities and resources... this results from the wide margin of appreciation States enjoy, as the Court has previously held, in difficult social and technical spheres... This consideration must be afforded even greater weight in the sphere of emergency relief in relation to a meteorological event, which is as such beyond human control, than in the sphere of dangerous activities of a man-made nature.

There must also be a proper judicial or administrative inquiry into alleged deficiencies which have led to a disaster of this nature.[85]

THE DUTY TO INVESTIGATE SUSPICIOUS DEATHS

In the *McCann* case, the Strasbourg Court observed that any general legal prohibition of arbitrary killing by agents of the State would be ineffective in practice in the absence of a procedure for reviewing the lawfulness of the use of lethal force by State authorities:

> The obligation to protect the right to life under this provision, read in conjunction with the State's general duty under Article 1 of the Convention to 'secure to everyone within their

[83] It will also cover adverse weather conditions. In *İlbeyi Kemaloğlu and Meriye Kemaloğlu v Turkey*, (App. 19986/06), 10 April 2012, the Court found that in circumstances where a primary school is exceptionally closed early due to bad weather conditions, it is not unreasonable to expect the school authorities to take basic precautions to minimize any potential risk and to protect the pupils. By neglecting to inform the municipality's shuttle service about the early closure of the school, the domestic authorities failed to take measures which might have avoided a risk to the right to life of the applicants' son who had died while walking home from school.

[84] *Budayeva and others v Russia*, (Apps. 15339/02, 21166/02, 20058/02, 11673/02, and 15343/02), 20 March 2008, ECHR 2008 (extracts).

[85] §§ 161–5.

> jurisdiction the rights and freedoms defined in [the] Convention', requires by implication that there should be some form of effective official investigation when individuals have been killed as a result of the use of force by, *inter alios*, agents of the State.[86]

In the *Ramsahai* case,[87] the Grand Chamber recapitulated the requirements of an investigation as follows:

> 324. In order to be 'effective' as this expression is to be understood in the context of Article 2 of the Convention, an investigation into a death that engages the responsibility of a Contracting Party under that Article must firstly be adequate. That is, it must be capable of leading to the identification and punishment of those responsible. This is not an obligation of result, but one of means. The authorities must have taken the reasonable steps available to them to secure the evidence concerning the incident. Any deficiency in the investigation which undermines its ability to identify the perpetrator or perpetrators will risk falling foul of this standard....
>
> 325. Secondly, for the investigation to be 'effective' in this sense it may generally be regarded as necessary for the persons responsible for it and carrying it out to be independent from those implicated in the events. This means not only a lack of hierarchical or institutional connection but also a practical independence.... What is at stake here is nothing less than public confidence in the state's monopoly on the use of force.[88]

The requirement for an effective investigation has formed a useful part of the Strasbourg Court's artillery, particularly in cases where the evidence is not sufficiently clear to justify a finding of deliberate killing by the State. In the *Kaya* case,[89] for example, the applicant's brother was found lying dead and riddled with bullets in a field near his village in south-east Turkey. The respondent State claimed that he was a terrorist who had been killed during a battle with security forces. Witnesses from the village—none of whom, however, were prepared to testify before the Commission's fact-finding delegation—allegedly said that he was an ordinary, unarmed farmer who had been shot by the soldiers without justification or provocation. Only a rudimentary post-mortem had been performed before the body was handed over for burial to the villagers, and the public prosecutor who subsequently took over the inquiry appeared to have accepted without question the military's version of events, omitting to take statements from witnesses or collect any forensic evidence. In these circumstances the Commission and Court, examining the case some years later and hampered by the reluctance of witnesses to come forward,[90] were unable to establish clearly what had taken place or to find for the applicant on his complaint that his brother had been deliberately killed by the soldiers. The Strasbourg Court did, however, find a breach of Article 2 on the basis that the domestic investigation into the death had been inadequate.[91]

The Court has explained[92] that the essential purpose of such investigation is to secure the effective implementation of the domestic laws which protect the right to life and, in those cases involving State agents or bodies, to ensure their accountability for deaths

[86] *McCann and others v United Kingdom*, (App. 18984/91), 27 September 1995, Series A No 324, (1996) 21 EHRR 97, § 161.

[87] *Ramsahai and others v The Netherlands*, (App. 52391/99), 15 May 2007 [GC], (2008) 46 EHRR 983, ECHR 2007-nyr.

[88] §§ 323–5.

[89] *Kaya v Turkey*, (App. 22729/93), 19 February 1998, (1999) 28 EHRR 1, ECHR 1998-I.

[90] See ch.2 for details of the Strasbourg organs' fact-finding powers.

[91] See also *Akpinar and Altun v Turkey*, (App. 56760/00), 27 February 2007, ECHR 2007-III; *Osmanoğlu v Turkey*, (App. 48804/99), 24 January 2008; and *Beker v Turkey*, (App. 27866/03), 24 March 2009.

[92] See, for example, *Hugh Jordan v United Kingdom*, (App. 24746/94), 4 May 2001, (2003) 37 EHRR 52, ECHR 2001-III, §§ 105 and following.

occurring under their responsibility. What form of investigation will achieve those purposes may vary in different circumstances. However, whatever mode is employed, the authorities must act of their own motion, once the matter has come to their attention. They cannot leave it to the initiative of the next of kin either to lodge a formal complaint or to take responsibility for the conduct of any investigative procedures. The procedural aspect of Article 2 can, in this way, be distinguished from the obligation under Article 13 to provide an effective remedy. Put bluntly, Article 2 appears to be most concerned with an official investigation leading to the establishment of criminal liability, whereas the focus of Article 13 is the provision of a civil remedy to the victim or his or her relatives, to enable them to seek compensation.[93]

More recently in *Varnava and others v Turkey*[94] the Grand Chamber has returned to the issue of effective investigations for disappearances. This case concerned the disappearance of a number of Cypriot nationals during the Turkish military operations in northern Cyprus in 1974. As the disappearances occurred in life-threatening circumstances where the conduct of military operations was accompanied by widespread arrests and killings, the Grand Chamber found that Article 2 imposes a continuing obligation on the Government to account for the whereabouts and fate of the missing men:

> Whether they died, in the fighting or of their wounds, or whether they were captured as prisoners, they must still be accounted for. Article 2 must be interpreted in so far as possible in light of the general principles of international law, including the rules of international humanitarian law which play an indispensable and universally-accepted role in mitigating the savagery and inhumanity of armed conflict.... The Court therefore concurs with the reasoning of the Chamber in holding that in a zone of international conflict Contracting States are under obligation to protect the lives of those not, or no longer, engaged in hostilities. This would also extend to the provision of medical assistance to the wounded; where combatants have died, or succumbed to wounds, the need for accountability would necessitate proper disposal of remains and require the authorities to collect and provide information about the identity and fate of those concerned, or permit bodies such as the ICRC to do so.[95]

The Grand Chamber in *Cyprus v Turkey*[96] had previously found that the United Nations Committee on Missing Persons (CMP)'s procedures did not meet the standard of investigation required by Article 2 and the Grand Chamber in *Varnava* saw no reason to differ from that conclusion. Thus it found a continuing violation of Article 2 on account of the failure of the Turkish authorities to conduct an effective investigation into the fate of the nine men who disappeared in life-threatening circumstances.

Similar considerations have been in play in relation to widespread disappearances in the Northern Caucasus. In the context of disappearances that took place in Chechnya and Ingushetia between 1999 and 2006, the Court has identified a number of common shortcomings of the criminal investigations:

> delays in the opening of the proceedings and in the taking of essential steps; lengthy periods of inactivity; failure to take vital investigative steps, especially those aimed at the identification and questioning of the military and security officers who could have witnessed or participated in the abduction; failure to involve the military prosecutors even where there was sufficient evidence of the servicemen's involvement in the crimes; inability to trace the

[93] See *Öneryildiz v Turkey*, (App. 48939/99), 30 November 2004 [GC], (2005) 41 EHRR 325, ECHR 2004-XII.

[94] *Varnava and others v Turkey*, (App. 16064/90, 16065/90, 16066/90, 16068/90, 16069/90, 16070/90, 16071/90, 16072/90 and 16073/90), 18 September 2009 [GC], ECHR 2009.

[95] § 185.

[96] *Cyprus v Turkey*, (App. 25781/94), ECHR 2001 IV. [GC], §§ 13–18.

> vehicles, their provenance and passage through military roadblocks; belated granting of victim status to the relatives; and failure to ensure public scrutiny by informing the next of kin of the important investigative steps and by granting them access to the results of the investigation.[97]

In a number of cases, the Court has concluded that the combination of these factors has rendered the criminal investigations ineffective.[98] In *Aslakhanova and others v Russia*, the Court held that the situation 'must be characterised as resulting from systemic problems at the national level, for which there is no effective domestic remedy. It affects core human rights and requires the prompt implementation of comprehensive and complex measures.'[99] The Court therefore provided some guidance on measures to be taken, as a matter of urgency, by the Russian authorities to address the issue of the systemic failure to investigate disappearances in the Northern Caucasus.

For an investigation into alleged unlawful killing by State agents to be effective and to comply with Article 2, it must be carried out by someone who is fully independent of those implicated in the events[100] on the basis of objective evidence.[101] The investigation must be capable of leading to a determination of whether the force used in such cases was justified in the circumstances and to the identification and punishment of those responsible.[102] This entails that the authorities must have taken the reasonable steps available to them to secure the evidence concerning the incident, including eyewitness testimony, forensic evidence, and, where appropriate, an autopsy which provides a complete and accurate record of injury and an objective analysis of clinical findings, including the cause of death.[103] In *Mikayil Mammadov v Azerbaijan*[104] the investigation into a suicide was undermined by the authorities' failure to question the suicide victim before her death in hospital even though they were aware that she had suffered life-threatening injuries which made her survival uncertain. The Court took the view that in these circumstances, the authorities were 'obliged to act in a prompt and diligent manner in order to try to obtain evidence which would no longer be available after her death' and had failed to do this.[105] The investigation must be carried out promptly, in order to maintain public confidence in the authorities' adherence to the rule of law and to prevent any appearance of collusion in or tolerance of unlawful acts.[106] For the same reasons, the investigation must, to a certain

[97] *Aslakhanova and others v Russia*, (Apps. 2944/06 and 8300/07, 50184/07, 332/08, and 42509/10), 18 December 2012, § 123.

[98] See, for example, *Vakhayeva and others v Russia*, (App. 1758/04), 29 October 2009; *Shokkarov and others v Russia*, (App. 41009/04), 3 May 2011; and *Umarova and others v Russia*, (App. 25654/08), 31 July 2012.

[99] *Aslakhanova and others v Russia*, (Apps. 2944/06 and 8300/07, 50184/07, 332/08, 42509/10), 18 December 2012, § 217.

[100] *Güleç v Turkey*, (App. 21593/93), 27 July 1998, (1999) 28 EHRR 121, ECHR 1998-IV; and *Ögur v Turkey*, (App. 21594/93), 20 May 1999; (2001) 31 EHRR 912, ECHR 1999-III.

[101] *Ergi v Turkey*, (App. 23818/94), 28 July 1998, (2001) 32 EHRR 388, ECHR 1998-IV.

[102] *Kaya v Turkey*, (App. 22729/93), 19 February 1998, (1999) 28 EHRR 1, ECHR 1998-I; and *Ögur v Turkey*, (App. 21594/93), 20 May 1999, (2001) 31 EHRR 912, ECHR 1999-III.

[103] *Salman v Turkey*, (App. 21986/93), 27 June 2000, (2002) 34 EHRR 425, ECHR 2000-VII; *Tanrikulu v Turkey*, (App. 23763/94), 8 July 1999 [GC], (2000) 30 EHRR 950, ECHR 1999-IV; and *Gül v Turkey*, (App. 22676/93), 14 December 2000, (2002) 34 EHRR 719.

[104] *Mikayil Mammadov v Azerbaijan*, (App. 4762/05), 17 December 2009.

[105] § 130.

[106] *Yasa v Turkey*, (App. 22495/93), 2 September 1998; (1999) 28 EHRR 408, ECHR 1998-VI; *Çakici v Turkey*, (App. 23657/94), 8 July 1999, (2001) 31 EHRR 133; *Tanrikulu v Turkey*, (App. 23763/94), 8 July 1999 [GC], (2000) 30 EHRR 950, ECHR 1999-IV; and *Mahmut Kaya v Turkey*, (App. 22535/93), 28 March 2000, ECHR 2000-III.

degree, be open to public scrutiny, and the relatives of the deceased must always have the opportunity to become involved.[107]

These requirements are illustrated by the *Ramsahai* case, which concerned the shooting of a suspect by the police.[108] Having found that the killings did not involve more force than was strictly necessary, the Strasbourg Court focused on aspects of the investigation which followed. Violations of Article 2 were found in only two respects: by thirteen votes to four that the investigation was inadequate; and by sixteen votes to one that the investigation was not sufficiently independent. On the former point, the Grand Chamber concluded that there had been a failure to test the hands of the police officers for gunshot residue, and to stage any reconstruction of the incident; no examination of the weapons or ammunition of the two officers had been undertaken. Furthermore there was no adequate photograph of the injuries suffered by Ramsahai; the officers had not been kept separate after the incident; and they had not been questioned until nearly three days later. The dissenting judges considered that a defect in the investigative procedure only gave rise to a violation of Article 2 if it was such as to undermine the capacity of the investigation to establish the facts surrounding the death or the liability of the person involved. That was not the case here. In respect of the second finding of a violation of Article 2, the Grand Chamber concluded that the delay of over fifteen hours before the investigation was handed over to someone unconnected with the police force to which the officers were attached meant that the investigation was not sufficiently independent. The dissenting judge did not consider that the delay had tainted the independence of the investigation, since it had not adversely impacted upon its effectiveness. There does not appear, on the facts of the case, to have been any suggestion that the Dutch police had acted in bad faith or were attempting to cover up any wrongdoing. What is striking from this judgment is the level of detail required of the process of investigation following the fatal shooting by the police.[109] This is standard-setting of a high order, and might prove to be impracticable or overly costly to apply, particularly in remote regions.

In the United Kingdom, investigations into suspicious deaths usually take the form of inquests, which are public hearings into the facts conducted by independent judicial officers (coroners), normally sitting with a jury. Judicial review lies from procedural decisions by coroners and in respect of any mistaken directions given to the jury. In the *McCann* case[110] the Strasbourg Court found that the inquest held into the deaths of three terrorists shot dead by British soldiers in Gibraltar satisfied the procedural obligation contained in Article 2, as it provided a detailed review of the events surrounding the killings and gave the relatives of the deceased the opportunity to examine and cross-examine witnesses involved in the operation. More recently, however, in a series of judgments concerning killings by the security forces in Northern Ireland,[111] the Strasbourg Court found violations of Article 2 based on flaws in the inquests.[112]

[107] *Güleç v Turkey*, (App. 21593/93), 27 July 1998, (1999) 28 EHRR 121, ECHR 1998-IV; *Ögur v Turkey*, (App. 21594/93), 20 May 1999, (2001) 31 EHRR 912, ECHR 1999-III; and *Mojsiewiew v Poland*, (App. 11818/02), 24 March 2009.

[108] *Ramsahai and others v The Netherlands*, (App. 52391/99), 15 May 2007 [GC], (2008) 46 EHRR 983, ECHR 2007-nyr. See also *Giuliani and Gaggio v Italy*, (App. 23458/02), 25 August 2009 [GC], ECHR 2011 (extracts).

[109] See *Ramsahai*, §§ 399–431.

[110] *McCann and others v United Kingdom*, (App. 18984/91), 27 September 1995, Series A No 324, (1996) 21 EHRR 97; see earlier in this chapter.

[111] *Hugh Jordan v United Kingdom*, (App. 24746/94), 4 May 2001, (2003) 37 EHRR 52, ECHR 2001-III; *McKerr v United Kingdom*, (App. 28883/94), 4 May 2001, (2002) 34 EHRR 553, ECHR 2001-III; *Kelly and others v United Kingdom*, (App. 30054/96), 4 May 2001; *Shanaghan v United Kingdom*, (App. 37715/97), 4 May 2001; *McShane v United Kingdom*, (App. 43290/98), 28 May 2002, (2002) 35 EHRR 523; and *Finucane v United Kingdom*, (App. 29178/95), 1 July 2003, (2003) 37 EHRR 656, ECHR 2003-VIII.

[112] See M. Requa and G. Anthony, 'Coroners, controversial deaths, and Northern Ireland's past conflict' [2008] PL 443.

The son of the applicant in the *Hugh Jordan* case, for example, had been shot and killed by a British police officer. However, this police officer was not a compellable witness under the Northern Irish inquest rules, and declined to give evidence or to be cross-examined, thus seriously detracting from the inquest's power to establish the facts. Moreover, the Northern Irish system also differed from that used in Gibraltar in the *McCann* case (and applicable in England and Wales) in that the jury could not enter a verdict, such as 'unlawful killing'; all it could do was to give the identity of the deceased and the date, place, and direct cause of death. Since the inquest could not, therefore, play an effective role in the identification or prosecution of any criminal offences which might have occurred, the Strasbourg Court found that it fell short of the requirements of Article 2. The Court also criticized the lack of advance disclosure of witness statements to the deceased's family and the delay in the proceedings: over eight years after the death, the inquest had still not come to a conclusion.[113]

The requirement of an independent investigation when the respondent State is an occupying power was considered in the case of *Al-Skeini and others v United Kingdom*[114] involving six deaths in Al-Basrah, southern Iraq in 2003. The relatives of the first four applicants were shot by British soldiers; the son of the fifth applicant was beaten by British soldiers and then forced into a river where he drowned; the son of the sixth applicant died while detained at a British military base. The Court acknowledged the practical problems caused to the investigatory authorities by the fact that the UK was an occupying power in a foreign and hostile region in the immediate aftermath of invasion and war. While the Court recognized that in such circumstances the procedural duty under Article 2 must be applied realistically, taking into account specific problems faced by investigators, it also noted that in order for any investigation into acts allegedly committed by occupying forces to be effective, it was particularly important that the investigating authority was, and was seen to be, operationally independent of the military chain of command.[115]

For three of the applicants' relatives, the investigation process remained entirely within the military chain of command and was limited to taking statements from the soldiers involved. The Grand Chamber immediately concluded that this fell short of the procedural requirements of Article 2, and, indeed, the UK Government accepted this conclusion. In respect of two of the applicants' relatives, there was an investigation by the Special Investigation Branch into their deaths but the Court found that this was also not sufficient to comply with the requirements of Article 2 because this body was not, during the relevant period, operationally independent from the military chain of command. On this point, the Grand Chamber agreed with the domestic court that the fact that the Special

[113] In *Finucane v United Kingdom*, (App. 29178/95), 1 July 2003, (2003) 37 EHRR 656, ECHR 2003-VIII, the inquest was inadequate because it was limited to identifying the man who shot the applicant's husband (a lawyer who had represented a number of Republican suspects), and could not examine the evidence which suggested that members of the Royal Ulster Constabulary had in some way solicited the killing. See, on the lack of independence of the Royal Ulster Constabulary (RUC) in relation to the investigation of certain deaths in Northern Ireland, *Reavey v United Kingdom*, (App. 34640/04), 27 November 2007.

[114] *Al-Skeini and others v United Kingdom*, (App. 55721/07), 7 July 2011 [GC], ECHR 2011.

[115] This case is also of significance in the context of the right to life due to its contribution to the evolving jurisprudence on extraterritorial jurisdiction under the Convention. As discussed in ch.5, the Grand Chamber held that the UK's assumption of authority and responsibility for the maintenance of security in south-east Iraq during its occupation meant that it exercised authority and control over individuals killed in the course of security operations there. All of the applicants' deceased relatives were thus regarded as falling within the jurisdiction of the UK. There are still some unanswered questions in relation to extraterritorial jurisdiction and the Court's interpretation of the concept may well further evolve in the future, but its extension in this case can only strengthen the Convention's ability to protect the life of those killed by foreign forces or in the course of occupation by another State.

Investigation Branch was not free to decide for itself when to start and cease an investigation and reported in the first instance to the military chain of command, meant that it could not be seen as sufficiently independent from the soldiers implicated in the events to satisfy the requirements of Article 2.[116] Even though one of the applicants had received a substantial sum in settlement of his civil claim and an admission of liability on behalf of the Army, there was never a full and independent investigation into the circumstances of his son's death, and thus the procedural requirements of Article 2 had not been satisfied. Only in relation to the final applicant's relative's death, where a full, public inquiry was nearing completion, was Article 2 fully satisfied.[117]

While the early cases have concerned investigations into deaths allegedly caused by a State's security forces, more recently the Court has dealt with cases concerning the investigation of deaths which have occurred in more routine circumstances. It has already been noted that a State is responsible for the proper medical care of prisoners,[118] and others who come into the State's care.[119] The Convention case-law on investigations apply as much to such circumstances as to cases involving the use of force by members of the security forces. Those requirements extend to a death following treatment in hospital of an ordinary member of the public. The *Šilih* case[120] concerned a 21-year-old man who was being treated for urticaria. He had an allergic reaction to one of the drugs administered to treat his condition, and subsequently died. The case concerned the enquiries into the circumstances of the death, and any liability for it. In Slovenia, this can be done through both criminal and civil proceedings. The man's parents used both processes, which proceeded at a snail's pace. This was not a case of absence of procedures, but of the way the procedures had operated in the case of this man's death. The Grand Chamber emphasized the need for a prompt response, especially to a sudden death in a hospital setting. In addition to the excessive length of both sets of proceedings, there were other deficiencies in the operation of the procedure and there was a violation of Article 2.

Despite early dicta to the contrary,[121] it now appears that the obligation to investigate is not confined to cases where it can be established that the death was caused by agents of the State, but also arises wherever life has been lost in circumstances potentially engaging the responsibility of the State.[122] In the *Menson* case,[123] the applicants' brother died after he had been set on fire by four white youths. The applicants did not allege that the State had in any way caused the death, or that the authorities knew, or should have known, that

[116] § 172.

[117] It will apparently not breach Article 2 if soldiers who have been convicted of murder following the shooting of a civilian are, having regard to exceptional circumstances, retained as serving members of the armed forces on their release from custody (*McBride v United Kingdom*, (App. 1396/06), Decision of 9 May 2006, ECHR 2006-V).

[118] *Gagiu v Romania*, (App. 63258/00), 24 February 2009.

[119] *Mojsiejew v Poland*, (App. 11818/02), 24 March 2009.

[120] *Šilih v Slovenia*, (App. 71463/01), 9 April 2009 [GC], (2009) 49 EHRR 996, ECHR 2009-nyr.

[121] See, for example, *Kurt v Turkey*, (App. 24276/94), 25 May 1998; (1999) 27 EHRR 373, ECHR 1998-III, § 107.

[122] *Öneryildiz v Turkey*, (App. 48939/99), 30 November 2004 [GC], (2005) 41 EHRR 325, ECHR 2004-XII, § 91.

[123] *Menson and others v United Kingdom*, (App. 47916/99), Decision of 6 May 2003, ECHR 2003-V. See also *Yasa v Turkey*, (App. 22495/93), 2 September 1998, (1999) 28 EHRR 408, ECHR 1998-VI, (death caused by unknown assailant); *Ögur v Turkey*, (App. 21594/93), 20 May 1999, (2001) 31 EHRR 912, ECHR 1999-IV, (death caused by warning shot fired into the air by a soldier); *Calvelli and Ciglio v Italy*, (App. 32967/96), 17 January 2002 [GC], ECHR 2002-I, (death caused by negligent medical treatment); *Öneryildiz v Turkey*, (App. 48939/99), 30 November 2004, (2005) 41 EHRR 325, ECHR 2004-XII, (death caused by the negligent operation of a waste disposal site); and *Dodov v Bulgaria*, (App. 59548/00), 17 January 2008, (2008) 47 EHRR 932, ECHR 2008, (presumed death following disappearance of woman with Alzheimer's disease from a State-run nursing home).

he was at risk of violence. The Strasbourg Court held, nonetheless, that the absence of any direct State responsibility for Menson's death did not exclude the applicability of Article 2. By requiring a Contracting Party to take appropriate steps to safeguard the lives of those within its jurisdiction,[124] Article 2(1) imposed a duty to secure the right to life by putting in place effective criminal law provisions to deter the commission of offences against the person, backed up by law enforcement machinery for the prevention, suppression, and punishment of breaches of such provisions. In the *Menson* case, since the applicants' brother sustained life-threatening injuries in suspicious circumstances, this obligation required by implication that there should be some form of effective official investigation, capable of establishing the cause of the injuries and the identification of those responsible with a view to their punishment. Despite serious shortcomings in the initial police reaction to the attack—which the applicants claimed to have arisen from the racist attitudes of the Metropolitan Police—the killers had eventually been prosecuted and convicted. The respondent State's duty under Article 2 had, therefore, been satisfied.

By contrast, the respondent State in the *Angelova and Iliev* case[125] had not satisfied its duty to investigate and prosecute those who had committed murder. A 28-year-old man of Roma origin had been attacked by a group of teenagers and fatally stabbed. The initial action of the police was prompt and a number of youths were brought into custody. But the investigation was complicated by allegations from one of the suspects that the attack had been racially motivated; some of those arrested changed their evidence. The investigation stalled, and there was a period of nearly four years when nothing happened at all, and for which no reasonable explanation could be provided. The positive obligation to investigate, and where appropriate prosecute,[126] requires 'promptness and reasonable expedition' especially where the death appeared to follow a racially motivated attack.[127]

MEDICAL TERMINATION OF PREGNANCY AND THE RIGHTS OF THE UNBORN CHILD

Unlike Article 4 of the American Convention on Human Rights, which provides that the right to life must be protected 'in general, from the moment of conception', Article 2 of the Convention is silent as to the temporal limitations of the right to life and, in particular, does not define 'everyone' ('*toute personne*') whose 'life' is protected by the Convention.

In *X v United Kingdom*[128] the Commission considered an application by a man complaining that his wife had been allowed to have an abortion on health grounds. While it accepted that the potential father could be regarded as the 'victim' of a violation of the right to life, it considered that the term 'everyone' as used in the Convention could not apply prenatally, but observed that 'such application in a rare case—e.g. under Article 6, paragraph 1—cannot be excluded'.[129] The Commission added that the general usage of the term 'everyone' and the context in which it was used in Article 2 of the Convention did not include the unborn. As to the term 'life' and, in particular, the beginning of life,

[124] *LCB v the United Kingdom*, (App. 23413/94), 9 June 1998, (1998) 27 EHRR 212, ECHR 1998-III; see earlier in this chapter.

[125] *Angelova and Iliev v Bulgaria*, (App. 55523/00), 26 July 2007, (2008) 47 EHRR 236, ECHR 2007-IX.

[126] See also *Nikolova and Velichkova v Bulgaria*, (App. 7888/03), 20 December 2007, (2009) 48 EHRR 915, §§ 58–64, and 75.

[127] §§ 97–8.

[128] App. 8416/79, *X v United Kingdom*, Decision of 13 May 1980, (1980) 19 DR 244.

[129] § 7. For such an application in connection with access to a court, see App. 24844/94, *Reeve v United Kingdom*, Decision of 30 November 1994, (1995) 79-A DR 146.

the Commission noted a 'divergence of thinking on the question of where life begins' and added:

> While some believe that it starts already with conception, others tend to focus upon the moment of nidation, upon the point that the foetus becomes 'viable', or upon live birth.[130]

The Commission went on to examine whether Article 2 was:

> to be interpreted: as not covering the foetus at all; as recognising a 'right to life' of the foetus with certain implied limitations; or as recognising an absolute 'right to life' of the foetus.

Although it did not express an opinion on the first two options, it categorically ruled out the third interpretation, having regard to the need to protect the mother's life, which could not be separated from that of the unborn child:

> The 'life' of the foetus is intimately connected with, and it cannot be regarded in isolation of, the life of the pregnant woman. If Article 2 were held to cover the foetus and its protection under this Article were, in the absence of any express limitation, seen as absolute, an abortion would have to be considered as prohibited even where the continuance of the pregnancy would involve a serious risk to the life of the pregnant woman. This would mean that the 'unborn life' of the foetus would be regarded as being of a higher value than the life of the pregnant woman.[131]

In the case of *H v Norway*,[132] concerning an abortion carried out on non-medical grounds against the father's wishes, the Commission added that Article 2 required a Contracting Party not only to refrain from taking a person's life intentionally but also to take appropriate steps to safeguard life. It considered that it did not have to decide 'whether the foetus may enjoy a certain protection under Article 2, first sentence', but did not exclude the possibility that 'in certain circumstances this may be the case notwithstanding that there is in the Contracting Parties a considerable divergence of views on whether or to what extent Article 2 protects the unborn life.' It further noted that in such a delicate area the Contracting Parties had to have a certain discretion, and concluded that the mother's decision, taken in accordance with Norwegian legislation, had not exceeded that discretion.

The reluctance to decide when Article 2's protection begins continued in *Vo* v France.[133] This case raised the new issue of whether, apart from cases where the mother has requested an abortion, harming a foetus should be treated as a criminal offence in the light of Article 2 of the Convention, with a view to protecting the right to life of the foetus. Hospital staff confused the identity of the applicant, who was six months pregnant and had come in for a routine check-up, with that of another woman with the same family name who wished to have her intra-uterine device (IUD) removed. As a result of the doctors' negligence the applicant lost her unborn child. She was unable to bring criminal proceedings against the doctors, because, under French law, a foetus could not be the victim of unintentional homicide.

The Strasbourg Court avoided coming to any firm conclusion on the question:

> [T]he Court is convinced that it is neither desirable, nor even possible as matters stand, to answer in the abstract the question whether the unborn child is a person for the purposes of Article 2 of the Convention ("*personne*" in the French text). As to the instant case, it considers it unnecessary to examine whether the abrupt end to the applicant's pregnancy falls

[130] § 12. [131] § 19.

[132] App. 17004/90, *H v Norway*, Decision of 19 May 1992, (1992) 73 DR 155.

[133] *Vo v France*, (App. 53924/00), 8 July 2004 [GC], (2005) 40 EHRR 259, ECHR 2004-VIII. For discussion, see A. Plomer, 'A Foetal Right to Life? The Case of *Vo v France*' (2005) 5 HRLR 311.

> within the scope of Article 2, seeing that, even assuming that that provision was applicable, there was no failure on the part of the respondent State to comply with the requirements relating to the preservation of life in the public-health sphere.[134]

It was able to justify this avoidance of the key question by acknowledging that there was a lack of consensus across Europe on the nature and status of the foetus, although it did recognize that 'it may be regarded as common ground between States that the embryo/foetus belongs to the human race. The potentiality of that being and its capacity to become a person—enjoying protection under the civil law, moreover, in many States, … —require protection in the name of human dignity, without making it a 'person' with the 'right to life' for the purposes of Article 2.'[135] The Court took the view that even assuming that the foetus gained some protection from Article 2, French law offered sufficient protection in the form of the criminal offence of unintentionally causing injury to the mother, and the possibility of bringing civil proceedings for damages. Some commentators feel that this discussion of whether Article 2 would have been violated on the facts of the case is inappropriate in the absence of a definitive answer to the preliminary question of whether the provision is even applicable to a foetus.[136] On the other hand, it is a pragmatic side-stepping of an eternally contentious question and one that is duplicated in the Court's approach to the potentially related question of whether the Convention recognizes a right to an abortion under Article 8.[137]

EUTHANASIA AND THE QUALITY OF LIFE

Since the judgment in the *Pretty* case,[138] it is clear that the right to life in Article 2 does not include a 'right to die'. The applicant suffered from an untreatable motor-neurone disease. Her muscles were becoming progressively weaker, so that at the time of the application she was paralysed from the neck down, had virtually no decipherable speech, and had to be fed through a tube, although her intellect and capacity to make decisions were unimpaired. Her life expectancy was very poor, and the final stages of the disease were expected to be distressing and undignified. She wished her husband to be permitted to assist her suicide without risk of prosecution. The Strasbourg Court observed that the consistent emphasis in its case-law had been the obligation of the State to protect life. Article 2 was unconcerned with issues to do with the quality of life or self-determination.[139]

[134] § 85.

[135] § 84. This use of the concept of human dignity to imply two levels of protection for human life under the Convention is considered further in E. Wicks, 'The Meaning of Life: Dignity and the Right to Life in International Human Rights Treaties' (2012) 12 HRLR 199. It is criticized in A. Plomer, 'A Foetal Right to Life? The Case of *Vo v France*' [2005] HRLR 311, p. 317.

[136] See E. Wicks, *Human Rights and Healthcare* (Hart Publishing, Oxford 2007), 183–4. Judge Costa, dissenting, suggested that had 'Article 2 been considered to be entirely inapplicable, there would have been no point… in examining the question of foetal protection and the possible violation of Article 2…' (Judge Costa's Separate Opinion, § 10.)

[137] In App. 6959/75, *Brüggemann and Scheuten v Federal Republic of Germany*, Report of 12 July 1977, (1977) 10 DR 100, the Commission denied such a right, holding that pregnancy was not solely a private matter. In more recent cases, the Court has affirmed this approach (*A, B & C v Ireland*, (App. 25579/05), 16 December 2010) and afforded States a wide margin of appreciation in how to regulate this area. The Court has, however, been increasingly willing to find procedural violations of Article 8 in respect of an inability to access abortions, or challenge refusals of access. See, for example, *A, B & C v Ireland* and *Tysiac v Poland*, (App. 5410/03), 20 March 2007, (2007) 45 EHRR 42. This issue will be discussed more fully in the context of Art. 8.

[138] *Pretty v United Kingdom*, (App. 2346/02), 29 April 2002, (2002) 35 EHRR 1, ECHR 2002-III.

[139] See, on euthanasia generally, Council of Europe, *Euthanasia. Volume I: Ethical and human aspects* (Council of Europe Publishing, Strasbourg 2003); *Volume II: National and European perspectives*, (Council of

Currently, there are four Member States of the Council of Europe (Switzerland, Belgium, the Netherlands, and Luxembourg) which allow medical practitioners to prescribe lethal drugs, subject to specific safeguards,[140] but there have not, to date, been any admissible cases under Article 2 brought by a friend or relative complaining about euthanasia carried out by a doctor or authorized by a Contracting Party,[141] although there have been cases brought under Article 8 challenging a State's failure to permit assisted dying.[142] The applicant in the *Pretty* case argued that a failure to acknowledge a right to die under the Convention would place such countries which do permit assisted suicide in breach of the Convention. The Strasbourg Court refused to consider this proposition in the abstract, and remarked that, even if circumstances prevailing in a particular country which permitted assisted suicide were found not to infringe Article 2 of the Convention, that would not assist the applicant in establishing 'the very different proposition—that the United Kingdom would be in breach of its obligations under Article 2 if it did not allow assisted suicide...'[143] There is little doubt that other provisions of the Convention are better suited to arguments about legalized assisted dying (such as Articles 3 and 8). Whether Article 2 can, or will, be used to prevent such steps remains open to debate. Certainly in *Haas v Switzerland*, the Court made clear that Article 2 'obliges the national authorities to prevent an individual from taking his or her own life if the decision has not been taken freely and with full understanding of what is involved.'[144] The relationship between Article 2 and Article 8 in this context will need to be further developed in future cases.

CONCLUDING REMARKS

After a slow start, the body of judgments concerning the right to life has now taken its place among the richest and most dynamic of all the Convention case-law. The broad lines, both procedural and substantive, of the prohibition on unlawful killing by agents of the State have been established, although no doubt further detail will emerge as different factual situations are placed before the Court. There remain questions of scope in relation to the beginning and end of life which seem likely to worry the Court for some time to come. However, it is in connection with the positive obligation to take measures to safeguard lives that the greatest scope for innovation remains, and it will be interesting to see how far the Strasbourg Court considers it possible to extend the protection afforded by Article 2 without placing too great a burden on the State.

Europe Publishing, Strasbourg 2004). See also J. Griffiths, H. Weyers, and M. Adams, *Euthanasia and Law in Europe* (Hart, Oxford 2008); D. Morris, 'Assisted suicide under the European Convention on Human Rights: a Critique' [2003] EHRLR 65; H. Nys, 'Physician Involvement in a Patient's Death: A Continental European Perspective' (1999) 7 Medical Law Review 208.

[140] *Koch v Germany*, (App. 497/09), Judgment of 19 July 2012, § 26.

[141] In *Glass v United Kingdom*, (App. 61827/00), 9 March 2004, (2004) 39 EHRR 341, ECHR 2004-II, the applicants complained about the administration, against the wishes of his parents, of life-shortening morphine-based pain-killers to a very severely disabled child. The Court emphasized in its admissibility decision that there was no evidence that the doctors who prescribed the drugs intended to hasten the child's death; they wished only to alleviate his suffering; and indeed the child survived and was able to return home from hospital. For this reason the applicants' complaint under Article 2 was declared inadmissible and the complaint was examined only under Article 8. The Court found a violation of that provision, on the ground that the hospital authorities should have sought a court ruling before giving the child diamorphine.

[142] In addition to *Pretty* itself, see *Haas v Switzerland*, (App. 31322/07), Judgment of 20 January 2011, ECHR 2011; *Koch v Germany*, (App. 497/09) Judgment of 19 July 2012; *Gross v Switzerland*, (App. 67810/10), 14 May 2013.

[143] *Pretty v United Kingdom*, (App. 2346/02), 29 April 2002, (2002) 35 EHRR 1, ECHR 2002-III. The Strasbourg Court also rejected the applicant's complaints under Articles 3, 8, and 14 about the ban on assisted suicide.

[144] *Haas v Switzerland*, (App. 31322/07), Judgment of 20 January 2011, ECHR 2011, § 54.

9

PROHIBITION OF TORTURE

INTRODUCTION

Article 3 is the shortest in Section I of the Convention stating simply: 'No one shall be subjected to torture or to inhuman or degrading treatment or punishment.' The fundamental character of the prohibition is affirmed by the fact that no derogation in respect of its provisions is permitted even in time of war or public emergency.[1]

The Strasbourg Court has been consistent in its maintenance of the absolute nature of Article 3 despite the pressure from States to dilute this protection in regard to cases concerning the threat from terrorism. This is well illustrated by the *Chahal* case.[2] The United Kingdom wished to deport Chahal, a Sikh separatist, to India arguing that he had been involved in terrorist activities and posed a risk to the national security of the United Kingdom. The Strasbourg Court said:

> Article 3 enshrines one of the most fundamental values of democratic society. The Court is well aware of the immense difficulties faced by States in modern times in protecting their communities from terrorist violence. However, even in these circumstances, the Convention prohibits in absolute terms torture or inhuman or degrading treatment or punishment, irrespective of the victim's conduct.[3]

Despite attempts to persuade the Strasbourg Court that the interests of the community as a whole may be taken into account in deciding whether to remove a person whose continued presence might be seen to be a threat to the host country, the Grand Chamber in the *Saadi* case has re-affirmed the absolute nature of the prohibition:

> As the prohibition of torture and inhuman and degrading treatment or punishment is absolute, irrespective of the victim's conduct . . . the nature of the offence allegedly committed by the applicant is therefore irrelevant for the purposes of Article 3 . . .[4]

[1] On Article 3, see generally A. Reidy, *The Prohibition of Torture: A Guide to the implementation of Article 3 of the European Convention on Human Rights*, Human Rights Handbooks, No. 6 (Council of Europe Publishing, Strasbourg 2003); A. Cassese, 'Prohibition of Torture and Inhuman or Degrading Treatment or Punishment' in R. Macdonald, F. Matscher, and H. Petzold, *The European System for the Protection of Human Rights* (Martinus Nijhoff, Dordrecht 1993), 225; H. Danelius, 'Protection against Torture in Europe and the World' in R. Macdonald, F. Matscher, and H. Petzold, *The European System for the Protection of Human Rights* (Martinus Nijhoff, Dordrecht 1993), at 263; N. Rodley and M. Pollard, *The Treatment of Prisoners under International Law* (OUP, Oxford 2009); S. Levinson, *Torture. A Collection* (OUP, Oxford 2004); and J. Murdoch, *The Treatment of Prisoners: European standards* (Council of Europe Publishing, Strasbourg 2006).

[2] *Chahal v United Kingdom*, (App. 22414/93), 15 November 1996, (1997) 23 EHRR 413, ECHR 1996-V.

[3] § 80.

[4] *Saadi v Italy*, (App. 37201/06), 28 February 2008 [GC], (2009) 49 EHRR 730, ECHR 2008-nyr, § 127.

The Strasbourg Court described the argument based on the balancing of the risk of harm if the person is removed against their dangerousness to the host State as 'misconceived'.[5] Nor was there any merit in the argument that the risk of ill-treatment should be stronger in those cases where the continued presence of the person in the host State presented a security risk; this was not compatible with the absolute nature of Article 3.[6] But the assessment of the real risk of ill-treatment in the country of destination will always be a rigorous one.[7]

The absolute nature of Article 3 was again underlined in the *Gäfgen* case[8]. Gäfgen kidnapped the son of a German banker for a ransom. He was arrested, and unknown to the police, he had already killed the boy. The police officers in charge of the interrogation believed the boy's life was in grave danger and made threats of violence against Gäfgen in order to extract information about where the boy was held. Gäfgen told the police where the boy was and the police retrieved the boy's body along with other evidence. Gäfgen was convicted of the boy's murder. The police officers were found guilty under German law of using coercion. They received a small fine. The Strasbourg Court recognized that the police acted in order to save the boy's life but noted:

> . . . it is necessary to underline that, having regard to the provision of Article 3 and to its long-established case-law . . . the prohibition on ill-treatment of a person applies irrespective of the conduct of the victim or the motivation of the authorities. Torture, inhuman or degrading treatment cannot be inflicted even in circumstances where the life of an individual is at risk . . . Article 3, which has been framed in unambiguous terms, recognises that every human being has an absolute, inalienable right not to be subjected to torture or to inhuman or degrading treatment under any circumstances, even the most difficult. The philosophical basis underpinning the absolute nature of the right under Article 3 does not allow for any exceptions or justifying factors or balancing of interests, irrespective of the conduct of the person concerned and the nature of the offence at issue.[9]

After addressing the issues of definition which arise under Article 3, this chapter explores a number of specific areas where Article 3 has been applied by the Commission and the Court. It will then address positive obligations developed by the Court, evidential issues connected with proving conduct falling within the Article. One disappointing development is the frequency with which the Court finds violations of Article 3. This reflects only in part its increasing willingness to find violations in a broader range of situations than in earlier years.[10]

DEFINING THE TERMS

Article 3 covers both punishment and treatment. Punishment is given its ordinary meaning, but it is not normally necessary to distinguish between treatment and punishment. Punishment and treatment are often not subject to separate analysis, since in many cases punishment must involve treatment. Sometimes the Strasbourg Court simply categorizes the punishment as 'inhuman or degrading treatment' taken together.[11]

[5] § 139.

[6] § 140. See, generally, D. Moeckli, '*Saadi v Italy*: The Rules of the Game Have *Not* Changed' (2008) 8 HRLRev 534.

[7] *NA v United Kingdom*, (App. 25904/07), 17 July 2008, (2009) 48 EHRR 337, ECHR 2008-nyr.

[8] *Gäfgen v Germany*, (App. 22978/05), 1 June 2010.

[9] § 107.

[10] Most notably in relation to various conditions of detention. See later in this chapter.

[11] *II v Bulgaria*, (App. 44082/98), 9 June 2005. See also *Mayzit v Russia*, (App. 63378/00), 20 January 2005.

ARTICLE 3 IS ONLY CONCERNED WITH CONDUCT WHICH ATTAINS 'A MINIMUM LEVEL OF SEVERITY'

In order for conduct to fall within Article 3, it must 'attain a minimum level of severity'.[12] This test will apply whatever the category of conduct in issue. The effect of setting a significant threshold is that trivial complaints, and even activity which is undesirable or illegal, will not fall within the scope of the prohibition in Article 3 unless it causes sufficiently serious suffering or humiliation to the victim. However, in the *Selmouni* case,[13] the Strasbourg Court indicated that interpretation of the Convention as a living instrument could result in acts classified in the early case-law as inhuman or degrading treatment being classified as torture in the future. Presumably, it would follow that conduct which previously had not attained the threshold for categorization as inhuman or degrading treatment might be so categorized in the future.

In the *Jalloh* case,[14] the Grand Chamber restated the Court's long-standing view:

> According to the Court's well-established case-law, ill-treatment must attain a minimum level of severity if it is to fall within the scope of Article 3. The assessment of this minimum level of severity is relative; it depends on all the circumstances of the case, such as the duration of the treatment, its physical and mental effects and, in some cases, the sex, age and state of health of the victim....[15]

So, for example, attacks on an applicant's honesty and way of life which were motivated by racial discrimination constitute an aggravating factor when considering whether treatment accorded to him reached the minimum level of severity.[16] But in another case, the Strasbourg Court found that strip searches of visitors (one of whom had a learning difficulty) to a prison, which were not carried out in accordance with national rules in a number of respects and caused the individuals significant distress, did not reach the minimum level of severity to fall within Article 3, though they did constitute a violation of Article 8.[17] The Strasbourg Court subjects allegations of violations of Article 3 to a particularly thorough scrutiny even if there have been domestic proceedings and investigations into the allegations. The enquiries in the national legal order must themselves be very thorough, and represent a genuine attempt to find out what happened and who may be responsible for any reprehensible conduct.[18]

THE CONCEPT OF AN ADMINISTRATIVE PRACTICE

Where the factual evidence shows that the complained of action, even though it is unlawful, has been repeated time and again by agents of the State, and where there has been official tolerance of the conduct at more senior level, this has come to be known as an

[12] *Ireland v United Kingdom*, 18 January 1978, Series A No 25, (1979–80) 2 EHRR 25, § 162; and *Tyrer v United Kingdom*, 25 April 1978, Series A No 26, (1979–80) 2 EHRR 1, § 30.

[13] *Selmouni v France*, (App. 25803/94), 28 July 1999 [GC], (2000) 29 EHRR 403, ECHR 1999-V, § 101. See also M. Addo and N. Grief, 'Is there a policy behind the decisions and judgments relating to Article 3 of the European Convention on Human Rights?' (1995) 20 ELRev 178.

[14] *Jalloh v Germany*, (App. 54810/00), 11 July 2006 [GC], (2007) 44 EHRR 667, ECHR 2006-IX.

[15] § 67. See also *Kafkaris v Cyprus*, (App. 21906/04), 12 February 2008 [GC], (2009) 49 EHRR 877, ECHR 2008-nyr, § 95.

[16] *Moldovan and others v Romania*, (Apps. 41138/98 and 64320/01), 12 July 2005, (2007) 44 EHRR 302, ECHR 2005-VII, § 111.

[17] *Wainwright v United Kingdom*, (App. 12350/04), 26 September 2006, (2007) 44 EHRR 809, ECHR 2006-X.

[18] See, for example, *Muradova v Azerbaijan*, (App. 22684/05), 2 April 2009, §§ 99 and 101.

'administrative practice.' In *Ireland v United Kingdom*, the Strasbourg Court characterized an administrative practice as:

> an accumulation of identical or analogous breaches which are sufficiently numerous and inter-connected to amount not merely to isolated incidents or exceptions but to a pattern or system....[19]

This has a double significance. First, at the stage of admissibility, the usual requirement to exhaust domestic remedies may well be disregarded.[20] Secondly, on consideration of the merits, the finding of an administrative practice, implying official tolerance of the pattern of conduct, is clearly far more serious than an isolated incident of improper conduct by individuals.

DEFINING TORTURE

The United Nations General Assembly's definition of torture in the 1975 Declaration provides a helpful starting point in stating that:

> Torture constitutes an aggravated and deliberate form of cruel, inhuman and degrading treatment or punishment.[21]

The United Nations built on the Declaration with the Convention Against Torture (UNCAT) containing a more detailed definition of torture:

> ... the term 'torture' means any act by which severe pain or suffering, whether physical or mental, is intentionally inflicted on a person for such purposes as obtaining from him or a third person information or a confession, punishing him for an act he or a third person has committed or is suspected of having committed, or intimidating or coercing him or a third person, or for any reason based on discrimination of any kind, when such pain or suffering is inflicted by or at the instigation of or with the consent or acquiescence of a public official or other person acting in an official capacity. It does not include pain or suffering arising only from, inherent in or incidental to lawful sanctions.[22]

The UN Convention clearly differentiates between torture and other forms of ill-treatment. Inhuman and degrading treatment is covered by Article 16 which states that Contracting Parties shall undertake to prevent acts of cruel, inhuman or degrading treatment not amounting to torture, where such acts are committed or instigated with the consent or acquiescence of a public official or a person acting in an official capacity.[23] This distinction has important consequences under the UN Convention as prohibitions of State action and the legal obligations placed on States are only applicable to torture under Article 1.[24]

[19] *Ireland v United Kingdom*, 18 January 1978, Series A No 25, (1979–80) 2 EHRR 25, § 159. See also *Caraher v the United Kingdom*, (App. 24520/94), 11 January 2000, ECHR 2000-I, which summarizes the case-law on administrative practice.

[20] Since legal action in respect of a single incident may not address the repetitive nature of the conduct:, *Donnelly and others v United Kingdom*, (Apps. 5577–83/72) 5 April 1973, (1973) 16 *Yearbook* 212. *Manole and others v Moldova*, (App. 13936/02), 17 September 2009, § 84-85, See further ch.2.

[21] UNGA Res. 3452 (XXX) of 9 December 1975, Declaration on the protection of all persons from being subjected to torture and other cruel, inhuman or degrading treatment or punishment, Art. 1.

[22] United Nations Convention Against Torture and Other Cruel, Inhuman or Degrading Treatment or Punishment 1984, Art. 1.

[23] United Nations Convention Against Torture and Other Cruel, Inhuman or Degrading Treatment or Punishment 1984, Art. 16.

[24] See M. Evans, 'Getting to Grips with Torture', (2002) ICLQ 51(2), 365–383.

In contrast, Article 3 of the European Convention on Human Rights clearly prohibits all three forms of ill-treatment in the Article. However a finding of torture may be relevant to the assessment of damages under Article 41 of the Convention as well as impacting on the admissibility of evidence under Article 6.[25]

The definition of torture was discussed at length in the Commission's Report in the *Greek* case on the alleged violations of Article 3 by the Greek Government after the revolution of 21 April 1967.[26] However, the leading authority is the judgment of the Strasbourg Court in *Ireland v United Kingdom*, which concluded that:

> ... it was the intention that the Convention with its distinction between torture and inhuman treatment should by the first of these terms attach a special stigma to deliberate inhuman treatment causing very serious and cruel suffering.[27]

The distinction between torture and inhuman treatment is frequently one of degree. In every case the determination of whether there has been torture, inhuman or degrading treatment must be decided in the light of all the circumstances of the case. In *Ireland v United Kingdom*, the Strasbourg Court suggested that the following factors were relevant in determining the existence of inhuman treatment: the duration of the treatment, its physical or mental effects, and the sex, age, and state of health of the victim.[28] In the *Tyrer* judgment, the Court said that the nature and context of the punishment itself, and the manner and method of its execution should be considered in determining whether a punishment constituted degrading treatment.[29] The threshold of seriousness required and the need to consider the relative nature of the conduct in context indicate that the prohibition in Article 3 is not a static one, but receives a living interpretation and must be considered in the light of present-day circumstances.[30]

In *Ireland v United Kingdom*,[31] the Irish Government alleged that persons in custody in Northern Ireland had been subjected to treatment which constituted torture and inhuman and degrading treatment and punishment within the meaning of Article 3 of the Convention and that such treatment constituted an administrative practice. In issue, in particular, were the five techniques for interrogating detained persons in depth, consisting of covering their heads with hoods, obliging them to stand for long periods against a wall with the limbs outstretched, subjecting them to intense noise, depriving them of sleep, and feeding them on a diet of bread and water. After a committee of inquiry in the United Kingdom had looked into these techniques and consideration by Privy Counsellors, the Prime Minister announced in March 1972 that the interrogation techniques would be discontinued. The Commission's Report of February 1976 concluded that the five techniques amounted to torture and inhuman treatment in breach of Article 3.[32] The Irish Government referred the case to the Court which gave judgment in 1978. Rather to the surprise of many, it concluded that the five techniques did not amount to torture, though they did constitute inhuman and degrading treatment. The case is especially important for its contribution to the case-law on the definition

[25] See ch.13 with regard to the difference between torture and other forms of ill-treatment when the Court is examining the use of confession and other evidence, *see Gäfgen v Germany*, (App. 22978/05), 1 June 2010; *El Haski v Belgium*, (App. 649/08), 25 September 2012.

[26] App. 3321/67, *Denmark v Greece*; App. 3322/67, *Norway v Greece*; App. 3323/67, *Sweden v Greece*; and App. 3344/67, *Netherlands v Greece* ('the *Greek* case'), Report of 18 November 1969, (1969) 12 *Yearbook* 1, 186–510.

[27] *Ireland v United Kingdom*, 18 January 1978, Series A No 25, (1979–80) 2 EHRR 25, § 167.

[28] § 162. [29] *Tyrer v United Kingdom*, 25 April 1978, Series A No 26, (1979–80) 2 EHRR 1, § 30.

[30] *Selmouni v France*, (App. 25803/94), 28 July 1999, (2000) 29 EHRR 403, ECHR 1999-V, § 101.

[31] *Ireland v United Kingdom*, 18 January 1978, Series A No 25, (1979–80) 2 EHRR 25.

[32] (1976) 19 *Yearbook* 512, 774–6.

of the terms used in Article 3, but it contains many mixed signals. While the majority limited the finding to inhuman and degrading treatment, several judges in the minority concluded that the five techniques amounted to torture and the British judge, Sir Gerald Fitzmaurice, in a powerful, but often considered partial, dissenting opinion concluded that they did not amount even to inhuman and degrading treatment.[33]

In the *Aksoy* case,[34] the Strasbourg Court, for the first time, found a Contracting Party guilty of torture. The applicant had been stripped naked, with his arms tied together behind his back, and suspended by his arms. The Court considered that this form of treatment must have been deliberately inflicted, and was of such a serious and cruel nature that it could only be described as torture.[35] In coming to this conclusion, the Court affirmed what it had said in *Ireland v United Kingdom* and noted:

> In order to determine whether any particular form of ill-treatment should be qualified as torture, the Court must have regard to the distinction drawn in Article 3 between this notion and that of inhuman or degrading treatment. As it has remarked before, this distinction would appear to have been embodied in the Convention to allow the special stigma of 'torture' to attach only to deliberate inhuman treatment causing very serious and cruel suffering.[36]

Findings of torture have since been made in many other cases against a number of Contracting Parties. This greater willingness to categorize conduct as torture was signalled in the *Selmouni* case.[37] The case concerned ill-treatment in France of persons suspected of involvement in drug-trafficking. The applicant was, over a number of days, exposed to severe beatings, made to run along a corridor with police officers on either side to trip him up, invited to suck a police officer's penis, urinated upon, and threatened with a blowlamp and then a syringe. The Strasbourg Court concluded, unanimously, that the physical and mental violence, considered as a whole caused severe pain and suffering that was particularly serious and cruel, and was properly categorized as torture. It is almost certain that if similar facts to those in *Ireland v United Kingdom* came before the Strasbourg Court today, it would have no hesitation in categorizing the interrogation techniques as torture.

Unsurprisingly, repeated beating and rape of a witness by the police has been found to amount to torture.[38] It is particularly shocking that such conduct could happen in one of the Contracting Parties to the European Convention.[39]

DEFINING INHUMAN TREATMENT

Inhuman treatment need not necessarily be deliberate and includes suffering that arises out of conditions of detention.[40] All the circumstances of the case must be considered. The Strasbourg Court has repeatedly said:

[33] See M. O'Boyle, 'Torture and Emergency Powers under the European Convention on Human Rights' (1977) 71 AJIL 674; and D. Bonner, '*Ireland v United Kingdom*' (1978) 27 ICLQ 897. Note that in 1997, the United Nations Committee Against Torture found similar techniques amounted to torture (Concluding Observations of the Committee Against Torture, Israel (A/52/44, paras. 253-260, 09/05/97). As noted the UK discontinued the techniques in 1972. However, these techniques have been used by UK troops implicated in the death of Baha Mousa and other incidents in Iraq, see *The Report of the Baha Mousa Inquiry*, September 2011: Volume I–III accessible at: www.bahamousainquiry.org.

[34] *Aksoy v Turkey*, (App. 21987/93), 18 December 1996, (1997) 23 EHRR 553, ECHR 1996-VI.

[35] § 64. [36] § 63.

[37] *Selmouni v France*, (App. 25803/94), 28 July 1999, (2000) 29 EHRR 403, ECHR 1999-V, § 101.

[38] *Maslova and Nalbandov v Russia*, (App. 839/02), 24 January 2008, ECHR 2008-nyr.

[39] See also *Aydin v Turkey*, (App. 23178/94), (1997) 25 EHRR 251.

[40] *Labita v Italy*, (App. 26772/95), 6 April 2000 [GC], (2008) 46 EHRR 1228, ECHR 2000-IV, § 120.

> Treatment has been held by the Court to be 'inhuman' because, *inter alia*, it was premeditated, was applied for hours at a stretch and caused either actual bodily injury or intense physical and mental suffering, and also 'degrading' because it was such as to arouse in its victims feelings of fear, anguish and inferiority capable of humiliating and debasing them. In order for a punishment or treatment associated with it to be 'inhuman' or 'degrading', the suffering or humiliation involved must in any event go beyond that inevitable element of suffering or humiliation connected with a given form of legitimate treatment or punishment. The question whether the purpose of the treatment was to humiliate or debase the victim is a further factor to be taken into account but the absence of any such purpose cannot conclusively rule out a finding of a violation of Article 3.[41]

It seems that beatings by the police will not attain the threshold to constitute torture where they occur 'over a short period of heightened tension and emotions' and where there are no aggravating factors, such as an aim to extract a confession, or conduct with racist motivation. Such conduct will, however, constitute inhuman treatment.[42]

The following situations have been found by the Court to amount to inhuman treatment:[43] ill-treatment in detention, deportation or extradition where there is a real risk of inhuman treatment in the proposed country of destination, anxiety caused by failure to carry out a proper investigation into a disappearance, and destruction of personal property.

Sometimes the Strasbourg Court does not distinguish between inhuman and degrading treatment. So in the case of *II v Bulgaria*,[44] the Strasbourg Court categorized simply as 'inhuman and degrading treatment' the detention of an individual for three months in a very small cell without any natural light or satisfactory ventilation, coupled with poor sanitary facilities and no provision for spending time out of his cell.[45]

In the *Öcalan* case,[46] the Court concluded that the imposition of the death penalty after an unfair trial would constitute a breach of Article 2; and this conclusion informed their finding that the imposition of the death penalty after an unfair trial would also constitute inhuman treatment.[47] The Court has further found that the death penalty is in itself a violation of Article 3, amounting to inhuman treatment.[48]

DEFINING DEGRADING TREATMENT

As noted earlier, it has sometimes been said that degrading treatment requires the presence of gross humiliation before others or being driven to act against will or conscience. However, the Strasbourg Court has stated on several occasions that gross humiliation, as the purpose of the acts in issue, is not always a necessary ingredient of degrading treatment.[49] Nor is intention to

[41] *T & V v United Kingdom*, (Apps. 24888/94 and 24724/94), 16 December 1999 [GC], (2000) 30 EHRR 121, ECHR 1999-IX, § 71. See also *Jalloh v Germany*, (App. 54810/00), 11 July 2006 [GC], (2007) 44 EHRR 667, ECHR 2006-IX, § 68.

[42] See, for example, *Egmez v Cyprus*, (App. 30873/96), 21 December 2000, (2002) 34 EHRR 753, ECHR 2000-XII, § 78.

[43] See further later in this chapter.

[44] *II v Bulgaria*, (App. 44082/98), 9 June 2005. See also *Mayzit v Russia*, (App. 63378/00), 20 January 2005.

[45] On prison conditions, see further later in this chapter.

[46] *Öcalan v Turkey*, (App. 46221/99), 12 May 2005 [GC], (2005) 41 EHRR 985, ECHR 2005-IV.

[47] § 169. Note that in *Ilaşcu and others v Moldova and Russia*, (App. 48787/99), 8 July 2004 [GC], (2005) 40 EHRR 1030, ECHR 2004-VII, §§ 434–42, the Court found that living in the 'constant shadow of death' for some years by reason of a death sentence which had no legal basis or legitimacy, coupled with the conditions of the applicant's detention, amounted to torture.

[48] *Al Saadoon and Mufdhi v United Kingdom*, (App. 61498/08), 2 March 2010, § 121.

[49] See, for example, *Poltoratskiy v Ukraine*, (App. 38812/97), 29 April 2003, ECHR 2003-V, § 131.

humiliate.[50] But where humiliation or debasement is present, the threshold of severity would appear to require that the humiliation is severe. The process of investigation and discharge of homosexuals in the armed forces was found not to reach the requisite threshold in the *Smith and Grady* case.[51] The Court, however, noted that it would not exclude the possibility that treatment 'grounded upon a predisposed bias on the part of a heterosexual majority against a homosexual minority' could fall within the scope of Article 3.

The Commission has considered that racial discrimination could constitute degrading treatment.[52] In the *Marckx* case[53] the Court ruled that legal rules discriminating against illegitimate children did not constitute degrading treatment within Article 3, though the case might be decided differently if the same situation arose today. In *Cyprus v Turkey*[54] the Strasbourg Court found that Greek Cypriots living in the Karpas region of northern Cyprus had been subject to discriminatory treatment which attained a level of severity which amounted to degrading treatment.[55]

The *Moldovan* case[56] concerned the treatment by Romania of Romanian nationals of Roma origin, whose homes were destroyed with the involvement of State officials, who had also mismanaged the reconstruction programme such that the applicants and their families had been forced to live for a considerable period of time in 'cellars, hen-houses, stables, burned out shells, or to move in with friends and relatives in such overcrowded conditions that illness frequently occurred.'[57] The Strasbourg Court considered that a particularly serious violation of Article 8 of a continuing nature aggravated by racial motives constituted degrading treatment, since it involved an interference with the applicants' human dignity.

OBLIGATIONS CONCERNING THE REMOVAL OF PERSONS FROM THE STATE

In certain circumstances Article 3 can have an extraterritorial effect. In the *Soering* case,[58] the Strasbourg Court recognized that a Contracting Party may violate the obligations in Article 3 if its action exposes a person to the likelihood of ill-treatment in a place outside the jurisdiction of the Contracting Parties. The case concerned possible extradition to the United States where the 'death row phenomenon' was regarded as inhuman punishment. The Court made clear that the violation of the Convention in such circumstances is that of the sending State, and, by implication, the Court is not seeking to pass any judgment on a State which is not a party to the Convention.[59]

[50] *Peers v Greece*, (App. 28524/95), 19 April 2001, (2001) 33 EHRR 1192, ECHR 2001-III.

[51] *Smith and Grady v United Kingdom*, (Apps. 33985/96 and 33986/96), 27 September 1999, (2000) 29 EHRR 493, ECHR 1999-VI, §§ 120–3.

[52] Apps. 4403–19/70, 4422/70, 4434/70, 4476–8/70, 4486/70, 4501/70, 4526–30/70, *East African Asians v United Kingdom*, Decision of the Commission, 10 and 18 October 1970 (1970) 13 *Yearbook* 928; Report of the Commission, 14 December 1973 (1994) 78-A DR 5; Committee of Ministers Resolution DH (77) 2 of 21 October 1977 (1977) 20 *Yearbook* 642; and Committee of Ministers Resolution DH (94) 30 of 21 March 1994 (1994) 78-A DR 70, deciding to make the Report of the Commission public at the request of the United Kingdom Government; (1981) 3 EHRR 76, §§ 207–8 of the Report.

[53] *Marckx v Belgium*, 13 June 1979, Series A No 31, (1979–80) 2 EHRR 330.

[54] *Cyprus v Turkey*, (App. 25781/94), 10 May 2001, (2002) 35 EHRR 731, ECHR 2001-IV.

[55] §§ 302–311.

[56] *Moldovan and others v Romania*, (Apps 41138/98 and 64320/01), 12 July 2005, (2007) 44 EHRR 302, ECHR 2005-VII.

[57] § 90.

[58] *Soering v United Kingdom*, 7 July 1989, Series A No 161, (1989) 11 EHRR 439.

[59] § 91.

In the *Chahal* case,[60] the United Kingdom was precluded from returning a Sikh separatist to India, because the Court concluded that there would be a very real risk that the applicant would be the victim of ill-treatment at the hands of rogue elements within the Punjab Police.[61] The Court has also found that substantial grounds for believing there is a real risk to the applicant from private parties does not exclude the application of Article 3.[62]

The *D* case[63] presented a rather different set of circumstances. D was a national of St Kitts, who had been arrested at Gatwick Airport in possession of a large quantity of cocaine. While serving a prison sentence, he was discovered to be suffering from AIDS. As is normal, on completion of his prison sentence, he was subject to deportation back to St Kitts. He argued that he was in the advanced stages of the illness, medical services in St Kitts would be unable to provide treatment for his condition, and he had no relatives or friends in St Kitts who could care for him. This, he argued, would constitute treatment in breach of Article 3. The risk he had identified was, unlike the earlier cases, not a risk of intentional ill-treatment emanating from public authorities or private groups in his State of origin, but inherent inadequacies in the medical services in his home country. The Court emphasized the fundamental nature of the protection afforded by Article 3, and was clearly influenced by the consequences of the abrupt withdrawal of the medical and personal care afforded to him in the United Kingdom by the Terrence Higgins Trust, a leading AIDS charity. In the 'very exceptional circumstances'[64] of this case, the Court concluded that deportation to St Kitts would be a violation of Article 3 amounting to inhuman treatment.

In the *N* case,[65] the Grand Chamber clarified that the deportation of a person suffering from HIV or AIDS would not normally give rise to a violation of Article 3, even where the level of treatment available in the country of origin would be likely to fall far short of that enjoyed in the deporting State. The likelihood of a dramatically reduced life expectancy and the suffering attendant on dying from an AIDS-related disease would not amount to 'exceptional circumstances'. It would seem that only the removal of a person who was actually on the point of death, as in the *D* case, or possibly a pregnant woman whose child could be saved by anti-retroviral medication during pregnancy and immediately after birth, would give rise to a violation of Article 3. The Court in the *N* case stated that similar principles would apply in relation to the removal of a non-national suffering not just from AIDS or HIV but from any life-threatening physical or mental illness.[66]

In the *Jabari* case,[67] the Court considered that the deportation to Iran of a woman, who had been found to have had an adulterous relationship in that country in respect of which criminal proceedings had been instituted, would violate Article 3 because she would be at serious risk of punishment by stoning there. In an admissibility decision, the Court

[60] *Chahal v United Kingdom*, (App. 22414/93), 15 November 1996, (1997) 23 EHRR 413, ECHR 1996-V. The case was affirmed in *Saadi v Italy*, (App. 37201/06), 28 February 2008 [GC], (2009) 49 EHRR 730, ECHR 2008-nyr.

[61] See also *Ahmed v Austria*, (App. 25964/94), 17 December 1996, (1997) 24 EHRR 278.

[62] *HLR v France*, (App. 24573/94), 29 April 1997, (1998) 26 EHRR 29, ECHR 1997-III.

[63] *D v United Kingdom*, (App. 30240/96), 2 May 1997, (1997) 24 EHRR 423, ECHR 1997-III.

[64] § 54.

[65] *N v United Kingdom*, (App. 26565/05), 27 May 2008, ECHR 2008-nyr.

[66] See also *Bensaid v United Kingdom*, (App. 44599/98), 6 February 2001, (2001) 33 EHRR 205, ECHR 2001-I, where no violation was found. The dissenting judges in *N v United Kingdom* were critical of the Court's approach to establishing the threshold needed to engage Article 3. They argued that the Court had undermined the absolute nature of Article 3 by alluding to a balancing act between State considerations and the individual in Article 3 and including State resources as one of the circumstances to consider when deciding if Article 3 is engaged, *N v United Kingdom*, (App. 26565/05), 27 May 2008, ECHR 2008-nyr, Joint Dissenting Opinion Of Judges Tulkens, Bonello, and Spielmann.

[67] *Jabari v Turkey*, (App. 40035/98), 11 July 2000, ECHR 2000-VIII.

accepted that if a person deported to Nigeria could show a real risk of being subject to female genital mutilation, Article 3 would be engaged.[68]

There is nothing wrong in obtaining assurances from the receiving State that a person to be extradited will not be sentenced to death or life imprisonment, as in the *Olaechea Cahuas* case,[69] where Peru gave such an undertaking. In *Othman (Abu Qatada) v United Kingdom*,[70] the Court expanded on the criteria it will apply when considering diplomatic assurances from the receiving State. In examining the efficacy of assurances the Court will consider if the human rights situation in the receiving State excludes the use of assurances.[71] This would happen only in rare cases. If the situation does not exclude the use of assurances the court will examine several factors before accepting such assurances: whether assurances have been disclosed to the Court; whether the assurances are specific or general and vague; who has given the assurances and whether these can bind the receiving State, if the assurances come from the central government and bind local authorities; whether the assurances concern treatment which is legal or illegal in the receiving State; whether given by a Contracting State, the bilateral relations between the States in question; whether compliance with assurances can be objectively verified; whether there is effective protection against torture and the applicant's previous history in the receiving State; and, whether the assurances have been assessed by domestic courts in the sending State.[72] In *Othman*, the applicant argued that if the UK removed him to Jordan he would be subject to ill-treatment and would be put on trial based on evidence gained through torture. Jordan had given assurances to the UK of the applicant's safety and a fair trial. The Court accepted the assurances concerning ill-treatment but rejected the assurances given with regard to the risk of a flagrant denial of justice under Article 6 due to the use of torture evidence.[73]

In determining whether there would be a risk that a person would be subject to treatment falling within Article 3 if removed to another country, the Strasbourg Court will take account of reports of non-governmental organizations (such as Amnesty International),[74] but may conclude that such findings constitute a description of the general situation and do not support specific allegations made by applicants to the Strasbourg Court,[75] which will require corroboration by other evidence. Present circumstances, rather than the historical position, will always be decisive. In the *Mamatkulov and Askarov* case, the Grand Chamber stated the requirements as follows:

> In determining whether substantial grounds have been shown for believing that a real risk of treatment contrary to Article 3 exists, the Court will assess the issue in the light of all the material placed before it or, if necessary, material obtained *proprio motu*. Since the nature of the Contracting States' responsibility in cases of this kind lies in the act of exposing an individual to the risk of ill-treatment, the existence of the risk must be assessed primarily with reference to those facts which were known or ought to have been known to the Contracting State at the time of extradition; the Court is not precluded, however, from having regard to information which comes to light subsequent to the extradition. This may have value in

[68] *Collins and Akaziebe v Sweden*, (App. 23944/05), Decision of 8 March 2007, ECHR 2007-nyr, though there was no such risk established on the facts of this application.

[69] *Olaechea Cahuas v Spain*, (App. 24668/03), 10 August 2006, (2009) 48 EHRR 572, ECHR 2006-X.

[70] *Othman (Abu Qatada) v United Kingdom*, (App. 8139/09), 17 January 2012.

[71] § 188.

[72] § 189.

[73] See ch.12.

[74] *Saadi v Italy*, (App. 37201/06), 28 February 2008 [GC], (2009) 49 EHRR 730, ECHR 2008-nyr, § 138. See also *NA v United Kingdom*, (App. 25904/07), 17 July 2008, (2009) 48 EHRR 337, ECHR 2008-nyr.

[75] As it did in *Mamatkulov and Askarov v Turkey*, (Apps. 46827/99 and 46951/99), 4 February 2005 [GC], (2005) 41 EHRR 494, ECHR 2005-I.

confirming or refuting the appreciation that has been made by the Contracting Party of the well-foundedness or otherwise of an applicant's fears.[76]

Where the applicant has not been extradited or deported when the Court examines the case, the Court will assess the risk of ill-treatment at the time of the proceedings before the Court. This situation typically arises when deportation or extradition is delayed as a result of an indication by the Court of interim measures under rule 39 of the Rules of Court. Such an indication means more often than not that the Court does not yet have before it all the relevant evidence it requires to determine whether there is a real risk of treatment proscribed by Article 3 in the country of destination.[77] There has been a worrying increase in the number of occasions when a Contracting Party fails to comply with these interim measures, which will frequently result in a finding of a violation of Article 34.[78]

Where deportation of an unaccompanied young child is involved, there must be proper arrangements for the welfare of the child both throughout the journey and on arrival at the destination. Failure to put such arrangements in place will violate Article 3.[79]

The issue of the unlawful rendition of a person from one State to another has led to several cases before the Strasbourg Court, which examine the use of extraordinary rendition by the CIA involving the alleged complicity of European States in the removal of suspected terrorists to secret interrogation centres in non-European States. In *El-Masri v The Former Yugoslav Republic of Macedonia*,[80] the applicant lived in Germany. He was visiting Macedonia when he was held by Macedonian authorities, before being handed over to CIA agents at Skopje airport and flown to Afghanistan. As well as finding a substantive violation of Article 3 due to ill-treatment by the Macedonian authorities and acquiescence in ill-treatment by CIA agents, the Court also found Macedonia violated Article 3 for allowing the applicant to be flown to a place where there were substantial grounds for believing he was at real risk of ill-treatment.[81] Similar issues have arisen in cases brought against Russia where applicants were removed outside the normal processes of the law. In *Abdulkhakov v Russia*,[82] the Court noted that 'any extra-judicial transfer or extraordinary rendition, by its deliberate circumvention of due process, is an absolute negation of the rule of law and the values protected by the Convention. It therefore amounts to a violation of the most basic rights guaranteed by the Convention.'[83]

In a number of cases involving asylum seekers, the Court has held a Contracting State had violated Article 3. In *Hirsi Jaama and others v Italy*,[84] an Italian naval ship picked up asylum seekers at sea and returned them to Libya, where there was a risk they would be removed to Eritrea and Somalia. Once the Court established that the Italian naval ship's interdiction of the asylum seekers at sea was under the jurisdiction of the Convention it was held that Article 3 had been violated by the applicant's return to Libya and the risk of repatriation to Eritrea and Somalia. Apart from removal to non-Convention States, the

[76] § 69. [77] § 69. See also *N v Finland*, (App. 38885/02), 26 July 2005.

[78] For example, *Paladi v Moldova*, (App. 39806/05), 10 March 2009 [GC]. Note also the reported handover on 31 December 2008, in breach of interim measures ordered by the Strasbourg Court, to Iraqi authorities by British forces in Iraq of Faisal Al-Saadoon and Khalaf Mufdhi, who are accused of murdering two British soldiers: *Al Saadoon and Mufdhi v United Kingdom*, (App. 61498/08), 2 March 2010. See also *Mannai v Italy*, (App. 9961/10), 27 March 2012; *Abdulkhakov v Russia*, (App. 14743/11), 2 October 2012; *Rrapo v Albania*, (App. 58555/10), 25 September 2012; *Makharadze and Sikharulidze v Georgia*, (App. 35254/07), 22 November 2011.

[79] *Mubilanzila Mayeka and Kaniki Mitunga v Belgium*, (App. 13178/03), 12 June 2006, (2008) 46 EHRR 449, ECHR 2006-XI.

[80] *El-Masri v The Former Yugoslav Republic of Macedonia*, (App. 39630/09), 13 December 2012.

[81] The Court also found a procedural violation for a failure to investigate.

[82] *Abdulkhakov v Russia*, (App. 14743/11), 2 October 2012. [83] § 189.

[84] *Hirsi Jaama and others v Italy*, (App. 27765/09), 23 February 2012.

Court has also examined cases between Contracting States who are also members of the European Union. These cases are known as the 'Dublin' cases as under the EU 'Dublin system'[85] the EU Member State where the asylum seeker first enters and is registered is responsible for processing an asylum claim. If the asylum seeker moves to another State and claims asylum, that State may return the asylum seeker to the first State. The Court has found a number of cases which challenged return to another EU Member State as inadmissible. There has been an assumption that Member States would provide a safe return.[86] However, the Court will not defer from scrutinizing such returns and in *MSS v Belgium and Greece*[87] it found that Belgium violated Article 3 due to the real risk of ill-treatment to an asylum seeker if returned to Greece as the State responsible for the asylum claim of the applicant under the Dublin process. The Court examined the applicant's detention and living conditions when released from detention in Greece. It found not only that the conditions of detention for asylum seekers in Greece violated Article 3,[88] but that the situation of destitution that the applicant found himself in when released from detention was within the responsibility of the State. The Greek authorities knew about his situation and under a European Directive for the reception of asylum seekers[89] transposed into national law, Greece had accepted legal responsibilities for the treatment of asylum seekers. The inaction of the Greek authorities meant the applicant could not access his rights under Greek law. If Greece had examined his application for asylum promptly, the destitution in which the applicant found himself would not have arisen. His living conditions amounted to degrading treatment under Article 3.[90]

Cases concerning removal to a State where there is a real risk of ill-treatment have been important in expanding the application of Article 3 and have proved controversial, examining issues of sensitivity for states such as terrorism and asylum. The Court has been prepared to give close scrutiny to State behaviour in these cases, even where removal to a Contracting State is involved.[91] However, in areas that have resource implications such as health, the Court has been more reluctant to find violations except in the most extreme cases.

DISAPPEARANCES

A number of cases have addressed the application of Article 3 to situations where a close relative of the applicant has disappeared, and the events surrounding the disappearance

[85] Convention Determining the State Responsible for Examining Applications for Asylum Lodged in One of the Member States of the European Communities [1997] OJ C 254/1. (Dublin convention), replaced by Council Regulation (EC) No 343/2003 of 18 February 2003 establishing the criteria and mechanisms for determining the Member State responsible for examining an asylum application lodged in one of the Member States by a third-country national OJ L 50/1 (Dublin II regulation).

[86] *KRS v United Kingdom* (App. 32733/08), Decision of 2 December 2008, *Mohammed Hussein v Netherlands and Italy* (App. 27725/10) Decision of 2 April 2013.

[87] *MSS v Belgium and Greece*, (App. 30696/09), 21 January 2011.

[88] §§ 223–234, the Court noted the CPT and NGO reports into conditions in the detention centres for asylum seekers including overcrowding and poor sanitation; see also the Court's finding of violations in *S.D. v Greece*,(App. 53541/07), 11 June 2009, §§ 49–54, *A.A. v Greece*, (App. 12186/08), 22 July 2010, §§ 57–65.

[89] Council Directive 2003/9/EC of 27 January 2003 laying down minimum standards for the reception of asylum seekers. OJ L 31/18 (6 February 2003).

[90] §§ 249–264.

[91] The Strasbourg Court has ruled that removal of a person from Georgia to Russia would constitute a violation of Article 3 given the evidence of persecution in Russia of individuals of Chechen origin who have lodged applications with the Strasbourg Court. *Shamayev and others v Georgia and Russia*, (App. 36378/02), 12 April 2005, ECHR 2005-III.

have not been sufficiently investigated by the authorities.[92] The *Kurt* case,[93] which was an application by a mother in relation to her disappeared son, appears to be the first consideration by the Strasbourg Court of this issue under Article 3. The Court accepted that the uncertainty, doubt, and apprehension suffered by the applicant over a prolonged and continuing period caused her severe mental distress and anguish. The authorities failed to give serious consideration to her requests for information about his whereabouts. The Commission had concluded that this constituted inhuman and degrading treatment. The Court simply categorizes it as a breach of Article 3.

The Court in the *Çakici* case[94] established some general principles governing disappearance cases. The applicant claimed that his brother had been detained by the authorities in November 1993. He subsequently disappeared. The applicant said that in May 1996 he was told by the authorities that his brother had been killed in a clash with security forces in February 1995. The respondent State claimed that the brother had not been taken into custody, that he was a militant member of the PKK, and had been killed in February 1995 in a clash with security forces. Evidence was adduced that the father of the applicant and the applicant had, in December 1993, submitted a petition to the authorities requesting information about the whereabouts of the disappearance of the brother. Enquiries continued to be made, notably by the applicant in September 1994. The response of the authorities was simply to verify whether records contained the name of the applicant's brother. The applicant complained that the lack of information about his brother's disappearance constituted inhuman treatment towards himself. The Court said:

> Whether a family member is [a victim of treatment contrary to Article 3] will depend on the existence of special factors which gives the suffering of the applicant a dimension and character distinct from the emotional distress which may be regarded as inevitably caused to relatives of a victim of a serious human rights violation. Relevant elements will include the proximity of the family tie (in that context, a certain weight will attach to the parent–child bond), the extent to which the family member witnessed the events in question, the involvement of the family member in attempts to obtain information about the disappeared person and the way in which the authorities responded to those enquiries. The Court would further emphasize that the essence of such a violation does not so much lie in the fact of the 'disappearance' of the family member but rather concerns the authorities' reactions and attitudes to the situation when it is brought to their attention. It is especially in respect of the latter that a relative may claim directly to be a victim of the authorities' conduct.[95]

In the particular circumstances of this case, the Court concluded that there was no violation.[96]

The *Gongadze* case[97] is a shocking example of a violation of both Article 2 and Article 3 in relation to the disappearance of a political journalist in Ukraine. His widow reported his disappearance a day after he had gone missing. A decapitated corpse was subsequently

[92] For a definition of the phenomenon of disappearances, see ch.8. For an account of the cases against Russia arising from its conduct in Chechnya, see P. Leach, 'The Chechen Conflict: Analysing the Oversight of the European Court of Human Rights' [2008] EHRLR 732.

[93] *Kurt v Turkey*, (App. 24276/94), 25 May 1998, (1999) 27 EHRR 373, ECHR 1998-III. The Court appears to have drawn some inspiration from the decision of the United Nations Human Rights Committee in *Quinteros v Uruguay*, 21 July 1983, Case 107/1981, (1983) 38 UNGAOR Supp. 40 Annex XXI, § 14.

[94] *Çakici v Turkey*, (App. 23657/94), 8 July 1999 [GC], (2001) 31 EHRR 133, ECHR 1999-IV.

[95] *Çakici v Turkey*, (App. 23657/94), 8 July 1999 [GC], (2001) 31 EHRR 133, ECHR 1998-IV, § 98.

[96] See also *Timurtaş v Turkey*, (App. 23531/94), 13 June 2000, (2001) 33 EHRR 121, ECHR 2000-VI, §§ 91–8; *Taş v Turkey*, (App. 24396/94), 14 November 2000, (2001) 33 EHRR 325, §§ 77–80; and *Cyprus v Turkey*, (App. 25781/94), 10 May 2001 [GC], (2002) 35 EHRR 731, ECHR 2001-IV, §§ 154–8.

[97] *Gongadze v Ukraine*, (App. 34056/02), 8 November 2005, (2006) 43 EHRR 967, ECHR 2005-XI.

found, but there were announcements and denials by officials that this was the body of the missing man. It was eventually established that this was indeed his corpse. A subsequent investigation established that the journalist had been kidnapped and killed with the collusion of the most senior parliamentarians. The Strasbourg Court found that the attitude of the investigating authorities towards the applicant and her family constituted degrading treatment.[98] These cases continue to come before the Court.[99] In the *El Masri* case, the Court made it clear the importance of finding the truth in cases involving disappearance to the relatives and for the protection of human rights in general:

> the Court also wishes to address another aspect of the inadequate character of the investigation in the present case, namely its impact on the right to the truth regarding the relevant circumstances of the case. In this connection it underlines the great importance of the present case not only for the applicant and his family, but also for other victims of similar crimes and the general public, who had the right to know what had happened.[100]

DESTRUCTION OF HOMES AND POSSESSIONS

In the *Bilgin* case,[101] the Strasbourg Court found that destruction of the applicant's house and his possessions during operations by the security forces constituted inhuman treatment. The acts were deliberate and the operations of the security forces had been conducted with complete disregard for the safety and welfare of the applicant.

In the *Moldovan* case[102] the Court found that the involvement of State agents in the destruction of the homes of those of Roma origin coupled with failures of State agencies to prosecute those responsible and to manage the reconstruction of the destroyed homes effectively were motivated by racial discrimination. This constituted a serious violation of Article 8 of the Convention, which in turn constituted degrading treatment in breach of Article 3.

CORPORAL PUNISHMENT

The extent to which corporal punishment constitutes conduct in breach of Article 3 has been considered by the Strasbourg Court in a number of cases. The *Tyrer* case[103] concerned the imposition of the penalty of birching in the Isle of Man on a 15-year-old who had been convicted of assault on a senior pupil at his school. The punishment was administered by a police constable in private in the presence of the boy's father and a doctor. In concluding that the punishment of Tyrer constituted degrading treatment, the Court had regard to its character as 'institutionalized violence', to the fact that the punishment

[98] For further examples, see *Bazorkina v Russia*, (App. 69481/01), 27 July 2006, (2008) 46 EHRR 261; and *Varnava and others v Turkey*, (Apps. 16064–6/90 and 16068–73/90), 18 September 2009.

[99] Further examples of cases that have found violations of Article 3 against Russia in regard to disappearances in Chechyna, see *Gakayeva and others v Russia*, (Apps. 51534/08, 4401/10, 25518/10, 28779/10, 33175/10, 47393/10, 54753/10, 58131/10, 62207/10, and 73784/10), 10 October 2013; *Yandiyev and others v Russia*, (Apps. 34541/06, 43811/06 and 1578/07), 10 October 2013.

[100] *El-Masri v The Former Yugoslav Republic Of Macedonia*, (App. 39630/09), 13 December 2012, § 191.

[101] *Bilgin v Turkey*, (App. 23819/94), 16 November 2000, (2003) 35 EHRR 879.

[102] *Moldovan and others v Romania*, (Apps. 41138/98 and 64320/01), 12 July 2005, (2007) 44 EHRR 302, ECHR 2005-VII.

[103] *Tyrer v United Kingdom*, 25 April 1978, Series A No 26, (1979–80) 2 EHRR 1.

constituted an assault on the applicant's dignity and physical integrity, which may have had adverse psychological effects, and to the anguish of anticipating the punishment.[104]

The *Campbell and Cosans* case[105] concerned the use of corporal punishment in schools. In one case, the parent was unable to obtain an assurance that her son would not be subject to corporal punishment, and in the other the son, on his father's advice, presented himself for punishment but refused to accept it and was immediately suspended from school until such time as he was willing to accept the punishment. The form of corporal punishment in issue was the striking of the hand with a leather strap known as a 'tawse'. The Commission concluded that there was no violation of Article 3 in these cases. The Court noted that neither child had been subjected to corporal punishment. Nevertheless, 'provided it is sufficiently real and immediate, a mere threat of conduct prohibited by Article 3 may itself be in conflict with the provision.'[106] The Court, however, concluded that the suffering resulting from the treatment of the two boys did not meet the level inherent in the notion of degrading treatment. The Court went on to consider whether other provisions of the Convention had been violated.[107]

In the *Costello-Roberts* case[108] the Strasbourg Court ruled that the striking of the clothed buttocks of a seven-year-old boy with a rubber-soled gym shoe as an automatic punishment for accumulating five demerit points at his boarding school had no severe long-lasting effects and did not reach the level of severity necessary to bring the matter within Article 3. The Court did, however, have some misgivings about the automatic nature of the punishment and the delay of three days between the accumulation of the demerit points and the imposition of the penalty.

As in other cases, a careful judgment needs to be applied to the particular circumstances of each case. Corporal punishments which have a long-lasting effect and reach the threshold of severity required will violate Article 3, whether imposed in a public or a private school. The United Kingdom has responded to these judgments by passing legislation to prohibit corporal punishment in schools.

The *A* case[109] concerned the stepfather of a boy born in 1984, who in 1993 beat the boy with a garden cane using considerable force. The stepfather was prosecuted for assault occasioning actual bodily harm, but a jury acquitted him, apparently not accepting that the prosecution had proved that the beatings were other than for 'lawful correction' amounting to 'reasonable chastisement' which was a defence in English law. The Court concluded that the circumstances of this case meant that the applicant was not protected against treatment or punishment contrary to Article 3 by the United Kingdom, and consequently there was a violation of Article 3.

PROTECTION FROM DOMESTIC VIOLENCE

The Strasbourg Court has placed obligations on States to take steps to protect the victims of domestic violence. In *Opuz v Turkey*,[110] the applicant and her mother were threatened and assaulted over a long period of time by the applicant's husband. The women made complaints

[104] § 33.

[105] *Campbell and Cosans v United Kingdom*, 25 February 1982, Series A No 48, (1982) 4 EHRR 293.

[106] § 26. [107] See ch.16.

[108] *Costello-Roberts v United Kingdom*, 25 March 1993, Series A No 247-C, (1994) 19 EHRR 112.

[109] *A v United Kingdom*, (App. 25599/94), 23 September 1998, (1999) 27 EHRR 611, ECHR 1998-VI.

[110] *Opuz v Turkey*, (App. 33401/02), 9 June 2009. This case has been described as a landmark case in the Strasbourg Court as the Court went on to find a violation of Article 14 and in so doing recognized the gender

and then withdrew them under threats from the husband. No prosecution was brought until the husband stabbed the applicant seven times. He was fined for this. He then killed the applicant's mother. He was sentenced to life imprisonment but released pending appeal. The Court found violations of Articles 2 and 3 as the State had failed to prosecute and did not use protective measures available. The Court elaborated on domestic violence highlighting the scale of the problem of gender based violence in Europe. The Court stressed that:

> the issue of domestic violence, which can take various forms ranging from physical to psychological violence or verbal abuse, cannot be confined to the circumstances of the present case. It is a general problem which concerns all member States and which does not always surface since it often takes place within personal relationships or closed circuits and it is not only women who are affected. The Court acknowledges that men may also be the victims of domestic violence and, indeed, that children, too, are often casualties of the phenomenon, whether directly or indirectly. Accordingly, the Court will bear in mind the gravity of the problem at issue when examining the present case.[111]

It noted that the Turkish authorities discontinued investigations into the complaints because they were withdrawn. Importantly, the Court recognized a failure by the State to consider why the complaints were withdrawn and noted that an effective legal framework should be able to continue proceedings in the public interest.[112] In subsequent cases, the Court has found a violation of Article 3 where the State failed to prevent a husband returning to the family home despite a conviction for violence and sexual abuse of his children[113] and the failure of the State to protect by allowing the perpetrator of domestic violence to remain in the commonly owned apartment where domestic violence took place.[114]

ACTS IN THE COURSE OF ARREST AND POLICE DETENTION

The circumstances of arrest or detention in connection with court proceedings can fall within Article 3 where the humiliation or debasement to which it gives rise attains a special level, which significantly differs from that inherent in the process.[115] In some situations the conduct of the arresting and detaining officers will be subject to close scrutiny.[116]

Placing defendants who present no substantiated security risk in a metal cage in court for their trial will constitute a violation of Article 3.[117] The use of handcuffs in connection with a

based violence as a form of discrimination for the first time. See ch.24, See also P. Londono, 'Developing Human Rights Principles in Cases of Gender-based Violence: *Opuz v Turkey* in the European Court of Human Rights', (2009) 9 IJCL 793.

111 § 132. 112 § 145.

113 *E S and others v Slovakia*, (App. 8227/04), 15 September 2009.

114 *B v Moldova*, (App. 61382/09), 16 July 2013; for further domestic violence cases where a violation of Article 3 was found due to a failure to protect see *Valiuliene v Lithuania*, (App. 33234/07), 26 March 2013; *Eremia and others v Moldova*, (App. 3564/11), 28 May 2013. The Court has also found violations of other rights in domestic violence cases such as Article 2 (*Kontrova v Slovakia*, (App. 751/04), 31 May 2007) and Article 8 (*Kalucza v Hungary*, (App. 57693/10), 24 April 2012).

115 *Raninen v Finland*, (App. 20972/92), 16 December 1997, (1998) 26 EHRR 563, ECHR 1997-VIII, § 55.

116 As, for example, in *Olteanu v Romania*, (App. 71090/01), 14 April 2009.

117 *Ramishvili and Kokhreidze v Georgia*, (App. 1704/06), 27 January 2009, §§ 96–102; *Ashot Harutyunyan v Armenia*, (App. 34334/04), 15 June 2010, § 126; *Khodorkovskiy v Russia*, (App.5829/04), 31 May 2011, §§ 120–126. In contrast in *Titarenko v Ukraine*, (App. 31720/02), 20 September 2012, the Court found there was no violation where the applicant was a security risk and there was much less publicity surrounding his case.

lawful arrest or detention does not normally give rise to an issue under Article 3, provided that it does not entail the use of force or public exposure exceeding what is reasonably necessary in the particular circumstances of each case.[118] All the circumstances must be considered including any reasonable belief that the person concerned would resist arrest or seek to escape, or be a danger to themselves or others. But even where the arrest and detention is unlawful, the Court will not always be convinced that being handcuffed so adversely affects the applicant that the minimum level of severity is reached for Article 3 to bite. However, the use of handcuffs in the particular circumstances must not be disproportionate to the security risk. Their use in transferring a sick prisoner in a weak condition from prison to hospital coupled with other aspects of his treatment constituted inhuman and degrading treatment in one case.[119]

In the *Tomasi* case[120] the applicant had been subjected to considerable ill-treatment over a period of nearly two days while in police custody. He had been slapped, kicked, punched, and given forearm blows, made to stand for long periods and without support, had his hands handcuffed behind his back, been made to stand naked in front of an open window, been deprived of food, and threatened with a firearm. The respondent State was unable to offer any explanation for the injuries suffered by the applicant. But they argued that the injuries suffered by the applicant did not meet the level of severity necessary to constitute a violation of Article 3, and that there were particular circumstances obtaining in Corsica where there was significant terrorist activity. The Court did not accept these arguments, and concluded that there had been a violation of Article 3.[121]

The *Ribitsch* case[122] might be regarded as the first of the modern cases on physical assault while in police custody, since it couples the failure of the authorities to provide an explanation for the applicant's injuries with its finding of a violation of Article 3. It was not disputed that the applicant's injuries had been sustained during police detention, and the respondent State was found not to have satisfactorily established that they were caused other than as a result of his treatment in custody. The Court found that the applicant had been the victim of inhuman and degrading treatment.[123]

The *Jalloh* case[124] addresses the limits of investigation methods following arrest. Jalloh was suspected of involvement in drug dealing, and had been seen to swallow a small plastic bag. While in detention, a prosecutor authorized the use of an emetic in order to secure the regurgitation of the item which had been swallowed. Jalloh resisted, but the medication was administered by force, and a bag of cocaine was regurgitated. The applicant argued that the forcible administration of the emetic amounted to a breach of Article 3, particularly in the light of considerable medical evidence of the dangers of such a procedure. The Strasbourg Court affirmed the obligation of the Contracting Parties to protect the physical well-being of those in detention under suspicion of having committed offences. While any measure which is regarded as of therapeutic necessity cannot be regarded as inhuman or degrading, procedures designed to secure evidence from a suspect require further

[118] *Raninen v Finland*, (App. 20972/92), 16 December 1997, (1998) 26 EHRR 563, ECHR 1997-VIII, §§ 52–9. See also *Erdoğan Yağiz v Turkey*, (App. 27473/02), 6 March 2007, ECHR 2007-nyr, where a violation was found.

[119] *Mouisel v France*, (App. 67263/01), 14 November 2002, (2004) 38 EHRR 735, ECHR 2002-IX; *Salakhov and Islyamova v Ukraine*, (App 28005/08), 14 March 2013.

[120] *Tomasi v France*, 27 August 1992, Series A No 241-A, (1993) 15 EHRR 1.

[121] § 11. See also *Klaas v Germany*, 22 September 1993, Series A No 269, (1994) 18 EHRR 305.

[122] *Ribitsch v Austria*, 4 December 1995, Series A No 336, (1996) 21 EHRR 573.

[123] See also *Aksoy v Turkey*, (App. 21987/93), 18 December 1996, (1997) 23 EHRR 553, ECHR 1996-VI; and *Haci Özen v Turkey*, (App. 46286/99), 12 April 2007.

[124] *Jalloh v Germany*, (App. 54810/00), 11 July 2006 [GC], (2007) 44 EHRR 667, ECHR 2006-IX. For an analysis of the judgment see A. Ashworth, 'Case Comment, Human Rights: Article 3 – Article 6' (2007) Crim LR Sep, 717–721.

consideration. So, for example, the taking of blood or saliva samples contrary to a suspect's wishes will not constitute inhuman or degrading treatment. But procedures such as that in issue in the case require a weighing of all the risks of the procedure, its intrusiveness, the pain and suffering involved, the alternative procedures which may be available, the medical supervision involved, and the seriousness of the offence being investigated. In all the circumstances of this case, the Grand Chamber concluded by ten votes to seven that the procedure had amounted to inhuman and degrading treatment.[125]

CONDITIONS OF DETENTION

The fact and conditions of imprisonment are frequent sources of individual applications invoking Article 3. Few were considered by the Court in the early years, when the law was to be found in Commission decisions.[126] However, there has been a worrying increase in the number of cases coming before the Court. Several pilot judgments have been made by the Court in an attempt to address the systemic issues in some States.[127] The Court has also established a set of principles for determining when the conditions of detention might engage Article 3. In the *Poltoratskiy* case,[128] the Court, while acknowledging the inherent features of detention, said that conditions of detention must be compatible with respect for human dignity,[129] and that it is important that a detained person's health and well-being are adequately secured.[130] A similar approach is taken to the conditions of detention of those awaiting expulsion, or detained by the immigration authorities.[131]

In the *Valaşinas* case,[132] the applicant made many claims about the shortcomings of the prison regime to which he was subject. The Court did not find that the undeniably tough regime violated Article 3 since it did not reach the minimum level of severity to amount to degrading treatment; this included a period of fifteen days when the applicant was detained in a solitary confinement cell.[133] However, a specific incident in which the applicant had been obliged to strip naked in the presence of a woman prison officer, and in which his genitals and food were handled by a prison officer with bare hands, was considered to constitute degrading treatment.

In the *Aerts* case,[134] the applicant complained about the conditions in the psychiatric wing of the prison where he was in detention pending his trial for an assault on his

[125] Contrast *Bogumil v Portugal*, (App. 35228/03), 7 October 2008, where a surgical procedure to remove a packet of drugs was regarded as a therapeutic necessity.

[126] See, generally, N. Rodley, *The Treatment of Prisoners under International Law* (OUP, Oxford 1999).

[127] For example a pilot judgment relating to the lack of medical care in prisons in Georgia, *Poghosyan v Georgia*, (App. 9870/07), 24 February 2009; Pilot judgment relating to recurrent structural problem of inadequate facilities in detention, *Ananyev and others v Russia*, (Apps. 42525/07 and 60800/08), 10 January 2012; Pilot judgment relating to the problem of overcrowding in Italian prisons, *Torreggiani and others v Italy*, (App. 43517/09), 8 January 2013.

[128] *Poltoratskiy v Ukraine*, (App. 38812/97), 29 April 2003, ECHR 2003-V.

[129] On the concept of human dignity, see C. McCrudden, 'Human Dignity and Judicial Interpretation of Human Rights' (2008) 19 EJIL 655.

[130] § 132, referring to *Kudła v Poland*, (App. 30210/96), 26 October 2000 [GC], (2002) 25 EHRR 198, ECHR 2000-XI, §§ 92–4.

[131] *Dougoz v Greece*, (App. 40907/98), 6 March 2001, (2002) 34 EHRR 1480, ECHR 2001-II. See also *SD v Greece*, (App. 53541/07, 11 June 2009.

[132] *Valaşinas v Lithuania*, (App. 44558/98), 24 July 2001, ECHR 2001-VIII.

[133] Contrast *Nevmerzhitsky v Ukraine*, (App. 54825/00), 5 April 2005, ECHR 2005-II; and *Ostrovar v Moldova*, (App. 35207/03), 13 September 2005, where violations of Art. 3 were found.

[134] *Aerts v Belgium*, (App. 25357/94), 30 July 1998, (2000) 29 EHRR 50, ECHR 1998-V.

ex-wife with a hammer. The Committee for the Prevention of Torture[135] had reported critically on the psychiatric and therapeutic care available in the prison psychiatric wing, but did not categorize them as degrading. The Court considered that prolonged periods in the psychiatric wing would carry with them the risk of deterioration in a person's mental health. There was, however, for the Court no convincing evidence that the applicant's mental health had suffered and it was not established that the applicant had suffered treatment which could be classified as inhuman or degrading. In contrast, the Court found a violation in *MS v United Kingdom*,[136] where the applicant was held in police custody after an alleged assault on his aunt. The applicant was suffering from severe mental illness at the time of his arrest. Due to a lack of coordination between police and medical authorities, the applicant was held in the police station beyond the statutory limit for being held without charge and he was clearly in need of the appropriate medical treatment which he did not receive until the fourth day of custody. The delay led to the deterioration of the conditions in his cell which amounted to diminishing the applicant's dignity in a way which was degrading under Article 3.

In extreme cases, a convicted person's health may make imprisonment of itself a violation of Article 3,[137] as in the case of prisoners suffering from Wernicke-Korsakoff Syndrome.[138]

The placing of a juvenile in an adult prison for any significant length of time may well constitute a breach of Article 3.[139] The placing of a five-year-old in a Transit Centre, without facilities for children of this age, for two months pending her return from Belgium to the Democratic Republic of the Congo has been found to constitute inhuman treatment.[140]

In each case, as always, the facts must be viewed in the light of the circumstances as a whole. Thus the physical condition of the applicant may make treatment which would otherwise be lawful contrary to Article 3; conversely, the applicant's own conduct may exceptionally legitimize a degree of violence which would otherwise be prohibited. The case-law may conveniently be considered under a number of sub-headings.

PRISON CONDITIONS

The *Peers* case[141] concerned conditions in a prison in Greece. There had been a critical report by the Committee for the Prevention of Torture[142] in relation to the prison in question. It seemed that little had been done to improve the conditions in the prison. The Strasbourg Court concluded that confinement in a cell with no ventilation and no window at the hottest time of the year in circumstances where the applicant had to use the toilet in the presence of another and was present while the toilet was being used by his cell mate diminished his human dignity and amounted to degrading treatment. The poor state of prison facilities in some Contracting Parties remains a cause for concern. In the *Kadiķis*

135 See later in this chapter. 136 *MS v United Kingdom*, (App 24527/08), 3 May 2012.

137 *Tekin Yildiz v Turkey*, (App. 22913/04), 10 November 2005.

138 A brain disorder involving loss of specific brain functions caused by a thiamine deficiency, which may be brought about following hunger strikes.

139 See *Güveç v Turkey*, (App. 70337/01), 20 January 2009, where this situation resulted in serious psychological problems for the applicant. See also *Coselav v Turkey*, (App. 1413/07), 9 October 2012, where the Court found a violation of Article 2,where a juvenile prisoner committed suicide after being placed in an adult prison without appropriate medical or specialist care.

140 *Mubilanzila Mayeka and Kaniki Mitunga v Belgium*, (App. 13178/03), 12 June 2006, (2008) 46 EHRR 449, ECHR 2006-XI.

141 *Peers v Greece*, (App. 28524/95), 19 April 2001, (2001) 33 EHRR 1192, ECHR 2001-III.

142 See later in this chapter.

case,[143] the applicant complained that his cell, which had an area of six square metres, regularly held four or five people; it was poorly ventilated and had poor lighting; there were no exercise facilities; only one meal per day was provided; no drinking water was provided; there was no bedding or blankets; use of the toilet was restricted to three times a day and urgent needs were accommodated using a bottle and plastic bowl; and his family were allowed on only one occasion to provide him with items for personal hygiene and fresh clothing. The Strasbourg Court noted that the Committee for the Prevention of Torture had recommended a minimum of seven square metres of cell space per prisoner. The Court found these prison conditions to constitute degrading treatment in violation of Article 3.[144] In extreme cases, poor prison conditions, combined with aggravating circumstances, such as a failure to respond to a prisoner's mental health problems, could result in a finding that the overall prison regime constituted torture.[145]

TREATMENT OF DETAINEES, INCLUDING THE USE OF SOLITARY CONFINEMENT

Force-feeding a prisoner, where it could not be established that this was a medical necessity supported by genuine medical opinions, has been held to constitute torture.[146]

Strip searches which have no genuine relationship to security concerns and which are imposed on a prisoner can constitute degrading treatment.[147] Even where a process of strip searches can be justified for legitimate concerns over possession of prohibited articles or substances, the process must be administered in a manner which limits as far as possible the feelings of inferiority, anxiety, and humiliation which such procedures necessarily entail.[148]

A number of cases have questioned the practice of using solitary confinement. Solitary confinement of a prisoner which involves complete sensory isolation would constitute a form of inhuman treatment, although restrictions on association with other prisoners for security reasons, and limitations on visits, would not, of themselves, constitute inhuman punishment or treatment. It might well be otherwise when particular circumstances, such as the health of the individual or the duration of the restrictions, are considered.[149]

The Court's approach was explained in the *Van der Ven* case:

> In this context, the Court has previously held that complete sensory isolation, coupled with total social isolation, can destroy the personality and constitutes a form of inhuman treatment which cannot be justified by the requirements of security or any other reason. On the other hand, the removal from association with other prisoners for security, disciplinary or protective reasons does not in itself amount to inhuman treatment or degrading punishment.... In assessing whether such a measure may fall within the ambit of Article 3 in a given case, regard must

[143] *Kadiķis v Latvia (No. 2)*, (App. 62393/00), 4 May 2006.

[144] See also *Ciorap v Moldova*, (App. 12066/02), 19 June 2007. In *Torreggiani and others v Italy* (App. 43517/09) 8 January 2013,(pilot judgment) the Court called on Italy to redress the problem of overcrowding in Italian prisoners within one year of the judgment.

[145] *Sławomir Musial v Poland*, (App. 28300/06), 20 January 2009, § 95.

[146] *Nevmerzhitsky v Ukraine*, (App. 54825/00), 5 April 2005, ECHR 2005-II. See also *Ciorap v Moldova*, (App. 12066/02), 19 June 2007.

[147] See *Iwańczuk v Poland*, (App. 25196/94), 15 November 2001, (2004) 38 EHRR 148; *Lorsé and others v The Netherlands*, (App. 52750/99), 4 February 2003, (2003) 37 EHRR 105; *Van der Ven v The Netherlands*, (App. 50901/99), 4 February 2003, (2004) 38 EHRR 967, ECHR 2003-II; *Frérot v France*, (App. 70204/01), 12 June 2007, ECHR 2007-nyr; and *Savics v Latvia*, (App. 17892/03), 27 November 2012.

[148] *Frérot v France*, (App. 70204/01), 12 June 2007, ECHR 2007-nyr.

[149] *Öcalan v Turkey*, (App. 46221/99), 12 May 2005 [GC], (2005) 41 EHRR 985, ECHR 2005-IV, § 191.

be had to the particular conditions, the stringency of the measure, its duration, the objective pursued and its effects on the person concerned...[150]

The *Ramirez Sanchez* case[151] is a particularly striking example of the permissible use of solitary confinement. Ramirez Sanchez, better known as 'Carlos the Jackal'[152] was kept in solitary confinement for eight years and two months. But this lengthy regime had been subject to a rigorous process of assessment every three months which prevented its being arbitrary. Those assessments had taken account of medical reports on the applicant, none of which gave rise to any cause for concern. The applicant had had regular contact with a doctor, a priest, and his lawyers, and there were no restrictions on visits from members of his family, although they had never requested a visit. There was no evidence to suggest any intention to humiliate or debase the applicant. He was eventually transferred to more normal detention. The Court ruled that solitary confinement could never be imposed upon a prisoner indefinitely, but that was not the case here. By twelve votes to five, the Grand Chamber concluded that there was no violation of Article 3. The dissenting judges felt that neither the applicant's physical robustness nor his mental stamina could make solitary confinement of the nature and duration he had experienced acceptable under Article 3.

In the *A and others* case,[153] a number of foreign nationals suspected of involvement in terrorist plots had been interned without trial[154] in the United Kingdom because they could not be deported. They complained that their detention had violated Article 3, arguing that the high security conditions were inappropriate and damaging to their health; they also claimed that there was abnormal suffering associated with the indeterminate nature of their detention. While accepting the impact of the detention on the mental health of some of the detainees, the Grand Chamber concluded that it could not be said that they had no hope of release. The Court, however, sidestepped the conclusions of the Committee on the Prevention of Torture's conclusions that, at the time of their visit, the conditions amounted to inhuman and degrading treatment, by noting that nearly all the applicants had failed to use domestic proceedings to challenge those conditions, and so had failed to exhaust domestic remedies in this regard.[155] The Court's overall finding was that the treatment of the detainees did not reach the threshold of inhuman and degrading treatment.

In contrast, in two Polish cases, the Court found the isolation regime employed for 'dangerous' prisoners was a violation of Article 3 as they were held under the regime for several years in isolation without physical and mental stimulation and without a review of the regime.[156] The Court did consider the CPT report in these cases. In *X v Turkey*,[157] the Court found that the holding of a homosexual prisoner in solitary confinement for eight months was because of his sexual orientation and not used as a protective measure. The confinement therefore constituted inhuman and degrading treatment under Article 3.[158]

[150] *Van der Ven v The Netherlands*, (App. 50901/99), 4 February 2003, (2004) 38 EHRR 967, ECHR 2003-II, § 51. See also *Rohde v Denmark*, (App. 69332/01), 21 July 2005. (2006) 43 EHRR 325.

[151] *Ramirez Sanchez v France*, (App. 59450/00), 4 July 2006 [GC], (2007) 45 EHRR 1099, ECHR 2006-IX. See also *Rohde v Denmark*, (App. 69332/01), 21 July 2005, (2006) 43 EHRR 325.

[152] Who was serving a life sentence for the murder of two police officers, and who claimed to be a revolutionary by profession. He was suspected of involvement in a series of terrorist attacks.

[153] *A and others v United Kingdom*, (App. 3455/05), 19 February 2009 [GC], (2009) 49 EHRR 29, ECHR 2009-nyr.

[154] Following the filing of a derogation in respect of the rights to be found in Article 5.

[155] §§ 132–3.

[156] *Piechowicz v Poland*, (App. 20071/07), 17 April 2012; *Horych v Poland*, (App. 13621/08), 17 April 2012; see also *Savics v Latvia*, (App.17892/03), 27 November 2012.

[157] *X v Turkey*, (App. 246/26/09), 9 October 2012.

[158] The Court also found a violation of Article 14.

MEDICAL ATTENTION FOR DETAINEES

The Strasbourg Court has consistently ruled that all prisoners are entitled to conditions of detention which are compatible with human dignity. This includes having appropriate regard for their well-being.[159] Where mental health is in issue, Contracting Parties have been enjoined to take special account of the vulnerability of prisoners and their inability, in some cases, to complain coherently about their difficulties.[160] Very special measures will need to be put in place where a prisoner constitutes a suicide risk.[161] In one case, the Court ordered interim measures in the form of a requirement that the applicant be transferred from hospital to prison, somewhat controversially, found a violation where a transfer to prison took place and a transfer back to hospital took place three days later.[162]

The absence of facilities within a prison to meet the needs of a wheelchair user was found to constitute degrading treatment even though it was accepted that there was no intention to humiliate or debase the prisoner.[163] In the *Price* case,[164] the conditions in which a thalidomide victim was kept in prison were found to amount to degrading treatment. The applicant had been committed to prison for seven days for contempt of court;[165] she was detained both in a police cell and in prison for three and a half days. She was seriously disabled by her condition, and used a wheelchair. The Court concluded that her detention in conditions where she was dangerously cold, risked developing sores because her bed was too hard or unreachable, and was unable to get to the toilet or keep clean without the greatest of difficulties amounted to degrading treatment. Judge Bratza in a separate concurring opinion is scathing of the judicial authorities in committing the applicant to prison without determining in advance whether there were adequate facilities for meeting her special needs.

A complaint of a violation of Article 3 might arise from a failure to respond promptly and effectively to a prisoner's medical needs. The *Mouisel* case[166] concerned a prisoner suffering from chronic lymphocytic leukaemia who had been sentenced to fifteen years' imprisonment for armed robbery, kidnapping, and fraud. He raised a complaint that his continued detention and the conditions in which he had been detained violated Article 3. The Court acknowledged that a failure to provide appropriate medical treatment could bring the conduct of the authorities within the positive obligations of Article 3.[167] So, for example, in the *McGlinchey* case,[168] the respondent State was found to have breached the prohibition of inhuman and degrading treatment in Article 3 in failing to respond to the applicant's deteriorating condition. She was eventually admitted to hospital as an emergency case when she collapsed, but later died. McGlinchey suffered from asthma and

[159] *Kudła v Poland*, (App. 30210/96), 26 October 2000 [GC], (2002) 35 EHRR 11, ECHR 2000-XI, § 94; and *Paladi v Moldova* (App. 39806/05) 10 March 2009 [GC], §§ 71–2. For an example of a failure to provide an appropriate response to general medical needs, see *Khudobin v Russia*, (App. 59696/00), 26 October 2006, ECHR 2006-XII. For a pilot judgment relating to the lack of medical care in prisons in Georgia, see *Poghosyan v Georgia*, (App. 9870/07), 24 February 2009.

[160] *Renolde v France*, (App. 5608/05), 16 October 2008, (2009) 48 EHRR 969, § 120.

[161] *Rivière v France*, (App. 33834/03), 11 July 2006.

[162] *Paladi v Moldova*, (App. 39806/05), 10 March 2009 [GC], §§ 84–106; the Grand Chamber was split 9–8 on the violation of Article 34.

[163] *Vincent v France*, (App. 6253/03), 24 October 2006.

[164] *Price v United Kingdom*, (App. 33394/96), 10 July 2001, (2002) 34 EHRR 1285, ECHR 2001-VII.

[165] Under the remission system she was only incarcerated for three and a half days.

[166] *Mouisel v France*, (App. 67263/01), 14 November 2002, (2004) 38 EHRR 735, ECHR 2002-IX.

[167] § 40. See also *Logvinenko v Ukraine*, (App. 13448/07), Decision of 14 December 2010, where the applicant was not treated for HIV and tuberculosis.

[168] *McGlinchey and others v United Kingdom*, (App. 50390/99), 29 April 2003, (2003) 37 EHRR 821, ECHR 2003-V.

from heroin withdrawal. Similarly in *A.B v Russia*,[169] the State was found to have violated Article 3 where the prison authorities knew the applicant was HIV positive, kept him in deplorable conditions and did not provide adequate treatment. The Court found it particularly disturbing that the Government concluded that it was unnecessary to provide the anti-retoviral treatment required.

In the *Herczegfalvy* case,[170] the applicant, who had been convicted of offences of fraud and violence, complained that the medical treatment to which he had been subjected amounted to degrading treatment. He had been diagnosed as suffering from a mental illness, and was forcibly administered food and neuroleptics, isolated, and attached with handcuffs to his security bed for several weeks. The Commission concluded that there had been a violation of Article 3. Their decision was based on the conclusion that the treatment accorded to the applicant went beyond what was strictly necessary, and that it extended beyond the period necessary to serve its purpose (including the period of a week when he was handcuffed to his bed despite being unconscious). The Court affirmed that mental patients remain under the protection of Article 3, but that the 'established principles of medicine are…decisive in such cases; as a general rule, a measure which is therapeutic cannot be regarded as inhuman or degrading.'[171] But the Court would need to be satisfied as to the medical necessity for any particular form of treatment. In the present case, the Court considered this test to be met. On the facts as presented, the conclusions of the Court are surprising and the opinion of the Commission is to be preferred.

In the *Keenan* case,[172] the Court took a particularly robust view of the needs of a prisoner who was suffering from mental illness which included a risk of suicide. Keenan had been found hanged in his cell, and his mother as his next of kin claimed a violation of Article 3. A combination of poor medical notes, lack of effective monitoring of Keenan's health when he was a known suicide risk, and the imposition on him of seven days' segregation in the punishment block and an additional twenty-eight days added to his sentence constituted inhuman and degrading treatment.[173] He had committed suicide on his second day in segregation.

LENGTH OF DETENTION

The Court has said that a sentence whose severity bore no relationship to the offence could amount to an inhuman punishment.[174] Article 3 must, however, also be regarded as setting an absolute limit, based on respect for the human person, to what punishment is permissible, regardless of its label, and regardless also of the victim's own conduct. Article 3 should be considered as imposing an absolute prohibition of certain forms of punishment such as flogging, which are by their very nature inhuman and degrading. Within that limit, all the circumstances of the individual cases are relevant.

A particular issue has arisen in relation to life sentences, and whether the absence of any hope of release constitutes inhuman or degrading treatment. In the *Kafkaris* case,[175] the Strasbourg Court said that the imposition of a life sentence on an adult offender was not

[169] *A.B v Russia*, (App. 1439/06), 14 December 2010. See also *Salakhov and Islyamova v Ukraine*, (App. 28005/08), 14 March 2013, where the Court found a violation of Article 3 due to inadequate medical care in detention and in hospital, where the applicant was handcuffed. He died from an AIDS related illness two weeks after leaving hospital.

[170] *Herczegfalvy v Austria*, 24 September 1992, Series A No 242-B, (1993) 15 EHRR 437.

[171] § 82.

[172] *Keenan v United Kingdom*, (App. 27229/95), 3 April 2001, (2001) 33 EHRR 913, ECHR 2001-III.

[173] §§ 108–15.

[174] *Weeks v United Kingdom*, 2 March 1987, Series A No 114, (1988) 10 EHRR 293, § 47.

[175] *Kafkaris v Cyprus*, (App. 21906/04), 12 February 2008 [GC], (2009) 49 EHRR 877, ECHR 2008-nyr. See also *Léger v France*, (App. 19324/02), 11 April 2006, referred to the Grand Chamber but struck out of the list on 30 March 2009 following the death of the applicant.

in itself incompatible with any provision of the Convention.[176] However, the existence of some system for consideration of release[177] is a factor to be taken into account in assessing the compatibility of the sentence with Article 3. The Court has applied similar principles to extradition cases in finding no violation of Article 3, where the applicants argued that the possible sentences that would be imposed if convicted in the receiving State would amount to ill-treatement under Article 3.[178] In *Vinter and others v United Kingdom*,[179] the Grand Chamber found that the whole life sentence regime in the UK was incompatible with Article 3 as it provided an 'irreducible life sentence' and as such did not provide any prospect of release.[180] The Grand Chamber noted that the process of review should be included in the sentencing process. Notwithstanding significant developments in penal policy among the Contracting Parties, the Grand Chamber[181] found no violation of Article 3 under the system in Cyprus under which early release of those sentenced to life imprisonment rested entirely on the discretion of the executive.

POSITIVE OBLIGATIONS

In the *Moldovan* case,[182] The Strasbourg Court said:

> The obligation of the High Contracting Parties under Article 1 of the Convention to secure to everyone within their jurisdiction the rights and freedoms defined in the Convention, taken together with Article 3, requires States to take measures designed to ensure that individuals within their jurisdiction are not subjected to ill-treatment, including ill-treatment administered by private individuals. . . .[183]

Positive obligations under Article 3 would appear to involve two elements; the obligation to protect persons from ill-treatment by third parties and the procedural duty to carry out an effective investigation into ill-treatment.

POSITIVE OBLIGATION TO PROTECT AGAINST ILL-TREATMENT FROM THIRD PARTIES

First, there must be measures in the Contracting Party which constitute effective deterrence and protection. This will involve the categorization of many forms of conduct as criminal activity; this issue alone seldom troubles the Strasbourg Court. It is more often the operation in practice of the law which gives rise to concerns. In the *Okkali* case,[184] a 12-year-old boy had been beaten by police interrogators. The Court found a violation of Article 3 because the application of the criminal law had lacked rigour and so did not have a dissuasive effect capable of ensuring effective protection from inhuman and degrading treatment. In the earlier

[176] *Kafkaris v Cyprus*, (App. 21906/04), 12 February 2008 [GC], (2009) 49 EHRR 877, ECHR 2008-nyr, § 97.

[177] Which need not be a formal system of parole: § 104–5.

[178] *Harkins and Edwards v United Kingdom*, (Apps. 9146/07 and 32560/07), 17 January 2012; *Babar Ahmad and others v United Kingdom*, (Apps. 24027/07, 11949/08,36742/08, 66901/09, and 67534/09), 10 April 2012.

[179] *Vinter and others v United Kingdom*, (Apps. 66069/09, 130/10, 3896/10), 9 July 2013.

[180] In a concurring judgment United Kingdom, Judge Power Forde noted that the 'right to hope' is an important aspect of human dignity and to remove this would be degrading, § 1.

[181] *Kafkaris v Cyprus*, (App. 21906/04), 12 February 2008 [GC], (2009) 49 EHRR 877, ECHR 2008-nyr, By ten votes to seven. Followed in *Harkins and Edwards v United Kingdom*, (Apps. 9146/07 and 32560/07), 17 January 2012, § 140.

[182] *Moldovan and others v Romania*, (Apps. 41138/98 and 64320/01), 12 July 2005, (2007) 44 EHRR 302, ECHR 2005-VII.

[183] § 98.

[184] *Okkali v Turkey*, (App. 52067/99), 17 October 2006, ECHR 2006-XII.

A case,[185] which had concerned the availability of a defence of 'reasonable chastisement' in the context of the beating of a nine-year-old boy with a stick by his stepfather, the Court had ruled that children and other vulnerable individuals were entitled to State protection in the form of effective deterrence against beatings which constituted a serious breach of their personal integrity. Placing the burden of proof on the prosecution to establish beyond reasonable doubt that the beating went beyond the limits of reasonable chastisement, when the defence was raised, did not provide adequate protection.[186]

Where the conduct complained of is that of private parties, rather different considerations apply. The leading authorities are the cases of *Costello-Roberts*[187] and *A*.[188] The *Costello-Roberts* case concerned the use of corporal punishment in private schools, while the *A* case concerned the beating of a child by his stepfather. The Strasbourg Court ruled in both cases that Contracting Parties had an obligation under Article 3 to ensure that those within their jurisdiction are not subjected to treatment prohibited by Article 3, even where that treatment was meted out by private individuals.

The Court has restated this view in the *Z and others* case,[189] which concerned four children who had been subject to severe parental abuse known to the authorities in October 1987. The children had, however, not been taken into care until 1992. The respondent State did not contest the Commission's finding that the suffering of the children amounted to inhuman and degrading treatment, nor that it had failed to provide the children with adequate protection against such treatment. The Strasbourg Court made clear that the positive obligation on States is to take measures:

> to ensure that individuals within their jurisdiction are not subjected to torture or inhuman or degrading treatment, including such ill-treatment administered by private individuals... These measures should provide effective protection, in particular, of children and other vulnerable persons and include reasonable steps to prevent ill-treatment of which the authorities had or ought to have had knowledge.[190]

DUTY TO INVESTIGATE

The second requirement is for an effective investigation capable of leading to prosecution of well-founded allegations of ill-treatment.[191] The investigation must be thorough, expedient, and independent,[192] with the capacity to lead to the identification of the perpetrators whether agents of the State, or private individuals.[193] This includes an obligation to investigate allegations of racial discrimination.[194] The requirement of an effective investigation has given rise to a significant case-law.[195]

[185] *A v United Kingdom*, (App. 25599/94), 23 September 1998, (1999) 27 EHRR 611, ECHR 1998-VI.

[186] §§ 22–4; the need for amendment to the law as accepted by the respondent State before the Court. See also *Opuz v Turkey*, (App. 33401/02), 9 June 2009, where the Court found that the response of the authorities to complaints of domestic violence were 'manifestly inadequate'.

[187] *Costello-Roberts v United Kingdom*, 25 March 1993, Series A No 247-C, (1994) 19 EHRR 112.

[188] *A v United Kingdom*, (App. 25599/94), 23 September 1998, (1999) 27 EHRR 611, ECHR 1998-VI.

[189] *Z and others v United Kingdom*, (App. 29392/95), 10 May 2001 [GC], (2002) 34 EHRR 97, ECHR 2001-V.

[190] § 73. See also *Dordevic v Croatia*, (App. 41526/10), 24 July 2012.

[191] The requirements of investigations under Articles 2 and 3 are similar: see ch.8.

[192] *Akkoç v Turkey*, (Apps. 22947/93 and 22948/93), 10 October 2000, (2002) 34 EHRR 1173, ECHR 2000-X, § 118. See also *Mikheyev v Russia*, (App. 77617/01), 26 January 2006, §§ 107–10.

[193] See, for example, *Şečič v Croatia*, (App. 40116/02), 31 May 2007, (2009) 49 EHRR 408, ECHR 007-nyr.

[194] See *Assenov v Bulgaria* (1998) 28 EHRR 652.

[195] See earlier in this chapter for examples where a failure to investigate has led to a violation of Article 3 in cases concerning detention, domestic violence, and disappearances.

The Strasbourg Court has not been entirely consistent in spelling out the source of the obligation to conduct an effective investigation. In the *Aksoy* case,[196] the Court said that the obligation flowed from Article 13 requiring the State to provide an effective remedy in its national legal order.

In the *Sevtap Veznedaroglu* case[197] the Strasbourg Court recapitulated its case-law in the following terms, rooting the obligation more firmly within Article 3:

> [T]he Court reiterates that, where an individual raises an arguable claim that he has been seriously ill-treated by the police or other such agents of the State unlawfully and in breach of Article 3, that provision, read in conjunction with the State's general duty under Article 1 of the Convention to 'secure to everyone within their jurisdiction the rights and freedoms defined in... [the] Convention' requires by implication that there should be an effective official investigation capable of leading to the identification and punishment of those responsible.... If this were not the case, the general legal prohibition of torture and inhuman and degrading treatment and punishment, despite its fundamental importance, would be ineffective in practice and it would be possible in some cases for agents of the State to abuse the rights of those within their control with virtual impunity.[198]

The obligation is later described as a 'procedural obligation' which devolves on the State under Article 3.[199] Failures of the judicial authorities to take up investigations will also engage the obligation in Article 3.[200]

EVIDENTIAL ISSUES

Because a finding that a Contracting Party is guilty of torture, or even of inhuman and degrading treatment, carries a certain stigma, the Convention organs have required a very high standard of proof of the conduct, even using the term 'beyond reasonable doubt' in the *Ireland v United Kingdom* case.[201] In the *Nachova* case,[202] the Grand Chamber explained in more detail what it meant in using the term 'beyond reasonable doubt'. This is not simply the transplantation of any similar notion from the national legal orders, and the Court has no preconceived notion of procedural barriers to the admissibility of evidence:

> According to its established case-law, proof may follow from the coexistence of sufficiently strong, clear and concordant inferences or of similar unrebutted presumptions of fact. Moreover, the level of persuasion necessary for reaching a particular conclusion and, in this connection, the distribution of the burden of proof are intrinsically linked to the specificity of the facts, the nature of the allegation made and the Convention right at stake. The Court is also attentive to the seriousness that attaches to a ruling that a Contracting State has violated fundamental rights....[203]

[196] *Aksoy v Turkey*, (App. 21987/93), 18 December 1996, (1997) 23 EHRR 553, ECHR 1996-VI, § 98. See also *Assenov v Bulgaria*, (App. 24760/94), 28 October 1998, (1999) 28 EHRR 652, ECHR 1998-VIII, §§ 117–18.

[197] *Sevtap Veznedaroglu v Turkey*, (App. 32357/96), 11 April 2000, (2001) 33 EHRR 1412.

[198] § 32. [199] § 35.

[200] *Elci and others v Turkey*, (Apps. 23145 and 25091/94), 13 November 2003.

[201] *Ireland v United Kingdom*, 18 January 1978, Series A No 25, (1979–80) 2 EHRR 25, § 161. See generally, R. Wolfrum, 'The Taking and Assessment of Evidence by the European Court of Human Rights' in S. Breitenmoser and others, *Human Rights, Democracy and the Rule of Law. Liber amicorum Luzius Wildhaber*, (Nomos, Baden-Baden 2007), 915.

[202] *Nachova and others v Bulgaria*, (Apps. 43577/98 and 43579/98), 6 July 2005 [GC], (2006) 42 EHRR 933, ECHR 2005-VII. [203] § 147.

There will often be considerable dispute as to the facts where allegations of violations of Article 3 are brought before the Court. The victim may well not be in as strong a position as the Contracting Party in relation to the collection and presentation of evidence. The Court has been sensitive to this problem, while also recognizing that there must be compelling proof of a Contracting Party's failure before condemning it under the Article.[204]

As already noted, an obligation on the authorities to conduct a proper, timely, and conscientious investigation of allegations of ill-treatment by agents of the State is a feature of Article 3.[205] Failure to meet this obligation also has evidential implications. The starting point is that any allegations of ill-treatment must be supported by appropriate evidence.[206] The State will then be expected to offer some explanation as to the cause of injuries of which there is cogent evidence.[207] If they cannot do so, the Court will draw appropriate inferences from evidence that an applicant had suffered unexplained injuries during, for example, a period of police custody.[208]

The Strasbourg Court's approach to internal investigations can, accordingly, have a double sting in the tail. A failure to conduct a proper and timely investigation may itself constitute a violation of the Convention, but the absence of such an investigation is likely to make it difficult to provide a plausible explanation for injuries suffered by applicants and, in effect, supports the evidence of applicants.[209]

EUROPEAN CONVENTION FOR THE PREVENTION OF TORTURE

The European Convention for the Prevention of Torture and Inhuman and Degrading Treatment[210] came into force in February 1989. The Convention creates a monitoring mechanism in the form of a Committee which may make visits to any establishment in the territory of the Contracting Parties where persons are deprived of their liberty by a public authority. It aims at the prevention of torture rather than its repression and arises, according to the Preamble, from a conviction that:

> the protection of persons deprived of their liberty against torture and inhuman and degrading treatment or punishment could be strengthened by non-judicial means of a preventive character based on visits.

Examination of the *travaux préparatoires* reveals that there was considerable concern about possible conflicts between the work of the Committee for the Prevention of Torture

[204] For a critical discussion of evidential issues, see U. Erdal, 'Burden and standard of proof in proceedings under the European Convention' (2001) 26 ELRev HR 65.

[205] *Satik and others v Turkey*, (App. 31866/96), 10 October 2000.

[206] Reports by the Committee for the Prevention of Torture are increasingly being referred to by the Court in its judgments. See below in this chapter on the work of the Committee.

[207] *Tomasi v France*, 27 August 1992, Series A No 241-A, (1993) 15 EHRR 1, § 109. See also *Selmouni v France*, (App. 25803/94), 28 July 1999, (2000) 29 EHRR 403, ECHR 1999-V, § 87; and *Labita v Italy*, (App. 26772/95), 6 April 2000 [GC], (2008) 46 EHRR 1228, ECHR 2000-IV, § 131.

[208] See, for example, *Klaas v Germany*, 22 September 1993, Series A No 269, (1994) 18 EHRR 305, § 30; and *Mikheyev v Russia*, (App. 77617/01), 26 January 2006.

[209] See, for examples, *Hasan Kiliç v Turkey*, (App. 35044/97), 28 June 2005; *Karakaş and Yeşilirmak v Turkey*, (App. 43925/98), 28 June 2005; and *SB and HT v Turkey*, (App. 54430/00), 5 July 2005.

[210] ETS 126, and Protocols 1 and 2, ETS 151 and 152. For a commentary, see M. Evans and R. Morgan, *Preventing Torture. A Study of the European Convention for the Prevention of Torture and Inhuman or Degrading*

and the Commission and Court of Human Rights.[211] Happily this has not materialized, although there have been occasions where decisions of the Commission have taken the Committee by surprise.[212]

The existence of monitoring is designed to ensure that standards of treatment meet established human rights standards. The Committee has no judicial functions, but reports its findings and makes recommendations to the State concerned. These reports are confidential. They will remain unpublished unless the State requests their publication or the Committee by a two-thirds majority decides to make a public statement on a matter in the face of a State's failure to cooperate or refusal to make changes in the light of the Committee's recommendations. The Committee submits to the Committee of Ministers each year an overview report of its activities.

The norm has very much become for publication of the reports.[213] There is a growing tendency for the Strasbourg Court to refer to reports by the Committee in its decision-making. So in the *Aerts* case,[214] the Commission and the Court took note of the findings of the Committee in examining the conditions of detention in a particular psychiatric hospital. In a number of other cases, the Court has noted the conclusions of a report by the Committee, and has been influenced by those findings both in coming to its own conclusions on the facts and in giving consent to the requirements of Article 3.[215]

CONCLUDING REMARKS

It was only in December 1996 that the Strasbourg Court found a Contracting Party guilty of torture, but there has since been an upsurge in such findings.[216] Even more worrying has been the increase in findings of inhuman or degrading treatment. In 2012, there were findings of such treatment in 169 judgments against twenty-six Contracting Parties, with Russia, Romania, Turkey and Ukraine accounting for 103 of these judgments.[217] Some of these violations result from prison conditions, but many involve conduct which it is shocking should exist in Europe in the 21st century. The majority of the violations have been found against new Contracting Parties, who have some way to go to secure to those

Treatment (OUP, Oxford 1998); A. Cassese, 'A New Approach to Human Rights: The European Convention for the Prevention of Torture' (1989) 83 AJIL 128.

[211] Evans and Morgan, n.210.

[212] For example, the decision of the Commission (subsequently reversed by the Court) that airport holding centres for aliens were not places of detention for the purposes of Article 5 ECHR in App. 19776/92, *Amuur v France*, 10 January 1995, reversed by the Court, 25 June 1996; (1996) 22 EHRR 533, ECHR 1996-III; see Evans and Morgan, n.210, 371–4.

[213] Evans and Morgan, n.210, 198–203 and 339–41.

[214] *Aerts v Belgium*, (App. 25357/94), 30 July 1998, (2000) 29 EHRR 50, ECHR 1998-V, § 72 of the Commission's Report, and §§ 29–30, 42, and 62–5.

[215] See, for example, *Aksoy v Turkey*, (App. 21987/93), 18 December 1996, (1997) 23 EHRR 553, ECHR 1996-VI, § 46; *Aydin v Turkey*, (App. 23178/94), 25 September 1997, (1998) 25 EHRR 251, ECHR 1997-VI, §§ 49–50; *Dougoz v Greece* (App. 40907/98), 6 March 2001, (2002) 34 EHRR 1480, ECHR 2001-II, §§ 40–1 and 46; *Peers v Greece*, (App. 28524/95), 19 April 2001, (2001) 33 EHRR 1192, ECHR 2001-III, § 61 and 70–2; *Van der Ven v The Netherlands*, (App. 50901/99), 4, February 2003, (2004) 38 EHRR 967, ECHR 2003-II, §§ 32–4; *Mouisel v France*, (App. 67263/01), 14 November 2002, (2004) 38 EHRR 735, ECHR 2002-IX, § 47; *II v Bulgaria*, (App. 44082/98), 9 June 2005, §§ 37–46; *Salmanoğlu and Polattaş v Turkey*, (App. 15828/03), 17 March 2009; and *Piechowicz v Poland*, (App. 20071/07), 17 April 2012, *Horych v Poland*, (App. 13621/08), 17 April 2012.

[216] In 2012 the Strasbourg Court made findings of torture in 24 cases: one against Armenia, Belgium, Bulgaria, Bosnia Herzegovina, Greece, Slovakia, and Sweden, two against Macedonia, three against Italy, five against Ukraine and seven against Russia, European Court of Human Rights, violation by article and country, January 2013.

[217] Source: European Court of Human Rights, violation by article and country, January 2013.

within their jurisdiction even the most basic of human rights guarantees. What is also concerning is the spread of violations across over half the Member States.

The Strasbourg Court has kept faith with the absolute nature of the prohibition to be found in Article 3, and has resisted efforts by some Contracting Parties to introduce relative notions into the case-law relating to removal of persons to countries where there is a real risk that they will be exposed to ill-treatment. This is important in a climate where coping with terrorist threats puts respect for human rights under pressure. This is illustrated by the cases of extraordinary rendition coming before the Court and the robustness of the Court's response so far. It has clarified the use of diplomatic assurances and maintained the close scrutiny of bilateral agreements between States. The Court has also further recognized gender based violence as ill-treatment.

The focus on improving prison conditions is also to be welcomed. There has been something of a sea change in this area. Early cases were somewhat dismissive of complaints by prisoners about the conditions of their detention, and to some extent about features of their own treatment in particular circumstances. However, prompted by important standard-setting work by the Committee for the Prevention of Torture, the Strasbourg Court has delivered judgments, including pilot judgments, indicating the need for significant improvements in prison conditions which ensure the entitlement of prisoners to be treated with human dignity.

Perhaps the central message of the case-law examined in this chapter is the need for constant vigilance even among the countries of Europe in relation to one of the most fundamental of human rights.

10

PROTECTION FROM SLAVERY AND FORCED LABOUR

INTRODUCTION

Article 4 provides:

1. No one shall be held in slavery or servitude.
2. No one shall be required to perform forced or compulsory labour.
3. For the purposes of this Article the term 'forced or compulsory labour' shall not include:
   (a) any work required to be done in the ordinary course of detention imposed according to the provisions of Article 5 of this Convention or during conditional release from such detention;
   (b) any service of a military character or, in the case of conscientious objectors in countries where they are recognized, service exacted instead of compulsory military service;
   (c) any service exacted in case of an emergency or calamity threatening the life or well-being of the community;
   (d) any work or service which forms part of normal civic obligations.

Article 4(1) prohibits slavery and servitude; the wording shows that these are regarded as questions of status. Article 4(2), by contrast, prohibits forced or compulsory labour, and is intended to protect persons who are at liberty. Slavery and servitude are continuing—though not necessarily permanent—states, whereas forced labour may arise incidentally or on a temporary basis. The prohibitions of slavery and servitude are absolute (and outside any derogation under Article 15), but the prohibition of forced or compulsory labour is subject to the exemption for those forms of work or service expressly permitted under Article 4(3). No other substantive provision of the Convention is drafted in this way. The exceptions in Article 4(3)(a) and (b) are genuine exceptions, while the matters listed in Article 4(3)(c) and (d) are rather examples of obligations which cannot be said to fall within the definition of forced or compulsory labour.

It is not uncommon for allegations of violations of Article 4 to be attached to applications alleging violations of other Convention provisions. So, in the *Šijakova* case,[1] the applicants sought to argue (without success) that their children over the age of 18 who had joined the monastic order of the Macedonian Orthodox Church were in slavery. In the *Pearson* case,[2] the applicant, who was complaining that women reached State pensionable age at 60 while men did not do so until 65, argued unsuccessfully that a consequence of this differential age for entitlement to a State pension was forced labour for men. In the *Solovyev* case,[3] the Strasbourg

[1] *Šijakova and others v FYRM*, (App. 67914/01), Decision of 6 March 2003.

[2] *Pearson v United Kingdom*, (App. 8374/03), Decision of 27 April 2004.

[3] *Solovyev v Ukraine*, (App. 4878/04), 14 December 2006.

Court ruled as manifestly ill-founded a claim under Article 4(1) by a worker who had not received remuneration for the work he had done as an employee. He had secured a judgment for the unpaid wages, but the judgment remained unsatisfied.

Slavery and servitude are old-fashioned words suggesting practices which have long since ceased to exist. But the truth of the matter is that the modern manifestation of slavery and servitude is human trafficking, which exists on a significant scale worldwide. It exists within the Council of Europe countries in terms of countries of origin, transit, and destination.[4] The International Labour Organization has estimated that 2.45 million people are affected worldwide. The purpose of much of the traffic is sexual exploitation, but also includes forced labour or services. The practice affects women and children in particular.

SLAVERY OR SERVITUDE

DEFINITIONS

The prohibition of slavery and servitude is governed by numerous international treaties and there is now wide recognition that both are prohibited under customary international law.[5] The distinction between slavery and servitude is one of degree.[6] Slavery connotes being wholly in the legal ownership of another person,[7] while servitude is more limited though still connoting conditions of work or service wholly outside the control of the individual. The Commission's Report in the *Van Droogenbroeck* case said that:

> in addition to the obligation to provide another with certain services, the concept of servitude includes the obligation on the part of the 'serf' to live on another's property and the impossibility of changing his condition.[8]

The Strasbourg Court found that the situation in the *Siliadin* case[9] amounted to servitude but not slavery. The applicant had been brought to France from Togo by a relative of her father. She was then forced to work as a maid for some considerable time for fifteen hours a day, seven days a week. She had no personal resources, her papers had been confiscated,

[4] See general and country reports of the Council of Europe's Group of Experts on Action Against Trafficking in Human Beings (GRETA). GRETA is responsible for monitoring implementation of the Council of Europe Convention on Action against Trafficking in Human Beings. For example see GRETA's *Second General Report covering period 1 August 2011 to 31 July 2012* (Council of Europe, Strasbourg 4 December 2012). This report and other general and country reports and information can be found on the GRETA website at: www.coe.int/t/dghl/monitoring/trafficking/default_en.asp

[5] See Article 4 of the Universal Declaration of Human Rights, and P. Sieghart, *The International Law of Human Rights* (OUP, Oxford 1983), 54–5.

[6] None of the major human rights instruments defines slavery and servitude. A definition of slavery can be found in Article 1 of the Slavery Convention of 1926 as follows: 'Slavery is the status or condition of a person over whom any or all of the powers attaching to the right of ownership are exercised.' Servitude is broadly defined in Article 7 of the Supplementary Convention on the Abolition of Slavery, the Slave Trade, and Institutions and Practices Similar to Slavery of 1956 by reference to a variety of practices listed in Article 1 of that Convention.

[7] In *M and others v Italy*, (App. 40020/03), 31 July 2012, the Court examined the issue of payment upon marriage as a transfer of ownership amounting to slavery. It held that in the circumstances, the exchange of money could reasonably be viewed as a gift, a tradition common to many cultures.

[8] *Van Droogenbroeck*, Report of 9 July 1980, Series B, No. 44.

[9] *Siliadin v France*, (App. 73316/01), 26 July 2005, (2006) 43 EHRR 287, ECHR 2005-VII. See also V. Mantouvalou, 'Servitude and Forced Labour in the 21st Century: The Human Rights of Domestic Workers' (2006) 35 ILJ 395; and H. Cullen, '*Siliadin v France*: Positive Obligations under Article 4 of the European Convention on Human Rights' (2006) 6 HRLRev 585.

she was afraid of contacting the authorities because of her irregular immigration status, and was vulnerable and isolated. The Court considered that the applicant could not be said to be owned by the couple in the strict sense, but her lack of freedom and the requirement that she work such long hours on every day of the week meant that she had been held in servitude.

In *C.N and V v France*,[10] the Court noted that servitude was an aggravated form of compulsory labour. Servitude is distinguished from compulsory labour by the victim's feeling that the situation cannot change and is permanent. It is sufficient that these feelings are based on objective criteria or caused or maintained by those responsible for the situation.[11] The two victims in the case were distinguished. Both girls were brought from Burundi to work for a family. One victim stayed at home all day to do domestic labour, and never left the home for fear of arrest and deportation. This was held to be servitude as the victim feared her situation was permanent. In contrast, her sister was allowed to go to school and do her homework, obtaining good marks. She was not in servitude, given her ability to leave the home and change her situation with education. Importantly, the Court has also noted in *C.N. v United Kingdom*[12] that *domestic* servitude may have a distinct meaning under Article 4, separate from issues surrounding human trafficking. Domestic servitude 'involves a complex set of dynamics, involving both overt and more subtle forms of coercion, to force compliance.' In this case, the authorities dealt with the applicant's allegations as a trafficking case, whereas the Court held that the police investigation into the applicant's claims should have focused primarily on her domestic situation. The absence of a criminal offence of domestic servitude meant the State failed in its positive obligation to protect the applicant. The finding of the Court somewhat qualifies the general reference to trafficking and servitude in *Siliadin* and suggests that although servitude can be a consequence of human trafficking,[13] a more nuanced approach should be taken towards domestic servitude.

HUMAN TRAFFICKING

CONVENTION ON ACTION AGAINST TRAFFICKING IN HUMAN BEINGS

Siliadin was significant for its general recognition of the modern phenomenon of trafficking in people.[14] The case was decided at the same time as the Council of Europe adopted the Convention on Action against Trafficking in Human Beings in 2005.[15] As at 1 October 2013, there were forty ratifications, and three signatures not followed by ratification. Four countries have not signed this Convention.[16] The Convention is the first to recognize explicitly that human trafficking is a violation of human rights and an offence to the

[10] *C.N and V v France*, (App. 67724/09), 11 Oct 2012. [11] § 91.

[12] *C.N. v United Kingdom*, (App. 4239/08), 13 November 2012, § 80.

[13] See later *Rantsev v Cyprus and Russia*, (App. 25965/04), 7 January 2010.

[14] However, see earlier; the general application of trafficking legislation to domestic servitude can be questioned given the finding in *C.N v United Kingdom*, (App. 4239/08), 13 November 2012, § 80, which distinguished domestic servitude from human trafficking.

[15] ETS 197, which entered into force on 1 February 2008. There is a particularly detailed Explanatory Report to the Convention. See also S. Egan, 'Protecting the victims of trafficking: problems and prospects' [2008] EHRLR 106.

[16] As of 30 November 2013, Russia, Czech Republic, Monaco, and Liechtenstein had not signed the 2005 Convention.

dignity and integrity of human beings. Parties to the Convention are required to implement national measures to prevent trafficking, particularly by ensuring that all activities linked to trafficking are made criminal offences, and to discourage demand, as well as to develop facilities to support victims of trafficking. Parties are also required to cooperate internationally to tackle the problem. The effectiveness of the Convention is secured through the monitoring mechanisms contained in Part VII. A Group of Experts on action against trafficking (GRETA) was established with responsibility for monitoring the activities of the Contracting Parties. There are also provisions ensuring that action by Council of Europe countries dovetails with international action to address the problem of human trafficking.

Since the *Siliadin* case and the adoption of the 2005 Convention, the Strasbourg Court has been asked to examine the relationship between human trafficking and Article 4, in the light of the growth of human trafficking and the development of anti-trafficking measures. In *Rantsev v Cyprus and Russia*,[17] the victim's daughter died in suspicious circumstances in Cyprus, after she had been brought from Russia as an 'artiste'. A Cypriot report noted that these women often worked as prostitutes and that they were under coercion from their employers with threats of violence.[18] The Court noted that it has rarely been called upon to examine Article 4 but emphasized the increased prevalence of human trafficking and measures to combat it as illustrated by the 2005 Convention. As the European Convention on Human Rights is a living instrument, and 'in light of the proliferation of both trafficking itself and of measures taken to combat it', the Court considered:

> it appropriate in the present case to examine the extent to which trafficking itself may be considered to run counter to the spirit and purpose of Article 4 of the Convention such as to fall within the scope of the guarantees offered by that Article without the need to assess which of the three types of proscribed conduct are engaged by the particular treatment in the case in question.[19]

By not attempting to link particular treatment to one of the three forms of conduct in Article 4, the Court has moved away from the more semantic approach of *Siliadin* to recognizing the broader context of human trafficking as a threat to human dignity. In view of its obligation to interpret the Convention as a living instrument, the Court concluded 'that trafficking itself, within the meaning of Article 3(a) of the Palermo Protocol and Article 4(a) of the Anti-Trafficking Convention, falls within the scope of Article 4 of the Convention.'[20] The Court thus incorporated the definition of these specific conventions into the Court's jurisprudence.[21]

POSITIVE OBLIGATIONS

In the light of the development of international instruments concerning human trafficking, the Strasbourg Court was asked in *Siliadin*[22] to consider whether France had afforded sufficient protection to the applicant under its positive obligations, since slavery and servitude were not classified as criminal offences under French criminal law. The couple who had kept the applicant in servitude had been acquitted when charged with the offences of wrongfully obtaining unpaid or insufficiently paid services from a vulnerable

[17] *Rantsev v Cyprus and Russia*, (App. 25965/04), 7 January 2010. [18] § 85.

[19] § 279. [20] § 282.

[21] As noted in *M and others v Italy and Bulgaria*, (App. 40020/03), 31 July 2012.

[22] *Siliadin v France*, (App. 73316/01), 26 July 2005, (2006) 43 EHRR 287, ECHR 2005-VII.

or dependent person. The Court noted a recommendation of the Parliamentary Assembly which had regretted the failure of Contracting Parties to make domestic slavery an offence under their criminal law in concluding that France had failed to meet its positive obligations under the Convention to afford the applicant effective protection against servitude.

In ruling that Article 4 requires Contracting Parties to take measures to suppress the problem of forced labour, the Strasbourg Court took a significant step to breathe new life into Article 4 by acknowledging the obligations placed on States by international conventions to take measures to protect victims of trafficking. Since *Siliadin* the Court has expanded on the substance of what is an appropriate legal framework to protect victims in addition to an adequate criminal law. A State should provide relevant training for law enforcement and immigration officials, immigration rules should address trafficking, and there should be an effective regulation of businesses used as cover for trafficking.[23]

The Court has also expanded the type of positive obligations that may be placed on a State under Article 4. It has found that the State also has a positive duty to protect victims and prevent harm to potential victims. The State should take operational measures where:

> the State authorities were aware, or ought to have been aware, of circumstances giving rise to a credible suspicion that an identified individual had been, or was at real and immediate risk of being, trafficked or exploited within the meaning of Article 3(a) of the Palermo Protocol and Article 4(a) of the Anti-Trafficking Convention. In the case of an answer in the affirmative, there will be a violation of Article 4 of the Convention where the authorities fail to take appropriate measures within the scope of their powers to remove the individual from that situation or risk.[24]

The Court acknowledged that any burden on the State must not be disproportionate given operational policies and resources. However, States should endeavour to protect victims within their territories and put preventative policies and practices in place.[25] Like Articles 2 and 3, the Court has further found that there is a procedural obligation to investigate under Article 4, where there is a 'credible suspicion' of a violation of Article 4.[26] The steps necessary for an effective investigation are similar to those developed by the Court under Article 2.[27] However, the Court has added a specific obligation on States in the context of human trafficking which reflects the international instruments on trafficking. In *Rantsev*, the Court noted the international dimension to human trafficking involving the treatment of persons over borders.[28] In this context, the duty to investigate goes further than the need for an effective domestic investigation and also includes cross border cooperation between States in the investigation of trafficking. In *Rantsev*, the Court held that Russia as the state of origin of the victim of human trafficking in this case, failed to properly investigate the recruitment of the victim's daughter and so had failed to fulfill its procedural obligations.[29]

[23] *Rantsev v Cyprus and Russia*, (App. 25965/04), 7 January 2010, § 284–287. The Court found that Cyprus had failed to provide an effective legal framework to protect the victim. However Russia had not violated Article 4 on this point, bearing in mind its restricted competence on the particular facts. The Court found a violation of Article 4 due to a failure to provide an effective legal protection in both *CN and V v France*, (App. 67724/09), 11 October 2012 and *CN v United Kingdom*, (App. 4239/08), 13 November 2012, § 80.

[24] *Rantsev v Cyprus and Russia*, (App. 25965/04), 7 January 2010, § 286.

[25] § 287, this specific obligation is in line with the Palermo Protocol 2000, signed by both Cyprus and Russia.

[26] *CN v United Kingdom*, (App. 4239/08), 13 November 2012, § 69; *Rantsev v Cyprus and Russia* (App. 25965/04), 7 January 2010 § 288.

[27] See ch.8.

[28] *Rantsev v Cyprus and Russia*, (App. 25965/04), 7 January 2010, § 290.

[29] *Rantsev v Cyprus and Russia*, (App. 25965/04), 7 January 2010, §§ 307–9. In contrast in *M and others v Italy and Bulgaria*, (App. 40020/03), 31 July 2012, the Court found that Bulgaria cooperated with Italy and assisted the applicants in the case.

The recent case-law of the Court and the expansion of positive obligations has substantially developed Article 4 to reflect the problem of 'modern day slavery' as elucidated in international instruments on human trafficking.

FORCED OR COMPULSORY LABOUR

Article 4(2) provides that no one shall be required to perform forced or compulsory labour, but Article 4(3) provides for certain exceptions. The Strasbourg Court has said:

> The Court reiterates that paragraph 3 of Article 4 is not intended to 'limit' the exercise of the right guaranteed by paragraph 2, but to 'delimit' the very content of that right, for it forms a whole with paragraph 2 and indicates what 'the term "forced or compulsory labour" shall not include' (ce qui 'n'est pas consideré comme "travail forcé ou obligatoire"'). This being so, paragraph 3 serves as an aid to the interpretation of paragraph 2. The four sub-paragraphs of paragraph 3, notwithstanding their diversity, are grounded on the governing ideas of the general interest, social solidarity and what is normal in the ordinary course of affairs.[30]

The expression 'forced or compulsory labour' is taken from a Convention of the International Labour Organization (ILO), Convention No. 29 of 1930, subsequently supplemented by another ILO Convention, the Abolition of Forced Labour Convention of 1957. It seems reasonable to rely, for the interpretation of Article 4, on the work of the ILO organs in defining the term for the purposes of the ILO Conventions, and the Commission and the Court has in fact done so.[31] The Commission and the Court has imported two key elements into the concept of forced or compulsory labour. First, the work must be performed by the worker involuntarily. Secondly, either the requirement to do the work must be unjust or oppressive or the work itself involves avoidable hardship.[32]

The issue of forced or compulsory labour was extensively examined by the Commission in the controversial *Iversen* case.[33] A law passed in Norway in 1956 provided that dentists might be required for a period of up to two years to take a position in a public dental service. Some members of the Opposition had objected to the Bill on the ground that it introduced a compulsory direction of labour which was contrary to the Norwegian Constitution and to Article 4 of the Convention. The respondent State, however, rejected these arguments and maintained that this direction of labour was necessary to implement a public dental service. The applicant, Iversen, was directed under the Act to take up for one year the position of dentist in the Moskenes district in northern Norway. He eventually accepted the post, but after some months he gave it up and left. He was subsequently convicted and sentenced under the Act, and his appeal was dismissed by the Supreme Court.

In his application to the Commission, he alleged that the Act, and the order assigning him to the district of Moskenes, were contrary to Article 4 of the Convention. Exceptionally, the Commission's decision on admissibility records a divided vote: it held by a majority of six votes to four that the application was inadmissible. The majority considered that the service of Iversen in Moskenes was not forced or compulsory labour within the meaning

[30] *Karlheinz Schmidt v Germany*, 18 July 1994, Series A No 291-B; (1994) 18 EHRR 513, § 22.

[31] See for example *Van der Mussele v Belgium*, 23 November 1983, Series A No 70, (1984) 6 EHRR 163, *Graziani-weiss v Austria*, (App. 31950/06), 18 October 2012.

[32] See App. 4653/70, *X v Federal Republic of Germany*, Decision of 1 April 1974 (1974), 17 *Yearbook* 148; App. 8410/78, *X v Federal Republic of Germany*, Decision of 13 December 1979, (1980) 18 DR 216; and App. 9322/81, *X v Netherlands*, Decision of 3 May 1983, (1983) 32 DR 180.

[33] App. 1468/62, *Iversen v Norway*, Decision of 17 December 1963, (1963) 6 *Yearbook* 278.

of Article 4 of the Convention. However, the majority was itself divided; four members of the majority considered that the service of Iversen in Moskenes was manifestly not forced or compulsory labour under Article 4(2), and therefore found it unnecessary to express any opinion on the applicability of Article 4(3), while the other two members of the majority considered that that service was reasonably required of him in an emergency threatening the well-being of the community and was therefore authorized under Article 4(3).

The concept of forced or compulsory labour was analysed by the four members of the majority as follows:

> The concept cannot be understood solely in terms of the literal meaning of the words, and has in fact come to be regarded in international law and practice, as evidenced in part by the provisions and application of ILO Conventions and Resolutions on Forced Labour, as having certain elements... [namely] that the work or service is performed by the worker against his will and, secondly, that the requirement that the work or service be performed is unjust or oppressive or the work or service itself involves avoidable hardship.[34]

On this analysis the service required of Iversen was held not to be forced or compulsory labour under Article 4(2); the requirement to perform that service was not unjust or oppressive since the service, although obligatory:

> ...was for a short period, provided favourable remuneration, did not involve any diversion from chosen professional work, was only applied in the case of posts not filled after being duly advertised, and did not involve any discriminatory, arbitrary, or punitive application.

However, even if the element of oppressiveness could be said to be absent in this case, it is doubtful how far it is a necessary constituent of forced labour as generally understood in international law and practice. The ILO Forced Labour Convention No. 29 of 1930 in fact defines the term 'forced or compulsory labour', for the purposes of that Convention, simply as 'all work or service which is exacted from any person under the menace of a penalty and for which the said person has not offered himself voluntarily';[35] but that Convention did not prohibit such work or service if it forms part of normal civic obligations in a self-governing country, or is exacted in execution of a penal sentence, or exacted in an 'emergency requiring the mobilization of manpower for essential work of national importance'. Article 4(3) of the European Convention, as seen above, contains similar provisions.

In the *Iversen* case, as already stated, the reasoning of the other two members of the Commission who voted for inadmissibility was based on Article 4(3); they held that the service of Iversen was service reasonably required of him in an emergency threatening the well-being of the community. The respondent State had made no substantial submissions on this point but as part of the general background of the case had explained that the northern districts of Norway had a deplorable lack of social services, which seriously affected the social and health conditions of these communities; thus, while there was in Oslo in 1946 one dentist per 650 inhabitants, the ratio in three of the northern provinces was one dentist per 13,000, 6,000, and 5,500 inhabitants respectively. Moreover, adequate dental care was rendered even more difficult by the enormous distances, the difficulties of communication, and the arctic weather conditions prevailing during the winter months.

While these considerations may have made it difficult for the Norwegian authorities to find any alternative practical solution to the problem, it is by no means clear that they are relevant to the provisions of Article 4, which, unlike many of the later Articles, contains no escape clause 'for the protection of health'. The opinion of the two members of the

[34] (1963) 6 *Yearbook* 278, 328.

[35] Art. 2(1). See *Van der Mussele v Belgium*, 23 November 1983, Series A No 70, (1984) 6 EHRR 163, §§ 32–3.

Commission referred to above is open to criticism; for it seems doubtful whether the situation in northern Norway could be described as an 'emergency' or 'calamity' as required by Article 4(3)(c). These terms suggest some sudden overwhelming natural disaster, not the permanent social, climatic, and geographical conditions however serious they may be.

The minority of the Commission was rightly of the opinion that the application was not manifestly ill-founded, and that it should be declared admissible. The minority found that the conditions under which Iversen was required to perform his work, although it was paid and was only for a limited time, did not exclude the possibility of its being forced or compulsory labour, since it was imposed subject to penal sanctions; and that the question of the applicability of Article 4(3)(c) of the Convention required further examination.

It is hard to escape the conclusion that the Commission's decision to reject the application was influenced by political considerations. The case had caused considerable controversy in Norway and the decision coincided with a decision of the respondent State to renew its declaration accepting the Commission's competence under former Article 25 for a period of only one year.[36]

In the *Talmon* case,[37] the applicant complained that a requirement that he look for and accept employment deemed suitable for him as a condition of entitlement to unemployment benefit amounted to a requirement that he undertake forced or compulsory labour. He claimed that the only suitable employment for himself was work as an 'independent scientist and social critic'. The Commission declared the application manifestly ill-founded since it did not raise any issues under Article 4. Though this is an unremarkable case, the question may be posed as to the severity of the sanction for non-performance before something becomes compulsory or forced labour.

Since the *Talmon* case, the Court has stated that it considers the application of Article 4(2) in light of the underlying objectives of the Article and considering all the circumstances.[38] It has noted that when examining duties placed on a member of a particular profession it will consider whether the duties fall outside the ambit of the normal professional activities, whether services are remunerated or compensated, whether the duties are based on social solidarity, and whether the burden imposed is disproportionate.[39] The Court has also noted that Article 4(3) serves as an interpretive aid for Article 4(2) as the four sub-paragraphs under Article 4(3) 'are grounded on the governing ideas of the general interest, social solidarity and what is normal in the ordinary course of affairs.'[40]

[36] (1963) 6 *Yearbook* 26. See also H. G. Schermers, 'European Commission of Human Rights: The Norwegian Dentist Case on Compulsory Labour' [1964] *Nederlands Tijdschrift voor International Recht* 366.

[37] App. 30300/96, *Talmon v Netherlands*, Decision of 26 February 1997; [1997] EHRLR 448. See also *X v Netherlands* (1976) 7 DR 161, *Schuitemaker v Netherlands*, (App. 15906/98), Decision of 4 May 2010, where the Court held a similar case inadmissible. A condition to find suitable employment placed on the applicant with regard to receiving unemployment benefit did not amount to compulsory labour under Article 4 See also the United Kingdom case of *R (on the application of Reilly and another) v Secretary of State for Work and Pensions* [2013] UKSC 68, which found that regulations requiring unpaid work for a prescribed period whilst claiming jobseekers allowance did not violate Article 4. The judgment reviewed the case-law cited in this section, see §§ 77-91 of the judgment.

[38] *Steindel v Germany*, (App. 29878/07), Admissibility Decision of 14 September 2010; *Graziani-weiss v Austria*, (App. 31950/06), 18 October 2012.

[39] *Van der Mussele v Belgium*, 23 November 1983, Series A No 70, (1984) 6 EHRR 163, para 39, see also *Graziani-weiss v Austria*, (App. 31950/06), 18 October 2012, § 38. In *CN and V v France*, (App. 67724/09), 11 October 2012 the court noted that 'disproportionate burden' can also be used to distinguish between domestic tasks in the family home which could be reasonably required and compulsory labour (§ 74).

[40] *Graziani-weiss v Austria*, (App. 31950/06), 18 October 2012, § 37.

PRISON LABOUR

Article 4(3)(a) excludes from the term 'forced or compulsory labour' 'any work required to be done in the ordinary course of detention imposed according to the provisions of Article 5 of this Convention or during conditional release from such detention'.

In a group of applications[41] from persons detained in various prisons in Germany, the Commission examined the scope of this provision. The applicants complained that during their detention in prison they were subjected to forced and compulsory labour without receiving adequate payment and without being insured under the social security laws.

The Commission has regularly rejected applications by prisoners claiming higher payment for their work or claiming the right to be covered by social security systems.[42] The present applicants, however, raised a new point in complaining also that part of the work required of them during their detention was performed on behalf of private firms under contracts concluded with the prison administration; this system, they alleged, constituted a state of slavery for the prisoners concerned. However, the Commission examined this complaint primarily under Article 4(3)(a), that is, in relation to forced or compulsory labour. After an exceptionally detailed investigation of the background of this provision, and a survey of the practice in the Contracting Parties, the Commission found that the form of prison labour of which the applicants complained clearly appeared to fall within the framework of work normally required from prisoners within the meaning of Article 4(3)(a).

In *Stummer v Austria* a man who had spent many years in prison complained that the exclusion of prisoners from eligibility to be affiliated to the old-age pension system for work performed violated Article 4.[43] The Grand Chamber noted that this was the first time the Court had to address the issue since the Commission had dismissed the German cases. It examined the validity of the Commission reasoning in the light of present day conditions, applying the living instrument principle.[44] The Court acknowledged that there had been a developing consensus in Member States regarding penal policy and prison work. The European Prison Rules 2006 noted that prisoners should be included in national social security systems. However, the Court went on to find that although there was a clear consensus on the link between prison work and social security, only a small number of Member States affiliated working prisoners to pension schemes. There was not enough consensus to constitute a divergence from the Commission findings.[45] There was no violation. The majority decision reflects a narrow view of the present consensus as noted by Judge Tulkens' dissent in the case, accusing the majority of failing to provide proper supervision of State practice.[46] Judge Tulkens noted that forty years had passed since the Commission findings and there had been a consensus on the need to normalize prisoner's work. He did not agree that it was now normal to require a prisoner to work without affiliation to the pension system. He noted the nature of prison has changed with an increasing number of elderly inmates and that the majority had failed to recognize this.[47]

It may be thought that the exemption under Article 4(3)(a) of 'work required to be done in the ordinary course of detention imposed according to the provisions of Article 5' can

[41] Apps. 3134/67, 3172/67, and 3188–3206/67, *Twenty-one Detained Persons v Federal Republic of Germany*, Decision of 6 April 1968, (1968) 11 *Yearbook* 528.

[42] (1968) 11 *Yearbook* 528, 552.

[43] *Stummer v Austria*, (App. 37452/02), 7 July 2011.

[44] § 127–129.

[45] § 130–134.

[46] Partly dissenting judgment of Judge Tulkens (§ 10).

[47] § 6.

arise only if all the provisions of Article 5 have been observed. In the *Vagrancy* cases[48] the Commission had expressed the view that the work that the applicants were required to do was not justified under Article 4 because there had been a breach of Article 5(4). The Strasbourg Court, however, held that while there was a breach of Article 5(4), there was no breach of Article 4 because the vagrants were lawfully detained under Article 5(1)(e).[49] This is a perplexing decision since Article 5 must be read as a whole, and it would seem that any breach of paragraphs (1)–(4) would render the arrest or detention unlawful. It is not sufficient to say that the detention is justified under one provision of the Convention if it is unlawful under another provision. Nor does Article 4(3)(a) itself differentiate between the provisions of Article 5. On this point, therefore, the view of the Commission is to be preferred to that of the Court.

MILITARY SERVICE

Article 4(3)(b) excludes 'any service of a military character' from the prohibition of forced or compulsory labour.

In the '*Sailor Boys*' case[50] four applicants aged 15 and 16 had joined the British army or naval forces for a period of nine years to be calculated from the age of 18. They had subsequently applied for discharge from the service but, in spite of repeated requests, discharge had been refused. They alleged, *inter alia*, a violation of their right under Article 4(1) not to be held in servitude.

The Commission also considered the case under Article 4(2) but found that any complaint that the applicants' service constituted 'forced or compulsory labour' must be rejected as being manifestly ill-founded in view of the express provision of Article 4(3)(b). That provision, according to the Commission, wholly excluded *voluntary* military service from the scope of Article 4(2); and, by the omission of the word 'compulsory' which appeared in the ILO Convention, 'it was intended to cover also the obligation to continue a service entered into on a voluntary basis.'[51]

The respondent State submitted that the exclusion of military service in Article 4(3)(b) was to be understood as applying equally to slavery and servitude in paragraph (1). Any argument to the contrary necessarily involved the anomalous conclusion that, although no service of a military character can be forced or compulsory labour under the Convention, military service may amount to the more oppressive condition of slavery or servitude. The applicants, however, rightly pointed out that the drafters of the Article clearly intended that there should be an absolute prohibition against servitude or slavery, but only a qualified prohibition against forced or compulsory labour.

The Commission found that generally the duty of soldiers who enlist after the age of majority to observe the terms of their engagement, and the ensuing restriction of their freedom and personal rights, do not amount to an impairment of rights which could come under the terms 'slavery or servitude'; and that the young age at which the applicants entered the services could not in itself attribute the character of 'servitude' to the normal condition of a soldier.

With regard to the young age of enlistment, the applicants referred to the special protection of minors provided for in all legal systems in respect of 'their own possibly

[48] *De Wilde, Ooms and Versyp v Belgium*, 18 June 1971, Series A No 12, (1979–80) 1 EHRR 373. See ch.11.

[49] § 89.

[50] App. 3435–3438/67, *W, X, Y, and Z v United Kingdom*, Decision of 19 July 1968, (1968) 11 *Yearbook* 562.

[51] (1968) 11 *Yearbook* 562, 594.

unconsidered engagements'. The Commission pointed out that the applicants' parents had given their consent and that:

> the protection of minors in other fields of law consists exactly in the requirement of parental consent and also in the existence of the principle that an engagement entered into by the minor will be void without such consent but valid and binding if the consent has been duly given.

The Commission did not, however, refer to another element in the protection of minors, frequently found in domestic legal systems, which enables minors, in certain circumstances, to decide for themselves on reaching the age of majority whether to continue or to repudiate their undertaking.

The applications were thus finally rejected as inadmissible but subsequently revised Navy Service Regulations were introduced in the United Kingdom under which boy entrants could decide at the age of 18 to leave the navy after three years' adult service, that is, at the age of 21.

In addition to military service, Article 4(3)(b) also authorizes service required to be performed by conscientious objectors in lieu of compulsory military service.[52]

MILITARY SERVICE AND ARTICLE 9

In several Commission cases,[53] the Commission found that a violation of the right to freedom of conscience, thought, and religion under Article 9 could not be argued in connection to conscientious objection. The Commission found that Article 4(3) prevented the use of Article 9. The Court was asked to review the Commission findings for the first time in *Bayatyan v Armenia*.[54] The Chamber affirmed the reasoning of the previous case-law. However, the Grand Chamber disagreed. Using the living instrument principle the Court noted the changed consensus in Europe concerning conscientious objection. It also referred to the *travaux préparatoires* of the Convention, noting that:

> the Travaux Préparatoires confirm that the sole purpose of sub-paragraph (b) of Article 4 § 3 is to provide a further elucidation of the notion "forced or compulsory labour". In itself it neither recognises nor excludes a right to conscientious objection and should therefore not have a delimiting effect on the rights guaranteed by Article 9.[55]

The shift to recognizing the applicability of Article 9 to military service underlines the general consensus and policies of the Contracting States with regard to providing alternative forms of military service and the influence of other international instruments such as the EU Charter on Fundamental Rights and those of the UN which are discussed explicitly in *Bayatyan*.[56]

EMERGENCIES

Article 4(3)(c) takes outside the prohibition in Article 4(2) service exacted in case of an emergency or calamity threatening the life or well-being of the community. As noted

[52] App. 2299/64, *Grandrath v Federal Republic of Germany*, App. 2299/64 Report of Commission, 12 December 1966; Decision of Committee of Ministers, 29 June 1967, (1967) 10 *Yearbook* 626.

[53] For example *Grandrath v Federal Republic of Germany*, App. 2299/64 Report of Commission, 12 December 1966; Decision of Committee of Ministers, 29 June 1967, (1967) 10 *Yearbook* 626.

[54] *Bayatyan v Armenia*, (App. 233459/03), 7 July 2011, ECHR 2011; see also ch.17.

[55] § 100.

[56] §§ 105–8.

earlier, in the *Iversen* case, some members of the Commission felt that this would encompass a shortage of dentists in remote parts of Norway. The better view is that it involves the work needed to deal with an acute and temporary emergency. Examples might be tackling a forest fire, or assisting in the evacuation of those threatened by some natural disaster. In requiring any service under this provision, the authorities would, of course, be required to have regard to a person's capacity for the work involved. In the absence of this exception, Contracting Parties would need to invoke Article 15 before the people could be required to assist in an emergency; the requirements of Article 15 are more strictly drawn than those set out in Article 4(3)(c). Nevertheless, the threshold for using the provision in Article 4(3)(c) does seem to be significant.

CIVIC OBLIGATIONS

Article 4(3)(d) authorizes 'any work which forms part of normal civic obligations'. This differs from the service encompassed within Article 4(3)(c) in that there need be no emergency. The test is one of normality in the sense of what might reasonably be expected of a particular individual in a particular situation. The distinction will usually be one of degree, but quite where the boundary is remains to be established. In one case[57] the Commission concluded that the obligation of the holder of shooting rights in a hunting district to take part in the gassing of fox holes could be justified either under paragraph (c) or (d). In another case, the Strasbourg Court was easily satisfied that jury service is a normal civic obligation.[58]

The question has been raised whether the Austrian system of legal aid was compatible with Article 4 of the Convention.[59] The applicant, a lawyer practising in Vienna, complained that he was compelled, contrary to Article 4, to act as unpaid defence counsel for a person who lacked the means to pay counsel's fees. Under the legal aid system, a lawyer was required to offer his services and was subject to disciplinary sanctions if he refused to do so. He was paid no fee and was reimbursed for practically none of his expenses. In return for these services, the respondent State paid annually to the Bar Association a fixed lump sum which was used for charitable purposes, especially for old-age pensions for lawyers no longer in practice; but there was no legal right to such benefits.

In the proceedings on admissibility, the respondent State submitted, *inter alia*, that lawyers, by voluntarily choosing their profession, accept the obligation to act under the legal aid system, and that consequently this was not compulsory labour, but a consequence of their own free decision. Further, even if it did constitute compulsory labour it formed part of normal civic obligations under Article 4(3)(d). The applicant replied that the obligation was limited to the legal profession, and within that profession applied only to counsel; consequently it could not be regarded as part of normal civic obligations. The Commission declared the application admissible, but there was subsequently a friendly settlement.

It would seem that the interpretation of 'normal' civic obligations requires a comparison with the practice in comparable professions in other Contracting Parties. Article 4(3)(d) contains the clearest invitation in the Convention to consider current practice as a standard of interpretation.

[57] App. 9686/82, *S v Federal Republic of Germany*, Decision of 4 October 1984 (1985) 39 DR 90.

[58] *Zarb Adami v Malta*, (App. 17209/02), 20 June 2006, (2007) 44 EHRR 49, ECHR 2006-VIII.

[59] App. 4897/71, *Gussenbauer v Austria*, Decision of 22 March 1972, (1973) 42 CD 41 and App. 5219/71, *Gussenbauer v Austria*, Decision of 14 July 1972, (1973) 42 CD 94. See also App. 4653/70, *X v Federal Republic of Germany*, Decision of 1 April 1974, (1974) 17 *Yearbook* 148.

The issue of the normal incidents of professional work in the context of the free representation of indigents was considered by the Court in the *Van der Mussele* case.[60] The requirement in issue was that of Belgian law under which pupil barristers were required to represent indigent defendants without a fee or reimbursement of expenses. Failure to undertake this work could result in a refusal to admit the person to the Belgian Bar. The Strasbourg Court did not accept at face value the Commission's conclusion that the applicant had consented in advance to the situation. The Court's decision makes clear that the second requirement of forced or compulsory labour, namely that the character of the work to be performed must be unjust or oppressive, is very much a subsidiary criterion. As noted, the Court's approach is to have regard to all the circumstances of the case in the light of the purpose of Article 4. Having regard to the nature of the work which fell within the normal ambit of the work of an advocate, to the advantage of the pupil barrister of undertaking this work as part of professional training, and to the fact that the burden was not disproportionate, the Court concluded that there was no compulsory labour in this case for the purposes of Article 4(2) and so it did not need to consider whether the representation of indigents was a normal civic obligation for pupil barristers falling within Article 4(3)(d). The absence of any fee or reimbursement of expenses was regretted by the Court, but did not alone render the work forced or compulsory labour.[61] In *Steindel v Germany*,[62] the applicant was a doctor in private practice. Every medical practitioner in the region was required to be part of an out-of-hours emergency service and failure to take part would lead to disciplinary proceedings. The applicant argued that this amounted to compulsory labour. However, the Court held the case inadmissible, partly on the basis that the obligation was founded on a concept of civil solidarity and fell within the ambit of normal professional activities.

ARTICLE 4 AND ARTICLE 14

Article 14 of the Convention prohibits discrimination in areas within the ambit of the Convention.[63] This has caused particular difficulties in relation to Article 4.

The difficulty arises because of the unusual structure of Article 4. If the matters referred to in Article 4(3) are outside the scope of Article 4, can they ever be used as the basis for an argument that there has been discrimination in the way a Contracting Party regulates the activity?

In the *Van der Mussele* case,[64] the Strasbourg Court found that a requirement to undertake pro bono work without fee as a pupil advocate did not constitute forced labour under Article 4(2). But the Court went on to consider an argument based on discrimination between the groups required to undertake such legal work. The Court appears to have justified this by categorizing the work as 'abnormal' if there was discrimination in the groups or individuals required to undertake the work. In the event no such discrimination was found.

Karlheinz Schmidt v Germany[65] concerned an application complaining that a requirement in Germany that a person serve as a fireman or pay a fire service levy in lieu of service was discriminatory in that it applied to men but not to women, taking Article 4 together with Article 14.[66] Where the applicant lived, there was no shortage of volunteer firemen,

[60] *Van der Mussele v Belgium*, 23 November 1983, Series A No 70, (1984) 6 EHRR 163.

[61] Judgment has been affirmed in *Bucha v Slovakia*, (App. 43259/07), 20 September 2011, where the Court held the application inadmissible. See also *Graziani-weiss v Austria*, (App. 31950/06), 18 October 2012.

[62] *Steindel v Germany*, (App. 29878/07), Admissibility decision of 14 September 2010.

[63] See ch.24.

[64] *Van der Mussele v Belgium*, 23 November 1983, Series A No 70, (1984) 6 EHRR 163.

[65] *Karlheinz Schmidt v Germany*, 18 July 1994, Series A, No 291-B, (1994) 18 EHRR 513.

[66] See ch.24 on Art. 14.

and so the requirement was to pay the fire service levy. The Strasbourg Court considered that compulsory fire service constituted normal civic obligations within the meaning of Article 4(3)(d), and that the compensatory charge was so closely linked to compulsory fire service that it also fell within Article 4. The Court then went on to consider the issue of discrimination raised by the applicant. The Court found a violation of Article 14 read with Article 4(3)(d) despite that paragraph taking the matters included within its terms outside the protection afforded by Article 4.

In the *Zarb Adami* case,[67] the applicant successfully argued that practice in relation to the requirement to serve as a juror in Malta which resulted in very few women serving as jurors constituted unlawful discrimination when Article 4 was read together with Article 14, despite the categorization of jury service as a normal civic obligation. Judges Bratza and Garlicki, in two concurring opinions, express some dissatisfaction at the reasoning of the majority, and the reasoning of the Strasbourg Court in the earlier cases. Both judges, however, consider that there is a line of reasoning which permits these cases to be regarded as falling within the ambit of Article 4.[68] Judge Garlicki said:

> ...I believe that it is possible to read Article 4, taken as a whole, in a broader way, not only as prohibiting any forms of compulsory labour but also as regulating State prerogatives in establishing different forms of compulsory work and services. In other words, Article 4 may also be read as setting a general framework of duties which may be imposed on an individual. Article 4 empowers the State to establish such duties and services but—by the very fact of their enumeration—Article 4 absorbs (includes) them into the realm of the Convention. One of the consequences of such inclusion is that those duties and services must be formulated in a manner compatible with the Convention, its Article 14 included.[69]

CONSENT

Consent cannot make slavery or servitude which would otherwise be prohibited under Article 4(1) lawful. In the '*Sailor Boys*' case[70] the respondent State argued that an essential feature of servitude is that it has been forced upon a person against his will, in circumstances where he has no genuine freedom of choice.[71] However, Article 4(1) should be construed as prohibiting also the voluntary acceptance of servitude. As the Commission had observed, 'Personal liberty is an inalienable right which a person cannot voluntarily abandon.'[72] Indeed, a proposal to add the qualification 'involuntary' to servitude was rejected by the drafters of the Supplementary Convention on Slavery 1956 and of the United Nations Covenant on Civil and Political Rights precisely on the ground that 'it should not be possible for any person to contract himself into bondage.'[73] This interpretation is further supported by the judgment of the Strasbourg Court in the *Vagrancy* cases.[74]

However, it is less clear, in view of the terms 'forced' and 'compulsory', whether a voluntary undertaking would exclude the applicability of Article 4(2). It has already been seen that one of the elements of work which is prohibited is its performance by workers against their will; but the question remains whether a person who has voluntarily accepted

[67] *Zarb Adami v Malta*, (App. 17209/02), 20 June 2006, (2007) 44 EHRR 49, ECHR 2006-VIII.

[68] Indeed Judge Bratza would have found the violation to be of Article 14 read in conjunction with Article 4, rather than Article 14 read in conjunction with Article 4(3)(d).

[69] Concurring Opinion of Judge Garlicki.

[70] Apps. 3435–3438/67, *W, X, Y, and Z v United Kingdom*, Decision of 19 July 1968, (1968) 11 *Yearbook* 562.

[71] (1968) 11 *Yearbook* 562, 576.

[72] Report of the Commission in the *Vagrancy Cases*, 19 July 1969, Series B No 10, 91.

[73] UN Doc. A/2929, 33.

[74] *De Wilde, Ooms and Versyp v Belgium*, 18 June 1971, Series A No 12, (1979–80) 1 EHRR 373. See ch.11.

an obligation can be compelled to continue in circumstances which, objectively viewed, would constitute forced or compulsory labour. The question raised is that of the severity of the sanction before the activity could be said to be compulsory or forced.

In the *Iversen* case the respondent State contended that the applicant had freely accepted the conditions of service, that he knew of the effect of the Norwegian legislation and voluntarily entered into an agreement with the competent authorities, and in particular that by his conversations with officials in the Ministry for Social Affairs and his consent to being posted in Moskenes, the relationship between the applicant and the Ministry had assumed a contractual nature which excluded any application of Article 4 of the Convention.[75] The Commission, however, did not refer to this aspect of the case in its decision.

In the '*Sailor Boys*' case, however, the Commission appeared to attach great importance to the fact that not only the applicants but also their parents had initially given their consent. This view, again, may be open to doubt in view of the Court's judgment in the *Vagrancy* cases and the issues of principle underlying that judgment, which were not fully apparent in the Commission's reasoning. In *Graziani-weiss v Austria*,[76] the applicant objected to being made the legal guardian of a minor. The Court noted that although there was an element of prior consent in the applicant's professional choice as a lawyer, this element alone is not determinative when examining whether he had been forced to undertake compulsory labour and so did not exclude the applicability of Article 4,[77] throwing further doubt on the Commission's findings.

CONCLUDING REMARKS

The Strasbourg Court has clarified and expanded on the application of Article 4 to reflect the international and domestic developments in the area of forced labour, servitude, and trafficking. The judgment in *Bayatyan v Armenia*[78] which found that Article 4 did not prevent the application of Article 9 to military service was very much influenced by the changing consensus and international developments in regard to conscientious objection and is to be welcomed. In contrast, the Court has taken a more cautious approach to prisoner's rights with regard to prison work, despite a developing European consensus.[79] This is an area that may be open to a more purposive approach in the future.

The Trafficking Convention has been signed in all but four of the Contracting Parties. As a result, the Strasbourg Court has expanded on the principle set out in the *Siliadin* case in order to interpret Article 4 in the light of the obligations set out in the Trafficking Convention. That has been a welcome use of the principle of interpreting the Convention as a living instrument in order to strengthen efforts within the Council of Europe to combat the scourge of trafficking in human beings. The Court has also underlined the need for States to distinguish trafficking from domestic servitude in cases where domestic servitude raises complex issues for the applicant.

Although the number of cases coming before Strasbourg is still relatively small in comparison to other Articles in the Convention, the Court's explicit interpretation of Article 4 to address human trafficking and the expansion of positive obligations on States to protect victims, prevent further trafficking, to investigate where there is a 'credible suspicion' of trafficking, and to cooperate with other States should make it easier for victims of human trafficking to access the protection of the European Convention on Human Rights at domestic and European level.

75 App. 1468/62, *Iversen v Norway*, Decision of 17 December 1963, (1963) 6 *Yearbook* 278, 308.

76 *Graziani-weiss v Austria*, (App. 31950/06), 18 October 2012.

77 § 40.

78 *Bayatyan v Armenia*, (App. 233459/03), 7 July 2011, ECHR 2011 see also ch.17.

79 *Stummer v Austria*, (App. 37452/02), 7 July 2011.

11

PERSONAL LIBERTY AND SECURITY

INTRODUCTION

The Strasbourg Court frequently prefaces its consideration of Article 5 cases with the following words:

> The Court stresses the fundamental importance of the guarantees contained in Article 5 for securing the right of individuals in a democracy to be free from arbitrary detention at the hands of the authorities. It has stressed in that connection that any deprivation of liberty must not only have been effected in conformity with the substantive and procedural rules of national law but must equally be in keeping with the very purpose of Article 5, namely to protect the individual from arbitrary detention. In order to minimize the risks of arbitrary detention, Article 5 provides a corpus of substantive rights intended to ensure that the act of deprivation of liberty be amenable to independent judicial scrutiny and secures the accountability of the authorities for that measure.[1]

The object of Article 5 is to guarantee liberty of the person,[2] and in particular to provide guarantees against arbitrary arrest or detention. It seeks to achieve this aim by excluding any form of arrest or detention without lawful authority and proper judicial control.

STRUCTURE OF ARTICLE 5

Article 5 takes a somewhat different approach from corresponding provisions in other human rights treaties. For example, Article 9 of the International Covenant on Civil and Political Rights simply prohibits arbitrary arrest or detention.[3] The structure of Article 5, however, sets out a general right to liberty followed by a prohibition on deprivation of liberty save in the circumstances specified in Article 5(1)(a) to (f). These will be construed narrowly.[4] If a respondent State cannot demonstrate that a measure falls within one of these sub-paragraphs then there is a violation of Article 5. If a measure does fall within

[1] Taken from *Bazorkina v Russia*, (App. 69481/01), 27 July 2006, (2008) 46 EHRR 261, § 146.

[2] M. Mancovei, *The right to liberty and security of the person: a Guide to the implementation of Article 5 of the European Convention on Human Rights*, Human Rights Handbooks, No. 5 (Council of Europe Publishing, Strasbourg 2004).

[3] Article 9 (1) of the ICCPR (1966) states: 'Everyone has the right to liberty and security of the person. No one shall be subjected to arbitrary arrest or detention. No one shall be deprived of his liberty except on such grounds and in accordance with such procedures as are established by law.' For a discussion on freedom from arbitrary detention generally and a comparison of the ICCPR and ECHR see S. Shah, 'Administration of Justice' in D. Moeckli, S. Shah, and S. Sivakumaran. *International Human Rights Law* (2nd edn) (OUP, Oxford 2014), 259–269.

[4] *Lexa v Slovakia*, (App. 54334/00), 23 September 2008, §§ 118–19.

one of these sub-paragraphs, then Article 5(1) also requires any deprivation of liberty to be lawful.[5]

Article 5(2)–(4) sets out certain rights for persons who have been detained.[6] Article 5(2) and Article 5(4) apply to all detainees, whereas Article 5(3) applies only to persons detained pending trial on criminal charges. Article 5(5) contains an enforceable right to compensation to everyone who has been the victim of arrest or detention in contravention of the provisions of Article 5.

Derogations under Article 15 from the obligations in Article 5 are permitted.[7]

The first sentence of Article 5 provides that everyone has the right to liberty and security of person; the meaning of 'security' in Article 5 is, however, uncertain.[8] The question was raised, but not resolved, in the *East African Asians* cases.[9] On the normal principles of interpretation, the term 'security' should be given a meaning independent of 'liberty', but the remainder of the provision is concerned exclusively with deprivation of liberty. The matter appeared to have been finally resolved in the *Bozano* case,[10] where the Strasbourg Court's reasoning indicated that the primary focus of Article 5 is the deprivation of liberty.[11] In cases involving the disappearance of prisoners, however, the Court has made greater use of the terminology of 'liberty and security of person', because of uncertainty as to the continuing detention of the disappeared person and the suspicion that he or she may have been executed.[12]

WHAT AMOUNTS TO A DEPRIVATION OF LIBERTY?

The second sentence of the provision states that no one shall be 'deprived of his liberty' save in the circumstances described. What constitutes a 'deprivation of liberty'? Confinement to a locked prison cell clearly constitutes such a deprivation, but less absolute forms of restriction can be more problematic. Article 2 of Protocol 4 protects the right to leave a country and to move freely within one,[13] so it has been necessary for the Strasbourg Court to draw a line between deprivations of liberty within the meaning of Article 5, and restrictions on freedom of movement. As the case-law shows, this distinction is more a matter of degree and intensity than of nature or substance.[14] In deciding whether a restriction on freedom falls within the scope of Article 5, the Strasbourg Court will look at such factors as the type, duration, effects, and manner of implementation of the measure in question.

[5] See later in this chapter.

[6] For a discussion of aspects of the protection afforded by Article 5 in criminal proceedings, see generally S. Trechsel, *Human Rights in Criminal Proceedings* (OUP, Oxford 2005).

[7] See ch.4. See also *A and others v United Kingdom*, (App. 3455/05), 19 February 2009 [GC], (2009) 49 EHRR 29, ECHR 2009-nyr.

[8] See R. Powell, 'The right to security of person in European Court of Human Rights jurisprudence' [2007] EHRLR 649.

[9] App. 4626/70, *East African Asians v United Kingdom*, Decision of 6 March 1978, (1978) 13 DR 5.

[10] *Bozano v France*, 18 December 1986, Series A No 111, (1987) 9 EHRR 297.

[11] See especially § 54.

[12] See, for example, *Timurtaş v Turkey*, (App. 23531/94), 13 June 2000, (2001) 33 EHRR 121, ECHR 2000-VI, § 106; *Çiçek v Turkey*, (App. 25704/94), 27 February 2001, (2003) 37 EHRR 464, § 169; and *Ibragimov and others v Russia*, (App. 34561/03), 29 May 2008, § 117. See also *El Masri v Republic of Macedonia*, (App. 39630/09), 13 December 2012, § 231, where the Court underlined the importance of the procedural safeguards of Article 5 for 'personal security of the person' in cases involving disappearances.

[13] See ch.23.

[14] *Guzzardi v Italy*, 6 November 1980, Series A No 39, (1981) 3 EHRR 333, § 93.

The *Guzzardi* case[15] is the classic example of a borderline case. The applicant was ordered, on suspicion of being a member of the Mafia, to remain on a small island near Sardinia for sixteen months. Although there was no perimeter fence, he was not allowed to leave an area of two and a half square kilometres containing a village inhabited solely by other men subject to the same type of residence order, and he had to keep a curfew and report to the police twice a day. His wife and child were not prevented from living with him, but the available accommodation was cramped and dilapidated and thus unsuitable for a family. Although he was allowed to work, there were few employers on the island and he was unable to find a job. He had to seek the permission of the police before making a telephone call or seeing an outside visitor. Any breach of these conditions was punishable by incarceration. The Strasbourg Court, comparing Guzzardi's situation to that of a person kept in an open prison, found that there had been a deprivation of liberty for the purposes of Article 5.

There is no deprivation of liberty if the applicant consents to detention. However, the Court will examine the concrete situation of the person involved. The applicant in the *HL* case[16] was severely autistic, unable to speak and prone to bouts of agitation and self-harm. His doctors decided that it was in his best interests to be admitted to hospital for a while; since he did not resist, he was admitted as an 'informal' patient, under no legal obligation to remain in hospital. He remained in the hospital on this basis for just over three months; thereafter, following national legal proceedings, he was compulsorily detained. He complained under Article 5(1) about his time as an 'informal' patient. The Court did not find it determinative that the applicant had been compliant and never attempted, or expressed the wish, to leave, considering that 'the right to liberty is too important in a democratic society for a person to lose the benefit of Convention protection for the single reason that he may have given himself up to be taken into detention'. Instead, it found the key factor to have been that the health care professionals treating and managing the applicant exercised complete and effective control over his care and movements, and he was not, in reality, free to leave, since had he made such an attempt there was evidence that the doctors would immediately have detained him under compulsory powers. There had, therefore, been a deprivation of liberty.[17] In *Stanev v Bulgaria*,[18] the Court underlined the importance of assessing the concrete situation by restating that the protection of Article 5 would be undermined if an applicant loses the protection of the Convention on the basis that he initially gave himself up to detention.[19]

The applicants in the *Amuur* case[20] were refugees from Somalia who had travelled via Kenya and Syria to Paris-Orly Airport. They were refused entry to France on the ground that their passports had been falsified and for twenty days, before being sent back to Syria, they were shuttled by the police between a nearby hotel, one of the floors of which had been let as a transit zone to the Ministry of the Interior, and the *Espace* lounge of the airport. The Court rejected the respondent State's argument that, since the applicants had been free at any time to return to Syria or any other country which would have accepted

[15] *Guzzardi v Italy*, 6 November 1980, Series A No 39, (1981) 3 EHRR 333.

[16] *HL v United Kingdom*, (App. 45508/99), 5 October 2004, (2005) 40 EHRR 761, ECHR 2004-IX. See also *Ashingdane v United Kingdom*, 28 May 1985, Series A No 93, (1985) 7 EHRR 528. *Storck v Germany*, (App. 61603/00), 16 June 2005, (2006) 43 EHRR 96, ECHR 2005-V.

[17] See also *Enhorn v Sweden*, (App. 56529/00), 25 January 2005, (2005) 41 EHRR 633, ECHR 2005-I, discussed later in this chapter. Contrast *HM v Switzerland*, (App. 39187/98), 26 February 2002, (2004) 38 EHRR 314, ECHR 2002-II.

[18] *Stanev v Bulgaria*, (App 36760/06), 17 January 2012.

[19] § 119.

[20] *Amuur v France*, (App. 19776/92), 25 June 1996, (1996) 22 EHRR 533, ECHR 1996-III.

them, the holding measures to which they had been subjected did not amount to a deprivation of liberty.

Cases involving members of the armed forces have also thrown up some problems of definition. The *Engel* case[21] concerned the penalties which could be imposed on conscripted Dutch soldiers. There were grades of arrest: the lower grades involved confinement to barracks, while 'strict arrest' involved detention in locked cells. The Court considered that a different regime might well be applicable to the armed forces, and went on to find that the light forms of arrest did not amount to deprivations of liberty, although strict arrest would. Similarly, once an individual is detained in prison, additional restrictions on his or her liberty, imposed for disciplinary reasons, will not usually give rise to any issue under Article 5(1), although sufficiently severe cases could breach Article 3.[22]

In *Shimovolos v Russia*[23] the Court found that, where the applicant was forcibly taken to a police station to be questioned about his future involvement in a protest, this amounted to a deprivation of liberty despite being detained in the police station for no more than 45 minutes.

The Court has subsequently adopted a more restrictive approach to 'deprivation of liberty' under Article 5. In *Austin and others v United Kingdom*,[24] protests had been held in London which had led to some disorder. As part of the police operation, part of the demonstration was cordoned off (known as kettling) and those who were inside the cordon were not allowed to leave until some hours later. One applicant was a protester whilst the others had been caught up in the cordon but were not part of the demonstrations. The Government argued that the cordoning did not amount to a deprivation of liberty as the purpose of the police action had to be taken into account in determining if a deprivation had taken place. The Court accepted the Government's arguments in finding that there had not been a deprivation of liberty. It found that:

> It is important to note, therefore, that the measure was imposed to isolate and contain a large crowd, in volatile and dangerous conditions. As the Government pointed out…, the police decided to make use of a measure of containment to control the crowd, rather than having resort to more robust methods, which might have given rise to a greater risk of injury to people within the crowd…The Court finds no reason to depart from the judge's conclusion that in the circumstances the imposition of an absolute cordon was the least intrusive and most effective means to be applied. Indeed, the applicants did not contend that, when the cordon was first imposed, those within it were immediately deprived of their liberty.[25]

The Court considered the purpose of the police actions relevant to whether there was a 'deprivation of liberty' under Article 5. The Court noted that this decision was based on the 'specific and exceptional' facts of the case.[26] This was a situation of force majeure, where there was an imminent risk of violence and injury to those present. The Court had to be creative in its approach to 'deprivation of liberty' in order to allow crowd control that was not arbitrary and was continually assessed as necessary by the police.

[21] *Engel and others v Netherlands*, (Apps. 5100/71, 5101/71, 5102/71, 5354/72, and 5370/72), 8 June 1976, Series A No 22, (1979–80) 1 EHRR 647.

[22] See ch.9.

[23] *Shimovolos v Russia*, (App. 30194/09), 21 June 2011. Similarly in *Foka v Turkey*, (App. 28940/95), 24 June 2008, the Court found that the detention of the applicant in the police station for a few hours, where she was taken forcibly, amounted to deprivation of liberty. In *Gillan and Quinton v United Kingdom*, (App. 4158/05), 12 January 2010, § 57 the Court suggested that a stop and search by police for 30 minutes could amount to a deprivation. However, the Court did not make a finding on Article 5 as it found it unnecessary to do so, as it found a violation under Article 8.

[24] *Austin and others v United Kingdom*, (Apps. 39692/09, 40713/09, and 41008/09), 15 March 2012.

[25] § 66.

[26] § 68.

However the dissenting opinions in the case note that this is not how 'deprivation of liberty' has previously been interpreted. The purpose of the State action has been a part of the deliberation on whether a deprivation is justified under Article 5(1)(a)–(f) and not whether there has been a 'deprivation'. The dissent expressed concern with the majority's argument that in crowd control cases, the maintenance of law and order can be taken into account in deciding if there is a deprivation, as this 'appears dangerous to us in that it leaves the way open for carte blanche and sends out a bad message to police authorities.'[27]

As noted by the dissent, the decision in *Austin* may make it easier for a State to argue that Article 5 is inapplicable by allowing States to argue for a balancing exercise when determining 'deprivation', which may introduce added grounds for actions and so undermine the exclusive grounds for a deprivation of liberty specifically set out by the Convention. Despite the Court acknowledging this is an exceptional case, the dissent's concerns may be justified. However, in a subsequent judgment,[28] the Court unanimously found a violation of Article 5, where the applicants were Chechen refugees held for several hours by the police in Georgia. The Government argued that checks were being carried out on Chechen refugees due to the prevailing security situation. However, although the Court was not specifically commenting on whether there was a deprivation, it made it clear that Article 5(1) was to be narrowly construed:

> The Court reiterates, however, that even taking into account the special circumstances of the case, Article 5 § 1 does not permit a balance to be struck between the individual's right to liberty and the State's interest in addressing security threats. The Government's argument is inconsistent with the principle that paragraphs (a) to (f) of Article 5 § 1 amount to an exhaustive list of exceptions and that only a narrow interpretation of these exceptions is compatible with the aims of Article 5. If detention does not fit within the confines of the paragraphs as interpreted by the Court, it cannot be made to fit by an appeal to the need to balance the interests of the State against those of the detainee.[29]

It is yet to be seen what impact the *Austin* decision may have on future case law, but the pronouncements of the court post *Austin* have reiterated the restrictiveness of Article 5 without referring to *Austin*. It may remain an exceptional case.

THE LAWFULNESS OF THE DEPRIVATION OF LIBERTY

A deprivation of liberty which does not fall within one of the six categories listed in Article 5(1) will breach the Convention.[30] It is not, however, sufficient merely to come within one of the permitted grounds of detention. The deprivation of liberty must also be 'lawful' and carried out 'in accordance with a procedure prescribed by law'. 'Lawfulness' in Article 5(1) carries the same meaning as 'in accordance with law' in Articles 8–11.[31]

In the *Amuur* case,[32] guidelines under French law concerning the holding of asylum seekers in the international zone of an airport were contained in an unpublished Ministry of the Interior circular. This circular was not available to asylum seekers or their lawyers,

[27] Joint Dissenting Opinion of Judges Tulkens, Spielmann, and Garlicki, § 7.

[28] *Baisuev and Anzorov v Georgia*, (App. 39804/04), 18 December 2012. [29] § 60.

[30] *Saadi v United Kingdom*, (App. 13229/03), 29 January 2008, (2008) 47 EHRR 427, ECHR 2008-nyr, § 67.

[31] *Steel and others v United Kingdom*, (App. 24838/94), 23 September 1998, (1998) 28 EHRR 603, ECHR 1998-VII; and ch.14.

[32] *Amuur v France*, (App. 19776/92), 25 June 1996, (1996) 22 EHRR 533, ECHR 1996-III.

contained no guarantees against arbitrary detention, and did not provide for review by the national courts. The law was not sufficiently clear and accessible. Similarly, in the *Baranowski* case,[33] the Court found deficiencies in the Polish law on pre-trial detention. In 1993, when the applicant was arrested, it was the practice in Poland that, once a bill of indictment had been lodged, the accused could continue to be detained on remand until trial without the need for a court order. The Court found that this practice of maintaining detention on the basis of the indictment was not founded on any specific legislative provision or case-law but stemmed from the absence of clear rules. It did not, therefore, satisfy the test of foreseeability.[34] Furthermore, the fact that without a court order the detention could continue for an unlimited and unpredictable period was contrary to the principle of legal certainty and open to arbitrariness and abuse.

As the *Baranowski* judgment indicates, even where the national law has been complied with, the deprivation of liberty will not be 'lawful' if national law allows for arbitrary or excessive detention. In the *Erkalo* case[35] the applicant was detained in a mental hospital pursuant to a court order. When the order expired there was, because of an administrative error, a period of two months during which the applicant continued to be detained before a new order was granted by the court. Although, under the Dutch Code of Criminal Procedure, the detention was not unlawful in these circumstances, the Court held that the lack of administrative and judicial safeguards—demonstrated by the fact that the absence of any legal basis for the detention came to light only when the applicant himself applied to court—rendered the detention arbitrary and thus unlawful under Article 5(1).[36]

The Court has also had to determine the lawfulness of detention under international legal obligations. In *Medvedyev and others v France*,[37] French authorities detained the applicants at sea, after intercepting their ship and charged the applicants with conspiracy to import drugs. The Court examined the 1982 UN Convention of the Law of the Sea and a diplomatic note from Cambodia allowing the French to board the ship (under a Cambodian flag). It decided that the Convention and the agreement could not represent a clearly defined legal basis. There was therefore a violation of Article 5.[38]

THE CONCEPT OF ARBITRARINESS

It is axiomatic that the essence of Article 5 is to protect the individual against arbitrary detention. Even a detention which is lawful under national law will be a breach of Article 5 if it is arbitrary. Such a situation would arise where the authorities have acted in bad faith or used deception, as in the *Čonka* case,[39] where Romany families were tricked into presenting themselves at a police station with the promise that their asylum applications would be completed, only to be served with deportation papers and taken into immediate custody. The Grand Chamber has spelled out the key principles relating to arbitrariness in

[33] *Baranowski v Poland*, (App. 28358/95), 28 March 2000, ECHR 2000-III.

[34] See, similarly, *Hilda Hafsteinsdottir v Iceland*, (App. 40905/98), 8 June 2004 and *Creanga v Romania*, (App. 29226/03), 23 February 2012.

[35] *Erkalo v Netherlands*, (App. 23807/94), 2 September 1998, (1999) 28 EHRR 509, ECHR 1998-VI.

[36] The Court reached a similar conclusion in *HL v United Kingdom*, (App. 45508/99), 5 October 2004, (2005) 40 EHRR 761, ECHR 2004-IX. See also *Varbanov v Bulgaria*, (App. 31365/96), 5 October 2000.

[37] *Medvedyev and others v France*, (App. 3394/03), 29 March 2010; see also *Al Jedda v United Kingdom*, (App. 27021/08), 07 July 2011, §§ 98–109.

[38] By ten votes to seven.

[39] *Čonka v Belgium*, (App. 51564/99), 5 February 2002, (2002) 34 EHRR 1298, ECHR 2002-I, see also *Creanga v Romania*, (App. 29226/03), 23 February 2012.

its judgment in the *Saadi* case.[40] The Court stressed the following points. Both the order to detain and the execution of the detention must genuinely conform with the purpose of detention as set out in Article 5(1); a failure to ensure that there is some relationship between the ground of permitted deprivation of liberty and the conditions of detention will render the deprivation arbitrary. The Strasbourg Court will also assess whether detention was necessary to achieve its stated aim. Detention should be seen as a remedy of last resort, and lesser measures must be considered and found to be insufficient to safeguard either the individual or the public interest. It follows that the duration of any detention will also be a relevant factor in considering whether it was, or has become, arbitrary in nature. In *James, Wells and Lee v United Kingdom*,[41] the Court found that rehabilitation is part of any indeterminate sentencing scheme for dangerous prisoners. Delays in providing prisoners held under such a scheme with access to the appropriate treatment courses needed in order to demonstrate rehabilitation meant that the prisoners could not demonstrate elimination of risk which was the reason for their continued detention. These delays meant the detention after the prisoners' determinate sentence had expired was arbitrary under Article 5(1).

Where the detention is for the purpose specified in Article 5(1)(b), (d), or (e), the notion of arbitrariness requires an assessment to be made of the necessity of detention for the stated aim.[42] The requirement is somewhat different in relation to detention following conviction by a competent court under Article 5(1)(a), since the choice of detention as a sentence and its duration are matters for the national court rather than the Strasbourg Court.[43] The Court has adopted a similar position in relation to detention with a view to deportation in Article 5(1)(f), provided that the detention does not continue for an unreasonable length of time, and that deportation proceedings are conducted with due diligence.[44] The Court has said that the same consideration applies where the detention is for the purpose of preventing an unauthorized entry into the country.[45]

POSITIVE OBLIGATIONS

The development of positive obligations[46] under Article 5 has lagged somewhat behind its development under other Articles of the Convention, most notably Articles 2, 3, and 8. That position has largely been remedied by the Strasbourg Court's judgment in the *Storck* case.[47] The applicant, who was born in 1958, had spent much of her life in hospitals and psychiatric institutions. One of the issues raised in her application concerned her detention in a locked ward in a private psychiatric clinic for nearly two years from July 1977 to April 1979. The police had assisted in her return to the clinic when she had escaped. An action for damages which she later instituted was, following appeals, unsuccessful. The Strasbourg Court found that the responsibility of the respondent State arose for three reasons: first, the police had assisted in her return to the clinic; secondly, the courts

[40] *Saadi v United Kingdom*, (App. 13229/03), 29 January 2008 [GC], (2008) 47 EHRR 427, ECHR 2008-nyr, §§ 67–74.

[41] *James, Wells and Lee v United Kingdom*, (Apps. 25119/09, 57715/09 and 57877/09), 18 September 2012.

[42] § 70.

[43] Provided that the detention follows and has a sufficient causal connection with a lawful conviction: § 71

[44] § 72. [45] §§ 73–4.

[46] Save for those expressly provided for in the provision: see A. Mowbray, *The Development of Positive Obligations under the European Convention on Human Rights by the European Court of Human Rights* (Hart, Oxford 2004), ch.4. Note also the requirements to record detentions, and to investigate unacknowledged detentions referred to earlier in this chapter.

[47] *Storck v Germany*, (App. 61603/00), 16 June 2005, (2006) 43 EHRR 96, ECHR 2005-V.

had rejected her claims; and thirdly, the State had positive obligations under Article 5. The Court said:

> Article 5(1), first sentence,... must... be considered as laying down a positive obligation on the State to protect the liberty of its citizens. Any conclusion to the effect that this was not the case would not only be inconsistent with the Court's case-law, notably under Articles 2, 3 and 8 of the Convention. It would, moreover, leave a sizeable gap in the protection from arbitrary detention which would be inconsistent with the importance of personal liberty in a democratic society. The State is, therefore, obliged to take measures providing effective protection of vulnerable persons, including reasonable steps to prevent the deprivation of liberty of which the authorities have or ought to have knowledge...[48]

To the extent that earlier pronouncements[49] might be taken to indicate that there are no, or only very limited, positive obligations arising under Article 5, those decisions should not be regarded as so deciding.[50] In the *Rantsev* case involving human trafficking, the Court found that the State's responsibility is engaged where it fails to prevent a loss of liberty which is imposed on a victim by private individuals.[51] The Court has further developed procedural obligations under Article 5, especially the need for investigations in cases involving disappearances.[52] In *Varnava v Turkey*,[53] the Court made it clear that where there is an arguable claim that an applicant had been taken into custody and had not subsequently been seen, it is incumbent on the state to carry out an effective investigation.[54]

The question has also risen as to the State's obligations to apply Article 5 where it is under positive obligations flowing from other Convention Articles such as Article 2 and Article 3. In *Jendrowski v Germany*[55] the Court considered the relationship of positive obligations under Article 5 with those arising in the same situation under Articles 2 and 3. The applicant, a convicted rapist, was challenging his continued detention. Whilst acknowledging a State's obligation to protect persons within its jurisdiction under Articles 2 and 3 and noting that they considered the applicant was at risk of reoffending, the Court nevertheless stated that the Court has:

> repeatedly held that the scope of any positive obligation on State authorities to take preventive operational measures to protect individuals from the criminal acts of another individual must take into consideration the need to ensure that the authorities exercise their powers to control and prevent crime in a manner which fully respects the due process and other guarantees which legitimately place restraints on the scope of their action, including the guarantees contained, in particular, in Article 5 of the Convention.[56]

UNACKNOWLEDGED DETENTION

Unacknowledged deprivation of liberty constitutes a serious violation of Article 5.[57] The Strasbourg Court frequently says in such cases:

[48] *Storck*, § 102.

[49] *Nielsen v Denmark*, 28 November 1988, Series A No 144, (1989) 11 EHRR 175; *Koniarska v United Kingdom*, (App. 33670/96), Decision of 12 October 2000.

[50] See A. Campbell, 'Positive obligations under the ECHR: deprivation of liberty by private actors' (2006) 10 *Edinburgh Law Review* 399.

[51] *Rantsev v Cyprus and Russia*, (App. 25965/04), 7 January 2010, §§ 319–21.

[52] See earlier *Idalova and Idalov v Russia*, (App. 41515/04), 5 February 2009. See also. *El Masri v Republic of Macedonia*, (App. 39630/09), 13 December 2012.

[53] *Varnava v Turkey*, (App. 16064/90), 18 September 2009.

[54] § 208.

[55] *Jendrowski v Germany*, (App. 30060/04), 14 April 2011.

[56] § 36. This line of reasoning by the Court was emphasized by the dissent in *Austin v United Kingdom* (Apps. 39692/09, 40713/09 and 41008/09), 15 March 2012.

[57] *Timurtaş v Turkey*, (App. 23531/94), 13 June 2000, (2001) 33 EHRR 121, ECHR 2000-VI, § 103.

> The unacknowledged detention of an individual is a complete negation of these guarantees and discloses a most grave violation of Article 5. Bearing in mind the responsibility of the authorities to account for individuals under their control, Article 5 requires them to take effective measures to safeguard against the risk of disappearance and to conduct a prompt and effective investigation into an arguable claim that a person has been taken into custody and has not been seen since....[58]

The characteristics of unacknowledged deprivations are a failure by the State to account for the whereabouts of a person taken into their custody. This requires the formal recording of information as to the identity of the person detained and the person detaining him or her, the date, time, duration, and location of the detention, and the reasons for the detention.[59] As noted, where complaints are made of unacknowledged detentions, there is a positive obligation on the State to conduct an investigation to determine the whereabouts of the missing person.[60]

PERMITTED PRE-TRIAL DETENTION

Article 5(1)(c) allows for the arrest and pre-trial detention of a person in the following terms:

> the lawful arrest or detention of a person effected for the purpose of bringing him before the competent legal authority on reasonable suspicion of having committed an offence or when it is reasonably considered necessary to prevent his committing an offence or fleeing after having done so;

Article 5(3) adds to the safeguards for such persons by providing:

> Everyone arrested or detained in accordance with the provisions of paragraph (1)(c) of this article shall be brought promptly before a judge or other officer authorized by law to exercise judicial power and shall be entitled to trial within a reasonable time or to release pending trial. Release may be conditioned by guarantees to appear for trial.

Article 5(1)(c) can be broken down into a number of separate conditions, all of which must be present in order for the arrest or detention to be acceptable under the Convention. Thus, the arrest or detention must be 'lawful'; it must be effected for the purpose of bringing the detainee 'before the competent legal authority'; and the detainee must reasonably be suspected of having committed an offence or of being about to commit an offence or abscond having committed an offence.

The expression 'competent legal authority' has been held to carry the same meaning as 'judge or other officer authorized by law to exercise judicial power' in Article 5(3);[61] this meaning is considered in more detail later in this chapter.

It has long been established that these provisions do not permit any form of preventive detention.[62] It is not acceptable to detain someone for a crime not yet committed.[63]

[58] *Bazorkina v Russia*, (App. 69481/01), 27 July 2006, (2008) 46 EHRR 261, § 146.

[59] *Çiçek v Turkey*, (App. 25704/94), 27 February 2001, (2003) 37 EHRR 464, § 165. *Varnava v Turkey* (App. 16064/90), 18 September 2009.

[60] For an example of such cases arising from Russian conduct in Chechnya, see *Idalova and Idalov v Russia*, (App. 41515/04), 5 February 2009. See also *El Masri v Republic of Macedonia*, (App. 39630/09), 13 December 2012 arising from extraordinary rendition.

[61] *Schiesser v Switzerland*, 4 December 1979, Series A No 34, (1979–80) 2 EHRR 417.

[62] *Engel and others v Netherlands*, (Apps. 5100/71, 5101/71, 5102/71, 5354/72, and 5370/72), 8 June 1976, Series A No 22, (1979–80) 1 EHRR 647, § 69; *Al Jedda v United Kingdom*, (App. 27021/08), 7 July 2011.

[63] *Lawless v Ireland*, 1 July 1961, Series A No 3, (1979–80) 1 EHRR 15, §§ 13–14; and *Ječius v Lithuania* (App. 34578/97), 31 July 2000, (2002) 35 EHRR 400, ECHR 2000-IX. For argument to the contrary, see

As long as, at the time of the arrest or detention, the intention to bring the suspect to court is there, it is immaterial whether or not in the event he is actually brought to court or charged,[64] although too long a period of preliminary detention without judicial control may give rise to an issue under Article 5(3).

The word 'offence' in Article 5(1)(c) carries an autonomous meaning, identical to that of 'criminal offence' in Article 6,[65] and the 'offence' must be specific and concrete. Although the classification of the offence under national law is one factor to be taken into account, the nature of the proceedings and the severity of the penalty at stake are also relevant.[66] Thus, for example, detention under close arrest on charges of desertion from the British army,[67] carrying a maximum penalty of two years' imprisonment, falls within Article 5(1)(c), although such military offences lie outside the mainstream English criminal law.

There will, accordingly, be very few cases falling within the second two alternatives in paragraph 1(c). Since the words 'when it is reasonably considered necessary to prevent [the detained person] committing an offence' do not authorize general preventive detention, evidence of intention on the part of the detainee to commit a concrete offence will be necessary. However, in most European countries, acts preparatory to the commission of a crime are themselves categorized as offences. Such evidence would, therefore, usually be sufficient to bring the detainee within the first limb: arrest or detention upon 'reasonable suspicion of having committed an offence'. Similarly any arrest or detention falling within the third limb—'to prevent [the detainee]...fleeing after having [committed an offence]'—will also fall within the first.

The requirement that the arrest and detention must be dependent upon the existence of reasonable suspicion that an offence has been committed means that there must be facts or information which would satisfy an objective observer.[68] The standard of proof required for making an arrest is lower than that required for a criminal charge and subsequently a conviction.[69] In the *Fox, Campbell and Hartley* case,[70] the applicants argued that the interpretation by the courts of emergency legislation as requiring only a subjective test of honest belief that the person detained was a terrorist was incompatible with Article 5(1)(c). The Strasbourg Court found that in the context of the special problems presented in combating terrorism a lower standard of 'reasonable suspicion' might be acceptable, but that some objectively realistic grounds would still be needed. Since the respondent State had not provided any evidence on which it could be shown that there was any basis for the suspicion that the applicants were terrorists, the Strasbourg Court found a violation of Article 5(1)(c). In the *Labita* case[71] it held that the uncorroborated hearsay evidence of an anonymous informant was not enough to found 'reasonable suspicion' of the applicant's involvement in Mafia-type activities. In the *O'Hara* case,[72] the applicant was arrested on suspicion of having committed a sectarian murder, and released without charge after six days and thirteen hours. The applicant complained of unlawful arrest, assault, and

C. Macken, 'Preventive Detention and the Right to personal Liberty and security under Article 5 ECHR' (2006) 10 *The International Journal of Human Rights* 195. However, the interpretation given in *Lawless* has been affirmed in recent case-law, see *Ostendorf v Germany*, (App. 15598/08), 7 March 2013, §§ 65–8.

[64] *Labita v Italy*, (App. 26772/95), 6 April 2000 [GC], (2008) 46 EHRR 1228, ECHR 2000-IV, § 155.

[65] See ch.12.

[66] *Benham v United Kingdom*, (App. 19380/92), 10 June 1996, (1996) 22 EHRR 293, ECHR 1996-III.

[67] *Hood v United Kingdom*, (App. 27267/95), 18 February 1999, (2000) 29 EHRR 365, ECHR 1999-I.

[68] *Erdagöz v Turkey*, (App. 21890/93), 22 October 1997, (2001) 32 EHRR 443, ECHR 1997-VI.

[69] *Erdagöz v Turkey*, (App. 21890/93), 22 October 1997, (2001) 32 EHRR 443, ECHR 1997-VI. § 51.

[70] *Fox, Campbell and Hartley v United Kingdom*, 30 August 1990, Series A No 182, (1991) 13 EHRR 157.

[71] *Labita v Italy*, (App. 26772/95), 6 April 2000 [GC], (2008) 46 EHRR 1228, ECHR 2000-IV.

[72] *O'Hara v United Kingdom*, (App. 37555/97), 16 October 2001, (2002) 34 EHRR 812, ECHR 2001-X.

ill-treatment before the national courts, where the arresting officer gave evidence that he had made the arrest after having been told by a superior officer at a briefing that the applicant was suspected of the murder. It emerged during the Strasbourg proceedings that the briefing had been based on information from four separate informants, who had previously been proved reliable and whose information about the murder had been consistent. The Court held that this was sufficient to found a 'reasonable suspicion' that the applicant was involved.

Article 5(3) guarantees certain rights to persons arrested or detained in accordance with the provisions of Article 5(1)(c). The first part of Article 5(3) is concerned with rights immediately on arrest (the arrest period); the second part deals with detention on remand (the remand period), that is, following charge.[73]

THE ARREST PERIOD

According to Article 5(3), any person arrested on suspicion of having committed a criminal offence has the right to be brought 'promptly' before 'a judge or other officer authorized by law to exercise judicial power'. In contrast to the right to judicial review of the legality of the detention under Article 5(4), which may be conditional on the application of the detained person, the right under Article 5(3) is to be brought promptly before a judge: it is the duty of a Contracting Party on its own initiative to see that this is done.[74]

There has been considerable case-law on the meaning of 'promptly' in this context, particularly in connection with applicants detained on suspicion of involvement in terrorism.[75] States as diverse as the United Kingdom and Turkey have invoked the need to hold terrorist suspects *incommunicado* for some time following arrest, because of the risk that other members of the terrorist organization could destroy evidence or put the lives of witnesses or even judges in danger. Conversely, judicial safeguards are of particular importance in connection with emotive crimes of this nature, when the police and prosecution are likely to be under pressure to secure convictions and may be tempted to use unorthodox means to secure confessions. The purpose of this provision is to protect those held in custody from ill-treatment.[76]

The Strasbourg Court has never put a finite limit on the acceptable length of preliminary detention, since it considers that this must depend on the circumstances in each case. Some guidance is, however, provided by the *Brogan* case,[77] which indicates that the period in issue is a matter of a few days. The applicants were detained under special provisions enabling the Secretary of State for Northern Ireland to extend an initial forty-eight-hour period of detention. The shortest length of detention after arrest was four days and six hours and the longest was six days and sixteen hours. All the applicants were released without charge. The Government claimed these measures were necessary as they needed extra time to question terrorist suspects who had been trained in counter-interrogation techniques. Even taking account of the particular situation at that time in Northern Ireland, the Court regarded all cases as violations of the requirements of Article 5(3).

[73] These are distinct rights which are not necessarily temporally linked: *TW v Malta*, (App. 25644/94), 29 April 1999 [GC], (2000) 29 EHRR 185, § 49; and *McKay v United Kingdom*, (App. 543/03), 3 October 2006 [GC], (2007) 44 EHRR 827, ECHR 2006-X, §§ 31–47.

[74] *McKay v United Kingdom*, (App. 543/03), 3 October 2006 [GC], (2007) 44 EHRR 827, ECHR 2006-X, § 34.

[75] See E. Myjer, 'The plain meaning of the word "promptly"', in P. Mahoney and others, *Protecting Human Rights: The European Perspective. Studies in Memory of Rolv Ryssdal* (Carl Heymanns, Köln 2000), 975.

[76] *Öcalan v Turkey* [GC], (App. 46221/99), § 103, ECHR 2005-IV; *Aksoy v Turkey*, judgment of 18 December 1996, *Reports* 1996-VI; *Ladent v Poland*, (App. 11036/03), 18 March 2008, §§ 73-4.

[77] *Brogan and others v United Kingdom*, 29 November 1988, Series A No 145-B, (1989) 11 EHRR 117.

The nature of what constitutes an acceptable length of time before being brought before a judge is further illustrated in *Ipek and others v Turkey*.[78] The applicants were minors. Despite the fact that the period of detention before being brought before a judge was less than four days and the case involved terrorism, the Court held that there was a violation of Article 5 as the fact the applicants were minors meant additional safeguards should have been in place to prevent abuse.[79]

The United Kingdom's response to the *Brogan* judgment was not to repeal the law allowing for extended periods of pre-charge detention; instead it filed a derogation under Article 15 of the Convention, claiming that, in view of the existence of 'an emergency threatening the life of the nation' this part of Article 5(3) should not be applied in Northern Ireland. When the same extended detention provisions came before the Court in the *Brannigan and McBride* case[80] the respondent State conceded that they were not consistent with Article 5(3), but the Court found that the derogation was valid and that there was no violation.[81]

Even where a Contracting Party has derogated from its Article 5(3) obligations the Court retains a power of review. The applicant in the *Aksoy* case[82] was arrested on suspicion of involvement with the PKK, and detained *incommunicado* for fourteen days under emergency provisions in force in south-east Turkey. The respondent State claimed that there was no violation because it had filed an Article 15 derogation in view of Kurdish separatist violence which had given rise to an 'emergency threatening the life of the nation'. The Court accepted that there was such an emergency, but ruled that, even taking into account the difficulty of investigating terrorist offences, fourteen days was too long to hold a suspect without judicial supervision and without access to a lawyer, doctor, or friend. The Court also found the applicant had been tortured during this period, underlining the role of Article 5(3) in attempting to safeguard suspects against abuse.

In the *Medvedyev* case,[83] the Court considered that the thirteen days it took to take the applicants to France and before a judge after they were intercepted at sea for suspected drug smuggling was within an acceptable length of time, given the distance from France, the weather, and the state of the ship.

A number of cases have considered the character of the 'other officer authorized by law to exercise judicial power'.[84] The 'officer' need not be a judge but must display judicial attributes sufficient to protect the rights of the detained person. Most importantly, he or she must be independent of the executive and the parties to the case.[85] Thus a District Attorney who has been involved in indicting and prosecuting the accused cannot fulfil the role of judicial 'officer' under Article 5(3).[86] When assessing independence, the

[78] *Ipek and others v Turkey*, (Apps. 17019/02 and 30070/02), 3 February 2009.

[79] § 36. See also *Kandzhov v Bulgaria*, (App. 68294/01), 6 November 2008, where there were no special circumstances justifying the prolonged detention of three days and 23 hours before being brought before a judge.

[80] *Brannigan and McBride v United Kingdom*, 26 May 1993, Series A No 258-B, (1994) 17 EHRR 539.

[81] In February 2001 the United Kingdom lifted the derogation, in the light of the Northern Irish peace process. A new derogation to Art. 5(1)(f) was filed on 18 December 2001 following the September 11 attacks, which was lifted on 8 April 2005. See also *A and others v United Kingdom*, (App. 3455/05), 19 February 2009 [GC], ECHR 2009-nyr.

[82] *Aksoy v Turkey*, (App. 21987/93), 18 December 1996, (1997) 23 EHRR 553, ECHR 1996-VI.

[83] *Medvedyev v France*, (App. 3394/03), 29 March 2010, by eleven votes to eight. A number of dissenting judges argued that the State could have taken other measures such as taking a judicial officer to the applicants or transporting the applicants back on a naval ship. Joint Partly Dissenting opinion of Judges Tulkens, Bonello, Zupančič, Fura, Spielmann, Tsotsoria, Power, and Poalelungi.

[84] Summarized in *McKay v United Kingdom*, (App. 543/03), 3 October 2006 [GC], (2007) 44 EHRR 827, ECHR 2006-X, §§ 35–40.

[85] *Schiesser v Switzerland*, 4 December 1979, Series A No 34, (1979–80) 2 EHRR 417.

[86] *Huber v Switzerland*, (App. 12794/87), 23 October 1990, Series A No 188.

appearance of the situation from the viewpoint of an outside observer is decisive: if it appears that the 'officer' may intervene in subsequent criminal proceedings on behalf of the prosecution, his or her independence and impartiality may be open to doubt. In the *Assenov* case,[87] the Strasbourg Court therefore held that the prosecutor who authorized the applicant's continued detention on remand could not provide sufficient guarantees of independence, since he could in theory have taken over the prosecution of the subsequent criminal proceedings. Military disciplinary regimes in several countries have led to violations of Article 5(3), since the Strasbourg Court's autonomous interpretative approach brings many military offences within the scope of Article 5 paragraphs (1)(c) and (3). In the *Hood* case,[88] for example, the Court found that the British system whereby the accused soldier's commanding officer remanded him in close arrest was incompatible with Article 5(3) since the same officer was likely to play a central role in the ensuing prosecution and trial by court martial. Similarly, the lack of complete impartiality of the Dutch *auditeur militeur* and the Belgian counterpart took them outside the provision.[89]

The 'officer' must adopt a procedure which meets the normal requirements of due process. This includes hearing representations from the detainee at an oral hearing and deciding, by reference to legal criteria, whether or not the detention is justified.[90] If detention is not justified, the 'officer' must have the power to order release.[91] When examining justification for detention, the 'officer' will examine the lawfulness of the detention and whether there is reasonable suspicion that the person has committed an offence. There is no automatic obligation for the review to decide on the release of the detained person for reasons outside of the lawfulness of the detention or the absence of reasonable suspicion.[92]

THE RIGHT TO RELEASE PENDING TRIAL AND TRIAL WITHIN A REASONABLE TIME

Article 5(3) requires those kept in detention to be brought to trial within a reasonable time; there is a presumption in favour of release.[93] The drafting of Article 5(3) is ambiguous. Read together with Article 5(1) it appears to permit the detention on remand of any person reasonably suspected of having committed an offence—that is, any person likely to stand trial—as long as the trial takes place within a reasonable time, a right in any case guaranteed by Article 6(1). Such an interpretation would, however, be at odds with the purpose of Article 5 which is, broadly, to limit detention to those circumstances where it

[87] *Assenov v Bulgaria*, (App. 24760/94), 28 October 1998, (1998) 28 EHRR 652, ECHR 1998-VIII. And see also *Pantea v Romania*, (App. 33343/96), 3 June 2003, ECHR 2003-VI.

[88] *Hood v United Kingdom*, (App. 27267/95), 18 February 1999, (2000) 29 EHRR 365, ECHR 1999-I.

[89] *De Jong, Baljet and Van den Brink v Netherlands*, 22 May 1984, Series A No 77, (1986) 8 EHRR 20, *Van der Sluijs, Zuiderfeld and Klappe v Netherlands*, 22 May 1984, Series A No 78, (1991) 13 EHRR 461; *Duinhoff and Duif v Netherlands*, 22 May 1984, Series A No 79, (1991) 13 EHRR 478, and *Pauwels v Belgium*, 26 May 1988, Series A No 135, (1989) 11 EHRR 238. See also *Brincat v Italy*, 26 November 1992, Series A No 249-A, (1993) 16 EHRR 591, concerning the Italian deputy public prosecutor.

[90] *Assenov v Bulgaria*, (App. 24760/94), 28 October 1998, (1999) 28 EHRR 652, ECHR 1998-VIII, § 146; *Caballero v United Kingdom*, (App. 32819/96), 8 February 2000, (2000) 30 EHRR 643, ECHR 2000-II; *Sabeur ben Ali v Malta*, (App. 35892/97), 29 June 2000, (2002) 34 EHRR 693.

[91] See, for example, *Aquilina v Malta*, (App. 25642/94), 29 April 1999 [GC], (1999) 29 EHRR 185, ECHR 1999-III.

[92] *McKay v United Kingdom*, (App. 543/03), 3 October 2006 [GC], (2007) 44 EHRR 827, ECHR 2006-X, § 36–40.

[93] *McKay v United Kingdom*, (App. 543/03), 3 October 2006 [GC], (2007) 44 EHRR 827, ECHR 2006-X, § 41.

is strictly necessary in the public interest and to provide guarantees to detainees against arbitrariness. Moreover, it would mean that the Convention allowed for pre-trial detention in many more cases than most national European legal systems, where it is usually necessary to show some ground such as a risk of absconding or tampering with evidence before it is possible to lock up a person who, although accused of an offence, is innocent until proved guilty. The Strasbourg Court has therefore rejected this reading and, in a clear example of the purposive interpretative approach, has held in a series of judgments that not only the initial arrest, but also the continuing *detention* must be justified, as long as it lasts, by adequate grounds; and that, independently of those grounds, its *duration* must also not exceed a reasonable time. Reasonableness will be assessed in the light of all the circumstances of the case, which will include examination of the reason put forward by the respondent State.[94] It is also a requirement that the continuing need for detention is considered, since a detention which is initially justified may cease to be so with the passage of time.[95] Suspicion that the detained person has committed an offence, while a necessary condition, does not suffice to justify detention continuing beyond a short initial period, even where the accused is charged with a particularly serious crime and the evidence against him is strong.[96] The Court has never elaborated an exhaustive list of grounds which could justify pre-trial detention; each case is to be judged on its own particular merits.

Thus, as far as the need for pre-trial detention is concerned, the Strasbourg Court understands its role essentially as one of reviewing whether the reasons given by the national courts for refusing release are adequate and sufficient.[97] In each case, the national courts must assess the need for detention with reference to the particular facts. For this reason a British law which automatically denied release on bail to a person charged with a serious violent crime if he had already been convicted of such a crime was incompatible with Article 5(3).[98]

The ground most frequently relied upon by national courts is the risk of absconding. But the risk must be substantiated in each case.[99] It is not sufficient for the national authorities simply to point to the fact that the accused would receive a long prison sentence if convicted as evidence that he or she would be likely to disappear,[100] although this may be a relevant consideration. The applicant in the *Barfuss* case[101] was charged with fraudulently obtaining a number of large bank loans and faced a heavy sentence. The decisions of the Czech courts refusing his applications for bail referred in addition to the fact that he had contacts in Germany, and that if he fled there it would be impossible to continue with the prosecution because there was no extradition agreement between Germany and the Czech Republic. This reasoning was held by the Strasbourg Court to be sufficient for the purposes of Article 5(3).

Where the danger of absconding can be avoided by bail or other guarantees, the accused must be released, and there is an obligation on the national authorities to consider such alternatives to detention.[102] Moreover, in those countries which have the system of bail on

[94] *McKay*, § 43. [95] § 44.

[96] *Tomasi v France*, 27 August 1992, Series A No 241-A, (1993) 15 EHRR 1; *Ječius v Lithuania*, (App. 34578/97), 31 July 2000, (2002) 35 EHRR 400, ECHR 2000-IX.

[97] *Prencipe v Monaco*, (App. 43378/06), 16 July 2009, § 74.

[98] *Caballero v United Kingdom*, (App. 32819/96), 8 February 2000, (2000) 30 EHRR 643, ECHR 2000-II.

[99] In *Kundla v Poland*, (App. 30210/96), 26 October 2000, the risk of absconding was found to be relevant during the early period of detention but had receded later and so a violation of Article 5(3) arose.

[100] See, for example, *Muller v France*, (App. 21802/93), 17 March 1997, ECHR 1997-II.

[101] *Barfuss v Czech Republic*, (App. 35848/97), 31 July 2000, (2002) 34 EHRR 948.

[102] *Wemhoff v Germany*, 27 June 1968, Series A No 7, (1979–80) 1 EHRR 55, § 15 of 'The Law'; *Jablonski v Poland*, (App. 33492/96), 21 December 2000, (2003) 36 EHRR 455.

financial sureties, the amount of the sureties must not be excessive, and must be fixed by reference to the purpose for which they are imposed, namely to ensure that this particular defendant appears for trial.[103] The sum must never be set exclusively by reference to the seriousness of the charge without considering the accused's financial circumstances. The Court took an interesting position on the amount of the surety in *Mangouras v Spain*.[104] The applicant was a Greek national who was detained for trial for his part in causing a large oil spill from his ship off the coast of Spain. The surety was set extremely high at three million euros. The Government argued that given his lack of ties to Spain, the fear of absconding and the gravity of the offence as well as his professional relationship with those paying the surety, a high amount was justified. The Court agreed. Whilst reiterating that the sum set should be based on ensuring that the applicant appears for trial and should consider the applicant's circumstances, the Court noted that the loss caused by the applicant and the gravity of the offence are relevant factors. Given the professional relationship that the applicant had with those paying his surety (employers and insurers) and the nature of the oil spill, at a time of great environmental concern in Europe, these new realities should be taken into account when applying Article 5(3). In the present case the professional environment which provided the setting for the actions in question and the considerable environmental damage caused meant the State was justified in imposing a surety that was beyond the means of the applicant to pay.[105]

Another common ground invoked to justify pre-trial detention is the risk of re-offending prior to trial. Again, the national court judgments must show that this risk was substantiated: reference to past crimes may not be sufficient.[106] There must be some evidence of a propensity to re-offend.[107] In the *Assenov* case[108] the authorities were entitled to rely on this ground since the applicant was charged with a long series of thefts, some of which had allegedly been committed subsequent to his initial arrest and questioning by the police.

Other grounds which have been accepted by the Strasbourg Court as capable of justifying detention are the risk of suppression of evidence,[109] and of collusion, that is, contacting other defendants or witnesses to agree on a false version of events.[110] In *Sarban v Moldova*,[111] the Government attempted to justify the continued detention of the applicant on all three grounds discussed above (risk of absconding, re-offending, and collusion) with little evidence to demonstrate how they applied to the applicant's case. Unsurprisingly, the Court found a violation of Article 5(3).[112]

The right to trial within a reasonable time under Article 5(3) can be invoked only by those detained until trial. If a person is released at any stage before the trial, the situation is governed by Article 6(1) alone. Provided the relevant periods are sufficiently long, there is nothing to prevent a detainee from making claims under both provisions. The relevant period under Article 5(3) begins with arrest or detention. The question when the

[103] *Neumeister v Austria*, 27 June 1968, Series A No 8, (1979–80) 1 EHRR 91, §§ 13–14 of 'The Law'; *Punzelt v Czech Republic*, (App. 31315/96), 25 April 2000, (2001) 33 EHRR 1159.

[104] *Mangouras v Spain*, (App. 12050/04), 28 September 2010.

[105] §§ 88–92. Majority judgment by ten votes to seven. The dissenting opinions argued that the Court had failed to properly consider the applicant's ability to pay and his personal situation. Joint Dissenting Opinion of Judges Rozakis, Bratza, Bonello, Cabral Barreto, David Thór Björgvinsson, Nicolaou and Bianku.

[106] *Muller v France*, (App. 21802/93), 17 March 1997, ECHR 1997-II.

[107] *Matznetter v Austria*, 10 November 1969, Series A No 10, (1979–80) 1 EHRR 198, § 9 of 'The Law'.

[108] *Assenov v Bulgaria*, (App. 24760/94), 28 October 1998, (1999) 28 EHRR 652, ECHR 1998-VIII.

[109] *Wemhoff v Germany*, 27 June 1968, Series A No 7, (1979–80) 1 EHRR 55, §§ 13–14 of 'The Law'.

[110] *Ringeisen v Austria*, 16 July 1971, Series A No 13, (1979–80) 1 EHRR 455, § 107.

[111] *Sarban v Moldova*, (App. 3456/05), 4 October 2005; see also *Manulin v Russia*, (App. 26676/06), 11 April 2013, §§ 60–2.

[112] §§ 101–4.

Article ceases to apply is more complicated, since some European legal systems regard all detention as provisional until the conviction and sentence are confirmed by the final appeal court. In its judgment in the *B* case,[113] the Strasbourg Court ruled that, despite the provision of Austrian law that sentence becomes final only with the determination of any appeal, the applicant's detention on remand came to an end for the purposes of the Convention with the finding of guilt and sentencing at first instance. If an applicant brings a case based on separate periods of detention then these are not treated as a whole period for the purpose of admissibility to the Court under the six month rule.[114] Each period of detention will be dealt with separately. However, if a first period of detention based on the same legal proceeding as a subsequent period of detention is excluded due to the case not being lodged in time with the Court, any examination of subsequent proceedings (that are admissible) by the Court can take into account all periods of detention when deciding if the reasons for detention are sufficient and relevant.[115]

Just as the start and end points of the period to be considered under Article 5(3) are different from those relevant for Article 6(1), so the assessment of what length of time is 'reasonable' differs for the two Articles. In its *Wemhoff* judgment the Court said:

> *It is... mainly in the light of the fact of the detention* of the person being prosecuted that national courts... must determine whether the time that has elapsed, for whatever reason, before judgment is passed on the accused has at some stage exceeded a reasonable limit, that is to say imposed a greater sacrifice than could, in the circumstances of the case, reasonably be expected of a person presumed to be innocent.[116]

Consequently Article 5(3) requires that there must be 'special diligence' in bringing the case to trial if the accused is detained.[117] A detained person is entitled to have the case given priority and conducted with particular expedition.[118]

The Strasbourg Court applies a broad two-stage approach. It will first determine whether the grounds relied upon by the national authorities were adequate, until the very end, to justify remanding the accused in custody. If the detention was justified in principle, the Court will then examine the conduct of the prosecution to ensure that the pre-trial detention was not unnecessarily prolonged.[119] Periods of inactivity by the national authorities lasting more than a few months are usually taken by the Court as a sign of lack of diligence, particularly if the overall duration of the detention was long. By way of example, the Court has generally found periods of pre-trial detention lasting from two and a half[120] to nearly five years[121] to be excessive. However, the Court has stated that a shorter period of time may still be excessive, depending on the specific context of the detention. In *Shishkov v Bulgaria*,[122] an overall pre-trial detention period of seven months and three weeks was held to be unjustified

[113] *B v Austria*, 28 March 1990, Series A No 175, (1991) 13 EHRR 20.

[114] Art. 35 of the ECHR, see ch.2.

[115] *Idalov v Russia*, (App. 5826/03), 22 May 2012, §§ 116–136.

[116] *Wemhoff v Germany*, 27 June 1968, Series A No 7, (1979–80) 1 EHRR 55, § 5 of 'The Law' (emphasis added).

[117] *Stögmüller v Germany*, 10 November 1969, Series A No 9, (1979–80) 1 EHRR 155, § 5 of 'The Law'.

[118] *Wemhoff v Germany*, 27 June 1968, Series A No 7, (1979–80) 1 EHRR 55, § 17 of 'The Law'.

[119] *Contrado v Italy*, (App. 24143/95), 24 August 1998, Reports of Judgements and Decisions 1998-V, where the Court found a detention period of two years, seven months and seven days was not excessive, noting the complex nature of the investigation by the prosecutor's office and the number of witnesses interviewed and called to the trial. The applicant was an alleged member of the Mafia and the Court recognized the complexity of bringing such a case to Court.

[120] *Punzelt v Czech Republic*, (App. 31315/96), 25 April 2000, (2001) 33 EHRR 1159. Compare *Pantano v Italy*, (App. 60851/00), 6 November 2003. See also *Moiseyev v Russia*, (App. 62936/00), 9 October 2008.

[121] *PB v France*, (App. 38781/97), 1 August 2000.

[122] *Shishkov v Bulgaria*, (App. 38822/97), ECHR 2003-I (extracts).

as the authorities had applied a statutory presumption of detention if there was a risk of absconding, re-offending, or collusion where offences were of a certain gravity. There was a failure to examine the individual circumstances of the applicant. The Court noted that it

> is not unmindful of the fact that the majority of length-of-detention cases decided in its judgments concern longer periods of deprivation of liberty and that against that background seven months and three weeks may be regarded as a relatively short period in detention. Article 5 § 3 of the Convention, however, cannot be seen as authorising pre-trial detention unconditionally provided that it lasts no longer than a certain period. Justification for any period of detention, no matter how short, must be convincingly demonstrated by the authorities.[123]

THE REMAINING PERMITTED GROUNDS OF DETENTION

DETENTION AFTER CONVICTION BY A COMPETENT COURT: ARTICLE 5(1)(A)

Article 5(1)(a) permits 'the lawful detention of a person after conviction by a competent court'. It is the *detention* which must be 'lawful', not the *conviction*. The lawfulness of the detention ends when the term of imprisonment to which the person has been sentenced finishes. So continuing a person's detention beyond the period of their sentence will constitute a violation of Article 5.[124] Although many applications to the Strasbourg Court allege that they have been convicted of crimes they did not commit, the Court has no power under Article 5(1)(a) to examine whether the evidence adduced before the national courts was sufficient for a finding of guilt. Similarly, if an appeal against conviction is successful, the quashing of the conviction does not render the previous detention unlawful; and the same applies to acquittal following a retrial.[125]

The sentencing body must be a 'competent court'. 'Competent' means that it must have the power under national law to order the detention in question and 'court' carries the same meaning as in Article 5(4): the body must possess a judicial character and follow a fair procedure.[126] In the *Stoichkov*[127] case, the Court found that there was a lack of a 'competent' court due to the fact that his conviction by a domestic court with the proper judicial character was unfair as he was tried 'in absentia'. He was not allowed to go before the Court for a fresh determination.

In the *Ilaşcu* case,[128] the applicants were convicted and sentenced to detention pending execution by the Supreme Court of the break-away 'Moldavian Republic of Transdniestria', which was not recognized as a State under international law. The Strasbourg Court observed that in certain circumstances a court belonging to the judicial system of an entity not recognized under international law might be regarded as a tribunal 'established by

[123] § 66.

[124] *Pilla v Italy*, (App. 64088/00), 2 March 2006.

[125] App. 3245/67, *X v Austria*, Decision of 4 February 1969, (1969) 12 *Yearbook* 206, 236.

[126] *De Wilde, Ooms and Versyp v Belgium*, (Apps. 2832/66, 2835/66, and 2899/66), 18 November 1970, Series A No 12, (1979–80) 1 EHRR 373, § 78; *Engel and others v Netherlands*, (Apps. 5100/71, 5101/71, 5102/71, 5354/72, and 5370/72), 8 June 1976, Series A No 22, (1979–80) 1 EHRR 647, § 68.

[127] *Stoichkov v Bulgaria*, (App. 9808/02), 24 March 2005.

[128] *Ilaşcu and others v Moldova and Russia*. (App. 48787/99), 8 July 2004 [GC], (2005) 40 EHRR 1030, ECHR 2004-VII.

law' provided that it formed part of a judicial system operating on a 'constitutional and legal basis' reflecting a judicial tradition compatible to the Convention, in order to enable individuals to enjoy the Convention guarantees. The Transdniestrian court, however, did not belong to such a system, and operated in a patently arbitrary and unfair manner. The Court accordingly found that none of the applicants had been convicted by a 'court', and that a sentence of imprisonment passed by a judicial body such as the 'Supreme Court of the MRT' at the close of proceedings like those conducted in the instant case, could not be regarded as 'lawful detention' ordered 'in accordance with a procedure prescribed by law'.

In cases where the 'court' is in a non-Convention State, it is not necessary for it to have followed the strict requirements of Article 6 when making the order for detention, as long as it has not acted in 'flagrant denial of justice'.[129]

'Conviction', like 'court', carries an autonomous meaning under the Convention, and can include a finding of guilt in respect of what is classified as a disciplinary or administrative offence under national law.[130] The deprivation of liberty must flow directly from the conviction. In the *Van Droogenbroeck* case[131] the sentence of the court involved imprisonment for two years followed by a further ten years following release during which the convicted person was 'placed at the Government's disposal', meaning that he could be detained by executive order. The Strasbourg Court considered that there was a sufficient causal connection between the original conviction and the recall during the ten-year period.

The applicant in the *Weeks* case[132] had been sentenced to life imprisonment following an assault because he was considered dangerous. He was released on licence, then recalled to prison after becoming violent. The Strasbourg Court considered that the deprivation of liberty which arose when Weeks's licence was revoked was sufficiently closely linked to the original conviction to meet the requirements of Article 5(1)(a). The same was not true in the *Stafford* case,[133] where the applicant, a convicted murderer, was sentenced to life imprisonment, as is mandatory for all cases of murder in the United Kingdom. He was released on licence in 1979, after having served the punitive element of the life sentence (the 'tariff'). Some fifteen years later he was convicted of fraud and sentenced to a short term of imprisonment. On the expiry of that sentence, the Home Secretary refused to allow his release, claiming that Stafford should continue to be detained under the original life sentence, because there was a risk that he would commit further offences of dishonesty. The Strasbourg Court abandoned its earlier case-law, which had held that the imposition of the mandatory life sentence authorized the State to detain that person for any length of time, at any point, throughout the rest of his or her life. Instead, it found that national law had evolved, to the extent that it recognized that the mandatory life sentence did not impose imprisonment for life as a punishment. After the expiry of the tariff, only considerations of dangerousness, linked to the original murder conviction, could justify the revocation of the licence. The Court could not accept that a decision-making power by the executive to detain the applicant on the basis of perceived fears of future non-violent criminal conduct unrelated to his original murder conviction accorded with the spirit of the Convention, with its emphasis on the rule of law and protection from arbitrariness.

[129] *Drozd and Janousek v France*, 26 June 1992, Series A No 240, (1992) 14 EHRR 745.

[130] *Engel and others v Netherlands*, (Apps. 5100/71, 5101/71, 5102/71, 5354/72, and 5370/72), 8 June 1976, Series A No 22, (1979–80) 1 EHRR 647.

[131] *Van Droogenbroeck v Belgium*, 24 June 1982, Series A No 50, (1982) 4 EHRR 443.

[132] *Weeks v United Kingdom*, 2 March 1987, Series A No 114, (1988) 10 EHRR 293. A separate complaint of a violation of Article 5(4) was successful: see later.

[133] *Stafford v United Kingdom*, (App. 46295/99), 28 May 2002 [GC], (2002) 35 EHRR 1121, ECHR 2002-IV.

The detention after the expiry of the fraud sentence was not, therefore, justified under Article 5(1)(a).

In a series of cases against Germany, it has been held that 'preventative detention' of dangerous offenders after conviction was a violation of Article 5. Applying the principles above, the Court examined the retrospective change in the law extending the length of detention after the end of the determinate part of their sentence, which was decided after the original sentence had been passed. This retrospective change to the original sentence was held to break the link between the original sentence and the continuing detention.[134] Where the preventative detention was not applied retrospectively, the Court has upheld such sentences.[135]

The English provision permitting the Court of Appeal to determine that the time spent in prison pending an unmeritorious appeal shall not form part of the sentence being served was in issue in the *Monnell and Morris* case.[136] The Commission concluded that there had been a breach of Article 5, but the Court disagreed. The rule created a disincentive to unmeritorious appeals, thereby assisting the speedier handling of deserving cases; and trial within a reasonable time is one of the objectives of Article 6.[137] Possible loss of time was therefore an integral part of the criminal appeal process following conviction of an offender and so was permissible under Article 5(1)(a).

Again, since the Strasbourg Court is not an appeal court against decisions of national courts, it will not substitute its own views on the appropriateness of a sentence for those of the national authorities. Thus, the applicants in the cases of *T* and *V*[138] failed to persuade the Strasbourg Court that their detention following their convictions, aged 11, for murdering a toddler when they were aged ten, was contrary to Article 5(1). In common with all children convicted of murder in England and Wales they were sentenced to an indeterminate period of detention ('during Her Majesty's pleasure'). It was argued on their behalf that to impose the same sentence on all child murderers, regardless of their age or circumstances, was arbitrary and therefore 'unlawful'. The Court, however, held that since the applicants' sentences complied with English law and followed conviction by a competent court, no issue arose under Article 5, although it did indicate that very long periods of detention in respect of juveniles might be inconsistent with Article 3 of the Convention.[139]

DETENTION OF A PERSON FOR FAILURE TO COMPLY WITH AN OBLIGATION PRESCRIBED BY LAW: ARTICLE 5(1)(B)

Article 5(1)(b) permits:

> the lawful arrest or detention of a person for non-compliance with the lawful order of a court or in order to secure the fulfilment of any obligation prescribed by law;

The first limb authorizes detention for non-compliance with the lawful order of a court. This could mean, *inter alia*, arrest to secure attendance in court following a failure to

[134] *M v Germany*, (App. 19359/04), 10 May 2010, (2010) 51 EHRR 41; *Kallweit v Germany*, (App. 17792/07), 13 January 2011; *Mautes v Germany*, (App. 20008/07), 13 January 2011; *Schummer v Germany*, (App. 27360/04), 13 January 2011; *Jedrowiak v Germany*, (App. 30060/04), 14 April 2011; and *Haidn v Germany*, (App. 6587/04), 13 January 2011.

[135] *Schmitz v Germany*, (App. 30493/04), 9 June 2011.

[136] *Monnell and Morris v United Kingdom*, 2 March 1987, Series A No 115, (1988) 10 EHRR 205.

[137] See ch.12.

[138] *T v United Kingdom*, (App. 24724/94); and *V v United Kingdom*, (App. 24888/94), 16 December 1999 [GC], (2000) 30 EHRR 121, ECHR 1999-IX.

[139] See ch.9.

comply with a summons,[140] or imprisonment for failure to pay a fine[141] or to comply with an injunction or a child custody or maintenance order.[142] In the *Steel* case,[143] the applicant hunt saboteurs had been ordered by the magistrates' court to agree to be bound over to keep the peace for a period of twelve months. Their imprisonment for refusing to enter into this promise of future good conduct was held by the Strasbourg Court to fall within the scope of the first limb of Article 5(1)(b).[144]

The second limb authorizes detention to secure the fulfilment of any obligation prescribed by law. In the *Benham* case[145] the applicant's imprisonment for failing to pay local taxes was held to fall within this part of Article 5(1)(b).

Detention under this ground must always be proportionate to the aim pursued. Detention cannot be used for a purpose other than that which the measure purports to fulfil. In *Khodorkovskiy v Russia*,[146] the applicant was detained as a witness as part of an investigation into Russian companies (the Yukos investigations). However, when he was questioned as a witness, he was immediately charged with an offence. Coupled with the manner and timing of his detention as a witness, the Court found that the real intent of the witness summons was to bring the applicant to an area where it would be more convenient to charge him. This led to a violation of Article 5 as the measure used to detain the applicant was used to achieve a different aim than the one put forward by the Government. In the *Vasileva* case,[147] the applicant, a 65-year-old woman, was arrested following a dispute with an inspector on a bus as to whether or not she had a valid ticket, and detained in police custody for over twenty-four hours because she refused to give them her name and address as required by Danish law. The moment she complied with this obligation, she was released. The Strasbourg Court accepted, therefore, that the applicant had been detained in order to 'secure the fulfilment' of an obligation as required by Article 5(1)(b) of the Convention. It went on, however, to examine 'whether in the circumstances of the present case a reasonable balance was struck between the importance of securing the fulfilment of the obligation in general and the importance of the right to liberty'. Taking into account (1) the nature of the obligation arising from the relevant legislation including its underlying object and purpose; (2) the characteristics of the person being detained and the particular circumstances leading to the detention; and (3) the length of the detention, it concluded that a proper balance had not been struck between the need to secure the fulfilment of the obligation and the right to personal liberty.[148]

Imprisonment for debt may be permitted by Article 5(1)(b). However, for those Contracting Parties which have ratified the Fourth Protocol to the Convention, a restriction on detention in such cases is introduced by Article 1 of that Protocol.[149]

[140] App. 32206/96, *GK v Austria*, Decision of 16 October 1996.

[141] App. 28188/95, *Tyrell v United Kingdom*, Decision of 4 September 1996.

[142] App. 26109/95, *Santa Cruz Ruiz v United Kingdom*, Decision of 22 October 1997.

[143] *Steel and others v United Kingdom*, (App. 24838/94), 23 September 1998, (1998) 28 EHRR 603, ECHR 1998-VII.

[144] See also *Ostendorf v Germany*, (App. 15598/08), 7 March 2013, where the Court held that a failure to comply with an order with regard to restrictions on an applicant attending a football match due to hooliganism was held to comply with Article 5.

[145] *Benham v United Kingdom*, (App. 19380/92), 10 June 1996, (1996) 22 EHRR 293, ECHR 1996-III.

[146] *Khodorkovskiy v Russia*, (App. 5829/04), 31 May 2011.

[147] *Vasileva v Denmark*, (App. 52792/99), 25 September 2003, (2005) 40 EHRR 681. See also Apps. 8022/77, 8025/77, 8027/77, *McVeigh and others v United Kingdom*, Decision of 18 March 1981, (1982) 25 DR 15.

[148] Contrast *Novotka v Slovakia*, (App. 47244/99), Decision of 4 November 2003.

[149] Which provides: 'No one shall be deprived of his liberty merely on the ground of inability to fulfil a contractual obligation.'

DETENTION OF MINORS: ARTICLE 5(1)(D)

Article 5(1)(d) permits:

> the detention of a minor by lawful order for the purpose of educational supervision or his lawful detention for the purpose of bringing him before the competent legal authority;

This clause authorizes detention in two distinct sets of circumstances. The first limb covers orders requiring compulsory attendance at school which might otherwise amount to a deprivation of liberty under Article 5(1). There is no requirement that the order should be that of a court; the making of such orders by an administrative authority is not excluded. In such cases however the person subject to the order will be entitled to seek a review of that order under Article 5(4).[150] The second limb of paragraph (1)(d) allows minors to be brought before the judicial or administrative authority, which is to decide whether or not to order their detention. The paragraph thus clearly authorizes the exercise of the jurisdiction of juvenile courts in non-criminal cases.

The age at which a person ceases to be a minor has not been definitively established. The Council of Europe has adopted a resolution recommending Member States in principle to reduce the age of majority from 21 to 18,[151] but the adoption of the age of 18 as the age of majority has not been universal under national legal systems. In the *Koniarska* case,[152] the Strasbourg Court held that the applicant was a minor until the age of 18 and that Article 5(1)(d) permitted her detention for educational supervision up to that age, even though the school-leaving age in the United Kingdom is 16. It would appear, therefore, that 'minor' is to be given an autonomous meaning under the Convention, independent of the age of majority under national law.

The *Bouamar* case[153] concerned the detention of a 16-year-old boy with a disturbed personality. He had displayed behavioural problems and was detained in an adult prison for nine periods each of up to fifteen days because the authorities had been unable to find a suitable juvenile institution able to accept him immediately. The Belgian Government sought to argue that the detention was for educational supervision, but this argument failed since no genuine educational facilities had been made available for him. The Court concluded that an interim custody measure prior to placement involving supervized education was not precluded by Article 5(1)(d) but that the shuttling between prison and other arrangements totalling 119 days of detention in a 291-day period did violate the provision.[154]

In contrast, the applicant in the *Koniarska* case,[155] a 17-year-old girl, had been diagnosed as suffering from a psychopathic disorder and was placed in a specialist, secure, residential facility for seriously disturbed young people. She submitted that this detention was not for the purpose of educational supervision, but was instead ordered as a containment measure, any education offered being purely incidental. However, the Strasbourg Court held that the words 'educational supervision' should not be equated rigidly with notions of classroom teaching but could also be seen as embracing other aspects of local authority care, particularly where, as was the case with the applicant, an extensive range of classes was made available.[156]

[150] See later in this chapter.

[151] Resolution CM(72) 29 of the Committee of Ministers of the Council of Europe.

[152] *Koniarska v United Kingdom*, (App. 33670/96), Decision of 12 October 2000.

[153] *Bouamar v Belgium*, 29 February 1988, Series A No 129, (1989) 11 EHRR 1.

[154] §§ 51–3. See, similarly, *DG v Ireland*, (App. 39474/98), 16 May 2002.

[155] *Koniarska v United Kingdom*, (App. 33670/96), Decision of 12 October 2000.

[156] In *Ichin and others v Ukraine*, (App. 28189/04 and 28192/04), 21 December 2010, the Court reiterated that educational supervision encompasses more than a classroom setting. In this case it did not include a juvenile holding facility where there was no evidence of educational provision.

The specific provisions relating to minors in Article 5(1)(d) do not preclude the application to them of arrest and detention under any of the other sub-paragraphs of Article 5(1), such as detention consequent upon conviction or as persons of unsound mind.

VULNERABLE GROUPS: ARTICLE 5(1)(E)

Article 5(1)(e) permits:

> the lawful detention of persons for the prevention of the spreading of infectious diseases, of persons of unsound mind, alcoholics or drug addicts or vagrants;

Article 5(1)(e) draws together a disparate group[157] whose detention might be justified on grounds of social protection: those with infectious diseases, persons of unsound mind, alcoholics, drug addicts, and vagrants. There is no requirement that the detention should be imposed by a court; it may be ordered by an administrative authority, although such an order will be subject to judicial control under paragraph (4).

VAGRANTS

Since the judgment of the Strasbourg Court in the *Vagrancy* cases in 1971,[158] there have been few cases concerning this permitted ground of detention, probably because as standards evolve in Europe it appears increasingly repugnant forcibly to detain people merely because they are homeless. It is difficult to imagine many such cases where the detention would not in reality be prompted by some other aspect of the vagrant's conduct or condition, such as criminal offending, addiction, or mental illness.

The case of vagrancy is exceptional because 'vagrants' are detained for their *previous* rather than *present* condition, so that there is no obvious trigger for release. In the *Vagrancy* cases, two of the applicants had been placed at the disposal of the respondent State for the astonishingly long period of two years (they were both released earlier), while the third was placed at its disposal indefinitely (although in practice under Belgian law this meant one year). Unless a general limit to the length of detention can be inferred from the practice of the Contracting Parties, so as to render longer periods 'arbitrary', the only control in the Convention would appear to be that the detention must not be so lengthy as to constitute inhuman or degrading treatment under Article 3. It is, however, likely that if another such case were to come before the Strasbourg Court today, in line with the case-law on the detention of mental patients and alcoholics, it would read into this provision an implied requirement that the detention be proved strictly necessary for the welfare of the vagrant or the protection of the public.

MENTAL ILLNESS

The approach adopted by the Strasbourg Court to provide protection for persons detained by reason of mental illness has been to establish a framework of procedural tests which must be satisfied. In the *Winterwerp* case[159] the Court established three tests. First, the presence

[157] Using labels that now look somewhat dated.

[158] *De Wilde, Ooms and Versyp v Belgium*, (Apps. 2832/66, 2835/66, and 2899/66), 18 November 1970, Series A No 12, (1979–80) 1 EHRR 373.

[159] *Winterwerp v Netherlands*, (App. 6301/73), 24 October 1979, Series A No 33, (1979–80) 2 EHRR 387. See also *Stanev v Bulgaria*, (App. 36760/06), 17 January 2012.

of 'unsound mind' must be determined by objective medical evidence; secondly, the mental illness must result in a condition making detention necessary for the protection of the patient or others; thirdly, the detention must be justified on a continuing basis. It has since added a fourth requirement: there must be some relationship between the ground of detention relied upon under Article 5(1) and the place and conditions of detention. Thus, persons detained because of mental illness must be held in a hospital or clinic, and not in a prison where the treatment and therapy required is unavailable.[160] Provided the *Winterwerp* criteria are fulfilled, the condition making detention necessary does not have to be based on medical treatment. The Court has held that 'the detention of a mentally disordered person may be necessary not only where the person needs therapy, medication or other clinical treatment to cure or alleviate his condition, but also where the person needs control and supervision to prevent him, for example, causing harm to himself or other persons.'[161]

In the *Varbanov* case,[162] the Strasbourg Court found a violation based on the fact that the applicant, who had a history of threatening behaviour, had been committed to psychiatric hospital for a period of twenty days on the order of a prosecutor in the absence of any medical evidence of mental illness. Although the Court observed that in an urgent case where immediate committal was believed to be necessary for safety reasons it might be acceptable under Article 5(1)(e) to arrest the patient first and get a medical appraisal shortly thereafter,[163] in Varbanov's case there was no evidence of danger and no psychiatric evaluation was ever undertaken throughout the time of his detention.

The developing nature of medical understanding of mental illness, together with the fact that individuals suffering from certain psychiatric conditions, if released, may pose a danger not only to themselves but also to the community, has meant that there is a certain deference to national authorities in their evaluation of the medical evidence in connection with the second and third limbs of the *Winterwerp* test.[164] Even where the evidence shows that the detained person is no longer suffering from mental illness, it does not automatically follow that he or she should immediately and unconditionally be released back into the community. The Court made this approach clear in the *Johnson* case,[165] although it also emphasized that the exercise of official caution cannot justify delaying release indefinitely. The applicant had been properly detained, but his condition improved and he was found on the medical evidence no longer to be mentally ill. But the authorities considered that he was not yet ready to live on his own in the community. His discharge from hospital was made conditional on his residence under supervision in a hostel. However, because of a combination of the limited number of hostel places and the applicant's negative attitude, which deterred the few available hostels from taking him, no place was found for him and his release from hospital was delayed for four years, until the Tribunal ordered his unconditional release. The applicant argued that from the time of the review at which he was found no longer to be suffering from mental illness, his detention had not been in conformity with Article 5(1)(e) and he should have been immediately and unconditionally released. The Court rejected this submission, declaring that such a rigid approach to

[160] *Aerts v Belgium*, (App. 25357/94), 30 July 1998, (1999) 29 EHRR 50, ECHR 1998-V. *Ashingdane v United Kingdom*, 28 May 1985, Series A No 93, (1985) 7 EHRR 528.

[161] *Stanev v Bulgaria*, (App. 36760/06), 17 January 2012, § 46; see also *Hutchison Reid v United Kingdom*, (App. 50272/99), § 52, ECHR 2003-IV.

[162] *Varbanov v Bulgaria*, (App. 31365/96), 5 October 2000, ECHR 2000-X.

[163] As occurred in, for example, *Herz v Germany*, (App. 44672/98), 12 June 2003.

[164] See *Luberti v Italy*, 23 February 1984, Series A No 75, (1984) 6 EHRR 440, § 27. The criteria also apply to recall of patients who have been detained in mental hospitals: see *X v United Kingdom*, 24 October 1981, Series A No 46, (1982) 4 EHRR 188.

[165] *Johnson v United Kingdom*, (App. 22520/93), 24 October 1997, (1997) 27 EHRR 296, ECHR 1997-VII.

the interpretation of the third *Winterwerp* condition would place an unacceptable degree of constraint on the national authorities' discretion, given that the assessment of full recovery from mental illness was not a certain science and that premature, unsupervised release might be risky in some cases. The national authorities had based their decision on the medical evidence before it and it had not been unreasonable to make the applicant's release conditional on residence in a hostel. However, once this condition had been imposed, the onus was on the authorities to make sure that a hostel place was available. In fact, the lack of a hostel place and the continuing insistence that the applicant could only be released to a hostel led to the indefinite deferral of his release, until he was unconditionally discharged four years after the authorities had first found him free of mental illness. This delay, together with the lack of adequate procedural safeguards—it was not possible for the applicant to petition the authorities between annual reviews—gave rise to a violation of Article 5(1).

Because of the need for specialist expertise and the near impossibility of the Strasbourg Court itself attempting to assess medical evidence, the requirement of procedural 'lawfulness' is particularly important in connection with the detention of the mentally ill. In the *Varbanov* case,[166] as well as finding the applicant's detention unlawful for lack of supporting medical opinion, the Strasbourg Court found an additional ground of violation in that, at the time of the committal, Bulgarian law did not contain any express provision empowering a prosecutor to order compulsory confinement for the purpose of psychiatric evaluation. There was an instruction issued by the Minister of Health, implying that prosecutors had such powers, but this lacked the requisite clarity to conform with the standard of 'lawfulness' under the Convention.

Persons detained as being mentally unsound are normally detained for an indefinite period, although often with a right to periodical review. Article 5(4), discussed later, is therefore of great importance for mental patients, for it will frequently be the case that initial detention in hospital is justified, but the need for continuing detention may be more questionable.

ALCOHOLICS AND THOSE SUFFERING FROM INFECTIOUS DISEASE

As with all the other terms describing vulnerable groups in Article 5(1)(e), the word 'alcoholic' carries an autonomous Convention meaning. The Court gave some indication as to how it should be interpreted in the first case to come before it concerning detention for drunkenness.[167] The applicant, a partially sighted pensioner, was apprehended by the police at a post office where he was complaining that his post box had been opened and emptied. He was taken to a sobering-up centre, where he was certified by a doctor as being 'moderately intoxicated' and held for six and a half hours. The Court observed that in common usage the word 'alcoholic' denotes a person who is addicted to alcohol. There was, however, a link with the other categories in sub-paragraph (e), in that the detention of individuals in these groups could be justified only where it was necessary for medical treatment or on grounds of social policy to prevent a risk of danger to themselves or to the public. Having regard to the rule in the Vienna Convention on the Law of Treaties that in interpreting a treaty it is necessary to look at its object and purpose,[168] the Court found

[166] *Varbanov v Bulgaria*, (App. 31365/96), 5 October 2000, ECHR 2000-X.

[167] *Witold Litwa v Poland*, (App. 26629/95), 4 April 2000, (2001) 33 EHRR 1267, ECHR 2000-III.

[168] See ch.4.

that this purpose would be defeated if the provision allowed for the detention only of those suffering from the clinical condition of alcoholism, but not for non-alcoholics whose conduct under the influence of drink gave rise to a danger to the safety of themselves or others. This approach was confirmed by the *travaux préparatoires*, which included reference to 'drunkenness'. The applicant's arrest and detention therefore in principle fell within the scope of Article 5(1)(e). However, the Court found that there had been a violation of Article 5(1) because there was no evidence that the applicant had behaved in such a way as to pose a threat to himself or others or that the draconian measure of detention was necessary in the light of the rather trivial facts of the case. An individual could not be deprived of his liberty for being an 'alcoholic' unless other, less severe, measures had been considered and found to be insufficient to safeguard the individual or public interest.

The Court followed these principles in its first judgment concerning detention 'for the prevention of the spreading of infectious diseases'.[169] The applicant, who was HIV positive, was ordered to be held in compulsory hospital isolation over a period of almost seven years; because he kept escaping, he was in fact deprived of his liberty for about eighteen months. Under the Swedish Infectious Diseases Act, the county medical officer had issued the applicant with various instructions aimed at preventing the spread of the disease, such as a requirement to inform all medical practitioners and prospective sexual partners that he was HIV positive and to abstain from consuming such an amount of alcohol that his judgement would thereby be impaired and others put at risk of being infected with HIV. The applicant claimed that as soon as he found out about his condition he stopped having sex, and although he continued drinking, there was no evidence that he did so to excess. He did, however, refuse voluntarily to see a psychiatrist. The national courts ordered his confinement because they considered there was reasonable cause to suspect that the applicant, if released, would fail to comply with the medical officer's instructions. The Court found that the essential criteria when assessing the 'lawfulness' of the detention of a person 'for the prevention of the spreading of infectious diseases' were whether the spreading of the infectious disease was dangerous for public health or safety, and whether detention of the person infected was the last resort in order to prevent the spreading of the disease, less severe measures having been considered and found to be insufficient to safeguard the public interest. Given that the applicant had, to a large extent, complied with the medical officer's instructions, his detention was not held to have been essential and there had been a violation of Article 5(1).

DETENTION IN CONNECTION WITH DEPORTATION OR EXTRADITION: ARTICLE 5(1)(F)

Article 5(1)(f) permits:

> the lawful arrest or detention of a person to prevent his effecting an unauthorized entry into the country or of a person against whom action is being taken with a view to deportation or extradition.

The first limb is for the prevention of an unauthorized entry into the country, and the second is where detention is required where action is being taken to deport or extradite someone.

The Grand Chamber considered the first limb for the first time only in 2008 in the *Saadi* case.[170] The Court concluded that the presence of an asylum seeker in a country was

[169] *Enhorn v Sweden*, (App. 56529/00), 25 January 2005, (2005) 41 EHRR 633, ECHR 2005-I.

[170] *Saadi v United Kingdom*, (App. 13229/03), 29 January 2008 [GC], (2008) 47 EHRR 427, ECHR 2008-nyr, §§ 61–6.

not authorized on presentation of a claim for asylum to the authorities. The consequence is that a Contracting Party could detain an asylum seeker, or indeed any person seeking immigration, until that person's entry has been authorized. However, such detention must remain compatible with the overall purpose of Article 5 and not be arbitrary. The Grand Chamber said:

> To avoid being branded as arbitrary... such detention must be carried out in good faith; it must be closely connected to the purpose of preventing unauthorized entry of the person to the country; the place and conditions of detention should be appropriate, bearing in mind that 'the measure is applicable not to those who have committed criminal offences but to aliens who, often fearing for their lives, have fled from their own country...; and the length of the detention should not exceed that reasonably required for the purpose pursued.[171]

Applying these principles, the Strasbourg Court found no violation of Article 5(1) where the respondent State had initially not detained an applicant for asylum, but subsequently detained him in a reception centre for asylum seekers for seven days.[172] However, the Court has found a violation of Article 5 where an unaccompanied minor was detained in an adult detention centre for illegal migrants, with no adaptions made to consider the extreme vulnerability of the child in this situation.[173]

In order to comply with the second limb of this provision, the detained person must be the object of action 'with a view to deportation or extradition'. There is no need for the State to establish that the detention was reasonably considered necessary in order to prevent the person from absconding or from committing an offence—in contrast to the position of a person detained under Article 5(1) paragraphs (c), (b), or (e).[174]

In the *A and others* case,[175] the Grand Chamber was not satisfied that the detention of a number of the applicants fell within Article 5(1)(f), as claimed by the respondent State, since it could not be said that they were being detained with a view to deportation or extradition. As the Grand Chamber noted, the derogation which the United Kingdom had filed in respect of Article 5(1) was based on the proposition that deportation or extradition was not possible because of the risk of ill-treatment in the country of destination.

In addition, as long as the *detention* is 'lawful', it is immaterial for the purposes of Article 5(1)(f) whether the underlying *decision to expel* can be justified under national or Convention law.[176] This interpretation follows from the wording of Article 5(1)(f) and is consistent with the principle that in assessing compliance with Article 5(1)(a) the Strasbourg Court will not itself examine whether there was sufficient evidence to support the applicant's conviction. Thus in the *Chahal* case,[177] even though the Court found that the decision to expel the applicant to India was contrary to Article 3 of the Convention because he would run a real risk of torture or illegal killing, his detention for six years prior to the Court's judgment was permissible under Article 5(1)(f).

[171] § 74.

[172] See also *Riad and Idiab v Belgium*, (Apps. 29787/03 and 29810/03), 24 January 2008, ECHR 2008-nyr, for an example of a case where the Court decided that the respondent State had not acted in good faith.

[173] *Mubilanzila Mayeka and Kaniki Mitunga v Belgium*, (App. 13178/03), ECHR 2006-XI, § 103. The Court also found a violation of Article 3 in this case.

[174] *Chahal v United Kingdom*, (App. 22414/93), 15 November 1996, (1997) 23 EHRR 413, ECHR 1996-V, § 112; *Čonka v Belgium*, (App. 51564/99), 5 February 2002, (2002) 34 EHRR 1298, ECHR 2002-I, § 38.

[175] *A and others v United Kingdom*, (App. 3455/05), 19 February 2009 [GC], (2009) 49 EHRR 29, ECHR 2009-nyr, §§ 161–72.

[176] *Chahal v United Kingdom*, (App. 22414/93), 15 November 1996, (1997) 23 EHRR 413, ECHR 1996-V, § 112.

[177] *Chahal v United Kingdom*, (App. 22414/93), 15 November 1996, (1997) 23 EHRR 413, ECHR 1996-V.

It follows that, in the absence of any procedural irregularity or official arbitrariness such as to render the detention unlawful,[178] the only way for an applicant to establish a breach of this provision is to show that, throughout or for some part of his detention, he was not truly the object of deportation or extradition action. One way of establishing this is to show that the authorities did not pursue the expulsion proceedings with 'due diligence' and that they thereby allowed the detention to be unnecessarily prolonged.[179] In the *Kolompar* case[180] delays of over two years and eight months awaiting deportation were found not to constitute a violation of Article 5 since the delays were not attributable to the action of the authorities. Even more strikingly, as mentioned earlier, the Court found no violation of Article 5(1) in the *Chahal* case,[181] where the applicant, a Sikh separatist accused of terrorism by the British Government, had been detained for over six years pending the completion of the national and Strasbourg proceedings. This period included a delay of over seven months while the Home Office considered and rejected an application for refugee status and a further six months for the Home Office to make a fresh decision after the first had been quashed by judicial review. The Court found that these delays were justified in view of the importance of the issues in the case—the respondent State alleged that intelligence information showed that Chahal's continued residence in England raised a threat to British national security, whereas Chahal denied these accusations and claimed that he would run a risk of torture or illegal execution if returned to India. Hasty decision-making in such a case would not, in the Court's view, benefit either the applicant or the general public. However, perhaps the *Chahal* case should be regarded as exceptional; six years does seem a very long time to imprison a person who has not been proved to have committed even the most insignificant criminal offence, and in such circumstances it is arguable that a high standard of speed and diligence should be expected of the authorities.

As detention on the basis of Article 5(1)(f) is only lawful as long as deportation proceedings are in progress, the Court has examined the lawfulness of detention where the Court has imposed an interim measure under Rule 39, suspending the proceedings for the removal of the applicant. The Court has found that continued detention whilst an interim measure is in place does not necessarily make detention unlawful provided that the authorities still envisage expulsion at a later stage, so that 'action is being taken' despite the suspended proceedings, and on condition that detention must not be unreasonably prolonged.[182] In *Keshmiri v Turkey (No2)*[183] the Court found that there had been prolonged detention after an interim order was put in place, during which time no steps were taken to find an alternative solution. The Court also noted that it had found a violation of Article 3 if the applicant was returned to Iran or Iraq and the State had not taken any steps to ascertain whether the applicant could be sent elsewhere. This amounted to a violation of Article 5. In contrast, the Court has found that detention after the imposition of an interim measure by the Court was lawful where the applicant was detained in accordance

[178] See, for example, *Čonka v Belgium*, (App. 51564/99), 5 February 2002, (2002) 34 EHRR 1298, ECHR 2002-I, where the Roma applicants' arrest and detention pending deportation was in breach of Article 5(1) because the authorities had tricked them into reporting to the police station by issuing them with a summons stating that their attendance was necessary 'to complete the asylum process'; and see the discussion of arbitrariness in *Chahal*.

[179] *A and others v United Kingdom*, (App. 3455/05), 19 February 2009, § 164.

[180] *Kolompar v Belgium*, 24 September 1992, Series A No 235-C, (1993) 16 EHRR 197, §§ 37–43.

[181] *Chahal v United Kingdom*, (App. 22414/93), 15 November 1996, (1997) 23 EHRR 413, ECHR 1996-V.

[182] *Gebremedhin [Gaberamadhien] v France*, (App. 25389/05), ECHR 2007-V; *S.P. v Belgium*, (App. 12572/08), 14 June 2011; *Keshmiri v Turkey (No2)*, (App. 22426/10), 17 January 2012; *Azimov v Russia*, (App. 67474/11), 18 April 2012.

[183] *Keshmiri v Turkey (No2)*, (App. 22426/10), 17 January 2012, § 34; see also *Azimov v Russia*, (App. 67474/11), 18 April 2012.

with domestic law and his detention was reviewed on a monthly basis.[184] In *A and others v United Kingdom*,[185] the applicants were detained under deportation laws as they could not be deported due to a risk of torture under Article 3. The Court noted that the detention period was not as long as in *Chahal*, but in *Chalal*, the Government had acted diligently in order to determine the compatibility of Chahal's removal. The same could not be said in this case. The Court held a violation of Article 5.[186]

Where the applicant does not have travel documents and cannot be deported without them similar principles apply.[187] Where an applicant does not cooperate in ascertaining his identity where there are no travel documents, the State can 'detain such an alien for a reasonable time in order to ensure his or her participation at scheduled interviews with the police or with other authorities, notably since such arrangements usually require preparation and/or summoning of other people for example interpreters, representatives at embassies or personnel trained to perform language tests.'[188] In contrast, the Court found a violation where the applicant could not be returned to Algeria due to a lack of documents and the unwillingness of the applicant to cooperate.[189] In this case, the Court found that the State did not act with the due diligence necessary to justify continued detention in view of deportation. They did not pursue the matter vigorously or negotiate with the Algerian authorities. Unlike in *Chahal* and *Agnisson*, the State had not taken steps to allow for deportation. Detention cannot be justified if deportation is no longer feasible.[190]

NOTIFICATION OF THE REASONS FOR ARREST OR DETENTION

Article 5(2) embodies the elementary safeguard that those deprived of their liberty should know why. It provides:

> Everyone who is arrested shall be informed promptly, in a language which he understands, of the reasons for his arrest and of any charge against him.

Consequently any person arrested or detained must be told promptly and in simple language the essential factual and legal basis for the detention. This will enable detainees to apply to challenge the lawfulness of the detention if they so wish. Whether the obligation is met will be determined in the light of all the circumstances of each case.[191] This provision applies in respect of *everyone* who is arrested or detained. It may be compared with Article 6(3)(a), which provides that everyone charged with a criminal offence must be informed promptly, in a language which he or she understands, and in detail, of the nature and cause of the accusation against him or her. The information to which a person is entitled under Article 6 is more specific and more detailed than that required by Article 5, because it is necessary to enable the accused to prepare a defence. For the purposes of Article 5(2), on the other hand, it is sufficient if detainees are informed in general terms of the reasons for the arrest and of any charge against them.[192] The question of the timing of notification was raised in the *Murray*

[184] *Al Hanchi v Bosnia and Herzegovina* (App. 48205/09) 15 November 2011.

[185] *A and others v United Kingdom*, (App. 3455/05), ECHR 2009.

[186] §§ 162–172.

[187] *Agnisson v Denmark*, (App. 39964/08), 4 October 2001.

[188] *Agnisson v Denmark*, (App. 39964/08), 4 October 2001.The Court held that the application was inadmissible.

[189] *Louled Massoud v Malta*, (App. 24340/08), 27 July 2010.

[190] §§ 64–70; see also *Mikolenko v Estonia*, (App. 10664/05), 8 October 2009, §§ 64–5.

[191] *Kerr v United Kingdom*, (App. 40451/98), Decision of 7 December 1999.

[192] *Nielsen v Denmark*, (App. 343/57), Decision of 2 September 1959, (1958–9) 2 *Yearbook* 412, 462.

case.[193] The Strasbourg Court noted that whether the content and promptness of the information given to the detainee was sufficient depended on the special features of each case. An interval of a matter of hours between arrest and interrogation, during which the reasons for her arrest were brought to her attention, could not be regarded as failing to be prompt.

On occasion, however, the circumstances of the arrest may speak for themselves, as the Strasbourg Court found to have been the case in the *Dikme* case.[194] The applicant had presented false identity papers to the police and had been arrested immediately the police discovered the forgery. Whether or not the police gave reasons, the Court found that the applicant could not complain under Article 5(2) that he had been ignorant of the grounds for his arrest. In the *Kerr* case,[195] the applicant was informed at the time of his arrest of the anti-terrorist legislation under which he was detained. The Court held that a bare indication of the legal basis for an arrest could not, on its own, be sufficient for the purposes of Article 5(2), but that since, immediately after his arrest, the applicant was questioned about his suspected involvement in a recent bomb explosion at a military barracks, his membership of a proscribed organization, and about the use he had made of items seized by the police from his house, in particular computer equipment and the information stored on the computer, the reasons for his detention must have been sufficiently clear to him for the purposes of Article 5(2).

TESTING THE LEGALITY OF THE DETENTION

Article 5(4) provides for a legal review of the legality of any detention:

> Everyone who is deprived of his liberty by arrest or detention shall be entitled to take proceedings by which the lawfulness of his detention shall be decided speedily by a court and his release ordered if the detention is not lawful.

The right to judicial review under Article 5(4) covers all forms of arrest and detention. The 'court' to which the detained person has access for the purposes of Article 5(4) does not have to be a 'court of law of the classic kind integrated within the standard judicial machinery of the country'.[196] It must, however, be a body of a 'judicial character' offering certain procedural guarantees.[197] Thus the 'court' must be independent both of the executive and of the parties to the case.[198] It must have the power to order release if it finds that the detention is unlawful; a mere power of recommendation is insufficient.[199]

THE NATURE OF THE JUDICIAL REVIEW

The scope of the proceedings required by Article 5(4) was the subject of comment in the *E* case:

> Article 5(4) does not guarantee a right to judicial review of such a scope as to empower the court on all aspects of the case, including questions of pure expediency, to substitute its own

[193] *Murray v United Kingdom*, 28 October 1994, Series A No 300-A, (1995) 19 EHRR 193.

[194] *Dikme v Turkey*, (App. 20869/92), 11 July 2000, ECHR 2000-VIII.

[195] *Kerr v United Kingdom*, (App. 40451/98), Decision of 7 December 1999.

[196] *Weeks v United Kingdom*, 2 March 1987, Series A No 254, (1988) 10 EHRR 293, § 61.

[197] *De Wilde, Ooms and Versyp v Belgium*, (Apps. 2832/66, 2835/66, and 2899/66), 18 November 1970, Series A No 12, (1979–80) 1 EHRR 373.

[198] *Neumeister v Austria*, 27 June 1968, Series A No 8, (1979–80) 1 EHRR 91, § 24 of 'The Law'.

[199] See, for example, *Singh v United Kingdom* (App. 23389/94), 21 February 1996, ECHR 1996-I, § 65; *Curley v United Kingdom*, (App. 32340/96), 28 March 2000; *Benjamin and Wilson v United Kingdom*, (App. 28212/95), 26 September 2002; 36 EHRR 1.

> discretion for that of the decision-making authority. The review should, however, be wide enough to bear on those conditions which are essential for the 'lawful' detention of a person according to Article 5(1).[200]

It follows, therefore, that if a person is detained under Article 5(1)(c) of the Convention, the 'court' must be empowered to examine whether or not there is sufficient evidence to give rise to a reasonable suspicion that he or she has committed an offence, because the existence of such a suspicion is essential if detention on remand is to be 'lawful' under the Convention.[201] Similarly, in the case of a person detained on grounds of mental ill-health, the reviewing 'court' must assess the legality of the detention in the light of the *Winterwerp* criteria discussed earlier.[202] It should be noted that unlike the procedure for judicial review under Article 5(3), there is no requirement for an automatic judicial review under Article 5(4).[203] However in cases where an applicant is detained in a mental health setting and lacks capacity to initiate proceedings, the Court has found on several occasions that an effective regulatory framework of review is necessary to ensure that those who lack capacity can pursue an independent legal remedy to challenge continuing detention at 'reasonable intervals'.[204] This framework should ensure legal guarantees appropriate to the deprivation in question and should include some form of representation.[205] The joint partly dissenting opinion in *Stanev*,[206] suggested that the Court should consider placing a positive obligation on States to provide a review procedure to assess measures restricting legal capacity, especially where the applicant is unable to comprehend the consequences of a review or is unable to initiate it.[207]

The scope of review required with regard to a person detained under paragraph 5(1)(f) appears uncertain. The Court has found that immigration bail proceedings do not fall under Article 5(4).[208]

In the *Chahal* judgment,[209] as has been seen, the Court held that all that was needed to ensure that the detention was 'lawful' under this provision was proof that action was being taken with a view to deportation; absent arbitrariness, it was immaterial for the purposes of Article 5(1) whether or not the underlying decision to expel was justified or whether there was any evidence that the detention was necessary to prevent the proposed deportee from absconding or committing a crime, for example. It might be assumed, therefore, that all that could be expected from the 'court' reviewing the legality of the detention under Article 5(4) would be a determination of the fact that deportation proceedings were genuinely under way. However, the Court went on to hold in the *Chahal* judgment that the bail and habeas corpus proceedings brought by the applicant in the English courts were deficient under Article 5(4) because the courts were unable to look behind the Secretary

[200] *E v Norway*, 29 August 1990, Series A No 181, (1990) 17 EHRR 30, § 50.

[201] See, for example, *Nikolova v Bulgaria*, (App. 31195/96), 25 March 1999 [GC], (2001) 31 EHRR 64, ECHR 1999-II; *Grauslys v Lithuania*, (App. 36743/97), 10 October 2000, (2002) 34 EHRR 1084; and *A and others v United Kingdom*, (App. 3455/05), 19 February 2009 [GC], ECHR 2009-nyr.

[202] Habeas corpus and judicial review proceedings in the High Court are therefore insufficient for the purposes of Article 5(4): *HL v United Kingdom*, (App. 45508/99), 5 October 2004, (2005) 40 EHRR 761, ECHR 2004-IX.

[203] *Shtukaturov v Russia*, (App. 44009/05), 27 March 2008.

[204] *Milhailovs v Latvia*, (App. 35939/10), 27 March 2013, §§ 154–9; *Shtukaturov v Russia*, (App. 44009/05), 27 March 2008; *Kedzior v Poland*, (App. 45026/07), 16 October 2012.

[205] *Stanev v Bulgaria*, (App. 36760/06). 17 January 2012, § 171.

[206] *Stanev v Bulgaria*, (App. 36760/06). 17 January 2012.

[207] Joint Partly Dissenting Opinion of Judges Tulkens, Spielmann, and Laffranque.

[208] *Ismail v United Kingdom*, (App. 48078/09), 17 September 2013.

[209] *Chahal v United Kingdom*, (App. 22414/93), 15 November 1996; (1997) 23 EHRR 413, ECHR 1996-V, § 112.

of State's assertions that national security would be at risk if Chahal was at liberty so as to determine the question themselves in the light of all the available evidence. The Court went so far as to refer to a procedure used in Canada in such cases, which it suggested would ensure compliance with Article 5(4), whereby all evidence relating to national security was aired before the court deciding on the legality of the detention in the presence of a security-cleared counsel instructed by the detainee.

In the *A and others* case,[210] the Grand Chamber found a violation of Article 5(4) in relation to two of the detainees. The Strasbourg Court considered the arrangements under which the Special Immigration Appeals Commission (SIAC) could consider both open material, which was disclosed to the detainee, and closed material which was disclosed neither to the detainee nor to his or her legal advisers. Instead the closed material was disclosed to a special advocate appointed by the respondent State's Solicitor General to act on behalf of the detainee, and who could make submissions to SIAC on both matters of procedure and substance. Once the special advocate had seen closed material, he or she was not permitted to have any contact with the detainee. The essence of the special advocate procedure was accepted as balancing the need for disclosure and the risk of compromising national security. However, the operation of the system must not leave a detainee in the position of being unable to challenge the allegations against them because the open material was of such a general nature that it lacked sufficient specificity to enable this to be done. That was the case in relation to the two detainees in respect of whom a violation of Article 5(4) was found.

As far as procedural requirements are concerned, Article 5(4) does not always require the same guarantees as would be necessary under Article 6(1) for criminal or civil litigation. The proceedings must generally be capable of commencement on the application of the person deprived of his or her liberty,[211] though automatic reference to review of a judicial character will also suffice. The form of procedure followed may vary depending on the nature of the detention under review and the relevant issues before the 'court'.[212] An adversarial oral hearing with legal representation is always required, however, in cases of detention under Article 5(1)(c) or where the continued legality of the detention depends on an assessment of the applicant's character or mental state.[213] In the *Lamy* case,[214] the Court considered that the failure to make documents available promptly to the applicant's lawyer precluded the possibility of an effective challenge to statements which formed the basis of the decision to detain, giving rise to a violation of Article 5(4).

The requirement for review by a 'court' prompted a spate of applications from former Communist countries where under the old regime it was common for the prosecuting authorities to be empowered to decide virtually all questions relating to pre-trial detention, with the possibility of only limited recourse to a court. In Bulgaria, for example, in the mid-1990s, a person detained on remand on the decision of the prosecutor was entitled to contest his detention in court only once, even if the detention continued for two years or more. Since the frequency of this periodic review was inadequate, and since

[210] *A and others v United Kingdom*, (App. 3455/05), 19 February 2009 [GC], (2009) 49 EHRR 29, ECHR 2009-nyr, §§ 202–24.

[211] There was a violation of Article 5(4) in *Rakevich v Russia*, (App. 58973/00), 28 October 2003, because under Russian law the applicant, a mental patient, was unable herself to apply to have her continuing detention judicially reviewed, but had instead to rely on the initiative of the hospital authorities.

[212] See, for example, *Niedbala v Poland*, (App. 27915/95), 4 July 2000, § 66.

[213] *Assenov v Bulgaria*, (App. 24760/94), 28 October 1998, (1999) 28 EHRR 652, ECHR 1998-VIII; *Niedbala v Poland*, (App. 27915/95), 4 July 2000; *Grauslys v Lithuania*, (App. 36743/97), 10 October 2000; *Wloch v Poland*, (App. 27885/98), 19 October 2000, (2002) 34 EHRR 229.

[214] *Lamy v Belgium*, 30 March 1989, Series A No 151, (1989) 11 EHRR 529.

the prosecution was not an independent 'court' for the purposes of Article 5(4), the Court found a violation in the *Assenov* case.[215] During the same period in Poland, although a person detained on remand could apply to a court, neither the detained person nor his lawyer was entitled to attend the hearing or be informed of the prosecutor's reasons for opposing release, leading the Strasbourg Court to find violations in a number of cases.[216]

WHEN ARE REVIEWS REQUIRED?

Article 5(4) provides that 'the lawfulness of [the] detention shall be decided *speedily*' (emphasis added). There are two aspects to this requirement: first, the opportunity for legal review must be provided soon after the person is taken into detention (and thereafter, as discussed below, at reasonable intervals if necessary); secondly, the review proceedings must be conducted with due diligence.

In each case, the question whether the review has been completed sufficiently 'speedily' depends on all the circumstances. In a case of a straightforward bail application by a man detained on suspicion of drug-trafficking, for example, the Court held that three weeks was too long.[217] Longer periods might be acceptable in more complex cases—for example, where it is necessary to seek medical reports in respect of a detained mental patient—but, given the importance of the right to liberty, there is still a pressing obligation on the authorities to deal quickly with such applications for release. In the *Baranowski* case,[218] for example, the fact that it took a court deciding a bail application six weeks to obtain a report from a cardiologist and a further month to obtain evidence from a neurologist and a psychiatrist was evidence of lack of due diligence and gave rise to a violation of Article 5(4).

In many cases, the examination carried out by the court which first makes the order for detention is sufficient for the purposes of Article 5(4). This is so, for example, where a person convicted of a criminal offence is sentenced to a determinate term of imprisonment.

Where, however, the justification for a prolonged period of detention is liable to vary over time, the detained person is entitled under Article 5(4) to apply for judicial review of the detention's continued legality at intervals. This proposition was first enunciated in cases of indefinite detention under mental health legislation,[219] but has been extended to cases where continuing detention is conditioned upon a view that the person is dangerous in a broader sense, and even to cases of detention on remand.[220] In *Bezicheri v Italy*, the Court underlined the need for a review of pre-trial detention at short intervals. In this case a month's interval between reviews would be reasonable.[221]

In the United Kingdom, all prisoners serving life sentences (either mandatory life imprisonment for murder or a discretionary life sentence for some other offence), are entitled, once

[215] *Assenov v Bulgaria*, (App. 24760/94), 28 October 1998, (1999) 28 EHRR 652, ECHR 1998-VIII.

[216] *Niedbała v Poland*, (App. 27915/95), 4 July 2000, (2000) 33 EHRR 1137; *Trzaska v Poland*, (App. 25792/94), 11 July 2000; *Wloch v Poland*, (App. 27785/95), 19 October 2000, (2002) 34 EHRR 229; and see *Grauzinis v Lithuania*, (App. 37975/97), 10 October 2000, (2002) 35 EHRR 144, for a similar problem in Lithuania.

[217] *Rehbock v Slovenia*, (App. 29462/95), 28 November 2000, ECHR 2000-XII; and see also *GB v Switzerland*, (App. 27426/95), 30 November 2000, (2002) 34 EHRR 265 (32 days to decide the bail application of terrorist suspect was too long).

[218] *Baranowski v Poland*, (App. 28358/95), 28 March 2000, ECHR 2000-III.

[219] *Herczegfalvy v Austria*, 24 September 1992, Series A No 242-B, (1993) 15 EHHR 437 *Kolanis v United Kingdom*. (App. 517/02), ECHR 2005-V.

[220] *De Jong, Baljet and van der Brink v Netherlands*, (Apps. 8805/79, 8806/79, and 9242/81), 22 May 1984, Series A No 77, (1986) 8 EHRR 20; and *Bezicheri v Italy*, (App. 11400/85), 25 October 1989, Series A No 164, (1990) 12 EHRR 210.

[221] *Bezicheri v Italy*, (App. 11400/85), 25 October 1989, Series A No 164, (1990) 12 EHRR 210.

the punitive part of the sentence (the 'tariff') has expired,[222] to periodic review to determine whether they are still too dangerous to be released into the community.[223] The same applies to juveniles sentenced to be detained 'during Her Majesty's pleasure'.[224] The review must be effective, in the sense of taking proper account of the original concerns which led to the detention, and it should also be conducted judicially, in a procedurally fair manner, and speedily. In the *Oldham* case[225] the Court held that a two-year interval between reviews of detention following the applicant's recall to prison was too long to be 'speedy'.

AN ENFORCEABLE RIGHT TO COMPENSATION

Article 5(5) provides that:

> Everyone who has been the victim of arrest or detention in contravention of the provisions of this article shall have an enforceable right to compensation.

It is not clear why special provision is made for compensation for a breach of Article 5(1)–(4), when there is no such special provision in relation to the other rights guaranteed by the Convention, and when there is a general provision under Article 13 requiring an effective remedy for any violation.

Although any breach of Article 5 established by national courts or by Convention organs will, in the absence of an enforceable right to compensation under national law, give rise in addition to a breach of Article 5(5),[226] relatively few applicants invoke this provision before the Court, perhaps because by the time they get to Strasbourg most applicants are more interested in seeking damages under Article 41.

In the *Fox, Campbell and Hartley*[227] and *Brogan*[228] cases, for example, the Court found this provision to have been breached since there was no rule of Northern Irish law which would have provided compensation for the arrest and prolonged initial detention of the applicants under the prevention of terrorism legislation. The Court came to the same conclusion in the *Hood* case,[229] where the applicant, a soldier, was unable to claim compensation before the English courts in respect of the fact that his commanding officer, who was not sufficiently independent for the purposes of Article 5(3), had authorized his detention in close arrest.

[222] And the 'tariff' itself must be set by a judge: *Stafford v United Kingdom*, (App. 46295/99), 28 May 2002 [GC], (2002) 35 EHRR 1121, ECHR 2002-IV; *T v United Kingdom* (App. 24724/94) and *V v United Kingdom* (App. 24888/94), 16 December 1999 [GC], (2000) 30 EHRR 121, ECHR 1999-IX.

[223] *Thynne, Wilson and Gunnell v United Kingdom*, (Apps. 11787/85, 11978/86, and 12009/86), 25 October 1990, Series A No 190, (1991) 13 EHRR 666; *Stafford v United Kingdom*, (App. 46295/99), 28 May 2002 [GC], (2002) 35 EHRR 1121, ECHR 2002-IV; *Benjamin and Wilson v United Kingdom*, (App. 28212/95), 26 September 2002, (2003) 36 EHRR 1; *James, Wells and Lee v United Kingdom*, (Apps. 25119/09, 57715/09, and 57877/09), 18 September 2012.

[224] *Hussain v United Kingdom*, (App. 21928/93), 21 February 1996, (1996) 22 EHRR 1, ECHR 1996-I; *Singh v United Kingdom* (App. 23389/94), 21 February 1996, ECHR 1996-I.

[225] *Oldham v United Kingdom*, (App. 36273/97), 26 September 2000, (2001) 31 EHRR 34, ECHR 2000-X.

[226] See, for example, *Houtman and Meeus v Belgium*, (App. 22945/07), 17 March 2009; and *A and others v United Kingdom*, (App. 3455/05), 19 February 2009 [GC], ECHR 2009-nyr.

[227] *Fox, Campbell and Hartley v United Kingdom*, (Apps. 12244/86, 12245/86, and 12383/86), 30 August 1990, Series A No 182, (1991) 13 EHRR 157.

[228] *Brogan and others v United Kingdom*, (Apps. 11209/84, 11234/84, 11266/84, and 11386/85), 29 November 1988, Series A No 145-B, (1989) 11 EHRR 117.

[229] *Hood v United Kingdom*, (App. 27267/95), 18 February 1999, (2000) 29 EHRR 365, ECHR 1999-I.

CONCLUDING REMARKS

The right to liberty is of fundamental importance. As well as the value to the individual of liberty in itself, many of the other rights protected by the Convention are to a certain extent conditional upon it. It becomes possible to interfere with and place limitations on the autonomy of detainees in every imaginable way; for example, they may only send and receive letters if this is allowed by those holding them, and their detention may leave them vulnerable to torture and execution.[230] It is, therefore, regrettable that the text of Article 5 of the Convention is rather confused and unclear. Instead of using a multiplicity of expressions—'competent court' in 5(1)(a), 'court' in 5(1)(b) and 5(4), 'competent legal authority' in 5(1)(c), and 'judge or other officer authorized by law to exercise judicial power' in 5(3)—would it not have been possible for those drafting this provision to use one term consistently? And what is to be made of the apparent overlap of limitations on pre-trial detention in paragraphs 1(c) and 3, and of the rights to judicial review in paragraphs 3 and 4?

In their approach to the interpretation of Article 5, the Strasbourg Court has done much to overcome these problems. Most of the basic principles under Article 5 are now clearly established. Nonetheless, this is a Convention Article that is repeatedly violated by many Contracting Parties. Corruption and political pressure on judges can in some countries mean that individuals are detained pre-trial even where there is no reasonable suspicion of criminal conduct. In parts of central and eastern Europe, Soviet traditions have been hard to dispel, and criminal suspects are still detained almost as a matter of course, even where the national court has not clearly identified any real ground for refusing bail. Under-resourced legal systems and long delays in coming to trial can mean that individuals who have not been convicted of any wrongdoing are detained for year after year.[231] Those States which have bad records in relation to unjustified and excessively lengthy pre-trial detention under Article 5(3), moreover, are frequently also States which the Strasbourg Court has found under Article 3 to provide inhuman and degrading conditions of detention. The problems are clearly linked, both in terms of the suffering caused to detainees and the solution available to those Contracting Parties. Given this, the concern of the dissenting judges in the *Austin* case may be justified if States who already violate Article 5 attempt to extend the reasons for deprivation of liberty by emphasizing the 'purpose' of the State acts. However, the Court has consistently emphasized that a State cannot claim its need to protect persons under Articles 2 and 3 to justify detention outside of the obligations set forth in Article 5.

The interpretation and application of the right to compensation in Article 5(5) remains undeveloped.

[230] See *Aksoy v Turkey*, (App. 21987/93), 18 December 1996, (1997) 23 EHRR 553, ECHR 1996-VI, § 76.

[231] As in, for example, *Kauczor v Poland*, (App. 45219/06), 3 February 2009.

12

THE RIGHT TO A FAIR TRIAL IN CIVIL AND CRIMINAL CASES

INTRODUCTION

Article 6 is an omnibus provision, which has been described as 'a pithy epitome of what constitutes a fair administration of justice'.[1] The rights protected by the Article occupy a central place in the Convention system. A fair trial, in civil and criminal cases alike, is a basic element of the notion of the rule of law and part of the common heritage, according to the Preamble, of the Contracting Parties.

While Article 6(2) and (3)[2] contain specific provisions setting out 'minimum rights' applicable only in respect of those charged with a criminal offence, Article 6(1) applies both to civil and criminal proceedings.

The text of Article 6(1) reads:

> In the determination of his civil rights and obligations or of any criminal charge against him, everyone is entitled to a fair and public hearing within a reasonable time by an independent and impartial tribunal established by law. Judgment shall be pronounced publicly but the press and public may be excluded from all or part of the trial in the interests of morals, public order or national security in a democratic society, where the interests of juveniles or the protection of the private life of the parties so require, or to the extent strictly necessary in the opinion of the court in special circumstances where publicity would prejudice the interests of justice.

Article 6 is the provision of the Convention most frequently invoked by applicants to Strasbourg.[3] As with other provisions of the Convention, many of the terms used in Article 6(1) bear 'autonomous' meanings and require interpretation. It is therefore hardly surprising that there is substantial case-law on the provision's application. It would not be possible, within the scope of this book, to give a comprehensive account of this case-law, and the present chapter is intended only to provide an overview of some of the more important and interesting aspects.

[1] N. Mole and C. Harby, *The right to a fair trial: a Guide to the implementation of Article 6 of the European Convention on Human Rights*, Human Rights Handbooks, No. 3 (Council of Europe Publishing, Strasbourg 2006). See also J. Cremona, 'The public character of trial and judgment in the jurisprudence of the European Court of Human Rights' in F. Matscher and H. Petzold, *Protecting Human Rights: The European Dimension: Studies in Honour of Gérard J. Wiarda* (Carl Heymanns, Köln 1990), 107. See also L. Loucaides, 'Questions of Fair Trial under the European Convention on Human Rights' (2003) 3 HRLRev 27.

[2] Considered in ch.13.

[3] In 2012, out of 1,423 judgments finding a violation of at least one Convention provision, 493 concerned the right to a fair trial and a further 456 concerned the length of proceedings: European Court of Human Rights, *Annual Report 2012* (Council of Europe Publishing, Strasbourg 2013), 132. The Court is now dealing with a smaller proportion of Article 6 cases under the Court's priority policy, see ch.2.

THE SCOPE OF ARTICLE 6(1)

THE 'FOURTH INSTANCE' DOCTRINE

Every month the Strasbourg Court receives many hundreds of letters complaining about the decisions reached by national courts in civil and criminal trials. Many of these applications are, however, based on a fundamental misconception of the Convention system. The Court has no jurisdiction under Article 6 to reopen national legal proceedings or to substitute its own findings of fact, or the application of national law to them, for the conclusions of national courts.[4] The Court's task with regard to a complaint under Article 6 is to examine whether the proceedings, taken as a whole, were fair and complied with the specific safeguards stipulated by the Convention. Unlike a national court of appeal, it is not concerned under Article 6 with the questions whether the conviction was safe, the sentence appropriate, the award of damages in accordance with national law, and so on. And a finding by the Court that an applicant's trial fell short of the standards of Article 6 does not have the effect of quashing the conviction[5] or overturning the judgment, as the case may be.

The Court calls this principle the 'fourth instance' doctrine, because it is *not* to be seen as a third or fourth instance of appeal from national courts. It is important to bear the doctrine in mind when considering whether a particular factual situation based on criminal or civil proceedings raises any issue under Article 6.

WHAT IS A 'CRIMINAL CHARGE'?

Article 6(1) applies 'in the determination of [a person's] civil rights and obligations or of any criminal charge against him'. As with other key expressions used in the Convention, the Court has ruled that the concept of a 'criminal charge' must bear an 'autonomous' meaning, independent of the categorizations employed within the national legal orders. In this way, it is possible to achieve uniformity of approach throughout Europe and prevent States from avoiding Convention controls by classifying offences as disciplinary, administrative, or civil matters.

The *Engel* case[6] concerned action taken against members of the armed forces in respect of offences, such as insubordination, classified in the Netherlands as disciplinary in nature. The Court stated that relevant considerations in establishing whether the matter should be seen as involving the determination of a 'criminal charge' for the purposes of Article 6 were threefold: (1) the classification of the proceedings under national law; (2) the essential nature of the offence; and (3) the nature and degree of severity of the penalty that could be imposed having regard in particular to any loss of liberty, a characteristic of criminal liability.

The Court also considered the group to whom the legislation applied (small and closely defined groups of potential offenders are suggestive of a disciplinary or administrative procedure rather than a mainstream criminal offence). Short periods of imprisonment are not sufficient in themselves to bring Article 6 into play: Engel's punishment of two days of

[4] It follows, therefore, that an application pending before the Strasbourg Court is not a ground for a stay of execution in national proceedings: see the English decision in *Locabail (UK) Ltd v Waldorf Investment Corp and others*, [2000] HRLR 623, 25 May 2000, Chancery Division.

[5] See ch.13.

[6] *Engel and others v Netherlands*, (Apps. 5100/71, 5101/71, 5102/71, 5354/72, and 5370/72), 8 June 1976, Series A No 22, (1979–80) 1 EHRR 647.

strict arrest was insufficiently severe, in the absence of other criminal characteristics, to be regarded as a criminal penalty. The national classification is however important. If a matter is classed as criminal under national law, this will be enough to bring it within the scope of Article 6, even if it is relatively trivial.

The Grand Chamber has endorsed and applied this methodology in the *Ezeh and Connors* case.[7] The applicants were convicted rapists serving sentences of imprisonment who committed offences contrary to the Prison Rules—threatening to kill a probation officer, in one case, and colliding with a prison officer during exercise in the other. They were tried by the Prison Governor, without legal aid or representation, and sentenced to additional days of custody—forty for the first applicant and seven days for the second applicant. The Court, applying the *Engel* criteria, noted that the offences were classified as disciplinary under national law and applied only to prisoners, although they also corresponded to the offences of making a threat to kill and assault under the mainstream criminal law. The nature and severity of the punishment were decisive in leading the Court to hold that the offences were 'criminal' for the purposes of Article 6: under national law there was a legal right to remission, and the loss of remission or additional days of imprisonment amounted to new deprivations of liberty over and above the rape sentences.[8] The Court emphasized in this connection that what was important in deciding whether the applicant faced a 'criminal charge' was the penalty that was 'liable to be imposed', which could be determined with reference to the statutory maximum, which was forty-two days for each offence. In these circumstances, the deprivations of liberty which were liable to be, and which actually were, imposed on the applicants were not sufficiently inconsequential as to displace the presumed criminal nature of the charges against them.[9] The Court did not give a fixed lower limit at which a sentence of imprisonment would be too short to bring a disciplinary charge into the criminal sphere, although it did refer to the decision in the *Engel* case that two days was not enough.[10]

In the *Ezeh and Connors* case, the respondent State argued that the special need to maintain discipline in prisons entailed that prison governors should be allowed a certain flexibility in awarding punishment of loss of remission, following proceedings which need not necessarily comply with Article 6. The Court took note of these submissions, but considered that there were other sanctions available to prison governors which would be adequate to keep up discipline without bringing Article 6 into operation.

The *Matyjek* case[11] concerned the nature of the proceedings in which the applicant had been found to have lied in making a declaration about his involvement with Poland's security services between 1944 and 1990 under lustration laws. The underlying purpose of lustration legislation is to require declarations about such prior involvement so that such matters cannot be the source of the blackmailing of public officials. A final judgment that a person had lied in a lustration declaration disqualified them from public office for a period of ten years. In its admissibility decision, the Strasbourg Court reiterated its earlier case-law,

[7] *Ezeh and Connors v United Kingdom*, (Apps. 39665/98 and 400086/98), 9 October 2003 [GC], (2004) 39 EHRR 1, ECHR 2003-X.

[8] The Court in effect overruled *Campbell and Fell v United Kingdom*, (Apps. 7819/77 and 7878/77), 28 June 1984, Series A No 80, (1985) 7 EHRR 165. See also *Findlay v United Kingdom*, (App. 22107/93), 25 February 1997, (1997) 24 EHRR 221, ECHR 1997-I; *Hood v United Kingdom*, (App. 27267/95), 18 February 1999 [GC], (2000) 29 EHRR 365, ECHR 1999-I; *Benham v United Kingdom*, (App. 19380/92), 10 June 1996, (1996) 22 EHRR 293, ECHR 1996-III; and *Steel and others v United Kingdom*, (App. 24838/94), 23 September 1998, (1998) 28 EHRR 603, ECHR 1998-VII.

[9] § 129. [10] § 129.

[11] *Matyjek v Poland*, (App. 38184/03), Decision of 30 May 2006, ECHR 2006-VII; 24 April 2007, ECHR 2007-nyr.

but emphasized that the second and third criteria established in the *Engel* case were alternative and not necessarily cumulative. A cumulative approach remained appropriate, however, where separate analysis of each criterion did not make it possible to reach a clear conclusion.[12] Applying these criteria, the Court concluded that the lustration proceedings in issue constituted criminal charges.

In the *Öztürk* case[13] the German authorities had decided as a matter of policy to take certain less serious motoring offences, punishable by fine, out of the criminal sphere. The majority of the Court found, applying the *Engel* criteria, that the purpose of the fine was both deterrent and punitive and this sufficed to show the criminal nature of the matter for Convention purposes. The process of decriminalization in the national law did not affect the classification under the Convention.[14] A strong dissenting group of five felt, however, that the decision did not adequately reflect the trend towards decriminalization of minor offences in several European countries and the fact that it was in the interests of the accused to remove certain types of conduct from the stigma of criminality. Recognizing the legitimacy of these significant changes would, for them, take such matters outside the ambit of criminal law.

AT WHAT STAGES OF CRIMINAL PROCEEDINGS DOES ARTICLE 6(1) APPLY?

The protection of Article 6 starts from the time when a person is charged with a criminal offence. This is not, however, necessarily the moment when formal charges are first made against a person suspected of having committed an offence. For, as previously noted, the protection of Article 6 does not depend on the particular features of the system of criminal investigation and prosecution, which may and do vary considerably between the Contracting Parties. Moreover, as the object of Article 6 is to protect a person throughout the criminal process, and since formal charges may not be brought until a fairly advanced stage of an investigation, it is necessary to find a criterion for the opening of criminal proceedings which is independent of the actual development of the procedure in a specific case.

The Court has defined a 'charge' for the purposes of Article 6(1) as 'the official notification given to an individual by the competent authority of an allegation that he has committed a criminal offence.'[15] It may, however, 'in some instances take the form of other measures which carry the implication of such an allegation and which likewise substantially affect the situation of the suspect.'[16]

Article 6(1) covers the whole of the proceedings in issue, including appeal proceedings and the determination of sentence.[17]

[12] § 47. In its consideration of the merits, the Court found a violation of Art. 6(1), taken in conjunction with Art. 6(3).

[13] *Öztürk v Germany*, (App. 8544/79), 21 February 1984, Series A No 73, (1984) 6 EHRR 409.

[14] The Court has similarly found, against other States, that motoring and other offences, despite local classification as 'administrative', are 'criminal' for the purposes of Article 6: *Schmautzer v Austria*, (App. 15523/89), 23 October 1995, Series A No 328-A, (1995) 21 EHRR 511; *Malige v France*, (App. 27812/95), 23 September 1998, (1999) 28 EHRR 578, *Meftah and others v France*, (App. 32991/96), 26 July 2002; and see also *Lauko v Slovakia*, (App. 26138/95), 2 September 1998 (nuisance); *Canady v Slovakia*, (App. 18268/03), 20 October 2009 (insult during legal proceedings); *Bendenoun v France*, 24 February 1994, Series A No 284, (1994) 18 EHRR 54; *AP, MP and TP v Switzerland*, (App. 19958/92), 29 August 1997, (1998) 26 EHRR 541; *Segame SA v France*, (App. 4837/06), 7 June 2012; and *Steininger v Austria*, (App. 21539/07), 17 April 2012 (tax offences).

[15] *Eckle v Germany*, (App. 8130/78), 15 July 1982, Series A No 51, (1983) 5 EHRR 1, § 73.

[16] *Foti v Italy*, (Apps. 7604/76, 7719/76, 7781/77, and 7913/77), 10 December 1982, Series A No 56, (1983) 5 EHRR 313, § 52.

[17] *Eckle v Germany*, (App. 8130/78), 15 July 1982, Series A No 51, (1983) 5 EHRR 1, §§ 76–7; *Phillips v United Kingdom*, (App. 41087/98), 5 September 2001, ECHR 2001-VII.

Thus, in the *Delcourt* case,[18] Article 6(1) was found to be applicable to proceedings before the Belgian Court of Cassation. The respondent State had argued that the Court of Cassation did not deal with the merits of cases submitted to it, but the Court found that although the judgment of the Court of Cassation could only confirm or quash a decision, and not reverse or replace it, it was still 'determining' a criminal charge.

The cases of *T* and *V*[19] raised questions about the applicability of Article 6(1) to a sentencing procedure. The applicants had been convicted at the age of eleven of murdering a two-year-old the year before. As with all children convicted in England and Wales of murder, they were sentenced to be detained 'during Her Majesty's pleasure'. This is an indeterminate sentence: a period of detention, 'the tariff', is served to satisfy the requirements of retribution and deterrence, and thereafter it is legitimate to continue to detain the offender only if this appears to be necessary for the protection of the public. At the time of the applicants' conviction, the tariff was set by the Home Secretary. The Court held that the tariff-fixing procedure amounted to the fixing of a sentence and that there had been a violation of Article 6(1) since the Home Secretary was not 'an independent and impartial tribunal'.

Proceedings which take place after conviction and sentence have become final fall outside Article 6. Thus this provision does not cover an application by a convicted prisoner for release on probation or parole,[20] or for a new trial,[21] or for review of his sentence after the decision has become *res judicata*.[22] Nor does Article 6(1) apply on an application for provisional release pending trial[23] nor to proceedings following a decision that an applicant is unfit to plead to a criminal charge.[24]

WHAT ARE 'CIVIL RIGHTS AND OBLIGATIONS'?

The definition of 'civil rights and obligations' has proved more problematic.

First, it is clear that there must be a 'right' (or an 'obligation'). Thus, for example, questions relating to the making of an *ex gratia* payment by the State would not attract the protection of Article 6 because there is no 'right' to such a payment. In *Boulois v Luxembourg*,[25] the Court found that prison leave under national law was not a right but a privilege as the permission for prison leave was discretionary with no remedy provided under the relevant law. Although discretion is not decisive when finding a measure is not a right, in this case the wording of the legislation led to such a conclusion.[26] Secondly, the right (or obligation) must exist under national law: this point is dealt with in more detail later in the section on 'access to court'. Thirdly, the right (or obligation) must be 'civil' in nature, and it is in connection with this aspect of the definition that the real difficulties arise.

[18] *Delcourt v Belgium*, (App. 2689/65), 17 January 1970, Series A No 11, (1979–80) 1 EHRR 355.

[19] *T v United Kingdom*, (App. 24724/94) and *V v United Kingdom* (App. 24888/94), 16 December 1999 [GC], (2000) 30 EHRR 121, ECHR 1999-IX.

[20] *X v Austria*, (App. 606/59), Decision of 19 September 1961 (1961) 4 *Yearbook* 340; App. 1760/63, *X v Austria*, Decision of 23 May 1966, (1966) 9 *Yearbook* 166; App. 4133/69, *X v United Kingdom*, Decision of 13 July 1970, (1970) 13 *Yearbook* 780.

[21] *Fischer v Austria*, (App. 27569/02), Decision of 6 May 2003.

[22] *X v Austria*, (App. 1237/61), Decision of 5 March 1962 (1962) 5 *Yearbook* 96, 102.

[23] *Neumeister v Austria*, (App. 1936/63), 27 June 1968, Series A No 8, (1979–80) 1 EHRR 91, §§ 22 and 23 of 'The Law'; *Matznetter v Austria*, (App. 2178/64), 10 November 1969, Series A No 10, (1979–80) 1 EHRR 198, § 13 of 'The Law'.

[24] *Antoine v United Kingdom*, (App. 62960/00), Decision of 13 May 2003.

[25] *Boulois v Luxembourg*, (App. 37575), 3 April 2012.

[26] The Grand Chamber overruled the Chamber in this case (fifteen votes to two – the dissent noted the increasing consensus in Europe with regard to the importance of prisoners leave with regard to prisoners' reintegration to society).

It is evident that this phrase covers ordinary civil litigation between private individuals, relating, for example, to actions in tort, contract, and family law. The Court has extended the scope of the provision to cover interim measures such as interlocutory judgments issued by civil courts, where a civil right or obligation is at issue and the granting of the interim measure effectively determines the dispute.[27] The Court justified this change from previous case-law by underlining the backlog in justice systems throughout Europe and that in practice interim proceedings often decide the merits of a case.[28] It is more difficult, however, to determine whether Article 6(1) should apply also to disputes between individuals and the State rather than private law. If, for example, a public authority expropriates my land, do I have the right to a court hearing? Does the term cover only private rights to the exclusion of public law matters?[29]

From the start, the Court and Commission took the view that, as with the definition of 'criminal charge', the question whether a dispute relates to 'civil rights and obligations' could not be answered solely by reference to the way in which it is viewed under the national law of the respondent State; the concept has an 'autonomous' meaning under the Convention.[30] Any other approach would have allowed Contracting Parties to circumvent fair trial guarantees under Article 6(1) simply by classifying various areas of the law as 'public' or 'administrative' and would have risked creating disparity in the protection of human rights throughout Europe.

While this refusal to be tied by national law definitions is no doubt correct, it does give rise to uncertainty as to whether a particular type of dispute is included. Although the Court has, from time to time, appeared to base itself on various elements such as the economic nature of the right concerned, it has never attempted to elaborate universal criteria, comparable to the *Engel* criteria for a 'criminal offence',[31] by which to identify 'civil rights and obligations', preferring instead to decide the matter on a case-by-case basis. The closest it has come to giving general guidance is to repeat that while the national law position is not totally without importance, the substantive content, character, and effects of the right concerned are more decisive.

The Strasbourg Court first considered the interpretation of 'civil rights and obligations' in the *Ringeisen* case.[32] The dispute in question involved an application by Ringeisen for approval of the transfer to him, from a private person, of certain plots of land in Austria. He alleged that the Regional Real Property Transactions Commission which had heard his appeal against the decision of the District Commission, was biased, and consequently that it was not an impartial tribunal as required by Article 6(1).

The majority of the Commission concluded that Article 6(1) did not apply because the expression 'civil rights and obligations' should be construed restrictively as including only disputes between private individuals and not any proceedings in which the citizen is confronted by a public authority. In contrast, the Court held that Article 6(1) was applicable (although it had not been violated because there was no evidence of bias). As to the interpretation of Article 6(1), it held as follows:[33]

[27] *Micallef v Malta*, (App. 17056/06), 15 October 2009. [28] § 79.

[29] For a detailed consideration of the legislative history of the provision, see P. Van Dijk, 'The interpretation of "civil rights and obligations" by the European Court of Human Rights—one more step to take' in F. Matscher and H. Petzold, *Protecting Human Rights: The European Dimension: Studies in Honour of Gérard J. Wiarda* (Carl Heymanns, Köln 1990), 131–43.

[30] App. 1931/63, *X v Austria*, (App. 1931/63), Decision of 2 October 1964, (1964) 7 *Yearbook* 212 at 222; *König v Germany*, (App. 6232/73), 28 June 1978, Series A No 27, (1979–80) EHRR 170; and see, *Maaouia v France*, (App. 39652/98), 5 October 2000 [GC], (2001) 33 EHRR 1037, ECHR 2000-X, § 34.

[31] See earlier in this chapter.

[32] *Ringeisen v Austria*, (App. 2614/65), 16 July 1971, Series A No 13, (1979–80) 1 EHRR 455.

[33] § 94.

> For Article 6, paragraph (1), to be applicable to a case ('contestation') it is not necessary that both parties to the proceedings should be private persons, which is the view of the majority of the Commission and of the Government. The wording of Article 6, paragraph (1), is far wider; the French expression 'contestations sur (des) droits et obligations de caractère civil' covers all proceedings the result of which is decisive for private rights and obligations. The English text, 'determination of... civil rights and obligations', confirms this interpretation.

The character of the legislation which governs how the matter is to be determined (civil, commercial, administrative law, etc.) and that of the authority which is invested with jurisdiction in the matter (ordinary court, administrative body, etc.) are therefore of little consequence.

When Ringeisen purchased property from the Roth couple, he had a right to have the contract for sale which they had made with him approved if he fulfilled, as he claimed to do, the conditions laid down in the Act. Although it was applying rules of administrative law, the Regional Commission's decision was to be decisive for the relations in civil law ('de caractère civil') between Ringeisen and the Roth couple. This is enough to make it necessary for the Court to decide whether or not the proceedings in the case complied with the requirements of Article 6, paragraph (1), of the Convention.

Following its decision in the *Ringeisen* case, the Strasbourg Court has adopted an increasingly liberal interpretation of the concept of civil rights and obligations. Thus, in another early case,[34] it held that proceedings which involved the withdrawal of an authority to run a medical clinic and an authorization to practise medicine were within the scope of Article 6(1). This was so even though the function of the body which had taken the decision was to act in the interests of public health and to exercise responsibilities borne by the medical profession towards society at large. Similarly, in the *Pudas* case,[35] where the applicant's licence to operate a taxi on specified routes was revoked as part of a programme of rationalization which would have involved the replacement of one of his routes by a bus service, the Court rejected the respondent State's argument that, since the revocation of the licence depended essentially on an assessment of policy issues not capable of, or suited to, judicial control, the matter did not involve the determination of civil rights and obligations. Instead the Court held, unanimously, that the public law features of the case did not exclude the matter from the scope of Article 6(1), which applied since the revocation of the licence affected the applicant's business activities.

Questions relating to children taken into public care;[36] the expropriation of property by public authorities;[37] objections to and the enforcement of planning and decisions and the environment;[38] the withdrawal of licences to serve alcohol[39] and to work a gravel pit; disciplinary proceedings resulting in suspension from medical[40] and legal[41] practice; a

[34] *König v Germany*, (App. 6232/73), 28 June 1978, Series A No 27, (1979–80) 2 EHRR 170. See also *Kraska v Switzerland*, (App. 13942/88), 19 April 1993, Series A No 254-B, (1994) 18 EHRR 188.

[35] *Pudas v Sweden*, (App. 10426/83), 27 October 1987, Series A No 125, (1988) 10 EHRR 380.

[36] *McMichael v United Kingdom*, (App. 16424/90), 24 February 1995, Series A No 307-B, (1995) 20 EHRR 205.

[37] *Sporrong and Lönnroth v Sweden*, (Apps. 7151/75 and 7152/75), 23 September 1982, Series A No 52, (1983) 5 EHRR 35; and *Bodén v Sweden*, (App. 10930/84), 27 October 1987, Series A No 125, (1988) 10 EHRR 36; *Zanatta v France* (App. 38042/97), 28 March 2000.

[38] *Mats Jacobsson v Sweden*, (App. 11309/84), 28 June 1990, Series A No 180-A, (1991) 13 EHRR 79; *Bryan v United Kingdom*, (App. 19178/91), 9 September 1997, Series A No 335-A, (1995) 21 EHRR 342; *Taskin v Turkey*, (App. 49517/99), Judgment of 4 December 2003, ECHR 2003-X.

[39] *Tre Traktörer AB v Sweden*, (App. 10873/84), 7 July 1989, Series A No 159, (1991) 13 EHRR 309.

[40] *Fredin v Sweden*, (App. 12033/86), 18 February 1991, Series A No 192, (1991) 13 EHRR 784.

[41] *Le Compte, van Leuven and de Meyere v Belgium*, (Apps. 6878/75 and 7238/75), 23 June 1981, Series A No 43, (1982) 4 EHRR 1.

journalist's access to information for the purposes of publication,[42] and conditions of detention[43] have all been held to be sufficiently 'civil' in nature to fall within the scope of Article 6(1).

Disputes concerning liability to tax, despite their pecuniary consequences, have been held to be public law issues to which Article 6(1) does not apply.[44] It might be thought that social security is another such issue. However, in the *Feldbrugge* case,[45] which concerned a claim for sickness benefits, the Strasbourg Court concluded by a majority of ten to seven that Article 6(1) applied. It considered that, although the character of the legislation, the compulsory nature of insurance against certain risks, and the assumption by public bodies of responsibility for ensuring social protection were public law characteristics, these were outweighed by the personal and economic nature of the asserted right by the applicant, the connection with a contract of employment, and the similarities with insurance under ordinary law. In the *Deumeland* case,[46] decided the same day, the Court reached the same conclusion as regards the right to a widow's supplementary pension following the death of her husband in an industrial accident.[47]

Until the *Salesi* judgment,[48] it was not clear whether this interpretation would extend to non-contributory types of social assistance, which are not based on any 'contract' between the State and the individual and are harder to compare to private law insurance schemes. In the *Salesi* case, however, which concerned a dispute over entitlement to a disability allowance financed entirely from public funds and not dependent on the payment of contributions, the Court found that Article 6(1) applied.[49] It appeared to rely on two factors: first, the fact that entitlement to the allowance was a right under national law, derived from statute, which the applicant could assert in an ordinary civil court and which was not dependent on an exercise of State discretion; secondly, the fact that, as a result of being denied the allowance, the applicant had suffered an interference with her means of subsistence. This second factor was sufficient to make the right 'civil' for the purposes of the Convention.

The same arguments could perhaps be applied to certain rights of aliens to enter and stay in States of which they are not nationals. Rights such as the right to asylum are governed by international and national law and are not within the discretion of the State to withhold; moreover, a decision to expel an alien can have the most serious consequences on his or her economic and personal welfare. However, the Commission consistently rejected all such applications as inadmissible under Article 6(1),[50] and this approach

[42] *Shapovalov v Ukraine*, (App. 45835/05), 31 October 2012.

[43] *Ganci v Italy*, (App. 41576/98), 30 October 2003, ECHR 2003-XI; *Musumeci v Italy*, (App. 33695/96), 11 January 2005.

[44] *Charalambos v France*, (App. 49210/99), Decision of 8 February 2000; *Vidacar S.A. and Obergrup S.L. v Spain*, (Apps. 41601/98, 41775/98), Decision of 20 April 1999.

[45] *Feldbrugge v Netherlands*, (App. 8562/79), 29 May 1986, Series A No 99, (1986) 8 EHRR 425.

[46] *Deumeland v Germany*, (App. 9384/81), 29 May 1986, Series A No 100, (1986) 8 EHRR 448. See also *Schouten and Meldrum v Netherlands*, (Apps. 19005/91 and 19006/91), 9 December 1994, Series A No 304, (1995) 19 EHRR 432.

[47] See also, similarly, *Schuler-Zgraggen v Switzerland*, (App. 14518/89), 24 June 1993, Series A No 263, (1993) 16 EHRR 405, relating to invalidity pension.

[48] *Salesi v Italy*, (App. 13023/87), 23 February 1993, Series A No 257-A, (1998) 26 EHRR 187, § 19. For a similar progression in the scope of the notion of 'possessions' under Article 1 of Protocol 1 to encompass claims for non-contributory benefits see *Stec and others v United Kingdom*, (Apps. 65731/01 and 65900/01), Decision of 6 July 2005 [GC], (2005) 41 EHRR SE18, ECHR 2005-X.

[49] See also *Mennitto v Italy*, (App. 33804/96), 3 October 2000 [GC], (2002) 34 EHRR 1122, ECHR 2000-X.

[50] See the citations in the *Maaouia v France*, (App. 39652/98), 5 October 2000 [GC], (2001) 33 EHRR 1037, ECHR 2001-X, § 35.

was confirmed by the Strasbourg Court in the *Maaouia* case.[51] The applicant, a Tunisian national, complained about the length of the proceedings he had brought to overturn an order excluding him from France. In this case the Court did not consider the economic or personal effect of exclusion on the individual concerned, but instead attempted to determine the intention of the Contracting Parties who had drafted and signed the Convention. Despite the fact that Protocol 7 to the Convention was adopted only in November 1984, after the Commission had already expressed the view that a decision to deport a person does 'not involve a determination of his civil rights and obligations or of any criminal charge against him' within the meaning of Article 6(1), the Court decided that the creation of this Protocol, which contains procedural guarantees applicable to the expulsion of aliens, indicated that the Contracting Parties did not regard such proceedings as being governed by Article 6.

Disputes about access to election documentation raised by election observers are not proceedings concerned with the determination of civil rights and obligations.[52]

The Court's emphasis on the character of the right in question and its effects on the individual has created difficulties in classifying employment-related claims brought by civil servants against their employer, the State. The Court initially held that 'disputes relating to the recruitment, careers and termination of service of civil servants are as a general rule outside the scope of Article 6(1)'.[53] This principle was soon perceived as unsatisfactory, however, since it left everyone working in the public sector without the protection of Article 6(1) and led to disparity between the Member States of the Council of Europe because the type of employees categorized as 'civil servants' varies from State to State; in some countries, for example, teachers are 'civil servants' whereas they are assimilated with private sector employees in others.

The Court's case-law, therefore, witnessed a gradual whittling away of this sweeping exclusion. In a series of cases involving, for example, pension[54] and salary[55] disputes, it was held that where the claim in issue related to a 'purely' or 'essentially' economic right, Article 6(1) applied. Where, however, the claim principally called into question the authorities' discretionary powers, Article 6(1) did not apply.

Once again, the Court's approach proved unworkable. Almost any employment dispute will have economic consequences for the employee and it proved difficult to draw the line between cases falling within Article 6(1) and those excluded without creating uncertainty and injustice. In the *Neigel* case,[56] for example, the proceedings brought by the applicant centred on the authorities' refusal to reinstate her to a permanent post in the civil service, but the Court held that it concerned her recruitment and career and that Article 6(1) was not applicable; her claim for lost salary was insufficient to bring it within the scope of that provision because in order to succeed with this claim she needed first to prove that the refusal to reinstate her had been unlawful.

One of the first acts of the new Court was to attempt to rectify this situation. In the *Pellegrin* judgment[57] the Grand Chamber set out a new test for determining the application of Article 6(1) to civil service employment disputes, based on the nature of the

[51] *Maaouia v France*, (App. 39652/98), 5 October 2000 [GC], (2001) 33 EHRR 1037, ECHR 2000-X.

[52] *Geraguyn Khorhurd Patgamavorakan Akum v Armenia*, (App. 11721/04), Decision of 11 May 2009.

[53] *Massa v Italy*, (App. 14399/88), 24 August 1993, Series A No 265-B, (1994) 18 EHRR 266, § 26.

[54] *Massa v Italy*, (App. 14399/88), 24 August 1993, Series A No 265-B, (1994) 18 EHRR 266; and *Francesco Lombardo v Italy*, (App. 11519/85), 26 November 1992, Series A No 249-B, (1996) 21 EHRR 188.

[55] *De Santa v Italy*, (App. 25574/94); *Lapalorcia v Italy*, (App. 25586/94); *Abenavoli v Italy*, (App. 25587/94), 2 September 1997.

[56] *Neigel v France*, (App. 18725/91), 17 March 1993.

[57] *Pellegrin v France*, (App. 28541/95), 8 December 1999 [GC], (2001) 31 EHRR 651, ECHR 1999-VIII.

employee's duties and responsibilities. The only disputes now excluded from the scope of Article 6(1) are 'those which are raised by public servants whose duties typify the specific activities of the public service in so far as the latter is acting as the depository of public authority responsible for protecting the general interests of the State or other public authorities'.[58] This principle allows the State to protect its interests by giving it virtually a free hand (as far as Article 6 is concerned) in hiring and firing core civil servants, such as diplomats, policy-makers, policemen, and soldiers,[59] while protecting the rights of the thousands of others (cleaners, nurses, teachers, and so on) whose jobs, to all intents and purposes, are identical to those of their counterparts in the private sector.[60]

That judgment, however, is not the end of the story, since the application of the functional criterion was acknowledged by the Court in a later case to be capable of anomalous results.[61] Accordingly the Strasbourg Court extended its decision in the *Pellegrin* case as follows:

> To recapitulate, in order for the respondent State to be able to rely before the Court on the applicant's status as a civil servant in excluding the protection embodied in Article 6, two conditions must be fulfilled. First, the State in its national law must have expressly excluded access to a court for the post or category of staff in question. Secondly, the exclusion must be justified on objective grounds in the State's interest. The mere fact that the applicant is in a sector or department which participates in the exercise of power conferred by public law is not in itself decisive. In order for the exclusion to be justified, it is not enough for the State to establish that the civil servant in question participates in the exercise of public power or that there exists, to use the words of the Court in the *Pellegrin* judgment, a 'special bond of trust and loyalty' between the civil servant and the State, as employer. It is also for the State to show that the subject matter of the dispute in issue is related to the exercise of State power or that it has called into question the special bond. Thus, there can in principle be no justification for the exclusion from the guarantees of Article 6 of ordinary labour disputes, such as those relating to salaries, allowances or similar entitlements, on the basis of the special nature of relationship between the particular civil servant and the State in question. There will, in effect, be a presumption that Article 6 applies. It will be for the respondent Government to demonstrate, first, that a civil-servant applicant does not have a right of access to a court under national law and, second, that the exclusion of the rights under Article 6 for the civil servant is justified.[62]

In conclusion, then, it can be seen that the expression 'civil rights and obligations' has come to encompass many areas which are frequently regarded by national systems as part of public or administrative law. While this extension of the protection offered by Article 6(1) can only be welcomed, it is on occasion difficult to discern any consistent principle in the Court's case-law. This lack of principle can make it difficult for Contracting Parties to determine the extent of their obligations under Article 6(1) and for citizens to know their rights. Moreover, certain inconsistencies can appear difficult to defend. What, for example, is the fundamental difference between entitlement to a tax allowance and entitlement to a

[58] § 66. [59] See, for example, *Batur v Turkey*, (App. 38604/97), Decision of 4 July 2000.

[60] See, for example, *Frydlender v France*, (App. 30979/96), 27 June 2000 [GC], ECHR 2000-VII; *Procaccini v Italy*, (App. 31631/96), 30 March 2000; *Satonnet v France*, (App. 30412/96), 2 August 2000; *Castanheira Barros v Portugal*, (App. 36945/97), 26 October 2000; *Lambourdière v France* (App. 37387/97), 2 August 2000; *Martinez-Caro de la Concha Casteneda and others v Spain*, (App. 42646/98), Decision of 7 March 2000; *Kajanen and Tuomaala v Finland*, (App. 36401/97), Decision of 18 October 2000.

[61] *Eskelinen and others v Finland*, (App. 63235/00), 19 April 2007 [GC], (2007) 45 EHRR 985, ECHR 2007-IV, § 51.

[62] § 62. For an example of the application of the new criteria, see *Czetković v Serbia*, (App. 17271/04), 10 June 2008, §§ 36–8. See also *Cudak v Lithuania*, (App. 15869/02), 23 March 2010 §§ 42–4.

social security benefit which could justify holding the latter to fall within the scope of 'civil rights and obligations' but not the former?

THE NEED FOR A DISPUTE

Article 6(1) requires not only that the matter concern civil rights or obligations, but that there be a dispute (*contestation*, from the French text of Article 6(1)) concerning the particular rights or obligations. In the *Benthem* judgment[63] the Strasbourg Court reviewed the case-law on this requirement and summarized its content as follows:

> (a) Conformity with the spirit of the Convention requires that the word 'contestation' (dispute) should not be 'construed too technically' and should be 'given a substantive rather than a formal meaning'...
> (b) The 'contestation' (dispute) may relate not only to 'the actual existence of a... right' but also to its scope or the manner in which it may be exercised... It may concern both 'questions of fact' and 'questions of law'...
> (c) The 'contestation' (dispute) must be genuine and of a serious nature...
> (d) ...'the... expression "contestations sur (des) droits et obligations de caractère civil" [disputes over civil rights and obligations] covers all proceedings the result of which is decisive for [such] rights and obligations.'... However, 'a tenuous connection or remote consequences do not suffice for Article 6(1)...: civil rights and obligations must be the object—or one of the objects—of the 'contestation' (dispute); the result of the proceedings must be directly decisive for such a right."

Thus, for example, in the *Fayed* case,[64] the Court held that an investigation by inspectors appointed by the Department of Trade and Industry into the applicants' take-over of Harrods did not attract the protection of Article 6, despite the applicants' argument that their reputations (a civil right) had been at stake. The Court found that the purpose of the inquiry had been to ascertain and record facts which might subsequently be used as the basis for action by other competent authorities—prosecuting, regulatory, disciplinary, or even legislative. It was satisfied that the functions performed by the inspectors were essentially investigative and that they had not been empowered to make any legal determination as to criminal or civil liability concerning the Fayed brothers.

Article 6(1) continues to apply to all stages of legal proceedings for the 'determination of... civil rights and obligations', not excluding stages subsequent to judgment on the merits. For example, in the *Robins* case[65] the Court held that proceedings to determine the costs liability of the unsuccessful party to civil litigation should be seen as a continuation of the principal dispute, and had therefore to be decided within a reasonable time.

RIGHT OF ACCESS TO COURT

One of the rights which has been developed out of the provisions of Article 6 is the right of access to a court for the determination of a particular civil issue.

The Court first recognized this right in the *Golder* case in 1975.[66] In a clear application of the 'effective rights' interpretation technique, it held that the detailed fair trial guarantees

[63] *Benthem v Netherlands*, (App. 5548/80), 23 October 1985, Series A No 97, (1986) 8 EHRR 1, § 32.

[64] *Fayed v United Kingdom*, (App. 17101/90), 21 September 1994, Series A No 294-B, (1994) 18 EHRR 393.

[65] *Robins v United Kingdom*, (App. 22410/93), 23 September 1997, (1998) 26 EHRR 527, ECHR 1997-V.

[66] *Golder v United Kingdom*, (App. 4451/70), 21 February 1975, Series A No 18, (1979–80) 1 EHRR 524.

under Article 6 would be useless if it were impossible to start court proceedings in the first place. The applicant was detained in an English prison where serious disturbances broke out. He was accused of assault by a prison officer and wished to bring proceedings for defamation in order to have his record cleared, but this was precluded by the Prison Rules. Though not without limitation, the Court concluded that Article 6(1) contained an inherent right of access to court, observing:

> In civil matters one can scarcely conceive of the rule of law without there being a possibility of access to the courts.... The principle whereby a civil claim must be capable of being submitted to a judge ranks as one of the universally recognized fundamental principles of law; the same is true of the principle of international law which forbids the denial of justice. Article 6(1) must be read in the light of these principles.[67]

The right of access to court is not absolute: it is open to States to impose restrictions on would-be litigants, as long as these restrictions pursue a legitimate aim and are not so wide-ranging as to destroy the very essence of the right.[68] For example, orders preventing vexatious litigants from commencing or pursuing claims without leave are not usually in breach of Article 6(1), since such orders pursue the aim of preserving court time and resources for deserving cases and since the litigant would be granted leave to pursue a meritorious action.[69] But it is not open to a Contracting Party to refuse to accept process starting actions, notwithstanding the permissibility under national law of filing actions by electronic means. In the *Lawyer Partners* case[70] the respondent State refused to accept details on DVDs as a means of starting multiple actions claiming that it lacked the resources to process actions submitted in this way notwithstanding the permissibility of filing action by electronic means. The case was clear cut, partly because the national constitutional court had also concluded that the authorities could not refuse to accept actions filed in this way. The Court has also recognized the importance of access to a court for those declared legally incapacitated. In *Stanev v Bulgaria*,[71] the Court found that the denial of access to a court to challenge the declaration of incapacity of the partially incapacitated applicant was under the circumstances a violation of Article 6(1). The Court noted the growing European consensus on the right, in principle, to direct access to a court for those mentally incapacitated.[72]

In the *Stubbings* case,[73] the Strasbourg Court ruled that the provisions of the Limitation Act 1960, requiring actions for damages for trespass against the person to be started within three years of the alleged injury or the victim's 18th birthday, were not a disproportionate restriction on the right of access to court, even though the applicants, victims of child sexual abuse, had been unable to bring proceedings within the time limit because of the effects of repressed memory syndrome. Limitation periods were held to pursue the legitimate aim of ensuring legal certainty and finality, while still allowing litigants some

[67] §§ 34–5.

[68] *Ashingdane v United Kingdom*, (App. 8225/78), 28 May 1985, Series A No 93, (1985) 7 EHRR 528; see also *Markovic and others v Italy*, (App. 1398/03), 14 December 2006 [GC], (2007) 44 EHRR 1045, ECHR 2006-XIV.

[69] App. 11559/85, *H v United Kingdom*, Decision of 2 December 1985, (1985) 45 DR 281.

[70] *Lawyer Partners AS v Slovakia*, (Apps. 54252/07 and 14 others), 16 June 2009.

[71] *Stanev v Bulgaria*, (App. 36760/06), Decision of 17 January 2012.

[72] §§ 243–5. The Court refers to the 2006 United Nations Convention on the Rights of Persons with Disabilities and Recommendation No. R (99)4 of the Committee of Ministers of the Council of Europe on principles concerning the legal protection of incapable adults, which recommend that adequate procedural safeguards be put in place to protect legally incapacitated persons to the greatest extent possible.

[73] *Stubbings and others v United Kingdom*, (Apps. 22083/93 and 22095/93), 22 October 1996; (1997) 23 EHRR 213, ECHR 1996-IV.

opportunity to come to court. However, their application to particular facts can result in their being a disproportionate response.[74]

The right of access to a court must not only exist in theory, it must also be effective. This means, for example, that if a poor litigant wishes to bring court proceedings which are meritorious but so complex as to be impossible to pursue without professional legal assistance, the State must provide legal aid if this is 'indispensable for an effective access to court'.[75] A similar principle applies where the needy party is the defendant to the action. The Court explained in a case brought by two environmental protesters sued for libel by the hamburger chain McDonald's:

> The question whether the provision of legal aid is necessary for a fair hearing must be determined on the basis of the particular facts and circumstances of each case and will depend *inter alia* upon the importance of what is at stake for the applicant in the proceedings, the complexity of the relevant law and procedure and the applicant's capacity to represent him or herself effectively...[76]

Because the 'McLibel Two' were defending their freedom of expression, a right considered important under the Convention system, and risked having a substantial sum of damages awarded against them, and because the case was extraordinarily complex and cumbersome to defend, the criteria discussed were fulfilled and there was a violation of Article 6(1).[77]

The right to bring a claim to court applies only in respect of rights provided for by the national law; it is not possible through Article 6(1) to challenge the substantive *content* of national law. Sometimes, however, it can be difficult to decide whether a particular rule of national law negates a substantive right, or simply forms a procedural impediment to access to court such as to raise an issue under Article 6(1). This has been the case with the rules under English law providing that certain professions are immune from civil suit. In the *Osman* case[78] a member of the applicants' family was shot and killed by a stalker. The applicants claimed that the police had negligently failed to protect them, despite the presence of clear warning signs from the killer. They started negligence proceedings against the police in the English courts, but these were struck out by the Court of Appeal which held that, in light of House of Lords case-law, no action could lie against the police in negligence in the investigation and suppression of crime because public policy (the desire to save police resources for fighting crime rather than fighting court cases) required an immunity from suit. Before the Strasbourg Court, the British Government argued that Article 6(1) did not apply, because the exclusionary rule applied by the Court of Appeal meant that the applicants had no substantive right under national law against the police.

In a controversial decision, the Strasbourg Court held that Article 6(1) was applicable. It observed that English common law had long accorded a plaintiff the right to bring proceedings in negligence. Faced with such a claim, it was for the national court to determine whether the defendant owed the plaintiff a duty of care; in other words, whether the damage caused had been foreseeable, whether there existed a relationship of proximity

[74] *Stagno v Belgium*, (App. 1062/07), 7 July 2009.

[75] *Airey v Ireland*, (App. 6289/73), 9 October 1979, Series A, No 32, (1979–80) 2 EHRR 305, § 26.

[76] *Steel and Morris v United Kingdom*, (App. 68416/01), 15 February 2005, (2005) 41 EHRR 403, ECHR 2005-II, § 61.

[77] This finding should be contrasted with that in *McVicar v United Kingdom*, (App. 46311/99), 7 May 2002; (2002) 35 EHRR 566; ECHR 2002-III, where the Court found that the journalist defending libel proceedings was able to mount an effective case without legal representation.

[78] *Osman v United Kingdom*, (App. 23452/94), 28 October 1998, (2000) 29 EHRR 245, ECHR 1998-VIII.

between the parties, and whether it was fair, just, and reasonable to impose a duty of care in the circumstances. The rule applied by the Court of Appeal—giving the police a certain, limited immunity from suit on policy grounds—did not automatically doom the proceedings to failure from the start, but instead in principle allowed the national court to make a considered assessment as to whether or not the rule should be applied in that particular case. The Court therefore concluded that the applicants had a right under English law, derived from the law of negligence, to seek an adjudication on the admissibility and merits of their claim against the police, but that the rule giving the police immunity from suit acted as a watertight, irrebuttable defence and was thus disproportionate.

In the later *Z and others* case,[79] the Court, while not expressly overruling its judgment in *Osman*, conceded that its reasoning there 'was based on an understanding of the law of negligence... which has to be reviewed in the light of the clarifications subsequently made by the domestic courts'.[80] The applicants were five children who had been badly neglected and abused by their parents. During a period of over five years, despite being aware of the situation, the local authority took no steps to remove the children from their parents' care. The applicants subsequently started proceedings against the local authority, claiming damages for negligence and/or breach of statutory duty and arguing that the local authority's failure to act had resulted in their psychological damage. The proceedings were struck out as revealing no cause of action, and the applicants appealed to the Court of Appeal and, finally, the House of Lords.[81] In its judgment the House of Lords examined, *inter alia*, whether the local authority had owed the applicants a duty of care. It was accepted that the damage to the applicants had been foreseeable, and that there was a relationship of proximity between the parties. The House of Lords did not, however, consider that it would be just and reasonable to impose a duty of care in the circumstances, in view of the interdisciplinary nature of the statutory system of child protection, and the extraordinarily difficult and delicate task faced by social services in such situations. If liability in damages were to be imposed, it was feared that local authorities would adopt a more cautious and defensive approach to their duties, which would not be in the interests of children generally.

The Strasbourg Court found that Article 6(1) applied, since, prior to the judgment of the House of Lords, there had been no national decision indicating whether or not a local authority owed children a duty of care in such circumstances; until that judgment, therefore, the applicants had had an arguable claim to a civil right under English law. This aspect of the Court's reasoning alone would appear to contradict its *Osman* judgment, since by the time the applicants in *Osman* started proceedings the House of Lords had already established that no negligence action could lie against the police in respect of their acts and omissions in the investigation and suppression of crime. Moreover, when the Court in *Z and others* went on to examine whether there had been a violation of Article 6, it found that the applicants had not in fact been deprived of access to court, since they had been able to bring their claims before the national courts, culminating in a detailed consideration by the House of Lords as to whether a novel category of negligence actions should be developed.[82]

[79] *Z and others v United Kingdom*, (App. 29392/95), 10 May 2001 [GC], (2002) 34 EHRR 97; ECHR 2001-V.

[80] § 100. [81] *X and others v Bedfordshire County Council*, [1995] 2 AC 633.

[82] The Court did, however, find violations of Articles 3 and 13 based on the local authority's failure to act and the lack of any effective domestic remedy. The distinction between the absence of a substantive national legal right (when Article 6(1) does not apply) and a procedural restriction on a litigant's ability to sue on the basis of an existing right (when Article 6(1) applies and may be violated where the restriction is disproportionate) was re-examined in *Roche v United Kingdom*, (App. 32555/96), 19 October 2005 [GC], (2006) 42 EHRR 599; ECHR 2005-X. This was a case brought by conscripts who participated in medical tests during the 1950s and have been unable to claim damages because the State enjoys immunity under s. 10 of the Crown Proceedings Act 1947.

The Grand Chamber had the opportunity to review its approach to the right of access to a court in the *Markovic* case.[83] The case concerned claims made in Italy by relatives of citizens of Serbia and Montenegro who had been killed in a NATO air strike on Belgrade. Italy had provided the air bases from which the aircraft had taken off in order to carry out the bombing raids in which the relatives of the applicants were killed. The Italian Court of Cassation concluded that it had no jurisdiction to consider the claims. The applicants then argued that they had been denied access to a court in breach of Article 6. The Strasbourg Court affirmed that the distinction between substantive limitations and procedural bars determines the scope of the guarantees under Article 6.[84] The Court continued:

> Where... the superior national courts have analysed in a comprehensive and convincing manner the precise nature of the impugned restriction, on the basis of the relevant Convention case-law and principles drawn therefrom, this Court would need strong reasons to differ from the conclusion reached by those courts by substituting its own views for those of the national courts on the question of interpretation of domestic law... and by finding, contrary to their view, that there was arguably a right recognized by domestic law.[85]

Applying these principles, the Grand Chamber concluded by ten votes to seven that there was no violation of Article 6. The effect is that the guarantee of a fair trial in Article 6 does not extend to the determination of claims for damages which national law classifies as political acts which are not justiciable before the national courts. The seven dissenting judges concluded that, in contrast to the detailed considerations which had been given to the arguments of the parties in the litigation in the *Z and others* case,[86] the Italian courts had not sought to balance the competing interests at stake and had not explained with sufficient clarity why the fact that the acts complained of were of a political nature should defeat their civil action. This lack of consideration and explanation meant that there had not been a proper consideration of the issues in the national legal order. The minority judgment does not mean that the Italian courts did have jurisdiction, but simply that they had failed to analyse the claims in a comprehensive and convincing manner.[87]

The right of access to court has a more limited application in the criminal sphere. There is no right under Article 6 to have criminal proceedings brought against a suspected offender, for example, and no right as such to an appeal. Where, however, an appeal procedure is provided by national law, it must comply with Article 6[88] and access to it must not be blocked disproportionately or unfairly. Thus the rule under French law that a convicted person may bring an appeal in cassation only if he surrenders to custody was found to be a disproportionate restriction on access to court in the *Papon* case.[89] The Court also found a violation of this right in a case against the Netherlands,[90] where the applicant company

[83] *Markovic and others v Italy*, (App. 1398/03), 14 December 2006 [GC], (2007) 44 EHRR 1045, ECHR 2006-XIV.

[84] § 94.

[85] § 95. See *Roche v United Kingdom*, (App. 32555/96), 19 October 2005 [GC], (2006) 42 EHRR 599; ECHR 2005-X.

[86] *Z and others v United Kingdom*, (App. 29392/95), 10 May 2001 [GC], (2002) 34 EHRR 97, ECHR 2001-V, and see earlier in this chapter.

[87] See also the application of Article 6(1) involving access to a court in cases involving issues of State immunity; *Cudak v Lithuania*, (App. 15869/02), 23 March 2010; *Sabeh El Leil v France*, (App. 34869/05), 29 June 2011; *Wallishauser v Austria*, (App. 156/04), 17 July 2012; *Oleynikov v Russia*, (App. 3670304), 13 March 2013; *Stichting Mothers of Srebrenica and others v Netherlands*, (App. 65542/12), 11 June 2013.

[88] *Delcourt v Belgium*, (App. 2689/65), 17 January 1970, Series A No 11, (1979–80) 1 EHRR 355.

[89] *Papon v France*, (App. 54210/00), 25 July 2002, (2004) 39 EHRR 217, ECHR 2002-XII. For a similar case see *Scoppola v Italy No.2*, (App. 10249/03), 17 September 2009.

[90] *Marpa Zeeland B.V and Metal Welding B.V v The Netherlands*, (App. 46300/99), 9 November 2004, (2005) 40 EHRR 407, ECHR 2004-X.

had been persuaded to withdraw its appeal against sentence on the basis of assurances from the Advocate General that the penalty would, in any event, be reduced. By the time the company discovered that these assurances would not be followed through, the withdrawal of the appeal had become irrevocable.

THE EFFECTIVENESS OF COURT PROCEEDINGS

Linked to the principle of access to court is another fundamental aspect of the rule of law: that a final court judgment should be effective.

This is obviously true in criminal as in civil cases. The Grand Chamber found a violation of Article 6 in the *Assanidze* case[91] where the applicant, the former mayor of Batumi, the capital of the Ajarian Autonomous Republic, was convicted of a number of criminal offences and imprisoned in the Ajarian Autonomous Republic. Even when he had subsequently been acquitted of all charges by the Georgian courts, the Ajari authorities refused to release him. The Court observed that:

> The guarantees afforded by Article 6 of the Convention would be illusory if a Contracting State's national legal or administrative system allowed a final, binding judicial decision to acquit to remain inoperative to the detriment of the person acquitted. It would be inconceivable that paragraph 1 of Article 6, taken together with paragraph 3, should require a Contracting State to take positive measures with regard to anyone accused of a criminal offence... and describe in detail procedural guarantees afforded to litigants—proceedings that are fair, public and expeditious—without at the same time protecting the implementation of a decision to acquit delivered at the end of those proceedings. Criminal proceedings form an entity and the protection afforded by Article 6 does not cease with the decision to acquit...[92]

The non-execution of civil judgments appears to be an endemic problem in much of eastern Europe—particularly in cases where the State is the judgment debtor—and there have been many judgments finding violations of Article 6 on this ground.[93]

In the second *Burdov* case,[94] the Strasbourg Court adopted a pilot judgment following the finding of a violation of Article 6(1) and of Article 1 of Protocol 1 on account of the prolonged failure of the Russian authorities to enforce certain national judgments ordering monetary payments by the authorities. The respondent State was required to set up an effective domestic remedy to secure adequate redress for non-enforcement or delayed enforcement of judgments, and to grant such redress within one year for all victims of non-payment of judgment debts.

The right to effective court proceedings also entails that once a civil judgment or a criminal acquittal has become final and binding, there should be no risk of its being overturned. In the *Ryabykh*[95] case the Court explained:

[91] *Assanidze v Georgia*, (App. 71503/01), 8 April 2004 [GC], (2004) 39 EHRR 653, ECHR 2004-II.

[92] § 182.

[93] See, among many examples, *Hornsby v Greece*, (App. 18357/91), 19 March 1997, (1997) 24 EHRR 250; *Burdov v Russia*, (App. 59498/00), 7 May 2002, (2004) 38 EHRR 639, ECHR 2002-III; *Jasuniene v Lithuania*, (App. 41510/98), 6 March 2003; *Shmalko v Ukraine*, (App. 60750/00), 20 July 2004; and *Popov v Moldova*, (App. 74153/01), 18 January 2005. In *Pini, Bertani, Manera and Atripaldi v Romania*, (Apps. 78028/01 and 78030/01), 22 June 2004, (2005) 40 EHRR 312; ECHR 2004-V, where the Court found a violation where the State had not acted to enforce a judgment requiring a private children's home to hand children over to their adoptive parents.

[94] *Burdov v Russia (No. 2)*, (App. 33509/04), 15 January 2009, (2009) 49 EHRR 22, ECHR 2009-nyr.

[95] *Ryabykh v Russia*, (App. 52854/99), 24 July 2003, (2005) 40 EHRR 615, ECHR 2003-IX; §§ 51–2.

> ... One of the fundamental aspects of the rule of law is the principle of legal certainty, which requires, among other things, that where the courts have finally determined an issue, their ruling should not be called into question.... Legal certainty presupposes respect for the principle of *res judicata*..., that is the principle of the finality of judgments. This principle insists that no party is entitled to seek a review of a final and binding judgment merely for the purpose of obtaining a rehearing and a fresh determination of the case. Higher courts' power of review should be exercised to correct judicial errors and miscarriages of justice, but not to carry out a fresh examination. The review should not be treated as an appeal in disguise, and the mere possibility of there being two views on the subject is not a ground for re-examination. A departure from that principle is justified only when made necessary by circumstances of a substantial and compelling character.

THE OVERALL REQUIREMENTS OF A FAIR HEARING

Much of what will be said later in this chapter will deal with the specific features of a fair trial set out in Article 6(1), but there is also an overriding requirement that the proceedings should be fair. Compliance with specific rights set out in Article 6 will not alone guarantee that there has been a fair trial. It is not possible to state in the abstract the content of the requirement of a fair hearing; this can be considered only in the context of the proceedings as a whole, including any appeal proceedings.[96] A number of specific ingredients of a fair trial have, however, emerged from the case-law.

PROCEDURAL EQUALITY

The concept of 'equality of arms' (*égalité des armes*) was first mentioned in the *Neumeister* case,[97] and has been a feature of Article 6(1) ever since. It requires a fair balance between the parties and applies to both civil and criminal cases.[98] In the context of civil cases between private parties, 'equality of arms' does not have to be absolute. There is no duty on the State, for example, to provide legal aid to an impecunious litigant to such a level as to bring him or her into total parity with a wealthy opponent.[99] What matters is that parties are afforded a reasonable opportunity to present their case—including their evidence—under conditions that do not place them at a substantial disadvantage *vis-à-vis* the other side.[100] Thus, in criminal proceedings, if the prosecution enjoys a significant procedural advantage—such as the chance for the *avocat général* to make submissions to the Court of Cassation in the absence of representatives of the defence—there will not be a reasonable equality of arms between the parties.[101] By way of another, rather glaring, example, the Court found a violation of Article 6(1) in criminal proceedings where the defence lawyer

[96] *Fedje v Sweden*, (App. 12631/87), 26 September 1991, Series A No 212-C, (1994) 17 EHRR 14; and *Kostovski v Netherlands*, (App. 11454/85), 20 November 1989, Series A No 166, (1990) 12 EHRR 434.

[97] *Neumeister v Austria*, (App. 1936/63), 27 June 1968, Series A No 8, (1979–80) 1 EHRR 91.

[98] *Steel and Morris v United Kingdom*, (App. 68416/01), 15 February 2005, (2005) 41 EHRR 403, ECHR 2005-II, § 59.

[99] § 62.

[100] *Dombo Beheer BV v Netherlands*, (App. 14448/88), 27 October 1993, Series A No 274-A, (1994), 18 EHRR 213, § 33, *Marc-Antoine v France*, (App. 54984/09), Decision of 4 June 2013.

[101] *Borgers v Belgium*, (App. 12005/86), 30 October 1991, Series A No 214, (1993) 15 EHRR 92.

was made to hang around for fifteen hours before finally being given a chance to plead his case in the early hours of the morning.[102]

AN ADVERSARIAL PROCESS AND DISCLOSURE OF EVIDENCE

Closely related to equality of arms is the right to have an adversarial trial. This means 'the opportunity for the parties to have knowledge of and comment on the observations filed or evidence adduced by the other party'.[103]

In order for the adversarial process to work effectively, it is important, in civil and criminal proceedings, that relevant material is available to both parties. Security considerations will not justify blanket restrictions on the availability of such evidence where it affects the interests of a litigant, since there are means which can accommodate legitimate security concerns while offering a substantial measure of procedural justice to a litigant.[104]

The Court explained the principle as it applies in criminal proceedings in its *Rowe and Davis* judgment:[105]

> It is a fundamental aspect of the right to a fair trial that criminal proceedings, including the elements of such proceedings which relate to procedure, should be adversarial and that there should be equality of arms between the prosecution and defence. The right to an adversarial trial means, in a criminal case, that both prosecution and defence must be given the opportunity to have knowledge of and comment on the observations filed and the evidence adduced by the other party.... In addition Article 6(1) requires... that the prosecution authorities should disclose to the defence all material evidence in their possession for or against the accused.

The entitlement to disclosure of relevant evidence is not, however, an absolute right. In criminal (and sometimes also in civil) proceedings there may be competing factors, such as national security, or the need to protect witnesses at risk of reprisals, or to keep secret police methods of investigation of crime, which must be weighed against the rights of the accused. In some cases it may be necessary to withhold certain evidence from the defence so as to preserve the fundamental rights of another individual or to safeguard an important public interest. However, as the Court emphasized in *Rowe and Davis*, only such measures restricting the rights of the defence which are strictly necessary are permissible under Article 6(1).

In accordance with the 'fourth instance' doctrine, the Court will not itself review whether or not an order permitting non-disclosure was justified in any particular case. Instead, it examines the decision-making procedure to ensure that it complied, as far as possible, with the requirements of adversarial proceedings and equality of arms and incorporated adequate safeguards to protect the interests of the accused.

In the *Rowe and Davis* case the prosecution had unilaterally decided, without consulting the trial judge, to withhold evidence in its possession about the existence and role of an informer. This man, who was one of the main prosecution witnesses at the applicants' trial on charges of armed robbery and murder, had, unbeknown to the defence or the judge, received a substantial reward for assisting the prosecution authorities. The applicants were convicted and appealed, and at this stage the prosecution notified the Court of Appeal about the withheld material. The Court of Appeal inspected it and held a hearing to decide

[102] *Makhfi v France*, (App. 59335/00), 19 October 2004.

[103] *Ruiz-Mateos v Spain*, (App. 12952/87), 23 June 1993, Series A No 262, (1993) 16 EHRR 505, § 63.

[104] *Dağtekin and others v Turkey*, (App. 70516/01), 13 March 2008.

[105] *Rowe and Davis v United Kingdom*, (App. 28901/95), 16 February 2000 [GC], (2000) 30 EHRR 1, ECHR 2000-II, § 60.

whether it should be disclosed, but the defence were not permitted to attend this hearing and were never allowed to see the evidence or informed of its nature or content.

The Strasbourg Court decided that the procedure before the Court of Appeal was not sufficient to satisfy the requirements of Article 6(1). The rights of the defence would have been adequately protected if the trial judge had had the opportunity to examine the withheld evidence and make the decision on disclosure.[106] However, the Court took the view that, unlike the trial judge, who saw the witnesses give their testimony and was fully versed in all the evidence and issues in the case, the judges in the Court of Appeal were dependent for their understanding of the possible relevance of the undisclosed material on transcripts of the Crown Court hearings and on the account of the issues given to them by prosecuting counsel. In addition, the first instance judge would have been in a position to monitor the need for disclosure throughout the trial, assessing the importance of the undisclosed evidence at a stage when new issues were emerging, when it might have been possible through cross-examination seriously to undermine the credibility of key witnesses and when the defence case was still open to take a number of different directions or emphases. In contrast, the Court observed, the Court of Appeal was obliged to carry out its appraisal *ex post facto* and might even, to a certain extent, have unconsciously been influenced by the jury's verdict of guilty into underestimating the significance of the undisclosed evidence.

In the *Edwards and Lewis* case,[107] it was the trial judge who reviewed all the evidence which the prosecution sought not to disclose. In the particular circumstances of the case, however, this created a problem of inequality of arms. Each applicant had applied to have the prosecution case against him struck out for abuse of process on the ground that he had been entrapped into committing the offence by undercover police officers. As a matter of English procedural law, the trial judge must determine, as a question of fact and taking into account such matters as the accused's past criminal record and any evidence concerning his dealings with the police, whether or not it is established on the balance of probabilities that the police improperly incited the offence. The problem arose under Article 6 because the same trial judge had already examined, in the absence of any representative of the defence, the prosecution's undisclosed evidence, which had to be disclosed only if it was likely to be of assistance to the defence case. Because of the secret nature of this procedure the defence were unable to know whether or not the undisclosed evidence was in fact harmful to the accused's allegations of entrapment, and, if so, whether the evidence was accurate or could have been rebutted. For example, it was subsequently revealed in the case of Edwards that the undisclosed evidence suggested that he had for some time before the police operation been involved in drug trafficking: an allegation which was of material relevance to the judge's decision on entrapment and one which the defendant strongly denied.

A REASONED DECISION

A reasoned decision, while not expressly required by Article 6, is implicit in the requirement of a fair hearing, which has been recognized by the Court.[108] If a court gives some reasons, then prima facie the requirements of Article 6 in this respect are satisfied, and this

[106] As occurred in the cases of *Jasper v United Kingdom*, (App. 27052/95), 16 February 2000, (2000) 30 EHRR 97; and *Fitt v United Kingdom*, (App. 29777/96), 16 February 2000, (2000) 30 EHRR 223, ECHR 2000-II, where the Court found no violation.

[107] *Edwards and Lewis v United Kingdom*, (Apps. 39647/98 and 40461/98), 27 October 2004 [GC], (2005) 40 EHRR 593, ECHR 2004-X.

[108] *Van de Hurk v Netherlands*, (App. 16034/90), 19 April 1994, Series A No 288, (1994) 18 EHRR 481, § 61. See also *Ruiz-Torija v Spain*, (App. 18390/91), 9 December 1994, Series A No 303-A, (1994) 19 EHRR 553; and *Hiro Balani v Spain*, (App. 18064/91), 9 December 1994, Series A No 303-B, (1994) 19 EHRR 566.

presumption is not upset simply because the judgment does not deal specifically with one point considered by an applicant to be material. On the other hand, if, for example, an applicant were to show that the court had ignored a fundamental defence, which had been clearly put before it and which, if successful, would have discharged him in whole or in part from liability, then this would be sufficient to rebut the presumption of a fair hearing. Refusal to address a ground of appeal submitted by an appellant, which is cogent and relevant, and could have an effect on the outcome of the case, will also constitute a breach of Article 6(1).[109]

This analysis applies *a fortiori* to criminal proceedings. Thus, where a convicted person has the possibility of an appeal, the lower court must state in detail the reasons for its decision, so that on appeal from that decision the accused's rights may be properly safeguarded.[110] However, under a jury system, the reasoning of the jury may not be accessible or published. The use of a lay jury was challenged in *Taxquet v Belgium*.[111] The applicant had been convicted of the murder of a government minister by a jury. No reasons were given by the jury. The Court noted the divergence in legal systems in Europe and that States have considerable discretion in the choice of legal systems. The Court found:

> the Convention does not require jurors to give reasons for their decision.... Nevertheless, for the requirements of a fair trial to be satisfied, the accused, and indeed the public, must be able to understand the verdict that has been given; this is a vital safeguard against arbitrariness...[112]

Safeguards may include judicial guidance or questions given to the jury which form the framework for the decision.

In the *Gorou* case,[113] the Grand Chamber indicated that the elaboration of reasons must be related to the nature of the dispute before the court, and that the Strasbourg Court will take account of judicial practice in the national legal orders. This would justify only a brief decision in cases where a civil party joined in criminal proceedings was seeking to secure the filing of an appeal by the public prosecutor following an acquittal in the criminal proceedings.

APPEARANCE IN PERSON

It depends on the nature of the proceedings whether a failure to allow the individual accused or civil litigant to attend in person will constitute a violation of Article 6(1).[114] In the *Kremzow* case,[115] the applicant was represented by a lawyer at the hearing of his appeal against sentence, but was not himself brought to court from prison. The Strasbourg Court made it clear that, as a general rule, accused persons should always be present at their trial. It further held that the applicant should have been enabled to attend the hearing of his appeal against sentence, since an increase from twenty years to life imprisonment was in issue, and an assessment of the applicant was to take place. The Court said:

> These proceedings were thus of crucial importance for the applicant and involved not only an assessment of his character and state of mind at the time of the offence but also his

[109] *Luka v Romania*, (App. 34197/02), 21 July 2009.

[110] App. 1035/61, *X v Federal Republic of Germany*, Decision of 17 June 1963, (1963) 6 *Yearbook* 180, 192.

[111] *Taxquet v Belgium*, (App. 926/05), 16 November 2010.

[112] §§ 91–2. Ireland, France, and the UK had been third party interveners in the case due to the extensive use of juries in these legal systems. The Court found a violation in this case due to the lack of safeguards.

[113] *Gorou v Greece (No. 2)*, (App. 12686/03), 20 March 2009 [GC], ECHR 2009-nyr.

[114] And, in criminal cases, Article 6(3)(c): see ch.14.

[115] *Kremzow v Austria*, (App. 12350/86), 21 September 1993, Series A No 268-B, (1994) 17 EHRR 322.

> motive. In circumstances such as those of the present case, where evaluations of this kind were to play such a significant role and where their outcome could be of major detriment to him, it was essential to the fairness of the proceedings that he be present during the hearing of the appeals and afforded the opportunity to participate in it together with his counsel.[116]

In contrast, no issue arose under Article 6 by virtue of Kremzow's absence during the appeal court's consideration of his plea of nullity, since he was represented and the nature of the hearing did not require him to be there.

The same principles apply in civil proceedings. Thus the individual concerned should be allowed to attend where, for example, an assessment of his or her character or state of health is directly relevant to the formation of the court's opinion, as in the case of a parent seeking access to a child[117] or a claimant seeking disability benefits.[118]

EFFECTIVE PARTICIPATION

It is not, however, sufficient that the criminal defendant or civil party is present in court. He or she must, in addition, be able effectively to participate in the proceedings. In one criminal case,[119] the applicant was slightly deaf and had not been able to hear some of the evidence given at trial. The Strasbourg Court did not, however, find a violation of Article 6(1) in view of the fact that the applicant's counsel, who could hear all that was said and was able to take his client's instructions at all times, chose for tactical reasons not to request that the accused be seated closer to the witnesses.

The applicants in the *T* and *V* cases[120] were eleven years old at the time of their trial for the murder of a two-year-old child. The proceedings were held in a blaze of publicity, in a packed courtroom, and there was medical evidence to show that both boys were suffering from post-traumatic stress at the time. The Strasbourg Court found violations of Article 6(1), commenting that it was highly unlikely that the applicants would have felt sufficiently uninhibited, in the tense courtroom and under public scrutiny, to have consulted with their lawyers during the trial. A later case[121] involved an 11-year-old boy with a long history of offending who was tried for robbery in the Crown Court. In contrast to the *T* and *V* trial, the case had attracted no publicity and a modified procedure had been adopted in an attempt to make the trial less intimidating; for example, the judge and barristers left off their wigs and gowns, plenty of breaks were taken and the applicant was allowed to sit with his social worker. The Strasbourg Court nonetheless found a violation of Article 6(1) on the ground that the applicant had been found to have the intellectual capacity of a child aged six to eight, and appeared to have little understanding of the nature of the proceedings or what was at stake. The Court concluded that:

> ... when the decision is taken to deal with a child, such as the applicant, who risks not being able to participate effectively because of his young age and limited intellectual capacity, by way of criminal proceedings rather than some other form of disposal directed primarily at determining the child's best interests and those of the community, it is essential that he

116 § 67. See also *Lagardere v France*, (App. 18851/07), 12 April 2012, where the applicant's guilt was declared two years after his death.

117 *X v Sweden*, (App. 434/58), Decision of 30 June 1959, (1958–9) 2 *Yearbook* 354, at 370.

118 *Salomonsson v Sweden*, (App. 38978/97), 12 November 2002.

119 *Stanford v United Kingdom*, (App. 16757/90), 23 February 1994, Series A No 282-A.

120 *T v United Kingdom*, (App. 24724/94) and *V v United Kingdom*, (App. 24888/94), 16 December 1999 [GC], (2000) 30 EHRR 121, ECHR 1999-IX.

121 *SC v United Kingdom*, (App. 60958/00), 15 June 2004, (2005) 40 EHRR 226, ECHR 2004-IV.

be tried in a specialist tribunal which is able to give full consideration to and make proper allowance for the handicaps under which he labours, and adapt its procedure accordingly.[122]

THE SPECIFIC REQUIREMENTS OF ARTICLE 6(1)

AN INDEPENDENT AND IMPARTIAL TRIBUNAL ESTABLISHED BY LAW

Article 6(1) guarantees the right to a fair trial before 'an independent and impartial tribunal established by law'. There cannot be a fair criminal or civil trial before a court which is, or appears to be, biased against the defendant or litigant, and the fair trial guarantees are meaningless if the tribunal's decision is liable to be overturned by some other authority which does not offer such guarantees.[123]

The Strasbourg Court is concerned both with the subjective and objective elements of independence and impartiality. The subjective element involves an enquiry into whether the personal conviction of a judge in a particular case raises doubts about his or her independence or impartiality. The judge's lack of bias is presumed unless there is evidence to the contrary and there are exceedingly few cases where subjective bias has been established since in practice such evidence can be very hard to come by. The objective element involves determination of whether, in terms of structure or appearance, a party's doubts about the tribunal's independence and impartiality may be legitimate.[124]

This applies whenever a member of a tribunal knows one of the parties to or witnesses at a trial. In the *Pullar* case,[125] for example, by sheer coincidence one of the jurors selected to try a case of corruption had previously been employed by the leading prosecution witness. The Strasbourg Court did not consider that this gave rise to a problem under Article 6(1), because a detailed examination of the juror's relationship with the witness—who had dismissed him from his job—did not demonstrate that the juror would be predisposed to believe his testimony.[126]

Care is also required, particularly in Continental criminal justice systems, where a judge has had some involvement in the pre-trial stages of the process. If this is routine pre-trial supervision of the case, there will be no breach of Article 6(1), but if the nature of the decision could suggest some pre-judging of the substantive issue, a violation of Article 6(1) could arise.[127]

In one case,[128] five of the nine jurors who served in the trial of a defamation action brought by way of private prosecution were members of the political party which was the principal target of the allegedly defamatory material. The jury selection procedures

[122] § 35.

[123] *Van de Hurk v Netherlands*, (App. 16034/90), 19 April 1994, Series A No 288, (1994) 18 EHRR 481.

[124] See generally *Piersack v Belgium*, (App. 8692/79), 1 October 1982, Series A No 53, (1983) 5 EHRR 169, and *Hauschildt v Denmark*, (App. 10486/83), 24 May 1989, Series A No 154, (1990) 12 EHRR 266. The principles have been affirmed in *Micallef v Malta*, (App. 17056/06), 15 October 2009, and *Harabin v Slovakia* (App. 58688/11), Decision of 20 November 2012.

[125] *Pullar v United Kingdom*, (App. 22399/93), 10 June 1996, (1996) 22 EHRR 391, ECHR 1996-III.

[126] See also *Langborger v Sweden*, (App. 11179/84), 22 June 1989, Series A No 155, (1990) 12 EHRR 416.

[127] As in *Hauschildt v Denmark*, (App. 10486/83), 24 May 1989, Series A No 154, (1990) 12 EHRR 266; see also *De Cubber v Belgium*, (App. 9186/80), 26 October 1984, Series A No 86, (1985) 7 EHRR 236; *Ben Yaacoub v Belgium*, (App. 9976/82), 27 November 1987, Series A No 127-A, (1991) 13 EHRR 418; *Fey v Austria*, (App. 14396/88), 24 February 1993, Series A No 255, (1993) 16 EHRR 387; and *Nortier v Netherlands*, (App. 13924/88), 24 August 1993, Series A No 267, (1993) 17 EHRR 273.

[128] *Holm v Sweden*, (App. 14191/88), 25 November 1993, Series A No 279-A, (1994) 18 EHRR 79.

complied with the requirements of Swedish law; attempts by the applicant to have those jurors disqualified who were members of the political party failed. The Strasbourg Court found that the links between the defendants and the five jurors could give rise to misgivings as to their objective independence and impartiality; this in turn rendered the independence and impartiality of the court questionable and there was a violation of Article 6(1).

This judgment may be less far-reaching than at first sight appears.[129] In essence, there was a failure by the national procedures to achieve their objective of removing from the jury those with an interest in the outcome of the litigation. Wider applications, such as complaints about trial by a jury whose composition does not correspond to the ethnic origin of the defendant, are unlikely to succeed unless the particular facts of the case show that the defendant's concerns about racism in the tribunal are objectively justified.

In the *Sander* case,[130] for example, the defendant was Asian. In the course of his trial in the Crown Court a member of the jury sent a note to the judge alleging that two fellow jurors had been making openly racist remarks and jokes and expressing the fear that the defendant would be convicted, not on the evidence, but because he was Asian. The judge adjourned the case, asking each member of the jury to consider overnight whether he or she felt able to try the case without prejudice. The following morning the judge received two letters from the jury. The first, signed by all the jurors including the one who had sent the complaint, refuted the allegation of racism. The second letter was written by a single juror who explained that he might have been the one responsible for making the racist jokes. He apologized for causing offence and declared that, in truth, he was not in the slightest racially biased. The judge decided not to dismiss the jury—despite a request from the defence—but instead directed them on the importance of their task and the trial continued, culminating in the applicant's conviction.

The Strasbourg Court, finding a violation of Article 6(1), held that, viewed objectively, the collective letter from the jury could not have been sufficient to dispel the applicant's fears, because the jurors would have been unlikely openly to admit to racism. Nor could his fears have been allayed by the judge's direction, however trenchant, because racist views could not be changed overnight. This judgment demonstrates, perhaps, the evolution of the Court's understanding of racism: in the earlier *Gregory* case,[131] with almost identical facts, the Court found that the judge's direction had been adequate to guarantee the jury's impartiality.

In the recent case of *Hanif and Khan v United Kingdom*[132] the applicants were convicted of drug offences. At trial, one of the jurors was a police officer. The applicants challenged the evidence given by one of the police officers at the trial. During the trial, the police officer on the jury informed the judge that he knew the police officer giving evidence. He had worked with him several times but not in the same station and he did not know him socially. The judge questioned the police officer on the jury and decided he could continue on the jury. The Court declined the opportunity to decide if a police officer on a jury would always lead to a violation but rather decided the case on its particular facts.

The Court found that in these particular circumstances there was a violation of Article 6. The dispute involving the police evidence was central to the case and the judicial questioning of the jury was not enough to displace the risk that the juror might favour the police evidence. The concerns of the applicants were objectively justified.

[129] And see, in contrast, *AB Kurt Kellermann v Sweden*, (App. 41579/98), 26 October 2004; and *Pabla KY v Finland*, (App. 47221/99), 22 June 2004, ECHR 2004-V.

[130] *Sander v United Kingdom*, (App. 34129/96), 9 May 2000, (2001) 31 EHRR 1003, ECHR 2000-V.

[131] *Gregory v United Kingdom*, (App. 22299/93), 25 February 1997, (1998) 25 EHRR 577.

[132] *Hanif and Khan v United Kingdom*, (App. 52999/08), 20 December 2011.

In other cases, the defect in the tribunal derives not from the personality, behaviour or prior involvement of one particular member, but from more formal concerns about the body's structure, powers, and composition. Relevant factors here are the manner of appointment and duration of office of the adjudicators[133] and the existence of guarantees against outside interference,[134] as well as the appearance of independence.[135] The use of lay judges sitting with legally qualified judges is not, of itself, objectionable, particularly where the expertise which the lay judges bring to the proceedings can be helpful. But the system must offer sufficient guarantees of the independence of the lay judges. They must not be removable from office at will, and their other roles must not conflict with their judicial functions.[136]

In the *Findlay* case[137] the Strasbourg Court examined the independence and impartiality of an army court martial. Under the legislation then in force, a court martial in the United Kingdom was convened on an ad hoc basis by a senior officer in the defendant's regiment. The convening officer not only appointed all the officers who sat as judges in the court martial, he also appointed the prosecuting and defending officers, prepared the evidence against the accused, and had the power to quash or vary the court's decision. It is not, therefore, surprising that Strasbourg Court found that the court martial was not 'independent and impartial'.[138]

The *Incal* case[139] was also concerned with the effect of the participation of military personnel in the criminal justice system. The applicant, a civilian, was convicted of disseminating Kurdish separatist propaganda by a National Security Court. These courts, composed of two civilian judges and a legally trained army officer, were set up specifically to deal with offences against Turkey's territorial integrity and national security. The Strasbourg Court found a violation of Article 6(1) on the basis that, given the nature of the charges against him and the fact that he was a civilian, the applicant could legitimately fear that the reason for including a military judge on the tribunal was to lead it to be unduly influenced by considerations which had nothing to do with the evidence in the case. The presence of a military judge on the panel determining Abdullah Öcalan's culpability for numerous terrorist offences led the Grand Chamber to find a violation of Article 6(1), even though the military judge had been replaced, before the verdict was reached, by a civilian who had sat as a substitute.[140]

The requirements of independence and impartiality apply equally in civil cases. In a group of related cases,[141] the Strasbourg Court found that the presence of civil servants

[133] *Le Compte, van Leuven and de Meyere v Belgium*, (Apps. 6878/75 and 7238/75), 23 June 1981, Series A No 43, (1982) 4 EHRR 1, § 55.

[134] *Piersack v Belgium*, (App. 8692/79), 1 October 1982, Series A No 53, (1983) 5 EHRR 169, § 27.

[135] *Delcourt v Belgium*, (App. 2689/65), 17 January 1970, Series A No 11, (1979–80) 1 EHRR 355.

[136] *Luka v Romania*, (App. 34197/02), 21 July 2009.

[137] *Findlay v United Kingdom*, (App. 22107/93), 25 February 1997, (1997) 24 EHRR 221, ECHR 1997-I.

[138] The Grand Chamber found in 2003 that the new procedure, as amended by the Army Act 1998, complies with Article 6: see *Cooper v United Kingdom*, (App. 48843/99), 16 December 2003 [GC], (2004) 39 EHRR 171, ECHR 2003-XII; compare *Grieves v United Kingdom*, (App. 57067/00), 16 December 2003, (2004) 39 EHRR 51, ECHR 2003-XII.

[139] *Incal v Turkey*, (App. 22678/93), 9 June 1998; (2000) 29 EHRR 449, ECHR 1998-IV. *Ergin v Turkey (No. 6)*, (App. 47533/99), § 41, 5 May 2006 and *Martin v United Kingdom*, (App. 40426/98), Decision of 7 September 1999.

[140] *Öcalan v Turkey*, (App. 46221/99), 12 May 2005 [GC], (2005) 41 EHRR 985, ECHR 2005-IV.

[141] *Ettl and others v Austria*, (App. 9273/81), 23 April 1987, Series A No 117, (1988) 10 EHRR 255; *Erkner and Hofauer v Austria*, (App. 9616/81), 23 April 1987, Series A No 117, (1987) 9 EHRR 464; and *Poiss v Austria*, (App. 9816/82), 23 April 1987, Series A No 117, (1988) 10 EHRR 231; compare *Sramek v Germany*, (App. 8791/79), 22 October 1984, Series A No 84, (1985) 7 EHRR 351.

on adjudicating tribunals did not, of itself, taint the tribunal provided that there were appropriate guarantees of their independence, including a prohibition on public authorities from giving them instructions concerning the exercise of the judicial function.[142] Moreover, in certain circumstances even where the first instance tribunal is not sufficiently independent, the availability of judicial review by an Article 6 compliant court will remedy the earlier defect.[143]

PUBLIC HEARINGS

Publicity is seen as one guarantee of the fairness of trial; it offers protection against arbitrary decisions and builds confidence by allowing the public to see justice being administered.[144] To answer the question whether there has been a public hearing within the meaning of Article 6(1), it is necessary to consider the proceedings as a whole. For example, the absence of a public hearing on appeal or cassation raises an issue under Article 6(1) only if the superior court is 'determining' an issue, which is not the case in legal systems where the appeal or cassation court carries out a supervisory role, in the sense that decisions of earlier hearings can be overturned only on points of law, requiring a further hearing in the court below.[145] In the *Axen* case,[146] for example, there was a public first instance hearing of a personal injuries claim, but the appeal was heard *in camera*, pursuant to a scheme to reduce the workload of the courts. This did not violate Article 6(1), since the proceedings taken as a whole could be regarded as public. The role of the appeal court was limited to dismissal of the appeal on points of law, thus making the decision of the first instance court final.[147]

In England and Wales, applications for leave to appeal against conviction or sentence are normally heard in private, and the position is similar in other countries. It would seem that this is permissible if such applications can be regarded as a step in the appellate process, and if there is a right to an appeal, heard in public, against the refusal of the application. Similarly, in civil cases, interlocutory proceedings which are held in private may be permissible subject to corresponding conditions.[148]

Article 6(1) contains a list of limitations to the right to a public hearing on grounds of public policy, national security, privacy, or where strictly necessary in the interests of justice, but these are to be tightly construed. The applicant in the *Riepan* case[149] was tried for offences committed in prison in a special hearing room in the prison. The public was not excluded, but no steps were taken to let anyone know that the hearing would take place. The Strasbourg Court held that only in rare cases could security concerns justify excluding the public. It observed that a trial would comply with the requirement of publicity only if the public was able to obtain information about its date and place and if this place was easily accessible. In many cases these conditions would be fulfilled by holding the hearing

[142] *Tsfayo v United Kingdom*, (App. 60860/00), 14 November 2006, (2009) 48 EHRR 457, §§ 40–9.

[143] Compare, for example, *Edwards v United Kingdom*, (App. 13071/87), 16 December 1992, Series A No 247-B, (1993) 15 EHRR 417, and *Rowe and Davis v United Kingdom*, (App. 28901/95), 16 February 2000 [GC], (2000) 30 EHRR 1, ECHR 2000-II; or *Bryan v United Kingdom*, (App. 19178/91), 22 November 1995, Series A No 335-A, (1996) 21 EHRR 342; with *Kingsley v United Kingdom*, (App. 35605/97), 7 November 2000, (2001) 33 EHRR 288, ECHR 2000-IV.

[144] *Pretto and others v Italy*, (App. 7984/77), 8 December 1983, Series A No 71, (1984) 6 EHRR 182.

[145] *Pretto and others v Italy*, (App. 7984/77), 8 December 1983, Series A No 71, (1984) 6 EHRR 182.

[146] *Axen v Germany*, (App. 8273/88), 8 December 1983, Series A No 72, (1984) 6 EHRR 195.

[147] See also *Sutter v Switzerland*, (App. 8209/78), 22 February 1984, Series A No 74, (1984) 6 EHRR 272.

[148] *X v United Kingdom*, (App. 3860/68), Decision of 16 May 1969 (1970) 30 CD 70.

[149] *Riepan v Austria*, (App. 35115/97), 14 November 2000, ECHR 2000-XII, § 34.

in a normal courtroom large enough to accommodate spectators. The holding of a trial outside a regular courtroom, in particular in a place like a prison to which the general public usually has no access, presented a serious obstacle to its public character, and the State was under an obligation to take compensatory measures to ensure that the public and the media were informed and granted effective access.

By way of contrast, the hearings at issue in the *P and B* case[150] were to determine the residence of children. According to the Family Proceedings Rules applicable in England and Wales, the presumption is that such hearings should be held in chambers, although the judge has a discretion to hold a public hearing if one of the parties requests this and shows that there are strong grounds for doing so. The respondent State relied on the proviso in Article 6(1) that 'the press and public may be excluded from all or part of the trial...where the interests of juveniles or the private life of the parties so require, or to the extent strictly necessary in the opinion of the court in special circumstances where publicity would prejudice the interests of justice.' The Strasbourg Court agreed, commenting that proceedings concerning the residence of children were:

> prime examples of cases where the exclusion of the press and public may be justified in order to protect the privacy of the child and parties and to avoid prejudicing the interests of justice. To enable the deciding judge to gain as full and accurate a picture as possible of the advantages and disadvantages of the various residence and contact options open to the child, it is essential that the parents and other witnesses feel able to express themselves candidly on highly personal issues without fear of public curiosity or comment.

PUBLIC JUDGMENTS

Article 6(1) also gives a right, in civil and criminal cases, to the public pronouncement of the judgment. There have been a number of cases concerning the precise meaning to be given to the words 'pronounced publicly'.[151] Fairly early on, the Strasbourg Court decided that it was not necessary for the judgment actually to be read out in open court and that States enjoyed a discretion as to the manner in which judgments would be made public. In the leading case of *Pretto*,[152] for example, the applicant complained that the judgment of the Court of Cassation on appeal had not been pronounced at a public hearing. The Strasbourg Court stressed the need to take account of the entirety of the proceedings. Furthermore, although the Court of Cassation's decision had not been pronounced in open court, anyone could consult or obtain a copy of it. There had therefore been no violation of Article 6(1). The form of publicity to be given to a judgment had to be assessed in the light of the special features of the proceedings in question and by reference to the object and purpose of Article 6(1).[153]

The requirement in Article 6(1) for public pronouncement of judgments, unlike that for a public hearing, is not expressed to be subject to any limitations. In the *P and B* case,[154] however, the Strasbourg Court agreed with the respondent State that it would frustrate the purpose of holding child residence hearings in private—namely, to protect the privacy of the children and their families and to promote justice—if judgments were freely

[150] *P and B v United Kingdom*, (Apps. 36337/97 and 35974/97), 24 April 2001, (2002) 34 EHRR 529, ECHR 2001-III.

[151] In the French text, 'doit être rendu publiquement.'

[152] *Pretto and others v Italy*, (App. 7984/77), 8 December 1983, Series A No 71, (1984) 6 EHRR 182.

[153] § 26. For a judgment affirming these criteria see *Fazliyski v Bulgaria*, (App. 40908/05), 16 April 2013.

[154] *P and B v United Kingdom*, (Apps. 36337/97 and 35974/97), 24 April 2001, (2002) 34 EHRR 529, ECHR 2001-III; see also earlier, in relation to 'public hearings'.

available to the public. It held that the requirements of Article 6(1) were satisfied in child residence cases because anyone who could establish an interest could, with the leave of the court, consult or obtain a copy of the full text of the orders and/or judgments of first instance courts, and that the judgments of the Court of Appeal and of first instance courts in cases of special interest were routinely published, thereby enabling the public to study the manner in which the courts generally approach such cases and the principles applied in deciding them.

The Court has stated that in national security cases, some limitations may be justified but these should not negate the protection afforded by Article 6:

> even in indisputable national security cases, such as those relating to terrorist activities, some States had opted to classify only those parts of the judicial decisions whose disclosure would compromise national security or the safety of others, thus illustrating that there existed techniques which could accommodate legitimate security concerns without fully negating fundamental procedural guarantees such as the publicity of judicial decisions.[155]

JUDGMENT IN A REASONABLE TIME

Excessive length of legal proceedings is the single most common complaint received by the Strasbourg Court. The Grand Chamber has encapsulated the requirements of judgment within a reasonable time as follows:

> 43. ... [The Court] reiterates that the 'reasonableness' of the length of proceedings must be assessed in the light of the circumstances of the case and with reference to the following criteria: the complexity of the case, the conduct of the applicant and of the relevant authorities and what was at stake for the applicant in the dispute....
>
> 45. The Court reiterates that it is for the Contracting States to organize their legal systems in such a way that their courts can guarantee to everyone the right to a final decision within a reasonable time in the determination of his civil rights and obligations....[156]

The right under Article 6(1) to 'a fair and public hearing within a reasonable time' may be compared with the right under Article 5(3) to trial within a reasonable time. However, while the right guaranteed under Article 5(3) applies only to persons detained on remand on a criminal charge, the scope of Article 6(1) is wider, extending to civil and criminal cases alike, and in criminal cases it applies whether the accused is detained or at liberty. The latter factor is important in assessing the reasonableness of the period, since, as stated earlier, Article 5(3) requires that there must be 'special diligence' in bringing the case to trial if the accused is detained. The object of the provision in Article 6(1) is to protect the individual concerned from living too long under the stress of uncertainty and, more generally, to ensure that justice is administered without delays which might jeopardize its effectiveness and credibility.[157]

In civil cases there is usually no problem in deciding when the period to be taken into consideration started: this is usually the date on which proceedings were initiated, for example by the issuing of a summons or writ.[158] In criminal cases, time begins to run as soon as the accused is officially notified of an allegation that he has committed a criminal offence; this may occur on a date prior to the case coming before the trial court, such as

[155] *Raza v Bulgaria*, (App. 31465/08), 11 February 2010, § 53; *Fazliyski v Bulgaria*, (App. 40908/05), 16 April 2013, § 69.

[156] *Frydlender v France*, (App. 30979/96), 27 June 2000 [GC], (2001) 31 EHRR 1152, ECHR 2000-VII, §§ 43 and 45.

[157] *Bottazzi v Italy*, (App. 34884/97), 28 July 1999, ECHR 1999-V.

[158] *Šakanovič v Slovenia*, (App. 32989/02), 13 March 2008, §§ 35–6.

the date of arrest, the date when the person concerned was officially notified that he would be prosecuted, or the date when preliminary investigations were opened.[159] The period to be taken into consideration lasts until the final determination of the case, and therefore includes appeal or cassation proceedings, proceedings to assess damages or sentence, and enforcement proceedings.[160] The State can be held responsible only for delays which are attributable to it; if the parties to the litigation or the defendant in a criminal case have caused or contributed to the delay, those periods of time are not taken into account.

As noted earlier, the reasonableness of the length of proceedings is assessed in the light of all the circumstances of the case, having regard in particular to the complexity of the issues before the national courts, the conduct of the parties to the dispute and of the relevant authorities, and what was at stake for the applicant.[161] For example, in a case where the applicant sought compensation from the State for having negligently infected him with HIV, 'special diligence' was required in view of the fact that the applicant was dying of AIDS.[162] Similarly, delays are less likely to be tolerable where the dispute concerns access between a parent and child, given the irreversible damage which can be done to such a relationship through lack of contact.[163]

The Court is called upon to determine more complaints about the unreasonable length of proceedings than any other type of case under the Convention. In the *Bottazzi* case[164] in 1999 it observed that the frequency with which violations of this provision were found against Italy reflected a continuing situation that had not been remedied, constituting a practice of systematic human rights breaches incompatible with the Convention.[165]

Applications complaining about the excessive length of proceedings in the national legal order are among the most numerous before the Strasbourg Court.[166] The result is that the Strasbourg Court's docket gets clogged up with repetitive cases which require formal adjudication. One response to such cases has been the use of variants of the pilot judgment procedure.[167] In the *Lukenda* case[168] the length of proceedings in Slovenia was identified as a systemic problem. The Strasbourg Court urged Slovenia to address the problem 'that has resulted from inadequate legislation and inefficiency in the administration of justice.'[169] The Court added:

> To prevent future violations of the right to a trial within a reasonable time, the Court encourages the respondent State to either amend the existing range of legal remedies or add new remedies so as to secure genuinely effective redress for violations of that right.[170]

This is a variant of the pilot judgment procedure since other pending cases before the Strasbourg Court were *not* adjourned while remedies were found within the national legal order for the look-alike cases. Indeed the Strasbourg Court subsequently produced around 200 further judgments against Slovenia in the look-alike cases where application had been

[159] *Eckle v Germany*, (App. 8130/78), 15 July 1982, Series A No 51, (1983) 5 EHRR 1.

[160] *Crowther v United Kingdom*, (App. 43741/00), 9 February 2005, § 24.

[161] *Frydlender v France*, (App. 30979/96), 27 June 2000, (2001) 31 EHRR 1152, ECHR 2000-VII, § 43; and *Davies v United Kingdom*, (App. 42007/98), 16 July 2002, (2002) 35 EHRR 720, § 26.

[162] *A and others v Denmark*, (App. 20826/92), 8 February 1996, (1996) 22 EHRR 458.

[163] *H v United Kingdom*, (App. 9580/81), 8 July 1987, Series A No 120, (1988) 10 EHRR 95.

[164] *Bottazzi v Italy*, (App. 34884/97), 28 July 1999, ECHR 1999-V.

[165] See also developments under Art. 13 noted in ch.7.

[166] Venice Commission, *Can Excessive Length of Proceedings be Remedied?* (Council of Europe Publishing, Strasbourg 2007).

[167] Described in ch.2.

[168] *Lukenda v Slovenia*, (App. 23032/02), 6 October 2005, (2008) 47 EHRR 728, ECHR 2005-X.

[169] § 93. [170] § 98.

made to the Strasbourg Court.[171] Following the judgment in the *Lukenda* case, the Slovenian Government established the Lukenda Project to address the problem, and passed legislation in 2006 to this end. In a later case, the Strasbourg Court expressed itself satisfied that the 2006 legislation did address the problem and required future applicants complaining of failure to deliver judgment in a reasonable time to use the remedies provided under the new legislation. Failure to do so would result in dismissal of their applications for failure to exhaust domestic remedies.[172]

In a pilot judgment against Germany,[173] the Court declined to stay similar pending cases, finding that 'continuing to process all length of proceedings cases in the usual manner will remind the respondent State on a regular basis of its obligation under the Convention and in particular resulting from this judgment.'[174] The Court found that Germany had ignored a large number of previous Strasbourg judgments dating back to 2006,[175] which may explain its apparent exasperation with Germany in relation to the continuing violation under Article 6.

In the *Scordino* case[176] the Strasbourg Court laid down certain conditions which it would expect national courts to establish in order to address problems about the speed of judicial proceedings.[177] The best solution is prevention, but where concerns arose, there should be a remedy designed to expedite proceedings which are lingering. This is more satisfactory than a system of compensation for proceedings which go on too long. States with systemic problems[178] are praised for introducing procedures both for seeking the expediting of proceedings and for awarding compensation where delays are excessive. But it may not be necessary to introduce both types of procedure.[179]

WAIVING RIGHTS

It is possible to waive some, but probably not all, of the rights under Article 6. One example is the right of a criminal defendant to be present at trial.[180] In a case involving a criminal trial, the Strasbourg Court said:

> Neither the letter nor the spirit of Article 6 of the Convention prevents a person from waiving of his own free will, either expressly or tacitly, the entitlement to the guarantees of a fair trial.... However, if it is to be effective for Convention purposes, a waiver of the right to take part in the trial must be established in an unequivocal manner and be attended by minimum safeguards commensurate to its importance.... Furthermore, it must not run counter to any important public interest....[181]

[171] E. Friberg, 'Pilot Judgments from the Court's Perspective' in Council of Europe, *Towards Stronger Implementation of the European Convention on Human Rights at National Level* (Council of Europe, Strasbourg 2008), 86, 91. See also *Scordino v Italy (No. 1)*, (App. 36813/97), 26 March 2006 [GC], (2007) 45 EHRR 207; ECHR 2006-V.

[172] *Korenjak v Slovenia*, (App. 463/03), Decision of 15 May 2007.

[173] *Rumpf v Germany*,(App. 46344/06), 2 September 2010.

[174] § 75, At the time of the decision, there were 55 similar cases against Germany pending before the Court.

[175] See §§ 65–9 which lists approximately 40 previous judgments, including a decision of a three judge committee on repetitive cases.

[176] *Scordino v Italy (No. 1)*, (App. 36813/97), 29 March 2006 [GC], (2007) 45 EHRR 207, ECHR 2006-V.

[177] §§ 182–9.

[178] Austria, Croatia, Spain, Poland, and the Slovak Republic are named: § 186.

[179] For a study of the effectiveness of national remedies in respect of excessive length of proceedings, see Venice Commission, *Can Excessive Length of Proceedings be Remedied?* (Council of Europe Publishing, Strasbourg 2007).

[180] For a similar waiver in a civil case, see *Zumtobel v Austria*, (App. 12235/86), 21 September 1993, Series A No 268-A, (1994) 17 EHRR 116.

[181] *Sejdovic v Italy*, (App. 56581/00), 1 March 2006 [GC], ECHR 2006-II, § 86. See also *Jones v United Kingdom*, (App. 30900/02), Decision of 9 September 2003. see also *Idalov v Russia*, (App. 5826/03), 22 May 2012.

An accused who absconds before trial cannot, for example, be said to have impliedly, through his conduct, waived the right to trial in his presence unless this was a clearly foreseeable consequence of his actions. Thus, in the *Jones* case,[182] where the possibility of trying a defendant *in absentia* had not been clearly established under English law at the time of the trial, the applicant, as a layman, could not have been expected to appreciate that his failure to attend on the date set for the start of the trial would result in his being tried and convicted in his absence and in the absence of legal representation. In a case concerning Italy,[183] the applicant could waive his rights to a full criminal trial and opted instead for a summary procedure, therefore getting the benefit of a reduced sentence. However after the applicant had chosen the summary procedure, Italy changed the law and removed the reduced sentence for murder. The Court held that this made the criminal proceedings unfair as the applicant was deprived of the advantages of the waiver and although he could withdraw from the agreement, it would only mean a return to a full trial and the possibility of a longer sentence. The Court noted that:

> although the Contracting States are not required by the Convention to provide for simplified procedures, where such procedures exist and have been adopted, the principles of fair trial require that defendants should not be deprived arbitrarily of the advantages attached to them.[184]

EXTRATERRITORIAL EFFECT

In the *Soering* judgment the Court observed that:

> The right to a fair trial in criminal proceedings, as embodied in Article 6 holds a prominent place in a democratic society. The Court does not exclude that an issue might exceptionally be raised under Article 6 by an extradition decision in circumstances where the fugitive has suffered or risks suffering a flagrant denial of a fair trial....[185]

It appears, therefore, that the extraterritorial application of Article 6 is limited to the criminal sphere. In the Court's case-law, the term 'flagrant denial of justice' has been synonymous with a trial which is manifestly contrary to the provisions of Article 6 or the principles embodied therein. The Court has indicated that the following circumstances would amount to a 'flagrant denial of justice': conviction in absentia with no possibility subsequently to obtain a fresh determination of the merits of the charge; a trial which is summary in nature and conducted with a total disregard for the rights of the defence; detention without any access to an independent and impartial tribunal to have the legality of the detention reviewed; deliberate and systematic refusal of access to a lawyer, especially for an individual detained in a foreign country.[186]

The applicants in the *Mamatkulov and Askarov* case[187] were charged with terrorist offences in Uzbekistan and fled to Turkey, where they were arrested and extradited.[188] After their return to Uzbekistan they were tried and convicted in private, without being

[182] *Jones v United Kingdom*, (App. 30900/02), Decision of 9 September 2003. See also *Sejdovic v Italy*, (App. 56581/00), 1 March 2006 [GC], ECHR 2006-II.

[183] *Scoppola v Italy No.2*, (App. 10249/03), 17 September 2009.

[184] § 139.

[185] *Soering v United Kingdom*, (App. 14038/88), 7 July 1989, Series A No 161, (1989) 11 HRR 439, § 113.

[186] *Othman (Abu Qatada) v United Kingdom*, (App. 8139/09), 17 January 2012, § 259.

[187] *Mamatkulov and Askarov v Turkey*, (Apps. 46827/99 and 46951/99), 4 February 2005 [GC], (2005) 41 EHRR 494, ECHR 2005-I.

[188] Contrary to the Court's request to Turkey under Rule 39 of the Rules of Court: see further ch.2.

given any access to their lawyers, and sentenced to long terms of imprisonment. They argued before the Strasbourg Court that, in extraditing them, Turkey had violated Article 6. The Grand Chamber held that, in principle, the extraditing State's responsibility could be engaged under Article 6 in these circumstances, but then bizarrely went on to find that since the risk of a flagrant denial of justice in the receiving State had to be assessed at the date of extradition, and since there was at that point—but only because Turkey rushed through the extradition contrary to the Court's request to wait until it had decided the case—very little available evidence about what awaited the applicants in Uzbekistan, there had been no violation. The view of the four dissenting members of the Grand Chamber is much to be preferred. They clarified that:

> What constitutes a 'flagrant' denial of justice has not been fully explained in the Court's jurisprudence but the use of the adjective is clearly intended to impose a stringent test of unfairness going beyond mere irregularities or lack of safeguards in the trial procedures such as might result in a breach of Article 6 if occurring within the Contracting State itself.... In our view, what the word 'flagrant' is intended to convey is a breach of the principles of fair trial guaranteed by Article 6 which is so fundamental as to amount to a nullification, or destruction of the very essence, of the right guaranteed by that Article.

The minority went on to find that documents available from Amnesty International before the extradition took place demonstrated substantial grounds for concluding that self-incriminating evidence extracted by torture was routinely used to secure guilty verdicts in Uzbekistan and that suspects were frequently detained and interrogated for many days without being given access to a lawyer. Given that the Turkish Government had not sought or received any assurances from Uzbekistan that the applicants would be given a fair trial, the Court should have found Turkey to have been in breach of Article 6.

The Court again addressed the issue of the removal of an applicant to another State where there is a risk of a violation of Article 6 in the *Othman*[189] case. The Court used the language of the minority in *Mamatkulov and Askarov* in stating that a 'flagrant denial of justice' means a nullification or destruction of the very essence of Article 6. As noted earlier, the Court elucidated some examples from the case-law of what would amount to a flagrant denial of justice including conviction in absentia, summary trial with no defence rights, detention without review, and no access to a lawyer. It went on to find that the use of evidence obtained by torture would also amount to a flagrant denial of justice.[190] The Court noted the stringent nature of the test for a flagrant denial of justice as there had not been a finding of a violation of Article 6 in removal cases since *Soering*.[191] It also distinguished *Othman* from *Mamatkulov and Askarov*,[192] on the grounds that the *Mamatkulov and Askarov* complaints were general and unspecified and dealt with an interim measure under Rule 39.[193] The Court found that the applicant had to show that there was a real risk of the use of evidence obtained by torture being used in a future trial if he was sent back to Jordan. On examination of the evidence, the Court found there was a real risk of torture evidence being used and so there was a flagrant denial of justice.[194]

The *Othman* judgment reflects the preferable dissenting opinion in *Mamatkulov and Askarov* and by setting the standard of proof placed on the applicant as a 'real risk' of a

[189] *Othman (Abu Qatada) v United Kingdom*, (App. 8139/09), 17 January 2012.

[190] §§ 259–67.

[191] *Soering v United Kingdom*, 7 July 1989, Series A No. 161, § 113.

[192] *Mamatkulov and Askarov v Turkey* (Apps. 46827/99 and 46951/99) 4 February 2005 [GC], (2005) 41 EHRR 494, ECHR 2005-I.

[193] §§ 284–5.

[194] §§ 281–5. The Court did not accept diplomatic assurances given to the UK by Jordan that the applicant would receive a fair trial, see ch.9.

flagrant denial of justice if removed from the State, the Court recognized the difficulties of gaining evidence in these cases.

CONCLUDING REMARKS

The Strasbourg Court's case-law on the right to a fair trial is extensive and has had a significant impact. For the individual concerned, a finding of a violation by the Court can lead to criminal proceedings being reopened or, in civil cases, the award of damages.[195] Perhaps more importantly, States all over Europe have amended and improved their legal procedures to comply with the Court's rulings. The perennial problem of excessive length of proceedings is beginning to be addressed in a systematic fashion in a number of Contracting Parties.

There are, however, limitations to the scope of the Court's review under Article 6. First, like the rest of the Convention, this provision protects only against violations imputable to the State; if unfairness is caused in legal proceedings by the negligence or misconduct of a lawyer (a private person), rather than, for example, the courts, no issue can arise.[196] Secondly, in accordance with the principle of subsidiarity and the 'fourth instance' doctrine, the Strasbourg Court has no power under Article 6 to substitute its own assessment of the evidence in a case for that of the national courts, and in connection with certain procedural matters, such as the need to call a particular witness, it will take issue with national courts only in exceptional circumstances.[197] Article 6 cannot be used as a vehicle to criticize the *content* of national law and the Court's interpretation of the expressions 'criminal charge' and 'civil rights and obligations', though extensive, does not embrace all types of legal proceedings.

Some of these lacunae are filled by other provisions in the Convention and Protocols. Article 1 of Protocol 7, for example, provides certain procedural rights to an alien lawfully resident in the territory of a State and facing expulsion. In addition, the Strasbourg Court has read procedural guarantees into some of the substantive rights under the Convention—the right to family life under Article 8, for example, requires that a fair procedure be followed when a child is taken into public care and, in accordance with Article 13, an effective domestic remedy must be provided in respect of all arguable breaches of the Convention.[198]

Chapter 13 is concerned with certain additional rights which arise in the context of criminal law and procedure.

[195] See ch.2.

[196] *Tripodi v Italy*, (App. 13743/88), 22 February 1994, Series A No 281-B, (1994) 18 EHRR 295.

[197] *Thomas v United Kingdom*, (App. 19354/02), Decision of 10 May 2005.

[198] See *Z and others v United Kingdom*, (App. 29392/95), 10 May 2001 [GC], (2002) 34 EHRR 97, ECHR 2001-V, and, in respect of the procedural guarantees available to asylum seekers, *Chahal v United Kingdom*, (App. 22414/93), 15 November 1996, (1997) 23 EHRR 413, ECHR 1996-V. See also ch.7.

13

ASPECTS OF THE CRIMINAL PROCESS

INTRODUCTION

This chapter examines the fair trial guarantees specific to criminal proceedings.[1] These are principally contained in paragraphs (2) and (3) of Article 6, although certain aspects of the right to a fair trial in Article 6(1) which apply only in criminal proceedings are also considered here. The second part of the chapter is concerned with the rule against retrospective legislation in Article 7 of the Convention, and a number of additional rights connected with the criminal process introduced by Articles 2 to 4 of Protocol 7.

THE SCOPE OF ARTICLE 6(2) AND (3)

Article 6, paragraphs (2) and (3) provide:

> 2. Everyone charged with a criminal offence shall be presumed innocent until proved guilty according to law.
> 3. Everyone charged with a criminal offence has the following minimum rights:
>   (a) to be informed promptly, in a language which he understands and in detail, of the nature and cause of the accusation against him;
>   (b) to have adequate time and facilities for the preparation of his defence;
>   (c) to defend himself in person or through legal assistance of his own choosing or, if he has not sufficient means to pay for legal assistance, to be given it free when the interests of justice so require;
>   (d) to examine or have examined witnesses against him and to obtain the attendance and examination of witnesses on his behalf under the same conditions as witnesses against him;
>   (e) to have the free assistance of an interpreter if he cannot understand or speak the language used in court.

Articles 6(2) and (3) apply to 'everyone charged with a criminal offence'. As with the expression 'in the determination…of any criminal charge against him' in Article 6(1),[2] the Court has adopted an autonomous interpretation, independent of the categorization of legal proceedings under national law.

In order to decide whether a person can be said to be 'charged with a criminal offence' within the meaning of Article 6, paragraphs (2) and (3), the Strasbourg Court has regard to the same *Engel* criteria[3] that it applies when assessing whether proceedings are 'in the

[1] See S. Trechsel, *Human Rights in Criminal Proceedings* (OUP, Oxford 2005). [2] See ch.12.

[3] *Engel and others v Netherlands*, (Apps. 5100/71, 5101/71, 5102/71, 5354/72, and 5370/72), 8 June 1976, Series A No 22, (1979–80) 1 EHRR 647; and see ch.12.

determination of any criminal charge' in paragraph (1). Indeed, there does not appear to be any significant difference between the scope of the two expressions except as regards the duration of the proceedings covered. In the *Phillips* case[4] the Court explained:

> [W]hilst it is clear that Article 6(2) governs criminal proceedings in their entirety, and not solely the examination of the merits of the charge... the right to be presumed innocent under Article 6(2) arises only in connection with the particular offence 'charged'. Once an accused has properly been proved guilty of that offence, Article 6(2) can have no application in relation to allegations made about the accused's character and conduct as part of the sentencing process, unless such accusations are of such a nature and degree as to amount to the bringing of a new 'charge' within the autonomous Convention meaning.

It can be presumed that the same is true of the application of Article 6(3). In contrast, Article 6(1) applies throughout criminal proceedings in their entirety, including sentencing.[5]

FAIR TRIAL GUARANTEES IN CRIMINAL CASES

In addition to the safeguards discussed in Chapter 12, which are necessary to a greater or lesser degree in both civil and criminal proceedings, the Strasbourg Court has held that a person charged with a criminal offence enjoys, *inter alia*, certain additional rights, some of which are considered below. The five rights set out in Article 6(3) are stated to be minimum rights in criminal cases.

POLICE METHODS OF INVESTIGATION

Even before charges are brought against an accused, unfairness on the part of the police responsible for the investigation against him or her may be sufficient to give rise to a violation of Article 6(1). In the *Teixeira de Castro* case,[6] for example, the applicant was offered money by undercover police officers to supply them with heroin. Although he had no previous criminal record, the applicant did have contacts who were able to get hold of drugs, and, tempted by the money, he complied with the officers' request. He was subsequently charged and convicted of a drugs offence. There was no evidence that the trial proceedings in themselves were unfair, but the Strasbourg Court held that, since the police officers appeared to have instigated the offence, which would not otherwise have been committed, from the outset the applicant was deprived of a fair trial in breach of Article 6(1). The Court contrasted the officers' actions with those of 'true' undercover agents, who conceal their identities in order to obtain information and evidence about crime, without actively inciting it; the second type of situation would not normally in itself give rise to any issue under Article 6.[7]

It is only in rare and extreme cases that the Strasbourg Court considers unlawful behaviour by the police or investigators sufficient in itself to bring the trial into breach of Article

[4] *Phillips v United Kingdom*, (App. 41087/98), 5 September 2001, ECHR 2001-VII. [5] See ch.12.

[6] *Teixeira de Castro v Portugal*, (App. 25829/94), 9 June 1998, (1999) 28 EHRR 101, ECHR 1998-IV.

[7] See *Lüdi v Switzerland*, (App. 12433/86), 15 June 1992, Series A No 238, (1993) 15 EHRR 440; *Eurofinacom v France*, (App. 58753/00), Decision of 17 September 2004, ECHR 2004-VII; and *Gorgievski v FYR of Macedonia*, (App. 18002/02), 16 July 2009. *Edwards and Lewis v United Kingdom*, (App. 39647/98 and 40461/98), 27 October 2004, ECHR 2004-X.

6. If the domestic courts choose to accept the prosecution evidence, the Strasbourg Court will usually accept that decision,[8] unless the abuse of process has been fundamental (as in *Teixeira de Castro* and the other cases on entrapment) or has in some way rendered the evidence against the accused unreliable (as in cases about the breach of the right to silence or the use of evidence gained through ill treatment, considered later.)

So, for example, in the *Khan* case,[9] the police had installed a hidden listening device in a hotel and obtained a recording of the applicant discussing a drugs deal. At the time of the investigation and trial there was no legislation in the United Kingdom governing the use of such apparatus by the police; in consequence, the Court found that Article 8 of the Convention had been violated.[10] It declined, however, the applicant's invitation to find that Article 6(1) had also been breached by virtue of the unlawful methods employed during the investigation. Instead, the Court examined the fairness of the proceedings as a whole and found no violation of Article 6(1), referring to the fact that the applicant had been afforded the opportunity to contest the authenticity of the recording and its admission in evidence. It had reached a similar conclusion in the *Schenk* case[11] where the obtaining of a tape recording by the police was unlawful not only according to the Convention, but also under domestic law.

The applicant in the *Allan* case[12] was suspected of shooting the manager of a convenience store during a robbery. During his interviews with the police he elected to remain silent. The police, frustrated with the lack of evidence, began secretly recording the applicant's conversations in prison with his girlfriend and co-accused. When it appeared that the recordings, although containing some incriminating statements, would not be enough to convict the applicant, they put him in a cell with a long-standing informant, whom they had carefully coached in the art of extracting information. After four months of shared custody, the informant was able to produce a 60-page statement regarding his conversations with the applicant, which was used at the latter's trial for murder.

The Strasbourg Court, following its *Khan* judgment, found that since the domestic courts had considered the recordings of the applicant's conversations with his girlfriend and co-accused to be reliable, their use at trial was not in breach of Article 6. Interestingly, however, the Court found that, in contrast to the position in *Khan*, the admissions allegedly made by the applicant to his informant cell-mate, and which formed the main or decisive evidence against him at trial, were not spontaneous and unprompted statements volunteered by the applicant, but were induced by persistent questioning. The informant, at the insistence of the police, had channelled their conversations into discussions of the murder in circumstances which could be regarded as the functional equivalent of interrogation, without any of the safeguards which would attach to a formal police interview, including the attendance of a solicitor and the issuing of the usual caution, and in circumstances where the applicant was feeling vulnerable and open to pressure. The Court concluded that the information gained by the informant had been obtained in defiance of the applicant's will and its use at trial impinged on his right to silence:

> While the right to silence and the privilege against self-incrimination are primarily designed to protect against improper compulsion by the authorities and the obtaining

[8] In accordance with the 'fourth instance' doctrine: see *Allan v United Kingdom*, (App. 48539/99), 5 November 2002, (2003) 36 EHRR 143, ECHR 2002-IX, § 42.

[9] *Khan v United Kingdom*, (App. 35294/97), 12 May 2000, (2001) 31 EHRR 1016; see also *Chalkley v United Kingdom*, (App. 63881/00), 12 June 2003, (2003) 37 EHRR 680; and *Perry v United Kingdom*, (App. 63737/00), 17 July 2003, (2004) 39 EHRR 76, ECHR 2003-IX.

[10] The procedure was not 'in accordance with law': see ch.14.

[11] *Schenk v Switzerland*, (App. 10862/84), 12 July 1988, Series A No 140, (1991) 13 EHRR 242.

[12] *Allan v United Kingdom*, (App. 48539/99), 5 November 2002, (2003) 36 EHRR 143, ECHR 2003-IX.

> of evidence through methods of coercion or oppression in defiance of the will of the accused, the scope of the right is not confined to cases where duress has been brought to bear on the accused or where the will of the accused has been directly overborne in some way. The right, which the Court has previously observed is at the heart of the notion of a fair procedure, serves in principle to protect the freedom of a suspected person to choose whether to speak or to remain silent when questioned by the police. Such freedom of choice is effectively undermined in a case in which, the suspect having elected to remain silent during questioning, the authorities use subterfuge to elicit, from the suspect, confessions or other statements of an incriminatory nature, which they were unable to obtain during such questioning and where the confessions or statements thereby obtained are adduced in evidence at trial.[13]

The following section is concerned with further aspects of the right to silence.

THE RIGHT TO SILENCE, THE PRINCIPLE AGAINST SELF-INCRIMINATION, AND THE PRESUMPTION OF INNOCENCE

Although it is not specifically mentioned in Article 6 of the Convention, the Strasbourg Court has held[14] that the right to silence and the right not to incriminate oneself are generally recognized international standards which lie at the heart of the notion of a fair criminal procedure under Article 6(1). These rights are closely linked to the principle enshrined in Article 6(2), that a person accused of a crime is innocent until proved guilty according to law.

As Lord Mustill has observed,[15] the 'right to silence' is a composite term which in fact encompasses a number of separate rights. He identified the following as protected, to a greater or lesser degree, by English law:

> (1) A general immunity, possessed by all persons and bodies, from being compelled on pain of punishment to answer questions posed by other persons or bodies.
> (2) A general immunity, possessed by all persons and bodies, from being compelled on pain of punishment to answer questions the answers to which may incriminate them.
> (3) A specific immunity, possessed by all persons under suspicion of criminal responsibility whilst being interviewed by police officers or others in similar positions of authority, from being compelled on pain of punishment to answer questions of any kind.
> (4) A specific immunity, possessed by accused persons undergoing trial, from being compelled to give evidence, and from being compelled to answer questions put to them in the dock.
> (5) A specific immunity, possessed by persons who have been charged with a criminal offence, from having questions material to the offence addressed to them by police officers or persons in a similar position of authority.
> (6) A specific immunity...possessed by accused persons undergoing trial, from having adverse comment made on any failure (a) to answer questions before the trial, or (b) to give evidence at the trial.

[13] § 51.

[14] *Saunders v United Kingdom*, (App. 19187/91), 17 December 1996, (1997) 23 EHRR 313, ECHR 1996-VI.

[15] *R. v Director of Serious Fraud Office, ex parte Smith*, [1992] 3 WLR 66.

The right not to incriminate oneself can include protection against the requirement to produce documents, as well as the right not to make statements or admissions.[16]

In the *Saunders* case[17] the applicant had been forced, through the threat of imprisonment for failure to answer questions, to give evidence to government-appointed investigators about an allegedly illegal share-support scheme. Transcripts of his interviews with the inspectors were subsequently used by the prosecution in criminal proceedings against him. The Strasbourg Court, which had found in an earlier judgment[18] that Article 6 did not apply to investigations of this kind, did not find any breach of the Convention arising from the inspectors' compulsory powers *per se*. However, it held that the subsequent use by the prosecution at the applicant's criminal trial of transcripts of the interviews violated his right to silence.

In its *Saunders* judgment the Court observed that the rationale of the right to silence and the principle against self-incrimination lies in the protection of the accused against improper compulsion by the authorities, thereby contributing to the avoidance of miscarriages of justice. The right not to incriminate oneself, in particular, presupposes that the prosecution in a criminal case should seek to prove its case against the accused without resort to evidence obtained through methods of coercion or oppression in defiance of the will of the accused. On the basis of this explanation, the Court drew a distinction between the right of an accused person to remain silent, which is protected by the Convention, and the use in criminal proceedings of material which might be obtained from the accused through the use of compulsory powers but which has an existence independent of the will of the suspect, such as documents acquired pursuant to a warrant, breath, blood and urine samples, and bodily tissue for the purpose of DNA testing, which is not inconsistent with Article 6.[19]

This distinction between documents, which can be said to have an 'independent existence' and statements or admissions was revisited by the Grand Chamber in the *Jalloh* case.[20] On his arrest on suspicion of dealing in drugs, Jalloh was seen to swallow a plastic bag. On authorization of the public prosecutor, an emetic was forcibly administered which resulted in Jalloh's regurgitating one bag which was found to contain cocaine. He complained that the use at his trial of this evidence violated his rights under Article 6 not to incriminate himself. The Grand Chamber noted that it could be said that the bag of cocaine was evidence which had an existence independent of the will of the accused, but found a number of features of the case which distinguished it from that line of authority. The compulsory administration of emetics was used to retrieve the material against the will of the accused, and the degree of force required was considerable, and was found to violate Article 3.[21] Summarizing its position the Strasbourg Court said:

> In order to determine whether the applicant's right not to incriminate himself has been violated, the Court will have regard, in turn, to the following factors: the nature and degree of compulsion used to obtain the evidence; the weight of the public interest in the investigation

[16] *JB v Switzerland*, (App. 31827/96), 3 May 2001, ECHR 2001-III. See also *Funke and others v France*, (App. 10828/84), 25 February 1993, Series A No 256-A, (1993) 16 EHRR 297.

[17] *Saunders v United Kingdom*, (App. 19187/91), 17 December 1996; (1997) 23 EHRR 313, ECHR 1996-VI.

[18] *Fayed v United Kingdom*, (App. 17101/90), 21 September 1994, Series A No 294-B, (1994) 18 EHRR 393.

[19] This distinction was adopted and applied by the Privy Council in *Brown v Stott* [2001] 2 WLR 817 where it held that a statutory requirement to provide a breath specimen when suspected of driving with excess alcohol, with a maximum penalty of a £1,000 fine or six months' imprisonment for non-compliance, was not incompatible with Article 6(2). See also App. 8239/78, *X v Netherlands*, (1979) 16 DR 184, where the Commission came to a similar conclusion.

[20] *Jalloh v Germany*, (App. 54810/00), 11 July 2006 [GC], (2007) 44 EHRR 667, ECHR 2006-IX.

[21] The prohibition of torture, and inhuman or degrading treatment. See ch.9.

and punishment of the offence at issue; the existence of any relevant safeguards in the procedure; and the use to which any material so obtained is put.[22]

By eleven votes to six, the Grand Chamber found that Article 6 had been violated.

There is also considerable case-law under paragraphs (1) and (2) of Article 6 on the extent to which a criminal court may draw an inference of guilt from an accused's silence. This is the aspect of the right to silence referred to at point (6) in Lord Mustill's list quoted earlier, and the question is also relevant to the presumption of innocence, which requires that the burden of proving an offence lies on the prosecution.

The applicant in the *Telfner* case[23] was convicted of an offence involving a hit-and-run driving incident. The victim of the incident had been able to give the police the make and registration number of the car, but could not identify the driver. The applicant elected not to give evidence at trial, and the prosecution case relied almost entirely on the findings of the police that the applicant was the principal user of the car (registered in his mother's name) and had not been at home at the time of the accident. The Strasbourg Court held that, although it might be permissible for a court to draw an inference of guilt from an accused's silence, where the evidence adduced was so strong that the only common-sense inference to be drawn was that the accused had no answer to the case against him, in the instant case the evidence for the prosecution was extremely weak. In requiring the applicant to provide an explanation, without having first established a convincing prima facie case against him, the courts in effect shifted the burden of proof from the prosecution to the defence, giving rise to a violation of Article 6(2).

The *O'Halloran and Francis* case[24] concerned requirements under English legislation that the registered keeper must provide evidence of who was the driver of a vehicle caught by a roadside speed camera. Failure to comply is an offence. The question before the Strasbourg Court was whether the compulsion to make statements which might incriminate a person or lead to their incrimination is compatible with Article 6 of the Convention. The Court, relying on the test it had laid down in the *Jalloh* case,[25] concluded that there was no violation of this provision. Owners of motor vehicles know they are subject to a regulatory regime, and only limited information was required under the legislation in issue.[26]

In the *John Murray* case[27] the Court found that it was compatible with Article 6(1) for the trial judge (who sat alone, without a jury) to draw an inference of guilt from the fact that the applicant had remained silent under police questioning and at trial. The evidence against him was strong and, in accordance with Article 3 of the Criminal Evidence (Northern Ireland) Order 1988, he had been warned at the time of his arrest that he did not have to say anything, but that his failure to mention any fact which he subsequently relied on in his defence might be treated in court as supporting the case against him.

It is clear, therefore, that the Court does not consider that the drawing of inferences from an accused's silence is in itself incompatible with Article 6, as long as judicial

[22] *Jalloh v Germany*, (App. 54810/00), 11 July 2006 [GC], (2007) 44 EHRR 667, ECHR 2006-IX, § 117.

[23] *Telfner v Austria*, (App. 33501/96), 20 March 2001, (2002) 34 EHRR 207.

[24] *O'Halloran and Francis v United Kingdom*, (Apps. 15809/02 and 25624/02), 29 June 2007 [GC], (2008) 46 EHRR 397, ECHR 2008-nyr.

[25] *Jalloh v Germany*, (App. 54810/00), 11 July 2006 [GC], (2007) 44 EHRR 667, ECHR 2006-IX, see earlier in this chapter.

[26] For a contrasting case, see *Krumpholz v Austria*, (App. 1321/05), 18 June 2010, where the Court found that a conviction for a speeding offence where the applicant was forced to say who was driving was a violation of Article 6 due to the lack of procedural safeguards.

[27] *Murray (John) v United Kingdom*, (App. 18731/91), 8 February 1996, (1996) 22 EHRR 29, ECHR 1996-I.

safeguards operate to ensure fairness. In the *Condron* case[28] it found a violation of Article 6(1), because the trial judge failed to direct the jury that they could draw an adverse inference only if satisfied that the applicants' silence at the police interview could only sensibly be attributed to their having no answer to the accusations against them, or none that would stand up to cross-examination. The applicants were heroin addicts and suffering from withdrawal at the time of their interviews with the police on suspicion of drug dealing. Although they were cautioned by the investigating officers that it might harm their defence if they failed to mention something which they might later rely on in court, and were found by a police doctor to be fit for questioning, they made no comment on the advice of their solicitor, who disagreed with the doctor's assessment.

This case illustrates the Court's tendency to assess the fairness of proceedings looked at as a whole, rather than to formulate rigid procedural rules.[29] If the trial judge had exercised his discretion properly, no unfairness would have been caused to the accused. It was, however, impossible for the Court of Appeal to rectify the problem (without ordering a retrial) because of the difficulty of assessing the extent to which the jury had been influenced by the misdirection.

THE BURDEN OF PROOF AND STATUTORY PRESUMPTIONS

In the *Salabiaku* case,[30] the Court was asked to consider the compatibility with Article 6(2) of a law reversing the burden of proof in respect of certain elements of an offence. The applicant had been found in possession of illegal drugs at a Paris airport. He was not, however, charged with and convicted of an offence of simple possession, but instead with offences of smuggling and importation, which include an element of knowledge or intent. The French Customs Code setting out the offences stated generally that 'the person in possession of contraband goods shall be deemed liable for the offence.' The Court rejected the Commission's opinion that Article 6(2) merely provided a procedural guarantee to be observed by the courts, and held that the provision also placed a duty on legislators to respect the rights of the accused when framing offences. It observed, generally, that:

> Presumptions of fact or of law operate in every legal system. Clearly, the Convention does not prohibit such presumptions in principle. It does, however, require the Contracting States to remain within certain limits in this respect as regards criminal law.

The Court underlined that it was not its task to consider legislation *in abstracto*, and instead examined the facts of the particular case. It found that the presumption created by the Code and applied to the applicant was not irrebuttable, since the courts which had dealt with the applicant had followed case-law to the effect that once the fact of possession had been established by the prosecution, the burden shifted to the defence to prove, if they could, that the accused was the victim of '*force majeure*' or for some reason could not have been expected to know about the goods in his possession, in which case he would have been acquitted. The courts had examined all the evidence, including evidence that the applicant

[28] *Condron v United Kingdom*, (App. 35382/97), 2 May 2000, (2001) 31 EHRR 1, ECHR 2000-IV.

[29] For a further example see *Sievert v Germany*, (App. 29881/07), 19 July 2012, § 67, where the Court noted that the Court examined the proceedings as a whole and whether there were counterbalancing factors that enable the proceedings to be fair under Article 6.

[30] *Salabiaku v France*, (App. 10519/83), 7 October 1988, Series A No 141-A, (1991) 13 EHRR 379. See also *Hoang v France*, (App. 13191/87), 25 September 1992, Series A No 243, (1993) 16 EHRR 53; *Radio France and others v France*, (App. 53984/00), 30 March 2004, (2005) 40 EHRR 706, ECHR 2004-X; and *Phillips v United Kingdom*, (App. 41087/98), 5 September 2001, ECHR 2001-VII.

had shown no surprise when the drugs were discovered in his suitcase, and had found him guilty without relying on the statutory presumption. In these circumstances, there had been no violation of Article 6(2).

It is interesting to speculate as to what type of reversed burden of proof the Court would find inconsistent with Article 6. The *Telfner, John Murray*, and *Condron* cases underline that Article 6(1) and (2) require the prosecution at least to establish prima facie that the accused has committed an offence, and that it is permissible for a court to draw an inference of guilt from the accused's failure to provide an explanation only where this is the sole common-sense conclusion to be drawn. The legislation under examination in the *Salabiaku* case placed the onus on the prosecution to establish possession of prohibited goods, and then required the court to infer that the accused had knowledge of them, in the absence of proof to the contrary. Again, particularly having regard to the way in which this law was actually applied in the applicant's case, it might be said that the reversal of the burden of proof only went so far as to permit the court to draw a 'common-sense' inference.

In the *Phillips* case which concerned confiscation of assets from a convicted drug trafficker, the statutory presumption came into operation once the prosecution had established (1) that the accused had derived some benefit from drug-trafficking (which must in many cases follow almost automatically from his or her conviction for the offence which triggers the confiscation procedure); and (2) that the accused had owned property or incurred expenditure at any time since his conviction or during the period of six years before the date on which the criminal proceedings were commenced. The burden then passed to the accused to prove that the property or expenditure did not represent the proceeds of drug-trafficking.

Owning property and spending money are activities undertaken by almost everyone in western society and, unlike possessing illegal drugs, are not prima facie unlawful. In finding no violation of Article 6(1), the Court appears to have been influenced by the fact that had the applicant's account of his financial dealings been true, it would not have been difficult for him to rebut the statutory assumption; most people who, for example, buy a house, are able to show where the money came from without great difficulty. The Court indicated that 'an issue relating to the fairness of the procedure might arise in circumstances where the amount of a confiscation order was based on the value of assumed hidden assets', presumably because of the difficulty which would be involved in disproving the existence and source of unspecified and unsubstantiated articles. The Court's acceptance of the reversed burden of proof in this case might also be explained by the fact that it operated in the context of a procedure analogous to sentencing, to enable the national court to assess the amount at which a confiscation order should properly be fixed. It is possible that if a similarly sweeping presumption were applied to facilitate a court in finding a person guilty of an offence, this might give rise to a violation of Article 6(1) and (2).

OTHER ASPECTS OF THE PRESUMPTION OF INNOCENCE

Article 6(2) is not merely concerned with the burden of proof. It also prohibits the authorities from saying or doing anything which indicates that they believe a person is guilty of an offence, unless or until guilt is proven.[31] This does not prevent the authorities from informing the public about criminal investigations in progress, but it does require them to be discreet and circumspect in order to preserve the presumption of innocence. So a reference, without qualification, at a press conference conducted by senior officials that a person was an accomplice to murder amounted to a declaration of guilt in breach of

[31] *Borovský v Slovakia*, (App. 24528/02), 2 June 2009.

Article 6(2).[32] In this case the Strasbourg Court for the first time indicated that the protection of Article 6(2) may be infringed not only by a judge or a court, but also by other public authorities.

In a group of related cases,[33] statements were made, after criminal proceedings had been discontinued and where the defendants were seeking reimbursement of expenses, indicating some probability that the defendants were guilty. On close analysis, the Court concluded that the terms used by the judges described a state of suspicion rather than a finding of guilt. Article 6(2) had not been violated. This issue was taken up in the *Sekanina* case.[34] Sekanina had been tried and acquitted for the murder of his wife, then brought proceedings for reimbursement of costs and compensation for detention on remand for just over a year. The claim for compensation was dismissed on the ground that his acquittal had not dispelled the suspicion of his having committed the murder. The respondent State argued that the indications given by the court merely referred to the continued existence of suspicion, which had been accepted in earlier cases, and did not reflect the opinion that Sekanina was guilty. The Court unanimously distinguished the earlier cases which concerned the discontinuance of proceedings before a final determination, whereas the present case concerned proceedings following an acquittal. The statements made by the national court were inconsistent with the presumption of innocence.[35]

In contrast, the Court found no violation in a similar case involving proceedings following a conviction that had been overturned by the Court of Appeal in the UK. In *Allen v United Kingdom*,[36] the applicant had been convicted of the manslaughter of her child. The Court of Appeal found the expert medical evidence unreliable and so acquitted the applicant, stating that the time that had passed and the fact the applicant had served her sentence meant that there was no need for a retrial. Her application for compensation for a miscarriage of justice was refused. She challenged this decision. This was dismissed by the High Court as the Court of Appeal had not found that she should be acquitted due to 'reasonable doubt' but that the new evidence 'created the possibility' that she may have been acquitted. The applicant argued that the High Court reasoning violated her presumption of innocence under Article 6.

The Court noted that following from the post-*Sekanina* case-law there is:

> no single approach to ascertaining the circumstances in which that Article will be violated in the context of proceedings which follow the conclusion of criminal proceedings. As illustrated by the Court's existing case-law, much will depend on the nature and context of the proceedings in which the impugned decision was adopted.[37]

The Court also noted that the language used by the decision maker was of critical importance when assessing decisions such as these. The Court found that her acquittal was not based on the merits of the case but was more akin to the discontinuing of proceedings. The Court concluded that neither the rules for compensation nor the wording of the decision had violated

[32] *Allenet de Ribemont v France*, (App. 15175/89), 10 February 1995, Series A No 308, (1996) 22 EHRR 582. See, more recently, *Lavents v Latvia*, (App. 58442/00), 28 November 2002; and *YB and others v Turkey*, (Apps. 48173/99 and 48319/99), 28 October 2004; compare *Zollmann v United Kingdom*, (App. 62902/00), Decision of 27 November 2003.

[33] *Lutz v Germany*, (App. 9912/82), 25 August 1987, (1988) 10 EHRR 182; *Nölkenbockhoff v Germany*, (App. 10300/83), 25 August 1987, (1988) 10 EHRR 163.

[34] *Sekanina v Austria*, (App. 13126/87), 25 August 1993, Series A No 266-A, (1994) 17 EHRR 221.

[35] See, in a similar vein, *Baars v Netherlands*, (App. 44320/98), 28 October 2003, (2004) 39 EHRR 538; *Del Latte v Netherlands*, (App. 44760/98), 9 November 2004; and *Capeau v Belgium*, (App. 42914/98), 13 January 2005. ECHR 2005-I.

[36] *Allen v United Kingdom*, (App. 25424/09), 12 July 2013.

[37] § 125.

Article 6. The English Courts had not commented on whether the applicant would be likely to be acquitted or convicted in a retrial or whether the evidence indicated guilt or innocence. It was for a jury in English criminal law to determine guilt or innocence and the Court of Appeal had not impinged on this role.[38]

The Court has found that the use of a dock or metal cage during legal proceedings may in some circumstances be degrading under Article 3, depending on grounds such as the security risk posed by the applicant and the amount of publicity surrounding the proceedings.[39] However, the Court has not yet found that the use of the dock or cage undermines the presumption of evidence. In the *Titarenko* case,[40] the applicant argued that the use of a cage prevented him from communicating properly with his lawyer. The Court rejected the argument, finding that the use of the cage was proportionate given the security risks, that although communication was limited he could still communicate with his lawyer if necessary and he had not raised the issue before the domestic court. Other jurisdictions have removed the dock, with concerns expressed about an interference with the right to consult a lawyer, as well as issues surrounding dignity.[41] The absence of the dock in some European States[42] and the removal of metal cages in States such as Armenia and Georgia[43] may indicate an increasing concern about the impact of the dock on dignity and the presumption of innocence, though the Strasbourg Court has maintained the principle of examining the proceedings as a whole to consider if they are unfair.[44]

USE OF EVIDENCE OBTAINED BY TORTURE

Article 15 of the United Nation's Convention against Torture provides:[45]

> Every State Party shall ensure that any statement which is established to have been made as a result of torture shall not be invoked as evidence in any proceedings, except against a person accused of torture as evidence that the statement was made.

There is no corresponding provision in the European Convention, but it is not surprising that the Strasbourg Court has read such an obligation into Article 6. The issue was touched on in the *Jalloh* case,[46] although that case concerned not statements, but physical evidence: cocaine regurgitated following the forcible administration of an emetic. In the course of its judgment, the Strasbourg Court said:

> ...different considerations apply to evidence recovered by a measure found to violate Article 3. An issue may arise under Article 6 § 1 in respect of evidence obtained in violation

[38] §§ 131–6.

[39] See ch.9. *Ramishvili and Kokhreidze v Georgia*, (App. 1704/06), 27 January 2009, §§ 96–102; *Ashot Harutyunyan v Armenia*, (App. 34334/04), 15 June 2010, § 126; *Khodorkovskiy v Russia*, (App. 5829/04), 31 May 2011, §§ 120–6; *Titarenko v Ukraine*, (App. 31720/02), 20 September 2012; *Svinarenko and Slyadnev v Russia*, (Apps. 32541/08 and 43441/08), 11 December 2012 (referred to Grand Chamber 29 April 2013).

[40] *Titarenko v Ukraine*, (App. 31720/02), 20 September 2012.

[41] In USA see *Commonwealth v Boyd*, 92 A.705 (Pa.1914), US Court of Appeal for the First Circuit; *Young v Callahan*, 700 F.2d 32, 36.

[42] Such as Denmark and the Netherlands, see L. Mulcahy, 'Putting the Defendant in Their Place. Why do we still use the Dock in criminal proceedings?' (2013) 53*Brit J of Criminology*, 1159–1136.

[43] As noted in *Ashot Harutyunyan v Armenia*, (App. 34334/04), 15 June 2010, § 118.

[44] Several European States including the UK continue to use the dock in legal proceedings indicating that there may be concern about its use but as yet no consensus. See L. Mulcahy, 'Putting the Defendant in Their Place. Why do we still use the Dock in criminal proceedings?' (2013) 53*Brit J of Criminology*, 1159–1136 for a discussion on the use of the dock in the UK and other jurisdictions.

[45] See generally, T. Theniel, 'The admissibility of evidence obtained by torture under international law' (2006) 17 EJIL 349.

[46] *Jalloh v Germany*, (App. 54810/00), 11 July 2006 [GC], (2007) 44 EHRR 667, ECHR 2006-IX.

> of Article 3 of the Convention, even if the admission of such evidence was not decisive in securing the conviction (see *İçöz v. Turkey* (dec.), no. 54919/00, 9 January 2003; and *Koç v. Turkey* (dec.), no. 32580/96, 23 September 2003). The Court reiterates in this connection that Article 3 enshrines one of the most fundamental values of democratic societies. Even in the most difficult circumstances, such as the fight against terrorism and organised crime, the Convention prohibits in absolute terms torture and inhuman or degrading treatment or punishment, irrespective of the victim's conduct. Unlike most of the substantive clauses of the Convention, Article 3 makes no provision for exceptions and no derogation from it is permissible under Article 15 § 2 even in the event of a public emergency threatening the life of the nation...[47]

The Court dealt directly with evidence obtained by ill-treatment in the *Gäfgen* case.[48] The applicant complained that his conviction was based, in part, on evidence obtained from him under duress. He had been threatened by two police officers with serious violence to his person in an interaction lasting about ten minutes. In response to these threats, he had led the police to the place where a body had been left. He argued that the 'real' evidence flowing from the initial confession and the finding of the body should have been excluded from his trial. The Court found that he had suffered inhuman treatment and that the absolute nature of Article 3 meant no statement extracted under ill-treatment should be used in a trial. However, the Court differentiated between torture and other forms of ill-treatment. All evidence gathered through torture whether from the confession or flowing from it are excluded. If the victim suffers inhuman or degrading treatment the initial confession is excluded. However, if the evidence flowing from it is not relied upon to find guilt then the overall trial can still held to be fair.[49] In *Gäfgen*, the Court found no violation of Article 6. The distinction between a confession and evidence flowing from the confession was criticized by the dissenting opinions, who took a more holistic approach by describing the evidence gathering process as an 'organic whole'.[50] The Court applied *Gäfgen* in *Alchagin v Russia*.[51] The applicant had confessed to theft and was later convicted. He claimed his confession was made following inhuman and degrading treatment. The Court found that the confession was indeed made under such duress, but went on to find that the trial was not rendered unfair. The applicant had made later confessions and had the benefit of legal representation when he made the statement and could have challenged the admissibility during the trial. Therefore there were safeguards in place to ensure a fair trial. However, this seems to be an exceptional case, where the presence of a lawyer when the statement was made as well as the other safeguards distinguished the case from several other cases where a violation was found.[52]

[47] § 99.

[48] *Gäfgen v Germany*, (App. 22978/05), 1 June 2010 which involved the kidnap for ransom of a child, who was subsequently murdered.

[49] § 172-178. The majority opinion can be said to reflect the distinction made in national legal systems, for example see in England and Wales, sections 76 and 78 of the Police and Criminal Evidence Act 1984 (c.60); Section 76 concerns the exclusion of confession evidence due to the use of oppressive means to obtain it or unreliability, whereas section 78 gives the court discretion to exclude evidence having regard to all the circumstances, including as to how it was obtained, where its inclusion would have such an adverse effect on the fairness of proceedings that the Court should not admit it.

[50] Joint Partly Dissenting Opinion of Judges Rozakis, Tulkens, Jebens, Ziemele, Bianku and Power, § 5.

[51] *Alchagin v Russia*, (App. 20212/05), 7 January 2012; see also *El Haski v Belgium*, (App. 649/08), 25 September 2012, where the Court applied the principle outlined in *Gäfgen* to third party evidence, § 85.

[52] The Court has found a violation of Article 6 in similar cases were there has been an absence of legal counsel and use of confession evidence without any safeguards *Yaremenko v Ukraine*, (App. 32092/02), 12 June 2008, §§ 74–81; *Pavlenko v Russia*, (App. 42371/02), 1 April 2010, §§ 97–120; *Shishkin v Russia*, (App. 18280/04), 7 July 2011, §§ 148–52.

The Court examined the use of incriminating third party statements in *Kaciu and Katorri v Albania*.[53] The second applicant in the case objected to the use of the first applicant's statement against her. The court found that the first applicant's statement had been illicited by ill-treatment without safeguards and so there was a violation of Article 6. With regard to the use of his statement against the second applicant, the Court noted the Grand Chamber decision in *Othman*[54] where it found the use of torture evidence could lead to a 'flagrant denial of justice' and concluded:

> that the admission in evidence of incriminating statements obtained from a third party as a result of torture renders the proceedings as a whole unfair, irrespective of whether such evidence was decisive for securing the applicant's own conviction. Such evidence should not be afforded the cloak of legality and used at the trial of and for the conviction of the accused as that would irretrievably damage the fairness of the trial.[55]

In *El Haski v Belgium*,[56] the Court examined the use of evidence gained from third parties outside of the State, in this case Morocco. The court noted that if the evidence arises from a legal system that does not offer 'meaningful guarantees of an independent, impartial and serious examination of allegations of torture or inhuman and degrading treatment, it will be necessary and sufficient for the complainant... to show that there is a "real risk" that the impugned statement was thus obtained.'[57] The State must then investigate to determine if there is a risk.

PROMPT NOTIFICATION OF THE CHARGES AND INTERPRETATION

The possibility for an accused to know the case against him is essential to the preparation of a defence. The duty on the State under Article 6(3)(a) is more explicit than the requirement of notification of the reason for detention in Article 5(2), and demands prompt information in a language the accused understands and in detail. Article 6(3)(e) grants the right to free interpretation if a person cannot understand or speak the language used in court. This issue has often been raised in conjunction with the right to notification of the charges and the two issues will be considered together.

Whereas the right to publicly funded legal assistance does not arise in every case, interpretation, where necessary, must be provided free regardless of the means of the defendant and must extend to the translation or interpretation of all documents or statements in the proceedings which it is essential for the defendant to understand in order to have the benefit of a fair trial.[58]

The applicant in the *Cuscani* case[59] was the Italian manager of 'The Godfather Restaurant' in Newcastle. He was prosecuted for serious tax offences, carrying a substantial prison sentence, and pleaded guilty. At the sentencing hearing the applicant's counsel told the judge that the applicant's 'English is poor and his Italian is very Southern'. The proceedings were adjourned, but at the next hearing no interpreter was present, contrary to the judge's

[53] *Kaciu and Katorri v Albania*, (Apps. 33192/07 and 33194/07), 25 June 2013.

[54] *Othman (Abu Qatada) v United Kingdom*, (App. 8139/09), 17 January 2012.

[55] § 128.

[56] *El Haski v Belgium*, (App. 649/08), 25 September 2012.

[57] § 88.

[58] *Luedicke, Belkacem and Koç v Germany*, (Apps. 6210/73, 6877/75, and 7132/75), 28 November 1978, Series A No 29, (1979–80) 2 EHRR 149. See also *Öztürk v Germany*, (App. 8544/79), 21 February 1984, Series A No 73, (1984) 6 EHRR 409 and *Kamasinski v Austria*, (App. 9783/82), 19 December 1989, Series A No 168, (1991) 13 EHRR 36.

[59] *Cuscani v United Kingdom*, (App. 32771/96), 24 September 2002, (2003) 36 EHRR 11. See also *Brozicek v Italy*, (App. 10964/84), 19 December 1989, Series A No 167, (1990) 12 EHRR 371.

order. The applicant's counsel, however, informed the judge that he thought it would be all right to proceed because the applicant's brother was present and had quite good English, and they would 'make do and mend'. The Court, finding a violation of Article 6(1)(e), held that the judge was 'the ultimate guardian of the fairness of the proceedings' and should not have been satisfied with the defence counsel's assurances, particularly since it was apparent that counsel himself had difficulty in communicating with his client.

The *Kamasinski* case[60] concerned an American charged with offences in Austria. He was provided with an interpreter during the pre-trial stages of the criminal process and a lawyer who was a registered English language interpreter was appointed to represent him at his trial. He nevertheless complained that he had not received English translations of the indictment. The Court held that Article 6(3)(a) did not require that the notification of the charge be given in writing nor translated in written form. In some cases, a difficulty could arise under the provision if no written translation of the indictment was provided, but in the circumstances of the present case, it was clear that the oral explanations provided to the applicant in his first language constituted sufficient information of the charges against him.

An accused person whose own conduct has been the principal cause of his not receiving notification of the charges against him cannot complain under Article 6(3)(a).[61] Discrepancies resulting from a clerical error in the statement of the provision which is the basis of the charge will not amount to a violation of the provision.[62]

The Court has found that an interpreter should be provided during pre-trial proceedings including the investigation stage, unless it is demonstrated in the light of the circumstances of the case, that there are compelling reasons to restrict access.[63] It has also found that illiterate detainees require additional protection, for example in cases where the State claims the detainee waived her right to a lawyer.[64]

TIME AND FACILITIES TO RUN A DEFENCE

The obligation in Article 6(3)(b) that those charged with a criminal offence are to have adequate time and facilities for the preparation of a defence is linked to the right in Article 6(3)(c) to personal representation or legal assistance. There are comparatively few cases in which Article 6(3)(b) alone has resulted in a violation of the Convention.

A pragmatic view is taken of the nature of the right. For example, where an accused person's lawyer has access to documentation, but not the accused himself, there will be no breach of the provision,[65] and a failure by the court to comply with a procedural request will not give rise to a breach if it seems that the procedure would not have served a useful purpose.[66]

The applicant in the *Hadjianastassiou* case[67] wished to challenge in the Court of Cassation the legality of proceedings in the Court of Appeal. The Court of Appeal's decision had been read out in summary form on 22 November 1985, but the full reasons were not disclosed until 10 January 1986. The time limit for applying to the Court of Cassation

60 *Kamasinski v Austria*, (App. 9783/82), 19 December 1989, Series A No 168, (1991) 13 EHRR 36.

61 *Hennings v Germany*, (App. 12129/86), 16 December 1992, Series A No 215-A, (1993) 16 EHRR 83, § 26.

62 *Gea Catalán v Spain*, (App. 19160/91), 10 February 1995, Series A No 309, (1995) 20 EHRR 266.

63 *Diallo v Sweden*, (App. 13205/07), 5 January 2010; *Saman v Turkey*, (App. 35292/05), 5 April 2011.

64 *Saman v Turkey*, (App. 35292/05), 5 April 2011, § 35.

65 *Kamasinski v Austria*, (App. 9783/82), 19 December 1989, Series A No 168, (1991) 13 EHRR 36.

66 *Bricmont v Belgium*, (App. 10857/84), 7 July 1989, Series A No 158, (1990) 12 EHRR 217.

67 *Hadjianastassiou v Greece*, (App. 12945/87), 16 December 1992, Series A No 252-A, (1993) 16 EHRR 219.

was five days from the date of the Court of Appeal's judgment (in November), and after the expiry of the time limit applicants were barred from expanding upon any legal argument. The Strasbourg Court concluded that the rights of the defence had been restricted to such a degree that there had been a violation of Article 6(3)(b) taken in conjunction with Article 6(1).

LEGAL ASSISTANCE

Article 6(3)(c) provides that 'everyone charged with a criminal offence' has three minimum rights: (1) to defend himself in person, or (2) to defend himself through legal assistance of his own choosing, and (3) if he has not sufficient means to pay for legal assistance, to be given it free when the interests of justice so require. The aim of this provision is to ensure that defendants have the possibility of presenting an effective defence.[68]

Only shortcomings in legal representation which are imputable to the State authorities can give rise to a violation of Article 6(3)(c). In the *Tripodi* case,[69] the applicant's lawyer was ill and unable to attend a hearing before the Court of Cassation, which refused his request for an adjournment and determined the matter in his absence, on the basis of written pleadings. It appeared that the lawyer had done little to ensure that he was replaced for the day of the hearing but the Strasbourg Court, looking at the proceedings as a whole, found no violation.

The rights in Article 6(3)(c) are capable of applying pre-trial, since absence of legal representation at this stage could in certain circumstances affect the fairness of the proceedings as a whole.[70] In the *Öcalan* case[71] the applicant, the leader of the PKK, was detained on a small island in the Marmara Sea near Istanbul pending trial for numerous terrorist offences. The island was declared a military zone and access to it was strictly controlled. The applicant was denied contact with his lawyers for the first week of his detention, during which time he was extensively questioned and made a number of admissions. Subsequently, the applicant was allowed to consult with his lawyers, but for two one-hour periods a week, and only within hearing of the prison guards. Neither the applicant nor his lawyers were given sight of the voluminous case-file until very shortly before the hearing. The overall effect of these difficulties so restricted the rights of the defence that the principle of a fair trial was contravened, giving rise to a violation of Article 6(1), taken together with Article 6(3)(b) and (c).

The right to see a lawyer in the early stages of a police investigation is not absolute, and, where there is a good reason, can be subjected to restrictions. In the *John Murray* case[72] the respondent State argued that the problems involved in investigating terrorist offences justified the denial of contact between the applicant and a lawyer during the first 48 hours of police questioning, but the Court disagreed. Since Northern Irish law permitted an inference of guilt to be drawn from the applicant's silence under police questioning, the refusal of a lawyer had deprived him of a fair trial.

The decision was affirmed in *Salduz v Turkey*,[73] with the Court using similar language that it has applied when discussing the other aspects of defence rights such as the presumption of innocence.

[68] *Goddi v Italy*, (App. 8966/80), 9 April 1984, Series A No 76, (1984) 6 EHRR 457.

[69] *Tripodi v Italy*, (App. 13743/88), 22 February 1994, Series A No 281-B, (1994) 18 EHRR 295.

[70] *Imbrioscia v Switzerland*, (App. 13972/88), 24 November 1993, Series A No 275, (1994) 17 EHRR 441.

[71] *Öcalan v Turkey*, (App. 46221/99), 12 May 2005 [GC], (2005) 41 EHRR 985, ECHR 2005-IV.

[72] *Murray (John) v United Kingdom*, (App. 18731/91), 8 February 1996; (1996) 22 EHRR 29, ECHR 1996-I.

[73] *Salduz v Turkey*, (App. 36391/02), 20 November 2008.

> the Court finds that in order for the right to a fair trial to remain sufficiently 'practical and effective'..., Article 6 § 1 requires that, as a rule, access to a lawyer should be provided as from the first interrogation of a suspect by the police, unless it is demonstrated in the light of the particular circumstances of each case that there are compelling reasons to restrict this right. Even where compelling reasons may exceptionally justify denial of access to a lawyer, such restriction—whatever its justification—must not unduly prejudice the rights of the accused under Article 6.[74]

The *Poitrimol* case[75] concerned a rule of criminal procedure which allowed the appeal courts to refuse to hear an appeal against conviction where the accused was a fugitive from justice and declined to attend. The Strasbourg Court ruled that a person does not lose his right to the benefit of legal assistance by virtue of his own absence from court. Although it was permissible to have sanctions to secure the attendance of the accused in court, in Poitrimol's case the refusal to hear his lawyer was disproportionate and there was a violation of Articles 6(1) and 6(3)(c) taken together.

The Strasbourg Court has held that 'where the deprivation of liberty is at stake, the interests of justice in principle call for legal representation', and if the defendant cannot afford to pay for this himself, public funds must be available as of right.[76] It will normally be in the interests of justice for a person to receive representation on an appeal where a substantial prison sentence is involved and there is a real issue to be considered.[77] Where an initial refusal of legal aid has taken place, and such an issue emerges, there should be a procedure for further considering the grant of legal assistance.[78] Where an appeal court is called upon to make a full assessment both factually and legally of the defendant's guilt or innocence on a serious charge, personal attendance as well as representation will be required for the proceedings to comply with Article 6(3)(c).[79]

While the national authorities 'should, as a rule, endeavour to choose a lawyer in whom the defendant places confidence',[80] the accused does not have an unlimited veto where his legal representation is publicly funded. In the *Croissant* case,[81] the national court had appointed three lawyers to assist in the defence of the applicant, who was charged with various criminal offences arising out of his activities as lawyer to various members of the Red Army Faction; the trial had political overtones. Croissant objected to the assignment of one of the lawyers, whom he alleged had been assigned to ensure that the trial proceeded without interruption rather than to protect his interests. There was no evidence to show that the relationship was so strained as to make a proper defence impossible, and the Strasbourg Court found no violation of Article 6(3)(c) either in the appointment of multiple counsel nor in the appointment of counsel against the wishes of the defendant.

[74] § 55.

[75] *Poitrimol v France*, (App. 14032/88), 23 November 1993, Series A No 277-A, (1994) 18 EHRR 130. See also *Lala v Netherlands*, (App. 14861/89), 22 September 1994, Series A No 297-A, (1994) 18 EHRR 586 and *Pelladoah v Netherlands*, (App. 16737/90), 22 September 1994, Series A No 297-B, (1994) 19 EHRR 81.

[76] *Benham v United Kingdom*, (App. 19380/92), 10 June 1996; (1996) 22 EHRR 293, ECHR 1996-III.

[77] *Granger v United Kingdom*, (App. 11932/86), 28 March 1990, Series A No 174, (1990) 12 EHRR 469; *Boner v United Kingdom*, (App. 18711/91), 28 October 1994, (1995) 19 EHRR 246; and *Maxwell v United Kingdom*, (App. 18949/91), 28 October 1994, Series A No 300–C, (1995) 19 EHRR 97. See also *Quaranta v Switzerland*, (App. 12744/87), 24 May 1991, Series A No 205.

[78] *Granger v United Kingdom*, (App. 11932/86), 28 March 1990, Series A No 174, (1990) 12 EHRR 469; *Boner v United Kingdom*, (App. 18711/91), 28 October 1994, (1995) 19 EHRR 246; and *Maxwell v United Kingdom*, (App. 18949/91), 28 October 1994, Series A No 300–C, (1995) 19 EHRR 97. See also *Quaranta v Switzerland*, (App. 12744/87), 24 May 1991, Series A No 205.

[79] *Sibgatullin v Russia*, (App. 32156/02), 23 April 2009.

[80] *Croissant v Germany*, (App. 13611/88), 25 September 1992, Series A No 237-B, (1993) 16 EHRR 135, § 7.

[81] *Croissant v Germany*, (App. 13611/88), 25 September 1992, Series A No 237-B, (1993) 16 EHRR 135, § 7.

In the *Sejdovic* case,[82] the Strasbourg Court has elaborated the Convention requirements for representation by counsel where defendants are tried in their absence. It stressed the fundamental importance of adequate defence even for those not present at their trial. While it is appropriate to discourage unwarranted absences, any sanctions for failure to attend must not be disproportionate in the circumstances of the case. Sejdovic had been declared a fugitive by the Italian courts and tried in his absence; it appeared that he had not been given notice of the case against him. He was furthermore deprived of the opportunity to ask for the proceedings against him to be reopened. There had been a violation of Article 6.

WITNESSES AND EVIDENCE

Article 6(3)(d) grants a number of rights in respect of defence witnesses: to secure their attendance and to examine their evidence on the same basis as the witnesses against the accused. This provision must be considered in the context of both the accusatorial system—where it is for the parties, subject to the control of the court, to decide which witnesses they wish to call—and the inquisitorial system—where the court decides for itself which witnesses it wishes to hear. In the former system, the witnesses are examined and cross-examined by the parties or their representatives, although additional questions may be put by the judge, while in the latter system witnesses are examined by the court.

Article 6(3)(d) is intended to ensure, under each system, that the accused is placed on a footing of equality with the prosecution as regards the calling and examination of witnesses,[83] but it does not give defendants a right to call witnesses without restriction.[84] Moreover, in accordance with the 'fourth instance' doctrine, it is normally for the national courts to decide whether it is necessary or advisable to call a witness, and, provided the principle of equality has been respected, the Strasbourg Court would find a violation only in exceptional circumstances.[85] A court can therefore refuse to hear a witness for the reason that his statement would be irrelevant,[86] and, even where the evidence is relevant, the court fulfils its obligation if it takes all appropriate steps to try to ensure the appearance of the witness.[87]

The Strasbourg Court has been called upon to decide a number of cases in which the prosecution in criminal trials has relied upon the evidence of anonymous witnesses. The applicant in the *Doorson* case[88] had been convicted of drugs offences on the evidence of a number of anonymous witnesses. He had not been permitted to see these witnesses since they claimed to be frightened of reprisals, but during the course of the appeal proceedings his lawyer had been present while they were questioned by the investigating judge and had had an opportunity to put questions to them himself, and the investigating judge had drawn up a full report for the Court of Appeal explaining her reasons for considering that the witnesses could be relied upon. The Court found that it was justifiable to protect the rights of the witnesses to respect for their life, liberty, and security of person (as secured by various provisions in the Convention) by preserving their anonymity and

[82] *Sejdovic v Italy*, (App. 56581/00), 1 March 2006 [GC], ECHR 2006-II.

[83] *Bönisch v Austria*, (App. 8658/79), 6 May 1985, Series A No 92, (1987) 9 EHRR 191.

[84] Or to have hearsay statements admitted in evidence when the witness is no longer able to remember crucial events: *Thomas v United Kingdom*, (App. 19354/02), Decision of 10 May 2005.

[85] *Bricmont v Belgium*, (App. 10857/84), 7 July 1989, Series A No 158, (1990) 12 EHRR 217.

[86] *Wiechert v Federal Republic of Germany*, (App. 1404/62), Decision of 7 March 1964 (1964) 7 *Yearbook* 104, 112.

[87] *Thomas v United Kingdom*, (App. 19354/02), Decision of 10 May 2005.

[88] *Doorson v Netherlands*, (App. 20524/92), 26 March 1996, (1996) 22 EHRR 330.

that the difficulties this caused for the defence had been adequately counterbalanced by the procedures followed by the investigating judge. Nonetheless, the Court observed that it would never be acceptable for a conviction to be based solely or to a decisive extent on anonymous statements.[89]

In the *Al-Khawaja and Tahery* case,[90] the Court clarified the meaning of 'sole and decisive' in regard to use of such evidence. In the first case the evidence in question was the read statement of the victim of an alleged sexual assault who had subsequently committed suicide. In the second case, the evidence which was read out was not of an anonymous witness, but of an identified witness who had been too scared to attend the trial and give evidence. In neither case could this evidence be subject to cross-examination. The Strasbourg Court indicated that in all cases, the starting point for the Court's assessment is whether the defendant has had an opportunity to test or to have evidence tested, whether during the investigation or at trial, in circumstances where the conviction is based solely or to a decisive degree on that evidence.[91] However, the Court went on to examine the meaning of 'decisive' in this context. The Court retained the rule as outlined in *Doorson*. However, it noted that it should not be applied inflexibly and the Court should consider the context of the use of evidence before finding a violation. If the evidence of absent witnesses can justifiably be used then it is not automatically a violation if it is the 'sole and decisive' evidence agent the applicant. In such circumstances, the Court will submit the proceedings to stringent scrutiny and consider counterbalancing factors with regard to the fairness of proceedings. As the Court noted:

> Because of the dangers of the admission of such evidence, it would constitute a very important factor to balance in the scales, to use the words of Lord Mance in *R. v. Davis*... and one which would require sufficient counterbalancing factors, including the existence of strong procedural safeguards. The question in each case is whether there are sufficient counterbalancing factors in place, including measures that permit a fair and proper assessment of the reliability of that evidence to take place. This would permit a conviction to be based on such evidence only if it is sufficiently reliable given its importance in the case.[92]

In the case before them, the two statements which were read out were regarded as the decisive basis for the conviction. In the first applicant's case there was sufficient counterbalancing safeguards to find there was no violation of Article 6, but there was a violation in the second applicant's case given the lack of sufficient counterbalancing safeguards to avoid a violation of Article 6(1) read with Article 6(3)(d).

The *Perna* case[93] applied similar principles to the admission of documentary evidence, as well as requests that particular persons are called to give evidence. The Grand Chamber, in a unanimous decision, affirmed that the admissibility of evidence is primarily a matter for regulation by national law. In dealing with complaints relating to such matters the Strasbourg Court is concerned to ascertain whether the proceedings as a whole were fair.[94]

[89] See also *Saidi v France*, (App. 14647/89), 20 September 1993, Series A No 261-C, (1994) 17 EHRR 251, A similar issue arose in the *Van Mechelen and others v Netherlands*, (Apps. 21363/94, 21364/94, 21427/93, and 22056/93), 23 April 1997, (1998) 25 EHRR 647, ECHR 1997-III, concerning uncorroborated evidence of police officers. The Court distinguished this case from the *Doorson* case in view of the particular problems, which arise where police officers give evidence anonymously. It therefore found a violation of Articles 6(1) and 3(d) taken together.

[90] *Al-Khawaja and Tahery v United Kingdom*, (Apps. 26766/05 and 22228/06), 15 December 2011.

[91] § 118, referring to *Lucà v Italy*, (App. 33354/96), 27 February 2001, ECHR 2001-II, § 40.

[92] § 147. For application of the more flexible sole and decisive rule see *Gani v Spain*, (App. 61800/08), 19 February 2013.

[93] *Perna v Italy*, (App. 48898/99), 6 May 2003 [GC], (2004) 39 EHRR 563, ECHR 2003-V.

[94] § 29.

It will be for the person complaining that a trial has been unfair to show why it is important for the witnesses concerned to be heard and their evidence must be necessary for the establishment of the truth. The applicant had not established these matters and the Grand Chamber unanimously found no violation of Article 6(1) and (3)(d) of the Convention.

In criminal proceedings concerning accusations of sexual abuse, particularly where the complainant is a child, the Court has held that certain measures may be taken to protect him or her, provided that such measures can be reconciled with an adequate and effective exercise of the rights of the defence. Thus in the *SN* case[95] the Court found no violation of Article 6 paragraphs 1 and 3(d) taken together where a schoolteacher had been convicted of sexually assaulting her ten-year-old pupil virtually solely on the basis of a videotaped interview of the boy with a specially trained police officer. Under Swedish law in such cases child complainants are rarely called to give evidence in court because of the traumatizing effect this might have on them. The Court found that it was sufficient for the purposes of Article 6 that the applicant's counsel could have attended the interview or given the police officer any questions which the defence wanted to be put to the boy.

THE PRINCIPLE OF LEGALITY

The Convention is not merely concerned with the procedural fairness of criminal trials. Article 7 is concerned with the substantive criminal law and embodies the principle of legality, which stipulates that no one should be convicted or punished except in respect of a breach of a pre-existing rule of law.[96] There are two main aspects to this principle. First, Article 7 prohibits legislatures and courts from creating or extending the law so as to criminalize acts or omissions which were not illegal at the time of commission or omission, or to increase a penalty retroactively. Secondly, it requires that the criminal law should be clearly defined;[97] this second aspect of the principle is almost a precondition of the first, since the more precisely drafted an offence is, the less scope there is for creative judicial interpretation and nasty courtroom surprises for defendants.

Article 7 states:

1. No one shall be held guilty of any criminal offence on account of any act or omission which did not constitute a criminal offence under national or international law at the time when it was committed. Nor shall a heavier penalty be imposed than the one that was applicable at the time the criminal offence was committed.
2. This Article shall not prejudice the trial and punishment of any person for any act or omission which, at the time when it was committed, was criminal according to the general principles of law recognised by civilised nations.

APPLICABILITY OF ARTICLE 7

The terms 'criminal offence' and 'penalty' in Article 7 carry autonomous meanings independent of the characterization under domestic law. The question whether any particular act amounts to a conviction for a 'criminal offence' is determined by reference to the '*Engel*

[95] *SN v Sweden*, (App. 34209/96), 2 July 2002, ECHR 2002-V; see also *Magnusson v Sweden*, (App. 53972/00), Decision of 6 December 2003.

[96] *Nullum crimen, nulla poena sine lege*; best paraphrased in English as: only the law can define a crime and prescribe a penalty.

[97] The Strasbourg Court has said that 'the criminal law must not be extensively construed to an accused's detriment': *Achour v France*, (App. 67335/01), 29 March 2006 [GC], (2007) 45 EHRR 9, ECHR 2006-IV, § 41.

criteria':[98] principally the classification in domestic law, the nature of the offence itself, and the nature and severity of the sentence which can be imposed.[99] Similar considerations apply in deciding whether a measure amounts to a 'penalty'. As the Strasbourg Court observed in the *Welch* case:[100]

> The wording of Article 7(1), second sentence, indicates that the starting point in any assessment of the existence of a penalty is whether the measure in question is imposed following conviction for a 'criminal offence'. Other factors that may be taken into account as relevant in this connection are the nature and purpose of the measure in question; its characterisation under national law; the procedures involved in the making and implementation of the measure; and its severity.

The applicant in that case was arrested for drugs offences committed in November 1986. The Drug Trafficking Offences Act 1986 came into force in January 1987; it introduced confiscation orders intended to ensure that those convicted of drugs offences could not retain the profits of drugs-related activity. The retroactive effect of the confiscation order imposed on the applicant was not in dispute; the only question before the Strasbourg Court was whether such an order could properly be described as a 'penalty'. The Court rejected the respondent State's argument that the order was preventive, rather than punitive, observing that 'the aims of prevention and reparation are consistent with a punitive purpose and may be seen as constituent elements of the very notion of punishment.' It concluded that Welch faced more 'far-reaching detriment' as a result of the confiscation order than that to which he would have been exposed at the time he committed the offences, and that there had, therefore, been a violation of Article 7.

In the *Adamson* case[101] the Court was called upon to decide whether inclusion on a register of known sex offenders constituted a 'penalty'. Under the Sex Offenders Act 1997, which entered into force on 1 September 1997, any person convicted after that date of one of the sexual offences listed in the Act, or any person already serving a sentence of imprisonment for such an offence at the date of commencement, was required, after his release, to register with the police and keep them informed of any change of name or address. In holding that this requirement did not amount to a 'penalty', the Court found it relevant that its purpose was not to punish sex offenders, but to contribute towards a lower rate of re-offending. It noted that the obligation to register was imposed as a matter of law, with no additional procedure, following conviction of a sexual offence. Although failure to register constituted a criminal offence, punishable by imprisonment, independent proceedings would have to be brought against a defaulter in which his degree of culpability in defaulting would be taken into account in sentencing. Finally, the Court did not consider that the obligation to notify the police of the information required by the Act could, in itself, be regarded as severe. The applicant had expressed the fear that his inclusion on the register would lead to vigilante-style attacks on him or his family, but the Court dismissed this concern because it had not been provided with any evidence to suggest that the applicant would be put at risk in this way.

RETROACTIVE CRIMINALIZATION

The Convention was drafted in the aftermath of the Second World War, and presumably those responsible for framing Article 7 had in mind events in Germany and other parts

[98] See ch.12. [99] *Brown v United Kingdom*, (App. 38644/97), Decision of 24 November 1998.

[100] *Welch v United Kingdom*, (App. 17440/90), 9 February 1993, Series A No 307-A.

[101] *Adamson v United Kingdom*, (App. 42293/98), Decision of 26 January 1999.

of Europe in the 1930s, when newly imposed totalitarian regimes promulgated retroactive laws, making criminal without warning acts which had been lawful under democratic rule. Following the fall of the Berlin Wall in November 1989, the change of administration in many eastern and central European countries was almost as extreme, with democratic governments being elected in the place of Communist dictatorships. Quite naturally, these changes were frequently accompanied by a strong desire to bring to justice those responsible for the worst excesses of the old regimes.

Faced with a similar situation following the fall of Nazi Germany in 1945, the international community developed the 'Nuremberg principles', which permitted individuals to be prosecuted for acts so heinous as to be classified as 'crimes against humanity', even if these same acts had not been criminal according to Nazi legislation and practice. These principles are reflected in the second paragraph of Article 7.[102]

In two applications against Germany the Strasbourg Court was required to examine whether it was compatible with Article 7(1) for the courts of the unified Federal Republic to convict men in respect of acts which, in the submission of the applicants, had not been criminal according to the law and practice of the German Democratic Republic (GDR). The three applicants in the case of *Streletz, Kessler and Krenz v Germany*[103] had occupied senior positions in the GDR State apparatus. After unification, the first two applicants were convicted of incitement to commit intentional homicide and the third applicant was convicted of intentional homicide as an indirect principal on the grounds that, as they had participated in high-level decisions on the GDR's border-policing regime, they shared responsibility for the deaths of a number of young people who had attempted to flee to West Berlin between 1971 and 1989 and had been killed by landmines or by shots fired by East German border guards. The applicant in the case of *K-HW*[104] had served as a soldier in the GDR border guard and, in 1973, when he was twenty years old, had shot and killed a fugitive attempting to swim to West Berlin.

The German courts which convicted the applicants did not rely on the argument that the acts in question had amounted to 'crimes against humanity' or had been criminal according to the general principles of international law. Instead they held that the acts had been prohibited by GDR law on the dates they were committed. They relied on the fact that the GDR had ratified the United Nations' International Covenant on Civil and Political Rights (which guarantees, *inter alia*, the right to life and the right to freedom of movement) and enacted a number of statutory provisions protecting the right to life and restricting the use of lethal force for the prevention of serious crime. The practice of the East German authorities, however, for which the applicants in the *Streletz* case had been partly responsible, was to encourage border guards to disregard the legislation and to annihilate border violators. In the event of a successful crossing, the guards on duty could expect to be the subject of an investigation by the military prosecutor.

In the *Streletz* case the Strasbourg Court observed that GDR statute law, together with the provisions of the international treaties ratified by it, had provided a clear prohibition on disproportionate and arbitrary killing. It was not open to the applicants to argue that,

[102] In *Papon v France*, (App. 54210/00), Decision of 15 November 2001, ECHR 2001-XII, the Court rejected the applicant's argument that at his trial for war crimes it had been a breach of Article 7 for the national court to reverse its case-law and adopt a broader interpretation of Article 6 of the Nuremberg Statute, removing the need to prove intent on the part of an accessory to such an offence to serve as an instrument of the Nazis' totalitarian policy. See also *Kononov v Latvia*, (App. 36376/04), 17 May 2010, for an example of a war crimes case.

[103] *Streletz, Kessler and Krenz v Germany*, (Apps. 34044/96, 35532/97, and 44801/98), 22 March 2001 [GC], (2001) 33 EHRR 751, ECHR 2001-II.

[104] *K-HW v Germany*, (App. 32701/97), 22 March 2001, (2003) 36 EHRR 1081, ECHR 2001-II.

in the light of GDR State practice, their convictions as accessories to murder had not been foreseeable, since they themselves had to a large extent been responsible for the disparity between the legislation and the practice.

The Court's finding of no violation of Article 7 in the *K-HW* case appears somewhat harsher (and three of the seventeen judges in the Grand Chamber dissented from it). The applicant had been a young and junior soldier; he had undergone a process of indoctrination and had been ordered to protect the border 'at all costs'; he knew that he would be subject to investigation if he allowed a fugitive successfully to escape from East Germany. However, the Court held that the GDR statute law was accessible to all, and that 'even a private soldier could not show total, blind obedience to orders which flagrantly infringed not only the GDR's own legal principles but also internationally recognized human rights.'[105]

Perhaps more convincing is the argument put by Sir Nicolas Bratza in his concurring opinion:

> I accept... that the situation in the GDR was such that the applicant could hardly have foreseen at the time that his actions would result in his prosecution for the offence of intentional homicide. But this is a very different question from the one facing the Court, namely whether the applicant could reasonably have foreseen that his actions amounted to such an offence. While this question may be open to differing opinions, I can find no reason to depart from the considered opinion of the national courts that opening fire on a defenceless person, who was attempting to swim away from East Berlin and who posed no threat to life or limb, so clearly breached any principle of proportionality that it was foreseeable that it violated the legal prohibition on killing.

The issue of war crimes has troubled the Strasbourg Court in recent years. Such cases can turn on detailed consideration of the factual conclusions. In *Kononov v Latvia*,[106] the applicant, a Latvian, was a member of a Soviet partisan brigade in Latvia during the Second World War. At that time Latvia was a Soviet Republic and was governed by Soviet law. A number of partisans were killed. A partisan brigade, of which the applicant was allegedly a member, carried out reprisals on those whom they believed informed the Germans about the partisans, also killing other members of the men's families. There was some dispute as to whether the men and their families were participants in hostilities. After Latvian independence from Russia, the Soviet laws were replaced by the 1922 Constitution. Latvia retained the 1961 Criminal Code but inserted a new clause with regard to war crimes. The applicant was charged under the Code with war crimes and after two trials was found guilty. He argued that his conviction violated Article 7 as the actions were not war crimes and were statute barred under the criminal code.

The Chamber found that on the evidence the allegations did not amount to war crimes and so the prosecution of the applicant under the criminal court was statute-barred.[107] However the Grand Chamber disagreed. It found that the status of the applicant and the villagers whether combatants or participants in the conflict meant that their execution could amount to a war crime. It also found that by May 1944 war crimes 'were defined as acts contrary to the laws and customs of war and that international law had defined the basic principles underlying, and an extensive range of acts constituting, those crimes. States were at least permitted (if not required) to take steps to punish individuals for such crimes, including on the basis of command responsibility.'[108] It went on to examine the specific war crimes that applicant was accused of committing. It concluded that the State's

[105] § 75. [106] *Kononov v Latvia*, (App. 36376/04), 17 May 2010.
[107] *Kononov v Latvia*, (App. 36376/04), 24 July 2008. [108] § 213.

use of provisions of international humanitarian law was applicable in this case and that the events did amount to war crimes. The Grand Chamber then considered if these were statute barred. It found that in 1944, a Court would have had to rely on international law to prosecute the applicant and that international law at the time was silent on the issue of limitations. It concluded that since international law has never placed limitations on war crimes then the applicant's prosecution was not statute barred and so should have been foreseeable to the applicant 'as even the most cursory reflection by the applicant, would have indicated that, at the very least, the impugned acts risked being counter to the laws and customs of war as understood at that time and, notably, risked constituting war crimes for which, as commander, he could be held individually and criminally accountable.'[109]

In the *Korbely* case,[110] the Strasbourg Court was called upon to consider whether events in October 1956 in Budapest in which the applicant was involved constituted with sufficient accessibility and foreseeability crimes against humanity under the Geneva Convention. The Strasbourg Court re-affirmed the requirement that an offence must be clearly defined in law:

> This requirement is satisfied where the individual can know from the wording of the relevant provision—and, if need be, with the assistance of the courts' interpretation of it and with informed legal advice—what acts and omissions will make him criminally liable. The Court has thus indicated that when speaking of 'law' Article 7 alludes to the very same concept as that to which the Convention refers elsewhere when using that term, a concept which comprised written as well as unwritten law and implies qualitative requirements, notably those of accessibility and foreseeability.[111]

The Grand Chamber concluded that the law in the Geneva Convention was accessible since the Geneva Conventions had been proclaimed in Hungary by a national legislative measure. But whether the requirement of foreseeability was met turned on the meaning of a crime against humanity in 1956. Careful analysis of the provision and its understanding in Hungary suggested that it was 'open to question whether the constituent elements of a crime against humanity were satisfied in the present case'.[112] The Strasbourg Court has also been called upon to consider prosecutions flowing from events in Bosnia. In the *Jorgic* case,[113] the applicant took issue with his conviction for genocide, arguing that the German courts had adopted an interpretation of genocide which did not have a basis either in German law or international law. The Strasbourg Court concluded that the interpretation adopted by the national court was supported both by the Genocide Convention and by a number of German scholars. Furthermore the interpretation was reasonably foreseeable on receipt of proper advice. There was no violation of Article 7. A second area of enquiry was also needed in order to ascertain whether one of the victims of the killing by the applicant was 'taking no active part in the hostilities' which was a requirement to bring him within the protection of the Geneva Convention. This issue had not been fully addressed by the national courts. This meant that it could not be shown that it was foreseeable that the applicant's acts constituted a crime against humanity under international law, and there had been a violation of Article 7 of the Convention.

The second part of Article 7(1) prohibits the retrospective application of a heavier penalty that existed at the time the criminal offence was committed. In the *Welch* case,[114] the Court found that the imposition of a confiscation order on conviction for drug offences

[109] § 238. See concurring and dissenting judgments for a contrasting opinion on the nature of international law in 1944.

[110] *Korbely v Hungary*, (App. 9174/02), 19 September 2008 [GC], ECHR 2008-nyr.

[111] § 70.

[112] § 85.

[113] *Jorgic v Germany*, (App. 74613/01), 12 July 2007, ECHR 2007-IX.

[114] *Welch v United Kingdom*, (App. 17440/90), 9 February 1993, Series A No 307-A.

was a retrospective heavier penalty as the legislation governing the orders was introduced after the offence was committed.[115] In *Del Rio Prada v Spain*,[116] the applicant was found guilty of serious terrorist offences and received several prison sentences, up to a maximum of thirty years, from which remission was to be calculated. However following a change in judicial interpretation of the rules, remission was calculated for every separate sentence, effectively meaning the applicant would have to spend longer in prison. The Court noted that there was a distinction between the scope of the penalty and the rules governing the execution of a penalty. The latter does not fall under Article 7.[117] On the facts, the Court determined that the judicial reinterpretation of the remission rules did fall under the scope of the penalty and therefore did violate Article 7. This decision was criticized by the dissenting opinions, which noted that it departed from settled case-law such as *Kafkaris*[118] on the discretion to be given to States with regard to changes in the execution of a sentence.[119]

The question has arisen as to whether Article 7 contains a guarantee of the right to a more lenient penalty provided in law subsequent to an offence. The Commission had answered the question in the negative, reflecting the position of the International Covenant on Civil and Political Rights.[120] However in *Scoppola v Italy (no 2)*,[121] the Court departed from the Commission Decision and concluded that Article 7 not only guarantees the non-retrospectiveness of more stringent criminal law but also the retrospectiveness of more lenient criminal law. The Court came to its conclusion based on the growing consensus in international and domestic law, illustrated by the European Union's Charter of Fundamental Rights and decisions of the Court of Justice of the European Union (CJEU) as well as the International Criminal Court.[122] However, the dissenting opinion notes the *travaux préparatoires* of the Convention and previous case-law in arguing the majority went beyond its powers to widen the interpretation of Article 7 and have rewritten Article 7 to comply with what they thought it ought to have been rather than respecting the limits set by the Convention provisions.[123]

CLARITY OF CRIMINAL LEGISLATION

It follows from the rule against retrospective legislation under Article 7 that legal provisions which interfere with individual rights must be adequately accessible and formulated with sufficient precision to enable the citizen to regulate his conduct. The Strasbourg Court's approach towards such cases under Article 7 is identical to that used to determine whether a provision authorizing an interference with the right to private and family life under Article 8 or to freedom of religion or expression under Articles 9 and 10 is sufficiently precise as to render the interference 'in accordance with the law'.[124] The condition

[115] See also *Ecer and Zeyrek v Turkey*, (Apps. 29295/95 and 29363/95), 27 February 2001, ECHR 2001-II; *Mihai Toma v Romania*, (App. 1051/06), 24 January 2012.

[116] *Del Rio Prada v Spain*, (App. 42750/09), 21 October 2013.

[117] See *Kafkaris v Cyprus*, (App. 21906/04), 12 February 2008 [GC], (2009) 49 EHRR 877, ECHR 2008-nyr.; *M v Germany*, (App. 19359/04), 17 December 2009, ECHR 2009.

[118] See *Kafkaris v Cyprus*, (App. 21906/04), 12 February 2008 [GC], (2009) 49 EHRR 877, ECHR 2008-nyr.; *M v Germany*, (App. 19359/04),17 December 2009, ECHR 2009.

[119] *Del Rio Prada v Spain*, (App. 42750/09), 21 October 2013, Joint Partly Dissenting Opinion Of Judges Mahoney And Vehabović.

[120] *X v Germany*, (App. 7900/77), Commission Decision of 6 March 1978, *Decisions and Reports* (DR) 13.

[121] *Scoppola v Italy (no 2)*, (App. 10249/03), 17 September 2009.

[122] §§ 103–9.

[123] Partly Dissenting Opinion of Judge Nicolaou, joined by Judges Bratza, Lorenzen, Jočiené, Villiger, and Sajó.

[124] See ch.14, and see *Custers, Deveaux and Turk v Denmark*, (Apps. 11843/03, 11847/03, and 11849/03), 3 May 2007.

is satisfied where the individual can know from the wording of the relevant provision and, if need be, with the assistance of the national courts' interpretation of it, what acts and omissions will make him liable.[125]

While it has been argued that certain offences known to English law, such as those based on dishonesty, public mischief, or conspiring to corrupt public morals may be inconsistent with Article 7,[126] the Strasbourg case-law shows that a crime has to be very loosely defined indeed before the Court will find a violation of this provision.[127]

In the *Kokkinakis* case,[128] for example, the applicant, a Jehovah's witness, was convicted under a Greek law which prohibited proselytism. 'Proselytism' was defined in the statute as meaning:

> in particular, any direct or indirect attempt to intrude on the religious beliefs of a person of a different religious persuasion, with the aim of undermining those beliefs, either by any kind of inducement or promise of an inducement or moral support or material assistance, or by fraudulent means or by taking advantage of his inexperience, trust, need, low intellect or naïvety.

The applicant contended that this provision was so widely defined that it could encompass almost any attempt to convert a person to another religious faith. The Strasbourg Court noted that the wording of many statutes is not absolutely precise and that the need to avoid excessive rigidity and to keep pace with changing circumstances means that many laws were inevitably couched in fairly vague terms. However, the settled national case-law interpreting the statute was sufficiently clear to enable Kokkinakis to regulate his conduct in the matter.[129]

Article 7 does not merely prohibit retrospective law-making by the legislature or executive, it also prohibits extension of the application of the criminal law by the judiciary.[130] Nonetheless, the Strasbourg Court has shown itself prepared to give national courts considerable leeway in this respect, recognizing that:

> however clearly drafted a legal provision may be, in any system of law, including criminal law, there is an inevitable element of judicial interpretation. There will always be a need for elucidation of doubtful points and for adaptation to changing circumstances. Indeed, in the…Convention States, the progressive development of the criminal law through judicial law-making is a well entrenched and necessary part of legal tradition. Article 7 of the Convention cannot be read as outlawing the gradual clarification of the rules of criminal liability through judicial interpretation from case to case, provided that the resulting development is consistent with the essence of the offence and could reasonably be foreseen.[131]

The applicant in the *CR* case[132] was convicted of the attempted rape of his wife. At the time he tried to force her to have sex, and indeed until the judgments of the Court of Appeal and House of Lords in his case, it was an established rule of common law that a man could not rape his wife, because in getting married a woman was deemed to have consented

[125] *Kokkinakis v Greece*, (App. 14307/88), 25 May 1993, Series A No 260-A, (1994) 17 EHRR 397, § 52.

[126] See *Shaw v Director of Public Prosecutions* [1962] AC 220; *Knuller (Publishing, Printing and Promotions) Limited v Director of Public Prosecutions* [1973] AC 435; *R. v Pattni, Dhunna, Soni and Poopalarajah* [2001] Crim LR 570.

[127] For an examples, see *Liivik v Estonia*, (App. 12157/05), 25 June 2009.

[128] *Kokkinakis v Greece*, (App. 14307/88), 25 May 1993, Series A No 260-A, (1994) 17 EHRR 397, § 52.

[129] See also *Baskaya and Okçuoglu v Turkey*, (Apps. 23536/94 and 24408/94), 8 July 1999, (2001) 31 EHRR 292, ECHR 1999-IV.

[130] *X v Austria*, (App. 1852/63), Decision of 22 April 1965 (1965) 8 *Yearbook* 190, 198.

[131] *CR v United Kingdom*, (App. 20190/92), 2 November 1995, Series A No 335-C, (1996) 21 EHRR 363, § 34.

[132] *CR v United Kingdom*, (App. 20190/92), 2 November 1995, Series A No 335-C, (1996) 21 EHRR 363, § 34.

once and for all to intercourse with her husband. A number of exceptions to this principle had been developed—for example, where the couple had separated by court order or deed of agreement—but these did not apply in the applicant's case. The Court of Appeal and House of Lords both refused his appeal against conviction, holding that the rule was unacceptable in modern Britain and should be held inapplicable.

Despite the fairly overwhelming evidence that the domestic courts' judgments represented a reversal, rather than a clarification, of the law, the Strasbourg Court rejected the applicant's complaint under Article 7, holding that 'judicial recognition of the absence of immunity had become a reasonably foreseeable development of the law'.

Perhaps the true explanation for the Court's decision was its understandable repugnance for the rule conferring immunity from rape charges to husbands. As it observed:

> The essentially debasing character of rape is so manifest that the result of the decisions of the Court of Appeal and the House of Lords—that the applicant could be convicted of attempted rape, irrespective of his relationship with the victim—cannot be said to be at variance with the object and purpose of Article 7 of the Convention, namely to ensure that no one should be subjected to arbitrary prosecution, conviction or punishment.... What is more, the abandonment of the unacceptable idea of a husband being immune against prosecution for rape of his wife was in conformity not only with a civilised concept of marriage but also, above all, with the fundamental objectives of the Convention, the very essence of which is respect for human dignity and human freedom.[133]

The Court's reasoning appears to overlook the fact that most criminal laws are directed at behaviour which offends against human dignity and freedom. While the removal of the immunity from English law is to be welcomed, the rule of law would have been better respected if Parliament had carried out the reform with purely prospective effect.[134]

The issue of the quality of the law is well illustrated in the *Kafkaris* case.[135] Kafkaris had been convicted of a contract killing; he had placed explosive beneath a car which had killed a man and his two children. He was sentenced to life imprisonment under the provisions of the Cyprus Criminal Code. Regulations on the effect of the sentence indicated that this would be for a term of twenty years with the possibility of early release for good behaviour. In litigation not involving the applicant, the Regulations were declared unconstitutional. The effect was to increase operative length of the applicant's sentence to a whole life term without the possibility of early release. By fifteen votes to two, the Grand Chamber found a violation of Article 7 by reason of the deficiency in the quality of the law applicable at the material time, and by sixteen votes to one that there had been no violation in relation to the complained of retrospective application of a longer sentence and removal of the possibility of remission. The Grand Chamber considered that the sentence of life imprisonment was provided for in the Criminal Code and was the only basis for the imposition of this sentence. By contrast, the Regulations in issue concerned the manner in which the sentence would be executed. The penalty of life imprisonment under the Criminal Code could not be regarded at the time as amounting only to twenty years in prison.[136] However, at the material time, the distinction between the scope of a life sentence and its manner of execution was 'not immediately apparent'[137] and this constituted a breach of Article 7.

[133] § 42.

[134] Rather than the matter being dealt with by judicial decisions on the content of the common law.

[135] *Kafkaris v Cyprus*, (App. 21906/04), 12 February 2008 [GC], (2009) 49 EHRR 877, ECHR 2008-nyr.

[136] § 149. There is a particularly trenchant criticism of the reasoning of the majority in the dissenting opinion of Judge Borrego.

[137] § 148.

RECIDIVISM

The *Achour* case[138] concerned French legislation which provided that those committing a second offence of the same nature would incur a longer sentence. Prior to 1 March 1994 the period within which the second offence had to be committed for a person to be regarded as a recidivist was five years from the expiry of a prison sentence. From 1 March 1994 the period was extended to ten years. Achour had completed a sentence for drug trafficking on 12 July 1986. He was sentenced for a further offence in respect of which proceedings had begun on 11 December 1995. This was outside the five-year period provided for in the earlier law, but within the ten-year period in the later law. He argued that this violated Article 7.

The Strasbourg Court noted that 'matters relating to the existence of [rules on recidivism], the manner of their implementation, and the reasoning behind them' was a matter for policy decisions in the respondent State.[139] The Court concluded, by sixteen votes to one, that, notwithstanding the extension of the period within which the second offence was committed, it was foreseeable that the applicant could be regarded as a recidivist with the consequences for the length of his sentence on committing the repeat offence. It seems significant that recidivism was seen as an aggravating factor in relation to a particular individual and not in relation to the nature of the offence committed.[140]

PROTOCOL 7

Protocol 7 includes a number of additional rights in respect of the criminal process: a rule against double jeopardy, the right to an appeal, and the right to compensation following a miscarriage of justice.[141]

THE RULE AGAINST DOUBLE JEOPARDY

Article 4 of Protocol 7 provides:

1. No one shall be liable to be tried or punished again in criminal proceedings under the jurisdiction of the same State for an offence for which he has already been finally acquitted or convicted in accordance with the law and penal procedure of that State.
2. The provisions of the preceding paragraph shall not prevent the reopening of the case in accordance with the law and penal procedure of the State concerned, if there is evidence of new or newly discovered facts, or if there has been a fundamental defect in the previous proceedings, which could affect the outcome of the case.
3. No derogation from this Article shall be made under Article 15 of the Convention.

The Explanatory Memorandum to Protocol 7 resolves some aspects of the wording of the provision. A conviction or acquittal becomes final, according to the Memorandum, when 'no further ordinary remedies are available or when the parties have exhausted such remedies or have permitted the time limit to expire without availing themselves of these.'

[138] *Achour v France*, (App. 67335/01), 29 March 2006 [GC], (2007) 45 EHRR 9, ECHR 2006-IV.

[139] § 44.

[140] *In personam* rather than *in rem* in the words of the Court. There is a helpful concurring opinion of Judge Zupančič. The Court has found that a State may apply procedural changes in a manner that may be to the detriment of the applicant as long as it does not involve arbitrariness *Scoppola v Italy (no 2)*, (App 10249/03), 17 September 2009; see also *Previti v Italy*, (App. 1845/08), 12 February 2013.

[141] The United Kingdom is not a signatory to this Protocol. For an up-to-date list of ratifications see http://conventions.coe.int.

There is no intention in the wording of the Article to preclude cases being reopened in favour of the convicted person, but the prohibition on double jeopardy does not preclude a person being subject to several different types of procedure in relation to the same conduct, for example, to civil proceedings for compensation in addition to a criminal trial. In *Margus v Croatia*,[142] the Court found that amnesty laws had been wrongly applied to the applicant with regard to alleged war crimes. This defect in proceedings fell under the second part of Article 4 of Protocol 7.

The application of the Article is limited to proceedings in a single State. The Explanatory Memorandum notes that the international application of the prohibition is adequately covered in the European Convention on Extradition of 1957, the European Convention on the International Validity of Criminal Judgments of 1970, and the European Convention on the Transfer of Proceedings in Criminal Matters of 1972.

The Strasbourg Court has stated that the aim of Article 4 of Protocol 7 'is to prohibit the repetition of criminal proceedings that have been concluded by a final decision.'[143] The scope of Article 4 has been clarified by the Grand Chamber in the *Sergey Zolotukhin* case.[144] The Grand Chamber was influenced by the text of corresponding provisions in the Covenant on Civil and Political Rights, and the American Convention on Human Rights, in concluding that the Article should be interpreted as prohibiting the prosecution or trial of an individual for a second offence where that second prosecution or trial arose from 'identical facts or facts which are substantially the same, and the guarantee comes into play where a new set of proceedings is instituted after a prior acquittal or conviction has acquired the status of *res judicata*.'[145]

THE RIGHT TO AN APPEAL

Article 2 of Protocol 7 provides:

1. Everyone convicted of a criminal offence by a tribunal shall have the right to have his conviction or sentence reviewed by a higher tribunal. The exercise of this right, including the grounds on which it may be exercised, shall be governed by law.
2. This right may be subject to exceptions in regard to offences of a minor character, as prescribed by law, or in cases in which the person concerned was tried in the first instance by the highest tribunal or was convicted following an appeal against acquittal.

The explanatory report indicates that the reference to a tribunal in paragraph (1) is designed to exclude from its ambit any conviction resulting from a decision of a non-judicial organ. There is no explanation as to the relationship of this provision with Article 6, which would seem to require that the determination of criminal charges is by an independent tribunal. Paragraph (2) allows limitations to be placed on the right, and excludes it altogether in certain situations. It is unclear how the provision accommodates systems, like that of England and Wales, which in many cases require leave to be obtained before an appeal may be pursued. The explanatory report indicates that the intention was to view application for leave to appeal as a form of review under the provision, though it is at least arguable that the words of the text do not achieve this.

[142] *Margus v Croatia*, (App. 4455/10), 13 November 2012 (pending before Grand Chamber).

[143] *Nikitin v Russia*, (App. 50178/99), 20 July 2004, (2005) 41 EHRR 149, ECHR 2004-VIII, § 35; followed in *Fadin v Russia*, (App. 58079/00), 27 October 2006; and *Xheraj v Albania*, (App. 37959/02), 29 July 2008. See also *Ruotsalainen v Finland*, (App. 13079/03), 16 June 2009.

[144] *Sergey Zolotukhin v Russia*, (App. 14939/03), 10 February 2009 [GC], ECHR 2009-nyr.

[145] §§ 82–3.

The *Galstyan* case[146] concerned a prosecution and conviction for a public order offence. The applicant claimed that he had no right of appeal under Article 2 of Protocol 7, while the respondent State argued that a procedure for review did exist. The Strasbourg Court indicated that where an offence is found to be of a criminal character within Article 6 of the Convention, it also attracts the provisions of Article 2 of Protocol 7.[147] The procedure on which the respondent State relied lacked 'any clearly defined procedure or time limits and consistent application in practice.' Such a review was not compatible with the requirements of Article 2 of Protocol 7.[148]

COMPENSATION FOR A MISCARRIAGE OF JUSTICE

Article 3 of Protocol 7 provides:

> When a person has by final decision been convicted of a criminal offence and when subsequently his conviction has been reversed, or he has been pardoned, on the ground that a new or newly discovered fact shows conclusively that there has been a miscarriage of justice, the person who has suffered punishment as a result of such conviction shall be compensated according to the law or the practice of the State concerned, unless it is proved that the non-disclosure of the unknown fact in time is wholly or partly attributable to him.

The right to compensation is narrowly drafted, but the provision is reasonably self-explanatory. It is intended only to cover the clearest cases of miscarriages of justice where the miscarriage cannot be said to be wholly or partly the fault of the person punished. The scope of the reference to the 'practice' of the State in the provision is unclear. It suggests that *ex gratia* arrangements may be permissible. The right to compensation for victims of arrest or detention in breach of the requirements of Article 5 refers to 'an enforceable right to compensation', which is an altogether clearer phrase.

It is clear that the Strasbourg Court will require the conditions set out in the Article to be fully met, especially that the conviction has been reversed on the grounds that a new or newly discovered fact shows conclusively that there has been a miscarriage of justice.[149]

[146] *Galstyan v Armenia*, (App. 26986/03), 15 November 2007.
[147] § 120.
[148] § 126, affirmed in *Gasparyan v Armenia (No 2)*, (App. 22571/05), 16 September 2009.
[149] See *Matveyev v Russia*, (App. 26601/02), 3 July 2008.

14

LIMITATIONS COMMON TO ARTICLES 8–11

INTRODUCTION

This chapter is about the express limitations to be found in the second paragraphs of Articles 8 to 11. The Convention does not contain a single approach to limiting the scope of the rights it protects; rather it uses a number of different techniques. There is provision in Article 15 for derogating from some of the protected rights in times of war or public emergency threatening the life of the nation.[1] Secondly, some of the Articles themselves define conduct as outside the protection of the Article in which the right is enumerated when it might otherwise be viewed as within it. So, Article 2(2) excludes deprivation of life from the scope of the right to life when it results from the use of force which is no more than absolutely necessary in one of three defined situations.[2] Similarly Article 4(3) provides that certain types of work, and military service, do not constitute forced or compulsory labour.[3] Article 5 spells out exhaustively the circumstances in which a deprivation of liberty will be permissible.[4] The third technique adopted for limiting the scope of Convention rights can be found in Articles 8 to 11 which make provision for limitations where certain qualifying conditions are satisfied.[5]

Each of Articles 8–11 sets out a Convention right in the first paragraph, but then qualifies it by listing limitations, or restrictions as the Court sometimes describes them, in the second paragraph. Though there are some differences of detail in the nature of the limitations arising under each Article, there is sufficient commonality of approach to justify a collective consideration of these limitations before examining the substantive rights protected under each of these Articles.[6] The justification for these limitations is sometimes

[1] See ch.6. [2] See ch.8. [3] See ch.10. [4] See ch.11.

[5] Similar or analogous limitations can be found elsewhere in the Convention; for example, in Article 2 of Protocol 4 and Article 1 of Protocol 7. It can also be argued that the Strasbourg Court has construed the protection of property rights in Article 1 of Protocol 1 as requiring a similar approach: see ch.20.

[6] See generally, S. Greer, *The Exceptions to Articles 8 to 11 of the European Convention on Human Rights* (Council of Europe Publishing, Strasbourg 1997); J. Viljanen, '*The European Court of Human Rights as a Developer of General Doctrines of Human Rights Law. A Study of the Limitations Clauses of the European Convention on Human Rights* (Tampereen yliopisto, Tampere 2003); B. Hovius, 'The Limitations Clauses of the European Convention on Human Rights and Freedoms and Section 1 of the Canadian Charter of Rights and Freedoms: A Comparative Analysis' (1987) 6 YEL 1; A. McHarg, 'Reconciling Human Rights and the Public Interest: Conceptual Problems and Doctrinal Uncertainty in the Jurisprudence of the European Court of Human Rights' (1999) 62 MLR 671; L. Wildhaber, 'The "Margin of Appreciation" in National Law and the Law of the Strasbourg Institutions', Address to Conference of Presidents of the Supreme Courts and Attorneys General of the Member States of the European Union, London 1 June 2000; S. Greer, 'Constitutionalizing Adjudication under the European Convention on Human Rights' (2003) 23 OJLS 405; S. Greer, '"Balancing" and the European Court of Human Rights: a Contribution to the Habermas-Alexy Debate' (2004) 63 CLJ 412; and J. Sweeney, 'Margins of Appreciation: Cultural Relativity and the European Court of Human Rights in the Post-Cold War Era' (2005) 54 ICLQ 459.

said to arise because of the need to balance the interest of the community against the interests of the individual. This has led some to characterize the exceptions as public interest exceptions to Convention rights. One commentator has observed:

> The relationship between human rights and public interest exceptions is one of the most important issues in contemporary human rights jurisprudence. Not only is the interpretation given to exceptions a key determinant of the utility of rights in practice, but this is also the area in which the political or value-laden nature of the choices facing the court is most obvious, raising questions as to the legitimacy of judicial rather than democratic decision-making.[7]

It is also worth just briefly mentioning the restrictions on the political activities of aliens which may arise under Article 16. Article 16 provides:

> Nothing in Articles 10, 11 and 14 shall be regarded as preventing the High Contracting Parties from imposing restrictions on the political activity of aliens.

This is potentially a very restrictive provision, which could be used to exclude from the application of the Convention those within the jurisdiction of the Contracting States who otherwise enjoy the protection of the Convention. It is not a blanket derogation from the requirements of Articles 10, 11, and 14, but merely permits derogation from the rights contained in those Articles which relate to political activity. However, it is not easy to see how objectionable conduct by those who are not nationals of the State would fall outside the widely drafted limitations contained in those provisions. This may explain why the provision is rarely used and has never been fully considered by the Strasbourg Court.[8]

EXPRESS LIMITATIONS: SOME GENERAL POINTS

The second paragraphs of Articles 8–11 allow for interference by the authorities with the protected rights under certain prescribed conditions. There are two basic principles concerning the restrictions on the rights guaranteed. The first principle is that only the restrictions expressly authorized by the Convention are allowed. That principle is nowhere stated explicitly, but it is presupposed by the whole system of the Convention. Further, it is presupposed, in particular, by the second basic principle, which is expressly stated by Article 18. This principle is that 'the restrictions permitted under this Convention to the said rights and freedoms shall not be applied for any purpose other than those for which they have been prescribed.'

The requirement that restrictions must, in every case, be justified by an express provision of the Convention is significant. It enables the Strasbourg Court to control the

[7] A. McHarg, 'Reconciling Human Rights and the Public Interest: Conceptual Problems and Doctrinal Uncertainty in the Jurisprudence of the European Court of Human Rights' (1999) 62 MLR 671, 695.

[8] In *Piermont v France*, (Apps. 15773/89 and 15774/89), 27 April 1995, Series A, No.314, the Court found that the applicant's possession of the nationality of a Member State of the European Union and her status as a member of the European Parliament did not allow Article 16 to be raised against her, The Partly Dissenting Opinion of Judges Ryssdal, Matscher, Sir John Freeland and Jungwiert, however, took the view that a German national could indeed be an alien in the eyes of French law and that, therefore, Article 16 was at least relevant to this case. It was noted, however, that account must be taken of the increased internationalization of politics in modern circumstances and of the interest which an MEP may legitimately have in the affairs of a Community territory. Thus even the dissenting judges acknowledged that limits may have to be admitted to the restrictions on the political activity of aliens permissible under Article 16.

alleged interference by reference to those express provisions. In dealing with exceptions to Convention rights, the Court adopts a narrow interpretation.[9] In the *Sidiropoulos* case, which concerned the limitations to Articles 11, the Strasbourg Court noted that 'exceptions to freedom of association must be narrowly interpreted, such that the enumeration of them is strictly exhaustive and the definition of them necessarily restrictive.'[10] The same is true of all the limitations to Articles 8 to 11.

Greer has suggested that the justifications for the limitations expressed in these Articles can be divided into those which protect public interests (national security, territorial integrity, the economic well-being of the nation, health and morals, and disorder or crime) and those which protect private interests (maintaining the authority and impartiality of the judiciary, protecting the rights and freedoms of others, and preventing the disclosure of information received in confidence).[11] Such a distinction is, however, somewhat artificial, since some of the interests said to be private interests are clearly intended to serve a public purpose, such as maintaining the authority and impartiality of the judiciary. Most commentators agree that there is a considerable diversity of treatment of individual cases by the Strasbourg organs,[12] and that the Strasbourg Court's decisions tend to be very fact specific.

The Strasbourg Court adopts a three-part inquiry where a Contracting Party seeks to rely on a limitation in one of the Convention Articles. First, it determines whether the interference is in accordance with, or prescribed by, law, then it looks to see whether the aim of the limitation is legitimate in that it fits one of the expressed heads in the particular Article, and finally it asks whether the limitation is in all the circumstances necessary in a democratic society. In making this assessment, the Strasbourg Court will consider whether a Contracting Party has based its decision 'on an acceptable assessment of the relevant facts.'[13] Central to this determination is the proportionality of the interference in securing the legitimate aim. Only the minimum interference with the right which secures the legitimate aim will be permitted. The essence of each of the restrictions is that the interests of society as a whole override the interests of the individual. In cases involving this balancing of values, the question frequently before the Strasbourg Court will be whether the interference goes beyond what is necessary in a democratic society.

The Strasbourg Court does not always follow this three-part inquiry. In some cases, it moves directly to the question of whether an interference can be regarded as necessary in a democratic society without determining whether the complained-of measure was taken in accordance with law for a legitimate aim. In such cases, the Strasbourg Court will indicate that its decision does not require it to determine whether a State measure was in accordance with law or served a legitimate aim.[14] The reason for this approach would seem to be twofold. Sometimes it is difficult for the Court to call into question a respondent State's good faith in imposing restrictions on a Convention right; and sometimes it is hard for the

[9] See, for example, *Klass v Germany*, (App. 5029/71), 6 September 1978, Series A No 28, (1979–80) 2 EHRR 214, § 42; and *The Observer and The Guardian v United Kingdom*, (App. 13585/88), 26 November 1991, Series A No 216, (1992) 14 EHRR 153, § 59.

[10] *Sidiropoulos and others v Greece*, (App. 26695/95), 10 July 1998, (1999) 27 EHRR 633, ECHR 1998-IV, § 38.

[11] S. Greer, *The Exceptions to Articles 8 to 11 of the European Convention on Human Rights* (Council of Europe Publishing, Strasbourg 1997).

[12] For example, A. McHarg, 'Reconciling Human Rights and the Public Interest: Conceptual Problems and Doctrinal Uncertainty in the Jurisprudence of the European Court of Human Rights' (1999) 62 MLR 671, 683–4.

[13] *Gorzelik and others v Poland*, (App. 44158/98), 17 February 2004 [GC], (2005) 40 EHRR 76, ECHR 2004-I, § 96.

[14] For a clear example of such an approach, see *Christian Democratic People's Party v Moldova*, (App. 28793/02), 14 February 2006, (2007) 45 EHRR 392, ECHR 2006-II.

Court to find a breach of national law if the national authorities have acted on the basis that national law has been complied with.

A REQUIRED LEGAL BASIS FOR THE INTERFERENCE

First it must be shown that any restriction imposed on one of the Convention rights is in each case 'in accordance with the law',[15] or 'prescribed by law'.[16] The difference in the language used in Article 8 when compared with Articles 9–11 is immaterial;[17] the French text of the Convention reads *prévue(s) par la loi* in all cases.[18]

The Strasbourg Court, building on the Commission's case-law, has established a three-fold test for determining whether an interference is in accordance with law. First, it must be established that the interference with the Convention right has some basis in national law.[19] Secondly, the law must be accessible; and, thirdly, the law must be formulated in such a way that a person can foresee, to a degree that is reasonable in the circumstances, the consequences which a given action will entail. This is known as the test of foreseeability.[20] The requirements of accessibility and foreseeability have been described as the 'quality of law' requirements.[21]

The references to 'law' are, of course, to national law, and the Strasbourg Court must accept the interpretation of national law adopted by the national courts, unless there are very strong reasons for disagreeing.[22] This is not because the Court is not a 'fourth instance', or higher court of appeal above the national courts. It is rather because questions of national law are for the Court simply questions of fact.

There is no requirement that the law be statutory; it can be unwritten law. In the *Sunday Times* case[23] it was the common law of contempt that was in issue. In the *Barthold* case[24] it was the rules of the Veterinary Surgeons' Council, which had authority to make professional rules. In the *Slivenko* case[25] it was a Treaty between Latvia and Russia relating to the

[15] Art. 8(2) of the Convention. The same language is used in Arts. 2(3) and (4) of Protocol 4, and Art. 1(1) of Protocol 7. What is said here is relevant to consideration of those provisions of the Convention.

[16] Arts. 9(2), 10(2), and 11(2). The same language is used in Art. 2(2) of Protocol 7. What is said here is relevant to consideration of those provisions of the Convention.

[17] See *Sunday Times v United Kingdom*, (App. 6538/74), 26 April 1979, Series A No 30, (1979–80) 2 EHRR 245, § 48.

[18] Art. 1 of Protocol 1 requires interferences to be 'subject to the conditions provided for by law', which raises similar issues to those discussed in this section.

[19] For examples of cases in which the Court could find no relevant law, see *Djavit An v Turkey*, (App. 20652/92), 20 February 2003, (2005) 40 EHRR 1002, ECHR 2003-III; and *Mikhaylyuk and Petrov v Ukraine*, (App. 11932/02), 10 December 2009. In *Republican Party of Russia v Russia*, (App. 12976/07), 12 April 2011 the domestic courts had relied on a provision which was not in force at the material time which the Court confirmed could not therefore serve as a lawful basis for the interference with the applicant's Art. 11 rights.

[20] See, for example, *Huvig v France*, (App. 11105/84), 24 April 1990, Series A No 176-B, (1990) 12 EHRR 528, § 26; and *S and Marper v United Kingdom*, (Apps. 30562/04 and 30566/04), 4 December 2008 [GC], (2009) 48 EHRR 1169; ECHR 2008-nyr, § 99.

[21] For example, *Al-Nashif v Bulgaria*, (App. 50963/99), 20 June 2002, (2003) 36 EHRR 655, § 121.

[22] *Roche v United Kingdom*, (App. 32555/96), 19 October 2005 [GC], (2006) 42 EHRR 599; ECHR 2005-X, § 120. This was a case on restrictions to access to a court under Article 6, but the same principles must apply under Articles 8 to 11.

[23] *Sunday Times v United Kingdom*, (App. 6538/74), 26 April 1979, Series A No 30, (1979–80) 2 EHRR 245.

[24] *Barthold v Germany*, (App. 8734/79), 23 March 1985, Series A No 90, (1985) 7 EHRR 383.

[25] *Slivenko v Latvia*, (App. 48321/99), 9 October 2003 [GC], (2004) 39 EHRR 490, ECHR 2003-X.

withdrawal of Russian troops from the country. In the '*Bosphorus Airways*' case[26] it was a European Community Regulation.

The character of the law imposing the limitations was considered in the *Sunday Times* case.[27] It is not alone enough that the law qualifies as such in the national legal system (though if it does not, any defence a Contracting Party seeks to mount is certain to fail), it must also display additional qualities. First, the law must be adequately accessible: the citizen must be able to have an indication that is adequate in the circumstances of the legal rules applicable to a given case. Secondly, a norm cannot be regarded as 'law' unless it is formulated with sufficient precision to enable citizens to regulate their conduct: they must be able—if need be with appropriate advice—to foresee, to a degree that is reasonable in the circumstances, the consequences which a given action may entail.[28] The Strasbourg Court went on to explain that the requirement of foreseeability was not designed to secure absolute certainty, so that no interpretation would be required in determining the scope of application of the law. However, a certain level of clarity is required. In the *Vogt* case[29] the Court said that the level of precision required:

> depends to a considerable degree on the content of the instrument in question, the field it is designed to cover and the number and status of those to whom it is addressed.[30]

Issues of legal certainty were crucial in *Ternovszky v Hungary*[31] in which the Court stated that the right to choice in matters of child delivery must include the legal certainty that the choice is lawful and not subject to sanctions, directly or indirectly. The issue of health professionals assisting home births was found by the Court to be surrounded by legal uncertainty within Hungary. A Government Decree sanctioned health professionals who carried out activities within their qualifications in a manner which is incompatible with the law or their licence, and in at least one case proceedings were instituted against a health professional for having assisted home birth. The Court concluded that the lack of legal certainty and the threat to health professionals limited the choices of the applicant considering home delivery and was incompatible with the notion of foreseeability.

These requirements can be problematic in cases where they relate to the interests of national security. In the *Malone* case,[32] the Strasbourg Court stressed that the law must indicate the scope of any discretion of the executive with regard to the interception of communications and the manner of its exercise with sufficient clarity to give the individual protection against arbitrary interference. The law of England and Wales was so obscure and subject to such differing interpretations, particularly in respect of the dividing line between conduct covered by legal rules and that covered by executive discretion that it lacked the minimum degree of legal protection required to qualify as 'law' for the purposes of the Convention. In the *Halford* case,[33] there was no regulation of interceptions of calls made on telecommunications systems outside the public network. Telephone calls made on a private network by Alison Halford when Assistant Chief Constable with the Merseyside Police were intercepted; this constituted a violation of Article 8, since the interference with respect for her private life and correspondence was not in accordance with the law.

[26] *'Bosphorus Airways' v Ireland*, (App. 45036/98), 30 June 2005 [GC], (2006) 42 EHRR 1, ECHR 2005-VI.

[27] *Sunday Times v United Kingdom*, (App. 6538/74), 26 April 1979, Series A No 30, (1979–80) 2 EHRR 245.

[28] § 49. [29] *Vogt v Germany*, (App. 17851/91), 26 September 1995, (1996) 21 EHRR 205.

[30] § 48. [31] *Ternovszky v Hungary*, (App. 67545/09), 14 December 2010.

[32] *Malone v United Kingdom*, (App. 8691/79), 2 August 1984, Series A No 82, (1985) 7 EHRR 14; and *Liberty v United Kingdom*, (App. 58243/00), 1 July 2008, (2009) 48 EHRR 1.

[33] *Halford v United Kingdom*, (App. 20605/92), 25 June 1997, (1997) 24 EHRR 523, ECHR 1997-III.

In the *Leander* case,[34] which concerned security checks on certain government personnel, the Strasbourg Court recognized that the requirement of foreseeability could not be the same in the context of security checks on personnel as in other fields. Nevertheless, the law had to be sufficiently clear in regard to the circumstances and conditions which justified secret checks. The Swedish law met these standards.

However, in *Shimovolos v Russia*[35] the creation and maintenance of a surveillance database and the procedure for its operation were governed by a ministerial order which was not published and was not accessible to the public. While the Court acknowledged that, in the special context of secret measures of surveillance, the accessibility and foreseeability requirements cannot mean that an individual should be able to foresee when the authorities are likely to resort to secret surveillance, it is nevertheless 'essential to have clear, detailed rules on the application of secret measures of surveillance, especially as the technology available for use is continually becoming more sophisticated. The law must be sufficiently clear in its terms to give citizens an adequate indication of the conditions and circumstances in which the authorities are empowered to resort to any measures of secret surveillance and collection of data.'[36] These requirements were not met in the present case and thus the interference with the applicant's rights under Article 8 was not 'in accordance with the law'. The Court also noted the need for safeguards which it said should be set out in statute law to avoid abuses. These must include the nature, scope, and duration of the possible measures; the grounds required for ordering them; the authorities competent to permit, carry out and supervise them; and the kind of remedy provided by the national law.[37]

Two cases against the United Kingdom further illustrate the application of the requirement of identifiability, accessibility, and foreseeability in determining whether an interference is 'prescribed by law'. The *Steel* case[38] concerned the imposition of a requirement to be bound over to keep the peace on those charged with, and convicted of, breaches of the peace. The Strasbourg Court concluded that a liability to be bound over to keep the peace was sufficiently clear where such a requirement was imposed after a finding that a person had committed a breach of the peace, despite its being couched in vague and general terms. In the particular circumstances it would be clear that those bound over were agreeing to refrain from causing further, similar, breaches of the law for the period for which they agreed to be bound over.[39] The facts before the Strasbourg Court in the *Hashman and Harrup* case[40] were, arguably, significantly different. The applicants had been involved in activities designed to disrupt a fox-hunt. They were brought before the magistrates' court by way of complaint that they should be required to enter into a recognizance to keep the peace and be of good behaviour. They were so bound over. On a complaint that the measures constituted an interference with their freedom of expression, the Court considered whether binding over to keep the peace as a means of controlling anti-social behaviour was 'prescribed by law'. Here the Court regarded the law as being too vague; the binding over orders were not in the nature of a sanction for past unlawful conduct; the notion of conduct *contra bonos mores*[41] was too vague to meet the requirement of predictability of

[34] *Leander v Sweden*, (App. 9248/81), 26 March 1987, Series A No 116, (1987) 9 EHRR 433.

[35] *Shimovolos v Russia*, (App. 30194/09), 21 June 2011. [36] § 68. [37] § 68.

[38] *Steel and others v United Kingdom*, (App. 24838/94), 23 September 1998, (1999) 28 EHRR 603, ECHR 1998-VII. [39] §§ 76 and 94.

[40] *Hashman and Harrup v United Kingdom*, (App. 25594/94), 25 November 1999, (2000) 30 EHRR 241, ECHR 1999-VIII.

[41] Defined as behaviour which is 'wrong rather than right in the judgment of contemporary fellow citizens': § 38.

application. It could not be said that what the applicants were being bound over not to do must have been apparent to them. The dissenting judge disagreed, noting that the binding over order placed an 'unmistakable obligation on the applicants, namely to refrain from any offensive and deliberate action which would disturb the lawfully organized activity of others engaged in fox-hunting.'[42] The distinction between a case where there is conduct of which the applicants were convicted which rendered the binding over foreseeable, and one where there is conduct leading to a complaint but no conviction, is a particularly narrow one.

It will be important for all of the consequences of the domestic legal provisions to be foreseeable. In *Kurić and others v Slovenia*,[43] the Grand Chamber found that, while accessible domestic law meant that the applicants would be able to foresee that by failing to apply for Slovenian nationality, they would be treated as aliens, they could not reasonably have expected that their status as aliens would entail the unlawfulness of their residence on Slovenian territory. The extreme measure of 'erasure', which could not have been foreseen, was carried out automatically, without prior notification and without the applicants being given the opportunity to challenge it. In the Court's view, the absence of any notification could have led the applicants to believe that their status as residents had remained unchanged and that they could continue residing and working in Slovenia. The Grand Chamber also noted that there was a legal vacuum in the domestic legislation at the time since there was no legal provision regulating the transition of the legal status of the 'erased' to the status of aliens living in Slovenia. The applicants were therefore not in a position to foresee the measure complained of, nor to envisage its repercussions to their private and family life.

The recent case of *Vyerentsov v Ukraine*[44] concerned the application of Soviet legislation on the procedure for holding peaceful demonstrations by the Ukrainian authorities in the absence of the Ukraine's own legislative framework to implement its Constitutional rules on freedom of assembly. Whilst the Court accepted that 'it may take some time for a country to establish its legislative framework during a transitional period, it cannot agree that a delay of more than twenty years is justifiable, especially when such a fundamental right as freedom of peaceful assembly is at stake.'[45] Domestic legislation prescribed a penalty for breaches of the procedure for organizing and holding demonstrations and thus the impugned arrest had a basis in domestic law which was accessible. However, the procedure relied upon by the authorities (which derived from a Soviet decree), was not formulated with sufficient precision to enable the applicant to foresee, to a degree that was reasonable in the circumstances, the consequences of his actions.

Finally, the quality of law requirements may necessitate appropriate procedural safeguards. In *Sanoma Uitgevers B.V. v The Netherlands*[46] the Court reiterated that any interference with the right to protection of journalistic sources must be attended with legal procedural safeguards commensurate with the importance of the principle at stake. The most vital such safeguard is the guarantee of review by a judge or other independent and impartial decision-making body. On the facts of the case before it, the investigating judge's involvement lacked any legal basis and performed only an advisory role. The Court described this situation as 'scarcely compatible with the rule of law'[47] and concluded that the quality of the law was deficient in that there was no procedure with adequate legal safeguards to enable an independent assessment as to whether the interest of the criminal

[42] Dissenting opinion of Judge Baka.

[43] *Kurić and others v Slovenia*, (App. 26828/06), 26 June 2012 [GC], ECHR 2012 (extracts).

[44] *Vyerentsov v Ukraine*, (App. 20372/11), 11 April 2013. [45] § 55.

[46] *Sanoma Uitgevers B.V. v The Netherlands*, (App. 38224/03), 14 September 2010 [GC]. [47] § 98.

investigation overrode the public interest in the protection of journalistic sources. While in this case, safeguards against abuse were considered in the context of 'prescribed by law', sometimes they will be considered by the Court under the heading of what is 'necessary in a democratic society'.[48]

SPECIFIED LEGITIMATE AIMS

Table 14.1 maps the legitimate aims to be found in the second paragraphs of Article 8–11 of the Convention. Article 10 on freedom of expression has the longest list of limitations, and Article 9 on freedom of thought, conscience, and religion the shortest list of limitations. In modern times, it looks anomalous that the interests of national security are not listed in Article 9. There is also considerable overlap between some of the restrictions. There are also some differences of wording which do not appear to be particularly significant.

For example, national security is almost certainly broad enough to incorporate territorial integrity, though that is only mentioned in Article 10. It is also interesting to note that the economic well-being of the country is only listed in Article 8, which suggests that economic considerations cannot base restrictions on the rights protected by Articles 9–11. Given the case-law on trade union rights under Article 11, that omission might be questioned by some. Articles 8, 10, and 11 refer to the prevention of disorder or crime, whereas Article 9 alone refers to the protection of public order and does not mention the prevention of disorder or crime. But the concepts of protecting public order, and preventing disorder and crime, are probably much the same in terms of a Contracting Party's aims in imposing restrictions on the rights contained in Articles 8 to 11.

Once the Court is satisfied that any restriction has a legal basis which meets the requirements of 'law' under the Convention provisions, it will go on to consider whether the restriction is for one of the specified legitimate aims.[49] The justifications set out in the Convention provisions are exhaustive, but also quite comprehensive in the range of interests which may be brought into play. It has proved very easy for a Contracting State to bring its action within one of the stated exceptions, and the Strasbourg Court seldom has to spend much time analysing the nature of the limitation to satisfy itself that it falls within one of them;[50] indeed, it frequently finds that a measure is justified by reference to several specific aims. There are cases where the Strasbourg Court doubts the applicability of a claim by a Contracting Party. So, in the *Sidiropoulos* case,[51] Greece sought to justify refusal to register an association on the grounds that it was 'upholding Greece's cultural traditions and historical and cultural symbols.' [52] The Strasbourg Court was not persuaded that such a ground fell within the legitimate aims set out in Article 11(2), but was nevertheless able to find other legitimate aims served by the measures adopted by the respondent State.

The Court does, however, adopt a rigorous, though variable, approach to the issues of necessity and proportionality in relation to the measures taken to secure the legitimate

[48] As in *Avilkina and others v Russia*, (App. 1585/09), 6 June 2013.

[49] See generally P. Kempees, '"Legitimate aims" in the case-law of the European Court of Human Rights' in P. Mahoney and others, *Protecting Human Rights: The European Perspective. Studies in Memory of Rolv Ryssdal* (Carl Heymanns, Köln 2000), 659.

[50] Claims by the respondent State are only rarely contested by applicants.

[51] *Sidiropoulos and others v Greece*, (App. 26695/95), 10 July 1998, (1999) 27 EHRR 633, ECHR 1998-IV.

[52] § 37.

Table 14.1 Express limitations in Articles 8–11

Article 8 *Right to respect for private and family life*	Article 9 *Freedom of thought, conscience and religion*	Article 10 *Freedom of expression*	Article 11 *Freedom of assembly and association*
in accordance with law	prescribed by law	prescribed by law	prescribed by law
necessary in a democratic society	necessary in a democratic society	necessary in a democratic society	necessary in a democratic society
interests of national security		interests of national security	interests of national security
		interests of territorial integrity	
interests of public safety	interests of public safety	interests of public safety	interests of public safety
interests of economic well-being of the country			
prevention of disorder or crime	protection of public order	prevention of disorder or crime	prevention of disorder or crime
protection of health or morals	protection of health or morals	protection of health or morals	protection of health or morals
		protection of the reputation of others	
protection of the rights and freedoms of others	protection of the rights and freedoms of others	protection of the rights of others	protection of the rights and freedoms of others
		preventing the disclosure of information received in confidence	
		maintaining the authority and impartiality of the judiciary	

aim. What follows are simply some illustrations of cases in which reliance has been placed on a particular ground.

THE INTERESTS OF NATIONAL SECURITY

The interests of national security are listed in Articles 8, 10, and 11, but omitted from Article 9.[53] National security is a broad concept. Kempees summarizes the scope of this

[53] See *Nolan and K v Russia*, (App. 2512/04), 12 February 2009.

limitation as measures protecting 'the safety of the State against enemies who might seek to subdue its forces in war or subvert its government by illegal means' including those features which make it a democracy.[54]

In the *Zana* case[55] the Strasbourg Court regarded measures taken by Turkey to deal with the security situation in south-east Turkey as measures for the protection of national security.

The *Klass* case[56] concerned the legitimacy of secret surveillance. The Strasbourg Court accepted that the German measures fell within the national security exception, since democratic societies found themselves threatened by highly sophisticated forms of espionage and by terrorism, and needed to undertake secret surveillance to counter such threats.

In the *Rekvényi* case[57] the Court accepted, in the context of a challenge that the provisions violated Article 10, that a constitutional ban on political activities and party affiliation by police officers could be imposed 'for the protection of national security and public safety and the prevention of disorder'. Several aims were also relied upon by the respondent Government in *Republican Party of Russia v Russia*[58] to justify the applicant's dissolution for failure to comply with the requirements of minimum membership and regional representation, namely protecting the democratic institutions and constitutional foundations of the Russian Federation, securing its territorial integrity, and guaranteeing the rights and legitimate interests of others. The Court reiterated that 'the defence of territorial integrity is closely linked with the protection of "national security"...while the protection of a State's democratic institutions and constitutional foundations relates to "the prevention of disorder", the concept of "order" within the meaning of the French version of Article 11 encompassing the "institutional order".'[59] The Court was prepared to accept that the contested statutory requirements and the applicant's dissolution for failure to comply with them were intended to protect national security, prevent disorder, and guarantee the rights of others.

Although the Court does not usually scrutinize the Government's reliance upon national security as a legitimate aim too closely, it is sometimes prepared to do so:

> even where national security is at stake, the concepts of lawfulness and the rule of law in a democratic society require that measures affecting fundamental human rights must be subject to some form of adversarial proceedings before an independent body competent to review the reasons for the decision and relevant evidence, if need be with appropriate procedural limitations on the use of classified information. The individual must be able to challenge the executive's assertion that national security is at stake. While the executive's assessment of what poses a threat to national security will naturally be of significant weight, the independent authority must be able to react in cases where invoking that concept has no reasonable basis in the facts or reveals an interpretation of "national security" that is unlawful or contrary to common sense and arbitrary.[60]

In the absence of this in the case of *Nolan and K. v Russia*, the Court was unable to discern any concrete findings of fact corroborating the Government's argument that the applicant's religious activity posed a threat to national security.

[54] P. Kempees, '"Legitimate aims" in the case-law of the European Court of Human Rights' in P. Mahoney and others, *Protecting Human Rights: The European Perspective. Studies in Memory of Rolv Ryssdal* (Carl Heymanns, Köln 2000), 662.

[55] *Zana v Turkey*, (App. 18954/91), 25 November 1997, (1999) 27 EHRR 667, ECHR 1997-VII, § 49.

[56] *Klass v Germany*, (App. 5029/71), 6 September 1978; Series A No 28, (1979–80) 2 EHRR 214.

[57] *Rekvényi v Hungary*, (App. 25390/94), 20 May 1999, (2000) 30 EHRR 519, ECHR 1999-III, § 41.

[58] *Republican Party of Russia v Russia*, (App. 12976/07), 12 April 2011.

[59] § 101.

[60] *Nolan and K. v Russia*, (App. 2512/04), 12 February 2009, § 71.

Furthermore, the Court emphasized that the exceptions to freedom of religion listed in Article 9(2) 'must be narrowly interpreted, for their enumeration is strictly exhaustive and their definition is necessarily restrictive' and noted that national security is not listed as a legitimate aim in that provision. In the Court's view, 'Far from being an accidental omission, the non-inclusion of that particular ground for limitations in Article 9 reflects the primordial importance of religious pluralism as "one of the foundations of a 'democratic society' within the meaning of the Convention" and the fact that a State cannot dictate what a person believes or take coercive steps to make him change his beliefs.'[61] Therefore, the interests of national security could not serve as a justification for the measures taken by the Russian authorities against the applicant.

THE INTERESTS OF TERRITORIAL INTEGRITY

This ground, which is surprisingly only mentioned specifically in Article 10, is often linked to national security as in the *Zana* case.[62] The Court has chosen to couple territorial integrity closely with issues of national security, thus reducing the effect of its specific mention only in Article 10. The interests of territorial integrity would seem to require some threat of violence or disorder before resort can be made to this ground. Turkish arguments that a limitation justified on grounds of territorial integrity involved issues relating to the preservation of national unity as an idea[63] were rejected.

THE INTERESTS OF PUBLIC SAFETY

Few cases have raised questions of limitations based solely on public safety, and the Strasbourg Court does not appear to have relied exclusively on this head, though frequently, as in the *Rekvényi* case discussed earlier, reliance is placed on public safety alongside national security and the prevention of disorder. In one case,[64] the Commission upheld resort to public safety in a case where it was argued that married people should be able to continue their married life in prison. A more easily sustained case could be made under the prevention of disorder or crime head.

The ground was raised and accepted in the *Buckley* case,[65] which concerned the refusal of planning permission to a gypsy for caravans to be used as homes. The requirement of planning permission was said in this case to be 'aimed at furthering highway safety, the preservation of the environment and public health'. The Court accepted that these came within the exceptions relating to public safety, the economic well-being of the country, the protection of health, and the protection of the rights of others.

Public safety is often viewed as being synonymous with public order. In the *Metropolitan Church of Bessarabia* case, which concerned the system in Moldova under which only recognized religions could be practised, the Strasbourg Court said:

> The Court considers that States have the power to inquire into whether a movement or association is using supposedly religious aims in order to pursue activities that may harm the population or public safety.

[61] § 73.

[62] *Zana v Turkey*, (App. 18954/91), 5 November 1997, (1999) 27 EHRR 667, § 49; *Republican Party of Russia v Russia*, (App. 12976/07), 12 April 2011, § 101.

[63] And so justifying restrictions on freedom of expression, see, for example, *Arslan v Turkey*, (App. 23462/94), 8 July 1999, (2001) 31 EHRR 264.

[64] App. 8166/78, *X and Y v Switzerland*, 3 October 1978, (1979) 13 DR 241, 243.

[65] *Buckley v United Kingdom*, (App. 20348/92), 25 September 1996, (1997) 23 EHRR 101, ECHR 1996-IV, §§ 62–3.

> In view of the circumstances of the case, the Court holds that the impugned interference did in this case pursue a legitimate aim under Article 9(2) namely the protection of order and public safety.[66]

Recently, in *Sabanchiyeva and others v Russia*[67] the applicants complained about the authorities' refusal to return the bodies of their deceased relatives. Relying upon the Government's concerns about the risk of increasing inter-ethnic and religious tension, the Court agreed that this measure could be considered as having been taken in the interests of public safety, as well as for the prevention of disorder, and for the protection of the rights and freedoms of others.

FOR THE ECONOMIC WELL-BEING OF THE COUNTRY

This legitimate aim is mentioned only in Article 8, which suggests that economic considerations may not underpin limitations to the rights in Articles 9, 10, and 11. The omission of this specific head from Article 11 is worth noting.[68]

The protection of the economic well-being of the country was referred to in the *Gillow* case,[69] which concerned the requirement to have permission from the authorities to occupy a home in Guernsey. The Strasbourg Court accepted the respondent State's arguments that it was permissible to 'maintain the population within limits that permit the balanced economic development of the island'.[70] In the *Berrehab* case, the Strasbourg Court concluded that the deportation of a Moroccan citizen on his divorce from a Dutch national could legitimately be based on the economic well-being of the country since the respondent State was concerned 'because of population density, to regulate the labour market'.[71]

The *Miailhe* case[72] concerned the exercise of search and seizure powers of people's homes by customs authorities. The applicants argued that there had been a violation of Article 8. The Strasbourg Court considered that the interferences with the rights protected in Article 8 were in the interests of the economic well-being of the country. Similarly in the *Funke* case[73] the Court was faced with a complaint of a violation of Article 8 arising from searches of the applicant's home in connection with enquiries into financial dealings with foreign countries contrary to French law. The Court concluded that the interferences pursued a legitimate aim of being in the interest of the economic well-being of the country.

An order to vacate a flat, under Croatian laws regulating ownership which allowed an owner to seek repossession of his or her property when the possessor has no legal grounds for possession, was found to pursue the legitimate aim of the economic well-being of the country in *Orlić v Croatia*.[74] In *Kryvitska and Kryvitskyy v Ukraine*,[75] since the authorities

[66] *Metropolitan Church of Bessarabia v Moldova*, (App. 45701/99), 14 December 2001, (2002) 35 EHRR 306, ECHR 2001-XII, § 113. See also *Leela Förderkreis EV v Germany*, (App. 58911/00), 6 November 2008, (2009) 49 EHRR 117, § 94 (an Article 9 case).

[67] *Sabanchiyeva and others v Russia*, (App. 38450/05), 6 June 2013.

[68] Nor is it mentioned in Article 2 of Protocol 4, although Article 2(4) of that Protocol does include limitations 'justified by the public interest'; this is a phrase not used in Articles 8 to 11 and may be wide enough to include economic interests.

[69] *Gillow v United Kingdom*, (App. 9063/80), 24 November 1986, Series A No 109, (1986) 11 EHRR 355.

[70] § 54.

[71] *Berrehab v Netherlands*, (App. 10730/84), 21 June 1988, Series A No 138, (1989) 11 EHRR 322, § 26.

[72] *Miailhe v France*, (App. 12661/87), 25 February 1993, Series A No 256-C, (1993) 16 EHRR 332.

[73] *Funke v France*, (App. 10828/84), 25 February 1993, Series A No 256-A, (1993) 16 EHRR 297.

[74] *Orlić v Croatia*, (App. 48833/07), 21 June 2011.

[75] *Kryvitska and Kryvitskyy v Ukraine*, (App. 30856/03), 2 December 2010.

sought vacation of a property in order to gain profit, the Court accepted that eviction was seen as benefiting the economic well-being of the country. *Yordanova and others v Bulgaria*[76] established that improvement of the urban environment by removing unsightly and substandard buildings and replacing them with modern dwellings meeting the relevant architectural and technical requirements is a legitimate aim in the interests of economic well-being and the protection of the health and the rights of others. In the *Hatton* case,[77] the Strasbourg Court seems to have accepted that night flights 'contribute at least to a certain extent to the general economy', though it was acknowledged that it was difficult to draw a clear line between the interests of the airlines and that of the economic interests of the country as a whole. In *Zammit Maempel v Malta*[78] the Court accepted this legitimate aim in the context of regulation of firework displays at a village feast which generated an amount of income and which therefore, at least to a certain extent, aided the general economy.

THE PREVENTION OF DISORDER OR CRIME

Articles 8, 10, and 11 refers to the prevention of disorder or crime, whereas Article 9 refers to the prevention of public disorder. Little seems to turn on the difference of wording,[79] since the concept of order, of which the opposite is disorder, is probably somewhat wider than the concept of 'public order'.[80] What is, however, clear is that disorder and crime are different concepts. In *Van Der Heijden v The Netherlands*[81] the Court confirmed that the prevention of crime concept encompasses the securing of evidence for the purpose of detecting and prosecuting crime. Similarly in the *S and Marper* case, the Court accepted that a system of retaining DNA samples and fingerprints served the aim of preventing crime, although it found that the scheme in place in the United Kingdom was too far-reaching and disproportionate.[82]

The prevention of disorder or crime is the most frequently raised justification before the Strasbourg Court, and the most frequently accepted by it. This is unsurprising since many complaints involve penal measures, whose underlying purpose is the prevention of disorder or crime. For example, in *Piechowicz v Poland*[83] restrictions on contact between the applicant and his common-law wife while he was in prison were based on the fact that she was indicted together with the applicant in the criminal proceedings against him and thus could be regarded as applied in pursuance of the prevention of disorder or crime.

An example of how easy this legitimate aim can be to apply is provided by the case of *Dadouch v Malta*[84] where the Court seemed to have some doubts about its relevance: 'While it is difficult to perceive how the refusal to register the applicant's marriage could prevent bigamy or ensure certainty in respect of personal status as submitted by the

[76] *Yordanova and others v Bulgaria*, (App. 25446/06), 24 April 2012, § 113.

[77] *Hatton v United Kingdom*, (App. 36022/97), 8 July 2003 [GC], (2003) 37 EHRR 611, ECHR 2003-VIII, § 126.

[78] *Zammit Maempel v Malta*, (App. 24202/10), 22 November 2011.

[79] Article 1 of Protocol 7 refers to 'public order', and Article 2 of Protocol 4 uses the French phrase *ordre public*.

[80] See *Engel and others v Netherlands*, (Apps. 5100/71, 5101/71, 5102/71, 5354/72, and 5370/72), 8 June 1976, Series A No 22, (1979–80) 2 EHRR 647, § 98.

[81] *Van Der Heijden v The Netherlands*, (App. 42857/05), 3 April 2012 [GC], § 54.

[82] *S and Marper v United Kingdom*, (Apps. 30562/04 and 30566/04), 4 December 2008 [GC], (2009) 48 EHRR 1169; ECHR 2008. See further below in this chapter, and the discussion of the case in ch.16.

[83] *Piechowicz v Poland*, (App. 20071/07), 17 April 2012.

[84] *Dadouch v Malta*, (App. 38816/07), 20 July 2010.

Government... the Court is prepared to accept that national regulation of the registration of marriage may serve the legitimate aim of the prevention of disorder and the protection of the rights of others, as contended by the Government.'[85]

In the *Otto-Preminger Institute* case[86] the Strasbourg Court accepted that the provisions of the Austrian Penal Code which permitted seizure of a film considered to offend the religious sensibilities of Roman Catholics were 'intended to suppress behaviour directed against objects of religious veneration that is likely to cause "justified indignation" '[87] and so operated to prevent public disorder.

'Prevention of disorder' may encompass broader issues than public disorder, however. An interesting view was taken of the 'prevention of disorder' in *Republican Party of Russia v Russia*[88] where the Court stated that 'the protection of a State's democratic institutions and constitutional foundations relates to "the prevention of disorder", the concept of "order" within the meaning of the French version of Article 11 encompassing the "institutional order".'[89]

THE PROTECTION OF HEALTH OR MORALS

This limitation is frequently cited as the justification for interferences with Convention rights.[90] Once again, two rather disparate interests are combined, but it is clear that the limitation may operate for the protection of health or for the protection of morals; it does not have to be for the protection of both.

The protection of health is often relied upon in the context of public health. For example, a programme of compulsory vaccination may pursue the legitimate aim of protection of health,[91] as too may measures to cope with the hazards associated with an unlawful settlement of makeshift houses lacking sewage and sanitary facilities.[92] Protection of health may also, however, refer to individual health and not just to the protection of public health.[93] In *Jehovah's Witnesses of Moscow and others v Russia*[94] the refusal of blood transfusions on religious grounds was found to be relevant to a legitimate aim of protection of health. In this case, domestic courts had found that under the influence of the applicant community its members had refused transfusions of blood and/or blood components even in difficult or life threatening circumstances. The Strasbourg Court noted that, according to the judgments of the Russian courts, the dissolution of the applicant community was necessary to prevent it from breaching the rights of others, inflicting harm on its members, damaging their health, and impinging on the well-being of children. Therefore, the interference pursued the legitimate aims of the protection of health and the rights of others under Articles 9 and 11.

The notion of the protection of morals seems to have been regarded as referring to sexual morality, when that is not a necessary constraint of the language used. The classic example is the seizure of *The Little Red Schoolbook* which gave rise to the *Handyside* case.[95]

[85] § 54.

[86] *Otto-Preminger Institute v Austria*, (App. 13470/87), 20 September 1994, Series A No 295-A, (1995) 19 EHRR 34.

[87] § 48.

[88] *Republican Party of Russia v Russia*, (App. 12976/07), 12 April 2011.

[89] § 101.

[90] See generally C. Nowlin, 'The Protection of Morals under the European Convention for the Protection of Human Rights and Fundamental Freedoms' (2002) 24 HRQ 264.

[91] *Solomakhin v Ukraine*, (App. 24429/03), 15 March 2012.

[92] *Yordanova and others v Bulgaria*, (App. 25446/06), 24 April 2012.

[93] *Eriksson v Sweden*, (App. 11373/85), 22 June 1989, Series A No 156, (1990) 12 EHRR 183, §§ 66–7.

[94] *Jehovah's Witnesses of Moscow and others v Russia* (App. 302/02)10 June 2010.

[95] *Handyside v United Kingdom*, (App. 5493/72), 7 December 1976, Series A No 24, (1979–80) 1 EHRR 737.

The Strasbourg Court was called upon to consider whether the conviction of individuals who had published a reference book targeted at children of school age containing advice on sexual and other matters violated the guarantee of freedom of expression in Article 10. The Court readily accepted that the issues raised here related to the protection of morals in the sense that the protection of morals entailed the safeguarding of the moral standards of society as a whole. A similar view was taken in a case involving the confiscation of a number of sexually explicit paintings.[96]

Perhaps a different approach was adopted in the *Dudgeon* case,[97] in which the Court was called upon to decide whether the continuing criminalization, in Northern Ireland, of certain sexual activities between consenting male adults in private constituted a breach of Article 8 of the Convention. Elsewhere in the United Kingdom, such acts no longer constituted criminal offences. In its judgment the Strasbourg Court said:

> The Convention right affected by the impugned legislation protects an essentially private manifestation of the human personality.... There is now a better understanding, and in consequence an increased tolerance, of homosexual behaviour to the extent that in the great majority of the member States of the Council of Europe it is no longer considered to be necessary or appropriate to treat homosexual practices of the kind now in question as in themselves a matter to which the sanctions of the criminal law should be applied.... Although members of the public who regard homosexuality as immoral may be shocked, offended or disturbed by the commission by others of private homosexual acts, this cannot on its own warrant the application of penal sanctions when it is consenting adults alone who are involved.[98]

The Strasbourg Court could not see that criminalization of the acts in question was required to preserve moral standards, though it is equally the case that the Court was able to find a common European standard in relation to the conduct in question. The case may be contrasted with the Court's judgment in the *Laskey, Jaggard and Brown* case.[99] This case concerned sado-masochistic practices undertaken by men in private, and arguably was on all fours with the circumstances in the *Dudgeon* case in terms of private manifestations of human personality. Nevertheless, the Strasbourg Court did not regard the criminalization of acts of a sado-masochistic nature[100] as in breach of Article 8. The Court failed to grasp the nettle of considering the limits of State interference in private consensual conduct as a breach of respect for the personal autonomy of individuals. It may have been influenced by the arguments relating to the protection of health having regard to the nature of the injuries inflicted by the participants upon one another. In a later case (not involving concerns about 'public health considerations'), the Court followed the approach in the *Dudgeon* case in confirming that there was a violation of Article 8 in applying criminal sanctions to consensual sexual conduct between men in private.[101] However, in *Stübing v Germany*[102] the criminal prohibition of consensual sexual intercourse between consanguine adult siblings was accepted to be aimed at the protection of morals and of the rights of others, an

[96] *Müller and others v Switzerland*, (App. 10737/84), 24 May 1988, Series A No 132, (1991) 13 EHRR 212.

[97] *Dudgeon v United Kingdom*, (App. 7525/76), 22 October 1981, Series A No 45, (1982) 4 EHRR 149.

[98] § 60.

[99] *Laskey, Jaggard and Brown v United Kingdom*, (Apps. 21627/93, 21826/93, and 21974/93), 19 February 1997, (1997) 24 EHRR 39, ECHR 1997-I.

[100] And the refusal of a defence of consent to them in the United Kingdom. For a more liberal approach towards sado-masochistic role play, see *Pay v United Kingdom*, (App. 32792/05), Decision of 16 September 2008.

[101] *ADT v United Kingdom*, (App. 35765/97), 31 July 2000, (2001) 31 EHRR 33, ECHR 2000-IX.

[102] *Stübing v Germany*, (App. 43547/08), 12 April 2012.

approach that again failed to engage with the crux of the debate between private actions and public morality.

The protection of morals will include different considerations dependent upon the specific moral values of a State. Thus in *A, B, C v Ireland*[103] the Grand Chamber acknowledged that the right to life of the unborn is one aspect of the legitimate aim of the protection of morals in Ireland (and not in many other Contracting States). The Court accepted that the restrictions on lawful abortion were based on 'profound moral values concerning the nature of life'.[104] This approach enabled the Grand Chamber to avoid the need to determine whether the term 'others' in Article 8(2) extends to the unborn.

THE PROTECTION OF THE REPUTATION OF OTHERS

The protection of the reputation of others is only mentioned in Article 10,[105] which concerns freedom of expression. Articles 8 and 9 refer to the protection of the rights and freedoms of others, while Article 10 refers to the protection of the reputation or rights of others. Little seems to turn on the different form of wording, but the subordination of freedom of expression for the protection of the reputation of others probably justifies specific reference in Article 10. It is commonly cited in Article 10 cases.[106]

In the *Lindon* case,[107] writers and publishers of a book presented as a novel were convicted of defamation or complicity in defamation. The book tells the story of the trial of Ronald Blistier, a *Front National* militant, for the killing of a young man of North African descent. The book is based on a real-life trial for murders of black men. Jean-Marie Le Pen[108] had declared that the case was a put-up job to discredit the *Front National.* It was not contested in the case that the French legislation on which the convictions of the writers and publishers were based was for the protection of the reputation of others.[109] It is accordingly clear that the protection of the reputation of others is not simply that of individuals but also of various kinds of organization.[110]

This ground was used, somewhat controversially, as the basis for upholding the German Unfair Competition Act in the *Jacubowski* case.[111] A provision seeking to protect the reputation of others does not at first sight appear to have anything to do with protecting commercial interests.

The Court has confirmed that it is generally for the national courts to determine whether an impugned statement is capable of affecting a plaintiff's reputation. Therefore in *Karsai v Hungary*[112] the Court would not depart from the conclusions of the national courts even when the applicant disputed whether the impugned statement could be understood to have referred to the plaintiff.

[103] *A, B and C v Ireland*, (App. 25579/05), 16 December 2010 [GC], ECHR 2010.

[104] § 241.

[105] As part of the phrase 'for the reputation or rights of others'.

[106] See further ch.18.

[107] *Lindon, Otchakovsky-Laurens and July v France*, (Apps. 21279/02 and 36448/02), 22 October 2007 [GC], (2008) 46 EHRR 761, ECHR 2007-XI.

[108] Leader of the *Front National*, a far-right nationalist party in France, which campaigns against immigration, particularly from North Africa.

[109] Jean-Marie Le Pen and the *Front National* party.

[110] See, for example, *Schmidt v Austria*, (App. 513/05), 17 July 2008, where it was the reputation of the Vienna Food Inspection Agency which was in issue.

[111] *Jacubowski v Germany*, (App. 15088/89), 23 June 1994, Series A No 291, (1995) 19 EHRR 64. See also *Barthold v Germany*, (App. 8734/79), 23 March 1985, Series A No 90, (1985) 7 EHRR 383, and *Markt Intern Verlag GmbH and Klaus Beermann v Germany*, (App. 10572/83), 20 November 1989, Series A No 165, (1990) 12 EHRR 161. See discussion of these cases in ch.18.

[112] *Karsai v Hungary*, (App. 5380/07), 1 December 2009.

THE PROTECTION OF THE RIGHTS OR FREEDOMS OF OTHERS

This too is a frequently raised limitation, which covers a wide range of matters. There can often be an overlap between this aim and other specified aims.

The limitation was used in the *Otto-Preminger Institute* case[113] where the showing of the offending film was considered to breach the right to respect for religious feelings when the rights in Articles 9 and 10 were read together.[114]

This limitation has also been applied frequently in child-care cases, where it is readily accepted that national legislation for placing children in care serves the purpose of 'protecting the rights and freedoms of others': in this case the child.[115]

The existence of this ground shows just how open-ended the limitations can be. The range of rights which might be protected is not limited. This may be useful. For example, it enabled the Strasbourg Court in the *Chappell* case[116] to regard search warrants,[117] designed to discover items produced in breach of intellectual property rights which could then be seized, as falling within the limitations to Article 8.[118] In *MGN Limited v The United Kingdom*[119] the Court accepted that a conditional fee arrangement with recoverable success fees sought to achieve the legitimate aim of the widest public access to legal services for civil litigation funded by the private sector and thus the protection of the rights of others within the meaning of Article 10(2) of the Convention. In *Maskhadova and others v Russia*[120] the rights and freedoms of others included the need to minimize the informational and psychological impact of terrorist acts on the population, including the weakening of its propaganda effect and the need to protect the feelings of relatives of the victims of the terrorist acts in question.

THE PREVENTION OF THE DISCLOSURE OF INFORMATION RECEIVED IN CONFIDENCE

Article 10(2) contains two additional limitations. The first relates to measures for preventing the disclosure of information received in confidence. Interestingly in the *Weber* case,[121] where the applicant had been fined for breaching the confidentiality of the judicial investigation, the Strasbourg Court regarded the limitation as designed to protect the authority and impartiality of the judiciary, rather than on this ground. This suggests that this limitation is seen as rather more concerned with material received in confidence outside the courtroom.

A clear example of the use of this legitimate aim can be found in the *Autronic* case,[122] which concerned the reception and re-transmission of televised material from the Soviet Union which was intended for reception only within the Soviet Union. The Strasbourg

[113] *Otto-Preminger Institute v Germany*, (App. 13470/87), 20 September 1994, Series A No 295-A, (1995) 19 EHRR 34.

[114] §§ 46–8.

[115] See, for example, *Johansen v Norway*, (App. 17383/90), 7 August 1996, (1997) 23 EHRR 33, ECHR 1996-III.

[116] *Chappell v United Kingdom*, (App. 10461/83), 30 March 1989, Series A No 152, (1990) 12 EHRR 1.

[117] Anton Piller orders.

[118] Further examples of the use of this ground can be found in the *Spycatcher* cases: *Observer and Guardian v United Kingdom*, (App. 13585/88), 26 November 1991, Series A No 216, (1992) 14 EHRR 153; and *Sunday Times v United Kingdom (No. 2)*, (App. 13166/87), 26 November 1991, Series A No 217, (1992) 14 EHRR 229. See ch.18.

[119] *MGN Limited v The United Kingdom*, (App. 39401/04), 18 January 2011.

[120] *Maskhadova and others v Russia*, (App. 18071/05), 6 June 2013.

[121] *Weber v Switzerland*, (App. 11034/84), 22 May 1990, Series A No 177, (1990) 12 EHRR 508.

[122] *Autronic Ag v Switzerland*, (App. 12726/87), 22 May 1990, Series A No 178, (1990) 12 EHRR 485.

Court regarded the Swiss measure as serving the aim of preventing the disclosure of confidential information.[123] A more recent example is *Stoll v Switzerland*[124] in which the applicant's conviction for publication of 'secret official deliberations' pursued the legitimate aim of preventing the disclosure of information received in confidence.

MAINTAINING THE AUTHORITY AND IMPARTIALITY OF THE JUDICIARY

Article 10(2) also permits limitations justified as maintaining the authority and impartiality of the judiciary. Resort to this ground for interferences with the rights contained in Article 10 is relatively rare. Where the interests of the judiciary are concerned it is more usual to rely upon the protection of the reputation or rights of others. In one case,[125] the applicant company complained that the grant of injunctions by the Austrian authorities prohibiting the publication of a photograph of a suspect violated the rights in Article 10. The injunctions were granted on the basis that they were intended to protect the suspect against insult and defamation and against violations of the presumption of innocence. The Strasbourg Court concluded that this met the aim of protecting the reputation of others and also served to maintain the authority and impartiality of the judiciary.[126] In the *Schöpfer* case,[127] the Court accepted that a penalty imposed upon a lawyer by a professional body in respect of a lawyer's inflammatory criticisms of the judiciary pursued the legitimate aim of maintaining the authority and impartiality of the judiciary, while in *Žugić v Croatia*[128] the imposition of a fine for contempt of court pursued a legitimate aim of maintaining the authority of the judiciary.

However, in the *Wille* case,[129] the Strasbourg Court appears to have been uncertain in its application of this legitimate aim. The case concerned a complaint by a former politician that, following a lecture he had given on constitutional law, the monarch of Liechtenstein had written to him announcing his intention not to appoint the applicant to political office again. The applicant complained that this was a violation of Article 10. The Strasbourg Court appears somewhat hesitant both over whether the measure was prescribed by law and over the underlying objective of the measure. It was argued that the measure was required to maintain public order and to promote civil stability, and to preserve judicial independence and impartiality. The Court did not find it necessary to consider these issues but proceeded on the assumption that the measure was prescribed by law and pursued a legitimate aim in deciding that such a measure was not necessary in a democratic society.[130]

THE LIMITATION MUST BE NECESSARY IN A DEMOCRATIC SOCIETY

THE BASIC TEST

In addition to being lawful and serving a legitimate purpose, the restriction must be 'necessary in a democratic society'[131] for serving that purpose. Establishing that the measure

[123] § 59. [124] *Stoll v Switzerland*, (App. 69698/01), 10 December 2007, ECHR 2007-V.

[125] *News Verlags GmbH and CoKG v Austria*, (App. 31457/96), 11 April 2000, (2001) 31 EHRR 246, ECHR 2000-I.

[126] §§ 44–5. See also *Falter Zeitschriften Gmbh v Austria (No. 2)*, (App. 3084/07), 18 September 2012.

[127] *Schöpfer v Switzerland*, (App. 25054/94), 20 May 1998, (2001) 33 EHRR 845, ECHR 1998-III.

[128] *Žugić v Croatia*, (App. 3699/08), 31 May 2011.

[129] *Wille v Liechtenstein*, (App. 28396/95), 28 October 1999, (2000) 30 EHRR 558, ECHR 1999-VII.

[130] §§ 53–6.

[131] Articles 8(2), 9(2), 10(2) and 11(2).

is necessary in a democratic society involves showing that the action taken is in response to a pressing social need, and that the interference with the rights protected is no greater than is necessary to address that pressing social need. The latter requirement is referred to as the test of proportionality. This test requires the Strasbourg Court to balance the severity of the restriction placed on the individual against the importance of the public interest. The classic formulation of the test is to be found in the *Silver* case:

> (a) the adjective 'necessary' is not synonymous with 'indispensable', neither has it the flexibility of such expressions as 'admissible', 'ordinary', 'useful', 'reasonable' or 'desirable';
> (b) the Contracting States enjoy a certain but not unlimited margin of appreciation in the matter of the imposition of restrictions, but it is for the Court to give the final ruling on whether they are compatible with the Convention;
> (c) the phrase 'necessary in a democratic society' means that, to be compatible with the Convention, the interference must, *inter alia*, correspond to a 'pressing social need' and be 'proportionate to the legitimate aim pursued';
> (d) those paragraphs of Articles of the Convention which provide for an exception to a right guaranteed are to be narrowly construed.[132]

THE MARGIN OF APPRECIATION AND PROPORTIONALITY

In deciding whether action is necessary in a democratic society, the notion of the State's margin of appreciation has arisen and can often be troublesome.[133] To what extent should the Strasbourg organs defer to a Contracting Party's interpretation of the situation it faces in allowing a limitation on the rights guaranteed by the Convention?[134]

The scope of the margin of appreciation will sometimes be broad and sometimes narrow depending on the nature of the rights in issue, or on the balancing of competing rights.[135] The doctrine is of relevance both in considering the scope of a Contracting Party's choices when interfering with a right protected by Articles 8–11,[136] and in considering the steps which a Contracting Party must take to guarantee the rights protected for individuals within their jurisdiction.[137] It is not easy to provide a definition of the doctrine which applies in every case, and the concept has been regarded as indeterminate and its application difficult to predict. The concept would appear to be a sliding scale whose application will depend on its context. One commentator has observed:

> ...the margin of appreciation varies not only in relation to different exceptions, but in relation to the *same* exceptions in different contexts.

[132] *Silver v United Kingdom*, (Apps. 5947/72, 6205/73, 7052/75, 7061/75, 7107/75, 7113/75, and 7136/75), 25 March 1983, Series A No 61, (1983) 5 EHRR 347, § 97.

[133] See, especially, Y. Arai-Takahashi, *The Margin of Appreciation Doctrine and the Principle of Proportionality in the Jurisprudence of the ECHR* (Intersentia, Antwerp 2002); A. McHarg, 'Reconciling Human Rights and the Public Interest: Conceptual Problems and Doctrinal Uncertainty in the Jurisprudence of the European Court of Human Rights' (1999) 62 MLR 671; G. Letsas, *A Theory of Interpretation of the European Convention on Human Rights* (OUP, Oxford 2007), ch.4; A. Legg, *The Margin of Appreciation in International Human Rights Law* (OUP, Oxford 2012); and G. Itzcovich, 'One, None and One Thousand Margins of Appreciations: The *Lautsi* Case' (2013) 13 HRLR 287.

[134] The doctrine is also relevant when consideration is given to the validity of derogations under Article 15. See ch.6, and *A and others v United Kingdom*, (App. 3455/05), 19 February 2009 [GC], (2009) 49 EHRR 29, ECHR 2009, §§ 173–4.

[135] The appropriate width of the margin can be a matter of heated contention between a Contracting State and the Court, as has recently been apparent in the context of the prisoner voting ban in the UK. This issue is discussed fully in ch.22.

[136] Negative obligations.

[137] Positive obligations.

> A final layer of uncertainty arises from inconsistency as to the order in which the various elements of the *Handyside/Silver/Lingens* framework are addressed, if indeed they are addressed at all. Thus, is the nature of democratic necessity distinct from or part of the assessment of proportionality? Does the margin of appreciation apply to states' assessment of what the public interest requires, or to the balance to be struck between individuals and the collective, or both?... Rather than being a 'test' in the conventional dispositive sense, therefore, the *Handyside/Silver/Lingens* framework provides a set of highly imprecise justificatory strategies which can be used to support a number of approaches to the issue.[138]

In the *Handyside* case[139] the Strasbourg Court said:

> By reason of their direct and continuous contact with the vital forces of their countries, State authorities are in principle in a better position than the international judge to give an opinion on the exact content of these requirements as well as on the 'necessity' of a 'restriction' or 'penalty' intended to meet them.[140]

In considering whether a Contracting Party has gone beyond what the situation requires:

> The Court's supervisory functions oblige it to pay the utmost attention to the principles characterizing a 'democratic society'.[141]

In the *Refah Partisi* case,[142] the Strasbourg Court explored the characteristics of a democratic society in the light of its earlier case-law.[143] From this discussion it is possible to discern that the Court regards the qualities of pluralism, tolerance, broad-mindedness, equality, liberty, and encouraging self-fulfilment as important ingredients of any democracy, together with freedom of religion, expression and assembly, and the right to a fair trial.

A few general principles relating to the breadth of the margin of appreciation to be applied have been established.

Where a particularly important facet of an individual's existence or identity is in issue under Article 8, the Strasbourg Court will be less likely to accept that a Contracting Party should be afforded a broad discretion.

One example is the *X and Y* case,[144] which concerned a young mentally handicapped girl who had been seriously sexually assaulted. Because of a lacuna in Dutch law, it was not possible for criminal proceedings to be instituted, although she could have brought a civil claim for damages. While recognizing that in principle Contracting Parties enjoyed a margin of appreciation when it came to the choice of means calculated to secure respect for private life between individuals, the Court ruled that the precise nature of the Contracting Party's obligation would depend on the particular aspect of private life in issue. This was a case where 'fundamental values and essential aspects of private life' (that is, a woman's right to physical integrity and freedom from sexual assault) were at stake. Since it was of vital importance to protect women from interference of this kind, the Contracting Party could not be allowed a great deal of discretion: effective deterrence, in the form of criminal sanctions, was indispensable.[145]

[138] A. McHarg, 'Reconciling Human Rights and the Public Interest: Conceptual Problems and Doctrinal Uncertainty in the Jurisprudence of the European Court of Human Rights' (1999) 62 MLR 671, 688.

[139] *Handyside v United Kingdom*, (App. 5493/72), 7 December 1976, Series A No 24, (1979–80) 1 EHRR 737.

[140] § 48. [141] § 26.

[142] See J. Merrills, *The Development of International Law by the European Court of Human Rights* (MUP, Manchester 1993), ch.8, 'Human rights and democratic values' at 125–50. For a detailed discussion of the qualities of a democratic society by the Court, see *Refah Partisi (the Welfare Party) v Turkey*, (Apps. 41340/98, 41342/98, and 41344/98), 13 February 2003 [GC], (2003) 37 EHRR 1, ECHR 2003-II.

[143] §§ 86–95.

[144] *X and Y v Netherlands*, (App. 8978/80), 26 March 1985, Series A No 91, (1986) 8 EHRR 235.

[145] §§ 24 and 27.

Similarly, in *Z v Finland*,[146] while accepting that individual interests could sometimes be outweighed by the public interest in the investigation and prosecution of crime, the Strasbourg Court emphasized the fundamental importance of protecting the confidentiality of medical data, for the sake of personal privacy and to preserve confidence in the medical profession and health services. It found that measures including the disclosure of the applicant's medical records without her consent in the course of criminal proceedings against her husband amounted to a violation of Article 8.

A similar balancing exercise was undertaken in the *Dudgeon* case,[147] where the complaint was that certain forms of homosexual activity were prohibited by the criminal law. Although the tendency is to allow a wide margin to a Contracting Party where questions of morality are in issue, the applicable criminal law inhibited the applicant from enjoying 'a most intimate aspect of private life' and the Strasbourg Court therefore required particularly serious reasons to be shown before it would accept that this interference was 'necessary'.

In some cases, the interests of two private parties will be in issue, as in the *Evans* case,[148] which concerned a conflict between the wish of a woman to become pregnant using embryos frozen at an earlier date, and the wish of her former partner that the embryos not be used. United Kingdom law requires the consent of both man and woman for the use of such embryos. The Grand Chamber could find no uniform European approach to the new moral and ethical issues presented by the case, and considered that the legislative scheme in the UK had been the product of much consideration, consultation, and debate. In such circumstances it was appropriate to afford the respondent State a wide margin of appreciation.

Conflicting rights were also in issue in *Axel Springer AG v Germany*[149] where the Court noted that the outcome of an application should not, in principle, vary according to whether it has been lodged with the Court under Article 10 of the Convention by the publisher who has published an offending article or under Article 8 of the Convention by the person who was the subject of that article. In the Court's view, the margin of appreciation should in principle be the same in both cases. By this, the Court means that the margin should be considerably wide and thus where the balancing exercise between Articles 8 and 10 has been undertaken by the national authorities in conformity with the criteria laid down in the Court's previous case-law, the Court would require strong reasons to substitute its view for that of the domestic courts.[150] In areas of morality,[151] the scope of the margin is likely to be wide, since there is among the Contracting States no uniform conception of morals. This is illustrated by the *Handyside* case concerning *The Little Red Schoolbook*,[152] and also explains how its publication could be accepted in some Contracting States but not others. It may also explain the decision in the *Otto-Preminger Institute* case.[153] The location of the cinema in a predominantly Roman Catholic area, where a film was shown that would be deeply offensive to devout Roman Catholics, appears to have been an important factor

[146] *Z v Finland*, (App. 22009/93), 25 February 1997, (1998) 25 EHRR 371, ECHR 1997-I.

[147] *Dudgeon v United Kingdom*, (App. 7525/76), 22 October 1981, Series A No 45, (1982) 4 EHRR 149.

[148] *Evans v United Kingdom*, (App. 6339/05), 10 April 2007 [GC], (2008) 46 EHRR 728, ECHR 2007-IV, §§ 77–82.

[149] *Axel Springer AG v Germany*, (App. 39954/08), 7 February 2012.

[150] § 88. Despite the margin of appreciation enjoyed by the respondent State in this case, the Court still found a violation.

[151] As noted earlier, much of the case-law is concerned with sexual morality.

[152] *Handyside v United Kingdom*, (App. 5493/72), 7 December 1976, Series A No 24, (1979–80) 1 EHRR 737.

[153] *Otto-Preminger Institute v Austria*, (App. 13470/87), 20 September 1994, Series A No 295-A, (1995) 19 EHRR 34.

in the Strasbourg Court's decision that the interference with the rights in Article 10 was justified.

Though at first sight the Strasbourg Court may appear to grant a wider margin of appreciation where positive obligations are in issue, this is often more apparent than real, since it will often be the case that the nature of the right in respect of which positive obligations are argued is finely balanced against the wider interests of the whole community.[154] In some of the earlier cases involving transsexuals which have come before it, the Strasbourg Court had allowed Contracting Parties a wide margin of appreciation, despite the fact that the same 'intimate aspect of private life' (an individual's sexual identity) was in issue here as in *Dudgeon*.

In the *Rees* case,[155] for example, the Strasbourg Court was asked to decide whether the respondent State was under a positive obligation to allow the entry in the register of births relating to the applicant and his birth certificate to be altered to reflect his change of sex from female to male. In the view of the Court, since the 'particular features [of transsexualism] [had] been identified and examined only fairly recently' and there was no European consensus to how such individuals should be treated, a wide margin of appreciation was permitted. In contrast, as the Strasbourg Court had observed in the *Dudgeon* case:

> [I]n the great majority of the member States of the Council of Europe it is no longer considered necessary or appropriate to treat homosexual practices of the kind now in question as in themselves a matter to which the sanctions of the criminal law should be applied; the Court cannot overlook the marked changes which have occurred in this regard in the domestic law of the member States.[156]

In the *X, Y and Z* case,[157] the Strasbourg Court again pointed to the lack of any common European standard, when it ruled that a failure to allow a female-to-male transsexual to be registered as the father of a child born by artificial insemination to his female partner did not violate Article 8. Although in the past it had held that Article 8 required Contracting Parties to establish legal mechanisms to reinforce a child's stability within the family, these earlier cases had been concerned with family ties between biological parents and their children. Since there was no generally shared approach among the Contracting Parties with regard to either the granting of parental rights to transsexuals or the manner in which the social relationship between a child conceived by artificial insemination by donor and the 'social father' should be reflected in law, and since the law in these fields at national level appeared to be in a transitional stage, it was not for the Court to adopt or impose any single viewpoint; in other words, the respondent State had to be afforded a wide margin of appreciation.

These cases, where a wide margin of appreciation is allowed because of a lack of common ground in Europe, can be seen as further examples of the principle that the nature of the individual right determines the breadth of the margin, since a divergence in national law may indicate that the nature and degree of importance of the individual interest is still in the process of being understood, recognized, and accepted. There is sometimes a discrepancy between a State's view of the lack of common ground and that of the Court. For example, in *Alekseyev v Russia*,[158]in the context of the width of the margin in respect of a ban on Gay

[154] See *Monory v Romania and Hungary*, (App. 71099/01), 5 April 2005, (2005) 41 EHRR 771, § 72.

[155] *Rees v United Kingdom*, (App. 9532/81), 17 October 1986, Series A No 106, (1987) 9 EHRR 56, §§ 37–8; and see also the *Cossey v United Kingdom*, (App. 10843/84), 27 September 1990, Series A No 184, (1991) 13 EHRR 622.

[156] *Dudgeon v United Kingdom*, (App. 7525/76), 22 October 1981, Series A No 45, (1982) 4 EHRR 149, § 60.

[157] *X, Y and Z v United Kingdom* (App. 21830/93), 22 April 1997, (1997) 24 EHRR 143, ECHR 1997-II.

[158] *Alekseyev v Russia*, (App. 4916/07, 25924/08, and 14599/09), 21 October 2010.

Pride marches, the Court noted that 'the Government claimed a wide margin of appreciation in granting civil rights to people who identify themselves as gay men or lesbians, citing the alleged lack of European consensus on issues relating to the treatment of sexual minorities. The Court cannot agree with that interpretation.'[159] The Court then gave examples of topics on which there is a European consensus such as the abolition of criminal liability for homosexual relations between adults, homosexuals' access to service in the armed forces, and equal ages of consent under criminal law for heterosexual and homosexual acts. While the Court acknowledged there remain certain issues where no European consensus has been reached, such as granting permission to same-sex couples to adopt a child and the right to marry, it noted that such an absence of consensus was of no relevance to the present case because 'conferring substantive rights on homosexual persons is fundamentally different from recognising their right to campaign for such rights. There is no ambiguity about the other Member States' recognition of the right of individuals to openly identify themselves as gay, lesbian or any other sexual minority, and to promote their rights and freedoms, in particular by exercising their freedom of peaceful assembly.'[160]

Usually when the Court identifies the emergence of a European consensus on a particular issue, it does so in order to narrow the margin of appreciation granted to the respondent State. It deviated from that approach, however, in *A, B and C v Ireland*[161] where it clearly acknowledged a consensus on the regulation of abortion: 'In the present case, and contrary to the Government's submission, the Court considers that there is indeed a consensus amongst a substantial majority of the Contracting States of the Council of Europe towards allowing abortion on broader grounds than accorded under Irish law.'[162] However, in a departure from its usual practice, the Grand Chamber did not regard that consensus as narrowing the broad margin of appreciation enjoyed by Ireland. This was because there was still no consensus on the related question of the scientific and legal definition of the beginning of life. In the Court's words, 'Since the rights claimed on behalf of the foetus and those of the mother are inextricably interconnected... the margin of appreciation accorded to a State's protection of the unborn necessarily translates into a margin of appreciation for that State as to how it balances the conflicting rights of the mother.'[163]

As the dissenting judges noted, 'According to the Convention case-law, in situations where the Court finds that a consensus exists among European States on a matter touching upon a human right, it usually concludes that that consensus decisively narrows the margin of appreciation which might otherwise exist if no such consensus were demonstrated.'[164] These judges were concerned, and rightly so, about the implications of the majority's departure from this well-established approach. They explained that the majority's approach of considering that profound moral views 'can override the European consensus, which tends in a completely different direction, is a real and dangerous new departure in the Court's case-law.'[165] It may be that the explicit recognition of an emerging consensus is a sign, as it was in the transsexual cases discussed earlier, that the Court's toleration of a State out of step with the consensus may soon draw to an end.

[159] § 83.

[160] § 84. [161] *A, B and C v Ireland*, (App. 25579/05), 16 December 2010 [GC], ECHR 2010.

[162] § 235. In particular, the Court noted that the first and second applicants could have obtained an abortion on request (according to certain criteria including gestational limits) in some 30 Contracting States; the first applicant could have obtained an abortion justified on health and well-being grounds in approximately 40 Contracting States; and the second applicant could have obtained an abortion justified on well-being grounds in some 35 Contracting States. [163] § 237.

[164] Joint Partly Dissenting Opinion of Judges Rozakis, Tulkens, Fura, Hirvelä, Malinverni and Poalelungi, § 5.

[165] § 9.

In some cases, the width of the margin allowed to Contracting Parties depends not so much on the importance to the individual of the rights concerned, but rather on the nature of the general interest with which they conflict. As the Strasbourg Court remarked in the *Dudgeon* case, 'the scope of the margin of appreciation is not identical in respect of each of the aims [set out in the second paragraph of Article 8] justifying restrictions on a right.'[166]

Thus, in the *Laskey, Jaggard and Brown* case,[167] where the applicants complained of having been prosecuted and convicted for offences of assault and wounding arising from consensual sado-masochistic activities, the Strasbourg Court judgment means that Contracting Parties are entitled to seek to regulate practices involving the infliction of physical harm:

> The determination of the level of harm that should be tolerated by the law in situations where the victim consents is in the first instance a matter for the State concerned since what is at stake is related, on the one hand, to public health considerations and to the general deterrent effect of the criminal law, and, on the other, to the personal autonomy of the individual.

National security is another area where Contracting Parties are allowed a wide margin, since the protection of large numbers of people is in issue and the information on which such decisions are based is frequently highly sensitive. Thus, in the *Klass* case,[168] the Strasbourg Court, which accepted that the sophistication of modern terrorism entailed that some system of secret surveillance over post and telecommunications might in exceptional circumstances be necessary, allowed a certain discretion to the national legislature as to how such a system should be organized and controlled: it was 'certainly not for the Court to substitute for the assessment of the national authorities any other assessment of what might be the best policy in this field.' Nonetheless, in view of the encroachment on individual rights inherent in such a system, Contracting Parties could not be afforded an unlimited licence but had to satisfy the Court that adequate and effective safeguards were in place.

In the *Leander* case,[169] the applicant complained that he had been excluded from employment in the civil service because he had been registered as a security risk by the police. Since it was undoubtedly necessary, for security reasons, for Contracting Parties to have laws enabling the secret collection and storage of information and to use it when assessing the suitability of candidates for employment in sensitive posts, and since Leander's private life was not affected except in so far as he was prevented from gaining employment as a civil servant (a right which was not as such enshrined in the Convention), the Strasbourg Court accepted that the respondent State should enjoy a wide margin of appreciation, both in assessing the existence of a pressing social need and in choosing the means for achieving the legitimate aim of protecting national security.[170]

It is not only in cases involving national security that the Strasbourg Court allows a wide margin in recognition of the practical realities of certain types of State activity. In child-care cases, for example, the national authorities may frequently be called upon to make extremely difficult and delicate decisions rapidly, for the benefit of the child. In these circumstances, the scope of the discretion allowed to the Contracting Party will vary,

[166] *Dudgeon v United Kingdom*, (App. 7525/76), 22 October 1981, Series A No 45, (1982) 4 EHRR 149, § 52.

[167] *Laskey, Jaggard and Brown v United Kingdom*, (Apps. 21627/93, 21826/93, and 21974/93), 19 February 1997, (1997) 24 EHRR 39, ECHR 1997-I.

[168] *Klass v Germany*, (App. 5029/71), 6 September 1978, Series A No 28, (1979–80) 2 EHRR 214, §§ 48–50.

[169] *Leander v Sweden*, (App. 9248/81), 26 March 1987, Series A No 116, (1987) 9 EHRR 433.

[170] § 59.

depending both on the urgency of the case and the competing interests at stake. Thus, the Strasbourg Court recognizes that the authorities enjoy a wide margin of appreciation in assessing the necessity of taking a child into care. In such cases it considers that it would not be appropriate for it to substitute its own judgment, reached with the benefit of hindsight but without direct contact with the individuals concerned or the prevailing social and cultural conditions.[171] On the other hand, decisions taken in this area often prove to be irreversible: children who have been taken away from their parents may in the course of time establish new bonds which should not be disrupted by renewed parental contact. There is, accordingly, an even greater call than usual for protection against arbitrary interferences.[172] The Strasbourg Court therefore sees its role predominantly as one of reviewing the quality of the decision-making process, including whether relevant and sufficient reasons were given[173] and the parents were consulted if possible.[174] A stricter scrutiny is, however, called for in relation to any further measures such as restrictions on access, not only because these could eradicate the family life shared between parent and child,[175] but also because the public interest in protecting the child carries less weight once the child is in a safe place.

Another area where the Strasbourg Court in principle allows a wide margin to the national authorities is town and country planning. As with the national security and child-care cases, the reasons for this are twofold. First, the public interest, in safeguarding a pleasant environment, is weighty. Secondly, such measures require an appreciation of local, social, economic, and environmental conditions, which the national authorities are best placed to assess.[176] Thus, in the *Gillow* case,[177] the Strasbourg Court took the view that 'the Guernsey legislature is better placed than the international judge to assess the effects of any relaxation of the housing controls.' However, the discretion of a Contracting Party in this field is not unlimited, particularly where important Convention rights, such as the right to respect for a 'home', are in issue. As in the child-care cases referred to earlier, the Strasbourg Court will pay particular attention to the procedural safeguards in the decision-making process in determining whether the impugned measure falls within the margin of appreciation.[178]

The *Hatton* case[179] concerned an alleged breach of Article 8 arising from exposure to aircraft noise. The Grand Chamber, reversing the decision of the Chamber,[180] concluded that there was no breach of Article 8. The Grand Chamber was faced with conflicting arguments on the margin of appreciation. The applicants argued that there was a narrow margin of appreciation since rights under Article 8 were in issue, whereas the United Kingdom

[171] *Olsson v Sweden (No. 2)*, (App. 13441/87), 27 November 1992, Series A No 250, (1994) 17 EHRR 134, § 90.

[172] *W v United Kingdom*, (App. 9749/82), 8 July 1987, Series A No 121, (1988) 10 EHRR 29.

[173] *Hokkanen v Finland*, (App. 19823/92), 23 September 1994, Series A No 299-A, (1994) 19 EHRR 139, § 55.

[174] *W v United Kingdom*, (App. 9749/82), 8 July 1987, Series A No 121, (1988) 10 EHRR 29.

[175] *Johansen v Norway*, (App. 17383/90), 7 August 1996, (1997) 23 EHRR 33, ECHR 1996-III, § 64.

[176] And see also *Powell and Rayner v United Kingdom*, (App. 9310/81), 21 February 1990, Series A No 172, (1990) 12 EHRR 355, § 44, where the Court ruled that it should not 'substitute for the assessment of the national authorities any other assessment of what might be the best policy in this difficult social and technical sphere [the regulation of aircraft noise]. This is an area where the Contracting States are to be recognized as enjoying a wide margin of appreciation.'

[177] *Gillow v United Kingdom*, (App. 9063/80), 24 November 1986, Series A No 109, (1986) 11 EHRR 355, § 56.

[178] *Buckley v United Kingdom*, (App. 20348/92), 25 September 1996, (1997) 23 EHRR 101, ECHR 1996-IV, § 76.

[179] *Hatton v United Kingdom*, (App. 36022/97), 8 July 2003 [GC], (2003) 37 EHRR 611, ECHR 2003-VIII; see also J. Hyam, '*Hatton v United Kingdom* in the Grand Chamber: One Step Forward, Two Steps Back?' [2003] EHRLR 631.

[180] *Hatton v United Kingdom* (App. 36022/97), 2 October 2001, (2001) 34 EHRR 1.

argued that the margin was wide since the case concerned matters of general policy. The Grand Chamber's answer was as follows:

> The Court must consider whether the Government can be said to have struck a fair balance between [the economic interests of the country as a whole] and the conflicting interests of the persons affected by noise disturbances, including the applicants. Environmental protection should be taken into consideration by Governments in acting within their margin of appreciation and by the Court in its review of that margin, but it would not be appropriate for the Court to adopt a special approach in this respect by reference to a special status of environmental human rights. In this context the Court must revert to the question of the scope of the margin of appreciation available to the State when taking policy decisions of the kind at issue.[181]

This approach has been criticized by one commentator for focusing on the circumstances in which the infringement had arisen rather than by reference to the nature of the infringement.[182] However, it should be noted that the Strasbourg Court does not always focus on the effect of the interference on the right in issue, but sometimes focuses on the exception which has been invoked.

Letsas[183] helpfully draws a distinction between two uses of the term 'margin of appreciation'. The first, which he labels the substantive concept, addresses the relationship between individual freedoms and collective goals.[184] The second, which he labels the structural concept, addresses the intensity of review by the Strasbourg Court.[185] Letsas observes:

> It is my view that much of the confusion and controversy surrounding the margin of appreciation is due to the Court's failure to distinguish between these two ideas in its case-law. The Court uses the same term ... both for saying that the applicant did not, as a matter of human rights, have the right he or she claimed, and for saying that it will not substantively review the decision of national authorities as to whether there has been a violation.[186]

The significance of the margin of appreciation in examining the requirement that any restriction be necessary in a democratic society cannot be underestimated. It will be at the heart of nearly all the cases coming before the Strasbourg Court.[187] It is also often the subject of disagreement between the majority and dissenting opinions. Sometimes this is due to a disagreement on the specific issue that is subject to a margin. For example, in *Hristozov and others v Bulgaria*[188] the Court gave a wide margin of appreciation to the respondent State to strike an appropriate balance between private and public interests in the context of the availability of unauthorized medicinal products. A number of dissenting judges criticized this approach. The dissenting opinion of Judge De Gaetano joined by Judge Vučinić highlighted the specific issues raised in the present case and their suitability to fall within a wide margin:

[181] *Hatton v United Kingdom*, (App. 36022/97), 8 July 2003 [GC], (2003) 37 EHRR 611, ECHR 2003-VIII, § 122.

[182] J. Hyam, '*Hatton v United Kingdom* in the Grand Chamber: One Step Forward, Two Steps Back?' [2003] EHRLR 631, 638.

[183] G. Letsas, *A Theory of Interpretation of the European Convention on Human Rights* (OUP, Oxford 2007), ch.4.

[184] 85; typified by the limitation clauses in Articles 8–11.

[185] 91; typified by those cases where the Strasbourg Court refuses to intervene because there is no European consensus.

[186] 81.

[187] R. MacDonald, 'The margin of appreciation in the jurisprudence of the European Court of Human Rights' in *Le Droit International à l'heure de sa Codification: études en l'honneur de Roberto Ago* (Giuffré, Milan 1987), 187.

[188] *Hristozov and others v Bulgaria*, (App. 47039/11 and 358/12), 13 November 2012, ECHR 2012 (extracts).

> I...agree that matters of health care policy are, in principle, within the margin of appreciation of the domestic authorities, who are best placed to assess priorities, use of resources and social needs...However, the issue in the present case is a considerably narrower one, and does not involve the allocation of resources. No financial considerations or imperatives were involved. The applicants were not calling upon the State to pay for this treatment...They were simply asking for the State to 'get out of the way' and allow them access to an experimental product which would be provided to them free of charge. In the instant case, therefore, the Court should have determined the applicable margin of appreciation by reference to factors that are more specific to the situation at hand...and in particular to the applicants' critical medical condition and the available prognosis.[189]

The partly dissenting opinion of Judge Kalaydjieva reiterated that the margin of appreciation is an instrument to facilitate the assessment of the necessity and proportionality of interferences with the Convention rights and is not 'a general waiver of the duty of States to respect them.' This is an important distinction to be born in mind in future cases, particularly in the context of State pressure to expand the role of the margin. The Brighton Declaration illustrates the States' fondness for the discretion accorded to them by means of the margin of appreciation. This important document encourages the Court to give 'great prominence to and apply consistently' the principles of subsidiarity and the margin of appreciation and concludes that a reference to these two principles should be included in the Preamble to the Convention.[190] An interpretive tool that has proved controversial in its justification and implementation may in the future be elevated to a foundational principle of the Convention.

CONCLUDING REMARKS

The application of the limitations to be found in Articles 8 to 11 (and elsewhere in the Convention) arises with great frequency. Since the majority of cases turn on whether the limitation is 'necessary in a democratic society', the margin of appreciation doctrine is at the heart of the review by the Strasbourg Court of decisions made by Contracting Parties. This brings into play the doctrine of proportionality. It would seem that the margin of appreciation goes to the legitimacy of the aim of the interference in meeting a pressing social need, whereas the doctrine of proportionality concerns the means used to achieve that aim. The two doctrines are, however, intertwined, and many cases illustrate how the principle of proportionality has been used to show that a Contracting Party has gone beyond its margin of appreciation. As a device to protect the value pluralism that is central to the European Convention system, the doctrine has served its purpose well. As a device for providing predictability of outcome in any given case, it remains an indeterminate and elusive doctrine full of complexity in its operation.

[189] Dissenting opinion of Judge De Gaetano joined by Judge Vučinić, § 3.

[190] High Level Conference on the Future of the European Court of Human Rights: Brighton Declaration (accessible here: http://hub.coe.int/20120419-brighton-declaration), § 12.

15

PROTECTING FAMILY LIFE

INTRODUCTION

This and Chapter 16 consider the development of the rights protected by Article 8, which is one of the most open-ended provisions of the Convention.[1] Article 8 provides:

> 1. Everyone has the right to respect for his private and family life, his home and his correspondence.
> 2. There shall be no interference by a public authority with the exercise of this right except such as is in accordance with the law and is necessary in a democratic society in the interests of national security, public safety or the economic well-being of the country, for the prevention of disorder or crime, for the protection of health or morals, or for the protection of the rights and freedoms of others.

The protection of the family, as the fundamental unit of society, figures at more than one place in the Convention. Article 12 guarantees the right to marry and to found a family, while Article 8 prohibits, in principle, and subject to the provisions of paragraph (2), interference with an existing family unit. Article 2 of the First Protocol deals with an important aspect of the rights of parents in relation to their children's education. It provides for the right of parents to ensure such education in conformity with their own religious and philosophical convictions.[2]

The right to marry and found a family may be considered as a particular form of family life, but it is separately protected in Article 12, which provides:

> Men and women of marriageable age have the right to marry and found a family, according to the national laws governing the exercise of this right.

Article 5 of Protocol 7 adds to the rights in Article 12 by providing for equality of rights and responsibilities of a private law character between spouses, and in their relations with their children.

The rights protected by Articles 8 and 12, and Article 5 of Protocol 7, are somewhat disparate. However, the fact that the rights in Article 8 are grouped together in the same Article strengthens the protection given by that Article, since each right is reinforced by its context. Thus, the right to respect for family life, the right to respect for private life, and the right to respect for the home and correspondence may be read together as guaranteeing collectively more than the sum of their parts. Subject to that important point, it is now possible to categorize the rights protected by Article 8 in providing a synthesis of the case-law of the Strasbourg Court. This chapter considers matters related to family

[1] See generally D. Feldman, 'The developing scope of Article 8 of the European Convention on Human Rights' [1997] EHRLR 265; C. Warbrick, 'The structure of Article 8' [1998] EHRLR 32; and U. Kilkelly, *The right to respect for private and family life: a Guide to the implementation of Article 8 of the European Convention on Human Rights*, Human Rights Handbooks No. 1 (Council of Europe Publishing, Strasbourg 2003).

[2] See ch.21.

life, while the following chapter focuses on the protection of private life, as well as respect for the home and correspondence. As with a number of Articles, the rights contained in the first paragraph are subject to the limitations set out in the second paragraph. In many cases, the interference will be justifiable on the basis of these limitations.[3]

DEFINING FAMILY LIFE

Respect for family life requires identification of what constitutes a family.[4] The existence, or absence, of family life is essentially a question of fact.[5] A mother and father and children who are dependent on them, including illegitimate and adopted children, constitute a family. Indeed, the Strasbourg Court has said that 'the mutual enjoyment by parent and child of each other's company constitutes a fundamental element of family life.'[6] De facto family ties can arise where parties are living together outside marriage.[7]

It is implicit in the Strasbourg Court's judgment in the *Marckx* case that marriage gives rise to a presumption of family life between the husband and wife,[8] even if the couple have not set up home together.[9] In relation to children, family life exists between children and their parents (whether married or not) from the moment of the child's birth. The family ties exist even where the parents are not living together at the time of the child's birth.[10] Only in exceptional circumstances will this bond between parent and child be broken and family life cease to exist.[11] It is a violation of Article 8 to deny a mother the opportunity to enable recognition of the biological father of her child; a legal presumption that the husband is the father of a child born in wedlock which cannot be denied by the mother may violate Article 8.[12] The Court has confirmed that persons divested of legal capacity retain 'a vital interest, protected by the Convention, in establishing the biological truth about an important aspect of their private and family life and having it recognised in law.'[13] Thus the State had failed to discharge its positive obligation to guarantee the applicant's right to respect for his private and family life when it prevented a person lacking capacity from establishing his paternity of a child, even though both he and the child's mother agreed that he was the child's biological father. In *Ahrens v Germany*[14] the applicant alleged that the domestic courts' refusal to allow him to challenge another man's legal paternity had violated his Article 8 right to respect for his family life. The Court, however, was unconvinced that 'family life' was engaged here. It observed that the relationship between the applicant and the mother of his child had ended approximately one year before the child

[3] For a discussion of the limitations in Articles 8–11, see ch.14.

[4] See J. Liddy, 'The concept of family life under the ECHR' [1998] EHRLR 15; and U. Kilkelly, *The Child and the European Convention on Human Rights* (Ashgate, Dartmouth 1999), ch.7.

[5] *K & T v Finland*, (App. 25702/94), 12 July 2001, (2003) 36 EHRR 255, ECHR 2001-VII, § 150.

[6] *B v United Kingdom*, (App. 9840/82), 8 July 1987, Series A No 121, (1988) 10 EHRR 87, § 60.

[7] *Johnston and others v Ireland*, (App. 9697/82), 18 December 1986, Series A No 112, (1987) 9 EHRR 203, § 25.

[8] *Marckx v Belgium*, (App. 6833/74), 13 June 1979, Series A No 31, (1979–80) 2 EHRR 330.

[9] But note the somewhat odd decision in *Şerife Yiğit v Turkey*, (App. 3976/05), 20 January 2009 [GC], where a religious marriage was not recognized for certain purposes because Turkish law provided that a religious ceremony performed by an imam did not give rise to any commitments towards third parties or the State.

[10] *Berrehab v Netherlands*, (App. 10730/84), 21 June 1988, Series A No 138, (1989) 11 EHRR 322, § 21 and *Keegan v Ireland*, (App. 16969/90), 26 May 1994, Series A No 290, (1994) 18 EHRR 342, § 44.

[11] *Gül v Switzerland*, (App. 23218/94), 19 February 1996, (1996) 22 EHRR 93, ECHR 1996-I, § 32.

[12] *Kroon and others v Netherlands*, (App. 18535/91), 27 October 1994, Series A No 297-C, (1995) 19 EHRR 263, and see further ch.16.

[13] *Krušković v Croatia*, (App. 46185/08), 21 June 2011, § 34.

[14] *Ahrens v Germany*, (App. 45071/09), 22 March 2012.

was conceived and that ensuing relations were of a purely sexual nature. There was no indication that they envisaged founding a family together and no signs of any commitment of the applicant towards the child before it was born. Under these circumstances, the Court said that it was not convinced that the applicant's decision to demand a paternity test and to bring an action aimed at establishing his paternity were sufficient to bring the relationship between himself and the child within the scope of family life.[15] The Court may have been influenced in its conclusion by the existence of a family relationship between the child and her legal father, who was living together with the child's mother and providing parental care on a daily basis. There was no doubt, however, that the matter fell within the applicant's 'private life' and was thus covered by Article 8, although there was held to be no violation in this case.

A similar approach was taken in *Kautzor v Germany*[16] even though in this case the applicant was married to the child's mother at the time of conception. As he had never seen the child and there had never been a close personal relationship between him and the child, the Court was reluctant to regard this as an established family life, although the private life element of Article 8 was again engaged. In both cases, the lack of a consensus across Europe on the issue of the determination of a child's legal status meant that a wide margin of appreciation had to be accorded to the States on such matters.

However the Court was more sympathetic to the biological father in *Anayo v Germany*.[17] The refusal of the German courts to grant the applicant access to his biological children on the ground that he had no social and family relationship with them was found to violate Article 8. In deciding whether family life existed in this case, the Court noted that the fact that the applicant had never met the children, and thus had not yet established a family relationship with them, could not be held against him:

> the Court has found that intended family life may, exceptionally, fall within the ambit of Article 8 in cases in which the fact that family life has not been established is not attributable to the applicant...This applies, in particular, to the relationship between a child born out of wedlock and the child's biological father, who are inalterably linked by a natural bond while their actual relationship may be determined, for practical and legal reasons, by the child's mother and, if married, by her husband. In the present case, the applicant did not yet have any contact with his biological children because their mother and their legal father, who were entitled to decide on the twins' contacts with other persons... refused his requests to allow contact with them. Moreover, under the provisions of German law... the applicant could neither acknowledge paternity nor contest Mr B.'s paternity so as to become the twins' legal father. Therefore, the fact that there was not yet any established family relationship between him and his children cannot be held against him.[18]

In the Court's view, the applicant had demonstrated interest in and commitment to the children; had expressed his wish to have contacts with his children both before and after their birth; and although the applicant and the children's mother had never cohabited, their relationship had lasted some two years and was therefore not, in the words of the Court, 'merely haphazard'.[19] For these reasons, the Court was not prepared to exclude the possibility that refusal of access to the children was an interference with the applicant's family life.[20]

[15] § 59. [16] *Kautzor v Germany*, (App. 23338/09), 22 March 2012.

[17] *Anayo v Germany*, (App. 20578/07), 21 December 2010. [18] § 60. [19] § 61.

[20] The Court noted that the domestic court had failed to consider whether contact between the children and the applicant would be in the children's best interests. Therefore the Court found that the domestic court had failed to fairly balance the competing rights involved and thus the reasons given for refusing the applicant contact with his children had not been 'sufficient' for the purposes of paragraph 2 of Article 8.

Perhaps surprisingly, in the subsequent judgment of *Schneider v Germany*[21] the Court applied a similar approach in a case in which it had not been established whether the applicant was indeed the biological father of the child.

Adoption places the adoptive parents in the same position as biological parents for the purposes of the protection of family life, even where there has been little contact with the adopted child and where the adoption is contested.[22]

Relationships between brothers and sisters, taken together with those between parents and children are also covered.[23] In some circumstances, relations with grandparents may be protected under Article 8.[24] More remote relationships are generally not close enough to constitute family relationships protected by Article 8, though they might nevertheless fall within the sphere of private life.

In deciding whether a relationship between unmarried adults constitutes family life, the Strasbourg Court has identified a number of factors which should be taken into account:

> ...whether the couple live together, the length of their relationship and whether they have demonstrated their commitment to each other by having children together or by any other means...[25]

Same-sex couples have also been recognized as enjoying a family life under Article 8. In *Schalk and Kopf v Austria*,[26] the Court explicitly recognized that 'a rapid evolution of social attitudes towards same-sex couples has taken place in many member States'[27] and because of this it considered that it would be 'artificial' to maintain the view from previous cases that a same-sex couple can enjoy only a 'private life' and not a 'family life' under Article 8. It concluded that 'the relationship of the applicants, a cohabiting same-sex couple living in a stable de facto partnership, falls within the notion of "family life", just as the relationship of a different-sex couple in the same situation would.'[28]

The *Poluhas Dödsbo* case[29] concerned a complaint about a refusal to permit the removal by the widow of an urn containing the ashes of her husband from one town in Sweden to another. The Strasbourg Court did not consider it necessary to classify whether this constituted an aspect of family life or private life, although it did regard Article 8 as applying to the situation.

The Strasbourg Court's pronouncements on the nature of the family suggest that there is a hierarchy of relationships. At the top of the hierarchy is the traditional heterosexual relationship of married couples, moving through parenting between non-married couples down to more removed family relationships at the bottom of the hierarchy. This was demonstrated in the case of *Van Der Heijden v The Netherlands*.[30] This case concerned an attempt to compel the applicant to give evidence in criminal proceedings against her long-standing companion

[21] *Schneider v Germany*, (App. 17080/07), 15 September 2011.

[22] *Pini and others v Romania*, (Apps. 78028/01 and 78030/01), 22 June 2004, (2005) 40 EHRR 312, ECHR 2004-V, §§ 136–48.

[23] *Moustaquim v Belgium*, (App. 12313/86), 18 February 1991, Series A No 193, (1991) 13 EHRR 802, § 36.

[24] See *Vermeire v Belgium* (App. 12849/87), 29 November 1991, Series A No 214-C, (1993) 15 EHRR 488, which concerned exclusion of a granddaughter from the estate of a grandparent because of the illegitimate nature of the kinship; and *Bronda v Italy*, (App. 40/1997/824/1030), 9 June 1998, *Reports of Judgments and Decisions* 1998-IV.

[25] *Al-Nashif v Bulgaria*, (App. 50963/99), 20 June 2002, (2003) 36 EHRR 655, § 112. See also *Kroon and others v Netherlands*, (App. 18535/91), 27 October 1994, Series A No 297-C, (1995) 19 EHRR 263, § 30; and *X, Y and Z v United Kingdom*, (App. 21830/93), 22 April 1997, (1997) 24 EHRR 143, ECHR 1997-II, §§ 36–7.

[26] *Schalk and Kopf v Austria*, (App. 30141/04), 24 June 2010, ECHR 2010.

[27] § 93.

[28] § 94. See also *X and others v Austria*, (App. 19010/07), 19 February 2013 [GC], ECHR 2013.

[29] *Elli Poluhas Dödsbo v Sweden*, (App. 61564/00), 17 January 2006, ECHR 2006-I.

[30] *Van Der Heijden v The Netherlands*, (App. 42857/05), 3 April 2012.

with whom the Court acknowledged she enjoyed a 'family life'. The Court recognized that there were two competing public interests at issue in this case: the public interest in the prosecution of serious crime and the public interest in the protection of family life from State interference. The State's balancing of those competing interests by means of providing that persons in the applicant's position who wished to avail themselves of testimonial privilege had to have registered their relationship formally, or be legally married, was not in violation of Article 8. The Court explained the difference it perceived between long-standing relationships falling within 'family life' and a formal marriage or registered partnership:

> The Court does not accept the applicant's suggestion that her relationship with Mr A., being in societal terms equal to a marriage or a registered partnership, should attract the same legal consequences as such formalised unions. States are entitled to set boundaries to the scope of testimonial privilege and to draw the line at marriage or registered partnerships. The legislature is entitled to confer a special status on marriage or registration and not to confer it on other de facto types of cohabitation. Marriage confers a special status on those who enter into it; the right to marry is protected by Article 12 of the Convention and gives rise to social, personal and legal consequences... Likewise, the legal consequences of a registered partnership set it apart from other forms of cohabitation. Rather than the length or the supportive nature of the relationship, what is determinative is the existence of a public undertaking, carrying with it a body of rights and obligations of a contractual nature. The absence of such a legally binding agreement between the applicant and Mr A. renders their relationship, however defined, fundamentally different from that of a married couple or a couple in a registered partnership...[31]

Thus, despite recent acknowledgment of the evolution of 'family' relationships to include same-sex couples, there remains a hierarchy in terms of the protection to be offered to formal as opposed to less formal relationships.

POSITIVE OBLIGATIONS AND FAMILY LIFE

The wording of Article 8(1) differs from the wording of Articles 2 to 7. It refers to a right to respect for private and family life, home, and correspondence. The notion of 'respect' is a relatively imprecise one, but the Commission and the Strasbourg Court have applied an interpretation which serves to give effect to the continuing evolution of concepts of privacy and family life.[32] Article 8 prohibits arbitrary interferences by a Contracting Party into respect for family and private life, the home, and correspondence.

Positive obligations under Article 8 can arise in two types of situations. The first is where a Contracting Party must take some action to secure respect for the rights included in the Article, as distinct from simply refraining from interfering with the rights protected. Examples of this type of case are the immigration cases where a Contracting Party must allow a person to enter or remain in the country. The second type of situation is where a duty arises for a Contracting Party to protect an individual from interferences by other individuals.

An increasing number of cases in which violations of Article 8 are raised concerns positive obligations, although these arise more frequently in the context of the protection

[31] § 69.

[32] See G. Cohen-Jonathan, 'Respect for private and family life' in R. Macdonald, F. Matscher, and H. Petzold, *The European System for the Protection of Human Rights* (Martinus Nijhoff, Dordrecht 1993), 405.

of private life. There are many illustrations of such cases appearing in this chapter and Chapter 16.

A RIGHT TO REPRODUCE BY MEANS OF ASSISTED REPRODUCTION?

Given the rapid developments in assisted reproductive technology, it is not surprising that the Court has faced the question of whether Article 8's right to respect for family life encompasses a right to reproduce using such technology. *S.H. and others v Austria*[33] concerned the prohibition of all egg donation and sperm donation for the purposes of IVF in Austria. A Chamber of the Court found this to be a violation of the Article 8 rights of two couples for whom these options represented the only chance of having a child genetically related to one of them. However the Grand Chamber allowed Austria a wide margin of appreciation on the basis that there is still no European consensus on such issues:

> Since the use of IVF treatment gave rise then and continues to give rise today to sensitive moral and ethical issues against a background of fast-moving medical and scientific developments, and since the questions raised by the case touch on areas where there is not yet clear common ground amongst the member States, the Court considers that the margin of appreciation to be afforded to the respondent State must be a wide one.[34]

The Grand Chamber recognized that the right of a couple to conceive a child and to make use of medically assisted procreation for that purpose is protected by Article 8, as such a choice is an expression of private and family life. (The Court did not distinguish between these two concepts in this case.) Although it gave a wide margin to Austria due to consensus on this issue still emerging, it did warn that this is a fast-moving area which must be kept under review.[35]

A complete ban on IVF will be harder to defend. For example, the Inter-American Court of Human Rights recently found Costa Rica in violation of the American Convention on Human Rights (ACHR) for its complete ban on IVF which it found to be a disproportionate interference with the rights to private and family life of infertile people.[36] Further issues of reproductive rights will be discussed in Chapter 16 in the context of private life.[37]

CUSTODY, ACCESS, AND CARE PROCEEDINGS

Many applications under Article 8 concern the relationships of parents and children after marriage breakdown or other family crisis. The issue may arise after the separation or divorce of the parents, when the courts make an order concerning the custody of, or access to, the children. Or it may arise when children are taken into the care of the public authorities.

In these situations, the State authorities are required to balance a number of rights, which may compete or conflict with each other. Each parent, and to a lesser degree other family members such as grandparents,[38] has a right to respect for his or her family ties

[33] *S.H. and others v Austria*, (App. 57813/00), 3 November 2011 [GC], ECHR 2011. [34] § 97.

[35] § 118.

[36] *Caso Artavia Murillo and others v Costa Rica* (Serie C, No. 257) (Inter-American Court of Human Rights).

[37] See especially the discussion of *Evans v United Kingdom*, (App. 6339/05), 10 April 2007 [GC], (2008) 46 EHRR 728, ECHR 2007-IV involving a conflict of rights.

[38] *Bronda v Italy*, (App. 22430/93), 9 June 1998, (2001) 33 EHRR 81, ECHR 1998-IV, § 59.

with the child under Article 8. The child, similarly, has a right to respect for his or her family life. But the best interests of the child may not be in staying with the birth parents. The State also has duties under Articles 8 and 3 to protect the child from emotional, sexual, and physical abuse, and this may mean removing the child quickly from a bad home environment.[39] In all such cases, the overriding interest is the child's safety and well-being.[40]

Unlike the Strasbourg judges, the national social workers and courts will usually have had direct contact with all the people concerned, often at the stage when care measures are being envisaged or immediately after their implementation. The Strasbourg Court will not be so well placed to assess the personalities, needs, and capacities of the parents and children, and in any event, by the time the case gets to Strasbourg, irreversible decisions may have been made. In assessing the 'necessity' of the measures, the Court does not, therefore, attempt to substitute itself for the domestic authorities but instead reviews their decisions, looking particularly to see whether the reasons given were relevant and sufficient and that the procedure was fair, to ensure that the authorities have not exceeded their margin of appreciation.[41]

This margin of appreciation varies from case to case, depending on the nature of the issues and the seriousness of the interests at stake. The State authorities enjoy a broad margin when it comes to assessing the necessity of taking a child into care, although the fact that a child could be placed in a more beneficial environment for his or her upbringing will not on its own justify a compulsory measure of removal.[42] The margin is, however, narrower in respect of any further limitations which carry the risk of entirely destroying the relationship between parent and child, such as restrictions on access visits or other forms of contact.[43] This can be seen, for example, in the recent case of *Ageyevy v Russia*.[44] The applicants claimed that the sudden removal of their adopted children, the revocation of the adoption, and the continued lack of access to the children violated their Article 8 rights. As the children were initially removed from the applicants' care due to a perceived threat to their life or health, this was held by the Court to be a justified interference with the applicants' right to respect for family life. However, the subsequent revocation of the adoption was not justified as it had not been shown that the measure corresponded to any overriding requirement in the children's best interests.

The applicants in the *K & T* case[45] were a mother and her male partner. The mother had a history of severe psychotic mental illness and had been hospitalized on a number of occasions. She had two young children from previous relationships and became pregnant again by the second applicant. In the light of expert reports which indicated that the older child's mental health would be damaged by continued contact with her mother, a court order was made placing the older child in her father's care and allowing only very limited, supervised, access to the mother. The applicants subsequently voluntarily placed the younger child, who was showing behavioural problems, in a children's home. There was evidence that the mother behaved inappropriately during visits to the children's home and that the child was disturbed following her visits. Immediately after the third child was

[39] *Z and others v United Kingdom*, (App. 29392/95), 10 May 2001 [GC], (2002) 34 EHRR 97, ECHR 2001-V.

[40] *K & T v Finland*, (App. 25702/94), 12 July 2001 [GC], (2003) 36 EHRR 255, ECHR 2001-VII, § 173.

[41] *Olsson v Sweden (No.2)*, (App. 13441/87), 27 November 1992, Series A No 250, § 90; and *K & T v Finland*, (App. 25702/94), 12 July 2001 [GC], (2003) 36 EHRR 255, ECHR 2001-VII, § 154.

[42] *K & T v Finland*, (App. 25702/94), 12 July 2001 [GC], (2003) 36 EHRR 255, ECHR 2001-VII, § 173.

[43] *Johansen v Norway*, (App. 17383/90), 7 August 1996; (1997) 23 EHRR 33, ECHR 1996-III; and *K & T v Finland*, (App. 25702/94), 12 July 2001 [GC], (2003) 36 EHRR 255, ECHR 2001-VII, § 155.

[44] *Ageyevy v Russia*, (App. 7075/10), 18 April 2013.

[45] *K & T v Finland*, (App. 25702/94), 12 July 2001 [GC], (2003) 36 EHRR 255, ECHR 2001-VII.

born, emergency care orders were made in respect of the baby and the second child. The baby was taken to a children's home within hours of birth and the other child's placement in the home became compulsory. The father was allowed to visit and care for the baby in the home without restriction. The mother, who was again hospitalized for mental health reasons, was allowed to visit the baby if accompanied by a psychiatric nurse. Subsequently a care plan was drawn up placing both the younger children together with foster parents. The father applied for custody of the baby, but his application was refused because, in the light of his continuing relationship with the mother, it was not considered that he would be able properly to care for the baby or guarantee her safety. The applicants were allowed only monthly supervised access visits, to allow the children to settle down with their new family. By the time the children had been in their foster home for a little over a year, the mother's health improved and she had a fourth child, whom she was allowed to keep, and she and her partner applied to have the other children returned to their care. The application was refused.

The Grand Chamber examined all of the compulsory measures we have discussed separately and the case therefore provides useful guidance as regards a range of restrictions on parental rights. In respect of the emergency care orders, it accepted that it might not always be possible, because of the urgency of the situation or fears about the parents' reactions, to associate them in the decision-making process or give them prior warning. However, the State authorities had to show that a careful assessment of the impact of the proposed care measure on the parents and the children, as well as of the possible alternatives to taking the children into public care, was carried out prior to the implementation of such a measure. The Court emphasized that the taking of a newborn baby into public care at the moment of its birth is an extremely harsh measure, likely to cause great distress to any mother, and requiring extraordinarily compelling reasons in justification. It was not satisfied that such reasons had been shown to exist in the instant case. Both the mother and the baby were in hospital care at the time. The authorities had known about the forthcoming birth for months in advance and were well aware of the mother's mental problems, so that the situation was not an emergency in the sense of being unforeseen. When such a drastic measure was contemplated, it was incumbent on the national authorities first to examine whether alternative methods of protecting the baby would be feasible. There was no evidence that alternatives to removal had been considered.

The Court also criticized the State authorities for failing to take sufficient steps to reunite the family despite evidence of an improvement in the mother's health. In this connection it placed emphasis on 'the guiding principle whereby a care order should be regarded as a temporary measure, to be discontinued as soon as circumstances permit'.[46] It continued by observing that:

> 178. ... The positive duty to take measures to facilitate family reunification as soon as reasonably feasible will begin to weigh on the competent authorities with progressively increasing force as from the commencement of the period of care, subject always to its being balanced against the duty to consider the best interests of the child.
>
> 179. In the instant case, the Court notes that enquiries were made in order to ascertain whether the applicants would be able to bond with the children.... They did not, however, amount to a serious or sustained effort directed towards facilitating family reunification such as could reasonably be expected for the purposes of Article 8 § 2—especially since they constituted the sole effort on the authorities' part to that effect in the seven years during which the children have been in care. The minimum

[46] *K & T*, § 178.

> to be expected of the authorities is to examine the situation anew from time to time to see whether there has been any improvement in the family's situation. The possibilities of reunification will be progressively diminished and eventually destroyed if the biological parents and the children are not allowed to meet each other at all, or only so rarely that no natural bonding between them is likely to occur. The restrictions and prohibitions imposed on the applicants' access to their children, far from preparing a possible reunification of the family, rather contributed to hindering it. What is striking in the present case is the exceptionally firm negative attitude of the authorities....[47]

Where a care order is implemented in an inappropriate manner, as, for example, where children are dispersed over some distance which renders the objective of reuniting the family difficult to achieve, there may be a violation of respect for family life by such action.[48] A similar conclusion was reached where, for a period of six years, a mother's access to her daughter was restricted and she had no enforceable visiting rights under a regime designed ultimately to reunite the family.[49]

In the *RK and AK* case,[50] the applicants, who were Pushto speakers and had difficulties in speaking and understanding English, brought their two-month-old daughter to the hospital with a fracture to her arm. The parents were interviewed without an interpreter by a consultant paediatrician, who concluded that it was a non-accidental injury. When the child was ready to be discharged from hospital, a care order was made placing her in the care of her aunt, who lived near the parents. The parents were permitted supervised access. They contested the care order but, following a hearing where they gave evidence through an interpreter, the judge concluded that they were lying and were concealing information about how the child had come by the injury. Some months later the child sustained another fracture while in her aunt's care. Further tests were carried out and she was diagnosed with brittle bone disease. Further expert reports confirmed that this was likely to have been the cause of the first injury and the care order was discharged. The applicants complained about the care order under Article 8. The Court found no violation, commenting that:

> ...mistaken judgments or assessments by professionals do not *per se* render child-care measures incompatible with the requirements of Article 8. The authorities, medical and social, have duties to protect children and cannot be held liable every time genuine and reasonably-held concerns about the safety of children *vis-à-vis* members of their families are proved, retrospectively, to have been misguided.[51]

There may also be a violation of Article 8 if no adequate steps are taken to enable a non-custodial parent to have access to a child.[52] Where paternal access is sought to a child born outside marriage, securing family life for the father can involve competing interests with the mother and with the child. In the *Elsholz* case,[53] the Strasbourg Court stressed the wide margin of appreciation to be accorded to the national authorities in assessing the

[47] §§ 178–9.

[48] *Olsson v Sweden (No. 1)*, (App. 10465/83), 24 March 1988, Series A No 130, (1989) 11 EHRR 259.

[49] *Eriksson v Sweden*, (App. 11373/85), 22 June 1989, Series A No 156, (1990) 12 EHRR 183. See also *Margareta and Roger Andersson v Sweden*, (App. 12963/87), 25 February 1992, Series A No 226-A, (1992) 14 EHRR 615. Contrast *Rieme v Sweden*, (App. 12366/86), 22 April 1992, Series A No 226-B, (1992) 16 EHRR 155, and *Olsson v Sweden (No.2)*, (App. 13441/87), 27 November 1992, Series A No 250. See also *Johansen v Norway*, (App. 17383/90), 7 August 1996; (1997) 23 EHRR 33, ECHR 1996-III; and *L v Finland*, (App. 25651/94), 27 April 2000; (2001) 31 EHRR 737.

[50] *RK and AK v United Kingdom*, (App. 38000/05), 30 September 2008.

[51] § 36.

[52] *Nuutinen v Finland*, (App. 32842/96), 27 June 2000; (2002) 34 EHRR 358, ECHR 2000-VIII.

[53] *Elsholz v Germany*, (App. 25735/94), 13 July 2000 [GC], (2002) 34 EHRR 1412, ECHR 2000-VIII.

necessity to take a child into care, but that a narrower margin would apply where access by the absent parent following a family breakdown was involved. The views of the child will be particularly important, but expert psychological evidence should be available to evaluate such views. If such safeguards are not present, then the involvement of the father in crucial decisions relating to his access to his child will not alone be sufficient to meet the requirements of respect for the family life of himself and his child. This approach has been approved by a majority judgment of the Grand Chamber.[54] Whether the decision-making process sufficiently protects the interests of a parent will depend upon the circumstances of each case. The Grand Chamber in the *Sommerfield* case[55] did not regard it as necessary to obtain an expert psychological report where views had been expressed by a daughter at the ages of 10, 11, and 13. Three dissenting judges considered that the Convention did require such evidence even in the case of a child of this age.

The applicant in the *Keegan* case[56] was the father of a daughter by his unmarried partner. The case concerned the adoption of the daughter against the wishes of the natural father, who complained that this violated his rights under Article 8. The relationship between the mother and father had broken down shortly after the mother had become pregnant. The father visited the newborn baby at the nursing home where she was born, but was subsequently denied access when he tried to visit the child at the home of his former partner's parents. The mother made arrangements for the child to be adopted, and the child was subsequently placed by a registered adoption society with prospective adoptive parents. The applicant was advised of these actions by letter from his former partner after the child had been placed with the prospective adoptive parents. The applicant sought appointment from the courts as guardian of the child, and to be granted custody of the child, which was opposed by the mother and the prospective adoptive parents. The decision was eventually made by the Irish courts that the child should remain with the adoptive parents and an adoption order was subsequently made in respect of the child.

Noting that the birth of the child was not the result of casual sex but 'was the fruit of a planned decision taken in the context of a loving relationship', the Strasbourg Court concluded that there was family life in this case.[57] The question was whether a process of adoption which allowed no involvement by the father could be justified. The Strasbourg Court found that the procedure could not be justified by the limitations in paragraph (2). The Court was clearly influenced by the existence of a sequence of events the outcome of which 'was likely to prove to be irreversible'.[58] The Strasbourg Court places great stress on the quality of the procedure by which adoption decisions are taken, because decisions on adoption are generally irreversible. The procedure must involve participation by the biological parent even where that parent has a severe mental illness.[59]

The Court has also implied procedural requirements into Article 8 in relation to care proceedings. In *A.K. and L. v Croatia*[60] the first applicant had been divested of her parental rights and she argued that she was intellectually incapable of participating in or understanding the court proceedings that did so. The Court considered the procedural requirements in such a situation:

> It is true that Article 8 contains no explicit procedural requirements, but this is not conclusive of the matter. The relevant considerations to be weighed by a local authority in reaching

[54] *Sahin v Germany*, (App. 30943/96), 8 July 2003 [GC], ECHR 2003-VIII.

[55] *Sommerfield v Germany*, (App. 31871/96), 8 July 2003 [GC], (2004) 38 EHRR 756, ECHR 2003-VIII.

[56] *Keegan v Ireland*, (App. 16969/90), 26 May 1994, Series A No 290, (1994) 18 EHRR 342.

[57] §§ 44–5. [58] § 55. See also *Todorova v Italy*, (App. 33932/06), 13 January 2009.

[59] *X v Croatia*, (App. 11223/04), 17 July 2008.

[60] *A.K. and L. v Croatia*, (App. 37956/11), 8 January 2013. In *R.P. v United Kingdom*, (App. 38245/08), 9 October 2012, the Court examined a similar factual scenario from the stand point of Article 6.

decisions on children in its care must perforce include the views and interests of the natural parents. The decision-making process must therefore, in the Court's view, be such as to ensure that their views and interests are made known to, and duly considered by, the local authority and that they are able to exercise in due time any remedies available to them. In the Court's view, what therefore has to be determined is whether, having regard to the particular circumstances of the case and notably the serious nature of the decisions to be taken, the parents have been involved in the decision-making process, seen as a whole, to a degree sufficient to provide them with the requisite protection of their interests. If they have not, there will have been a failure to respect their family life and the interference resulting from the decision will not be capable of being regarded as necessary within the meaning of Article 8...'[61]

The applicant had a mild mental disability, a speech impediment, and a limited vocabulary. The Court noted the irony of these issues being regarded by the national authorities as grounds to fear that she would not be able to teach her child to speak properly, and yet not sufficient reason to provide her with legal representation when trying to argue her case in proceedings concerning her parental rights.[62] The Court concluded that there were no adequate safeguards at any stage of the process of severing her parental ties and found a violation of Article 8.

In *Y.C. v The United Kingdom*,[63] a care and placement order removing a child from the applicant's care was clearly an interference with her right to respect for family life but was justified under Article 8(2) as it did not exceed the margin of appreciation afforded to the respondent State and the reasons for the decision were relevant and sufficient. In this case, the Court further clarified the relevant factors to consider in the making of such decisions:

in seeking to identify the best interests of a child and in assessing the necessity of any proposed measure in the context of placement proceedings, the domestic court must demonstrate that it has had regard to, inter alia, the age, maturity and ascertained wishes of the child, the likely effect on the child of ceasing to be a member of his original family and the relationship the child has with relatives.[64]

Often in respect of care decisions, time will be of the essence. In *Kopf and Liberda v Austria*,[65] the applicants claimed that the belated decision of the Austrian courts on their request for the right to visit their former foster child breached their right to respect for their family life and the Court agreed. Although the domestic courts had fairly balanced the conflicting interests in the case, the fact that the proceedings were so lengthy, taking in total three and a half years to conclude, had a direct and adverse impact on the applicants' position. Therefore the State had failed to comply with its duty under Article 8 to deal diligently with the applicants' request for visiting rights.

In the context of care decisions, the Court sometimes has the difficult task of balancing parental rights against the best interests of the child, which is recognized to be the primary consideration. In *Vojnity v Hungary*[66] the withdrawal of the applicant's access rights in respect of his son on the basis of his religious beliefs was held to amount to a violation of Article 14 in conjunction with Article 8. The Court reiterated that 'the rights to respect for family life and religious freedom as enshrined in Articles 8 and 9 of the Convention, together with the right to respect for parents' philosophical and religious convictions in education, as provided in Article 2 of Protocol No. 1 to the Convention, convey on parents the right to communicate and promote their religious convictions in the bringing

[61] § 63. [62] § 73. [63] *Y.C. v The United Kingdom*, (App. 4547/10), 13 March 2012.
[64] § 135. [65] *Kopf and Liberda v Austria*, (App. 1598/06), 17 January 2012.
[66] *Vojnity v Hungary*, (App. 29617/07), 12 February 2013.

up of their children.'[67] The Court did not accept the Government's argument concerning the threat to the child's psychological health from the applicant's proselytism. While the Court acknowledged that the expert appointed by the District Court considered that the applicant's participation in the boy's life was harmful, it concluded that 'no convincing evidence was presented to substantiate a risk of actual harm, as opposed to the mere unease, discomfort or embarrassment which the child may have experienced on account of his father's attempts to transmit his religious beliefs.'[68] Arguably, it is a judgment in which parental rights are rather more evident than the rights of the child.

INTERNATIONAL CHILD ABDUCTION CASES

In recent years, the Court has increasingly had to consider the right to respect for family life in the context of international child abduction scenarios. It has made clear in a number of cases that the States' obligations under Article 8 in this context are to be interpreted in harmony with the general principles of international law, with particular account to be given to the provisions of the Hague Convention on the Civil Aspects of International Child Abduction 1980. In *Neulinger and Shuruk v Switzerland*[69] the first applicant was found to have abducted her son from Israel to Switzerland. The Swiss courts sought to enforce the child's return to his father in Israel, but the first applicant and her son (the second applicant) argued that this would infringe their right to respect for family life. The Grand Chamber agreed, on the basis that it was not convinced that the child's best interests would be served by the enforcement of the return order as he would be uprooted again from his home environment.

Šneersone and Kampanella v Italy[70] concerned a complaint by a mother and her son that the Italian courts' decisions ordering the son's return to Italy from Latvia were contrary to his best interests as well as in violation of international and Latvian law. The Court reiterated the principles apparent from *Neulinger and Shuruk*:

> In this area the decisive issue is whether a fair balance between the competing interests at stake – those of the child, of the two parents, and of public order – has been struck, within the margin of appreciation afforded to States in such matters…, bearing in mind, however, that the child's best interests must be the primary consideration…. "The child's interests" are primarily considered to be the following two: to have his or her ties with his or her family maintained, unless it is proved that such ties are undesirable, and to be allowed to develop in a sound environment…[71]

In this case, the Court concluded that the son's return to his father in Italy was not necessary in a democratic society. Relevant factors included that the child and his father had no language in common, he had never lived without his mother, and his mother was unable to move to Italy with him. While the domestic authorities have a margin of appreciation in determining the child's best interests, the supervision of this margin by the Strasbourg Court in cases of child abduction seems to be exceptionally close.

Portraying the other side of the issue of the return of an abducted child is the case of *Shaw v Hungary*.[72] The applicant complained that the Hungarian authorities failed to take timely and adequate measures for him to be reunited with his daughter following her abduction to France. The Court reiterated that in cases of child abduction, 'the adequacy

[67] § 37. [68] § 38.

[69] *Neulinger and Shuruk v Switzerland*, (App. 41615/07), 6 July 2010 [GC], ECHR 2010.

[70] *Šneersone and Kampanella v Italy*, (App. 14737/09), 12 July 2011. [71] § 85.

[72] *Shaw v Hungary*, (App. 6457/09), 26 July 2011.

of a measure is to be judged by the swiftness of its implementation, as the passage of time can have irremediable consequences for relations between the child and the parent who does not live with him or her.'[73] Almost eleven months passed between the abduction and the delivery of the enforceable final judgment ordering the return of the child. The Court acknowledged that the passage of time may in some situations require a reassessment of the child's ties to his or her parents and their environments, but that was not the case here. The bottom line in issues concerning the enforcement of an abducted child's return seems to be that the guarantees in Article 8 will apply in a manner subject to the child's best interests.[74] This can also be seen in *Karrer v Romania*[75] where domestic courts had rejected the first applicant's request for the return of her abducted daughter (the second applicant) on the ground that the return would expose the child to physical and psychological harm. The Strasbourg Court explained its approach:

> the Court must ascertain whether the domestic courts conducted an in-depth examination of the entire family situation and of a whole series of factors, in particular of a factual, emotional, psychological, material and medical nature, and made a balanced and reasonable assessment of the respective interests of each person, with a constant concern for determining what the best solution would be for the abducted child in the context of an application for his return to his country of origin.[76]

In this case, the Court concluded that the decision-making process at domestic level was flawed because no in-depth analysis was conducted with a view to assessing the child's best interests and in addition the first applicant was not given the opportunity to present his case in an expeditious manner.

THE RIGHT TO ADOPT

The Strasbourg Court has held that the Convention does not include a right to adopt a child.[77] Adoption means 'providing a child with a family, not a family with a child'[78] Where there are competing interests between those of the child and of those seeking to adopt, then the best interests of the child will be key in determining how those competing interests are to be resolved.

The circumstances of the *Pini* case[79] are rather sad. Two Italian couples had agreed to adopt Romanian children who had been placed for adoption following their abandonment by their parents. Adoption orders were made when the children were nine years old; they had had very little contact with their adoptive parents and the adoption orders were challenged in the Romanian courts by the CEPSB,[80] and by the children. It seems that the adoption was not the wish of the children (who by this time were more than ten years old).

[73] § 66. [74] § 75.

[75] *Karrer v Romania*, (App. 16965/10), 21 February 2012. [76] § 40.

[77] *Fretté v France*, (App. 36515/97), 26 February 2002, (2004) 38 EHRR 438, ECHR 2002-I. This case concerned a situation where an application to adopt had been rejected solely on the basis of the applicant's sexual orientation; the complaint was raised under Art. 14 read in conjunction with Art. 8. [78] § 42.

[79] *Pini and others v Romania* (Apps. 78028/01 and 78030/01), 22 June 2004, (2005) 40 EHRR 312, ECHR 2004-V.

[80] Poiana Soarelui Educational Centre in Braşov, which was an agency with whom the Child Welfare Board had placed the children when they were abandoned. See § 130 for a brief description of the role of CEPSB. There is a suggestion that the Centre was opposed to the adoption of Romanian children by non-nationals.

This was to have a decisive impact upon the Strasbourg Court's conclusions on compliance with Article 8. The Court said:

> The Court has consistently held that particular importance must be attached to the best interests of the child in ascertaining whether the national authorities have taken all the necessary steps that can reasonably be demanded to facilitate the reunion of the child and his or her parents. In particular, it has held in such matters that the child's interests may, depending on their nature and seriousness, override those of the parent.... The Court considers that it is even more important that the child's interests should prevail over those of the parents in the case of a relationship based on adoption, since, as it has previously held, adoption means 'providing a child with a family, not a family with a child'.[81]

The Strasbourg Court concluded that the Romanian authorities had not violated Article 8 in the manner in which it dealt with the applicants' efforts to secure the delivery of the children to them.

The *Emonet* case[82] involved the loss, on adoption, of the parental tie between a mother and daughter under provisions of Swiss law. The applicants were the child, the biological mother, and her cohabitee. Isabelle's mother was living with Roland Emonet, but he was not the father of Isabelle. She had divorced Isabelle's father in 1985 and he died in 1994. Isabelle came to regard Roland as her father and they wished to be a family in the eyes of the law. But the effect of the adoption of Isabelle by Roland was that the parental tie between Isabelle and her mother came to an end. Despite their objections, the Swiss courts refused to make any accommodations to the situation. The position would have been different if Roland and Isabelle's mother had married, but they were cohabiting. According to the Court, respect for the applicants' family life required both the biological and social realities to be taken into account. The automatic and permanent loss of parental rights by the mother in the circumstances of this case served no one's interests, and this situation had not been foreseen in the law. There was a violation of Article 8.

More recently, cases have arisen concerning second parent adoption within same-sex couples—i.e. the situation where one partner has a child and the other partner wishes to adopt the child in order to share legal parentage. The Grand Chamber had already confirmed that the refusal of adoption on the basis of sexuality was a violation of Article 14 in conjunction with Article 8.[83] In *X and others v Austria*[84] the applicants alleged that they had been discriminated against in comparison with different-sex couples because second-parent adoption was legally impossible for a same-sex couple. The Grand Chamber reiterated that the relationship of a cohabiting same-sex couple living in a stable de facto relationship falls within the notion of 'family life'.[85] It then referred to the admissibility decision in *Gas and Dubois v France*[86] in which the relationship between two women who were living together and had entered into a civil partnership, and the child conceived by one of them by means of assisted reproduction but being brought up by both of them, constituted 'family life' within the meaning of Article 8 of the Convention, but the refusal of second-parent adoption was not a violation of that Article because French law only allowed married couples to share parentage in this way. By contrast, in the *X* case, Austrian law did permit heterosexual couples to achieve second-parent adoption and therefore the

[81] *Pini and others v Romania*, (Apps. 78028/01 and 78030/01), 22 June 2004, (2005) 40 EHRR 312, ECHR 2004-V, §§ 155–6.

[82] *Emonet and others v Switzerland*, (App. 39051/03), 13 December 2007, (2009) 49 EHRR 234, ECHR 2007-XIV.

[83] *E.B. v France*. (App. 43546/02). 22 January 2008 [GC].

[84] *X and others v Austria*, (App. 19010/07), 19 February 2013 [GC], ECHR 2013.

[85] See *Schalk and Kopf v Austria*, (App. 30141/04), 24 June 2010.

[86] *Gas and Dubois v France*, (App. 25951/07) 31 August 2010, ECHR 2012.

refusal of this opportunity for same-sex couple amounted to discrimination under Article 14 in conjunction with Article 8. The Grand Chamber did acknowledge the moral complexity of the issue, noting that it was aware 'that striking a balance between the protection of the family in the traditional sense and the Convention rights of sexual minorities is in the nature of things a difficult and delicate exercise, which may require the State to reconcile conflicting views and interests perceived by the parties concerned as being in fundamental opposition.'[87] However, in this case it rejected Austria's claim for a wide margin of appreciation because it viewed the matter as one of discrimination on the basis of sexual orientation which admits only a very narrow margin, The contentious nature of the decision is nicely illustrated by the argument of the seven dissenting judges who felt that the majority went beyond the usual limits of the evolutive method of interpretation, anticipating social change rather than recognizing it. Despite the inclusion of same-sex couples in the Convention's conception of family, there appears to remain some moral discomfort within the Court and many Contracting States in providing equal protection for family life irrespective of sexual orientation.

INHERITANCE RIGHTS

In the *Marckx* case[88] the Strasbourg Court accepted that rights of succession between near relatives came within the sphere of family life.

In the *Pla and Puncernau* case,[89] the Strasbourg Court faced, for the first time, a case involving inheritance rights in the private sphere, that is, in the context of the freedom to leave property to persons of your choice. The dispute arose in the context of a will made in Andorra which, as interpreted by the courts of Andorra, operated to exclude adopted children from succession. It was argued that the sole purpose of the contested clause in the will was to exclude only illegitimate children from entitlement to inherit the testatrix's property. Though the applicants claimed a violation of Article 8 taken alone, as well as of Article 8 when read in conjunction with Article 14, the Court begins by dealing with the second complaint first 'since the issue of alleged discriminatory treatment... is at the heart of the applicants' complaint'.[90] The Strasbourg Court is at pains to stress that it bases its decision on the interpretation by the Andorran courts of the will in issue, and not with the freedom of the testatrix to dispose of her property as she wished. The Court, by five votes to two, concluded that there had been a violation of Article 8 when read with Article 14. The national court's interpretation amounted to a judicial deprivation of an adopted child's inheritance rights; it was 'blatantly inconsistent with the prohibition of discrimination established by Article 14'. It was not therefore necessary to consider separately the question of whether there had been a violation of Article 8 taken alone.

Many cases involving rights of inheritance are pleaded under Article 1 of Protocol 1 and Article 14.[91]

THE FAMILY LIFE OF NON-NATIONALS

Action by the authorities, such as expelling a person from a country, or refusing to admit someone, may result in separation of husband and wife, or of parents and children. When

[87] § 151.

[88] *Marckx v Belgium*, (App. 6833/74), 13 June 1979, Series A No 31, (1979–80) 2 EHRR 330.

[89] *Pla and Puncernau v Andorra*, (App. 69498/01), 13 July 2004, (2006) 42 EHRR 522, ECHR 2004-VIII.

[90] § 42. [91] See ch.24 on Art.14.

expulsion or refusal of admission is the source of the complaint, that action of itself cannot constitute a breach of the Convention. The Convention does not guarantee, at any rate outside the Fourth Protocol, any right to reside in a particular country. The Strasbourg Court has repeatedly stated that 'no right of an alien to enter or reside in a particular country is as such guaranteed by the Convention.'[92] But, as in the *East African Asians* cases,[93] the question may arise whether, for example, a refusal of admission infringes some other right which is guaranteed. Thus, while the right to reside in a particular country is not, as such, guaranteed by the Convention, it is necessary to examine complaints of expulsion or of refusal of admission in relation to Article 8 where such a measure might disrupt the family unit. The interests of preserving family life may also be relevant when decisions to deport someone arise. Such questions can involve the protection of private life as well as of family life.[94]

Where there has been an interference with family life by reason of an exclusion or deportation, that decision must be made 'in accordance with law', which requires a legal basis that is accessible and foreseeable. There must be some measures of legal protection in domestic law against arbitrary action by the authorities. The Strasbourg Court refers to this as the 'quality of law criterion'.[95] The level of protection provided within the national legal order will depend on the nature and extent of the interference with family life.[96] Safeguards will be required even in cases involving national security, since the individual must be able to challenge the executive's assertion that national security is at stake.[97]

In the *CG* case[98] a Turkish national living in Bulgaria with his wife and daughter was made the subject of a deportation order and summarily deported to Turkey. It was said that his residence permit was withdrawn because he was a threat to national security; he was, in fact, believed to be involved in drug dealing. The Strasbourg Court considered that, in this context, Article 8 required that deportation measures should be subject to some form of adversarial proceedings before an independent authority competent to scrutinize the reasons put forward for the deportation. The information in that case was the result of secret surveillance procedures which may themselves have been in breach of Article 8. In finding a violation of Article 8, the Strasbourg Court said:

> While actions taken in the interests of national security may, in view of the sensitivity of the subject-matter, attract considerably less in terms of guarantees than might otherwise be the case, an expulsion designed to forestall lesser evils such as run-of-the-mill criminal activities may have to be reviewed in proceedings providing a higher degree of protection of the individual.[99]

[92] For example, *Al-Nashif v Bulgaria*, (App. 50963/99), 20 June 2002, (2003) 36 EHRR 655, § 114.

[93] Apps. 4403–19/70, 4422/70, 4434/70, 4476–8/70, 4486/70, 4501/70, 4526–30/70, *East African Asians v United Kingdom*, Decision of the Commission, 10 and 18 October 1970, (1970) 13 *Yearbook* 928; Report of the Commission, 14 December 1973, (1994) 78-A DR 5; Committee of Ministers' Resolution DH (77) 2 of 21 October 1977, (1977) 20 *Yearbook* 642; and Committee of Ministers' Resolution DH (94) 30 of 21 March 1994, (1994) 78-A DR 70, deciding to make the Report of the Commission public at the request of the United Kingdom Government.

[94] *Dalia v France*, (App. 26102/95), 19 February 1998, (2001) 33 EHRR 26, ECHR 1998-I, §§ 43–5; and *Slivenko v Latvia*, (App. 48321/99), 9 October 2003 [GC], (2004) 39 EHRR 490, ECHR 2003-X, § 95; and see discussion in ch.16.

[95] *Al-Nashif v Bulgaria*, (App. 50963/99), 20 June 2002, (2003) 36 EHRR 655, § 121.

[96] *PG and JH v United Kingdom*, (App. 44787/98), 25 September 2001, ECHR 2001-IX, § 46.

[97] *Al-Nashif v Bulgaria*, (App. 50963/99), 20 June 2002, (2003) 36 EHRR 655, §§ 123–4.

[98] *CG and others v Bulgaria*, (App. 1365/07), 24 April 2008. See also *Lupsa v Romania*, (App. 10337/04), 8 June 2006, ECHR 2006-VII; and *Liu v Russia*, (App. 42086/05), 6 December 2007.

[99] *CG*, § 45.

There was patently in this case an absence of protection from arbitrary action by the State.

The *Al-Nashif* case[100] concerned a stateless man of Palestinian origin who was living in Bulgaria with his wife and children. He was prosecuted and subsequently deported seemingly for engaging in certain religious activities: teaching the Muslim religion without authority and being linked to a fundamentalist organization. The basis of the decision to deport was not made known to the applicant or his lawyers, and the decisions could be taken without following any form of adversarial process. The Strasbourg Court by four votes to three determined that there was a lack of required safeguards against arbitrary action. The dissenting judges were concerned at the elevation of the procedural requirements to a separate issue, noting that earlier case-law had regarded the quality of the decision-making process as a matter going to the question of the proportionality of the decision to deport.

If the quality of law criterion is satisfied, the Strasbourg Court will go on to consider whether the deportation or exclusion serves a legitimate aim. This has not generally proved problematic. In the most commonly met cases in which the applicant has become involved in some criminal activity, the measure will serve the purpose of being for the prevention of disorder or crime.

Finally, the Strasbourg Court will decide whether the deportation or exclusion is necessary in a democratic society, which requires the Contracting Party to show that the action is justified by a pressing social need and is proportionate to the aim pursued.[101] In the *Boultif* case,[102] the Strasbourg Court laid down guiding principles in order to examine whether a measure of expulsion was necessary in a democratic society:

> In assessing the relevant criteria in such a case, the Court will consider the nature and seriousness of the offence committed by the applicant; the duration of the applicant's stay in the country from which he is going to be expelled; the time which has elapsed since the commission of the offence and the applicant's conduct during that period; the nationalities of the various persons concerned; the applicant's family situation, such as the length of the marriage; other factors revealing whether the couple lead a real and genuine family life; whether the spouse knew about the offence at the time when he or she entered into a family relationship; and whether there are children in the marriage and, if so, their age. Not least, the Court will also consider the seriousness of the difficulties which the spouse would be likely to encounter in the applicant's country of origin, although the mere fact that a person might face certain difficulties in accompanying her or his spouse cannot in itself preclude expulsion.[103]

Boultif was an Algerian national living in Switzerland with his Swiss wife. He was prosecuted, convicted, and imprisoned for the offences of robbery and damage to property (committed sixteen months after his entry into Switzerland) which are described as 'particularly ruthless and brutal'. His behaviour in prison appears to have been exemplary, and he was in work following his release from prison. His residence permit was then withdrawn; he moved to Italy. The Strasbourg Court considered that the seriousness of his offence in terms of his being a continuing danger was mitigated by his conduct in prison and on his release. The Court then considered whether the family could establish their family life elsewhere. Algeria was considered but rejected: the wife had

[100] *Al-Nashif v Bulgaria*, (App. 50963/99), 20 June 2002, (2003) 36 EHRR 655.

[101] *Mehemi v France*, (App. 25017/94), 26 September 1997, (2000) 30 EHRR 739, ECHR 1997-VI, § 34; and *Dalia v France* (App. 26102/95), 19 February 1998, (2001) 33 EHRR 26, ECHR 1998-I, § 52.

[102] *Boultif v Switzerland*, (App. 54273/00), 2 August 2001, (2001) 33 EHRR 1179, ECHR 2001-IX.

[103] § 48. See also *Amrollahi v Denmark*, (App. 56811/00), 11 July 2002, § 35.

never lived there, and though she speaks French did not speak Arabic. It could not be expected that she would follow her husband to Algeria. The establishment of family life in Italy was also considered, but the applicant's current residence in Italy was unlawful and the Court did not consider that family life could be established there. The Court concluded, unanimously, that there had been a serious impediment to family life, since it was practically impossible for the applicant to live his family life outside Switzerland. The interference was accordingly not proportionate to the aim of the prevention of disorder and crime.[104]

The question of the nature and extent of a person's family life will be determined in the light of the position obtaining at the time when any exclusion order becomes final.[105] The *Maslov* case[106] concerned the deportation of a seventeen-year-old who had lived in Austria since the age of six and had been convicted of a string of burglaries. The Grand Chamber ruled that, although Article 8 provides no absolute protection against expulsion for any category of non-national, including those where were born in the host country or moved there in their early childhood, very serious reasons would be required for the removal of a settled migrant who has lawfully spent all or the major part of his or her childhood and youth in the host country.[107]

In the *Moustaquim* case[108] the applicant, a Moroccan national, who had lived in Belgium since the age of two, was successful in arguing that deportation would interfere with his family life by depriving him of contact with his parents and brothers and sisters.[109]

In the *Nasri* case,[110] the Strasbourg Court ruled that execution of a deportation order against an Algerian national violated his right to family life, because it would be disproportionate in the exceptional circumstances of the particular case. The applicant was deaf and without speech from birth, had lived virtually all his life in France with his parents and eight siblings, was illiterate, could not read, and did not know a recognized sign language, but had been convicted of gang rape.

In the *Al-Nashif* case, the Strasbourg Court said:

> Where immigration is concerned, Article 8 cannot be considered to impose on a State a general obligation to respect the choice by married couples of the country of their matrimonial residence and to authorize family reunion in its territory.
>
> However, the removal of a person from a country where close members of his family are living may amount to an infringement of the right to respect for family life as guaranteed by Article 8(1) of the Convention.[111]

[104] For an example of a case where consideration of these factors resulted in a decision that there was no violation of Article 8, see *Üner v Netherlands*, (App. 46410/99), 18 October 2006 [GC], (2007) 45 EHRR 421, ECHR 2006-XII.

[105] *Maslov v Austria*, (App. 1638/03), 23 June 2008 [GC], ECHR 2008, § 61.

[106] *Maslov v Austria*, (App. 1638/03), 23 June 2008 [GC], ECHR 2008. See also R. Cholewinski, 'Strasbourg's "Hidden Agenda"? The Protection of Second-Generation Migrants from Expulsion under Art. 8 of the ECHR' (1994) 3 NQHR 287.

[107] § 75; the Strasbourg Court joins consideration of rights flowing from family life and private life in this judgment.

[108] *Moustaquim v Belgium*, (App. 12313/86), 18 February 1991, Series A No 193, (1991) 13 EHRR 802.

[109] See also *Beldjoudi v France*, (App. 12083/86), 26 March 1992, Series A No 234-A, (1992) 14 EHRR 801; *Djeroud v France*, (App. 13446/87), 23 January 1991, Series A No 191-B, (1992) 14 EHRR 68; *Boughanemi v France* (App. 22070/93) 24 April 1996, (1996) 22 EHRR 228, ECHR 1996-II; and *Gül v Switzerland*, (App. 23218/94), 19 February 1996; (1996) 22 EHRR 93, ECHR 1996-I.

[110] *Nasri v France*, (App. 19465/92), 13 July 1995, Series A No 324, (1996) 21 EHRR 458. See also *Ezzouhdi v France*, (App. 47160/99), 6 February 2001; and *Boultif v Switzerland*, (App. 54273/00), 2 August 2001, (2001) 33 EHRR 1179, ECHR 2001-IX.

[111] *Al-Nashif v Bulgaria*, (App. 50963/99), 20 June 2002, (2003) 36 EHRR 655, § 114.

The Strasbourg Court has recognized the State's margin of appreciation in such cases, but has increasingly subjected this to supervision at the European level. This will involve a consideration of whether the exclusion measure strikes a fair balance between the individual's rights under the Convention and the wider interests of the community.[112]

In *Nunez v Norway*[113] the applicant argued that her breaches of Norwegian immigration law could not justify her being separated from her two minor children. The applicant, after having first been deported from Norway in March 1996 with a two-year-prohibition on re-entry due to a criminal conviction, defied that prohibition by re-entering the country in July 1996 with the use of a false identity and travel document. On the basis of her misleading information, she was subsequently granted a work permit and a settlement permit. The Court acknowledged the strong public interest in the applicant's expulsion from Norway upon discovery of her deceit, but was ultimately not satisfied that the Norwegian authorities had acted within their margin of appreciation when seeking to strike a fair balance between that public interest and the applicant's need to be able to remain in Norway in order to maintain her contact with her two children in their best interests. It held that the applicant's expulsion from Norway with a two-year re-entry ban would entail a violation of Article 8.

This can be contrasted with the case of *Antwi and others v Norway*.[114] In this case, the first applicant used a forged passport and birth certificate stating a false identity when he applied for a work and residence permit in Norway as an EEA citizen, and subsequently for renewal of those permits and for citizenship. He and his wife both originally came from Ghana and the Court found no obstacle preventing her from accompanying the first applicant to their country of origin and continuing their family life there. Their ten year old child's links to Ghana were minimal and the Court accepted that it would probably be difficult for her to adapt to life in Ghana and that implementation of the expulsion order would not be beneficial to her. However, the Court found that there were no insurmountable obstacles in the way of the applicants all settling together in Ghana or, at the least, to maintaining regular contact. The exceptional circumstances of *Nunez* were distinguished, not least because of the more prompt proceedings in the present case, and Norway was found to have acted within its margin of appreciation.

When considering whether there exists an effective family life, the Strasbourg Court (and, in its time, the Commission) normally requires two elements: a close relationship; and one between persons who have been living together at the time of, or shortly before, the alleged interference. Over time the Strasbourg Court has developed a notion of the core or nuclear family whose unity is protected under Article 8 independently of the length of its existence.[115] By contrast, wider family ties have been recognized as forming part of private life, but such ties only come into existence after the passage of time and tend to become more significant the longer a person has lived in a country and developed the wider network of family ties.[116]

Similar considerations may apply to decisions on entry. If it is doubtful whether the family could establish itself elsewhere, and members of the family are seeking to join other members of the family in the territory of a Contracting Party, then the complaint must

[112] *Maslov v Austria*, (App. 1638/03), 23 June 2008 [GC], ECHR 2008, § 76.

[113] *Nunez v Norway*, (App. 55597/09), 28 June 2011.

[114] *Antwi and others v Norway*, (App. 26940/10), 14 February 2012.

[115] *X v Croatia*, (App. 11223/04), 17 July 2008, § 37.

[116] See D. Thym, 'Respect for Private and Family Life under Article 8 ECHR in Immigration Cases: a Human Right to Regularize Illegal Stay?' (2008) 57 ICLQ 87. See also discussion in relation to the protection of private life and immigration issues in ch.16.

be examined on the merits. This was the situation in two applications in the first group of *East African Asians* cases.[117] In each of the two, the applicant had been refused permission to enter the United Kingdom from Uganda to join his wife, who had lawfully entered the UK, in one case with six children, some time previously. The complaints were declared admissible, but shortly afterwards all the applicants in this group of cases were admitted for permanent residence.

The conclusion seems to be that the Convention does not *guarantee* the right to family life in a particular country, but only an effective family life as such, no matter where. This principle, however, appears to be modified in the case of the relationships between parents and their children if the latter are not admitted to the country where the former have their residence.

It would seem to follow that, while the admission of a person to permanent residence may not imply any obligation to admit the spouse (present or future), it may imply an obligation to admit any dependent children. The issue of the admission of spouses of those permanently settled was raised by the Strasbourg Court in the *Abdulaziz, Cabales and Balkandali* cases[118] where three women applicants lawfully and permanently settled in the United Kingdom who had subsequently married husbands from their countries of origin complained that the refusal of the British authorities to permit their husbands to join them in the UK constituted a violation of Article 8. In the face of a submission from the UK that the issue raised concerned immigration control for which Protocol 4 (to which the UK is not a party) alone made provision, the Court stated that the Convention and its Protocols must be read as a whole; it did not follow that because a Contracting Party had not ratified a part of the Convention concerned with immigration that those parts of the Convention to which they were a party and which touched on measures taken in that field would not be applicable. The Court noted that the nature of the application was that the wives (who were settled in the UK) were complaining that they were threatened with deprivation of the society of their spouses.

The UK advanced two further arguments. First, there was no family life to protect, since the couples had never established homes together; and, secondly, there was no obstacle to the couples living together in the countries of their husband's residence and the claim was, in effect, a claim to choose their country of residence. The Court recalled that it had said in the *Marckx* case[119] that Article 8 presupposes the existence of a family, but considered that marriage established a family life between husband and wife that was protected by the Convention even if the couple had not yet set up home together. Cohabitation was seen as a normal incident of marriage; all three couples had cohabited, and one had a son. This was sufficient to establish the family life protected by the Article. The Strasbourg Court, differing from the Commission, went on to consider whether there was a violation of Article 8 taken alone in these circumstances. The Court confirmed that in the circumstances presented by the applicants, there was no violation of Article 8 taken alone:

> The duty imposed by Article 8 cannot be considered as extending to a general obligation on the part of a Contracting State to respect the choice by married couples of the country of

[117] Apps. 4403–19/70, 4422/70, 4434/70, 4476–8/70, 4486/70, 4501/70, 4526–30/70, *East African Asians v United Kingdom*, Decision of the Commission, 10 and 18 October 1970, (1970) 13 *Yearbook* 928, at 1004; see also Report of the Commission, 14 December 1973, (1994) 78-A DR 5; Committee of Ministers Resolution DH (77) 2 of 21 October 1977, (1977) 20 *Yearbook* 642; and Committee of Ministers Resolution DH (94) 30 of 21 March 1994, (1994) 78-A DR 70.

[118] *Abdulaziz, Cabales and Balkandali v United Kingdom*, (Apps. 9214/80, 9473/81, and 9474/81), 28 May 1985, Series A No 94, (1985) 7 EHRR 471.

[119] *Marckx v Belgium*, (App. 6833/74), 13 June 1979, Series A No 31, (1979–80) 2 EHRR 330.

their matrimonial residence and to accept the non-national spouses for settlement in that country.[120]

A final point that has arisen in some of these cases is whether the immigration laws involve an element of discrimination based on sex which might raise an issue under Article 14 taken together with Article 8. In the UK, as in other European countries, the rule is frequently applied that a woman may normally be admitted to join her husband, but that only exceptionally may a man be admitted to join his wife. In the *East African Asians* cases, the Government submitted that the place of residence of a family is normally the place of residence of the husband, and that Article 8 does not safeguard any right for husband and wife to live together permanently in any other place than the place of residence of the husband, or at a place where he is entitled to be.[121] The question is whether such differential treatment of men and women in this field is justifiable under Article 14, or whether it constitutes discrimination under that Article.

The question of discrimination on grounds of sex was also raised in the *Abdulaziz, Cabales and Balkandali* cases[122] since it was easier for a man settled in the UK to be joined by his wife than for a woman to be joined by her husband. The Court found a violation of Article 8 taken together with Article 14.

Where a marriage ends, immigration issues can also arise. In the *Berrehab* case[123] a Moroccan national became divorced from his Dutch wife; the couple had a daughter who was born after the couple had ceased living together, though Mr Berrehab saw her regularly over a number of years. Following the divorce, he was then refused a residence permit and complained that this violated his family life under Article 8. The Strasbourg Court held that Article 8 was applicable and rejected an argument that Berrehab could travel from Morocco to the Netherlands to see his daughter. The Dutch authorities relied on the exception in paragraph (2) in the interests of public order. The Court concluded that the exclusion of Berrehab in these circumstances was excessive in protecting public order and so constituted a violation of Article 8.

THE FAMILY LIFE OF PRISONERS

Applicants detained in prison have frequently complained of interference with the right to respect for family life. Some have complained that they have been refused permission to have visits from their children.[124] The Commission frequently rejected such complaints under paragraph (2), for example on the ground that such interference with family life was necessary for the prevention of crime.[125]

The issue was raised before the Strasbourg Court in the *Boyle and Rice* case in the context of a complaint of a violation of Article 13.[126] The Court said:

> When assessing the obligations imposed on the Contracting Parties by Article 8 in relation to prison visits, regard must be had to the ordinary and reasonable requirements of

[120] *Abdulaziz, Cabales and Balkandali v United Kingdom*, (Apps. 9214/80, 9473/81, and 9474/81), 28 May 1985, Series A No 94, (1985) 7 EHRR 471, § 68.

[121] (1970) 13 *Yearbook* 928, 978, cf. 1004.

[122] *Abdulaziz, Cabales and Balkandali v United Kingdom*, (Apps. 9214/80, 9473/81, and 9474/81), 28 May 1985, Series A No 94, (1985) 7 EHRR 471.

[123] *Berrehab v Netherlands*, (App. 10730/84), 21 June 1988, Series A No 138, (1989) 11 EHRR 322.

[124] See, for example, *Ostrovar v Moldova*, (App. 35207/03), 13 September 2005.

[125] App. 1983/63, *X v Netherlands*, Decision of 13 December 1965, (1966) 18 CD 19; cf. App. 2515/65, *X v Federal Republic of Germany*, Decision of 23 May 1966, (1966) 20 CD 28.

[126] *Boyle and Rice v United Kingdom*, (Apps. 9659/82 and 9658/82), 27 April 1988, Series A No 131, (1988) 10 EHRR 425.

> imprisonment and to the resultant degree of discretion which the national authorities must be allowed in regulating a prisoner's contact with his family.[127]

The Court found that there was no arguable complaint where a prisoner in the lowest security category was allowed twelve visits a year of one hour's duration.[128]

The *Moiseyev* case[129] concerned an applicant convicted and sentenced to four years and six months' imprisonment in a strict security correctional colony. Initially no visits from his family were permitted during the first nine months following his arrest. Thereafter two visits per month of one hour each were allowed. During these visits, he was separated from his wife and daughter by a glass partition and a prison warden was present. For periods totalling seven months while his appeals were being examined, visits were suspended altogether. The Strasbourg Court found that the refusal of family visits had not been determined by reference to a law whose application was foreseeable, since the law conferred an unfettered discretion on the investigator without defining in any way the circumstances in which visits could be refused.

The Strasbourg Court next considered the limitations on the frequency and duration of visits. Such limitations were, in the circumstances of this case, not proportionate to the aim of preventing disorder or crime. The applicant's circumstances could be distinguished from certain Italian cases which involved imprisoned Mafia members.[130] Finally, the Court ruled that separation of visitors by a glass screen could only be justified if there was an established security risk.[131] The imposition of such a measure was disproportionate and constituted a violation of Article 8.

Similarly, in *Piechowicz v Poland*[132] the Court reiterated that it is an essential part of a detainee's right to respect for family life that the authorities enable him or, if need be, assist him in maintaining contact with his close family. The denial of contact with the applicant's common law wife for over two years was held not to be necessary in a democratic society in order to prevent crime, despite her being indicted in the same proceedings as the applicant. While the Court acknowledged that some restrictions would be justified in permitting visits from his young son, the blanket refusal of visit permissions for a period of nine months and subsequently for two months was similarly excessive and not justified under Article 8(2).

A refusal to grant compassionate leave to attend the funeral of the prisoner's father may breach respect for family life in Article 8.[133] Similarly, a refusal to allow a prisoner to visit his seriously injured daughter in the hospital and subsequently to provide a timely and adequate reply to his request to attend her funeral in plain clothes was found to have violated Article 8.[134] The Grand Chamber has given further consideration to the family life of prisoners in the *Dickson* case.[135] The applicants were a married couple. Kirk Dickson had been convicted of murder in 1994 and sentenced to life imprisonment with a direction that the minimum term to be served was fifteen years. He met Lorraine through a prison pen-pal network while he was in prison, and in 2001, they married. The couple requested

[127] § 74.

[128] See also *Messina v Italy, (No. 2)*, (App. 25498/94), 28 September 2000, ECHR 2000-X.

[129] *Moiseyev v Russia*, (App. 62936/00), 9 October 2008.

[130] Such as *Messina v Italy, (No. 2)*, (App. 25498/94), 28 September 2000, ECHR 2000-X.

[131] *Ciorap v Moldova*, (App. 12066/02), 19 June 2007, § 117.

[132] *Piechowicz v Polandi*, (App. 20071/07), 17 April 2012.

[133] *Czarnowski v Poland*, (App. 28586/03), 20 January 2009.

[134] *Giszczak v Poland*, (App. 40195/08), 29 November 2011.

[135] *Dickson v United Kingdom*, (App. 44362/04), 4 December 2007 [GC], (2008) 46 EHRR 927, ECHR 2007-XIII.

artificial insemination facilities to enable them to have a child together, arguing that a combination of the length of his sentence and her age meant that this was the only way in which they could have a child. The Secretary of State has a discretion in such matters, but did not consider that there were exceptional circumstances which would warrant granting the application. It was refused. The applicants complained of a violation of Article 8 and 12.[136] The Grand Chamber ruled, citing its judgment in the *Hirst* case,[137] that automatic forfeiture of rights should not attend imprisonment purely on the ground that public opinion might be offended by accommodations made for prisoners, although it did accept that maintaining public confidence in the penal system had a role to play in the establishment of penal policy. Equally, the Grand Chamber acknowledged that consideration of the welfare of any child conceived in the circumstances of this case was relevant. The Grand Chamber was, however, clearly influenced by the fact that 30 Contracting Parties permitted conjugal visits,[138] although it did not consider that Contracting Parties were under any obligation to make provision for such visits. In concluding by twelve votes to five that there had been a violation of Article 8, the Grand Chamber felt that the exceptional circumstances threshold had been set too high, and that there had not been any proper consideration of the balance to be struck. Furthermore the policy was not embodied in primary legislation, which meant that the various competing interests had never been fully weighed, nor proportionality assessed, by Parliament.

The Court has taken a similar approach to the rights of prisoners when considering applications claiming a breach of Article 12 on account of domestic authorities' refusal to grant them leave to marry in prison.[139] The Court confirmed that prisoners continue to enjoy the fundamental human rights and freedoms that are not contrary to the sense of deprivation of liberty, including the right to marry, and that any additional limitation must be justified by the authorities. Such limitations could be justified on the basis of security but not merely on the basis of public opinion. The Court found violations of Article 12 on the basis that the national authorities had failed to strike a fair balance of proportionality between the various public and individual interests at stake. Article 12 will now be considered in more detail.

THE RIGHT TO MARRY AND FOUND A FAMILY

Article 12 guarantees the right to marry and to found a family. These rights are not subject to limitations of the kind set out in paragraph (2) of Articles 8 to 11. Instead, limitations are to be found in the provision that men and women of marriageable age have the right to marry and to found a family, 'according to the national laws governing the exercise of this right'.

The scope of this qualification is not clear. It is evident that the exercise of the rights guaranteed cannot be wholly governed by national law. In that case, the protection of Article 12 would extend only to cases where there was a breach of national law. But the purpose of the Convention, here as elsewhere, is to guarantee certain human rights irrespective of the provisions of national law.[140] The correct view, therefore, is that Article 12

[136] The Grand Chamber ruled that no separate issue under Article 12 arose.

[137] *Hirst v United Kingdom (No. 2)*, (App. 74025/01), 6 October 2005 [GC], (2006) 42 EHRR 849, ECHR 2005-IX; discussed in ch.16.

[138] Which, of course, obviated the need to making artificial insemination facilities available.

[139] *Frasik v Poland*, (App. 22933/02) 5 January 2010, ECHR 2010 (extracts); *Jaremowicz v Poland*, (App. 24023/03), 5 January 2010.

[140] See Opsahl, 'The Convention and the right to respect for family life, particularly as regards the unity of the family and the protection of the rights of parents and guardians in the education of children' in A. H. Robertson, *Privacy and Human Rights* (MUP, Manchester 1973), 182.

imposes an obligation to recognize, both in principle and in practice, the right to marry and to found a family. This obligation implies that the restrictions placed on these rights by national law must be imposed for a legitimate purpose, for example, to prevent polygamy or incest, and must not go beyond a reasonable limit to attain that purpose. On the other hand, the precise scope of the restrictions may vary among the Contracting Parties, as does, for example, marriageable age.

In the *B and L* case[141] the Strasbourg Court was asked to consider the rules in the United Kingdom which prohibited a marriage between a father-in-law and a daughter-in-law unless the former husband and the mother of the former husband had died. The purpose of the restriction was to protect the integrity of the family by preventing sexual rivalry between parents and children. There had already been proposals in the United Kingdom for amending the law to lift the prohibition, since it was considered that the ban served no useful purpose of public policy. The Strasbourg Court concluded that there had been a violation of Article 12.

The issue of the right to marry for non-EEA nationals was considered in the case of *O'Donoghue and others v The United Kingdom*.[142] The applicants alleged that the existence of the Certificate of Approval scheme and its application to them constituted a disproportionate interference with their Article 12 rights. This scheme (in various formats) required non-EEA nationals to submit an application to the Secretary of State for the Home Department for a Certificate of Approval before being permitted to marry in the United Kingdom. The Court found such a requirement was not inherently objectionable and that Contracting States may properly impose reasonable conditions on the right of a third-country national to marry in order to ascertain whether the proposed marriage is one of convenience and, if necessary, to prevent it. However, the Court was concerned that the decision whether or not to grant a Certificate of Approval was not based solely on the genuineness of the proposed marriage, but rather on whether the applicant had sufficient leave to remain. The Court also found that a blanket prohibition, without any attempt being made to investigate the genuineness of the proposed marriages, restricted the right to marry to such an extent that the very essence of the right was impaired, and that even the existence of an exception on compassionate grounds did not remove the impairment of the essence of the right, as this was an exceptional procedure which was entirely at the discretion of the Secretary of State. Furthermore, a fee of £295 also impaired the right to marry and thus the UK was in violation of Article 12.

In this case, the Court clearly explained the different types of limitations justified under Articles 8 and 12 respectively. It explained that 'in examining a case under Article 12 the Court would not apply the tests of "necessity" or "pressing social need" which are used in the context of Article 8 but would have to determine whether, regard being had to the State's margin of appreciation, the impugned interference has been arbitrary or disproportionate.'[143]

Article 14 is also of special importance in relation to Article 12, since it prohibits discrimination not only, for example, on racial or religious grounds, but also on grounds of sex. Thus, in relation to marriage and the founding of a family, there must be no discrimination between men and women. Not all forms of differential treatment constitute discrimination so that there is no requirement that marriageable age, for example, should

[141] *B and L v United Kingdom*, (App. 36536/02), 13 September 2005, (2006) 42 EHRR 195.

[142] *O'Donoghue and others v The United Kingdom*, (App. 34848/07), 14 December 2010, ECHR 2010 (extracts).

[143] § 84.

be the same for both men and women but all differential treatment must be examined by reference to its purpose and justification to ensure that it is not unlawful.

In two cases against the United Kingdom,[144] the Strasbourg Court concluded that the provisions of national law under which the allocation of sex to that registered at birth was fixed and determined the sex of the partner a person could marry impaired the essence of the right to marry in the case of transsexuals. Such provisions accordingly constituted a breach of Article 12.[145]

In the case of *Schalk and Kopf v Austria*[146] the Grand Chamber was asked to consider the application of the right to marry to same-sex couples. The applicants complained that they were discriminated against as, being a same-sex couple, they were denied the possibility to marry or to have their relationship otherwise recognized by law. The Court first took a textual interpretation of Article 12's statement that 'Men and women of marriageable age have the right to marry':

> The Court observes that, looked at in isolation, the wording of Article 12 might be interpreted so as not to exclude the marriage between two men or two women. However, in contrast, all other substantive Articles of the Convention grant rights and freedoms to 'everyone' or state that 'no one' is to be subjected to certain types of prohibited treatment. The choice of wording in Article 12 must thus be regarded as deliberate. Moreover, regard must be had to the historical context in which the Convention was adopted. In the 1950s marriage was clearly understood in the traditional sense of being a union between partners of different sex.[147]

The applicants argued that Article 12 should be interpreted in light of modern day conditions. The Court distinguished this case from its earlier decisions on transsexuals but it noted that Article 9 of the European Union Charter of Fundamental Rights deliberately dropped the mention of 'man and woman' in respect of the right to marry. In light of this, the Court concluded that it would no longer consider that the right to marry in Article 12 must in all circumstances be limited to marriage between two persons of the opposite sex, but that the question whether or not to allow same-sex marriage would be left to regulation by the national law of the Contracting State.[148] The Court noted in this regard that 'marriage has deep-rooted social and cultural connotations which may differ largely from one society to another' and thus the Court 'must not rush to substitute its own judgment in place of that of the national authorities, who are best placed to assess and respond to the needs of society.'[149]

The applicants also alleged an infringement of Article 14, taken in conjunction with Article 8 but, despite the Court's important step forward in the protection of the rights of homosexuals, there was no violation of the Convention found in this case. The Court noted that as Article 12 does not impose an obligation to grant same-sex couples access to marriage, Article 14 taken in conjunction with Article 8, a provision of more general

[144] *Goodwin v United Kingdom*, (App. 28957/95), 11 July 2002 [GC], (2002) 35 EHRR 447, ECHR 2002-VI, and *I. v United Kingdom*, (App. 25680/94), 11 July 2002 [GC], (2003) 36 EHRR 967.

[145] For earlier case-law, see *Rees v United Kingdom*, (App. 9532/81), 17 October 1986, Series A No 106, (1987) 9 EHRR 56; *Cossey v United Kingdom*, (App. 10843/84), 27 September 1990, Series A No 184, (1991) 13 EHRR 622; and *Sheffield and Horsham v United Kingdom*, (Apps. 22885/93 and 23390/94), 30 July 1998, (1999) 27 EHRR 163, ECHR 1998-V.

[146] *Schalk and Kopf v Austria*, (App. 30141/04), 24 June 2010. For discussion, see L. Hodson, 'A Marriage By Any Other Name? *Schalk and Kopf v Austria*' (2011) 11 HRLR 170, and F. Hamilton, 'Why the Margin of Appreciation is Not the Answer to the Gay Marriage Debate' [2013] EHRLR 47.

[147] § 55.

[148] § 61.

[149] § 62.

purpose and scope, cannot be interpreted as imposing such an obligation either. In relation to alternative means of legal recognition of same-sex partnerships, the Court regarded this as falling within the category of 'evolving rights with no established consensus, where States must also enjoy a margin of appreciation in the timing of the introduction of legislative changes'.[150] Thus Austria was not in violation for only introducing legally recognized partnerships in 2010.

While the right to marry and the right to found a family are two separate rights, it seems from the wording of the Article that only married heterosexual couples can claim the right to found a family. If the Article had been worded 'Everyone has the right to marry and to found a family', it might have been easier to infer that unmarried people or same sex couples also had the right to found a family. It may be significant, also, that the Article ends with a reference to 'this right', rather than 'these rights', thus apparently envisaging a close connection between the two.[151] But even if unmarried persons may have no right under Article 12 to found a family, the term 'family' in Article 8 has a wider meaning as we have seen.

The right of men and women, once married, to found a family may be subject to increasing strain in a society preoccupied with the dangers of overpopulation. Article 12 plainly does not preclude the provision of family planning services; at the other extreme, sterilization carried out in dubious circumstances may well involve a violation of Articles 8 and 12 of the Convention.[152] Fiscal incentives for marriage have been held to be acceptable under Article 14 when read with Article 1 of Protocol 1.[153] A temporary prohibition on remarriage within three years after divorce imposed under Swiss law applicable at the time on the spouse held responsible for the breakdown of the marriage was held to violate Article 12 as being disproportionate to the legitimate aim being pursued, namely protecting the institution of marriage and the rights of others.[154]

Several applications have sought to read into the provisions of Articles 8 and 12 a right to divorce. In the *Johnston* case[155] the Strasbourg Court concluded that the right to divorce cannot be derived from the provisions of Article 12, and it would accordingly be inconsistent to interpret the extent of the positive obligations flowing from Article 8 to include a right to divorce. However, if national legislation allows divorce, Article 12 will secure for divorced persons the right to remarry without unreasonable restrictions. In *V.K. v Croatia*[156] the applicant complained that the lengthy divorce proceedings had impaired his right to marry again. The Court found a violation of Article 12 on the basis that the failure of the domestic authorities to conduct the divorce proceedings left the applicant in a state of prolonged uncertainty which amounted to an unreasonable restriction of his right to marry.

[150] § 105.

[151] Contrast the wording of the European Union Charter of Fundamental Rights which provides in Article 9, 'The right to marry and the right to found a family shall be guaranteed in accordance with the national laws governing the exercise of these rights.' See also C. McGlynn, 'Families and the European Union Charter of Fundamental Rights: progressive change or entrenching the status quo?' (2001) 26 ELRev 582.

[152] *KH and others v Slovakia*, (App. 32881/04), 28 April 2009, (2009) 49 EHRR 857 and *VC v Slovakia*, (App. 18968/07), Decision of 16 June 2009, ECHR 2011 (extracts).

[153] *Burden v United Kingdom*, (App. 13378/05), 29 April 2008 [GC], (2008) 47 EHRR 857, ECHR 2008-nyr.

[154] *F v Switzerland*, (App. 11329/85), 18 December 1987, Series A No 128, (1988) 10 EHRR 411.

[155] *Johnston and others v Ireland*, (App. 9697/82), 18 December 1986, Series A No 112, (1987) 9 EHRR 203.

[156] *V.K. v Croatia*, (App. 38380/08), 27 November 2012.

EQUALITY BETWEEN SPOUSES

Article 5 of Protocol 7 provides:

> Spouses shall enjoy equality of rights and responsibilities of a private law character between them, and in their relations with their children, as to marriage, during marriage and in the event of its dissolution. This article shall not prevent States from taking such measures as are necessary in the interests of children.

The rights protected under this Article are of a private law character, and the Articles have no application to public law areas, such as tax, social security, labour laws, or the criminal law. It is only spouses who are protected, so the position of those about to marry remains governed wholly by Article 12. The Article should not be regarded as having any application to the disposition of property in the event of a dissolution of the marriage, nor does it imply any obligation on a Contracting Party to provide for dissolution of the marriage.[157]

CONCLUDING REMARKS

This chapter has mainly considered those cases where the Strasbourg Court has rooted its judgment in the protection of family life. Though the Court does not always make a clear distinction between the protection of private life and family life, and rightly views the protection of the Article taken as a whole as potentially providing broader protection than its individual elements might if taken alone, it is now possible to divide the Strasbourg Court's case-law into those cases primarily concerned with family life and those primarily concerned with private life. The following chapter considers the Strasbourg Court's case-law on private life, home, and correspondence.

In this chapter, we have seen that the Strasbourg Court has added a procedural superstructure to Article 8 which provides safeguards for individuals in relation to interferences with their family life. These procedural safeguards must enable national decision-makers to consider the competing interests that will frequently be at the heart of interferences with family life. Decision-making which is sensitive to the protection of family life is unlikely to result in the finding of a violation of Article 8, but it remains surprising how often Contracting Parties have given insufficient consideration to the balancing of the right to respect for family life with their internal policy preferences. In recent years, the potential conflicts between respect for traditional family units and the rights of all persons to respect for their own family life irrespective of whether that family meets traditional expectations has increasingly presented difficult questions to the Strasbourg Court. The recognition of same-sex couples as enjoying a 'family life' has been a vital and positive development in the jurisprudence but the issue of discrimination on the grounds of sexual orientation is far from over and further decisive steps are likely to be needed in the near future.

[157] Explanatory memorandum to Protocol 7, Council of Europe Document H(84)5, at 12.

16

PROTECTING PRIVATE LIFE, THE HOME, AND CORRESPONDENCE

INTRODUCTORY REMARKS

The scope of the protection of private life under the Convention is being increasingly explored in the Strasbourg Court's case-law. It was suggested some years ago that the Convention protects the individual, under this head, against attacks on physical or mental integrity or moral or intellectual freedom, attacks on honour and reputation, the use of a person's name, identity, or likeness, being spied upon, watched, or harassed, and the disclosure of information protected by the duty of professional secrecy.[1] This has proved to be the case.

In a compelling, analysis, Moreham has proposed that the Strasbourg Court's case-law on private life can be synthesized into five categories: freedom from interference with physical and psychological integrity; freedom from unwanted access to and collection of information; freedom from serious environmental pollution; the right to be free to develop one's identity; and the right to live one's life in the manner of one's choosing.[2] This analysis, with slight modification, is adopted in this chapter in presenting an exposition of the way in which the Strasbourg Court has developed the right to private life. Moreham's analysis also largely incorporates the concept of the right to respect for the home and correspondence into the protection of private life, since where you live and your communications with others and theirs with you are essential ingredients of a social life in a community. Nevertheless, there remain one or two aspects of respect for the home and correspondence which are more conveniently addressed separately from the five areas in Moreham's synthesis.

DEFINITIONS

PRIVATE LIFE

In 1976, the Commission defined private life as follows:

> For numerous Anglo-Saxon and French authors the right to respect for 'private life' is the right to privacy, the right to live as far as one wishes, protected from publicity.... In the

[1] C. Velu, 'The European Convention on Human Rights and the Right to Respect for Private Life, the Home and Communications' in A. H. Robertson, *Privacy and Human Rights* (MUP, Manchester 1973), 12.

[2] N. Moreham, 'The right to respect for private life in the European Convention on Human Rights: a re-examination' [2008] EHRLR 44, 45. See also J. Marshall, *Personal Freedom through Human Rights Law? Autonomy, Identity and Integrity under the European Convention on Human Rights* (Martinus Nijhoff, Leiden 2009).

> opinion of the Commission however, the right to respect for private life does not end there. It comprises also, to a certain degree, the right to establish and develop relationships with other human beings especially in the emotional field, for the development and fulfilment of one's own personality.[3]

Cohen-Jonathan observes:

> One can consider anything having to do with personal health, philosophical, religious or moral beliefs, family and emotional life, friendships and, subject to reservations, professional and material life as part of private life.[4]

The Strasbourg Court had occasion to comment on the meaning of 'private life' in the *Niemietz* case,[5] which concerned the question of whether a search of law offices violated Article 8. The Court observed:

> The Court does not consider it possible or necessary to attempt an exhaustive definition of the notion of 'private life.' However, it would be too restrictive to limit the notion to an 'inner circle' in which the individual may live his own personal life as he chooses and to exclude therefrom entirely the outside world not encompassed within that circle. Respect for private life must also comprise to a certain degree the right to establish and develop relationships with other human beings. There appears, furthermore, to be no reason of principle why this understanding of the notion of 'private life' should be taken to exclude activities of a professional or business nature since it is, after all, in the course of their working lives that the majority of people have a significant, if not the greatest, opportunity of developing relationships with the outside world.... Thus, especially in the case of a person exercising a liberal profession, his work in that context may form part and parcel of his life to such a degree that it becomes impossible to know in what capacity he is acting at a given moment of time.[6]

In the *Peck* case, the Strasbourg Court recapitulated its approach to the scope of private life:

> Private life is a broad term not susceptible to exhaustive definition. The Court has already held that elements such as gender identification, name, sexual orientation and sexual life are important elements of the personal sphere protected by Article 8. That Article also protects a right to identity and personal development, and the right to establish and develop relationships with other human beings and the outside world and it may include activities of a professional or business nature. There is, therefore, a zone of interaction of a person with others, even in a public context, which may fall within the scope of 'private life'....[7]

In concluding that mental health must also be regarded as a crucial part of private life associated with the aspect of moral identity, the Strasbourg Court again stated that private life is a broad term 'not susceptible to exhaustive definition' but will protect such important elements of the personal sphere as 'gender identification, name and sexual orientation and sexual life'.[8]

[3] App. 6825/74, *X v Iceland*, Decision of 18 May 1976, (1976) 5 DR 86. See also L. Doswald-Beck, 'The Meaning of the "Right to respect for Private Life" under the European Convention on Human Rights' (1983) 4 HRLJ 283, and L. Loucaides, 'Personality and Privacy under the European Convention on Human Rights' (1990) 61 BYIL 175.

[4] G. Cohen-Jonathan, 'Respect for private and family life' in Macdonald, Matscher, and Petzold, *The European System for the Protection of Human Rights* (Martinus Nijhoff, Dordrecht 1993), 405, 407. See also H. Tomás Gómez-Arostegui, 'Defining Private Life under the European Convention on Human Rights by Referring to Reasonable Expectations' (2005) 35 *California Western International Law Journal* 153.

[5] *Niemietz v Germany*, (App. 13710/88), 16 December 1992, Series A No 251-B, (1993) 16 EHRR 97.

[6] § 29. See also *Bigaeva v Greece*, (App. 26713/05), 28 May 2009, § 23.

[7] *Peck v United Kingdom*, (App. 44647/98), 28 January 2003, (2003) 36 EHRR 719; ECHR 2003-I, § 57.

[8] *Bensaid v United Kingdom*, (App. 44599/98), 6 February 2001, (2001) 33 EHRR 205; ECHR 2001-I, § 47.

The Strasbourg Court uses the term 'physical and moral integrity of the person' as within the concept of private life.[9] The Court has stated on a number of occasions that private life includes a right to identity and personal development, and to establish personal relationships. In the *Odièvre* case, the Grand Chamber said:

> Matters of relevance to personal development include details of a person's identity as a human being and the vital interest protected by the Convention in obtaining information necessary to discover the truth concerning important aspects of one's personal identity, such as the identity of one's parents, birth, and in particular the circumstances in which a child is born, forms part of a child's, and subsequently the adult's, private life guaranteed by Article 8 of the Convention.[10]

A criminal conviction in itself will not constitute an interference with private life. In *Gillberg v Sweden*,[11] the applicant was a university professor who was convicted of misuse of office for refusing to comply with a court order requiring him to grant access to research materials. The Grand Chamber rejected his complaint that this conviction amounted to an interference with his private life, holding that Article 8 cannot be relied on in order to complain of a loss of reputation which is the foreseeable consequence of one's own actions, such as the commission of a criminal offence. While the Court accepted that the protection of an individual's moral and psychological integrity is an important aspect of Article 8, the applicant's conviction was held to be a foreseeable application of the relevant offence and furthermore that offence had no obvious bearing on the right to respect for 'private life' given that it concerned professional acts and omissions by public officials in the exercise of their duties.[12]

Although the increasingly broad concept of private life has in many cases been taken to include issues relating to the home and correspondence, the right to respect for home and correspondence remain specified features in the text of Article 8. Consideration of the definitions of these terms in the case-law of the Strasbourg Court continues to be warranted.

HOME

Applications relating specifically to this aspect of Article 8 have not been numerous; many issues have involved a combination of private life and home. Also, many issues which might otherwise have fallen within its provisions have been considered under Article 1 of Protocol 1.[13] In the *Greek* case,[14] Article 8 was violated by the suspension of the right to respect for the home in the Greek Constitution, and by 'the consequent disregard of this right, in particular by the practice of the Greek authorities of carrying out arrests at night.'[15]

[9] *Stubbings and others v United Kingdom*, (Apps. 22083/93 and 22095/93), 22 October 1996, (1997) 23 EHRR 213, ECHR 1996-IV, § 59.

[10] *Odièvre v France*, (App. 42326/98), 13 February 2003 [GC], (2004) 38 EHRR 871; ECHR 2003-III, § 29.

[11] *Gillberg v Sweden*, (App. 41723/06), 3 April 2012 [GC].

[12] A different approach is taken in cases where the criminal conviction impacts directly upon a core element of private life, such as sexuality and family relationships: *Laskey, Jaggard and Brown v United Kingdom*, (Apps. 21627/93, 21826/93, and 21974/93), 19 February 1997, (1997) 24 EHRR 39, ECHR 1997-I (sado-masochism); *Stübing v Germany*, (App. 43547/08), 12 April 2012 (incest).

[13] See ch.20.

[14] (App. 3321/67), *Denmark v Greece*, (App. 3322/67), *Norway v Greece*, (App. 3323/67), *Sweden v Greece*, (App. 3344/67), *Netherlands v Greece*, ('the *Greek* case'), Report of 18 November 1969, (1969) 12 *Yearbook* 1.

[15] (1969) 12 *Yearbook* 152–3.

Article 8 requires Contracting Parties to guarantee respect for the home.[16] This does not appear to include a right to a home,[17] nor to a particular home.[18] But it does cover a requirement that Contracting Parties protect the physical security of a person's actual home and belongings there.[19] So deliberate destruction of homes by the security forces is a particularly grave and unjustified interference with the rights in Article 8.[20] In *Cyprus v Turkey*,[21] the refusal of the authorities in the occupied part of northern Cyprus to allow displaced Greek Cypriots to return to their homes there constituted a continuing violation by Turkey of Article 8.[22] The 'multitude of adverse circumstances' which attended the daily lives of Greek Cypriots living in the Karpas region[23] of northern Cyprus violated their right to respect for their private and family life and home under Article 8.[24]

A broad view is taken of what is a person's home. It can include the business premises of a professional person,[25] or a caravan site used as a home in breach of planning permission.[26]

CORRESPONDENCE

Correspondence covers written materials including materials sent through the post, as well as telephonic communications and email.[27] What appears to characterize 'correspondence' as distinct from materials constituting 'expression' within Article 10 is direct communication to another. Applications concerning interference with correspondence have mainly been brought by those in prison,[28] and in relation to various surveillance techniques, most notably telephone tapping,[29] but in the latter case the right to respect for correspondence is almost always taken together with private life. Interference with correspondence has also arisen in the context of bankruptcy proceedings.[30] The application of a rule in Italian bankruptcy law that all correspondence had to be handed over to the trustee in bankruptcy, which lasted for a period of over fourteen years, was found in the circumstances of this case to constitute an interference with the applicant's correspondence which violated Article 8.

[16] For the substantive nature of the guarantee, see later in this chapter.

[17] See Commission's decision in App. 159/56, *X v Germany*, (1955–7) 1 *Yearbook* 202, concerning a claim that the Article required a State to provide a home for a refugee.

[18] See Commission's decision in App. 31600/96, *Burton v United Kingdom*, 15 September 1996, (1996) 22 EHRR CD135 concerning a claim by a gypsy to be permitted to live her last days in a caravan according to gypsy tradition.

[19] *Novoseletskiy v Ukraine*, (App. 47148/99), 22 February 2005, (2006) 43 EHGRR 1139, ECHR 2005-II.

[20] *Selçuk and Asker v Turkey*, (Apps. 23184/94 and 23185/94), 24 April 1998, (1998) 26 EHRR 477, ECHR 1998-II, § 86.

[21] *Cyprus v Turkey*, (App. 25781/94), 10 May 2001 [GC], (2002) 35 EHRR 731; ECHR 2001-IV. See also *Xenides-Arestis v Turkey*, (App. 46347/99), 22 December 2005.

[22] § 175.

[23] This perhaps should, more appropriately, have been referred to by the Strasbourg Court as the 'Karpasi region' of Cyprus, since this is the way in which the region is described by Greek Cypriots.

[24] *Cyprus v Turkey*, (App. 25781/94), 10 May 2001 [GC], (2002) 35 EHRR 731; ECHR 2001-IV, § 296.

[25] *Niemietz v Germany*, (App. 13710/88), 16 December 1992, Series A No 251-B, (1993) 16 EHRR 97, §§ 30–1.

[26] *Buckley v United Kingdom*, (App. 20348/92), 25 September 1996, (1997) 23 EHRR 101, ECHR 1996-IV, § 54. See also *Gillow v United Kingdom*, 24 November 1986, Series A No 109. (1989) 11 EHRR 335, § 46.

[27] *Copland v United Kingdom*, (App. 62617/00), 3 April 2007, (2007) 45 EHRR 858, ECHR 2007-IV.

[28] See later in this chapter.

[29] See later in this chapter.

[30] *Luordo v Italy*, (App. 32190/96), 17 July 2003, (2005) 41 EHRR 547; ECHR 2003-IX. See also *Campagnano v Italy*, (App. 77955/01), 23 March 2006, ECHR 2006-IV.

POSITIVE OBLIGATIONS AND PRIVATE LIFE

The Strasbourg Court has frequently referred to positive obligations in the context of respect for private life within Article 8. However, where positive obligations are in issue, there is a considerable margin of appreciation for a Contracting Party as to how it regulates a particular area.[31] In the *Hatton* case in 2003, the Grand Chamber indicated that the approach to positive obligations was essentially the same as where there were interferences:

> Article 8 may apply in environmental cases whether the pollution is directly caused by the State or whether State responsibility arises from the failure properly to regulate private industry. Whether the case is analysed in terms of a positive duty on the State to take reasonable and appropriate measures to secure the applicants' rights under paragraph 1 of Article 8 or in terms of an interference by a public authority to be justified in accordance with paragraph 2, the applicable principles are broadly similar. In both contexts regard must be had to the fair balance that has to be struck between the competing interests of the individual and of the community as a whole; and in both contexts the State enjoys a certain margin of appreciation in determining the steps to be taken to ensure compliance with the Convention. Furthermore, even in relation to the positive obligations flowing from the first paragraph of Article 8, in striking the required balance the aims mentioned in the second paragraph may be of a certain relevance.[32]

It follows that the dividing line between negative and positive obligations under Article 8 is a fine one. The current position of the Strasbourg Court is summarized by the Grand Chamber as follows:

> 70. The Court recalls that, although the object of Article 8 is essentially that of protecting the individual against arbitrary interference by the public authorities, it does not merely compel the State to abstain from such interference. In addition to this primarily negative undertaking, there may be positive obligations inherent in an effective respect for private and family life. These obligations may involve the adoption of measures designed to secure respect for private and family life even in the sphere of the relations of individuals between themselves. The boundaries between the State's positive and negative obligations under Article 8 do not lend themselves to precise definition. The applicable principles are nonetheless similar. In particular, in both instances regard must be had to the fair balance to be struck between the competing interests...[33]

The Strasbourg Court went on to indicate that, in some cases, the analysis of a situation as involving positive or negative obligations would be very similar, since the essential question is whether a fair balance has been struck.[34] The similarity of the approach to positive and negative obligations has arisen because the Strasbourg Court has indicated that, in determining the balance to be struck between the interests of the community and the interests of the individual, the aims referred to in Article 8(2) 'may be of a certain relevance.'[35]

[31] See *Rees v United Kingdom*, (App. 9532/81), Series A No 106, (1987) 9 EHRR 56, §§ 37 and 44, and the discussion of this issue in ch.16.

[32] *Hatton and others v United Kingdom*, (App. 36022/97), 8 July 2003 [GC], (2003) 37 EHRR 611, ECHR 2003-VIII, § 98. See also *Dickson v United Kingdom*, (App. 44362/04), 4 December 2007 [GC], (2008) 46 EHRR 927, ECHR 2007-XIII.

[33] *Dickson v United Kingdom*, (App. 44362/04), 4 December 2007 [GC], (2008) 46 EHRR 927, ECHR 2007-XIII, § 70. See also *Codarcea v Romania*, (App. 31675/04), 2 June 2009.

[34] § 71.

[35] *Babylonová v Slovakia*, (App. 69146/01), 20 June 2006, (2008) 46 EHRR 183, ECHR 2006-VIII.

In *A, B and C v Ireland*,[36] the Court further clarified the factors that are relevant for the assessment of the content of the positive obligations under Article 8:

> Some factors concern the applicant: the importance of the interest at stake and whether 'fundamental values' or 'essential aspects' of private life are in issue... and the impact on an applicant of a discordance between the social reality and the law, the coherence of the administrative and legal practices within the domestic system being regarded as an important factor in the assessment carried out under Article 8... Some factors concern the position of the State: whether the alleged obligation is narrow and defined or broad and indeterminate...and the extent of any burden the obligation would impose on the State...[37]

Because of the way in which the Strasbourg Court has brought together the questions to be considered in relation to positive and negative obligations, cases involving positive obligations are not treated separately, but are considered within the headings which follow.

FREEDOM FROM INTERFERENCE WITH PHYSICAL AND PSYCHOLOGICAL INTEGRITY

INTERFERENCE WITH THE PERSON

In the *YF* case, which concerned, in part, a gynaecological examination against the will of the woman concerned, the Strasbourg Court said:

> The Court observes that Article 8 is clearly applicable to these complaints, which concern a matter of 'private life', a concept which covers the physical and psychological integrity of a person.... It reiterates in this connection that a person's body concerns the most intimate aspect of private life. Thus, a compulsory medical intervention, even if it is of minor importance, constitutes an interference with this right....[38]

Inappropriate strip searching of persons visiting someone in prison will also constitute a violation of Article 8, even though the treatment falls short of that within the scope of Article 3.[39]

In *Gillan and Quinton v The United Kingdom*[40] the Court considered the use of stop and search powers by the police. The relevant domestic law was Sections 44-47 of the Terrorism Act 2000 which permitted a uniformed police officer to stop any person within a specific geographical area and physically search the person and anything carried by him or her. The police officer was permitted to request the removal of headgear, footwear, outer clothing, and gloves. The search would take place in public and failure to submit to it amounted to a criminal offence. The Court considered that the use of these coercive powers to require an individual to submit to a detailed search of his person, his clothing and his personal belongings amounted to a clear interference with the right to respect for private life. It dismissed any suggestion that because the search was undertaken in a public place it rendered Article 8 inapplicable, holding instead that 'the public nature of the search may, in certain cases, compound the seriousness of the interference because of an element of humiliation and embarrassment.'[41] The Court distinguished this power to stop

[36] *A, B and C v Ireland*, (App. 25579/05), 16 December 2010 [GC], ECHR 2010. [37] § 248.

[38] *YF v Turkey*, (App. 24209/94), 22 July 2003, (2004) 39 EHRR 715; ECHR 2003-IX, § 33.

[39] *Wainwright v United Kingdom*, (App. 12350/04), 26 September 2006, (2007) 44 EHRR 809; ECHR 2006-X, §§ 41–9.

[40] *Gillan and Quinton v The United Kingdom*, (App. 4158/05), 12 January 2010, ECHR 2010 (extracts).

[41] § 63.

and search from the searches undertaken at airport security on the basis that a passenger can avoid these by leaving the airport while the applicants in this case had no such option to avoid the search.

In relation to whether this interference was in accordance with the law, the applicants argued that the provisions conferred an unduly wide discretion on the police, both in terms of the authorization of the power to stop and search and its application in practice. Under the Terrorism Act 2000, a senior police officer was empowered to authorize any constable in uniform to stop and search a pedestrian in any area specified by him within his jurisdiction if he 'considers it expedient for the prevention of acts of terrorism'. The Court noted that 'expedient' means no more than 'advantageous' or 'helpful' and that there was no requirement at the authorzation stage that the stop and search power be considered 'necessary' and therefore no requirement of any assessment of the proportionality of the measure.[42] The Court was also concerned about the breadth of the discretion conferred on the individual police officer as 'Not only is it unnecessary for him to demonstrate the existence of any reasonable suspicion; he is not required even subjectively to suspect anything about the person stopped and searched.'[43] One consequence of this in the Court's view is that 'in the absence of any obligation on the part of the officer to show a reasonable suspicion, it is likely to be difficult if not impossible to prove that the power was improperly exercised.'[44] Therefore the Court concluded that both the powers of authorisation and confirmation as well as those of stop and search under the 2000 Act were not sufficiently circumscribed nor were they subject to adequate legal safeguards against abuse and were therefore not 'in accordance with the law'.

Where conduct, such as child sexual abuse, is in issue, there is a positive obligation on the State to provide protection from such grave interferences with private life. This will not, however, require unlimited civil actions where the conduct is adequately covered by criminal law sanctions. In a case against the Netherlands,[45] the Strasbourg Court considered an application made on behalf of a mentally disabled girl aged 16, who had been raped while in a privately run home for the those with special needs. The law of the Netherlands did not recognize a complaint unless made by the victim in person. If she lacked capacity, the criminal law could take no cognizance of the alleged offence. It appeared that there was no similar bar on the use of the civil law. The family argued that this violated respect for the private life of their daughter, and there was no dispute as to the applicability of the Article, since the concept of private life covers the physical and moral integrity of the person, including their sexual life.[46] The absence of protection by the criminal law in so serious a case was found to be a violation of Article 8. A similar issue arose in the *MC* case.[47] The applicant complained that the law in Bulgaria did not provide effective protection against rape and sexual abuse, since only cases where the victim had resisted actively were prosecuted. The Strasbourg Court considered that the Contracting Parties have positive obligations inherent in Articles 3 and 8 to enact legislation effectively punishing rape and to apply them in practice through effective investigation and prosecution.[48]

The extensive positive obligations imposed upon Contracting States to protect physical integrity have also been evident in more recent cases. For example, in *A. v Croatia*[49] the State's positive obligations under Article 8 to protect the applicant from domestic violence were in issue. The Court confirmed that under Article 8 States have 'a duty to protect the

[42] § 80. [43] § 83. [44] § 86.

[45] *X and Y v Netherlands*, (App. 8978/80), 26 March 1985, Series A No 91, (1986) 8 EHRR 235.

[46] § 22.

[47] *MC v Bulgaria*, (App. 39272/98), 4 December 2003, (2005) 40 EHRR 459, ECHR 2003-XII.

[48] §§ 148–53. [49] *A. v Croatia*, (App. 55164/08), 14 October 2010.

physical and moral integrity of an individual from other persons. To that end they are to maintain and apply in practice an adequate legal framework affording protection against acts of violence by private individuals.'[50] Furthermore, it was not sufficient that the national courts had imposed measures upon the perpetrator of the violence, such as periods of detention, and psychiatric or psycho-social treatment, because these measures had not been enforced. The Court noted that the aim of restraining and deterring the offender from causing further harm could not be achieved without the sanctions imposed being enforced. Therefore the State had failed to satisfy its positive obligation to ensure the applicant's right to respect for private life.

In *Georgel and Georgeta Stoicescu v Romania*[51] the applicant complained about the attack on her by a pack of stray dogs, submitting that this was due to the failure by the authorities to implement adequate measures against the numerous stray dogs in Bucharest. The Court recognized that the problem of stray dogs in Bucharest had become a public health and safety issue. It acknowledged that the State would enjoy a wide margin of appreciation on this issue, but significantly it also noted that the Convention is intended to safeguard rights that are 'practical and effective' and that this remains true in cases 'where a general problem for the society reaches a level of gravity such that it becomes a serious and concrete physical threat to the population.'[52] In such a case, it is incumbent on the public authorities to act in good time, in an appropriate and consistent manner. The Court concluded that the lack of sufficient measures taken by the Romanian authorities in addressing the issue of stray dogs, combined with their failure to provide appropriate redress to the applicant as a result of the injuries sustained, amounted to a breach of the State's positive obligations under Article 8.

The use of corporal punishment in schools has been examined by the Strasbourg Court in a number of complaints of violations of Article 3.[53] Comments in the *Costello-Roberts* case[54] suggest that certain aspects of schooling and school discipline might attract protection under Article 8 additional to that afforded by Article 3. The Court recognized that even the act of 'sending a child to school necessarily involved some degree of interference with his or her private life', though it is not clear that such interference would entail adverse effects for the person's physical or moral integrity. Indeed, in this case the Court concluded that the disciplinary regime at the independent preparatory boarding school, which included the possibility of being beaten on the bottom with a rubber-soled gym shoe, did not come within the scope of the prohibition in Article 8. But the Strasbourg Court did not exclude 'the possibility that there might be circumstances in which Article 8 could be regarded as affording in relation to disciplinary measures a protection which goes beyond that given by Article 3.'[55]

SEARCHES OF PROPERTY

A number of Article 8 cases concern respect for private life and the home in the context of the legitimacy of searches of either the home or business premises.

The *Chappell* case[56] challenged the use of Anton Piller orders under English law. Anton Piller orders represent a common law development of interlocutory measures in civil

[50] § 60. [51] *Georgel and Georgeta Stoicescu v Romania*, (App. 9718/03), 26 July 2011.

[52] § 59. [53] See ch.9.

[54] *Costello-Roberts v United Kingdom*, (App. 13134/87), 25 March 1993, Series A No 247-C, (1994) 19 EHRR 112.

[55] § 36. That view is supported by the approach of the Court in *Wainwright v United Kingdom*, (App. 12350/04), 26 September 2006, (2007) 44 EHRR 809; ECHR 2006-X, §§ 41–9.

[56] *Chappell v United Kingdom*, (App. 10461/83), 30 March 1989, Series A No 152, (1990) 12 EHRR 1.

proceedings, *inter alia*, enabling a search of premises to take place often with the object of seizing material produced in breach of a copyright or trademark. The Strasbourg Court concluded that the search of the applicant's home authorized by the order constituted an interference with respect for his home. The aim, namely, to protect the rights of others, was legitimate and the order met the requirements of Article 8 as being in accordance with law. The necessary safeguards existed to ensure that action was only taken where it was necessary in a democratic society. The undertaking given by solicitors for plaintiffs seeking such an order was sufficient to ensure the proper supervision of the implementation of any order granted by the court.

The *Niemietz* case[57] concerned a search of a lawyer's office under warrant from the court in order to establish the true identity of a person who had signed himself Klaus Wegner which was believed to be a pseudonym. The Strasbourg Court concluded that the interference was in accordance with law and pursued the legitimate aim of being for the prevention of crime and the protection of the rights of others, but went on to consider whether it was necessary in a democratic society. The Court found that the interference was out of all proportion to the aim pursued, in that it impinged on professional secrecy and that searches of lawyer's offices in Germany had not been surrounded by any special procedural safeguards.[58]

The *Funke* case[59] involved consideration of the legitimacy of search of the applicants' homes by customs officers in France in connection with alleged exchange control irregularities. The aim was legitimate in that it could be said to be for the economic well-being of the country and the prevention of crime. Once again the issue came down to determination of whether the interferences were necessary in a democratic society. There must always be adequate safeguards against abuse, but this was not so in the present case. The customs authorities had very wide powers, including exclusive competence to assess the expediency, number, length, and scale of searches. There was no requirement to obtain a judicial warrant. This resulted in a situation in which the restrictions and limitations provided for in the law were too lax and full of loopholes for the interferences to be strictly proportionate to the legitimate aim pursued. The situation in the case of Funke was made worse in that the customs authorities never lodged any complaint against him alleging an offence against the exchange control regulations.

A search which is authorized under national law where there are special procedural safeguards will violate Article 8 if it can be shown that the underlying purpose is to find out a journalist's sources through his lawyer, since this will have repercussions on rights under Article 10 of the Convention.[60] The Strasbourg Court will expect that search warrants are not drafted in terms which are too wide and do not give any indication of the reasons for the search. This is particularly so where the search is of premises of those who have not been accused of any offence.[61] Equally the Court will expect the national authorities to have shown reasonable care in ensuring that the target of a forcible entry to property remains at that property. In the *Keegan* case,[62] the applicants (in whom the police had no interest at all) had been living at the address for about six months prior to the forcible

[57] *Niemietz v Germany*, (App. 13710/88), 16 December 1992, Series A No 251-B, (1993) 16 EHRR 97.

[58] See also *Buck v Germany*, (App. 41604/98), 28 April 2005, (2006) 42 EHRR 440; ECHR 2005-IV, for an example of a 4:3 decision of a Chamber finding a violation of Art. 8 in the context of the search of business premises in order to ascertain the identity of the driver of car caught speeding in a radar trap.

[59] *Funke and others v France*, (App. 10828/84), 25 February 1993, Series A No 256-A, (1993) 16 EHRR 297.

[60] *Roemen and Schmit v Luxembourg*, (App. 51772/99), 25 February 2003, ECHR 2003-IV, §§ 64–71.

[61] See, for example, *Ernst and others v Belgium*, (App. 33400/96), 15 July 2003.

[62] *Keegan v United Kingdom*, (App. 28867/03), 18 July 2006, (2007) 44 EHRR 716; ECHR 2006-X.

and dramatic search which took place of their home. Once their error was discovered, the police were duly apologetic and repairs were carried out to the applicants' home. There was nevertheless a breach of Article 8; basic steps to check the connection between the address and the offence as at the time of the search had not been effectively carried out, and the entry and search had caused significant fear and alarm to innocent people.

Entries and searches, including recording and retaining personal details and photographing individuals which are properly applied under anti-terrorist legislation are unlikely to give rise to successful complaints under Article 8, since they will normally be easily justified as measures for the prevention of crime.[63]

SURVEILLANCE AND INTERCEPTION OF COMMUNICATIONS

A group of cases has concerned the extent to which Article 8 protects the citizen from various forms of surveillance, which might include the opening of correspondence or listening to telephone communications. The whole area of covert surveillance is one where advances in technology present increasing threats to the private life of the individual. The Strasbourg Court is not unaware of the need for vigilance in the light of an increasingly sophisticated technology.[64] The Court has decided that it is not only the party whose telephone line is tapped who has standing to complain, but also third parties whose conversations are intercepted.[65] Although the existence of intelligence services with powers of secret surveillance is tolerated under Convention principles, the practices of such services must be shown to be necessary for safeguarding democratic institutions, and any interference must be supported by relevant and sufficient reasons and be proportionate to the aims pursued.[66]

The *Klass* case[67] raised the question of the compatibility of German law with Article 8. The applicants objected that the German law on surveillance did not oblige the authorities to notify the persons subject to the surveillance after the event and did not provide any system of remedies for the ordering and execution of such measures. The Court agreed with the Commission that the applicants could claim to be victims of a violation of the Convention as required under former Article 25.[68] On the substantive complaint, the Strasbourg Court considered that telephone conversations came within the ambit of 'private life' and the concept of 'correspondence'. As in so many cases under Article 8, the Court concluded that surveillance could constitute an interference, that it was in accordance with law, and that it could serve a legitimate aim, but the key question was whether the interference was necessary in a democratic society. The answer to this question turned on the existence and adequacy of safeguards against possible abuse; this is a theme which constantly appears in such cases. The German conditions were considered to be appropriately restrictive and to be within the State's margin of appreciation. The test laid down by the Strasbourg Court was as follows:

[63] *Murray v United Kingdom*, (App. 14310/88), 28 October 1994, Series A No 300-A, (1995) 19 EHRR 193.

[64] *Kopp v Switzerland* (App. 23224/94), 25 March 1998, (1999) 27 EHRR 91, § 72. See also *PG and JH v United Kingdom*, (App. 44787/98), 25 September 2001, ECHR 2001-IX; and *Copland v United Kingdom*, (App. 62617/00), 3 April 2007, (2007) 45 EHRR 858, ECHR 2007-IV.

[65] *Lambert v France*, (App. 23618/94), 24 August 1998, (2000) 30 EHRR 346, ECHR 1998-V.

[66] *Segerstedt-Wiberg and others v Sweden*, (App. 62332/00), 6 June 2006, (2007) 44 EHRR 14, ECHR 2006-VII, § 88; see also *Rotaru v Romania*, (App. 28341/95), 4 May 2000 [GC], ECHR 2000-V.

[67] *Klass and others v Germany*, 6 September 1978, Series A No 28, (1979–80) 2 EHRR 214.

[68] See ch.2.

> The Court must be satisfied that, whatever system of surveillance is adopted, there exist adequate and effective guarantees against abuse. This assessment has only a relative character: it depends on all the circumstances of the case, such as the nature, scope and duration of the possible measures, the grounds required for ordering such measures, the authorities competent to permit, carry out and supervise such measures, and the kind of remedy provided by the national law.[69]

The Strasbourg Court expressed mild concern that supervisory control was not exercised by a judge, but noted that initial control under the German legislation was effected by an 'official qualified for judicial office and by the control provided by the Parliamentary Board and the G 10 Commission'.[70] The Court concluded that, taking judicial notice of technical advances in the means of espionage and surveillance, and of the development of terrorism in Europe, the German system for controlling covert surveillance met the requirements of Article 8 of the Convention.

In subsequent cases, the Court has tended to consider the adequacy of safeguards as a matter going to the 'lawfulness' of the measure in question rather than its proportionality. It would defeat the purpose of secret surveillance if individuals were able to pinpoint exactly when the police were likely to be listening in on their conversations and adapt their behaviour accordingly, and the Court has not interpreted Article 8 to require that this information should be provided to individuals, either before, during, or after they have been the subject of surveillance measures. On the other hand, however, secret powers of surveillance are open to abuse by the State authorities.[71] The Court has therefore held that, to comply with Article 8, national law should provide fairly detailed guidelines as to the circumstances when surveillance is allowed and any individual measure of surveillance must comply with national law. While national law need not be entirely clear in all its detail, it must not give the executive an unfettered or excessively broad discretion. The law must indicate the scope of any discretion conferred on the competent authorities and the manner of its exercise with sufficient clarity to give the individual adequate protection against arbitrary interference. In relation to secret measures of surveillance, the Court has developed the following minimum safeguards that should be set out in statute law in order to avoid abuses of power: the nature of the offences which may give rise to an interception order; a definition of the categories of people liable to have their telephones tapped; a limit on the duration of telephone tapping; the procedure to be followed for examining, using, and storing the data obtained; the precautions to be taken when communicating the data to other parties; and the circumstances in which recordings may or must be erased or the tapes destroyed.[72]

The French system for authorizing telephone-tapping was examined in the *Huvig* and *Kruslin* cases.[73] Since the French Courts had consistently viewed various provisions of the

[69] *Klass and others v Germany*, (App. 5029/71), 6 September 1978, Series A No 28, (1979–80) 2 EHRR 214, § 50.

[70] § 56. A revised version of the German G10 law was considered in *Weber and Saravia v Germany*, (App. 54934/00), Decision of 29 June 2006, and found to contain sufficient safeguards.

[71] *Rotaru v Romania*, (App. 28341/95), 4 May 2000 [GC], ECHR 2000-V.

[72] *Rotaru v Romania*, (App. 28341/95), 4 May 2000 [GC], ECHR 2000-V; *Weber and Saravia v Germany*, (App. 54934/00), Decision of 29 June 2006; and *Liberty and others v United Kingdom*, (App. 58243/00), 1 July 2008, (2009) 48 EHRR 1.

[73] *Huvig v France*, (App. 11105/84), 24 April 1990, Series A No 176-B, (1990) 12 EHRR 528; *Kruslin v France*, (App. 11801/850), 24 April 1990, Series A No 176-B, (1990) 12 EHRR 547; *Valenzuela Contreras v Spain*, (App. 27671/95), 30 July 1998, (1999) 28 EHRR 483; ECHR 1998-V; *Liberty and others v United Kingdom*, (App. 58243/00), 1 July 2008, (2009) 48 EHRR 1; and *Bykov v Russia*, (App. 4378/02), 10 March 2009 [GC], ECHR 2009.

Code of Criminal Procedure as authorizing the carrying out of telephone-tapping by a senior police officer on a warrant issued by an investigating judge, the Strasbourg Court regarded the practice as being in accordance with law. But the Court went on to say that to be fully in accordance with the law, the quality of the law must be such as to provide safeguards against what is a serious interference with private life. The French system was very short on processes to prevent abuse, with key aspects of the process not adequately defined, such as the categories of person liable to have their telephones tapped or the nature of the offences which warranted such measures. There was consequently a violation of Article 8.[74]

Obviously a telephone tap without obtaining legal authority where such a procedure is provided for will amount to a violation of Article 8, as in one case, where a senior police officer colluded in obtaining a recording of a telephone conversation in a manner inconsistent with the requirements of French law.[75]

The *Malone* case[76] concerned the law of England and Wales on the interception of communications on behalf of the police for the purposes of the prevention and detection of crime. Interception involved both postal and telephonic communication. The practice of 'metering' also came under scrutiny. Metering involves the use of a meter check printer which registers the number dialled on a particular telephone and the time and duration of each call. It does not record speech. James Malone was an antiques dealer, who was charged and convicted of handling stolen goods. The investigation had involved the interception of Malone's telephone calls. He also complained that his telephone line had been metered. At the time there was no overall statutory code governing the interception of postal and telephone communications. Metering was essentially a system by which the Post Office checked that customers were correctly charged, though it was admitted in the proceedings that the Post Office did on occasion cooperate with the police in metering a telephone line if 'the information is essential to police enquiries in relation to serious crime and cannot be obtained from other sources.' [77] The absence of a proper statutory code governing interception of communications proved fatal to the respondent State's defence of the case. The Court said:

> [I]t cannot be said with any reasonable certainty what elements of the powers to intercept are incorporated in legal rules and what elements remain within the discretion of the executive. In view of the attendant obscurity and uncertainty as to the state of the law in this essential respect,...the law of England and Wales does not indicate with reasonable clarity the scope and manner of exercise of the relevant discretion conferred on the public authorities. To that extent, the minimum degree of legal protection to which citizens are entitled under the rule of law in a democratic society is lacking.[78]

The interferences with James Malone's communications were therefore in breach of Article 8 in that they were not 'in accordance with the law'. The Strasbourg Court came to a similar conclusion in relation to the practice of metering.

The UK responded to the *Malone* judgment with the passage of the Interception of Communications Act but this legislation failed to regulate the interception of communications on private networks. The *Halford* case[79] concerned the interception of telephone calls

[74] See also *Herczegfalvy v Austria*, (App. 10533/83), 24 September 1992, Series A No 242-B, (1993) 15 EHRR 437, § 91.

[75] *A v France*, (App. 14838/89), 23 November 1993, Series A No 277-B, (1994) 17 EHRR 462. See also *MM v The Netherlands*, (App. 39339/98), 8 April 2003, (2004) 39 EHRR 414.

[76] *Malone v United Kingdom*, (App. 8691/79), 2 August 1984, Series A No 82, (1985) 7 EHRR 14.

[77] *Malone*, § 56. [78] § 79.

[79] *Halford v United Kingdom*, (App. 20605/92), 25 June 1997, (1997) 24 EHRR 523, ECHR 1997-III.

made by Alison Halford, Assistant Chief Constable of the Merseyside Police, both in her office and at home. The Strasbourg Court rejected an argument by the British Government that Article 8 did not apply because the applicant could have no reasonable expectation of privacy in relation to calls made from her office, recalling its earlier case-law as set out earlier. The Court concluded that telephone conversations came within the scope of 'private life' and 'correspondence' in Article 8. The interception of office telephone calls was not in accordance with law since there was no regulation of interception of calls outside the public network; and there was a violation in relation to telephone calls from her office. However, the Court was not satisfied that the applicant had proved on the balance of probabilities that there was interception of calls made from her home. Accordingly there was no violation in this regard. The Court noted that the applicant was complaining of measures of surveillance actually applied to her, and not, as in *Klass*, that the very possibility of telephone interceptions violated her Article 8 rights.

The Interception of Communications Act also allowed the executive to intercept communications passing between the United Kingdom and any individual or transmitter located outside the United Kingdom. This was subsequently the subject of the *Liberty* case.[80] The law was drafted in very broad terms: there was no limitation on the type of communications which could be intercepted.[81] Once captured, the applicants claimed that the data were filtered using an electronic search engine. Search terms were devised by officials. The only legal requirement was that material could only be searched for, listened to, or read, if it fell within very broad categories, such as material helpful for the detection of crime or the prevention of terrorism. The law required the Government Minister to 'make such arrangements as he consider[ed] necessary' to ensure that material which did not fall within one of these broad categories was not examined and that any data which were examined were disclosed and reproduced only to the extent necessary, but these 'arrangements' were not made public. Although the respondent State maintained that there was a Code of Practice, it was secret, and there were no statutory limitations on the type of information collected or the way in which it could be used, shared, or stored. There was therefore a violation of Article 8.

Other cases highlighted other issues with the UK system. The storing of information concerning a person's private life in a secret police register interferes with the right to respect for private life guaranteed by Article 8.[82] The potentially pervasive extent of telephone surveillance and data collection by the State is illustrated by the facts and judgment in the *Copland* case,[83] which concerned the monitoring of telephone, email, and internet usage of an employee of a further education college in order to determine whether she was making excessive use of the facilities for personal purposes. The respondent State argued that the college's powers to do 'anything necessary or expedient' for the purposes of providing further education included the monitoring activities. The Strasbourg Court did not find this at all persuasive: all the more so since subsequent legislation did make provision for monitoring of employee communications by employers. The monitoring was not in accordance with law and there was a violation of Article 8. The *Kahn* case[84] concerned another lacuna at the time in the national law of the UK. The applicant was convicted of a serious drugs offence after the police had used secret listening devices to obtain evidence

[80] *Liberty and others v United Kingdom*, (App. 58243/00), 1 July 2008, (2009) 48 EHRR 1.

[81] For example, all communications passing through cables under the sea between the UK and mainland Europe.

[82] *Hewitt and Harman v United Kingdom*, (App. 12175/86), 9 May 1989, (1992) 14 EHRR 657.

[83] *Copland v United Kingdom*, (App. 62617/00), 3 April 2007, (2007) 45 EHRR 858, ECHR 2007-IV.

[84] *Khan v United Kingdom*, (App. 39394/97), 12 May 2000, (2001) 31 EHRR 1016, ECHR 2000-V.

against him. At the time the only regulatory measures were non-binding Home Office guidelines which were not directly accessible to members of the public.

Finally, in *Kennedy v United Kingdom*[85] the domestic law was found to be compatible with Article 8. The applicant complained that his communications were being unlawfully intercepted in order to intimidate him and undermine his business activities, in violation of Article 8, and more generally challenged the regime established under Regulation of Investigatory Powers Act 2000 (RIPA) for authorizing interception of internal communications. RIPA provided that interception can only take place where the Secretary of State believes that it is necessary in the interests of national security, for the purposes of preventing or detecting serious crime or for the purposes of safeguarding the economic well-being of the UK. The Court found that the applicant had failed to demonstrate a reasonable likelihood that there was actual interception in his case but, following its approach in *Klass* and *Malone*, it was prepared to consider the complaint concerning the very existence of measures permitting secret surveillance. However, it concluded that the domestic legal provisions 'indicate with sufficient clarity the procedures for the authorisation and processing of interception warrants as well as the processing, communicating and destruction of intercept material collected. The Court further observes that there is no evidence of any significant shortcomings in the application and operation of the surveillance regime.'[86] It therefore found no violation of Article 8 in respect of RIPA.

Collection and storage of data by means of a GPS device may also amount to an interference with private life. In *Uzun v Germany*[87] the applicant alleged that the surveillance measures he had been subjected to, in particular his observation via GPS, and the use of the data obtained thereby in criminal proceedings against him, had violated his right to respect for his private life. The Court confirmed that the systematic collection and storing of data by security services on particular individuals constituted an interference with private lives. It noted that GPS surveillance is different in nature from other methods of visual or acoustical surveillance which disclose more information on a person's conduct, opinions, or feelings and thus are more susceptible to interfering with private life. However, as the investigation authorities had systematically collected and stored data on the applicant for three months by attaching a GPS device to his car, and then used it to draw up a pattern of the applicant's movements in order to make further investigations and to collect additional evidence at the places the applicant had travelled to, which was later used at the criminal trial against the applicant, the Court found that there had been an interference with the applicant's private life. The interference was justified in this case, however, as the Court was satisfied that it was proportionate to the aim pursued.

RECORDING AND DISSEMINATING IMAGES

In the *Von Hannover* case,[88] the Strasbourg Court recapitulated its views on the use of photographs:

> 50. The Court reiterates that the concept of private life extends to aspects relating to personal identity, such as a person's name..., or a person's picture.... Furthermore, private life, in the Court's view, includes a person's physical and psychological integrity; the guarantee afforded by Article 8 of the Convention is primarily intended to ensure the

[85] *Kennedy v United Kingdom*, (App. 26839/05), 18 May 2010. [86] § 169.

[87] *Uzun v Germany*, (App. 35623/05), 2 September 2010, ECHR 2010 (extracts).

[88] *Von Hannover v Germany*, (App. 59320/00), 24 June 2004, (2005) 40 EHRR 1, ECHR 2004-VI. See also *Reklos and Davourlis v Greece*, (App. 1234/05), 15 January 2009.

development, without outside interference, of the personality of each individual in his relations with other human beings.... There is therefore a zone of interaction of a person with others, even in a public context, which may fall within the scope of 'private life'....

52. As regards photos, with a view to defining the scope of the protection afforded by Article 8 against arbitrary interference by public authorities, the European Commission of Human Rights had regard to whether the photographs related to private or public matters and whether the material thus obtained was envisaged for a limited use or was likely to be made available to the general public....[89]

The applicant in this case was Princess Caroline of Monaco who complained that failed attempts in judicial proceedings in Germany to control the publication there of photographs of herself constituted a violation of her right to respect for her private life. The Strasbourg Court grappled with the tension between the right to privacy and freedom of expression in Article 10 of the Convention, but noted that both Articles permit limitations for the protection of the rights and reputation of others, which they considered took on particular importance in this context. The touchstone was whether publication was justified by considerations of public concern:

The Court considers that a fundamental distinction needs to be made between reporting facts—even controversial ones—capable of contributing to a debate in a democratic society relating to politicians in the exercise of their functions, for example, and reporting details of the private life of an individual who, moreover, as in this case, does not exercise official functions. While in the former case the press exercises its vital role of 'watchdog' in a democracy by contributing to 'impart[ing] information and ideas on matters of public interest', it does not do so in the latter case.[90]

This test is certainly not, in the view of the Strasbourg Court, satisfied where the sole purpose of publication of the photographs is to satisfy the curiosity of readers about the private life of a particular person. This does not contribute to any debate of general interest to society. The conditions under which the applicant could secure protection of her right to privacy in the German courts did not strike a fair balance between the competing interests in this case. There was a violation of Article 8.

The German courts took note of the Court's approach in this case. In *Von Hannover v Germany (No. 2)*[91] the applicants complained of the refusal by the German courts to grant an injunction against any further publication of a photo that had appeared in 2002 in two German magazines. The Grand Chamber was satisfied that the German courts had taken account of the approach required in Strasbourg cases such as the first *Von Hannover* case and that they had carefully balanced the right of the publishing companies to freedom of expression against the right of the applicants to respect for their private life. In line with this case-law, the German Courts had attached fundamental importance to the question whether the photos had contributed to a debate of general interest and to the circumstances in which the photos had been taken. The Court found no violation here.

The *Sciacca* case[92] develops this approach in relation to the ordinary person, as distinct from someone in the public eye. This aspect 'enlarges the zone of interaction which may fall within the scope of private life...'[93] It did not matter that the applicant was at the time the subject of criminal proceedings. Photographs of the applicant, which had apparently

[89] §§ 50 and 52. [90] *Von Hannover*, § 63.

[91] *Von Hannover v Germany (No. 2)*, (App. 40660/08 and 60641/08), 7 February 2012 [GC] ECHR 2012.

[92] *Sciacca v Italy*, (App. 50774/99), 11 January 2005, (2006) 43 EHRR 400, ECHR 2005-I.

[93] § 29.

been provided by a State agency, were reproduced in newspapers. The Strasbourg Court found a violation because the use of the photographs for this purpose was not in accordance with law; the supply of the photographs in the case before the Strasbourg Court was not within such provisions as existed in Italy. In the *Khuzhin* case,[94] the use on a television programme of photographs of three brothers charged with serious offences was held to have no information value in itself, and, in such cases, there had to be compelling reasons for interfering with the applicants' right to respect for their private life. No such justification could be found; the brothers were in custody and not fugitives, and the use of the photograph added nothing to the forthcoming trial. There was a violation of Article 8.

Disseminating the photograph of a person the police wished to interview as a witness but describing him as a 'wanted person' will violate Article 8.[95]

Mosley v The United Kingdom[96] required the Court to consider whether Article 8 requires State law to provide for an opportunity to seek an injunction prior to publication of material violating the right to respect for private life. The applicant complained that the UK had violated its positive obligations under Article 8 by failing to impose a legal duty on the News of the World newspaper to notify him in advance of publication of material which violated his right to respect for private life in order to allow him the opportunity to seek an interim injunction and thus prevent publication. In considering this, the Court recognized the dangers of the general nature of the duty called for, especially its implications for freedom of expression which would not be limited to the sensationalist reporting at issue in this case but extend to political reporting and serious investigative journalism.[97] For this reason, the Court granted the UK a wide margin and concluded that there had been no violation of Article 8.

In terms of a pre-notification requirement, the Court noted that there would have to be a public interest exception to such a requirement and that even in the applicant's own case (which concerned sexual activities which the newspaper claimed indicated Nazi overtones) the public interest exception would apply, or at least a reasonable belief that it applied would suffice. Furthermore, the Court noted that a pre-notification requirement would only be as strong as the sanctions imposed for failing to observe it. A regulatory or civil fine would be unlikely to deter newspapers from publishing private material without pre-notification, while criminal sanctions or punitive fines would, in the Court's view, 'create a chilling effect which would be felt in the spheres of political reporting and investigative journalism, both of which attract a high level of protection under the Convention.'[98] The Court concluded that Article 8 does not require a legally binding pre-notification requirement.

The Strasbourg Court has begun to comment on the impact of closed-circuit television (CCTV) in public places. In the *Peck* case,[99] the Court noted that the monitoring of the actions of an individual in a public place by the use of photographic equipment does not give rise to an interference with a person's private life.[100] However, most CCTV cameras are linked to video recording facilities. The Court acknowledged that such recordings, and the systematic or permanent nature of the record, may give rise to interferences with private life. But in this case, the applicant was not complaining about the CCTV recording itself, but about its release to the local press as an example of the success of CCTV monitoring. The applicant had at the time been severely depressed, and was identifiable on the

94 *Khuzhin and others v Russia*, (App. 13470/02), 23 October 2008.

95 *Nikolaishvili v Georgia*, (App. 37048/04), 13 January 2009.

96 *Mosley v The United Kingdom*, (App. 48009/08), 10 May 2011. 97 § 121. 98 § 129.

99 *Peck v United Kingdom*, (App. 44647/98), 28 January 2003, (2003) 36 EHRR 41; ECHR 2003-I.

100 § 59.

CCTV recording carrying a kitchen knife with which he subsequently attempted to slit his wrists. He accepted that being seen on the CCTV system, which led to police intervention, may have saved his life.

There was a violation of Article 8 in this case, since there had been no attempt to obtain Peck's consent to the showing of the recording, and the local authority did not appear to have considered disguising the applicant's identity. The violation was not mitigated in any way by the subsequent media appearances of Peck as a means of raising his concerns about the use of the video recording.

The circumstances of the *Perry* case were somewhat different, but also unusual.[101] The applicant was suspected of committing armed robberies. He refused to participate in identification parades. He was then covertly filmed in the police station using the custody suite cameras which had been especially adjusted for this purpose. The video footage was used for identification purposes, and contributed to securing his conviction. In the course of its judgment, the Court said:

> ...the normal use of security cameras *per se* whether in the public street or on premises, such as shopping centres or police stations where they serve a legitimate and foreseeable purpose, do not raise issues under Article 8(1) of the Convention.[102]

But the unusual and irregular manner of using these facilities in this case (which breached national rules of criminal procedure on identification evidence in a number of respects) meant that there had been a violation of Article 8.

So, it is clear that the use of CCTV cameras in public places, or places to which the public have ready access such as shopping centres and police stations, and the recording of the images they see, do not engage Article 8. However, the use to which the recordings are put may, in the particular circumstances of each case, constitute an interference with the rights protected by Article 8. Such actions will need to have a proper legal base, a legitimate aim, and be necessary in a democratic society.

THE COLLECTION, STORAGE, AND USE OF PERSONAL DATA

The collection of information by officials of the State about individuals without their consent will interfere with their private life, as will its use, for example, in court proceedings. Examples include covert measures, such as the keeping of secret files. There may be an interference with private life even when the information kept on file relates to 'public' activities such as membership of organizations or participation in politics. This is because, as previously mentioned, it is not always easy to draw a clear line between 'private' and 'public' activities. However, the Strasbourg Court has also said that 'public information can fall within the scope of private life where it is systematically collected and stored in files held by the authorities'.[103] An interference with private life can also arise from overt measures, such as official censuses and the collection and retention of fingerprints, photographs, or genetic material by the police.[104]

[101] *Perry v United Kingdom*, (App. 63737/00), 17 July 2003, (2004) 39 EHRR 76, ECHR 2003-IX.

[102] § 40. [103] *Rotaru v Romania*, (App. 28341/95), 4 May 2000 [GC], ECHR 2000-V, § 43.

[104] *S and Marper v United Kingdom*, (App. 30562/04), 4 December 2008 [GC], (2009) 48 EHRR 1169; ECHR 2008.

The *Leander* case[105] established that the storage of information is capable of resulting in a breach of the right to respect for private life, although in the particular circumstances of that case, it did not because there were appropriate safeguards. The case concerned the 'personnel control procedure' applicable to navy employees in Sweden. This had resulted in the applicant's being found unsuitable for particular employment, and he complained of an interference in his private life. The procedure involved the maintenance of a secret police register containing information concerning his private life. The Strasbourg Court found the Swedish law setting up the system sufficiently clear and precise as to its ambit to meet the requirements of the Convention that interferences with private life be in accordance with law. This left the question of whether the system was necessary in a democratic society in the interests of national security. Where national security is involved the margin of appreciation allowed to the Contracting Party is a wide one, but there must nevertheless be safeguards for the citizen. There was, in fact, in this case an elaborate system of safeguards, which met the requirements of the Convention.

Safeguards were, however, found to be lacking in the *Turek* case.[106] The applicant had lost his job when a negative security clearance was issued under lustration legislation[107] and his legal challenge to the issue of that negative security clearance were frustrated because key evidence was kept secret. The Court accepted that, particularly in proceedings relating to the operation of state security agencies, there might be legitimate grounds for limiting access to documents. However, this argument carried little weight, since the lustration proceedings were concerned with events during the communist era, rather than any security concerns of the modern State. There was a breach of Article 8 because there were insufficient safeguards to enable the applicant to secure effective protection of his right to respect for his private life.

The *Rotaru* case[108] concerned complaints by a Romanian lawyer that information going back more than fifty years had been held concerning him by the intelligence services, and that there were no procedures by which he could seek to refute some of that information. The Romanian system had some basis in law, but the requirement of foreseeability was not satisfied. There were no apparent limits on the exercise of the powers by the State to collect and store the information; there was no procedure under which the subject of the information could consult it, find out its nature, or seek to correct it. The failure of the national law to indicate with reasonable clarity the scope and manner of the exercise of the State's powers, and the interference with the applicant's private life was not 'in accordance with law' resulting in a violation of Article 8.

The placement of the applicant on a Sex Offenders Register after being sentenced to fifteen years' imprisonment for the rape of a minor was considered in *Gardel v France*.[109] The Court took the view that the need for safeguards is all the greater where the protection of personal data undergoing automatic processing is concerned, not least when such data are used for police purposes. These safeguards should ensure that such data are relevant and not excessive in relation to the purposes for which they are stored; that they are preserved in a form which permits identification of the data subjects for no longer than is required

[105] *Leander v Sweden*, 26 March 1987, Series A No 116, (1987) 9 EHRR 433; see also *Rotaru v Romania*, (App. 28341/95), 4 May 2000 [GC], ECHR 2000-V; and *Amman v Switzerland*, (App. 27798/95), 16 February 2000 [GC], (2000) 30 EHRR 843, ECHR 2000-II.

[106] *Turek v Slovakia*, (App. 57986/00), 14 February 2006, (2007) 44 EHRR 861, ECHR 2006-II.

[107] Legislation concerned with declarations by people who had been involved with State security agencies under communist regimes.

[108] *Rotaru v Romania*, (App. 28341/95), 4 May 2000 [GC], ECHR 2000-V.

[109] *Gardel v France*, (App. 16428/05), 17 December 2009, ECHR 2009.

for the purpose for which those data are stored, and that they afford adequate guarantees to ensure that retained personal data are efficiently protected from misuse and abuse.[110] It was satisfied that such safeguards existed in this case and that the domestic authorities had struck a fair balance between the competing private and public interests at stake.

The retention without limit of time of DNA samples and fingerprints in part of the UK was at issue in the *S and Marper* case.[111] S, a juvenile, and Marper had both had DNA samples and fingerprints taken. In S's case, he was acquitted of all charges against him, and in Marper's case, the case against him was formally discontinued. However, under English law, the DNA samples and fingerprints were kept on record despite their requests that they be destroyed. Both complained that this constituted a violation of their right to private life under Article 8. The Strasbourg Court regarded the retention of DNA samples as having a more important impact on private life than fingerprints, but nevertheless the retention of each constituted an interference with private life. The Strasbourg Court had some reservations about the quality of law requirements in relation to the statutory provision permitting retention of this material, but drew no formal conclusion on this issue. The Strasbourg Court accepted that the retention of these personal data could be said to be for the prevention of crime, and so the compatibility of the scheme fell to be determined on an analysis of whether retention of the personal data in the circumstances of this case was necessary in a democratic society. The Court looked for something approaching a European consensus, and noted that the great majority of Contracting Parties required samples to be removed or destroyed within a certain period following acquittal or discharge of those from whom the samples had been taken. The system in England, Wales, and Northern Ireland[112] appeared to be the only one among the Contracting Parties which allowed the indefinite retention of such material in relation to a person of any age suspected of any recordable offence. The Court was not persuaded by an argument that the UK was more advanced than other countries in its use of DNA profiling. There was a risk of stigmatization, and feelings of stigmatization, in such a system, which was particularly acute in the case of juveniles. A fair balance of competing interests had not been struck and there was a unanimous finding by the Grand Chamber of a breach of Article 8.

The *Craxi* case[113] shows that dissemination by newspapers of information collected by a public authority in circumstances where those newspapers must have obtained the information from the public authority without any procedural safeguards constitutes a breach of Article 8. Disclosure of information obtained in compliance with Article 8 may still amount to a violation. Thus in *Drakšas v Lithuania*[114] the Court found that while the interception of the applicant's telephone conversations was necessary in a democratic society to safeguard national security and prevent crime, the subsequent disclosure of the conversations on national television was not necessary and was in violation of Article 8.

The circumstances in the *LL* case[115] were rather different. In contested divorce proceedings in France, the wife adduced medical reports concerning the husband which indicated that he was an alcoholic and prone to domestic violence. The husband denied this.

[110] § 62.

[111] *S and Marper v United Kingdom*, (App. 30562/04), 4 December 2008 [GC], (2009) 48 EHRR 1169; ECHR 2008.

[112] The position in Scotland permits retention, initially for three years, of such data only in the case of adults charged with violent or sexual offences.

[113] *Craxi v Italy (No. 2)*, (App. 25337/94), 17 July 2003, (2004) 38 EHRR 995.

[114] *Drakšas v Lithuania*, (App. 36662/04), 31 July 2012.

[115] *LL v France*, (App. 7508/02), 10 October 2006, ECHR 2006-XI.

Somewhat earlier in *Z v Finland*[116] the Strasbourg Court had ruled that the protection of medical data is of fundamental importance to a person's enjoyment of private life, and that respecting the confidentiality of such information was of paramount importance.[117] Though the Court accepted that the interests of the community in disclosure of such information might outweigh the right to confidentiality, the context will determine the extent of a Contracting Party's margin of appreciation in authorizing disclosure. In the *LL* case, the Court found that the use of the disputed medical report was not proportionate to the legitimate aim of protecting the rights and freedoms of others.

A similar approach was adopted more recently in *Avilkina and others v Russia.*[118] The applicants alleged that the disclosure of their medical files to the prosecutor's office amounted to a violation of their right to respect for their private life. The Court reiterated that the protection of personal data, including medical information, is of fundamental importance to a person's enjoyment of the right to respect for his or her private and family life guaranteed by Article 8 and that respecting the confidentiality of health data is a vital principle in the legal systems of all the Contracting Parties to the Convention.[119] While the interests in protecting the confidentiality of medical data may be outweighed by the interest of investigating and prosecuting crime and in the publicity of court proceedings, in this case the applicants were not suspects or accused in any criminal investigation. The prosecutor was merely conducting an inquiry into the activities of the applicants' Jehovah's Witness religious organization in response to complaints received by his office. The Court found there was no pressing need for the disclosure and that no less intrusive means of obtaining the information sought had been attempted. The Court concluded that the collection of the confidential medical information by the prosecutor's office was not accompanied by sufficient safeguards to prevent disclosure inconsistent with the respect for the applicants' private life guaranteed under Article 8.

In serious cases, the Contracting Parties will have a positive obligation to compel disclosure of a person's identity which might otherwise be regarded as a confidential matter. So, in the *KU* case,[120] the respondent State was found to be in breach of Article 8 when it had no framework for compelling an internet service provider to disclose the identity of a customer who had posted an advertisement of a sexual nature on an internet dating site pretending to be the applicant, a twelve-year-old boy, and soliciting an intimate relationship with a male.

The duty of confidentiality in relation to records lawfully held has also been the subject of proceedings before the Strasbourg Court.[121] Though the disclosure of which the applicant complained (of her health records in connection with a social security claim) was found not to be a violation of Article 8, the Court noted:

> The Court reiterates that the protection of personal data, particularly medical data, is of fundamental importance to a person's enjoyment of his or her right to respect for private and family life as guaranteed by Article 8 of the Convention. Respecting the confidentiality of health data is a vital principle in the legal systems of all the Contracting Parties to the Convention. It is crucial not only to respect the sense of privacy of a patient but also to preserve his or her confidence in the medical profession and in the health services in general. The domestic law must afford appropriate safeguards to prevent any such communication

[116] *Z v Finland*, (App. 22009/93), 25 February 1997, (1998) 25 EHRR 371, ECHR 1997-I.

[117] § 95. [118] *Avilkina and others v Russia*, (App. 1585/09), 6 June 2013. [119] § 45.

[120] *KU v Finland*, (App. 2872/02), 2 December 2008, (2009) 48 EHRR 1237.

[121] *MS v Sweden*, (App. 20837/92), 27 August 1997, (1999) 28 EHRR 313, ECHR 1997-IV. See also *Z v Finland*, (App. 22009/93), 25 February 1997, (1998) 25 EHRR 371, ECHR 1997-I.

or disclosure of personal health data as may be inconsistent with the guarantees in Article 8 of the Convention.[122]

FREEDOM TO DEVELOP ONE'S IDENTITY

PARENTAL LINKS AND CHILDHOOD

Article 8 may assist children to know and understand their childhood. Though there is no right of access to care records and a refusal of complete access does not amount to an interference with family life, nevertheless a system which allows disclosure of care records to children formerly in care only with the consent of contributors but makes no provision for considering the reasonableness of any refusal of consent will go beyond the margin of appreciation permitted by the Article.[123] The Strasbourg Court has sometimes classified these issues as relating to family life, and sometimes to private life. All the cases are, however, considered in this chapter since they adopt a common approach both for children seeking to establish who their biological parents are, as well as cases in which fathers have sought to establish or contest paternity.

The Grand Chamber revisited the question of resolving competing interests of confidentiality and openness in the context of the provision of information for adopted children about their biological family in the *Odièvre* case.[124] The factual situation was very simple. An adopted child, who had attained the age of majority, was seeking information about her biological family. She had been abandoned by her natural mother who had requested that the birth be kept secret. In France, the effect of a declaration like that signed by the mother at birth resulted in a permanent inability of the child to learn the identity of her biological mother.[125] The applicant was only able to obtain non-identifying information about her biological family, from which she learned that she had three brothers. The Court considered that access to such information fell within the ambit of private life in Article 8. The Strasbourg Court recognized that the two competing interests of the mother for confidentiality and of the grown-up child for information are not easily reconciled. The Court, after rather slender reasoning, concluded that the respondent State had not breached Article 8 and had not overstepped its margin of appreciation in dealing with the competing interests which it faced. This was a majority decision by ten judges from which seven judges dissented in a powerfully argued joint dissenting opinion. They agreed that a balance had to be struck, but considered that the majority had not had proper regard to developments in understanding the needs of adopted children to trace their natural parents. Furthermore, the French legislation effectively gave the natural mother a 'right of veto' 'condemning the child to lifelong ignorance'.[126] The dissenting judges concluded that, if a system of anonymous births is to be retained, a Contracting Party has a positive obligation to establish an independent authority with the power to decide whether or not to grant access.

The *Jäggi* case[127] shows the Strasbourg Court in rather more sympathetic mood towards a person seeking to establish who his father was. In this case it was a 67-year-old man who was seeking authorization for a DNA test to be carried out on the remains of the person

[122] *MS v Sweden*, § 41.

[123] *Gaskin v United Kingdom*, (App. 10454/83), 7 July 1989, Series A No 160, (1990) 12 EHRR 36; *MG v United Kingdom*, (App. 39393/98), 24 September 2002, (2003) 36 EHRR 22.

[124] *Odièvre v France*, (App. 42326/98), 13 February 2003 [GC], (2004) 38 EHRR 871; ECHR 2003-III.

[125] The Joint Dissenting Opinion records that 'no other legislative system is so weighted in favour of maternal anonymity' (§ 13).

[126] § 7 of the Joint Dissenting Opinion.

[127] *Jäggi v Switzerland*, (App. 58757/00), 13 July 2006, (2008) 47 EHRR 702, ECHR 2006-X.

he claimed to be his father. The refusal of the authorities to permit this was a violation of respect for his private life; the Court observed that 'an individual's interest in discovering his parentage does not disappear with age, quite the reverse.'[128]

A procedural barrier to establishment of paternity was found to be a violation of Article 8 in the *Phinikaridou* case.[129] There had been a deathbed confession to the applicant, then aged 52, by her mother telling her the name of her biological father. An absolute limitation period in the national legal order resulted in the rejection of efforts by the applicant to secure judicial recognition of paternity. The application of so rigid a time limit, without any exceptions and regardless of the circumstances, impaired the very essence of the right to respect for private life.

The *Shofman* case[130] concerned a father's action contesting paternity. Some two years after a child was born, of whom the applicant believed he was the father, it was established through DNA tests that he was not. He immediately began divorce proceedings and proceedings to contest the paternity of the child. The paternity suit was dismissed because the national law set a one-year time limit from the date on which the putative father was informed that he had been registered as the father. This time limit had passed by the time the applicant discovered that he was not the child's father. The Strasbourg Court found a violation of respect for the private life of the applicant, since it was not necessary in a democratic society to establish an inflexible time limit. Although practice in other Contracting Parties was not uniform, it was possible in some States in exceptional circumstances to bring paternity challenge proceedings out of time. The existence of such exceptions did not defeat what was accepted as a legitimate aim of time limits to balance legal certainty in family relations and the interests of the child.

The facts of the *Paulík* case[131] are rather sad. The applicant had a sexual relationship with a woman in 1966; she subsequently gave birth to a daughter. Under provisions of national law at the time, he was presumed to be the father and was so regarded. An order to pay maintenance for the child was made, with which the applicant complied. The applicant maintained contact with her. In 2004, the applicant's 'daughter (who was by now married and had a family of her own which was financially supported by the applicant) had an argument with him over his financial contribution, and proposed that paternity be re-tested. A DNA test established that the applicant was not the father. The applicant then sought to initiate proceedings in the national courts to challenge his paternity of the 'daughter'. The 'daughter' indicated that she had no objection to his denial of paternity. The national authorities nevertheless regarded the establishment of paternity which had occurred many years earlier to be irreversible. The Strasbourg Court found a violation of Article 8 in that there was no procedure 'for bringing the legal position into line with the biological reality' and this did not benefit anyone.[132]

The circumstances of the *Różański* case[133] were the reverse; the applicant was seeking to establish that he was the father of a child. The circumstances involved a number of changes of mind by both the applicant and the mother of the child, and ultimately the applicant got nowhere in his attempts to get proceedings under way (partly because the proceedings required the consent of the mother) which would determine the paternity of the child in question. The Strasbourg Court characterized the issue as one concerning the applicant's

[128] § 40. [129] *Phinikaridou v Cyprus*, (App. 23890/02), 20 December 2007, ECHR 2007-XIV.

[130] *Shofman v Russia*, (App. 74826/01), 24 November 2005, (2007) 44 EHRR 741.

[131] *Paulík v Slovakia*, (App. 10699/05), 10 October 2006, (2008) 46 EHRR 142, ECHR 2006-XI.

[132] § 46.

[133] *Różański v Poland*, (App. 55339/00), 18 May 2006, (2007) 45 EHRR 625. See also *Mizzi v Malta*, (App. 26111/02), 12 January 2006, (2008) 46 EHRR 529, ECHR 2006-I.

right to family life. There was a violation of Article 8 in that there was no proper investigation by the national authorities of the applicant's assertion that he was the biological father of the child.

Issues of recognition of parenthood have also afflicted transsexuals. The *X, Y and Z* case[134] concerned X, a female-to-male transsexual, who lived in a permanent stable relationship with Y. Y underwent artificial insemination by an anonymous donor and gave birth to a child, Z. X sought registration as the father of the child. The Registrar-General advised that only a biological man could be regarded as the father for the purposes of registration, though the child could bear X's last name and that X would be entitled to a personal tax allowance in respect of the child provided he could show that he maintained the child. X went ahead and sought to register himself as the father of the child but was not permitted to do so. In considering the complaint of a violation of Article 8, the Strasbourg Court considered that de facto family ties linked the three applicants and so Article 8 was applicable. The Court noted that the issues raised in this case were different from those raised in the earlier transsexual cases, and concerned recognition of parenthood in cases where there had been artificial insemination by a donor. Since there was no common ground on these issues among the Contracting Parties, a wide margin of appreciation should be accorded to individual States. Had a fair balance been struck between the competing interests of the individual and those of the community as a whole? After considering the arguments on both sides, the Court concluded that there was no obligation falling on the United Kingdom formally to recognize X as the father of Z, and there was no violation of Article 8. Four dissenting judges would have found a violation of Article 8, while one further judge would have found a violation of Article 14 taken in conjunction with Article 8, and one further judge would have found violations of Article 8 and Article 14.

CULTURAL IDENTITY

Personal autonomy is an important principle underlying the interpretation of Article 8 and the provision therefore is capable of encompassing many different aspects of a person's physical and social identity, including an individual's ethnic identity. A series of cases has concerned the rights of gypsies. The *Buckley* case[135] concerned the refusal of planning permission to enable a gypsy to live in a caravan on her own land. The Strasbourg Court rejected a suggestion that respect for the home was only engaged where the home had been established lawfully. A refusal of planning permission constituted an interference which was in accordance with law, and planning legislation was accepted to serve the interests of the economic well-being of the country, the protection of health, and the protection of the rights of others. In considering whether the interference is necessary in a democratic society, the Court noted, in concluding that there was no violation of Article 8, that the process by which decisions were made had to be fair:

> Whenever discretion capable of interfering with the enjoyment of a Convention right such as the one at issue in the present case is conferred on national authorities, the procedural safeguards available to the individual will be especially material in determining whether the respondent State has, when fixing the regulatory framework, remained within the margin of its appreciation. Indeed, it is settled case-law that, whilst Article 8 contains no explicit procedural requirements, the decision-making process leading to measures of interference

[134] *X, Y and Z v United Kingdom*, (App. 21830/93), 22 April 1997, (1997) 24 EHRR 143, ECHR 1997-II.

[135] *Buckley v United Kingdom*, (App. 20348/92), 25 September 1996, (1997) 23 EHRR 101.

must be fair and such as to afford due respect to the interests safeguarded to the individual by Article 8.[136]

Judgment was given in January 2001 in five further cases against the United Kingdom concerning planning and enforcement measures taken against gypsies in respect of their occupation on their own land of caravans as their homes.[137] The cases contain a wealth of information on domestic and international texts on gypsies. The facts of these cases were broadly similar. The applicants were gypsies by birth and had lived a travelling lifestyle. They bought land with the intention of living on it in caravans; they moved onto the land and applied for planning permission, which was refused. Enforcement notices were served requiring the use of the land for residential purposes to cease. The Grand Chamber referred to its decision in the *Buckley* case, and noted that it was 'in the interests of legal certainty, foreseeability and equality before the law that it should not depart, without good reason, from precedents laid down in previous cases' though due regard should be had to changing conditions and any emerging consensus among the Contracting Parties.[138] The Court considered the measures in issue to affect the applicants' private and family life, and home. There had been an interference with those rights which was in accordance with law, and in the interests of protecting the rights of others. The question was therefore whether the interference was necessary in a democratic society. The applicants relied heavily on the growing international consensus about the importance of providing legal protection of the rights of minorities, and an obligation to protect their security, identity, and lifestyle. The respondent State stressed the importance of planning controls in balancing the needs of the individual and the community, and that national authorities were better placed to make the necessary judgments on these issues. The Court came down in favour of the respondent State; the decisions on planning matters had been taken after weighing the various competing interests, and there were adequate procedural safeguards for the applicants. The Court was influenced by the fact that the homes were initially established unlawfully, that is, without the required planning permission.[139] A dissenting opinion of seven judges would have found a violation of Article 8 on the grounds that there is an international consensus which is sufficiently concrete that gypsies require special protection in respect of their right to respect for home, private and family life, which has a dimension beyond environmental concerns. Such concerns when weighed against the interference in the applicants' rights did not disclose a pressing social need. The dissenting judges denied that their decision was tantamount to excluding gypsies from the system of planning control.

In the *Connors* case,[140] the Strasbourg Court found that the lack of procedural safeguards surrounding the summary eviction of gypsies from a local authority gypsy site breached Article 8 of the Convention. The only basis for the eviction appeared to be some concern that a member of the family was a 'magnet for trouble'. In the course of its judgment, the Strasbourg Court noted:

> The vulnerable position of gypsies as a minority means that some special consideration should be given to their needs and their different lifestyle both in the relevant regulatory framework and in reaching decisions in particular cases. . . .[141]

[136] § 76.

[137] *Chapman v United Kingdom*, (App. 27238/95), (2001) 33 EHRR 399; ECHR 2001-I; *Beard v United Kingdom*, (App. 24882/94), (2001) 33 EHRR 442; *Coster v United Kingdom*, (App. 24876/94), (2001) 33 EHRR 479; *Lee v United Kingdom*, (App. 25289/94), (2001) 33 EHRR 677; and *Smith (Jane) v United Kingdom*, (App. 25154/94), (2001) 33 EHRR 712; all 18 January 2001 [GC].

[138] *Chapman*, § 70.

[139] *Chapman*, § 102.

[140] *Connors v United Kingdom*, (App. 66746/01), 27 May 2004, (2005) 40 EHRR 189.

[141] § 84.

A statutory scheme permitting the summary eviction of gypsies was a disproportionate response to the problems local authorities faced. It could not be shown that the scheme was used to ensure a turnover of vacant pitches (so sustaining a nomadic lifestyle) nor to prevent families from becoming long-term residents.[142]

In *Aksu v Turkey*[143] the applicant alleged that three publications—a book entitled *The Gypsies of Turkey* and two dictionaries—contained expressions and definitions which offended his Roma/Gypsy identity. The Grand Chamber noted that 'any negative stereotyping of a group, when it reaches a certain level, is capable of impacting on the group's sense of identity and the feelings of self-worth and self-confidence of members of the group. It is in this sense that it can be seen as affecting the private life of members of the group.'[144] The Grand Chamber considered whether the respondent Government had complied with their positive obligation under Article 8 to protect the applicant's private life from alleged interference by the author of the publications. In considering this, the Court gave significant weight to Article 10's protection for freedom of expression and concluded that the Turkish authorities had not overstepped their margin of appreciation in balancing the two relevant rights.

In *Ciubotaru v Moldova*,[145] the applicant claimed that there had been a violation of Article 8 due to the fact that when collecting and recording information concerning his identity the Moldovan authorities had refused to register his Romanian ethnic identity and forced on him an ethnic identity with which he did not identify. The Court reiterated that an individual's ethnic identity constitutes an essential aspect of his or her private life and identity and noted that this would be particularly true in the current social setting of the Republic of Moldova, where the problem of ethnic identity had been the subject matter of social tension and heated debate. In addition, in that State an individual's recorded ethnic identity is decisive for the determination of the ethnic identity of his or her children and later generations. The Court had no doubt, therefore, that the refusal to register the applicant's Romanian ethnic identity fell within the ambit of 'private life' under Article 8. In considering whether the interference was proportionate, the Court was willing to accept that it be open to authorities to refuse a claim to be officially recorded as belonging to a particular ethnicity where such a claim is based on purely subjective and unsubstantiated grounds, but in this case took the view that the applicant had been confronted with a legal requirement which made it impossible for him to adduce any evidence in support of his claim.[146] The State had thus failed in its positive obligation to secure to the applicant the effective respect for his private life.

A rather different issue faced the Court in *Kurić and others v Slovenia*[147] in which the applicants alleged that they had been arbitrarily deprived of their status as permanent residents after Slovenia had declared its independence in 1991. The applicants' names were 'erased' from the Register of Permanent Residents, together with the names of more than 25,000 other former SFRY (Socialist Federal Republic of Yugoslavia) citizens who had citizenship of one of the other republics and permanent residence in Slovenia. As the applicants failed to submit requests for Slovenian citizenship by a certain date, they became aliens and were also deprived of their residence status in Slovenia. In the view of the Grand Chamber, the applicants could not have reasonably expected that

[142] For a wide-ranging article on the human rights of travellers, see R. Sandland, 'Developing a Jurisprudence of Difference: The Protection of the Human Rights of Travelling Peoples by the European Court of Human Rights' (2008) 8 HRLRev 475.

[143] *Aksu v Turkey*, (App. 4149/04 and 41029/04), 15 March 2012 [GC], ECHR 2012.

[144] § 58.

[145] *Ciubotaru v Moldova*, (App. 27138/04), 27 April 2010.

[146] § 57.

[147] *Kurić and others v Slovenia*, (App. 26828/06), 26 June 2012 [GC], ECHR 2012 (extracts).

this status as aliens would entail the unlawfulness of their residence on Slovenian territory and would lead to such an extreme measure as the 'erasure' which was carried out automatically and without prior notification. The Court found there was a legal vacuum in the legislation at the time since no procedure was put in place for ex-SFRY citizens holding the citizenship of one of the other republics to request permanent residence permits. It concluded, therefore, that Slovenian legislation and administrative practice which resulted in the 'erasure' lacked the requisite standards of foreseeability and accessibility required under Article 8(2).

The Grand Chamber also concluded that the measures were not necessary in a democratic society to achieve the legitimate aim of the protection of national security. It noted the implications of the measure for the applicants who, prior to Slovenia's declaration of independence, had been lawfully residing in Slovenia for several years:

> Owing to the 'erasure', they experienced a number of adverse consequences, such as the destruction of identity documents, loss of job opportunities, loss of health insurance, the impossibility of renewing identity documents or driving licences, and difficulties in regulating pension rights. Indeed, the legal vacuum in the independence legislation... deprived the applicants of their legal status, which had previously given them access to a wide range of rights.[148]

The Court concluded that Slovenia should have taken steps to regularize the residence status of former SFRY citizens in order to ensure that failure to obtain Slovenian citizenship would not disproportionately affect the Article 8 rights of the 'erased'. This important case confirms that legal personality is a fundamental aspect of personal identity protected under the right to respect for private life in Article 8. Judge Vučinić, in his partly dissenting opinion, went so far as to describe the actions of Slovenia as 'a legalistic means of ethnic cleansing'.

NAMES

Some international conventions make explicit reference to names.[149] The European Convention is silent on this issue, but both the Commission and the Court have held that regulation of names falls within the ambit of private life. This includes the choice of a child's forenames by their parents.[150]

In the *Burghartz* case,[151] the applicants were Swiss nationals who had married in Germany. They chose the wife's last name, Burghartz, as their family name under the provisions of the German Civil Code. On returning to Switzerland, they applied to use Burghartz as their family name, and Mr Burghartz sought to use the name Schnyder Burghartz. The applications were turned down. Under Swiss law, the wife was permitted to use her family name before that of her husband. An appeal in respect of the use of the name Burghartz as the family name succeeded, but Mr Burghartz was denied the use of his family name before Burghartz.

[148] § 356.

[149] Art. 24(2) of the International Covenant on Civil and Political Rights, Arts. 7 and 8 of the Convention on the Rights of the Child, and Art. 18 of the American Convention on Human Rights. For a Community law case concerning names, see Case C-168/91, *Konstantinidis v Altensteig-Standesamt*, [1993] ECR-I 2755. See generally H. Greve, '"What's in a Name?" The Human Right to a Recognized Individual Identity' in S. Breitenmoser and others, *Human Rights, Democracy and the Rule of Law. Liber Amicorum Luzius Wildhaber* (Nomos, Baden Baden 2007), 295.

[150] *Guillot v France*, (App. 22500/93), 24 October 1996, ECHR 1996-V.

[151] *Burghartz v Switzerland*, (App. 16213/90), 22 February 1994, Series A No 280-B, (1994) 18 EHRR 101.

The Strasbourg Court ruled that a person's name as a means of personal identification and of linking to a family concerns family and private life under Article 8. Nevertheless the State has an interest in regulating the use of names. In this case, the different treatment accorded to men and women in the use of names constituted a violation of Article 8 taken in conjunction with the non-discrimination provision in Article 14.[152]

In another case[153] a Finnish national challenged the refusal of the Finnish authorities to permit him to change his last name. The Strasbourg Court considered whether there was an interference in this case, and noted that there is a distinction between a situation in which the State refuses to permit a name to be changed and in which the State requires a name to be changed. The distinction is between the positive and negative obligations of States under the Convention. The Court went on:

> Despite the increased use of personal identity numbers in Finland and in other Contracting States, names retain a crucial role in the identification of people. Whilst therefore recognizing that there may exist genuine reasons prompting an individual to wish to change his or her name, the Court accepts that legal restrictions on such a possibility may be justified in the public interest; for example in order to ensure accurate population registration or to safeguard the means of personal identification and of linking the bearers of a given name to a family.[154]

In the absence of common ground among the Contracting Parties, the Strasbourg Court allowed Finland a wide margin of appreciation. There was no interference with the rights in Article 8(1) in this case because the sources of inconvenience to the applicant were not sufficient to raise an issue of failure to respect his private life; there were also alternative names which the authorities would have permitted him to use.

A violation was, however, found in the *Johansson* case.[155] The applicants wished to name their son 'Axl' in a manner which did not comply, in relation to the form of spelling, with the Finnish legislation on names. While the Strasbourg Court accepted that the protection of children from being given an unsuitable name, which might open them to ridicule, or be a mere expression of parental whimsy, and the preservation of national naming practices are in the public interest, the broad discretion accorded to the Contracting Parties was not without limit. In the absence of compelling evidence that a name would have negative consequences for the preservation of the cultural and linguistic identity of Finland, there was a violation of Article 8 in the interference with the choice of name by the parents.

TRANSSEXUALS

Transsexuals[156] have long been assertive in using Article 8 to secure recognition of their gender identity in some of the Contracting States. This line of cases provides an excellent case study of both the interpretation of the Convention as a living instrument and the development of positive obligations for Contracting Parties under the European Convention, though the law now appears well settled following the Strasbourg Court's judgments in two cases against the UK in 2002.[157]

[152] See ch.24.

[153] *Stjerna v Finland*, (App. 18131/91), 25 November 1994, Series A No 299-B, (1997) 24 EHRR 195.

[154] § 39.

[155] *Johansson v Finland*, (App. 10163/02), 6 September 2007, (2008) 47 EHRR 369, ECHR 2007-X.

[156] See Council of Europe and the International Commission on Civil Status, *Transsexualism in Europe* (Council of Europe Publishing, Strasbourg 2000). See also A. Campbell and H. Lardy, 'Transsexuals—the ECHR in Transition' (2003) 54 NILQ 209.

[157] *Goodwin v United Kingdom*, (App. 28957/95), 11 July 2002 [GC], (2002) 35 EHRR 447; ECHR 2002-VI; and *I v United Kingdom*, (App. 25680/94), 11 July 2002 [GC], (2003) 36 EHRR 967. For the earlier case-law, see

The tide turned with the unanimous judgments of the Grand Chamber in the *Goodwin* and *I* cases,[158] which concerned post-operative male-to-female transsexuals. The *Goodwin* case raised the inability of Goodwin to change her gender as recorded in a number of official government records, while the *I* case raised the issue of change to a birth certificate. Though there was not yet evidence of a common European approach, the Court concluded that there was:

> the clear and uncontested evidence of a continuing international trend in favour not only of increased social acceptance of transsexuals but of legal recognition of the new sexuality of post-operative transsexuals.[159]

It was significant that the Strasbourg Court had, in earlier cases, 'signalled its consciousness of the serious problems facing transsexuals and stressed the importance of keeping the need for appropriate legal measures in the area under review.'[160] Goodwin is a male-to-female transsexual who had undergone gender re-assignment surgery, and lived as a woman. But for legal purposes in the United Kingdom, she remained classified as a man. The situation was far from a minor inconvenience; it resulted in feelings of vulnerability, humiliation, and anxiety. The Strasbourg Court considered that, where medical services in a Contracting Party provided for gender re-assignment surgery with a view to creating a biological identity of the gender the person perceives that he or she has, it was illogical to refuse to recognize the legal implications of such treatment. The Court undertook a detailed analysis of current knowledge of the phenomenon of gender dysphoria, and noted that there was not yet a universal approach to the disorder. This meant that Contracting Parties would enjoy a wide margin of appreciation, but that margin is not without its limits. The Grand Chamber observed:

> Nonetheless, the very essence of the Convention is respect for human dignity and human freedom. Under Article 8 of the Convention in particular, where the notion of personal autonomy is an important principle underlying the interpretation of its guarantees, protection is given to the personal sphere of each individual, including the right to establish details of their identity as individual human beings.... In the twenty first century the right of transsexuals to personal development and to physical and moral security in the full sense enjoyed by others in society cannot be regarded as a matter of controversy requiring the lapse of time to cast clearer light on the issues involved. In short, the unsatisfactory situation in which post-operative transsexuals live in an intermediate zone as not quite one gender or the other is no longer sustainable.[161]

Once the Strasbourg Court had reached that position, it was inevitable, in the light of the earlier cases, that it would find that there was a violation of Article 8.[162]

Despite the significant development in the Strasbourg Court's position as reflected in these cases, new issues relating to the rights of transsexuals under Article 8 nevertheless continue to emerge. Under the legislation in the United Kingdom following these cases, a system of certification of gender has been introduced, but married parties can only obtain

Van Oosterwijck v Belgium, (App. 7654/76), 6 November 1980, Series A No 40, (1981) 3 EHRR 557; *Rees v United Kingdom*, (App. 9532/81), 17 October 1986, Series A No 106, (1987) 9 EHRR 56; *Cossey v United Kingdom*, (App. 10843/84), 27 September 1990, Series A No 184, (1991) 13 EHRR 622; *B. v France*, (App. 13343/87), 25 March 1992, Series A No 232-C, (1994) 16 EHRR 1; and *Sheffield and Horsham v United Kingdom* (Apps. 22885/93 and 23390/94), 30 July 1998, (1999) 27 EHRR 163, ECHR 1998-V.

[158] *Goodwin v United Kingdom*, (App. 28957/95), 11 July 2002 [GC], (2002) 35 EHRR 447; ECHR 2002-VI; and *I v United Kingdom*, (App. 25680/94), 11 July 2002 [GC], (2003) 36 EHRR 967.

[159] *Goodwin*, § 85; and *I*, § 65. [160] *Goodwin*, § 75. [161] *Goodwin*, § 90.

[162] The United Kingdom has responded by passing the Gender Recognition Act 2004.

a full certificate where annulment of the marriage is obtained. In the *Parry* case,[163] following gender re-assignment of one of the parties to a marriage, neither party wished to seek annulment of the marriage, and complained that their failure to be eligible for a full certificate constituted a violation of Article 8. The Court ruled the application inadmissible on the grounds that it was not disproportionate. It was noted that the parties could continue their relationship as a civil partnership. In *H. v Finland*[164] the applicant complained that her right to private and family life had been violated when the full recognition of her new gender was made conditional on the transformation of her marriage into a civil partnership. The Court ruled that the effects of the Finnish system had not been shown to be disproportionate and that a fair balance has been struck between the competing interests of the applicant's right to respect for her private life by obtaining a new female identity number and the State's interest to maintain the traditional institution of marriage intact. There had been no violation of Article 8. The case has been referred to the Grand Chamber.

In the *Van Kück* case,[165] the applicant argued that court decisions in Germany which confirmed decisions that the costs of hormone treatment and gender re-assignment surgery were not reimbursable by her health insurance company violated her rights under Article 8. The Strasbourg Court considered the applicant's complaints both under Article 6 and under Article 8. Violations of both Articles were found by a majority of four votes to three. The case is not authority for the proposition that all medical costs connected with hormone treatment and surgery are to be met by public health systems, since the decision turns on the manner in which the Court of Appeal in Germany characterized the applicant's condition as one of her own making, and required her to show, beyond a level that was proportionate in the case, the genuineness of her medical condition and the need for treatment for it.

In the *Grant* case[166] the Strasbourg Court found a violation of Article 8 where the national authorities refused to recognize the applicant's status as a woman for the purpose of entitlement at the age of 60 to a State retirement pension, whereas the pensionable age for a man was 65.[167]

HOMOSEXUALITY

In the *Dudgeon* case[168] the applicant complained that, under the law in force in Northern Ireland, he was liable to criminal prosecution on account of his homosexual conduct and that he had experienced fear, suffering, and psychological distress directly caused by the very existence of the laws in question, including fear of harassment and blackmail. He further complained that, following a search of his house, he was questioned by the police about certain homosexual activities and that personal papers belonging to him were seized during the search and not returned until more than a year later. Dudgeon alleged that, in breach of Article 8, he had suffered, and continued to suffer, an unjustified interference with his right to respect for his private life. In Northern Ireland, but not, as a result of changes in the law, elsewhere in the United Kingdom, the offences were committed whether the act took place in

[163] *Parry v United Kingdom*, (App. 42971/05), 28 November 2006, ECHR 2006-XV.

[164] *H. v Finland*, (App. 37359/09), 13 November 2012.

[165] *Van Kück v Germany*, (App. 35968/97), 12 June 2003, (2003) 37 EHRR 973; ECHR 2003-VII. See also *Schlumpf v Switzerland*, (App. 29002/06), 9 January 2009.

[166] *Grant v United Kingdom*, (App. 32570/03), 23 May 2006, (2007) 44 EHRR 1, ECHR 2006-VII.

[167] But the entitlement to such recognition only arose from 5 September 2002, the date of the Court's judgment in the *Goodwin* case.

[168] *Dudgeon v United Kingdom*, (App. 7525/76), 22 October 1981, Series A No 45, (1982) 4 EHRR 149.

public or in private, whatever the age or relationship of the participants involved, and whether or not the participants consented. The Strasbourg Court said:

> [T]he maintenance in force of the impugned legislation constitutes a continuing interference with the applicant's right to respect for his private life (which includes his sexual life) within the meaning of Article 8, paragraph (1). In the personal circumstances of the applicant, the very existence of this legislation continuously and directly affects his private life ... either he respects the law and refrains from engaging—even in private with consenting male partners—in prohibited sexual acts to which he is disposed by reason of his homosexual tendencies, or he commits such acts and thereby become liable to criminal prosecution.[169]

The question was whether the interference was justified under paragraph (2). There was no doubt that the limitation was in accordance with the law, but a more contentious issue was whether the prohibition in the law of Northern Ireland was 'necessary in a democratic society' for 'the protection of morals' or the 'protection of the rights and freedoms of others'. The Court accepted that some degree of regulation of male homosexual conduct, as indeed of other forms of sexual conduct, by means of the criminal law can be justified as 'necessary in a democratic society', and recalled that the national authorities have a margin of appreciation in assessing this necessity. Nevertheless, any restriction must be proportionate to the legitimate aim pursued. This was particularly striking in a situation where the law of Great Britain and Northern Ireland differed, even though they were constituent parts of the same State. Despite the acknowledged conservatism of society in Northern Ireland, as compared to other parts of the United Kingdom, the Court did not consider that there remained any justification for keeping the prohibitory law on the statute book. The Court did not consider that decriminalization implied approval of the conduct regulated previously by the criminal law. Taking all the circumstances into account, the maintenance in force of the criminal sanctions for homosexual conduct between adult males in private was disproportionate to the aims sought to be achieved and violated Article 8 of the Convention.[170]

A similar approach was taken in the *Norris* case[171] which concerned legislation in effect in Ireland, and in the *Modinos* case,[172] which concerned the law of Cyprus.[173]

Two cases decided in 1999 addressed the issue of whether a discharge from the Royal Navy solely on the grounds of the applicants' homosexuality and in pursuance of the Ministry of Defence policy to exclude homosexuals from the armed forces violated their right to a private life.[174] The Strasbourg Court found that the exclusion of homosexuals from the armed forces was in accordance with law, and could be said to be in the interests of national security and for the prevention of disorder, but concluded that the exclusion in the case of the applicants was not necessary in a democratic society. A detailed consideration of the issue had been conducted by the British Government by its Homosexuality Assessment Policy Team (HAPT) which concluded that the policy should be maintained. The Court was clearly influenced by the policies of other Contracting Parties. Although the margin of appreciation to the State was acknowledged, the Court considered that,

[169] *Dudgeon*, § 41. [170] §§ 60–1.

[171] *Norris v Ireland*, (App. 10581/83), 26 October 1988, Series A No 142, (1991) 13 EHRR 186.

[172] *Modinos v Cyprus*, (App. 10570/89), 22 April 1993, Series A No 259, (1994) 16 EHRR 485.

[173] See also P. van Dijk, 'The Treatment of Homosexuals under the European Convention on Human Rights' in K. Waaldijk and A. Clapham, *Homosexuality: A European Community Issue* (Martinus Nijhoff, Dordrecht 1993), 179.

[174] *Smith and Grady v United Kingdom*, (Apps. 33985/96 and 33986/96), 27 September 1999, (2000) 29 EHRR 493; ECHR 1999-VI; and *Lustig-Prean and Beckett v United Kingdom*, (Apps. 31417/96 and 32377/96), 27 September 1999, (2000) 29 EHRR 548. See also *Perkins and R v United Kingdom*, (Apps. 43208/98 and

where the restrictions concerned 'a most intimate part of an individual's private life', particularly serious reasons would be required before such interferences would fall within the limitations in Article 8(2).[175] These decisions are to be welcomed and show that the Court's assessment of a State's margin of appreciation requires substantiated specific examples of the risks asserted by the State which are claimed to justify an interference with private life.

In the *Sutherland* case[176] the applicant successfully argued before the Commission that United Kingdom legislation which fixed the minimum age of consent for homosexual conduct by men at the age of 18 rather than at the age of 16 which was the age of consent applicable to a woman constituted a violation of Article 8 when read with Article 14 prohibiting discrimination.[177] The Commission concluded that this was so. The case was subsequently struck out of the list following amendment of the UK legislation on the age of consent for homosexuals.[178]

SADO-MASOCHISM

The issue of the criminalization of specific sexual practices of some homosexual men was considered in the *Laskey, Jaggard and Brown* case.[179] Three men were convicted of assault and wounding arising from sado-masochistic practices between consenting adults and taking place wholly in private. The men argued that the decision of the House of Lords refusing a defence of consent to the practices in which they had engaged constituted violations of their right to respect for their private life. No justification for the interference could be sustained under the Convention. They also argued that there was discrimination in comparison to other acts likely to cause greater harm and cited the availability of the defence of consent in the sport of boxing as an example.

The Strasbourg Court accepted that the regulation of the conduct in question was in accordance with law, and that it could be said to be for the protection of health or morals. Some hesitation can be detected in the decision of the majority, which noted that, although sexual orientation and activity concern an intimate aspect of private life, 'not every sexual activity carried out behind closed doors necessarily falls within the scope of private life'.[180] However, the Court proceeded on the assumption that the activities in issue formed part of private life. Given the nature of the activities, the Court allowed the State a wide margin of appreciation since the activities involved the infliction of physical harm; it did not matter that the context was in the course of sexual conduct. The Court rejected the suggestion by the applicants that they had been singled out because they were homosexuals, noting the comment of the trial judge that the unlawful conduct would be dealt with equally whether it arose between homosexuals, heterosexuals, or bisexuals.[181] The Strasbourg Court concluded that the measures were necessary in a democratic society for the protection of health, and did not find it necessary to address the issue of whether the interference could also be justified for the protection of morals.

44875/98), 22 October 2002; and *Beck, Copp and Bazeley v United Kingdom*, (Apps. 48535/99, 48536/99, and 48537/99), 22 October 2002.

175 *Smith and Grady*, § 89; *Lustig-Prean*, § 82.

176 *Sutherland v United Kingdom*, (App. 25186/94), Decision of the Commission of 21 May 1996; Judgment of the Court of 27 March 2001 [GC].

177 On Article 14, see ch.24.

178 Sexual Offences (Amendment) Act 2000 which entered into force on 8 January 2001.

179 *Laskey, Jaggard and Brown v United Kingdom*, (Apps. 21627/93, 21826/93, and 21974/93), 19 February 1997, (1997) 24 EHRR 39, ECHR 1997-I.

180 § 36. In a short and trenchant concurring opinion, Judge Pettiti concludes that Article 8 was not applicable in this case.

181 § 47.

The case may usefully be contrasted with the *ADT* case,[182] which involved the prosecution for gross indecency of a male homosexual arising from sexual conduct[183] involving up to four other men which had been recorded on videotape for the private use of the applicant. Here the Court readily characterized the activity as falling within the private life of those involved. It was appropriate to apply a narrow margin of appreciation; 'the absence of any public health considerations and the purely private nature of the behaviour'[184] did not justify the application of criminal sanctions. The Court was unanimous in finding that there had been a violation of Article 8.

Whereas the Strasbourg Court has found it relatively easy to require the decriminalization of homosexual conduct between consenting adults in private because of the general consensus on this issue among the Contracting Parties, the Court appears less comfortable when dealing with the extreme forms of sexual gratification in issue in the *Laskey* case, and can be criticized for responding with extreme caution.[185] In so far as the fact that the conduct was recorded on videotape may have been relevant, that seems not now to be significant in the light of the decision in *ADT*. That must be right.

The *Pay* case[186] concerned the dismissal of a probation officer whose sexual preferences included bondage, domination, and sado-masochism. He had some business interests connected with these preferences, which included a website. He also engaged in sexual activities in a private members' club which involved male domination over submissive women. This public performance aspect of his sexual activities was claimed by the applicant to be a fundamental part of his sexual expression rather than a mere adjunct to it. He argued that his dismissal violated his right to respect for his private life. An issue arose as to whether the applicant had, by his performances in the private club (which had been video-recorded) resulted in his having waived his Article 8 rights. The Strasbourg Court did not find it necessary to determine this point, but went on to find the application to be manifestly ill-founded. The applicant's unwillingness to accept that his sexual activities, coupled with his business interests, might compromise his work as a probation officer whose work included work with sexual offenders, led the Court to conclude that his dismissal was not a disproportionate response on the part of the authorities.

INCEST

The Court does not regard the criminalization of incest between consenting adults to amount to a violation of Article 8. This was considered in the case of *Stübing v Germany*.[187] The applicant had been placed in a children's home at the age of three and adopted at the age of seven, after which he had no contact with his family of origin. When he re-established contact with that family at the age of 23, he discovered that he had a 16 year old sister and soon after commenced a sexual relationship with her. They lived together for several years and had four children together. He was convicted of incest on three separate occasions. The applicant argued that these convictions interfered with his right to respect for private and family life. The Court found no consensus between the Member States as to whether the consensual commitment of sexual acts between adult siblings should be criminally sanctioned, although it did recognize a broad consensus that 'sexual relationships between siblings are neither accepted by the legal order nor by society as a whole.'[188] As the case concerned a question

[182] *ADT v United Kingdom*, (App. 35765/97), 31 July 2000, (2001) 31 EHRR 33; ECHR 2000-IX.
[183] Oral sex and mutual masturbation.
[184] *ADT*, § 38.
[185] See L. Moran, '*Laskey v The United Kingdom*: Learning the Limits of Privacy' (1998) 61 MLR 77.
[186] *Pay v United Kingdom*, (App. 32792/05), Decision of 16 September 2008.
[187] *Stübing v Germany*. (App. 43547/08), 12 April 2012.
[188] § 61.

about the requirements of morals, the Court granted Germany a wide margin of appreciation in determining how to confront incestuous relationships between consenting adults, even though the decision concerned an intimate aspect of private life. Given the domestic courts' careful consideration of the issue, the Court unanimously found there to be no violation of Article 8. What is missing from this judgment is any recognition of the complexity of the concept of 'family' in the light of care placements, adoption, and (although not relevant here) modern assisted reproduction techniques.

IMMIGRATION ISSUES AND PRIVATE LIFE

A comparatively recent development has been the extension of the Strasbourg Court's case-law on private life within Article 8 to offer a degree of protection to certain migrants.[189] Chapter 15 considered how the Court's case-law on family life provides a degree of protection against adverse immigration decisions where family life would be affected; it noted that in immigration questions, the notion of the core family has been introduced. In the *Slivenko* case,[190] the Grand Chamber acknowledged that removal of persons from a country had the capacity to adversely affect 'the network of personal, social and economic relations that make up the private life of every human being.'[191] The applicants were the wife and daughter of a former Soviet army officer of Russian origin who wished to remain in Latvia. The wife, Tatjana Slivenko, was born in 1959 in Estonia, and moved to Latvia at the age of one month; the daughter, Karina, was born in 1981 in Latvia. The husband served in the Russian army until 1994; he moved to Russia in 1996, but his wife and daughter remained in Latvia. The attempts of the wife and daughter to contest a deportation order were unsuccessful, and Tatjana and Karina moved to Russia in 1999 to join the father. Tatjana's parents remained in Latvia, and became seriously ill; the terms of the deportation order prevented Tatjana and Karina from entering Latvia for five years from 1996.

Tatjana Slivenko could not rely on family life (in relation to her relationship as an adult child with her parents), and so the case turned on the long-term residence with its establishment of a network of personal, social, and economic relations as the basis of the Court's decision that there had been a violation of Article 8. The Latvian authorities had overstepped the margin of appreciation, and the removal of Tatjana and Karina was not proportionate.

The *Sisojeva* case[192] also concerned Russian nationals living in Latvia.[193] The case was, however, not directly about deportation, since the Latvian authorities had given assurances that they would not proceed with deportation. The residence status of the applicants rested on a series of temporary residence permits; this, they argued, placed them in a position of insecurity and legal uncertainty which interfered with their private life. The Grand Chamber's decision was to strike the case out of the list in so far as it related to Article 8. The respondent State had offered to regularize the residence of the applicants by the time the Court came to consider the issue, but the Court's judgment makes it clear that the effects of uncertainty in relation to immigration status can interfere with private life, but

[189] This section draws on an analysis of this case-law in D. Thym, 'Respect for Private and Family Life under Article 8 ECHR in Immigration Cases: a Human Right to Regularize Illegal Stay?' (2008) 57 ICLQ 87.

[190] *Slivenko v Latvia*, (App. 48321/99), 9 October 2003 [GC], (2004) 39 EHRR 490, ECHR 2003-X. See generally G. Guliyeva, 'Lost in transition: Russian-speaking non-citizens in Latvia and the protection of minority rights in the European Union' (2008) 33 ELRev 843.

[191] § 96.

[192] *Sisojeva and others v Latvia*, (App. 60654/00), 15 January 2007 [GC], (2007) 45 EHRR 753, ECHR 2007-II.

[193] Though one of the applicants was stateless.

went on to observe that the Convention did not guarantee any right to a particular type of residence permit. That was a matter for the discretion of the Contracting Parties.[194]

Thym argues convincingly that these cases signal the Court's 'new readiness to extend the protective reach of Article 8 ECHR in the field of immigration'[195] and are not limited to the particular facts of Russian minorities in the Baltic States.

Article 8 may also be engaged when steps are taken to prevent someone from leaving a country. In the *Iletmiş* case[196] the applicant, who lived in Germany, was arrested in Turkey on a visit to his family members there. On his release, his passport was not returned to him. His wife and children were at the time in Germany; they left Germany to join him in Turkey. He was subsequently acquitted of the offences with which he had been charged. He complained that the retention of his passport which prevented him from leaving the country amounted to a violation of his private and family life under Article 8. The Strasbourg Court considered that this was a case concerning private life. Although preventive measures such as confiscation of a passport can constitute measures permitted by Article 8(2), there is always the requirement that the confiscation, and its continuation, are necessary in a democratic society. The confiscation in this case went on for far too long. The Court observed:

> At a time when freedom of movement, particularly across borders, is considered essential to the full development of a person's private life, especially when, like the applicant, the person has family, professional and economic ties in several countries, for a State to deprive a person under its jurisdiction of that freedom for no reason is a serious breach of its obligations.[197]

A.A. v United Kingdom[198] involved an applicant who had arrived in the UK from Nigeria at the age of 13 and was convicted of rape at the age of 15. After serving two years detention, he obtained A-levels, and an undergraduate and postgraduate degree in the UK, while appealing against a deportation order. The Court found that deportation after his seven years at liberty would be disproportionate to the legitimate aim of prevention of crime. It should be noted, however, that the finding of a violation in this case is due to its exceptional facts and private life issues do not normally weigh heavily in the balance where deportation is considered to be conducive to the public interest.[199]

HEALTH AND MEDICAL PROCEDURES

The right to respect for private life also encompasses a right to be informed about health risks to which persons have been exposed, and issues relating to access to particular medical procedures. It will also cover the use of medical procedures to which the person has not consented, but this generally falls under the heading of freedom from interference with the person discussed earlier in this chapter. Issues can also arise in relation to consent by a parent to the medical treatment of a child.

[194] § 91. See also *Kaftailova v Latvia*, (App. 59643/00), 7 December 2007 [GC]; and *Shevanova v Latvia*, (App. 58822/00), 7 December 2007 [GC].

[195] D. Thym, 'Respect for Private and Family Life under Article 8 ECHR in Immigration Cases: a Human Right to Regularize Illegal Stay?' (2008) 57 ICLQ 87, 111.

[196] *Iletmiş v Turkey*, (App. 29871/96), 6 December 2005, ECHR 2005-XII.

[197] § 50.

[198] *A.A. v United Kingdom*, (App. 8000/08), 20 September 2011.

[199] Compare, for example, *MS v United Kingdom* (dec), (App. 56090/08), 16 October 2012.

The *Glass* case[200] concerned disputes which arose between doctors and the mother of a severely mentally and physically disabled child. The mother had made it clear that she was opposed to the admission of morphine or diamorphine to her son, which the doctors considered necessary to relieve distress when they considered that he was in the terminal phase of respiratory failure. Such medication was administered despite her opposition. The Strasbourg Court concluded that the decision to impose treatment in the face of the mother's objections constituted an interference with respect for the child's private life, and, in particular, his right to physical integrity. The interference had not been necessary in a democratic society since the hospital could have made, but failed to make, an early application to the courts for their determination of whether the administration of such powerful medication was in the best interests of the child.

Even more disturbing are cases involving the sterilization of women of Roma origin, where doubts exist in the circumstances of the case whether the consent to sterilization was properly given.[201] In *V.C. v Slovakia*,[202] the applicant was sterilized in a public hospital immediately after giving birth. The doctors considered the procedure to be necessary, as a future pregnancy entailed serious risks to her life and that of her child. The applicant was a mentally competent adult patient, therefore her informed consent was needed and she was asked to give her consent in writing two and a half hours after she had been brought to hospital, when she was in the process of labour. She was not fully informed and was given no chance to reflect. The Court regarded such an approach as 'not compatible with the principles of respect for human dignity and human freedom embodied in the Convention'.[203] In light of its finding that the sterilization was in breach of the applicant's rights under Article 3 of the Convention, the Court did not consider it necessary to examine this complaint separately under Article 8. Nonetheless, it did consider whether Slovakia had complied with its positive obligation under Article 8 to put in place effective legal safeguards to protect the reproductive health of women of Roma origin in particular, and found a violation in this regard.

Abuse of mental health procedures will also engage Article 8. In a case with unedifying facts involving the use of mental health procedures to remove a person's legal capacity so that the mother could claim possession of property the applicant had inherited from his grandmother,[204] the Strasbourg Court found a violation of the right to respect for private life arising from the failure of the proceedings in which the applicant's mental capacity was considered to afford him protection.

It will be hard to establish a violation of Article 8 in respect of a denial of specific medical treatment. In *Hristozov and others v Bulgaria*[205] the applicants argued that the authorities' refusal to give them authorization to use an experimental anti-cancer product limited their capacity to choose, in consultation with their doctors, the way in which they should be medically treated with a view to possibly prolonging their lives. The product had not been authorized in any country, but had been allowed for so-called 'compassionate use' in a number of countries. The Court described the interest at stake for the applicants as 'the freedom to opt, as a measure of last resort, for an untested treatment which may carry risks but which the applicants and their doctors consider appropriate to their circumstances, in an attempt to save their lives'.[206] It recognized countervailing public interests,

[200] *Glass v United Kingdom*, (App. 61827/00), 9 June 2004, (2004) 39 EHRR 341; ECHR 2004-II.

[201] *KH and others v Slovakia*, (App. 32881/04), 28 April 2009, (2009) 49 EHRR 857.

[202] *V.C. v Slovakia*, (App. 18968/07), 8 November 2011, ECHR 2011 (extracts).

[203] § 112.

[204] *Shtukaturov v Russia*, (App. 44009/05), 27 March 2008, ECHR 2008.

[205] *Hristozov and others v Bulgaria*, (App. 47039/11 and 358/12), 13 November 2012, ECHR 2012 (extracts).

[206] § 120.

however, and thought it appropriate that a wide margin of appreciation should be given to the State especially as regards the detailed rules it lays down with a view to achieving a balance between competing public and private interests. Bulgaria had not exceeded that wide margin of appreciation in determining that medicinal products which have not been authorized in Bulgaria, could only be used if those products had already been authorized in another country.[207] There was no violation of Article 8, nor of Articles 2 or 3, indicating how reluctant the Court is to intervene on issues such as this.

In the *Guerra* case,[208] the Strasbourg Court found a violation of a positive obligation to provide information to local residents of the dangers to those living about one kilometre away from a factory producing fertilizers which had been classified as presenting a high risk of causing severe environmental pollution with attendant health hazards. There is, in such circumstances, a positive obligation of the State to provide essential information which would enable individuals to assess the risks they and their families might face if they continued to live so close to the source of the risk. This principle of entitlement of access to information has been extended to a general entitlement of access to medical records, which may only be curtailed in clearly defined and justifiable circumstances.[209]

Access to records and to personal information may well prove to be an area where the requirements of Article 8 increasingly impose positive obligations on a Contracting Party. An interesting set of circumstances was presented to the Court in the *McGinley and Egan* case.[210] The applicants had been stationed on or near Christmas Island and took part in the line-up procedure during atmospheric nuclear tests.[211] They sought increases of their war pensions on the basis that they had developed medical conditions caused by their exposure to radiation. They believed that documents in the possession of the Government would assist them, but were refused access to them. They claimed that non-disclosure of records constituted an unjustifiable interference with their private lives. The Court concluded that Article 8 did apply:

> Where a Government engages in hazardous activities, such as those in issue in the present case, which might have hidden adverse consequences on the health of those involved in such activities, respect for private and family life under Article 8 requires that an effective and accessible procedure be established which enables such persons to seek all relevant and appropriate information.[212]

There was, however, in this case no violation, since there was a procedure under the Pensions Appeal Tribunal Rules of Procedure under which the applicants could have requested the documents which had not been used.[213]

[207] The Dissenting Opinion of Judge De Gaetano joined by Judge Vučinić made the sensible point that, while matters of resource allocation in health care policy are within the margin of appreciation of the domestic authorities, the issue in the present case was a considerably narrower one: 'The applicants were not calling upon the State to pay for this treatment…They were simply asking for the State to "get out of the way" and allow them access to an experimental product which would be provided to them free of charge. In the instant case, therefore, the Court should have determined the applicable margin of appreciation by reference to factors that are more specific to the situation at hand…and in particular to the applicants' critical medical condition and the available prognosis.' (§ 3).

[208] *Guerra and others v Italy*, (App. 14967/89), 19 February 1998, (1998) 26 EHRR 357, ECHR 1998-I.

[209] *KH and others v Slovakia*, (App. 32881/04), 28 April 2009, (2009) 49 EHRR 857.

[210] *McGinley and Egan v United Kingdom*, (Apps. 21825/93 and 23414/94), 9 June 1998, (1999) 27 EHRR 1, ECHR 1998-III; ECHR 2000-I (revision).

[211] Service personnel were ordered to line up in the open and to face away from the explosions with their eyes closed and covered until twenty seconds after the blast.

[212] *McGinley and Egan v United Kingdom*, (Apps. 21825/93 and 23414/94), 9 June 1998, (1999) 27 EHRR 1, ECHR 1998-III; ECHR 2000-I (revision), § 101.

[213] A subsequent request for revision on the basis that the procedure under the Pensions Appeal Tribunal rules would not have secured the relevant documents failed by five votes to two: see *McGinley and Egan v United Kingdom*, (Apps. 21825/93 and 23414/94) (Revision request), 28 January 2000; ECHR 2000-I.

The *Roche* case[214] concerned a former soldier who developed health problems which he believed to be related to his participation in 1962 and 1963 in tests at a military defence establishment working on chemical weapons of various kinds. He complained that his difficulties in getting access to information about the tests raised issues under Article 8. In the particular circumstances of this case, the Grand Chamber was unanimous in concluding that there had not been:

> an effective and accessible procedure enabling the applicant to have access to all relevant and appropriate information that would allow him to assess any risk to which he had been exposed....[215]

REPRODUCTIVE RIGHTS

The question of whether a foetus enjoys the protection of the right to life under Article 2 remains undecided. It is not surprising, therefore, that there have been an increasing number of challenges to States' regulation of abortion under Article 8's right to respect for private life.[216] Curiously, the Court seems to share the Commission's confusing approach to the question of whether pregnancy is a private issue. In the 1977 case of *Bruggemann and Scheuten v Germany*, the European Commission of Human Rights held that 'pregnancy cannot be said to pertain uniquely to the sphere of private life.' In the Commission's view, not every regulation of abortion amounted to an interference with the right to respect for private life of the mother, resulting in the unsatisfactory position that pregnancy is to be regarded under the ECHR as an aspect of, but not solely of, a woman's private life. The Court has confirmed this approach in a number of cases, most recently reiterating in the *A, B, C* case that that 'Article 8 cannot be interpreted as meaning that pregnancy and its termination pertain uniquely to the woman's private life as, whenever a woman is pregnant, her private life becomes closely connected with the developing foetus.'[217] This approach appears markedly different from the Court's usual approach of recognizing that an interference falls within the concept of private life and then considering whether it is justified under Article 8(2) due to competing public interests.

In *Tysiąc v Poland*[218] the applicant's pregnancy (her third) and delivery constituted a risk to her eyesight. She wished to have the pregnancy terminated for this reason, but she was unable to persuade doctors to approve this. In Poland, medical terminations of pregnancy remain a criminal offence save for certain exceptions which include danger to the mother's life or health. She had the child and her eyesight deteriorated badly after the delivery. The Strasbourg Court found that the operation of the national legislation failed to distinguish between cases where there is full agreement between the woman and the doctors, and cases where there is no agreement; there was no particular and timely procedural framework for resolving differences of opinion. This created for the applicant a situation of prolonged uncertainty. A violation of Article 8 was found by six votes to one. The case is significant in terms of procedural obligations in respect of abortion. The next case to reach the Court raised both procedural and substantive complaints.

214 *Roche v United Kingdom*, (App. 32555/96), 19 October 2005 [GC], (2006) 42 EHRR 599, ECHR 2005-X.

215 § 167.

216 For an interesting review of the recent cases, see D. Fenwick, '"Abortion Jurisprudence" at Strasbourg: Deferential, Avoidant and Normatively Neutral?' [2013] *Legal Studies* 1.

217 *A, B and C v Ireland*, (App. 25579/05), 16 December 2010 [GC], ECHR 2010, § 213. See also *Tysiąc v Poland*, (App. 5410/03), 20 March 2007, (2007) 45 EHRR 947, ECHR 2007-IV; *Vo v France*, (App. 53924/00), 8 July 2004 [GC], (2005) 40 EHRR 259, ECHR 2004-VIII.

218 *Tysiąc v Poland*, (App. 5410/03), 20 March 2007, (2007) 45 EHRR 947, ECHR 2007-IV.

In *A, B and C v Ireland*[219] the three applicants had all obtained abortions in the UK due to being unable to do so in Ireland. The first two applicants complained under Article 8 about the prohibition of abortion for health and well-being reasons in Ireland while the third applicant complained about the failure to implement the constitutional right to an abortion in Ireland in the case of a risk to the life of the woman.

In respect of the first two applicants, the key question for the Court was whether the criminal prohibition of abortion, for all reasons other than a risk to the woman's life, was a violation of Article 8's right to respect for private life. The Court acknowledged that 'the acute sensitivity of the moral and ethical issues raised by the question of abortion' tended to suggest that a wide margin would be appropriate, but it noted that a European consensus on the issue would negate this conclusion. The Court found that there was 'indeed a consensus amongst a substantial majority of the contracting States of the Council of Europe towards allowing abortion on broader grounds than accorded under Irish law'.[220] However, in a surprising departure from its previous practice, the Court did not use that emerging consensus to narrow the width of the margin to be accorded to Ireland. This is because it found the consensus to be specific to the issue of the availability of abortion and held that there was still no consensus on when life begins. Therefore, the Court felt justified in offering Ireland a wide margin of appreciation to determine the extent to which it would protect the right to life of the unborn.

Six judges dissented on this point[221] arguing that the lack of consensus on when life begins is not pertinent to the case. They argue that the fact that the Court acknowledged a consensus on the balancing of the right to life of the foetus with the rights of the mother should have significantly reduced Ireland's margin of appreciation. These dissenting judges point out that this case is 'the first time that the Court has disregarded the existence of a European consensus on the basis of "profound moral views"'. They argue that to consider that such moral views 'can override the European consensus, which tends in a completely different direction, is a real and dangerous new departure in the Court's case-law.'[222]

In light of the wide margin granted to Ireland, the Court concluded that the prohibition of abortion on health and well-being grounds was consistent with Article 8 because there is a right to lawfully travel abroad for an abortion, and the prohibition is based on 'the profound moral views of the Irish people as to the nature of life'.[223] The apparent contradiction in these two points is ignored by the Court.

The third applicant's complaint was analysed under the positive obligation aspect of Article 8. The question for the Court was whether there existed a positive obligation on Ireland to provide an effective and accessible procedure allowing the third applicant to establish her entitlement to a lawful abortion. While there was a constitutional acknowledgment of the legality of an abortion to save the mother's life, there had been no legislative implementation of that exception to the general prohibition of abortion and the Court was not convinced that either a constitutional action nor an ordinary medical consultation process sufficed. In the Court's view, the lack of legislative implementation of the risk to life exception had resulted 'in a striking discordance between the theoretical right to a lawful abortion in Ireland on the grounds of a relevant risk to a woman's life and the reality of its practical implementation.'[224]

[219] *A, B and C v Ireland*, (App. 25579/05), 16 December 2010 [GC], ECHR 2010. See E. Wicks, '*A, B, C v Ireland*: Abortion Law under the European Convention on Human Rights' (2011) 11 HRLR 556.

[220] § 235.

[221] Judges Rozakis, Tulkens, Fura, Hirvelia, Malinverni, and Poalelungi.

[222] § 9 of dissenting opinion.

[223] § 241.

[224] § 164.

It is clear, therefore, that Article 8 not only requires a State to refrain from interference with a woman's right to make her own choices about pregnancy which cannot be justified under Article 8(2), but also to ensure that an effective and accessible procedure is in place so that a pregnant woman can realistically exercise all of the options lawfully open to her. The issue of the appropriate balance between protection of the foetus and respect for a pregnant woman's self-determination, and health, remains one on which a wide margin of appreciation is given to States. Arguably, however, the recognition of a European consensus in this case hints at a more interventionist Court in future abortion cases.[225]

Two further cases on abortion, both involving Poland, have been considered by the Court under Article 8. In *R.R. v Poland*[226] the applicant complained that her right to respect for her private life, specifically her psychological and moral integrity, had been violated by the Polish authorities' failure to provide her with access to genetic tests to determine whether the foetus was affected with a genetic disorder and also by the absence of a comprehensive legal framework to guarantee her rights. The Court considered the case as one concerning the State's positive obligations, despite its acknowledgment in the *A, B, C* case that prohibition of the termination of pregnancies sought for reasons of health and/or well-being can amount to an interference with the right to respect for private life. In *R.R.*, the Court took the view that it was not access to abortion as such which was primarily in issue, but rather timely access to a medical diagnostic service that would make it possible to determine whether the conditions for lawful abortion existed. The Court also distinguished this case from other cases where the applicants complained about denial of access to certain health services for reasons of insufficient funding or availability. No objective reasons had been given as to why the genetic tests were not carried out immediately after the suspicions as to the foetus' condition had arisen but only after a lengthy delay. Polish legislation permitted an abortion to be carried out before the foetus is capable of surviving outside the mother's body if prenatal tests or other medical findings indicate a high risk that the foetus will be severely and irreversibly damaged or suffer from an incurable life-threatening ailment. Therefore, the Court recognized that access to full and reliable information on the foetus' health was a necessary prerequisite for a legally permitted possibility to have an abortion to arise. This led the Court to reiterate its finding in *Tysiąc* that once the State has adopted statutory regulations allowing abortion in some situations, it must not structure its legal framework in a way which would limit real possibilities to obtain it: 'if the domestic law allows for abortion in cases of foetal malformation, there must be an adequate legal and procedural framework to guarantee that relevant, full and reliable information on the foetus' health is available to pregnant women.'[227]

Polish regulation of abortion was again challenged in *P. and S. v Poland*.[228] In this case, the applicants complained about the absence of a comprehensive legal framework guaranteeing timely and unhindered access to abortion under the conditions set out by the applicable laws. The first applicant was a minor who was pregnant following a rape. The Court identified the difficulties she had faced in obtaining an abortion:

> The events surrounding the determination of the first applicant's access to legal abortion were marred by procrastination and confusion. The applicants were given misleading and

[225] Compare the Court's approach in the transsexual cases: *Rees v United Kingdom*, (App. 9532/81), 17 October 1986, Series A No 106, (1987) 9 EHRR 56; *Cossey v United Kingdom*, (App. 10843/84), 27 September 1990, Series A No 184, (1991) 13 EHRR 622; *Sheffield and Horsham v United Kingdom* (Apps. 22885/93 and 23390/94), 30 July 1998, (1999) 27 EHRR 163, ECHR 1998-V; *Goodwin v United Kingdom*, (App. 28957/95), 11 July 2002 [GC], (2002) 35 EHRR 447; ECHR 2002-VI; and *I v United Kingdom*, (App. 25680/94), 11 July 2002 [GC], (2003) 36 EHRR 967.

[226] *R.R. v Poland*, (App. 27617/04), 26 May 2011, ECHR 2011 (extracts).

[227] § 200.

[228] *P. and S. v Poland*, (App. 57375/08), 30 October 2012.

> contradictory information. They did not receive appropriate and objective medical counselling which would have due regard to their own views and wishes. No set procedure was available to them under which they could have their views heard and properly taken into consideration with a modicum of procedural fairness.[229]

The Court concluded that effective access to reliable information on the conditions for the availability of lawful abortion, and the relevant procedures to be followed, is directly relevant for the exercise of personal autonomy, and thus found that the Polish authorities had failed to comply with their positive obligations under Article 8.[230]

Beyond the medical termination of pregnancy, other issues involving reproductive rights have come before the Court under Article 8. *Evans v United Kingdom* concerned a potential right to reproduce.[231] In this case, the Grand Chamber acknowledged that respect for private life 'incorporates the right to respect for both the decisions to become and not to become a parent.'[232] Natalie Evans wished to have children; her partner at the time also wished to have children by her. It was discovered that she had ovarian tumours for which the treatment was the removal of her ovaries with the consequence that she would be unable to have children. The couple decided to create and freeze embryos for later use. The relationship subsequently broke down, and the partner decided that he no longer wished the embryos to be used. Where consent is withdrawn, the embryos must be destroyed. Natalie Evans sought to have the embryos preserved, since this was her only opportunity of becoming a biological parent.[233] She argued that there was a breach of her Article 8 rights to respect for her private life in the requirement for continuing consent by the man for the use of the embryos.

The Grand Chamber by thirteen votes to four concluded that there was no violation of Article 8. The position under national law was clear; both parties had been made aware of the regime when they undertook the creation of the embryos. There was a clash of rights here: between respect for the private life of the woman to choose to become pregnant, and the private life of the man to choose not to become a parent with a woman with whom his relationship had ended. The Strasbourg Court was clearly aware of the dilemma, but, in the absence of a uniform approach among the Contracting Parties, and in the face of a clear scheme which had been put to both the man and the woman, concluded that the national legislation (which had been the product of much reflection, consultation, and debate) struck a reasonable balance between the competing interests at stake. The Grand Chamber has confirmed in *S.H. and others v Austria*[234] that the right of a couple to conceive a child and to make use of medically assisted procreation for that purpose is protected by Article 8, as such a choice is an expression of private and family life. A wide margin of appreciation will be appropriate.

Ternovszky v Hungary[235] concerned the circumstances of giving birth. The applicant complained that the ambiguous legislation on home birth dissuaded health professionals from assisting her when giving birth at home, which amounted to a discriminatory

[229] § 108.

[230] The Court also found a violation of Article 8 in respect of the public disclosure of information about the applicants' case which was neither lawful nor served a legitimate interest.

[231] *Evans v United Kingdom*, (App. 6339/05), 10 April 2007 [GC], (2008) 46 EHRR 728, ECHR 2007-IV; see also M. Ford, 'Evans v United Kingdom: what implications for the jurisprudence of pregnancy?' (2008) 8 HRLRev 171.

[232] § 71.

[233] As noted in ch.2, the Strasbourg Court ordered interim measures to preserve the embryos pending the determination of the case before the Strasbourg Court.

[234] *S.H. and others v Austria*, (App. 57813/00), 3 November 2011 [GC], ECHR 2011. The case is discussed in more detail in ch.15 under the topic of family life.

[235] *Ternovszky v Hungary*, (App. 67545/09), 14 December 2010.

interference with her right to respect for her private life. The Court confirmed that 'the circumstances of giving birth incontestably form part of one's private life'[236] and the State must ensure a proper balance between societal interests and individual rights. In the context of home birth, this implies that the mother is entitled to a legal and institutional environment that enables her choice, except where other rights render necessary the restriction thereof. The Court concluded that the matter of health professionals assisting home births was surrounded by legal uncertainty in Hungary and prone to arbitrariness. The situation was therefore incompatible with the notion of 'foreseeability' and hence with that of 'lawfulness' under Article 8(2).

ASSISTED DYING

Issues relating to euthanasia and assisted suicide have also been argued under Article 8. In the *Pretty* case,[237] the applicant was concerned that her husband should be immune from prosecution if he were to assist her suicide, and sought to challenge the blanket ban on assisted suicide in the United Kingdom. Although the Strasbourg Court found no violation of respect for the right to private life having regard to the limitations set out in Article 8(2),[238] it did observe:

> The applicant in this case is prevented by law from exercising her choice to avoid what she considers will be an undignified and distressing end to her life. The Court is not prepared to exclude that this constitutes an interference with her right to respect for her private life as guaranteed under Article 8(1) of the Convention.

The Court has had opportunities to develop upon its comments in *Pretty* on the application of Article 8 to assisted suicide in three recent cases. In *Haas v Switzerland*[239] the applicant suffered from a serious bipolar disorder. He had twice attempted suicide unsuccessfully and sought to obtain 15 grams of sodium pentobarbital, which is available only on prescription, in order to end his life with the assistance of Dignitas. He was refused the lethal substance and claimed that his right to choose the time and manner of his death was not respected in contravention of Article 8.

The Court confirmed that an individual's right to decide by what means and at what point his or her life will end is one of the aspects of the right to respect for private life within the meaning of Article 8. However, it emphasized that this case did not concern the freedom to die and possible immunity for a person providing assistance with a suicide, as the *Pretty* case had done. Instead, the subject of dispute was whether the State must ensure that the applicant can obtain a lethal substance without a medical prescription, by way of derogation from the applicable legislation, in order to commit suicide painlessly and without risk of failure. The Court observed that, in contrast to the *Pretty* case, the applicant was not physically incapable of committing suicide and sought to impose upon the State a right to a more dignified suicide. The Court considered the applicant's request from the perspective of a positive obligation on the State to take the necessary measures to permit a dignified suicide. As the Convention must be read as a whole, it recognized the relevance of Article 2 in this context, which imposes a duty on State authorities to protect vulnerable

[236] § 22.

[237] *Pretty v United Kingdom*, (App. 2346/02), 29 April; 2002, (2002) 35 EHRR 1, ECHR 2002-III.

[238] Relying heavily on a State's margin of appreciation: see §§ 68–78.

[239] *Haas v Switzerland*. (App. 31322/07), 20 January 2011, ECHR 2011. See I. Black, 'Suicide Assistance for Mentally Disordered Individuals in Switzerland and the State's Positive Obligation to Facilitate Dignified Suicide' (2012) 20 Medical Law Review 157.

persons against actions by which they endanger their own lives. The Court clarified that it took the view that Article 2 'obliges the national authorities to prevent an individual from taking his or her own life if the decision has not been taken freely and with full understanding of what is involved.'[240] Therefore, it held that Article 2 obliges States to establish a procedure capable of ensuring that a decision to end one's life does indeed correspond to the free wish of the individual concerned and it considered that Switzerland's requirement for a medical prescription, issued on the basis of a full psychiatric assessment, was a means enabling this obligation to be met.[241] The Court also noted that such regulations 'are all the more necessary in respect of a country such as Switzerland, where the legislation and practice allow for relatively easy access to assisted suicide.'[242]

The lack of consensus across the Council of Europe with regard to an individual's right to decide how and when his or her life should end means that States will enjoy a considerable margin of appreciation in this area. Therefore, the Court concluded that, even assuming that the States have a positive obligation to adopt measures to facilitate the act of suicide with dignity, the Swiss authorities had not failed to comply with this obligation in the instant case. It should be noted, however, that despite mention of a wide margin of appreciation, the Court's judgment seems to set out a clear limitation on the facilitation of assisted dying, namely that safeguards must be put in place to ensure that the individual is making a free and informed choice about how to die.

The Court has had further opportunities to consider these challenging issues. In *Koch v Germany*,[243] the applicant's wife had suffered from total sensorimotor quadriplegia, which meant that she was almost completely paralysed and needed artificial ventilation and constant care and assistance from nursing staff. According to medical assessment, she had a life expectancy of at least fifteen more years but she wished to end her life by committing suicide with the applicant's help. She requested fifteen grams of pentobarbital of sodium from the German authorities to enable her to commit suicide at her home but was refused. Instead she and the applicant travelled approximately ten hours to Switzerland and she died there with the assistance of Dignitas. The applicant alleged that the refusal to grant his late wife authorization to acquire a lethal dose of drugs violated his right to respect for private and family life and he further complained about the domestic courts' refusal to examine the merits of his complaint. The Court found that the German courts had refused to examine the merits of the applicant's motion on the ground that he could neither rely on his own rights, nor did he have standing to pursue his late wife's claim after her death. The Court did not regard that refusal to examine the merits of the applicant's complaint as serving any legitimate interest under Article 8(2) and thus there was a violation of the procedural aspect of Article 8.

The issue of obtaining a lethal dose of sodium pentobarbital was again raised in *Gross v Switzerland*[244] where the Court found that the lack of guidelines as to whether and under which circumstances a doctor is entitled to issue a prescription for sodium pentobarbital to a patient who, like the applicant, is not suffering from a terminal illness was 'likely to have a chilling effect on doctors who would otherwise be inclined to provide someone such as the applicant with the requested medical prescription.'[245] The Court concluded that Swiss law, while providing the possibility of obtaining a lethal dose of sodium pentobarbital on medical prescription, did not provide sufficient guidelines ensuring clarity as to the extent of this right and there was therefore a violation of Article 8.

[240] § 54. [241] § 58. [242] § 57. [243] *Koch v Germany*, (App. 497/09), 19 July 2012.
[244] *Gross v Switzerland*, (App. 67810/10), 14 May 2013. [245] § 65.

The Court declined to offer any guidance on the substance of such guidelines and thus this series of cases on the States' obligations in respect of assisted dying remain somewhat ambiguous. As with the equally emotive question of abortion, the Court is more comfortable imposing procedural standards than seeking to impose substantive ones. There is now no doubt that choices about how to die, including seeking a dignified death by means of suicide, fall within the protection of Article 8 but States have a wide margin of appreciation, as well as conflicting obligations under the right to life, and thus it appears unlikely that a right to a specific means of death will be upheld under Article 8 in the foreseeable future.

PROTECTION OF ONE'S LIVING ENVIRONMENT

It seems that the use of Article 8 as a means of generating environmental rights is heavily circumscribed. The current position is perhaps best summed up in the words of the Strasbourg Court itself in the *Kyrtatos* case:

> ... according to its established case-law, severe environmental pollution may affect individuals' well-being and prevent them from enjoying their homes in such a way as to affect their private and family life adversely, without, however, seriously endangering their health.... Yet the crucial element which must be present in determining whether, in the circumstances of a case, environmental pollution has adversely affected one of the rights safeguarded by paragraph 1 of Article 8 is the existence of a harmful effect on a person's private or family sphere and not simply the general deterioration of the environment. Neither Article 8 nor any of the other Articles of the Convention are specifically designed to provide general protection of the environment as such; to that effect, other international instruments and domestic legislation are more pertinent in dealing with this particular aspect.[246]

A number of complaints arising from nuisance caused by adjacent commercial activity have been made under Article 1 of Protocol 1,[247] but a better basis for complaint may be Article 8.[248] In the *López Ostra* case[249] the applicant complained that the operations of a liquid and solid waste management plant operated by a group of tanneries twelve metres from her home which released 'gas fumes, pestilential smells and contamination' harmful to health violated respect for her home guaranteed by Article 8. The Strasbourg Court found that Article 8 was applicable and stressed the need to strike a fair balance between the competing interests of the individual and of the community as a whole. Despite the relatively wide margin of appreciation enjoyed by the State, this was a case where the level of nuisance borne by the applicant exceeded that which would be viewed as reasonable when weighing the competing interests.

The *Guerra* case[250] concerned the risks associated with the operation of a chemical factory producing fertilizer and other chemical compounds. The applicants all lived about a kilometre from the factory. The Court concluded that the direct effect of emissions from

[246] *Kyrtatos v Greece*, (App. 41666/98), 22 May 2003, (2005) 40 EHRR 390; ECHR 2003-VI, § 52.

[247] See ch.20.

[248] See Council of Europe, *Environmental Protection and the European Convention on Human Rights*, Human Rights File No. 21 (Council of Europe Publishing, Strasbourg 2005). See also Council of Europe, *Overview of the case-law of the European Court of Human Rights in environmental matters*, DH–DEV(2004)002rev; and Council of Europe, *Elements on the Protection of Human Rights and the Environment*, DH–DEV(2005)001.

[249] *López Ostra v Spain*, (App. 16798/90), 9 December 1994, Series A No 303-C, (1995) 20 EHRR 277. See also *Branduse v Romania*, (App. 6586/03), 7 April 2009 (smells from a tip).

[250] *Guerra and others v Italy*, (App. 14967/89), 19 February 1998, (1998) 26 EHRR 357, ECHR 1998-I.

the factory was that the applicants' private and family life was involved. This was, however, a case where a State's positive obligations were engaged; the question was whether the national authorities had taken the necessary steps to ensure effective protection of the applicants' rights under Article 8. The Court concluded that the failure of the authorities to provide timely information concerning the nature of the risks associated with the factory's activities denied the applicants the opportunity to assess the risks to themselves and their families if they continued to live close to the factory. There was accordingly a violation of Article 8.

In the *Fadeyeva* case[251] the Court concluded that the positive obligations under Article 8 might require a State to re-house those living close to industrial plants where the level of toxic emissions was shown to be hazardous to health.

Where an activity presents risks to the environment which might impact upon the personal lives of those living nearby, there must be a genuine and procedurally fair environmental impact assessment, otherwise there will be a failure to respect the private life of those persons.[252] Though the Strasbourg Court commonly states that Article 8 contains no explicit procedural requirements, it has read in a requirement for proper procedures in environmental cases. In the *Taşkin* case, it said:

> Where a State must determine complex issues of environmental and economic policy, the decision-making process must firstly involve appropriate investigations and studies in order to allow them to predict and evaluate in advance the effects of those activities which might damage the environment and infringe individuals' rights and to enable them to strike a fair balance between the various conflicting interests at stake.... The importance of public access to the conclusions of such studies and to information which would enable members of the public to assess the danger to which they are exposed is beyond question.... Lastly, the individuals concerned must also be able to appeal to the courts against any decision, act or omission where they consider that their interests or their comments have not been given sufficient weight in the decision-making process...[253]

The problems of aircraft noise were first raised before the Strasbourg Court under Article 8 in the *Powell and Rayner* case as possible violations of the right to respect for their private life and homes.[254] The Court noted that any violation of the Article would arise as a breach of the State's positive obligations since Heathrow Airport is not owned or operated by the State. Having regard to the measures taken to control night flights and noise from the airport, the Court concluded that there was no serious ground on which a violation of the UK's positive obligations could be maintained.

The *Hatton* case[255] also concerned complaints that the noise from night flights for those living in the vicinity of Heathrow Airport constituted a violation of their rights under Article 8, and was ultimately considered by a Grand Chamber. The Court considered that this was a case in which they had to consider whether the UK Government had met its positive obligations to take reasonable and appropriate measures to secure the applicants' rights under Article 8. The Court noted that the earlier cases in which environmental

251 *Fadeyeva v Russia*, (App. 55723/00), 9 June 2005, (2007) 45 EHRR 295, ECHR 2005-IV.

252 *Taşkin v Turkey*, (App. 46117/99), 10 November 2004, (2006) 42 EHRR 1127, ECHR 2004-X.

253 § 119. See also *Giacomelli v Italy*, (App. 59909/00), 2 November 2006, (2007) 45 EHRR 871, ECHR 2006-XII.

254 *Powell and Rayner v United Kingdom*, (App. 9310/81), 21 February 1990, Series A No 172, (1990) 12 EHRR 355.

255 *Hatton and others v United Kingdom*, (App. 36022/97), 8 July 2003 [GC], (2003) 37 EHRR 611; ECHR 2003-VIII. See also J. Hyam, '*Hatton v United Kingdom* in the Grand Chamber: One Step Forward, Two Steps Back?' [2003] EHRLR 632.

rights had been in issue turned on the failure of the State to comply with some aspect of the regime operating in the national legal order:

> ... in *López Ostra* the waste treatment plant at issue was illegal in that it operated without the necessary licence, and it was eventually closed down. In *Guerra*, too, the violation was founded on an irregular position at the domestic level, as the applicants had been unable to obtain information that the State was under a statutory obligation to provide.[256]

A distinguishing feature in the *Hatton* case was that the domestic regime had been tested in the national legal order and found to be compatible with it. The Strasbourg Court accepted that night flying would be in the interests of the economic well-being of the country as a whole, and rejected an approach in the context of environmental rights which would accord them a special status. Having regard to the balance of competing interests, the national authorities could not be said to have overstepped their margin of appreciation. No violation of Article 8 was found, reversing the decision of the Chamber. Five dissenting judges felt that the interpretation of the Convention as a living instrument required greater weight to be given to environmental protection in balancing the interests of the State and those of the individual:

> After all, as in this case, what do human rights pertaining to the privacy of the home mean if day and night, constantly or intermittently, it reverberates with the roar of aircraft engines?[257]

However, a failure by the authorities to police effectively noise nuisance caused by night clubs and bars in breach of the conditions under which they were permitted to operate, which prevents a person from sleeping and causes insomnia, will constitute a breach of Article 8.[258]

PROTECTION OF THE HOME

Many cases involving housing and the home will fall to be considered under Article 1 of Protocol 1.[259] But it is clear that aspects of security of tenure under landlord and tenant laws can involve issues touching on respect for the home.[260] The *McCann* case[261] illustrates the protection afforded. The applicant and his wife were tenants of a home rented to them by a local authority. The marriage broke down in circumstances where the husband was allegedly guilty of domestic violence. The wife and the children were re-housed, and the husband moved back into the home. The wife was then asked to end the joint tenancy by signing a notice to quit. She did this, but a week later sought to retract it; she had not appreciated that the effect would be to remove her former husband's right to live in the property. He said he needed the space to enable his children to visit. The local authority were reluctant to let him remain because of their policy not to assist those who had been involved in domestic violence. In possession proceedings, it was ruled that the applicant had no defence because of the termination of his tenancy as a result of the wife's notice to quit.

[256] § 120.

[257] Joint Dissenting Opinion of Judges Costa, Ress, Türmen, Zupančič, and Steiner, § 12.

[258] *Moreno Gómez v Spain*, (App. 4143/02), 16 November 2004, (2005) 41 EHRR 899, ECHR 2004-X. It is significant that the conduct which caused the difficulties was a breach of the conditions under which the night clubs and bars were permitted to operate.

[259] See ch.20.

[260] See *Larkos v Cyprus*, (App. 29515/95), 18 February 1999 [GC], (2000) 30 EHRR 597; ECHR 1999-I.

[261] *McCann v United Kingdom*, (App. 19009/04), 13 May 2008, (2008) 47 EHRR 913.

The Strasbourg Court found a violation of Article 8 because, under the summary eviction procedure, the applicant had lost his home in circumstances when he had no opportunity to have the proportionality of the measure determined by an independent tribunal. Where a person lacks legal capacity and her home is at risk, Contracting Parties must ensure that procedures affecting a person's home reflect the need to protect their interests. Specific justification would be required where a time limit operated to prevent a vulnerable person from participating effectively in proceedings under which she was deprived of her home. The principle of legal certainty would not be violated by very limited exceptions to the operation of time limits designed to serve the interests of legal certainty.[262]

The leading case on housing rights under Article 8 is the *Gillow* case.[263] Mr and Mrs Gillow sought to challenge under Article 8 the restrictive system of licences for the occupation of housing on Guernsey. The couple had acquired a house on Guernsey during a period of employment there, which had subsequently been let while the couple were working elsewhere than Guernsey. They returned to occupy it, but were refused the requisite licence and were prosecuted and convicted for unlawful occupation under Guernsey law. The Strasbourg Court considered that there was an interference with respect for the home, which was in accordance with law. The legislation restricting who could live on the island was accepted as having a legitimate aim. Was the interference necessary in a democratic society? The Strasbourg Court concluded that on its terms, there was no violation of Article 8 as far as the contested legislation *per se* was concerned. But the Court went on to consider whether the manner of its application to Mr and Mrs Gillow violated Article 8. On the particular facts of the case, the Court concluded that the refusal of both temporary and permanent licences to occupy their home and the conviction and fine imposed were disproportionate to the legitimate aim of the legislation and so constituted a violation of Article 8.

PROTECTION OF PRISONERS' CORRESPONDENCE

Article 8 has been used as a vehicle for addressing a number of prisoners' rights, particularly the rights of correspondence of those detained in prison.[264] 'Correspondence' refers primarily, but not exclusively, to communication in writing. Article 8 prohibits, subject to the exceptions in paragraph (2), any form of interference with correspondence, whether by censorship or otherwise. Prisoners' letters may be stopped or intercepted. There may be censorship of incoming and of outgoing letters. Or there may be a restriction on the number of letters that may be written. The subject may be treated in two parts: restrictions on the correspondence of prisoners, and other detained persons; and restrictions on correspondence with defence counsel. Often, of course, interference with prisoners' letters can be justified on one of the grounds stated in paragraph (2), as being necessary, for example, for the prevention of crime, or for the protection of the rights of others.[265]

The leading case is the *Golder* case.[266] Golder was serving a term of imprisonment for robbery. There was a riot in Parkhurst Prison and Golder was wrongly accused of being

[262] *Zehetner v Austria*, (App. 20082/02), 16 July 2009.

[263] *Gillow v United Kingdom*, (App. 9063/80), 24 November 1986, Series A No 109, (1989) 11 EHRR 335.

[264] See also European Prison Rules 1987; see generally N. Loucks, *Prison Rules: A Working Guide. The Millenium* [sic] *Edition* (Prison Reform Trust, London 2000).

[265] App. 3717/68, *X v Ireland*, 6 February 1970, (1970) 31 CD 96.

[266] *Golder v United Kingdom*, (App. 4451/70), 21 February 1975, Series A No 18, (1979–80) 1 EHRR 524.

involved in it. Certain letters he wrote concerning the consequences of the allegation were stopped by the prison governor because he had not raised his complaints internally first; his petition to the Home Secretary asking for a transfer and requesting permission to consult a lawyer with a view to bringing civil proceedings in respect of the allegations against him were rejected. The effect of this was to bar him from communicating with a lawyer about his complaints. The Strasbourg Court concluded that there was an interference with the applicant's correspondence, and went on to consider whether the interference could be justified under the second paragraph of Article 8. The issue was whether the interference was 'necessary' for one of the grounds set out in the paragraph. This must, said the Court, be considered 'having regard to the ordinary and reasonable requirements of imprisonment'.[267] The Court concluded that there was no justification for a restriction on Golder's right to communicate with a lawyer with a view to seeking advice in connection with possible civil proceedings.[268]

The position which appears to have emerged from the case-law is that freedom of correspondence for prisoners will be protected to a high degree. The Strasbourg Court requires the national law authorizing the interference to be drafted with precision in order to meet the requirement that the interference is in accordance with law.[269] The Court will also require the clearest evidence that the action taken is proportionate to the aim of the limitation of freedom of correspondence. Exceptional circumstances will need to be present before control can be exercised over correspondence between prisoners with serious medical conditions and their doctors.[270] Stopping or censoring letters containing what are regarded as derogatory remarks about the prison authorities will not be justified.[271] The position is neatly summarized in the words of the Court:

> The Court recognizes that some measures of control over prisoners' correspondence is not of itself incompatible with the Convention, but the resulting interference must not exceed what is required by the legitimate aim pursued.[272]

In the *Campbell* case[273] Campbell, who had been convicted of assault and murder and sentenced to life imprisonment with a recommendation that he serve not less than twenty years in prison, complained that his correspondence with his lawyer concerning a number of civil matters was opened and read by the prison authorities. The Strasbourg Court concluded that there had been an interference which was in accordance with law with the aim of preventing disorder or crime. Once again the consideration came down to determining whether the interference was necessary in a democratic society. The Court saw:

> no reason to distinguish between the different categories of correspondence with lawyers which, whatever their purpose, concern matters of a private and confidential character. In principle, such letters are privileged under Article 8.[274]

[267] § 45. See also *Campbell and Fell v United Kingdom*, (Apps. 7819/77 and 7878/77), 28 June 1984, Series A No 80, (1985) 7 EHRR 165.

[268] See also *Silver and others v United Kingdom*, (Apps. 5947/72, 6205/73, 7052/75, 7061/75, 7107/75, 7113/75, and 7136/75), 25 March 1983, Series A No 61, (1983) 5 EHRR 347.

[269] For examples of cases where the national law left the authorities too much latitude and so did not meet the requirement, see *Domenichini v Italy*, (App. 15943/90), 21 October 1996; *Petra v Romania* (App. 27273/95), 24 August 1998; and *Moiseyev v Russia*, (App. 62936/00), 9 October 2008.

[270] *Szuluk v United Kingdom*, (App. 36936/05), 2 June 2009, ECHR 2009.

[271] *Pfeifer and Plankl v Austria*, (App. 10802/84), 25 February 1992, Series A No 227, (1992) 14 EHRR 692.

[272] § 46.

[273] *Campbell v United Kingdom*, (App. 13590/88), 25 March 1992, Series A No 223, (1993) 15 EHRR 137.

[274] § 48.

The opening of mail might be justified to determine whether it contained any illicit enclosure, but that would not extend to reading the letter. This could be guaranteed by opening the letter in the presence of the prisoner. The reading of any letters between lawyer and prisoner could only be justified where the authorities have reasonable cause to believe that the privilege is being abused. In the *Campbell* case, the Court concluded that there was no pressing social need for the opening and reading of Campbell's correspondence with his solicitor.

It is vital to distinguish the different elements involved in 'control' of correspondence, and to differentiate quite clearly the grounds of exception permitted under Article 8(2).

Some aspects of the control of prisoners' correspondence would present no difficulties on this analysis. The stopping of a particular letter could obviously be justified in a particular case on one of the grounds mentioned in paragraph (2) (for example, 'for the prevention of crime') if the object of the letter were for example to effect an escape from prison. This in turn would justify, on the same ground, the reading by prison authorities of all letters, both incoming and outgoing. Finally, the fact that all letters may have to be read by prison authorities, who are responsible for good order in prisons, might in turn be said to justify the imposition of a limit to the number of letters which a prisoner may send or receive. In each case, however, the interference would have to be properly justified on one of the grounds stated in paragraph (2), and the reasons given by the authorities ascertained and assessed on this basis.

A clear legal justification for the interference will be essential. In *Mehmet Nuri Özen and others v Turkey*,[275] the prison authorities had refused to forward the applicants' letters to their addressees because they were unable to understand the letters written in Kurdish and were not prepared to pay for their translation into Turkish. The Court concluded that this interference with the applicants' correspondence was not in accordance with the law.

The correspondence of detained persons with their defence counsel is specially privileged. This follows from Article 6(3)(b) of the Convention which guarantees to everyone charged with a criminal offence the right to have adequate time and facilities for the preparation of his defence. This provision applies equally to proceedings on appeal.

The *Schönenberger and Durmaz* case[276] concerned the stopping of a letter from a lawyer instructed by the wife of Durmaz, who had been arrested and was being held in custody. Despite the letter's having been received, the district prosecutor kept it from Durmaz, who then had a lawyer assigned to him as an indigent. The lawyer's letter had urged Durmaz to make no statement to the authorities. The issue before the Court was whether the interference which had taken place was necessary in a democratic society. The respondent State argued that the stopping of the letter was necessary because the advice jeopardized the proper conduct of pending criminal proceedings by inviting the suspect not to make a statement. The Strasbourg Court noted that the advice contained in the letter did not amount to any exhortation to act unlawfully; it did not pose a threat to the normal conduct of the prosecution. Nor was it relevant that the lawyer had at the time of sending the letter been instructed by Durmaz's wife. The Court was unanimous in finding that there was a violation of Article 8.

In the case of *Piechowicz v Poland*,[277] the Court explained the importance of the lawyer-client correspondence:

[275] *Mehmet Nuri Özen and others v Turkey*, (Apps. 15672/08, 24462/08, 27559/08, 28302/08, 28312/08, 34823/08, 40738/08, 41124/08, 43197/08, 51938/08, and 58170/08), 11 January 2011.

[276] *Schönenberger and Durmaz v Switzerland*, (App. 11368/85), 20 June 1988, Series A No 137, (1989) 11 EHRR 202.

[277] *Piechowicz v Poland*, (App. 20071/07), 17 April 2012.

> the Court would recall that any person who wishes to consult a lawyer should be free to do so under conditions which favour full and uninhibited discussion. For that reason the lawyer-client relationship is, in principle, privileged. The Court has many times stressed the importance of a prisoner's right to communicate with counsel out of earshot of the prison authority. By analogy, the same applies to the authorities involved in the proceedings against him. Indeed, if a lawyer were unable to confer with his client without such surveillance and receive confidential instructions from him, his assistance would lose much of its usefulness, whereas the Convention is intended to guarantee rights that are practical and effective. It is not in keeping with the principles of confidentiality and professional privilege attaching to relations between a lawyer and his client if their correspondence is susceptible to routine scrutiny by individuals or authorities who may have a direct interest in the subject matter contained therein. The reading of a prisoner's mail to and from a lawyer should only be permitted in exceptional circumstances when the authorities have reasonable cause to believe that the privilege is being abused in that the contents of the letter endanger prison security or the safety of others or are otherwise of a criminal nature. What may be regarded as 'reasonable cause' will depend on all the circumstances but it presupposes the existence of facts or information which would satisfy an objective observer that the privileged channel of communication was being abused.[278]

In *Yefimenko v Russia*[279] the Court did not discern any justification for the routine inspection of the applicant's correspondence and found that the relevant provisions of Russian law failed to afford a measure of legal protection against arbitrary interference by public authorities with the applicant's right to respect for his correspondence. Furthermore, in relation to inspection of correspondence between the applicant and the Court, the Court recognized that 'it was incumbent on the national authorities to put in place a framework for avoiding any unjustified "chilling" effect on the effective exercise of a right of individual application before the Court and for avoiding the risk of various forms of direct or indirect influence on the prisoner impairing his opportunities to communicate with the Court.'[280] It concluded that Russia has failed to comply with its obligations under Article 34 of the Convention which imposes an obligation on a Contracting State not to hinder the right of the individual to present and pursue a complaint effectively with the Court.

CONCLUDING REMARKS

The range of rights protected under the umbrella of private life under Article 8 is now very wide indeed, and the range of rights may not yet be fully explored. Topical issues such as the use of social media, press intrusion,[281] and unprecedented levels of state surveillance[282] are likely to present difficult dilemmas to the Court over the next few years. The concept of a private life, free from interference from others, seems increasingly under threat and Article 8 is at the forefront of the Court's protection of individual freedom across Europe. The analysis offered in this chapter seeks to bring some coherence to a large body of case-law in a context where the Strasbourg Court continues to indicate that

[278] § 239.

[279] *Yefimenko v Russia*, (App. 152/04), 12 February 2013. A request for referral to the Grand Chamber is pending.

[280] § 164.

[281] See the Leveson Inquiry, its report, and the subsequent political and public debate about press regulation. The report can be read at: www.levesoninquiry.org.uk/about/the-report/

[282] Details of secret mass surveillance programmes run by the US and British governments was revealed by the whistleblowing of Edward Snowden in 2013. See: www.theguardian.com/world/the-nsa-files.

private life is not susceptible of an exhaustive definition. It is now abundantly clear that private life is not just about notions of privacy in its traditional sense. What does emerge is that the distinction between negative and positive obligations in this context is becoming increasingly blurred, and that the procedural dimension to decision-making affecting rights within the ambit of private life is taking on greater importance. Procedures in this context must offer an effective means for national authorities to consider and reflect upon the private life dimension to situations ranging from artificial insemination to permits for large-scale projects with the capacity to harm the environment.

17

FREEDOM OF THOUGHT, CONSCIENCE, AND RELIGION

INTRODUCTION

The Court frequently emphasizes the importance of the rights protected by Article 9. It has held that 'freedom of thought, conscience and religion is one of the foundations of a 'democratic society' within the meaning of the Convention.'[1] There are two aspects of this. First, particularly when it comes to religious belief, for the individual believer the freedom to believe and to worship may be the core element of his or her personality. Any unjustified interference with this right will have a detrimental effect on the individual concerned, requiring him or her to deny what he or she considers most important. In addition, it is important for the wider society to ensure that the right is safeguarded. Democracy, as understood within the Convention system, is about plurality and choice—the 'marketplace of ideas.' In a democracy, as a safeguard against the imposition of any one, totalitarian, viewpoint, we all need access to information and to a wide range of differing opinions. This applies to information and opinion about politics and other subjects of public interest, but also to information about more fundamental philosophical, religious and non-religious, explanations and approaches to life. As the Court said in its first judgment under Article 9, the right to freedom of religion 'is also a precious asset for atheists, agnostics, sceptics and the unconcerned. The pluralism indissociable from a democratic society, which has been dearly won over the centuries, depends on it.'[2] However, closer scrutiny of the case-law reveals that the Court's approach to what constitutes an interference with the right to manifest religion or belief, and when such an interference is justifiable, can be inconsistent and loosely reasoned.

Article 9 provides:

1. Everyone has the right to freedom of thought, conscience and religion; this right includes freedom to change his religion or belief and freedom, either alone or in community with others and in public or private, to manifest his religion or belief, in worship, teaching, practice and observance.
2. Freedom to manifest one's religion or beliefs shall be subject only to such limitations as are prescribed by law and are necessary in a democratic society in the interests of public safety, for the protection of public order, health or morals, or for the protection of the rights and freedoms of others.[3]

[1] *Kokkinakis v Greece*, (App. 14307/88), 25 May 1993, Series A No 260-A, (1994) 17 EHRR 397, § 31.

[2] *Kokkinakis v Greece*, (App. 14307/88), 25 May 1993, Series A No 260-A, (1994) 17 EHRR 397, § 31.

[3] See generally J-F. Renucci, *Article 9 of the European Convention on Human Rights. Freedom of thought, conscience and religion*, Human Rights Files No. 20 (Council of Europe Publishing, Strasbourg 2005); J. Murdoch, *Freedom of thought, conscience and religion: a guide to the implementation of Article 9 of the European Convention on Human Rights*, Human Rights Handbooks, No. 9 (Council of Europe Publishing, Strasbourg 2007); M. Evans, *Religious Liberty and International Law in Europe* (CUP, Cambridge 1998); and C. Evans, *Freedom of Religion under the European Convention on Human Rights* (OUP, Oxford 2001).

The freedoms guaranteed are closely related to the freedom of expression guaranteed by Article 10,[4] and to Article 11 since many religions and belief systems expect some form of community worship or association. Religious education, which is a subject of special difficulty, is dealt with by Article 2 of the Protocol 1.[5]

THE SCOPE OF ARTICLE 9

DEFINING RELIGION OR BELIEF

Article 9(1) protects two aspects of freedom of religion, belief and conscience: first, the right to believe whatever you want and freely to change your belief. This right is expressed, by the text of Article 9, to be absolute and unfettered. Secondly, Article 9 protects the right to manifest religion or belief, through worship, teaching, practice, and observance. Since the manifestation of religion or belief can have an impact on others, this right is qualified by paragraph 2 of Article 9. Virtually all the applications to the Court relate to alleged interferences with the right to manifest religion or belief, since the democratic State does not tend to get involved when it comes to what a person believes within the privacy of his or her mind.

The protection of Article 9 extends to a wide range of convictions and philosophies, not limited to, for example, religious belief. However, in the recent *Eweida* case, the Court confirmed that 'The right to freedom of thought, conscience and religion denotes views that attain a certain level of cogency, seriousness, cohesion and importance.'[6] This means that mere ideas or opinions will not constitute a belief. The borderline can frequently be difficult to draw, since belief is, of course, inherently subjective. In the *Pretty* case,[7] the Court rejected the applicant's argument that the threatened prosecution of her husband for assisting her suicide was an interference with her ability to manifest her belief in the notion of assisted suicide for herself. But the Court did not offer a definition of religion or belief; it merely said that not all opinions or convictions constitute beliefs in the sense protected by Article 9(1), and that her claims did not involve a form of manifestation of a religion or belief.[8]

Both the Commission and the Strasbourg Court have adopted a broad approach to what amounts to religions or beliefs. So the following have been accepted as religions or beliefs: Christian denominations of many kinds[9] including Jehovah's Witnesses[10] and the Salvation Army,[11] Judaism,[12] Islam,[13] Hinduism,[14] Sikhism,[15] and Buddhism.[16] Less mainstream belief systems have also been recognized, such as atheism,[17] Druidism,[18] the

[4] See *Otto-Preminger Institute v Austria*, (App. 13470/87), 20 September 1994, Series A No 295-A, (1994) 19 EHRR 34, § 47; and *Wingrove v United Kingdom*, (App. 17419/90), 25 November 1996, (1997) 24 EHRR 1, ECHR 1996-V, §§ 47–8.

[5] See ch.21.

[6] *Eweida and others v United Kingdom*, (App. 48420/10, 59842/10, 51671/10, and 36516/10), 15 January 2013, ECHR 2012 (extracts), § 81.

[7] *Pretty v United Kingdom*, (App. 2346/02), 29 April 2002, (2002) 35 EHRR 1, ECHR 2002-III.

[8] § 82.

[9] App. 11045/84, *Knudsen v Norway*, Decision of 8 March 1985, (1985) 42 DR 247.

[10] *Kokkinakis v Greece*, (App. 14307/88), 25 May 1993, Series A No 260-A, (1994) 17 EHRR 397; and *Manoussakis and others v Greece*, (App. 18748/91), 26 September 1996, (1997) 23 EHRR 387, ECHR 1996-IV.

[11] *Moscow Branch of the Salvation Army v Russia*, (App. 72881/01), 5 October 2006, (2007) 44 EHRR 912, ECHR 2006-XI.

[12] App. 10180/82, *D v France*, Decision of 6 December 1983, (1983) 35 DR 199.

[13] App. 16278/90, *Karaduman v Turkey*, Decision of 3 May 1993, (1993) 74 DR 93.

[14] App. 20490/92, *ISKCON and others v United Kingdom*, Decision of 8 March 1994, (1994) 76-A DR 41.

[15] App. 8121/78, *X v United Kingdom*, Decision of 6 March 1982, (1982) 28 DR 5, 38.

[16] App. 5442/72, *X v United Kingdom*, Decision of 20 December 1974, (1974) 1 DR 41.

[17] App. 10491/83, *Angelini v Sweden*, Decision of 3 December 1986, (1986) 51 DR 41.

[18] App. 12587/86, *Chappell v United Kingdom*, Decision of 14 July 1987, (1987) 53 DR 241.

Divine Light Zentrum,[19] and the Osho movement.[20] Even the controversial Church of Scientology has been accepted as falling within the scope of the Article.[21]

In one case involving a prisoner,[22] the Commission held that it did not have sufficient evidence to substantiate the applicant's claim to being a 'light worshipper' whose rights under Article 9 had been violated.[23] In another case where a prisoner applicant claimed that he was being denied the practice of the Wicca religion in prison, the question of the recognition of Wicca as a religion did not arise since the applicant had not mentioned any facts making it possible to establish the existence of the religion.[24] Evans comments on this case that it raises questions about when applicants can be expected to adduce evidence to establish that their claimed religion is a known religion, and what evidence the Commission (and now the Strasbourg Court) would find acceptable to sustain such a conclusion.[25] However, the Court has confirmed that 'the State's duty of neutrality and impartiality is incompatible with any power on the State's part to assess the legitimacy of religious beliefs or the ways in which those beliefs are expressed.'[26] Thus all religious ideas that are cogent and coherent—i.e. internally logical—and important to the individual—i.e. central to his approach to life—are protected. Issues of whether a religion should be characterized as a cult, for example, do not arise at this point and would only be relevant to questions of the proportionality of any interference.[27]

DEFINING A 'MANIFESTATION' OF RELIGION OR BELIEF

Freedom of thought, conscience, and religion includes freedom to manifest one's religion or belief.[28] The general right to freedom of thought, conscience, and religion protected by Article 9(1) is absolute. The manifestation of religion or belief is, however, subject to the limitations set out in paragraph (2), where 'necessary in a democratic society in the interests of public safety, for the protection of public order, health or morals, or for the protection of the rights and freedoms of others'. The dividing line between interferences with freedom of religion or belief and its manifestation is a fine one in some cases. All measures taken to impose restrictions on the manifestation of religion or belief must be in accordance with law, that is, have an identifiable legal basis and be sufficiently clear that persons will know how to regulate their behaviour.[29] In the past, the Strasbourg Court

[19] App. 8118/77, *Omkarananda and the Divine Light Zentrum v Switzerland*, Decision of 19 March 1981, (1981) 25 DR 105.

[20] *Leela Förderkreis E.V and others v Germany*, (App. 58911/00), 6 November 2008, (2009) 49 EHRR 117.

[21] App. 7805/77, *Pastor X and the Church of Scientology v Sweden*, Decision of 5 May 1979, (1979) 22 *Yearbook* 244; and *Church of Scientology Moscow v Russia*, (App. 18147/02), 5 April 2007.

[22] See later in this chapter for specific comment on prisoners and Article 9.

[23] App. 4445/70, *X v Germany*, Decision of 1 April 1970, (1970) 37 CD 119.

[24] App. 7291/75, *X v United Kingdom*, Decision of 4 October 1977, (1977) 11 DR 55.

[25] C. Evans, *Freedom of Religion under the European Convention on Human Rights* (OUP, Oxford 2001), 58.

[26] *Eweida and others v United Kingdom*, (Apps. 48420/10, 59842/10, 51671/10, and 36516/10), 15 January 2013, ECHR 2013 (extracts), § 81. See also *Manoussakis and others v Greece*, (App. 18748/91), 26 September 1996, (1997) 23 EHRR 387, ECHR 1996-IV, § 47.

[27] See later in this chapter.

[28] See P. Cumper, 'The public manifestation of religion or belief: challenges for a multi-faith society in the twenty-first century' in A. Lewis and R. O'Dair, *Law and Religion* (OUP, Oxford 2001), 311.

[29] For example of cases, where the Strasbourg Court decided that there was no foundation in law, see *Kuznetsov and others v Russia*, (App. 184/02), 11 January 2007, (2009) 49 EHRR 355 (interfering with a religious assembly of Jehovah's Witnesses); and *Igor Dmitrijevs v Latvia*, (App. 61638/00), 30 November 2006 (refusal to allow a prisoner applicant to attend the prison's religious services).

has tended to adopt a narrow view of the manifestation of religion or beliefs, so that only those manifestations which are the objectively necessary outward displays of the religion or beliefs have been protected.[30]

In the recent case of *Eweida*, however, the Court explained its current view:

> In order to count as a 'manifestation' within the meaning of Article 9, the act in question must be intimately linked to the religion or belief. An example would be an act of worship or devotion which forms part of the practice of a religion or belief in a generally recognised form. However, the manifestation of religion or belief is not limited to such acts; the existence of a sufficiently close and direct nexus between the act and the underlying belief must be determined on the facts of each case.[31]

Thus in this case, the Court had no hesitation in recognizing that a wish to wear a crucifix, and to do so openly, was a manifestation of religious beliefs. This approach to the issue of manifestation is a welcome development which avoids problematic issues of determining whether acts such as displaying a crucifix are required by Christian belief. There remains however much room for interpretation as to whether a close and direct nexus between the act and the belief can be based upon a purely subjective interpretation of religion.

A distinction must be drawn between the holding and communication of a belief, and acts motivated by the belief but not central to its expression. Thus, although pacifism has been held to fall within the scope of Article 9 as a belief, the Commission did not consider that an applicant was able to challenge her conviction and sentence resulting from the distribution of leaflets indicating opposition to the policy of the United Kingdom Government in Northern Ireland, since the leafleting 'did not manifest her belief in the sense of Article 9(1).'[32] In another case, the Commission received a complaint that a decision of the Market Court in Sweden, restricting the terms used in advertisements for the sale by the Church of Scientology of the Hubbard Electrometer, violated Article 9. The Hubbard Electrometer was described by the applicants as a religious artefact used to measure the electrical characteristics of the 'static field' surrounding the body. The Commission distinguished between words in publicity material related to the beliefs of the Church and words aimed at selling, which were not within Article 9(1) since they were 'more a manifestation of a desire to market goods for profit than the manifestation of a belief in practice.'[33]

Compliance with dietary laws is another aspect of the manifestation of religious belief, and was considered by the Strasbourg Court in the case of *Cha'are Shalom Ve Tsedek v France*.[34] The applicant association represented a group of ultra-orthodox Jews who refused to eat any meat which was not certified as '*glatt*', meaning that the animal had been ritually slaughtered and that the lungs had been examined for impurities. The French authorities authorized a number of slaughterhouses administered by a body representing the majority of Jews in France, which ensured that meat was prepared in such a way as to be kosher, but not '*glatt*', but the respondent State refused to allow the applicant to set up its own slaughterhouses. The Strasbourg Court found that, since '*glatt*' meat imported from Belgium was available in France, there had been no interference with the applicant

[30] This is most noticeable in the case-law relating to the religious freedom of prisoners, which is discussed later in this chapter.

[31] *Eweida and others v United Kingdom*, (Apps. 48420/10, 59842/10, 51671/10, and 36516/10), 15 January 2013, ECHR 2013 (extracts), § 82.

[32] App. 7050/75, *Arrowsmith v United Kingdom*, Decision of 12 October 1978 (1980) 19 DR 5.

[33] App. 7805/77, *Pastor X and the Church of Scientology v Sweden*, Decision of 5 May 1979, (1979) 22 *Yearbook* 244, 250.

[34] *Cha'are Shalom Ve Tsedek v France*, (App. 27417/95), 27 June 2000, ECHR 2000-VII.

association's members' right to freedom to manifest their religion. Arguably this factor would have been more pertinent to a proportionality determination than to the question of whether there was an interference.

Clearly, dismissing someone from employment[35] solely because of their religious beliefs will violate Article 9.[36] This will be an infringement of freedom of religion, rather than its manifestation. But Article 9 does not, of itself, give any entitlement to time off work for religious festivals. In the *Kosteski* case,[37] the applicant complained of a breach of Article 9 when he was fined for taking time off work to observe Muslim religious festivals. The accommodations at his place of work required him to substantiate his claims that he was a practising Muslim, and he had declined to do so. It was not disproportionate to make this requirement of him. Nor was it a breach of Article 9 when read with Article 14 (prohibiting discrimination), since it was not unreasonable to require him to substantiate his claim to be a practising Muslim. The Court adopted a similar approach in *Franceso Sessa v Italy*,[38] where the applicant was a lawyer who complained about the refusal to adjourn a hearing scheduled on a Jewish holiday. The Court was not convinced that this amounted to a restriction on the applicant's right to freely manifest his faith. The applicant had not shown that pressure had been exerted on him to change his religious belief or to prevent him from manifesting his religion or beliefs. Even if there had been an interference with the applicant's right guaranteed under Article 9(1), such interference had been justified on grounds of the protection of the rights and freedoms of others, and in particular the public's right to the proper administration of justice and the principle that cases be heard within a reasonable time.

The Strasbourg Court ruled as manifestly ill-founded a complaint that prosecution of pharmacists for refusing to supply contraceptives breached their right to manifest their religious beliefs. It was legitimate to limit the manifestation of religious beliefs in the professional sphere, and there was no evidence that the applicants could not manifest their religious beliefs without interference outside that sphere.[39] The position was clarified in the recent case of *Eweida and others v United Kingdom*.[40] The third applicant, Ms Ladele, was a registrar of births, deaths and marriages. As a Christian, she held the view that marriage is the union of one man and one woman for life and believed that same-sex unions are contrary to God's will. She refused to agree to be designated as a registrar of civil partnerships, and ultimately lost her job due to this refusal. The fourth applicant, Mr McFarlane, worked for Relate as a counsellor. He refused to commit himself to providing psycho-sexual counselling to same-sex couples, which also resulted in the loss of his job. The Court confirmed that these two applications involved a conflict of rights, namely the right of the applicants to manifest their religious beliefs and the rights of homosexuals to equal treatment, although the Court generally allows the national authorities a wide margin of appreciation when it comes to striking a balance between competing Convention rights. While no violation of Article 9 was found in respect of these two applicants, this recent case clarifies that an interference with the Article 9 right to manifest religious beliefs may arise within an employment context.

[35] Where that employment has no special characteristics which might be considered to warrant a narrower view.

[36] *Ivanova v Bulgaria*, (App. 52435/99), 12 April 2007, (2008) 47 EHRR 1173, ECHR 2007-IV.

[37] *Kosteski v the Former Yugoslav Republic of Macedonia*, (App. 55170/00), 13 April 2006, (2007) 45 EHRR 712.

[38] *Francesco Sessa v Italy*, (App. 28790/08), 3 April 2012.

[39] *Pichon and Sajous v France*, (App. 49853/99), Decision of 2 October 2001, ECHR 2001-X.

[40] *Eweida and others v United Kingdom*, (Apps. 48420/10, 59842/10, 51671/10, and 36516/10), 15 January 2013, ECHR 2013 (extracts). For discussion, see M. Pearson, 'Article 9 at a Crossroads: Interference Before and After *Eweida*' (2013) 13 HRLR 580.

In respect of the fourth applicant, the Court took into account that Mr McFarlane had voluntarily enrolled on Relate's post-graduate training programme in psycho-sexual counselling, while knowing that Relate operated an Equal Opportunities Policy and that it would not be possible to filter clients on the ground of sexual orientation. While this was not regarded as determinative of the question of whether there had been an interference, the Court did regard the applicant's decision to enter into a contract of employment and to undertake responsibilities which he knows will have an impact on his freedom to manifest his religious belief, as a matter to be weighed in the balance when assessing whether a fair balance was struck.[41] The joint partly dissenting opinion of Judges Vučinić and De Gaetano makes the point that there is an important distinction between Mr McFarlane who joined Relate knowing that it adopted an Equal Opportunities Policy, and Ms Ladele who was employed as a Registrar before civil partnerships were legalized.[42] The Court did not give any weight to this distinction, however, and thus it remains difficult to establish a violation of Article 9 for workplace requirements. One applicant in *Eweida* was successful in this context, however, and this will be discussed further in the section on religious dress and symbols.

PROSELYTISM

According to Article 9, freedom to manifest one's religion is not only exercisable in community with others, 'in public' and within the circle of those whose faith one shares, but can also be asserted 'alone' and 'in private'; furthermore, it includes in principle the right to try to convince one's neighbour, for example through 'teaching', failing which, moreover, 'freedom to change [one's] religion or belief', enshrined in Article 9, would be likely to remain a dead letter.[43] Note that there is no right to manifest conscience,[44] though most such claims could almost certainly be framed in terms of manifestation of beliefs. The case-law, discussed later in this chapter, concerning conscientious objection to military service may be classified in this way.

The applicants in the *Kokkinakis* case[45] were Jehovah's Witnesses engaged in evangelical activity, including calling at houses to persuade the occupiers to join them. They had the misfortune to call upon the wife of an Orthodox priest, who reported them to the police, since in Greece proselytism (defined as attempting to convert believers away from the Orthodox religion)[46] is a criminal offence. The applicants were arrested, charged, and subsequently convicted and fined.

The Strasbourg Court concluded that the Greek law against proselytism was sufficiently clearly drafted for the purposes of Article 9(2) and that it pursued the legitimate aim of protecting the rights and freedoms of others. This left consideration of whether the limitation was necessary in a democratic society. A fine distinction is made in this part of the majority's judgment. Bearing Christian witness—an interesting phrase—is described as

[41] § 109.

[42] This seems to be an important and relevant distinction, although the joint opinion is undermined by some regrettable comments that criticize the public authority for its approach 'which clearly favoured "gay rights" over fundamental human rights'. The dilemma is more accurately described as a conflict between two different fundamental rights.

[43] *Kosteski v the Former Yugoslav Republic of Macedonia*, (App. 55170/00), 13 April 2006, (2007) 45 EHRR 712.

[44] But see P. Edge, 'Current Problems in Article 9 of the European Convention on Human Rights' [1996] *Juridical Review* 42 which might be taken to suggest to the contrary.

[45] *Kokkinakis v Greece*, (App. 14307/88), 25 May 1993, Series A No 260-A, (1994) 17 EHRR 397.

[46] *Kokkinakis v Greece*, (App. 14307/88), 25 May 1993, Series A No 260-A, (1994) 17 EHRR 397.

true evangelism, and is contrasted with 'improper proselytism', described as 'a corruption or deformation of it which was not compatible with respect for freedom of thought, conscience and religion'. The Greek action violated Article 9 because there was no evidence that the applicants had attempted to convince the householder by improper means. The conviction was accordingly not justified by a pressing social need.

An example of what the Strasbourg Court considers 'improper proselytism' was provided by the *Larissis and others* case.[47] The applicants were officers in the Greek air force who were convicted of proselytism after complaints from soldiers under their command that they had attempted to persuade the soldiers to become Jehovah's Witnesses. The Court decided that the Greek authorities had been justified in taking measures to protect the junior airmen from the applicants, in view of the fact that the hierarchical and claustrophobic nature of life within the armed forces might make it difficult for a subordinate to rebuff the approaches of an individual of superior rank or to withdraw from a conversation initiated by him. There was a risk of indoctrination.

The Strasbourg Court emphasized that not every discussion about religion or other sensitive matters between individuals of unequal rank would justify a Contracting Party in taking repressive measures under Article 9(2). However, such justification would arise wherever there was evidence of harassment or the application of undue pressure in abuse of power.

Similar issues had arisen in the *Kalaç* case.[48] The applicant was a judge advocate in the Turkish air force. He was compulsorily retired partly on the grounds that his conduct and attitude 'revealed that he had adopted unlawful fundamentalist opinions.' The respondent State argued that his retirement did not constitute an interference with the applicant's freedom to practise his religion, but that his manifestation of his religious beliefs was, as a member of the armed forces, incompatible with the requirement for loyalty to the secular foundation of the Turkish State. The Strasbourg Court found no violation of Article 9. As a member of the armed forces, there were no limitations on his ability to 'fulfil the obligations which constitute the normal forms through which a Muslim practises his religion.'[49] A Contracting Party, however, remained free to regulate certain conduct which would not be objectionable outside the context of the hierarchy of the armed forces.

RELIGIOUS DRESS AND SYMBOLS

Schools are also hierarchical structures, and teachers are in a powerful position to influence the children in their charge. The applicant in the *Dahlab* case[50] was a teacher in a Swiss state school for four- to eight-year-olds. She converted to Islam and began wearing the Islamic headscarf to school. Although there was no evidence that she had spoken about religion to her pupils, the Strasbourg Court considered that the Swiss authorities were justified in forbidding her from wearing the Islamic headscarf at work, consistent with their policy of maintaining religious neutrality in schools. The Court held that seeing their teacher wearing the Islamic headscarf might have a 'proselytizing effect' on children at a young and impressionable age, and would transmit negative messages to them about lack of equality between the sexes. It does not appear to have given much weight to the argument that the experience of being taught by a woman in traditional Islamic dress

[47] *Larissis and others v Greece*, (Apps. 23772/94, 26377/94, and 23678/94), 24 February 1998, (1999) 27 EHRR 329, ECHR 1998-I.

[48] *Kalaç v Turkey*, (App. 20704/92), 1 July 1997, (1999) 27 EHRR 552, ECHR 1997-V.

[49] § 29.

[50] *Dahlab v Switzerland*, (App. 42393/98), Decision of 15 February 2001, ECHR 2001-V; *Dogru v France*, (App. 27058/05), 4 December 2008.

might have passed on to the children positive messages about the equality of different religious and cultural groups. The Court did not attempt to determine what it meant to the applicant to wear the headscarf or, for example, whether she would consider herself obliged to retire from her teaching post in the public sector if required to remove it. The balancing exercise for the proportionality test was, therefore, too one-sided.

The prohibition of wearing the Islamic headscarf in Turkish universities was raised in the *Leyla Şahin* case.[51] The applicant had been a medical student at Istanbul University. The Grand Chamber recognized the significance of secularism in Turkey, and recalled that, in countries where several religions coexist, it may be necessary to place restrictions on the manifestation of religious beliefs in order to reconcile the interests of different groups and to ensure that everyone's beliefs are respected. There was, accordingly, a need for a margin of appreciation in the regulation of the wearing of religious dress or symbols in teaching institutions. The Grand Chamber, in concluding that there was no violation of Article 9, said:

> ...it is the principle of secularism, as elucidated by the [Turkish] Constitutional Court..., which is the paramount consideration underlying the ban on the wearing of religious symbols in universities. In such a context, where the values of pluralism, respect for the rights of others and, in particular, equality before the law of men and women are being taught and applied in practice, it is understandable that the relevant authorities should wish to preserve the secular nature of the institution concerned and so consider it contrary to such value to allow religious attire, including, as in the present case, the Islamic headscarf, to be worn.[52]

It is trite to observe that different Contracting Parties adopt different approaches to the wearing of the Islamic headscarf.[53] But it can be argued that this decision is limited to the special circumstances in Turkey. That is not to be uncritical of the Strasbourg Court, which has failed to spell out exactly what the requirements of secularism are, and how the collective commitment to secularism can be balanced against the wish of some Muslim women to wear the headscarf as a symbol of their religious beliefs. The judgment of the Court in the *Leyla Şahin* case can be criticized for concluding that the wearing of the headscarf by an individual constitutes a form of indoctrinating others. These different views are taken up in the sole dissenting opinion in this case. Judge Tulkens considers that the judgment of the Court displays a lack of European supervision here, in the face of arguments by the applicant that she supported the principle of secularism and had no intention to challenge it by wearing a headscarf. The dissenting judge also observes that no other Contracting Party has a ban on wearing religious symbols which extends to higher education. Judge Tulkens is critical of the reasoning of the majority in linking the issue to one of sexual equality and notes that a decision of the German Constitutional Court had

[51] *Leyla Şahin v Turkey*, (App. 44774/98), 10 November 2005 [GC], (2007) 44 EHRR 99, ECHR 2005-IX. See also M. Evans, *Manual on the Wearing of Religious Symbols in Public Areas* (Strasbourg, 2009); A. Vakulenko, 'Islamic Dress in Human Rights Jurisprudence: A Critique of Current Trends' (2007) 4 HRLRev 717; and J. Marshall, 'Conditions for Freedom? European Humans Law and the Islamic Headscarf Debate' (2008) 30 HRQ 631. See also *Dogru v France*, (App. 27058/05), 4 December 2008, (2009) 49 EHRR 179; and *Kervanci v France*, (App. 31645/04), 4 December 2008.

[52] § 116. See also *Aktas ve France*, (App. 43563/08); *Bayrak v France*, (App. 14308/08); *Gamaleddyn v France*, (App. 18527/08); *Ghazal v France*, (App. 29134/08); *J Singh v France*, (App. 25463/08); and *R Singh v France*, (App. 27561/08); Decisions of 17 July 2009, all declaring applications concerning the wearing of conspicuous religious symbols to be manifestly ill-founded.

[53] See generally I. Gallala, 'The Islamic Headscarf: An Example of Surmountable Conflict between *Sharî'a* and the Fundamental Principles of Europe' (2006) 12 ELJ 593; and S. Langlaude, 'Indoctrination, Secularism, Religious Liberty and the ECHR' (2006) 55 ICLQ 929.

indicated that wearing the headscarf had no single meaning. It would be logical to argue (as Judge Tulkens observes) that, if sexual equality was at issue here, and if the wearing of the headscarf indicated the subordination of women, there would be a violation of equality principles by those Contracting Parties which did *not* ban the headscarf.

The issue of religious dress was considered again more recently in *Ahmet Arslan v Turkey*.[54] The applicants had received criminal convictions for wearing religiously prescribed clothing in a public place. The circumstances of this case were distinguished from those in *Şahin* in that this case involved private individuals dressing in a religious manner in a public street rather than in an official building and, unlike in *Şahin*, there was no question of proselytism or of pressure being exerted on others. The Court declined to give Turkey a wide margin of appreciation, as it had done in *Şahin* and found a violation of Article 9. Whether the Court will take the same position in respect of a ban on the wearing of the burka in public[55] remains to be seen but the return to a wide margin of appreciation in the context of religious dress worn by ordinary citizens in a public space will be hard to reconcile with the approach in *Ahmet Arslan*.[56]

Christian insignia have also been the subject of cases before the Strasbourg Court in recent years. In *Lautsi v Italy*[57] the applicant complained that her two children attended a State school in which a crucifix was displayed in every classroom and that this was contrary to the principle of secularism in which she wished to educate her children. In finding no violation of the Convention by Italy, the Grand Chamber focused entirely upon Article 2 of Protocol 1 rather than Article 9. The distinguishing of displaying crucifixes in a classroom from the wearing of an Islamic headscarf by a teacher in the earlier case of *Dahlab* has significant implications for future cases under Article 9, however. While the banning of the wearing of an Islamic headscarf by a teacher of young children was within the State's margin of appreciation in *Dahlab*, in *Lautsi* the Court was keen to assert that 'the presence of crucifixes is not associated with compulsory teaching about Christianity.'[58]

While it is certainly true that distinctions between different States will be appropriate due to the wide discrepancies in the role of religion across European States, and that the questions facing the Court were not the same in these two cases, there is arguably less difference between a teacher wearing an Islamic headscarf and a state school displaying crucifixes than is suggested in the Court's judgment. The number of interveners in this case, and the emphasis of many of them on the principle of subsidiarity, effectively illustrate the outcry with which the Chamber's earlier decision finding a violation in *Lautsi* had been met. The Court has to walk a very tight line between upholding freedom of religion and respecting the constitutional position of state religions. Ronchi observes that: 'Without engaging in a much clearer definition of what a passive symbol is, the court distinguishes between *Dahlab* and *Lautsi;* in so doing, it creates a sort of 'presumption of indoctrination' for the Islamic headscarf, whereas the crucifix, owing to its intrinsic nature as passive symbol, can be placed by public powers wherever they wish and this will never be considered as a form

[54] *Ahmet Arslan v Turkey*, (App. 41135/98), 23 February 2010.

[55] Such bans currently exist in France, Belgium, and the Netherlands. *S.A.S. v France*, (App. 43835/11), about the wearing of a burka in public, was scheduled to be heard by the Grand Chamber on 27 November 2013.

[56] For two interesting discussions of this point, see G. Van der Schyff & A. Overbeeke, 'Exercising Religious Freedom in the Public Space: a Comparative and European Convention Analysis of General Burqa Bans' (2011) *European Constitutional Law Review* 424 and M. Hunter-Henin, 'Why the French don't like the Burqa: Laicite, National Identity and Religious Freedom' (2012) ICLQ 613.

[57] *Lautsi v Italy*, (App. 30814/06), 18 March 2011 [GC], ECHR 2011 (extracts), 50 EHRR 42. For discussion, see B. Schlutter, 'Crucifixes in Italian Classrooms: *Lautsi v Italy*' [2011] EHRLR 715.

[58] § 74.

of indoctrination.'[59] This may overstate the point but it nevertheless highlights a potential, and troublesome, reading of the Grand Chamber's judgment in *Lautsi* which can only harm the Court's efforts to treat all religious beliefs across Europe with equal respect and tolerance.

The Court recently returned to the issue of crucifixes in the case of *Eweida and others v United Kingdom*[60] in which two applicants argued that their employer's ban on wearing crucifixes had infringed their right to manifest their religious belief as Christians. A further two applicants complained about sanctions taken against them by their employers as a result of their concerns about performing services which they considered to condone homosexual union. Ms Eweida worked for British Airways whose previous uniform policy prohibited the wearing of any jewellery, including a crucifix, on the outside of clothing. The company subsequently changed its policy. Ms Chaplin was a nurse employed by the Royal Devon and Exeter NHS Foundation Trust. Its uniform policy prohibited all necklaces on the grounds of health and safety. This factor proved crucial in the Court's reasoning. It found that this was a legitimate reason for restricting the second applicant's freedom to manifest her beliefs by means of wearing a cross on a chain and regarded this as a field where the domestic authorities must be allowed a wide margin of appreciation. The Court held that the 'hospital managers were better placed to make decisions about clinical safety than a court, particularly an international court which has heard no direct evidence.'[61] For Ms Eweida, however, the Court did find a violation of Article 9 on the basis that the domestic courts had not struck a fair balance between the applicant's desire to manifest her religious belief and British Airways' wish to project a certain corporate image. The Strasbourg Court held that the domestic courts accorded the company's aim too much weight. This conclusion was supported by the fact that exceptions had been made for other religious dress, such as turbans and hijabs, and by the fact that the company subsequently changed its policy.

MANIFESTATION OF RELIGION AND BELIEF BY PRISONERS

There have been a number of complaints by prisoners of interference with religious liberty. It remains doubtful how far a prisoner can claim under Article 9 facilities to practise a religion which is not generally practised in that Contracting Party. Where a British prisoner complained of the absence of the services of a Church of England priest in a German jail, the Commission appears to have considered that a German Protestant pastor might have been sufficient to comply with Article 9 in such a case.[62] The Commission stated that a refusal by the prison authorities to provide special food required by a religion which was not a religion usually practised in that State was permitted under Article 9(2).[63] Nor, in the Commission's opinion, did Article 9 impose any obligation to put at the disposal of prisoners books which they consider necessary for the exercise of their religion or for the development of their philosophy of life.[64] The Commission could, however, have considered this complaint under Article 10 of the Convention, or even under Article 2 of Protocol 1. In the same case, the applicant's complaint that the prison authorities had refused him

[59] P. Ronchi, 'Crucifixes, Margin of Appreciation and Consensus: the Grand Chamber ruling in *Lautsi v Italy*' (2011) *Ecclesiastical Law Journal* 287, 294.

[60] *Eweida and others v United Kingdom*, (Apps. 48420/10, 59842/10, 51671/10, and 36516/10), 15 January 2013, ECHR 2013 (extracts).

[61] § 99.

[62] App. 2413/65, *X v Federal Republic of Germany*, Decision of 16 December 1966, (1967) 23 CD 1, 8.

[63] Not published. See Case Law Topics No. 1, *Human Rights in Prison*, 31.

[64] App. 1753/63, *X v Austria*, Decision of 15 February 1965, (1965) 8 *Yearbook* 174, 184.

permission to grow a beard, as prescribed by his religion, was rejected under Article 9(2). The respondent State had submitted, somewhat curiously, that the refusal was justified as being necessary in order to be able to identify the prisoner. The decision is not satisfactory.

One application[65] concerned a Buddhist prisoner who was refused permission to send out articles for publication in a Buddhist magazine. He claimed that the exchange of ideas with his fellow Buddhists was an element in the exercise of his religion, and alleged a violation of Article 9. The Commission noted that the prison authorities had tried to find a Buddhist minister for him and, when they had been unable to do so, allowed him an extra letter each week to communicate with a fellow Buddhist. The Commission found that the applicant had failed to prove that communication with other Buddhists was a necessary, as distinct from important, part of the practice of his religion. Consequently the application was manifestly ill-founded.

In another application[66] the prison authorities refused to allow a prisoner to retain a copy of *Tai Chi Ch'ua and I Ching (A Choreography of Body and Mind)* because it contained an illustrated section on the martial arts and self-defence, which they considered would be dangerous if used against others. The Commission concluded that there had been an interference with the applicant's freedom of religion, but that it was justified under the limitations in Article 9(2). Again the application was manifestly ill-founded.

In one extraordinary case, an Indian, of Sikh ethnic origin and religion, found himself imprisoned for breaking nine windows in a University Senate House during a degree ceremony. He refused to wear prison clothes and spent twenty-three months dressed only in a towel or a blanket. His refusal to wear clothes led to his isolation from other prisoners and he refused to clean out his cell. He complained, *inter alia*, of violations of Article 9. The Commission ruled that Article 9 does not imply any right for prisoners to wear their own clothes and that the applicant had failed to show any reason within Article 9 why he should not wear prison clothes. The Commission was prepared to accept that his religion might require a practice of high-class Sikhs of not cleaning floors and that an interference with his rights under Article 9 in this respect might have arisen. However, the Commission went on to hold that any such interference would be justified as necessary in a democratic society under the limitations recognized by Article 9(2).[67] Accordingly the application was in this respect manifestly ill-founded.

The reported cases taken together give the impression that the Commission was somewhat unsympathetic to complaints of interference with religious freedom by prisoners. As Evans notes,[68] there is a hint in some of the cases involving prisoners that they may be using personal beliefs as a means of seeking privileges which would not otherwise be available. She argues that such doubts should perhaps be tackled more directly. This would avoid a situation in which an unreasonable threshold for establishing the requirements of a particular set of beliefs might arise for those sincerely holding them, while recognizing that in some circumstances, a more searching enquiry is appropriate. She says:

> In cases where fraud may be suspected the precise nature of the evidence that would be required to demonstrate insincerity would differ from case to case, but the burden of proof should be on the State to show some reason to think that the person is using religious or other belief fraudulently in order to obtain an advantage to which he or she would not otherwise be entitled.[69]

[65] App. 5442/72, *X v United Kingdom*, Decision of 20 December 1974, (1975) 1 DR 41.

[66] App. 6886/75, *X v United Kingdom*, Decision of 18 May 1976, (1976) 5 DR 100.

[67] App. 8121/78, *X v United Kingdom*, Decision of 6 March 1982 (1982) 28 DR 5, 38.

[68] C. Evans, *Freedom of Religion under the European Convention on Human Rights* (OUP, Oxford 2001), 57–9.

[69] § 59.

The Court has demonstrated a rather more sympathetic approach to demands from prisoners in at least one case. In *Jakobski v Poland*,[70] a Buddhist prisoner complained about the failure to provide him with a meat-free diet while in prison. The Court regarded the applicant's decision to adhere to a vegetarian diet as motivated or inspired by his religion and thus falling within the scope of Article 9, rejecting Poland's argument that vegetarianism was not a vital tenet of Buddhism. The Court proceeded to find a violation on the basis that the authorities had failed to strike a fair balance between the interests of the prison authorities and those of the applicant. In particular, the Court was 'not persuaded that the provision of a vegetarian diet to the applicant would have entailed any disruption to the management of the prison or to any decline in the standards of meals served to other prisoners.'[71] Such an approach stands in stark contrast to the earlier admissibility decisions by the Commission.

However, *Kovaļkovs v Latvia*,[72] an admissibility decision by the Court, showed greater parallels to the Commission's approach. The applicant complained in general terms that he had been denied the ability to follow the religious customs of his faith in Vaishnavism. The Court focused on the applicant's purported inability to read religious literature, to meditate and to pray because of being placed in a cell together with other prisoners and on the fact that incense sticks were taken away from his cell, all of which it regarded as motivated or inspired by a religion and not unreasonable. It concluded that, taking into account the State's margin of appreciation, these impugned interferences were necessary in a democratic society for the protection of the rights and freedoms of others. This legitimate aim was relevant due to a number of factors, such as potential financial implications having an indirect impact on the quality of treatment of other inmates; the wish of other prisoners not to be disturbed by the applicant's religious rituals; and the need to limit the types of objects that may be kept in prison cells.[73] The interference was proportionate with these legitimate aims because it was not such as to completely prevent the applicant from manifesting his religion. The Court took the view that 'having to pray, read religious literature and to meditate in the presence of others is an inconvenience, which is almost inescapable in prisons, yet which does not go against the very essence of the freedom to manifest one's religion.' As the prison authorities had, on at least one occasion, offered the applicant the use of separate premises for performing religious rituals and the applicant had refused that offer, the Court was satisfied that the balance between the legitimate aims and the 'minor' interference with the applicant's freedom to manifest his religion had been achieved.[74] The applicant's complaints concerning Article 9 of the Convention were held to be inadmissible as manifestly ill-founded.

CONSCIENTIOUS OBJECTION TO MILITARY SERVICE

Considerable problems arise in balancing the competing interests where a Contracting Party requires a citizen to behave in a manner contrary to his beliefs in pursuit of a more obviously useful social aim. Compulsory military service is a prime example, since in a number of Contracting Parties[75] it is still considered necessary to safeguard national

[70] *Jakobski v Poland*, (App. 18429/06), 7 December 2010. [71] § 52.

[72] *Kovaļkovs v Latvia* (dec), (App. 35021/05), 31 January 2012. [73] § 64. [74] § 67.

[75] For example, Albania, Austria, Bulgaria, Cyprus, Denmark, Estonia, Finland, Germany, Greece, Norway, Poland, Romania, Russia, Sweden, Switzerland, Turkey, and Ukraine are understood to require military service, though many permit substitute service.

security even in peacetime, while many pacifists find it objectionable in the extreme. Moreover, Article 4(3)(b) expressly excludes from the prohibition on forced or compulsory labour, 'any service of a military character or, in the case of conscientious objectors where they are recognized, service exacted instead of compulsory military service'.

Two conclusions seem to follow from the wording of Article 4(3)(b). First, since it speaks of conscientious objectors 'in countries where they are recognized', it seems that Contracting Parties are not obliged, under Article 9, to recognize a right to conscientious objection. Secondly, since it makes express provision for substitute service, it follows that where conscientious objectors are permitted to perform substitute service in lieu of military service, they cannot claim, under Article 9, exemption from substitute service. Hence no one is entitled under Article 9 to exemption on grounds of conscience either from military service or from substitute service.[76] The issue was examined by the Commission in the *Grandrath* case.[77] The applicant was a Jehovah's Witness who objected, for reasons of conscience and religion, not only to performing military service but also to any kind of substitute service. The German authorities recognized him as a conscientious objector but required him to perform substitute civilian service. When he refused to do so, criminal proceedings were instituted and he was convicted and sentenced to eight months' imprisonment, a sentence which was reduced on appeal to six months.

In the Commission's opinion, there were two aspects to be considered under Article 9.[78] First, there was the question of whether civilian service would have restricted the applicant's right to manifest his religion. The Commission considered that, given the nature of the service in question, it would not in fact have interfered either with the private and personal practice of his religion or with his duties to his religious community, which were in any case a spare-time activity. Secondly, the Commission examined whether Article 9 had been violated by the mere fact that the applicant had been required to perform a service which was contrary to his conscience or religion. It concluded that, having regard to the provisions of Article 4, objections of conscience did not, under the Convention, entitle a person to exemption from substitute service.

Initially the Court heard cases on subsidiary aspects of the right to conscientious objection[79] but it finally had the opportunity to consider this important issue in *Bayatyan v Armenia*.[80] The applicant was a Jehovah's Witness who was arrested, convicted, and

[76] App. 17086/90, *Autio v Finland*, Decision of 6 December 1991, (1992) 72 DR 245.

[77] App. 2299/64, *Grandrath v Federal Republic of Germany*, Report of Commission, 12 December 1966, Decision of Committee of Ministers, 29 June 1967, (1967) 10 *Yearbook* 626; see also App. 5591/72, *X v Austria*, Decision of 2 April 1973 (1973) 43 CD 161, and App. 7705/76, *X v Federal Republic of Germany*, Decision of 5 July 1977, (1978) 9 DR 196.

[78] App. 2299/64, *Grandrath v Federal Republic of Germany*, Report of Commission, 12 December 1966, Decision of Committee of Ministers, 29 June 1967, (1967) 10 *Yearbook* 626, 672.

[79] For example, in the *Thlimmenos* case (App. 34369/97), 6 April 2000, (2001) 31 EHRR 411, ECHR 2000-IV) the applicant, another Greek Jehovah's Witness, had been convicted of the criminal offence of 'insubordination' as a result of his refusal to wear a military uniform. He was subsequently refused permission to practise as an accountant, in accordance with a law excluding anyone with a criminal record from the profession. The Court did not examine the proportionality of the criminal measures—since the applicant did not complain about them—but it did find that the accountancy ban amounted to a violation of Articles 9 and 14 taken together. In *Tsirlis and Kouloumpas v Greece*, (Apps. 19233/91 and 19234/91), 29 May 1997, (1998) 25 EHRR 198, the Strasbourg Court found a violation of Art. 5(1) arising from the imprisonment of two Jehovah's Witnesses' ministers for refusing to do military service, on the basis that the detention was 'unlawful' under Greek law. It did not find it necessary to examine the complaint under Arts. 9 and 14 of the Convention. See also *Valsamis v Greece*, (App. 21787/93), 18 December 1996, (1997) 24 EHRR 294, ECHR 1996-VI, where the Court decided that requiring the children of Jehovah's Witnesses to attend a military parade did not offend against their pacifist beliefs.

[80] *Bayatyan v Armenia*, (App. 23459/03), 7 July 2011 [GC], ECHR 2011.

imprisoned for his refusal to perform military service on conscientious grounds. The Grand Chamber rejected the previous Commission case-law which had read Article 9 as being qualified by Article 4(3)(b) and instead took an evolutive approach to Article 9 which would bring it into line with a trend among Council of Europe Member States to recognize the right to conscientious objection. By the time of the judgment, only Azerbaijan and Turkey remained outside of the consensus (as even Armenia itself had recognized such a right subsequent to the applicant's release from prison).[81] The Court also recognized other important developments concerning recognition of the right to conscientious objection in various international fora, including in the interpretation by the UNHRC of the provisions of the ICCPR (Articles 8 and 18). Therefore, in accordance with the 'living instrument' approach to interpretation of the Convention, the Court declined to read Article 9 in conjunction with Article 4(3)(b) and instead applied it on its own terms.

The Grand Chamber started by noting that Article 9 does not explicitly include a right to conscientious objection, but held that 'opposition to military service, where it is motivated by a serious and insurmountable conflict between the obligation to serve in the army and a person's conscience or his deeply and genuinely held religious or other beliefs, constitutes a conviction or belief of sufficient cogency, seriousness, cohesion and importance to attract the guarantees of Article 9.'[82] The applicant's objection to military service in the present case was regarded as motivated by his religious beliefs which the Court noted were 'genuinely held and were in serious and insurmountable conflict with his obligation to perform military service.'[83] Most Council of Europe States which have compulsory military service have introduced alternatives in order to reconcile the possible conflict between individual conscience and military obligations. In the Court's view, a State which has not introduced such alternatives enjoys only a limited margin of appreciation and must advance convincing and compelling reasons to justify any interference.[84] The lack of any alternative to military service in Armenia at the relevant time meant that the restriction on the applicant's right to manifest his religious beliefs could not be regarded as a proportionate limitation of his Article 9 rights. Thus the Court found a violation, holding that the applicant's conviction had constituted an interference which was not necessary in a democratic society within the meaning of Article 9.

The Court concluded that the system in Armenia at the relevant time failed to strike a fair balance between the interests of society as a whole and those of the applicant and it emphasized that 'respect on the part of the State towards the beliefs of a minority religious group like the applicant's by providing them with the opportunity to serve society as dictated by their conscience might, far from creating unjust inequalities or discrimination as claimed by the Government, rather ensure cohesive and stable pluralism and promote religious harmony and tolerance in society.'[85] The judgment is a welcome, if overdue, recognition of an important element of the manifestation of many religious beliefs.[86] The narrow margin of appreciation given to Armenia in this case is both welcome and unusual, but clearly explainable on the facts due to the strong consensus among European States on the recognition of a right to conscientious objection. Areas on which there is far less consensus still dominate the Article 9 case-law.

[81] § 103–104.

[82] § 110. [83] § 111. [84] § 123. [85] § 126.

[86] Since *Bayatyan*, the Court has found similar violations in relation to conscientious objection in *Erçep v Turkey*, (App. 43965/04), 22 November 2011 and *Savda v Turkey*, (App. 42730/05), 12 June 2012.

IMMIGRATION ISSUES AND FREEDOM OF RELIGION

In the *El Majjaoui* case[87] a mosque in The Netherlands, which served Muslims from the local Moroccan community, had recruited an imam from abroad, but failed to secure a work permit for him. The individual and the mosque argued that there was a breach of Article 9 in the refusal to provide a work permit for the imam. The Chamber had relinquished the case to the Grand Chamber, but, by the time the case came before the Grand Chamber, a subsequent application for a work permit had been successful. The Grand Chamber struck the case out of its list. In so doing, the Grand Chamber expressed its agreement with a Commission decision[88] that Article 9 does not guarantee foreign nationals a right to obtain a residence permit for work, even if the employer is a religious association.

Immigration issues were again raised in *Nolan and K v Russia*.[89] The applicant came to Russia in 1994 on an invitation of the Unification Church, a religious association officially registered in Russia. He was granted leave to stay which was subsequently extended on an annual basis through invitation from the Unification Church until 2002 when the Russian authorities banned his re-entry to the State on the basis of national security. Although the Russian Government claimed that the threat to national security arose from the applicant's activities rather than his religious beliefs, it produced no evidence to support this. Furthermore, Article 9(2) (unlike the second paragraphs in Articles 8, 10, and 11) did not include the interests of national security as a legitimate aim for an interference with the right to manifest a religion or belief. The Court was adamant that Article 9(2) would be strictly interpreted:

> 73 ....in so far as the Government relied on the protection of national security as the main legitimate aim of the impugned measure, the Court reiterates that the exceptions to freedom of religion listed in Article 9 § 2 must be narrowly interpreted, for their enumeration is strictly exhaustive and their definition is necessarily restrictive... Far from being an accidental omission, the non-inclusion of that particular ground for limitations in Article 9 reflects the primordial importance of religious pluralism as "one of the foundations of a 'democratic society' within the meaning of the Convention" and the fact that a State cannot dictate what a person believes or take coercive steps to make him change his beliefs...

As the Russian Government had not put forward a plausible legal and factual justification for the applicant's exclusion from Russia, and in light of the Concept of National Security of the Russian Federation, as amended in January 2000, which declared that the national security of Russia should be ensured in particular through opposing 'the negative influence of foreign religious organisations and missionaries', the Court found unanimously that there had been a violation of the applicant's right to manifest his religion.

Article 9 is unlikely to be of assistance in the context of expulsion. The *Z and T* case[90] concerned a couple who had left Pakistan in October 2001 in the face of attacks on Christian churches in Bahwalpur, and travelled to the United Kingdom where they claimed asylum. When their applications were unsuccessful, they argued that they would be unable to live openly and freely as Christians if they were returned to Pakistan, and that this violated

[87] *El Majjaoui & Stichting Touba Moskee v The Netherlands*, (App. 25525/03), 20 December 2007 [GC].

[88] App. 32168/96, *Hüsnü Öz v Germany*, Decision of 3 December 1996.

[89] *Nolan and K v Russia*, (App.2512/04), 12 February 2009.

[90] *Z and T v United Kingdom*, (App. 27034/05), Decision of 28 February 2006, ECHR 2006-III.

Article 9. In deciding that the application was inadmissible, the Strasbourg Court ruled that it was highly unlikely that Article 9 could ever be used for this purpose, since the sort of risk in relation to the exercise of religious beliefs which might justify a prohibition on removal would almost certainly fall within Articles 2 or 3. The Court observed:

> ...protection is offered to those who have a substantiated claim that they will either suffer persecution for, inter alia, religious reasons or will be at real risk of death or serious ill-treatment, and possibly flagrant denial of a fair trial or arbitrary detention because of their religious affiliation (as for any other reason). Where...an individual claims that on return to his own country he would be impeded in his religious worship in a manner which falls short of those proscribed levels, the Court considers that very limited assistance, if any, can be derived from Article 9 by itself. Otherwise it would be imposing an obligation on Contracting States effectively to act as indirect guarantors of freedom of worship for the rest of the world.

A RIGHT NOT TO MANIFEST A RELIGION

Article 9 also prevents a Contracting Party from imposing obligations on citizens in relation to participation in national life which offend their religious beliefs, unless these obligations are necessary in a democratic society. A State-imposed obligation found not to serve a pressing social need was examined in the case of *Buscarini and others*.[91] The applicants had been elected as Members of the San Marino Parliament. Before taking office they were required to swear an oath 'on the Holy Gospels' to uphold the Constitution. The Strasbourg Court held that this was tantamount to requiring elected representatives of the people to swear allegiance to a particular religion, and was not, therefore, compatible with Article 9. In many Contracting Parties an affirmation is accepted in place of an oath where there is a requirement to take an oath in connection with some public office.[92]

In *Dimitras v Greece* the issue of oaths was raised once more.[93] The applicants who had all been summoned to appear in court as witnesses or complainants in criminal proceedings, complained that they were asked to take the oath by placing their right hands on the Bible. They then had to inform the authorities that they were not Orthodox Christians and that they preferred to make a solemn declaration instead. The Court found that this presumption that a witness was an Orthodox Christian was difficult to reconcile with freedom of religion as it required those individuals to give details of their religious convictions in order to rectify that presumption and avoid having to take a religious oath. The Court unanimously found a violation of the applicants' Article 9 rights.

In *Sinan Işik v Turkey*[94] the applicant, who stated that he was a member of the Alevi religious community, complained that he had to carry an identity card on which his religion was indicated as Islam. The Court referred once more to the negative aspect of the right to manifest one's religion or beliefs, namely an individual's right not to be obliged to disclose his or her religion or beliefs and not to be obliged to act in such a way that it is possible to conclude that he or she holds—or does not hold—such beliefs.[95] The Court found a violation of Article 9 by Turkey. As the card was frequently used in everyday life, it required the applicant to disclose his religious beliefs against his will every time he used it.[96] The Court

[91] *Buscarini and others v San Marino*, (App. 24645/94), 18 February 1999, (2000) 30 EHRR 208, ECHR 1999-I.

[92] As, for example, in the case of the judicial oath in the United Kingdom.

[93] *Dimitras v Greece*, (App. 42837/06), 3 June 2010.

[94] *Sinan Işik v Turkey*, (App. 21924/05), 2 February 2010, ECHR 2010.

[95] § 41. See also *Alexandridis v Greece*, (App. 19516/06), 21 February 2008.

[96] § 50.

also reiterated that it is not for the State authorities to assess the applicant's religion and that its efforts to do so, by labelling the applicant's religious beliefs as 'Islam', were in breach of the State's duty of neutrality and impartiality.[97]

The negative aspect of the right to manifest a religion arose once more in *Grzelak v Poland*[98] where the applicant had chosen not to attend religious education classes at school and had not been offered any alternative ethics classes, leading to the absence of a mark for 'religion/ethics' on successive school reports. The Court found that this amounted to a form of unwarranted stigmatization of the applicant and that the State's margin of appreciation was exceeded in this matter as the very essence of the applicant's right not to manifest his religion or convictions under Article 9 of the Convention was infringed. It thus found a violation of Article 14 taken in conjunction with Article 9. In these recent cases the importance of the protection offered by Article 9 for non-believers, as declared in the early case of *Kokkinakis*,[99] has come to the fore of the Court's reasoning.[100]

THE RECOGNITION AND AUTHORIZATION OF RELIGIOUS ORGANIZATIONS

The Court has held that a religious association may exercise on behalf of its members the rights guaranteed by Article 9 of the Convention, taken alone and in conjunction with Article 14.[101] The status of religion within the Contracting Parties varies considerably.[102] Some States have established religions,[103] while others have de facto State religions.[104] By contrast some States are explicitly secular.[105] The German Constitution provides that there shall be no State church. In a number of Contracting Parties,[106] there are provisions for official recognition of religious organizations. The most obvious policy obstructing the manifestation of religion or belief is action by a Contracting Party refusing to recognize a religious grouping. Serious and unexplained delays in granting recognition to a religious association under national law will constitute a violation of Article 9.[107] The application of such laws is coming under challenge in the context of Articles 9 and 11.

The rather loose definition of religion inevitably raises the question of the borderline between a religion and a sect, which the Strasbourg organs may view with some distrust even though any issues arising under Article 9 are likely to relate to the manifestation of the belief, which are subject to the limitations set out in Article 9(2). Interestingly, as Renucci notes, the Commission has never used the word 'sect'.[108] The Strasbourg Court

[97] § 46. [98] *Grzelak v Poland*, (App. 7710/02), 15 June 2010.

[99] *Kokkinakis v Greece*, (App. 14307/88), 25 May 1993, Series A No 260-A, (1994) 17 EHRR 397.

[100] *Lautsi v Italy*, (App. 30814/06), 18 March 2011 [GC], ECHR 2011 (extracts), 50 EHRR 42, discussed earlier in the context of religious insignia, would also fall within this category of cases, although in that case the balance between the manifestation of the religious beliefs of the majority and a minority's desire for a secular education was struck rather differently.

[101] *Leela Förderkreis e. V. and others v Germany*, (App. 58911/00), 6 November 2008, § 79 and *Ásatrúarfélagid v Iceland* (dec.), (App. 22897/08), 18 September 2012, § 26.

[102] See C. Evans, *Freedom of Religion under the European Convention on Human Rights* (OUP, Oxford 2001), ch.2, section 2.2. [103] For example, the United Kingdom, Iceland, and Norway.

[104] For example, the Orthodox Church in Greece.

[105] The constitutions of both France and Turkey contain explicit commitments to secularism.

[106] Predominantly but not exclusively the new democracies of central and eastern Europe.

[107] *Religionsgemeinschaft der Zuegen Jehovas and others v Austria*, (App. 40825/98), 31 July 2008.

[108] J-F. Renucci, *Article 9 of the European Convention on Human Rights. Freedom of thought, conscience and religion*, Human Rights Files No. 20 (Council of Europe Publishing, Strasbourg 2005), 17.

has, however, in its judgments in the *Manoussakis* case[109] and in the *Kalaç* case,[110] used the word 'sect' and 'sects', but very much in passing (though also in a pejorative sense). The question was presented more squarely in a case against France, though ultimately it was not necessary to provide an answer to the question of what constitutes a sect which is outside the scope of the protection of Article 9.[111] Jehovah's Witnesses in France complained that the publication of two reports of a parliamentary commission, and a legislative bill to strengthen preventive and punitive actions against sectarian groups, had seriously jeopardized the exercise of its freedom of religion. A law had been passed in June 2001 in this area. Jehovah's Witnesses had been named in one of the reports as a dangerous sect. The Strasbourg Court concluded that the application was an attempt to call into question the compatibility, in the abstract, of French proposals (which were devoid of any legal effect), and the applicants could not establish that they were a victim, or even a potential victim of a violation of Article 9.

The notion that sects are bad was at the heart of the *Leela Förderkreis E.V* case.[112] The case concerned associations in Germany which belonged to the Osho movement, better known to many under its former label, the Bhagwan movement. The German authorities became concerned about the potential danger these associations could be to the personal development and social relations of young people. An information campaign was undertaken which described the Osho movement in pejorative terms.[113] The complaints of the associations wound their way to the Bundesverwassungsgericht, which upheld the legality of the information campaign, including its use of language. The associations complained that the campaign constituted an interference with their right to manifest their religion. The Strasbourg Court accepted that the activities of the associations constituted a manifestation of the associations' beliefs, and proceeded, without determining the issue one way or another, on the basis that the information campaign constituted an interference with that right. The Court accepted that the German Basic Law, which included a duty to impart information on subjects of public concern, was wide enough to provide a legal base for its actions. It was clear that the German authorities were acting for a legitimate aim.[114] The majority of five concluded that the information campaign had not gone beyond what was necessary in a democratic society in the circumstances in which there was some conflict and tension in German society about the increasing number of new religions and ideological movements. Somewhat controversially, the Strasbourg Court added:

> ...such a power of preventive intervention on the State's part is also consistent with the Contracting Parties' positive obligations under Article 1 of the Convention to secure the rights and freedoms of persons within their jurisdiction. Those obligations relate not only to any interference that may result from acts or omissions imputable to agents of the State or occurring in public establishments, but also to interference imputable to private individuals within non-State entities....[115]

Where issues relating to the recognition of a religion are raised, the Strasbourg Court has adopted a policy of reading Articles 9 and 11 as closely interlinked. The starting point is

[109] *Manoussakis and others v Greece*, (App. 18748/91), 26 September 1996, (1997) 23 EHRR 387, ECHR 1996-IV, § 39.

[110] *Kalaç v Turkey*, (App. 20704/92), 1 July 1997, (1999) 27 EHRR 552, ECHR 1997-V, § 26.

[111] *The Christian Federation of Jehovah's Witnesses in France v France*, (App. 53430/99), Decision of 6 November 2001, ECHR 2001-XI.

[112] *Leela Förderkreis E.V and others v Germany*, (App. 58911/00), 6 November 2008, (2009) 49 EHRR 117.

[113] Describing them as 'sects', 'youth sects', 'psycho-sects', and 'psycho-groups'.

[114] For the protection of public safety, public order, and the protection of the rights and freedoms of others: § 94.

[115] § 99.

freedom of association with others, but the context is freedom of religion. This approach is most clearly spelled out in the *Moscow Branch of the Salvation Army* case.[116] The Salvation Army had been registered in Russia as a religious organization with status as a legal entity since May 1992. In 1997 a new law entered into force which required religious organizations to re-register and to ensure that their articles of association conformed to the new law. Despite litigation in the Russian courts, the Salvation Army failed to secure re-registration, and the Russian authorities then took action for dissolution of the Moscow Branch. The applicant complained of a violation of Articles 9 and 11. The Strasbourg Court reiterated the centrality of religious freedom in a democratic society and continued:

> ...the autonomous existence of religious communities is indispensable for pluralism in a democratic society, and is thus an issue at the very heart of the protection which Article 9 affords. The State's duty of neutrality and impartiality, as defined in the Court's case-law, is incompatible with any power on the State's part to assess the legitimacy of religious beliefs (see Metropolitan Church of Bessarabia..., and Hasan and Chaush v Bulgaria [GC], no. 30985/96, § 62, ECHR 2000-XI).[117]

The Strasbourg Court then reiterates that the right to form an association is an inherent part of the rights protected by Article 11, and observes:

> While in the context of Article 11 the Court has often referred to the essential role played by political parties in ensuring pluralism and democracy, associations formed for other purposes, including those proclaiming or teaching religion, are also important to the proper functioning of democracy.[118]

The Court stressed that the need for any regulation of associations in order to protect the State's institutions and citizens must be used sparingly in the context of a strict interpretation of the limitations to freedom of association. The Strasbourg Court considered that there had been an interference with the applicant's rights under Article 11 when read in the light of Article 9. In this context there was only a limited margin of appreciation for the respondent State. The Court then examined the two main grounds put forward for the refusals of recognition: that the branch was subordinate to a foreign national. While the Russian law prohibited foreign nationals from being founders of Russian religious organizations, it did not extend to prohibition of local branches of such religions. Where there was a situation in which a church's headquarters were abroad, there was simply an additional requirement that the articles of association of the foreign governing body were also filed. The Court concluded that the foreign origins of the local branch could not constitute a relevant and sufficient ground for refusing registration under the Russian law. The second objection was that the Salvation Army was organized on hierarchical grounds; indeed it had been described by the Moscow Justice Department as a 'paramilitary organization'. The Court found no basis from the lawful activities of the Salvation Army over a period of seven years, nor in its religious organization, to suggest that it advocated a violent change in the respondent State's constitutional foundations and so undermined State security or integrity. The findings to this effect by Russian authorities were without any evidentiary basis and so were an arbitrary ground of interference. The Strasbourg Court concluded that the Russian authorities had not acted in good faith and had neglected their duty of neutrality and impartiality towards the Salvation Army. The unanimous decision of the Chamber was that there was a violation of Article 11 when read in the light of Article 9.[119]

[116] *Moscow Branch of the Salvation Army v Russia*, (App. 72881/01), 5 October 2006, (2007) 44 EHRR 912, ECHR 2006-XI. See also *Verein der Freunde der Christengemeinschaft and others v Austria*, (App. 76581/01), 26 February 2009.

[117] § 58.

[118] § 61.

[119] See also *Church of Scientology Moscow v Russia*, (App. 18147/02), 5 April 2007, (2008) 46 EHRR 304.

A similar case involving Russia came before the Court in 2010. *Jehovah's Witnesses of Moscow and others v Russia*[120] concerned a decision by the Russian courts to dissolve the applicant community and to ban its activities. As a result, the applicant community ceased to exist as a registered religious organization and the individual applicants, being its members, were divested of their right to manifest their religion in community with others. The Court described such a blanket ban on the activities of a religious community belonging to a known Christian denomination as 'an extraordinary occurrence'[121] and was unconvinced by the reasons put forward by Russia to justify its actions. It held that the Russian courts had not adduced relevant and sufficient reasons to prove any of its conclusions, namely that the applicant community forced families to break up; that it infringed the rights and freedoms of its members or third parties; that it incited its followers to commit suicide or refuse medical care; that it impinged on the rights of non-Witness parents or their children; or that it encouraged members to refuse to fulfil any duties established by law. Furthermore, even if there had been compelling reasons for the interference, the sanction pronounced by the domestic courts was excessively severe:

> 159. ...The judgments of the Russian courts put an end to the existence of a religious community made up of approximately 10,000 believers and imposed an indefinite ban on its activities unlimited in time or scope. This was obviously the most severe form of interference, affecting, as it did, the rights of thousands of Moscow Jehovah's Witnesses who were, as a consequence, denied the possibility of joining with fellow believers in prayer and observance. Therefore, even if the Court were to accept that there were compelling reasons for the interference, it finds that the permanent dissolution of the applicant community, coupled with a ban on its activities, constituted a drastic measure disproportionate to the legitimate aim pursued.

The Court did not overlook the trend emerging in Russia under the Religions Act 1997 of denying re-registration to religious organizations which were described as 'non-traditional religions', including The Salvation Army and the Church of Scientology, as well as Jehovah's Witnesses.[122] The Court pointed out that this differential treatment remains a matter of concern for the Parliamentary Assembly of the Council of Europe.[123]

A variation on this theme arose in *Kimlya and others v Russia*[124] where two Scientology groups were refused registration as 'religious organisations' within the meaning of the Russian Religions Act, thus denying them legal personality, because they had not existed for a period of at least fifteen years. As the Court noted, a religious group without legal personality cannot possess or exercise the rights associated with legal-entity status, such as the rights to own or rent property, to maintain bank accounts, to hire employees, and to ensure judicial protection of the community, its members and its assets. In the Court's view, those rights are essential for exercising the right to manifest one's religion.[125] The restricted status afforded to 'religious groups' under the Religions Act did not allow members of such a group to establish places of worship, hold religious services in places accessible to the public, produce, obtain and distribute religious literature, or create educational institutions. Therefore, such a restricted status did not enable members of religious groups to enjoy effectively their right to freedom of religion, rendering such a right illusory and theoretical.[126]

[120] *Jehovah's Witnesses of Moscow and others v Russia*, (App. 302/02), 10 June 2010. [121] § 155.

[122] See *Church of Scientology Moscow v Russia*, (App. 18147/02), 5 April 2007, § 97, and *Moscow Branch of the Salvation Army v Russia*, (App. 72881/01), 5 October 2006, ECHR 2006-XI, § 97. [123] § 157.

[124] *Kimlya and others v Russia*, (Apps. 76836/01 and 32782/03), 1 October 2009, ECHR 2009.

[125] § 85. [126] § 86.

The interference with the applicants' Article 9 rights was not necessary in a democratic society as they had been denied registration as religious organizations merely because of the automatic operation of a legal provision that prevented all religious groups which had not existed for at least fifteen years from obtaining legal-entity status. The Russian Government had not identified any pressing social need which the impugned restriction served or any relevant and sufficient reasons which could justify the lengthy waiting period that a religious organization had to endure prior to obtaining legal personality.[127]

Similar issues were raised in *Religionsgemeinschaft der Zeugen Jehovas and others v Austria*[128] and the Court noted that a prolonged wait before granting legal personality to a religious organization can amount to a violation of Article 9, even if auxiliary associations were created with legal personality during that period and did not suffer interference by the authorities.[129] The first applicant, the Jehovah's Witnesses in Austria, had been granted legal personality as a registered religious community, a private-law entity, but wished to become a religious society, a public-law entity that enjoys privileged treatment in many areas. The Court held that all religious groups which so wished must have a fair opportunity to apply for this special status and the criteria established must be applied in a non-discriminatory manner.[130] The imposition of a waiting period before the organization could obtain this status as a public-law body was considered by the Court who concluded that it 'could accept that such a period might be necessary in exceptional circumstances such as would be in the case of newly established and unknown religious groups. But it hardly appears justified in respect of religious groups with a long-standing existence internationally which are also long established in the country and therefore familiar to the competent authorities, as is the case with the Jehovah's Witnesses.'[131] Accordingly, it also found a violation of Article 14 of the Convention taken in conjunction with Article 9.

In a later case, *Jehovas Zeugen in Österreich v Austria*,[132] the applicant community complained that it had been discriminated against in the exercise of its rights under Article 9 because, as a religious community, it had been subject to laws concerning the employment of foreigners and tax from which recognized religious societies had been exempted. Again the Court found a violation of Article 14 taken in conjunction with Article 9.[133]

The *Metropolitan Church of Bessarabia v Moldova* case also concerned recognition of a church.[134] Moldova refused to recognize the Metropolitan Church of Bessarabia in circumstances where only religions recognized by the respondent State may be practised in Moldova. In finding a violation of Article 9, the Strasbourg Court took the opportunity to restate both the role of the State in the regulation of religious activities, and the relationship of the freedom protected by Article 9 with certain other freedoms:

> 117. The Court further observes that in principle the right to freedom of religion for the purposes of the Convention excludes assessment by the State of the legitimacy

[127] § 100.

[128] *Religionsgemeinschaft der Zeugen Jehovas and others v Austria*, (App. 40825/98), 31 July 2008.

[129] § 79. [130] § 92. [131] § 98.

[132] *Jehovas Zeugen in Österreich v Austria*, (App. 27540/05), 25 September 2012.

[133] See also *Association les Temoins de Jehovah v France*, (App. 8916/05), 30 June 2011.

[134] *Metropolitan Church of Bessarabia v Moldova*, (App. 45701/99), 14 December 2001; (2002) 35 EHRR 306, ECHR 2001-XII. See also *Biserica Adevărat Ortodoxă din Moldova and others v Modlova*, (App. 952/03), 27 February 2007. For an example of a dispute in which Article 9 was pleaded but where the Strasbourg Court determined the case by reference to rights arising under Article 6, see *Canea Catholic Church v Greece*, (App. 25528/94), 16 September 1997, (1999) 27 EHRR 521. Renucci suggests that the Court has displayed a tendency to sidestep some questions arising under Article 9 by preferring to decide cases under other Articles to the detriment of Article 9: see J-F. Renucci, *Article 9 of the European Convention on Human Rights. Freedom of thought, conscience and religion*, Human Rights Files No. 20 (Council of Europe Publishing, Strasbourg 2005), 36–41.

of religious beliefs or the ways in which those beliefs are expressed. State measures favouring a particular leader or specific organs of a divided religious community or seeking to compel the community or part of it to place itself, against its will, under a single leadership, would also constitute an infringement of the freedom of religion. In democratic societies the State does not need to take measures to ensure that religious communities remain or are brought under a unified leadership.... Similarly, where the exercise of the right to freedom of religion or of one of its aspects is subject under domestic law to a system of prior authorisation, involvement in the procedure for granting authorisation of a recognised ecclesiastical authority cannot be reconciled with the requirements of paragraph 2 of Article 9....

The earlier *Manoussakis* case[135] had concerned Jehovah's Witnesses living in Crete. They rented a room for the purpose of conducting activities, such as meetings and weddings, connected with their beliefs as Jehovah's Witnesses. They were subsequently prosecuted and convicted for having established and operated a place of worship without the authorizations required by law. Though the Strasbourg Court is at pains to indicate that it will not pass judgment on a generalized complaint by the applicants about policies of the respondent State which might affect the practice of their religion by Jehovah's Witnesses, on the specific issues it did consider there was some doubt about whether the interference with their rights under Article 9 was prescribed by law. The Court reviewed the national legislation on the granting of authorization for the use of premises for the practice of religious beliefs, and noted that the State had tended to use the system of authorization 'to impose rigid, or indeed prohibitive, conditions on practice of religious beliefs by certain non-orthodox movements, in particular Jehovah's Witnesses.'[136] The Court, like the Commission, concluded that the conviction of which the applicants complained had such a direct effect on their freedom of religion that it could not be regarded as proportionate to the aim pursued and so was not necessary in a democratic society. The Court also indicated that intervention in the procedure for authorization of the established church—in this case the Greek Orthodox Church—could not be reconciled with the provisions in Article 9(2).[137]

However, a specific system for authorization of the use of premises for religious purposes must be distinguished from the application of generally applicable legal provisions concerning planning consent. In the latter case, it will be rather easier to justify the application of planning requirements which affects the use of premises for religious purposes.[138]

Non-recognition of a religion by the State does not, however, deprive adherents of that religion from the protection of Article 9, since such an approach would mean that the State could exclude certain beliefs by withholding recognition. Punishing those who manifest religious beliefs which have not been recognized by the State constitutes a violation of Article 9.[139]

POSITIVE OBLIGATIONS

In the *Hasan and Chaush* case[140] the Strasbourg Court observed that:

[w]ere the organizational life of the [religious] community not protected by Article 9 of the Convention, all other aspects of the individual's freedom of religion would become vulnerable.

[135] *Manoussakis and others v Greece*, (App. 18748/91), 26 September 1996, (1997) 23 EHRR 387, ECHR 1996-IV.

[136] § 48. [137] §§ 51–3.

[138] *Vergos v Greece*, (App. 65501/01), 24 June 2004, (2005) 41 EHRR 913.

[139] *Masaev v Moldova*, (App. 6303/05), 12 May 2009.

[140] *Hasan and Chaush v Bulgaria*, (App. 30985/96), 26 October 2000 [GC], (2002) 34 EHRR 1339, ECHR 2000-XI.

In the *Father Basil* case,[141] the Strasbourg Court condemned as a violation of Article 9 the failure of the Georgian authorities to ensure tolerance of the exercise by the applicants (a group of Jehovah's Witnesses) of their right to freedom of religion in the face of a violent and outrageous attack on worshippers and their place of worship by Father Basil (a defrocked Orthodox priest) and a group of extremists.

Recent judgments confirm that there are, indeed, circumstances where, in order to comply with Article 9, the State has to take positive measures, and these may represent a greater willingness on the part of the Court to scrutinize States' purported justifications for interfering with religious expression. In *Eweida*, the Court acknowledged that:

> Where, as for the first and fourth applicants, the acts complained of were carried out by private companies and were not therefore directly attributable to the respondent State, the Court must consider the issues in terms of the positive obligation on the State authorities to secure the rights under Article 9 to those within their jurisdiction... Whilst the boundary between the State's positive and negative obligations under the Convention does not lend itself to precise definition, the applicable principles are, nonetheless, similar. In both contexts regard must be had in particular to the fair balance that has to be struck between the competing interests of the individual and of the community as a whole, subject in any event to the margin of appreciation enjoyed by the State...[142]

In its judgment in the *Otto-Preminger Institute* case, the Strasbourg Court ruled that Contracting Parties have positive obligations under Article 9 to 'ensure the peaceful enjoyment of the rights guaranteed under Article 9 to the holders of those beliefs and doctrines', though it also recognized that the pluralism inherent in the Convention values meant that those holding religious beliefs 'cannot reasonably expect to be exempt from all criticism' and must 'tolerate and accept the denial by others of their religious beliefs and even the propagation by others of doctrines hostile to their faith.'[143] This means that Contracting Parties have a responsibility to ensure tolerance between the rival factions between and within religious and belief groups.[144] In the *Leela Förderkreis E.V* case,[145] the Strasbourg Court, in a case where the authorities had run an information campaign using pejorative terms about associations belong to the Osho movement, somewhat controversially based its decision to find no violation of Article 9 on the positive duty of Contracting Parties to provide information about matters of concern to its people.

The applicant in the *Serif* case[146] enjoyed the support of part of the Muslim community in Thrace, and was elected Mufti (religious leader), despite the fact that another Mufti had already been appointed by the respondent State. The applicant was subsequently convicted of the criminal offences of having usurped the functions of a minister of a 'known religion' and having publicly worn the uniform of such a minister without having the right to do so. The respondent State argued before the Strasbourg Court that the authorities had had

[141] *97 members of the Gldani Congregation of Jehovah's Witnesses and 4 others v Georgia*, (App. 71156/01), 3 May 2007, (2008) 46 EHRR 613, ECHR 2007.

[142] *Eweida and others v United Kingdom*, (App. 48420/10, 59842/10, 51671/10, and 36516/10) 15 January 2013, ECHR 2013 (extracts), § 84. See also *Jakobski v Poland*, (App. 18429/06), 7 December 2010; *Ahmet Arslan v Turkey*, (App. 41135/98), 23 February 2010.

[143] *Otto-Preminger Institute v Austria*, (App. 13470/87), 20 September 1994, Series A No 295-A, (1994) 19 EHRR 34.

[144] *Serif v Greece*, (App. 38178/97), 4 December 1999, (2001) 31 EHRR 561, ECHR 1999-IX, § 53. See also *Metropolitan Church of Bessarabia v Moldova*, (App. 45701/99), 14 December 2001, (2002) 35 EHRR 306, ECHR 2001-XII.

[145] *Leela Förderkreis E.V and others v Germany*, (App. 58911/00), 6 November 2008, (2009) 49 EHRR 117.

[146] *Serif v Greece*, (App. 38178/97), 4 December 1999, (2001) 31 EHRR 561, ECHR 1999-IX.

to intervene in order to avoid the creation of tension between different religious groups in the area. The Court, finding a violation of Article 9, observed that tension between competing religious groups was an unavoidable consequence of pluralism, but that the role of the authorities in such a situation was not to remove the cause of the tension, thereby eliminating pluralism, but instead to ensure tolerance between the rival factions.[147] In a democratic society, it commented, there was no need for the State to take measures to ensure that religious communities remained or were brought under a unified leadership. In the *Hasan and Chaush* case,[148] where the Bulgarian authorities were found to have similarly interfered in the affairs of the Muslim community, the Court declared a violation of Article 9 based on the arbitrary nature of the relevant legislation, which gave an almost unfettered power to the executive to appoint the person of its choice as Chief Mufti.[149]

CONCLUDING REMARKS

The pursuit of multiculturalism and peaceful co-habitation of different religious groups within society has frequently proved challenging. The history of Europe is littered with examples of extreme religious intolerance and, indeed, the European Convention was conceived in the immediate aftermath of the persecution and genocide of the adherents of one religion, Judaism, in the hope that it would help to prevent such an atrocity ever taking place again. For many believers, religious faith is central to their existence and their most important defining characteristic. The Court is correct, therefore, to stress in its case-law the duty of the State as a guarantor of pluralism and the fundamental nature of the rights to freedom of belief and freedom to manifest religion. The case-law can, however, be criticized as lacking in any detailed formulation of principles and concepts. The Strasbourg Court has yet to define 'religion' or to elaborate any guidelines as to how mainstream or established a religion has to be before it requires recognition by the State. While the Court has accepted that restrictions might be permissible to prevent religious pressure being placed on individuals by their superiors in hierarchical structures, it has not attempted to elaborate any general guidelines as to when attempts at conversion become abusive, what constitutes a 'cult' or when the State should step in to protect children or other vulnerable individuals from violations of human rights carried out in the name of religion. Nor has it explained what types of non-religious 'beliefs' will gain protection under Article 9. In addition, the case-law regarding the extent to which restrictions can be placed on the manifestation of religious belief is not consistent. These are all difficult questions, but that is precisely why the Court's guidance is needed.

[147] See also *Metropolitan Church of Bessarabia v Moldova*, (App. 45701/99), 14 December 2001, (2002) 35 EHRR 306, ECHR 2001-XII; and *Holy Synod of the Bulgarian Orthodox Church (Metropolitan Inokentiy) v Bulgaria*, (Apps. 412/03 and 35677/04), 22 January 2009.

[148] *Hasan and Chaush v Bulgaria*, (App. 30985/96), 26 October 2000 [GC], (2002) 34 EHRR 1339, ECHR 2000-XI.

[149] See also *Svyato-Mykhaylivska Parafiya v Ukraine*, (App. 77703/01), 14 June 2007, which concerned registration issues where a religious organization wished to changed the leadership of the church to which it is affiliated, and arbitrary action by the authorities.

18

FREEDOM OF EXPRESSION

INTRODUCTION

In its seminal judgment in the *Handyside* case, the Strasbourg Court emphasized the importance of the rights protected by Article 10, which, it said, 'constitutes one of the essential foundations of a democratic society, one of the basic conditions for its progress and for the development of every man.'[1] There is a link with Article 9 on freedom of thought, conscience, and religion, since expression of personal beliefs and ideas is for many an inherent part of the holding of those beliefs and ideas. Article 11 also has relevance, since individuals may wish to come together to express their ideas either in private or in public, as does Article 8 where issues of privacy overlap with the rights protected by Article 10. Given its foundational aspect, it is, therefore, perhaps surprising that the list of restrictions is longer than for other Articles of the Convention. The Article also, uniquely, makes specific reference to duties and responsibilities in the exercise of the rights the Article protects.[2]

Article 10 provides,

1. Everyone has the right to freedom of expression. This right shall include freedom to hold opinions and to receive and impart information and ideas without interference by public authority and regardless of frontiers. This article shall not prevent States from requiring the licensing of broadcasting, television or cinema enterprises.
2. The exercise of these freedoms, since it carries with it duties and responsibilities, may be subject to such formalities, conditions, restrictions or penalties as are prescribed by law and are necessary in a democratic society, in the interests of national security, territorial integrity or public safety, for the prevention of disorder or crime, for the protection of health or morals, for the protection of the reputation or rights of others, for preventing the disclosure of information received in confidence, or for maintaining the authority and impartiality of the judiciary.

The right to freedom of expression set out in the Article's first paragraph, including freedom to hold opinions and to receive and impart information and ideas[3] without interference by the State, is extremely broad. All forms of expression are included, through any medium: this includes paintings,[4] books,[5] cartoons,[6] films,[7] video-recordings,[8] statements

[1] *Handyside v United Kingdom*, (App. 5493/72), 7 December 1976, Series A No 24, (1979–80) 1 EHRR 737, § 48.

[2] See generally, M. Macovei, *Freedom of expression: a guide to the implementation of Article 10 of the European Convention on Human Rights*, Human Rights Handbooks No. 2 (Council of Europe Publishing, Strasbourg 2004).

[3] *Autronic AG v Switzerland*, (App. 12726/87), 22 May 1990, Series A No 178, (1990) 12 EHRR 485.

[4] *Müller v Switzerland*, (App. 10737/84), 24 May 1988, Series A No 133, (1991) 13 EHRR 212.

[5] *Handyside v United Kingdom*, (App. 5493/72), 7 December 1976, Series A No 24, (1979–80) 1 EHRR 737.

[6] *Leroy v France*, (App. 36109/03), 2 October 2008.

[7] *Otto-Preminger Institute v Austria*, (App. 13470/87), 20 September 1994, Series A No 295-A, (1994) 19 EHRR 34.

[8] *Monnat v Switzerland*, (App. 73604/01), 21 September 2006, ECHR 2006-X.

in radio interviews,[9] information pamphlets,[10] and the internet;[11] and with any content, including incitement to hatred,[12] and pornography.[13]

To quote again from the *Handyside* case:

> [Article 10] is applicable not only to 'information' or 'ideas' that are favourably received or regarded as inoffensive or as a matter of indifference, but also those that offend, shock or disturb the State or any sector of the population. Such are the demands of that pluralism, tolerance and broadmindedness without which there is no 'democratic' society.[14]

However, as is explicitly recognized in the text of Article 10(2), and by the Strasbourg Court in its case-law, free expression, particularly by way of the mass media, is a powerful tool, carrying special duties and responsibilities. If it is vital to protect the right to free expression because of its power to promote democracy, uncover abuses, and advance political, artistic, scientific, and commercial development, it is also important to recognize that free expression can equally be used to incite violence, spread hatred, and impinge on individual privacy and safety. The Court's case-law is an attempt to strike the proper balance between these competing interests.[15]

The majority of cases concerning Article 10 are brought by persons who have received some penalty for defaming or insulting other people. When considering whether such a penalty constitutes a violation of Article 10 the Strasbourg Court will take into account a number of factors, including the function fulfilled by the author and the subject, whether the impugned expression consists of a statement of fact or a value judgment, and the severity of the penalty.[16]

WHAT CONSTITUTES AN INTERFERENCE WITH FREE EXPRESSION?

The Strasbourg Court takes a broad view of what constitutes an interference with free expression. At its most obvious this includes executive orders preventing publication[17] or the confiscation of published material.[18] Article 10(2) makes clear that 'penalties' as well as 'restrictions', 'conditions', and 'formalities' must be justified. The 'penalties' referred to can include criminal sanctions,[19] damages in a civil action,[20] reprimands in disciplinary

[9] *Barthold v Germany*, (App. 8734/79), 23 March 1985, Series A No 90, (1985) 7 EHRR 383.

[10] *Open Door Counselling and Dublin Well Woman v Ireland*, (Apps. 14234/88 and 14235/88), 29 October 1992, Series A No 246, (1993) 15 EHRR 244.

[11] *Perrin v United Kingdom*, (App. 5446/03), Decision of 18 October 2005, ECHR 2005-XI. See also *Times Newspapers Ltd (Nos. 1 and 2) v United Kingdom*, (Apps. 3002/03 and 23676/03), 10 March 2009.

[12] *Jersild v Denmark*, (App. 15890/89), 24 September 1994, Series A No 298, (1994) 19 EHRR 1; *Vejdeland v Sweden*, (App. 1813/07), 9 February 2012.

[13] *Wingrove v United Kingdom*, (App. 17419/90), 25 November 1996, (1997) 24 EHRR 1.

[14] *Handyside v United Kingdom*, (App. 5493/72), 7 December 1976, Series A No 24, (1979–80) 1 EHRR 737, § 48.

[15] See E. Barendt, *Freedom of Speech* (OUP, Oxford 2005).

[16] For a critical comment on the development of the case-law in this area, see G. Millar, 'Whither the spirit of Lingens?' [2009] EHRLR 277.

[17] See the 'Spycatcher' cases: *The Observer and Guardian Newspapers Ltd v United Kingdom*, (App. 13585/88), 26 November 1991, Series A No 216, (1992) 14 EHRR 153 and *Sunday Times v United Kingdom (No 2)*, (App. 13166/87), 26 November 1991, Series A No 217, (1992) 14 EHRR 229.

[18] *Vereniging Weekblad Bluf! v Netherlands*, (App. 16616/90), 9 February 1995, Series A No 306-A, (1995) 20 EHRR 189.

[19] *Zana v Turkey*, (App. 18954/91), 25 November 1997, (1999) 27 EHRR 667, ECHR 1997-VII.

[20] *Tolstoy Miloslavsky v United Kingdom*, (App. 18139/91), 13 July 1995, Series A No 316-B, (1995) 20 EHRR 442.

proceedings,[21] or dismissals, at least when the person in question is a public sector employee.[22] Other forms of post-publication measures can also constitute interferences if they have a chilling effect on future expression. For example, the Strasbourg Court has held that attempts to uncover journalistic sources, either by search order[23] or by disclosure order,[24] are interferences requiring justification under Article 10(2). In response to an applicant's argument under Article 8, that the State should require the media to give prior notice to the subjects of media stories about their private life, the Court found that the imposition of pre-publication notifications could have a chilling affect on the media and so would not impose such a requirement.[25] Refusal to authorize the performance of a play constitutes a restriction on freedom of expression,[26] as can confiscation of written materials intended to be given to others in order to impart information and ideas.[27] A prohibition on wearing the five-pointed red star, as the symbol of the international workers' movement falls within the ambit of Article 10.[28] Revocation of a call-up for military service can be an interference with freedom of expression.[29]

LIMITATIONS ON FREEDOM OF EXPRESSION

Certain restrictions are expressly allowed. Article 10(1) itself provides that Contracting Parties may require the licensing of broadcasting, television, or cinema enterprises. Moreover, in common with Articles 8, 9, and 11, Article 10 includes a second paragraph which permits a Contracting Party to limit the right set out in the first paragraph, provided that such limitations are 'prescribed by law', and 'necessary in a democratic society' in pursuit of one of the specified aims.[30]

The situations in which a restriction may be justifiable include the need to protect important public interests—such as national security, territorial integrity, freedom from crime and disorder, health and morality, and the authority and impartiality of the judiciary—and also other individual rights, such as a person's right to privacy or reputation. The margin of appreciation allowed to Contracting Parties in restricting freedom of expression will vary depending on the purpose and nature of the limitation and of the expression in question. As the Strasbourg Court made clear in its *Handyside* judgment,

[21] *Steur v Netherlands*, (App. 39657/98), 28 October 2003, (2004) 39 EHRR 706, ECHR 2003-XI; *Frankowicz v Poland*, (App. 53025/99), 16 December 2008; and *Wojtas-Kaleta v Poland*, (app. 20436/02), 16 July 2009.

[22] *Vogt v Germany*, (App. 17851/91), 26 September 1995, Series A No 323, (1996) 21 EHRR 205; *Fuentes Bobo v Spain*, (App. 39293/98), 29 February 2000; and *Guja v Moldova*, (App. 14277/04), 12 February 2008 [GC], ECHR 2008-nyr.

[23] *Roemen and Schmit v Luxembourg*, (App. 51772/99), 25 February 2003, ECHR 2003-IV, §§ 47 and 57; *Ressiot and others v France*, (App. 15054/07), 28 June 2012; and *Nagla v Latvia*, (App. 73469/10), 16 July 2013.

[24] *Goodwin v United Kingdom*, (App. 17488/90), 27 March 1996, (1996) 22 EHRR 123, ECHR 1996-II, § 28. See also *Nordisk Film & TV A/S v Denmark*, (App. 40485/02), Decision of 8 December 2005, ECHR 2005-XIII; and *Telegraaf Media Nederland Landelijke Media B V and others v Netherlands*, (App. 39315/06), 22 November 2012.

[25] *Mosley v United Kingdom*, (App. 48009/08), 10 May 2011, § 132.

[26] *Ulusoy and others v Turkey*, (App. 34797/03), 3 May 2007.

[27] *Foka v Turkey*, (App. 28940/95), 24 June 2008, §§ 102–9.

[28] *Vajnai v Hungary*, (App. 33629/06), 8 July 2008. No issue appears to have been raised in this case that this was the manifestation of a personal belief, which would, of course, fall within Article 9. So it seems that secular insignia will be treated differently from religious insignia. See also *Donaldson v United Kingdom*, (App. 56975/09), 25 January 2011, where the wearing of an Easter Lily by an Irish Republican prisoner was held to be covered by Article 10(1).

[29] *Erdel v Germany*, (App. 30067/04), Decision of 13 February 2007, ECHR 2007-II.

[30] See ch.14.

'every "formality", "condition", "restriction" or "penalty" imposed in this sphere must be proportionate to the legitimate aim pursued.'[31]

On the other side of the balance, to be weighed against the importance of the aim pursued by the restriction, is the nature of the expression restricted. The Strasbourg Court takes into account the fact that, in the context of effective political democracy and respect for human rights mentioned in the Preamble to the Convention, freedom of expression not only is important in itself, but also plays a central role in the protection of the other rights under the Convention. Thus the Court consistently gives a higher level of protection to publications and speech which contribute towards social and political debate, criticism, and information—in the broadest sense. Artistic and commercial expression,[32] in contrast, receive a lower level of protection.

This is illustrated in the case of *Mouvement Raelien Suisse v Switzerland*.[33] The applicant group wished to place a poster in a public place. The poster contained pictures of extraterrestrials and a spaceship and displayed the movement's website address and telephone number. The authorization was denied. The group also advocated 'sensual meditation' which it was argued was linked to paedophilia. The organization also believed in 'geniocracy' (a political system based on intelligence) which involves an advocacy of human cloning. The Grand Chamber found by a majority[34] that there was no violation of Article 10. The Court examined the type of expression under scrutiny. It decided that the applicant's views could not be classified as political speech and were more akin to advertising, though there was no inducement to buy a product. It stated the poster and website had a 'certain proselytising function'.[35] It is unclear from the majority reasoning where this expression fits in to the traditional categories used by the Court. The dissenting opinions were critical of this definition of the 'type' of expression, with one judge describing the type of expression as more akin to philosophical debate.[36]

Other important factors to take into account include the extent of the restriction and the form of the expression. The Court will scrutinize prior restraints on expression more closely, because of their inherent dangers.[37] Such restraints will require safeguards against their misuse. A ban on the publication and distribution of a newspaper, for example, will be compatible with the Convention only if there is a particularly strict framework of legal rules regulating the scope of the ban and ensuring the effectiveness of judicial review to prevent the possibility of abuse.[38] The Court will also look at whether the applicants had alternate means of expression.[39]

As for the form of the expression, the Strasbourg Court has acknowledged that account must be taken of the fact that audio-visual media have a more immediate and powerful effect than print media.[40] In general, more restrictive measures will be permissible in relation to the audio and visual media, because the potential for damage is greater.[41] The

[31] *Handyside v United Kingdom*, (App. 5493/72), 7 December 1976, Series A No 24, (1979–80) 1 EHRR 737, § 48.

[32] *Vgt Verein gegen Tierfabriken v Switzerland*, (App. 24699/94), 28 June 2001, (2002) 34 EHRR 159, ECHR 2001-VI, § 71.

[33] *Mouvement Raelien Suisse v Switzerland*, (App. 16354/06), 13 July 2012.

[34] Nine votes to eight.

[35] § 52.

[36] Dissenting Opinion of Judge Pinto De Albuquerque.

[37] See *Mosley v United Kingdom*, (App. 48009/08), 10 May 2011, § 132.

[38] *Çetin and others v Turkey*, (Apps. 40153/98 and 40160/98), 13 February 2003, ECHR 2003-III; see also *Gawęda v Poland*, (App. 26229/95), 14 March 2002, (2004) 39 EHRR 90, ECHR 2002-II.

[39] *Appleby and others v United Kingdom*, (App. 44306/98), ECHR 2003-VI; and *Mouvement Raelien Suisse v Switzerland*, (App. 16354/06), 13 July 2012.

[40] *Pedersen and Baadsgaard v Denmark*, (App. 49017/99), 17 December 2004 [GC], (2006) 42 EHRR 486, ECHR 2004-XI, § 79; and *Editorial Board of Parvoye Delo and Shtekel v Ukraine*, (App. 33014/05), 5 May 2011.

[41] *Murphy v Ireland*, (App. 44179/98), 10 July 2003, (2004) 38 EHRR 212, ECHR 203-IX, § 74.

Court has recently had to examine cases involving the internet. It has noted that regulation of the print media will differ from that of the internet given the internet serves billions of users worldwide. The risk of the violation of rights such as Article 8 is higher than in the printed press.[42] However, the internet also enhances freedom of expression. The Court stated in a case involving alleged defamation on a newspaper's website that:

> In light of its accessibility and its capacity to store and communicate vast amounts of information, the Internet plays an important role in enhancing the public's access to news and facilitating the dissemination of information generally. The maintenance of Internet archives is a critical aspect of this role…[43]

The Court examined the restriction of access to internet sites for the first time in *Yildirim v Turkey*.[44] The applicant had established a google site in order to publish his academic research. Access to google sites were blocked by a court order as part of criminal proceedings against another google user. The Court examined the law on internet restrictions throughout Europe and although they concluded there was no clear consensus as to the form of permissible restrictions due to the rapidly changing nature of the medium, the Court underlined the fact that the:

> Internet has now become one of the principal means by which individuals exercise their right to freedom of expression and information, providing as it does essential tools for participation in activities and discussions concerning political issues and issues of general interest.[45]

Even though the measure in question was a restriction rather than a wholesale ban, it was held to be a violation of Article 10.[46] In a dissenting opinion in *Mouvement Raelien Suisse v Switzerland*[47] the judge noted that 'the Internet being a public forum par excellence, the State has a narrow margin of appreciation with regard to information disseminated through this medium. This is even more the case as regards hyperlinks to web pages that are not under the de facto or de jure control of the hyperlinker.'[48] The dissent disagreed with the majority in this case that the poster in question should not be authorized as it held a link to a website that contained ideas linked to paedophilia and cloning. The indirect relationship between the hyperlink and future content of a website the hyperlinker cannot control, casts doubt on the necessity to restrict a poster which contains the hyperlink. [49]

The Court has found that the form of expression includes the language in which it is expressed. In the *Sendikasi* case,[50] the trade union in question promoted education in a mother tongue, which in this case was Kurdish. An order for the dissolution of the Union was made on the grounds the promotion of Kurdish threatened the integrity of the State. The Court found a violation of Article 10 stating that 'Article 10 encompasses the freedom to receive and impart information and ideas in any language which affords the opportunity to take part in the public exchange of cultural, political and social information and ideas of all kinds.'[51]

[42] *Editorial Board of Parvoye Delo and Shtekel v Ukraine*, (App. 33014/05), 5 May 2011.

[43] *Times Newspapers limited (No1 and 2) v United Kingdom*, (Apps. 3002/03 and 23676/03), 10 March 2009, § 27.

[44] *Yildirim v Turkey*, (App. 3111/10), 18 December 2012.

[45] § 55.

[46] A violation on the grounds the measure was not prescribed by law: § 57.

[47] *Mouvement Raelien Suisse v Switzerland*, (App. 16354/06), 13 July 2012.

[48] Judge Pinto De Albuquerque.

[49] Joint Dissenting Opinion of Judges Sajó, Lazarova Trajkovska and Vučinić.

[50] *Egítím ve Bilím Emekçileri Sendikasi v Turkey*, (App. 20641/05), 25 September 2012.

[51] § 71. See also *Sukran Aydin and others v Turkey*, (App. 49197/06), 22 January 2013 concerning the right of private parties to use a non-official language during an election campaign. A criminal penalty for doing so was held to be a violation of Article 10.

The Court has also examined the use of public space to express ideas. In *Appleby v United Kingdom*,[52] the Court found that there is no right to unrestricted access to all public forums. In this case the applicant wanted to have access to a shopping mall owned by a private company. There was no positive obligation on the State in this case to ensure access, especially when other means of dissemination were available. In *Women on the Waves v Portugal*,[53] *Appleby* was distinguished as the case involved the access of a ship to Portuguese territorial waters which were by their nature an open, public space. In *Mouvement Raelien Suisse v Switzerland*,[54] the Court held that access to a public square could be restricted especially in relation to an advertising or information campaign. However, in a strong dissent, the majority were criticized for failing to insist on the need for neutrality from the State and the need for:

> equal access for all individuals and entities that are not expressly prohibited. It is certainly necessary to combat the dangers and excesses of sects and a State may have to ban associations that seriously contravene democratic values. However, it is difficult to accept that a lawful association, with a website that has not been prohibited, should be prevented from promoting its ideas through posters that are not unlawful in themselves. As to the argument whereby, in accepting a poster campaign in public space, the municipal authorities would be endorsing or tolerating the opinions at issue, we find this not only rather unrealistic in relation to the current role of such authorities, but also dangerous. That would be tantamount to arguing, a contrario, that freedom of expression in public space could be restricted solely for the reason that the authorities disagree with the ideas conveyed. Article 10 of the Convention would then risk becoming inoperative.[55]

The Strasbourg Court now adopts a formulaic description of its role in assessing whether a Contracting Party's reliance on the restrictions in the second paragraph of the Article is compatible with Article 10:

> 45. ... The Court's task, in exercising its supervisory jurisdiction, is not to take the place of the competent national authorities but rather to review under Article 10 the decisions they delivered pursuant to their power of appreciation. This does not mean that the supervision is limited to ascertaining whether the respondent State exercised its discretion reasonably, carefully and in good faith; what the Court has to do is to look at the interference complained of in the light of the case as a whole and determine whether the reasons adduced by the national authorities to justify it are 'relevant and sufficient' and whether it was 'proportionate to the legitimate aim pursued'. In doing so, the Court has to satisfy itself that the national authorities applied standards which were in conformity with the principles embodied in Article 10 and, moreover, that they relied on an acceptable assessment of the relevant facts. ...[56]

INCITEMENT TO VIOLENCE AND HATE SPEECH

In the *Gündüz* case, the Court said:

> ... tolerance and respect for the equal dignity of all human beings constitute the foundations of a democratic, pluralistic society. That being so, as a matter of principle it may be

[52] *Appleby and others v United Kingdom*, (App. 44306/98), ECHR 2003-VI.

[53] *Women on the Waves v Portugal*, (App. 31276/05), 3 February 2009.

[54] *Mouvement Raelien Suisse v Switzerland*, (App. 16354/06), 13 July 2012.

[55] Joint Dissenting Opinion of Judges Tulkens, Sajó, Lazarova Trajkovska, Bianku, Power-Forde, Vučinić, and Yudkivska, § 11; see similar criticism in Joint Dissenting Opinion of Judges Sajó, Lazarova Trajkovska and Vučinić and Judge Pinto De Albuquerque.

[56] *Lindon, Otchakovsky-Laurens and July v France*, (Apps. 21279/02 and 36448/02), 22 October 2007[GC] (2008) 46 EHRR 761, ECHR 2007-XI, §§ 45–6.

> considered necessary in certain democratic societies to sanction or even prevent all forms of expression which spread, incite, promote or justify hatred based on intolerance (including religious intolerance), provided that any 'formalities', 'conditions', 'restrictions' or 'penalties' imposed are proportionate to the legitimate aim pursued.
>
> Furthermore . . . there can be no doubt that concrete expressions constituting hate speech, which may be insulting to particular individuals or groups, are not protected by Article 10 of the Convention.[57]

In practice the Strasbourg Court has not maintained any clear distinction between statements that 'spread, incite, promote or justify hatred based on intolerance' and 'concrete expressions constituting hate speech'. The Court, and the Commission in its time, have relied on Article 17 of the Convention,[58] and on the limitations set out in Article 10(2), as interchangeable justifications for declaring inadmissible complaints where the expression in question incites violence or hatred based on intolerance.[59]

In determining whether or not a statement constitutes such an incitement, context is very important. A statement is less likely to be interpreted as an incitement to violence if it is reported to a well-informed audience as part of a pluralistic debate. So, for example, the *Jersild* case[60] concerned the broadcast on Danish television of a programme in which a group of self-confessed racist youths made extremely offensive remarks about black people. The presenter and the head of the news section were prosecuted and convicted. The Strasbourg Court was satisfied that the presentation of the item was not intended to propagate racist views, but to address an issue of some public interest. The broadcast was part of a serious Danish news programme and was intended for a well-informed audience. Taking account of all these factors, the penalties imposed on the presenter and the head of the news section were not necessary in a democratic society for the protection of the rights of others.

If the context is one of conflict and tension, on the other hand, particular caution will be required of the media. In such situations journalists bear special responsibilities and duties, because they can become 'a vehicle for the dissemination of hate speech and violence'.[61] The majority of the Grand Chamber considered that the *Sürek (No. 1)* case was an example of this. The applicant was the owner of a newspaper who was prosecuted and fined for publishing readers' letters about the Kurdish conflict. These letters condemned the military actions of the authorities in south-east Turkey and accused them of brutal suppression of the Kurdish people in their struggle for independence and freedom. One of the letters alleged that the State had connived in imprisonment, torture, and killing of

[57] *Gündüz v Turkey*, (App. 35071/97), 4 December 2003, (2005) 41 EHRR 59, ECHR 2003-XI, § 40.

[58] See ch.6.

[59] See, for example, *Remer v Germany*, Decision of 6 September 1995, (1995) 82 DR 117; App. 25062/94, *Honsik v Austria*, Decision of 18 October 1995, (1995) 83 DR 77; App. 31159/96, *Marais v France*, Decision of 24 June 1996, (1996) 86 DR 184; *Witzsch v Germany*, (App. 32307/96), Decision of 20 April 1999; *Schimanek v Austria*, (App. 41448/98), Decision of 1 February 2000; *Hizb Ut-Tahir and others v Germany*, (App. 31098/08), 12 June 2012; *Kasymakhunov and Saybatalov v Russia*, (Apps. 26261/05 and 26377/06), 14 March 2013, §§ 102–14.

[60] *Jersild v Denmark*, (App. 15890/89), September 24, 1994, Series A No 298, (1994) 19 EHRR 1.

[61] *Erdogdeu and Ince v Turkey*, (Apps. 25067/94 and 25068/94), 8 July 1999 [GC], ECHR 1999-IV, § 54; and see the series of judgments of the Grand Chamber on the same day: *Sürek and Özdemir v Turkey*, (Apps. 23927/94 and 24277/94), 8 July 1999 [GC]; *Sürek v Turkey (No. 1)*, (App. 26682/95), 8 July 1999 [GC], ECHR 1999-IV; *Sürek v Turkey (No. 2)*, (App. 24122/94), 8 July 1999 [GC]; *Sürek v Turkey (No. 4)*, (App. 24762/94), 8 July 1999 [GC]; and see also *Ceylan v Turkey*, (App. 23556/94), 8 July 1999 [GC], (2000) 30 EHRR 73, ECHR 1999-IV and *Okçuoglu v Turkey*, (App. 24246/94), 8 July 1999 [GC]. Politicians and other public figures must also act responsibly, because of their power to influence the public mood: *Zana v Turkey*, (App. 18954/91), 25 November 1997, (1999) 27 EHRR 667, ECHR 1997-VII.

dissidents in the name of the protection of democracy and the Republic. The other letter referred to two massacres which the writer claimed were intentionally committed by the authorities as part of a strategic campaign to eradicate the Kurds, and concluded:

> [T]he struggle of our people for national freedom in Kurdistan has reached a point where it can no longer be thwarted by bloodshed, tanks and shells. Every attack launched by the Turkish Republic to wipe out the Kurds intensifies the struggle for freedom. The bourgeoisie and its toadying press, which draw attention every day to the brutalities in Bosnia-Herzegovina, fail to see the brutalities committed in Kurdistan. Of course, one can hardly expect reactionary fascists who call for a halt in the brutalities in Bosnia-Herzegovina to call for a halt in the brutalities in Kurdistan.
>
> The Kurdish people, who are being torn from their homes and their fatherland, have nothing to lose. But they have much to gain.

The Strasbourg Court emphasized that there was limited scope under Article 10(2) for restrictions on political speech or on debate on matters of public interest, and that the boundaries of permissible criticism were wider with regard to the government than in relation to a private citizen or even a politician. The Contracting Parties should display restraint in resorting to criminal proceedings, particularly where other means were available for replying to unjustified criticism. Nevertheless, in the Court's view, the letters amounted to 'an appeal to bloody revenge by stirring up base emotions and hardening already embedded prejudices which have manifested themselves in deadly violence'. In view of the tense security situation in south-east Turkey, the authorities were justified in penalizing the publisher. The case was by no means clear-cut. Six of the seventeen judges in the Grand Chamber dissented, on the ground, broadly, that it had not been established that there was a real risk of the letters, inciting hatred or violence.[62]

Cases involving Turkey have continued to come before the Court.[63] In *Faruk Temel v Turkey*,[64] the applicant was the Chair of a legal political party. At a press meeting, he read out a statement criticizing the US's involvement in Iraq, the solitary confinement of a terrorist leader, and the disappearances of persons in police custody. He was convicted of disseminating propaganda. The Court found that overall, his speech had not incited others to violence and so there was a violation of Article 10.

There are some historical facts which are still so sensitive that attempts to deny or revise them would be considered hate speech and removed from the protection of Article 10 by Article 17. The applicant in the *Garaudy* case,[65] for example, was an historian who wrote a book which denied various aspects of the Holocaust. The Strasbourg Court observed:

> There can be no doubt that denying the reality of clearly established historical facts, such as the Holocaust, as the applicant does in his book, does not constitute historical research akin to a quest for the truth. The aim and the result of that approach are completely different, the real purpose being to rehabilitate the National-Socialist regime and, as a consequence, accuse the victims themselves of falsifying history. Denying crimes against humanity is therefore one of the most serious forms of racial defamation of Jews and of incitement to

[62] In contrast see *Otegi Mondragon v Spain*, (App. 2034/07), 15 March 2011, where the Court found that the statement calling the King of Spain the Commander in Chief of an army responsible, inter alia, for the torture of Basque activists in an area where there has been a history of violence was not incitement to violence and there was a violation of Article 10.

[63] For examples see *Urper and others v Turkey*, (Apps. 14526/07 et al) 20 October 2009; *Cox v Turkey*, (App. 2933/03), 20 May 2010; *Dink v Turkey*, (App. 2668/07), 14 September 2010; *Altuğ Taner Akçam v Turkey*, (App. 27520/07), 25 October 2011; *Gudenoglu and others v Turkey*, (Apps. 42599/08 et al), 29 January 2013.

[64] *Faruk Temel v Turkey*, (App. 16853/05), 1 February 2011.

[65] *Garaudy v France*, (App. 65831/01), Decision of 24 June 2003, ECHR 2003-IX.

> hatred of them. The denial or rewriting of this type of historical fact undermines the values on which the fight against racism and anti-Semitism are based and constitutes a serious threat to public order. Such acts are incompatible with democracy and human rights because they infringe the rights of others. Its proponents indisputably have designs that fall into the category of aims prohibited by Article 17 of the Convention.[66]

The Strasbourg Court has so far declined to extend this category of clearly established historical facts beyond the Holocaust.[67] Hence, it has held that Articles that exculpated Marshal Pétain[68] from any wrongdoing in the Second World War and a book that cast doubt on the account of heroes of the Resistance[69] were not removed from the protection of Article 10 by Article 17. Nor, in a very different context, was the publication of a book which appeared to advocate the use of prohibited drugs.[70]

The dividing line between material which incites violence and that which merely offends is a fine one to be determined in all the circumstances of the case.[71] So a cartoon published in a Basque newspaper two days after the devastating attacks on the United States on 11 September 2001, which seemed to glorify the conduct of the attackers, and which attracted a fine and a requirement to publish the court's judgment gave rise to no violation of Article 10.[72] The Strasbourg Court considered that the drawing assumed a special significance both by reason of the proximity in time to the terrorist attacks in the United States, and its publication in the Basque region. Taken together this increased the propensity of the drawing to stir up violence and public disorder. The nature of the penalty had been modest, and the action of the French authorities was not disproportionate.[73]

In *Vedjeland v Sweden*,[74] for the first time the Court examined whether homophobic literature amounted to hate speech. The applicants had placed leaflets in the lockers of school children, which made various derogatory statements concerning homosexuality. The Court found that the State was justified in imposing penalties on the applicants for 'agitation against a national group'. The Court reiterated that:

> inciting to hatred does not necessarily entail a call for an act of violence, or other criminal acts. Attacks on persons committed by insulting, holding up to ridicule or slandering specific groups of the population can be sufficient for the authorities to favour combating racist speech in the face of freedom of expression exercised in an irresponsible manner... In this regard, the Court stresses that discrimination based on sexual orientation is as serious as discrimination based on 'race, origin or colour'.[75]

Whilst acknowledging that the aim of the leaflets may have been to start a debate about the lack of objectivity in Swedish schools, the Court agreed with the State that the leaflets were unnecessarily offensive and were aimed at children. The Court did not go as far as labelling the leaflets 'hate speech' and so excluded the case under Article 17.

[66] *Garaudy*, p.23.

[67] Although in *Ivanov v Russia*, (App. 35222/04), Decision of 20 February 2007, the Court did rule that 'a general vehement attack on one ethnic group [Jews]' was so at odds with the requirements of tolerance that Article 17 deprived the applicant of the benefit of the protection afforded by Article 10.

[68] *Lehideux and Isorni v France*, (App. 24662/94), 23 September 1998, (2000) 30 EHRR 665.

[69] *Chauvy and others v France*, (App. 64915/01), 29 June 2004, (2005) 41 EHRR 610, ECHR 2004-VI.

[70] *Palusiński v Poland*, (App. 62414/00), Decision of 3 October 2006, ECHR 2006-XIV, 9.

[71] *Féret v Belgium*, (App. 15615/07), 16 July 2009.

[72] *Leroy v France*, (App. 36109/03), 2 October 2008.

[73] For an example of a case where the reverse was true, see *Orban and others v France*, (App. 20985/05), 15 January 2009. See also *Otegi Mondragon v Spain*, (App. 2034/07), 15 March 2011.

[74] *Vedjeland v Sweden*, (App. 1813/07), 9 February 2012.

[75] § 55.

Several judges concurred with the majority opinion, but on the basis that the leaflets were targeted at children rather than the comments amounting to incitement to hatred. They argued the Court had gone too far in allowing the State to classify offensive speech as incitement.[76] In contrast, several judges criticized the majority for not going far enough. They believed that this was a missed opportunity to underline that homophobic expression is contrary to the spirit of the Convention. They accused the majority of taking an American approach to expression,[77] which Europeans cannot afford to do. They noted that Europe's:

> tragic experience in the last century demonstrates that racist and extremist opinions can bring much more harm than restrictions on freedom of expression. Statistics on hate crimes show that hate propaganda always inflicts harm, be it immediate or potential. It is not necessary to wait until hate speech becomes a real and imminent danger for democratic society.[78]

The different concurring opinions of the judges in *Vedjeland* demonstrates that the Court has yet to develop bright lines between what amounts to offence, incitement, and hate speech.

THE PRESS AS THE 'WATCHDOG' OF DEMOCRACY

The Strasbourg Court has repeatedly emphasized that the press act as a 'public watchdog' in a democratic society.[79] Although they must not overstep certain bounds and may be regulated,[80] they have a duty nevertheless to impart information and ideas on all matters of public interest.[81] Not only does the press have the task of imparting such information and ideas, the public also has a right to receive them. As a result, the national margin of appreciation is limited when the author of the expression in question is a journalist, fulfilling his social duty to impart information and ideas on matters of public concern. Journalists should even be free to use a degree of exaggeration and provocation.[82]

The Strasbourg Court has also recognized that other associations, such as environmental campaign groups, fulfil a role, similar to that of the press, in stimulating public discussion.[83] As a result, the Court will be careful to ensure that any penalty imposed on them

[76] Concurring Opinion of Judge Spielmann, joined by Judge Nussberger, Concurring Opinion of Judge Boštjan M. Zupančič.

[77] See Concurring Opinion of Judge Boštjan M. Zupančič and his discussion of the American approach in *Snyder v Phelps* et al, 562 U.S.(2011) with regard to homophobic speech.

[78] Concurring Opinion of Judge Yudkivska, joined by Judge Villiger, § 11.

[79] *Goodwin v United Kingdom*, (App. 17488/90), 27 March 1996, (1996) 22 EHRR 123, ECHR 1996-II, § 39.

[80] There are limitations that can be placed on the press, see later in this chapter with regard to the need to protect the Article 8 rights of individuals. This is illustrated in the UK where evidence of illegal activities such as 'phone hacking' by newspapers has led to criminal proceedings and a public inquiry recommending greater oversight of the press. There is a debate about what kind of regulation is acceptable in a democratic society, see *The Leveson Inquiry: The Report into the Culture, Practices and Ethics of the Press*, 29 November 2012, accessible at: www.official-documents.gov.uk/document/hc1213/hc07/0780/0780.asp.

[81] *Thorgeir Thorgeirson v Iceland*, (App. 13778/88), 25 June 1992, Series A No 239, (1992) 14 EHRR 843, § 63; *Jersild v Denmark*, (App. 15890/89), 23 September 1994, Series A No 298, (1994) 19 EHRR 1, § 31; and *De Haes and Gijsels v Belgium*, (App. 19983/92), 24 February 1997, (1997) 25 EHRR 1, ECHR 1997-I, § 37.

[82] *Prager and Oberschlick v Austria*, (App. 15974/90), 26 April 1995, Series A No 313, (1996) 21 EHRR 1, § 38.

[83] *Steel and Morris v United Kingdom*, (App. 68416/01), 15 February 2005, (2005) 41 EHRR 403, ECHR 2005-II, § 95. *Társaság A Szabadságjogokért v. Hungary*, (App. 37374/05), 14 April 2009 § 27.

does not have a disproportionate 'chilling effect' on their ability to contribute to the public debate.

Lawyers, however, are expected to be circumspect in their expression, especially when they are acting in litigation:

> 45. The Court reiterates that the special status of lawyers gives them a central position in the administration of justice as intermediaries between the public and the courts. Such a position explains the usual restrictions on the conduct of members of the Bar. Moreover, the courts—the guarantors of justice, whose role is fundamental in a State based on the rule of law—must enjoy public confidence. Regard being had to the key role of lawyers in this field, it is legitimate to expect them to contribute to the proper administration of justice, and thus to maintain public confidence therein....
>
> 46. ...While lawyers too are certainly entitled to comment in public on the administration of justice, their criticism must not overstep certain bounds. In that connection, account must be taken of the need to strike the right balance between the various interests involved, which include the public's right to receive information about questions arising from judicial decisions, the requirements of the proper administration of justice and the dignity of the legal profession....[84]

The function of the subject in society is also important. Penalties imposed for criticizing the government of a State will require extremely strong justification. As the Strasbourg Court said in the *Castells* case:[85]

> The limits of permissible criticism are wider with regard to the Government than in relation to a private citizen, or even a politician. In a democratic system the actions or omissions of the Government must be subject to the close scrutiny not only of the legislative and judicial authorities but also of the press and public opinion. Furthermore, the dominant position which the Government occupies makes it necessary for it to display restraint in resorting to criminal proceedings, particularly where other means are available for replying to the unjustified attacks and criticisms of its adversaries or the media.

This includes not only members of the government but Heads of State[86] including States which have a Monarchy.[87] It is not just the State that has to be tolerant. The limits of acceptable criticism are wide in regard to all politicians, whether or not they are in the government, because they knowingly lay themselves open to the scrutiny of the press and public.[88] The same holds for criticism of civil servants acting in an official capacity;[89] and similar principles apply to other persons who have voluntarily entered the public arena: for example prominent businesspeople, who are actively involved in the affairs of large public companies,[90] or persons and associations that participate in a public debate.[91]

[84] *Nikula v Finland*, (App. 31611/96), 21 March 2002, (2004) 38 EHRR 944, ECHR 2002-II, §§ 45–6. See also *Morice v France*, (App. 29369/10), 11 July 2013.

[85] *Castells v Spain*, (App. 11798/85), 23 April 1992, Series A No 236, (1992) 14 EHRR 445, § 46.

[86] *Eon v France*, (App. 26118/10), 14 March 2013; *Tusalp v Turkey*, (App. 32131/08), 21 May 2012.

[87] *Otegi Mondragon v Spain*, (App. 2034/07), 15 March 2011.

[88] *Dichand and others v Austria*, (App. 29271/95), 26 February 2002, § 39. See also *Scharsach and News Verlagsgesellschaft mbH v Austria*, (App. 39394/98), 13 November 2003, (2005) 40 EHRR 569, ECHR 2003-XI; and *Kuliş v Poland*, (App. 15601/02), 18 March 2008.

[89] *July and SARL Libération v France*, (App. 20893/03), 14 February 2008.

[90] *Fayed v United Kingdom*, (App. 17101/90), 21 September 1994, Series A No 294-B, (1994) 18 EHRR 393. See also *Verlagsgruppe News GmbH v Austria (No. 2)*, (App. 10520/02), 14 December 2006.

[91] *Nilsen and Johnsen v Norway*, (App. 23118/93), 25 November 1999 [GC], ECHR 1999-VIII, § 52; and *Jerusalem v Austria*, (App. 26958/95), 27 February 2001, (2003) 37 EHRR 567, ECHR 2001-II, § 39.

Of course, even public figures are entitled to some privacy, however, and since there is little public benefit to be derived from exposing certain aspects of a politician's private life, the national authorities may be justified in taking preventive measures.[92]

The scope for attacking public servants is narrower than politicians because they do not knowingly lay themselves open to close scrutiny of their every word and deed to the extent to which politicians do and because they must enjoy public confidence in conditions free of undue perturbation if they are to be successful in performing their tasks.[93] The Strasbourg Court is particularly protective of judges. Article 10(2) expressly authorizes limitations for maintaining the authority and impartiality of the judiciary, and the Court has frequently held that, in order to maintain public confidence in the judiciary, judges should be protected from unjustified, destructive, and untrue attacks.[94] However, judges will lose this protection if they enter political life.[95]

If the person attacked is a public servant, the Strasbourg Court will pay particular attention to whether the attacks were professional or personal. Public servants and judges should be expected to endure criticism but not insult. So, for example, the Court found a violation in a case[96] where the applicant journalists had criticized in virulent terms the Court of Appeal judges who had awarded custody of two children to their father, a notary who had been accused by his ex-wife of child abuse. The journalists had been sued in defamation by the judges and ordered to pay nominal damages. The Strasbourg Court placed reliance on the fact that the Articles had been well researched and had formed part of a public debate which had been taking place in Belgium at the time on incest, child abuse, and judicial reactions to these problems. By contrast, the Court found no violation in the *Barfod* case,[97] where the applicant had been convicted of criminal defamation following his publication of an article questioning the impartiality of two lay judges. The attack on the judges in this case had been personal and destructive, and the applicant had not been prevented from voicing criticism of the judgment, rather than of the judges themselves.

In the *Steel and Morris* case, the subject of the defamation was the fast-food chain, McDonald's. The applicants sought to argue that large multinational companies, like McDonald's, should never be able to bring defamation proceedings. However, the Strasbourg Court rejected this argument. It held that, although the limits of acceptable criticism are wide in the case of such companies (because they inevitably and knowingly lay themselves open to close scrutiny of their acts), national authorities were entitled to afford companies some protection from defamation because there is a public interest in protecting the commercial success and viability of companies, not only for the benefit of shareholders and employees, but also for the wider economic good.[98]

The Strasbourg Court makes a critical distinction between value judgments and statements of fact. Value judgments cannot be proved. A requirement, in defamation proceedings, that a defendant prove the truth of a value judgment will violate his right to freedom

[92] *Tammer v Estonia*, (App. 41205/98), 6 February 2001, (2003) 37 EHRR 857, ECHR 2001-I. See also *Standard Verlags GmbH v Austria (No. 2)*, (App. 21277/05), 4 June 2009.

[93] *Lešník v Slovakia*, (App. 35640/97), 11 March 2003, ECHR 2003-IV, § 53.

[94] *Skalka v Poland*, (App. 43425/98), 27 May 2003, § 40. See also *Perna v Italy*, (App. 48898/99), 6 May 2003 [GC], (2004) 39 EHRR 563, ECHR 2003-V; and *Morice v France*, (App. 29369/10), 11 July 2013.

[95] *Hrico v Slovakia*, (App. 49418/99), 20 July 2004, § 46.

[96] *De Haes and Gijsels v Belgium*, (App. 19983/92), 24 February 1997; (1997) 25 EHRR 1, ECHR 1997-I.

[97] *Barfod v Denmark*, (App. 11508/85), 22 February 1989, Series A No 149, (1991) 13 EHRR 493.

[98] *Steel and Morris v United Kingdom*, (App. 68416/01), 15 February 2005, (2005) 41 EHRR 403, ECHR 2005-II, § 94.

of expression, protected by Article 10.[99] However, that does not mean that defendants can express any opinions, no matter how damaging, without any evidence to support them. Even value judgments will require, at the very least, some basis in fact.[100] Factual statements, on the other hand, are susceptible of proof. In general, it will be reasonable, in the interests of protecting the rights and reputations of others, to require defendants in defamation proceedings to prove the truth of factual statements that they have made.[101] However, they should be given the chance to do so. The protection of the rights and reputation of others will not normally justify a rule that prevents defendants from pleading justification in their defence.[102]

There are some statements of fact which it is in the interest of the public to hear but which are impossible to prove. For example, many important newspaper stories come from sources that would not be prepared to give evidence in defamation proceedings. As a result, the Strasbourg Court has recognized that there are some circumstances where the interests of society require that defendants in defamation proceedings be exempted from their ordinary duty to verify statements of fact. In considering whether those circumstances exist, the Court will have regard to the nature and degree of the defamation and the reliability of any sources.[103] The conduct of the defendant will be important. The Court will examine, *inter alia*, whether the defendant conducted a reasonable amount of research before making the defamatory statement,[104] whether the allegations were presented in a reasonably balanced manner,[105] and whether the person defamed was given the opportunity to defend himself or herself.[106]

The Strasbourg Court will judge for itself whether the statement was a value judgment or a statement of fact.[107] That determination can be very controversial.[108] In the *Pedersen and Baadsgard* case,[109] for example, the applicants produced two television programmes concerning the conviction of a person for murder. The programme strongly criticized the conduct of the police and, in particular, the Chief Superintendent, who was identified by name. A witness was interviewed, who claimed that she had provided an alibi for the convicted person, which the police had ignored. The applicants then showed a photograph of the Chief Superintendent and asked a series of rhetorical questions, such as:

> Was it [the named Chief Superintendent] who decided that the report should not be included in the case? Or did he and the Chief Inspector of the Flying Squad conceal the witness's statement from the defence, the judges and the jury?

[99] *Lingens v Austria*, (App. 9815/82), 8 July 1986, Series A No 103, (1986) 8 EHRR 407, § 46; *Oberschlick v Austria*, (App. 11662/85), 23 May 1991, Series A No 204, (1994) 19 EHRR 389, § 63; and *Ukrainian Media Group v Ukraine*, (App. 72713/01), 29 March 2005, (2006) 43 EHRR 499.

[100] *Dichand and others v Austria*, (App. 29271/95), 26 February 2002, § 52; and *Otegi Mondragon v Spain*, (App. 2034/07), 15 March 2011.

[101] *McVicar v United Kingdom*, (App. 46311/99), 7 May 2002, (2002) 35 EHRR 566, ECHR 2002-III, § 87.

[102] *Colombani and others v France*, (App. 51279/99), 25 June 2002, ECHR 2002-V, § 66. See also *Sorguç v Turkey*, (App. 17089/03), 23 June 2009, § 33.

[103] *Bladet Tromsø and Stensaas v Norway*, (App. 21980/93), 20 May 1999 [GC], (2000) 29 EHRR 125, ECHR 1999-III, § 66; and *McVicar v United Kingdom*, (App. 46311/99), 7 May 2002, (2002) 35 EHRR 566, ECHR 2002-III, § 84; *Lithia Publishing Company Ltd and Constantinides v Cyprus*, (App. 17550/03), 22 May 2008.

[104] *Prager and Oberschlick v Austria*, (App. 15974/90), 26 April 1995, Series A No 313, (1996) 21 EHRR 1, § 37.

[105] *Bergens Tidende and others v Norway*, (App. 26132/95), 2 May 2000, (2001) 31 EHRR 430, ECHR 2000-IV, § 57.

[106] § 58.

[107] *Stojanovic v Croatia*, (App. 23160/09), 9 September 2013, where the Court disagreed with the domestic court in finding the applicant made a statement of fact. There was not enough proof to come to this conclusion.

[108] For a very odd majority decision by four votes to three which turned on the characterization of the offending material as fact or value judgment, see *Schmidt v Austria*, (App. 513/05), 17 July 2008.

[109] *Pedersen and Baadsgaard v Denmark*, (App. 49017/99), 17 December 2004 [GC], (2006) 42 EHRR 486, ECHR 2004-XI.

Nine out of the seventeen members of the Grand Chamber found that these rhetorical questions amounted to statements of fact, which the applicants had failed to prove. They considered that the nature and degree of the defamation was very serious (as the applicants had identified the Chief Superintendent on national television and accused him of committing a serious criminal offence) and that the applicants had not taken sufficient steps to verify the truth of the witness's story. As a result, they found that there was no violation of Article 10. The remaining eight judges, on the other hand, considered the questions posed by the applicants to be 'value judgments or provocative hypotheses', for which there was a sufficient factual basis. The dissent in the case and the outcome of other cases before the Court[110] highlights the problematic nature of the distinction that is drawn by the Court between a value judgement and a statement of fact.

The Court has controversially examined defamatory remarks made on a news portal.[111] However the comments were not made by the owners of the portal but by third parties who could leave comments on news stories on the news site. The applicants Delfi AS, owned a large internet news portal in Estonia. At the end of the news articles there were the words 'add your comment' and fields for comments, the commenter's name, and his or her email address. Comments left by others could be accessed in a separate area. The comments were uploaded automatically and were not edited or moderated by the applicant. The articles received about 10,000 readers' comments every day. Many of these were under false names.

There was a system of notify-and-take-down, where any reader could mark a comment as insulting and the comment was removed expeditiously. There was also a system of automatic deletion of comments that included certain obscene words. A victim of a defamatory comment could also directly notify the applicant, in which case the comment was removed immediately. The applicant had made efforts to advise users that the comments were not its opinion and that the authors of comments were responsible for their content. After running a story about a company destroying public ice roads, 185 comments were left by users, twenty of them making threats or were offensive against the company. After about six weeks the company's lawyers requested that the comments be taken down. The applicants took the comments down on the same day as the request.

Despite these measures taken by the applicant, the Court held that the finding of the domestic courts that the applicants pay minimal damages to the company was not a violation of Article 10. The Estonian Courts held an EU Directive that provides protection for the hosts of news portals such as the applicants was inapplicable and the Strasbourg Court found that it was within the discretion of the State as to how to interpret EU legislation in its laws.[112] It went on to find that the measures taken were not enough to avoid liability for the comments. The applicants had control over the comments once they were posted and were aware that there may be negative comments from anonymous users who the company could not sue. In conclusion the Court held:

> in particular the insulting and threatening nature of the comments, the fact that the comments were posted in reaction to an article published by the applicant company in its professionally-managed news portal run on a commercial basis, the insufficiency of the measures taken by the applicant company to avoid damage being caused to other parties' reputations and to ensure a realistic possibility that the authors of the comments will be held liable, and the moderate sanction imposed on the applicant company, the Court... in

[110] Such as see *Schmidt v Austria*, (App. 513/05), 17 July 2008.

[111] *Delfi AS v Estonia*, (App. 64569/09), 10 October 2013, not yet final as of 30 November 2013.

[112] § 74.

> the present case the domestic courts' finding that the applicant company was liable for the defamatory comments posted by readers on its Internet news portal was a justified and proportionate restriction on the applicant company's right to freedom of expression.[113]

As the Court has previously noted, the internet is an important forum for the dissemination of ideas and opinions. However, the Court had to find a balance between protection of expression and the need to protect persons from personal abuse, and invasion of privacy. The judgment of the Court may be of concern to news portal and internet sites that post users' comments. It may be necessary for these sites to consider whether to allow anonymous posting and therefore a question arises as to whether a lack of anonymity will have a 'chilling effect'. The Court also avoided differentiating between the portal as a mere host of content or a publisher of it. It left this to the State to decide.

THE CONFLICT WITH THE RIGHT TO PRIVATE LIFE

See Chapters 14 and 16 for further discussion of this area.

The Strasbourg Court initially established some guidelines on the use of photographs in relation to rights protected by Article 8 in the *Von Hannover* case.[114] The Strasbourg Court has also addressed the question in the context of Article 10, noting the relationship between the two Articles. The balancing exercise required is a tricky one for all concerned.[115] When does an expectation of respect for private life get trumped by the right of the general public to be informed, through publication of photographs of the person concerned, of a matter of public interest? When will a photograph in addition to words contribute to a debate of general interest?

The applicant in the *Von Hannover* case[116] was Princess Caroline of Monaco. She complained about the publication in German magazines of paparazzi photographs of her eating in restaurants, playing with her children, and enjoying herself on holiday. She sought an injunction in the German courts to prevent the publication of further photographs. The German Constitutional Court, however, refused an injunction. The Strasbourg Court observed that:

> Although freedom of expression also extends to the publication of photos, this is an area in which the protection of the rights and reputation of others takes on particular importance. The present case does not concern the dissemination of 'ideas', but of images containing very personal or even intimate 'information' about an individual. Furthermore, photos appearing in the tabloid press are often taken in a climate of continual harassment which induces in the person concerned a very strong sense of intrusion into their private life or even of persecution.[117]

The Court drew a 'fundamental distinction' between the reporting of facts capable of contributing to a debate in a democratic society relating to politicians in the exercise of their functions, where the press exercised an important 'watchdog' role, and the reporting of details of an individual's private life, where it did not. Although the public right to be

[113] § 94.

[114] *Von Hannover v Germany* (App. 59320/00), 24 June 2004, (2005) 40 EHRR 1, ECHR 2004-VI.

[115] As in *Egeland and Hanseid v Norway*, (App. 34438/04), 16 April 2009.

[116] *Von Hannover v Germany* (App. 59320/00), 24 June 2004, (2005) 40 EHRR 1, ECHR 2004-VI.

[117] § 59.

informed could in some extend to aspects of the private life of public figures, particularly politicians, that was not the case here.[118] In *MGN Limited v United Kingdom*,[119] the Court held there was no violation where the domestic courts found a breach of confidence when the newspaper printed stories about the supermodel Naomi Campbell's history of drug abuse and treatment for drug addiction. It held that the stories about drug abuse were already in the public domain. It was the additional information about the model's treatment for addiction that interfered with her privacy.[120]

In a further two cases involving Von Hannover[121] and in the *Axel Springer AG* case,[122] the Court further elucidated on the factors it will consider when balancing the protection of the private life of the applicant with the need to protect freedom of expression. In *Axel Springer*, the applicant newspaper printed articles about the arrest of a well-known television actor for possession of drugs. The actor played a police officer in a television series. The actor claimed the articles had violated his private life and the domestic courts had imposed an injunction on the newspaper prohibiting any future stories on the actor's arrest. The Court noted the rights under Article 8 and Article 10 are accorded equal respect and so when balancing the rights the Court would consider:

- contribution to a debate of general interest;
- how well known is the person concerned and what is the subject of the report;
- prior conduct of the person concerned;
- method of obtaining the information and its veracity;
- content, form, and consequences of the publication;
- severity of the sanction imposed.

In the present case, the Court found that the injunctions were a violation of Article 10 as the actor was well known in his role as a police officer, he had revealed details of his private life in previous interviews, the police and prosecutor were the source of the stories, the stories focused on the actor's arrest and did not make unsubstantiated allegations, and the injunctions could have a chilling effect.[123]

In the *Armonienė* case,[124] the Strasbourg Court held that, even where the national courts uphold an individual's claim to privacy against the press, there will be a breach of Article 8 if the damages awarded are too low. The applicant was the widow of a man who was not a public figure of any kind. He was, however, named in an article on the front page of the biggest Lithuanian newspaper. The article, which also included his address, claimed that he had AIDs and had fathered a child with an unmarried mother who was also HIV positive.

[118] See also *Hachette Filipacchi Associés v France*, (App. 71111/01), 14 June 2007, (2009) 49 EHRR 515, ECHR 2007-VII, where the Court was divided when examining the publication of photographs of a murdered politician just after his assassination, which distressed his family. The magazine was ordered to publish a statement stating the family had found the publication distressing. The Court held this was not a violation of Article 10, though the dissent thought that the nature of the photograph (face down), the fact it was widely disseminated on television and was not prurient meant there was a violation of Article 10.

[119] *MGN Limited v United Kingdom*, (App. 39401/04), 18 January 2011.

[120] § 150–155. The Court did find a violation as it found the success fees the applicant had to pay were excessive.

[121] *Von Hannover v Germany (No.2)*, (App. 40660/08), 7 February 2012 and (App. 8772/10), 19 September 2013.

[122] *Axel Springer AG v Germany*, (App. 39954/08), 7 February 2012.

[123] §§ 96–110, the Court found by twelve votes to five for a violation. The dissent argued that the domestic courts had examined the criteria and carried out the balancing exercise. The Court should not substitute its view for the decision of the Court. Dissenting Opinion of Judge López Guerra joined by Judges Jungwiert, Jaeger, Villiger, and Poalelungi.

[124] *Armonienė v Lithuania*, (App. 36919/02), 25 November 2008.

The Lithuanian court found that the newspaper article was unfounded and had damaged the applicant's reputation, health, and relationships, but that it had not been deliberately malicious. It awarded the maximum amount of damages permitted by law in the absence of proof of malice, approximately €3,000. The Strasbourg Court found that there had been an 'outrageous abuse of press freedom' causing substantial harm and found the statutory restriction on the judge's power to award damages to breach Article 8.

SEVERITY OF ANY PENALTY

The severity of the penalty imposed will often be important. Large awards of damages in civil proceedings can, in themselves, be enough to violate Article 10,[125] particularly if they are out of proportion to the income of the applicant and there is no evidence of any financial damage to the person defamed.[126] If damages are awarded by juries, the judiciary will be required to exercise a certain amount of control over the level of those damages so as to keep them within reasonable bounds.[127]

Similarly, if applicants are punished for their freedom of expression by way of a criminal sanction, the Strasbourg Court will examine whether that sanction was necessary and appropriate. In so doing, the Court will have regard to the seriousness of the offence and the previous record of the applicant.[128] Sentences of imprisonment will be particularly hard to justify. Indeed the Court has said, in the *Cumpănă* case, that imprisoning a journalist for defamation, when the context is a debate on a matter of legitimate public interest, requires the presence of exceptional circumstances, 'notably where other fundamental rights have been seriously impaired, as, for example, in the case of hate speech or incitement to violence'.[129] Such a sentence creates an unacceptable chilling effect on journalistic freedom of expression.[130]

There are some situations where any penalty, no matter how light, will violate Article 10. In the *Eon* case,[131] the applicant was convicted of an offence and given a suspended fine of €30 for insulting the Head of State. He had waved a placard reading 'Casse toi pov'con' ('Get lost, you sad prick'), a phrase used by President Sarkozy when a farmer had refused to shake his hand. The phrase was widely disseminated in the media and on the internet and became a matter of public debate. The Court, found that although the fine was small, the case was part of a debate of public interest in France and the law in question may have had a chilling effect on freedom of expression, especially the use of satire, which plays an important role in debating matters of public concern.[132]

In some cases the conduct of the applicant in adopting 'an exceedingly casual attitude' to national proceedings in which a penalty is imposed may influence the Court in its determination of the proportionality of the measures in issue.[133]

[125] *MGN Limited v United Kingdom*, (App. 39401/04), 18 January 2011.

[126] *Steel and Morris v United Kingdom*, (App. 68416/01), 15 February 2005, (2005) 41 EHRR 403, ECHR 2005-II, §§ 96–7.

[127] *Tolstoy Miloslavsky v United Kingdom*, (App. 18139/91), 13 July 1995, Series A No 316-B, (1995) 20 EHRR 442, § 50.

[128] *Skalka v Poland*, (App. 43425/98), 27 May 2003, § 41.

[129] *Cumpănă and Mazăre v Romania*, (App. 33348/96), 17 December 2004 [GC], (2005) 41 EHRR 200, ECHR 2004-X, § 115.

[130] *Ricci v Italy*, (App. 30210/06), 8 October 2013 where the Court found that a four month prison sentence for breaching confidentiality by airing a television programme from another television channel without its permission or the permission of the participants, was an excessive penalty and a violation of Article 10.

[131] *Eon v France*, (App. 26118/10), 14 March 2013.

[132] See also *Steur v Netherlands*, (App. 39657/98), 28 October 2003, (2004) 39 EHRR 706, ECHR 2003-XI.

[133] *Ivanciuc v Romania*, (App. 18624/03), Decision of 8 September 2005, ECHR 2005-XI.

LEGAL AID TO DEFEND DEFAMATION PROCEEDINGS

The Strasbourg Court has had to consider whether (and when) Article 10 requires the defendants in defamation proceedings to be provided with legal aid. The applicant in the *McVicar* case[134] was a journalist who alleged, in an article for a magazine, that the athlete Linford Christie had used banned performance-enhancing drugs. Christie sued him for defamation. During most of the proceedings the applicant represented himself because he could not afford legal fees and because legal aid was not available for defamation. The jury found that he had not proved the truth of the allegation and he was ordered to pay for the costs of the action and made subject to an injunction forbidding him from publishing the allegation again. McVicar claimed that the lack of legal aid was a violation of his right to a fair trial and his right to freedom of expression. The Court rejected these arguments, noting that he was an experienced and well-educated journalist, that the issues in the case were relatively simple and that he had had the assistance of a specialist defamation lawyer for at least some of the case.

In the *Steel and Morris* case, the applicants were a part-time bar worker and a former postal worker receiving social security benefits. They were associated with London Greenpeace, an environmental group that published a pamphlet that made various defamatory allegations about the fast-food chain McDonald's. The subsequent defamation proceedings brought by McDonald's (dubbed the 'McLibel trial') ran for two and a half years and became the longest in English history. The trial at first instance lasted 313 court days and was preceded by twenty-eight interlocutory proceedings. The appeal hearing lasted twenty-three days. The factual case involved 40,000 pages of documentary evidence and 130 oral witnesses on scientific issues such as nutrition, diet, degenerative disease, and food safety, some of which were considered too complex for a jury to assess. Once again the applicants were not entitled to legal aid and, although they received considerable assistance from lawyers acting *pro bono*, they acted alone for the bulk of the proceedings. The Court relied on the extraordinary length and complexity of the case in finding that, in this particular case, the lack of legal aid did violate the applicants' right to freedom of expression (as well as their right to a fair trial).[135]

CONFIDENTIAL INFORMATION

Article 10 guarantees the freedom to receive as well as impart information, but it does not confer a right of access to information.[136] Although the Strasbourg Court appears increasingly ready to find an obligation on the State to provide information to concerned individuals included in the right to respect for private life under Article 8,[137] Article 10, in contrast, is directed at proscribing interference by a public authority between a willing

[134] *McVicar v United Kingdom*, (App. 46311/99), 7 May 2002, (2002) 35 EHRR 566, ECHR 2002-III.

[135] *Steel and Morris v United Kingdom*, (App. 68416/01), 15 February 2005, (2005) 41 EHRR 403, ECHR 2005-II, §§ 59–72 and 75.

[136] *Leander v Sweden*, (App. 9248/81), 26 March 1987, Series A No 116, (1987) 9 EHRR 433; and *Gaskin v United Kingdom*, (App. 10454/83), 7 July 1989, Series A No 160, (1990) 12 EHRR 36. Compare Art. 19 of the Covenant on Civil and Political Rights.

[137] See ch.16.

giver and a willing recipient. But it will be a violation of Article 10 for a Contracting Party to refuse to grant access to documents once a national court has made an order for this to happen.[138] The Court has also not ruled out that Article 10 includes the right of the individual not to impart confidential information if ordered by a Court, but that the question should be addressed in the circumstances of each case. In *Gillberg v Sweden*[139] the applicant refused to release confidential research findings after being ordered to do so by the Court. He argued that he had a negative right not to impart information. However on the facts the Court found that the research findings belonged to the university for which he worked and his research was not akin to a journalist sources or to a lawyer's duty of confidentiality. There was no violation of Article 10.

In the *Hadjianastassiou* case[140] the Strasbourg Court made it clear that the State was to be afforded a very wide margin of appreciation when the protection of national security was in issue. The applicant had been convicted and sentenced for having disclosed military secrets. The leaked information was of very minor importance, but the Court concluded that any disclosure of State secrets was apt to a compromise national security and found no violation.

In two cases concerning the publication of Peter Wright's book *Spycatcher*,[141] the newspapers concerned complained of a violation of Article 10 arising from the action by the Attorney General in bringing breach of confidence actions and seeking injunctions restraining publication of extracts of the book. Of particular significance was a decision of the Court of Appeal that the injunctions against *The Observer* and *The Guardian* bound all the media within the jurisdiction of the English courts and that any publication or broadcast of the *Spycatcher* material would constitute a criminal contempt of court. Despite the arrival in the United Kingdom of copies of the book imported from outside the country, the injunctions were kept in force until October 1988. For the first period[142] the Strasbourg Court ruled by fourteen to ten that the risk of material prejudicial to the security services existed and that this justified the imposition of injunctions. For the remaining period, the decision was unanimous that there was a violation of Article 10; the material could no longer be regarded as likely to prejudice the security services since the book was freely circulating in the United States.

The Court has also examined the use of copyright material on the internet. In *Ashby Donald and others v France*,[143] the applicants were fashion photographers who had taken photographs at a fashion show and then put them on their website with the intention of selling them. This was held to be an infringement of copyright of the fashion houses. The Court upheld the right of the State to enforce the copyright law. Similarly, in a case involving the file sharing website 'Pirate Bay', the Court found the case inadmissible as there were weighty reasons for the State to protect the property rights of the copyright holders.[144]

[138] *Kenedi v Hungary*, (App. 31475/05), 26 May 2009.

[139] *Gillberg v Sweden*, (App. 41723/06), 3 April 2012.

[140] *Hadjianastassiou v Greece*, (App. 12945/87), 16 December 1992, Series A No 252-A, (1993) 16 EHRR 219, §§ 38–47.

[141] *Observer and Guardian v United Kingdom*, (App. 13585/88), 26 November 1991, Series A No 216), (1992) 14 EHRR 153; and *Sunday Times v United Kingdom (No. 2)*, (App. 13166/87), 26 November 1991, Series A No 217, (1992) 14 EHRR 229. See also *Blake v United Kingdom*, (App. 68890/01), Decision of 25 October 2005, ECHR 2005-XII.

[142] From July 1986 to July 1987.

[143] *Ashby Donald and others v France*, (App. 36769/08), 10 January 2013.

[144] *Neij and Sunde Kolmisoppi v Sweden*, (App. 40397/12), 19 February 2013.

WHISTLE-BLOWERS

In a number of cases where civil servants had publicly criticized their employers and suffered disciplinary measures,[145] the Commission accepted that State employees and service personnel have a special 'duty of discretion', meaning that their freedom to criticize government policies in a public manner is curtailed. Nonetheless, restrictive measures must be proportionate, and the motives of the person disclosing the information and the ability to substantiate his or her criticisms are relevant considerations. Criticisms which are made to a more limited audience, for example the commanding officer of military personnel, require a greater degree of tolerance, even if expressed in strong terms.[146]

The *Guja* case[147] was the first to deal explicitly with the practice of whistle-blowing.[148] The applicant was the head of the press office in the Moldovan Prosecutor General's Office. There were concerns about corruption in the practices of law enforcement agencies. Guja saw a letter from a very senior politician which sought to bring pressure on the prosecutor to terminate pending prosecutions against certain police officers. A report concerning two such letters was published in a newspaper, and Guja admitted that he had given copies to the press. He argued that he had acted in good faith, that the letters were not confidential, and that he had acted in line with the President's anti-corruption drive. The applicant was dismissed from his employment, and his legal proceedings seeking reinstatement failed. He complained of a violation of Article 10. The Grand Chamber, in a unanimous judgment finding a violation of Article 10, said:

> 72. ... the Court notes that a civil servant, in the course of his work, may become aware of in-house information, including secret information, whose divulgation or publication corresponds to a strong public interest. The Court thus considers that the signalling by a civil servant or an employee in the public sector of illegal conduct or wrongdoing in the workplace should, in certain circumstances, enjoy protection. This may be called for where the employee or civil servant concerned is the only person, or part of a small category of persons, aware of what is happening at work and is thus best placed to act in the public interest by alerting the employer or the public at large....
>
> 73. In the light of the duty of discretion [owed by a civil servant], disclosure should be made in the first place to the person's superior or other competent authority or body. It is only where this is clearly impracticable that the information could, as a last resort, be disclosed to the public.... In assessing whether the restriction on freedom of expression was proportionate, therefore, the Court must take into account whether there was available to the applicant any other effective means of remedying the wrongdoing which he intended to uncover.[149]

Two key factors would be considered by the Court in assessing the proportionality of the interference with Article 10 rights. The first is the level of the public interest in the

[145] See, for example, App. 18597/92, *Haseldine v United Kingdom*, Decision of 13 May 1992.

[146] *Grigoriades v Greece*, (App. 24348/94), 25 November 1997, (1999) 27 EHRR 464, ECHR 1997-VII.

[147] *Guja v Moldova*, (App. 14277/04), 12 February 2008 [GC], ECHR 2008-nyr. See also *Juppala v Finland*, (App. 18620/03), 2 December 2008, § 42 which concerned a good faith disclosure to a doctor about possible child abuse which resulted in the informant being found guilty of defamation.

[148] The term is derived from the practice of English police officers in times gone by of blowing their whistles to draw attention to criminal activity. Whistle-blowing has typically come to refer to the practice of an insider communicating evidence of misconduct and claiming exemption from sanctions for breaching an employer's confidence.

[149] *Guja v Moldova*, (App. 14277/04), 12 February 2008 [GC], ECHR 2008-nyr, §§ 72–3.

disclosed information, and whether this overrides the confidentiality of the information. The second factor is the authenticity of the information which is disclosed. There is a heavy burden on the disclosing party to ensure the accuracy and reliability of the information disclosed. Whistle-blowers will also be expected to show that they have acted in good faith, and not from any sense of personal grievance, or expectation of personal advantage. The Court will examine alternative channels for making the disclosure and the detriment to the employer. As in other aspects of the application of Article 10, the severity of any penalty imposed upon the whistle-blower will need to be weighed in the balance. [150]

In the *Guja* case, the Court distinguished its judgment in the *Stoll* case.[151] In the latter case, a journalist obtained a confidential document written by the Swiss Ambassador to the United States discussing the strategy which might be adopted by the Swiss authorities in negotiating a settlement of compensation claims for Holocaust victims for unclaimed assets deposited in Swiss bank accounts. It was assumed that the journalist had acquired the document in breach of official secrecy. He then wrote an article in a newspaper critical of the ambassador, which disclosed some of the contents of the confidential document. He was fined 800 Swiss francs for publishing secret official deliberations. The Swiss Press Council found that the publication had been legitimate, but was critical of the content, which made the ambassador's comments appear sensational and shocking. The journalist complained of a violation of Article 10. The Grand Chamber clearly found this a challenging case. They were faced with a conflict not between a private interest and a public interest, but rather between two public interests: 'the interest of readers in being informed on a topical issue and the interest of the authorities in ensuring a positive and satisfactory outcome to the diplomatic negotiations being conducted.'[152] Reversing the Chamber judgment, the Grand Chamber, by twelve votes to five, concluded that there had been no violation of Article 10. In making its assessment, the Grand Chamber considered the issue at stake, namely the dissemination of confidential information on a matter of considerable public interest, the nature of the interests at stake, the review of the sanction on the journalist by the national courts, the conduct of the journalist, and the severity of the penalty. The overwhelming sense in reading the judgment of the Court is that it was very heavily influenced by the interest in protecting the confidentiality of information within the diplomatic service in order to ensure the proper functioning of international relations. In her concurring opinion, Judge Ziemele was critical of the majority in singling out the interests of the respondent State in this way, and their basing their conclusions on the capacity of the disclosure to undermine diplomatic negotiations as distinct from its actual impact. The dissenting judges view the judgment as 'a dangerous and unjustified departure from the Court's well-established case-law' in giving far too great a weight to the confidential nature of the document. In a contrasting case involving a request for the release of information concerning surveillance carried out by the intelligence services in Romania,[153] the Court found a violation. The distinguishing feature of this case from *Stoll* may be the fact that the case involved the alleged illegal activities of an intelligence service in an ex-communist State and so the disclosures were important to the protection of democracy within the State. This prevailed over the need to maintain public confidence in the organization.

[150] The Court affirmed this criteria for assessing violation in whistle-blower cases in *Heinisch v Germany*, (App. 28274/08), 21 July 2011, §§ 71–92.

[151] *Stoll v Switzerland*, (App. 69698/01), 10 December 2007 [GC], ECHR 2007-XIV. See also *Kudeshkina v Russia*, (App. 29492/05), 26 February 2009.

[152] § 116.

[153] *Bucur and Toma v Romania*, (App. 40238/02), 8 January 2013.

The Strasbourg Court has also made judgments which support journalistic enquiry. In the *Damann* case,[154] a journalist was prosecuted, convicted on appeal, and fined for inciting another to disclose an official secret. The journalist, as part of his investigation into a spectacular robbery, had obtained information from an administrative assistant in the prosecutor's office about whether certain individuals had any previous criminal convictions. The journalist did not use the information in any published material; he had been prosecuted after he had shown a police officer the information he had received. The Strasbourg Court noted that it was dealing with a journalist's research in investigating a potential story for publication. The Court noted that the provider of the information had not been tricked, threatened or pressurized into providing the information, and the journalist had not published the information (and so there was no interference with the rights of others). In all the circumstances, the conviction and light penalty were such as to have a chilling effect on journalists undertaking research inherent in the task of newspaper reporting; the interference was not necessary in a democratic society. There was a risk that such action would inhibit the role of the press as a public watchdog on matters of public interest.

OBSCENITY AND BLASPHEMY

In the *Handyside* case the Strasbourg Court noted that there was no uniform European concept of 'morality' and made it clear that Contracting Parties would enjoy a wide margin of appreciation in assessing whether measures were required to protect moral standards.[155]

This approach was followed in the *Müller* case,[156] which concerned an exhibition of contemporary art including three paintings depicting sexual acts, seized by the authorities on the grounds that they were obscene. The Strasbourg Court found that it was not unreasonable for the Swiss courts to have found the paintings liable to offend the sense of sexual propriety of persons of ordinary sensitivity. As a result, the imposition of fines did not violate Article 10.

The expression under consideration in the *Wingrove* case[157] was a video made by the applicant portraying a woman, dressed as a nun and described in the credits as 'Saint Teresa' (of Avila), having an erotic fantasy involving the crucified figure of Christ. The video was refused a certificate for distribution by the British Board of Film Classification on the grounds that it appeared to contravene the British blasphemy law, in that the Board considered that its public distribution would outrage and insult the feelings of believing Christians. The Strasbourg Court did not consider that there was yet sufficient common ground in the legal and social orders of the Contracting Parties to conclude that a system allowing a State to impose restrictions on the propagation of material on the basis that it was blasphemous was, in itself, incompatible with the Convention. A wider margin of appreciation was generally available to Contracting Parties when regulating freedom of expression in relation to matters liable to offend intimate personal convictions within the sphere of morals or, especially, religion, since the authorities were in a better position

[154] *Damann v Switzerland*, (App. 77551/01), 25 April 2006.

[155] *Handyside v United Kingdom*, (App. 5493/72), 7 December 1976, Series A No 24, (1979–80) 1 EHRR 737, § 43; and *Peta Deutschland v Germany*, (App. 43481/09), 8 November 2012.

[156] *Müller and others v Switzerland*, (App. 10737/84), 24 May 1988, Series A No 133, (1991) 13 EHRR 212. See also *Otto-Preminger Institute v Austria*, (App. 13470/87), 20 September 1994, Series A No 295-A, (1995) 19 EHRR 34.

[157] *Wingrove v United Kingdom*, (App. 17419/90), 25 November 1996, (1997) 24 EHRR 1; ECHR 1996-V.

than the international judge to assess what was likely to cause offence to believers in each country. Having viewed the film itself, the Strasbourg Court concluded that the reasons given by the British authorities to justify the measures taken could be considered as both relevant and sufficient for the purposes of Article 10(2).

However, in the *Vereinigung Bildener Künstler* case,[158] the Strasbourg Court, by four votes to three, found a violation of Article 10 where the Austrian authorities had prohibited the continued exhibition of a large collage on display in a public gallery, which depicted public and religious figures engaged in sexual activity.[159] The Court seems to have been influenced by the fact that the art installation was 'some sort of counter-attack against the Austrian Freedom Party'.[160] The dissenting opinions of Judges Spielmann and Jebens took the view that the artwork lost its protection under Article 10 because of its failure to respect the human dignity of certain of those portrayed.[161]

One of the problems of the cases concerned with obscenity and blasphemy (particularly the latter) is that the earlier case-law of the Strasbourg Court came very close to establishing a right not to be insulted by others in relation to religious feelings. This is certainly one conclusion that can be drawn from the Court's approach to the film *Das Liebeskonzil* in the *Otto-Preminger* case,[162] and to the film 'Visions of Ecstasy' in the *Wingrove* case.[163] A preferable way to deal with such cases would be to offer no protection to the advocacy of religious hatred.[164]

There is a line of cases which suggests that the Strasbourg Court is not fully wedded to the notion of protecting a right not to be insulted by others in relation to religious feelings, but is rather concerned with respect for freedom of expression on the one hand while securing the right of others to respect for their freedom of thought, conscience, and religion. Someone writing critically about religion, but without advocating or inciting hatred, does not interfere with the rights protected by Article 9. There is therefore little to balance. The beginnings of this approach can be seen in the *IA* case,[165] in which the Strasbourg Court found by four votes to three no violation of Article 10 where the Turkish authorities had convicted of blasphemy the author of a book which contained critical remarks about aspects of Islam. The Court draws on its judgments in the *Otto-Preminger* and *Wingrove* cases in noting that 'as a matter of principle it may be considered necessary to punish improper attacks on objects of religious veneration.'[166] But the Court does go on to indicate that the judgment of the Court is based not on 'comments that offend or shock, or a "provocative" opinion, but also [constitute] an abusive attack on the Prophet of Islam.'[167] The joint opinion of the dissenting judges invited the Court to reconsider the case-law in this

[158] *Vereinigung Bildener Künstler v Austria*, (App. 68354/01), 25 January 2007, (2008) 47 EHRR 189, ECHR 2007-II.

[159] For a graphic description of the artwork, see the dissenting opinion of Judge Loucaides.

[160] *Vereinigung Bildener Künstler*, § 34.

[161] On the concept of human dignity, see C. McCrudden, 'Human Dignity and Judicial Interpretation of Human Rights' (2008) 19 EJIL 655.

[162] *Otto-Preminger Institute v Austria*, (App. 13470/87), 20 September 1994, Series A No 295-A, (1994) 19 EHRR 34. See also App. 8710/79, *Gay News Ltd and Lemon v United Kingdom*, Decision of 7 May 1982, (1082) 5 EHRR 123, § 11.

[163] *Wingrove v United Kingdom*, (App. 17419/90), 25 November 1996, (1997) 24 EHRR 1.

[164] See J. Temperman, 'Blasphemy, Defamation of Religions and Human Rights Law' (2008) 26 NQHR 517, especially 533–44. See also Art. 20(2) of the International Covenant on Civil and Political Rights which provides: 'Any advocacy of national, racial or religious hatred that constitutes incitement to discrimination, hostility or violence shall be prohibited by law.'

[165] *IA v Turkey*, (App. 42571/98), 13 September 2005, (2007) 45 EHRR 703, ECHR 2005-VIII.

[166] § 24. [167] § 28.

area which 'seems to place too much emphasis on conformism or uniformity of thought and to reflect an overcautious and timid conception of freedom of the press.'[168]

By contrast, in the *Giniewski* case,[169] the Strasbourg Court unanimously found a violation of Article 10 as a result of the prosecution of an author for defamation. The offending material was a critical analysis of Pope John Paul II's encyclical 'The splendour of truth'. The Court characterized the material as not being gratuitously offensive, insulting, or inciting disrespect or hatred.[170] The *Klein* case[171] concerned a response by a journalist and film critic to protests by Archbishop Sokol about the showing of, and publicity for, the film '*The People vs. Larry Flint*'. This resulted in complaints. Criminal proceedings were brought against the applicant; he was convicted. His appeals were unsuccessful. The Strasbourg Court unanimously found a violation of Article 10, noting that the applicant's comments 'neither interfered with the right of believers to express and exercise their religion nor did it denigrate the content of their religious faith....'[172]

The Strasbourg Court was spared the difficulty of adjudicating on the twelve cartoons of the prophet Mohammad published in the Danish newspaper *Morgenavisen Jyllands-Posten*,[173] when it ruled that the applicants had no standing to complain about their publication.[174] Had the merits of that controversy come before the Strasbourg Court, it is certainly arguable that the publication of the cartoons did not interfere in any way with freedom of religion, and freedom to manifest religious beliefs. This would have left the Strasbourg Court to elaborate the concept of insult to a religion, and the dividing line between the expression of views, here in art form, which are offensive to many Muslims but legitimate under Article 10, and matters which are likely to incite religious hatred which are not. The case would also have required the Strasbourg Court to consider positive obligations, since the complaint was that the Danish authorities had not intervened to prevent or punish the publication of the cartoons, when they should have done in order to respect their religious sensitivities.

ADVERTISEMENTS

The Strasbourg Court has recognized that advertising performs a useful function in society, namely to provide individuals with the means of discovering the characteristics of services and goods on offer.[175] Nevertheless, it may sometimes be restricted, especially to prevent unfair competition and untruthful or misleading advertising.[176] National authorities will have a wide margin of appreciation when the advertisements are purely commercial.[177] That margin will be reduced where the advertisements serve a wider public interest.

[168] § 8 of joint dissenting opinion.

[169] *Giniewski v France*, (App. 64016/00), 31 January 2006, (2007) 45 EHRR 589, ECHR 2006-I.

[170] § 52. [171] *Klein v Slovakia*, (App. 72208/01), 31 October 2006. [172] § 52.

[173] Which resulted in an international uproar arising from the taboo on representations of the prophet widely held among Muslims, though not apparently spelled out in the Koran.

[174] *Ben el Mahi and others v Denmark*, (App. 5853/06), Decision of 8 February 2006, ECHR 2006-XV. For comment on this saga, see K. Boyle, 'The Danish Cartoons' (2006) 24 NQHR 185; and D. Keane, 'Cartoon Violence and Freedom of Expression' (2008) 30 HRQ 845.

[175] See M. Hertig Randall, 'Commercial Speech under the European Convention on Human Rights: Subordinate or Equal?' (2006) 6 HRLRev 53.

[176] *Casado Coca v Spain*, (App. 15450/89), 24 February 1994, Series A No 285-A, (1994) 18 EHRR 1, § 51.

[177] *Vgt Verein gegen Tierfabriken v Switzerland*, (App. 24699/94), 28 June 2001, (2002) 34 EHRR 159, ECHR 2001-VI, § 71.

The cases of *Casado Coca*[178] and *Barthold*[179] illustrate this well. Casado Coca was a member of the Spanish Bar who was disciplined by the Barcelona Bar Council for placing advertisements in newspapers. The Strasbourg Court found that the rules which prevented him advertising fell within the national authorities' margin of appreciation. Barthold, on the other hand, was a veterinary surgeon, who published an article explaining the treatment he had given to a cat outside normal office hours and arguing that a regular night service should be provided in Hamburg. His name and clinic address was given. A private association against unfair competition complained that the article breached the professional rules on advertising of veterinary surgeons. An injunction restraining future similar publications was obtained against him. In finding a violation, the Strasbourg Court relied principally on the fact that the issue raised in the article was one of genuine public interest.

Sometimes the question of whether or not an advertisement serves a wider public interest may be very delicate. In the *Tierfabriken* case,[180] for example, the applicant took out an advert protesting against the treatment of pigs. The advertisement depicted a noisy hall with pigs in small pens, gnawing at the iron bars. The accompanying voice stated, *inter alia*, that the rearing of pigs in such circumstances resembled concentration camps. The association was prevented from broadcasting the advertisement because of a domestic law against political advertising. The Strasbourg Court accepted that a ban on political advertising might be justified in certain circumstances. However, it noted that the applicant was not a powerful financial group and concluded that, in the particular circumstances of the case, the reasons for the ban were not relevant and sufficient.

In the *Murphy* case[181] the applicant was a pastor attached to the Irish Faith Centre who wanted to broadcast an advertisement for the screening of a film on the evidence for the resurrection. However, he was prevented from doing so because of a domestic law against religious advertising. The Strasbourg Court found no violation of Article 10. It distinguished the *Tierfabriken* case on the grounds that national authorities had a wider margin of appreciation in relation to religious matters as they are liable to offend personal convictions.

The two cases are not easy to reconcile. Even taking into account the sensitivity of religion as a topic (especially in Ireland), Murphy's advertisement was unlikely to offend anyone. The Strasbourg Court in *Murphy* relied, instead, on the respondent State's argument that a provision which allowed the filtering, on a case by case basis, of unacceptable or excessive religious advertising would be difficult to apply fairly, objectively, and coherently. Why should it be any easier to filter political advertising on a case by case basis?

In a controversial decision given the variations in practice among the Contracting Parties, the Strasbourg Court ruled unanimously in the *TV Vest* case[182] that the prohibition in Norway on political advertisements on television breached Article 10. The terms of the judgment do not seem to be limited to the particular facts of that case, which concerned a penalty imposed on the television station and the political party.[183] The judgment

[178] *Casado Coca v Spain*, (App. 15450/89), 24 February 1994, Series A No 285-A, (1994) 18 EHRR 1, § 51.

[179] *Barthold v Germany*, (App. 8734/79), 25 March 1985, Series A No 90, (1975) 7 EHRR 383.

[180] *Vgt Verein gegen Tierfabriken v Switzerland*, (App. 24699/94), 28 June 2001, (2002) 34 EHRR 159, ECHR 2001-VI. See also *Verein Gegen Tierfabriken Schweiz (VgT) v Switzerland (No. 2)*, (App. 32772/02), 30 June 2009 [GC], ECHR 2009-nyr, in which the Grand Chamber found a violation of Article 10 arising from the continuing failure of the respondent State to permit the broadcasting of the commercial.

[181] *Murphy v Ireland*, (App. 44179/98), 10 July 2003, (2004) 38 EHRR 212, ECHR 2003-IX.

[182] *TV Vest AS and Rogaland Pensjonistparti v Norway*, (App. 21132/05), 11 December 2008, (2009) 48 EHRR 1206.

[183] The Pensioners Party, which is a small party polling in local and regional elections 1.3 per cent of the votes on a national basis.

emphasized the permanent and absolute nature of the ban which applied only to television, the importance of political speech, and the lack of any content in the impugned broadcast 'liable to offend intimate personal convictions within the sphere of morals and religion'.[184] This enabled the Court to distinguish its judgment in the *Murphy* case. The judgment may have caused concern in those Contracting Parties which ban paid political advertising.[185] However, the Court has since upheld a legislative ban on paid political advertising in the UK. In *Animal Defenders International v United Kingdom*,[186] the Strasbourg Court found that a ban of an advertisement against the use of animals in advertising was proportionate. It found that a general measure such as the ban on political advertising could be proportionate. The Court examined the legislative choices made by the State. The more convincing the justifications for a general measure, the less important its impact in an individual case.[187] The Court found that the scrutiny by the domestic bodies, the limitation of the ban to paid, political advertising on television and radio, the availability of alternate media and the risk of abuse and arbitrariness if the limitation was widened to social advocacy groups meant the general measure was proportionate.[188] It rejected the applicant's argument that the broadcast media was not as open to the influence of powerful wealthy interest groups as it was once was. It noted that despite a move away from broad prohibitions, there was still a lack of consensus in Europe on the regulation of political advertising. The Court did not explicitly overrule the *TV Vest* case,[189] but used the lack of consensus in States to give the UK a margin of appreciation as to how it implemented restrictions on political advertising.

The concurring opinion of Judge Bratza agreed with the focus on the general measure and expressed his doubts about the *Tierfabriken*[190] judgment. He thought *Murphy* preferable.[191] However, the dissenting opinion preferred *Tierfabriken* and could not see how an almost identical prohibition in *Tierfabriken* was a violation but there was not a violation in the UK. They are critical of what they see as double standards when the Court should be setting minimum standards. They found that the measures were disproportionate. They argued that parliamentary debate and scrutiny of a general measure does not guarantee compatibility with Convention rights and democracy is not helped by well-intentioned paternalism.[192]

BROADCASTING

Broadcasting is subject to greater regulation than the written word, since Article 10(1) includes the power to license broadcasting, cinema, and television enterprises. The purpose of the licensing can be broad,[193] but there is a duty to ensure that the rights under Article 10 remain protected.[194]

[184] § 64. [185] §§ 24–7 contain a comparative analysis of the position in the Contracting Parties.

[186] *Animal Defenders International v United Kingdom*, (App. 48876/08), 22 April 2013. The Court found a violation by nine votes to eight.

[187] § 109. [188] §§ 119–22.

[189] *TV Vest AS and Rogaland Pensjonistparti v Norway*, (App. 21132/05), 11 December 2008, (2009) 48 EHRR 1206.

[190] *Vgt Verein gegen Tierfabriken v Switzerland*, (App. 24699/94), 28 June 2001, (2002) 34 EHRR 159, ECHR 2001-VI. [191] Concurring Opinion of Judge Bratza, § 4.

[192] Joint Dissenting Opinion of Judges Ziemele, Sajó, Kalaydjieva, Vučinić and De Gaetano.

[193] App. 4515/70, *X and the Association of Z v United Kingdom*, Decision of 12 July 1971, (1971) 14 *Yearbook* 538.

[194] App. 9297/81, *X Association v Sweden*, Decision of 1 March 1982, (1982) 28 DR 204; and *Centro Europa 7 S.R.L. and Di Stefano v Italy*, (App. 38433/09), 7 June 2012.

In the *Groppera Radio* case,[195] Groppera Radio broadcast radio programmes from Italy to listeners in Switzerland. They failed to comply with a Swiss Ordinance prohibiting cable retransmission of such programmes. The Court ruled that the object, purpose, and scope of the third sentence of Article 10(1) had to be considered in the context of the article as a whole, and in particular the limitations in Article 10(2). No violation was found in the case.

The *Informationsverein Lentia* case[196] concerned five applications for broadcasting licences (one for television and four for radio) which were refused, because the Austrian Broadcasting Corporation held a monopoly. The Austrian Government relied on the third sentence of paragraph (1), or, in the alternative, on the limitations in paragraph (2), and argued that the monopoly enabled the State to regulate the technical aspects of audio-visual activities and to determine their place and role in modern society. The Court found a violation of Article 10, observing that the State is the 'ultimate guarantor' of pluralism, and that a public broadcasting monopoly could not be justified. This reasoning was further outlined in *Manole and others v Moldova*.[197] The State owned broadcaster, TRM, was the most watched television broadcaster in Moldova. It did not have a monopoly as there were private broadcasters. However, its news programme were the most watched, especially among rural communities who had little access to cable or satellite television. The applicants were employees of TRM. They alleged that there was undue political interference with the reporting of news on TRM. As reporters, they had gone on strike and were disciplined.

The Court reiterated the necessary of the State to ensure pluralism:

> Where a State does decide to create a public broadcasting system, it follows from the principles outlined above that domestic law and practice must guarantee that the system provides a pluralistic service. Particularly where private stations are still too weak to offer a genuine alternative and the public or State organisation is therefore the sole or the dominant broadcaster within a country or region, it is indispensable for the proper functioning of democracy that it transmits impartial, independent and balanced news, information and comment and in addition provides a forum for public discussion in which as broad a spectrum as possible of views and opinions can be expressed.[198]

The Court noted the Council of Europe's Committee of Ministers has made several recommendations on the independence and regulation of the media.[199] In this case, the freedom of expression of the applicants had been violated as the State had failed to guarantee pluralism by not having an adequate legal framework in place that would have prevented the editorial policy of TRM being controlled by the political organ of the Government. A change in the law did not redress the problem, as given that one party controlled the organs of the State, the rules for appointments to a new body to oversee TRM did not prevent political bias. The case underlines the positive obligation on the State to ensure pluralism and prevent political interference that may undermine this.

[195] *Groppera Radio AG and others v Switzerland*, (App. 10890/84), 28 March 1990, Series A No 173, (1990) 12 EHRR 321.

[196] *Informationsverein Lentia v Austria*, (Apps. 13914/88, 15041/89, 15717/89, 15779/89, and 17207/90), 24 November 1993, Series A No 276, (1994) 17 EHRR 93.

[197] *Manole and others v Moldova*, (App. 13936/02), 17 September 2009.

[198] § 101.

[199] For example Committee of Ministers Recommendation No. R(96)10 on 'The Guarantee of the Independence of Public Service Broadcasting' (Council of Europe 1996); Recommendation Rec(2000)23 on 'The Independence and Functions of Regulatory Authorities for the Broadcasting Sector' (Council of Europe 2000), See also, Resolution No. 1 on The Future of Public Service Broadcasting Fourth European Ministerial Conference on Mass Media Policy, Prague, 7–8 December 1994.

In regulating broadcasting, a Contracting Party must take care not to infringe the right of a person to receive information. In the *Autronic* case,[200] the Swiss Government had refused permission for a company specializing in home electronics to receive programmes from a Soviet satellite. There was a violation of Autronic's rights under Article 10.

In one unusual case,[201] the right to receive information was held to include the right of an Iraqi family living in Stockholm to have a satellite dish in apparent breach of the terms of their tenancy agreement in order to be able to receive television programmes in Arabic and Farsi. There was no other means of their obtaining such media, and they had been evicted from their home. There is a hint in the Court's judgment that the safety reasons put forward by the landlord and accepted by the courts were spurious.

POSITIVE OBLIGATIONS

In the context of Article 10, the Strasbourg Court has in the past been somewhat circumspect about referring to the positive obligations of the Contracting Parties, but it is clear that positive obligations do arise in relation to securing to all the rights of freedom of expression enshrined in the provision. This includes ensuring pluralism in broadcasting.[202] As we have seen, in some circumstances, there is an obligation to provide some form of legal assistance to those defending defamation proceedings.[203]

Freedom to receive information may also involve positive obligations, but the precise parameters of this obligation are not clear. There is authority to support the proposition that the freedom to receive information prohibits a Contracting Party from restricting a person from receiving information that others are willing to impart, but that this does not extend to a positive obligation to disseminate information of its own motion.[204]

Positive obligations do include providing a legal framework that protects expression such as the enforcement of a court order to provide information.[205] In *Dink v Turkey*,[206] Dink was a journalist who wrote several articles on the Armenian people in Turkey and was charged with denigrating the Turkish nation. He was later shot dead. The Court found that the State had an obligation to create a favourable environment for participation in public debate by all the persons, free from fear. In the case, the State had failed to protect the applicant's freedom of expression. The Court has found this extends to private parties where the State may have to provide redress for actions such as employment dismissals.[207]

200 *Autronic AG v Switzerland*, (App. 12726/87), 22 May 1990, Series A No 178, (1990) 12 EHRR 485.

201 *Khurshid Mustafa and Tarzibachi v Sweden*, (App. 23883/06), 16 December 2008.

202 See, for example, *Fuentes Bobo v Spain*, (App. 39293/98), 29 February 2000; *Vgt Verein gegen Tierfabriken v Switzerland*, (App. 24699/94), 28 June 2001, (2002) 34 EHRR 159, ECHR 2001-VI.; *Manole and others v Moldova*, (App. 13936/02), 17 September 2009, § 99; and *Centro Europa 7 S.R.L. and Di Stefano v Italy*, (App. 38433/09), 7 June 2012,

203 *Steel and Morris v United Kingdom*, (App. 68416/01), 15 February 2005, (2005) 41 EHRR 403, ECHR 2005-II.

204 *Roche v United Kingdom*, (App. 32555/96), 19 October 2005 [GC], (2006) 42 EHRR 599, ECHR 2005-X, §§ 172–3. But note that access to information has largely been considered to date under Article 8: see ch.16.

205 *Youth Initiative for Human Rights v Serbia*, (App. 48135/06), 25 June 2013; *Frăsilă And Ciocîrlan v Romania*, (App. 25329/03), 10 December 2012.

206 *Dink v Turkey*, (App. 2668/07), 14 September 2010.

207 *Palomo Sanchez and others v Spain*, (App. 28995/06), 12 September 2011. Although no violation was found where the applicants claimed dismissal due to trade union activities, the Court acknowledged that there was a positive obligation on the State to provide redress if necessary.

It is also arguable that the State may be under an obligation to provide public space for expression. In *Appleby v United Kingdom*,[208] the Court found there was no violation of Article 10 where the applicant argued that the State should guarantee access to a public space in a privately owned shopping mall. However the Court did not rule out the possibility that the State would be under a positive obligation to regulate property rights to protect Article 10. In *Mouvement Raelien Suisse v Switzerland*[209] the Court did not examine the regulation of posters in a public space as a positive obligation. However, Judge Bratza noted that the regulation of a specific public space and power of the State to authorize posters in the area could be construed as involving a positive obligation on the State. However, this does not allow an unrestricted access to public space.[210]

CONCLUDING REMARKS

The Strasbourg Court has repeatedly emphasized the vital role that freedom of expression, and the free press in particular, have to play in a democratic society. The expansion of the Council of Europe in the last twenty-five years has served to prove the point. The media in central and eastern Europe were instrumental in bringing down totalitarianism, and continue to form a vital safeguard in the new democracies, throughout Europe.

It remains surprising how frequently the criminal law, or the law of defamation, is used to control various forms of expression among the Contracting Parties. This seems to be the key battleground between applicants and the Contracting Parties in many applications made to the Strasbourg Court, despite clear guidance to the Contracting Parties in the judgments of the Court. The Court has also been asked to examine the nature of hate speech, incitement and offence and has attempted, not always successfully, to define clear approaches to these issues. There is also the issue of the internet and social media which is increasingly coming before the Court in areas such as the clash with private life, defamation, copyright, and State restrictions on access. This is a rapidly developing area and the Court will have to continue to apply and develop the principles it has established for more traditional media.

[208] *Appleby v United Kingdom*, (App. 44306/98), ECHR 2003-VI.

[209] *Mouvement Raelien Suisse v Switzerland*, (App. 16354/06), 13 July 2012.

[210] Concurring Opinion of Judge Bratza.

19

FREEDOM OF ASSEMBLY AND ASSOCIATION

INTRODUCTION

Article 11 includes a somewhat disparate range of rights, and spans the divide between, on the one hand, civil and political rights, and, on the other economic and social rights. The case-law of the Strasbourg Court now ensures that the right to peaceful assembly in Article 11, especially when read with Article 10 of the Convention, provides a right to peaceful protest. The remainder of the article concerns association, but can be divided into three distinct areas: the protection of political parties; the protection of other associations; and a bundle of trade union rights. As noted in Chapter 17, Article 11 when read with Article 9 provides protection for religious associations.[1]

The text of Article 11 reads:

1. Everyone has the right to freedom of peaceful assembly and to freedom of association with others, including the right to form and to join trade unions for the protection of his interests.
2. No restrictions shall be placed on the exercise of these rights other than such as are prescribed by law and are necessary in a democratic society in the interests of national security or public safety, for the protection of health or morals or for the protection of the rights and freedoms of others. This article shall not prevent the imposition of lawful restrictions on the exercise of these rights by members of the armed forces, of the police or of the administration of the state.

Assembly and association are clearly interlinked. A group of persons could not form an effective association if they had no right to meet. Freedom of assembly includes the right to meet both in private and in public. In its public aspect, it largely constitutes what this chapter refers to as the right to peaceful protest.

POSITIVE OBLIGATIONS

The Strasbourg organs have long held that there are positive obligations to secure the effective enjoyment of the rights contained in Article 11.[2] In the *Plattform 'Ärzte für das Leben'* case,[3] an association of doctors which campaigned against medical termination of pregnancy with a view to securing changes in the Austrian legislation complained of violations of Article 11 when two demonstrations were disrupted by counter-demonstrations despite

[1] See, for example, *Moscow Branch of the Salvation Army v Russia*, (App. 72881/01), 5 October 2006, (2007) 44 EHRR 912, ECHR 2006-XI.

[2] *Christians against Racism and Fascism v United Kingdom*, (App. 8440/78), Decision of 16 July 1980, (1980) 21 DR 138.

[3] *Plattform 'Ärzte für das Leben' v Austria*, 21 June 1988, Series A No 139, (1991) 13 EHRR 204.

a significant police presence. One issue which arose in the case was the extent to which a Contracting Party is required under Article 11 to intervene to secure conditions permitting the exercise of the right. The Strasbourg Court said:

> Genuine, effective freedom of peaceful assembly cannot... be reduced to a mere duty on the part of the State not to interfere: a purely negative conception would not be compatible with the object and purpose of Article 11.... Article 11 sometimes requires positive measures to be taken, even in the sphere of relations between individuals, if need be.[4]

In the *Djavit An* case, the Court simply said:

> ...the Court considers that, although the essential objective of Article 11 is to protect the individual against arbitrary interference by public authorities with the exercise of the rights protected, there may in addition be positive obligations to secure the effective enjoyment of these rights....[5]

It is clear that positive obligations apply in the fields both of the right to peaceful assembly and of freedom of association:

> ...the Court has often reiterated that the Convention is intended to guarantee rights that are not theoretical or illusory, but practical and effective.... It follows from that finding that a genuine and effective respect for freedom of association cannot be reduced to a mere duty on the part of the State not to interfere; a purely negative conception would not be compatible with the purpose of Article 11 nor with that of the Convention in general. There may thus be positive obligations to secure the effective enjoyment of the right to freedom of association... even in the sphere of relations between individuals.... Accordingly, it is incumbent upon public authorities to guarantee the proper functioning of an association or political party, even when they annoy or give offence to persons opposed to the lawful ideas or claims that they are seeking to promote. Their members must be able to hold meetings without having to fear that they will be subjected to physical violence by their opponents. Such a fear would be liable to deter other associations or political parties from openly expressing their opinions on highly controversial issues affecting the community. In a democracy the right to counter-demonstrate cannot extend to inhibiting the exercise of the right of association....[6]

The Court has also reiterated that the State is under a positive obligation to protect private employees from dismissal

> ...there is also a positive obligation on the authorities to provide protection against dismissal by private employers where the dismissal is motivated solely by the fact that an employee belongs to a particular political party (or at least to provide the means whereby there can be an independent evaluation of the proportionality of such a dismissal in the light of all the circumstances of a given case).[7]

PEACEFUL PROTEST

OVERVIEW

Article 11 provides for the right of peaceful assembly. It is questionable whether the word 'peaceful' is really needed, given the limitations for which provision is made in the second

[4] § 32.

[5] *Djavit An v Turkey*, (App. 20652/92), 20 February 2003, (2005) 40 EHRR 1002, ECHR 2003-III, § 57.

[6] *Ouranio Toxo and others v Greece*, (App. 74989/01), 20 October 2005, (2007) 45 EHRR 277, ECHR 2005-X, § 37. See also *Redfearn v United Kingdom*, (App. 47335/06), 6 November 2012, § 43.

[7] *Redfearn v United Kingdom*, (App. 47335/06), 6 November 2012, § 43.

paragraph of the Article. It is, however, clear that an assembly will not be other than peaceful simply because it is considered likely to, or does, provoke a violent response in others, provided that those complaining of violations of Article 11 remain peaceful in their own intentions and behaviour.[8] Where this is in issue, the Strasbourg Court will determine whether on the evidence before it those involved in the organization of the prohibited meetings had violent intentions.[9] This is one context in which the positive obligations of the Contracting Parties come into play. They will be expected, so far as reasonable and practicable, to police any demonstrations in order to avoid disorder and violence.[10] But there is no immunity from prosecution for unlawful actions during the course of the demonstration, nor for participation in an unauthorized demonstration.[11] The Strasbourg Court has come to read Article 11 with Article 10 in establishing the parameters of the right of peaceful assembly. If the essence of the applicant's complaint relates to participation in a demonstration, the Strasbourg Court will consider the case under Article 11 rather than Article 10;[12] Article 10 is regarded as a *lex generalis*, while Article 11 is regarded as a *lex specialis*.[13] The case-law can legitimately be regarded as now providing a right to peaceful protest.

While recognizing the difficulties of definition, Mead helpfully offers a typology of protest.[14] The distinction between freedom of expression and freedom of assembly is found in the attempt at persuasion in a public context. For Mead there are four criteria which constitute the hallmarks of protest as distinct from simply an expression of ideas. First, the activity must be politically participative. Secondly, the protest is directed towards a body that is capable of implementing, or preventing, the change. Thirdly, the subject matter of the protest must transcend the individual.[15] Finally, protest runs alongside and outside formal political party structures. Against this background, Mead proposes four types of protest: static assemblies, processions, peaceful persuasion, and obstructive direct action. Mead's conclusions are arguably overstated in stating that Contracting Parties 'crack down on peaceful demonstrations and processions',[16] and that, when admissibility decisions are taken into account, 'applications claiming a violation of the right to protest have largely been unsuccessful'.[17] Typically Contracting Parties succeed in justifying interference with demonstrations on the grounds of preventing disorder.

[8] *Ziliberberg v Moldova*, (App. 61821/00), 4 May 2004; and *Galstyan v Armenia*, (App. 26986/03), 15 November 2007.

[9] *Stankov and the United Macedonian Organisation Ilinden v Bulgaria*, (Apps. 29221/95 and 29225/95), 2 October 2001, ECHR 2001-IX, §§ 76–8; *Gun and others v Turkey*, (App. 8029/07), 18 June 2013.

[10] *Christians against Racism and Fascism v United Kingdom*, (App. 8440/78), Decision of 16 July 1980, (1980) 21 DR 138; and *Plattform 'Ärzte für das Leben' v Austria*, 21 June 1988, Series A No 139, (1991) 13 EHRR 204, §§ 34–8.

[11] *Galstyan v Armenia*, (App. 26986/03), 15 November 2007, § 115.

[12] But the Court is not wholly consistent in this regard; for an example of cases which seem to relate to protest as much as to expression, see *Açik and others v Turkey*, (App. 31451/03), 13 January 2009; *Berladir and others v Russia*, (App. 34302/06), 10 July 2012 as an example of where the Court discussed Article 11 but reiterated in was doing so in the light of Article 10.

[13] *Ezelin v France*, (App. 11800/85), 26 April 1991, Series A No 202, (1992) 14 EHRR 362, §§ 34–5; and *Galstyan v Armenia*, (App. 26986/03), 15 November 2007, §§ 95–6, *Schwabe and M.G. v Germany*, (Apps. 8080/08 and 8577/08), 1 December 2011, §§ 99–101.

[14] D. Mead, 'The right to peaceful protest under the European Convention on Human Rights—a content study of Strasbourg case-law' [2007] EHRLR 345; see also D. Mead, *The New Law of Peaceful Protest. Rights and Regulation in the Human Rights Act Era* (Hart, Oxford 2009).

[15] Though Mead acknowledges just how difficult the dividing line is to draw in this context, he finds it helpful to test whether the protest is motivated by self-interest or altruism. Note however that Article 11 does not exclude the self-interested protest.

[16] D. Mead, 'The right to peaceful protest under the European Convention on Human Rights—a content study of Strasbourg case-law', [2007] EHRLR 345, 354.

[17] D. Mead, [2007] EHRLR 345, 354. There are, however, very many reasons why applications may be declared inadmissible; such decisions do not necessarily involve acceptance that the conduct of the respondent State was justified.

AUTHORIZATION AND NOTIFICATION OF DEMONSTRATIONS

There is no prohibition on Contracting Parties requiring authorization for, or notification of, demonstrations. This will not be regarded as encroaching on the right to peaceful assembly if its purpose is to enable the authorities to take reasonable and appropriate measures in order to guarantee the smooth running of the demonstration, whatever its nature.[18] But such systems must operate fairly and in accordance with law. In *Vyerentsov v Ukraine*,[19] the Court held that transitional laws stemming from the Soviet regime and local regulations governing the right to assembly did not provide a sufficient legal basis. The Court recognized that some discretion was left to the State with regard to transitional provisions from Soviet rule. However, over twenty years was too long a time to allow transition from Soviet rule when a fundamental right such as Article 11 is in question.

Any penalties for failure to comply with the administrative requirements for obtaining authorization must not be disproportionate. So, in the *Sergey Kuznetsov* case,[20] the imposition of even a modest fine for submitting a notice eight days in advance of a small-scale demonstration rather than the ten days required was found to be a violation of Article 11.[21]

There must not be an overreaction to a demonstration for which no notification has been provided; the touchstone is a combination of tolerance and proportionality.[22] A refusal of authorization can itself constitute an interference, as can prohibitions on demonstrations,[23] since refusals are capable of having 'a chilling effect on the applicants and other participants in assemblies' and could have discouraged:

> ... other persons from participating in the assemblies on the ground that they did not have official authorization and that, therefore, no official protection against possible hostile counter-demonstrations would be ensured by the authorities.[24]

A similar approach will be taken where a demonstration is ordered to disperse; a decision to disperse an assembly must be justified.[25] Ordering a demonstration to disperse simply because there has been a failure to notify the authorities in advance is likely to constitute a violation of Article 11, especially if there is no evidence to suggest that the demonstration presents any real danger to public order.[26] The authorities, usually the police, must not be heavy-handed. The touchstone is always tolerance where demonstrators do not engage in acts of violence. Where the heavy-handed approach of the authorities causes tensions to rise, and violence to break out, that will not usually protect the respondent State from successful complaints that Article 11 has been violated.[27]

[18] *Sergey Kuznetsov v Russia*, (App. 10877/04), 23 October 2008, § 42; *Berladir and others v Russia*, (App. 34302/06), 10 July 2012, § 40; see also *Gun and others v Turkey*, (App. 8029/07), 18 June 2013.

[19] *Vyerentsov v Ukraine*, (App. 20372/11), 11 April 2013.

[20] *Sergey Kuznetsov v Russia*, (App. 10877/04), 23 October 2008.

[21] It seems to be significant that this defect was only noticed six weeks after the demonstration had taken place.

[22] *Oya Ataman v Turkey*, (App. 74552/01), 5 December 2006, ECHR 2006-XV; *Balçik and others v Turkey*, (App. 25/02), 29 November 2007; and *Saya and others v Turkey*, (App. 4327/02), 7 October 2008. See *Éva Molnár v Hungary*, (App. 10346/05), 7 October 2008, for a case where the intervention of the authorities did not fall foul of Article 11.

[23] See *Stankov and the United Macedonian Organisation Ilinden v Bulgaria*, (Apps. 29221/95 and 29225/95), 2 October 2001, ECHR 2001-IX.

[24] *Baczkowski and others v Poland*, (App. 1543/06), 3 May 2007, (2009) 48 EHRR 475, ECHR 2007-VI, § 67. See also *Patyi and others v Hungary*, (App. 5529/05), 7 October 2008.

[25] *Friedl v Austria*, (App. 15225/89), Decision of 30 November 1992.

[26] *Bukta and others v Hungary*, (App. 25691/04), 17 July 2007, ECHR 2007-IX.

[27] *Nurettin Aldemir and others v Turkey*, (Apps. 32124/02, 32126/02, 32129/02, 32132/02, 32133/02, 32137/02, and 32138/02), 18 December 2007.

In the *Cisse* case,[28] a group of around 300 illegal immigrants, most of African origin, occupied a church in Paris in order to draw attention to the difficulties of securing reviews of their immigration status in France. The occupation went on for two months. Ten occupants went on hunger strike. Concerns arose about the sanitary conditions in the church, although the parish priest made no complaint to the authorities. The church was evacuated in a somewhat heavy-handed manner by the authorities. The applicant, one of the occupants, complained of a violation of Article 11. The Strasbourg Court emphasized that illegal immigrants present in France enjoyed the right to peaceful assembly under Article 11, but, although the judgment of the Court makes critical comments about the heavy-handed evacuation of the church, no violation of Article 11 was found. It was open to the authorities to restrict the protest on the grounds of protecting order after tolerating the occupation for some two months.[29]

Where an issue is particularly sensitive, it may be possible for a Contracting Party to ban all demonstrations relating to a particular issue in particular places.[30] In the *Milan Rai, Gill Allmond and 'Negotiate Now'* case,[31] the applicants complained about a refusal to permit them to hold a demonstration in Trafalgar Square, even though they were offered the opportunity to hold the demonstration in Hyde Park. A policy decision had been taken to refuse all requests for demonstrations relating to Northern Ireland in Trafalgar Square 'founded on the concern to avoid the use of the square by those supporting the use of violence.' It was conceded that this was not the purpose of the proposed demonstration, but the Commission concluded that 'where complex issues arise as to the causes of the conflict and any possible solutions' the policy of the British Government could be considered legitimate in seeking to prevent disorder and in protecting the rights and freedoms of others. A different conclusion might be reached in a case where a proposed alternative venue did not enable those wishing to demonstrate to achieve their objectives in holding the proposed demonstration.

The *Ollinger* case[32] provides guidance on how the authorities in the Contracting Parties should deal with the risks of counter-demonstrations. The applicant, a member of the Green Party, notified the authorities that he would be holding a small meeting at the Salzburg municipal cemetery on All Saints Day in front of the war memorial as a commemoration of the Salzburg Jews killed in the Second World War. He noted that the meeting would coincide with a gathering of *Kameradschaft IV*, who would be commemorating the deaths of SS soldiers killed in the Second World War. The response of the authorities was to prohibit Ollinger's meeting because of the risk of disturbances. An appeal against the decision failed. A complaint to the Constitutional Court also failed, although it was ruled that the approach of the police authorities had been too narrow. However, the wider view was that the prohibition was required by the State's positive obligations under Article 9 of the Convention. All Saints Day was an important religious holiday which was characterized by visits to cemeteries to commemorate the dead, and there had been disturbances in previous years between meetings organized by the applicant and those organized by *Kameradschaft IV*.

[28] *Cisse v France*, (App. 51346/99), 9 April 2002, ECHR 2002-III.

[29] For another case where initial tolerance of the situation appears to have been significant, see *Barraco v France*, (App. 31684/05), 5 March 2009.

[30] *Rassemblement Jurassien and Unité Jurassienne v Switzerland*, (App. 8191/78), Decision of 10 October 1979, (1979) 17 DR 108.

[31] *Milan Rai, Gill Allmond and 'Negotiate Now' v United Kingdom*, (App. 25522/94), Decision of 6 April 1995. See also *Arthur Pendragon v United Kingdom*, (App. 31416/96), Decision of 19 October 1998, which concerned a four-day ban on demonstrations within a four mile radius of Stonehenge.

[32] *Ollinger v Austria*, (App. 76900/01), 29 June 2006, (2008) 46 EHRR 849, ECHR 2006-IX.

The question before the Strasbourg Court was whether the authorities had struck a fair balance between the interests of the two groups wishing to hold demonstrations on the same day in the same place. The Strasbourg Court had doubts about whether the competing interests had been fairly weighed, though it agreed that it would be too narrow a view simply to ban the counter-demonstration to protect the initial demonstration. The Court was not convinced that the ban was required to protect ordinary visitors to the cemetery, nor was it convinced that it was unreasonable and impracticable to police the two demonstrations to avoid disorder. The Austrian authorities had failed to strike a fair balance, and there was a violation of Article 11.

In *Faber v Hungary*,[33] the Court was asked to examine police actions during two opposing demonstrations. An anti-fascist organisation held a demonstration in Budapest to protest against racism. At the same time, a right wing political party assembled in an area near the demonstration to express their views. The applicant was standing silently near the anti-fascist demonstration and close to the right wing demonstration when he was arrested for holding an Arpad (Arrow Cross) flag. He was standing near the steps leading to the Danube embankment at a location where large numbers of Jews were killed by the Arrow Cross regime in 1944/45. Although the case was dealt with by the Court under Article 10 in conjunction with Article 11, similar principles used in *Ollinger* were applied. The Court noted that the State has a wide margin of appreciation when policing demonstrations and counter-demonstrations, but noted:

> If every probability of tension and heated exchange between opposing groups during a demonstration were to warrant its prohibition, society would be faced with being deprived of the opportunity of hearing differing views on any question which offends the sensitivity of the majority opinion…The Court would add that a demonstration may annoy or give offence to persons opposed to the ideas or claims that it is seeking to promote. The participants must, however, be able to hold the demonstration without having to fear that they will be subjected to physical violence by their opponents; such a fear would be liable to deter associations or other groups supporting common ideas or interests from openly expressing their opinions on highly controversial issues affecting the community. In a democracy the right to counter-demonstrate cannot extend to inhibiting the exercise of the right to demonstrate.[34]

In this case, the Court whilst balancing the competing interests of the two demonstrations, found that although the display of the flag may have disturbed protestors in the anti-fascist demonstration, there was no evidence that it would lead to public disorder. The display of the flag itself was not enough to amount to a justification for the interference of the right. Whilst symbols of a totalitarian regime may be restricted depending on the context of the display, this was not the case here.[35]

It would seem that there is no right to hold demonstrations on private property such as a shopping mall. Although the *Appleby* case[36] was decided primarily under Article 10, the Strasbourg Court indicates that a Contracting Party is not obliged to make provision for rights under Articles 10 and 11 to be exercisable in 'quasi-public' places such as shopping malls which are in private ownership. The Strasbourg Court was influenced not only by trends in the case-law of the Supreme Court in the United States, but also by the factual situation in which the applicants were able to seek signatures to their petition and

[33] *Faber v Hungary*, (App. 40721/08), 24 October 2012. [34] § 38.

[35] § 58. The Court noted its finding under Article 10 with regard to Holocaust denial, see ch.18.

[36] *Appleby and others v United Kingdom*, (App. 44306/98), 6 May 2003, (2003) 37 EHRR 783, ECHR 2003-VI.

distribute leaflets in the public spaces leading to the shopping mall, and had been able to secure permission to have a stand within a hypermarket in the shopping mall.

Restrictions on movement within a Contracting Party in exercise of the freedom of peaceful assembly may constitute a violation of Article 11. The *Yeşilgöz* case[37] concerned a trip by members of an association to a part of Turkey. They were prevented from entering the region, because there was a state of emergency in effect. While the Strasbourg Court recognized that the political atmosphere was a factor of some weight which could be taken into account, it noted further that no reasons had been given for refusing entry to the members of the association, and there was nothing to indicate that the visit would exacerbate the emergency in the region. The visit was described as a fact-finding visit. Similar issues arose in the *Djavit An* case.[38] The applicant is a Cypriot national of Turkish origin who lives in Nicosia, north of the green line. He is a member of the Movement for an Independent and Federal Cyprus. There is a Turkish Cypriot coordinating committee in the north of the island, and a Greek Cypriot coordinating committee in the south of the island. The applicant was unable to obtain permission to cross the green line in order to participate in bi-communal meetings. He complained of a violation of Article 11. Despite objections that the real issue in the case related to freedom of movement, the Strasbourg Court considered the case under Article 11 as an aspect of freedom of assembly, which includes the right to have private and public meetings. The refusal of permission to cross the green line to attend bi-communal meetings interfered with the Article 11 right. The respondent State could not show how this refusal was prescribed and regulated by law, and there was, accordingly, a violation of Article 11.

UNLAWFUL CONDUCT BY DEMONSTRATORS

Obstructive direct action always runs the risk of involving some unlawful activity on the part of the protesters. This can be illustrated by the facts of the *Drieman* case.[39] The applicants were members of Greenpeace who had been prosecuted and convicted for activities in the Norwegian exclusive economic zone designed to disrupt whaling. They complained that this constituted a breach of Articles 10 and 11. The Strasbourg Court did not consider it necessary to determine whether the matters complained of fell within Article 10 or Article 11. The complaints were inadmissible. The applicants had been able to protest in general for a period of around one month about the resumption of whaling in Norwegian waters, whereas the convictions related to two specific incidents of conduct which breached Norwegian law; that conduct—seeking to block whaling vessels with manoeuvres in zodiac dinghies—constituted 'a form of coercion forcing the whalers to abandon their lawful activity.'

The *Plattform 'Ärzte für das Leben'* case[40] is somewhat anomalous in that the Strasbourg Court was considering whether Article 13 had been violated, since the Commission had ruled that the complaint based on Article 11 was inadmissible. The only way into Article 11 was accordingly to consider whether it was arguable that Article 11 was engaged. The Strasbourg Court's judgment is not wholly satisfactory, since its reasoning suggests that the case was indeed arguable under Article 11. The Court does examine the nature of the respondent State's conduct in policing the demonstration, and concludes that the police

[37] *Yeşilgöz v Turkey*, (App. 45454/99), 20 September 2005.

[38] *Djavit An v Turkey*, (App. 20652/92), 20 February 2003, (2005) 40 EHRR 1002, ECHR 2003-III.

[39] *Drieman and others v Norway*, (App. 33678/96), Decision of 4 May 2000.

[40] *Plattform 'Ärzte für das Leben' v Austria*, 21 June 1988, Series A No 139, (1991) 13 EHRR 204.

response was reasonable. It then concluded that no 'arguable claim that Article 11 was violated has thus been made out; Article 13 therefore did not apply in the instant case.'[41] The case is, however, frequently cited as authority for the proposition that Article 11 protects a demonstration that may annoy or give offence to persons opposed to the ideas and claims the demonstration seeks to promote.[42]

The *Ezelin* case[43] is rather more helpful. It establishes that exercising the right to peaceful assembly does not protect the demonstrator from sanctions for violence or disorder which ensues but that any sanctions which relate primarily to the fact of demonstrating must be proportionate. The case concerned an application by a lawyer, who was Vice-Chairman of the Trade Union of the Guadeloupe Bar, complaining that the French courts had imposed a disciplinary penalty by way of reprimand on him because he had taken part in a demonstration protesting at the use of the Security and Freedom Act in Guadeloupe, and had failed to express his disapproval of insults uttered by other demonstrators against the judiciary. In assessing the proportionality of the sanction, the Strasbourg Court noted that it was to a certain extent symbolic, because it did not prevent the applicant from practising as a lawyer. However, it observed that:

> The proportionality principle demands that a balance be struck between the requirements of the purposes listed in Article 11(2) and those of the free expression of opinions, by word, gesture or even silence by persons assembled on the streets or in other public places. The pursuit of a just balance must not result in *avocats* being discouraged, for fear of disciplinary sanctions, from making clear their beliefs on such occasions.[44]

The penalty exceeded that which was necessary in a democratic society, since Ezelin had not himself committed any reprehensible act at all during the demonstration.

The *Galstyan* case[45] involved the imposition of a much more severe penalty: three days' detention. The applicant had been present at a large rally protesting about the conduct of recent elections in Armenia. He was arrested for obstructing traffic and behaving in an anti-social way, and subsequently convicted for violating public order by making a loud noise. The Strasbourg Court ruled that the imposition of the sanction for being present and proactive at the demonstration impaired the very essence of the right to freedom of peaceful assembly, and there was a violation of Article 11. It will be particularly difficult for a Contracting Party to show that a penalty imposed essentially for attendance at a demonstration for which authorization has been given can be justified. Respondent States are likely to argue that a public order offence has been committed,[46] but the Strasbourg Court will consider whether such claims are justified and are not simply the direct consequences of participation in the demonstration.[47] Such measures would strike at the 'very essence of the right to freedom of peaceful assembly'.[48]

The Court has also examined the detention of protestors on their way to a protest. In the *Schwabe and M.G* case,[49] the applicants were on their way to protest at a G8 summit. They were stopped and searched by the police. They had banners asking for 'freedom for

[41] § 39.

[42] As in *Stankov and the United Macedonian Organisation Ilinden v Bulgaria*, (Apps. 29221/95 and 29225/95), 2 October 2001, ECHR 2001-IX, § 86.

[43] *Ezelin v France*, 26 April 1991, Series A No 202, (1992) 14 EHRR 362.

[44] § 52.

[45] *Galstyan v Armenia*, (App. 26986/03), 15 November 2007; see also *Kudrevičius and others v Lithuania*, (App. 37553/05), 26 November 2013.

[46] As in *Ashughyan v Armenia*, (App. 33268/03), 17 July 2008.

[47] See *Çetinkaya v Turkey*, (App. 75569/01), 27 June 2006.

[48] *Ashughyan v Armenia*, (App. 33268/03), 17 July 2008, § 93.

[49] *Schwabe and M.G. v Germany*, (Apps. 8080/08 and 8577/08), 1 December 2011.

all prisoners' and 'free all now', and the police stated they resisted arrest. The applicants argued that their detention was to prevent them attending the protest rather than prevent a criminal offence. The Court found that the evidence of the possible violent intentions of the applicants was ambiguous at best and they had no previous convictions. It noted that the possibility of violent protesters joining a peaceful protest did not remove the protection of Article 11. It went on to find that the G8 protest was concerned with issues of important public interest and that the five-day detention of the applicants was disproportionate when considering the aim of public safety. The Court had already found the detention was unlawful under Article 5 and that less restrictive measures could have been taken such as removal of the banners.[50]

It may also be a violation of Article 11 if there is a conviction for the organization of a protest where there has been violence, but the organizers were not involved and the intention had been for a peaceful protest. In the *Gun and others*[51] case, the applicants organized a protest against the continued detention of Ocalan, the leader of the PKK, which is designated as a terrorist organization in Turkey. The protests were suspended. However the applicants organized a meeting where a press statement was read out. The police ordered the demonstrators to disperse but allowed the statement to be read and the protest broke up peacefully. However clashes did occur between the police and about ten demonstrators who did not include the applicants. The applicants were convicted for organizing the protest and were given an eighteen-month prison sentence and a fine.

The Court noted that the police had tacitly tolerated the protest and the evidence suggested there was no intention to use violence at the protest. The applicants were not charged with specific violence or inciting violence. The State had not shown enough evidence to justify a fear of violence at the protest, there had been no investigation held to find the actual perpetrators of the violence, and the sentence was excessive. There was therefore a violation of Article 11.[52]

A particularly strict view will be taken of attempts to restrict demonstrations, which can be regarded as the legitimate activities of a political party. The *Christian Democratic People's Party* case[53] concerned demonstrations organized by the applicant political party against Government proposals to make the study of the Russian language compulsory in schools for children aged seven or over. The authorities, on receipt of the notification of the demonstration, changed the proposed venue without giving any reasons for the change of location. Demonstrations went ahead at the original location on several days. As a consequence the authorities suspended some of the political activities[54] of the applicant party for one month. The Strasbourg Court considered the issue of whether this response was necessary in a democratic society without prejudice to the issues of whether the measure was in accordance with law and justified as being for a legitimate reason. The Strasbourg Court said:

> In view of the essential role played by political parties in the proper functioning of democracy, the exceptions set out in Article 11 are, where political parties are concerned, to be

[50] *Schwabe and M.G. v Germany*, § 118, see also *Halcobyan and others v Armenia*, (App. 34320/04), 10 April 2012; and *Kasparov and others v Russia*, (App. 21613/07), 3 October 2013.

[51] *Gun and others v Turkey*, (App. 8029/07), 18 June 2013.

[52] *Gun and others v Turkey*, (App. 8029/07), 18 June 2013, §§ 77–85.

[53] *Christian Democratic People's Party v Moldova*, (App. 28793/02), 14 February 2006, (2007) 45 EHRR 392, ECHR 2006-II.

[54] Cited in the separate opinion (partly concurring and partly dissenting) as using the mass media, disseminating propaganda and agitation, carrying out bank transactions or other operations, and participating in elections.

> construed strictly; only convincing and compelling reasons can justify restrictions on such parties' freedom of association. In determining whether a necessity within the meaning of Article 11 § 2 exists, the Contracting States have only a limited margin of appreciation, which goes hand in hand with rigorous European supervision.... It therefore follows that the Court must scrutinize very carefully the necessity for imposing a ban on a parliamentary political party's activities, even a ban of fairly short duration.[55]

The respondent State had submitted video recordings of the demonstrations, but these failed to assist its case. They showed that the demonstrations were essentially peaceful affairs, and there was nothing which could be regarded as an incitement to public violence. The Strasbourg Court ruled that 'only very serious breaches such as those which endanger political pluralism or fundamental democratic principles could justify a ban on the activities of a political party.'[56]

There are, however, special responsibilities placed upon elected officials which might be regarded as requiring circumspection in their actions in exercise of their rights under Article 11. This can be illustrated by the admissibility decision in the *Osmani* case.[57] Osmani had been elected mayor of Gostivar. The local council subsequently decided that the Albanian and Turkish flags should fly alongside the Macedonian flag in front of the town hall. Similar provision was made for the flying of flags on other public buildings on public holidays. The Constitutional Court was asked to consider the validity of the decision, and ultimately decided that it was unconstitutional. In the meantime, Osmani had organized a public meeting which was inflammatory in that only the flag of the Republic of Albania was flown and at which Osmani made a speech inciting the crowd not to accept the decision of the Constitutional Court, and promising that Gostivar would become an Albanian town. Two days later, there were violent scenes at the town hall. Osmani organized armed shifts to protect the Albanian flag. Sometime later there were further violent clashes at the town hall when police removed the flags from the town hall. Three people died. Osmani was prosecuted and convicted of a number of offences and sentenced to imprisonment. His appeals failed. He then complained to the Strasbourg Court that there had been a violation of Article 11. In finding the application to be manifestly ill-founded, the Strasbourg Court indicates that freedom of peaceful assembly is of particular importance for an elected representative of the people, but also notes the context and conduct of the applicant in the case before them. The applicant had breached his duties as an elected public official in refusing to uphold decisions of the Constitutional Court, and in becoming actively involved in the planning and setting up of headquarters and armed shifts for the protection of the flag of the Republic of Albania. His conduct was not the expression of personal political opinion, but constituted the stirring up of hatred and intolerance in a very sensitive inter-ethnic situation.

CONCLUSION ON PEACEFUL ASSEMBLY

The case-law on peaceful assembly provides a good illustration of the relationship between positive and negative obligations. A Contracting Party is permitted to regulate peaceful assembly in a manner which facilitates it. This includes a positive obligation to police peaceful protests in a manner which enables the protesters to get their message across effectively. In

[55] *Christian Democratic People's Party*, § 68.

[56] § 76. See also *Güneri and others v Turkey*, (Apps. 42853/98, 43609/98, and 44291/98), 12 July 2005.

[57] *Osmani and others v the Former Yugoslav Republic of Macedonia*, (App. 50841/99), Decision of 11 October 2001, ECHR 2001-X.

taking action to address disorder which will arise from time to time, the Contracting Parties may be called upon to justify their action as dealing with disorder rather than seeking to impose sanctions simply by reason of the protests having taken place. Some of the case-law does indicate that some Contracting Parties fail to get the balance right between proper regulation and improper repression.

DEFINING ASSOCIATIONS

Article 11 protects the right to 'freedom of association with others'. Put broadly, and subject to the provisos set out in the second paragraph, this constitutes the right to choose whether or not to form and join associations such as political parties and trade unions, and also other organizations, such as lodges of Freemasons.[58]

The case-law on freedom of association addresses three core types of association: (1) political parties; (2) trade unions; and (3) other associations. The essence of freedom of association is that 'citizens should be able to create a legal entity in order to act collectively in a field of mutual interest.'[59] So it is inherent in the concept of freedom of association that there is a right to form associations, and for those associations to be recognized in the national legal orders. If the issue arises, it will be for the Strasbourg Court to decide whether an applicant constitutes an association for the purposes of Article 11:

> The term 'association'...possesses an autonomous meaning; the classification in national law has only relative value and constitutes no more than a starting point.[60]

In the *Chassagnou* case, the French Government had argued that *associations communales de chasse agréés*[61] were public law associations with the powers of public authorities and so fell outside the concept of associations in Article 11. But the Strasbourg Court, while accepting the public law aspect of the associations, concluded that they were groupings of private individuals who wished to pool their land for the purpose of hunting. They were accordingly associations within the scope of Article 11. However, professional regulatory bodies set up by statute which remain integrated within State structures will not be associations for the purposes of Article 11,[62] particularly where there is no corresponding prohibition on establishing an association of professionals in the private sector.[63]

Where an issue arises as to whether an association is a public law or a private law association, the Strasbourg Court will look to see which characteristics predominate. The issue arose in the *Sigurjónsson* case,[64] which concerned the required membership of '*Frami*' as a precondition to obtaining a licence to operate a taxi. The association had both public law and private law characteristics. It exercised certain functions under the legislation applicable to the provision of taxi services, but was also fully autonomous in determining

[58] *NF v Italy*, (App. 37119/97), 2 August 2001, (2002) 35 EHRR 106, ECHR 2001-IX; and *Grande Oriente d'Italia di Palazzo Giustiniani v Italy*, (App. 35972/97), 2 August 2001, (2002) 34 EHRR 629, ECHR 2001-VIII.

[59] *Gorzelik and others v Poland*, (App. 44158/98), Chamber judgment of 20 December 2001, (2004) 38 EHRR 77, § 55; the decision was upheld in the Grand Chamber on 17 February 2004, (2005) 40 EHRR 76, ECHR 2004-I.

[60] *Chassagnou and others v France*, (Apps. 25088/94, 28331/95, and 28443/95), 29 April 1999 [GC], (2000) 29 EHRR 615, ECHR 1999-III, § 100.

[61] Approved municipal hunters' associations.

[62] *Le Compte, Van Leuven and de Meyere v Belgium*, (Apps. 6878/75 and 7238/75), 23 June 1981, Series A No 43, (1982) 4 EHRR 1, §§ 63–5.

[63] *Albert and Le Compte v Belgium*, (Apps. 7299/75 and 7496/86), 10 February 1983, Series A No 58, (1983) 5 EHRR 533.

[64] *Sigurdur A. Sigurjónsson v Iceland*, (App. 16130/90), 30 June 1993, Series A No. 264, (1993) 16 EHRR 462.

its own aims and procedures. In particular, it exercised a number of functions designed to protect the interests of its members, and so operated much like a trade union. The Strasbourg Court did not decide that it was a trade union, but concluded that its character was predominantly that of a private law organization and so constituted an association for the purposes of Article 11.[65]

The Strasbourg Court has found no difficulties in regarding political parties as being associations for the purposes of Article 11:

> ...even more persuasive than the wording of Article 11, in the Court's view, is the fact that political parties are a form of association essential to the proper functioning of democracy. In view of the importance of democracy in the Convention system,... there can be no doubt that political parties come within the scope of Article 11.[66]

REGISTRATION

There is nothing improper in Contracting Parties requiring registration of associations, whatever their purpose, although any decision to refuse registration will be an interference with the freedom of association which will require justification. The *Sidiropoulos* case[67] concerned applicants of Macedonian ethnic origin who were living in Greece; they sought to register an association with broad objectives to promote Macedonian historical and cultural heritage. The refusal was based on a perceived incompatibility between the association's objects and the Greek national interest, in particular suggestions that the association disputed the Greek identity of the region of Macedonia. On appeal, the refusal was upheld on the ground that the true intention of the founders of the association was to undermine the territorial integrity of Greece. The Strasbourg Court accepted that the refusal was grounded in law and met one of the legitimate aims set out in Article 11(2), but did not agree that refusal to register (a fundamental interference with freedom of association) was necessary in a democratic society. The Court recognized that the founders of the association regarded themselves as belonging to a minority in Greece, but this could not be regarded as constituting a threat to democratic society. There was a violation of Article 11.

Similarly in a case against Bulgaria,[68] an organization wished to re-register after previously being dissolved in a manner that was found by the Strasbourg Court in a previous judgment to be a violation of Article 11.[69] The Court applied the principles established in the previous case-law including the necessity of protecting pluralism and the limited margin of appreciation States have when attempting to justify a decision to not register an association. Separatist ideology was not a justifiable ground for a failure to register an

[65] §§ 31–2.

[66] *United Communist Party of Turkey and others v Turkey*, (App. 19392/92), 30 January 1998, (1998) 26 EHRR 121, ECHR 1998-I, § 25.

[67] *Sidiropoulos and others v Greece*, (App. 26695/95), 10 July 1998, (1999) 27 EHRR 633, ECHR 1998-IV. See also *Stankov and the United Macedonian Organisation Ilinden v Bulgaria*, (Apps. 29221/95 and 29225/95), 2 October 2001, ECHR 2001-IX; and *Association of Citizens Radko and Paunkovski v The Former Yugoslav Republic of Macedonia*, (App. 74651/01), 15 January 2009, which concerned dissolution of Macedonian associations.

[68] *United Macedonian Organisation Ilinden and others v Bulgaria (no.2)*, (App. 34960/04), 18 October 2011.

[69] *Stankov and the United Macedonian Organisation Ilinden v Bulgaria*, (Apps. 29221/95 and 29225/95), 2 October 2001, ECHR 2001-IX; see also *United Macedonian Organisation Ilinden – PIRIN and others v Bulgaria*, (App. 59489/00), 20 October 2005, §§ 58–62 and in a previous case where the State failed to register the organization, *United Macedonian Organisation Ilinden and others v Bulgaria*, (App. 59491/00), 19 January 2006.

association.[70] In this case, the reasons given where not sufficient to be a proportionate measure and so violated Article 11.

The national law regarding registration must be clear in order to comply with the lawfulness requirement under Article 11. In the *Church of Scientology Moscow* case,[71] the applicant Church was repeatedly refused registration on the ground, among other things, that it had submitted an incomplete set of documents. Despite requests, the authorities would never specify which documents were missing. This procedure was repeated until the deadline for registration expired. In the subsequent proceedings brought by the Church, the District Court held that the applicant had not complied with national law in that the application for re-registration only included copies, rather than originals, of the charter and registration certificate. The Strasbourg Court found a breach of Article 11 because the domestic law was not 'formulated with sufficient precision to enable the citizen to foresee the consequences which a given action may entail and to regulate his or her conduct accordingly.' [72] The requirement to submit the original documents did not follow from the text of the national law, and no other regulatory documents which might have set out such a requirement were referred to in the domestic proceedings. It was not mentioned in the grounds for the refusal advanced by the Moscow Justice Department or in the Presidium's decision remitting the matter for a new examination, but appeared for the first time in the District Court's judgment. In these circumstances, the Court was unable to find that the domestic law was formulated with sufficient precision enabling the applicant to foresee the adverse consequences which the submission of copies would entail.

POLITICAL PARTIES

In the case of the *United Communist Party of Turkey*[73] the Strasbourg Court rejected the respondent State's argument that Article 11 applied only to trade-union-type associations, and held that political parties also fell within its scope and were, indeed, entitled to a high level of protection because of their important role in any democracy.

The Party had been dissolved by the Turkish Constitutional Court on the grounds, first, that the word 'Communist' in the title was objectionable and, secondly, because the Party's manifesto had distinguished between the 'Turkish' and the 'Kurdish' nations; in Turkey, the promotion of separatism is unconstitutional. The Strasbourg Court considered that a political party's choice of name could not in principle justify a measure as drastic as dissolution in the absence of other relevant and sufficient circumstances. On the second point, since the Party had advocated a political, rather than a violent, solution to the Kurdish problem, and one of the principal characteristics of democracy was the possibility of resolving a country's problems through dialogue, there could be no justification for hindering a political group solely because it sought to debate in public the situation of part of the State's population and to take part in the nation's political life in order to find,

[70] *United Macedonian Organisation Ilinden and others v Bulgaria (no.2)*, (App. 34960/04), 18 October 2011, §§ 36–38.

[71] *Church of Scientology Moscow v Russia*, (App. 18147/02), 5 April 2007, (2008) 46 EHRR 304.

[72] § 92.

[73] *United Communist Party of Turkey and others v Turkey*, (App. 19392/92), 30 January 1998, (1998) 26 EHRR 121, ECHR 1998-I. See generally H. Cullen, 'Freedom of Association as a Political Right' (1999) 24 ELRev HR/30; and M. Koçak and E. Örücü, 'Dissolution of Political Parties in the Name of Democracy: cases from Turkey and the European Court of Human Rights' (2003) 9 EPL 399.

according to democratic rules, solutions capable of satisfying everyone concerned.[74] The dissolution of the Party was, therefore, disproportionate and contrary to Article 11.[75] The Strasbourg Court views pluralism as being at the heart of the concept of democracy, which it upholds; political parties are seen as vital participants in the process of debate and dialogue which underpins participatory democracy.

The Court has also found that a State may interfere in the internal affairs of a political party where an association has failed to comply with reasonable legal formalities or due to prolonged internal conflict in the organization. However, in *Republican Party of Russia v Russia*,[76] where no official complaints had been made about the political party in question, the Court found that any such interference should be proportionate and the authorities:

> should not intervene in the internal organisational functioning of associations to such a far-reaching extent as to ensure observance by an association of every single formality provided by its own charter.[77]

In December 1999, following a survey of the practice among countries which cooperate with the Commission, the Venice Commission[78] adopted a set of guidelines on the dissolution of political parties.[79] The guidelines recognized that:

> Prohibition or dissolution of political parties can be envisaged only if it is necessary in a democratic society and if there is concrete evidence that a party is engaged in activities threatening democracy and fundamental freedoms. This could include any party that advocates violence in all forms as part of its political programme or any party aiming to overthrow the existing constitutional order through armed struggle, terrorism or the organisation of any subversive activity.[80]

The guidelines themselves contain seven propositions, which may be summarized as follows:

(1) States should recognize the right of everyone to form political parties and to hold political opinions without interference by a public authority, although a requirement to register political parties will not of itself be considered a violation of this right.[81]

[74] The Court has applied similar principles to non-political associations, for example see *United Macedonian Organisation Ilinden and others v Bulgaria (no.2)*, (App. 34960/04), 18 October 2011.

[75] The Strasbourg Court reached similar conclusions in relation to the dissolution of Turkish political parties in the following cases: *Socialist Party and others v Turkey*, (App. 21237/93), 25 May 1998, (1999) 27 EHRR 51, 1998-III; *Freedom and Democracy Party (OZDEP) v Turkey*, (App. 23885/94), 8 December 1999, (2001) 31 EHRR 674, ECHR 1999-VIII; and see also *Yazar and others v Turkey*, (Apps. 22723/93, 22724/93, and 22725/93), 9 April 2002, (2003) 36 EHRR 59, ECHR 2002-II; and *Dicle on behalf of the Democratic Party v Turkey*, (App. 25141/94), 10 December 2002. See also *Partidul Comunistilor v Romania*, (App. 46626/99), 3 February 2005, (2007) 44 EHRR 340, ECHR 2005-I.

[76] *Republican Party of Russia v Russia*, (App. 12976/07), 12 April 2011.

[77] § 87, The Court has applied similar principles to non-political parties, see *Tebieti Mühafize Cemiyyeti and Israfilov v Azerbaijan*, (App. 37083/03), 8 October 2009 ECHR 2009, § 78.

[78] The European Commission for Democracy through Law (known as the Venice Commission) was established within the framework of the Council of Europe and has come to be regarded as an internationally recognized independent legal think tank. See www.venice.coe.int.

[79] Guidelines on the Prohibition and Dissolution of Political Parties and Analogous Measures, adopted by the Venice Commission at its 41st plenary session in Venice, 10–11 December 1999, CDL-INF (2000) 1.

[80] § 10 of Explanatory Report attached to the guidelines.

[81] For an example of an unjustified refusal to register a political party, see *Linkov v Czech Republic*, (App. 10504/03), 7 December 2006; see also *Republican Party of Russia v Russia* (App. 12976/07) 12 April 2011. For a decision relating to funding arrangements for political parties, see *Parti Nationaliste Basque—Organisation Régionale d'Ipparalde v France*, (App. 71251/01), 7 June 2007, (2008) 47 EHRR 1037, ECHR 2007-VII.

(2) Any limitations on this right should be consistent with the provisions of the European Convention on Human Rights and other international treaties.

(3) Only political parties which advocate the use of violence as a political means to overthrow the democratic constitutional order should be susceptible of prohibition or dissolution. The advocacy of peaceful change is not alone a ground for prohibition or dissolution.

(4) A political party is not to be held responsible for the individual behaviour of its members which have not been sanctioned by the party.

(5) Prohibition or dissolution should be used with utmost restraint; less radical measures to deal with concerns should be explored before resorting to such measures.

(6) Legal measures directed to prohibition or dissolution should be a consequence of a judicial finding of unconstitutionality, be regarded as exceptional measures, be governed by the principle of proportionality, and be based on sufficient evidence of objectionable conduct attributable to the party itself.

(7) Prohibition or dissolution should be decided by the constitutional court or other appropriate judicial body in a procedure offering guarantees of due process.

In the *Refah Partisi* case,[82] the Grand Chamber, in what some regard as a controversial judgment,[83] unanimously took the view that it was compatible with Article 11 to dissolve the applicant political party, which at the time of dissolution had actually been in power for one year as part of a coalition government. The leaders of the *Refah Partisi* had declared their intention to establish a plurality of legal systems in Turkey based on differences in religious belief and to establish Islamic law (Sha'ria), a system of law which was in marked contrast to the values embodied in the Convention. The Grand Chamber held:

> ...that a political party may promote a change in the law or the legal and constitutional structures of the State on two conditions: firstly, the means used to that end must be legal and democratic; secondly, the change proposed must itself be compatible with fundamental democratic principles. It necessarily follows that a political party whose leaders incite to violence or put forward a policy which fails to respect democracy or which is aimed at the destruction of democracy and the flouting of the rights and freedoms recognized in a democracy cannot lay claim to the Convention's protection against penalties imposed on those grounds....
>
> The possibility cannot be excluded that a political party, in pleading the rights enshrined in Article 11 and also in Articles 9 and 10 of the Convention, might attempt to derive therefrom the right to conduct what amounts in practice to activities intended to destroy the rights or freedoms set forth in the Convention and thus bring about the destruction of democracy.... In view of the very clear link between the Convention and democracy..., no one must be authorized to rely on the Convention's provisions in order to weaken or destroy the ideals and values of a democratic society. Pluralism and democracy are based on a compromise that requires various concessions by individuals or groups of individuals, who must sometimes agree to limit some of the freedoms they enjoy in order to guarantee greater stability of the country as a whole....[84]

[82] *Refah Partisi (Prosperity Party) and others v Turkey*, (Apps. 41340/98, 41342/98, and 41344/98), 13 February 2003 [GC], (2003) 37 EHRR 1, ECHR 2003-II.

[83] K. Boyle, 'Human Rights, Religion and Democracy: The Refah Party Case' (2004) 1 *Essex Human Rights Review* 1. See also P. Macklem, 'Militant Democracy, Legal Pluralism, and the Paradox of Self-Determination' (2006) 4 *International Journal of Constitutional Law* 488.

[84] *Refah Partisi*, §§ 98–9.

Refah Partisi's policies and anti-secular stance could be considered dangerous for the rights and freedoms guaranteed by the Convention, and the real prospect that it would implement its programme after gaining power justified the Constitutional Court's action.

There are a number of startling features of this case. *Refah Partisi* had been in government as part of a coalition for twelve months when it was dissolved. It was a political party of long standing, which had polled the largest share of the votes (22 per cent) in the 1995 general election, and one of its members, Necmettin Erbakan, was Prime Minister. To dissolve such a party in such circumstances was, in the words of one commentator, to take 'the notion of "militant democracy", the measures permissible to defend democracy from being subverted through electoral politics, to a new level.'[85] The Grand Chamber accepted the assessment of the Turkish Constitutional Court that *Refah Partisi* was not committed to peaceful means and the change it advocated by its alleged conduct was such as to be incompatible with fundamental democratic principles. These concerns need to be set in the context of the deep commitment in the Turkish Constitution to secularism. The first constitution of modern Turkey in 1924 was committed to the 'six arrows' of Kemalism: nationalism, secularism, republicanism, populism, statism, and reformism.[86] The 1982 Constitution continues the commitment to secularism, and provides that no protection is to be afforded to activities contrary to the principle of the indivisibility of Turkey, and that there is to be no interference whatsoever by religious sacred feelings in State affairs and politics. Turkey's constitution commits it to be a democratic, secular, and social State governed by the rule of law and respect for human rights. At the heart of the objections to *Refah Partisi* was a concern that its hidden agenda was the conversion of the secular State into a religious State through the promotion of Islam. It is questionable whether there was sufficient evidence before the Court of anti-secular activities. The Strasbourg Court's comments on the tenets of Islam and on Sha'ria and their compatibility with the democratic principles enshrined in the Convention do seem somewhat insensitive.[87] As Boyle notes,[88] the judgment of the Grand Chamber can be read to suggest that peaceful advocacy of the tenets of Islam is unprotected under the European Convention. Boyle identifies the core issue raised by the discussion in this case of religion and secularism as follows:

> Can religion, democracy and human rights guarantees relate in ways that neither require the strict secularism as espoused in Turkey, nor the subordination of individual human rights to unchallengeable religious rules such as would result from shariah? Or may democracy and plurality of religion be accommodated only through the endorsement of secularism and the complete divorce of the religions of the electorate from political affairs? These questions undoubtedly constitute a new frontier of human right study, not just in multi-cultural Europe, but in the Middle East and in particular in the new Iraq.[89]

The Court applied the principles established in the *Refah Partisi* case in an arguably less controversial case against the Batasuna Parties in Spain.[90] The Batasuna Parties were dissolved by the Supreme Court on the grounds that their aims pursued activities inconsistent with

[85] K. Boyle, 'Human Rights, Religion and Democracy: The Refah Party Case' (2004) 1 *Essex Human Rights Review* 1, 2.

[86] See M. Koçak and E. Örücü, 'Dissolution of Political Parties in the Name of Democracy: Cases from Turkey and the European Court of Human Rights' (2003) 9 EPL 399, 407–9.

[87] As noted by Judge Kovler in his concurring opinion.

[88] K. Boyle, 'Human Rights, Religion and Democracy: The Refah Party Case' (2004) 1 *Essex Human Rights Review* 1, 12.

[89] § 16.

[90] *Herri Batasuna and Batasuna v Spain*, (Apps. 25803/04 and 25817/04), 30 June 2009.

democracy. Applying *Refah Partisi* the Court noted that whether the dissolution was necessary depended on:

> (i) whether there was plausible evidence that the risk to democracy, supposing it had been proved to exist, was sufficiently and reasonably imminent, and (ii) whether the acts and speeches imputable to the political party formed a whole which gave a clear picture of a model of society conceived and advocated by the party which was incompatible with the concept of a 'democratic society'.[91]

The Court found there was convincing evidence linking the parties to violent organizations such as ETA. The Court agreed unanimously that it was within the State's discretion to dissolve the parties, given their links to terrorist organizations.[92]

MEMBERSHIP OF A POLITICAL PARTY

In the *Redfearn* case,[93] the Court examined the issue of exclusion from employment due to membership of a political party. The applicant was a member of the British National Party (BNP), and was elected a councillor for the party in local elections. His main employment was as a bus driver and he worked for a private company, which carried out services for the local authority. BNP policies advocate an immigrant free UK and at the relevant time its membership was limited to white nationals. Many of the passengers on the buses were of Asian origin. After the applicant had been elected as a councillor for the BNP, his employment was terminated. The applicant argued that his political beliefs had never impacted on his professional activities and the company acknowledged that he never had any complaints made against him. The company argued that there was potential for problems arising from the applicant's political activities and his beliefs may have impacted negatively on their passengers, employees, and business. The UK does not include political belief as a protected characteristic in equality legislation and at the time of the case, did not include it as an exception to the rule that claims cannot be brought for unfair dismissal within the first year of employment and so his claim for unfair dismissal failed.

The Court underlined that with regard to positive obligations under Article 11 there may be sensitive social and economic factors, which mean that the State has a wide margin of appreciation. It will examine if measures taken by the State are 'reasonable and appropriate'. The Court noted that the company were placed in a difficult position due to the applicant's political beliefs. However, there was no evidence that the applicant's political beliefs had impacted on his work and it was admitted he was a good employee, It found that a claim for unfair dismissal would be an appropriate remedy but that the law in the UK was deficient in the protection it provided for employees in regard to association with a political party. The one year qualifying period for unfair dismissal meant he could not bring a case under the rules and nor did he fit into the exceptions which included race, religion, and sex but not political opinion. The Court held that the UK had to amend its law in such a way so that the Article 11 rights are effectively protected. However, in a dissenting opinion,[94] several judges believed the majority had expanded the positive obligation too far in requiring a free standing

[91] § 83.

[92] The Court applied similar principles to find no violation of Protocol 1, Article 3 where the applicant was barred from standing for election, as he was seen to be pursuing the policies of the Batasuna parties. *Etxeberria and others v Spain*, (Apps. 35579/03, 35613/03, 35626/03, and 35634/03), 30 June 2010.

[93] *Redfearn v United Kingdom*, (App. 47335/06), 6 November 2012.

[94] The case was decided by four votes to three. Joint Partly Dissenting Opinion of Judges Bratza, Hirvelä, and Nicolaou.

claim based on political belief with no temporal limitations. They held the UK was within its wide discretion in having a qualifying period and its exceptions to it. In Article 14 jurisprudence, the Court had accepted certain grounds for difference of treatment carried more weight[95] and so it should be open to the UK government to apply similar principles to the grounds for exceptions under employment legislation.

OTHER ASSOCIATIONS

The Strasbourg Court has interpreted Article 11 to include rights aimed at creating and preserving genuine democracy and freedom, not just in a party political sense, but also the freedom of citizens to pursue a vast array of interests such as culture, sport, and social and humanitarian assistance. Freedom of association includes the right to receive formal recognition for an association: an unreasonable refusal of registration, where this is required, will constitute a violation of Article 11. In assessing such cases, the Strasbourg Court has enunciated a number of general principles.[96] While Contracting Parties have a right to satisfy themselves that the aims and activities of an association are within the national law providing the scheme for registration, the decision on the application must be taken in a manner compatible with the Convention rights under Article 11. Inherent in the proper consideration of applications is recognition of the importance of pluralism to the proper functioning of democracy. This applies just as much in the case of associations formed other than for political purposes as for political parties. The implementation of the principle of pluralism must also recognize that unpopular or unorthodox expressions of opinion are a feature of the Convention right for individuals, and associations to which they belong, to express freely their ideas and opinions. Only convincing and compelling reasons can justify restrictions on freedom of association. As with political parties, refusal of recognition must always be grounded in conclusions based on convincing evidence that the association advocates the use of violence or undemocratic and unconstitutional means to secure its aims.[97]

The same position has been adopted where the conduct of the authorities in persistently returning documents seeking registration of an association amounts to a de facto refusal of registration. Blatant cases of delay in processing applications for registration are likely to be very difficult to defend, since the conduct will almost certainly not be 'prescribed by law'.[98]

Similar principles apply to the dissolution of an association. In *Vona v Hungary*,[99] the State dissolved an association and movement, which it found had initiated activities that were a danger to public order and encompassed discrimination against the Roma, a minority group. The movement had held military style marches through areas where a majority of inhabitants were Roma. The uniforms contained imagery associated with the fascist Arrow Cross who were responsible for Roma and Jewish massacres in World War Two. Speeches made by the movement contained anti-Roma and anti-Semitic content.

[95] See ch.24 and the weight given to certain grounds such as race and sex when considering justifications for difference of treatment.

[96] Summarized in *Zhechev v Bulgaria*, (App. 57045/00), 21 June 2007, §§ 34–6. See also *United Macedonian Organisation Ilinden and others v Bulgaria (no.2)*, (App. 34960/04), 18 October 2011, §§ 36–8.

[97] *Emin and others v Greece*, (App. 341344/05), 27 March 2008; and *Tourkiki Enosis Xanthis and others v Greece*, (App. 26698/05), 27 March 2008.

[98] *Ramazanova and others v Azerbaijan*, (App. 44363/02), 1 February 2007, (2008) 47 EHRR 407; and *Ismayilov v Azerbaijan*, (App. 4439/04), 17 January 2008.

[99] *Vona v Hungary*, (App. 35943/10), 9 July 2013.

The Court reiterated that the State has to demonstrate that there is a pressing need to dissolve an association under Article 11 but that where an organization's aims or practices may threaten democracy or advocate violence then it does not have to wait until such events happen before it acts. The Court further noted that the margin of appreciation is much narrower for political parties than for other associations, dependent on the circumstances:

> In view of the difference in the importance for a democracy between a political party and a non-political association, only the former deserves the most compelling scrutiny of the necessity of a restriction on the right to associate... This distinction has to be applied with sufficient flexibility. As to associations with political aims and influence, the level of scrutiny depends on the actual nature and functions of the association in view of the circumstances of the case.[100]

On the facts, the Court held the State acted within its margin of appreciation when it dissolved the association. It considered the association had not acted within the bounds of legal and peaceful activities:

> The demonstration by political protagonists of their ability and willingness to organise a paramilitary force goes beyond the use of peaceful and legal means of articulating political views. In view of historical experience – such as that of Hungary in the wake of Arrow Cross power – the reliance of an association on paramilitary demonstrations which express racial division and implicitly call for race-based action must have an intimidating effect on members of a racial minority, especially when they are in their homes as a captive audience.[101]

Freedom of association includes the right not to join an association as well as the right to form an association. The *Chassagnou* case[102] concerned membership of hunting associations in France. The applicants complained that, despite their opposition to hunting, they had been obliged to join a local hunting association. The effect was to permit hunting on their land. The Strasbourg Court considered the complaint under Article 11, when read with Article 9 because of the personal beliefs of the applicants that hunting was wrong. Given the French love of hunting, the issues before the Grand Chamber were sensitive. The Grand Chamber recognized the ethical issues raised by hunting, and therefore the need to strike a balance between rural tradition in France, and personal convictions. Detailed examination of the national law on the establishment of hunting associations showed considerable variation in practice and application. By twelve votes to five, the Grand Chamber concluded that there was a violation of Article 11:

> To compel a person by law to join an association such that it is fundamentally contrary to his own convictions to be as member of it, and to oblige him, on account of his membership of the association, to transfer his rights over the land he owns so that the association in question can attain objectives of which he disapproves, goes beyond what is necessary to ensure that a fair balance is struck between conflicting interests and cannot be considered proportionate to the aim pursued.[103]

In *Olafsson*[104] the Court was asked to examine the compulsory payment of industry fees to an employer's association when the applicant was not a member of that association. The applicant also argued that the association held political views that were opposite to

[100] § 58. [101] § 66.

[102] *Chassagnou and others v France*, (Apps. 25088/94, 28331/95, and 28443/95), 29 April 1999 [GC], (2000) 29 EHRR 615, ECHR 1999-III.

[103] § 117. See also *Schneider v Luxembourg*, (App. 2113/04), 10 July 2007.

[104] *Vorur Olafsson v Iceland*, (App. 20161/06), 27 April 2010.

his own views. The Court found that whilst the State has a margin of appreciation with regard to compulsory industry charges, there were inadequate safeguards with regard to the accountability and transparency of the funding of the association. It was not clear whether the members of the association were gaining an advantage by being funded by non-members like the applicant. There was a violation of Article 11.

Improper interference in the activities of an association may also breach Article 11. In the *Piroğlu and Karakaya* case,[105] the second applicant was convicted following a refusal to annul the membership of thirteen members of the Izmir Branch of the Human Rights Association. None of those named had been convicted of offences which would affect their membership of the association. It was conceded that those whose membership was required to be annulled had been taken into custody, but no charges had been brought. In such circumstances, the Strasbourg Court concluded that the authorities had not shown any legitimate reason why annulment of membership was required. It was a requirement of the Convention that national law afford a measure of protection against arbitrary interference by the public authorities with Convention rights.[106]

TRADE UNIONS

FREEDOM TO FORM AND JOIN TRADE UNIONS

The right to form and join trade unions is an aspect of the wider right to freedom of association set out in Article 11(1). It includes a positive obligation on the State to protect, through legislation, the union rights of workers in the private sector, as well as those employed by the State.[107] Article 11 is binding on the State as employer.[108] Inherent in any exercise of trade union rights is recognition of the legal personality of the union. In the *Tüm Haber Sen* case[109] the applicants, who were a trade union for public sector workers in the postal and telecommunications sector and its former president, complained that the dissolution of the union and consequent enforced cessation of its activities constituted a breach of Article 11. The Turkish authorities had ordered its dissolution on the grounds that it had been founded by civil servants and its members were civil servants.[110] The Strasbourg Court could find no pressing social need to prohibit the formation of trade unions by public sector workers and civil servants. There was a violation of Article 11.[111]

In contrast, the Court allowed the State to refuse to register a trade union in a religious organisation on the basis of religious autonomy. In the *Pästorul cel Bun* case [112] a number of Orthodox priests and lay members decided to form a trade union. The Church Diocese argued that even though the Priests were employed, the formation of a trade union without permission of the Archbishop was prohibited by the Romanian Orthodox Church, as

[105] *Piroğlu and Karakaya v Turkey*, (Apps. 36370/02 and 37581/02), 18 March 2008. [106] § 65.

[107] *Gustafsson v Sweden* (App. 15573/89), of 25 April 1996, (1996) 22 EHRR 409, ECHR 1996-II, § 45; Revision ECHR 1998-V.

[108] *Demir and Baykara v Turkey*, (App. 34503/97), 12 November 2008 [GC], (2009) 48 EHRR 1272, ECHR 2008-nyr, § 109; and *Tüm Haber Sen and Çinar v Turkey*, (App. 28602/95), 21 February 2006, (2008) 46 EHRR 374, ECHR 2006-II, § 29.

[109] *Tüm Haber Sen and Çinar v Turkey*, (App. 28602/95), 21 February 2006, (2008) 46 EHRR 374, ECHR 2006-II.

[110] See later in this chapter on the question of whether civil servants are members of the administration of the State within the final sentence of Article 11(2).

[111] See also *Demir and Baykara v Turkey*, (App. 34503/97), 12 November 2008 [GC], (2009) 48 EHRR 1272, ECHR 2008-nyr. [112] *Sindicatul 'Pästorul cel Bun' v Romania*, (App. 2330/09), 9 July 2013.

approved by government ordinance. The registration of the union was originally allowed by a domestic court but revoked on appeal.

The Romanian government underlined the need for the State to recognize religious autonomy and that members of the Church had a heightened degree of loyalty to the Church in which they had taken a vow of obedience. The applicant argued that they had a right to challenge the employment part of their relationship with the Church and that other trade unions had been recognized. The Chamber had found that there was a violation of Article 11. It recognized the autonomy of the Church but found that there was an employment contract in place which the domestic court had failed to consider properly given international standards regarding trade union rights.

However, a majority of the Grand Chamber found there was no violation.[113] It did agree with the Chamber that despite the heightened degree of loyalty owed by the members of the Church, this did not preclude them from trade union rights and there was an employment relationship.[114] The fact that the authorities had already recognized other trade unions in the Church underlined the employment relationship and the applicability of Article 11 to the church members. However, the Grand Chamber went on to note that the Church has protection under Article 9 with regard to its right to autonomy and to make decisions on how collective action might undermine that autonomy. This does not mean that further scrutiny is excluded. The Court stated that the authorities must:

> ...show, in the light of the circumstances of the individual case, that the risk alleged is real and substantial and that the impugned interference with freedom of association does not go beyond what is necessary to eliminate that risk and does not serve any other purpose unrelated to the exercise of the religious community's autonomy. The national courts must ensure that these conditions are satisfied, by conducting an in-depth examination of the circumstances of the case and a thorough balancing exercise between the competing interests at stake.[115]

The Court noted that the Romanian government had specifically recognized the autonomy of the Churches in Romania. Respect for autonomy includes remaining neutral and not acting as an arbiter between a Church and dissident movements within it. In this case, the domestic court was simply applying the principle of religious autonomy. The applicants had not followed the special procedures to set up a trade union and could not justify this. The review by the domestic court was 'plausible and substantial'.[116]

The Court has also found that the dissolution of a trade union because of its stated aims can only be justified for compelling reasons. In the *Sendikasi* case[117] an education union was dissolved by the Turkish State on the grounds that its aims, which included a principle that individuals could receive education in their mother tongue, were incompatible with democratic principles. The Court found a violation of Article 11 as it did not find compelling evidence that the aim as stated was a threat to democracy.

TRADE UNION RIGHTS

The Strasbourg Court has held that the words in Article 11, 'for the protection of his interests' cannot be devoid of meaning, and that it follows therefore that members of a trade

[113] By eleven votes to six. [114] § 143. [115] § 159.

[116] § 169, the dissenting opinions disagreed, finding on the facts that the applicants would not threaten the autonomy of the Church. Joint partly dissenting opinion of judges Spielmann, Villiger, López Guerra, Bianku, Møse, and Jäderblom.

[117] *Eğitim Ve Bilim Emekçileri Sendikasi v Turkey*, (App. 20641/05), 25 September 2012.

union have a right, in order to protect their interests, that the union be heard.[118] The union and its members must, moreover, be free, in one way or another, to seek to persuade the employer to listen to what it has to say on behalf of its members.[119] One way of forcing the employer to take notice is, of course, to strike.[120] The Court had adopted a cautious attitude, allowing a very wide margin of appreciation to Contracting Parties to decide the extent to which union rights should be recognized and protected under national law.[121] Thus, the Strasbourg Court had not initially been prepared to hold that Article 11 includes a right for a union to be consulted or recognized for collective bargaining.[122] In the United Kingdom, for example, it is entirely a matter of choice for the employer to decide whether or not to negotiate over pay and conditions collectively with a union, or directly with the individual employees, and this is compatible with Article 11. However, where there is no obligation under domestic law for the employer to deal with the union, if the right to organize collectively is to have any meaning:

> it must be possible for a trade union which is not recognized by an employer to take steps including, if necessary, organising industrial action, with a view to persuading the employer to enter into collective bargaining with it on those issues which the union believes are important for its members' interests. Furthermore, it is of the essence of the right to join a trade union for the protection of their interests that employees should be free to instruct or permit the union to make representations to their employer or to take action in support of their interests on their behalf. If workers are prevented from so doing, their freedom to belong to a trade union, for the protection of their interests, becomes illusory. It is the role of the State to ensure that trade union members are not prevented or restrained from using their union to represent them in attempts to regulate their relations with their employers.[123]

It follows, therefore, that the absence of any rule in English law to prevent an employer from bribing employees into giving up their Article 11 rights with a higher pay deal for those prepared to renounce union representation was in breach of the Convention.[124]

The right to strike and the consequences of doing so were considered in the *Schmidt and Dahlström* case[125] in which the applicants were a professor of law at the University of Stockholm and an officer in the Swedish army. They were members of unions which called selective strikes after the expiry of a collective agreement and the negotiation of its replacement. Neither went on strike, but as members of the 'belligerent' unions, they were

[118] *National Union of Belgian Police v Belgium*, 22 October 1975, Series A No 19, (1979–80) 1 EHRR 578; *Enerji Yapi-Yol Sen v Turkey*, (App. 68959/01), 21 April 2009.

[119] *Wilson and the National Union of Journalists and others v United Kingdom*, (Apps. 30668/96, 30671/96, and 30678/96), 2 July 2002, (2002) 35 EHRR 523, ECHR 2002-V, § 44.

[120] *Schmidt and Dahlström v Sweden*, 6 February 1976, Series A No 21, (1979–80) 1 EHRR 637; *Wilson and the National Union of Journalists and others v United Kingdom*, (Apps. 30668/96, 30671/96, and 30678/96), 2 July 2002, (2002) 35 EHRR 523, ECHR 2002-V, § 45.

[121] *Schmidt and Dahlström v Sweden*, 6 February 1976, Series A No 21, (1979–80) 1 EHRR 637; *Wilson and the National Union of Journalists and others v United Kingdom*, (Apps. 30668/96, 30671/96, and 30678/96), 2 July 2002, (2002) 35 EHRR 523, ECHR 2002-V, § 45.

[122] *National Union of Belgian Police v Belgium*, 22 October 1975, Series A No 19, (1979–80) 1 EHRR 578; *Swedish Engine Drivers' Union v Sweden*, 6 February 1976, Series A No 20, (1979–80) 1 EHRR 617; *Wilson and the National Union of Journalists and others v United Kingdom*, (Apps. 30668/96, 30671/96, and 30678/96), 2 July 2002, (2002) 35 EHRR 523, ECHR 2002-V, § 44. See now *Demir and Baykara v Turkey*, (App. 34503/97), 12 November 2008 [GC], (2009) 48 EHRR 1272, ECHR 2008-nyr, §§ 154.

[123] *Wilson and the National Union of Journalists and others v United Kingdom*, (Apps. 30668/96, 30671/96, and 30678/96), 2 July 2002, (2002) 35 EHRR 523, ECHR 2002-V, § 46.

[124] *Wilson and the National Union of Journalists and others v United Kingdom*, (Apps. 30668/96, 30671/96, and 30678/96), 2 July 2002, (2002) 35 EHRR 523, ECHR 2002-V, § 46.

[125] *Schmidt and Dahlström v Sweden*, 6 February 1976, Series A No 21, (1979–80) 1 EHRR 637.

denied certain retrospective benefits which were paid to members of other trade unions and to non-union employees who had not participated in the strikes. The Strasbourg Court concluded, first, that the rights enshrined in Article 11 did not include any rights to retroactivity of benefits, such as salary increases, resulting from a new collective agreement. Secondly, though the right to strike represents one of the most powerful means of protecting the interests of its members, such a right is subject to 'regulation of a kind that limits its exercise in certain instances'. There was thus no violation of Article 11 in the treatment accorded to the applicants.

CLOSED-SHOP ARRANGEMENTS

Article 11 did not originally prohibit the 'closed shop' system, whereby workers cannot be employed in a particular trade unless they are members of a particular union. The preparatory work on the Convention shows that, on account of the difficulties raised by the 'closed-shop' system, it was considered undesirable to include the principle set out in Article 20(2) of the Universal Declaration of Human Rights, that no one may be compelled to belong to an association.

In the *Young, James and Webster* case[126] the applicants complained that they had lost their jobs when they refused to join any of the unions within the closed-shop agreement and that this amounted to a violation of Article 11. The arrangement had been introduced after they had begun their employment with British Rail.[127] In this case, the Strasbourg Court sidestepped the question whether Article 11 encompassed the right not to be compelled to join a trade union, though it noted that the *travaux préparatoires* suggested that such a right had been deliberately excluded from the Convention. The closed-shop agreement at British Rail did, however, interfere with the applicants' right to form or join a trade union, since:

> a threat of dismissal involving loss of livelihood is a most serious form of compulsion and, in the present instance, it was directed against persons engaged by British Rail before the introduction of any obligation to join a particular trade union.[128]

In the Court's opinion, such a form of compulsion 'strikes at the very substance of the freedom guaranteed by Article 11'[129] and gave rise to a violation.

The issue was revisited in the *Sigurjónsson* case[130] where the applicant complained that the obligation on him to become a member of '*Frami*' in order to retain his licence to operate a taxicab violated his rights under Article 11. The Strasbourg Court reviewed the current statements on the right *not* to join an association and noted a 'growing measure of common ground' both within the Council of Europe and internationally. This led it to conclude:

> [T]he Convention is a living instrument which must be interpreted in the light of present-day conditions.... Accordingly, Article 11 must be viewed as encompassing a negative right of association. It is not necessary for the Court to determine in this instance whether this right is to be considered on an equal footing with the positive right.[131]

[126] *Young, James and Webster v United Kingdom*, 13 August 1981, Series A No 44, (1982) 4 EHRR 38.

[127] Sometimes referred to as post-entry requirements, as distinct from employments where it was known that there was a closed shop before the employment was taken up, which have been referred to as pre-entry arrangements.

[128] § 55. [129] § 55.

[130] *Sigurdur A Sigurjónsson v Iceland*, 30 June 1993, Series A No 264-A, (1993) 16 EHRR 462.

[131] § 35. But note that the Strasbourg Court did not, in this case, decide that '*Frami*' was a trade union.

The Court clearly disliked the degree of compulsion embedded in the provision and was not convinced that membership of '*Frami*' was necessary in order to achieve its objectives. It concluded that, notwithstanding Iceland's margin of appreciation, the measures complained of were disproportionate to the legitimate aim pursued.

The *Sibson* case[132] concerned an employee who resigned from his union following allegations of dishonesty and joined another union. His fellow employees voted in favour of a closed shop and threatened strike action if he continued to work at their depot. The employers sought to resolve the problem by transferring the applicant to another place of work. Another option was that he rejoin the union from which he had initially resigned. The applicant refused both options and resigned with immediate effect. The Strasbourg Court distinguished the *Young, James and Webster* case and found no violation of Article 11: the applicant had no strong objection to rejoining the union (he simply wanted an apology), and could, in any event, have kept his job by moving to another depot.

In the *Gustafsson* case[133] the applicant was an employer and restaurant owner, who refused to join one of the employers' associations established in Sweden for the purposes of collective bargaining with employees. Because of his refusal to enter into a collective agreement, his restaurant was the object of a union blockade which had a negative effect on his business. He complained that the respondent State should have provided some mechanism under national law whereby he could have terminated the union action.

The Strasbourg Court observed that in order to comply with the Swedish law on collective bargaining, it would not have been necessary for the applicant to join an employers' association. The law would have been satisfied, and the union action called off, if he had consented to sign a substitute agreement with his employees, recognizing their right to collective bargaining. The Court noted the special role and importance of collective agreements in the regulation of labour relations in Sweden, and the recognition of the legitimate character of collective bargaining included in a number of international instruments, including Article 6 of the European Social Charter, Article 8 of the 1966 International Covenant on Economic, Social and Cultural Rights, and Conventions nos. 87 and 98 of the International Labour Organisation. It concluded that the requirement on an employer to enter into a collective wage agreement fell within the respondent State's margin of appreciation under Article 11.

The distaste for closed-shop arrangements has been reinforced by a decision of the Grand Chamber in the *Sørensen and Rasmussen* case.[134] Both applicants had objected to being required to join a trade union as a condition of their employment. The judgment does not totally outlaw closed-shop arrangements but will make it very difficult for Contracting Parties to sustain such arrangements:

> In assessing whether a Contracting State has remained within its margin of appreciation in tolerating the existence of closed-shop agreements, particular weight must be attached to the justifications advanced by the authorities for them and, in any given case, the extent to which they impinge on the rights and interests protected by Article 11. Account must also be taken of changing perceptions of the relevance of closed-shop agreements for securing the effective enjoyment of trade union freedom. The Court sees no reason not to extend these considerations to both pre-entry and post-entry closed-shop agreements.[135]

[132] *Sibson v United Kingdom*, 20 April 1993, Series A No 258-A, (1994) 17 EHRR 193.

[133] *Gustafsson v Sweden*, (App. 15573/89), 25 April 1996, (1996) 22 EHRR 409, ECHR 1996-II; Revision, ECHR 1998-V.

[134] *Sørensen and Rasmussen v Denmark*, (Apps. 52562/99 and 52620/99), 11 January 2006 [GC], (2008) 46 EHRR 572, ECHR 2006-I.

[135] § 58.

That view is reinforced by the Strasbourg Court's conclusions following its survey of developments in Europe on the use of the closed shop:

> it appears that there is little support in the Contracting States for the maintenance of closed-shop agreements and that the European instruments referred to above clearly indicate that their use in the labour market is not an indispensable tool for the effective enjoyment of trade union freedoms.[136]

In the case of *Sørensen*, the Grand Chamber found by twelve votes to five, and in the case of *Rasmussen* by fifteen votes to two, that the respondent State had breached Article 11 in that it had failed to protect the applicants' right not to join a trade union.

THE CURRENT STATE OF THE LAW

The Strasbourg Court has summarized the development of its case-law on trade union rights as follows:

> 144. As a result of the foregoing, the evolution of case-law as to the substance of the right of association enshrined in Article 11 is marked by two guiding principles: firstly, the Court takes into consideration the totality of the measures taken by the State concerned in order to secure trade-union freedom, subject to its margin of appreciation; secondly, the Court does not accept restrictions that affect the essential elements of trade-union freedom, without which that freedom would become devoid of substance. These two principles are not contradictory but are correlated. This correlation implies that the Contracting State in question, whilst in principle being free to decide what measures it wishes to take in order to ensure compliance with Article 11, is under an obligation to take account of the elements regarded as essential by the Court's case-law.
>
> 145. From the Court's case-law as it stands, the following essential elements of the right of association can be established: the right to form and join a trade union . . . the prohibition of closed-shop agreements . . . and the right for a trade union to seek to persuade the employer to hear what it has to say on behalf of its members. . . .
>
> 146. This list is not finite. On the contrary, it is subject to evolution depending on particular developments in labour relations. In this connection it is appropriate to remember that the Convention is a living instrument which must be interpreted in the light of present-day conditions, and in accordance with developments in international law, so as to reflect the increasingly high standard being required in the area of the protection of human rights, thus necessitating greater firmness in assessing breaches of the fundamental values of democratic societies. In other words, limitations to rights must be construed restrictively, in a manner which gives practical and effective protection to human rights. . . .[137]

There is also a right to bargain collectively:

> . . . the Court considers that, having regard to the developments in labour law, both international and national, and to the practice of Contracting States in such matters, the right to bargain collectively with the employer has, in principle, become one of the essential elements

[136] § 75.

[137] *Demir and Baykara v Turkey*, (App. 34503/97), 12 November 2008 [GC], (2009) 48 EHRR 1272, ECHR 2008-nyr, §§ 144–6. The Court has reaffirmed these principles in *Sindicatul "Pastorul cel Bun" v Romania* (App. 2330/09) 9 July 2013. For discussion of trade union rights post the *Demir and Baykara* case see C. Barrow, 'Trade Union Rights in the United Kingdom and Article 11 of the European Convention: Past Failures and Future Possibilities' (2013) EHRLR (1), 56–71.

of the 'right to form and to join trade unions for the protection of [one's] interests' set forth in Article 11 of the Convention, it being understood that States remain free to organize their system so as, if appropriate, to grant special status to representative trade unions. Like other workers, civil servants, except in very specific cases, should enjoy such rights, but without prejudice to the effects of any 'lawful restrictions' that may have to be imposed on 'members of the administration of the State' within the meaning of Article 11 § 2—a category to which the applicants in the present case do not, however, belong....[138]

The recognition of the right to collective bargaining is an important step for the Court in the protection guaranteed to trade unions and within this it can be argued that the Court has recognized the right to strike in the exercise of collective bargaining, subject to justified restrictions.[139]

RESTRICTIONS ON PARTICULAR GROUPS OF WORKERS

Paragraph (2) of Article 11 contains the standard limitations which are common to Articles 8 to 11.[140] Additionally, it provides that:

> This article shall not prevent the imposition of lawful restrictions on the exercise of these rights by members of the armed forces, of the police or of the administration of the State.

The concept of 'lawfulness' in this provision is the same as that elsewhere in the Convention, requiring, in addition to conformity with domestic law, that the domestic law must be accessible, certain, and not arbitrary.[141]

There is a distinction to be drawn between members of the administration of the State, and civil servants, especially those employed in the municipalities.[142] It is not clear, however, whether interferences with the rights of association of civil servants in the specified groups must pursue a legitimate aim and be proportionate. The Commission, examining an application arising from the prohibition of trade union membership among civilian workers at the United Kingdom Government Communications Headquarters (GCHQ) in Cheltenham,[143] took the view that the sole requirements in such cases were that the restrictions be in accordance with national law and be free from arbitrariness.[144] In the *Vogt* case[145] the Strasbourg Court appeared to imply that such a measure would need to be proportionate, but left the question open, as it did in a case brought by a Hungarian police officer, who complained about an amendment to the Constitution prohibiting the police and members of the armed forces from joining political parties or engaging in political activities.[146] The Court did not need to consider the question under Article 11(2) since it

[138] § 154.

[139] *Enerji Yapi-Yol Sen v Turkey*, (App. 68959/1), 21 April 2009, § 32. See also *Danilenkov v Russia*, (App. 67336/01), 30 July 2009; *Kaya and Seyhan v Turkey*, (App. 30946/04), 15 September 2009.

[140] See ch.14.

[141] *Rekvényi v Hungary*, (App. 25390/94), 20 May 1999 [GC], (2000) 30 EHRR 519, ECHR 1999-III.

[142] *Demir and Baykara v Turkey*, (App. 34503/97), 12 November 2008 [GC], (2009) 48 EHRR 1272, ECHR 2008-nyr, § 97.

[143] *Council of Civil Service Unions and others v United Kingdom*, (App. 11603/85), Decision of 20 January 1987, (1987) 50 DR 228.

[144] 240 and 241.

[145] *Vogt v Germany*, 26 September 1995, Series A No 323, (1996) 21 EHRR 205, § 67.

[146] *Rekvényi v Hungary*, (App. 25390/94), 20 May 1999 [GC], (2000) 30 EHRR 519, ECHR 1999-III.

had already determined that the restriction was proportionate under Article 10, given in particular the problems Hungary had suffered in the past with a politicized police force.

The leading authority is now the decision of the Grand Chamber in the *Demir and Baykara* case.[147] This concerned the right of civil servants to form trade unions. Having regard to provisions in a number of international instruments, the Grand Chamber concluded that members of the administration of the State cannot be excluded from the scope of Article 11; at most they may be subject to lawful restrictions beyond those provided for elsewhere in the Article. Municipal civil servants will not normally fall within the special category and so any interference with their trade union rights will have to be justified under the usual limitations set out in Article 11(2).

The Court has held that it is permissible for a Contracting Party to restrict the political activity of local government officials,[148] but not to require them to renounce Freemasonry.[149] In the *Vogt* case[150] it found violations of Articles 10 and 11 where a West German teacher had been dismissed for membership of the Communist Party, given that she had not let her political beliefs affect her professional conduct in any way.[151] In a case involving police officers,[152] the Court held that the police, like all civil servants, have a duty of loyalty, reserve, and discretion to their employers. The police also should act in an impartial manner in public in order to maintain public trust. This has to be weighed against their trade union rights, which include the right to be heard.

CONCLUDING REMARKS

The case-law under Article 11 can, very broadly, be divided into two categories. The first, concerned with 'political' or 'democratic' rights, rely heavily on the principles developed by the Strasbourg Court under Article 10. The second type of case which arises under Article 11 relates to the employment-based rights to join, or refuse to join, a trade union. Here the Strasbourg Court's judgments were initially somewhat less confident, sometimes allowing the Contracting Parties such a wide margin of appreciation that it is difficult to discern any real content to the rights for practical purposes.

It must be remembered, however, that there is other international machinery for dealing with complaints concerning trade union rights, in particular under the conventions of the International Labour Organization[153] and under the European Social Charter. The provisions of the other international instruments are naturally more detailed, and within the International Labour Organization, in particular, a substantial body of law has been developed.

[147] *Demir and Baykara v Turkey*, (App. 34503/97), 12 November 2008 [GC], (2009) 48 EHRR 1272, ECHR 2008-nyr.

[148] *Ahmed and others v United Kingdom*, (App. 22954/93), 2 September 1998, (2000) 29 EHRR 1, ECHR 1998-VI.

[149] *Grande Oriente d'Italia di Palazzo Giustiniani v Italy*, (App. 35972/97), 2 August 2001, (2002) 34 EHRR 629, ECHR 2001-VIII.

[150] *Vogt v Germany*, 26 September 1995, Series A No 323, (1996) 21 EHRR 205. Contrast the admissibility decision in *Erdel v Germany*, (App. 30067/04), 13 February 2007, ECHR 2007-II.

[151] The Court applied a similar test in *Redfearn v United Kingdom*, (App. 47335/06), 6 November 2012, where the Court found that the applicant's political beliefs had not impacted on his professional activities for a private company that carried out services contracted out to it by the local authority.

[152] *Trade Union Of The Police In The Slovak Republic And others v Slovakia*, (App. 11828/08), 25 September 2012

[153] See L. Swepston, 'Human Rights Law and Freedom of Association: Development through ILO Supervision' (1998) 137 *International Labour Review* 169.

The Strasbourg Court could have reacted to this by deciding that it does not have the expertise, and that the Convention is not the most appropriate vehicle for settling complex socio-economic labour law questions.[154] However, the Court has arguably decided to look more closely at the case-law built up under other treaties, and apply the principles developed there. The recognition of collective bargaining and the protection of civil servants are two examples of the Court applying principles developed by other international bodies. It could be argued there is now an emerging uniformity in the field.[155]

[154] See the separate opinions in the *Gustafsson v Sweden* case, 25 April 1996, (1996) 22 EHRR 409, ECHR 1996-II; Revision, ECHR 1998-V.

[155] *Demir and Baykara v Turkey*, (App. 34503/97), 12 November 2008 [GC], (2009) 48 EHRR 1272, ECHR 2008-nyr; see also *Sindicatul 'Păstorul cel Bun' v Romania*, (App. 2330/09), 9 July 2013 which refers extensively to international standards in its reasoning, §§ 56–61.

20

PROTECTION OF PROPERTY

INTRODUCTION

The protection of property rights as human rights presents particular problems, and it is therefore not surprising that agreement could not be reached on their inclusion in the Convention as originally drafted.[1] A right to property is included in Article 1 of Protocol 1, but its content is broadly framed and the permissible restrictions are broad in scope. The beneficiaries of the guarantees in the Article are both individuals and business entities, including corporations. The Article has, consequently, taken on a commercial character and been used extensively by business in the advancement of its interests.

All the provisions of the Convention, including Articles 13 to 18, apply equally to the rights guaranteed by the First Protocol.[2] These rights are also subject in the same way to the control of the organs set up by the Convention.

Article 1 of the First Protocol provides:

> Every natural or legal person is entitled to the peaceful enjoyment of his possessions. No one shall be deprived of his possessions except in the public interest and subject to the conditions provided for by law and by the general principles of international law.
>
> The preceding provisions shall not, however, in any way impair the right of a State to enforce such laws as it deems necessary to control the use of property in accordance with the general interest or to secure the payment of taxes or other contributions or penalties.

Though drafted rather differently, the structure of the provision is similar to that found in Articles 8 to 11. There is a general right to peaceful enjoyment of possessions. Interferences can, however, be justified on the conditions set out in the Article which include references both to the 'public interest' and the 'general interest'; this is the test of proportionality that pervades the Convention's consideration of interferences and requires the balancing of the interests of the individual against the collective interest.

There is also a requirement in the Article that deprivations are 'subject to the conditions provided for by law'[3] and so the discussion of the notion of interferences being in

[1] See generally, A. Grgic and others, *The right to property under the European Convention on Human Rights: a guide to the implementation of the European Convention on Human Rights and its Protocols*, Human Rights Handbooks No. 4 (Council of Europe Publishing, Strasbourg 2007); H.G. Schermers, 'The International Protection of the Right of Property' in F. Matscher and H. Petzold (eds.), *Protecting Human Rights: The European Dimension. Essays in honour of Gérard J. Wiarda* (Carl Heymanns, Köln 1988), at 565; J. Frowein, 'The Protection of Property' in R. Macdonald, F. Matscher, and H. Petzold, *The European System for the Protection of Human Rights* (Martinus Nijhoff, Dordrecht 1993) at 515; A. Riza Coban, *Protection of Property Rights within the European Convention on Human Rights* (Ashgate, Aldershot 2004); and G. Ress, 'Reflections on the Protection of Property under the European Convention on Human Rights' in S. Breitenmoser and others, *Human Rights, Democracy and the Rule of Law. Liber amicorum Luzius Wildhaber*, (Nomos, Baden Baden 2007), 625.

[2] Protocol 1, Art. 5.

[3] *Prévues par la loi* in the French text.

accordance with law in relation to Articles 8 to 11 will also be relevant here.[4] The Article makes express provision for certain deprivations of property, though these must be in accordance with national law, in accordance with the general principles of international law, and in the public interest. It is also acknowledged that public authorities can control the use of property either in the general interest, or specifically to secure the payment of taxes or other contributions or penalties.

The Strasbourg Court has come to approach the protection of property rights using much the same methodology as it adopts in relation to complaints of violations of the rights protected by Articles 8 to 11. This secures a certain uniformity of approach in cases where a Contracting Party interferes with rights protected in the Convention, and seeks to offer a justification for this. However, the range of rights which falls within the concept of the 'public interest' and the 'general interest' is very wide indeed.[5]

The Court has repeatedly said that the Article comprises three distinct rules.[6] First, everyone is entitled to peaceful enjoyment of their possessions. Secondly, deprivation of possessions is subject to certain conditions. Finally, Contracting Parties are entitled to control the use of property where it is in the general interest. But these are not distinct rules, since the second and third rules relate to interferences with the peaceful enjoyment of possessions which may be justified in the general interest. This can be illustrated by the facts of the *Pye* case.[7] The applicants complained that the operation of the English land law rules on adverse possession meant that they had been deprived of property when land registered in their name was to be registered in the names of a couple who had occupied the land for twelve years. The Strasbourg Court categorizes the situation as one involving control over the use of land, whereas it might easily have been categorized as a deprivation.[8]

In the *Marckx* case,[9] the Strasbourg Court stated some general propositions on the scope of Article 1 of Protocol 1. It applies only to a person's existing possessions and gives no guarantee of a right to acquire possessions.[10] But the right to property does include the right to dispose of one's property.[11]

Once it has been established that the applicant has an interest which can be classified as a possession, the general approach of the Strasbourg Court is to consider first whether there has been a deprivation of possessions, followed by consideration of whether there has been a control of the use of possessions, since these are matters specifically dealt with by the Article. Only if there has been neither deprivation of possessions nor a control of

[4] See ch.14. For an example of a discussion of legality in the context of this Article, see *Bozcaada Kimisis Teodoku Rum Ortodoks Kilisesi Vafki v Turkey (No. 2)*, (Apps. 37639/03, 37655/03, 26736/04, and 42670/04), 3 March 2009; *Krstić v Serbia*, (App. 45394/06), 10 December 2013.

[5] Encompassing for example, the protection of nature and forests: *Turgut and others v Turkey*, (App. 1411/03), 8 July 2008, ECHR 2008-nyr; and the protection of natural heritage: *Anonymos Touristiki Etairia Xenodocheia v Greece*, (App. 35332/05), 21 February 2008.

[6] *Sporrong and Lönnroth v Sweden*, (Apps. 7151–2/75), 23 September 1982, Series A No 52, (1983) 5 EHRR 35, § 61. See, also *Hutten-Czapska v Poland*, (App. 35014/97), 19 June 2006 [GC], (2007) 45 EHRR 52, ECHR 2006-VIII, § 157; *Depalle v France*, (App. 24044/02), 29 March 2010, § 77; *Ališić and others v Bosnia and Herzegovina, Croatia, Serbia, Slovenia and the Former Yugoslav Republic of Macedonia*, (App. 60642/08), 6 November 2012 (Referral to Grand Chamber 18 March 2013), § 63, *Dzugayeva v Russia*, (App. 44971/04), 12 February 2013, § 23.

[7] *JA Pye (Oxford) Ltd and JA Pye (Oxford) Land Ltd v United Kingdom*, (App. 44302/02), 30 August 2007 [GC], (2008) 46 EHRR 1083, ECHR 2007-X.

[8] A point made in the joint dissenting opinion of Judges Rozakis, Bratza, Tsatsa-Nikolovska, Gyulumyan, and Šikuta, § 6.

[9] *Marckx v Belgium*, (App. 6833/74), 13 June 1979, Series A No 31, (1979–80) 2 EHRR 330.

[10] § 50. [11] § 63.

their use[12] does the Court consider, as a separate issue, whether there has been some other interference with the peaceful enjoyment of possessions. Such interferences will, however, only be unlawful if they are not in the general interest. The Court has brought together the tests it applies in relation to deprivations, the control of the use of property, and to other interferences with property, so that the questions the Court will ask in each of these circumstances raise essentially the same issues.

There has been a series of applications relating to the consequences of the reunification of Germany and the transition from totalitarian regimes to democratic structures in the countries of central and eastern Europe before the Strasbourg Court. In its judgments, the Grand Chamber has sought to establish the obligations of States in fairly managing a whole variety of schemes seeking to reverse injustices which arose from the regime in place before the advent of democracy.

POSITIVE OBLIGATIONS

The *Öneryildiz* case[13] concerned the loss of life and destruction of property as a result of unsafe conditions in a refuse tip, for which the respondent State was responsible. The Grand Chamber concluded that there was an obligation on States to take practical steps to avoid loss of property.[14] The obligation is very similar to that arising under Article 2. The *Budayeva* case[15] concerned a natural disaster rather than a disaster flowing from dangerous activities. There had been a mudslide which caused loss of life, and destruction of property. The authorities had known of the risk of mudslides in the area, but had not established any form of early warning system. This led the Court to conclude that a distinction should be drawn between the positive obligation to protect life and to protect property. Where there is a risk to life, the authorities must do everything to mitigate the risk, but where the risk is of destruction of property, 'the authorities enjoy a wider margin of appreciation.'[16] In the particular circumstances of the case, the respondent State had failed to comply with its positive obligations under Article 2, but not under Article 1 of Protocol 1. A similar distinction was drawn in respect of the obligation to conduct an inquiry into the disaster; there was a lesser obligation where destruction of property was involved.

The Court has emphasized that Article 1 of Protocol 1 may require 'measures which are necessary to protect the right of property…, even in cases involving litigation between individuals or companies.'[17] The Court has noted that where the circumstances of a case involve economic relations, obligations placed on the State may be more limited than in cases where the applicant faces a loss of possession due to negligence in the face of dangerous situations.[18] For example, the Court has established that positive obligations do not extend to a general obligation covering private debts.[19] However, the State may be engaged

[12] Or where the circumstances of the case are such that detailed categorization in this way is inappropriate: see, for example, *Solodyuk v Russia*, (App. 67099/01), 12 July 2005, § 29; and *Broniowski v Poland* (App. 31443/96), 22 June 2004 [GC], (2005) 40 EHRR 495, ECHR 2004-V.

[13] *Öneryildiz v Turkey*, (App. 48939/99), 30 November 2004 [GC], (2005) 41 EHRR 325, ECHR 2004-XII. See also *Dzugayeva v Russia*, (App. 44971/04), 12 February 2013, § 26.

[14] § 136.

[15] *Budayeva and others v Russia*, (Apps. 15339/02, 21166/02, 20058/02, 11673/02, and 15343/02), 20 March 2008, ECHR 2008-nyr.

[16] *Budayeva*, § 175.

[17] *Sovtransavto Holding v Ukraine*, (App. 48553/99), ECHR 2002-VII, §§ 54.

[18] *Kotov v Russia*, (App. 54522/00), 3 April 2012, § 111.

[19] § 111, see also *Kin-Stib and Majkić v Serbia*, (App. 12312/05), 20 April 2010, § 84.

in cases concerning enforcement procedures for debt recovery. In *Kotov v Russia*,[20] the applicant was owed money by a bank which went insolvent. He was listed as a creditor but did not receive the money owed due to lack of assets. He claimed the liquidator had acted unlawfully. The domestic courts dismissed his claim. The Court noted that the positive obligation on the State in these circumstances could be preventative or remedial. On the facts, the Court held there was no violation as the applicant could have sued the liquidator for damages after the end of the liquidation proceedings.[21]

Issues arising from the reunification of Germany, and from attempts to recover formerly owned property in some of the countries of central and eastern Europe, have generated a line of case-law on positive obligations. The Grand Chamber of the Court recapitulated the relevant principles in its judgment in the *Kopecký* case.[22] There is no duty falling on Contracting Parties to restore property taken by an earlier regime to its original owners; nor is there any restriction on their doing so. However, any scheme which is established will create a property right for those who meet the conditions of entitlement under the scheme, and will require that the scheme is Convention compliant. This will also be the case with any legislative scheme established prior to entry into force of the Convention, which is continued in operation following accession. The positive obligation has been stated to be to take timely and consistent action, which avoids an atmosphere of general uncertainty.[23] This includes a duty to put mechanisms in place to implement any legislative schemes devised by the State for restitution.[24]

The Strasbourg Court is adopting a similar approach in cases involving positive obligations to that which it adopts when negative obligations are in issue. In the *Broniowski* case, the Court examined the issue of compensation for land lost after the redrawing of Polish borders after the Second World War. The State established a compensation scheme. However, the applicant only received a small percentage of the value of land lost, after the State modified the scheme. The Grand Chamber said:

> ...the boundaries between the State's positive and negative obligations under Article 1 of Protocol 1 do not lend themselves to precise definition. The applicable principles are nonetheless similar. Whether the case is analysed in terms of a positive duty on the State or in terms of an interference by a public authority which requires to be justified, the criteria to be applied do not differ in substance. In both contexts regard must be had to the fair balance to be struck between the competing interests of the individual and of the community as a whole. It also holds true that the aims mentioned in that provision may be of some relevance in assessing whether a balance between the demands of the public interest involved and the applicant's fundamental right of property has been struck. In both contexts the State enjoys a certain margin of appreciation in determining the steps to be taken to ensure compliance with the Convention....[25]

Indeed in the *Broniowski* case, the Strasbourg Court noted that the behaviour of the State could be considered to be a hindrance to the effective exercise of Article 1 of Protocol 1, or as a failure to secure the implementation of the right. As the measures were not easy to classify in a single precise category, the Court declined to classify the contested measures

[20] *Kotov v Russia*, (App. 54522/00), 3 April 2012. [21] § 129–131.

[22] *Kopecký v Slovakia*, (App. 44912/98), 28 September 2004 [GC], (2005) 41 EHRR 944, ECHR 2004-IX. The 'restitution' cases are considered in more detail below.

[23] *Păduraru v Romania*, (App. 63252/00), 1 December 2005, §§ 92–3.

[24] *Catholic Archdiocese of Alba Iulia v Romania*, (App. 33003/03), 25 September 2012.

[25] *Broniowski v Poland*, (App. 31443/96), 22 June 2004, (2005) 40 EHRR 495, ECHR 2004-V, § 144. See also *Zolotas v Greece (No. 2)*, (App. 66610/09), 29 January 2013, § 40.

as engaging either positive or negative obligations, indicating that the Court would simply determine whether the conduct of the respondent State was justifiable.[26]

DEFINING POSSESSIONS

THE BASIC APPROACH

Possessions have been defined in broad terms by both the Commission and the Court. In this context, it is worth noting that the French text of the Convention uses the term '*biens*' which connotes a very broad range of property rights. The term has an autonomous meaning; it extends beyond physical goods, and covers a wide range of rights and interests which may be classified as assets.[27]

It is for the Strasbourg organs to determine what falls within the concept of possessions in the Article having regard to the classification of the matter under national law. Clearly both real and personal property[28] are within the notion of possessions, but the concept extends far beyond to all manner of things which have an economic value. So the Strasbourg organs have held that company shares are possessions.[29] A patent is also a possession,[30] as is an internet domain name.[31] Indeed, the provision is applicable to all intellectual property as such, including applications for registration of a trade mark.[32] Goodwill in a business constitutes possessions,[33] as does a licence to serve alcoholic beverages where this is vital to an applicant's business.[34] Telecommunications licences for providing internet and fixed telephone services are possessions.[35] Similarly a licence to extract gravel was regarded by the Strasbourg Court as a possession,[36] as was a licence to run a bonded warehouse.[37] The Court has also held that interests associated with exploiting a broadcasting licence amounted to a possession.[38] Fishing rights are possessions.[39] A planning permission is a possession.[40] But a driving licence is not a possession.[41] Tips

[26] § 146.

[27] *Gasus Dosier- und Fördertechnik GmbH v Netherlands*, 23 February 1995, Series A No 306-B, (1995) 20 EHRR 403, § 53.

[28] Often referred to as immovable and movable property.

[29] Apps. 8588/79 and 8589/79, *Bramelid & Malmström v Sweden*, Decision of 12 October 1982, (1982) 29 DR 64, and App. 11189/84, *Company S. & T. v Sweden*, Decision of 11 December 1988, (1987) 50 DR 121.

[30] App. 12633/87, *Smith Kline and French Laboratories Ltd v Netherlands*, Decision of 4 October 1990, (1990) 66 DR 70.

[31] *Paeffgen GmbH v Germany*, (Apps. 25379/02, 21688/05, 21722/05, and 21770/05), Decision of 18 September 2007.

[32] *Anheuser-Busch Inc. v Portugal*, (App. 73049/01), 11 January 2007 [GC], (2007) 45 EHRR 830, ECHR 2007-I.

[33] *Van Marle and others v Netherlands*, 26 June 1986, Series A No 101, (1986) 8 EHRR 483, § 41. But see also App. 10438/83, *Batelaan & Huiges v Netherlands*, Decision of 3 October 1984, (1985) 41 DR 170 to the effect that expectations lack the degree of certainty needed to constitute possessions.

[34] *Tre Traktörer Aktiebolag v Sweden*, 7 July 1989, Series A No 159, (1991) 13 EHRR 309, § 53.

[35] *Megadat.com SRL v Moldova*, (App. 21151/04), 8 April 2008, ECHR 2008-nyr, §§ 62–3.

[36] *Fredin v Sweden*, 18 February 1991, Series A No 192 (1991) 13 EHRR 784, § 40.

[37] *Rosenweig and Bonded Warehouses Ltd v Poland*, (App. 51728/99), 28 July 2005.

[38] *Centro Europa 7 S.r.l. and Di Stefano v Italy*, (App. 38433/09), 7 June 2012, § 179.

[39] App. 11763/85, *Banér v Sweden*, Decision of 9 March 1989, (1989) 60 DR 128; *Posti and Rahko v Finland*, (App. 27824/95), 24 September 2002, (2003) 37 EHRR 158, ECHR 2002-VII; and *Alatulkkila and others v Finland*, (App. 33538/96), 28 July 2005.

[40] *Pine Valley Developments Ltd and others v Ireland*, (App. 12742/87), 29 November 1991, Series A No 222, (1992) 14 EHRR 319.

[41] App. 9177/80, *X v Federal Republic of Germany*, Decision of 6 October 1981, (1982) 26 DR 255.

paid to waiters were held in one case not to constitute possessions of the waiters,[42] but compulsory deductions from the wages of those who are not members of the union for trade union activities will constitute an interference with possessions.[43] In another case, it was suggested that royal property may have a special status, but since the State had consistently treated the property in issue as private property, and had not established a distinct set of rules relating to royal property, the case was decided by the application of ordinary principles.[44]

In the *Öneryildiz* case,[45] the respondent State argued that unlawfully occupying land and building a home on it could not give rise to property rights within the Article. The applicant's home and its contents had been destroyed in a landslide following a methane explosion in a refuse tip; the authorities knew of the risks posed by the tip, but had taken no steps to make it safe. The Court rather sidestepped the issue by concluding that, although the applicant could show no property interest in the land, nevertheless he had a property interest in the house itself and its contents. This stemmed from the fact that the authorities knew they lived in the house and tolerated the situation. In a case[46] concerning the removal of a family from a home given to the applicants by the State whilst working for a State ministry, the Court again noted that the applicants lived in their home in 'good faith' and noted the:

> authorities' own manifest tolerance of the first applicant's exclusive, uninterrupted and open use of the cottage and the adjacent premises for more than ten years...The State never objected to the socio-economic and family environment established by the first applicant.[47]

In both cases, the applicants had a reasonable expectation[48] that they could remain in the homes. In contrast, in *Depalle v France*,[49] the Court held that the expectation of remaining in a home by the applicant was not reasonable. The applicant had purchased a house on public land, which was later designated for protection as a coastal area. The right to occupy the land was based on temporary permission being renewed regularly. When the new law protecting coastal areas was brought into force, the authorities refused to issue permission under the same conditions as before. The applicants should have anticipated that this might happen.[50]

The Strasbourg Court has also read Article 1 of Protocol 1 with Article 6 to provide a property right in an enforceable judgment against the State.[51]

LEASES AND LICENCES TO OCCUPY PROPERTY

Rights flowing from leases are accepted as possessions. In the *Mellacher* case,[52] it was not disputed that reductions in contractually agreed rents under rent control legislation

[42] *Nerva and others v United Kingdom*, (App. 42295/98), 24 September 2002, (2003) 36 EHRR 31, ECHR 2002-VIII. [43] *Evaldsson and others v Sweden*, (App. 75252/01), 13 February 2007.

[44] *The Former King of Greece and others v Greece*, (App. 25701/94), 23 November 2000 [GC], (2001) 33 EHRR 516, ECHR 2000-XII, §§ 65–6.

[45] *Öneryildiz v Turkey*, (App. 48939/99), 30 November 2004 [GC], (2005) 41 EHRR 325, ECHR 2004-XII.

[46] *Saghinadze and others v Georgia*, (App. 18768/05), 27 May 2012. [47] § 106.

[48] See later in this chapter with regard to legitimate expectations.

[49] *Depalle v France*, (App. 34044/02), 29 March 2010.

[50] See dissenting opinions, where the judges disagreed with the finding, given the applicant had lived in the house for fifty years and the house had been designated for occupation for over a century. Joint Dissenting Opinion of Judges Bratza, Vajić, David Thòr Björgvinsson, and Kalaydjieva.

[51] *Burdov v Russia*, (App. 59498/00), 7 May 2002, (2004) 38 EHRR639, ECHR 2002-III, and the pilot judgment in *Burdov v Russia (No. 2)*, (App. 33509/04), 15 January 2009, (2009) 49 EHRR 22; see also *Krstić v Serbia*, (App. 45394/06), 10 December 2013.

[52] *Mellacher v Austria*, (Apps. 10522/83, 11011/84, and 11070/84), 19 December 1989, Series A No 169, (1990) 12 EHRR 391, § 43.

constituted an interference with the applicants' enjoyment of their rights as owners of the rented properties.

Somewhat inconsistently with the broad interpretation of possessions taken in other contexts, the Court has drawn a narrow distinction between the basis on which individuals occupy property as their homes. In the *Larkos* case,[53] the Strasbourg Court sidestepped the issue when faced with a complaint by a government tenant that the differences in the levels of protection afforded under national law to private tenants and government tenants on termination of the lease violated Article 1 of Protocol 1 when read with Article 14 of the Convention.[54] The respondent State had argued that the applicant did not possess any interest in the property which constituted a possession falling within the scope of Article 1 of Protocol 1. The Court disposed of the case by finding a violation of Article 14 when read in conjunction with Article 8.

In an admissibility decision[55] the Court was faced with a situation in which a soldier in the provisional reserve force was allocated housing by the army. Following a change in the system for housing members of the military, the applicant was required to vacate the property and was evicted. The Court observed that the applicant did not have a lease, and that the arrangement could not be equated to 'an agreement under private law'. The Court went on to say:

> [The Court] points out that a right to live in a particular property not owned by the applicant does not constitute a 'possession' within the meaning of Article 1 of Protocol 1 .... Furthermore, allowing a 'user' such as the applicant (who was not even a tenant) to remain indefinitely in premises belonging to the State would prevent the authorities from performing their obligation to administer State property in accordance with their statutory and constitutional duties.[56]

The Court accordingly found the application to be inadmissible.[57] It is suggested that a more satisfactory approach would have been to recognize the applicant's property right in his housing, but to find that the interference was justified in the general interest.[58] This latter approach would be consistent with the *Saghinadze* case,[59] where the applicant was held to have a pecuniary interest because of a legitimate expectation of continued occupation, even where the applicant was not a tenant or owner.[60]

SOCIAL SECURITY PAYMENTS AND PENSIONS

Entitlements arising under pension and social security schemes have proved difficult to classify; the position was for some time unclear. A distinction had been drawn in the case-law between benefits which were paid on the basis of contributions, and those which were paid without reference to contributions. But the case-law did not always seem to maintain this

53 *Larkos v Cyprus*, (App. 29515/95), 18 February 1999 [GC], (2000) 30 EHRR 597, ECHR 1999-I.

54 Art. 14 provides protection against discrimination in matters within the scope of the Convention: see ch.24.

55 *JLS v Spain*, (App. 41917/98), Decision of 27 April 1999, ECHR 1999-V.

56 § 2.

57 The English law of property makes a clear distinction between tenants and licensees, but would regard licensees as entitled to protection of their property rights, though to a lesser extent than tenants. It is accordingly odd that the Court seemingly drew a distinction between a mere (lawful) user (likely to be characterized as a licensee under English Law) who has nothing which constitutes a possession within the Article, and a tenant who has a possession.

58 The applicant does not appear to have complained of a violation of his right to a home under Art. 8, presumably because an alternative home was made available to him.

59 *Saghinadze and others v Georgia*, (App. 18768/05), 27 May 2012.

60 See also *Ivan Panchenko v Ukraine*, (App. 10911/05), 10 December 2009.

distinction. However, the admissibility decision of the Grand Chamber in the *Stec* case[61] clarified matters.

An example of the ambiguity caused by the earlier case-law can be found in the *Gaygusuz* case.[62] Gaygusuz was a Turkish national who had worked in Austria, where he had paid contributions under the Austrian social security scheme. He had experienced periods of unemployment and periods when he was unfit for work. He applied for an advance on his retirement pension as a form of emergency assistance, but was refused because he was not an Austrian national. He complained that there had been a violation of Article 14 when read in conjunction with Article 1 of Protocol 1. The first question was whether the substance of the claim was a matter within the scope of the Article, since otherwise Article 14 could not be brought into play. Both the Commission and the Court concluded that the Article was applicable but for different reasons. The Commission concluded that the Article was brought into play because the obligation to pay 'taxes or other contributions' falls within its field of application.[63] The Court, however, concluded that the link with the obligation to pay taxes or other contributions was not required.[64] That was sufficient to engage the anti-discrimination provision in Article 14 and to find a violation since the discrimination between nationals and non-nationals was blatant. The Court took the same approach in the *Koua Poirrez* case.[65]

In the *Stec* case, the Grand Chamber accepted that the *Gaygusuz* case was ambiguous on the significance of contributions in bringing a claim within the scope of Article 1 of Protocol 1 for the purpose of claiming discriminatory treatment which breached Article 14 of the Convention. The Grand Chamber laid down a new approach, relying on an interpretation which renders the rights in the Convention practical and effective rather than theoretical and illusory.[66] The Grand Chamber also referred to the Court's case-law under Article 6 which had brought disputes concerning all forms of social security within the scope of that Article. The Court concluded that, whenever persons can assert a right to a welfare benefit under national law, Article 1 of Protocol 1 applies.[67] The Court goes on to note that the bringing of social security fairly and squarely within the scope of Article 1 of Protocol 1 does not create any right to acquire property nor does it include a right to a particular amount of benefit.[68] The Article is only applicable where national law provides for an entitlement to a social security benefit[69] and the applicant satisfies the legal conditions set down for the granting of a particular benefit.[70] However, if a Contracting Party does create rights to social security benefits, the benefit schemes must be operated in a manner which is compatible with the prohibition of discrimination set out in Article 14.[71]

[61] *Stec and others v United Kingdom*, (Apps. 65731/01 and 65900/01), Decision of 6 July 2005 [GC], (2005) 41 EHRR SE18, ECHR 2005-X.

[62] *Gaygusuz v Austria*, (App. 17371/90), 16 September 1996, (1997) 23 EHRR 364, ECHR 1996-IV.

[63] § 47 of the Commission Opinion. [64] § 41 of the Judgment.

[65] *Koua Poirrez v France*, (App. 40892/98), 30 September 2003, (2005) 40 EHRR 34, ECHR 2003-X, § 37. Other cases in the earlier line of authority include *Meyne-Moskalczuk and others v The Netherlands*, (App. 53002/99), Decision of 9 December 2003; *Van Den Bouwhuijsen and Schuring v The Netherlands*, (App. 44658/98), Decision of 16 December 2003; and *Kjartan Ásmundsson v Iceland*, (App. 60669/00), 12 October 2004, (2005) 41 EHRR 927, ECHR 2004-IX.

[66] See ch.4.

[67] *Stec and others v United Kingdom*, (Apps. 65731/01 and 65900/01), Decision of 6 July 2005 [GC], (2005) 41 EHRR SE18, ECHR 2005-X, §§ 50–1. This is affirmed in later cases, for example see, *Valkov v Bulgaria*, (App. 2033/04), 25 October 2011, § 84.

[68] See also *Maggio and others v Italy*, (App. 46286/09), 31 May 2011, § 55.

[69] *Carson and others v United Kingdom*, (App. 42184/05) ECHR 2010; *Raviv v Austria*, (App. 26266/05), 13 March 2012, § 61.

[70] *Richardson v the United Kingdom*, (App. 26252/08), Decision of 10 April 2012, §§ 17–18; *Damjanac v Croatia*, (App. 52943/10), 24 October 2013.

[71] See ch.24. See also *Carson and others v United Kingdom*, (App. 42184/05), ECHR 2010; *Stummer v Austria*, (App. 37452/02), 7 July 2011; *Raviv v Austria*, (App. 26266/05), 13 March 2012.

LEGAL CLAIMS, ASSETS, AND LEGITIMATE EXPECTATIONS

Various types of legal claims have been treated as possessions. Some of these cases are complex in their factual situations, making it difficult to draw general principles from them. What is clear is that there must be something which can be regarded as a legal claim. Thus a judgment debt will be a possession, so that quashing the judgment after it has become final will constitute an interference with the peaceful enjoyment of possessions.[72] Similarly a sufficiently established claim to a social tenancy agreement following disablement as a result of involvement in the emergency operations at the Chernobyl Nuclear Plant disaster of 1986 constituted a possession for the purposes of the Article.[73] Retrospective variation of the claimable heads of damages in the law of obligations constitutes an interference with possessions in relation to those with pending proceedings.[74]

In the *Van der Mussele* case,[75] the Court found that the absence of remuneration for legal services where a pupil lawyer had been required to represent a client without payment did not constitute an interference with possessions because no legal duty to pay remuneration ever arose, and the client's indigence meant that no assessment of fees could take place.[76]

The *Pine Valley Developments* case[77] concerned the impact of the annulment of a planning permission.[78] The Court in determining that there had been no violation of Article 1 of Protocol 1 was influenced by the element of risk inherent in a commercial venture in considering the proportionality of the State action which had resulted in the annulment of an earlier planning permission relating to an area 'zoned for the further development of agriculture so as to preserve a green belt'.[79]

In the *Stretch* case,[80] a local authority had granted an option to renew a lease, which was void since the local authority exceeded its powers in granting such an option. The act in excess of its powers was only discovered late in the day, and the applicant was in the later stages of negotiations with his sub-tenants. The Court regarded him as having a possession which could be protected by Article 1 of Protocol 1, since he had a legitimate expectation of exercising the option to renew which could be regarded as attached to the property rights he held under the lease.

In the *Gasus* case[81] the Court was faced with a situation in which the Dutch tax authorities had seized a concrete mixer from a buyer in order to enforce tax debts. The buyer had not yet paid the full price to the applicant company, which had the benefit of a retention of title clause. The Court considered that it made no difference whether the applicant company's right to the concrete mixer was a right of ownership or a 'security right *in rem*'.

[72] *Rybakh v Russia*, (App. 52854/99), 24 July 2003, (2005) 40 EHRR 615, ECHR 2003-IX.

[73] *Malinovskiy v Russia*, (App. 41302/02), 7 July 2005; and *Shpakovskiy v Russia*, (App. 41307/02), 7 July 2005.

[74] *Draon v France*, (App. 1513/03), 6 October 2005 [GC], (2006) 42 EHRR 807, ECHR 2005-IX; and *Maurice v France*, (App. 11810/03), 6 October 2005 [GC], (2006) 42 EHRR 885.

[75] *Van der Mussele v Belgium*, 23 November 1983, Series A No 70, (1984) 6 EHRR 163.

[76] Contrast the case of *Ambruosi v Italy*, (App. 31227/96), 19 October 2000, (2002) 35 EHRR 125, where a change in the rules on recovery of legal costs deprived a lawyer of fees, costs, and expenses due to him.

[77] *Pine Valley Developments Limited and others v Ireland*, (App. 12742/87), 29 November 1991, Series A No 222, (1992) 14 EHRR 319.

[78] It was an interference case rather than a deprivation case.

[79] *Pine Valley Developments Limited and others v Ireland*, (App. 12742/87), 29 November 1991, Series A No 222, (1992) 14 EHRR 319, § 59. See also *Håkansson and Sturesson v Sweden*, (App. 11855/85), 21 February 1990, Series A No 171, (1991) 13 EHRR 1, § 53.

[80] *Stretch v United Kingdom*, (App. 44277/98), 24 June 2003, (2004) 38 EHRR 196.

[81] *Gasus Dosier- und Fördertechnik GmbH v Netherlands*, 23 February 1995, Series A No 306-B, (1995) 20 EHRR 403.

Whatever view was taken, there was an interference with the peaceful enjoyment of its possessions.

The *Stran Greek Refineries* case[82] involved very large sums of money arising in connection with disputes surrounding the building of an oil refinery. Arbitration proceedings eventually took place, and an award was made. The arbitration award was subsequently declared void. The applicants complained of a violation of, among other Articles, Article 1 of Protocol 1, in that they had been deprived of the benefit of the award made in the arbitration proceedings. The Greek Government argued that there was no 'possession' involved here, since the arbitration award had a precarious legal basis and the award could not be equated with any right which might be recognized by such an award. The Court felt that the test was whether 'the arbitration award had given rise to a debt…that was sufficiently established to be enforceable.'[83] In the particular circumstances of the case, the Court concluded that the arbitration award was a final and binding award and did give rise to an enforceable debt, even though that right was revocable through the process of annulment of the award. There was therefore a possession within the meaning of Article 1 of Protocol 1.[84]

The *Pressos Compania Naviera* case revisited the issue in the context of claims in tort.[85] The dispute centred around claims arising following a collision at sea. Various parties concluded that the collision had arisen as the result of the negligence of the Belgian pilots on board the ships in question. A number of proceedings were brought. Legislation subsequently removed their causes of action retrospectively. The applicants claimed that this constituted an interference with their 'possessions'. The Commission concluded that there was nothing which constituted a possession; an action for damages simply raised the possibility of securing payment. Until there was an enforceable judgment, there was no debt and so no possession within the meaning of Article 1 of Protocol 1.

The Court disagreed, ruling that, having regard to the national law in issue, under the rules of tort, claims to compensation come into existence as soon as the damage occurs, and that a claim constituted an asset which was a possession within the meaning of Article 1 of Protocol 1.[86] The Court does not refer to its decision in *Stran Greek Refineries*, and it is difficult to see a distinction between the two cases which would justify different decisions. The mere expectation that a claim in tort will be determined in accordance with the general law of tort and give rise to an award of damages was sufficient to constitute a possession. A mere expectation is usually not sufficient to constitute a possession.

The Court could have resolved the uncertainty in the *National & Provincial Building Society* case,[87] but did not do so. The case concerned claims that changes to the system for the taxation of interest paid to savers with building societies deprived them of the possibility of securing refunds of taxation paid by them when the regulations were invalidated. Certain regulations were declared invalid, giving rise in the view of the building societies to claims for restitution of tax paid to the Government. These regulations were later retrospectively validated by subsequent legislation, which deprived the building societies of their claims for restitution.

[82] *Stran Greek Refineries and Stratis Andreadis v Greece*, 9 December 1994, Series A No 301-B, (1994) 19 EHRR 293. [83] § 59. [84] §§ 60–2.

[85] *Pressos Compania Naviera SA and others v Belgium*, (App. 17849/91), 20 November 1995, Series A No 332, (1996) 21 EHRR 301. [86] § 31.

[87] *National & Provincial Building Society, the Leeds Permanent Building Society and the Yorkshire Building Society v United Kingdom*, (Apps. 21319/93, 21449/93, and 21675/93), 23 October 1997, (1998) 25 EHRR 127, ECHR 1999-VII.

The issue was whether undetermined claims to restitution of monies paid constituted a possession. The Court, clearly aware of the case-law in the two earlier cases, sidestepped the definitional problem, and expressed 'no concluded view as to whether any of the claims asserted by the applicant societies could properly be considered to constitute possessions'.[88] The Court, however, proceeded 'on the working assumption that…the applicant societies did have possessions in the form of vested rights to restitution'.[89] Ultimately no breach of Article 1 of Protocol 1 was found. But a failure to pay default interest on overpaid tax over a period in excess of five years will constitute a violation of Article 1 of Protocol 1, even where the national law made no provision for payment of interest in such situations.[90]

What seemed to emerge from these authorities was that a legally acknowledged and enforceable debt is an asset (and so constitutes a possession within Article 1 of Protocol 1),[91] and that a legitimate expectation that an award of damages will be forthcoming on the application of the general law of obligations will also fall within the notion. Distinguishing the *Pressos Compania Naviera* case from the *National & Provincial Building Society* case requires the conclusion that in the former the expectation was 'legitimate' whereas in the latter it was not. In the *Gratzinger* case, the Grand Chamber said:

> …there is a difference between a mere hope of restitution, however understandable that hope may be, and a legitimate expectation, which must be of a nature more concrete than a mere hope and be based on a legal provision or a legal act such as a judicial decision….[92]

Indeed, the case-law concerning the restitution of property following the change from a totalitarian to a democratic regime in the countries of central and eastern Europe has led to something of a restatement of the law in this tricky area. The interest in issue in the *Pressos Compania Naviera* case has been explained in later case-law as being a legitimate expectation intimately linked to something which can be described as an asset, and the way in which the asset would be treated in the national legal order. What is required is a claim which is sufficiently established in the national legal order to constitute an asset for the applicant.[93] The Strasbourg Court has summarized the position as follows:

> …in certain circumstances, a 'legitimate expectation' of obtaining an 'asset' may also enjoy the protection of Article 1 of Protocol 1. Thus, where a proprietary interest is in the nature of a claim, the person in whom it is vested may be regarded as having a 'legitimate expectation' if there is a sufficient basis for the interest in national law, for example where there is settled case-law of the domestic courts confirming its existence (*Kopecký v Slovakia* [GC], no. 44912/98, § 52, ECHR 2004-IX). However, no legitimate expectation can be said to arise where there is a dispute as to the correct interpretation and application of domestic law and the applicant's submissions are subsequently rejected by the national courts (*Kopecký v Slovakia*, judgment cited earlier, § 50).[94]

[88] § 70. [89] § 70.

[90] *Eko-Elda AVEE v Greece*, (App. 10162/02), 9 March 2006, ECHR 2006-IV.

[91] See *Almeida Garrett, Mascarenhas Falcão and others v Portugal*, (Apps. 29813/96 and 30229/96), 11 January 2000, (2002) 34 EHRR 642, ECHR 2000-I.

[92] *Gratzinger and Gratzingerova v Czech Republic*, (App. 39794/98), Decision of 10 July 2002 [GC], ECHR 2002-VII, § 73. See also *Von Maltzan and others v Germany*, (Apps. 71916/01, 71917/01, and 10260/02), Decision of 2 March 2005 [GC], ECHR 2005-V.

[93] *Kopecký v Slovakia*, (App. 44912/98), 28 September 2004 [GC], (2005) 41 EHRR 944, ECHR 2004-IX, §§ 45–52. See also *Vilho Eskelinen and others v Finland*, (App. 63235/00), 19 April 2007 [GC], (2007) 45 EHRR 985, ECHR 2007-IV.

[94] *Anheuser-Busch Inc. v Portugal*, (App. 73049/01), 11 January 2007 [GC], (2007) 45 EHRR 830, ECHR 2007-I, § 65. This was reaffirmed in *Centro Europa 7 S.r.l. and Di Stefano v Italy*, (App. 38433/09), 7 June 2012, § 173.

In *Ramaer and Van Willigen v The Netherlands*,[95] the Court found the applicants' claims that they were entitled to the renewal of insurance contracts on terms that were at least as favourable as before were inadmissible. The Court differentiated the case from the *Pressos Compania Naviera* case[96] as the applicants in this case did not argue that existing claims were distinguished or reduced but focused on insurance claims that might accrue in the future.[97] The Court using the *Kopecký*[98]and *Gratzinger*[99] judgments stated that:

> The applicants' expectations were not based on a legal provision or a legal act such as a judicial decision. Rather, they were based on the hope to see their insurance contracts continued, or renewed, on terms no less favourable for them than those which they enjoyed previously. The Court has already drawn attention to the difference between a hope of securing an asset, however understandable that hope may be, and a legitimate expectation, which must be of a nature more concrete than a mere hope and be based on a legal provision or a legal act such as a judicial decision.[100]

DEPRIVATION OF PROPERTY

WHAT CONSTITUTES DEPRIVATION?

The essence of deprivation of property is the extinction of the legal rights of the owner.[101] This can arise in a number of circumstances. Where a claim is made that there has been a deprivation of property in the absence of a formal transfer of ownership, the Court will examine the realities of the situation in order to determine whether there has been a de facto expropriation.[102] An interference which does not constitute a formal or de facto expropriation may nevertheless constitute a means of control of the property which falls within Article 1 of Protocol 1. An obvious illustration is where a Contracting Party subjects property to a continuing tenancy at terms set by the State.[103]

In the *Sporrong and Lönnroth* case,[104] the presence of expropriation permits had the effect of imposing a long-term planning blight on the property in question and of reducing the selling price below normal market prices, but the Court concluded that the adverse impact on the property rights was not such as to make them disappear. There

[95] *Ramaer and Van Willigen v The Netherlands*, (App. 34880/12), Decision of 23 October 2012.

[96] *Pressos Compania Naviera SA and others v Belgium*, (App. 17849/91), 20 November 1995, Series A No 332, (1996) 21 EHRR 301.

[97] The Court also differentiated the case from *Gaygusuz v Austria*, (App. 17371/90), 16 September 1996, (1997) 23 EHRR 364, ECHR 1996-IV as in *Gaygusuz* the benefit the applicant was claiming was recognized in principle by the law but denied due to discriminatory practice.

[98] *Kopecký v Slovakia*, (App. 44912/98), 28 September 2004 [GC], (2005) 41 EHRR 944, ECHR 2004-IX.

[99] *Gratzinger and Gratzingerova v Czech Republic*, (App. 39794/98), Decision of 10 July 2002 [GC], ECHR 2002-VII.

[100] *Ramaer and Van Willigen v The Netherlands*, (App. 34880/12), Decision of 23 October 2012, § 81; see also *Veselinski v 'the former Yugoslav Republic of Macedonia'*, (App. 45658/99), and *Djidrovski v 'the former Yugoslav Republic of Macedonia'*, (App. 46447/99), 24 February 2009.

[101] See M. Pellonpää, 'Reflections on the notion of "deprivation of possessions" in Article 1 of the First Protocol of the European Convention on Human Rights', in P. Mahoney and others, *Protecting Human Rights: The European Perspective. Studies in Memory of Rolv Ryssdal* (Carl Heymanns, Köln 2000), 1087.

[102] *Sporrong and Lönnroth v Sweden*, (Apps. 7151–2/75), 23 September 1982, Series A No 52, (1983) 5 EHRR 35, § 63.

[103] As in *Ghigo v Malta*, (App. 31122/05), 26 September 2006.

[104] *Sporrong and Lönnroth v Sweden*, (Apps. 7151–2/75), 23 September 1982, Series A No 52, (1983) 5 EHRR 35.

was accordingly no deprivation of property in this case. The *Holy Monasteries* case has complex facts relating to the ownership of monasteries in Greece.[105] Many monasteries in Greece date their foundations to periods between the ninth and thirteenth centuries, and over the centuries they have accumulated considerable landholdings. In May 1987 a Greek law provided that the State would become the owner of the monasteries' property unless the monasteries proved their title to it in one of a number of specified ways. In some cases, the requirements would have been difficult for the monasteries to meet. In effect, there was a presumption that the property belonged to the State unless this was rebutted by the monasteries. One essential issue before the Court was whether this was a procedural device, as the respondent State argued, relating to the burden of proof of title to property, or whether it was, as the monasteries argued, a substantive provision whose effect is to transfer full ownership of the land in question to the Greek State.[106] The Court concluded that there had been a deprivation.[107]

In a series of cases against Italy,[108] taking possession of land with a view to its appropriation and starting building works on it without formal expropriation measures being taken constituted a deprivation of property which was incompatible with the applicants' Convention rights.

In the *Pressos Compania Naviera* case,[109] retrospective legislation which operated to deny the claimants an opportunity to sue in respect of claimed negligence by pilots which had led to collisions at sea was treated as a deprivation of property.

DESTRUCTION

Destruction of property plainly constitutes a deprivation of property.[110] A whole series of cases against Turkey related to the destruction of property in the course of clashes between the security forces and PKK sympathizers. A friendly settlement was reached on 22 March 2001 in 201 applications.[111]

The *Ayubov* case[112] concerned the alleged destruction of the applicant's house, its contents, and two cars which had been set on fire by armed men in camouflage uniforms who had arrived in military trucks. The Court concluded that they were agents of the State. The destruction of the applicant's property was a clear violation of Article 1 of Protocol 1.

EXPROPRIATIONS

As already noted, no formal expropriation is required for a deprivation of property to arise. But the distinction between deprivation and interference will be subtle. For a de facto deprivation through expropriation to arise, there must effectively be an extinction of

[105] *Holy Monasteries v Greece*, (Apps. 13092/87 and 13984/88), 9 December 1994, Series A No 301-A, (1995) 20 EHRR 1. [106] § 61. [107] § 66.

[108] *Carletta v Italy*, (App. 63861/00); *Colacrai v Italy*, (App. 63868/00); *Donati v Italy*, (App. 63242/00); and *La Rosa and Alba v Italy (No. 6) and (No. 8)*, (Apps. 63240/00 and 63285/00), 15 July 2005.

[109] *Pressos Compania Naviera SA and others v Belgium*, (App. 17849/91), 20 November 1995, Series A No 332, (1996) 21 EHRR 301; and see discussion of this case earlier in this chapter.

[110] See also *Handyside v United Kingdom*, (App. 5493/72), 7 December 1976, Series A No 24, (1979–80) 1 EHRR 737, §§ 62–3 (destruction of a book); *Akdivar v Turkey*, (App. 21893/93), 16 September 1996, (1997) 23 EHRR 143, ECHR 1996-IV, § 88 (destruction of a home); and *Isayeva, Yusupova and Bazayeva v Russia*, (Apps. 57947/00, 57948/00, and 57949/00), 24 February 2005, (2005) 41 EHRR 847, §§ 230–4 (destruction of cars and personal possessions in an air strike on a civilian convoy Grozny).

[111] Court of Human Rights, Information Note No. 28, March 2001, at 33.

[112] *Ayubov v Russia*, (App. 7654/02), 12 February 2009.

property rights. That did not arise in the *Sporrong and Lönnroth* case discussed earlier.[113] A similar conclusion was reached where rent control legislation limited the rental income of the owners of the property in question.[114]

The *Papamichalopoulos* case[115] is a good example of a de facto deprivation. The Greek Government had transferred land to the Greek Navy. Court proceedings had resulted in decisions that the land was not for disposal, but the Navy nevertheless established a naval base and holiday resort for officers on the land. The whole area was designated as a 'naval fortress'. The Court considered that the applicants remained the lawful owners of the land, but that there had been a de facto expropriation. Despite attempts to make amends after the restoration of democracy in Greece, no substitute land had been allocated to the applicants and this continued the violation of the right to peaceful enjoyment of their land.

Similarly in the *Hentrich* case,[116] a French law which permitted the revenue authorities to buy property which had been sold at below market value in order to discourage the practice was a de facto expropriation.

TEMPORARY OR PROVISIONAL DEPRIVATION

The *Handyside* case[117] establishes that temporary seizures do not constitute deprivations of property, though they may well constitute controls on the use of the property seized. In this case the material seized was a book which was considered to be obscene. Other examples of temporary seizures are provisional property confiscations in criminal proceedings;[118] provisional transfers of land as part of agricultural land consolidation proceedings;[119] and the seizure of an aircraft in which a consignment of cannabis had been found with a view to its forfeiture.[120]

CONDITIONS FOR PERMITTED DEPRIVATIONS

A deprivation falling within the first paragraph of Article 1 of Protocol 1 must meet three conditions to be justifiable under the provision:

- the measure providing for the deprivation must be in accordance with the conditions provided for by national law;

[113] *Sporrong and Lönnroth v Sweden*, (Apps. 7151–2/75), 23 September 1982, Series A No 52, (1983) 5 EHRR 35.

[114] *Mellacher v Austria*, (Apps. 10522/83, 11011/84, and 11070/84), 19 December 1989, Series A No 169, (1990) 12 EHRR 391, § 44; *Nobel v Netherlands*, (App. 27126/11), Decision of 2 July 2013.

[115] *Papamichalopoulos and others v Greece*, (App. 14556/89), 24 June 1993, Series A No 260-B, (1993) 16 EHRR 440. See also *Sarica and Dilaver v Turkey* (App. 11765/05) 27 May 2010, where the Court found that the land belonging to the applicant had been incorporated into a military zone was a de facto appropriation. The applicants were forced to take legal proceedings to get compensation. The law was unforeseeable and measures were arbitrary.

[116] *Hentrich v France*, (App. 13616/88), 22 September 1994, Series A No 296-A, (1994) 18 EHRR 440.

[117] *Handyside v United Kingdom*, (App. 5493/72), 7 December 1976, Series A No 24, (1979–80) 1 EHRR 737, § 62.

[118] *Raimondo v Italy*, (App. 12954/87), 22 February 1994, Series A No 281-A, (1994) 18 EHRR 237, §§ 29–30. See also *Jucys v Lithuania*, (App. 5457/03), 8 January 2008.

[119] *Erkner and Hofauer v Austria*, (App. 9616/81), 23 April 1987, Series A No 117, (1987) 9 EHRR 464, § 74; and *Wiesinger v Austria*, (App. 11796/85), 24 September 1991, Series A No 213, (1993) 18 EHRR 258, § 72.

[120] *Air Canada v United Kingdom*, (App. 18465/91), 5 May 1995, Series A No 316, (1995) 20 EHRR 150, §§ 28–33. See also *Islamic Republic of Iran Shipping Lines v Turkey*, (App. 40998/98), 13 December 2007, (2008) 47 EHRR 573, ECHR 2007-nyr.

- the general principles of international law must be respected;
- the deprivation must be in the public interest, and this will require a balancing of the public interest against individual rights.

The requirement that the measure must be in accordance with the conditions provided for by national law raises issues similar to those raised in relation to Articles 8 to 11.[121] This does not merely involve the identification of a national law authorizing the taking, but also involves some consideration of the quality of that law, so that there is protection against arbitrary action.[122] The law must accordingly be sufficiently precise and foreseeable in its consequences, and the deprivation must be surrounded by appropriate procedural guarantees. So in the *Hentrich* case,[123] which concerned the State's power to buy property sold at an undervalue, the absence of adversarial proceedings to challenge the State's right of pre-emption constituted a violation of Article 1 of Protocol 1.[124]

Of course, any taking which is in breach of national law will amount to a violation of Article 1 of Protocol 1.[125] However, it may be the way in which national law is applied that places an 'individual and excessive burden' on a person. This can be illustrated by the *Allard* case.[126] Certain property in Sweden was jointly owned by members of a family. Without the permission of the co-owners, a house was built on the land. When the dispute came before a national court, it resulted in a judicial decision that the house was to be removed. It was subsequently demolished. The applicant claimed that this constituted a deprivation of her property in breach of Article 1 of Protocol 1. The Strasbourg Court reiterated that a deprivation of property could be in the public interest even if the community at large gained no direct benefit from the deprivation. Maintaining a functioning system of co-ownership was considered to further the public interest.[127] But the manner of application of the law in this case went beyond what was necessary to secure that interest.

Deprivations of property must also evince respect for the general principles of international law, which require that non-nationals are protected against arbitrary expropriations and, in the case of lawful expropriations, are entitled to compensation for the loss of their property. The rule provides no protection for nationals of a State deprived of property by that State.[128] Once the Court had adopted this position, this requirement has proved to have little application in cases involving Article 1 of Protocol 1.

The public interest test will be at the heart of many cases arising under Article 1 of Protocol 1 as it is under many other claims of violations of Convention rights. In property cases, there is almost a presumption that a national measure is in the public interest. In the *James* case,[129] which concerned United Kingdom leasehold enfranchisement legislation, the Court said:

> The Court, finding it natural that the margin of appreciation available to the legislature in implementing social and economic policies should be a wide one, will respect the

[121] See in general ch.14.

[122] *James v United Kingdom*, (App. 8793/85), 21 February 1986, Series A No 98, (1986) 8 EHRR 123, § 67.

[123] *Hentrich v France*, (App. 13616/88), 22 September 1994, Series A No 296-A, (1994) 18 EHRR 440.

[124] § 42.

[125] As in *Iatridis v Greece*, (App. 31107/96), 25 March 1999 [GC], (2000) 30 EHRR 97, ECHR 1999-II; and *Minasyan and Semerjyan v Armenia*, (App. 27651/05), 23 June 2009.

[126] *Allard v Sweden*, (App. 35179/97), 24 June 2003, (2004) 39 EHRR 321, ECHR 2003-VII.

[127] § 52.

[128] Affirmed in *James v United Kingdom*, (App. 8793/85), 21 February 1986, Series A No 98, (1986) 8 EHRR 123, §§ 61–3; and in *Lithgow v United Kingdom*, (Apps. 9006/80, 9262/81, 9263/81, 9265/81, 9266/81, 9313/81, and 9405/81), 8 July 1986, Series A No 102, (1986) 8 EHRR 329, §§ 111–19.

[129] *James v United Kingdom*, (App. 8793/85), 21 February 1986, Series A No 98, (1986) 8 EHRR 123, § 46.

> legislature's judgment as to what is 'in the public interest' unless that judgment be manifestly without reasonable foundation. In other words, although the Court cannot substitute its own assessment for that of the national authorities, it is bound to review the contested measures under Article 1 of Protocol 1 and, in doing so, to make an enquiry into the facts with reference to which the national authorities acted.

In this case, the Court concluded that the United Kingdom system of leasehold enfranchisement under the Leasehold Reform Act 1967 was compatible with Article 1 of Protocol 1. Indeed, it is difficult to find a case in which the Court has not recognized the policy preferences of a State as providing a legitimate goal. But the Court has gone further than merely requiring the identification of a legitimate goal in determining whether a deprivation of property is in the public interest. The test of proportionality is also brought into play. A fair balance must be struck between the demands of the general interest of the community, and the individual's property rights. The latter cannot be expected to bear an individual and excessive burden in the particular circumstances of each case.[130]

The offering of compensation has come to play a crucial part in the consideration of proportionality, and is discussed later.

THE ISSUE OF COMPENSATION

Where there has been a deprivation of property, there is an expectation that compensation will be paid if the taking is to constitute a fair balance between the individual interest and the general interest,[131] and not to impose an excessive burden on the individual. A total lack of compensation will be justifiable only in exceptional circumstances.[132] In the *Holy Monasteries* case,[133] the Court restated the position established in its case-law:

> Compensation terms under the relevant legislation are material to the assessment whether the contested measure respects the requisite fair balance and, notably, whether it does not impose a disproportionate burden on the applicants. In this connection, the taking of property without payment of an amount reasonably related to its value will normally constitute a disproportionate interference and a total lack of compensation can be considered justifiable under Article 1 only in exceptional circumstances. Article 1 does not, however, guarantee a right to full compensation in all circumstances, since legitimate objectives of 'public interest' may call for less than reimbursement of the full market value.[134]

The existence of safeguards by which the reasonableness of the compensation can be checked can be important in showing that the burden on the individual is not excessive. The Strasbourg Court has indicated that legitimate objectives in the public interest may result in less than full compensation; and the protection of the historical and cultural heritage has been accepted as one such objective. But the scheme for determining compensation must be even-handed between the State and the individual. A violation was found in a case where depreciation in value arising from the listing property as having historical and cultural value could be taken into account but not an increase in its value arising from such classification.[135]

[130] § 50. See also *Gladysheva v Russia*, (App. 7097/10), 6 December 2011, §§ 76–7.

[131] See, for example, *NA v Turkey*, (App. 37451/97), 11 October 2005, (2007) 45 EHRR 287, ECHR 2005-X.

[132] As in *Jahn and others v Germany*, (Apps. 46720/99, 72203/01, and 72552/01), 30 June 2005 [GC], (2006) 42 EHRR 1084, ECHR 2005-VI; see later in this chapter. See also F. McCarthy, 'Deprivation without Compensation: the Exceptional Circumstance of *Jahn v Germany* [2007] EHRLR 295.

[133] *Holy Monasteries v Greece*, (Apps. 13092/87 and 13984/88), 9 December 1994, Series A No 301-A, (1995) 20 EHRR 1.

[134] § 71. See also *Pyrantiene v Lithuania*, (App. 45092/07), 12 November 2013.

[135] *Kozacioğlu v Turkey*, (App. 2334/03), 19 February 2009 [GC], ECHR 2009-nyr.

In a group of cases against Greece[136] an irrefutable presumption of benefit as a result of the compulsory purchase of property needed to build a new road which reduced the compensation payable was considered to place a disproportionate burden on the property owners. They were unable to argue that the work was of less, or even no, benefit to them.[137] Consideration of individual circumstances will not, however, always be a required feature of the calculation of compensation. In the *Lithgow* case,[138] the Court accepted that major nationalization programmes may require a standardized rather than an individual approach to the calculation of compensation, and, subject to the securing of a fair balance, a wide margin of appreciation will be allowed in the method for determining the calculation of the compensation payable. However, individual expropriations will require the Contracting Party to establish all the relevant factors for compensation, and must take into account the impact of the expropriation on the value of any remaining land.[139]

These principles apply just as much to situations where there is a transition from a planned economy to a market-oriented economy following the fall of communist regimes. So, in a case against Slovakia,[140] the compulsory leasing of allotments owned by an association of landowners at a very low rent, and their subsequent transfer to the tenants with compensation paid well below the market value of the land constituted a violation of Article 1 of Protocol 1. In relation to the calculation of compensation, the Strasbourg Court observed that there was a 'sliding scale' which balanced the scope and degree of importance of the public interest against the nature and amount of compensation provided to the owners.[141]

Long delays in the payment of compensation, particularly where there is high inflation or an inadequate payment of interest on the late payment, will also impose an excessive burden on the individual. In a line of cases against Turkey, violations were found where the land valuation was at a price obtaining at the date of the taking and where inflation was running at 70 per cent, but this had not been taken into account in the payments eventually made.[142]

RESTITUTION CASES

A line of case-law[143] has developed dealing with issues flowing from the reunification of Germany, and with restitution claims in the countries of central and eastern Europe. This justifies separate treatment of this class of case, which present challenges to the Court

[136] *Katikaridis and others v Greece*, (App. 19385/92), 15 November 1996, (2001) 32 EHRR 113, ECHR 1996-V; *Tsomtsos and others v Greece*, (App. 20680/92), 15 November 1996, ECHR 1996-V; and *Papachelas v Greece*, (App. 31423/96), 25 March 1999, (2000) 30 EHRR 923, ECHR 1999-II.

[137] *Papachelas v Greece*, (App. 31423/96), 25 March 1999 [GC], (2000) 30 EHRR 923, ECHR 1999-II, § 54.

[138] *Lithgow and others v United Kingdom*, (Apps. 9006/80, 9262/81, 9263/81, 9265/81, 9266/81, 9313/81, and 9405/81), 8 July 1986, Series A No 102, (1986) 8 EHRR 329, §§ 121–2.

[139] *Bistrovic v Croatia*, (App. 25774/05), 31 May 2007. The overall principles are recapitulated in *Scordino v Italy (No. 1)*, (App. 36813/97), 29 March 2006 [GC], (2007) 45 EHRR 207, ECHR 2006-V, §§ 93–8.

[140] *Urbárska Obec Trenčianske Biskupice v Slovakia*, (App. 74258/01), 27 November 2007, (2009) 48 EHRR 1139, ECHR 2007-XIII.

[141] § 126.

[142] *Akkuş v Turkey*, (App. 19263/92), 9 July 1997, (2000) 30 EHRR 365; literally dozens of other cases have been taken on this ground against a number of countries.

[143] The issues raised in restitution cases are not wholly new, since the Court has already had to consider some of the consequences of the Turkish intervention in Cyprus in terms of restitution of property: see *Loizidou v Turkey*, (App. 15318/89), 18 December 1996, (1996) 23 EHRR 513, ECHR 1996-VI; for a discussion see R. White, 'Tackling political disputes through individual applications' [1998] EHRLR 61. See also *Xenides-Arestis v Turkey*, (App. 46347/99), 22 December 2005.

by reason not only of the volume of cases, but also of the complex legal issues which are raised.

Certain principles emerge from the Court's case-law in cases of this kind. First, the Court will only be competent to examine applications to the extent that they relate to events occurring after the entry into force of the Convention for the respondent Contracting Party. Expropriations or confiscations which occurred before this date are outside the competence of the Court. Nor does a completed taking before the entry into force of the Convention for the respondent State give rise to any continuing situation of deprivation of a property right.[144] Secondly, where there is a procedure in national law for seeking recovery, those proceedings will be taken into account in determining whether there has been an interference with the applicant's property rights. But applicants must show that they have a property right which is being pursued in the national proceedings.[145] The mere hope of recognition of a former property right is not enough.[146] Furthermore, where the procedure for recovery of property is conditional, failure to fulfil that condition will extinguish any claimed property right. So in the *Malhous* case,[147] it was fatal to the applicant's claim that restitution proceedings in the Czech Republic were not available where the property had been transferred to other individuals who could establish that they had acquired a legal title to the property. That was precisely the situation in relation to the property he was seeking to recover. Furthermore the Court will be reluctant to go behind conclusions of the national courts that a condition has not been met.[148] The Strasbourg Court will not find violations where there have been irregularities or abuse of national regulations for which the applicants were responsible.[149]

The *Wittek* case[150] concerned an attempt by the applicants to recover title to their house in Leipzig, which they had given up as a condition of being permitted to leave the former German Democratic Republic. Their attempts to recover the property under national law failed, since it was well established that an agreement for sale could not be challenged in the civil courts if the dispute was over the restitution of property in the German Democratic Republic.[151] There had been, in the opinion of the Strasbourg Court, a thorough review of all the circumstances of the case by the national courts, and it could not be said that the applicants had suffered a disproportionate burden. There was no violation of Article 1 of Protocol 1.

The *Zvolský and Zvolská* case[152] concerned claims made by applicants who had been required to transfer property to a former owner. The applicants had, in 1967, acquired a farmhouse on a sale for value and adjoining agricultural land which the vendor had transferred to them without consideration.[153] At the time, release from an obligation to work

[144] *Malhous v Czech Republic*, (App. 33071/96), Decision of 13 December 2000 [GC], ECHR 2000-XII; and *Prince Hans-Adam II of Liechtenstein v Germany*, (App. 42527/98), 12 July 2001 [GC], ECHR 2001-VI. See also *von Maltzan, von Zitzweitz, Man Ferrostaal and Töpfer Stiftung v Germany*, (Apps. 71916/01, 71917/01, and 10260/02), Decision of 2 March 2005 [GC], ECHR 2005-V.

[145] *Malhous v Czech Republic*, (App. 33071/96), Decision of 13 December 2000 [GC], ECHR 2000-XII.

[146] *Gratzinger and Gratzingerova v Czech Republic*, (App. 39794/98), Decision of 10 July 2002 [GC], ECHR 2002-VII, § 73.

[147] *Malhous v Czech Republic*, (App. 33071/96), Decision of 13 December 2000 [GC], ECHR 2000-XII.

[148] *Jantner v Slovakia*, (App. 39050/97), 4 March 2003, where the issue was whether the applicant had, in fact, established a genuine permanent residence in Slovakia which was a condition of being able to obtain restitution.

[149] See *Velikovi and others v Bulgaria*, (Apps. 43278/98, 45437/99, 48014/99, 48380/99, 51362/99, 53367/99, 60036/00, 73465/01, and 194/02), 15 March 2007, (2009) 48 EHRR 640.

[150] *Wittek v Germany*, (App. 37290/97), 12 December 2002, (2005) 41 EHRR 1060, ECHR 2002-X.

[151] § 48.

[152] *Zvolský and Zvolská v Czech Republic*, (App. 46129/99), 12 November 2002, ECHR 2002-IX.

[153] Though it was argued that the applicants had paid a sum on top of the sale price of the farmhouse as compensation for his loss of the agricultural land.

for the socialist cooperative could only be achieved by transferring the land being worked; this was said to have been the vendor's motivation for the transfer. The applicants as the new owners were obliged as a condition of the purchase to give an undertaking to work for the cooperative as a replacement for the vendor. In 1991 the vendor signed a declaration that he had transferred the property of his own free will, but in 1993 nevertheless sought to recover the agricultural land, and obtained an order for its return to him. The applicants claimed that the Czech Republic had interfered with their property rights in breach of Article 1 of Protocol 1. The Court concluded that there was a basis in law for the restitution order and that it was in the public interest in that its purpose was to redress infringements of property rights which had occurred under the communist regime. The key question was whether a fair balance had been struck between the individual and community interest. As has already been noted, the absence of any compensation for a taking will require special justification. The Czech legislation had elected to deal with this issue without any ability to re-examine the circumstances surrounding individual transfers which had taken place. Cases such as this required some possibility for considering the competing claims of the former owner and the current owner in order to determine whether the transfer had genuinely infringed the former owner's property rights such that they should be given priority over the property rights of the current owner. There was a violation of the applicants' Convention rights.

The *Broniowski* case[154] concerned the long-term consequences of the re-drawing of the eastern border of Poland after the Second World War, which had resulted in the movement of large numbers of Polish citizens. Those who lost land were entitled to buy land from the State and to have the value of the abandoned land taken into account in the purchase price. However, the pool of land available to satisfy these claims was restricted by the exclusion of State agricultural and military property. This exclusion was subsequently held to be unconstitutional. Poland then sought to close off all such claims by deeming those who had received some compensation to be fully compensated, and to award 15 per cent of their entitlement to those who had received no compensation. The applicant was in this group and received only 2 per cent of the value of the property abandoned by his grandmother. No issue over the temporal application of the Convention arose, since the applicant clearly had an entitlement to compensation which was continuing, and which had been foreclosed by the Polish legislation in 2004. The Court decided this case as an interference with the applicant's peaceful enjoyment of possessions rather than as a deprivation of property. The Court accepted that a wide margin of appreciation was available to the State in circumstances such as this. In enunciating the general principles applicable in this case, the Grand Chamber said:

> ...the notion of 'public interest' is necessarily extensive. In particular, the decision to enact laws expropriating property or affording publicly funded compensation for expropriated property will commonly involve considerations of political, economic and social issues. The Court has declared that, finding it natural that the margin of appreciation available to the legislature in implementing social and economic policies should be a wide one, it will respect the legislature's judgments as to what is 'in the public interest' unless that judgment is manifestly without reasonable foundation. This logic applies to such fundamental changes of a country's system as the transition from a totalitarian regime to a democratic form of government and the reform of the State's political, legal and economic structure,

[154] *Broniowski v Poland*, (App. 31443/96), 22 June 2004, (2005) 40 EHRR 495, ECHR 2004-V; 28 September 2005 [GC] (friendly settlement), ECHR 2005-IX.

phenomena which inevitably involve the enactment of large-scale economic and social legislation.[155]

The Court accepted that, in complex political and economic circumstances such as those prevailing in Poland, entitlement to compensation may be severely restricted, but also indicated that the more stringent the restrictions the more compelling must be the reasons for the adoption of a particular scheme. In this case, the applicant's right to compensation had been rendered illusory, and then extinguished, by State conduct which could not be justified.

The Court went on to note that it had a further 167 applications relating to the same set of circumstances, and it was known that the scheme in issue affected nearly 80,000 people. The volume of potential cases was said to represent a 'threat to the future effectiveness of the Convention machinery'.[156] There was a systemic failure of the national legal order, which must be remedied as a consequence of the Court's judgment in this case.[157]

The *Hutten-Czapska* case[158] also concerned a situation which potentially affected very many people: around 100,000 landlords and between 600,000 and 900,000 tenants, and resulted in a pilot judgment. It concerned the imposition of tenancy agreements at very low levels of rent on property owners, which had occurred after the Second World War and had been maintained thereafter in one form or another. The applicant complained that the imposition of the tenancy agreements and the system of rent control deprived her of the opportunity to derive an income from the property, to cover the costs of the landlord's obligations, or to regain possession of her property (though she could sell it subject to any tenancy). The Strasbourg Court examined the claim as one involving the imposition of controls on the use of the property.[159] The Court considered that the measures had a proper legal base, and had a legitimate aim in the general interest. The Court then examined in considerable detail the issue of whether a fair balance had been struck. In concluding that there was a violation of the applicant's Convention rights, the Court was clearly influenced by a decision of the Polish Constitutional Court some five years earlier which had concluded that the rent control scheme had resulted in a disproportionate, unjustified, and arbitrary distribution of the social burden involved in housing reform, which had been effected mainly at the expense of landlords.

The *Jahn* case[160] concerned land in the former German Democratic Republic. In September 1945, owners of more than 100 hectares of land in the Soviet Occupied Zone of Germany had their property expropriated. This land was then distributed in plots averaging eight hectares to farmers who had little or no land of their own. Certain portions of the land had to be used for food production. The applicants were the heirs of such farmers. Following the fall of the Berlin Wall in November 1989, the negotiations on the reunification of Germany included the enactment of a law which permitted those to whom land had been distributed to acquire full title to it and to be able to dispose of it. This law became part of the law of the Federal Republic. The applicants' claims arose out of amendments to this law which required them to assign the property they had inherited to the German tax authorities without compensation, since they had not carried on an activity in the agricultural, forestry, or food-industry sector. This was a deprivation of property case.

155 § 149. 156 § 193.

157 The just satisfaction phase of the case was concluded with a judgment of 28 September 2005, ECHR 2005-IX.

158 *Hutten-Czapska v Poland*, (App. 35014/97), 19 June 2006 [GC], (2007) 45 EHRR 52, ECHR 2006-VIII; see also 28 April 2008 (friendly settlement), ECHR 2008-nyr.

159 See later in this chapter.

160 *Jahn and others v Germany*, (Apps. 46720/99, 72203/01, and 72552/01), 30 June 2005 [GC], (2006) 42 EHRR 1084, ECHR 2005-VI.

The Grand Chamber readily concluded that there was a legal basis for the deprivation, and that the law served the legitimate aim of correcting what the German Government viewed as unfair effects of the law that was amended. There was, accordingly, a need to consider whether a fair balance had been struck between the individual interest and the community interest. The Grand Chamber of the Court, differing from the decision of the Chamber, concluded that this was a case in which the absence of compensation was justifiable, since the application of the law which had been amended was to give the applicants a windfall gain rather than to deprive them of property they held.

In *Vistiņš and Perepjolkins v Latvia*,[161] the Court had to examine a complex appropriation of land by the State, which had previously been returned to owners under restitution laws, who had then donated the land to the applicants for services rendered. The land surrounded the Port of Riga. The State paid compensation but only at the price of the land in 1940. The Chamber treated the case as similar to *Jahn* and found no violation. However, the Grand Chamber disagreed and distinguished the case from *Jahn*. It stated that *Jahn* was an exceptional case and differed from the present case as first, the enactment of the legislation was different. *Jahn* was dealing with law passed by a communist regime, whilst this case considered a law passed by the democratic government. Secondly, the period of upheaval after the end of the communist regime was mainly passed in the present case, compared to the situation in *Jahn*. Finally, in *Jahn* a fair balance had been established given the specific situation and the need for social justice. The Grand Chamber questioned whether social justice was at issue here as the main beneficiary of the measures was the State.[162] On the facts, the lack of compensation meant there was no fair balance and therefore a violation. In contrast, the dissent agreed with the Chamber and argued that the majority should have recognized that the general framework applied in *Jahn* should be applicable to all transition States from the Soviet era:

> it cannot be denied that there are many differences between the factual situation in *Jahn* and that in the present case. However, *Jahn* remains applicable as a general framework which may and should be used when expropriations are closely connected to the process of transition.[163]

The *Kopecký* case[164] concerned an attempt to recover gold and silver coins. The applicant's father had been convicted in 1959 for keeping gold and silver coins, and the coins had been confiscated. In 1992 the conviction and all consequential decisions had been quashed by the Supreme Court under the Judicial Rehabilitation Act 1990. The applicant then claimed restitution of the coins under a 1991 statute, which provided for restitution of the specific property taken, not any substitute property. This statute contained a condition that the person seeking restitution must show where the coins were deposited as at 1 April 1991, the date on which the 1991 Act entered into force. Though the applicant had been successful at first instance, ultimately his claim failed because he could not meet the burden of proof in showing the location of the property sought as at 1 April 1991, though he had been able to show that the coins had been deposited with the Regional Administration of the Ministry of the Interior on 12 December 1958. The Grand Chamber concluded that this was a case which turned on whether the applicant had an 'asset', that is, a proprietary interest which has a sufficient basis in national law. The Court specifically

[161] *Vistiņš and Perepjolkins v Latvia*, (App. 71243/01), 25 October 2012.

[162] §§ 124–7.

[163] Joint Partly Dissenting Opinion of Judges Bratza, Garlicki, Lorenzen, Tsotsoria, and Pardalos, § 6; see also *Althoff and others v Germany*, (App. 5631/05), 8 December 2011, § 74, which the dissent argue is an example of the general application of *Jahn* to post reunification property rights in Germany.

[164] *Kopecký v Slovakia*, (App. 44912/98), 28 September 2004 [GC], (2005) 41 EHRR 944, ECHR 2004-IX.

disagreed with the Chamber that such an interest could arise where there was a 'genuine dispute' or an 'arguable case'. The Grand Chamber concluded that the applicant had no interest which constituted a 'possession' within the meaning of Article 1 of Protocol 1. Four dissenting judges took a different view. Three of them considered that the test applied by the Chamber was a proper one. Furthermore, the annulment of the confiscation order itself gave rise to a legitimate expectation that the applicant would be able to recover the confiscated property. Judge Strážnická considered that it was contrary to the purpose of restitution laws, on the one hand, to declare the existence of a remedy in respect of past infringements of the law, and, on the other hand, to eliminate the legitimate interest of entitled persons by burdening them with requirements that were impossible to fulfil. Other cases which had failed because a necessary condition had not been fulfilled could be distinguished from the present case; they had involved situations in which immovable property was in issue, the applicants did not meet the criteria for being treated as entitled persons, and the conditions (such as citizenship and residence) were ones with which they had a fair chance to comply.

The *Străin* case[165] was a rather more straightforward case. The applicants had been the owners of a house which was nationalized in 1950. In 1993 they brought an action seeking a declaration that the taking of the property was unlawful and an order for its restitution. Although it knew of the action for the recovery of the property (which had been converted into four apartments), the State-owned company which managed the property sold one of the apartments. The applicants sought, unsuccessfully, to have the sale declared void. They claimed that the sale in these circumstances constituted a taking of their property without compensation. The Court found a number of deficiencies: the Romanian law which had been applied did not meet the requirements established by the Court for it to constitute a proper legal base for the sale to a third party, and the Romanian Government had not put forward any legitimate aim for the measure;[166] nor had it adduced any exceptional circumstances justifying the absence of any compensation.

The *Pyrantiene* case[167] challenged restitution laws on a different basis. In this case, the applicant had bought a plot of land from the State in 1995 after the fall of the Communist regime. However, at the time of the sale, a claim for restitution by former owners was attached to the land and the sale was unlawful. It was declared void and she was awarded compensation for the price paid rather than the market value. The Court reiterated that the remedying of old injuries should not lead to disproportionate new wrongs.[168] The Court noted the need for good governance in such cases, which was not the case here. The State sold the land to the applicant without appropriate examinations being carried out. The Court noted the applicant had acted in good faith and could not have known about the claim on the land. As the compensation did not rectify the mistakes made by the State, there was a violation of Article 1 of Protocol 1.

An excessive delay in paying compensation awarded for the nationalization of property will also engage Article 1 of Protocol 1 since it constitutes an interference with the right to peaceful enjoyment of possession. Lack of funds was not a justification for the delay in meeting awards of compensation.[169]

[165] *Străin and others v Romania*, (App. 57001/00), 21 July 2005, ECHR 2005-VII. See also *Zwierzynski v Poland*, (App. 34049/96), 19 June 2001, (2004) 38 EHRR 122, ECHR 2001-VI.

[166] Though the Court seems to have been prepared to accept that it could have been for the protection of the rights of others, namely a purchaser in good faith.

[167] *Pyrantiene v Lithuania*, (App. 45092/07), 12 November 2013.

[168] § 50.

[169] *Scutari v Moldova*, (App. 20864/03), 26 July 2005.

CONTROLLING THE USE OF PROPERTY

SCOPE

The second paragraph of Article 1 of Protocol 1 preserves the power of the State to control the use of property whether in the general interest or 'to secure the payment of taxes or other contributions or penalties'. Many of the examples discussed earlier in this chapter on what constitutes a deprivation of property (and which fall short of deprivation) are examples of control on the use of property. So, seizure of obscene publications,[170] rent controls,[171] planning restrictions,[172] temporary seizure of property in criminal proceedings,[173] temporary seizure of an aircraft in connection with drugs enforcement legislation,[174] the withdrawal of a licence,[175] limitations on fishing rights,[176] retrospective tax legislation,[177] refusal to register applicants as certified accountants with adverse effects for their business,[178] limitation periods relating to adverse possession,[179] and the excessive length of bankruptcy proceedings during which time the applicant's ability to deal with his property was severely restricted,[180] and rendering a television set unusable when the compulsory subscription to the public television service is cancelled,[181] all constitute measures of control on the use of property. The Strasbourg Court also regards measures of confiscation, which amount to a deprivation of property, as also constituting control of the use of the property. This will involve consideration of whether a fair balance has been struck in confiscating the property between the interests of the community and respect for peaceful enjoyment of possessions.[182] The Strasbourg Court found the confiscation of a substantial sum of lawfully acquired United States dollars smuggled into Russia in breach of a requirement to declare such sums was a disproportionate penalty in the light of the imposition of a suspended prison sentence also imposed on the applicant.[183]

JUSTIFYING THE CONTROLS

As with all interferences with Convention rights, the measure which constitutes the interference must have a basis in national law, which will include European Union law. In a case

[170] *Handyside v United Kingdom*, (App. 5493/72), 7 December 1976, Series A No 24, (1979–80) 1 EHRR 737.

[171] *Mellacher v Austria*, (Apps. 10522/83, 11011/84, and 11070/84), 19 December 1989, Series A No 169, (1990) 12 EHRR 391.

[172] *Pine Valley Developments Limited and others v Ireland*, (App. 12742/87), 29 November 1991, Series A No 222, (1992) 14 EHRR 319.

[173] *Raimondo v Italy*, (App. 12954/87), 22 February 1994, Series A No 281-A, (1994) 18 EHRR 237; and *Vendittelli v Italy*, (App. 14804/89), 18 July 1994, Series A No 293-A, (1994) 19 EHRR 464.

[174] *Air Canada v United Kingdom*, (App. 18465/91), 5 May 1995, Series A No 316, (1995) 20 EHRR 150.

[175] *Tre Traktörer Aktiebolag v Sweden*, (App. 10873/84), 7 July 1989, Series A No 159, (1991) 13 EHRR 309; and (App. 12033/86), *Fredin v Sweden (No.1)*, 18 February 1991, Series A No 192, (1991) 13 EHRR 784.

[176] *Posti and Rahko v Finland*, (App. 27824/95), 24 September 2002, (2003) 37 EHRR 158, ECHR 2002-VII.

[177] *National & Provincial Building Society, the Leeds Permanent Building Society and the Yorkshire Building Society v United Kingdom*, (Apps. 21319/93, 21449/93, and 21675/93), 23 October 1997, (1998) 25 EHRR 127, ECHR 1997-VII.

[178] *Van Marle and others v Netherlands*, (Apps. 8543/79, 8674/79, 8675/79, and 8685/79), 26 June 1986, Series A No 101, (1986) 8 EHRR 483.

[179] *JA Pye (Oxford) Ltd and JA Pye (Oxford) Land Ltd v United Kingdom*, (App. 44302/02), 30 August 2007 [GC], (2008) 46 EHRR 1083, ECHR 2007-nyr.

[180] *Luordo v Italy*, (App. 32190/96), 17 July 2003, ECHR 2003-IX.

[181] *Faccio v Italy*, (App. 33/04), Decision of 17 April 2009.

[182] *Ismayilov v Russia*, (App. 30352/03), 6 November 2008, § 30.

[183] *Ismayilov v Russia*, (App. 30352/03), 6 November 2008, § 30. See also *Grifhorst v France*, (App. 28336/02), 26 February 2009; and *Moon v France*, (App. 39973/03), 9 July 2009.

concerning the impounding of an aircraft as part of the sanctions regime against Serbia and Montenegro, the Grand Chamber concluded that the underlying legal basis for measures which interfere with property rights may lie in EU law.[184]

Some of the early case-law suggested that, where a State can bring its actions within the scope of the second paragraph, there is no need for the balancing of interests to take place.[185] But later case-law has moved to a position where the fair balance test which applies to deprivations and other interferences is also applied to matters within the second paragraph of Article 1 of Protocol 1.[186]

The forfeiture and destruction of obscene materials is a justifiable measure within this second paragraph of Article 1.[187]

A similar view was taken of the forfeiture within the United Kingdom of Krügerrands.[188] In this case, the company had the misfortune to engage in business transactions in which they sold Krügerrands in exchange for a dishonoured cheque. They had the transaction declared void under German law and sought the recovery of the gold coins from the British customs authorities which had seized them. The Court considered the case one in which forfeiture did constitute a deprivation of property but was essentially a consequence of their illegal importation, the prohibition of which was a constituent element in a measure for the control of their use in the United Kingdom. Therefore it was necessary to consider only whether there had been compliance with the second paragraph of Article 1.

The *Gasus* case[189] concerned the seizure by the Dutch tax authorities of property from a company the title in which remained with its seller in Germany, since a retention of title clause prevented the passing of the property until all instalments of the purchase price had been paid. Such seizure was in accordance with the provisions of Dutch tax law. The complaint of the applicant company was that they had been deprived of their property in payment of a tax debt owed by a third party, that they were in no way responsible for causing the tax debt, and that they could not have been aware of it in agreeing to accept the price of the concrete mixer and ancillary equipment by instalments. Nevertheless, the Court concluded that this was a deprivation falling within the second paragraph of Article 1 of Protocol 1.

Later case-law has placed greater emphasis on the need to secure a fair balance between the individual interest and the general interest, though it has been acknowledged that a wide margin of appreciation will be accorded to States.[190] The modern approach can be illustrated by the *Chassagnou* case.[191] The applicants were opposed to hunting on ethical grounds. They had, nevertheless, been obliged to transfer hunting rights over their land to local hunters' associations, had been made members of the local association, and had

[184] *'Bosphorus Airways' v Ireland*, (App. 45036/98), 30 June 2005 [GC], (2006) 42 EHRR 1, ECHR 2005-VI.

[185] *Handyside v United Kingdom*, (App. 5493/72), 7 December 1976, Series A No 24, (1979–80) 1 EHRR 737, § 62.

[186] See *Pine Valley Developments Limited and others v Ireland*, (App. 12742/87), 29 November 1991, Series A No 222, (1992) 14 EHRR 319, §§ 57–9.

[187] See *Handyside v United Kingdom*, (App. 5493/72), 7 December 1976, Series A No 24, (1979–80) 1 EHRR 737, § 63.

[188] *AGOSI v United Kingdom*, (App. 9118/80), 24 October 1986, Series A No 108, (1987) 9 EHRR 1.

[189] *Gasus Dosier- und Fördertechnik GmbH v Netherlands*, (App. 15375/89), 23 February 1995, Series A No 306-B, (1995) 20 EHRR 403.

[190] *National & Provincial Building Society, the Leeds Permanent Building Society and the Yorkshire Building Society v United Kingdom*, (Apps. 21319/93, 21449/93, and 21675/93), 23 October 1997, (1998) 25 EHRR 127, ECHR 1997-VII, § 80; and *Mellacher v Austria*, (Apps. 10522/83, 11011/84, and 11070/84), 19 December 1989, Series A No 169, (1990) 12 EHRR 391, § 53.

[191] *Chassagnou and others v France*, (Apps. 25088/94, 28331/95, and 28443/95), 29 April 1999 [GC], (2000) 29 EHRR 615, ECHR 1999-III.

been unable to prevent hunting on their land. The measures were treated as falling within the second paragraph of Article 1, and are categorized as 'an interference with the... enjoyment of their rights as owners of property'.[192] The Court restated its established case-law that the second paragraph must be construed in the light of the principle laid down in the first sentence of Article 1, and went on to say that the interference must achieve a fair balance between the demands of the general interest of the community and the requirements of the protection of individuals' fundamental rights. The Court once again emphasized the wide margin of appreciation which the Contracting Parties enjoy, but tempered this with a restatement of the requirement of proportionality.[193] A violation of Article 1 of Protocol 1 was found in the case since the measures lacked proportionality.[194]

In *Suljagić v Bosnia and Herzegovina*[195] the applicant had deposited 'old foreign currency' in a bank in the Former Socialist Republic of Yugoslavia. The Bosnian government had enacted legislation to recompense deposits of old foreign currency. However the Court found that given the wide margin of appreciation, the legislation itself did not breach Article 1 of Protocol 1. However, a fair balance had not been achieved due to delays in implementation of the law. Following the finding of a violation in this respect, the Court noted that the measures affected a large number of people and that there were 1,350 similar applications on behalf of more than 13,500 applicants pending before the Court.[196] It applied the pilot judgment procedure.[197]

The *Spadea and Scalabrino* case[198] concerned the Italian system of postponing, suspending, or staggering the enforcement of eviction orders in order to avoid an upsurge in tenants having to find alternative homes because of the large number of leases which expired in 1982 and 1983. The Court concluded that the system operated as a control on the use of the property by the freeholders, but accepted that the legislation authorizing the delays in the enforcement of the eviction orders served the social purposes of protecting tenants on low incomes and of avoiding a risk of public disorder. A fair balance had been struck between the interests of the individual and the collective interest. But where the delays imposed an excessive burden amounting to some eleven years when the freeholders were kept out of their property, and where there was no possibility of getting compensation for the losses arising from their inability to gain possession of their property, that balance was not met and a breach of Article 1 of Protocol 1 was found.[199] In *Nobel and others v The*

[192] § 74. [193] § 75.

[194] See also *Hermann v Germany*, in contrast see *Chabauty v France*, (App. 57412/08), 4 October 2012 where a similar issue arose as had been decided in *Chassagnou and others v France*, (Apps. 25088/94, 28331/95, and 28443/95), 29 April 1999 [GC], (2000) 29 EHRR 615, ECHR 1999-III. However the Court found that there was no violation in this case. The difference in the balancing exercise was that the applicants did not oppose the hunting on their land for ethical reasons. Thus, the measure was not disproportionate given the wide margin of appreciation given to the State, §§ 55–7.

[195] *Suljagić v Bosnia and Herzegovina*, (App. 27912/02), 3 November 2009; see earlier case-law dealing with similar issues, for example *Jeličić v Bosnia and Herzegovina*, (App. 41183/02), 31 November 2006, ECHR 2006-XII.

[196] § 63.

[197] The Committee of Ministers closed the pilot judgment procedure on 8 June 2011, being satisfied with the remedial measures taken by the State (Res-54). In a similar and complex case involving old foreign currency, the Court found a violation by Slovenia and Serbia but not by other respondent States in *Ališić and others v Bosnia and Herzegovina, Croatia, Serbia, Slovenia and the former Yugoslav Republic of Macedonia*, (App. 60642/08), 6 November 2012 (Referred to Grand Chamber 18 March 2013) and again issued a pilot judgment.

[198] *Spadea and Scalabrino v Italy*, (App. 12868/87), 28 September 1995, Series A No 315-B, (1996) 21 EHRR 481.

[199] *Immobiliare Saffi v Italy*, (App. 22774/93), 28 July 1999 [GC], ECHR 1999-V. See also *Lunari v Italy*, (App. 21463/93), 11 January 2001; *PM v Italy*, (App. 24650/94), 11 January 2001; and *Tanganelli v Italy*, (App. 23424/98), 11 January 2001; see also *Lindheim and others v Norway*, (Apps. 13221/08 and 2139/10), 12 June 2012, where rent controls were held to be disproportionate given the excessive burden on the lessors under the lease condition imposed by the State, (App. 23424/94), 11 January 2001.

Netherlands,[200] the Court found inadmissible a claim by the applicants that rent controls which limited the rent they could charge were disproportionate. The Court found that the wide margin of appreciation meant the State were justified in having measures of rent control to meet the aim of social protection for tenants. The applicants knew of the controls when they bought the property and the controls were reasonable. In several cases challenging austerity measures introduced by States in order to access European Union funds,[201] the Court has found the applications inadmissible given the exceptional financial crisis faced by the States and the limited extent and temporary nature of cuts to State benefits.

In summary, three conditions need to be satisfied for a control on the use of property to be permissible under Article 1:

- the measure must have the character of law;
- the measure must be in the general interest, or be for the purpose of securing the payment of taxes or other contributions or penalties; and
- the measure must be deemed necessary by the State.

This modern approach has blurred somewhat the distinction between those measures constituting control of the use of property and those measures which are in the residual category of other interferences with peaceful enjoyment of possessions. It is also very close to the test for the permissibility of deprivation of property. Thus a unity of approach has developed in relation to all interferences with property rights.

OTHER INTERFERENCES WITH PEACEFUL ENJOYMENT OF POSSESSIONS

There remain cases which fall for consideration under a residual category of other interferences with peaceful enjoyment of possession. Although this right is guaranteed in the first sentence of the Article, the practice of the Court is to consider first whether there has been a deprivation, and then whether there has been a control on the use of property before considering whether there has been some other interference with the peaceful enjoyment of possessions. As indicated earlier, the Court has come to adopt a broad approach to the concept of the control of the use of property, leaving comparatively few cases to be considered under this head. The earlier case-law in which certain measures were considered to fall within this head would now almost certainly be considered as measures of control of the use of property. This is because the earlier case-law on the second paragraph of Article 1 did not require the State to show that the measure of control struck a fair balance between the individual and the collective interest.

For example, the system of expropriation permits in issue in the *Sporrong and Lönnroth* case[202] was considered to be an interference with the peaceful enjoyment of possessions, whereas now it would probably be regarded as a measure for the control of the use of property. A similar view would probably now be taken of land use plans,[203] though perhaps

[200] *Nobel and others v The Netherlands*, (App. 27126/11), Decision of 2 July 2013.

[201] *Koufaki and Adedy v Greece*, (Apps. 57665/12 and 57657/12), Decision of 7 May 2013; *Da Conceicao Mateus and Santos Janurio*, (Apps. 62235/12 and 57725/12), Decision of 8 October 2013.

[202] *Sporrong and Lönnroth v Sweden*, (Apps. 7151–2/75), 23 September 1982, Series A No 52, (1983) 5 EHRR 35.

[203] *Katte Klitsche de la Grange v Italy*, (App. 12539/86), 27 October 1994, Series A No 293-B, (1994) 19 EHRR 368.

land consolidation plans might still be regarded as interferences with peaceful possessions rather than measures for the control of their use.[204] In a case against Greece,[205] the applicants bought a plot of land and proposed to develop it by building a shopping centre, but the local authority decided to block the development though it did not have the funds to expropriate the land. A freeze on new building licences followed. Eventually the land was expropriated. The Court did not consider the early stages to constitute a deprivation of the property, since the owners' rights remained unaffected, nor was it a control of the use of property since the measures did not pursue such an aim. What was in issue was an interference with the peaceful use of possessions. There was no reasonable balance in this case between the rights of the owners and the environmental concerns of the local authority. Consequently, there was a violation of Article 1 of Protocol 1.

In a case where pension payments were made late in circumstances where their value had reduced significantly by the time of actual payment as a result of inflation and the devaluation of the Russian rouble, the Court found that there had been a violation of the right to peaceful enjoyment of possessions. An individual and excessive burden had fallen on the applicants.[206]

In determining whether an interference with the peaceful enjoyment of possessions is permissible, the Court now applies the same test as it has developed in relation to cases involving a deprivation of property, though this is articulated in somewhat different terms. In the *Broniowski* case, the Grand Chamber articulated the test in the following terms:

> Both an interference with the peaceful enjoyment of possessions and an abstention from action must strike a fair balance between the demands of the general interest of the community and the requirement of the protection of the individual's fundamental rights.
>
> The concern to achieve this balance is reflected in the structure of Article 1 of Protocol 1 as a whole. In particular, there must be a reasonable relationship of proportionality between the means employed and the aim sought to be realised by any measures applied by the State, including measures depriving a person of his or her possessions. In each case involving the alleged violation of that Article the Court must, therefore, ascertain whether by reason of the State's action or inaction the person concerned had to bear a disproportionate and excessive burden.[207]

These principles were applied in *NKM v Hungary.*[208] The Court examined the applicant's claim that the taxation on statutory severance pay given when employment with the civil service was terminated was a violation of Article 1 of Protocol 1. The Court found that the complex legal and factual issues raised by the case prevented the measure being classified in a precise category[209] and was therefore dealt with as an interference with the enjoyment of possessions. The Court went on to find the measure was disproportionate. The Court accepted the aim of 'social justice' in combination with the aim of redistribution of public money to be within the wide margin of appreciation given to the State when deciding on what is in the 'public interest'. It was also noted that it is within the State's margin of appreciation to decide what taxes or contributions are to be collected. However the Court did have serious doubts about the relevance of these aims to the applicant who was receiving statutory compensation and could not be held responsible for the fiscal problem the State

[204] See *Erkner and Hofauer v Austria*, (App. 9616/81), 23 April 1987, Series A No 117, (1987) 9 EHRR 464; and *Wiesinger v Austria*, (App. 11796/85), 24 September 1991, Series A No 213, (1993) 18 EHRR 258.

[205] *Pialopoulos and others v Greece*, (App. 37095/97), 15 February 2001, (2001) 33 EHRR 977.

[206] *Solodyuk v Russia*, (App. 67099/01), 12 July 2005.

[207] *Broniowski v Poland*, (App. 31443/96), 22 June 2004 [GC], (2005) 40 EHRR 495, ECHR 2004-V, § 150.

[208] *NKM v Hungary*, (App. 66529/11), 14 May 2013.

[209] § 43.

wished to remedy. However, the Court stated it did not need to decide on the adequacy of a measure that formally serves a social goal[210] as it would examine the measure to decide if a fair balance has been achieved. In the present case, an excessive burden was placed on the applicant compared to other civil servants in a similar position. The applicant's dismissal was followed by a period of unemployment and there was no transitional period for the applicant to adjust to the tax on severance pay which was introduced only a few weeks before her dismissal. The Court concluded that:

> it affected the applicant (and other dismissed civil servants in a similar situation) being in good-faith standing and deprived her of the larger part of a statutorily guaranteed, acquired right serving the special social interest of reintegration. In the Court's opinion, those who act in good faith on the basis of law should not be frustrated in their statute-based expectations without specific and compelling reasons.[211]

It should be noted that the concurring opinion noted that the case should not be seen as developing any new principles with regard to the application of the Convention to the area of the imposition of tax, which is for the State to decide. Only if the imposition of tax is applied in a particularly arbitrary way can the tax regime be challenged. Article 1 of Protocol 1 does not preclude the use of retrospective tax legislation.[212]

CONCLUDING REMARKS

The early case-law suggested a need to define with some precision the nature of the interference with property rights, because there were differences in the standards demanded of Contracting Parties, but the more modern case-law takes a very similar approach to all forms of interferences with property rights. Though the conditions for a lawful interference with the rights protected by Article 1 of Protocol 1 are perhaps not as stringent as those arising in relation to the rights protected by Articles 8 to 11, the Strasbourg Court has been influenced by the approach adopted there, and has required any measures of interference to meet a legitimate aim and to be proportionate in that it strikes a fair balance between the individual interest and the collective interest, and does not impose a disproportionate and excessive burden on the individual.

The rights protected in Article 1 of Protocol 1 have developed organically into something which is close to a general protection of property rights for both individuals and business enterprises. Contracting Parties are required to justify acts or omissions which interfere with freedom of property in terms of a fair balance between an individual interest and a collective interest, though establishing a legitimate and proportionate justification for the measures in issue has not proved to be particularly difficult for Contracting Parties. The Grand Chamber has been particularly active in this area and in developing the principles to be applied in a wide variety of situations, including major programmes in the countries of central and eastern Europe to provide redress for infringements of property rights, which arose in earlier times. However, just like Article 8, the development of the rights protected by Article 1 of Protocol 1 is almost certainly not yet complete.

[210] § 59. [211] § 75.

[212] Concurring Opinion of Judge Lorenzen joined by Judges Raimondi, and Jočiene.

21

THE RIGHT TO EDUCATION

INTRODUCTION

Article 2 of the Protocol 1 provides:

> No person shall be denied the right to education. In the exercise of any functions which it assumes in relation to education and teaching, the State shall respect the right of parents to ensure such education and teaching in conformity with their own religious and philosophical convictions.

As with the right to property, the inclusion of a right to education among the Convention rights proved to be controversial and complicated.[1] Even when agreement could be reached on the inclusion of the right in Article 2 of Protocol 1, a large number of reservations were entered in respect of it.[2]

All the provisions of the Convention, including Articles 13 to 18, apply equally to the rights guaranteed by the First Protocol.[3] These rights are also subject in the same way to the control of the organs set up by the Convention.

A number of general propositions can be made by way of introduction to the right enshrined in this Article. Though drafted as a negative formulation, it has been accepted that there is a right to education within existing provision, which applies to primary, secondary, and further or higher education. The concept of education is considered broadly. Most of the rights are enjoyed by the pupil or student, but parents have a separate right to respect for their own religious and philosophical convictions in the education of their children.

The main focus of the case-law has been on primary education, but it is now clear that the rights also relate to secondary and higher education,[4] and probably also professional education.[5] The Strasbourg Court has recognized that the right to education has links with the rights protected by Articles 8 to 10 of the Convention and needs to be interpreted consistently with the general spirit of the Convention as an instrument designed to maintain and promote the ideals and values of a democratic society.[6]

[1] A.H. Robertson, 'The European Convention on Human Rights—Recent Developments' (1951) BYBIL 359; and L. Wildhaber, 'Right to Education and Parental Rights' in R. Macdonald, F. Matscher, and H. Petzold (eds.), *The European System for the Protection of Human Rights* (Martinus Nijhoff, Dordrecht 1993), 531.

[2] Including a reservation by the United Kingdom. Even in 2013 there are reservations to Article 2 of Protocol 1 by Andorra, Azerbaijan, Bulgaria, Georgia, Germany, Ireland, Malta, Moldova, Romania, the former Yugoslav Republic of Macedonia, Turkey, and the United Kingdom and a Declaration by The Netherlands. See http://conventions.coe.int for a current list of reservations of Council of Europe instruments.

[3] Art. 5 of Protocol 1.

[4] *Leyla Şahin v Turkey*, (App. 44774/98), 10 November 2005 [GC], (2007) 44 EHRR 99, ECHR 2005-IX, § 141; *Mürsel Eren v Turkey*, (App. 60856/00), 7 February 2006, (2007) 44 EHRR 619, ECHR 2006-II, § 41; and *Irfan Temel and others v Turkey*, (App. 36458/02), 3 March 2009, § 39.

[5] *Kök v Turkey*, (App. 1855/02), 19 October 2006.

[6] *Kjeldsen, Busk Madsen and Pedersen v Denmark*, (Apps. 5095/71, 5920/72, and 5926/72), 7 December 1976, Series A No 23, (1979–80) 1 EHRR 711, § 54. See also *Valsamis v Greece*, (App. 21787/93), 18 December

Positive obligations are inherent in the obligations provided for in Article 2. This was recognized, in part, in the *Valsamis* case,[7] where the Strasbourg Court said that the obligation in the second sentence of the Article implies 'some positive obligations on the part of the State'. So, it would seem that Contracting Parties must strive to accommodate parental wishes flowing from religious or philosophical convictions. Whether that would extend to the funding, or even partial funding, of private schools where this is the only way in which respect for particular convictions could be secured is, as yet, an unanswered question. In a number of cases, the reservation filed in respect of the Article would, if found to be legitimate, protect the State.[8]

Where there is differential treatment in the provision of education, the non-discrimination provision in Article 14 frequently comes into play.[9]

THE RIGHT TO EDUCATION

The first and leading case on the right to education was the *Belgian Linguistic* case.[10] Six groups of applicants claimed that various aspects of the Belgian legislation governing the use of languages in schools were inconsistent with the Convention. The applicants, who were French-speaking residents in the Dutch-speaking part of Belgium and in the Brussels periphery, wanted their children to be educated in French. The Strasbourg Court decided that Article 2 did not include a right to be taught in the language of the parents' choice, nor a right of access to a particular school of the parents' choice. Ultimately, the Court found that the Belgian legislation failed to comply with the provisions of the Convention and Protocol in only one respect. It infringed Article 14 of the Convention,[11] read in conjunction with the first sentence of Article 2 of the First Protocol, in so far as it prevented certain children, solely on the basis of the residence of their parents, from having access to the French-language schools in certain communes on the periphery of Brussels. The law provided that the language of instruction in these communes was Dutch, but that French-speaking classes should be provided at the nursery and primary levels, on condition that it was asked for by sixteen heads of family. However, this education was not available to children whose parents lived outside these communes, even though there were no French-speaking schools in the communes where they lived. The Dutch classes, on the other hand, accepted all children, whatever the place of residence of the parents. Applying the criteria of discrimination which it elaborated in this case, the Court held that this differential treatment could not be justified under Article 14.

Although the wording of the Article is that 'no person shall be denied the right to education', the Strasbourg Court stated in the merits phase of the *Belgian Linguistic* case that the negative formulation meant that there was no obligation for the Contracting Parties to 'establish at their own expense, or to subsidize, education of any particular type or at any

1996, (1997) 24 EHRR 314, ECHR 1996-VI, § 25; and *Catan and others v Moldova and Russia*, (App. 43370/04), 19 October 2012.

[7] *Valsamis v Greece*, (App. 21787/93), 18 December 1996, (1997) 24 EHRR 294, ECHR 1996-VI, § 27.

[8] Where the reservation indicates that the provision of education was subject to national resource constraints. The Court has suggested a wide margin of appreciation in regard to resource allocation: *Tarantino and others v Italy*, (Apps 25851/09, 29204/09, and 64090/09), 2 April 2013.

[9] See ch.24.

[10] *Case relating to certain aspects of the laws on the use of languages in education in Belgium (Belgian Linguistic Case (No. 2)*, (Apps. 1474/62, 1677/62, 1691/62, 1769/63, 1994/63, and 2126/64), 23 July 1968, Series A No 6, (1979–80), 23 July 1968, Series A No 6, (1979–80) 1 EHRR 252 (cited in this chapter as the '*Belgian Linguistic* case').

[11] The prohibition on discrimination: see ch.24.

level'.[12] The Court went on to note that all the Contracting Parties have public education systems, and that Article 2 guaranteed the right, in principle, for pupils to 'avail themselves of the means of instruction existing at a given time'.[13] What this means is that the Article guarantees a right of access to existing educational provision, but Contracting Parties have a wide margin of appreciation as to the resources they devote to the system of education and as to its organization.[14]

The right of access is to the educational provision existing at any given time. The choice of provision is a matter for the Contracting Party, though it would seem that there is a right of persons to establish private schools.[15] Commission decisions have established that there is no obligation on a Contracting Party to provide selective education,[16] or schools offering education in the context of particular religious affiliations,[17] single-sex schools,[18] or separate schools for those with special educational needs.[19]

In the *Belgian Linguistic* case, the Strasbourg Court defined the scope of the right to education in the following terms:

> The first sentence of Article 2 of the Protocol consequently guarantees, in the first place, a right of access to educational institutions existing at a given time, but such access constitutes only a part of the right to education. For the 'right to education' to be effective, it is further necessary that, inter alia, the individual who is the beneficiary should have the possibility of drawing profit from the education received, that is to say, the right to obtain, in conformity with the rules in force in each State, and in one form or another, official recognition of the studies which he has completed.[20]

Dicta of the Court in the *Belgian Linguistic* case supports the view that the right to 'effective education' implies a duty on the State to provide schooling at least in the official language. In *Cyprus v Turkey*[21] the Cypriot Government complained that, although primary education was available in Greek in northern Cyprus, the 'Turkish Republic of Northern Cyprus' had closed down Greek secondary schools and that Greek Cypriot children living there had either to continue their secondary education in Turkish or English or to travel to the southern part of the island to attend Greek language schools. The Court observed that in the strict sense there was no denial of the right to education. Nonetheless, it found a violation of Article 2 of Protocol 1 because it considered that, having provided for primary education in Greek, it was unrealistic to expect children to switch to learning in another language once they reached secondary age. Having assumed responsibility for the provision of Greek-language primary schooling, the failure of the "Turkish Republic of

[12] § 3 under the heading 'B. Interpretation adopted by the Court'.

[13] § 3 under the heading 'B. Interpretation adopted by the Court'.

[14] *Tarantino and others v Italy*, (Apps. 25851/09, 29204/09, and 64090/09), 2 April 2013.

[15] *Kjeldsen, Busk Madsen and Pedersen v Denmark*, (Apps. 5095/71, 5920/72, and 5926/72), 7 December 1976, Series A No 23, (1979–80) 1 EHRR 711, § 50. See also *Jordebo Foundation of Christian Schools and Jordebo v Sweden*, (App. 11533/85),Decision of 6 March 1987, (1987) 51 DR 125; and App. 23419/94, *Verein Gemeinsam Lernen v Austria*, Decision of 6 September 1995, (1995) 82-A DR 41.

[16] *W and others v United Kingdom*, (Apps. 10228/92 and 10229/82), Decision of 6 March 1984, (1984) 37 DR 96.

[17] *X v United Kingdom*, (App. 7728/77), Decision of 2 May 1978, (1979) 14 DR 179.

[18] *W and others v United Kingdom*, (Apps. 10228/82 and 10229/82), Decision of 6 March 1984, (1984) 37 DR 96.

[19] *Simpson v United Kingdom*, (App. 14688/89), Decision of 4 December 1989, (1989) 64 DR 188; and *SP v United Kingdom*, (App. 28915/95), Decision of 17 January 1997.

[20] *Case relating to certain aspects of the laws on the use of languages in education in Belgium (Merits) Belgian Linguistic Case (No. 2)*, (Apps. 1474/62, 1677/62, 1691/62, 1769/63, 1994/63, and 2126/64), 23 July 1968, Series A No 6, (1979–80) 1 EHRR 252, § 4 under the heading 'B. Interpretation adopted by the Court'.

[21] *Cyprus v Turkey*, (App. 25781/94), 10 May 2001 [GC], (2002) 35 EHRR 731, ECHR 2001-IV.

northern Cyprus" authorities to make continuing provision for it at the secondary-school level had to be considered in effect to be a denial of the substance of the right at issue. The Court also rejected the idea that the availability of Greek-language schools in southern Cyprus would be sufficient to comply with the obligation under Article 2 of Protocol 1.[22]

In *Catan and others v Moldova and Russia*,[23] the Court affirmed the *Cyprus v Turkey* judgment when examining the use of language in schools in the disputed area of the Moldovan Republic of Transdniestria (MRT). The area declared its independence from Moldova in 1991 but it is not recognized internationally. Russia supported the MRT and had troops in the area. Moldovian is the official language of both Moldova and the MRT. However in the MRT a law in 1992 declared it had to be taught in the Cyrillic alphabet and not in Latin script, as was the case previously and is still the case in Moldova. Schools in the MRT were forbidden from using the Latin script. The applicants attended three schools in the MRT. One school made a request to use Latin script. Following this, teachers and children suffered abuse. Another school was evicted from its school building as it had failed to register. Eventually the school registered with the MRT. Another school attended by the applicants was threatened with closure for not registering with the MRT and had electricity and water supplies cut off. The Moldovan Government provided the school with transport and some facilities. The applicants complained under Article 2 of Protocol 1.

The Court held that Moldova were not in violation of Article 2. It had taken positive steps to attempt to protect the rights of the applicants including paying rent and salaries and providing new premises. However, the Court held that Russia had effective control in MRT. It held that the imposition of separatist ideology through the language laws was not a legitimate aim and further, that the applicants had a right to education in the recognized national language. In addition, there was a violation of Article 2 of Protocol 1 in regards to the parental right of respect for religious or philosophical convictions. Reading the Article in the light of Article 8, the parents were placed in the:

> invidious position of having to choose, on the one hand, between sending their children to schools where they would face the disadvantage of pursuing their entire secondary education in a combination of language and alphabet which they consider artificial and which is unrecognised anywhere else in the world, using teaching materials produced in Soviet times or, alternatively, subjecting their children to long journeys and/or substandard facilities, harassment and intimidation.[24]

Issues relating to access to education have been raised in a number of cases against States in central and eastern Europe. For example, the *Timishev* case[25] concerned a forced migrant who was an ethnic Chechen. His property in Grozny had been destroyed as a result of military operations and he was living in Nalchik. He was refused permanent residence in Nalchik by reason of his being a former resident of the Chechen Republic. His children were refused admission to a school in Nalchik, which they had previously attended, on the

[22] In relation to the first sentence of Article 2, a discontinuance of provision may constitute a violation. This means that there may be a positive obligation to continue educational provision in, for example, the language of a minority once that has been provided, even though there is no obligation to provide education in minority languages: *Cyprus v Turkey*, (App. 25781/94), 10 May 2001 [GC], (2002) 35 EHRR 731, ECHR 2001-IV, §§ 273–80.

[23] *Catan and others v Moldova and Russia*, (App. 43370/04), 19 October 2012.

[24] § 143.

[25] *Timishev v Russia*, (Apps. 55762/00 and 55974/00), 13 December 2005, (2007) 44 EHRR 776, ECHR 2005-XII. See also, *Catan and others v Moldova and Russia* (App. 43370/04, 8252/05, 18454/06) 19 October 2012 and numerous cases related to discrimination against the Roma community; *DH and others v Czech Republic*, (App. 57325/00), 13 November 2007 [GC], (2008) 47 EHRR 59, ECHR 2007-nyr; *Orşuş and others v Croatia*, (App. 15766/03), 16 March 2010; *Horvath and Kiss v Hungary*, (App. 11146/11), 29 January 2013.

grounds that he had no lawful right to remain in Nalchik, and that, since the schools were overcrowded, his request for admission of his children constituted an encroachment on the rights of other children. The Strasbourg Court considered this to be serious violation of Article 2. In *Ponomaryovi v Bulgaria*,[26] the Court examined the issue before it under Article 14 with Article 2 of Protocol 1. The applicants were two Russian nationals who moved to Bulgaria as young children. They had been given access to free schooling until near to the end of their secondary education when they were asked to pay fees. The Court found that although the State has discretion as to how it establishes education systems and that charging fees fell within that discretion, it had to guarantee effective access. The Court stated that in relation to the difference of treatment between nationals and non-nationals with regard to school fees, it:

> must solely determine whether, once a State has voluntarily decided to provide such education free of charge, it may deny that benefit to a distinct group of people.[27]

The Court went on to acknowledge the State's discretion in deciding on 'curtailing the use of resource-hungry public services.'[28] However, it noted that this discretion is qualified in regard to education as it is directly protected as a right in the Convention (unlike welfare or housing for example). It noted education is a:

> very particular type of public service, which not only directly benefits those using it but also serves broader societal functions. Indeed, the Court has already had occasion to point out that "[i]n a democratic society, the right to education... is indispensable to the furtherance of human rights [and] plays... a fundamental role...." Moreover, in order to achieve pluralism and thus democracy, society has an interest in the integration of minorities.[29]

On the facts it found that there was a violation of Article 14 with Article 2 of Protocol 1 as the applicants had not abused the education system, were young children when they arrived in Bulgaria, and were in the process of regularizing their immigration status.

In a group of cases involving the removal of gypsies from land where they had set up homes in breach of planning laws,[30] it was argued that the refusal to allow the families to remain on their own land resulted in their children being denied access to satisfactory education. In all three cases the Strasbourg Court found that the applicants had failed to substantiate their claims under this provision of the Convention and so there was no violation. The applications, however, signal the potential linkage between provisions of the Convention, though in most cases a requirement that a family moves its home would not result in schooling being unavailable to them if they were within the age range for which attendance at school was required by the State.

This linkage with other provisions of the Convention is also illustrated by the *Leyla Şahin* case,[31] which concerned the prohibition of the wearing of the Islamic headscarf in Turkish universities. The Grand Chamber found that there was no violation of Article 9 here and no separate violation of Article 2 of Protocol 1. The requirement not to wear a headscarf did not impair the essence of the right to education.

[26] *Ponomaryovi v Bulgaria*, (App. 5335/05), 21 June 2011. [27] § 53. [28] § 54. [29] § 55.

[30] *Coster v United Kingdom*, (App. 24876/94), (2001) 33 EHRR 479; *Lee v United Kingdom*, (App. 25289/94), (2001) 33 EHRR 677; and *Smith (Jane) v United Kingdom*, (App. 25154/94), (2001) 33 EHRR 712, all 18 January 2001 [GC].

[31] *Leyla Şahin v Turkey*, (App. 44774/98), 10 November 2005 [GC], (2007) 44 EHRR 99, ECHR 2005-IX. See also *Lautsi v Italy*, (App. 30814/06), 18 March 2011; and *Catan and others v Moldova and Russia*, (App. 43370/04), 19 October 2012.

REGULATING EDUCATION

In the *Campbell and Cosans* case,[32] the Strasbourg Court noted that the rights enshrined in the Article involved a duty on the State to regulate the provision of education:

> The right to education guaranteed by the first sentence of Article 2 by its very nature calls for regulation by the State, but such regulation must never injure the substance of the right nor conflict with other rights enshrined in the Convention or its Protocols.[33]

The *Belgian Linguistic* case recognized that effective education may require a Contracting Party to regulate education by requiring compulsory attendance at school. The Strasbourg organs have, however, consistently accorded to the Contracting Parties a wide margin of appreciation in the measures of regulation taken.[34] The Court has found that the margin of appreciation accorded to the State with regard to the regulation of education is narrower for primary education but is wider for secondary education and wider still for higher education.[35] However, the Court has noted that the discretion afforded to the State with regard to secondary education may be narrower today than it was previously:

> with more and more countries now moving towards what has been described as a "knowledge-based" society, secondary education plays an ever-increasing role in successful personal development and in the social and professional integration of the individuals concerned. Indeed, in a modern society, having no more than basic knowledge and skills constitutes a barrier to successful personal and professional development. It prevents the persons concerned from adjusting to their environment and entails far-reaching consequences for their social and economic well-being.[36]

Comments in the *Belgian Linguistic* case to the effect that the right to education involves a right to an effective education would seem to require Contracting Parties to maintain certain standards in education. This means that, whereas there may be universal entitlement to education up to a certain age, education beyond that age may be dependent upon the attainment of qualifications deemed necessary for the pursuit of more advanced education.[37] However, where the regulation operates as a denial of education, there will be a violation of the Article. So a provision in Scotland excluding a pupil from a State school because of a refusal to submit to corporal punishment exceeded the scope for reasonable regulation of education and amounted to a violation of the right to education in the first sentence of the Article.[38]

Basic procedural fairness prohibits a Contracting Party from acting in a totally arbitrary manner in relation to examination results within an established educational system. So, in the *Mürsel Erem* case,[39] it was a breach of Article 2 to refuse to accept some good results

[32] *Campbell and Cosans v United Kingdom*, (Apps. 7511/76 and 7743/76), 25 February 1982, Series A No 48, (1982) 4 EHRR 293.

[33] § 41.

[34] For example, as to the setting of the curriculum: see *Kjeldsen, Busk Madsen and Pedersen v Denmark*, (Apps. 5095/71, 5920/72, and 5926/72), 7 December 1976, Series A No 23, (1979–80) 1 EHRR 711, § 53.

[35] *Ponomaryovi v Bulgaria*, (App. 5335/05), 21 June 2011, § 56. The Court pointed out that the difference between the levels is set out in United Nations International Covenant of Civil and Political Rights as well as in Article 28 of the United Nations Convention on the Rights of the Child.

[36] *Ponomaryovi v Bulgaria*, (App. 5335/05), 21 June 2011,§ 57.

[37] *Glasewska v Sweden*, (App. 11655/85), Decision of 10 October 1985; (1985) 45 DR 300.

[38] *Campbell and Cosans v United Kingdom*, (Apps. 7511/76 and 7743/76), 25 February 1982, Series A No 48, (1982) 4 EHRR 293.

[39] *Mürsel Eren v Turkey*, (App. 60856/00), 7 February 2006, (2007) 44 EHRR 619, ECHR 2006-II.

following a series of poor results solely on the basis that they could not be explained by the prior poor results, and in the absence of any proof of cheating. However, the Court has recognized that some failures in procedures will not always amount to a violation of Article 2 of Protocol 1, as long as the State acts proportionately, considering the margin of appreciation in each case. Procedural fairness will also be examined with regard to exclusion or expulsion from school. In *Ali v United Kingdom*,[40] the applicant was excluded from his school whilst under police investigation for causing criminal damage to the school. There were several procedural irregularities; the school failed to set a time-limit for the initial period of exclusion, it failed to notify the applicant and his parents of their right of appeal to the governors of the school, the governors failed to hold a hearing and the period of exclusion was extended beyond the forty-five day maximum that was allowed under regulations. Despite this, the exclusion of the applicant was held to be proportionate given the ongoing criminal investigation, which hampered the applicant's return to school, and the alternative lessons offered. The applicant and his parents also refused to attend meetings with the school. The Court recognized that a permanent exclusion with no further access to full time education would be disproportionate but that was not the case here.[41] The judgment is notable because of the Court's explicit use of proportionality, noting that the test used is similar to that used in qualified rights under Articles 8 and 11[42] though there is no list of exclusive aims that applies to Article 2 of Protocol 1. This implies that the reasons given by the State for regulation are non-exhaustive.[43]

The system for the allocation of children to special schools must be fair, otherwise it runs the risk of violating Article 2 of Protocol 1 when read with Article 14 requiring equal treatment. The *DH* case[44] concerned the system in the Czech Republic for educating the children of Roma families. The applicants were children of Roma origin who had been assigned to special schools. The test which they had undertaken to establish their educational needs had been criticized by the European Commission against Racism and Intolerance (ECRI),[45] and by the Council of Europe Commissioner for Human Rights.[46] The applicants argued that the very high number of Roma children allocated to special schools as a result of the test provided strong evidence of indirect discrimination against this particular group. The Grand Chamber accepted that the statistical data did give rise to a strong presumption of indirect discrimination, which meant that it was for the respondent State to show that the difference in impact of the scheme was the result of objective factors unconnected with the racial origins of the applicants.[47] The Grand Chamber did not find the evidence of the respondent State satisfactory. Indeed the evidence suggested that there was bias in the educational tests, and that the parental consent to the allocation of places for their children in special schools was not an informed one, but in any event it was not possible to waive the right not to be subjected to racial discrimination.[48] The Grand Chamber concluded that the applicants, as members of a class, had suffered

[40] *Ali v United Kingdom*, (App. 40385/06), 11 January 2011. [41] §§ 55–64. [42] See ch.14.

[43] *Ali v United Kingdom*, (App. 40385/06), 11 January 2011, § 53.

[44] *DH and others v Czech Republic*, (App. 57325/00), 13 November 2007 [GC], (2008) 47 EHRR 59, ECHR 2007-nyr. See also *Sampanis and others v Greece*, (App. 32526/05), 5 June 2008; *Sampanis and others v Greece* (App. 59608/09) 11 December 2012 (continuing violation); *Orşuş and others v Croatia*, (App. 15766/03), 16 March 2010, (2009) 49 EHRR 572; *Horvath and Kiss v Hungary*, (App. 11146/11), 29 January 2013; *Lavida v Greece*, (App. 7923/10), 30 May 2013. For a wide-ranging discussion of the human rights of travellers, see R. Sandland, 'Developing a Jurisprudence of Difference: The Protection of the Human Rights of Travelling Peoples by the European Court of Human Rights' (2008) 8 HRLRev 475; Section D of the article discusses the *DH* case.

[45] See www.coe.int/t/e/human_rights/ecri/ for information on its work. [46] See ch.1.

[47] *DH and others v Czech Republic*, (App. 57325/00), 13 November 2007 [GC], (2008) 47 EHRR 59, ECHR 2007-nyr, § 195, see also ch.24. [48] § 204.

discrimination prohibited by the Convention, thus making it unnecessary to consider their cases on an individual basis.[49] There was a violation of Article 2 of Protocol 1 when read with Article 14.

The Court has also examined the regulation of access to higher education. As noted the margin of appreciation is wider for higher education than primary and secondary education.[50] In *Tarantino and others v Italy*,[51] the applicants argued that the entrance requirements imposed by the State on certain vocational degrees such as dentistry excluded them from access to higher education in the field of their choice. The applicants had to sit an entrance examination for a limited number of places. The State justified the requirements by arguing that there were a finite number of university places due to the need to maintain manageable class sizes and the need to regulate demand in the local employment market. The limitations on university places were applicable to both public and private universities. The Court examined the proportionality of the Italian Government's approach to limiting university places in certain professions. It considered the aim of achieving high levels of professionalism a legitimate one.[52] The Court noted that access to existing higher education institutions may depend on the availability of 'human, material and financial' resources and that the State should ensure equal treatment to those accessing higher education, which may involve a rigorous admissions policy applying to both public and private universities in order to ensure equality of treatment:

> In so far as the applicants complained that the same restrictions applied to private universities and therefore to instruction they were willing to pay for, it is undeniable that the resources for theoretical and practical education would in fact be largely dependent upon the private universities' human, material and financial capital and therefore on that basis it would be possible to have higher admission numbers without imposing an extra burden on the State and its structures. However, it is not irrelevant that the private sector in Italy is partly reliant on State subsidies. More importantly, in the present circumstances the Court cannot find disproportionate or arbitrary the State's regulation of private institutions as well, in so far as such action can be considered necessary to prevent arbitrary admission or exclusion and to guarantee equal treatment of persons. It reiterates that the fundamental right of everyone to education is a right guaranteed equally to pupils in State and independent schools, without distinction... Accordingly, the State has an obligation to regulate them so as to ensure that the Convention is complied with. In particular, the Court considers that the State is justified in being rigorous in its regulation of the sector – especially in the fields of study in question where a minimum and adequate education level is of utmost importance – in order to ensure that access to private institutions is not available purely on the basis of the financial means of candidates, irrespective of their qualifications and suitability for the profession.[53]

The Court found the measures proportionate given the aims and resources available. It is clear from the majority reasoning that a State has a positive obligation to ensure equal access to both public and private higher education establishments of those who meet the required criteria, irrespective of the wealth of the student.[54] In a case against Turkey[55]

[49] *DH*, § 209. [50] *Ponomaryovi v Bulgaria*, (App. 5335/05), 21 June 2011, § 57.

[51] *Tarantino and others v Italy*, (Apps. 25851/09, 29204/09, and 64090/09), 2 April 2013.

[52] As noted in *Ali v United Kingdom*, (App. 40385/06), 11 January 2011, there is no exhaustive list of aims attached to Article 2 of Protocol 1. [53] § 52.

[54] Partly Dissenting Opinion of Judge Pinto De Albuquerque. Judge Pinto De Albuquerque argued that the need to protect academic autonomy of private universities meant that the measures as applied to private universities were disproportionate. He did not refer to the equal treatment argument and instead focused on the right of the university to allow admittance to students at their own cost. The only ground for admittance should be merit, not market needs. [55] *Altinay v Turkey*, (App. 37222/04), 9 July 2013.

the State regulated access to vocational higher education degrees in communication by differentiating between general secondary schools and vocational schools. It did so by adding different co-efficients to the marks needed to gain entrance. This made it more difficult for those in vocational schools to pass the entrance exam. The Court held that there was no violation of Article 2 of Protocol 1, as the difference of treatment was proportionate to the aim of improving standards in higher education. However the introduction of new criteria after the applicant had begun attendance at the vocational school with no transitional provisions did amount to a violation of Article 14 with Article 2 of Protocol 1 as the measure was unforeseeable and there were no adjustments in the curriculum to reflect the changes.

SAFEGUARDING PLURALISM IN EDUCATION

The scope of the second sentence of the Article is much wider than the first, although it must be recalled that the Strasbourg Court has indicated that the two sentences of the Article must be read in the light of each other and of other provisions of the Convention. Indeed the Court has said that Article 2 is 'dominated' by its first sentence.[56] Its scope is wide because it is delimited by reference to the functions which a Contracting Party assumes in relation to education; many governments assume wide functions in relation to the regulation of education offered by both the State and by the private sector. The Court has described the purpose of the second sentence of Article 2 as follows:

> The second sentence of Article 2 aims in short at safeguarding the possibility of pluralism in education, which possibility is essential for the preservation of the 'democratic society' as conceived by the Convention.[57]

The rights protected by the second sentence are rights of parents, and so the focus will be on education provided before the children reach adulthood and can make their own decisions. The Strasbourg Court has also indicated that one of the purposes of the provision is to operate as a check against possible indoctrination:

> The State is forbidden to pursue an aim of indoctrination that might be considered as not respecting parents' religious and philosophical convictions. That is the limit that must not be exceeded.[58]

The effect of the second sentence of the Article on parental choice allows parents either to enrol their children in State education, to withdraw their children from the State system and educate them privately whether at a private school or at home,[59] or to enforce respect for their religious and philosophical convictions by alleging a violation of the second sentence of Article 2. It allows a significant parental influence on both the organization and content of educational provision.

[56] *Kjeldsen, Busk Madsen and Pedersen v Denmark*, (Apps. 5095/71, 5920/72, and 5926/72), 7 December 1976, Series A No 23, (1979–80) 1 EHRR 711, § 53. All the principles described in this section have been re-stated in *Folgerø v Norway*, (App. 15472/02), 29 June 2007 [GC], (2008) 46 EHRR 1147, ECHR 2007-VIII.

[57] *Kjeldsen, Busk Madsen and Pedersen v Denmark*, (Apps. 5095/71, 5920/72, and 5926/72), 7 December 1976, Series A No 23, (1979–80) 1 EHRR 711, § 50.

[58] § 53.

[59] Though this may be regulated by a Contracting Party, see, *Family H v United Kingdom*, (App. 10233/83), Decision of 6 March 1984, (1984) 37 DR 105.

The Strasbourg Court has ruled that the duty applies not to education viewed narrowly, but to the performance of all the functions assumed by the State, which will include the internal administration of the school.[60]

THE NATURE OF RELIGIOUS AND PHILOSOPHICAL CONVICTIONS

The leading authority on the nature of religious convictions is the *Valsamis* case,[61] which arose in the context of objections raised by a family of Jehovah's Witnesses. The Strasbourg Court recalled its case-law under Article 9 and acknowledged that Jehovah's Witnesses 'enjoy both the status of a "known religion" and the advantages flowing from that as regards observance'.[62] Thus, any person whose convictions can be described as those of a 'known religion' will be able to argue that they have religious convictions.

The leading authority on the nature of philosophical convictions is the *Campbell and Cosans* case.[63] The Strasbourg Court said:

> In its ordinary meaning the word 'convictions', taken on its own, is not synonymous with the words 'opinions' and 'ideas', such as are utilized in Article 10 of the Convention, which guarantees freedom of expression; it is more akin to the term 'beliefs'... appearing in Article 9—which guarantees freedom of thought, conscience and religion—and denotes views that attain a certain level of cogency, seriousness, cohesion and importance.
>
> As regards the adjective 'philosophical', it is not capable of exhaustive definition and little assistance as to its precise significance is to be gleaned from the travaux préparatoires....
>
> Having regard to the Convention as a whole..., the expression 'philosophical convictions' in the present context denotes, in the Court's opinion, such convictions as are worthy of respect in a 'democratic society' and are not incompatible with human dignity; in addition, they must not conflict with the fundamental right of the child to education, the whole of Article 2 being dominated by its first sentence.[64]

In a concurring Grand Chamber judgment in the *Lautsi* case,[65] it was noted that secularism is a philosophical conviction and is not the same as denominational neutrality. The Chamber judgment in the case was criticized for favouring secularism over other world views:

> Neutrality requires a pluralist approach on the part of the State, not a secularist one. It encourages respect for all world views rather than a preference for one. To my mind, the Chamber Judgment was striking in its failure to recognise that secularism (which was the applicant's preferred belief or world view) was, in itself, one ideology among others. A preference for secularism over alternative world views—whether religious, philosophical or otherwise—is not a neutral option. The Convention requires that respect be given to the first applicant's convictions insofar as the education and teaching of her children was

[60] *Campbell and Cosans v United Kingdom*, (Apps. 7511/76 and 7743/76), 25 February 1982, Series A No 48, (1982) 4 EHRR 293, § 33; *Lautsi v Italy*, (App. 30814/06), 18 March 2011, § 64: includes the organization of the school environment.

[61] *Valsamis v Greece*, (App. 21787/93), 18 December 1996, (1997) 24 EHRR 294, ECHR 1996-VI, re-affirmed in *Folgerø v Norway*, (App. 15472/02), 29 June 2007 [GC], (2008) 46 EHRR 1147, ECHR 2007-VIII.

[62] *Valsamis v Greece*, (App. 21787/93), 18 December 1996, (1997) 24 EHRR 294, ECHR 1996-VI, § 25.

[63] *Campbell and Cosans v United Kingdom*, (Apps. 7511/76 and 7743/76), 25 February 1982, Series A No 48, (1982) 4 EHRR 293.

[64] § 36. [65] *Lautsi v Italy*, (App. 30814/06), 18 March 2011.

concerned. It does not require a preferential option for and endorsement of those convictions over and above all others.[66]

THE NATURE OF THE DUTY TO RESPECT RELIGIOUS AND PHILOSOPHICAL CONVICTIONS

In the *Valsamis* case,[67] the Strasbourg Court explained its view of the nature of the duty to respect religious and philosophical convictions. The duty arose in relation not only to the content of education and the manner of its provision but also to the performance of all of the functions assumed by a Contracting Party.[68] Respect, said the Court, involves more than acknowledgment. Quite how this will convert into practice will involve the judgment of national authorities, but it would seem to require that genuine consideration is made to the possibility of accommodations which will avoid conflicts in the delivery and organization of education with the religious or philosophical convictions of parents.

The Strasbourg Court re-affirmed its earlier case-law that respect for democratic values did not mean that the views of the majority must always prevail. Although individual interests had to be subordinated to the views of the majority in some circumstances, a balance had to be achieved which ensured the fair and proper treatment of minorities and avoided any abuse of the position of the majority group.[69]

APPLICATION OF THE DUTY

The *Kjeldsen* case[70] concerned compulsory sex education in Denmark. Sex education had been an optional subject in Danish State schools for many years. In 1970 a law was enacted to make it obligatory in these schools. According to the law, sex education would not be presented as a separate subject, but would be integrated with the teaching of other subjects. The parents of a number of children objected that this law infringed their right to ensure education and teaching in conformity with their own religious and philosophical convictions. The Strasbourg Court concluded that compulsory sex education did not violate Article 2 in failing to respect the wishes of the parents. The Court stressed that there must be no attempt at indoctrination that might be regarded as not respecting the parents' religious or philosophical convictions. The information must be presented in 'an objective, critical and pluralistic manner'. The sex education programme in Denmark was considered to be 'within the bounds of what a democratic State may regard as the public interest'.[71]

[66] Concurring Opinion of Judge Power, for a detailed discussion of the *Lautsi* case and the concept of secularism and neutrality see D. McGoldrick, 'Religion in the European Public Square and in European Public Life' (2011) HRLRev 11(3), 451–502.

[67] *Valsamis v Greece*, (App. 21787/93), 18 December 1996, (1997) 24 EHRR 294, ECHR 1996-VI, re-affirmed in *Folgerø v Norway*, (App. 15472/02), 29 June 2007 [GC], (2008) 46 EHRR 1147, ECHR 2007-VIII. *Appel Irrgang and others v Germany*, (App. 45216/07), Decision of 6 October 2009; *Lautsi v Italy*, (App. 30814/06), 18 March 2011.

[68] *Valsamis v Greece*, (App. 21787/93), 18 December 1996, (1997) 24 EHRR 294, ERCHR 1996-VI, § 27; *Lautsi v Italy*, (App. 30814/06), 18 March 2011, § 64.

[69] *Valsamis v Greece*, (App. 21787/93), 18 December 1996, (1997) 24 EHRR 294, ERCHR 1996-VI, § 27; *Lautsi v Italy*, (App. 30814/06), 18 March 2011, § 64.

[70] *Kjeldsen, Busk Madsen and Pedersen v Denmark*, (Apps. 5095/71, 5920/72, and 5926/72), 7 December 1976, Series A No 23, (1979–80) 1 EHRR 711.

[71] See also *Dojan v Germany*, (App. 319/08), Admissibility Decision of 13 September 2011.

A different view was taken in relation to parents' objections to corporal punishment in the *Campbell and Cosans* case.[72] At issue here was what, at best, was a philosophical belief. The Strasbourg Court stated that a philosophical belief must relate to 'a weighty and substantial aspect of human life and behaviour'. The parental objection to corporal punishment met this standard since it concerned 'the integrity of the person, the propriety or otherwise of the infliction of corporal punishment and the exclusion of the distress which risk of such punishment entails'. The Court concluded that the United Kingdom had violated Article 2 of the Protocol when the school offered the parents in question no guarantee that their son would not be beaten, and no alternative education was available for him.

Compulsory attendance at a school parade to mark National Day in Greece[73] was at issue in the *Valsamis* case.[74] The applicants were a family of Jehovah's Witnesses; part of their religious beliefs involved opposition to events with military overtones. The daughter was punished by the school for not attending the school parade, even though the school had been advised that attendance would be inconsistent with the child's religious beliefs. Her parents complained that their wishes in respect of the family's religious convictions had not been respected. Though there is little that can be criticized in the Strasbourg Court's discussion of the content of religious convictions, their application to the facts of this case, which resulted in a finding that there was no violation of the Article, is unsatisfactory. The Court noted that the school had exempted the daughter from religious classes at the school, and went on to express surprise that 'pupils can be required on pain of suspension...to parade outside the school precincts on a holiday'.[75] It concluded that there was nothing in the requirement to attend the school parade which 'could offend the applicants' pacifist convictions to an extent prohibited by the second sentence of Article 2 of Protocol 1', because such celebrations serve both pacifist objectives and the public interest.[76] Perhaps the Court wished to send out a signal in this case that respect for religious and philosophical convictions would depend on an objective assessment of the situation, rather than simply seeking to ascertain whether the beliefs and the consequences of them were genuinely held.

The view of the two dissenting judges is to be preferred. They indicated that there was nothing to suggest that the beliefs of the family were unfounded and unreasonable. In the light of those beliefs the requirement of attendance was disturbing to the family and humiliating to the daughter. The applicant family was under no obligation to share the views of the majority on the value of the commemorative events of 28 October. Participation was not a neutral act, and it could not be said that attendance formed part of the usual school curriculum. The minority concluded that there had been a violation of the Article.

The possibility of exemptions from certain parts of the school curriculum as a means of respecting parental wishes arose in the *Hasan and Eylem Zengin* case[77] concerning classes in religious culture and ethics. The predominant form of Islam followed in Turkey is Hanafism, one of the four theological schools of Sunni Islam. The applicants, a father and his daughter, were adherents of Alevism, which is more closely related to Sufism. The

[72] *Campbell and Cosans v United Kingdom*, (Apps. 7511/76 and 7743/76), 25 February 1982, Series A No 48, (1982) 4 EHRR 293.

[73] On 28 October each year, which marks the outbreak of war between Greece and Fascist Italy on 28 October 1940, and so recognizes Greek attachment to values of democracy, liberty, and human rights.

[74] *Valsamis v Greece*, (App. 21787/93), 18 December 1996, (1997) 24 EHRR 294, ECHR 1996-VI. See also *Efstratiou v Greece*, (App. 24095/94), 18 December 1996.

[75] *Valsamis v Greece*, (App. 21787/93), 18 December 1996, (1997) 24 EHRR 294, § 31.

[76] *Valsamis v Greece*, (App. 21787/93), 18 December 1996, (1997) 24 EHRR 294, § 31.

[77] *Hasan and Eylem Zengin v Turkey*, (App. 1448/04), 9 October 2007, (2008) 46 EHRR 1060, ECHR 2007-XI. See also *Dojan v Germany*, (App. 319/08), 13 September 2013.

practice of Alevism differs significantly from that of Hanafism. Classes in religious culture and ethics taught in Turkish schools are deeply rooted in the Sunni tradition. The request of the applicants for exemption from such classes was unsuccessful.

The Strasbourg Court concluded that the complaint required it to consider, first, whether the syllabus for religious culture and ethics was taught in an objective, critical and pluralist manner, and, secondly, whether appropriate accommodations were available to respect the religious beliefs of parents. Examination of the aims of the syllabus and, to a certain extent, its content led the Strasbourg Court to conclude that the syllabus failed to respect the religious diversity which prevailed in Turkish society in that there was no teaching relevant to the Alevi faith, which had a significant following in Turkey. As such, the education failed to meet the criteria of objectivity and pluralism. This led to the question of exemptions. In Turkey the subject is compulsory, although there is a possibility for exemption for children 'of Turkish nationality who belong to the Christian or Jewish religion'.[78] The unanimous view of the Court was that the exemption procedure was not an appropriate means of addressing the structural problem with the religious education which had been identified by the Court.

The circumstances of the *Folgerø* case[79] concerned a revision to the way in which Christianity, other forms of religious belief, and various philosophies were taught in Norway. An integrated approach was adopted, but it was established that preponderant weight was given to Christianity in the form of cultural heritage and the Evangelical Lutheran Religion, which was the official State religion in Norway, of which 86 per cent of the population were members. The applicants were parents of children in primary schools who were members of the Norwegian Humanist Association. Partial exemption from the integrated subject was possible. The applicants had sought unsuccessfully to have their children exempted from the whole subject. The Grand Chamber decided to deal with the case under Article 2 of Protocol 1 rather than Article 9, which the applicants had also pleaded. The key issue was whether the possibility of partial exemption was sufficient to afford respect for the philosophical convictions of the parents. The question sharply divided the Grand Chamber by nine votes to eight. The majority noted that partial exemption gave rise to considerable problems. It required clear communication about the delivery of the content of the revised curriculum, and, more particularly, required the parents to disclose in some detail 'intimate aspects of their own religious and philosophical convictions'.[80] The possibility of separating activity from knowledge also concerned the majority, since the idea behind the exemption was to offer exemption from an activity but not from the underlying knowledge. The majority also rejected the alternative of the parents educating their children in the private sector, since 'the existence of such a possibility could not dispense the State from its obligation to safeguard pluralism in State schools which are open to everyone.'[81] The outcome was as follows:

> Against this background, notwithstanding the many laudable legislative purposes stated in connection with the introduction of the [the integrated] subject in the ordinary primary and lower secondary schools, it does not appear that the respondent State took sufficient care that information and knowledge included in the curriculum be conveyed in an objective, critical and pluralistic manner for the purposes of Article 2 of Protocol 1.[82]

[78] *Hasan and Eylem Zengin*, § 72.

[79] *Folgerø v Norway*, (App. 15472/02), 29 June 2007 [GC], (2008) 46 EHRR 1147, ECHR 2007-VIII. Certain issues in this case have also been considered by the United Nations Human Rights Committee: see C. Evans, 'Religious Education in Public Schools: An International Human Rights Perspective' (2008) 8 HRLRev 449.

[80] *Folgerø*, § 98. [81] § 101. [82] § 102.

The minority of eight judges disagreed both on the substance of the teaching of religion and other philosophies (which they did not feel gave an over-preponderance to Christianity) in the new syllabus, and on the intrusiveness into the beliefs of the objecting parents in relation to the securing of a partial exemption. They concluded:

> Against this background, we are satisfied that the respondent State, in fulfilling its functions in respect of education and teaching, had taken care that information or knowledge included in the curriculum of the [integrated] subject was conveyed in an objective, critical and pluralistic manner. It could not be said to have pursued an aim of indoctrination contrary to the parents' right to respect for their philosophical convictions and thereby transgressing the limits implied by Article 2 of Protocol 1.[83]

In *Lautsi v Italy*,[84] the applicant complained about the presence of crucifixes in the classroom, which violated her parental rights under Article 2 of Protocol 1. The Chamber[85] found a violation. It stated that the crucifix was a religious symbol which was placed in a classroom from which the pupils could only extract themselves by making disproportionate sacrifices. The State had failed in its duty of neutrality. The Chamber judgment was premised on the protection of the rights of the minority from indoctrination by the State. However, the Chamber failed to discuss and apply the margin of appreciation.[86] The Grand Chamber disagreed and found there had not been a violation. The State did have a margin of appreciation in its efforts to reconcile education with respect for the philosophical conviction of parents, as long as it was neutral and impartial and maintained pluralism. The Grand Chamber noted that this does not 'prevent States from imparting through teaching or education information or knowledge of a directly or indirectly religious or philosophical kind. It does not even permit parents to object to the integration of such teaching or education in the school curriculum',[87] as long as at the same time information is conveyed in an objective, critical, and pluralistic manner. The Court then went on to examine the relevant factors in deciding if there had been a violation. First, there was a lack of consensus amongst European States regarding religious symbols in State schools. It noted the *Folgerø* judgment[88] and that the setting of the curriculum in that case fell within the margin of appreciation. The Court then concluded that the crucifix on a wall is essentially a passive symbol whose influence on pupils was not comparable to speech or participation in religious activities. It further noted that all religions were tolerated within the school system in Italy. The Court finally noted that there was no proselytism in the school and the applicant maintained her ability to enlighten and advise her children. Given these facts, the Court held there was no indoctrination in this case.[89]

The concurring opinions in *Lautsi*[90] underline the sensitivity that surrounds the issue of religious and philosophical beliefs in the classroom. In one concurring opinion, it is noted that the balancing act between the rights of parents to have their religious and philosophical beliefs respected and the right of a large segment of a given society to display or teach a certain belief, parental rights are increasingly assuming less importance in a multi-cultural society where children are being exposed to different opinions outside

[83] Joint dissenting opinion of Judges Wildhaber, Lorenzen, Bîrsan, Kovler, Steiner, Borrego Borrego, Hajiyev, and Jebens.

[84] *Lautsi v Italy*, (App. 30814/06), 18 March 2011.

[85] *Lautsi v Italy*, (App. 30814/06), Chamber Judgment of 3 November 2009.

[86] For discussion on the Chamber judgment see D. McGoldrick, 'Religion in the European Public Square and in European Public Life' (2011) HRLRev 11(3), 451–502.

[87] § 62.

[88] *Folgerø v Norway*, (App. 15472/02), 29 June 2007 [GC], (2008) 46 EHRR 1147, ECHR 2007-VIII.

[89] §§ 63–77.

[90] *Lautsi v Italy*, (App. 30814/06), 18 March 2011.

the classroom and the home. The role of both the school and the parent are becoming less important:

> as a result of the changed composition of our societies, it is increasingly difficult for a State to cater for the individual needs of parents on educational issues. I would go as far as saying that its main concern, and this is a valid concern, should be to offer children an education which will ensure their fullest integration into the society in which they live and prepare them, in the best possible way, to cope effectively with the expectations that that society has of its members. Although this characteristic of education is not a new one – it has existed since time immemorial – it has recently acquired more obvious importance because of the particularities of our era and the composition of societies today. Again, the duties of the State have largely shifted from concerns of parents to concerns of society at large, thus reducing the extent of the parents' ability to determine, outside the home, the kind of education that their children receive.[91]

In a robust defence of a State's right to maintain its cultural identity and to choose what system of belief it may or may not adhere to, Judge Bonello argued that the State's obligation is to refrain from interfering in Lautsi's right to freedom of belief:

> With or without a crucifix on a schoolroom wall, the Lautsis enjoyed the most absolute and untrammelled freedom of conscience and religion as demarcated by the Convention. The presence of a crucifix in a State classroom might conceivably be viewed as a betrayal of secularism and an unjustifiable failure of the regime of separation between Church and State – but these doctrines, however alluring and beguiling, are nowhere mandated by the Convention, nor are they necessary constitutive elements of the freedoms of conscience and of religion. It is for the Italian authorities, not for this Court, to enforce secularism if they believe it forms part, or should form part, of the Italian constitutional architecture.[92]

Two judges dissented, agreeing with the Chamber that where schooling is compulsory and religious symbols are present, the school is not being as strictly neutral as it should be. Even with a margin of appreciation, there is a positive obligation on the State to not impose a religious belief on a pupil in a situation that is against their will.[93]

The *Lautsi*[94] judgment reiterates the principles discussed in earlier case-law but also demonstrates the controversial nature of the teaching of beliefs in the education system. The Chamber's judgment invoked strong criticism from Member States and religious organizations, including unsurprisingly the Vatican. It has been described as the case that has had the most widespread opposition in the history of the Strasbourg Court.[95] Ten Member States supporting Italy joined the Grand Chamber hearing and ten others declared that there were unhappy with the Chamber judgment. Several NGOs and a member group of the European Parliament also intervened and only two of these intervened on behalf of the applicant.[96] The main concern of the interveners was the Chamber's conflation of secularism and neutrality and the failure to recognize a State's discretion in this area.

Following this line of cases, it is not easy to provide a principled explanation for the outcomes. In the *Belgian Linguistic* case, the Strasbourg Court declined to guarantee education

[91] Concurring Opinion of Judge Rozakis joined by Judge Vajić.

[92] Concurring Opinion of Judge Bonello, § 2.9.

[93] Dissenting Opinion of Judge Malinverni joined by Judge Kalaydjieva.

[94] *Lautsi v Italy*, (App. 30814/06), 18 March 2011.

[95] D. McGoldrick, 'Religion in the European Public Square and in European Public Life' (2011) HRLRev 11(3), 472.

[96] D. McGoldrick, 'Religion in the European Public Square and in European Public Life' (2011) HRLRev 11(3), 473.

in a particular language. In the *Kjeldsen* case, the Court declined to strike down compulsory sex education in the light of parental objections. In the *Valsamis* case, the Strasbourg Court declined to strike down compulsory attendance at a national commemorative occasion with military overtones found to be objectionable to those with religious beliefs a central part of which included pacifism. However, in the *Campbell and Cosans* case, the Court upheld the parental objections to corporal punishment. One possible explanation is that corporal punishment involves the physical integrity of the individual, whereas sex education reflects the duty of the State to provide children with information. Language education arouses great political and constitutional sensitivities in some regions of Europe, and parading as part of a national commemoration was not considered inconsistent with pacifist beliefs when the overall objectives of the National Day were taken into consideration. Finally the *Folgerø* and *Lautsi* cases indicate how fine the lines will be between permissible and impermissible accommodations to the religious and philosophical beliefs of parents. What is clear is that the Court will allow the State discretion in its implementation of education, that the State must maintain pluralism and that the parental right to have teaching or the educational setting in accordance with their religious or philosophical beliefs will be premised on whether there is indoctrination from the State. Given the nature of today's society, Article 2 of Protocol 1 does not guarantee a right not to be exposed to beliefs that are contrary to one's own,[97] a point emphasized in the concurring judgment in *Lautsi*.[98]

EDUCATION FOR CONVICTED PRISONERS

Special difficulties may arise in relation to the right to education of convicted prisoners, especially since Article 2 contains no escape clause allowing interference in the interests of public order, security, or otherwise. However, so far the Commission and the Court have found applications arguing for the right to education in prison inadmissible. In *Epistatu v Romania*,[99] the applicant was serving a prison sentence. He had completed his compulsory education but wished to continue his high school studies in prison. The authorities refused his request due to resource issues but did provide alternate courses in which he could enrol. The Court found that the application was manifestly ill-founded under Article 2 of Protocol 1 and reiterated previous admissibility decisions[100] by stating that the fact that the applicant was:

> only prevented from continuing in full-time education during the period corresponding to . . . lawful detention after conviction by a court cannot be construed as a deprivation of the right to education within the meaning of Article 2 of Protocol No.1 to the Convention.[101]

The Court also noted that there was no obligation on the State to provide ad hoc courses in prison.[102] It noted that alternative courses had been made available.

The admissibility decisions illustrate the wide discretion given to States in the provision of education in prisons. The reasoning of the Strasbourg Court in the *Belgian Linguistic*

[97] *Folgerø v Norway*, (App. 15472/02), 29 June 2007 [GC], (2008) 46 EHRR 1147, ECHR 2007-VIII; and *Appel Irrgang and others v Germany*, (App. 45216/07), Decision of 6 October 2009.

[98] Concurring Opinion of Judge Rozakis joined by Judge Vajić.

[99] *Epistatu v Romania*, (App. 29343/10), 24 September 2013.

[100] *Durmaz and others*, (Apps. 46506/99, 46569/99, 46570/99, and 46939/99), 4 September 2001; *Georgiou v Greece*, (App. 45138/98), Decision of 13 January 2000, unreported; *Sorabjee v United Kingdom*, (App. 23938/94), Eur. Comm. HR, Decision of 23 October 1995, unreported.

[101] § 62.

[102] § 63. See *Natoli v Italy*, (App. 26161/95), Commission decision of 18 May 1998, unreported.

case could be applied in that the Contracting Parties have no positive obligation to subsidize or provide specific educational provision for prisoners, but may not take steps to interfere with it (by for example providing some form of training in prison). In this sense, the obligation under the first sentence of Article 2 may be much less susceptible to positive obligations on a Contracting Party than the obligation in the second sentence of the Article.

CONCLUDING REMARKS

The scope and protection of the Article has been discussed in relatively few cases compared to other rights in the Convention. However, some important principles have emerged. The State has a margin of appreciation in the establishment and regulation of education within its jurisdiction at any given time. This includes a margin of appreciation in relation to resource allocation, the setting of the curriculum and examinations, and the regulation of entry to higher education. However, once it has established educational institutions, it must guarantee equal treatment in access and non-discrimination in the delivery of education. The State must also guarantee to respect the rights of parents with regard to religious and philosophical convictions. In this area, controversial cases such as *Lautsi* underline the balancing act the Court must perform in a multicultural society. The *Lautsi* judgment did clarify the Court's thinking on the meaning of neutrality and secularism, and the explicit use of proportionality in recent case-law has made the reasoning of the Court more transparent. It is also clear that the question of religion in the classroom will be dealt with under Article 2 of Protocol 1 rather than Article 9. Given the living instrument principle and following *Lautsi*, the ability of a parent to object to educational activities or symbols in the classroom may become increasingly difficult unless there is compelling evidence of indoctrination by the State.

22

THE RIGHT TO FREE ELECTIONS

INTRODUCTION

Article 3 of Protocol 1 provides:

> The High Contracting Parties undertake to hold free elections at reasonable intervals by secret ballot, under conditions which will ensure the free expression of the opinion of the people in the choice of the legislature.

All the provisions of the Convention, including Articles 13 to 18, apply equally to the rights guaranteed by the First Protocol.[1] Article 3, like Articles 1 and 2 of Protocol 1, but to a lesser extent, reflects the difficulties which prevented these rights from being incorporated in the original text of the Convention. Those difficulties are preserved in an unsatisfactory text, which is the result of a compromise, and which continues to give rise to problems of interpretation.[2]

Article 3 of Protocol 1 'presupposes the existence of a representative legislature, elected at reasonable intervals, as the basis of a democratic society'.[3] It goes further than requiring free elections; it requires that the exercise of political power be subject to a freely elected legislature. Examination of the rights and freedoms guaranteed by the Convention has shown the importance of all those rights and freedoms being guaranteed by law, and of all restrictions on them being subject to the law. Article 3 of Protocol 1 underpins the whole structure of the Convention in requiring that laws should be made by a legislature responsible to the people.[4] Free elections are thus a condition of the 'effective political democracy' referred to in the Preamble, and of the concept of a democratic society which runs through the Convention. The Strasbourg Court has repeatedly stated that Article 3 of Protocol 1 'enshrines a characteristic of an effective political democracy'.[5]

[1] Art. 5 of Protocol 1.

[2] Contrast the drafting of Article 25 of the International Covenant on Civil and Political Rights. See also J. Cremona, 'The right to free election in the European Convention of Human Rights' in P. Mahoney and others, *Protecting Human Rights: The European Perspective. Studies in Memory of Rolv Ryssdal*, (Carl Heymanns, Köln 2000), 309.

[3] App. 3321/67, *Denmark v Greece*; App. 3322/67, *Norway v Greece*; App. 3323/67, *Sweden v Greece*; and App. 3344/67, *Netherlands v Greece* ('the *Greek* case'), Report of 18 November 1969, (1969) 12 *Yearbook* 1, 179.

[4] Article 3 is in force for 45 Contracting Parties. Monaco and Switzerland are not parties to Protocol 1.

[5] *Mathieu-Mohin and Clerfayt v Belgium*, 2 March 1987, Series A No 113, (1988) 10 EHRR 1, § 47; *United Communist Party of Turkey and others v Turkey*, (App. 19392/92), 30 January 1998, (1998) 26 EHRR 121, ECHR 1998-I, § 45; and *Matthews v United Kingdom*, (App. 24833/94), 18 February 1999, (1999) 28 EHRR 361, ECHR 1999-I, § 42. See also *Refah Partisi (The Welfare Party) v Turkey*, (Apps. 41340/98, 41342/92, 41343/98, and 41344/98), 13 February 2003 [GC], (2003) 37 EHRR 1, ECHR 2003-II, §§ 86–95; and *Ždanoka v Latvia*, (App. 58278/00), 16 March 2006 [GC], (2007) 45 EHRR 478, ECHR 2006-IV, §§ 96–101.

The obligation in Article 3 is expressed as an undertaking by the Contracting Parties rather than in the form of a right or prohibition. This had led to suggestions that, unlike other provisions of the Convention, it was intended that it should only be invoked by States and not by individuals. But the Strasbourg Court has ruled that the interpretation of the provision requires the recognition of individual rights:[6] the right to vote[7] and the right to stand as a candidate for election.[8]

Free elections imply a genuine choice. Hence, as the Commission stated in the *Greek* case, the suspension of political parties is also contrary to Article 3.[9] On the other hand, it is consistent with the Convention, in accordance with Article 17, to prohibit political parties with totalitarian aims. The Strasbourg Court has also said that Article 11 does not protect political parties whose aims are incompatible with the Convention:

> It necessarily follows that a political party whose leaders incite violence or put forward a policy which fails to respect democracy or which is aimed at the destruction of democracy and the flouting of the rights and freedoms recognized in a democracy cannot lay claim to the Convention's protection against penalties imposed on those grounds.[10]

The Grand Chamber of the Strasbourg Court has summarized the nature of the Court's test under Article 3 of the First Protocol as follows:[11]

> 103. The rights guaranteed under Article 3 of Protocol No. 1 are crucial to establishing and maintaining the foundations of an effective and meaningful democracy governed by the rule of law. Nonetheless, these rights are not absolute. There is room for 'implied limitations', and Contracting States must be given a margin of appreciation in this sphere. The Court re-affirms that the margin in this area is wide.... There are numerous ways of organising and running electoral systems and a wealth of differences, *inter alia*, in historical development, cultural diversity and political thought within Europe, which it is for each Contracting State to mould into its own democratic vision....
>
> 104. It is however for the Court to determine in the last resort whether the requirements of Article 3 of Protocol No. 1 have been complied with; it has to satisfy itself that the conditions imposed on the rights to vote or to stand for election do not curtail the exercise of those rights to such an extent as to impair their very essence and deprive them of their effectiveness; that they are imposed in pursuit of a legitimate aim; and that the means employed are not disproportionate.... In particular, any such conditions must not thwart the free expression of the people in the choice of the legislature—in other words, they must reflect, or not run counter to, the concern to maintain the integrity and effectiveness of an electoral procedure aimed at identifying the will of the people through universal suffrage....

The number of complaints of violations of Article 3 of Protocol 1 is increasing, and there is evidence that the Strasbourg Court is giving fresh emphasis to this provision as essential to the foundations of democratic legitimacy of the State. Many, but by no means all, of these

[6] *Ždanoka v Latvia*, (App. 58278/00), 16 March 2006 [GC], (2007) 45 EHRR 478, ECHR 2006-IV, § 102, affirming *Mathieu-Mohin and Clerfayt v Belgium*, 2 March 1987, Series A No 113, (1988) 10 EHRR 1. But note the dissenting opinion of Judge Rozakis in *Ždanoka*, which argues that Article 3 does not imply the individual rights but actually provides for them.

[7] Referred to as the active element of the individual rights arising under the provision.

[8] Referred to as the passive element of the individual rights arising under the provision.

[9] App. 3321/67, *Denmark v Greece*; App. 3322/67, *Norway v Greece*; App. 3323/67, *Sweden v Greece*; and App. 3344/67, *Netherlands v Greece* ('the *Greek* case'), Report of 18 November 1969, (1969) 12 *Yearbook* 1, 180.

[10] *Refah Partisi (The Welfare Party) v Turkey*, (Apps. 41340/98, 41342/92, 41343/98, and 41344/98), 13 February 2003 [GC], (2003) 37 EHRR 1, ECHR 2003-II, § 98. See also discussion of these issues in ch.19.

[11] *Ždanoka v Latvia*, (App. 58278/00), 16 March 2006 [GC], (2007) 45 EHRR 478, ECHR 2006-IV.

cases come from the new democracies of central and eastern Europe. Issues arising from new democratic rights have often related to eligibility both to vote and to stand for election having regard to a person's past history within a totalitarian regime.

IMPLIED RESTRICTIONS

Although there is no room for implied limitations under Articles 8 to 11, the Strasbourg Court has established that implied limitations have a central role to play in the application and interpretation of all aspects of Article 3 of Protocol 1.[12] No assistance can really be drawn from the list of express limitations in Article 8 to 11; any limitation compatible with the principle of the rule of law and the general objectives of the Convention will be permitted.[13] In assessing the compatibility of such restrictions with the provisions of Article 3, the Strasbourg Court does not apply the tests of necessity and a pressing social need, but rather considers whether there has been arbitrariness or a lack of proportionality, and whether the restriction has interfered with the free expression of the opinion of the people.[14]

WHAT IS THE LEGISLATURE?

The wording of Article 3 only encompasses elections to the legislature. This raises the question of what constitutes the legislature. The Commission consistently stated that the term must be interpreted in the light of both the institutions established by the constitutions of the Contracting Parties and the international undertakings affecting the legislative powers of the body under consideration.[15] The Strasbourg Court takes a similar view.[16]

Article 3 does not apply to the appointment of the Head of State. In *Paksas v Lithuania* the Grand Chamber confirmed that Article 3 of Protocol 1 applies only to the election of the 'legislature' and that the part of the applicant's complaint about his removal from office or disqualification from standing for the presidency was incompatible *ratione materiae* with the provisions of the Convention.[17] Nor does Article 3 apply to elections to organs of a professional body, such as the Royal Society for the Cultivation of Flower Bulbs, even if certain legislative power has been conferred on it.[18]

Much more problematic are issues of whether regional authorities constitute the legislature. Of the Member States of the Council of Europe, Switzerland is the clearest proof that Article 3 cannot be confined to the central power. It must extend to the Swiss cantons, which have a very high degree of autonomy, and to all provincial legislatures where there

[12] *Ždanoka v Latvia*, (App. 58278/00), 16 March 2006 [GC], (2007) 45 EHRR 478, ECHR 2006-IV, § 115.

[13] *Yumak and Sadak v Turkey*, (App. 10226/03), 8 July 2008 [GC], (2009) 48 EHRR 61, ECHR 2008-nyr, § 119.

[14] *Yumak and Sadak v Turkey*, (App. 10226/03), 8 July 2008 [GC], (2009) 48 EHRR 61, ECHR 2008-nyr, § 119.

[15] For example, in App. 11123/84, *Tête v France*, Decision of 9 December 1987, (1987) 54 DR 52.

[16] *Mathieu-Mohin and Clerfayt v Belgium*, 2 March 1987, Series A No 113, (1988) 10 EHRR 1, § 53; and *Matthews v United Kingdom*, (App. 24833/94), 18 February 1999, (1999) 28 EHRR 361, ECHR 1999-I, § 40.

[17] *Paksas v Lithuania*, (App. 34932/04), 6 January 2011 [GC], ECHR 2011 (extracts). See also App. 15344/89, *C-L and L Habsburg-Lothringen v Austria*, Decision of 14 December 1989, (1990) 64 DR 210, 219; *Guliyev v Azerbaijan*, (App. 35584/02), Decision of 27 May 2004; and *Boškoski v the former Yugoslav Republic of Macedonia*, (App. 11676/04), Decision of 2 September 2004.

[18] App. 9926/82, *X v Netherlands*, Decision of 1 March 1983, (1983) 32 DR 274.

is a measure of decentralization of power. The only federal States apart from Switzerland in the Council of Europe are Austria, Bosnia and Herzegovina, Germany, and Russia.

In one case where a convicted prisoner was refused permission to vote, his complaints related both to *Land* elections and to federal elections in Germany, and the Commission did not distinguish between them.[19] It would certainly be incorrect to exclude *Land* elections from the scope of Article 3.

Local government in the non-federal Contracting Parties may lack the necessary autonomy to constitute the legislature. However, it should be noted that the Strasbourg Court's decision in the *Ahmed* case is expressly stated to be without prejudice to the question of whether local government elections in the United Kingdom are within the scope of Article 3.[20] By contrast, the position of the devolved parliaments of Scotland and Wales would seem to be clearly within the concept of a legislature.[21]

A distinction can be drawn in all modern States between the legislative bodies which have supreme legislative powers, and subordinate authorities which are empowered only to enact subordinate legislation, however general it may be in its application. The term 'legislature', used without qualification in Article 3, should be interpreted as extending to a provincial legislature which has a degree of autonomy, but not to such subordinate authorities. This was the view taken by the Commission in the case of English Metropolitan county councils[22] which could not be considered the legislature, since their powers are derivative and are defined by legislation with certain activities requiring approval or consent. They did not 'possess an inherent primary rulemaking power'.[23] In the recent decision of *McLean and Cole v United Kindgom*[24] the Court confirmed that local elections do not fall within the scope of the Article.

The status of the European Parliament and the application of Article 3 to elections to it arose in the *Matthews* case.[25] The applicant was a British citizen living in Gibraltar, which is a dependent territory of the United Kingdom with its own legislature. The EC Treaty applies to Gibraltar, although the operation of parts of the EC Treaty is excluded in relation to Gibraltar under the terms of the Treaty of Accession. Elections to the European Parliament are governed by the Act Concerning the Election of the Representatives of the European Parliament by Universal Suffrage of 20 September 1976; this was signed by the ministers of foreign affairs of the Member States of the European Communities and attached to Council Decision 76/787.[26] The Act provided for elections to take place only in the territory of the UK but not in Gibraltar. The Strasbourg Court rejected the argument of the respondent State that the European Parliament should be excluded from the ambit of elections within the scope of Article 3 on the ground that it is a supranational rather than a national representative organ. The respondent State then argued that it lacked the

[19] App. 2728/66, *X v Federal Republic of Germany*, Decision of 6 October 1967, (1967) 10 *Yearbook* 336.

[20] *Ahmed and others v United Kingdom*, (App. 22954/93), 2 September 1998, (2000) 29 EHRR 1, ECHR 1999-VI, § 76. In *Hirst v United Kingdom (No.2)*, (App. 74025/01), Chamber Judgment of 30 March 2004, this judgment says in passing that local elections fall outside the scope of the Article: § 37. The judgment of the Grand Chamber of 6 October 2005 does not address this issue.

[21] Belgium and Spain are also among the Contracting Parties which operate systems of devolved government.

[22] App. 11391/85, *Booth-Clibborn and others v United Kingdom*, Decision of 5 July 1985, (1985) 43 DR 236.

[23] 248.

[24] *McLean and Cole v United Kindgom* (dec), (App. 12626/13 and 2522/12), 11 June 2013.

[25] *Matthews v United Kingdom*, (App. 24833/94), 18 February 1999; (1999) 28 EHRR 361, ECHR 1999-I. For a discussion of the case, see K. Muylle, 'Is the European Parliament a "Legislator"?' (2000) 6 EPL 243; and T. King, 'Ensuring human rights review of inter-governmental acts in Europe' (2000) 25 ELRev 79; and I. Canor, '*Primus inter pares*. Who is the ultimate guardian of fundamental rights in Europe?' (2000) 25 ELRev 3.

[26] [1976] OJ L278/5.

attributes of a legislature, which they defined as the power to initiate and adopt legislation.[27] After analysing the powers of the European Parliament and their impact upon Gibraltar, the Strasbourg Court concluded that the European Parliament constitutes 'part of the legislature of Gibraltar for the purposes of Article 3 of Protocol 1'.[28]

ELECTORAL SYSTEMS

The Grand Chamber has summarized the requirements of Article 3 in relation to the choice of electoral system as follows:

> The Court reiterates that the Contracting States enjoy a wide margin of appreciation when it comes to determination of the type of ballot through which the free expression of the opinion of the people in the choice of the legislature is mediated. In that regard, Article 3 of Protocol No. 1 goes no further than prescribing 'free' elections held at 'reasonable intervals' 'by secret ballot' and 'under conditions which will ensure the free expression of the opinion of the people'. Subject to that reservation, it does not create any 'obligation to introduce a specific system' such as proportional representation or majority voting with one or two ballots....[29]

A fair and proper electoral system under Article 3 requires a fair and proper system of voter registration, supported by effective electoral commissions.[30] Very weighty considerations will be needed to justify the disenfranchisement of sections of the electorate.[31] The way in which the outcome of elections is reviewed must also be fair and not arbitrary.[32] So the decision to annul the vote in four electoral divisions in elections in Ukraine in response to complaints about certain irregularities within those divisions was considered arbitrary and not proportionate to any legitimate aim.[33]

Although Article 3, in contrast to Article 21(3) of the Universal Declaration of Human Rights, does not refer expressly to universal suffrage, the Commission, reversing an earlier position, expressed the view that Article 3 implies recognition of universal suffrage.[34] The Strasbourg Court has agreed.[35] On the other hand, Article 3 is somewhat different in form from that in which the other rights in the Convention and Protocol are expressed. It does not provide in absolute terms that everyone has the right to vote. If a person complains that he or she is disqualified from voting, the Strasbourg Court's task is to consider whether such disqualification affects the free expression of the opinion of the people under Article 3.[36]

[27] The Parliament's most extensive legislative functions arise under the co-decision procedure set out in Article 251 EC, under which the European Parliament can block the progress of legislative measures proposed by the Commission and supported by the Council.

[28] *Matthews v United Kingdom*, (App. 24833/94), 18 February 1999; (1999) 28 EHRR 361, ECHR 1999-I, § 54. For the 2004 and 2009 elections to the European Parliament, Gibraltar was attached to the constituency covering Cornwall.

[29] *Yumak and Sadak v Turkey*, (App. 10226/03), 8 July 2008 [GC], (2009) 48 EHRR 61, ECHR 2008-nyr, § 110.

[30] *Georgian Labour Party v Georgia*, (App. 9103/04), 8 July 2008, ECHR 2008.

[31] *Georgian Labour Party v Georgia*, (App. 9103/04), 8 July 2008, ECHR 2008.

[32] See, for example, *Paschalidis, Koutmeridis and Zaharakis v Greece*, (Apps. 27863/05, 28422/05, and 28028/05), 10 April 2008.

[33] *Kovach v Ukraine*, (App. 39424/02), 7 February 2008, ECHR 2008.

[34] App. 2728/66, *X v Federal Republic of Germany*, Decision of 6 October 1967, (1967) 10 *Yearbook* 336, at 338; see also App. 5302/71, *X & Y v United Kingdom*, Decision of 11 October 1973, (1973) 44 CD 29, at 48.

[35] *Mathieu-Mohin and Clerfayt v Belgium*, 2 March 1987, Series A No 113, (1988) 10 EHRR 1, § 51.

[36] *Gitonas and others v Greece*, (Apps. 18747/91, 19376/92, 19379/92, 28208/95, and 27755/95), 1 July 1997, (1998) 26 EHRR 691, ECHR 1997-IV, § 39.

The formulation is important, if only because of the question of the effect of Article 14. The Commission accepted that certain categories of citizen may be excluded from voting, without the free expression of the opinion of the people being prejudiced. Thus, Belgians resident in the Congo complained unsuccessfully that they were denied the right to vote in the metropolis.[37] On the other hand, wider disqualifications, such as, for example, the disqualification of women, might be considered as affecting the free expression of the opinion of the people, even without regard to Article 14. An argument to this effect might be based on the general spirit of the Convention as well as the modern understanding of a democratic society.

In any event, it is clear that Switzerland regarded as an obstacle to ratification of the Convention and First Protocol the fact that women had only recently acquired the right to vote in federal legislative elections and did not have this right in certain of the cantons.[38] The former disability was removed by revision of the federal constitution.[39]

The scope of the rights embedded in Article 3 was considered in the *Mathieu-Mohin and Clerfayt* case.[40] The case concerned the complex rules operating in Belgian elections to ensure appropriate representation of the French-speaking and Dutch-speaking communities. Before considering the application of Article 3 to the particular facts of the case, the Strasbourg Court provided authoritative guidance on the scope of the rights protected by the Article. The Strasbourg Court approved the Commission's decisions in which it had held that the provision included a right of universal suffrage,[41] which embraced both the right to vote and the right to stand for election to the legislature.[42] But the Court went on to confirm that these rights are not absolute and that there is room for implied limitations. States enjoy a wide margin of appreciation as to the conditions they attach to the exercise of the right. However, the Court:

> has to satisfy itself that the conditions do not curtail the rights in question to such an extent as to impair their very essence and deprive them of their effectiveness; that they are imposed in pursuance of a legitimate aim; and that the means employed are not disproportionate.... in particular, such conditions must not thwart 'the free expression of the opinion of the people in the choice of the legislature'.[43]

The Strasbourg Court went on to declare that Article 3 does not create any obligation to introduce a specific system of elections and States enjoy a wide margin of appreciation in the choice of voting system. The key test is whether the chosen system provides for the free expression of the opinion of the people in the choice of the legislature.

The dissenting opinions related to the specific facts of the case, but a concurring opinion of Judge Pinheiro Farinha expressed reservations about the Court's approach to legislative systems which have two chambers. The majority had said that Article 3 applies 'to the election of the "legislature", or at least one of its chambers if it has two or more'.[44] Judge Pinheiro Farinha considered this wording 'inadequate and dangerous':

> As it stands, it would allow of a system at variance with 'the opinion of the people in the choice of the legislature' and might even lead to a corporative, elitist or class system which did not respect democracy.

[37] App. 1065/61, *X v Belgium*, Decision of 30 May 1961, (1961) 4 *Yearbook* 260.

[38] Federal Council's Report to the Federal Assembly on the Convention, (1969) 12 *Yearbook* 502, 509–10.

[39] But note that Switzerland is not a party to Protocol 1.

[40] *Mathieu-Mohin and Clerfayt v Belgium*, 2 March 1987, Series A No 113, (1988) 10 EHRR 1.

[41] App. 2728/66, *X v Federal Republic of Germany*, Decision of 6 October 1967, (1967) 10 *Yearbook* 336.

[42] Apps. 6745–46/76, *W, X, Y and Z v Belgium*, Decision of 30 May 1975, (1975) 18 *Yearbook* 244.

[43] *Mathieu-Mohin and Clerfayt v Belgium*, 2 March 1987, Series A No 113, (1988) 10 EHRR 1, § 52.

[44] *Mathieu-Mohin and Clerfayt*, § 53.

> In my opinion, we should say 'or at least of one of its chambers if it has two or more, on the twofold condition that the majority of the membership of the legislature is elected and that the chamber or chambers whose members are not elected does or do not have greater powers than the chamber that is freely elected by secret ballot.'

Some years ago the Liberal Party in the UK sought to challenge the simple majority voting system used in British elections on the grounds that it violated Article 3 when read in conjunction with Article 14 in that the effect of the chosen voting system was to give less weight to votes cast for Liberal Party candidates than for the Conservative or Labour Party candidates.[45] It was conceded by the applicants that the simple majority voting system could not be a violation of Article 3 when read alone, and the Commission noted that this concession was rightly made. But the Commission, in deciding that the application was manifestly ill-founded, also concluded that Article 3 when read in conjunction with Article 14 did not admit of the argument that there was any entitlement to the protection of equal voting influence for all voters.

The extent of Strasbourg supervision of electoral systems has been revisited by the Grand Chamber of the Strasbourg Court in the *Yumak and Sadak* case.[46] The applicants challenged the requirement in the Turkish electoral system for parties to reach a 10 per cent threshold of the national vote before they became entitled to representatives in the national Parliament. It was claimed that this threshold was the highest in Europe. The legitimacy of any national system will be judged in the context of 'the historical and political factors specific to each State.'[47] In the context of proportional representation systems, the Strasbourg Court acknowledged that thresholds served the purpose of avoiding excessive fragmentation and ensuring the emergence of a sufficiently clear and coherent political will.

In the context of the Turkish electoral system, the Grand Chamber accepted that the rules on thresholds served a legitimate aim: avoiding excessive and debilitating parliamentary fragmentation and strengthening governmental stability.[48] In considering the proportionality of the requirement, the Strasbourg Court noted that the threshold was the highest in Europe, but appears to conclude that the outcome of the elections of which the applicants complained was, in part, determined by the electoral strategy which had been adopted by their parties. The Court also noted certain observations made by the Constitutional Court in Turkey. The outcome was a finding by thirteen votes to four that there was that no violation of Article 3. However, there is a veiled warning that the threshold should be lowered.

Grosaru v Romania concerned the allocation of a parliamentary seat post-election and emphasized the need for clarity of electoral law in respect of the allocation of seats.[49] The applicant complained that the Romanian authorities had refused to allocate him a seat as a member of parliament representing the Italian minority in the parliamentary elections of 2000, despite the fact that he had secured the greatest number of votes at national level. The Italian Community seat was instead allocated to another candidate who had secured a large number of votes in a single constituency. The Court concluded that the lack of clarity of the electoral law as regards national minorities as well as the lack of sufficient guarantees as to the impartiality of the bodies responsible for examining the applicant's challenges impaired the very essence of the rights guaranteed by Article 3 of Protocol 1.[50]

[45] App. 8765/79, *Liberal Party, R and P v United Kingdom*, Decision of 18 December 1980, (1981) 21 DR 211.

[46] *Yumak and Sadak v Turkey*, (App. 10226/03), 8 July 2008 [GC], (2009) 48 EHRR 61, ECHR 2008.

[47] § 111. [48] § 125. [49] *Grosaru v Romania*, (App. 78039/01), 2 March 2010, ECHR 2010.

[50] § 57.

Issues related to the funding of political parties are more likely to give rise to issues under Article 11 than under Article 3 of Protocol 1.[51] Issues relating to media coverage of elections may be considered under Article 3, however. In *The Communist Party of Russia and others v Russia*, the applicants complained that the media coverage of the 2003 Russian elections had been biased, which had been detrimental to the opposition parties and candidates.[52] They argued that unequal media coverage had meant that the elections were not 'free' and were thus incompatible with Article 3 of Protocol 1. The applicants acknowledged that Russian law guaranteed neutrality of the broadcasting companies but argued that this was not respected in practice on the basis that TV coverage had been predominantly hostile to the opposition parties and candidates and that this was the result of political manipulation. The Russian Supreme Court had not been convinced of the existence of political manipulation and the Strasbourg Court concluded that it did not have sufficient evidence to discard the Supreme Court's conclusion on that point.

The Court proceeded, however, to question whether 'the State was under any positive obligation under Article 3 of Protocol No. 1 to ensure that media coverage by the State-controlled mass-media was balanced and compatible with the spirit of "free elections", even where no direct proof of deliberate manipulation was found.'[53] The Court concluded that the respondent State did take steps to guarantee some visibility of opposition parties and candidates on Russian TV and secure editorial independence and neutrality of the media. Although these arrangements did not secure de facto equality of all competing political forces in terms of their presence on TV screens, in light of the State's margin of appreciation, this did not amount to a failure to a violation of Article 3.

The case illustrates the close relationship between Article 3 of Protocol 1 and Article 10's protection for freedom of expression. The Court's acknowledgment of a State's positive obligations in this regard, extending beyond the avoidance of deliberate manipulation of the media, is significant, but the reluctance to restrict the margin of appreciation suggests that some degree of a lack of neutrality in media coverage of elections will be tolerated by the Court, especially where a domestic court has heard and rejected the complaint. The Court seems keen to emphasize, both in its remarks and final decision, that Article 3 'was not conceived as a code on electoral matters, designed to regulate all aspects of the electoral process.'[54]

THE RIGHT TO VOTE

It has long been the position of the Commission that the right to vote and the right to stand for election to the legislature may be subject to legitimate restrictions imposed by the State.[55] The Strasbourg Court has adopted the same position.[56] It takes a more rigorous approach to restrictions of the right to vote (the active aspect of the rights under Article 3), than in relation to the passive aspect of the right to stand for election. The Grand Chamber summarized the position in this way in the *Ždanoka* case:[57]

[51] See, for example, *Parti Nationaliste Basque—Organisation Régionale D'Iparralde v France*, (App. 71251/01), 7 June 2007, (2008) 47 EHRR 1037, ECHR 2007-VII.

[52] *The Communist Party of Russia and others v Russia*, (App. 29400/05), 19 June 2012.

[53] § 123.

[54] § 108.

[55] App. 6850/74, *X, Y and Z v Federal Republic of Germany*, Decision of 18 May 1976, (1976) 5 DR 90 and App. 11391/85, *Booth-Clibborn and others v United Kingdom*, 5 July 1985, (1985) 43 DR 236.

[56] *Mathieu-Mohin and Clerfayt v Belgium*, 2 March 1987, Series A No 113, (1988) 10 EHRR 1, § 52.

[57] *Ždanoka v Latvia*, (App. 58278/00), 16 March 2006 [GC], (2007) 45 EHRR 478, ECHR 2006-IV.

> ...while the test relating to the 'active' aspect of Article 3 of Protocol No. 1 has usually included a wider assessment of the proportionality of the statutory provisions disqualifying a person or a certain group of persons from the right to vote, the Court's test in relation to the 'passive' aspect of the above provision has been limited largely to a check on the absence of arbitrariness in the domestic procedures leading to disqualification of an individual from standing as a candidate...

Depriving persons abroad of the right to vote in their country of origin is permissible.[58] In *Sitaropoulos and Giakoumopoulos v Greece*, the applicants complained that the Greek legislature had not made the necessary arrangements enabling Greek expatriates to vote in parliamentary elections from their current place of residence.[59] A Chamber had found a violation of Article 3 of Protocol 1 but the Grand Chamber disagreed, noting that a variety of different approaches are adopted by States in respect of both whether, and how, citizens living abroad may exercise the right to vote. In *Shindler v United Kingdom*,[60] the Court found that the refusal to give a vote to expatriates who have not been resident in the UK for fifteen years or more was a proportionate restriction. However, permissible language requirements cannot be set at a disproportionately high level or be operated in an arbitrary manner with the effect that individuals are disenfranchised.[61] Any question of disqualification must be surrounded by procedural fairness and legal certainty.[62]

In the *Aziz* case[63] the Strasbourg Court found a violation of Article 3 where a Turkish Cypriot resident in the non-occupied south of the island was denied a vote on the ground that the constitutional arrangements[64] had provided for separate representation of the Greek Cypriot and Turkish Cypriot communities. The Court referred to a 'manifest lack of legislation resolving the ensuing problems.'[65]

In *Campagnano v Italy*, depriving persons of their vote simply by reason of being declared bankrupt was found to serve no purpose other than to belittle persons who had been made bankrupt irrespective of whether they had committed an offence. Such a provision was found not to serve any legitimate aim within Article 3 of Protocol 1.[66]

In an early case,[67] the Commission considered that depriving convicted prisoners of the right to vote did not violate the Convention. This was so even if the conviction is for conscientious objection to military service by a person who has refused to comply with the formalities for acquiring objector status.[68]

The fresh consideration of the issues arising from an automatic statutory ban on voting imposed on convicted prisoners ultimately came before the Grand Chamber in the

[58] App. 7730/76, *X v United Kingdom*, Decision of 28 February 1979, (1979) 15 DR 137.

[59] *Sitaropoulos and Giakoumopoulos v Greece*, (App. 42202/07), 15 March 2012, ECHR 2012.

[60] *Shindler v United Kingdom*, (App. 19840/09), 7 May 2013.

[61] *Podkolzina v Latvia*, (App. 46726/99), 9 April 2002, ECHR 2002-II. The applicant was a member of the Russian-speaking minority, whose language competence was in issue.

[62] *Podkolzina v Latvia*, (App. 46726/99), 9 April 2002, ECHR 2002-II; *Russian Conservative Party of Entrepreneurs and others v Russia*, (Apps. 55066/00 and 55638/00), 11 January 2007, (2008) 46 EHRR 863, ECHR 2007-I; *Krasnov and Skuratov v Russia*, (Apps. 17864/04 and 21396/04), 19 July 2007, (2008) 47 EHRR 1016, ECHR 2007-IX; and *Sarukhanyan v Armenia*, (App. 38978/03), 27 May 2008.

[63] *Aziz v Cyprus*, (App. 69949/01), 22 June 2004, (2005) 41 EHRR 164, ECHR 2004-V.

[64] Which had long since ceased to operate.

[65] *Aziz v Cyprus*, (App. 69949/01), 22 June 2004, (2005) 41 EHRR 164, ECHR 2004-V, § 29. The Court also found a separate violation of Article 14 when read in conjunction with Article 3 of Protocol 1.

[66] *Campagnano v Italy*, (App. 77955/01), 23 March 2006, ECHR 2006-IV.

[67] App. 2728/66, *X v Federal Republic of Germany*, Decision of 6 October 1967, (1967) 10 *Yearbook* 336.

[68] App. 9914/82, *H v Netherlands*, Decision of 4 July 1983, (1983) 33 DR 274.

Hirst case.[69] The applicant[70] complained that the blanket ban on voting in elections in the United Kingdom violated his rights under Article 3 of Protocol 1. The applicant argued that little thought had been given by the respondent State to the justification for the ban on voting, and earlier legislation had been consolidated without any debate on the question. The blanket ban was disproportionate and arbitrary. The respondent State noted that, among the Contracting States, eighteen countries imposed no restriction on the right of prisoners to vote, thirteen countries had a blanket ban, and twelve countries imposed some restrictions. It was argued that the purpose of the ban in the UK was a combined one in order to prevent crime, to punish offenders, and to enhance civic responsibility and respect for the rule of law. It only operated where an immediate custodial sentence was imposed and so was not disproportionate in effect since it was linked to the seriousness of the criminal conduct.

In determining that a blanket ban on voting went beyond a State's margin of appreciation, the Court took note of the discussion of similar issues in the Canadian Supreme Court.[71] The Strasbourg Court noted that the loss of voting rights plays no part in the sentencing process in the UK, and the Court could see no rational link between the deprivation of the vote and punishment for a crime. Nor was the Court convinced that the claim that the loss of the vote enhanced civic responsibility had merit; no similar bar was applied to those whose crime might be considered to be equally anti-social or 'uncitizen-like' upon whom no immediate custodial sentence was imposed. Though the Court clearly had serious doubts about the legitimacy of the aims put forward by the UK, it nevertheless refrained from determining that they were not legitimate, preferring to decide that the blanket ban was a disproportionate response to meeting those aims:

> The Court would observe that there is no evidence that the legislature in the United Kingdom has ever sought to weigh the competing interests or to assess the proportionality of a blanket ban on the right of convicted prisoners to vote.[72]

The Grand Chamber concluded that:

> a general, automatic and indiscriminate restriction on a vitally important Convention right must be seen as falling outside any acceptable margin of appreciation, however wide that margin might be....[73]

There had accordingly been a violation of Article 3.

Subsequently, the Court returned to the issue of the exclusion of prisoners from voting in *Frodl v Austria*.[74] The Austrian law adopted less of a blanket approach than the one in *Hirst* as, rather than applying automatically to all prisoners, it restricted disenfranchisement to those serving a prison sentence exceeding one year and only to convictions for offences committed with intent. The Court still found a violation of Article 3 of Protocol 1, however on the basis that the '*Hirst* test' not only precluded automatic and blanket restrictions but also as 'an essential element' required that 'the decision on disenfranchisement should be taken by a judge, taking into account the particular circumstances, and that there

[69] *Hirst v United Kingdom (No. 2)*, (App. 74025/01), 6 October 2005 [GC], (2006) 42 EHRR 849, ECHR 2005-IX.

[70] Who was serving a discretionary life sentence following his conviction for manslaughter.

[71] In *Sauvé v Attorney General of Canada (No.2)*, [2002] 3 SCR 519.

[72] *Hirst v United Kingdom (No. 2)*, (App. 74025/01), 6 October 2005 [GC], (2006) 42 EHRR 849, ECHR 2005-IX, § 79.

[73] § 82.

[74] *Frodl v Austria*, (App. 20201/04), 8 April 2010.

must be a link between the offence committed and issues relating to elections and democratic institutions.'[75] In the Court's view in *Frodl*, the purpose of these criteria is to ensure that 'such a measure is accompanied by specific reasoning given in an individual decision explaining why in the circumstances of the specific case disenfranchisement was necessary, taking the above elements into account.'[76] This onerous requirement was not mentioned in the next case to consider the issue of prisoner voting.

In *Greens and M.T. v United Kingdom*, the Court found another violation in respect of disenfranchisement of prisoners due to the UK's failure to execute the Court's judgment in *Hirst*.[77] It refers to the approach in *Frodl* but emphasizes that the Grand Chamber in *Hirst* declined to provide any detailed guidance as to the steps required by the UK and notes that the Court's own role is a subsidiary one,[78] presumably implying that the *Frodl* requirement of an individual decision by a judge was not necessarily required.

The saga continued in *Scoppola v Italy (No. 3)* in which a Chamber used the *Frodl* requirement to find Italy in violation for the removal of the applicant's right to vote which resulted from him being barred from public office, an ancillary penalty applied to any individual sentenced to life imprisonment or a prison sentence of five years or more.[79] Before the Grand Chamber, the UK was an intervening party and argued that the Court should revisit its decision in *Hirst*. This followed a parliamentary debate in which the UK members of parliament confirmed, by an overwhelming majority, the UK's existing blanket ban on prisoner voting.[80] The Grand Chamber declined to do as the UK Government wished in *Scoppola* and instead confirmed its judgment in *Hirst*. However, it did reject the more stringent requirements of the Chamber in *Frodl*:

> The Grand Chamber points out that the *Hirst* judgment makes no explicit mention of the intervention of a judge among the essential criteria for determining the proportionality of a disenfranchisement measure. The relevant criteria relate solely to whether the measure is applicable generally, automatically and indiscriminately within the meaning indicated by the Court (see paragraphs 85, 86 and 96 above). While the intervention of a judge is in principle likely to guarantee the proportionality of restrictions on prisoners' voting rights, such restrictions will not necessarily be automatic, general and indiscriminate simply because they were not ordered by a judge. Indeed, the circumstances in which the right to vote is forfeited may be detailed in the law, making its application conditional on such factors as the nature or the gravity of the offence committed.[81]

Furthermore, the Grand Chamber seemed intent on distancing itself from any suggestion that the question of disenfranchisement should be decided by the judicial rather than the legislative branch of government. It acknowledged that in *Hirst* it had noted the lack of reference to the issue of disenfranchisement by the criminal courts when sentencing but was at pains to point out that this aspect of its judgment had not been repeated in paragraph 82 which set out the criteria for assessing the proportionality of the impugned measure.[82] This might perhaps be viewed as an attempt at compromise by the Court given the heated political context in which the issue of prisoner voting is currently discussed.[83]

[75] § 34. [76] § 35.

[77] *Greens and M.T. v United Kingdom*, (App. 60041/08 and 60054/08), 23 November 2010, ECHR 2010 (extracts).

[78] § 113. [79] *Scoppola v Italy (No. 3)*, (App. 126/05), 22 May 2012.

[80] HC Debs, 10 Feb 2011, vol 523, col 493.

[81] *Scoppola v Italy (No. 3)*, (App. 126/05), 22 May 2012, § 99. [82] § 100.

[83] The issue has yet to be resolved in the UK. In a recent decision, the Supreme Court refused to depart from the reasoning in *Hirst* and *Scoppola*, noting that the Grand Chamber was unlikely to revise its view and concluding that 'There is on this point no prospect of any further meaningful dialogue between UK

Finally, the Grand Chamber concluded that the Italian system did not have the general, automatic, and indiscriminate character of the UK system held to be in violation in *Hirst* as prisoners serving short sentences were not disenfranchised. The Italian system, unlike that of the UK, was not disproportionate to what the Court acknowledges is a legitimate aim of preventing crime and enhancing civic responsibility and respect for the rule of law.[84] By contrast a Russian ban on voting that applied indiscriminately to all convicted prisoners was recently found to be a violation of Article 3 of Protocol 1.[85]

The indiscriminate nature of a voting ban was also the subject of the Court's criticism in *Alajos Kiss v Hungary*.[86] In this case, the applicant had lost his right to vote as the result of the imposition of an automatic, blanket restriction on the franchise of those under partial guardianship. The Court rejected the suggestion that an absolute bar on voting by any person under partial guardianship, irrespective of personal capacity, falls within the State's margin of appreciation. In addition to the general principle noted in *Hirst* that the margin of appreciation in this context is not all-embracing, the Court also recognized that 'if a restriction on fundamental rights applies to a particularly vulnerable group in society, who have suffered considerable discrimination in the past, such as the mentally disabled, then the State's margin of appreciation is substantially narrower and it must have very weighty reasons for the restrictions in question.'[87] Hungary was therefore found to be in violation of Article 3 of Protocol 1 for its automatic disenfranchisement of persons under partial guardianship.

The *Santoro* case[88] concerned the loss of voting rights by an individual regarded as 'socially dangerous' whom the Italian authorities had placed under special police supervision. One consequence was that the individual lost his right to vote. The Strasbourg Court does not take issue with the application of the provisions under which the applicant became disenfranchised, but does require that the administrative machinery for implementing the disqualification and for reinstating the individual on the electoral role does not involve undue delay. Where it does, there will be a violation of Article 3, as in this case.

THE RIGHT TO STAND FOR ELECTION

The Strasbourg Court, in the *Mathieu-Mohin and Clerfayt* case,[89] confirmed the long-held view of the Commission that States may impose certain restrictions on the right to stand for election. So a requirement that a certain number of signatures be obtained as qualification to stand as a candidate is a reasonable requirement.[90] A fair system of deposits will not violate the Convention.[91] Nor will restriction on the return of deposits and the reimbursement of election expenses in a system of proportional representation where the lists do

Courts and Strasbourg.' (per Lord Mance, § 34, *R (on the application of Chester) v Secretary of State for Justice; McGeoch v The Lord President of the Council and another* [2013] UKSC 63).

[84] For academic discussion, prior to the Grand Chamber judgment in *Scoppola*, see S. Briant, 'Dialogue, Diplomacy and Defiance: Prisoners' Voting Rights at Home and in Strasbourg' [2011] EHRLRev 243; C.R.G. Murray, 'Playing for Time: Prisoner Disenfranchisement under the ECHR after *Hirst v United Kingdom*' (2011) 22 *King's Law Journal* 309.

[85] *Anchugov and Gladkov v Russia* (App. 11157/04 and 15162/05), 4 July 2013.

[86] *Alajos Kiss v Hungary*, (App. 38832/06), 20 May 2010.

[87] § 42.

[88] *Santoro v Italy*, (App. 36681/97), 1 July 2004, (2006) 42 EHRR 705, ECHR 2003-I.

[89] *Mathieu-Mohin and Clerfayt v Belgium*, 2 March 1987, Series A No 113, (1988) 10 EHRR 1, § 52.

[90] App. 6850/74, *X, Y and Z v Federal Republic of Germany*, Decision of 18 May 1976, (1976) 5 DR 90.

[91] *Sukhovetskyy v Ukraine*, (App. 13716/02), 28 March 2006, (2007) 44 EHRR 1185, ECHR 2006-VI.

not obtain 5 per cent of the vote.[92] Restrictions which amount effectively to retrospective disqualifications from standing as a candidate will violate Article 3.[93]

The Greek rules prohibiting public officials from standing for election within a period of thirty-three months of holding public office were considered by the Strasbourg Court in the *Gitonas* case.[94] The applicants had stood for election, been elected, and had their election annulled by the Greek courts. The applicants argued that the Greek rules were imprecise and incoherent, and that far more senior posts did not carry the exclusion which applied to them. In a strongly factually based judgment, the Strasbourg Court disagreed with the Commission[95] in finding that there was no violation of Article 3.

Restrictions on the ability of certain local government officials to stand in local government elections in the United Kingdom were challenged in the *Ahmed* case.[96] In order to retain their posts in local government, the applicants all had to give up their political activities on behalf of political parties. They claimed that the requirement to do so breached, among other provisions, their right to full participation in the electoral process as guaranteed by Article 3 of Protocol 1. The regulations, they argued, had the effect of limiting without justification the electorate's choice of candidates. But the Court found no violation, accepting that the restrictions served the legitimate purpose of securing the political impartiality of civil servants.

Where the right to stand for election touches on the issue of individuals forming a political party, the Strasbourg Court has generally determined these issues under Article 11 and has, until recently, avoided addressing the question of whether the right to form and maintain a political party falls within the scope of Article 3 of Protocol 1.[97] However, in the *Sadak* case[98] the Strasbourg Court did consider the impact of Article 3 of Protocol 1 in a situation in which the dissolution of a political party[99] in Turkey had the automatic effect that the applicants forfeit their parliamentary seats. The Court found that such an immediate and automatic consequence of dissolution could not be regarded as 'proportionate to any legitimate aim relied on by the Government' and was 'incompatible with the very substance of the applicants' right to be elected and sit in Parliament under Article 3 of Protocol 1'. It infringed the 'sovereign power of the electorate who elected them as member of parliament.'[100]

[92] App. 11406/85, *Fournier v France*, Decision of 10 May 1988, (1988) 55 DR 130. See also *Gorizdra v Moldova*, (App. 53180/99), Decision of 2 July 2002. But note that refusal to return a deposit where a party has been improperly disqualified from an election will violate Article 1 of Protocol 1: *Russian Conservative Party of Entrepreneurs and others v Russia*, (Apps. 55066/00 and 55638/00), 11 January 2007, (2008) 46 EHRR 863, ECHR 2007-I, §§ 95–7.

[93] *Lykourezos v Greece*, (App. 33554/03), 15 June 2006, (2008) 46 EHRR 74, ECHR 2006-VIII.

[94] *Gitonas and others v Greece*, (Apps. 18747/91, 19376/92, 19379/92, 28208/95, and 27755/95), 1 July 1997; (1998) 26 EHRR 691, ECHR 1997-IV.

[95] Which had found a violation of Art. 3 by 9 votes to 8.

[96] *Ahmed and others v United Kingdom*, (App. 22954/93), 2 September 1998, (2000) 29 EHRR 1, ECHR 1998-VI.

[97] See discussion of cases involving political parties in ch.19. For examples of cases where the Court has not felt the need to consider applications under Art. 3 of Protocol 1, see *United Communist Party of Turkey and others v Turkey*, (App. 19392/92), 30 January 1998; (1998) 26 EHRR 121, ECHR 1998-I; *The Socialist Party and others v Turkey*, (App. 21237/93), 25 May 1998; (1999) 27 EHRR 51; and *Refah Partisi (The Welfare Party) v Turkey*, (Apps. 41340/98, 41342/92, 41343/98, and 41344/98), 13 February 2003 [GC], (2003) 37 EHRR 1, ECHR 2003-II.

[98] *Sadak and others v Turkey (No. 2)*, (Apps. 25144/94, 26149/95 to 26154/94, 27100/95, and 27101/95), 11 June 2002, (2003) 36 EHRR 396, ECHR 2002-IV. See also *Kavakçi v Turkey*, (App. 71907/01), 5 April 2007; *Silay v Turkey*, (App. 8691/02), 5 April 2007; and *Ilicak v Turkey*, (App. 15394/02), 5 April 2007.

[99] The Democracy Party *Demokrasi Partisi*.

[100] *Sadak and others v Turkey (No. 2)*, (Apps. 25144/94, 26149/95 to 26154/94, 27100/95, and 27101/95), 11 June 2002, (2003) 36 EHRR 396, ECHR 2002-IV, § 40.

The *Melnychenko* case[101] concerned rules operating in Ukraine for determining eligibility to stand for election. The authorities insisted upon residence in Ukraine as a condition of eligibility. The applicant was living in the United States, where he had applied for political asylum, but his officially registered address (*propiska)* remained in Ukraine. This was the standard basis for registration as a candidate in the elections. In the particular circumstances of the case, the Strasbourg Court concluded that the refusal to register his candidacy to stand for election was in breach of Article 3.

In *Sejdić and Finci v Bosnia and Herzegovina*, the applicants complained of their ineligibility to stand for election to the House of Peoples (the second chamber of the State parliament) and the Presidency of Bosnia and Herzegovina (the collective Head of State) on the ground of their Roma and Jewish origin.[102] The Constitution of Bosnia and Herzegovina is an unusual document as it is merely an annex to the General Framework Agreement for Peace in Bosnia and Herzegovina 1995 ('the Dayton Peace Agreement'). The Constitution requires a power-sharing approach between 'the constituent peoples' (i.e. Bosniacs, Croats, and Serbs). As the applicants did not wish to declare affiliation with any of the 'constituent peoples' due to their Roma and Jewish origin respectively, they were ineligible to stand for election to the House of Peoples and the Presidency. The Grand Chamber found that the applicants' ineligibility to stand for election to the House of Peoples lacked an objective and reasonable justification, due to the positive developments in the country since 1995, and therefore breached Article 14 taken in conjunction with Article 3 of Protocol 1. It also found a violation of the free-standing anti-discrimination right in Article 1 of Protocol 12 in respect of their exclusion from the Presidency (which would not fall within the ambit of Article 3 of Protocol 1). The Grand Chamber acknowledged that it may not yet be appropriate to abandon the power-sharing principle in its entirety but suggested that a compromise could be sought which would prevent other communities from being completely excluded. It also noted that the State had voluntarily committed to respect the principle of non-discrimination by acceding to the Convention, thereby recognising that the preservation of peace in the territory no longer required the limitation of fundamental rights.

A ban on eligibility to stand for election of those holding a nationality additional to that of the country in which the elections are being held was considered in *Tănase v Moldova*.[103] The applicant was a Moldovan politician of Romanian ethnicity who alleged that the prohibition on Moldovan nationals holding other nationalities sitting as members of Parliament violated his Article 3, Protocol 1 rights. The Moldovan Government argued that this restriction served the legitimate aim of ensuring loyalty to the State. The Grand Chamber was not entirely convinced of this argument given that opposition MPs were disproportionately effected by the restriction which had been introduced only one year before a general election. The Grand Chamber also noted that the Government have been unable to provide a single example of an MP with dual nationality showing disloyalty to the State of Moldova. The Grand Chamber declined to reach a conclusion on the existence of a legitimate aim, however, because it unanimously found the restriction to be disproportionate to any such aim pursued. The Court noted a European consensus to permit dual nationality MPs to sit in the legislature and, despite the peculiarities of Moldova's historical and political context (with a high proportion of dual nationals and having only recently become an independent State), it did not regard the Moldovan approach to be proportionate. This was largely because of the disproportionate impact upon parties in opposition to the Government which introduced the measure:

[101] *Melnychenko v Ukraine*, (App. 17707/02), 19 October 2004, (2006) 42 EHRR 784, ECHR 2004-X.

[102] *Sejdić and Finci v Bosnia and Herzegovina*, (Apps. 27996/06 and 34836/06), 22 December 2009, ECHR 2009.

[103] *Tănase v Moldova*, (App. 7/08), 27 April 2010 [GC], ECHR 2010.

> The Court must examine with particular care any measure which appears to operate solely, or principally, to the disadvantage of the opposition, especially where the nature of the measure is such that it affects the very prospect of opposition parties gaining power at some point in the future. Restrictions of this nature curtail the rights guaranteed by Article 3 of Protocol No. 1 to such an extent as to impair their very essence and deprive them of their effectiveness. The introduction of the prohibition in the present case shortly before elections, at a time when the governing party's percentage of the vote was in decline (see paragraphs 31 to 44 above), further militates against the proportionality of the measure.[104]

The Grand Chamber's judgment suggests that the Court will be careful to distinguish between restrictions based on securing loyalty to the State and those designed to secure loyalty to the State's current government.

The *Ždanoka* case[105] concerned the ineligibility of Tatjana Ždanoka to stand for election in Latvia by reason of her former membership of the Latvian Communist Party. This party had been declared unconstitutional by the Latvian authorities with the result that former active members of that party could not stand for election to the national parliament. The ban was indefinite in duration. The Latvian Government sought to justify the measure as meeting three aims: (1) it was a punitive measure for past conduct which displayed a lack of civic responsibility; (2) it was a preventive measure where past activities evidenced a risk of conduct likely to endanger democracy; and (3) her election might create an imminent danger for the State's constitutional order.

The Chamber judgment, finding a violation of Article 3 by five votes to two, was overturned on reference to the Grand Chamber in a thirteen votes to four judgment.

The Chamber[106] had accepted that barring a person's candidacy could be a legitimate punitive measure, but that the barring order should normally be temporary if it is to meet the requirement of proportionality. The aims relating to the protection of democratic values and the perceived threat to the State's constitutional order related to historical events in Latvia. The Court did not wish to become embroiled in historical controversy but did take as read the totalitarian and anti-democratic nature of the ruling Communist parties in the States of central and eastern Europe before 1990. However, there had been no ban on the activities of the political parties to which the applicant belonged until August 1991, and the Latvian Government had not taken legislative powers to provide for electoral ineligibility until the 1995 elections. This inevitably coloured the Court's view of the nature of the threat to democracy and the State's constitutional order arising from the activities of these parties. The evidence supplied did not indicate that the activities of the applicant were anti-democratic, though her ideas were diametrically opposed to certain policies of the Latvian Government. It followed that permanent ineligibility to stand for election was disproportionate to the aims pursued by the national measures, and its necessity in a democratic society had not been established. The Chamber found a violation of Article 3 of Protocol 1.

The Grand Chamber took a different view. This was not a punitive measure, but a preventive measure designed to:

> protect the integrity of the democratic process by excluding from participation in the work of a democratic legislature those individuals who had taken an active and leading role in a

[104] § 179.

[105] *Ždanoka v Latvia*, (App. 58278/00), 16 March 2006 [GC], (2007) 45 EHRR 478, ECHR 2006-IV. Contrast the judgment in *Ādamsons v Latvia*, (App. 3669/03), 24 June 2008, and see *Petkov and others v Bulgaria*, (Apps. 77568/01, 178/02, and 505/02), 11 June 2009.

[106] *Ždanoka v Latvia*, (App. 58278/00), 17 June 2004, (2005) 41 EHRR 659, ECHR 2004-IV.

party which was directly linked to the attempted violent overthrow of the newly established democratic regime.[107]

The national legislation was considered to be narrowly drafted by excluding only those who had 'actively participated' in the objectionable conduct. There was no reason to question the appreciation of the Latvian authorities that there was a threat to the new democratic order posed by a resurgence of ideas which could lead to the restoration of the former regime. In summary, the Strasbourg Court takes the view that this was a democracy defending itself. The dissenting judges considered that the indefinite ban on standing for election was problematic, but the majority too were alert to this question. The judgment of the Court notes that the Latvian Constitutional Court had indicated that a time limit should be placed on the restriction, and said that the Latvian Parliament 'must keep the statutory restriction under constant review, with a view to bringing it to an early end.'[108]

In the case of *Petkov and others v Bulgaria*, the three applicants were registered as candidates in the parliamentary elections to be held on 17 June 2001.[109] Prior to the election they were struck off the lists of candidates due to allegations that they had collaborated with the former State security agencies. The decisions to strike them off the lists were subsequently declared null and void by the Supreme Administrative Court. However, the electoral authorities did not restore their names to the lists, and as a result they could not run for Parliament. The Strasbourg Court found that there had been a violation of Article 3 of Protocol 1 due to the Bulgarian authorities' failure to reinstate the three applicants on the lists of candidates. The fact that the judgments were delivered only two days before the elections (and one even after them) was not a justifiable excuse for the Court as it regarded that those time pressures were largely of the authorities' own making.

Finally, it is important to note that electoral irregularities may negate the right to stand as a candidate in free elections. In *Namat Aliyev v Azerbaijan*, the applicant was a parliamentary candidate who complained that there had been a number of serious irregularities and breaches of electoral law in the constituency in which he stood.[110] He also complained that the domestic authorities, including the electoral commissions and courts, had failed to investigate his allegations. The Court started by rejecting the Government's argument that even if the applicant's allegations concerning election irregularities were true, it would not affect the ultimate result of the election. The Court emphasized that what was at stake in the present case was not the applicant's right to win the election in his constituency, but his right 'to stand for election in fair and democratic conditions, regardless of whether ultimately he won or lost' and that the Court's role in the present case was 'not to ascertain merely that the election outcome as such was not prejudiced, but to verify that the applicant's individual right to stand for election was not deprived of its effectiveness and that its essence had not been impaired.'[111]

The Court recognized that the claims made by the applicant were serious ones, including unlawful interference in the election process by local executive authorities, undue influence on voter choice, several instances of ballot-box stuffing, harassment of observers, irregularities in electoral rolls, and obvious discrepancies in the Precinct Electoral Commission (PEC) protocols showing a possible failure to account for as many as thousands of 'unused' blank ballots.[112] The Court confirmed that such irregularities were potentially capable of thwarting the democratic nature of the elections. It also emphasized the importance of a domestic system for effective examination of individual complaints

[107] *Z'danoka*, § 122. [108] § 135.
[109] *Petkov and others v Bulgaria*, (App. 77568/01, 178/02, and 505/02), 11 June 2009.
[110] *Namat Aliyev v Azerbaijan*, (App. 18705/06), 8 April 2010. [111] § 75. [112] § 78.

concerning electoral rights, which it regarded as one of the essential guarantees of free and fair elections:

> Such a system ensures an effective exercise of individual rights to vote and to stand for election, maintains general confidence in the State's administration of the electoral process and constitutes an important device at the State's disposal in achieving the fulfilment of its positive duty under Article 3 of Protocol No. 1 to hold democratic elections. Indeed, the State's solemn undertaking under Article 3 of Protocol No. 1 and the individual rights guaranteed by that provision would be illusory if, throughout the electoral process, specific instances indicative of failure to ensure democratic elections are not open to challenge by individuals before a competent domestic body capable of effectively dealing with the matter.[113]

The Azerbaijan domestic process had not satisfied these requirements. The domestic courts had relied on what the Court described as 'extremely formalistic reasons to avoid examining the substance of the applicant's complaints'.[114] In the circumstances of the present case, given the seriousness of the applicant's complaints and their relevance to Azerbaijan's compliance with its positive duty to hold free and fair elections, the Strasbourg Court regarded the rigid and overly formalistic approach as not justified under the Convention. The Court regarded the conduct and decisions of the electoral commissions and courts as giving an appearance of a lack of any genuine concern for the protection of the applicant's right to stand for election. This sufficed for it to conclude that the applicant's complaints were not effectively addressed at the domestic level and were dismissed in an arbitrary manner, amounting to a violation of Article 3 of Protocol 1.[115]

CONCLUDING REMARKS

After some initial uncertainty about the availability of individual petitions under Article 3 of Protocol 1, a significant case-law is developing on the nature of the legislature to which the Article refers, on the control of elections, on the circumstances in which individuals can be disenfranchised, and on the right to stand for election.

There has been considerable narrowing of the wide margin of appreciation referred to in the early cases now that the Strasbourg Court seems to be adopting a more robust test for interferences which States impose. This in turn has led to some political controversy, especially in the United Kingdom. As with other Articles of the Convention, the Strasbourg Court requires that procedural fairness surrounds decisions affecting the rights protected by the provision.

[113] § 81. [114] § 85.

[115] The Court has found numerous further instances where the interference with applicants' electoral rights by Azerbaijan fell foul of the standards required by Article 3 of Protocol 1. In some cases, this was due to the disqualification from running for election not being based on sufficient and relevant evidence and insufficient guarantees against arbitrariness: *Takishi v Azerbaijan*, (App. 18469/06), 28 February 2012; *Khanhuseyn Aliyev v Azerbaijan*, (App. 19554/06), 21 February 2012; *Abil v Azerbaijan*, (App. 16511/06), 21 February 2012. In other cases, a decision on the annulment of election results was regarded as arbitrary: *Hajili v Azerbaijan*, (App. 6984/06), 10 January 2012; *Mammadov v Azerbaijan (No. 2)*, (App. 4641/06), 10 January 2012; *Kerimli and Alibeyli v Azerbaijan*, (Apps. 18475/06 and 22444/06), 10 January 2012.

23

FREEDOM OF MOVEMENT

INTRODUCTION

Provisions of the Fourth and Seventh Protocols concern freedom of movement in the broadest sense. Article 2 of Protocol 4 concerns liberty of movement and freedom to choose a residence. Article 3 of the same Protocol prohibits the expulsion of nationals and enshrines the right of nationals to enter their own country, while Article 4 prohibits the collective expulsion of aliens. The provisions of Protocol 4, which are controversial in some States since they touch on issues of immigration policy, have not been ratified by all the parties to the Convention.[1] Finally, Article 1 of Protocol 7 provides that aliens are not to be expelled without due process of law.

As between the States parties to Protocol 4, its provisions are to be regarded as additional Articles of the Convention, and all the provisions of the Convention are to apply accordingly.[2] Article 5 of Protocol 4 and Article 6 of Protocol 7 make provision for a declaration concerning the application of the Protocol to dependent territories on the model of Article 56 of the Convention.

In addition, however, Article 5(4) of Protocol 4 provides that, for the purposes of Articles 2 and 3 of the Protocol, the territory of a State to which the Protocol applies by virtue of ratification, and each territory to which it applies by a declaration under Article 5, shall be treated as separate territories. The effect of this provision is that a State which ratifies the Protocol, and extends its application under Article 5 to its dependent territories, guarantees freedom of movement within each of those territories without also guaranteeing freedom of movement from one territory to another. The Committee of Experts explains paragraph 4 as follows:

> The Committee decided to add a paragraph 4 to Article 5 in order to take account of a problem which may arise in connection with States which are responsible for the international relations of overseas territories. Thus, for example, insofar as nationality is concerned, there is no distinction between the United Kingdom and most of the territories for whose international relations it is responsible; in relation to these territories and the United Kingdom there is a common citizenship, designated as 'citizenship of the United Kingdom and Colonies'.

Persons who derive the common nationality from a connection with one such territory do not, however, have the right to admission to, or have immunity from expulsion from, another such territory. Each territory has its own laws relating to admission to and expulsion from its territory. Under these laws admission can be refused to persons who, though they possess the common nationality, do not derive it from connection with the territory

[1] As at 30 November 2013, there are 43 parties to Protocol 4. Two countries (Turkey and the United Kingdom) have signed but not ratified the Protocol. Greece and Switzerland have not even signed the Protocol. See, for an example of a case where this was an issue, *Eugenia Michaelidou Developments Ltd and Michael Tymvios v Turkey*, (App. 16163/90), 31 July 2003.

[2] Art. 6(1) of Protocol 4.

in question, and in certain circumstances such persons can be expelled from that territory. Equally, persons who derive the common nationality from a connection with a dependent territory can in certain circumstances be refused admission to the United Kingdom or, if admitted, be expelled from the UK. What is said above is relevant to Article 3 of this Protocol, but a similar situation would arise as regards the interpretation of 'territory' for the purposes of Article 2.

Accordingly, it is desirable that the references in Articles 2 and 3 to the territory of a State should relate to the metropolitan territory and each non-metropolitan territory separately, and not to a single geographical entity comprising the metropolitan and other territories.

This interpretation would apply only to Article 2(1), and to Article 3 of Protocol 4.[3] Article 6(5) of Protocol 7 contains similar provisions.

MOVEMENT AND RESIDENCE

Article 2 of Protocol 4 provides:

1. Everyone lawfully within the territory of a State shall, within that territory, have the right to liberty of movement and freedom to choose his residence.
2. Everyone shall be free to leave any country, including his own.
3. No restrictions shall be placed on the exercise of these rights other than such as are in accordance with law and are necessary in a democratic society in the interests of national security or public safety, for the maintenance of the *ordre public*, for the prevention of crime, for the protection of health or morals, or for the protection of the rights and freedoms of others.
4. The rights set forth in paragraph 1 may also be subject, in particular areas, to restrictions imposed in accordance with law and justified by the public interest in a democratic society.

These provisions are based on Article 13(1) and (2) of the Universal Declaration of Human Rights, whose wording they follow closely. The right to return to the country of nationality, which is also included in Article 13(2) of the Universal Declaration, is dealt with separately by Article 3 of Protocol 4. While Article 2 deals with freedom of movement within a country, and the right to leave it, Article 3 precludes a State from expelling, or refusing to admit, its own nationals. Thus Article 2 applies to everyone, in relation to any country, but Article 3 applies only to nationals in relation to their own State.

The reference, in Article 2(1), to 'Everyone lawfully within the territory of a State' includes all that State's nationals present within its territory, since it follows from the provisions of Article 3 that, subject to the possible exception of extradition, the presence of persons in the State of which they are a national cannot be unlawful. As for persons who are not nationals, they are lawfully within the territory so long as they comply with any conditions of entry that may have been imposed. Such conditions may, of course, include restrictions as to the length of stay, after the expiry of which their presence will be unlawful. But it is argued that, subject to the limitations permitted under paragraphs 3 and 4, these conditions cannot, under Article 2(1), include any restrictions on their liberty of movement, or on their freedom to choose their residence.[4]

[3] Explanatory Reports on the Second to Fifth Protocols to the Convention, Strasbourg 1971, 55.

[4] See to the contrary, Explanatory Reports on the Second to Fifth Protocols to the Convention, Strasbourg 1971, 41.

The position is a little different in the case of asylum seekers, as the *Omwenyeke* case makes clear.[5] The freedom of movement of asylum seekers can be limited pending determination of their status under provisional authorizations. Presence in the territory is only lawful where the asylum seeker complies with the terms of the provisional authorization. So an asylum seeker present in Germany under a provisional authorization conditional on his remaining in the city of Wolfsburg did not have a right to freedom of movement outside that city. The asylum seeker would not be lawfully present in Germany when in breach of his provisional authorization.

The freedom to leave a country, under Article 2(2), is subject to the restrictions set out in paragraph 3. These restrictions are, of course, sufficient to preclude convicted prisoners from leaving the country in which they are detained. The reference to 'the maintenance of *ordre public*' in paragraph 3 was included, as is shown by the preparatory work, expressly to allow for the case of persons lawfully detained under Article 5.[6] Similarly, a person who has been detained with a view to deportation or extradition under Article 5(1)(f)[7] cannot claim the right to leave the country freely.[8]

The approach adopted by the Strasbourg Court in dealing with restrictions or limitations on the rights granted in Article 2(1) and (2) is very similar to that adopted when the Strasbourg Court is considering the limitations to be found in Articles 8 to 11.[9]

In the *Baumann* case,[10] the Strasbourg Court said:

> The Court reiterates that the right of free movement as guaranteed by paragraphs 1 and 2 of Article 2 of Protocol 4 is intended to secure to any person a right of liberty of movement within a territory and to leave that territory, which implies a right to leave for such a country of the person's choice to which he may be admitted.... It follows that liberty of movement prohibits any measure liable to infringe that right or to restrict the exercise thereof which does not satisfy the requirement of a measure which can be considered as necessary in a democratic society in the pursuit of the legitimate aims referred to in the third paragraph of the above-mentioned Article.[11]

In a later case, the Strasbourg Court said:

> Any measure restricting [the rights in Article 2] must be lawful, pursue one of the legitimate aims referred to in the third paragraph ... and strike a fair balance between the public interest and the individual's rights....[12]

Article 2 has been pleaded in a variety of circumstances, some of which appear quite fanciful. For example, admissibility decisions of the Strasbourg Court have ruled as inadmissible claims that security controls at airports constitute a restriction on free movement,[13] and that the need to avoid cigarette smoke in public restricts freedom of movement.[14] Rather more obvious situations have involved such matters as compulsory residence orders imposed in connection with criminal investigations, orders prohibiting a person's presence in a particular area, payment of tax and debts, national security, prevention of the

[5] *Omwenyeke v Germany*, (App. 44294/04), Decision of 20 November 2007, ECHR 2007-XII.

[6] Explanatory Reports on the Second to Fifth Protocols to the Convention, Strasbourg 1971, 41.

[7] See ch.11.

[8] App. 4436/70, *X v Federal Republic of Germany*, Decision of 26 May 1970, (1970) 13 *Yearbook* 1029.

[9] See ch.14.

[10] *Baumann v France*, (App. 33592/96), 22 May 2001, (2002) 34 EHRR 1041, ECHR 2001-V.

[11] § 61. [12] *Riener v Bulgaria*, (App. 46343/99), 23 May 2006, (2007) 45 EHRR 723, § 109.

[13] *Phull v France*, (App. 35753/03), Decision of 11 January 2005.

[14] *Botti v Italy*, (App. 77360/01), Decision of 2 December 2004.

removal of children or those with mental health issues without appropriate protection, and passport confiscations.

In one case,[15] an applicant who was subject to a compulsory residence order, which involved placing him under special police supervision, complained of a violation of the provision. The Commission ruled that the measures were an interference with his right of freedom of movement, but they were measures provided by law, which were necessary in a democratic society for the prevention of crime and maintenance of the *ordre public*. The measures were proportionate to a legitimate aim and the application was declared inadmissible.

In the *Raimondo* case,[16] the applicant, who was suspected of being a member of the Mafia, had been put under house arrest and placed under special police supervision. He complained that the special police supervision breached his rights under Article 2 of Protocol 4. The Strasbourg Court concluded that the measures fell short of a deprivation of liberty within the meaning of Article 5(1) and fell to be considered under Article 2 of the Protocol. The measures were, however, in its view justified as serving the aim of maintaining public order and for the prevention of crime; there was no lack of proportionality. However, for reasons which are not explained, there was a delay of eighteen days before the revocation of the special police supervision was notified to the applicant. For this period the interference with his rights under Article 2 of the Protocol was not in accordance with law nor was it necessary. There was to this extent a violation of the Article.[17]

The *Labita* case is a more dramatic example of a violation.[18] The applicant had been tried and acquitted of certain offences connected with Mafia-type activities. But the respondent State continued to keep in place special police supervision notwithstanding the acquittal, arguing that these were preventive measures to guard against the risk of future offences.[19] The Strasbourg Court concluded:

> [T]he Court considers that it is legitimate for preventive measures, including special supervision, to be taken against persons suspected of being members of the Mafia, even prior to conviction, as they are intended to prevent crimes being committed. Furthermore, an acquittal does not necessarily deprive such measures of all foundation, as concrete evidence gathered at trial, though insufficient to secure a conviction, may nonetheless justify reasonable fears that the person concerned may in the future commit criminal offences.[20]

However, in this case, the Strasbourg Court concluded that there was no such basis for the continuation of the measures, which were, consequently, a breach of Article 2 of Protocol 4.

In a series of cases involving Bulgaria,[21] the Court has examined the proportionality of travel restrictions on convicted prisoners who had left prison but were put under rehabilitation orders. The Court accepted that such measures may be necessary to prevent crime or maintain order. However in these cases, the ban was automatic and the individual circumstances of the applicant were not taken into account and were not reviewable by a Court. A general and automatic ban was not proportionate.

The *Baumann* case[22] concerned the seizure of a German passport in France by French police officers. At the time the passport holder was in Germany; he had been taken ill

[15] App. 12541/86, *Ciancimino v Italy*, Decision of 27 May 1991, (1991) 70 DR 103.

[16] *Raimondo v Italy*, 22 February 1994, Series A No 281-A; (1994) 18 EHRR 237.

[17] §§ 37–40.

[18] *Labita v Italy*, (App. 26772/95), 6 April 2000, (2008) 46 EHRR 1228, ECHR 2000-IV.

[19] As in the *Raimondo* judgment.

[20] *Labita v Italy*, (App. 26772/95), 6 April 2000, (2008) 46 EHRR 1228, ECHR 2000-IV, § 195.

[21] *Nalbankski v Bulgaria*, (App. 30943/04), 10 February 2011; *Sarkizov and others v Bulgaria*, (App. 37981/06), 17 April 2012; *Dimitar Ivanov v Bulgaria*, (App. 19418/07), 14 February 2012; and *Milen Kostov v Bulgaria*, (App. 40026/07), 3 September 2013.

[22] *Baumann v France*, (App. 33592/96), 22 May 2001, (2002) 34 EHRR 1041, ECHR 2001-V.

while staying in a hotel and moved from France to Germany for treatment. His passport was still in his hotel room and was seized when the police searched the hotel room. The passport was retained for some considerable time, but shortly after its seizure, the applicant was arrested by the German authorities, kept in custody by them, and subsequently tried and sentenced to imprisonment. The respondent State argued that the arrest and subsequent imprisonment in Germany meant that there had been no actual restriction on the applicant's freedom of movement. The Strasbourg Court considered that denial of the use of his passport constituted an interference with his right of movement. Since no action was taken by the French authorities against the applicant there was no justification for the continuing seizure of his passport. Though justified for a short initial period, the failure to return the passport thereafter constituted a violation of Article 2 of Protocol 4. Three judges added a partly dissenting opinion. For them, the factual situation presented by the applicant did not show any loss of movement in France; when the passport was seized in France, the applicant was already in Germany. The dissenting judges seem to take the view that the applicant could easily have obtained a replacement German passport from the German authorities, and so would not have suffered any restriction on his freedom of movement.

The *Napijalo* case[23] concerned the confiscation of a passport by the Croatian customs authorities at a border check when the applicant was crossing from Bosnia and Herzegovina into Croatia. He was alleged to have failed to declare certain goods he was bringing into Croatia; it was clear that this was a minor infringement, since a fixed penalty notice was issued for a sum equal to about €30, but the applicant could not pay this on the spot. It took the applicant just over two years to secure the return of his passport. He complained that this amounted to a violation of his freedom of movement under Article 2 of Protocol 4. The Strasbourg Court concluded that an unjustified confiscation of a passport constituted a violation of the rights protected by the Article. To be justifiable, such a measure must be in accordance with law and be a necessary measure in a democratic society for securing a legitimate aim. In this case, it was the continuing deprivation of the passport which amounted to a violation of Convention rights. No proceedings were ever instigated against the applicant in relation to customs violations.

Barring someone from having a passport without good reason may also constitute a violation of Article 2 of Protocol 4.[24] Where a ban was put in place for a good reason, it must be subject to periodic reassessment.

The *Riener* case[25] concerned a restriction on leaving Bulgaria arising from a tax debt. The Strasbourg Court accepted that this had a legal basis in Bulgarian law,[26] and was for a legitimate purpose, since Article 1 of Protocol 1 permits State parties to that Protocol to enact laws for the purpose of securing payment of taxes. The respondent State, however, failed to persuade the Strasbourg Court that the lengthy restriction on movement was proportionate, since it was applied automatically, was not systematically reviewed, and there was little evidence of attempts to recover the tax debt. The measure could only be justified as long as it served the aim of securing recovery of the tax debt; the restriction had become a de facto punishment. In *Khlyustov v Russia*,[27] the applicant had several travel bans imposed upon him for a failure to pay a debt. The ban was imposed by the bailiffs'

[23] *Napijalo v Croatia*, (App. 66485/01), 13 November 2003, (2005) 40 EHRR 735.

[24] *Ignatov v Bulgaria*, (App. 50/02), 2 July 2009.

[25] *Riener v Bulgaria*, (App. 46343/99), 23 May 2006, (2007) 45 EHRR 723.

[26] Though whether the law met the tests of foreseeability and clarity was regarded as closely linked to the issue of proportionality on which the case turned.

[27] *Khlyustov v Russia*, (App. 28975/05), 11 July 2013.

service. The Court found a violation of Article 2 of Protocol 4, as the measures should have been reviewed for proportionality throughout the length of the travel bans. The bailiffs' demands on which the bans were premised were based on the initial demand for payment of the debt and there was no reassessment of the justifications for the travel bans. In judicial reviews, the authorities did not assess the proportionality of the bans.

In what the Court described as a 'novel' case against Bulgaria,[28] the applicant, a Bulgarian national, had been deported from the US for working whilst on a student visa. Bulgaria had introduced penalties for immigration offences in other States. It imposed a two-year travel ban and the surrender of his passport. The State argued that the measure was in place due to migration from Bulgaria and to reassure other States with regard to Bulgarian migrants residing legally in other States. The Court found that even if it accepted this form of public order as a legitimate aim, the measure was not proportionate as the policy imposed a blanket ban. The Court accepted that an immigration measure such as this may be justified. However, it cannot be applied automatically without an examination of the individual circumstances in each case.[29]

Extending measures beyond the period for which restrictions on movement are strictly necessary recurs in the case-law. So, in the *Luordo* case[30] restricting the movement of a bankrupt beyond the period needed to secure assets for creditors constituted a violation of the Article.[31] But a more generous view of the conduct of a Contracting Party will be taken where the proceedings relate to criminal offences. In the *Federov and Federova* case,[32] the applicants had been charged with fraud, and the case had ping-ponged backwards and forwards between trial courts and the appellate courts for some years during which the applicants' movement was restricted. There was evidence that they had been given special permission to leave the district on two occasions. The Strasbourg Court did not consider that the actions of the Russian authorities to be disproportionate in this case. However, the Court may still find a measure relating to criminal proceedings disproportionate if there is no reassessment of the need for a travel restriction over the period of criminal proceedings.[33]

In the *Hajibeyli* case, the Strasbourg Court provided guidance on the approach to be taken in cases where restrictions on movement were connected with the investigation of criminal conduct. It is not simply a matter of considering the duration of the restriction:

> ...the Court considers that, in the present case, the comparative duration of the restriction, in itself, cannot be taken as the sole basis for determining whether a fair balance was struck between the general interest in the proper conduct of criminal proceedings and the applicant's personal interest in enjoying freedom of movement. The issue must be assessed according to all the special features of the case. The restriction may be justified in a given case only if there are clear indications of a genuine public interest which outweighs the individual's right to freedom of movement.[34]

[28] *Stamose v Bulgaria*, (App. 29713/05), 27 November 2012. [29] §§ 34–6.

[30] *Luordo v Italy*, (App. 32190/96), 17 July 2003, (2005) 41 EHRR 547, ECHR 2003-IX.

[31] See also *Ciaramella v Italy*, (App. 6597/03), Decision of 23 September 2004.

[32] *Federov and Federova v Russia*, (App. 31008/02), 13 October 2005, (2006) 43 EHRR 943. See also *Ivanov v Ukraine*, (App. 15007/02), 7 December 2006.

[33] *Makedonski v Bulgaria*, (App. 36036/04), 20 January 2011; see also *Pfeifer v Poland*, (App. 24733/04), Decision of 17 February 2011; and *Prescher v Bulgaria*, (App. 6767/04), 7 June 2011.

[34] *Hajibeyli v Azerbaijan*, (App. 16528/05), 10 July 2008, § 63; see also *Miazdzyk v Poland*, (App. 23592/07), 24 January 2012, where the Court held that the fact that the applicant was a foreign national and was not allowed to leave for even a short period to visit his children, together with the fact that the detention was lifted and held unnecessary meant that the measures were disproportionate.

The Strasbourg Court has accepted that a proportionate restriction on leaving a country may be imposed for reasons of national security.[35] The applicant complained of the five year ban on his travel abroad following his work on developing rocket and space devices. The Court indicated that the same tests applied where national security was in issue as in other cases of restrictions on travel abroad. Here the applicant had surrendered all classified material prior to his application to travel abroad, and was proposing to travel for the purely private purpose of visiting his father in Germany who was ill. The review available against a refusal to issue a passport in such circumstances was concerned with form rather than the merits of the reasons for the visit, and the respondent State failed to indicate how the restriction served the interests of national security. The Court clearly considered the ban on travel for this purpose as belonging to an earlier era in Russia, when interpersonal communications could be controlled much more easily. There was a violation of Article 2 of Protocol 4. Similarly in *Soltysyak v Russia*,[36] the Court held a travel ban on an ex-soldier who had worked on rocket test launches to be disproportionate. The Court noted that Russia remained the only ex-Soviet State in the Council of Europe to retain such blanket travel restrictions despite Russia's commitment to abolish such restrictions when it joined the Council of Europe.[37]

Two cases with very similar facts concern the ability of the Burgomaster of Amsterdam to impose a prohibition order restricting a person's presence in a particular area of Amsterdam as part of the crackdown on the public use of hard drugs.[38] There were some doubts about whether these orders were 'in accordance with law'[39] though the majority was satisfied that the appropriate tests were met. The applicant argued that the long-standing nature of these orders[40] impugned the pressing social need for such measures. The Strasbourg Court disagreed. In the particular circumstances of these cases, the imposition of the measures on the applicants did not violate the rights protected by Article 2 of Protocol 4.

The unjustified monitoring of movements and expulsion to a specific part of the national territory will be a violation of Article 2 of Protocol 4. The *Denizci* case[41] concerned restrictions on the movement of the applicants in the southern part of Cyprus and subsequent expulsion to the northern part of Cyprus. No lawful basis for the restrictions on the applicants' movements was put forward by the respondent State, and the Court concluded that there was an interference with the rights in Article 2 which were neither provided by law nor necessary.[42]

Similar circumstances have arisen in Russia in relation to residence registration. A requirement to report to the police every time a person wishes to change their place of residence or to visit family or friends away from their home constitutes an interference with the right to liberty of movement.[43] Local practices in violation of a ruling of the Constitutional Court which had stated that there was a legal duty to certify an applicant's

[35] *Bartik v Russia*, (App. 55565/00), 21 December 2006, ECHR 2006-XV.

[36] *Soltysyak v Russia*, (App. 4663/05), 10 February 2011.

[37] § 51.

[38] *Landvreugd v The Netherlands*, (App. 37331/97), 4 June 2002, (2003) 36 EHRR 1039; and *Olivieira v The Netherlands*, (App. 33129/96), 4 June 2002, ECHR 2002-IV.

[39] See the joint dissenting opinions in both cases.

[40] The provisions had been available as emergency measures for some eleven years at the time of their imposition on the applicants.

[41] *Denizci and others v Cyprus*, (Apps. 25316–25321/94, and 27207/95), 23 May 2001, ECHR 2001-V.

[42] §§ 400–6. The Strasbourg Court decided that its conclusions on the violation of Article 2 of Protocol 4 made it unnecessary to consider the complaint as a violation of Art. 3 of Protocol 4.

[43] *Tatishvili v Russia*, (App. 1509/02), 22 February 2007, (2007) 45 EHRR 1246, ECHR 2007-III, § 45.

intention to live at a specified address on presentation of a completed application also constituted violations of the right to free movement.[44]

A number of other cases have concerned freedom of movement within the Russian Federation, and among the countries of central and eastern Europe. In the *Timishev* case,[45] the applicant, who was an ethnic Chechen, complained that he had been stopped at a particular checkpoint en route to Nalchik, refused entry to a part of Russia, and had been obliged to make a 300-kilometre detour to complete his journey within the country. He argued that this was part of a policy of refusing entry to Chechens travelling by car. The Russian authorities claimed that he had tried to jump the queue at the checkpoint and been turned back for that reason. The Strasbourg Court found that the restriction on the applicant's movement was not 'in accordance with law', and there was a violation of Article 2 of Protocol 4. The Strasbourg Court went on to find a violation of Article 14 when read with Article 2 of Protocol 4 in that the restriction was based on ethnic considerations; he had been treated in a discriminatory manner.

THE PROHIBITION OF EXPULSION OF NATIONALS

As already stated, Article 3 precludes a State from expelling, or refusing to admit, its own nationals. Article 3(1) provides:

> No one shall be expelled, by means either of an individual or of a collective measure, from the territory of the State of which he is a national.

There is no provision for any restrictions to the rights guaranteed by Article 3, which is curious since the provision makes no exception for the practice of extradition. It is extraordinary that the explanatory report on Protocol 4 merely says that 'It was understood that extradition was outside the scope of this paragraph.'[46] Such understandings are not an adequate basis for drafting a legal text. In any event, on the accepted principles of treaty interpretation, this explanatory report cannot be invoked to interpret the text, since the text is clear and unambiguous.[47]

The European Convention on Extradition does not preclude the extradition of nationals, but provides that a Contracting Party shall have the right to refuse extradition of its nationals.[48] The extradition of nationals is prohibited by the law of many Member States of the Council of Europe.[49] But the Convention on Extradition permits a State to refuse the extradition of its nationals even if this would not be contrary to its own law. It would seem that States Parties to Protocol 4 are precluded from extraditing their nationals in the absence of a reservation to the contrary.[50]

The Commission has defined what constitutes expulsion, which occurs when a 'person is obliged permanently to leave the territory of the State... without being left the possibility

[44] *Tatishvili v Russia*, (App. 1509/02), 22 February 2007, (2007) 45 EHRR 1246, ECHR 2007-III, § 45.

[45] *Timishev v Russia*, (Apps. 55762/00 and 55974/00), 13 December 2005, (2007) 44 EHRR 776, ECHR 2005-XII. See also *Gartukayev v Russia*, (App. 71933/01), 13 December 2005; and *Bolat v Russia* (App. 14139/03), 5 October 2006, (2008) 46 EHRR 354, ECHR 2006-XI.

[46] Explanatory Reports on the Second to Fifth Protocols to the Convention, Strasbourg 1971, 47.

[47] Art. 31, Vienna Convention on the Law of Treaties, and see generally ch.4.

[48] ETS 24, Art. 6(1).

[49] For example, Cyprus, Germany, the Netherlands, and Switzerland.

[50] This view is not supported by J. Merrills and A. Robertson, *Human Rights in Europe* (MUP, Manchester 2001), 256.

of returning later'.[51] This definition neatly excludes extradition from the compass of expulsion under the Article.

It appears that the Committee of Experts which drafted Protocol 4 also considered the hypothesis of a State expelling one of its nationals after first depriving them of their nationality, but 'thought it was inadvisable in Article 3 to touch on the delicate question of the legitimacy of measures depriving individuals of nationality'.[52]

However, the effect of Article 3(1) must be to preclude a State from depriving persons of their nationality in order to expel them. Otherwise it would offer no adequate protection. The Commission, indeed, has gone further, and has considered whether it may be contrary to Article 3(1) to refuse to grant a person nationality if the object of the refusal is to be able to expel them. An applicant complained both of his imminent expulsion, and of the refusal of the German authorities to recognize him as a German citizen. The Commission stated that, although the Convention confers no right to a nationality as such, the question arose whether there existed, between the decision to refuse him nationality and the order for his expulsion, a causal connection creating the presumption that the refusal had as its sole object his expulsion from German territory. There was no evidence of that, however, in the case before them.[53]

In its admissibility decision in the *Slivenko* case,[54] the Strasbourg Court ruled that, while Article 3 secures an absolute and unconditional freedom from expulsion of a national, the grant of nationality was a matter for the national legal orders. While an arbitrary denial of nationality may under certain circumstances amount to an interference with rights under Article 8, no 'right to nationality' similar to that under Article 15 of the Universal Declaration of Human Rights is guaranteed by the Convention or its Protocols.[55]

THE RIGHT OF ENTRY TO THE TERRITORY OF THE STATE OF NATIONALITY

Similar considerations relating to the withdrawal of nationality apply to paragraph 2, which provides that:

> No one shall be deprived of the right to enter the territory of the State of which he is a national.

A State could not refuse persons nationality if they fulfil the conditions laid down by its law, or deprive such persons of their nationality, in order to be able to refuse them admission.

PROHIBITING THE COLLECTIVE EXPULSION OF ALIENS

Article 4 simply states, 'Collective expulsion of aliens is prohibited.' The Article does not regulate in any way the individual expulsion of aliens. Its scope is thus extremely limited.[56] The reasons given for this omission by the Committee of Experts are set out in the

[51] App. 6189/73, *X v Federal Republic of Germany*, Decision of 13 May 1974, (1974) 46 CD 214.

[52] Explanatory Reports on the Second to Fifth Protocols to the Convention, Strasbourg 1971, 47–8.

[53] App. 3745/68, *X v Federal Republic of Germany*, Decision of 15 December 1969, (1970) 31 CD 107.

[54] *Slivenko and others v Latvia*, (App. 48321/99), Decision of 23 January 2002, ECHR 2002-II.

[55] § 77.

[56] Issues relating to this provision are raised in *Georgia v Russia (I)*, (App. 13255/07). See Decision of 3 July 2009.

explanatory report.[57] One reason was that the matter had already been dealt with in the European Convention on Establishment. However, that Convention does not deal with the expulsion of aliens in general; it deals only with the expulsion of nationals of other States Parties to that Convention.[58] Possibly a difficulty for the governments was that if any rights were recognized in the Protocol in relation to the expulsion of aliens generally, then the rights granted on a reciprocal basis, under the Establishment Convention or under other treaties, to the nationals of other States Parties to those instruments might have had to be extended, through the effect of Article 14, to all aliens.

The case-law of the Commission and Court has attempted to define what constitutes a collective expulsion. The cases have raised the question as to when a series of individual expulsions can be regarded as a collective expulsion. The Commission appears to have concluded that where persons are expelled with others without their cases having received individual treatment, the expulsion will be collective.[59] The Strasbourg Court, citing its admissibility decision in an earlier case,[60] has given the following definition of collective expulsions:

> The Court reiterates its case-law whereby collective expulsion, within the meaning of Article 4 of Protocol No. 4, is to be understood as any measure compelling aliens, as a group, to leave a country, except where such a measure is taken on the basis of a reasonable and objective examination of the particular case of each individual alien of the group.... That does not mean that where the latter condition is satisfied the background to the execution of the expulsion orders plays no further role in determining whether there has been compliance with Article 4 of Protocol No. 4.[61]

In the *Čonka* case, four members of a single family had been expelled from Belgium; they were Slovakian nationals of Roma origin who had come to Belgium and claimed asylum. There had been some specific consideration of their individual circumstances, but it was clear from public statements that official arrangements had been made for the 'collective repatriation' to Slovakia of substantial numbers of Slovak nationals. Furthermore, a group of Slovak nationals had been required to attend at the police station at the same time; the orders requiring them to leave Belgium were couched in identical circumstances; there had been difficulties in the aliens making contact with a lawyer; and the asylum procedure had not been completed. All these factors led the Court to conclude that this was a case of collective expulsion rather than a series of individual expulsions; there were insufficient guarantees demonstrating that the personal circumstances of each of those concerned had been genuinely and individually taken into account. In a partly dissenting opinion, Judge Velaers did not find a violation of Article 4 of Protocol 4. In essence, he felt that the factors which gave rise to doubt about the genuineness of the consideration of the individual circumstances of each case did not lead to the conclusion that this was a collective expulsion:

> Repatriation as a group, an option the national authorities are free to choose for reasons of efficiency and economy, clearly cannot take place without prior preparation.[62]

A partly dissenting opinion by two other judges shares this view.[63]

[57] Explanatory Reports on the Second to Fifth Protocols to the Convention, Strasbourg 1971, 50–1.

[58] ETS 19, Art. 3.

[59] App. 7011/75, *Becker v Denmark*, Decision of 30 October 1975, (1976) 19 *Yearbook* 416; App. 14209/88, *A and others v Netherlands*, Decision of 16 December 1988, (1989) 59 DR 274.

[60] *Andric v Sweden*, (App. 45917/99), Decision of 23 February 1999.

[61] *Čonka v Belgium*, (App. 51564/99), 5 February 2002, (2002) 34 EHRR 1298, ECHR 2002-I, § 59.

[62] § 8 of Judge Velaers' partly dissenting opinion.

[63] Partly Dissenting Opinion of Judge Jungwiert, joined by Judge Kuris.

In a case against Cyprus,[64] a Syrian asylum seeker claimed he was part of a collective expulsion. He was detained along with 75 other Syrian asylum seekers, many of whom had been publically protesting about their treatment. He was one of those detained who was told he would be deported. The Court noted that the fact that a number of aliens are subject to similar decisions does not in itself lead to the conclusion that there is a collective expulsion. Where a case has been individually examined before a decision to remove a person from the territory is taken, it will be very difficult to establish that there is, in reality, a decision to expel a group of persons.[65] Despite the fact that a number of Syrians were brought at the same time to where they were detained, they were removed in groups, and the deportation order was couched in identical terms, the Court did not find a violation of Article 4 of Protocol 4. It seems the difference between this case and the *Čonka* decision was that the asylum procedure had been completed for those with deportation orders and so their individual circumstances had been assessed and the deportations were clearly linked to these assessments.[66] It may also reflect the minority view in *Čonka*.

These cases examined whether collective expulsion had taken place from the territory of the State. However, the Court has also examined if a collective expulsion can take place outside the territory of the State. In *Xhavara and others v Italy and Albania*,[67] Albanian nationals had attempted to enter Italy illegally on board an Albanian ship. The vessel was intercepted by an Italian warship approximately thirty-five nautical miles off the Italian coast. The Italian ship had attempted to prevent the Albanians from reaching Italian territory, leading to the death of fifty-eight people. The Court found that the application was inadmissabile as the applicants challenged an Italian law which had not been applied to their case. Therefore, the Court did not have to rule on the extraterritorial applicability of Article 4.

However, the Court did rule on the admissibility of Article 4 of Protocol 4 dealing with extraterritorial jurisdiction for the first time in another case against Italy. In *Hirsi Jaama and others v Italy*,[68] the Italian authorities intercepted Eritrean and Somali asylum seekers at sea who had left Libya for Italy. They brought them on board Italian naval ships and took them back to Libya. The Court decided that the applicants were under the extraterritorial jurisdiction of Italy.[69] The Government argued that Article 4 only applies if expulsion takes place from the national territory. However, the Court unanimously rejected the Government's arguments. The Court noted that unlike Articles 2 and 3 of Protocol 4 and Article 1 of Protocol 7, the wording of Article 4 does not explicitly limit the provision to those within the national territory of the State. The Court further noted that the Explanatory Report as well as the draft report of the Committee of Experts on the Protocol stated that the Protocol applies to those not domiciled in the State, just passing through the State, refugees, or stateless.[70] The Court noted the evolutive nature of the Convention and the need to make rights practical and effective:

> The economic crisis and recent social and political changes have had a particular impact on certain regions of Africa and the Middle East, throwing up new challenges for European States in terms of immigration control... If, therefore, Article 4 of Protocol No. 4 were to apply only to collective expulsions from the national territory of the States Parties to the

[64] *M A v Cyprus*, (App. 41872/10), 23 July 2013.

[65] *Sultani v France*, (App. 45223/05), 20 September 2007, ECHR 2007-X.

[66] *M A v Cyprus*, (App. 41872/10), 23 July 2013, §§ 252–5.

[67] *Xhavara and others v Italy and Albania*, (App. 39473/98), Decision of 11 January 2001.

[68] *Hirsi Jaama and others v Italy*, (App. 27765/09), 23 February 2012.

[69] §§ 70–82.

[70] §§ 174.

Convention, a significant component of contemporary migratory patterns would not fall within the ambit of that provision.[71]

The Court acknowledged the right of a State to control migratory flows but it cannot have recourse to practices that violate the Convention. On the facts, it was clear the applicants had no access to individual procedures to determine their status and that there was no-one on the Italian ships trained to carry out individual interviews nor were there interpreters or legal advisors.[72]

EXPULSION ONLY TO FOLLOW DUE PROCESS

Article 1 of Protocol 7 provides:

1. An alien lawfully resident in the territory of a State shall not be expelled therefrom except in pursuance of a decision reached in accordance with law and shall be allowed:
   a. to submit reasons against his expulsion
   b. to have his case reviewed; and
   c. to be represented for these purposes before the competent authority or a person or persons designated by that authority.
2. An alien may be expelled before the exercise of his rights under paragraph 1.a, b and c of this article, when such expulsion is necessary in the interests of public order or is grounded on reasons of national security.

This Article[73] provides certain limited procedural guarantees for those who are lawfully resident in one of the States which has ratified this provision in respect of decisions to expel them. Expulsion, according to the Explanatory Memorandum, is any measure compelling the departure of the person from the territory except extradition.[74] It is arguable that to be lawfully resident, a person must have passed through the necessary immigration procedures and have been admitted for residence rather than some more limited purpose, such as, perhaps a person admitted for a limited period as a student or a visitor. However, an admissibility decision under Article 2 of Protocol 4 suggests that a broader view may be taken, even though the words of Article 2 refer to a person as 'lawfully within the territory' while Article 1 of Protocol 7 uses the term 'lawfully resident in the territory'. The *Omwenyeke* case[75] suggests that a person is lawfully present where they are compliant with the terms of entry. So it would follow that a visitor is lawfully present while complying with the terms of any leave to enter for that purpose, but not thereafter. It remains to be seen whether the Strasbourg Court will define lawful residence under Article 1 of Protocol 7 differently from lawful presence under Article 2 of Protocol 4.

The *Lupsa* case[76] appears to be the first judgment under Article 1 of Protocol 7 by the Strasbourg Court. Lupsa was a national of Serbia who had lived in Romania for fourteen years, where he ran a business selling coffee. He was summarily deported on his return from travel outside Romania. In subsequent proceedings it was alleged that he

[71] §§ 176–177. [72] § 185.

[73] Protocol 7 has attracted 43 ratifications as at 30 November 2013; a further three countries (Germany, The Netherlands, and Turkey) have signed but not yet having ratified the Protocol. The UK is the only country not to sign this Protocol. [74] Explanatory Memorandum on the Seventh Protocol, 7.

[75] *Omwenyeke v Germany*, (App. 44294/04), Decision of 20 November 2007, ECHR 2007-XII.

[76] *Lupsa v Romania*, (App. 10337/04), 8 June 2006, (2008) 46 EHRR 810, ECHR 2006-VII. See to similar effect *Kaya v Romania*, (App. 33970/05), 12 October 2006; and *CG v Bulgaria*, (App. 1365/07), 24 April 2008, (2008) 47 EHRR 1117, ECHR 2008-nyr.

was an undesirable person engaged in activities capable of endangering national security. The Strasbourg Court found that the legal basis for his deportation had not afforded the minimum guarantees against arbitrary action.[77] In addition, the Romanian authorities had infringed the guarantees under Article 1(1)(a) and (b) of the provision; he had not been provided with the slightest intimation of the national security ground on which the authorities purported to base their decision, and his lawyer had not been afforded sufficient opportunity to study the case in order to guarantee a proper review of the decision.

Article 1 of Protocol 7 will be violated where there is no legal base for the deportation order.[78] The concept of action 'in accordance with law' has the same meaning as in other provisions of the Convention.[79]

The procedural guarantees are set out in self-explanatory manner in the Article,[80] which provides no protection of substance,[81] that is, relating to the grounds on which their expulsion might be sought. Nevertheless, the due process requirements themselves operate to preclude arbitrary decisions to expel.[82].

CONCLUDING REMARKS

Issues of free movement have thrown up a number of interesting and controversial issues, especially in relation to free movement in the new democracies of the Council of Europe. Complaints of violations of the freedom of movement provisions of Protocols 4 and 7 are frequently attached to complaints of violations of other provisions of the Convention. The Strasbourg Court tends to consider them towards the end of its decisions and judgments, often finding either that there is no substance to the complaint or that the factual context is the same as that considered under some other provision of the Convention. However, cases have continued to come before the Court from central and eastern Europe There will undoubtedly continue to be further developments in the case-law arising from the policies and practices of some of these States, as well as the issue of the interdiction at sea to prevent asylum seekers reaching the territory of European States, especially in southern Europe. The *Hirsi Jaama* judgment marked an important expansion of the protection from collective expulsion in the light of the continuing numbers of asylum seekers attempting to reach Europe.[83] As the concurring opinion of Judge Pinto notes, the case underlines the intersection between international refugee law and the European Convention of Human Rights.

[77] See also *Nolan and K v Russia*, (App. 2512/04), 12 February 2009.

[78] *Bolat v Russia* (App. 14139/03), 5 October 2006, (2008) 46 EHRR 354, ECHR 2006-XI; *Takush v Greece*, (App. 2853/09), Decision of 17 January 2012; *Ahmed v Romania*, (App. 34621/03), 13 July 2010.

[79] *CG v Bulgaria*, (App. 1365/07), 24 April 2008, (2008) 47 EHRR 1117, ECHR 2008-nyr, § 73; *Kaushal and others v Bulgaria*, (App. 1537/08), 2 December 2010, § 48.

[80] For further explanation, see Explanatory Memorandum on the Seventh Protocol.

[81] Other provisions of the Convention might assist, such as Arts. 3, 5(1)(f), 8, and 13.

[82] *Kaushal and others v Bulgaria*, (App. 1537/08), 2 December 2010, § 49; *Takush v Greece*, (App. 2853/09), 17 January 2012; *Ahmed v Romania*, (App. 34621/03), 13 July 2010.

[83] The number of asylum seekers attempting to reach southern Europe has increased, with the conflicts in the Middle East adding to the numbers arriving from African States. See UNHCR information and news on southern Europe available at: www.unhcr.org/pages/49e48e996.html.

24

FREEDOM FROM DISCRIMINATION

INTRODUCTION

Article 14 is an autonomous provision of the Convention, which contains a general prohibition of both direct and indirect discrimination in relation to the enjoyment of the rights guaranteed by the Convention and Protocols.[1] It is joined—for those Contracting Parties which have ratified it—by a more general equality provision in Protocol 12.[2]

Article 14 provides that:

> The enjoyment of the rights and freedoms set forth in this Convention shall be secured without discrimination on any ground such as sex, race, colour, language, religion, political or other opinion, national or social origin, association with a national minority, property, birth or other status.

The term 'Convention' includes the First, Fourth, Sixth, and Seventh Protocols, which themselves provide that all the provisions of the Convention apply to them.[3]

The enunciation of the principle of equality, and the prohibition of discrimination, were considered so fundamental as to be placed at the beginning of the Universal Declaration of Human Rights,[4] and of the United Nations Covenants on Economic, Social and Cultural Rights and on Civil and Political Rights.[5] These principles also have a prominent place in many national constitutions, for example in Article 3 of the German Basic Law, in the 'equal protection' clauses of the United States Constitution, and in the constitutions of many Commonwealth countries. Several international instruments prohibiting particular forms of discrimination, or discrimination in particular fields, have been drawn up, in the United Nations, in the International Labour Organization, in UNESCO, and elsewhere. There is thus a substantial body of law on the subject.

In considering allegations of violations of Article 14, there are four key questions. First, is the complaint within the 'scope' or 'ambit' of one of the substantive provisions of the Convention? Secondly, is the alleged reason for the discrimination one of the grounds listed in Article 14? Thirdly, can the applicants properly compare themselves with another class of persons which is treated more favourably? Fourthly, is the difference in treatment reasonably and objectively justified?

[1] See K. Partsch, 'Discrimination' in R. Macdonald, F. Matscher, and H. Petzold, (eds.) *The European System for the Protection of Human Rights* (Martinus Nijhoff, Dordrecht 1993), 571; and R. O'Connell, 'Cinderella comes to the Ball: Article 14 and the right to non-discrimination in the ECHR' (2009) 29 *Legal Studies* 211.

[2] ETS 177; in force since 1 April 2005. As at 1 December 2013 in force for 18 Contracting Parties. For current ratifications see http://conventions.coe.int. See further later in this chapter.

[3] Art. 5 of Protocol 1; Art. 6(1) of Protocol 4; Art. 6 of Protocol 6; and Art. 7 of Protocol 7.

[4] Arts. 1 and 2. [5] Arts. 2 and 3 of each Covenant.

POSITIVE OBLIGATIONS

The issue of positive obligations is somewhat different under Article 14 because of the requirement for the allegation of discrimination to fall within the ambit of one of the substantive Articles of the Convention. However, the Strasbourg Court has indicated that, whether the discrimination arises by some action or by a failure to ensure non-discrimination, the justification for the differential treatment must meet a legitimate aim and there must be a reasonable relationship of proportionality between that aim and its realization.[6] It is also inherent in the scheme of the Article that Contracting Parties are obliged to take steps to prevent discrimination falling within the ambit of the Article. This obligation manifests itself in the Court's conclusion that the right not to be discriminated against in the enjoyment of rights falling within the scope of the Convention will be violated where Contracting Parties fail to treat persons in different situations differently without any objective and reasonable justification for doing so.[7] However, in this context the Contracting Parties enjoy a considerable margin of appreciation in assessing whether and to what extent differences in otherwise similar situations justify a difference in treatment.[8]

An example of discrimination arising where there is a failure to treat different individuals or groups differently can be found in the *Thlimmenos* case, which concerned a conviction for refusal to serve in the armed forces by a Jehovah's Witness.[9] The applicant complained that, as a result of his conviction for the offence, he had been excluded from the profession of chartered accountant, and that the law failed to make any distinction between those convicted as a result of their religious beliefs and those convicted on other grounds. The applicant complained of a violation of Article 14 when taken together with Article 9 on freedom of thought, conscience, and religion. The Court, in finding a violation of Article 14 taken in conjunction with Article 9, extended its earlier case-law to situations where, without any objective and reasonable justification, a Contracting Party fails to treat differently persons whose situations are significantly different.[10] The Court has also found that the State has positive obligations in relation to the duty to protect persons from discriminatory harm[11] as well as the duty to investigate racial motives for State action.[12]

CONCEPTUAL ISSUES

Until the judgment of the Strasbourg Court in the *Belgian Linguistic* case,[13] there was some doubt as to the relationship between Article 14 and the Articles which define the other rights and freedoms guaranteed. Article 14 does not prohibit discrimination as such, in any

[6] *Posti and Rahko v Finland*, (App. 27824/95), 24 September 2002, (2003) 37 EHRR 158, ECHR 2002-VII.

[7] *Thlimmenos v Greece*, (App. 34369/97), 6 April 2000, (2001) 31 EHRR 411, ECHR 2000-IV.

[8] *Sommerfield v Germany*, (App. 31871/96), 8 July 2003 [GC], (2004) 38 EHRR 756, ECHR 2003-VIII, § 92.

[9] *Thlimmenos v Greece*, (App. 34369/97), 6 April 2000, (2001) 31 EHRR 411, ECHR 2000-IV.

[10] See also the development of indirect discrimination in *DH and others v Czech Republic*, (App. 57325/00), 13 November 2007 [GC], (2008) 47 EHRR 59, ECHR 2007-nyr.

[11] See for example *Opuz v Turkey*, (App. 33401/02), 9 June 2009.

[12] See *Nachova and others v Bulgaria*, (Apps. 43577/98 and 43579/98), 6 July 2005 [GC], (2006) 42 EHRR 933, ECHR 2005-VII.

[13] *Case relating to certain aspects of the laws on the use of languages in education in Belgium (Belgian Linguistic Case (No. 20)*, (Apps. 1474/62, 1677/62, 1691/62, 1769/63, 1994/63, and 2126/64), 23 July 1968, Series A No 6, (1979–80), 23 July 1968, Series A No 6, (1979–80) 1 EHRR 252 (cited in this chapter as the '*Belgian Linguistic* case').

context, but only in 'the enjoyment of the rights and freedoms set forth in this Convention'. On the other hand, did Article 14 only come into play if there had been a violation of one of those rights? The view that Article 14 had such a subsidiary role, advanced by the respondent State before the Court in the *Belgian Linguistic* case, derived some support from certain earlier decisions of the Commission.[14] However, this interpretation would, as the Commission itself argued in the *Belgian Linguistic* case, have deprived Article 14 of its effectiveness, and it was rejected by the Court. The breach of Article 14 does not presuppose the violation of the rights guaranteed by other Articles of the Convention. While it is true that this guarantee has no independent existence in the sense that under the terms of Article 14 it relates solely to 'rights and freedoms set forth in the Convention', a measure which in itself is in conformity with the requirements of a substantive Article enshrining the right or freedom in question may nevertheless infringe Article 14 when read in conjunction with it for the reason that it is of a discriminatory nature.

Thus, persons subject to the jurisdiction of a Contracting Party cannot draw from Article 2 of Protocol 1 the right to obtain from the public authorities the creation of a particular kind of educational establishment. Nevertheless, a Contracting Party which had set up such an establishment could not, in laying down entrance requirements, take discriminatory measures within the meaning of Article 14. In such cases there would be a violation of a guaranteed right or freedom as it is proclaimed by the relevant Article read in conjunction with Article 14. No distinctions should be made in this respect according to the nature of these rights and freedoms and of their correlative obligations, and whether the respect due to the right concerned implies positive action or mere abstention. This is clearly shown by the very general nature of the terms employed in Article 14; 'the enjoyment of the rights and freedoms set forth in this Convention shall be secured'.[15]

Thus to summarize, while there can never be a violation of Article 14 considered in isolation, there may be a violation of Article 14, considered together with another Article of the Convention, in cases where there would be no violation of that other Article taken alone. Discrimination is prohibited, not only in the restrictions permitted, but also in laws implementing the rights guaranteed, even if those laws go beyond the obligations expressly provided by the Convention.

A second, and more difficult, problem of interpretation raised by Article 14 was also dealt with by the Court in the *Belgian Linguistic* case. What forms of differential treatment constitute 'discrimination'? To argue that Article 14 prohibits all inequalities of treatment based on the grounds stated would lead to manifestly unreasonable results, since the inequality might actually be designed to benefit the less privileged class. For example, the provision of additional educational facilities for the children of poorer families would not necessarily constitute discrimination. On the other hand, if only certain forms of inequality are prohibited, by what objective criteria can they be identified? On this issue, the Court said:

> In spite of the very general wording of the French version ('*sans distinction aucune*'), Article 14 does not forbid every difference in treatment in the exercise of the rights and freedoms recognized. This version must be read in the light of the more restrictive text of the English version ('without discrimination'). In addition, and in particular, one would reach absurd results were one to give Article 14 an interpretation as wide as that which the French version seems to imply. One would, in effect, be led to judge as contrary to the Convention every one

[14] See M. Eissen, 'L'autonomie de l'article 14 de la Convention européenne des droits de l'homme dans la jurisprudence de la Commission', in *Mélanges Modinos* (Paris, 1968), 122.

[15] *Belgian Linguistic* case, (Apps. 1474/62, 1677/62, 1691/62, 1769/63, 1994/63, and 2126/64), 23 July 1968, Series A No 6, (1979–80) 1 EHRR 252, Section IB, § 9.

> of the many legal or administrative provisions which do not secure to everyone complete equality of treatment in the enjoyment of the rights and freedoms recognized. The competent national authorities are frequently confronted with situations and problems which, on account of differences inherent therein, call for different legal solutions; moreover, certain legal inequalities tend only to correct factual inequalities. The extensive interpretation mentioned above cannot consequently be accepted.
>
> It is important, then, to look for the criteria which enable a determination to be made as to whether or not a given difference in treatment, concerning of course the exercise of one of the rights and freedoms set forth, contravenes Article 14. On this question the Court, following the principles which may be extracted from the legal practice of a large number of democratic States, holds that the principle of equality of treatment is violated if the distinction has no objective and reasonable justification. The existence of such a justification must be assessed in relation to the aim and effects of the measure under consideration, regard being had to the principles which normally prevail in democratic societies. A difference of treatment in the exercise of a right laid down in the Convention must not only pursue a legitimate aim; Article 14 is likewise violated when it is clearly established that there is no reasonable relationship of proportionality between the means employed and the aim sought to be realised.[16]

The Court adopted, and applied in its examination of the legislation in question, the weaker of two alternative theses on the meaning of discrimination. On this weaker thesis, differential treatment is justified if it has an objective aim, derived from the public interest, and if the measures of differentiation do not exceed a reasonable relation to that aim.

A stronger thesis would be that differential treatment is justified only if, *without regard to the purpose of the measures in question*, the facts themselves require or permit differential treatment. This view of Article 14 was clearly formulated by a member of the Commission, Mr Balta, in an individual opinion in the *Grandrath* case.[17] He stated:

> In my view, the intention of Article 14 is to establish the principle of complete equality in the enjoyment of the rights and freedoms set forth in the Convention. This being so, enjoyment of those rights and freedoms may not be made subject to any kinds of discrimination other than those which are either inherent in the nature of the right in question or are designed to remedy existing inequalities.

The two theses both start from the idea that a difference of status, of sex, race, language, and so on, cannot of itself justify differential treatment; but whereas on the first thesis differential treatment might be justified by the purpose of the measures in question, on the second thesis it could only be justified if the difference of status implied certain objective factual differences which required or permitted different legal treatment. The distinction is of considerable practical importance, since, on the thesis adopted by the Strasbourg Court in the *Belgian Linguistic* case, it found a violation on only one aspect of the Belgian legislation; on the stronger thesis, other provisions might also have been inconsistent with the Convention.

Some examples of discrimination on certain of the grounds referred to in Article 14 has already been mentioned in earlier chapters: for example, in relation to sex and sexuality, under Article 8; to race, under Article 3; to language, under Article 2 of Protocol 1; and to religion, under Article 9; and in relation to property under Article 1 of Protocol 1.

[16] *Belgian Linguistic* case, Section IB, § 10.

[17] App. 2299/64, *Grandrath v Federal Republic of Germany*, Report of Commission, 12 December 1966; Decision of Committee of Ministers, 29 June 1967, (1967) 10 *Yearbook* 626.

Complaints under Article 14 are most frequently paired with Article 8, followed by Article 1 of Protocol 1, and Articles 10 and 6.

Finally, it should be noted that the grounds listed in Article 14 are not exhaustive. Discrimination based on any 'other status' is also prohibited. But precisely what is meant by a personal characteristic is one of the troublesome aspects of Article 14.[18] There is conflicting authority on the meaning and extent of 'other status'. A line of case-law seemed to suggest a narrow construction, meaning that where consideration of discrimination with regard to 'other status' is in issue, the basis of comparison must relate to a personal characteristic.[19] However another line of case-law developed which adopted a much wider approach. Taking into consideration the wide meaning that may be implied from the French text, *toute autre situation*, the *Engel*[20] case found that the list set out in Article 14 was merely illustrative and other status could include any situations including military rank, as was the case in *Engel*. The later case of *Rasmussen v Denmark*[21] noted that there is not even a need in some cases to determine which ground is being used.[22] The Court attempted to reconcile these two lines of authority in the *Carson* case,[23] where the Strasbourg Court accepted that residence, like domicile and nationality, is an aspect of personal status, and will ground a complaint of differential treatment. The Court combined both tests:

> It has established in its case-law that only differences in treatment based on a personal characteristic (or "status") by which persons or groups of persons are distinguishable from each other are capable of amounting to discrimination within the meaning of Article 14 ... However, the list set out in Article 14 is illustrative and not exhaustive, as is shown by the words "any ground such as" (in French "notamment")... It further recalls that the words "other status" (and a fortiori the French "toute autre situation") have been given a wide meaning so as to include, in certain circumstances, a distinction drawn on the basis of a place of residence. Thus, in previous cases the Court has examined under Article 14 the legitimacy of alleged discrimination based, inter alia, on domicile abroad... and registration as a resident... It is true that regional differences of treatment, resulting from the application of different legislation depending on the geographical location of an applicant, have been held not to be explained in terms of personal characteristics.... However, ... these cases are not comparable to the present case, which involves the different application of the same pensions legislation to persons depending on their residence and presence abroad.

It would seem from *Carson* that there is no formal requirement to establish a personal characteristic and personal status is a better term to describe those grounds which fall under 'other status'. This would include where the ground is based on personal choice. However, case-law since *Carson* has continued to use different approaches to 'personal status'. The

[18] For a discussion on the inconsistent approach of the Court to 'on grounds of other status' see J. Gerrards, 'The Discrimination Grounds of Article 14 of the European Convention on Human Rights' (2013) HRLawRev, 13:1, 99–124.

[19] See *Kjeldsen, Busk Madsen and Pedersen v Denmark*, (App. 5095/71, 5920/72, and 5926/72), 7 December 1976, Series A No 23, (1979–80) 1 EHRR 711, § 56. See also *Budak v Turkey*, (App. 57345/00), Decision of December of 7 September 2004, § 4.

[20] *Engel and others v the Netherlands*, (App. 5370/72), 8 June 1976, A22 (1976, 1 EHRR 674 § 72.

[21] *Rasmussen v Denmark*, (App. 8777/79), 28 November 1984, A87 (1984) 7 EHRR 647, § 34.

[22] See *Stubbings and others v United Kingdom*, (Apps. 22083/93 and 22095/93), 22 October 1996, (1997) 23 EHRR 213, ECHR 1996-IV, where the differential treatment related to the legal system's approach to providing a remedy for psychological harm resulting from child abuse and other types of actionable wrong; and *National & Provincial Building Society and others v United Kingdom*, (Apps. 21319/93, 21449/93, and 21675/93), 23 October 1997, (1998) 25 EHRR 127, ECHR 1997-VII, which concerned recovery of tax paid under invalidated tax regulations.

[23] *Carson and others v United Kingdom*, (App. 42184/05), 16 March 2010, ECHR 2010.

Clift[24] case found that the difference between sentencing regimes for prisoners fitted into Article 14, noting that there is no need for personal characteristics and instead examined the circumstances of the case. In contrast, in another UK case[25] the Court took a much narrower approach. The applicants claimed entitlement to a benefit given by the State even though they were living outside the UK. The Court held that acquiring a welfare benefit cannot be part of personal status as it was not innate. The Court has also sidestepped the issue of personal status for legal persons who are victims under the Convention by ignoring the grounds and focusing on differential treatment.[26]

The Court has clearly expanded the protection of Article 14 by including in other status, situations beyond innate personal characteristics, such as situations that could loosely be described as impacting on personal circumstances.[27] However, it will generally be easier to establish a situation as falling within Article 14 where the ground of differentiation is a personal characteristic. It is probably also true that different treatment which is based other than on a personal characteristic may be easier for the Contracting Party to justify.[28]

THE COURT'S METHODOLOGY

Over the years, the Strasbourg Court's methodology in dealing with complaints under Article 14 has developed considerably. At one time, there was much focus on whether there had been a violation of the substantive provision of the Convention claimed to be within the ambit of Article 14 before consideration of whether there was discrimination. If a violation of the substantive provision was found, there was a tendency not to consider that provision in conjunction with Article 14 in what one commentator describes as for 'reasons of procedural economy.'[29] The signal for a change to that approach was reinforced in an early decision of the Grand Chamber in the *Chassagnou* case:[30]

> Where a substantive Article of the Convention has been invoked both on its own and together with Article 14 and a separate breach has been found of the substantive Article, it is not generally necessary for the Court to consider the case under Article 14 also, though the position is otherwise if a clear inequality of treatment in the enjoyment of the right in question is a fundamental aspect of the case.[31]

This approach addresses a criticism which could be levelled at some early decisions of the Strasbourg organs where clear inequality of treatment had been ignored to the detriment

[24] *Clift v United Kingdom*, (App. 7205/07), 13 July 2010. See also *Laduna v Slovakia*, (App. 31827/02), 13 December 2011, where remand prisoners were held to have other status due to the legal status they were placed in, also see *Bah v United Kingdom*, (App. 5632807), 27 September 2011, which referred to *Clift* when finding immigration status was 'other status' under Article 14.

[25] *Springett and others v United Kingdom*, (App. 374726/05), Decision of 27 April 2010.

[26] See for example *Ozgurluk Ve Dayanisma Partisi (ODP) v Turkey*, (App. 7819/03), 10 May 2012.

[27] Personal status was described in this way in *Laduna v Slovakia*, (App. 31827/02), 13 December 2011, § 55, where the Court noted that being on remand is inextricably linked to personal characteristics.

[28] As in *Bah v United Kingdom*, (App. 5632807), 27 September 2011, where the Court found that immigration status comes under Article 14 but that there was an element of personal choice in that status, § 47. The Court noted that residence can be changed as a matter of choice: § 80.

[29] K. Partsch, 'Discrimination' in R. Macdonald, F. Matscher, and H. Petzold (eds.), *The European System for the Protection of Human Rights* (Martinus Nijhoff, Dordrecht 1993), 583.

[30] *Chassagnou and others v France*, (Apps. 25088/94, 28331/95, and 28443/95), 29 April 1999 [GC], (2000) 29 EHRR 615, ECHR 1999-III.

[31] § 89, although similar statements can be found in much earlier cases, see, for example, *Dudgeon v United Kingdom*, (App. 7525/76), 22 October 1981, Series A No 45, (1982) 4 EHRR 149, § 67.

of the development of the case-law on the prohibition of discrimination. When an allegation of a violation of a substantive provision of the Convention is coupled with an allegation that there has also been a violation of that Article when read with Article 14, there remain many cases where the Strasbourg Court does not find it necessary to address the complaint under Article 14, but there is an increasing number of cases in which the Court does choose to deal with this aspect of the applicant's complaints. Sometimes the Strasbourg Court does not consider the additional complaint involving discrimination because its response to the complaint under the substantive question would constitute reasonable and objective justification in relation to discrimination within Article 14.[32]

Where the essence of the complaint of a violation of the substantive provision is an act of discrimination, the Strasbourg Court begins by considering the allegation of a violation of Article 14 when read with the substantive provision. This can render it unnecessary to consider whether there has been a separate violation of the substantive Article. So, in the *Burghartz* case,[33] the applicants complained under Article 8 taken alone, and in conjunction with Article 14, that they had been refused consent to change their family surname and the husband's surname. The Court considered whether there had been a violation of Article 8 taken in conjunction with Article 14 first. The basis for doing so was said to be 'the nature of the complaints',[34] which was essentially a difference of treatment on the grounds of sex in relation to the use of names. The Court found a violation.

Sometimes, the Strasbourg Court finds a violation both of the substantive provision, and of that provision when read with Article 14. In the *Marckx* case,[35] the Court found violations of Article 8 taken alone in the process of recognition required of an unmarried mother to establish her maternity, and then went on to consider whether violations had occurred under Article 8 taken in conjunction with Article 14. It is difficult to see how these complaints were not in substance the same as those taken under Article 8 alone, but this was presumably one of those cases in which a 'clear inequality of treatment in the enjoyment of the right in question' arose as 'a fundamental aspect of the case'. Another example of a case in which a violation was found both of the substantive provision and of Article 14 is the *Bączkowski* case.[36] Members of an association whose objectives were to campaign on behalf of homosexual people were refused permission to organize a march in Warsaw. While the application was pending, the Mayor of Warsaw had made remarks in a newspaper interview to the effect that he would ban the march and that 'propaganda about homosexuality is not tantamount to exercising one's freedom of assembly'. The subsequent refusal of permission was purported to be based on concerns over road traffic management. The Strasbourg Court found that the decision was influenced by the remarks of the Mayor in the interview. A violation of Article 11 was found, but a violation of Article 14 read with Article 11 was also found on the grounds that the Mayor's statements indicated unlawful discrimination in the exercise of public powers.

In the *Aziz* case,[37] the Strasbourg Court found a violation of Article 3 of Protocol 1, and a violation of that Article when read with Article 14. The applicant was a Turkish Cypriot living in Nicosia who had been deprived of the opportunity to vote. After finding a violation of Article 3 of Protocol 1, the Court went on to consider the complaint under Article 14, noting that the complaint was 'not a mere restatement of the applicant's

[32] As in *Evans v United Kingdom*, (App. 6339/05), 10 April 2007 [GC], (2008) 46 EHRR 728, ECHR 2007-IV.

[33] *Burghartz v Switzerland*, (App. 16213/90), 22 February 1994, Series A No 280-B, (1994) 18 EHRR 101. See also *Ponomaryovi v Bulgaria*, (App. 633505), 21 June 2011.

[34] § 21.

[35] *Marckx v Belgium*, (App. 6833/74), 13 June 1979, Series A No 31, (1979–80) 2 EHRR 330.

[36] *Bączkowski and others v Poland*, (App. 1543/06), 3 May 2007, (2009) 48 EHRR 475, ECHR 2007-VI.

[37] *Aziz v Cyprus*, (App. 69949/01), 22 June 2004, (2005) 41 EHRR 164, ECHR 2004-V.

complaint' under the substantive Article.[38] There was discrimination between members of the Greek Cypriot and Turkish Cypriot communities for which there was no reasonable and objective justification. The case might usefully be contrasted with the *Eugenia Michaelidou Developments Ltd* case,[39] where the complaint concerned continuing denial of access to property in the occupied north of Cyprus. Having found a violation of Article 1 of Protocol 1, the Court declined to pronounce on allegations of violations of Article 14 when read with Article 1 of Protocol 1 since these allegations amounted to essentially the same complaints.[40]

In the *Nachova* case,[41] the Grand Chamber found violations both of Article 2 when read alone, and of Article 14 when read with Article 2. The applicants were relatives of two Roma men who had been shot and killed when they were on the run from the police. It was alleged that the killings were racially motivated, and that the authorities had failed in their duty to investigate the possible racist motivations in their killing. The Grand Chamber found that the investigation of the killings was inadequate and that this constituted a violation of the procedural aspect of Article 2.[42] In considering whether there was also a violation of Article 14 when read with Article 2, the Grand Chamber commented as follows:

> Owing to the interplay between the two provisions, issues such as those in the present case may fall to be examined under one of the two provisions only, with no separate issue arising under the other, or may require examination under both Articles. This is a question to be decided in each case on its facts and depending on the nature of the allegation made.[43]

The motivation for dealing with the complaint under Article 14 when read with Article 2 is not articulated beyond that statement, though it seems that the background of 'many published accounts of the existence in Bulgaria of prejudice and hostility against Roma'[44] may have been a significant factor. Another factor may have been the criticism the Court had received for failing to find a separate violation of Article 14 in cases involving race. In a robust dissenting opinion in *Anguelova v Bulgaria*,[45] Judge Bonello noted violations had been found in cases involving the Roma community under Article 2 and Article 3 but yet the Court had failed to highlight that racial discrimination was a fundamental aspect of these cases. He noted that the result of not using Article 14 was to conceal the systemic problem of discrimination in Europe:

> Leafing through the annals of the Court, an uninformed observer would be justified to conclude that, for over fifty years democratic Europe has been exempted from any suspicion of racism, intolerance or xenophobia. The Europe projected by the Court's case-law is that of an exemplary haven of ethnic fraternity, in which peoples of the most diverse origin coalesce without distress, prejudice or recrimination. The present case energises that delusion.[46]

Subsequent cases made the racial component much more explicit,[47] with the criticism of the Court in its examination of racial discrimination seemingly addressed in *Nachova*.

[38] § 36.

[39] *Eugenia Michaelidou Developments Ltd and Michael Tymvios v Turkey*, (App. 16163/90), 31 July 2003.

[40] Following the approach it had adopted in *Cyprus v Turkey*, (App. 25781/94), 10 May 2001 [GC], (2002) 35 EHRR 731, ECHR 2001-IV, § 199, but note the partly dissenting opinion of Judge Costa.

[41] *Nachova and others v Bulgaria*, (Apps. 43577/98 and 43579/98), 6 July 2005 [GC], (2006) 42 EHRR 933, ECHR 2005-VII.

[42] See ch.8.

[43] § 161.

[44] § 163. See later in this chapter for further comments on cases involving discrimination against minorities.

[45] *Anguelova v Bulgaria*, (App. 38361/97), 13 June 2002, ECHR 2002–IV.

[46] Partly Dissenting Opinion of Judge Bonello, § 2.

[47] See, for example, *Angelova and Iliev v Bulgaria*, (App. 55523/00), 26 July 2007, (2008) 47 EHRR 236; and *Cobzaru v Romania*, (App. 48254/99), 26 July 2007, (2008) 47 EHRR 288.

However, in cases concerning the sterilization of young Roma women in Slovakia,[48] the Court found a violation of Article 3 and then found there was no need to consider Article 14, despite evidence to suggest that the practice of sterilizing young women was particularly targeted at Roma women. The dissenting judge in the *V.C* case[49] noted that a failure to address Article 14 failed to recognize the structural problem in the State:

> Finding violations of Articles 3 and 8 alone in my opinion reduces this case to the individual level, whereas it is obvious that there was a general State policy of sterilisation of Roma women under the communist regime (governed by the 1972 Sterilisation Regulation), the effects of which continued to be felt up to the time of the facts giving rise to the present case.... The fact that there are other cases of this kind pending before the Court reinforces my personal conviction that the sterilisations performed on Roma women were not of an accidental nature, but relics of a long-standing attitude towards the Roma minority in Slovakia.[50]

In other cases involving the Roma community and race discrimination the Court has been rather inconsistent in its approach. In *Yordanova and others v Bulgaria*,[51] the Court found a violation under Article 8, noting that the eviction of Roma applicants from unlawfully built houses should involve the consideration of the minority group:

> In general, the underprivileged status of the applicants' group must be a weighty factor in considering approaches to dealing with their unlawful settlement and, if their removal is necessary, in deciding on its timing, modalities and, if possible, arrangements for alternative shelter. This has not been done in the present case.[52]

However, these factors were included in the examination of proportionality under Article 8 rather than using Article 14. In contrast in *Fedorchenko and Lozenko v Ukraine*[53] the Court found a violation of Article 2 and went on to find a violation of Article 14 with regard to the procedural failure to investigate. The case involved a fatal attack on a Roma dwelling so it may be suggested that the seriousness of the factual situation led to the Court to examine Article 14 separately. However, in another case[54] where there was an attack on Roma dwellings that led to a violation of Article 3 for a failure to investigate, there was no separate examination of Article 14. Apart from the difference in gravity of the acts in question in the two cases, it is difficult to discern why the failure to effectively investigate a case involving race was a fundamental aspect of one case and not the other. There is little explanation in *Koky* as to why Article 14 is not treated separately apart from the fact that the question of racial motives was covered under Article 3.[55] A better approach may be that where race is a fundamental issue in the case, the Court takes a consistent approach of using Article 14 to further highlight the racial discrimination that continues to persist in European States.

In very many cases, the Strasbourg Court concerns itself with four questions in making decisions on complaints under Article 14:[56]

- Does the complaint of discrimination fall within the scope of a protected right?
- Is the alleged reason for the discrimination one of the grounds listed in Article 14?

[48] *V.C v Slovakia*, (App. 18968/07), 8 November 2011; *N.B v Slovakia*, (App. 29518/10), 12 June 2012; *I.G and others v Slovakia*, (App. 15996/04), 13 November 2012.

[49] *V.C v Slovakia*, (App. 18968/07), 8 November 2011.

[50] Dissenting Opinion of Judge Mijovic.

[51] *Yordanova and others v Bulgaria*, (App. 25446/06), 24 April 2012.

[52] § 133.

[53] *Fedorchenko and Lozenko v Ukraine*, (App. 387/03), 20 September 2010.

[54] *Koky and others v Slovakia*, (App. 13624/03), 12 June 2012.

[55] § 243.

[56] See the Grand Chamber's statement of general principles in *Kafkaris v Cyprus*, (App. 21906/04), 12 February 2008 [GC], (2009) 49 EHRR 877, ECHR 2008-nyr, §§ 159–61.

- Can the applicants properly compare themselves with another class of persons which is treated more favourably?
- Is the difference of treatment capable of objective and reasonable justification?

Each of these questions will now be considered.

DOES THE COMPLAINT OF DISCRIMINATION FALL WITHIN THE SCOPE OF A PROTECTED RIGHT?

As noted, Article 14 only applies in respect of 'the enjoyment of the rights and freedoms as set forth' in the Convention, including its Protocols. But there is no requirement that there is a breach of another Convention right. An example of the modern formula used by the Strasbourg Court can be found in the *Kafkaris* case:[57]

> The Court reiterates that Article 14 of the Convention has no independent existence, since it has effect solely in relation to the rights and freedoms safeguarded by the other substantive provisions of the Convention and its Protocols. However, the application of Article 14 does not presuppose a breach of one or more of such provisions and to this extent it is autonomous.... A measure which in itself is in conformity with the requirements of the Article enshrining the right or freedom in question may however infringe this Article when read in conjunction with Article 14 for the reason that it is of a discriminatory nature.... Accordingly, for Article 14 to become applicable it suffices that the facts of a case fall within the ambit of another substantive provision of the Convention or its Protocols....[58]

In the *Stec* case,[59] the Court made it clear that there was no requirement under, for example, Article 1 of Protocol 1, to set up a system of social security or to pay welfare benefits of any particular kind or amount. However, if a State did decide to exceed its Convention commitments, and provide for the payment of a welfare benefit, it had to ensure that the terms of entitlement to the benefit were not discriminatory. The applicants in that case were complaining that different amounts of an industrial injury benefit were paid to men and women. When women reached the statutory retirement age of sixty, they became entitled to a lower rate of benefit. The statutory retirement age was sixty-five for men, however, so that men continued to be entitled to the higher rate of industrial injury benefit for a longer period. The Strasbourg Court held that although there was no obligation on the State under the Convention to provide for an industrial injury benefit, if such a benefit did exist, a person who was entitled to it under the terms of national law could claim it as a 'possession' within the meaning of Article 1 of Protocol 1. It therefore fell within the 'scope' of the Convention and Article 14 therefore applied.[60]

Similarly, in the *Belgian Linguistic* case,[61] the Strasbourg Court held that, although Article 2 of Protocol 1 did not place an obligation on the State to set up a publicly-funded

[57] *Kafkaris v Cyprus*, (App. 21906/04), 12 February 2008 [GC], (2009) 49 EHRR 877, ECHR 2008-nyr.

[58] § 159.

[59] *Stec and others v United Kingdom*, (Apps. 65731/01 and 65900/01), 12 April 2006 [GC], (2006) 43 EHRR 1017, ECHR 2006-VI. See also ch.20.

[60] See also *Runkee and White v United Kingdom*, (Apps. 42949/98 and 53134/99), 10 May 2007; *Carson and others v United Kingdom*, (App. 42184/05), ECHR 2010; *Stummer v Austria*, (App. 37452/02), 7 July 2011; *Raviv v Austria*, (App. 26266/05), 13 March 2012.

[61] *Belgian Linguistic* case, (Apps. 1474/62, 1677/62, 1691/62, 1769/63, 1994/63, and 2126/64), 23 July 1968, Series A No 6, (1979–80) 1 EHRR 252.

school of any particular kind, if the State did create such a school, it could not, in laying down entrance requirements, take discriminatory measures within the meaning of Article 14. Another example can be found in cases which raise issues surrounding adoption. There is no general right to adoption under Article 8, but where the State legislates for adoption it must do so in a non-discriminatory manner.[62]

An example of a complaint which was not found to fall within the scope of a Convention right is the *Haas* case.[63] The applicant was an illegitimate child; he knew who his father was, though his father had never recognized him as his son. Nevertheless, his father made regular payments towards his maintenance, visited him, and went on day trips with him. The father died intestate and his estate went to his nephew. The applicant claimed part of the estate, but the national courts refused to accept his claim to be the unrecognized son. The Court concluded that the complaint was not within the scope of Article 8; he had never lived with his father and the sporadic contacts did not constitute 'family life', nor had he taken steps to have his paternity recognized during his father's life.[64] Since the claim was not within the scope of Article 8, Article 14 issues could not be considered.

The Strasbourg Court generally takes a broad brush approach as to whether a claim falls within the ambit of one of the substantive Articles, and this can sometimes lead to considerable confusion about the outer limits of the operation of a particular Article.[65]

IS THE ALLEGED REASON FOR THE DISCRIMINATION ONE OF THE GROUNDS LISTED IN ARTICLE 14?

Article 14 includes a list of prohibited grounds of discrimination: 'sex, race, colour, language, religion, political or other opinion, national or social origin, association with a national minority, property, birth'. The list of prohibited grounds is not exhaustive, however, as the Article also states that discrimination based on 'other status' is prohibited.[66] The French version, 'toute autre situation', is even broader.

In the *Kjeldsen, Busk Madsen and Pedersen* case, the Strasbourg Court established that to fall within the concept 'other status', the difference in treatment had to be based on 'a personal characteristic by which persons or groups of persons are distinguishable from each other'.[67] The Court and Commission have held that such characteristics as illegitimacy,[68]

[62] *Frette v France*, (App. 36515/97), 26 February 2002, (2004) 38 EHRR 438 ECHR 2002-I; *EB v France*, (App. 43546/02), 22 January 2008 [GC], ECHR 2008-nyr; *Gas and Dubois v France*, (App. 29591/07), 15 March 2012.

[63] *Haas v The Netherlands*, (App. 36983/97), 13 January 2004, (2004) 39 EHRR 897, ECHR 2004-I. Contrast *Merger and Cros v France*, (App. 68864/01), 22 December 2004, dealing with the rights of an illegitimate child to inherit in a different situation.

[64] Which the Court, in the *Haas* case, hints might have brought the claim within the scope of 'private life' since it concerned the son's personal identity: § 42.

[65] See A. Baker, 'The Enjoyment of Rights and Freedoms: A New Conception of the "Ambit" under Article 14 ECHR' (2006) 65 MLR 714.

[66] See earlier in this chapter for uncertainties surrounding the application of 'other status'.

[67] *Kjeldsen, Busk Madsen and Pedersen v Denmark*, (App. 5095/71, 5920/72, and 5926/72), 7 December 1976, Series A No 23, (1979–80) 1 EHRR 711, § 56.

[68] *Marckx v Belgium*, (App. 6833/74), 13 June 1979, Series A No 31, (1979–80) 2 EHRR 330; *Fabris v France*, (App.1657408), 7 February 2013.

sexual orientation,[69] disability and health status[70], marital status,[71] country of domicile or residence,[72] immigration and refugee status,[73] remand and convicted prisoners,[74] and the suffering from the psychological harm caused by child abuse,[75] all constitute 'other status'.

The open-ended nature of the phrase 'other status'[76] can make it difficult to apply in some cases. The *Sidabras and Džautas* case[77] illustrates the differences of view which can arise. The case concerned the application of laws in Lithuania designed to restrict the activities of former KGB officers. Both had been dismissed from Government employment when it was established that they were former KGB employees. A consequence of the application of the legislation to them was a restriction on their applying for various jobs in the private sector for a period of ten years. They argued that this breached their rights under Article 8 either taken alone or when read with Article 14. The Strasbourg Court chose to consider the claims under Article 8 when read with Article 14 because the applicants 'alleged discrimination in this respect'.[78] The Court concluded that the complaints were within the scope of Article 8, and so considered the Contracting Party's compliance with Article 14. The Court recognized the legitimate interest of the Contracting Party in regulating employment conditions both in the public and private sectors, though the Convention does not guarantee a right of access to a particular profession. The Court also acknowledged that under Article 10 of the Convention a democratic State had 'a legitimate interest in requiring civil servants to show loyalty to the constitutional principles on which the society was founded.'[79] As it had in other cases,[80] the Court recognized the political context of the emergence of countries of central and eastern Europe from totalitarian regimes. The restrictions on the employment of former KGB employees could be seen as pursuing the aim of protecting national security, public safety, the economic well-being of the country, and the rights and freedoms of others. However, the restrictions which applied to employment in the private sector went beyond what was reasonably needed to secure those aims. The scheme lacked 'the necessary safeguards for avoiding discrimination and for guaranteeing adequate and appropriate judicial supervision of the imposition of such restrictions.'[81] No separate consideration of a violation of Article 8 was undertaken. There were two dissenting opinions. Judge Loucaides did not consider that people who had worked for the KGB and people who had not worked for the KGB could be said to be in 'analogous', 'similar', or 'relevantly similar' situations. Judge Thomassen took a similar view:

> The principle of non-discrimination, as it is recognized in European Constitutions and in International Treaties, refers above all to a denial of opportunities on grounds of personal

[69] *Sutherland v United Kingdom*, (App. 25186/94), Report of the Commission adopted on 1 July 1997, § 51.

[70] *Glor v Switzerland*, (App. 133044/04), 30 April 2009, *Kiyutin v Russia*, (App. 2700/10), 10 March 2011; *I.B v Greece*, (App. 552/10), 3 October 2013.

[71] *McMichael v United Kingdom*, (App. 16424/90), 24 February 1995, Series A No 307-B, (1995) 20 EHRR 205.

[72] *Johnston v Ireland*, (App. 9697/82), 18 December 1986, Series A No 112, (1987) 9 EHRR 203, §§ 59–61; *Darby v Sweden*, (App. 11581/85), 23 October 1990, Series A No 187, (1991) 13 EHRR 774, §§ 31–4.

[73] *Bah v United Kingdom*, (App. 5632807), 27 September 2011; *O'Donoghue and others v United Kingdom*, (App. 34838/07), 14 December 2010; *Hode and Abdi v United Kingdom*, (App. 22341/09), 6 November 2012.

[74] *Laduna v Slovakia*, (App. 31827/02), 13 December 2011.

[75] *Stubbings and others v United Kingdom*, (Apps. 22083/93 and 22095/93), 22 October 1996, (1997) 23 EHRR 213, ECHR 1996-IV.

[76] As discussed earlier in this chapter.

[77] *Sidabras and Džautas v Lithuania*, (Apps. 55480/00 and 59330/00), 27 July 2004, (2004) 42 EHRR 104, ECHR 2004-VIII. See also *Žickus v Lithuania*, (App. 26652/02), 7 April 2009.

[78] § 37. The discrimination was between those who were former KGB employees and those who were not: see § 41.

[79] § 52.

[80] Notably in cases concerning property rights: see ch.20.

[81] *Sidabras and Džautas*, § 59.

choices in so far as these choices should be respected as element's of someone's personality, such as religion, political opinion, sexual orientation and gender identity, or, on the contrary, on grounds of personal features in respect of which no choice at all can be made, such as sex, race, disability and age.

Working for the KGB in my opinion does not fall within either of those categories.

Both dissenting judges would have found a violation of Article 8 read alone in the circumstances of this case. Judge Mularoni appended a partly concurring opinion; she too would have preferred the Court to have considered the case under Article 8 when read alone, and would have found a violation. The case displays both some uncertainty about the nature of 'other status', the choice of comparator, and the circumstances in which it will be appropriate to take first the allegation of discrimination.

CAN THE APPLICANTS PROPERLY COMPARE THEMSELVES WITH ANOTHER CLASS OF PERSONS WHICH IS TREATED MORE FAVOURABLY?

The third question, in determining whether there has been a breach of Article 14, is whether the applicants can properly compare themselves with a class of persons who are treated more favourably. The Strasbourg Court has referred to the comparators being in 'similar situations',[82] or in 'relevantly similar situations',[83] or in 'analogous situations'.[84] The purpose of this test is to enable the Court to determine whether the less favourable treatment is attributable to one of the Article 14 prohibited grounds of discrimination, and not to other factors. For the test to function, the situation of the applicant and the comparator must be analogous in all material respects so that it can properly be concluded that the difference between them arises from an Article 14 ground.

The problem of comparing like with like is illustrated in the *Van der Mussele* case,[85] where the applicant argued unsuccessfully that the comparators were different professional groups. The Court considered that there were fundamental differences in the regulation of different professions that precluded their use as comparators in the case. The Court can perhaps be criticized for sometimes passing over detailed consideration of whether the comparators are in an analogous situation to the applicants, particularly where it seems likely that the Contracting Party will be able to show justification for the differential treatment. In fairness, it should be noted that the issue of whether the compared groups are truly in analogous situations can sometimes only be answered by considering whether their differential treatment can be justified.

In the *Burden* case,[86] the applicants were sisters who were living together in the same house. They argued that they were victims of discrimination, because they could not pass property between them on death free of inheritance tax, whereas property passing between spouses or civil partners was exempt. The issue was whether siblings, on the one

[82] *Marckx v Belgium*, (App. 6833/74), 13 June 1979, Series A No 31, (1979–80) 2 EHRR 330, § 32.

[83] *Fredin v Sweden*, (App. 12033/86), 18 February 1991, Series A No 192, (1991) 13 EHRR 784, § 60. This appears to be the currently favoured formulation: see *Burden v United Kingdom*, (App. 13378/05), 29 April 2008 [GC], (2008) 47 EHRR 857, ECHR 2008-nyr, § 60.

[84] *Stubbings and others v United Kingdom*, (Apps. 22083/93 and 22095/93), 22 October 1996, (1997) 23 EHRR 213, ECHR 1996-IV, § 71.

[85] *Van der Mussele v Belgium*, (App. 8919/80), 23 November 1983, Series A No 70, (1984) 6 EHRR 163.

[86] *Burden v United Kingdom*, (App. 13378/05), 29 April 2008 [GC], (2008) 47 EHRR 857, ECHR 2008-nyr.

hand, and spouses and civil partners, on the other hand, were in analogous positions. The Grand Chamber[87] concluded that they were not, because the relationships are qualitatively different. The relationship between siblings is a blood tie, and marriage or civil partnership is prohibited for those with such close blood ties. The relationship between couples who are married or register a civil partnership is a matter of choice, and a special status is thereby conferred upon that relationship. Since the sisters could not compare themselves with married couples or civil partners, they could not show any discrimination in breach of Article 14. The two dissenting judges considered that the justification for the inheritance tax exemption was the proximity of the relationship between the affected parties. That being so, it could not be the justification for refusing the exemption to the two sisters while allowing it for married couples and civil partners.[88]

The starting point is to consider whether applicants can show that they have been treated less favourably than the comparator group by reason of the characteristics identified. However, Article 14 also applies where there is indirect discrimination. This occurs where the same requirement applies to both groups, but where a significant number of one group is unable to comply with the requirement. As early as the *Belgian Linguistic* case, the Court indicated that the existence of discrimination might relate to the *effects* of State measures.[89] The Court's analysis does not use the terms direct and indirect discrimination, but rather focuses on whether the differential treatment alleged has no objective and reasonable justification.[90] That Article 14 covers indirect discrimination has been established beyond doubt in the *DH* case.[91]

IS THE DIFFERENCE OF TREATMENT CAPABLE OF OBJECTIVE AND REASONABLE JUSTIFICATION?

In the *Burden* case, the Grand Chamber said:

> ...a difference of treatment is discriminatory if it has no objective and reasonable justification; in other words, if it does not pursue a legitimate aim or if there is not a reasonable relationship of proportionality between the means employed and the aim sought to be realised. The Contracting State enjoys a margin of appreciation in assessing whether and to what extent differences in otherwise similar situations justify a different treatment,....[92]

In asserting a legitimate aim for the differential treatment, the respondent State must not only show the nature of the legitimate aim it is pursuing, but must also show by convincing evidence the link between the legitimate aim pursued and the differential treatment

[87] The Chamber judgment of 12 December 2006 had found no violation, but had left open the question of whether the sisters were in an analogous position to married couples or civil partners, indicating that, even if they were, the differential treatment could be justified.

[88] For other examples where the Court has not recognized a comparator, see, *Carson and others v United Kingdom*, (App. 42184/05), 16 March 2010 ECHR 2010; and *Aksu v Turkey*, (App. 4149/04), 15 March 2012.

[89] *Belgian Linguistic* case, (Apps. 1474/62, 1677/62, 1691/62, 1769/63, 1994/63, and 2126/64), 23 July 1968, Series A No 6, (1979–80) 1 EHRR 252, § 10 of Section IB.

[90] See, for example, *Abdulaziz, Cabales and Balkandali v United Kingdom*, (Apps. 9214/80, 9473/81, and 9474/81), 28 May 1985, Series A No 94, (1985) 7 EHRR 471, § 72.

[91] *DH and others v Czech Republic*, (App. 57325/00), 13 November 2007 [GC], (2008) 47 EHRR 59, ECHR 2007-nyr, §§ 175 and 184.

[92] *Burden v United Kingdom*, (App. 13378/05), 29 April 2008 [GC], ECHR 2008-nyr, § 60. Compare *Korelc v Slovenia*, (App. 28456/03), 12 May 2009.

challenged by the applicant.[93] As with the requirement to establish a legitimate claim under Article 8 to 11,[94] this is not generally a difficult hurdle for the respondent State to clear, particularly since the Court has held that the purpose of saving public money can be a legitimate aim under Article 14.[95]

In the *Gillow* case,[96] the Strasbourg Court accepted that preferential treatment for those with a strong attachment to Guernsey reflected in the island's restrictive housing laws was a legitimate aim, and found no breach of Article 14 read with Article 8. In the *Darby* case,[97] the Court concluded that the refusal to grant exemption from a church tax to a claimant not formally registered as a resident in Sweden on the grounds that their case for exemption was less strong than for those registered as formally resident and would give rise to administrative inconvenience, did not meet the requirement of being a legitimate aim, and accordingly found a violation of Article 14 read with Article 1 of Protocol 1.

In the *PM* case,[98] the Court did not accept that provisions of United Kingdom tax law which permitted married fathers to claim tax relief on maintenance payments after the breakdown of a marriage but did not allow unmarried fathers to claim such relief following the breakdown of a relationship outside marriage served a legitimate aim. The respondent State had sought to rely on the special regime of marriage as conferring specific rights and obligations for married persons. The Court responded by ruling that as a general rule unmarried fathers who have established family life with their children can claim equal rights of contact and custody with married fathers; the equal treatment requirement would extend to tax deductibility of maintenance payments.

In the *Abdulaziz, Cabales and Balkandali* case,[99] the Court concluded that the construction of immigration rules in such a way as to protect the domestic labour market was 'without doubt legitimate'[100] but that in its application the need to apply rules for this purpose which discriminated on grounds of sex could not be regarded, in fact, as sufficiently important to justify the difference of treatment.[101]

Again, as with Article 8 to 11, the breadth of the margin of appreciation allowed to the State—and thus the level of justification required from the State—will vary according to the circumstances, the subject matter, and its background. The case-law of the Court shows that not all grounds of discrimination are equally potent.[102] There are echoes of the case-law of the United States Supreme Court when it is dealing with the equal protection clause in the Fourteenth Amendment to the Constitution. Certain grounds of discrimination are inherently suspect and will be subject to particularly careful scrutiny. These include discrimination on grounds of sex, race, nationality, legitimacy, religion, and sexual orientation, where there is recognition that discrimination on such grounds is especially demeaning for those affected.

[93] *Larkos v Cyprus*, (App. 29515/95), 18 February 1999, (2000) 30 EHRR 597, ECHR 1999-I, § 31.

[94] See ch.14.

[95] *Andrejeva v Latvia*, (App. 55707/00), 18 February 2009 [GC], ECHR 2009-nyr, § 86. See also *Bah v United Kingdom*, (App. 5632807), 27 September 2011, where the Court noted that the State allocation of housing fell within a legitimate aim and the Court has noted on several occasions that the interests of children and the protection of the family are legitimate aims for the State to pursue, see for example *E.B v France*, (App. 43546/02), 22 January 2008; and *X v Austria*, (App. 19010/07), 19 February 2013.

[96] *Gillow v United Kingdom*, (App. 9063/80), 24 November 1986, Series A No 109, (1989) 11 EHRR 335.

[97] *Darby v Sweden*, (App. 11581/85), 23 October 1990, Series A No 187, (1991) 13 EHRR 774.

[98] *PM v United Kingdom*, (App. 6638/03), 19 July 2005, (2006) 42 EHRR 1015.

[99] *Abdulaziz, Cabales and Balkandali v United Kingdom*, (Apps. 9214/80, 9473/81, and 9474/81), 28 May 1985, Series A No 94, (1985) 7 EHRR 471.

[100] § 78.

[101] § 79.

[102] *Inze v Austria*, 28 October 1987, Series A No 126, (1988) 10 EHRR 394.

Where the differential treatment is between men and women,[103] on grounds of nationality,[104] on grounds of race,[105] on grounds of religion,[106] on grounds of legitimacy,[107] and on grounds of sexual orientation,[108] very weighty reasons are required to justify the differential treatment.

SEX AND GENDER

Where the basis for the difference of treatment is grounds of sex, the Contracting Parties enjoy no margin of appreciation and will find it very difficult to establish objective and reasonable justification. This can be illustrated by the *Karlheinz Schmidt* case.[109] The applicant complained that the system of requiring men to serve in the fire brigade or to pay a fire service levy in lieu violated Article 4 taken together with Article 14. The Court looked at the practicalities of the situation which was that men were not in practice required to serve, since there was no shortage of volunteers. But there remained the liability to pay the levy, which bore only on men and not on women. This difference of treatment on grounds of sex could hardly be justified.[110] Similarly in the *Markin* case,[111] the Court found that the exclusion of male military personnel from parental leave compared to female military personnel could not be justified either by a reference to the need to maintain the operational effectiveness of the armed forces or by reference to the State's attitudes to gender roles:

> The Court has already found that States may not impose traditional gender roles and gender stereotypes... Moreover, given that under Russian law civilian men and women are both entitled to parental leave and it is the family's choice to decide which parent should take parental leave to take care of the new-born child, the Court is not convinced by the assertion

[103] *Abdulaziz, Cabales and Balkandali v United Kingdom*, (Apps. 9214/80, 9473/81, and 9474/81), 28 May 1985, Series A No 94, (1985) 7 EHRR 471, § 78. See also *Van Raalte v Netherlands*, (App. 20060/92), 21 February 1997, (1997) 24 EHRR 503, ECHR 1997-I, § 39.

[104] *Gaygusuz v Austria*, (App. 17371/90), 16 September 1996, (1997) 23 EHRR 364, ECHR 1996-IV, § 42; and *Andrejeva v Latvia*, (App. 55707/00) 18 February 2009 [GC], ECHR 2009-nyr.

[105] *Timishev v Russia*, (Apps. 55762/00 and 55974/00), 13 December 2005, (2007) 44 EHRR 776, ECHR 2005-XII, § 58.

[106] *Hoffmann v Austria*, (App. 12875/87), 23 June 1993, Series A No 255-C, (1994) 17 EHRR 293, § 36. See also *Palau-Martinez v France*, (App. 64927/01), 16 December 2003, ECHR 2003-XII. However there was no violation found in *Eweida and others v United Kingdom*, (App. 4842/10), 15 January 2013.

[107] *Inze v Austria*, (App. 8695/79), 28 October 1987, Series A No 126, (1988) 10 EHRR 394, § 41. See also *Mazurek v France*, (App. 34406/97), 1 February 2000, ECHR 2000-II, § 49; *Camp and Bourimi v The Netherlands*, (App. 28369/95), 3 October 2000, (2002) 34 EHRR 1446, ECHR 2000-X, § 38; *Sommerfield v Germany*, (App. 31871/96), 8 July 2003 [GC], (2004) 38 EHRR 756, ECHR 2003-VIII, § 93; and *Fabris v France*, (App. 16574/08), 7 February 2013.

[108] At least where there is significant common ground among the Contracting Parties. See *Salgueiro da Silva Mouta v Portugal*, (App. 33290/96), 21 December 1999, (2001) 31 EHRR 1055, ECHR 1999-IX, (a custody case by the father of a daughter: violation found). See also *SL v Austria*, (App. 45330/99), 9 January 2003, (2003) 37 EHRR 799, ECHR 2003-I, (criminalization of certain homosexual conduct: violation found); *Karner v Austria*, (App. 40016/98), 24 July 2003, (2004) 38 EHRR 528, ECHR 2003-IX, (succession of tenancies between homosexual men: violation found); *BB v United Kingdom* (App. 53760/00), 10 February 2004, (2004) 39 EHRR 635, (different ages of consent for homosexual and heterosexual acts: violation found); and *E.B. v France*, (App. 43546/02), 22 January 2008 [GC], ECHR 2008-nyr (over-reliance on sexual orientation in authorization by single person to adopt: violation found).

[109] *Karlheinz Schmidt v Germany*, (App. 13580/88), 18 July 1994, Series A No 291-B, (1994) 18 EHRR 513.

[110] See also *Burghartz v Switzerland*, (App. 16213/90), 22 February 1994, Series A No 280-B, (1994) 18 EHRR 101, § 27; and *Schuler-Zgraggen v Switzerland*, (App. 14518/89), 24 June 1993, Series A No 263, (1993) 16 EHRR 405, § 67.

[111] *Konstantin Markin v Russia*, (App. 30078/06), 22 March 2012.

> that Russian society is not ready to accept similar equality between men and women serving in the armed forces.[112]

The Court also rejected the Government's argument that allowing women parental leave and not men amounted to positive discrimination in favour of women. In contrast, in the *Stec* case,[113] the Strasbourg Court held that it was permissible for the State authorities to treat men and women differently for the purposes of positive discrimination, in order to 'correct factual inequalities between them'. The Court accepted that the reason for introducing a differential age of entitlement to the State pension for men and women in the United Kingdom (65 for men and 60 for women) was to compensate women for the fact that, in general, they tended to spend longer periods of time than men out of paid employment and looking after children and other family members. It was therefore harder for women to build up the required number of qualifying years of National Insurance contributions. The difference in pensionable ages continued to be justified until such time as social conditions had changed so that women were no longer substantially prejudiced because of a shorter working life. This change, must, by its very nature, have been gradual, and it would be difficult or impossible to pinpoint any particular moment when the unfairness to men caused by differential pensionable ages began to outweigh the need to correct the disadvantaged position of women. According to the evidence before the Court, the State authorities had been within their margin of appreciation in deciding to wait until December 1991 before starting to move towards an equal pension age and in deciding to introduce the changes very gradually over a long period of time.

The Court has also used Article 14 to underline the importance of highlighting the gender discrimination involved in a failure to protect in cases of domestic violence. The Court found a violation of Article 14 for the first time in a case involving domestic violence in *Opuz v Turkey*.[114] The Court cited the United Nations Convention on the Elimination of Discrimination against Women and the United Nations Commission of Human Rights, stating that:

> bearing in mind its finding above that the general and discriminatory judicial passivity in Turkey, albeit unintentional, mainly affected women, the Court considers that the violence suffered by the applicant and her mother may be regarded as gender-based violence which is a form of discrimination against women. Despite the reforms carried out by the Government in recent years, the overall unresponsiveness of the judicial system and impunity enjoyed by the aggressors, as found in the instant case, indicated that there was insufficient commitment to take appropriate action to address domestic violence.[115]

The Court made a similar finding in *Eremia v Moldova*,[116] finding that the State had not simply failed to protect the applicant under Articles 3 and 8, but had also condoned the violence, reflecting a discriminatory attitude towards the applicant as a woman. The judgments in these cases have developed the Court's jurisprudence in line with other

[112] § 142.

[113] *Stec and others v United Kingdom*, (Apps. 65731/01 and 65900/01), 12 April 2006 [GC], (2006) 43 EHRR 1017, ECHR 2006-VI.

[114] *Opuz v Turkey*, (App. 33401/02), 9 June 2009, see ch. 9 with regard to a finding of ill treatment, see also P. Londono, 'Developing Human Rights Principles in Cases of Gender-based Violence: *Opuz v Turkey* in the European Court of Human Rights' (2009) 9 IJCL 793.

[115] *Opuz v Turkey*, (App. 33401/02), 9 June 2009, § 200.

[116] *Eremia v Moldova*, (App. 3564/11), 28 May 2011; see also *B v Republic of Moldova*, (App. 61382/09), 16 July 2013; and *Mudric v Republic of Moldova*, (App. 74839/10), 16 July 2013.

international bodies.[117] The judgments recognize the social and structural inequality that helps to perpetuate domestic violence against women.[118]

RACE AND ETHNICITY

The Strasbourg Court is taking an increasingly robust approach to cases where racial or ethnic motivation is involved.[119] As the Court has indicated, these are overlapping concepts. In the *Timishev* case, the Court said:

> Whereas the notion of race is rooted in the idea of biological classification of human beings into subspecies according to morphological features such as skin colour and facial characteristics, ethnicity has its origins in the idea of societal groups marked by common nationality, tribal affiliation, religious faith, shared language, or cultural and traditional origins and backgrounds.[120]

Discrimination on grounds of ethnicity is a form of racial discrimination, which is seen as a particularly serious form of discrimination. As a consequence, Contracting Parties are required to 'use all available means to combat racism', and no difference of treatment based on race or ethnicity is capable of being objectively justified.[121] The increasingly robust approach of the Strasbourg Court can be illustrated in a number of Roma cases[122] such as the *Šečič* case.[123] The applicant was a Croatian national of Roma origin. He was attacked and injured; his attackers shouted racist abuse at him while attacking him. The police investigation was extremely dilatory, lasting more than seven years. No one was brought to trial for the attack. The Strasbourg Court affirmed the positive obligation of Contracting Parties to use their best endeavours to investigate attacks, even by private parties, which involved racial hatred. A failure to make any distinction between such attacks and 'ordinary' violence was a failure to make a vital distinction, and may constitute unjustified treatment which breaches Article 14 when read with Article 3.[124] Such a violation was found in addition to a violation of Article 3 alone concerning the lack of an effective investigation.[125]

[117] For example the United Nations Committee on the Elimination of Discrimination Against Women (CEDAW), United Nations Special Rapporteur on violence against women, and the Committee of Ministers of the Council of Europe, see for example, Recommendation Rec(2002)5 of 30 April 2002 on the protection of women against violence.

[118] The Court has also applied Article 14 in several transgender cases *Schlumpf v Switzerland*, (App. 29022/06), 8 January 2009 (violation with regard to operation to change gender); *PV v Spain*, (App. 35159/09), 30 November 2010 (no violation with regard to contact proceedings); *H v Finland*, (App. 37359/09), 13 November 2012 (no violation with regard to impact of gender change on civil partnership–referred to Grand Chamber 29 April 2013).

[119] See further later in this chapter in relation to minorities.

[120] *Timishev v Russia*, (Apps. 55762/00 and 55974/00), 13 December 2005, (2007) 44 EHRR 776, ECHR 2005-XII, § 55.

[121] § 56–7.

[122] See earlier and later in this chapter, for example *Nachova and others v Bulgaria*, (Apps. 43577/98 and 43579/98), 6 July 2005 [GC], (2006) 42 EHRR 933, ECHR 2005-VII; *DH and others v Czech Republic*, (App. 57325/00), 13 November 2007 [GC], (2008) 47 EHRR 59, ECHR 2007-nyr.

[123] *Šečič v Croatia*, (App. 40116/02), 31 May 2007, (2009) 49 EHRR 408, ECHR 2007-VI. See also *97 members of the Gldani Congregation of Jehovah's Witnesses & 4 others v Georgia*, (App. 71156/01), 3 May 2007, (2008) 46 EHRR 30, ECHR 2007-V.

[124] § 67. See also *Angelova and Iliev v Bulgaria*, (App. 55523/00), 26 July 2007, (2008) 47 EHRR 236; and *Cobzaru v Romania*, (App. 48254/99), 26 July 2007, (2008) 47 EHRR 288. See also, the finding of a procedural violation of Article 3 with Article 14, which involved a Nigerian woman who was a prostitute. The decision was based on race but considered her vulnerability as a female prostitute, *B. S v Spain*, (App. 47159/08), 24 July 2012, § 62.

[125] See also *Bekos and Koutropoulos v Greece*, (App. 15250/02), 13 December 2005, (2006) 43 EHRR 22, ECHR 2005-XIII.

Even in less dramatic factual situations, the Strasbourg Court requires very weighty reasons for distinctions between nationals and non-nationals. In the *Andrejeva* case,[126] the Strasbourg Court held that, in the field of social security, differences in treatment between nationals and non-nationals would require very good reasons.[127]

OTHER STATUS

In relation to those characteristics that are not listed in the Article, the Court has elevated those that can be seen as personal characteristics or linked to them, to a similar status in terms of weighty reasons.

Sexual orientation

The Strasbourg Court first recognized the importance of the protection of sexual orientation under the substantive provisions such as Article 8.[128] However, applying the living instrument principle it has now recognized sexual orientation as a ground for discrimination under 'other status' requiring very weighty reasons to justify differential treatment and so avoid discrimination. This was first recognized in a case concerning custody[129] but has since been recognized in a range of areas such as criminal law,[130] tenancies,[131] social insurance,[132] and adoption. In adoption cases, such as *E. B v France*,[133] the Court has found that the rules governing adoption discriminated against single homosexuals wishing to adopt. However, in cases such as *Frette v France*[134] and *Gas and Dubois v France*,[135] the Court distinguished *E.B* in finding that the treatment of homosexual couples wishing to adopt in the circumstances of the case was not discriminatory compared to heterosexual couples in the same position.[136] There is also a developing body of cases dealing with same sex relationships. In these cases the Court has not gone as far as recognizing a right to same sex marriage as protected under the Convention. However it has found that where a State puts in place a legal protection for non-married couples, it must do so in a non-discriminatory way. In *Schalk and Koph v Austria*,[137] the Court did not find a violation of Article 14. It noted that recognition of same sex relationships did not lead to the right to the same legal recognition as marriage. However, it recognized an emerging consensus on the issue of regulation outside of marriage but this was not yet enough to narrow the margin of appreciation:

> The Court cannot but note that there is an emerging European consensus towards legal recognition of same-sex couples. Moreover, this tendency has developed rapidly over the past decade. Nevertheless, there is not yet a majority of States providing for legal recognition of same-sex couples. The area in question must therefore still be regarded as one of evolving

[126] *Andrejeva v Latvia*, (App. 55707/00) 18 February 2009 [GC], ECHR 2009-nyr.

[127] See also *Ponomaryovi v Bulgaria*, (App. 633505), 21 June 2011; and *Kuric and others v Slovenia*, (App. 26828/06), 26 June 2012.

[128] See ch.14.

[129] *Salgueiro da Silva Mouta v Portugal*, (App. 33290/96), 21 December 1999, (2001) 31 EHRR 1055, ECHR 1999-IX.

[130] *SL v Austria*, (App. 45330/99), 9 January 2003, (2003) 37 EHRR 799, ECHR 2003-I.

[131] *Karner v Austria*, (App. 40016/98), 24 July 2003, (2004) 38 EHRR 528, ECHR 2003-IX; and *Kozak v Poland*, (App. 13102/02), 2 March 2010.

[132] *P.B. and J.S. v Austria*, (App.18984/02), 22 July 2010.

[133] *E. B v France*, (App. 43546/02), 22 January 2008 [GC], ECHR 2008-nyr.

[134] *Frette v France*, (App. 36515/97), 26 February 2002, (2004) 38 EHRR 438 ECHR 2002-I.

[135] *Gas and Dubois v France*, (App. 29591/07), 15 March 2012.

[136] See *X v Austria*, (App. 19010/07), 19 February 2013, where the Court found a violation of Article 14 with regard to second parent adoption when comparing non-married heterosexual couples and non-married homosexual couples but no violation when comparing married heterosexual couples and non-married homosexual couples.

[137] *Schalk and Koph v Austria*, (App. 30141/04), 24 June 2010.

> rights with no established consensus, where States must also enjoy a margin of appreciation in the timing of the introduction of legislative changes.[138]

However three years later in *Vallianatos v Greece*,[139] the Court did find a violation of Article 14. The Court noted that a large number of European States have recognized same sex relationships in some legal form:

> The Court would point to the fact that, although there is no consensus among the legal systems of the Council of Europe member States, a trend is currently emerging with regard to the introduction of forms of legal recognition of same-sex relationships. Nine member States provide for same-sex marriage. In addition, seventeen member States authorise some form of civil partnership for same-sex couples. As to the specific issue raised by the present case..., the Court considers that the trend emerging in the legal systems of the Council of Europe member States is clear: of the nineteen States which authorise some form of registered partnership other than marriage, Lithuania and Greece are the only ones to reserve it exclusively to different-sex couples...In other words, with two exceptions, Council of Europe Member States, when they opt to enact legislation introducing a new system of registered partnership as an alternative to marriage for unmarried couples, include same-sex couples in its scope.[140]

The Court was not convinced by the State's reasoning for maintaining a difference of treatment given the situation in Europe. The Court also took a more robust approach to the margin of appreciation in *Vallianatos* than it did in the *Schalk* case, underlining in *Vallianatos* that differences based solely on sexual orientation are unacceptable.[141] The Court has taken a step forward in giving legal recognition to same sex relationships as Contracting States and non-European States increasingly move towards that position.[142]

Disability and health

The Strasbourg Court has also developed its case-law in relation to disability. In *Glor v Switzerland*,[143] the applicant had to pay taxes to the State as he could not perform compulsory military service or an alternative related occupation in lieu of service, as alternatives were only open to conscientious objectors. This was due to his disability. Those with severe disabilities were exempted. However, his disability was not severe enough to qualify for this exemption so he was treated the same as able-bodied persons who did not carry out compulsory duties. The Court found that this was discriminatory based on disability. By emphasizing that 'that special forms of civilian service tailored to the needs of people in the applicant's situation are perfectly envisageable,'[144] the Court was recognizing the 'social model' of disability, meaning it considered the applicant's access to civilian service rather than just his medical needs. The recognition of the 'social model' reflects the developments internationally in the protection of the rights of disabled people including the United Nations Convention on the Rights of Persons with Disabilities. This is further illustrated in two health related cases that have come before the Court, both dealing with HIV related illness.

[138] § 105; the dissent in the case argued that the State had failed to provide reasons for a difference of treatment and so there should be no room for a margin of appreciation: Joint Dissenting Opinion of Judges Rozakis, Spielmann, and Jebens.

[139] *Vallianatos v Greece*, (Apps. 29381/09 and 32684/09), 7 November 2013.

[140] § 91.

[141] § 77.

[142] For a discussion of the *Schalk* case and the legal position in non-European States see L. Hodson, 'A Marriage by Any Other Name? *Schalk and Kopf v Austria*' (2011) HR Law Rev 11:1, 170–179. Hodson notes that the UK intervened in the case to argue Articles 8 and 12 did not include same sex marriage. The UK has now changed that position, introducing the Marriage (Same Sex Couples) Act 2013.

[143] *Glor v Switzerland*, (App. 133044/04), 30 April 2009.

[144] § 95.

In *Kiyutin v Russia*[145] the applicant was from Uzbekistan. He was refused a residence permit in Russia as he had tested positive for HIV. The Court examined international developments in this area[146] and concluded that:

> a distinction made on account of one's health status, including such conditions as HIV infection, should be covered – either as a form of disability or alongside with it – by the term "other status" in the text of Article 14 of the Convention.[147]

The Court found a violation of Article 14 as it held that very weighty reasons were necessary before a justification for a difference of treatment could be established. The State had failed to demonstrate compelling reasons for the refusal to give a residence permit. The Court stated that:

> If a restriction on fundamental rights applies to a particularly vulnerable group in society that has suffered considerable discrimination in the past, then the State's margin of appreciation is substantially narrower and it must have very weighty reasons for the restrictions in question. The reason for this approach, which questions certain classifications per se, is that such groups were historically subject to prejudice with lasting consequences, resulting in their social exclusion. Such prejudice could entail legislative stereotyping which prohibited the individualised evaluation of their capacities and needs.[148]

The Court found that persons suffering from HIV fall into this category given the social stigma, negative stereotyping, and discrimination they have historically faced. The Court came to a similar finding in an employment related case, *I.B v Greece*.[149] The applicant had told work colleagues that he was HIV positive. Some of the colleagues and other staff asked the company to dismiss the applicant. The applicant was subsequently dismissed and his dismissal was upheld by the domestic Court. As in *Kiyutin*, the Court emphasized the need for effective participation of people in society. Although the judgment does not mention the UN Convention on Disability, the reasoning of the Court reflects the ethos of the Convention. The decisions on HIV related illness and the narrowing of the margin of appreciation in these cases is a step forward in the recognition of the need to remove social barriers that may prevent those with disabilities from exercising their rights fully under the Convention.

In contrast, where the difference of treatment is not based on an 'inherent' characteristic, it is likely that the Strasbourg Court will require a lower level of justification and allow a wider margin of appreciation to the State. Similarly, the margin of appreciation is usually wide when it comes to general measures of economic or social strategy.[150] Some examples include housing policy,[151] taxation,[152] and social security.[153]

[145] *Kiyutin v Russia*, (App. 2700/10), 10 March 2011.

[146] Such as Recommendation 1116 (1989) by the Parliamentary Assembly of the Council of Europe and the UN Convention on the Rights of Person with Disabilities.

[147] § 57. [148] § 63.

[149] *I.B v Greece*, (App. 552/10), 3 October 2013.

[150] As in, for example, *Stec and others v United Kingdom*, (Apps. 65731/01 and 65900/01), 12 April 2006 [GC], (2006) 43 EHRR 1017, ECHR 2006-VI; *Burden v United Kingdom*, (App. 13378/05), 29 April 2008 [GC], (2008) 47 EHRR 857, ECHR 2008-nyr; *Andrejeva v Latvia*, (App. 55707/00) 18 February 2009 [GC], ECHR 2009-nyr; *Bah v United Kingdom*, (App. 5632807), 27 September 2011; *O'Donoghue and others v United Kingdom*, (App. 34838/07), 14 December 2010; *Hode and Abdi v United Kingdom*, (App. 22341/09), 6 November 2012.

[151] *Gillow v United Kingdom*, (App. 9063/80), 24 November 1986, Series A No 109, (1989) 11 EHRR 335, § 66; and *Bah v United Kingdom*, (App. 5632807), 27 September 2011.

[152] *National & Provincial Building Society and others v United Kingdom*, (Apps. 21319/93, 21449/93, and 21675/93), 23 October 1997, (1998) 25 EHRR 127, § 88.

[153] *Carson and others v United Kingdom*, (App. 42184/05), 16 March 2010 ECHR 2010, *Stummer v Austria* (App. 37452/02) 7 July 2011.

The Court has held that:

> Because of their direct knowledge of their society and its needs, the national authorities are in principle better placed than the international judge to appreciate what is in the public interest on social or economic grounds, and the Court will generally respect the legislature's policy choice unless it is 'manifestly without reasonable foundation'.[154]

However, some of the Judges of the Strasbourg Court have questioned the width of the margin of appreciation given in cases involving economic arguments. Although in *Stummer v Austria*,[155] the majority found that there was no discrimination in the difference of treatment between prisoners and non-prisoners with regard to pension eligibility, the dissenting opinions criticized the majority's use of the margin of appreciation based on socio-economic arguments. The dissenting judges are critical of the Court for giving too much importance to economic arguments put forward by the States:

> With regard, firstly, to the legitimate aim pursued by the difference in treatment, the judgment refers to "preserving the economic efficiency and overall consistency of the old-age pension system by excluding from benefits persons who have not made meaningful contributions."...Although it is of course reasonable to take economic realities into account, it must nevertheless be acknowledged that there has been a gradual trend in the Court's recent case-law towards attaching considerable importance to them, sometimes to the detriment of fundamental rights (see N. v. the United Kingdom [GC], no. 26565/05, 27 May 2008; Burden v. the United Kingdom [GC], no. 13378/05, ECHR 2008...; and Carson and others v. the United Kingdom [GC], no. 42184/05, ECHR 2010.)[156]

The dissent goes on to note that there is an emerging consensus on prisoners' rights in Europe, including the inclusion of prisoners in social security systems. In their view, although the majority acknowledged an emerging consensus, too much weight was placed on economic arguments when the growing consensus meant the margin of appreciation should have been narrow, giving rise in this case to a violation.[157]

DISCRIMINATION AND MINORITIES

The Strasbourg Court's increasingly tough approach to discrimination cases involving differential treatment based to a decisive extent on race or ethnicity has already been noted. Those cases were decided on the individual circumstances presented.[158] The focus of attention in a number of cases has been systematic ill-treatment of those of Roma origin, where evidence of their ill-treatment in a number of Contracting Parties has come before the Strasbourg Court. A development in the case-law, which may be based upon recognition that minorities need special and collective protection if their human rights are to be respected, warrants a discussion distinct from reference to individual cases involving discrimination on racial or ethnic grounds.

[154] *Stec and others v United Kingdom*, (Apps. 65731/01 and 65900/01), 12 April 2006 [GC], (2006) 43 EHRR 1017, ECHR 2006-VI, § 52.

[155] *Stummer v Austria*, (App. 37452/02), 7 July 2011.

[156] Joint Partly Dissenting Opinion of Judges Tulkens, Kovler, Gyulumyan, Spielmann, Popović, Malinverni, and Pardalos, § 3.

[157] § 5.

[158] See, for example, *Timishev v Russia*, (Apps. 55762/00 and 55974/00), 13 December 2005, (2007) 44 EHRR 776, ECHR 2005-XII; *Angelova and Iliev v Bulgaria*, (App. 55523/00), 26 July 2007, (2008) 47 EHRR 236; and *Cobzaru v Romania*, (App. 48254/99), 26 July 2007, (2008) 47 EHRR 288.

The seminal case is the *D.H.* case.[159] The complaints arose in the context of the attempts by the respondent State to address the question of the education of children of Roma origin. The adopted solution was the creation of special schools. These were not, however, limited to Roma children; they were schools designated for children with learning difficulties who were unable to follow the ordinary school curriculum. Allocation to a special school was determined by an assessment made by a head teacher on the basis of tests which measured the child's intellectual capacity, and required the consent of the child's parent or guardian. Statistical evidence showed that more than half the pupils in the special schools were of Roma origin, and that in one of the school districts involved a child of Roma origin was twenty-seven times more likely to be in a special school than a child not of Roma origin. The applicants complained that the tests were not reliable, and that the parents had not been sufficiently informed to give consent to placement in a special school.

The Chamber judgment looked at the cases on an individual basis, and found no violation of the Convention. The Grand Chamber judgment took an entirely different approach to the case, treating the problem as a collective or systemic issue affecting Roma children in general, exemplified by the situations of the applicants in the case before them.

The Grand Chamber did not find that the authorities were motivated to discriminate; indeed there is some praise for the efforts made in the Czech Republic to address the issue.[160] But the segregated educational system was seen to be a source of concern. The Grand Chamber considered that the tests might well be culturally biased, and was influenced by critical reports from the European Commission against Racism and Intolerance (ECRI) and the Council of Europe's Commissioner for Human Rights. On the issue of parental consent, the Grand Chamber finds that there can be no waiver of the right not to be subjected to racial discrimination, even when that discrimination arose indirectly. By thirteen votes to four, the Grand Chamber finds a violation of Article 14 when read in conjunction with Article 2 of Protocol 1. This finding did not relate to individual cases, but to the applicants in general as members of the Roma community.[161] A key significance in this case is in treating indirect discrimination as a phenomenon and in addressing the phenomenon rather than focusing on individual complaints. This collective rather than individual approach could have implications for many areas of the Court's caseload. The reasoning of the majority in the case has been followed in subsequent cases involving the Roma community and education such as *Orsus v Croatia*[162] and *Horvath and Kiss v Hungary*.[163]

D.H has triggered a new approach to discrimination affecting minorities, and potentially to systemic problems of discrimination. Despite the robust dissenting criticism of

[159] *DH and others v Czech Republic*, (App. 57325/00), 13 November 2007 [GC], (2008) 47 EHRR 59, ECHR 2007-nyr. On this case, see R. Sandland, 'Developing a Jurisprudence of Difference: The Protection of the Human Rights of Travelling Peoples by the European Court of Human Rights' (2008) 8 HRLRev 475; and G. Hobcraft, 'Roma Children and Education in the Czech Republic: DH v Czech Republic: opening the door to indirect discrimination findings in Strasbourg' [2008] EHRLR 245.

[160] By the time of the judgment of the Grand Chamber legislation had abolished the system of special schools.

[161] There are strongly worded dissenting opinions, which castigate the Court for its collective approach and accuse it of usurping the functions of ECRI.

[162] *Orsus v Croatia*, (App. 15766/03), 16 March 2010, Judgment of Grand Chamber of nine votes to eight. Some of the dissent mirrored the dissent in *D.H.* Also, some judges agreed with the Chamber that the difference of treatment was based on language rather than race and so the State had a greater margin of appreciation.

[163] *Horvath and Kiss v Hungary*, (App. 11146/11), 29 January 2013; see also *Sampanis and others v Greece*, (App. 32526/05), 5 June 2008: *Sampani and others v Greece*, (App. 59608/09), 11 December 2012; *Lavida and others v Greece*, (App. 7973/10), 30 May 2013.

the majority decisions in *D.H* and *Orsus*, the recognition of indirect discrimination brings the Court and Convention in line with other international bodies and much domestic law. It does appear to open the door to something close to a class action before the Strasbourg Court. The Strasbourg Court has used the pilot judgment procedure in a case[164] involving Article 14 along with Articles 8 and 13. The case involved the re-classification of the applicants as non-nationals after the breakup of the old Yugoslav Republic with fewer rights than those foreign nationals who were not nationals under the old territorial boundaries. The case is one of direct discrimination based on national origin. However, the recognition of indirect discrimination by the Court may mean that the pilot judgment procedure is accessed in the future on the basis of a differential impact on a particular group in order to address systemic discrimination in a State.

THE BURDEN OF PROOF UNDER ARTICLE 14

Establishing differential treatment of a group in relevantly similar or analogous situations raises issues of evidence and proof. The practice of the Court is that it is for the applicant to show that there has been a difference of treatment, but that it is then for the respondent State to show that the difference in treatment can be justified.[165] There is, however, no formal burden of proof; nor are there formal rules of evidence. The Court will adopt conclusions that are supported by the free evaluation of all the evidence before it.[166] In the *D.H.* case,[167] the Grand Chamber observed:

> According to its established case-law, proof may follow from the coexistence of sufficiently strong, clear and concordant inferences or of similar unrebutted presumptions of fact. Moreover, the level of persuasion necessary for reaching a particular conclusion and, in this connection, the distribution of the burden of proof are intrinsically linked to the specificity of the facts, the nature of the allegation made and the Convention right at stake.[168]

The Grand Chamber also went on to note that a respondent State might be required to disprove an arguable allegation of discrimination.[169] Although statistics alone will not generally constitute evidence of discriminatory practices, in some cases the Court has relied upon statistics to establish a difference in treatment, especially in relation to discrimination between men and women.[170] In the *Zarb Adami* case,[171] statistical imbalances between the numbers of men and women serving as jurors was used to show differential treatment, even though the Maltese law made no distinction between the eligibility of men and women to serve as jurors. In the *D.H.* case, the Grand Chamber said that less strict evidential rules should apply in cases of alleged indirect discrimination,[172] and stressed the relevance of official statistics.[173] The Grand Chamber added:

[164] *Kuric and others v Slovenia*, (App.26828/06), 26 June 2012.

[165] *Chassagnou and others v France* (Apps. 25088/94, 28331/95, and 28443/95), 29 April 1999 [GC], (2000) 29 EHRR 615, ECHR 1999-III, §§ 91–2.

[166] *Nachova and others v Bulgaria*, (Apps. 43577/98 and 43579/98), 6 July 2005 [GC], (2006) 42 EHRR 933, ECHR 2005-VII, § 147, re-affirmed in *DH and others v Czech Republic*, (App. 57325/00), 13 November 2007 [GC], (2008) 47 EHRR 59, ECHR 2007-nyr, § 178.

[167] *DH and others v Czech Republic*, (App. 57325/00), 13 November 2007 [GC], (2008) 47 EHRR 59, ECHR 2007-nyr.

[168] § 178. [169] § 179. [170] § 180.

[171] *Zarb Adami v Malta*, (App. 17209/02), 20 June 2006, (2007) 44 EHRR 49, ECHR 2006-VIII.

[172] *DH and others v Czech Republic*, (App. 57325/00), 13 November 2007 [GC], (2008) 47 EHRR 59, ECHR 2007-nyr, § 186. [173] § 187.

> ... the Court considers that when it comes to assessing the impact of a measure or practice on an individual or group, statistics which appear on critical examination to be reliable and significant will be sufficient to constitute the prima facie evidence the applicant is required to produce. This does not, however, mean that indirect discrimination cannot be proved without statistical evidence.[174]

PROTOCOL 12: A GENERAL PROHIBITION OF DISCRIMINATION

Protocol 12 adds a general prohibition of discrimination to the prohibition of discrimination in relation to rights within the ambit of the Convention currently to be found in Article 14 of the Convention.[175]

Article 1 of Protocol 12 reads:

> 1. The enjoyment of any right set forth by law shall be secured without discrimination on any ground such as sex, race, colour, language, religion, political or other opinion, national or social origin, association with a national minority, property, birth or other status.
> 2. No one shall be discriminated against by any public authority on any ground such as those mentioned in paragraph 1.

The emphasis under Protocol 12 moves from a prohibition of discrimination to a recognition of a right of equality. The preamble to the Protocol refers to all persons being equal before the law and being entitled to the equal protection of the law, and expresses a commitment to the promotion of the equality of all persons through the collective prohibition of discrimination.

The Explanatory Report[176] states that the additional scope of the protection of Protocol 12 when compared with Article 14 relates to cases where a person is discriminated against:

> (1) in the enjoyment of any right specifically granted to an individual under national law;
> (2) in the enjoyment of a right which may be inferred from a clear obligation of a public authority under national law, that is, where a public authority is under an obligation under national law to behave in a particular manner;
> (3) by a public authority in the exercise of discretionary power (for example, granting certain subsidies);
> (4) by any other act or omission by a public authority (for example, the behaviour of law enforcement officers when controlling a riot).

The Explanatory Report goes on to note that it is unnecessary to specify which of the four examples given above comes within the first or second paragraph of Article 1 of Protocol

[174] § 188. For example see *Orsus v Croatia*, (App. 15766/03), 16 March 2010, where indirect discrimination was found due to the treatment in one specific area and not because of statistical evidence.

[175] For some background to Protocol 12, see G. Moon, 'The Draft Discrimination Protocol to the European Convention on Human Rights: A Progress Report' [2000] EHRLR 49. See also N. Grief, 'Non-discrimination under the European Convention on Human Rights: a Critique of the United Kingdom's Refusal to Sign and Ratify Protocol 12' (2002) 27 ELRev *Human Rights Survey* 3.

[176] Explanatory Report to Protocol No. 12 to the Convention for the Protection of Human Rights and Fundamental Freedoms. See also administrative opinion of the European Court of Human Rights of 6 December 1999 on the Protocol.

12, since the two paragraphs are complementary and their combined effect is to include all the circumstances listed. The Explanatory Report also notes that the emphasis on acts or omissions of public authorities should not be taken to exclude the possibility of positive obligations emerging from the new rights protected, just as they have emerged under many Articles of the current Convention.

Though there is significant overlap between the provisions, Article 1 of Protocol 12 is not drafted as a replacement for Article 14, and there is intended to be harmony of interpretation across the two provisions. Article 14 requires the applicant to show that there is differential treatment in an area within the ambit of the Convention rights. Article 1 of Protocol 12 requires the applicant to show that there is differential treatment in the enjoyment of any right set forth in national law. This will include rights granted by legislative measures, as well as rights granted by common law rules and by international law.[177] As with Article 14, the list of comparators given in the Article is illustrative only and not exhaustive. Until Protocol 12 is ratified by a much broader group of Contracting Parties, it is unlikely to play a significant role in the development of equality law under the Convention.[178]

There have been only a few cases that have reached the Court and been decided under Protocol 12. In *Sejdić and Finci v Bosnia and Herzegovina*,[179] the Court found a violation of Article 1 of Protocol 12 concerning elections to the presidency which did not fall under a Convention right. The Court stated that similar principles apply to the Protocol as are applied under Article 14:

> The notion of discrimination has been interpreted consistently in the Court's jurisprudence concerning Article 14 of the Convention. In particular, this jurisprudence has made it clear that "discrimination" means treating differently, without an objective and reasonable justification, persons in similar situations (see paragraphs 42-44 above and the authorities cited therein). The authors used the same term, discrimination, in Article 1 of Protocol No. 12. Notwithstanding the difference in scope between those provisions, the meaning of this term in Article 1 of Protocol No. 12 was intended to be identical to that in Article 14 (see the Explanatory Report to Protocol No. 12, § 18). The Court does not therefore see any reason to depart from the settled interpretation of "discrimination", noted above, in applying the same term under Article 1 of Protocol No. 12.[180]

In *Maktouf and Damjanović v Bosnia and Herzegovina*,[181] the Court held that different sentencing regimes in war crime trials held by different courts was not discriminatory. Applying Article 14 principles, the Court held that there were no grounds for discrimination that the applicants could claim applied to them. The Court then applied *Sejdić*, noting that the meaning of discrimination is identical in both provisions. In a case involving Croatia[182] dealing with the right to religion, the Court found Article 1 of Protocol 12 was applicable to part of the case but having found a violation of Article 14 with Article 9, did not find it necessary to consider the merits of the claim.

[177] The Explanatory Report states that, in the case of international law, this does mean that the Court of Human Rights will sit in judgment on compliance with international treaties.

[178] As at 1 December 2013 in force in eighteen Contracting Parties: Albania, Andorra, Armenia, Bosnia and Herzegovina, Croatia, Cyprus, Finland, Georgia, Luxembourg, Montenegro, the Netherlands, Romania, San Marino, Serbia, Slovenia, Spain, The Former Yugoslav Republic of Macedonia, and Ukraine.

[179] *Sejdić and Finci v Bosnia and Herzegovina*, (Apps. 27996/06 and 34836/06), 22 December 2009.

[180] § 55.

[181] *Maktouf and Damjanović v Bosnia and Herzegovina*, (Apps. 2312/08 and 34179/08), 18 July 2013.

[182] *Savez crkava "Riječ života" and others v Croatia*, (App. 7798/08), 9 December 2010. See also *Vučković and others v Serbia*, (App. 17153/11), 28 June 2012.

CONCLUDING REMARKS

Article 14 is an important provision of the Convention, but remains replete with difficulty in its application. As the case-law develops, it becomes less easy to predict when a matter will be regarded as falling within the scope of the Convention, what constitute relevantly similar situations, and when objective and reasonable justification can be established. There are cases where Contracting Parties seem to have an easy time in explaining the challenged measures, and others where they face an uphill struggle to escape condemnation under Article 14.

The lack of ratifications to Protocol 12 has not dissuaded the Court from developing protection under Article 14. With the development of indirect discrimination, there is now the prospect of a collective approach to discrimination at least in the field of the protection of minorities, and possibly in other cases where the discrimination is systemic. This may help address the underlying discrimination suffered by minorities such as the Roma. The expansion of the case-law with regard to domestic violence, sexual orientation, and disability also reflects the societal changes within Europe and beyond and may reinforce a less individualistic view of the Court towards discrimination, examining the impact of discriminatory practice on communities and groups as well as providing redress for the applicants.

One of the difficulties of Article 14 is the range of enumerated grounds of discrimination coupled with its open-ended nature by adding the words 'or other status'. The case-law shows the development of a delimitation between discrimination which can never, or hardly ever, be justified, and other areas of differential treatment where the heart of the debate will be about the legitimacy of choices made by Contracting Parties in State policies. Perhaps those conceptual issues which surrounded the *Belgian Linguistic* case need to be revisited in the hope of providing greater clarity outside those areas of discrimination which are regarded as deeply suspect.

PART 3

REFLECTIONS

25

RESULTS AND PROSPECTS

INTRODUCTORY REMARKS

The European Convention on Human Rights has attained a leading place in the development of international human rights protection. Over sixty years, the Strasbourg organs have built an admired human rights discourse from scratch. It has been regarded as a 'chapter in a developing European constitution'.[1] In its judgments, the Court itself has described the Convention as 'a constitutional instrument of European public order'.[2] The Convention system has become an integral part of the Council of Europe system; States wishing to become parties to the Statute of the Council of Europe are required to sign the Convention. Following the entry into force of Protocol 11, there is now a pan-European judicial system for the protection of human rights which applies to over 800 million people in forty-seven countries. The Court remains excellent value for money. The budget for 2013 is €66.8 million,[3] or €0.08 per head of population for the year.

The expansion of the Convention system to the new democracies of central and eastern Europe has brought with it new challenges.[4] Many of those countries had weak traditions of human rights protection, and in some of them, old traditions have led to a slow transition to respect for Convention rights within the national legal order. The result has been large numbers of applications made to the Strasbourg Court. In 2012, for example, six countries,[5] four of which are from central and eastern Europe, were the source of nearly 70 per cent of applications to the Strasbourg Court, with over 22 per cent of applications coming from Russia alone.[6] The cultural shift enlargement has brought is significant. Greer comments:

> No longer does [the Convention] express the identity of western European liberal democracy in contrast with the rival communist model of central and eastern Europe; it now provides an 'abstract constitutional identity' for the entire continent, especially for the former communist states recently received into membership.[7]

The principal achievement of the Convention has been the establishment of a formal system of legal protection available to individuals covering a range of civil and political rights,

[1] F. Jacobs, 'Human Rights in Europe: New Dimensions' (1992) 3 KCLJ 49, 50. See also R. Ryssdal, *Forty Years of the European Convention on Human Rights*, Address at Vienna on 18 January 1991, Council of Europe document Cour (91) 61, at 12; and Ryssdal, 'On the Road to a European Constitutional Court' in *Collected Courses of the Academy of European Law*, ii. bk. 2 (Martinus Nijhoff, Dordrecht 1993), 1.

[2] See, for example, *Loizidou v Turkey*, 23 March 1995, Series A No 310, (1995) 20 EHRR 99, § 75; and *Banković and others v Belgium and sixteen other States*, (App. 52207/99), Decision of 12 December 2001, (2007) 44 EHRR SE5, ECHR 2001-XII, § 80.

[3] Source: www.echr.coe.int.

[4] See C. Dupré, 'After Reforms: Human Rights Protection in Post-Communist States' [2008] EHRLR 621.

[5] Russia, Turkey, Italy, Ukraine, Serbia, and Romania.

[6] Analysis of Statistics 2012, available at: www.echr.coe.int/Documents/Stats_analysis_2012_ENG.pdf.

[7] S. Greer, *The European Convention on Human Rights. Achievements, Problems and Prospects*, (CUP, Cambridge 2006), 170–1. This book is a penetrating analysis of what the author calls in his preface the key successes and a cluster of systemic problems concerning the Convention and its application.

which has become the European standard. As arguably the most developed system of legal protection worldwide, it has also contributed to the development of the global definition and understanding of the substantive content of the rights it protects. It has been the model for the American Convention on Human Rights of 1969 and was a key text to which reference was made in the drafting of the African Charter on Human and Peoples' Rights. It has also been a reference point for courts in countries such as Australia, Canada, and India.[8]

Today, the Court faces an immense workload and increasing dissatisfaction of its role in some Contracting States, including the United Kingdom. Has the time come for the Court to seek changes which would embed its constitutional function more firmly in its institutional structures? Could Contracting Parties do more within their own national legal orders to reduce the flow of cases to the Strasbourg Court?

RESULTS

SUBSTANTIVE PROVISIONS

The catalogue of human rights in the European Convention is a statement of legal human rights,[9] that is, it consists of a system of rules, decisions, and principles. It confers rights, imposes duties, and establishes institutions to monitor and implement the specified rights and duties. The catalogue of rights in the European Convention is generally of civil and political rights based on liberal democratic ideals, though there are some rights, such as the provisions relating to education and property, and aspects of freedom of association, which touch on economic, social, and cultural rights.[10]

In November 1950, when the Convention was signed, there was little existing material defining the content of human rights. The key document was the Universal Declaration of Human Rights which had been adopted by the General Assembly of the United Nations in December 1948.[11] It would be many years before the United Nations International Covenant on Civil and Political Rights introduced a more detailed statement of civil and political rights coupled with measures of implementation. The Strasbourg system accordingly became a pioneer in the elaboration of the content of the rights declared in the Convention. The contribution to an understanding of the content and extent of the rights protected by the case-law of the Strasbourg Court, and to a lesser extent the decisions and reports of the European Commission, should not be underestimated both within the legal systems of the Contracting Parties to the Convention and beyond.

Every Article of Section I of the Convention has now spawned a significant case-law defining and clarifying the content of the rights protected. There is now a body of case-law imposing procedural requirements on Contracting Parties under Article 2 which provide additional guarantees that there will be proper respect for the right to life. Such requirements apply not only to those difficult circumstances where States face increasing threats of terrorist activity, but also to deaths arising in prisons and hospitals. Similar procedural

[8] R. Ryssdal, *Europe: the Roads to Democracy. The Council of Europe and the 'architecture' of Europe*, speech at Colloquy organized by the Secretary-General of the Council of Europe in Strasbourg, 18–19 September 1990, Council of Europe document Cour (90) 223, at 2.

[9] On the distinction between legal, political, and moral human rights, see D. Meuwissen, 'Human Rights and the End of History' in R. Lawson and M. de Blois (eds.), *The Dynamics of the Protection of Human Rights in Europe: Essays in Honour of Henry G. Schermers* (Martinus Nijhoff, Dordrecht 1994), at 293.

[10] Under the Council of Europe system, such rights are primarily the province of the European Social Charter; see D. Harris and J. Darcy, *The European Social Charter* (Transnational Publishers, New York 2001).

[11] General Assembly Resolution 217A of 10 December 1948, UNGAOR, 3rd session.

requirements have been imposed on Contracting Parties under Article 3. The definitions of torture and inhuman and degrading treatment under Article 3 have shaped State conduct, particularly in the methods for dealing with the threats of terrorist activity, and in procedures for considering the deportation or extradition of individuals.

In certain areas of internal military conflict, such as the conflicts in Chechnya and south-east Turkey, where national courts have for political reasons been unwilling or unable to defend human rights, the Strasbourg Court has been the only effective forum for establishing the facts relating to large numbers of extremely serious abuses, often amounting to war crimes, including murder, disappearances, torture, and the destruction of entire villages.[12]

Other examples of the impact of the Convention case-law can be found in the development of standards relating to the imposition of corporal punishment, and the conditions of detention. Various provisions of the Convention have interacted to produce a body of new protections for prisoners, for mental patients, and for transsexuals. The tendencies of the modern State to subject some within its jurisdiction to covert surveillance have been controlled by standards developed under the emerging case-law under Article 8.[13] Even in areas where State regulation has a clear role to play, the Court has insisted that such basic rights as freedom of expression are given equal weight with the urge to regulate and restrict. There is hardly an area of State regulation untouched by standards which have emerged from the application of Convention provisions to situations presented by individual applicants. For example, nationalizations and planning regulation must respect the right to property spelled out in the Convention. There is emerging case-law giving coherence and substance to the right to an effective remedy in the national legal order under Article 13, and the significance of the positive obligations imposed under various Articles continues to develop. The Court has not shirked the call to address systems in the countries of central and eastern Europe, and in the unified Germany, for dealing with property restitution issues which potentially affect many thousands of people.

National courts, even among the new Contracting Parties, frequently apply Convention case-law in determining issues before them. For example, research suggests that in Russia judges increasingly make reference to the Convention and the Court's case-law, despite a host of pressures to do otherwise.[14]

Since the Convention is subsidiary to the protection of human rights in national law, the task of the Strasbourg organs involves treading a delicate path between developing and enhancing the standards inherent in the Convention text, and respect for the choices which individual States must make in the face of specific situations. Many of the rights protected are subject to limitations. Setting the boundaries of those limitations has proved to be one of the most contentious aspects of the enforcement of the Convention provisions. Some critics of the Court accuse it of accommodating States too readily; others

[12] P. Leach, C. Paraskeva, and G. Uzelac, *International Human Rights and Fact-Finding. An analysis of the fact-finding missions conducted by the European Commission and Court of Human Rights* (London 2009), available at: www.londonmet.ac.uk/research-units/hrsj/.

[13] However, the recent revelations of massive covert surveillance by the United Kingdom in conjunction with the United States, Canada, New Zealand, and Australia, raise significant doubts as to whether the UK's involvement meets the Convention requirements. For details of the revelations, see www.theguardian.com/world/the-nsa-files.

[14] A. Trochev, 'All appeals lead to Strasbourg? Unpacking the impact of the European Court of Human Rights on Russia' (2009) 17 *Demokratizatsiya* 145, available at http://papers.ssrn.com/sol3/papers.cfm?abstract_id=1421342. See also H. Keller and A. Stone Sweet (eds.), *A Europe of Rights. The Impact of the ECHR on National Legal Systems* (OUP, Oxford 2008).

accuse the Court of judicial activism and complain that the Court does not give enough of a margin.[15]

PLACING THE INDIVIDUAL CENTRE STAGE IN ENFORCING CONVENTION RIGHTS

The European Convention system has succeeded in securing the acceptance of a machinery for the consideration of complaints from individuals, where they believe that their rights have been violated and where no remedy has been provided by the State. The willingness of States to become party to an exclusively judicial system served by a Court with automatic jurisdiction to receive complaints from individuals is remarkable. It is the more so when it is recalled that acceptance of any form of judicial settlement was initially very hesitant and that until comparatively recently reference to the Court was very much the exception. In its first forty years, the Court handed down 800 judgments; in its next ten years, it handed down 9,200 judgments. In the period 1959–2012 the Court delivered about 16,000 judgments. Finally, the maturing of the system has to be set in a context where the Court has at times been bold in its interpretation of the substantive provisions of the Convention.

The role of the individual applicant before the Strasbourg Court has been improved. Initially, the individual was little more than a bystander when cases came before the Court, but individuals are now the main enforcers of Convention rights.[16] However, the success of the Convention has brought with it an increase in the volume of individual applications, which has resulted in excessive delays in the determination of applications from high case-count countries. The volume of applications to the Court once threatened to overwhelm the institution, and itself pose a threat to the protection of human rights in Europe.

For many years, as the case-load increased, the Court was unable to dispose of as many applications as were lodged each year. For example, in 2011 around 64,500 applications were registered and just over 52,000 were disposed of by way of a judgment or decision, a deficit of over 12,500 applications which joined the already substantial backlog.[17] At the end of 2011 the number of registered applications stood at over 151,000 cases. However, once Protocol 14 finally entered into force in June 2010, significant changes could be made to the Court's treatment of manifestly inadmissible and repetitive cases. Manifestly inadmissible cases are now put before a Single Judge on the basis of brief reports prepared by Registry lawyers under the supervision of a non-judicial rapporteur, who is an experienced member of the Registry. Repetitive cases are communicated to the Government in a streamlined procedure which allows bulk communication of multiple applications and does not require submissions where the Government do not contest that a violation has occurred. Friendly settlement proposals are often made at the communication stage. As a consequence of the changes, such cases are now processed much more quickly and efficiently.

[15] For example, Lord Hoffmann has argued that 'In practice, the Court has not taken the doctrine of the margin of appreciation nearly far enough. It has been unable to resist the temptation to aggrandise its jurisdiction and to impose uniform rules on Member States.' ('The Universality of Human Rights' (2009) 125 LQR 416, 423-424.)

[16] Although NGOs play a much larger role than is widely perceived: L. Hodson, *NGOs and the Struggle for Human Rights in Europe* (Hart Publishing, Oxford 2010).

[17] European Court of Human Rights, *Analysis of Statistics 2011* (2012), available at: www.echr.coe.int.

The impact of these developments began to be felt in the course of 2012, when the Court's backlog started falling for the first time in years. By the end of 2012 the backlog stood at 128,100, a reduction of around 23,000 cases on the previous year, and by August 2013 it had fallen to approximately 119,650. This was achieved largely through disposal of significantly higher number of cases; the number of incoming cases remains high. Thus while the backlog remains substantial, the evidence suggests that it is finally under control.

In virtually all Contracting States, the Convention provisions have been incorporated into national law, although this has not, on the whole, reduced the incidence of applications to the Court. Indeed the number of applications demonstrates that more than half a century after the introduction of the Convention's catalogue of fundamental rights, there remain serious threats to their guarantee in very many Contracting States. Reactions to the terrorist attacks in the United States in September 2001, in Spain in March 2004, and in London in July 2005, show quite how fragile some rights which had come to be taken for granted are in times of international crisis.[18] In some Contracting Parties, national reflexes have kicked in which fallaciously suggest that human rights protections need to be lowered or removed in order to respond to the threat of terrorist outrages. The Strasbourg Court has stood firm in not allowing fundamental protections to be watered down.[19]

MAKING JUDGMENTS MORE EFFECTIVE

The Strasbourg Court, with the support of the Parliamentary Assembly and the Committee of Ministers, has developed pilot judgments which seek to address systemic abuses which come to light as a result of individual applications.[20] In two seminal cases against Poland,[21] the Grand Chamber of the Court extended the requirements the Convention imposes on Contracting Parties. In the first case, the Court ruled that Article 13 requires States to have a remedy in the national legal order for either avoiding excessive delays in the administration of justice, or for providing redress where such delays occur.[22] In the second case, the Court indicated, in the context of a property restitution case, that the remedy required in an individual application where a violation was found would extend to a requirement to provide a remedy for a class of individuals in the same situation. In both cases, the Court was requiring a remedy to a systemic defect in the national legal order; the effect of such decisions should be to reduce the number of repetitive claims[23] that are made to the Strasbourg Court. The pilot judgment procedure was clarified and codified in March 2011 when the Court added a new rule (Rule 61) to its Rules of Court clarifying how it handles potential systemic or structural violations of human rights. This procedure is likely to be used with greater frequency as the Strasbourg Court identifies more applications

[18] See generally Council of Europe, *Human Rights and the Fight against Terrorism. The Council of Europe Guidelines* (Council of Europe Publishing, Strasbourg 2005).

[19] For example, in re-affirming its judgment in the *Chahal* case in *Saadi v Italy*, (App. 37201/06), 28 February 2008 [GC], (2009) 49 EHRR 730, ECHR 2008, in requiring basic procedural guarantees for terrorist suspects in *A and others v United Kingdom*, (App. 3455/05), 19 February 2009 [GC], (2009) 49 EHRR 29, ECHR 2009, and in preventing deportation to a country where there was a real risk of the applicant facing a trial in which evidence obtained by torture would be admitted in *Othman (Abu Qatada) v The United Kingdom*, (App. 8139/09), 17 January 2012, ECHR 2012 (extracts).

[20] See ch.2.

[21] *Kudła v Poland*, (App. 30210/96), 26 October 2000 [GC], (2002) 35 EHRR 198, ECHR 2000-XI; and *Broniowski v Poland*, (App. 31443/96), 22 June 2004 [GC], (2005) 40 EHRR 495, ECHR 2004-V.

[22] See ch.23.

[23] Sometimes referred to as 'manifestly well-founded cases': see address by Luzius Wildhaber at the high level seminar on the reform of the European human rights system, held at Oslo on 18 October 2004: available at www.echr.coe.int.

which evidence systemic or structural problems within a national legal order which produces multiple applications. Pilot judgments raise new issues related to their enforcement, which, in turn, imposes new burdens on the Committee of Ministers. Despite these difficulties, pilot judgments are, without question, examples of the imaginative development of effective procedures within the Strasbourg Court which can be introduced without the need for treaty reform with its attendant problems of delay in implementation. A further such example is the 'priority policy' adopted by the Court in June 2009 under which more resources are concentrated on the most important category of cases.[24]

PROSPECTS

RELATIONSHIPS WITH OTHER INTERNATIONAL HUMAN RIGHTS PROCEDURES

The development of European standards runs the risk of producing conflict with other international agreements. The majority of the Contracting Parties to the European Convention are also party to international conventions on human rights protection having a global character.[25] The conflict has so far been avoided because generally the European standards have been more explicit and better developed than any global counterpart. It is also true that where other international bodies have been called upon to determine the content of rights protected, they have made reference to the deliberations of the European Court of Human Rights on similar issues; the Strasbourg Court is also making increasing reference to the text of corresponding human rights instruments, and to judgments and rulings in other procedures. The result has been that, to date, the other international regimes have provided a baseline of protection which the European Convention system has further developed as the minimum guarantee of protection in each of the Contracting States.[26] These, in turn, have been able in many cases to provide a higher level of protection than the minimum level required by the European Convention. Louise Arbour, speaking as United Nations Commissioner of Human Rights, has observed:

> In international law, there is a real risk of unnecessary fragmentation of the law, with different interpretative bodies taking either inconsistent, or worst, flatly contradictory views of the law, without proper acknowledgment of differing views, and proper analysis in support of the stated better position. In the field of human rights, these effects can be particularly damaging, especially when differing views are taken of the scope of the same State's obligations. Given the wide degree of overlap of substantive protection between the European Convention and, in particular, the International Covenant on Civil and Political Rights, the [Strasbourg] Court's use of UN materials diminishes the risk of inconsistent jurisprudence and enhances the likelihood of a better result in both venues.[27]

[24] High priority is given to urgent applications, those raising questions capable of having an impact on the effectiveness of the Convention system or raising an important question of general interest, and those which on their face raise as main complaints issues under Articles 2, 3, 4 or 5(1) of the Convention. See The Court's Priority Policy document, available at: www.echr.coe.int/Documents/Priority%20policy_ENG.pdf.

[25] See T. Opsahl, 'Ten years' coexistence Strasbourg—Geneva' in F. Matscher and H. Petzold (eds.), *Protecting Human Rights: The European Dimension. Essays in honour of Gérard Wiarda* (Carl Heymanns, Köln 1990), 431.

[26] See address by L. Arbour on the opening of the judicial year 2008 of the European Court of Human Rights, 25 January 2008.

[27] Address by L. Arbour on the opening of the judicial year 2008 of the European Court of Human Rights, 25 January 2008.

Despite such optimistic statements, there remains a risk of divergent interpretations of what appear at first sight to be the same human rights obligation expressed in different treaty texts.

EU ACCESSION

A subset of Contracting Parties to the European Convention constitute the European Union, which increasingly sees itself as a human rights organization, leading to potential difficulties in the evolving relationship between the two organizations and their courts. The development of the protection of human rights within the EU is well documented.[28] The relationship between the Strasbourg system and the EU is now at a crucial stage as the future accession of the EU to the Convention will bring new challenges, as well as opportunities. It should at least reduce the scope for conflict arising as a result of judgments of the Court of Justice.

Official talks on the EU's accession to the European Convention of Human Rights started on 7 July 2010, launched by Thorbjørn Jagland, the Secretary General of the Council of Europe, and Viviane Reding, Vice-President of the European Commission. Discussed since the late 1970s, the accession became a legal obligation under the Treaty of Lisbon, which entered into force on 1 December 2009. Authority for accession is now in place on both sides: Article 6(2) of the amended Treaty on European Union, and amended Article 59 of the Convention. On 5 April 2013 negotiators for the 47 Council of Europe Member States and the EU finalized the draft accession agreement of the European Union to the European Convention on Human Rights. It comprises:

(i) a draft Protocol to the Convention which will make the necessary amendments to the Convention to allow for EU participation in the Convention system;

(ii) a draft declaration to be made by the EU at the time of signature of the eventual Accession treaty;

(iii) a draft rule to be added to the Rules of the Council of Europe Committee of Ministers on execution of judgments; and

(iv) a draft model of Memorandum of Understanding between the EU and its Member States, agreeing the terms on which the EU will seek leave to intervene in Strasbourg proceedings against a Member State that involve a point of EU law.

Significantly, the draft agreement creates a co-respondent mechanism (by which, with the leave of the Strasbourg Court, the EU can become a co-respondent in a case when the respondent is a Contracting State and vice versa), and institutes a procedure by which, before Strasbourg rules on a case, the CJEU can first assess the compatibility of a provision of EU law with the Convention. It also gives members of the European Parliament the right to participate in the election of judges of the Strasbourg Court by the Parliamentary Assembly of the Council of Europe, including the election of an EU judge to sit on the Court.

Before accession occurs, further issues remain to be decided, including the means by which MEPs will participate in the Parliamentary Assembly; the participation of the EU in the work of the Council of Europe's Committee of Ministers on execution of judgments of the Strasbourg Court (since there is as yet no intention of the EU to formally join the

[28] See, for example, G. Harpaz, 'The European Court of Justice and its relations with the European Court of Human Rights: the quest for enhanced reliance, coherence and legitimacy' (2009) 46 CMLRev 105, and R.C.A. White, 'A New Era for Human Rights in the European Union?' (2011) 30 Yearbook of European Law 100.

Council of Europe); and the memorandum of understanding as to when the EU will seek leave to intervene in cases against its Member States remains to be agreed. It will also have to be determined which of the EU institutions will represent the Union before the Court (the Commission, it is thought). The CJEU still has to give its opinion on the revised agreement. Finally, and most importantly, since the draft Protocol to the Convention is an amending one, it requires the unanimous ratification of the 47 Member States of the Council of Europe. There is still a difficult political journey ahead, but the agreement on a draft treaty is a significant feat itself given the number of technical issues to deal with, as well a political opposition from the non-EU States. Accession of the EU to the ECHR will strengthen the protection of human rights in Europe, by ultimately submitting the EU and its legal acts to the jurisdiction of the European Court of Human Rights.

THE COURT'S RELATIONSHIP WITH STATE PARTIES

This is a challenging time for the relationship between the Court and some State Parties, most notably the United Kingdom. The former President of the Court has noted that 'the scale and tone of the current hostility directed towards the Court, and the Convention system as a whole, by the press, by members of the Westminster Parliament and by senior members of the Government has created understandable dismay and resentment among the judges in Strasbourg.'[29]

In light of this, and despite the reforms introduced in Protocol 14, further reform of the Strasbourg Court has become a pressing issue and was addressed in three recent High Level Conferences that resulted in three declarations: Interlaken Declaration of 19 February 2010; Izmir Declaration of 27 April 2011; and Brighton Declaration of 20 April 2012.[30] Increasingly the focus has shifted onto clarifying the relationship between national authorities and the Court. Thus, the Brighton Declaration, which stemmed from the High Level Conference on the Future of the Court and was the culmination of the UK's chairmanship of the Committee of Ministers, emphasizes that Contracting State Parties and the Court share responsibility for implementing the Convention. Perhaps the greatest challenge now facing the Strasbourg system is non-enforcement of the Court's judgments, as illustrated by the number of repetitive cases. The Brighton Declaration seeks to shift responsibility for securing human rights back to the States. This results in a focus on specific measures that States need to take in order to ensure effective implementation, but also, more controversially, on a perceived need for the Court to defer to national authorities.

The principle of subsidiarity is given significant prominence in the Brighton Declaration. The text encourages the Court to give 'great prominence to and apply consistently' the principles of subsidiarity and the margin of appreciation,[31] and it concludes that these principles should be added to the Preamble (for reasons of transparency and accessibility).[32] An earlier draft of the Brighton Declaration envisaged an amendment of the text of the Convention to explicitly mention the principles of subsidiarity and the margin of appreciation. The Declaration also emphasizes that, while it is for Court to decide on admissibility, there is a need to apply the admissibility criteria strictly and consistently not just to ensure 'efficient application of justice' but also 'to safeguard the respective roles

[29] N. Bratza, 'The Relationship Between the UK Courts and Strasbourg' [2011] EHRLR 505, 506.

[30] All three can be accessed via this link: www.echr.coe.int/Pages/home.aspx?p=court/reform&c=#n1365510045079_pointer.

[31] § 12(a).

[32] See M. Elliott, 'After Brighton: Between a Rock and a Hard Place' [2012] *Public Law* 619, for discussion.

of the Court and national authorities.'[33] Indeed, the Court is encouraged to be stricter in regarding an application as manifestly ill-founded if it 'raises a complaint that has been duly considered by a domestic court applying the rights guaranteed by the Convention in light of well-established case-law of the Court including on the margin of appreciation as appropriate, unless the Court finds that the application raises a serious question affecting the interpretation or application of the Convention.'[34] It is not only the Court that is urged to give greater priority to the principle of subsidiarity; the Committee of Ministers is also encouraged to apply the principle fully when considering how State Parties may choose to fulfill their obligations under the Convention.

Overall the Brighton Declaration seeks to reduce the workload of the Court, and ensure more effective implementation, by passing greater responsibility onto the State Parties to fully implement the Convention and asks the Strasbourg organs to trust the State Parties in doing so. Ironically, the sheer number of alleged violations committed by these States might urge caution in such an approach.

The addition to the Preamble envisaged by the Declaration is being implemented by means of Protocol 15 which will make the following addition to the Preamble once all State Parties have ratified it: 'Affirming that the High Contracting Parties, in accordance with the principle of subsidiarity, have the primary responsibility to secure the rights and freedoms defined in this Convention and the Protocols thereto, and that in doing so they enjoy a margin of appreciation, subject to the supervisory jurisdiction of the European Court of Human Rights established by this Convention.'[35] When in force, Protocol 15 will also remove the second safeguard clause from the 'no significant disadvantage' admissibility criterion in Article 35(3)(b).[36] The Brighton Declaration proposed this reform in order to further reflect the increasing emphasis on subsidiarity and the need to apply the admissibility criteria strictly. For the same reason, the time limit for admissibility of complaint is to be reduced by Protocol 15 from six months to four months.

2013 also saw the adoption of Protocol 16[37] which will allow the highest domestic courts and tribunals to request the Court to give advisory opinions on questions of principle relating to the interpretation or application of the rights and freedoms defined in the Convention or its Protocols. The Grand Chamber may refuse a request and must give reasons for doing so. The advisory opinions will not be binding.[38] The Preamble to Protocol 16 notes that the extension of the Court's competence to give advisory opinions will 'further enhance the interaction between the Court and national authorities and thereby reinforce implementation of the Convention, in accordance with the principle of subsidiarity.'

A CHANGING ROLE

One significant consequence of the Brighton Declaration's emphasis on the need for more effective national implementation is that it would enable the Court to 'focus its efforts on serious or widespread violations, systemic and structural problems, and important

[33] Brighton Declaration, § 12(c). [34] § 15(d).

[35] Article 1, Protocol 15, adopted 24 June 2013 (not yet in force).

[36] This provides the safeguard that 'no case may be rejected on this ground which has not been duly considered by a domestic tribunal.' See ch.2 for discussion.

[37] Protocol 16, adopted 6 May 2013 (not yet in force).

[38] For a discussion of this, and other differences between the EU preliminary ruling procedure and the European Convention advisory opinion procedure, see P Gragl '(Judicial) Love is Not a One Way Street: The EU Preliminary Reference Procedure as a Model for ECtHR Advisory Opinions under Draft Protocol No. 16' (2013) 38 ELRev 229.

questions of interpretation and application of the Convention, and hence would need to remedy fewer violations itself and consequently deliver fewer judgments.'[39] Such a suggestion would enhance the constitutional role of the Strasbourg Court.[40] Indeed, any long-term consideration of the development of the role of the Strasbourg Court has to grapple with the issue of its constitutional role. The challenge is in reconciling an increased constitutional role with the right of individual petition. The recent and current developments in Protocols 14–16 all retain a commitment to an open system of individual application (although the admissibility criteria are being incrementally tightened). No other constitutional court is so open to applicants. The paradigm of national constitutional courts is that they determine for themselves which cases they will hear. The underlying goal is to enable finite judicial resources to be matched to cases of the greatest significance.[41] What should not be forgotten, however, is the central role of individual petition in the ECHR system. During the drafting of the Convention in the late 1940s, this was recognised as the vital innovation of the European regional system:

> That the international machinery should be at the disposal of the victims is...the only means we have of persuading the men and women of Europe that something new has been done and that an advance has been achieved. We must say to them that even if the states take no further interest in them, and even if no one takes any action on their behalf, they may, by virtue of their dignity as men, avail themselves on their own behalf of an international organ of protection.[42]

With the huge expansion of the Convention to the States of central and eastern Europe, and the serious violations evident in some of those States, it would be a great pity to lose focus on this vital right of access to the Court for all men and women whose rights are trampled on, and voices ignored, by their own governments.

FINAL REMARKS

A former President of the European Court of Human Rights described the Court as emerging as a 'fully fledged international tribunal' which deals with diverse grievances brought to it by individuals which not only allege violations of the right to liberty or the right to the proper administration of justice, but also touch on 'some aspect of social, political or even economic life in the respondent Convention country.'[43]

[39] § 33.

[40] See W. Sadurski, 'Partnering with Strasbourg: Constitutionalization of the European Court of Human Rights, the Accession of Central and Eastern European States to the Council of Europe, and the Idea of Pilot Judgments' (2009) HRLRev 397, and S. Greer, *The European Convention on Human Rights. Achievements, Problems and Prospects* (CUP, Cambridge 2006), ch.7. For an overview of reform of the system under both the European Convention and the European Social Charter, see V. Mantouvalou and P. Voyatzis, 'The Council of Europe and the Protection of Human Rights: A System in Need of Reform' in S. Joseph and A. McBeth, *Research Handbook on International Human Rights Law* (Edward Elgar, Cheltenham 2010), available at http://ssrn.com/abstract=1360250.

[41] See discussion of this issue in the light of comments by some Strasbourg judges in R. White and I. Boussiakou, 'Voices from the European Court of Human Rights' (2009) 27 NQHR 167.

[42] G. Robertson, *Collected Edition of the Travaux Préparatoires* (The Hague, Martinus Nijhoff 1977), Vol. 2, p. 178, quoting Pierre-Henri Teitgen.

[43] R. Ryssdal, 'The European Court of Human Rights and Gérard Wiarda' in F. Matscher and H. Petzold (eds.), *Protecting Human Rights: The European Dimension. Essays in honour of Gérard Wiarda* (Carl Heymanns, Köln 1990), 1, 2.

Though there are certain to be Conventions setting detailed standards in particular areas, there will remain a central role for a more general catalogue of rights, which provides the essential core of fundamental rights which surrounds everyone within the jurisdiction of the Contracting States. That catalogue will be extended, and there will come a time when the substantive provisions of the Convention and its Protocols will need to be consolidated.

Together the Commission and the Court have ensured that the European Convention now provides the most sophisticated regional judicial architecture for the protection of human rights. Substance has been given to the rights in Section I of the Convention and the accompanying Protocols. The Contracting Parties have all accepted that individuals within their jurisdiction can raise a complaint before the Strasbourg Court if they believe that the State has not accorded them the protection guaranteed by the Convention. Those are huge achievements in the six decades since the Convention was signed. The signing of the European Convention on 4 November 1950 in the Palazzo Barberini represented a milestone in the protection of human rights in Europe. Over sixty years later the system introduced by the Convention continues to evolve as it faces up to the contemporary challenge of ensuring the continuing effectiveness and development of the protection of human rights for over 800 million people in forty-seven countries of a wider democratic Europe.

APPENDIX

TEXT OF THE EUROPEAN CONVENTION AND PROTOCOLS AS MODIFIED BY PROTOCOL 14

Entered into force: 1 June 2010

CONVENTION FOR THE PROTECTION OF HUMAN RIGHTS AND FUNDAMENTAL FREEDOMS

The governments signatory hereto, being members of the Council of Europe,

Considering the Universal Declaration of Human Rights proclaimed by the General Assembly of the United Nations on 10th December 1948;

Considering that this Declaration aims at securing the universal and effective recognition and observance of the Rights therein declared;

Considering that the aim of the Council of Europe is the achievement of greater unity between its members and that one of the methods by which that aim is to be pursued is the maintenance and further realisation of human rights and fundamental freedoms;

Reaffirming their profound belief in those fundamental freedoms which are the foundation of justice and peace in the world and are best maintained on the one hand by an effective political democracy and on the other by a common understanding and observance of the human rights upon which they depend;

Being resolved, as the governments of European countries which are like-minded and have a common heritage of political traditions, ideals, freedom and the rule of law, to take the first steps for the collective enforcement of certain of the rights stated in the Universal Declaration,

Have agreed as follows:

Article 1
Obligation to respect human rights

The High Contracting Parties shall secure to everyone within their jurisdiction the rights and freedoms defined in Section I of this Convention.

SECTION I RIGHTS AND FREEDOMS

Article 2
Right to life

(1) Everyone's right to life shall be protected by law. No one shall be deprived of his life intentionally save in the execution of a sentence of a court following his conviction of a crime for which this penalty is provided by law.

(2) Deprivation of life shall not be regarded as inflicted in contravention of this Article when it results from the use of force which is no more than absolutely necessary:

(a) in defence of any person from unlawful violence;

(b) in order to effect a lawful arrest or to prevent the escape of a person lawfully detained;

(c) in action lawfully taken for the purpose of quelling a riot or insurrection.

Article 3
Prohibition of torture

No one shall be subjected to torture or to inhuman or degrading treatment or punishment.

Article 4
Prohibition of slavery and forced labour

(1) No one shall be held in slavery or servitude.

(2) No one shall be required to perform forced or compulsory labour.

(3) For the purposes of this Article the term 'forced or compulsory labour' shall not include:

(a) any work required to be done in the ordinary course of detention imposed according to the provisions of Article 5 of this Convention or during conditional release from such detention;

(b) any service of a military character or, in the case of conscientious objectors in countries where they are recognised, service exacted instead of compulsory military service;

(c) any service exacted in case of an emergency or calamity threatening the life or well-being of the community;

(d) any work or service which forms part of normal civic obligations.

Article 5
Right to liberty and security

(1) Everyone has the right to liberty and security of the person. No one shall be deprived of his liberty save in the following cases and in accordance with a procedure prescribed by law:

(a) the lawful detention of person after conviction by a competent court;

(b) the lawful arrest or detention of a person for non-compliance with the lawful order of a court or in order to secure the fulfilment of any obligation prescribed by law;

(c) the lawful arrest or detention of a person effected for the purpose of bringing him before the competent legal authority on reasonable suspicion of having committed an offence or when it is reasonably considered necessary to prevent his committing an offence or fleeing after having done so;

(d) the detention of a minor by lawful order for the purpose of educational supervision or his lawful detention for the purpose of bringing him before the competent legal authority;

(e) the lawful detention of persons for the prevention of the spreading of infectious diseases, of persons of unsound mind, alcoholics or drug addicts or vagrants;

(f) the lawful arrest or detention of a person to prevent his effecting an unauthorised entry into the country or of a person against whom action is being taken with a view to deportation or extradition.

(2) Everyone who is arrested shall be informed promptly, in a language which he understands, of the reasons for his arrest and of any charge against him.

(3) Everyone arrested or detained in accordance with the provisions of paragraph (1)(c) of this article shall be brought promptly before a judge or other officer authorised by law to exercise judicial power and shall be entitled to trial within a reasonable time or to release pending trial. Release may be conditioned by guarantees to appear for trial.

(4) Everyone who is deprived of his liberty by arrest or detention shall be entitled to take proceedings by which the lawfulness of his detention shall be decided speedily by a court and his release ordered if the detention is not lawful.

(5) Everyone who has been the victim of arrest or detention in contravention of the provisions of this article shall have an enforceable right to compensation.

Article 6
Right to a fair trial

(1) In the determination of his civil rights and obligations or of any criminal charge against him, everyone is entitled to a fair and public hearing within a reasonable time by an independent and impartial tribunal established by law. Judgment shall be pronounced publicly but the press and public may be excluded from all or part of the trial in the interests of morals, public order or national security in a democratic society, where the interests of juveniles or the protection of the private life of the parties so require, or to the extent strictly necessary in the opinion of the court in special circumstances where publicity would prejudice the interests of justice.

(2) Everyone charged with a criminal offence shall be presumed innocent until proved guilty according to law.

(3) Everyone charged with a criminal offence has the following minimum rights:

(a) to be informed promptly, in a language which he understands and in detail, of the nature and cause of the accusation against him;

(b) to have adequate time and facilities for the preparation of his defence;

(c) to defend himself in person or through legal assistance of his own choosing or, if he has not sufficient means to pay for legal assistance, to be given it free when the interests of justice so require;

(d) to examine or have examined witnesses against him and to obtain the attendance and examination of witnesses on his behalf under the same conditions as witnesses against him;

(e) to have the free assistance of an interpreter if he cannot understand or speak the language used in court.

Article 7
No punishment without law

(1) No one shall be held guilty of any criminal offence on account of any act or omission which did not constitute a criminal offence under national or international law at the time when it was committed. Nor shall a heavier penalty be imposed than the one that was applicable at the time the criminal offence was committed.

(2) This Article shall not prejudice the trial and punishment of any person for any act or omission which, at the time when it was committed, was criminal according to the general principles of law recognised by civilised nations.

Article 8
Right to respect for private and family life

(1) Everyone has the right to respect for his private and family life, his home and his correspondence.

(2) There shall be no interference by a public authority with the exercise of this right except such as is in accordance with the law and is necessary in a democratic society in the interests of

national security, public safety or the economic well-being of the country, for the prevention of disorder or crime, for the protection of health or morals, or for the protection of the rights and freedoms of others.

Article 9
Freedom of thought, conscience and religion

(1) Everyone has the right to freedom of thought, conscience and religion; this right includes freedom to change his religion or belief and freedom, either alone or in community with others and in public or private, to manifest his religion or belief, in worship, teaching, practice and observance.

(2) Freedom to manifest one's religion or beliefs shall be subject only to such limitations as are prescribed by law and are necessary in a democratic society in the interests of public safety, for the protection of public order, health or morals, or for the protection of the rights and freedoms of others.

Article 10
Freedom of expression

(1) Everyone has the right to freedom of expression. This right shall include freedom to hold opinions and to receive and impart information and ideas without interference by public authority and regardless of frontiers. This article shall not prevent States from requiring the licensing of broadcasting, television or cinema enterprises.

(2) The exercise of these freedoms, since it carries with it duties and responsibilities, may be subject to such formalities, conditions, restrictions or penalties as are prescribed by law and are necessary in a democratic society, in the interests of national security, territorial integrity or public safety, for the prevention of disorder or crime, for the protection of health or morals, for the protection of the reputation or rights of others, for preventing the disclosure of information received in confidence, or for maintaining the authority and impartiality of the judiciary.

Article 11
Freedom of assembly and association

(1) Everyone has the right to freedom of peaceful assembly and to freedom of association with others, including the right to form and to join trade unions for the protection of his interests.

(2) No restrictions shall be placed on the exercise of these rights other than such as are prescribed by law and are necessary in a democratic society in the interests of national security or public safety, for the prevention of disorder or crime, for the protection of health or morals or for the protection of the rights and freedoms of others. This article shall not prevent the imposition of lawful restrictions on the exercise of these rights by members of the armed forces, of the police or of the administration of the State.

Article 12
Right to marry

Men and women of marriageable age have the right to marry and to found a family, according to the national laws governing the exercise of this right.

Article 13
Right to an effective remedy

Everyone whose rights and freedoms as set forth in this Convention are violated shall have an effective remedy before a national authority notwithstanding that the violation has been committed by persons acting in an official capacity.

Article 14
Prohibition of discrimination

The enjoyment of the rights and freedoms set forth in this Convention shall be secured without discrimination on any ground such as sex, race, colour, language, religion, political or other opinion, national or social origin, association with a national minority, property, birth or other status.

Article 15
Derogation in time of emergency

(1) In time of war or other public emergency threatening the life of the nation any High Contracting Party may take measures derogating from its obligations under this Convention to the extent strictly required by the exigencies of the situation, provided that such measures are not inconsistent with its other obligations under international law.

(2) No derogation from Article 2, except in respect of deaths resulting from lawful acts of war, or from Articles 3, 4 (paragraph 1) and 7 shall be made under this provision.

(3) Any High Contracting Party availing itself of this right of derogation shall keep the Secretary General of the Council of Europe fully informed of the measures which it has taken and the reasons therefor. It shall also inform the Secretary General of the Council of Europe when such measures have ceased to operate and the provisions of the Convention are again being fully executed.

Article 16
Restrictions on political activity of aliens

Nothing in Articles 10, 11 and 14 shall be regarded as preventing the High Contracting Parties from imposing restrictions on the political activities of aliens.

Article 17
Prohibition of abuse of rights

Nothing in this Convention may be interpreted as implying for any State, group or person any right to engage in any activity or perform any act aimed at the destruction of any of the rights and freedoms set forth herein or at their limitation to a greater extent that is provided for in the Convention.

Article 18
Limitation on use of restrictions on rights

The restrictions permitted under this Convention to the said rights and freedoms shall not be applied for any purpose other than those for which they have been prescribed.

SECTION II EUROPEAN COURT OF HUMAN RIGHTS

Article 19
Establishment of the Court

To ensure the observance of the engagements undertaken by the High Contracting Parties in the Convention and the protocols thereto, there shall be set up a European Court of Human Rights, hereinafter referred to as 'the Court'. It shall function on a permanent basis.

Article 20
Number of judges

The Court shall consist of a number of judges equal to that of the High Contracting Parties.

Article 21
Criteria for office

(1) The judges shall be of high moral character and must either possess the qualifications required for appointment to high judicial office or be jurisconsults of recognised competence.

(2) The judges shall sit on the Court in their individual capacity.

(3) During their term of office the judges shall not engage in any activity which is incompatible with their independence, impartiality or with the demands of a full-time office; all questions arising from the application of this paragraph shall be decided by the Court.

Article 22
Election of judges

(1) The judges shall be elected by the Parliamentary Assembly with respect to each High Contracting Party by a majority of votes cast from a list of three candidates nominated by the High Contracting Party.

Article 23
Terms of office and dismissal

(1) The judges shall be elected for a period of nine years. They may not be re-elected.

(2) The terms of office of judges shall expire when they reach the age of 70.

(3) The judges shall hold office until replaced. They shall, however, continue to deal with such cases as they already have under consideration.

(4) No judge may be dismissed from office unless the other judges decide by a majority of two-thirds that that judge has ceased to fulfil the required conditions.

Article 24
Registry and rapporteurs

(1) The Court shall have a registry, the functions and organisation of which shall be laid down in the rules of the Court.

(2) When sitting in a single-judge formation, the Court shall be assisted by rapporteurs who shall function under the authority of the President of the Court. They shall form part of the Court's registry.

Article 25
Plenary Court

The plenary Court shall:

(a) elect its President and one or two Vice-Presidents for a period of three years; they may be re-elected;

(b) set up Chambers, constituted for a fixed period of time;

(c) elect the Presidents of the Chambers of the Court; they may be re-elected;

(d) adopt the rules of the Court;

(e) elect the Registrar and one or more Deputy Registrars;

(f) make any request under Article 26, paragraph 2.

Article 26
Single-judge formation, committees, Chambers and Grand Chamber

(1) To consider cases brought before it, the Court shall sit in a single-judge formation, in committees of three judges, in Chambers of seven judges and in a Grand Chamber of seventeen judges. The Court's Chambers shall set up committees for a fixed period of time.

(2) At the request of the plenary Court, the Committee of Ministers may, by a unanimous decision and for a fixed period, reduce to five the number of judges of the Chambers.

(3) When sitting as a single judge, a judge shall not examine any application against the High Contracting Party in respect of which that judge has been elected.

(4) There shall sit as an *ex officio* member of the Chamber and the Grand Chamber the judge elected in respect of the High Contracting Party concerned. If there is none or if that judge is unable to sit, a person chosen by the President of the Court from a list submitted in advance by that Party shall sit in the capacity of judge.

(5) The Grand Chamber shall also include the President of the Court, the Vice-Presidents, the Presidents of the Chambers and other judges chosen in accordance with the rules of the Court. When a case is referred to the Grand Chamber under Article 43, no judge from the Chamber which rendered the judgment shall sit in the Grand Chamber, with the exception of the President of the Chamber and the judge who sat in respect of the High Contracting Party concerned.

Article 27
Competence of single judges

(1) A single judge may declare inadmissible or strike out of the Court's list of cases an application submitted under Article 34, where such a decision can be taken without further examination.

(2) The decision shall be final.

(3) If the single judge does not declare an application inadmissible or strike it out, that judge shall forward it to a committee or to a Chamber for further examination.

Article 28
Competence of committees

(1) In respect of an application submitted under Article 34, a committee may, by a unanimous vote,

(a) declare it inadmissible or strike it out of its list of cases, where such decision can be taken without further examination; or

(b) declare it admissible and render at the same time a judgment on the merits, if the underlying question in the case, concerning the interpretation or the application of the Convention or the Protocols thereto, is already the subject of well-established case-law of the Court.

(2) Decisions and judgments under paragraph 1 shall be final.

(3) If the judge elected in respect of the High Contracting Party concerned is not a member of the committee, the committee may at any stage of the proceedings invite that judge to take the place of one of the members of the committee, having regard to all relevant factors, including whether that Party has contested the application of the procedure under paragraph 1(b).

Article 29
Decisions by Chambers on admissibility and merits

(1) If no decision is taken under Article 27 or 28, or no judgment rendered under Article 28, a Chamber shall decide on the admissibility and merits of individual applications submitted under Article 34. The decision on admissibility may be taken separately.

(2) A Chamber shall decide on the admissibility and merits of inter-State applications submitted under Article 33. The decision on admissibility shall be taken separately unless the Court, in exceptional cases, decides otherwise.

Article 30
Relinquishment of jurisdiction to the Grand Chamber

Where a case pending before a Chamber raises a serious question affecting the interpretation of the Convention or the protocols thereto or where the resolution of a question before it might have a result inconsistent with a judgment previously delivered by the Court, the Chamber may, at any time before it has rendered its judgment, relinquish jurisdiction in favour of the Grand Chamber, unless one of the parties to the case objects.

Article 31
Powers of the Grand Chamber

The Grand Chamber shall

(a) determine applications submitted either under Article 33 or Article 34 when a Chamber has relinquished jurisdiction under Article 30 or when the case has been referred to it under Article 43;

(b) decide on issues referred to the Court by the Committee of Ministers in accord-ance with Article 46, paragraph 4; and

(c) consider requests for advisory opinions submitted under Article 47.

Article 32
Jurisdiction of the Court

(1) The jurisdiction of the Court shall extend to all matters concerning the interpretation and application of the Convention and the protocols thereto which are referred to it as provided in Articles 33, 34, 46 and 47.

(2) In the event of dispute as to whether the Court has jurisdiction, the Court shall decide.

Article 33
Inter-State cases

Any High Contracting Party may refer to the Court any alleged breach of the provisions of the Convention and the protocols thereto by another High Contracting Party.

Article 34
Individual applications

The Court may receive applications from any person, non-governmental organisation or group of individuals claiming to be the victim of a violation by one of the High Contracting Parties of the rights set forth in the Convention and the protocols thereto. The High Contracting Parties undertake not to hinder in any way the effective exercise of this right.

Article 35
Admissibility criteria

(1) The Court may only deal with the matter after all domestic remedies have been exhausted, according to the generally recognised rules of international law, and within a period of six months from the date on which the final decision was taken.

(2) The Court shall not deal with any individual application submitted under Article 34 that

(a) is anonymous; or

(b) is substantially the same as a matter that has already been examined by the Court or has already been submitted to another procedure of international investigation or settlement and contains no relevant new information.

(3) The Court shall declare inadmissible any individual application submitted under Article 34 if it considers that:

(a) the application is incompatible with the provisions of the Convention or the Protocols thereto, manifestly ill-founded, or an abuse of the right of individual application; or

(b) the applicant has not suffered a significant disadvantage, unless respect for human rights as defined in the Convention and the Protocols thereto requires an examination of the application on the merits and provided that no case may be rejected on this ground which has not been duly considered by a domestic tribunal.

(4) The Court shall reject any application which it considers inadmissible under this Article. It may do so at any stage of the proceedings.

Article 36
Third-party intervention

(1) In all cases before a Chamber or the Grand Chamber, a High Contracting Party one of whose nationals is an applicant shall have the right to submit written comments and to take part in the hearings.

(2) The President of the Court may, in the interest of the proper administration of justice, invite any High Contracting Party which is not a party to the proceedings or any person concerned who is not the applicant to submit written comments or take part in the hearings.

(3) In all cases before a Chamber or the Grand Chamber, the Council of Europe Commissioner for Human Rights may submit written comments and take part in hearings.

Article 37
Striking out applications

(1) The Court may at any stage of the proceedings decide to strike an application out of its list of cases where the circumstances lead to the conclusion that

(a) the applicant does not intend to pursue his application; or

(b) the matter has been resolved; or

(c) for any other reason established by the Court, it is no longer justified to continue the examination of the application.However, the Court shall continue the examination of the application if respect for human rights as defined in the Convention and the protocols thereto so requires.

(2) The Court may decide to restore an application to its list of cases if it considers that the circumstances justify such a course.

Article 38
Examination of the case

The Court shall examine the case together with the representatives of the parties and, if need be, undertake an investigation, for the effective conduct of which the High Contracting Parties concerned shall furnish all necessary facilities.

Article 39
Friendly settlements

(1) At any stage of the proceedings, the Court may place itself at the disposal of the parties concerned with a view to securing a friendly settlement of the matter on the basis of respect for human rights as defined in the Convention and the Protocols thereto.

(2) Proceedings conducted under paragraph 1 shall be confidential.

(3) If a friendly settlement is effected, the Court shall strike the case out of its list by means of a decision which shall be confined to a brief statement of the facts and of the solution reached.

(4) This decision shall be transmitted to the Committee of Ministers, which shall supervise the execution of the terms of the friendly settlement as set out in the decision.

Article 40
Public hearings and access to documents

(1) Hearings shall be public unless the Court in exceptional circumstances decides otherwise.

(2) Documents deposited with the Registrar shall be accessible to the public unless the President of the Court decides otherwise.

Article 41
Just satisfaction

If the Court finds that there has been a violation of the Convention or the protocols thereto, and if the internal law of the High Contracting Party concerned allows only partial reparation to be made, the Court shall, if necessary afford just satisfaction to the injured party.

Article 42
Judgments of Chambers

Judgments of Chambers shall become final in accordance with the provisions of Article 44, paragraph 2.

Article 43
Referral to the Grand Chamber

(1) Within a period of three months from the date of the judgment of the Chamber, any party to the case may, in exceptional cases, request that the case be referred to the Grand Chamber.

(2) A panel of five judges of the grand Chamber shall accept the request if the case raises a serious question affecting the interpretation or application of the Convention or the protocols thereto, or a serious issue of general importance.

(3) If the panel accepts the request, the Grand Chamber shall decide the case by means of a judgment.

Article 44
Final judgments

(1) The judgment of the Grand Chamber shall be final.

(2) The judgment of a Chamber shall become final.

(a) when the parties declare that they will not request that the case be referred to the Grand Chamber; or

(b) three months after the date of the judgment, if reference of the case to the Grand Chamber has not been requested; or

(c) when the panel of the Grand Chamber rejects the request to refer under Article 43.

(3) The final judgment shall be published.

Article 45
Reasons for judgments and decisions

(1) Reasons shall be given for judgments as well as for decisions declaring applications admissible or inadmissible.

(2) If a judgment does not represent, in whole or in part, the unanimous opinion of the judges, any judge shall be entitled to deliver a separate opinion.

Article 46
Binding force and execution of judgments

(1) The High Contracting Parties undertake to abide by the final judgment of the Court in any case to which they are parties.

(2) The final judgment of the Court shall be transmitted to the Committee of Ministers, which shall supervise its execution.

(3) If the Committee of Ministers considers that the supervision of the execution of a final judgment is hindered by a problem of interpretation of the judgment, it may refer the matter to the Court for a ruling on the question of interpretation. A referral decision shall require a majority vote of two thirds of the representatives entitled to sit on the Committee.

(4) If the Committee of Ministers considers that a High Contracting Party refuses to abide by a final judgment in a case to which it is a party, it may, after serving formal notice on that Party and by decision adopted by a majority vote of two thirds of the representatives entitled to sit on the Committee, refer to the Court the question whether that Party has failed to fulfil its obligation under paragraph 1.

(5) If the Court finds a violation of paragraph 1, it shall refer the case to the Committee of Ministers for consideration of the measures to be taken. If the Court finds no violation of paragraph 1, it shall refer the case to the Committee of Ministers, which shall close its examination of the case.

Article 47
Advisory opinions

(1) The Court may, at the request of the Committee of Ministers, give advisory opinions on legal questions concerning the interpretation of the Convention and the protocols thereto.

(2) Such opinions shall not deal with any question relating to the content or scope of the rights or freedoms defined in Section I of the Convention and the protocols thereto, or with any other question which the Court or the Committee of Ministers might have to consider in consequence of any such proceedings as could be instituted in accordance with the Convention.

(3) Decisions of the Committee of Ministers to request an advisory opinion of the Court shall require a majority vote of the representatives entitled to sit on the Committee.

Article 48
Advisory jurisdiction of the court

The Court shall decide whether a request for an advisory opinion submitted by the Committee of Ministers is within its competence as defined in Article 47.

Article 49
Reasons for advisory opinions

(1) Reasons shall be given for advisory opinions of the Court.

(2) If the advisory opinion does not represent, in whole or in part, the unanimous opinion of the judges, any judge shall be entitled to deliver a separate opinion.

(3) Advisory opinions of the Court shall be communicated to the Committee of Ministers.

Article 50
Expenditure on the Court

The expenditure on the Court shall be borne by the Council of Europe.

Article 51
Privileges and immunities of judges

The judges shall be entitled, during the exercise of their functions, to the privileges and immunities provided for in Article 40 of the Statute of the Council of Europe and in the agreements made thereunder.

SECTION III MISCELLANEOUS PROVISIONS

Article 52
Inquiries by the Secretary General

On receipt of a request from the Secretary General of the Council of Europe any High Contracting Party shall furnish an explanation of the manner in which its internal law ensures the effective implementation of any of the provisions of the Convention.

Article 53
Safeguard for existing human rights

Nothing in this Convention shall be construed as limiting or derogating from any of the human rights and fundamental freedoms which may be ensured under the laws of any High Contracting Party or under any other agreement to which it is a Party.

Article 54
Powers of the Committee of Ministers

Nothing in this Convention shall prejudice the powers conferred on the Committee of Ministers by the Statute of the Council of Europe.

Article 55
Exclusion of other means of dispute settlement

The High Contracting Parties agree that, except by special agreement, they will not avail themselves of treaties, conventions or declarations in force between them for the purpose of submitting, by way of petition, a dispute arising out of the interpretation or application of this Convention to a means of settlement other than those provided for in this Convention.

Article 56
Territorial application

(1) Any State may at the time of its ratification or at any time thereafter declare by notification addressed to the Secretary General of the Council of Europe that the present Convention shall, subject to paragraph 4 of this Article, extend to all or any of the territories for whose international relations it is responsible.

(2) The Convention shall extend to the territory or territories named in the notification as from the thirtieth day after the receipt of this notification by the Secretary General of the Council of Europe.

(3) The provisions of this Convention shall be applied in such territories with due regard, however, to local requirements.

(4) Any State which has made a declaration in accordance with paragraph 1 of this Article may at any time thereafter declare on behalf of one or more of the territories to which the declaration relates that it accepts the competence of the Court to receive applications from individuals, non-governmental organisations or groups of individuals as provided in Article 34 of the Convention.

Article 57
Reservations

(1) Any State may, when signing this Convention or when depositing its instrument of ratification, make a reservation in respect of any particular provision of the Convention to the extent that any law then in force in its territory is not in conformity with the provision. Reservations of a general character shall not be permitted under this Article.

(2) Any reservation made under this Article shall contain a brief statement of the law concerned.

Article 58
Denunciation

(1) A High Contracting Party may denounce the present Convention only after the expiry of five years from the date on which it became a party to it and after six months' notice contained in a notification addressed to the Secretary General of the Council of Europe, who shall inform the other High Contracting Parties.

(2) Such a denunciation shall not have the effect of releasing the High Contracting Party concerned from its obligations under this Convention in respect of any act which, being capable of constituting a violation of such obligations, may have been performed by it before the date at which the denunciation became effective.

(3) Any High Contracting Party which shall cease to be a member of the Council of Europe shall cease to be a Party to this Convention under the same conditions.

(4) The Convention may be denounced in accordance with the provisions of the preceding paragraphs in respect of any territory to which it has been declared to extend under the terms of Article 56.

Article 59
Signature and ratification

(1) This Convention shall be open to the signature of the members of the Council of Europe. It shall be ratified. Ratifications shall be deposited with the Secretary General of the Council of Europe.

(2) The European Union may accede to this Convention.

(3) The present Convention shall come into force after the deposit of ten instruments of ratification.

(4) As regard any signatory ratifying subsequently, the Convention shall come into force at the date of the deposit of its instrument of ratification.

(5) The Secretary General of the Council of Europe shall notify all the members of the Council of Europe of the entry into force of the Convention, the names of the High Contracting Parties who have ratified it, and the deposit of all instruments of ratification which may be effected subsequently.

Done at Rome, 4 November 1950.

Protocol to the Convention for the Protection of Human Rights and Fundamental Freedoms, as amended by Protocol No. 11

The governments signatory hereto, being members of the Council of Europe *Being resolved* to take steps to ensure the collective enforcement of certain rights and freedoms other than those already included in Section I of the Convention for the Protection of Human Rights and Fundamental Freedoms signed at Rome on 4 November 1950 (hereinafter referred to as 'the Convention'),

Have agreed as follows:

Article 1
Protection of property

Every natural or legal person is entitled to the peaceful enjoyment of his possessions. No one shall be deprived of his possessions except in the public interest and subject to the conditions provided for by law and by the general principles of international law.

The preceding provisions shall not, however, in any way impair the right of a State to enforce such laws as it deems necessary to control the use of property in accordance with the general interest or to secure the payment of taxes or other contributions or penalties.

Article 2
Right to education

No person shall be denied the right to education. In the exercise of any functions which it assumes in relation to education and to teaching, the State shall respect the right of parents to ensure such education and teaching in conformity with their own religious and philosophical convictions.

Article 3
Right to free elections

The High Contracting Parties undertake to hold free elections at reasonable intervals by secret ballot, under conditions which will ensure the free expression of the opinion of the people in the choice of the legislature.

Article 4
Territorial application

Any High Contracting Party may at the time of signature or ratification or at any time thereafter communicate to the Secretary General of the Council of Europe a declaration stating the extent to which it undertakes that the provisions of the present Protocol shall apply to such of the territories for the international relations of which it is responsible as are named therein. Any High Contracting Party which has communicated a declaration in virtue of the preceding paragraph may from time to time communicate a further declaration modifying the terms of any former declaration or terminating the application of the provisions of this Protocol in respect of any territory. A declaration made in accordance with this Article shall be deemed to have been made in accordance with paragraph 1 of Article 56 of the Convention.

Article 5
Relationship to the Convention

As between the High Contracting Parties the provisions of Articles 1, 2, 3 and 4 of this Protocol shall be regarded as additional articles to the Convention and all the provisions of the Convention shall apply accordingly.

Article 6
Signature and ratification

This Protocol shall be open for signature by the members of the Council of Europe, who are the signatories of the Convention; it shall be ratified at the same time as or after the ratification of the Convention. It shall enter into force after the deposit of ten instruments of ratification. As regards any signatory ratifying subsequently, the Protocol shall enter into force at the date of the deposit of its instrument of ratification.

The instruments of ratification shall be deposited with the Secretary General of the Council of Europe, who will notify all members of the names of those who have ratified.

Done at Paris, 20 March 1952.

[Protocol No. 2 becomes otiose, since the provisions on the Court's competence to give advisory opinions are incorporated in Articles 47 to 49 of the Convention]

[Protocol No. 3 has become otiose; it modified the procedure of the Commission by abolishing the system of sub-commissions]

Protocol No. 4 to the Convention for the Protection of Human Rights and Fundamental Freedoms securing certain rights and Freedoms other than those already included in the Convention and in the first Protocol thereto, as amended by Protocol 11

The governments signatory hereto, being members of the Council of Europe, *Being resolved* to take steps to ensure the collective enforcement of certain rights and freedoms other than those already included in Section I of the Convention for the Protection of Human Rights and Fundamental Freedoms signed at Rome on 4th November 1950 (hereinafter referred to as 'the Convention') and in Articles 1 to 3 of the First Protocol to the Convention, signed at Paris on 20th March 1952,

Have agreed as follows:

Article 1
Prohibition of imprisonment for debt

No one shall be deprived of his liberty merely on the ground of inability to fulfil a contractual obligation.

Article 2
Freedom of movement

(1) Everyone lawfully within the territory of a State shall, within that territory, have the right to liberty of movement and freedom to choose his residence.

(2) Everyone shall be free to leave any country, including his own.

(3) No restrictions shall be placed on the exercise of these rights other than such as are in accordance with law and are necessary in a democratic society in the interests of national security or public safety, for the maintenance of the *ordre public*, for the prevention of crime, for the protection of health or morals, or for the protection of the rights and freedoms of others.

(4) The rights set forth in paragraph 1 may also be subject, in particular areas, to restrictions imposed in accordance with law and justified by the public interest in a democratic society.

Article 3
Prohibition of expulsion of nationals

(1) No one shall be expelled, by means either of an individual or of a collective measure, from the territory of the State of which he is a national.

(2) No one shall be deprived of the right to enter the territory of the State of which he is a national.

Article 4
Prohibition of collective expulsion of aliens

Collective expulsion of aliens is prohibited.

Article 5
Territorial application

(1) Any High Contracting Party may, at the time of signature or ratification of this protocol, or at any time thereafter, communicate to the Secretary General of the Council of Europe a declaration stating the extent to which it undertakes that the provisions of this Protocol shall apply to such of the territories for the international relations of which it is responsible as are named therein.

(2) Any High Contracting Party which has communicated a declaration in virtue of the preceding paragraph may, from time to time, communicate a further declaration modifying the terms of any former declaration or terminating the application of the provisions of this Protocol in respect of any territory.

(3) A declaration made in accordance with this Article shall be deemed to have been made in accordance with paragraph 1 of Article 56 of the Convention.

(4) The territory of any State to which this Protocol applies by virtue of ratification or acceptance by that State, and each territory to which this Protocol is applied by virtue of a declaration by that State under this Article, shall be treated as separate territories for the purpose of the references in Articles 2 and 3 to the territory of a State.

(5) Any State which has made a declaration in accordance with paragraph 1 or 2 of this Article may at any time thereafter declare on behalf of one or more of the territories to which the declaration relates that it accepts the competence of the Court to receive applications from individuals, non-governmental organisations or groups of individuals as provided in Article 34 of the Convention in respect of all or any of Articles 1 to 4 of this Protocol.

Article 6
Relationship to the Convention

As between the High Contracting Parties the provisions of Articles 1 to 5 of this Protocol shall be regarded as additional Articles to the Convention, and the provisions of the Convention shall apply accordingly.

Article 7
Signature and ratification

(1) This Protocol shall be open for signature by the members of the Council of Europe who are signatories of the Convention; it shall be ratified at the same time as or after the ratification of the Convention. It shall enter into force after the deposit of five instruments of ratification. As regards any signatory ratifying subsequently, the Protocol shall enter into force at the date of the deposit of its instrument of ratification.

(2) The instruments of ratification shall be deposited with the Secretary General of the Council of Europe, who will notify all members of the names of those who have ratified.

Done at Strasbourg, 16 September 1963.

[Protocol No. 5 has become otiose; it concerned the procedure for the election of members of the Commission and Court]

Protocol No. 6 to the Convention for the Protection of Human Rights and Fundamental Freedoms Concerning the Abolition of the Death Penalty, as amended by Protocol 11

The Member States of the Council of Europe, signatory to this Protocol to the Convention for the Protection of Human Rights and Fundamental Freedoms, signed at Rome on 4 November 1950 (hereinafter referred to as 'the Convention'),

Considering that the evolution that has occurred in several Member States of the Council of Europe expresses a general tendency in favour of the abolition of the death penalty;

Have agreed as follows:

Article 1
Abolition of the death penalty

The death penalty shall be abolished. No-one shall be condemned to such penalty or executed.

Article 2
Death penalty in time of war

A State may make provision in its law for the death penalty in respect of acts committed in time of war or of imminent threat of war; such penalty shall be applied only in the instances laid down in the law and in accordance with its provisions. The State shall communicate to the Secretary General of the Council of Europe the relevant provisions of that law.

Article 3
Prohibition of derogations

No derogation from the provisions of this Protocol shall be made under Article 15 of the Convention.

Article 4
Prohibition of reservations

No reservation may be made under Article 57 of the Convention in respect of the provisions of this Protocol.

Article 5

Territorial application

(1) Any State may at the time of signature or when depositing its instrument of ratification, acceptance or approval, specify the territory or territories to which this Protocol shall apply.

(2) Any State may at any later date, by a declaration addressed to the Secretary General of the Council of Europe, extend the application of this Protocol to any other territory specified in the declaration. In respect of such territory the Protocol shall enter into force on the first day of the month following the date of receipt of such declaration by the Secretary General.

(3) Any declaration made under the two preceding paragraphs may, in respect of any territory specified in such declaration, be withdrawn by a notification addressed to the Secretary General. The withdrawal shall become effective on the first day of the month following the date of receipt of such notification by the Secretary General.

Article 6
Relationship to the Convention

As between the States Parties the provisions of Articles 1 to 5 of this Protocol shall be regarded as additional articles to the Convention and all the provisions of the Convention shall apply accordingly.

Article 7
Signature and ratification

The Protocol shall be open for signature by the Member States of the Council of Europe, signatories to the Convention. It shall be subject to ratification, acceptance or approval. A member State of the Council of Europe may not ratify, accept or approve this Protocol unless it has, simultaneously or previously, ratified the Convention. Instruments of ratification, acceptance or approval shall be deposited with the Secretary General of the Council of Europe.

Article 8
Entry into force

(1) This Protocol shall enter into force on the first day of the month following the date on which five Member States of the Council of Europe have expressed their consent to be bound by the Protocol in accordance with the provisions of Article 7.

(2) In respect of any member State which subsequently expresses its consent to be bound by it, the Protocol shall enter into force on the first day of the month following the date of the deposit of the instrument of ratification, acceptance or approval.

Article 9
Depositary functions

The Secretary General of the Council of Europe shall notify the Member States of the Council of:

(a) any signature;

(b) the deposit of any instrument of ratification, acceptance or approval;

(c) any date of entry into force of this Protocol in accordance with Articles 5 and 8;

(d) any other act, notification or communication relating to this Protocol.

Done at Strasbourg, 28 April 1983.

Protocol No. 7 to the Convention for the Protection of Human Rights and Fundamental Freedoms, as amended by Protocol No. 11

The Member States of the Council of Europe signatory hereto,

Being resolved to ensure the collective enforcement of certain rights and freedoms by means of the Convention for the Protection of Human Rights and Fundamental Freedoms signed at Rome on 4 November 1950 (hereinafter referred to as 'the Convention'),

Have agreed as follows:

Article 1
Procedural safeguards relating to expulsion of aliens

(1) An alien lawfully resident in the territory of a State shall not be expelled therefrom except in pursuance of a decision reached in accordance with law and shall be allowed:

(a) to submit reasons against his expulsion;

(b) to have his case reviewed; and

(c) to be represented for these purposes before the competent authority or a person or persons designated by that authority.

(2) An alien may be expelled before the exercise of his rights under paragraph 1 (a), (b) and (c) of this Article, when such expulsion is necessary in the interests of public order or is grounded on reasons of national security.

Article 2
Right of appeal in criminal matters

(1) Everyone convicted of a criminal offence by a tribunal shall have the right to have his conviction or sentence reviewed by a higher tribunal. The exercise of this right, including the grounds on which it may be exercised, shall be governed by law.

(2) This right may be subject to exceptions in regard to offences of a minor character, as prescribed by law, or in cases in which the person concerned was tried in the first instance by the highest tribunal or was convicted following an appeal against acquittal.

Article 3
Compensation for wrongful conviction

When a person has by a final decision been convicted of a criminal offence and when subsequently his conviction has been reversed, or he has been pardoned, on the ground that a new or newly discovered fact shows conclusively that there has been a miscarriage of justice, the person who has suffered punishment as a result of such conviction shall be compensated according to the law or the practice of the State concerned, unless it is proved that the non-disclosure of the unknown fact in time is wholly or partly attributable to him.

Article 4
Right not to be tried or punished twice

(1) No one shall be liable to be tried or punished again in criminal proceedings under the jurisdiction of the same State for an offence for which he has already been finally acquitted or convicted in accordance with the law and penal procedure of that State.

(2) The provisions of the preceding paragraph shall not prevent the reopening of the case in accordance with the law and penal procedure of the State concerned, if there is evidence of new or newly discovered facts, or if there has been a fundamental defect in the previous proceedings, which could affect the outcome of the case.

(3) No derogation from this Article shall be made under Article 15 of the Convention.

Article 5

Equality between spouses

Spouses shall enjoy equality of rights and relationships of a private law character between them, and in their relations with their children, as to marriage, during marriage and in the event of its dissolution. This Article shall not prevent States from taking such measures as are necessary in the interests of the children.

Article 6

Territorial application

(1) Any State may at the time of signature or when depositing its instrument of ratification, acceptance or approval, specify the territory or territories to which the Protocol shall apply and state the extent to which it undertakes that the provisions of this Protocol shall apply to such territory or territories.

(2) Any State may at any later date, by a declaration addressed to the Secretary General of the Council of Europe, extend the application of this Protocol to any other territory specified in the declaration. In respect of such territory the Protocol shall enter into force on the first day of the month following the expiration of a period of two months after the date of receipt of such notification by the Secretary General.

(3) Any declaration made under the preceding two paragraphs may, in respect of any territory specified in such declaration, be withdrawn or modified by a notification addressed to the Secretary General. The withdrawal or modification shall become effective on the first day of the month following the expiration of a period of two months after the date of receipt of such notification by the Secretary General.

(4) A declaration made in accordance with this Article shall be deemed to have been made in accordance with paragraph 1 of Article 56 of the Convention.

(5) The territory of any State to which this Protocol applies by virtue of ratification, acceptance or approval by that State, and each territory to which this Protocol is applied by virtue of a declaration by that State under this Article, may be treated as separate territories for the purpose of the reference in Article 1 to the territory of a State.

(6) Any State which has made a declaration in accordance with paragraph 1 or 2 of this Article may at any time thereafter declare on behalf of one or more of the territories to which the declaration relates that it accepts the competence of the Court to receive applications from individuals, non-governmental organisations or groups of individuals as provided in Article 34 of the Convention in respect of Articles 1 to 5 of this Protocol.

Article 7
Relationship to the Convention

As between the States Parties, the provisions of Article 1 to 6 of this Protocol shall be regarded as additional Articles to the Convention, and all the provisions of the Convention shall apply accordingly.

Article 8
Signature and ratification

This Protocol shall be open for signature by Member States of the Council of Europe which have signed the Convention. It is subject to ratification, acceptance or approval. A member State of the Council of Europe may not ratify, accept or approve this Protocol without previously or simultaneously ratifying the Convention. Instruments of ratification, acceptance or approval shall be deposited with the Secretary General of the Council of Europe.

Article 9
Entry into force

(1) This Protocol shall enter into force on the first day of the month following the expiration of a period of two months after the date on which seven Member States of the Council of Europe have expressed their consent to be bound by the Protocol in accordance with the provisions of Article 8.

(2) In respect of any member State which subsequently expresses its consent to be bound by it, the Protocol shall enter into force on the first day of the month following the expiration of a period of two months after the date of the deposit of the instrument of ratification, acceptance or approval.

Article 10
Depositary functions

The Secretary General of the Council of Europe shall notify all the Member States of the Council of Europe of:

(a) any signature;

(b) the deposit of any instrument of ratification, acceptance or approval;

(c) any date of entry into force of this protocol in accordance with Articles 6 and 9;

(d) any other act, notification or declaration relating to this Protocol.

Done at Strasbourg, 22 November 1984.

[Protocol No. 8 has become otiose; it concerned procedure of the 'old' Commission and Court]

[Protocol No. 9 has become otiose; it amended certain provisions of the Convention to improve the position of individual applicants]

[Protocol No. 10 has become otiose; it changes the majority required for a decision of the Committee of Ministers under the original Article 32]

[Protocol No. 11 is omitted; it amended the Convention and made transitional arrangements for the transfer of work from the Commission and Court to the 'new' Court]

Protocol No. 12 to the Convention for the Protection of Human Rights and Fundamental Freedoms

Entered into force on 1 April 2005

The Member States of the Council of Europe signatory hereto,

Having regard to the fundamental principle according to which all persons are equal before the law and are entitled to the equal protection of the law;

Being resolved to take further steps to promote the equality of all persons through the collective enforcement of a general prohibition of discrimination by means of the Convention for the

Protection of Human Rights and Fundamental Freedoms signed at Rome on 4 November 1950 (hereinafter referred to as 'the Convention');

Reaffirming that the principle of non-discrimination does not prevent States Parties from taking measures in order to promote full and effective equality, provided that there is an objective and reasonable justification for those measures.

Have agreed as follows:

Article 1
General prohibition of discrimination

(1) The enjoyment of any right set forth by law shall be secured without discrimination on any ground such as sex, race, colour, language, religion, political or other opinion, national or social origin, association with a national minority, property, birth or other status.

(2) No one shall be discriminated against by any public authority on any ground such as those mentioned in paragraph 1.

Article 2
Territorial application

(1) Any State may, at the time of signature or when depositing its instrument of ratification, acceptance or approval, specify the territory or territories to which this Protocol shall apply.

(2) Any State may at any later date, by a declaration addressed to the Secretary General of the Council of Europe, extend the application of this Protocol to any other territory specified in the declaration. In respect of such territory the Protocol shall enter into force on the first day of the month following the expiration of a period of three months after the date of receipt by the Secretary General of such declaration.

(3) Any declaration made under the two preceding paragraphs may, in respect of any territory specified in such declaration, be withdrawn or modified by a notification addressed to the Secretary General of the Council of Europe. The withdrawal or modification shall become effective on the first day of the month following the expiration of a period of three months after the date of receipt of such notification by the Secretary General.

(4) A declaration made in accordance with this article shall be deemed to have been made in accordance with paragraph 1 of Article 56 of the Convention.

(5) Any State which has made a declaration in accordance with paragraph 1 or 2 of this article may at any time thereafter declare on behalf of one or more of the territories to which the declaration relates that it accepts the competence of the Court to receive applications from individuals, non-governmental organisations or groups of individuals as provided by Article 34 of the Convention in respect of Article 1 of this Protocol.

Article 3
Relationship to the Convention

As between the States Parties, the provisions of Articles 1 and 2 of this Protocol shall be regarded as additional articles to the Convention, and all the provisions of the Convention shall apply accordingly.

Article 4
Signature and ratification

This Protocol shall be open for signature by Member States of the Council of Europe which have signed the Convention. It is subject to ratification, acceptance or approval. A member state of the Council of Europe may not ratify, accept or approve this Protocol without previously or simultaneously ratifying the Convention. Instruments of ratification, acceptance or approval shall be deposited with the Secretary General of the Council of Europe.

Article 5
Entry into force

(1) This Protocol shall enter into force on the first day of the month following the expiration of a period of three months after the date on which ten Member States of the Council of Europe have expressed their consent to be bound by the Protocol in accordance with the provisions of Article 4.

(2) In respect of any member state which subsequently expresses its consent to be bound by it, the Protocol shall enter into force on the first day of the month following the expiration of a period of three months after the date of the deposit of the instrument of ratification, acceptance or approval.

Article 6
Depositary functions

The Secretary General of the Council of Europe shall notify all the Member States of the Council of Europe of:

(a) any signature;

(b) the deposit of any instrument of ratification, acceptance or approval;

(c) any date of entry into force of this Protocol in accordance with Articles 2 and 5;

(d) any other act, notification or communication relating to this Protocol.

In witness whereof the undersigned, being duly authorised thereto, have signed this Protocol.

Done at Rome, 4 November 2000.

Protocol No. 13 to the Convention for the Protection of Human Rights and Fundamental Freedoms, Concerning the Abolition of the Death Penalty in all Circumstances, Signed at Vilnius on 3 May 2002

Entered into force on 1 July 2003

Preamble

The Member States of the Council of Europe signatory hereto,

Convinced that everyone's right to life is a basic value in a democratic society and that the abolition of the death penalty is essential for the protection of this right and for the full recognition of the inherent dignity of all human beings;

Wishing to strengthen the protection of the right to life guaranteed by the Convention for the Protection of Human Rights and Fundamental Freedoms signed at Rome on 4 November 1950 (hereinafter referred to as 'the Convention');

Noting that Protocol No. 6 to the Convention, concerning the Abolition of the Death Penalty, signed at Strasbourg on 28 April 1983, does not exclude the death penalty in respect of acts committed in time of war or of imminent threat of war;

Being resolved to take the final step in order to abolish the death penalty in all circumstances,

Have agreed as follows:

Article 1
Abolition of the death penalty

The death penalty shall be abolished. No one shall be condemned to such penalty or executed.

Article 2
Prohibition of derogations

No derogation from the provisions of this Protocol shall be made under Article 15 of the Convention.

Article 3
Prohibition of reservations

No reservation may be made under Article 57 of the Convention in respect of the provisions of this Protocol.

Article 4
Territorial application

1. Any State may, at the time of signature or when depositing its instrument of ratification, acceptance or approval, specify the territory or territories to which this Protocol shall apply.

2. Any State may at any later date, by a declaration addressed to the Secretary General of the Council of Europe, extend the application of this Protocol to any other territory specified in the declaration. In respect of such territory the Protocol shall enter into force on the first day of the month following the expiration of a period of three months after the date of receipt of such declaration by the Secretary General.

Any declaration made under the two preceding paragraphs may, in respect of any territory specified in such declaration, be withdrawn or modified by a notification addressed to the Secretary General. The withdrawal or modification shall become effective on the first day of the month following the expiration of a period of three months after the date of receipt of such notification by the Secretary General.

Article 5
Relationship to the Convention

As between the States Parties the provisions of Articles 1 to 4 of this Protocol shall be regarded as additional articles to the Convention, and all the provisions of the Convention shall apply accordingly.

Article 6
Signature and ratification

This Protocol shall be open for signature by Member States of the Council of Europe which have signed the Convention. It is subject to ratification, acceptance or approval. A Member State of the Council of Europe may not ratify, accept or approve this Protocol without previously or simultaneously ratifying the Convention. Instruments of ratification, acceptance or approval shall be deposited with the Secretary General of the Council of Europe.

Article 7
Entry into force

1. This Protocol shall enter into force on the first day of the month following the expiration of a period of three months after the date on which ten Member States of the Council of Europe

have expressed their consent to be bound by the Protocol in accordance with the provisions of Article 6.

2. In respect of any member State which subsequently expresses its consent to be bound by it, the Protocol shall enter into force on the first day of the month following the expiration of a period of three months after the date of the deposit of the instrument of ratification, acceptance or approval.

Article 8

Depositary functions

The Secretary General of the Council of Europe shall notify all the Member States of the Council of Europe of:

(a) any signature;

(b) the deposit of any instrument of ratification, acceptance or approval;

(c) any date of entry into force of this Protocol in accordance with Articles 4 and 7;

(d) any other act, notification or communication relating to this Protocol.

In witness whereof the undersigned, being duly authorised thereto, have signed this Protocol.

[Protocol 14 is omitted; it amended the Convention…]

Protocol No. 15 amending the Convention for the Protection of Human Rights and Fundamental Freedoms, Signed at Strasbourg 24 June 2013

Not yet in force

Preamble

The member States of the Council of Europe and the other High Contracting Parties to the Convention for the Protection of Human Rights and Fundamental Freedoms, signed at Rome on 4 November 1950 (hereinafter referred to as "the Convention"), signatory hereto,

Having regard to the declaration adopted at the High Level Conference on the Future of the European Court of Human Rights, held in Brighton on 19 and 20 April 2012, as well as the declarations adopted at the conferences held in Interlaken on 18 and 19 February 2010 and İzmir on 26 and 27 April 2011;

Having regard to Opinion No. 283 (2013) adopted by the Parliamentary Assembly of the Council of Europe on 26 April 2013;

Considering the need to ensure that the European Court of Human Rights (hereinafter referred to as "the Court") can continue to play its pre-eminent role in protecting human rights in Europe,

Have agreed as follows:

Article 1

At the end of the preamble to the Convention, a new recital shall be added, which shall read as follows:

"Affirming that the High Contracting Parties, in accordance with the principle of subsidiarity, have the primary responsibility to secure the rights and freedoms defined in this Convention and the Protocols thereto, and that in doing so they enjoy a margin of appreciation, subject to the supervisory jurisdiction of the European Court of Human Rights established by this Convention".

Article 2

(1) In Article 21 of the Convention, a new paragraph 2 shall be inserted, which shall read as follows:

"Candidates shall be less than 65 years of age at the date by which the list of three candidates has been requested by the Parliamentary Assembly, further to Article 22."

(2) Paragraphs 2 and 3 of Article 21 of the Convention shall become paragraphs 3 and 4 of Article 21 respectively.

(3) Paragraph 2 of Article 23 of the Convention shall be deleted. Paragraphs 3 and 4 of Article 23 shall become paragraphs 2 and 3 of Article 23 respectively.

Article 3

In Article 30 of the Convention, the words "unless one of the parties to the case objects" shall be deleted.

Article 4

In Article 35, paragraph 1 of the Convention, the words "within a period of six months" shall be replaced by the words "within a period of four months".

Article 5

In Article 35, paragraph 3, sub-paragraph b of the Convention, the words "and provided that no case may be rejected on this ground which has not been duly considered by a domestic tribunal" shall be deleted.

Final and transitional provisions

Article 6

(1) This Protocol shall be open for signature by the High Contracting Parties to the Convention, which may express their consent to be bound by:

(a) signature without reservation as to ratification, acceptance or approval; or

(b) signature subject to ratification, acceptance or approval, followed by ratification, acceptance or approval.

(2) The instruments of ratification, acceptance or approval shall be deposited with the Secretary General of the Council of Europe.

Article 7

This Protocol shall enter into force on the first day of the month following the expiration of a period of three months after the date on which all High Contracting Parties to the Convention have expressed their consent to be bound by the Protocol, in accordance with the provisions of Article 6.

Article 8

(1) The amendments introduced by Article 2 of this Protocol shall apply only to candidates on lists submitted to the Parliamentary Assembly by the High Contracting Parties under Article 22 of the Convention after the entry into force of this Protocol.

(2) The amendment introduced by Article 3 of this Protocol shall not apply to any pending case in which one of the parties has objected, prior to the date of entry into force of this Protocol, to a proposal by a Chamber of the Court to relinquish jurisdiction in favour of the Grand Chamber.

(3) Article 4 of this Protocol shall enter into force following the expiration of a period of six months after the date of entry into force of this Protocol. Article 4 of this Protocol shall not apply to applications in respect of which the final decision within the meaning of Article 35, paragraph 1 of the Convention was taken prior to the date of entry into force of Article 4 of this Protocol.

(4) All other provisions of this Protocol shall apply from its date of entry into force, in accordance with the provisions of Article 7.

Article 9

The Secretary General of the Council of Europe shall notify the member States of the Council of Europe and the other High Contracting Parties to the Convention of:

(a) any signature;

(b) the deposit of any instrument of ratification, acceptance or approval;

(c) the date of entry into force of this Protocol in accordance with Article 7; and

(d) any other act, notification or communication relating to this Protocol.

In witness whereof, the undersigned, being duly authorised thereto, have signed this Protocol. Done at Strasbourg, this 24th day of June 2013, in English and in French, both texts being equally authentic, in a single copy which shall be deposited in the archives of the Council of Europe. The Secretary General of the Council of Europe shall transmit certified copies to each member State of the Council of Europe and to the other High Contracting Parties to the Convention.

Protocol No. 16 to the Convention for the Protection of Human Rights and Fundamental Freedoms, Signed at Strasbourg 2 October 2013

Not yet in force

Preamble

The member States of the Council of Europe and other High Contracting Parties to the Convention for the Protection of Human Rights and Fundamental Freedoms, signed at Rome on 4 November 1950 (hereinafter referred to as "the Convention"), signatories hereto,

Having regard to the provisions of the Convention and, in particular, Article 19 establishing the European Court of Human Rights (hereinafter referred to as "the Court");

Considering that the extension of the Court's competence to give advisory opinions will further enhance the interaction between the Court and national authorities and thereby reinforce implementation of the Convention, in accordance with the principle of subsidiarity;

Having regard to Opinion No. 285 (2013) adopted by the Parliamentary Assembly of the Council of Europe on 28 June 2013,

Have agreed as follows:

Article 1

(1) Highest courts and tribunals of a High Contracting Party, as specified in accordance with Article 10, may request the Court to give advisory opinions on questions of principle relating to the interpretation or application of the rights and freedoms defined in the Convention or the protocols thereto.

(2) The requesting court or tribunal may seek an advisory opinion only in the context of a case pending before it.

(3) The requesting court or tribunal shall give reasons for its request and shall provide the relevant legal and factual background of the pending case.

Article 2

(1) A panel of five judges of the Grand Chamber shall decide whether to accept the request for an advisory opinion, having regard to Article 1. The panel shall give reasons for any refusal to accept the request.

(2) If the panel accepts the request, the Grand Chamber shall deliver the advisory opinion.

(3) The panel and the Grand Chamber, as referred to in the preceding paragraphs, shall include ex officio the judge elected in respect of the High Contracting Party to which the requesting court or tribunal pertains. If there is none or if that judge is unable to sit, a person chosen by the President of the Court from a list submitted in advance by that Party shall sit in the capacity of judge.

Article 3

The Council of Europe Commissioner for Human Rights and the High Contracting Party to which the requesting court or tribunal pertains shall have the right to submit written comments and take part in any hearing. The President of the Court may, in the interest of the proper administration of justice, invite any other High Contracting Party or person also to submit written comments or take part in any hearing.

Article 4

(1) Reasons shall be given for advisory opinions.

(2) If the advisory opinion does not represent, in whole or in part, the unanimous opinion of the judges, any judge shall be entitled to deliver a separate opinion.

(3) Advisory opinions shall be communicated to the requesting court or tribunal and to the High Contracting Party to which that court or tribunal pertains.

(4) Advisory opinions shall be published.

Article 5

Advisory opinions shall not be binding.

Article 6

As between the High Contracting Parties the provisions of Articles 1 to 5 of this Protocol shall be regarded as additional articles to the Convention, and all the provisions of the Convention shall apply accordingly.

Article 7

(1) This Protocol shall be open for signature by the High Contracting Parties to the Convention, which may express their consent to be bound by:

(a) signature without reservation as to ratification, acceptance or approval; or

(b) signature subject to ratification, acceptance or approval, followed by ratification, acceptance or approval.

(2) The instruments of ratification, acceptance or approval shall be deposited with the Secretary General of the Council of Europe.

Article 8

(1) This Protocol shall enter into force on the first day of the month following the expiration of a period of three months after the date on which ten High Contracting Parties to the Convention have expressed their consent to be bound by the Protocol in accordance with the provisions of Article 7.

(2) In respect of any High Contracting Party to the Convention which subsequently expresses its consent to be bound by it, the Protocol shall enter into force on the first day of the month following the expiration of a period of three months after the date of the expression of its consent to be bound by the Protocol in accordance with the provisions of Article 7.

Article 9

No reservation may be made under Article 57 of the Convention in respect of the provisions of this Protocol.

Article 10

Each High Contracting Party to the Convention shall, at the time of signature or when depositing its instrument of ratification, acceptance or approval, by means of a declaration addressed to the Secretary General of the Council of Europe, indicate the courts or tribunals that it designates for the purposes of Article 1, paragraph 1, of this Protocol. This declaration may be modified at any later date and in the same manner.

Article 11

The Secretary General of the Council of Europe shall notify the member States of the Council of Europe and the other High Contracting Parties to the Convention of:

(a) any signature;

(b) the deposit of any instrument of ratification, acceptance or approval;

(c) any date of entry into force of this Protocol in accordance with Article 8;

(d) any declaration made in accordance with Article 10; and

(e) any other act, notification or communication relating to this Protocol.

In witness whereof the undersigned, being duly authorised thereto, have signed this Protocol.

Done at Strasbourg, this 2nd day of October 2013, in English and French, both texts being equally authentic, in a single copy which shall be deposited in the archives of the Council of Europe. The Secretary General of the Council of Europe shall transmit certified copies to each member State of the Council of Europe and to the other High Contracting Parties to the Convention.

INDEX